T. S. ELIOT
COLLECTED PROSE

By T. S. Eliot

THE POEMS OF T. S. ELIOT
Volume 1: Collected and Uncollected Poems
Volume 2: Practical Cats and Further Verses
edited by Christopher Ricks and Jim McCue

COLLECTED POEMS 1909–1962
PRUFROCK AND OTHER OBSERVATIONS
THE WASTE LAND AND OTHER POEMS
FOUR QUARTETS
SELECTED POEMS
THE WASTE LAND:
A Facsimile and Transcript of the Original Drafts
edited by Valerie Eliot
INVENTIONS OF THE MARCH HARE:
Poems 1909–1917
edited by Christopher Ricks
THE ARIEL POEMS
THE WASTE LAND
ANNIVERSARY EDITION
OLD POSSUM'S BOOK OF PRACTICAL CATS
THE COMPLETE POEMS AND PLAYS

plays
MURDER IN THE CATHEDRAL
THE FAMILY REUNION
THE COCKTAIL PARTY
THE CONFIDENTIAL CLERK
THE ELDER STATESMAN

literary criticism
THE SACRED WOOD
SELECTED ESSAYS
THE USE OF POETRY AND THE USE OF CRITICISM
THE VARIETIES OF METAPHYSICAL POETRY
edited by Ronald Schuchard
TO CRITICIZE THE CRITIC
ON POETRY AND POETS
FOR LANCELOT ANDREWES
SELECTED PROSE OF T. S. ELIOT
edited by Frank Kermode

social criticism
THE IDEA OF A CHRISTIAN SOCIETY
NOTES TOWARDS THE DEFINITION OF CULTURE

letters
THE LETTERS OF T. S. ELIOT
Volume 1: 1898–1922; Volume 2: 1923–1925
edited by Valerie Eliot and Hugh Haughton
Volume 3: 1926–1927; Volume 4: 1928–1929;
Volume 5: 1930–1931; Volume 6: 1932–1933;
Volume 7: 1934–1935; Volume 8: 1936–1938;
Volume 9: 1939–1941
edited by Valerie Eliot and John Haffenden

prose
T. S. ELIOT COLLECTED PROSE
Volume 1: 1905–1928; Volume 2: 1929–1934;
Volume 3: 1935–1950; Volume 4: 1951–1966
edited by Archie Burnett

T. S. Eliot
COLLECTED PROSE

EDITED BY
ARCHIE BURNETT

VOLUME 2
1929–1934

faber

First published in 2024
by Faber & Faber Ltd, The Bindery,
51 Hatton Garden,
London, EC1N 8HN

Typeset by Donald Sommerville
Printed in Poland

All rights reserved

All writings by T. S. Eliot,
© Set Copyrights Limited 2024

The moral right of Archie Burnett to be identified
as editor of this work has been asserted in accordance with
Section 77 of the Copyright, Designs and Patents Act 1988

A CIP record for this book is available from the British Library

ISBN 978–0–571–29550–0

MIX
Paper | Supporting
responsible forestry
FSC® C018236

2 4 6 8 10 9 7 5 3 1

Contents

Guide to Using This Edition ... xi
Abbreviations ... xiii

THE PROSE

1929

American Critics	3
Introduction to Goethe	5
Turbervile's Ovid	8
Mr P. E. More's Essays	11
The Latin Tradition	14
A Commentary	16
[Works by Conan Doyle and A. K. Green]	19
Second Thoughts about Humanism	23
The Tudor Translators	23
The Elizabethan Grub Street	28
The Genesis of Philosophic Prose	33
A Commentary	38
Mr Barnes and Mr Rowse	41
[*Extraits d'un Journal* by Charles du Bos]	48
The Prose of the Preacher	48
Elizabethan Travellers' Tales	53
The Tudor Biographers	59
The Early Novel	63
Second Thoughts about Humanism	66
Preface	66
A Commentary	67
Experiment in Criticism	71
Tradition and Experiment in Present-Day Literature	71

1930

A Commentary	84
A Humanist Theory of Value	87
[*God* by J. Middleton Murry]	99

[*Baudelaire and the Symbolists* by Peter Quennell]	102
A Game at Chesse	104
Poetry and Propaganda	107
Religion without Humanism	117
Thinking in Verse	122
Rhyme and Reason	128
The Devotional Poets of the Seventeenth Century	133
A Commentary	139
In Memoriam	143
Mystic and Politician as Poet	143
The Minor Metaphysicals	149
John Dryden	154
Message to the Anglo-Catholic Congress in London	160
Second Message to the Anglo-Catholic Congress	160
A Commentary	161
Introduction	164
Introductory Essay	171
Arnold and Pater	176
Introduction	176
A Commentary	177
On Reading Einstein	179
Cyril Tourneur	185

1931

A Commentary	186
Thoughts After Lambeth	192
A Commentary	192
John Dryden I, II and III	199
If I Were a Dean	199
[*The Prospects of Humanism* by Lawrence Hyde]	202
A Commentary	203
[*Son of Woman* by John Middleton Murry]	209
[*Essays of a Catholic Layman in England* by Hilaire Belloc]	215
Thomas Heywood	216
Introduction	216
A Commentary	216
[*Fashion in Literature* by E. E. Kellett]	222
Preface	224
Donne in our Time	227

1932

A Commentary	236
Charles Whibley: A Memoir	242
Preface	242
Studies in Sanctity. VIII. George Herbert	244
Christianity and Communism	247
Mr Harold Monro: A Poet and his Ideal	254
Religion and Science: A Phantom Dilemma	256
The Search for Moral Sanction	261
A Commentary	267
Building up the Christian World	272
John Ford	278
A Commentary	278
Selected Essays 1917–1932	284
I Tradition and the Individual Talent	285
The Function of Criticism	292
II 'Rhetoric' And Poetic Drama	301
A Dialogue on Dramatic Poetry	309
Euripides and Professor Murray	323
Seneca in Elizabethan Translation	327
III Four Elizabethan Dramatists	359
Christopher Marlowe	366
Shakespeare and the Stoicism of Seneca	373
Hamlet	384
Ben Jonson	389
Thomas Middleton	400
Thomas Heywood	408
Cyril Tourneur	417
John Ford	426
Philip Massinger	435
IV Dante	448
V The Metaphysical Poets	484
Andrew Marvell	492
John Dryden	503
William Blake	513
Swinburne as Poet	518
VI Lancelot Andrewes	518
John Bramhall	528
Thoughts after Lambeth	535
VII Baudelaire	554
Arnold and Pater	564

Francis Herbert Bradley	575
Marie Lloyd	584
Wilkie Collins and Dickens	588
The Humanism of Irving Babbitt	596
Second Thoughts about Humanism	604
Charles Whibley	613
John Dryden The Poet the Dramatist the Critic	624
Dryden the Poet	624
Dryden the Dramatist	632
Dryden the Critic	641
A Commentary	650
From T. S. Eliot	655
Apology for the Countess of Pembroke	655

1933

A Commentary	656
A Commentary	660
Critical	665
A Commentary	667
Catholicism and International Order	672
[*Letters of Mrs Gaskell and Charles Eliot Norton*]	672
A Commentary	674
Housman on Poetry	678
The Modern Dilemma	680
The Use of Poetry and the Use of Criticism	685
Preface	685
Introduction	686
Apology for the Countess of Pembroke	700
The Age of Dryden	709
Wordsworth and Coleridge	716
Shelley and Keats	727
Matthew Arnold	737
The Modern Mind	747
Conclusion	760
Address By T. S. Eliot, '06	768

1934

A Commentary	774
Personality and Demonic Possession	780
After Strange Gods	781
Preface	781
I	783

II	784
III	795
Appendix	803
Le Morte Darthur	805
Tradition and Orthodoxy	809
Shakespeare Criticism	819
[Samuel Taylor Coleridge, 1772–1834]	829
A Commentary	829
The Story of the Pageant	832
A Commentary	833
[*The Oxford Handbook of Religious Knowledge*]	838
[*The Mystical Doctrine of St John of the Cross*]	839
[*A Christian Sociology for To-day*]	839
In Sincerity and Earnestness: New Britain as I See It	840
John Marston	842
The Problem of Education	842
A Commentary	845
Religious Drama and the Church	849
John Marston	852
What Does the Church Stand For?	862
Orage: Memories	864
Index of Article Titles	867

Guide to Using This Edition

This is a text-only edition, with the prose arranged in a single chronological sequence. However, the chronology has to be handled carefully in view of the fact that it was Eliot's practice to revise his work. (It is a shortcoming of Donald Gallup's indispensable 1969 bibliography that he does not always note that a reprinted text has also undergone revision: this means that all versions must be scrutinised for variants.) Where Eliot revised wording, even slightly, the latest revised version is printed at the point at which it appeared, and variants in wording are recorded there from the earlier version(s). An example: 'Tradition and the Individual Talent' was originally published in two parts in *The Egoist* in September and November/December 1919; both parts were combined and revised in *The Sacred Wood* (November 1920); and the text was further revised in *Selected Essays* (September 1932). Readers will find the text under *Selected Essays*, together with a record of the changes Eliot made at each stage. The earlier versions are recorded at the point at which they appeared, with an indication that they would undergo revision.

Even where revision involves merely putting a word in italics or quotation marks to introduce a new emphasis or attitude, this is regarded as a substantive change. In the few cases where revision also involves translation from French into English, variants are not recorded: translation itself constitutes a form of variation, and it would be difficult to decide, on the basis of often very slight differences of idiom and nuance, which variants are to be recorded and which not. Both the French and the English versions are printed in full, however. Textual variants are recorded below the latest revised text and variants are recorded by paragraph. Thus, '4 vast energy] energy' records that in paragraph 4, where the revised text has 'vast energy', the previously published text has 'energy'. Where the text was revised more than once, each variant is labelled. This edition aims to provide the most complete record available of Eliot's revisions to his authorised prose.

For the first time, page numbers in the text chosen for printing are inserted in a different font in editorial square brackets – for example [76], for convenience of reference to the original publications.

The conventions of all publications are regularised to Faber's house style. Block quotations are given in roman, single-spaced, and indented, and quotation marks at the beginning and end are not reproduced. Inconsistent punctuation for introducing block quotations (':—' as well as ':') is regularised to a colon. American spellings, when used, have been retained.

The numbers of volumes and issues of periodicals are given in arabic. Thus '2. 3' means 'volume 2, number 3'.

Obvious misprints, such as 'desert' for 'dessert', or 'writed' for 'writer', or beginning a sentence with 'they' instead of 'They', are silently corrected. It is not always possible to distinguish a misprint from an authorial error, but the following have been routinely corrected: passages in French (almost always a question of accents: Eliot's French was good, and it is hard to believe that in an article such as 'Marivaux' (Gallup C73), for instance, 'Corbiere' is followed within a few lines by 'Corbière', and hardly a single French accent is rendered correctly); names of persons ('Rubenstein' to 'Rubinstein', 'Weckerlin' to 'Weckherlin', the poet [Thomas] 'Grey' to 'Gray', [Sybil] 'Thorndyke' to 'Thorndike'); and titles of books (*Dorian Grey* to *Dorian Gray*, *Biographia Litteraria* to *Biographia Literaria*).

Eliot's misquotations, both of literature and of passages from books under review, are left uncorrected, in the interests of preserving what Eliot thought he was commenting on. Eliot on occasion makes use of terminology that will be offensive to contemporary readers, but has been retained in the text as originally published.

I have supplied or changed punctuation only where necessary, and have placed missing punctuation, as well as words, in editorial square brackets. One unusual practice in Eliot's punctuation has been highlighted by Jayme Stayer:[1] a comma inserted between subject and predicate:

What the poet has to say about poetry, will often be most valuable . . .

Even those of us who are not addressed, can agree that all 'sane' people are for peace.

Professor Stayer plausibly suggests that Eliot may be marking his sense of how a sentence should be delivered orally. It is often found when the grammatical subject is long. It causes no problems of comprehension, however, and I have therefore let such punctuation stand.

Archie Burnett
The Editorial Institute
Boston University

---

1 'Of Commas and Facts: Editing Volume 5 of *The Complete Prose*', *T. S. Eliot Studies Annual*, 2 (2018), 121–8.

Abbreviations

A.	*The Athenaeum* (see also *N&A*)
A&L	*Art and Letters*
ASG	*After Strange Gods* (London: Faber & Faber, 1934)
C.	*The Criterion*
CT	*The Church Times*
EAAM	T. S. Eliot, *Essays Ancient & Modern* (London: Faber & Faber, 1936)
ED	*Elizabethan Dramatists* (London: Faber & Faber, 1934)
EE	T. S. Eliot, *Elizabethan Essays* (London: Faber & Faber, 1934)
ER	*The English Review*
FLA	T. S. Eliot, *For Lancelot Andrewes: Essays on Style and Order* (London: Faber & Gwyer, 1928)
Gallup	*T. S. Eliot: A Bibliography*, by Donald Gallup (London: Faber & Faber, 1969)
HA	*The Harvard Advocate*
HJD	T. S. Eliot, *Homage to John Dryden: Three Essays on the Poetry of the Seventeenth Century* (London: The Hogarth Press, 1924)
HR	*The Hudson Review*
ICS	*The Idea of a Christian Society* (London: Faber & Faber, 1939)
IJE	*International Journal of Ethics*
JDPDC	*John Dryden The Poet the Dramatist the Critic* (London: Faber & Faber, 1932)
KEPB	T. S. Eliot, *Knowledge and Experience in the Philosophy of F. H. Bradley* (London: Faber & Faber, 1964)
King's	King's College Library, Cambridge
KR	*The Kenyon Review*
LM	*The London Magazine*
MG	*The Manchester Guardian* newspaper
N.	*The Nation*
N&A	*The Nation & Athenaeum*
NC	*The New Criterion*
NER	*New English Review*

NEW	*The New English Weekly*
NRF	*La Nouvelle Revue Française*
NS	*The New Statesman and Nation*
NTDC	*Notes Towards the Definition of Culture*
OPAP	T. S. Eliot, *On Poetry and Poets* (London: Faber & Faber, 1957; New York: Farrar, Straus & Cudahy, 1957)
SE	T. S. Eliot, *Selected Essays: 1917–1932* (London: Faber & Faber, 1932; 3rd UK edn: Faber & Faber, 1951, with supplementary material)
Spectator	*The Spectator*
SR	*The Sewanee Review*
SW	T. S. Eliot, *The Sacred Wood: Essays on Poetry and Criticism* (London: Methuen & Co., 1920)
T&T	*Time and Tide*
TCTC	T. S. Eliot, *To Criticize the Critic* (London: Faber & Faber, 1965; New York: Farrar, Straus & Giroux, 1965)
TES	*The Times Educational Supplement*
TLR	*The Little Review*
TLS	*The Times Literary Supplement* [London]
UPUC	T. S. Eliot, *The Use of Poetry and the Use of Criticism: Studies in the Relation of Criticism to Poetry in England* (London: Faber & Faber, 1933)

COLLECTED PROSE
1929–1934

1929

American Critics

Review of *The Reinterpretation of American Literature*, ed. Norman Foerster (1928). *TLS*, 1406 (10 Jan. 1929), 24. Unsigned. Gallup C275.

This book is a compilation of essays on related subjects, written on various occasions, but having something of the nature of a symposium, though the various authors do not criticise each other. It is of considerable general interest. The authors are chiefly of the academic world and of the younger generation; they represent the most intelligent aspect of contemporary American scholarship. During the last twenty years, and largely under the influence of Irving Babbitt at Harvard and his friends, a new type of American scholar has appeared. While the influence of President Eliot, of Harvard, dominated – roughly during the last quarter of the nineteenth century – the standards of American university scholarship were Teutonic. The degree of Doctor of Philosophy was all important; in the field of letters it was obtained by minute researches and *Forschungen*. The teacher of modern languages was well equipped with Gothic and Icelandic and Low Latin, but was often without any wide philosophic view of literature, and completely out of touch with the creative work of his own time. Now the tendency is to fly to the other extreme: no American college is without a course or two in contemporary literature, and even of contemporary American literature; and contemporary literature is perhaps given an exaggerated importance. It must be pointed out that the influence of Professor Babbitt has been to establish a just balance: not to disparage the scholarly research of such men as Kittredge and his pupils, which has borne good fruit in our time in the work of men like Professor John Livingstone Lowes, of Harvard, and, on the other hand, not to neglect contemporary literature, but to judge it by universal and severe criteria.

Mr Norman Foerster is one of the most brilliant of Mr Babbitt's disciples, and one of those nearest to the master. His recent work, *American Criticism* (which has not yet been published in England), contains, besides much sound criticism, an authoritative exposition of the 'New Humanism'. He has edited, with a preface, this collection of essays by colleagues of the American Literature Group of the Modern Language Association. These writers demand in unison a thorough revision of the traditional views of American literature and of the traditional methods of composing histories of American literature. As Mr Pattee's essay entitled 'A Call for a Literary Historian' (reprinted from the *American Mercury*) shows, they are much in sympathy with the modern school of American history and desire to co-operate with it. They seem to belong, furthermore, to what may be called (without too much emphasis on dates and ages) the third generation of modern American criticism. The first generation is represented by Irving Babbitt and Paul Elmer More (the former little known, the latter almost completely ignored, in this country). Theirs was the first attempt to de-provincialise America, to replace the fireside criticism of men like James Russell Lowell by the harder standards of Sainte-Beuve and Taine and Renan. There followed a more impatient group of critics of America, represented in the rougher sort by Mr Mencken with his *Prejudices* and *Americana* and in the genteeler sort by Mr Van Wyck Brooks with his *Wine of the Puritans* and his *Ordeal of Mark Twain*. The tendency of Mr Mencken was to exaggerate the value of everything contemporary which offended Boston – whether it offended the Puritan traditions of Beacon Hill or the views of the Irish-American bishopric; the tendency of Mr Brooks to be merely querulous. The third generation represents the disciples of the first generation: among general men of letters it is represented by Mumford, Munson, Allen Tate, among others; in the universities it is represented by Mr Foerster and his friends. It is one of the most interesting post-War phenomena of America. It could hardly exist, in its actual form, without the confidence and self-consciousness which the War aroused in America; but it represents also the sanest attempt to criticise and control this post-War America.

It is true, as these writers join in affirming, that there is no good history of American literature. It is also true, as they seem to be aware, that such a history would be very difficult to write. Barrett Wendell's monumental work, to which several of the writers refer sarcastically, is out of date; it was written from the point of view of old Boston, and was almost an admission, in a great many words, that there is no American literature. The most brilliant book, fragmentary, prejudiced, unbalanced as it is, and sometimes completely misleading, is certainly Mr D. H. Lawrence's dashing series of essays. Mr Lawrence's essay on Fenimore Cooper is the best thing ever written on Cooper; as might be expected, he is by no means so inspired about Poe and Hawthorne. What we are not sure that all the authors in this volume recognise is the isolated speciality of the task. Anyone who writes a history of American literature as *parallel* to English or French literature, or any other literature European or Asiatic, will be wrong, however moderate or just his claims for America may be. The justification for the history of American literature – instead of merely promoting the important Americans into a history of English literature – is that there is undoubtedly something American, and not English, about every American author. There is also something English about him, even when his ancestry is Swedish, German or Italian. An American writer, to write a first-rate history of American literature, must know far more about England, and even about the rest of Europe, than an Englishman needs to write a history of English literature, or a Frenchman to write a history of French literature. The case of Henry James is in point; James is understood by very few Americans and very few Englishmen. To understand James one should know the America that he knew at least as well as he knew it, and the England that he knew (and the rest of England) perhaps better than he knew it. The authors of this volume insist rightly that the history of American literature can only be written by an American who is not limited to the point of view of Boston or New York or Philadelphia or Chicago but who is what we may call a cosmopolitan-American, with equal knowledge and understanding of the whole country. But we should add that he must have this further intimate knowledge of Europe. The genuine history of American literature will be one which shall have importance in Europe as well as in America. Perhaps these are some of the reasons why it has not yet been written, and why Mr Lawrence's book, with all its faults, is still the best. There is some repetition, and much detail of little interest in itself, in this volume. But though only the expression of a desire for a history of American literature, it contains many hints of what is to come (Poe's critical abilities are at last being recognised) and deserves the study of every English critic.

Introduction to Goethe

Review of *Goethe and Faust: An Interpretation* by F. Melian Stawell and G. Lowes Dickinson (1929), and *Goethe's Faust* translated by Anna Swanwick (1928 edn).

N&A, 44. 15 (12 Jan. 1929), 527. Signed 'T. S. Eliot'. Gallup C276.

It is a pity that the first of these books should have to be offered for sale at fifteen shillings. I know quite well the size of the public and the costs of production; under present conditions no publisher would launch such a book at a lower price. But the authors express the desire to 'extend, in this country, the circle, still too narrow, of those who are interested in Goethe and his work'; and the persons among whom it is worth while to extend that interest will be mostly young and impecunious. We can only hope for a run on the lending libraries, or a wave of American enthusiasm, so that the publishers may be able to produce the book later at a lower price. For the authors know their subject with scholarship and zeal; they have not made their book in a hurry; and it introduces a study which really needs introduction.

The book is an introduction to Goethe through *Faust*, and an introduction to *Faust* by an ingenious mixture of commentary and translation. The translations are so good that I at first regretted that Miss Stawell and Mr Dickinson had not made two volumes, one the commentary and the other the complete translation of *Faust* which they say they have written. But a glance at Miss Swanwick's translation, excellent for its period (1850–78) convinced me that their method was the best for their purpose. Only earnest devotion to self-improvement could carry one through some of the dreary wastes in the second part of *Faust*; only the beauty of the verse makes it possible. There are large quantities of the Second Part which not the best of translations could make palatable. I hope that the Stawell-Dickinson translation will eventually appear; but when it does, its readers should reread the present volume first.

As the authors of this book are perfectly aware, Goethe, the object of passionate adoration to mid-Victorians, is at present in eclipse. It is highly desirable that he should again be admired and studied. But it is not merely a question of reviving a reputation; it is, at least in England and America, a matter of almost establishing a new one, so completely must critical opinion be revised. There have been good biographies, but for pure literary criticism, I suspect that we must wait for another generation to find the knowledge and understanding. That is not altogether our fault; the decline of interest in Goethe was an inevitable moment of history; and is connected with the reasons for which he is a writer of permanent greatness. Goethe is, as Mr Santayana made clear in an essay which is the nearest approach to a new critical opinion that I know, a philosophical poet. His philosophy, unfortunately, is that which the nineteenth century took up with, and it has therefore become too familiar to us in popular or degraded forms. Love, Nature, God, Man, Science, Progress: the post-Goethe versions of these terms are still current. But they are gradually being replaced: and as they are replaced, we shall be able to see Goethe more clearly and with more admiration.

It might be excessive to say that we cannot understand the nineteenth century without knowing Goethe; but it may be true to say that we cannot understand that century until we are able to understand Goethe. And perhaps the best way to understand many of the ideas of the nineteenth century is to go back behind them, to the man who expressed them best, and in whom they were fresh and new and enthusiastic. It is a useful exercise, for instance, to try to catch the original spirit of a passage like the following, which the present book quotes:

> Nature! We are surrounded by her, engulfed in her. . . . She creates fresh forms for ever; what is now, has never been before; what was, never comes back again – everything is new and yet still old . . . each of her works has a being of its own, each manifestation is a unique conception, and yet they all make one. . . . Every moment she begins an unending race, and every moment she is at the goal. . . . She has neither speech nor language; but she creates hearts and voices, and in them she feels and speaks. Love is her crown. . . .

On me this falls as dismal as a rural sermon. But it once had meaning, and it will have meaning again; not the meaning of something believed in, but the meaning of something which was once believed. What remains is the fact that Goethe said many such things better than anyone else has said them, and, indeed, thought and felt them better than anyone else has thought or felt them. If a passage like the foregoing seems to us to be nonsense, read the *Conversations with Eckermann*, in which is wisdom that every generation must respect. It would be a delusion to think that we can isolate the poetry of Goethe from his ideas; we cannot understand his feeling without taking his thought seriously.

Miss Stawell and Mr Dickinson have not attempted a critical revision of Goethe. Their book is an introduction, and they have done well to keep it so. There could be no better introduction to *Faust*. I applaud their attempt to revive interest in Goethe, not because I enjoy him, but because I wish I could do so, and because I regard my inability as an unfortunate limitation and prejudice. I cannot enjoy the Second Part of Faust, and to my mind the climax is an anti-climax. But if you do not enjoy it, you remain rather miserable because you do not. And this is not because it is a poem with a great reputation, and Goethe a poet with a greater reputation than that of any other poet in the two centuries in which he lived, but because one cannot escape the authentic feeling of greatness there.

The translations, as I said above, are wholly admirable, and really give some sensation of the original.

Turbervile's Ovid

Review of *The Heroycall Epistles of Ovid, Translated into English by George Turbervile*, edited with an Introduction and Glossary by Frederick Boas (1928).

TLS, 1407 (17 Jan. 1929), 40. Unsigned. Gallup C277.

A reprint of Turbervile's translation of the *Heroides* has long been due not only to the author but to every student of Tudor verse. Turbervile's translation of 1567 is memorable for two reasons: next to Golding's *Metamorphoses* and Marlowe's *Amores* it is the best Tudor translation of Ovid; and secondly, Turbervile is, with Golding, master of a verse form which it is very difficult to write well. The Cresset Press have spared no pains to give a well edited text and a handsome book. It is edited with introduction and glossary by Dr Boas; and it is illustrated by Miss Hester Sainsbury.

George Turbervile, if now obscure, was very respectably born, and very respectably educated at Winchester and at New College, of which he became a Fellow. He was the author of some original verse which was printed, and of several translations from Latin, French and Italian, but these translations from Ovid are his masterpiece. He was only twenty-seven when they appeared: at that age he becomes an historical figure, and disappears again into oblivion. The first three editions, of 1567, 1569 and 1570, were published by Henry Denham; the fourth, by John Charlewoode, was published in 1580; and the fifth, by Simon Strafford, in 1600. It is not surprising that there were no further editions: the seventeenth century, even at its beginning, hardly appreciated the fourteener measure. But during his own century Turbervile's translation appears to have enjoyed a deserved popularity, and probably fell into the hands of many writers who borrowed from Ovid through Turbervile. The present edition Dr Boas has based upon that of Charlewoode, as the differences are merely of 'typography, spelling, punctuation, and a number of verbal variants due chiefly to printers' errors'. Dr Boas expresses the hope that 'it will be found that [Turbervile's] work is not unworthy of being here presented, after 350 years, in this new dress.'

It is not only not unworthy, but highly meritorious, and even important. It is not only historically important, but the best translation of the *Heroides* in English. The versification is of three kinds. A few of the Epistles are done into a blank verse which is itself interesting; some are in the regular fourteener; but the most spirited, to our mind, is that in which a twelve-syllable line alternates with a fourteen. In the present edition, as in the original, the couplets are printed as quatrains. For example, the opening lines of *Dido to Aeneas*:

> Even so when fates doo call
> > ystretcht in moysted spring,
> Upon Meanders winding bankes
> > the snowish Swanne doth sing.
> Not for I thinke my wordes
> > may ought prevayle I wryte:
> For why? I know the haughty Gods,
> > at this my purpose spite.

This form, as used by Turbervile, has a surprising sprightliness and freedom from monotony, but he handles the true fourteener also as well as it can be handled. We are only now, with gradual increment of reprints, beginning to recognise the merits of this uncouth, peculiar form of verse. We can now recognise that the fourteener of Chapman's *Iliad* is not the true fourteener, but almost an exercise, with a different vocabulary, in an already archaic form. By the time that Chapman wrote, the English vocabulary had so altered that this metre was obsolete. To find the fourteener vocabulary, at its most typical and also (we must admit) sometimes at its worst, we can go to the *Tenne Tragedies of Seneca*. Our only complaint against Dr Boas's admirable introduction is that he gives the impression that Turbervile is extreme in quaintness where he is moderate. In apologising for the necessity for his excellent glossary Dr Boas says:

> Perhaps nothing is more striking in Turbervile's use of words than his predilection for colloquialisms, and for terms that have for us somewhat mean or grotesque associations. Sometimes these lend additional force to his version, as when Paris describes Menelaus as 'a rascall and a snudge', or 'that same unworthy patch.' But more often they break the spell of the poetry and bring us up with a jerk. Even allowing for the subtle changes in the associations of words between Tudor times and our own . . .

With all respect for Dr Boas's scholarship, he seems here to have exaggerated. For one thing, there were 'subtle changes' of the associations of words between very early Tudor and late Tudor (Elizabethan), or at least between early Tudor and Jacobean, which are to be considered before we contrast the Tudor language with our own. For another, these 'mean' and 'grotesque' terms belong to the early Tudor vocabulary; and the more we saturate ourselves in the period the less these terms 'break the spell of the poetry', for they are of the tissue of that poetry and of that metre. You find more of them in Turbervile's twelve and fourteen syllable verses than in his blank verse, interesting as the latter is; and to many persons Turbervile's twelve and fourteen syllable verses will seem more spirited than his blank verse. But in particular Turbervile is really moderate in grotesqueness. The examples that Dr Boas quotes can not only be paralleled but exceeded from the work of Heywood, Newton and the other translators of Seneca:

> O wanny jaws of Blancke Averne, eake Tartar dungeon grim,
> O Lethes lake of woful Soules the joy that therein swimme,
> And eake ye glummy Gulphes destroy, destroy me wicked wight
> And still in pit of pangues let me be plunged day and night.
> Now, now, come up ye Goblins grim from water creekes alow.

This is from Studley, a translator inferior to Heywood. It has charm, but it is much more grotesque than Turbervile. Turbervile is a classic English writer, in that he avoids the excesses of his own type of verse, though he writes it naturally and spontaneously.

Dr Boas concedes that Ovid's style 'has often a well-bred familiar ease, but is misrepresented by anything that savours of pedestrianism or rusticity'. We doubt whether the vocabulary of Turbervile, or even that of Studley, could be called 'rustic' by the standards of its own time. It has nothing to do with the deliberate and artificial rusticity of the *Shepherd's Calendar*. The statement is true of Ovid in general; but we might add that, in English translation, Ovid is equally misrepresented by anything that savours of modern scholarship or even of Augustan elegance. No one has translated Ovid better than Marlowe, who could not be called either rustic and pedestrian or pedantic; Golding follows next; but Turbervile is the third translator in the English language. It is open to question whether Miss Hester Sainsbury's undeniable talents might not have been better employed than in illustrating Turbervile. We should appreciate her ten illustrations better as a separate portfolio. There may be many persons able to enjoy both Turbervile and Miss Sainsbury; but some would prefer to enjoy them separately.

Mr P. E. More's Essays

Review of *The Demon of the Absolute* (New Shelburne Essays, Vol. I) by Paul Elmer More (1928).

TLS, 1412 (21 Feb. 1929), 136. Unsigned. Gallup C279.

Those who know Mr More as the author of the many volumes of 'Shelburne Essays', and of the five volumes entitled *The Greek Tradition*, will find that this first volume of 'New' Shelburne Essays is not merely a continuation of the old. In the former series, Mr More appears as a critic of the type of Sainte-Beuve, different from Sainte-Beuve by his wider range of literatures and his preoccupation with major, to the exclusion of minor, figures, and by a positive moral bent of Puritan origin. What connected these pieces of literary criticism was this moral interest, and the implications of his philosophic dualism. Since the last of the old series, Mr More has been following out the consequences of the Platonism which had always inspired his work, and in the latest of his *Greek Tradition* volumes, that on *Christ the Word*, has appeared as a champion of Athanasius and an interpreter of Greek to Anglican theology.

In this new volume he is not occupied with theology. The essay which gives the title to the book is much the longest and the most interesting; the second, called 'Modern Currents in American Literature', is an able criticism of some contemporary authors from the point of view of the older generation. The next four essays on Poe, Borrow, Trollope and Vaughan are studies in literary criticism; the last is the translation of an episode from the Mahábhárata. The new reader should be warned that the character of this book is miscellaneous, though the several items are excellent. For this reason we concentrate attention on the preface and the first essay, which together make up nearly a third of the volume.

The essay is a protest against certain modern tendencies in art and in philosophy, and it is to these tendencies that the author opposes his dualism. The demon of the absolute is for Mr More the spirit of heresy in all things: the human craving for unification which will push any theory to the extreme. There are, for the author of this book, certain absolute differences or gaps in the universe such as the gap between living and inanimate, or between mind and matter. In philosophy, we find that Mr More objects both to absolute idealism and to any form of materialism. In the theory of art, he devotes one chapter of this essay to attacking the doctrine of impressionism in criticism on the one hand, and that of absolute objective classification of works of art on the other hand. He points out, quite reasonably, that Anatole France's theory of critical caprice has very little relation to his practice, which was the exercise of a delicate sensibility trained by standards and traditions.

Mr More's comments on the absolute in literature and art are full of good sense, although somewhat distracted for English readers by his retorts to American critics of his own work. The section of this essay which has the most pertinence and the liveliest expression is that on 'The Phantom of Pure Science'. Mr More is naturally opposed to those modern developments of psychology of which Behaviourism is the extreme example and which would reduce ethics to biology. But he is also opposed to those scientists of whom Professor Whitehead is the most conspicuous, who would span the gulf between religion and science. This essay is one of the best pieces of criticism of the Whitehead philosophy that has been written. The author points out some of the most remarkable ambiguities in Professor Whitehead's theories, and asserts the uselessness of Professor Whitehead's God in religion:

> Formerly it was held that the human soul obeys the same laws as a stone; now we are to believe that a stone is of the same nature as the soul. In either case we avoid the discomfort of a paradoxical dualism and reduce the world to a monism which may plausibly call itself science, though as a matter of fact Mr Whitehead's theory, if carried out, would simply abolish science.... Mr Whitehead discards the traditional scientific materialism for an alternative doctrine of organism, that is, for a theory of *organic mechanism*. Well and good. But is it unkind to ask the use of talking about an organical explanation when you do not know what you mean by organism, or to hint that no very clear idea will be evoked by joining together two unknown quantities, organism and mechanism, and calling the world an organic mechanism?

In the essay from which we have just quoted Mr More has not elaborated his own theory of dualism explicitly. For that we must go to those parts of his work which deal directly with Plato and Platonism. We can go also to the work of his friend Professor Irving Babbitt, whose views in philosophy and literature are closely similar. We may further observe that the theories of More and Babbitt are very much in the current of the present time. Mr More's essay would, we think, be approved by Mr Wyndham Lewis, and his dualism is remarkably similar to the theory of discontinuity put forward by the late T. E. Hulme. In the remarkable posthumous volume of Hulme's notes which was published under the title of *Speculations*, Hulme outlined in a few rough notes a philosophy very similar to that of Mr More and Mr Babbitt. At the beginning of a draft entitled 'Humanism and the Religious Attitude' Hulme says:

One of the main achievements of the nineteenth century was the elaboration and universal application of the principle of continuity. The destruction of this conception is, on the contrary, an urgent necessity of the present.

Originally urged only by the few, it has spread – implicit in the popular conception of evolution – till it has attained the status of a category. We now absorb it unconsciously from an environment already completely soaked in it; so that we regard it, not as a principle, in the light of which certain regions of fact can be conveniently ordered, but as an inevitable constituent of reality itself. When any fact seems to contradict this principle, we are inclined to deny that the fact really exists. We constantly tend to think that the discontinuities in nature are only apparent, and that a fuller investigation would reveal the underlying continuity. This shrinking from a gap or jump in nature has developed to a degree which paralyses any objective perception, and prejudices our seeing things as they really are. For an objective view of reality we must make use both of the categories of continuity and discontinuity. Our principal concern, then, at the present moment, should be the re-establishment of the temper or disposition of mind which can look at a gap or chasm without shuddering.

This theory of gaps, as it may be called, points in the same direction as Mr More's dualism. Readers should not be deceived by Mr More's apparently antiquated terms, mind and matter. Whatever terms we may use, the attempt of the demon of the absolute is always to reduce mind to matter or matter to mind; and the inevitable reaction of common sense is to answer each resolution of that kind by a new division. The gap, for Mr More, as well as for Hulme, is much more than a mere distinction between mind and matter. They both assert in effect that there is a gap between psychology and ethics; and that any so-called reconciliation between religion and science is nugatory, because there are no common differences to be reconciled. The other essays in Mr More's book are all excellent; but anyone for whom the first essay is the introduction to Mr More's writings should be advised to turn next to his book on Plato.

The Latin Tradition

Review of *Founders of the Middle Ages* by Edward Kennard Rand (1928).

TLS, 1415 (14 Mar. 1929), 200. Unsigned. Gallup C280.

This book consists of a series of Lowell Lectures delivered in Boston in 1928. Though obviously lectures, or obviously to anyone who has ever lectured, reproduced (in the author's words) 'substantially as they were delivered', and though decidedly readable, these are not popular lectures; the subject is too limited and the author too learned. The eight chapters have, as in such a course of lectures they might be expected to have, eight topics: one is on St Ambrose, one on St Jerome, a third on a man on whom Professor Rand is one of the greatest living authorities – Boethius. The period of Christian culture treated is mainly the fourth, fifth and sixth centuries.

Though each lecture may be read by itself, for information on its special subject-matter, at least two theses run through the whole and connect the essays. One is that the attitude of the Church towards classical culture was always double – an attitude of disapproval of pagan literature and learning was offset by one of pious preservation and enjoyment, so that Dr Rand is able to insist upon the continuity of the classical tradition in Christianity. His other thesis appears more fitfully, and rather in the guise of jocular slaps at Mr Paul Elmer More. It will not be wholly intelligible to readers who do not know Mr More's great work on *The Greek Tradition*, and especially the volume entitled *Christ the Word*. We may explain briefly that Mr More's contention is for the superiority of the Greek over the Roman tradition in orthodox Christianity, for the superiority of Greek theology, down to Athanasius, over Roman theology, and that Mr More finds in Latin theology, at the same periods and through the Middle Ages, an excessive imprint of the Roman legal mind, over-refining and over-defining. Without entering into any theological controversy, or revealing his own point of view in these matters – for his book is strictly concerned with literary, not theological, criticism – Dr Rand presents himself as a champion of the Latin tradition. Hence such pleasant asperities as calling Mr More a 'Binitarian *contra mundum*'. But as Dr Rand does not really tackle Mr More in this book, we must leave them to wrangle the matter, if they will, on some other occasion; meanwhile reflecting that the difference may be partly due to Mr More's being more saturated in the Greek and Dr Rand in the Latin Christian literature.

There is no doubt that Dr Rand is a very fine scholar, and a scholar of intelligence and wide sympathies. Perhaps there is no first-rate Latinist, whose primary business it is to teach the Latin classics, who knows so well, and so *humanely*, the literature of Christian Rome. He shares the high view of humanism of his colleague Irving Babbitt, whom he quotes; and he carries his learning lightly and gracefully. His book, though crowded with suggestion, can be read through at a sitting. But each part, as we said, has its particular subject. In connexion with his first thesis, that of the continuity of pagan and Christian culture, he insists again and again upon the importance of Cicero to the early Christian writers. In one essay of much interest ('St Augustine and Dante') he takes pains to show the influence of classical culture, and particularly the influence of Cicero, upon Augustine, and through Augustine upon Dante. And Dr Rand is manifestly qualified in temper to sustain his own thesis, for he manifests throughout a balanced sympathy both with classical Roman thought and with the Catholic Church.

Dr Rand hardly touches upon the literature of the High Middle Ages, and therefore his essay on 'The New Poetry' is mainly a defence and exposition – and a persuasive one – of the poetry of Prudentius. The hymns of St Ambrose are the only hymns of the canonical Latin hymnology to come within his field in this book. This essay is full of curious and fertile suggestions. Dr Rand quotes a hymn of Ambrose,

> Inventor rutili, dux bone, luminis,
> Qui certis vicibus tempora dividis,
> Merso sole chaos ingruit horridum,
> Lucem reddite tuis Christe fidelibus.

To remind us that the author probably had in mind the line of Horace,

> Lucem redde tuae, dux bone, patriae.

The least satisfactory of the essays, good as it is, is that on 'St Ambrose the Mystic'. Like the essay on St Jerome, it is a capital introduction to the subject. But Dr Rand, who ought to know, and indeed does know, what medieval mysticism is, as he appreciates St Bernard and the Victorines, does not make out a very good case for St Ambrose as a mystic. 'A sure path to mysticism is through allegory,' he says. Mysticism is frequently allied to allegory; but it was a slip to call allegory a *path* to mysticism. What is most interesting in the essay is, again, the collocation of Ambrose with Cicero; but in choosing a title Dr Rand has for once gone astray. The book is to be commended to every student of letters; but in mentioning Dr Rand as one of the finest classical scholars and humanists of our time we may be permitted to add that we expect from him something more substantial than this book or than his charming little introduction to Ovid which was published a year or two ago.

A Commentary

C., 8. 32 (Apr. 1929), 377–81. Unsigned. Gallup C282.

THOUGHTS ON A GENERAL ELECTION

Everyone who cares for civilisation must dread and deplore that waste of time, money, energy and illusion which is called a General Election. No country pays so heavily for this undesirable luxury as Britain. In France political changes occur so frequently as to be indifferent; in America the recurrence of the malady is arranged every four years, and is rendered comparatively harmless by the fact that the results are usually known a year or two beforehand. But in Britain an election is still, more or less, what it pretends to be: its results cannot always be predicted. All that can be predicted this year is the usual waste of time, money and energy, a very small vote in consequence of the increased number of voters, and the return, known to Dryden, of 'old consciences with new faces'.

THE LITERATURE OF POLITICIANS

Once upon a time there was supposed to be a sort of gentlemanly accord, even occasionally a union, between politics and literature. That was in the days before politics had been associated rather with the principles of cricket – even that jolly political game has vanished. The terms [378] between politics and literature were so amiable that the statesman at least made some attempt to preserve the elements of prose style. Perhaps British statesmen once had more leisure, time to re-read their sentences, and even look up their words in a dictionary. Mr Lloyd George was always a busy little man. But it is no relief to turn from his periods to the dreary sermons of Mr Ramsay Macdonald. And if we proceed from bad to worse, we arrive at length at the prose style of Mr Winston Churchill. Beyond a certain point, degrees of inferiority are indifferent; and in this sense there can be nothing appreciably worse than the style of Mr Churchill's recent reminiscences in *The Times* newspaper. There may even be reason to fear that the Home Secretary, and perhaps all future Home Secretaries, may be so busy censoring English prose that they will have no time to study the art of writing and speaking it.

In our ideal Platonic Republic, of course, the country would be governed by those who can best write and speak its language – those, in other words, who can best think in that language.

THE POLITICS OF MEN OF LETTERS

Meanwhile, in spite of Monsieur Benda, men of letters will go on worrying about the principles of politics. They are in fact the only men who do worry about its principles. Mr Bernard Shaw and Mr H. G. Wells, though birds of the same nest, do not always agree; and the pair of them seem to have little in common with Mr Wyndham Lewis (*not* D. B. Wyndham Lewis). Yet they are all worried about politics, and they all incline in the direction of some kind of fascism. Mr Wells's fascism, it is true, is disguised behind the violent caricatures which he has drawn of Mussolini, and we do not suppose that he would be as well received in Italy as Mr Shaw. But it is merely that Mr Wells, during his afternoon naps, still dreams of Liberalism; while Mr Wells, in his morning [379] hours, makes hasty blue-prints of a really efficient administration. The aging Fabians, like the solitary artist, are more and more sympathetic towards some kind of autocracy.

This tendency deserves very serious consideration, for owing to the writings of these authors and others, it will become the instinctive attitude of thousands of unthinking people a few years hence. It will be sympathetic to the workman who does not want a vote which he shares with the young women on the street corner. At present, it is a natural attitude for the restive intellectual, and has considerable justification. There are qualifications to be drawn, however, before it is too late. The extreme of democracy – which we have almost reached – promises greater and greater interference with private liberty; but despotism might be equally despotic. There is a difference between democracy and self-government. In complete democracy, everyone in theory governs everyone else, as a kind of compensation for not being allowed to govern himself. The advantage of overt dictatorship is that the authority has to take the responsibility for its own actions; whereas under democracy it can always pretend that it is giving the people what the people demands. A rational government would be one which acted for itself in matters concerning which 'the people' is too ignorant to be consulted (and would not pretend otherwise); which acted for the people in matters in which the people does not know its own mind; which did as little governing as possible; and which left as large a measure of individual and local liberty as possible. There are of course many more matters in the modern world than ever before, in which a central government must exercise its authority over the whole country: a parish cannot be allowed to neglect its sanitation, or its insect pests, or its control of its part of a river, because that would cause injury to its neighbours. In the banking system – which is a form, and perhaps the most important [380] form, of government – some mediation has to be found between central authority and local independence.

We are in agreement with the eminent men of letters mentioned, in wishing to see the strengthening of central authority, the establishment of continuity in central policy, and its liberation from the humbug of pretending to act upon public opinion. Mr Wells's blue-print committees of experts represent of course the particular route that Mr Wells's mind has travelled: he retains a kind of Liberal optimism about Simon-commissions and Melchett-conventions. It is possible that Lord Melchett might be able to rule British industry entirely to its advantage. But Mr Wells would say that that is because Lord Melchett is an 'expert'; we should say that it is because Lord Melchett is the independent and intelligent Alfred Mond.

The men of letters seem to agree, and a great many obscure people will agree with them, that to have one fifty-thousandth part in choosing a representative (of whom one may know next to nothing) who himself will have only a small part in indicating the nomination of a Prime Minister who will himself be obliged to choose his Cabinet for various reasons, is a very poor kind of 'self-government' for a human being put in the world to form his own character and work out his own salvation. The ordinary man will add that it is difficult to choose between a Conservative Party which seems to have no programme, and a Labour Party which seems to have any number of inconsistent programmes. And the programme of a party on election-day is not necessarily the programme of the same party in office. All these reflections are common-place. We are not here concerned with the statistics of the coming election, but with the general state of mind five, ten or twenty years hence. If, as we believe, the indifference to politics as actually conducted is growing, then we must prepare a state of mind towards something other than the facile alternative of communist or fascist dictatorship.

[381] LAST THOUGHTS

After all, the purpose of government is, or should be, the happiness of the governed *in a good life*. But it is as immoral to *compel* a man to lead a good life – which of course being compulsory would not be really good – as to allow him to ruin himself. It is right to protect a man against his neighbours; but the reminder to Censorships is, that there is a very fine line of discrimination between the morality of protecting a man against his neighbours and the immorality of protecting him against himself.

[Works by Conan Doyle and A. K. Green]

Review of *The Complete Sherlock Holmes Short Stories* by Sir Arthur Conan Doyle (1929), and *The Leavenworth Case* by Anna Katharine Green (1928 edn).

C., 8. 32 (Apr. 1929), 552–6. Signed 'T. S. Eliot'. Gallup C283.
A superfluous comma after 'Police' in the penultimate paragraph
has been removed.

It might seem that Father Knox, in his definitive *Studies in Sherlock Holmes* (V, 'Essays in Satire', pp. 145 ff.) had said the last word on Sherlock Holmes: yet he overlooks several interesting points, and commits one gross error in saying that Rouletabille was the *natural* son of Ballmayer, when it is essential to the plot of *The Yellow Room* and *The Lady in Black* that he should be the *legitimate* son (his parents were married, if my memory is correct, in Cincinnati, Ohio); and says himself that a full examination would occupy two terms' lectures. There may therefore be a few matters still unexplored. One is this: why do these stories, in spite of their obvious defects from our present high standards of detective fiction, reread so much better than *The Leavenworth Case*?

I believe that *The Leavenworth Case* was the first detective story that I ever read; and that must be nearly thirty years ago. I wish that Messrs Gollancz, instead of merely reprinting it without explanations, had prefaced it with a biographical notice of Mrs Green, the author. She deserves that honour. It is true that she wrote only one other tale which at all approaches *The Leavenworth Case*, and I have forgotten its name; but she was deservedly popular towards the end of the nineteenth century, at a time when good detective fiction was not plentiful as blackberries. This book is still readable; but it is unfair to its author to present it among the fiction of the year without an explanation. It is still more interesting now, as a document upon sentimental taste in New York in the eighties and nineties, than as detective fiction.

We have now come to a point of time at which it begins to be possible to separate with some assurance the permanent from the transitory in detective fiction. We have two standard works by which to judge: *The Moonstone* of Wilkie Collins and *The Murder of Marie Roget* of Poe. *Edwin Drood* may be a third, but that would be in the same type as Collins. These stories are at least as interesting as they ever were. *Sherlock Holmes* is *almost* as interesting as he was, but with a distinct shade of difference; *The Leavenworth Case* has faded. Why?

The detective interest is a special one. *Marie Roget* is the purest of all detective stories, for it depends upon no 'human' interest [553] or interest of detail. Mr Croft, at his best, as in *The Cask*, succeeds by his thorough devotion to the detective interest; his characters are just real enough to make the story work; had he tried to make them more human and humorous he might have ruined his story. The love-interest in *The Cask*, is a postulate; it does not have to be developed, and puts no strain upon the author. But a writer may, like Collins – and that is his peculiar merit – reinforce detective interest by other interests. Collins had a wider gift for drama and fiction. The one thing not to do is to muddle the interests; as, to arouse detective hopes and provide only human satisfactions – or vice versa. It is here that Mrs Green failed. She did not realise that unless one can create permanent human beings, one had better leave one's figures as sketchy as possible. She had great ability of the detective fiction order, but no firm control. Possibly, for her time, the public was not educated up to *The Cask* or *The Benson Case*. Yet her contemporary, Holmes, survives.

Both books 'date', but there are two ways of dating. Sherlock Holmes reminds us always of the pleasant externals of nineteenth-century London. I believe he may continue to do so even for those who cannot remember the nineteenth century; though I cannot imagine what it would be like to read him for the first time in this volume, without the old illustrations. I wish that Messrs Murray would bring out another volume with the old illustrations: I cannot even remember the name of the artist: but I remember the hansom cabs, the queer bowlers, Holmes's fore-and-aft cap, Holmes in a frock coat after breakfast, Sir George Burnwell when he 'took down a life-preserver from the wall'. But in the Sherlock Holmes stories the late nineteenth century is always romantic, always nostalgic, and never merely silly.

It is a great convenience to the critic to be able to compare what he is writing about with something else. But I cannot think of anything to which to compare Sherlock Holmes. He does not seem to be descended from either Sergeant Cuff or Monsieur Dupin. His relationship to Lecoq is quite superficial. He has had, on the other hand, a numerous progeny. So has Professor Moriarty. Only Mycroft Holmes, that colossal genius, has, so far as I know, no descendants. In Arsène Lupin, even in Raffles, we distinguish the features of the Robin Hood type. But Holmes was always reticent about his family: in fact he has no family to be reticent about. Another, and perhaps the greatest of the Sherlock Holmes mysteries [554] is this: that when we talk of him we invariably fall into the fancy of his existence. Collins, after all, is more real to his readers than Cuff; Poe is more real than Dupin; but Sir A. Conan Doyle, the eminent spiritualist of whom we read in Sunday papers, the author of a number of exciting stories which we read years ago and have forgotten, what has he to do with Holmes? The only analogies are such as make the case more puzzling. We can think of Sam Weller without thinking of Dickens, or of Falstaff or

Hamlet without thinking of Shakespeare: yet we do not compare Conan Doyle with Dickens or Shakespeare. Even Holmes's reality is a reality of its own kind. Never is he impeccable. He employs the most incredible disguises: in a good modern detective story, such as Mr Freeman's, the author realises the need for apologising for disguises by explaining carefully how they were done. (sc. *Angelina Frood*). It was wrong of him to go mountain climbing in Switzerland when he could better have eluded Moriarty in London. The last two volumes show him in mental decay: he repeats himself; in *His Last Bow* he descends to the level of Bull-Dog Drummond; he repeats the name Carruthers for a new character, and again uses the name Lucas for another shady foreign gentleman of humble extraction. *The Lion's Mane* and *The Devil's Foot* are merely bits of natural history unworthy of a detective. And yet, if all the contemporary detective story writers brought out new books at the same time, and one of them was a new Holmes, it is the Holmes that we should read first.

It is of course, the dramatic ability, rather than the pure detective ability, that does it. But it is a dramatic ability applied with great cunning and concentration; it is not spilt about. The content of the story may be poor; but the form is nearly always perfect. We are so well worked up by the dramatic preparation that we accept the conclusion – even when, as in *The Red-Headed League*, it is perfectly obvious from the beginning. (By the way, was bank robbery subject to capital punishment at that epoch? or else why should John Clay, when caught, have exclaimed 'I'll swing for it'? This is one of the minor points which Father Knox seems to have overlooked. And what sort of garments did burglars wear, when Athelney Jones tore off Clay's accomplice's coat-tails?). Also, it must be remarked that the author (for we must mention Sir Arthur now and then) shows wisdom or instinct in keeping the sentimental interest down. Several times he trips: in *The Solitary Cyclist*, for instance, the phrase, 'we may save her from the worst fate that can befall a woman', [555] might date the story fifty years before it was written, as well as the 'forced marriage' which follows. In *The Second Stain* (the plot of which follows *The Naval Treaty*, precedes *The Bruce-Partington Plans*, and turns up again, reinforced by a comic page-boy who would make a good part for Ernie Lotinga, in *The Mazarin Stone* – and by the way, in the last of these, 'Count Negretto Sylvius' is a name unworthy of the inventor of Dr Roylott of Stoke Moran, as the personage is unworthy of the inventory of Professor Moriarty) in *The Second Stain*, I repeat, the Lady Hilda Trelawney Hope is a preposterous figure. *An indiscreet letter written before my marriage – a foolish letter, a letter of an impulsive, loving girl*: that sort of letter would not serve in a detective story now, though we sympathise with the author for what he had to be careful not to imply. But on the whole Sir Arthur kept the sentiment in its place; and it is superfluous sentiment that dates a detective story.

Now *The Leavenworth Case* is simply popping over with sentiment. And the sentimentality throws a spotlight upon every technical flaw in the plot.

> Seated in an easy chair of embroidered satin, but rousing from her half-recumbent position . . . I beheld a glorious woman. Fair, pale, proud, delicate; looking like a lily in the thick creamy-tinted wrapper that alternately clung to and swayed from her richly-moulded figure; with her Grecian front, crowned with the palest of pale tresses lifted and flashing with power . . . I held my breath in surprise, actually for the moment doubting if it were a living woman I beheld. . . . etc.

But this slumberous blonde is merely Mary; when it comes to her cousin, Eleanor,

> Here, description fails me; Eleanor Leavenworth must be painted by other hands than mine.

It is immediately certain that neither Mary nor Eleanor murdered old Mr Leavenworth: there is some dreadful mistake, and for most of the book, the toils close inexorably around the innocent. This sort of heroine belongs [not] to the Sherlock Holmes age, but to America, which was still apparently attached to the ideal heroine of the Wilkie Collins age. Sir Arthur never held up any of his tales with descriptions of this sort. *The Leavenworth Case* is a detective story of the period of transition. It has great merits. Mrs Green was so far as I know one of the first to use maps and drawings (before [556] Holmes used them) with an X to indicate the position of the body. She also had an expert to say whether a certain bullet came from a certain pistol. She was a thrilling writer in those days. And she has, I believe, influenced deeply the American, as distinct from the English, school of detective fiction. I seem to detect her influence upon even Mr Van Dine. In her later stories she inclined to over-elaborate machinery. In one called, I think, *The Circular Staircase*, people are killed by a leaden plummet which forms part of the ceiling decorations, and which is hauled up again into place by a wire; and there is an elaborate cryptogram hidden in some other preposterous place, which explains how to use the plummet. I recall a recent American tale in which a document which could easily have been left at a bank for safe custody is hidden behind a bookplate. Mr 'Van Dine', so far as I know the best of recent American detective writers, tends toward this vice (*videlicet* the turning of the key in *The Benson Case*, and the disposal of the revolver in *The Greene Case*).

But every writer owes something to Holmes. And every critic of The Novel who has a theory about the reality of characters in fiction, would do well to consider Holmes. There is no rich humanity, no deep and cunning psychology and knowledge of the human heart about him; he is obviously a formula. He has not the reality of any great character of Dickens or Thackeray or George Eliot or Meredith or Hardy; or Jane Austen or the Brontës or Virginia Woolf or James Joyce: yet, as I suggested, he is just as real to us as Falstaff or the Wellers. He is not even a very good detective. But I am not sure that Sir Arthur Conan Doyle is not one of the great dramatic writers of his age. And France, in the person of Arsène Lupin (about whom I hope to write at length) has rendered homage to him. What greater compliment could France pay to England, than the scene in which the great antagonists, Holmes and Lupin, are lying side by side on deckchairs on the Calais-Dover paquebot, and the London Commissioner of Police walks up and down the deck unsuspecting?

I do not wish to discourage the reading of Mrs Green's works. *The Leavenworth Case* is as well worth reading, for readers of current detective fiction, as any novel published since Mr Croft's *Starvel Farm*. Those who have not read it ought to read it; those who, like myself, have read it many years ago, will want to read it again.

Second Thoughts about Humanism

Publ. in *New Adelphi*, 2. 4 (June/Aug. 1929), [304]–10, and revised in *Hound and Horn*, 2. 4 (July/Sept. 1929), 339–50: Gallup C285.
Further revised in *SE*. See below, pp. 604–13.

The Tudor Translators

Listener, 1. 22 (12 June 1929), 833–4. Subheaded 'By T. S. Eliot'. Gallup C286.

In dealing with some of the greatest prose writers of the sixteenth and early seventeenth centuries, I do not mean to follow the method of history books. What I want to do is to give a kind of cross section of English prose at one time, mostly in the later years of Queen Elizabeth; and by putting one after other examples of very different kinds of writing, to illustrate the very great richness and variety of that prose. To me, the sixteenth and seventeenth centuries have always seemed the most exciting period of English literature, both in prose and verse. It was a time of many inventions, of very rapid development of every kind. In studying its prose, still more clearly than in studying its verse, we can watch the English mind learning to think and to speak: we see many people learning to think in English where before only a few people had thought in Latin and preparing a language in which anything could be expressed. I am not going to examine the whole process, but merely to try to show a few of the kinds of prose writing of the time, without which we should not have our literature or our language of to-day.

You may wonder at my beginning with translators, for translation does not seem to most people nowadays a particularly important part of literature. But the man who translated a famous Latin or Greek or French or Italian book into English was doing a different work, with different aims and standards, from the learned scholars who translate the classics nowadays. Their public was very different from the people who now read modern translations of Virgil or Tacitus in the Loeb Translation Series. Many of their readers were more like the novel-reading subscriber to a library when he takes home a novel translated from German or Scandinavian. He wants a good novel, and does not care much whether it be English, American, or a translation, except that in the latter he enjoys (or not) the local colour and foreign scenes. The Elizabethan reader of translations might or might not have heard of the author before he picked up the translation; but he read the book in the same spirit in which he would have read a book originally written in English. Obviously, the first task of the modern translator of a classical work is accuracy: if he mistranslates, or shows in any way that he is not a perfect master of the original language, the reviewer will find him out and denounce him directly. But if he translates into stale style, that is a minor fault; and scrupulous accuracy does not always allow a vivid style. That is inevitable, and it is right that a modern translation should be scholarly. But the Elizabethan translator had first of all to make a book that would interest readers of books. Sometimes, like Florio, who translated Montaigne, he happened to be so well qualified that we usually prefer to read him still in preference to modern translations; sometimes, like Adlington, who translated the *Golden Ass* of Apuleius (even the title is a translator's variation), the translation is so shameless as to be almost a different book. The differences between the King James' Authorised Bible and the modern Revised Bible only matter when some theological distinction is at issue, but Adlington's Apuleius is very different from Apuleius in Latin. It is quite certain that Adlington's knowledge of Latin was very poor, and that he depended upon a French translation, as he makes all the mistakes that the French translation made. It is natural that a popular thriller like the story of Apuleius, a genial tale of witchcraft and adventure comparable to *Dracula*, should be seized upon by a rogue of a translator who did not know his job; and that the Bible should be entrusted to the greatest scholars of the time, such as Bishop Andrewes: it is a fortunate accident that Montaigne should have been translated by a man who was at least bilingual. But what is important is that in Tudor times all of these people, from the eminent bishop who composed his own prayers in Greek and Hebrew, down to the hurried hack who translated from a translation, could write beautiful English.

They could do more than that. Their very freedom, in introducing to an eager public literary treasures for the first time, makes possible at best a kind of fidelity denied to the modern translator. They give the effect, and I imagine had much of the feeling, of men writing the books themselves; we often have the impression of men thinking the thoughts, and feeling the emotions of original authors. If you try yourself to translate from Latin or Greek, you are painfully aware of the differences between Latin or Greek ways of thinking and feeling and our own; even in translating a modern language into English, you are aware of the differences in mentality between any particular foreign people and your own. If you transmute the original too much, you falsify; but if you are painfully literal, you falsify, to the reader who does not know the original language, in a different way, and you do not even make sense. We know a great deal more about ancient Greece and Rome now, but the expansion of knowledge leaves less room for imagination. We have to use two terms: *translation* and *paraphrase*. In the former we are as faithful as possible, in the latter we are consciously unfaithful to the literal text, for the sake of catching the spirit and making English prose or verse with it. The Tudor translation was between translation and paraphrase.

Now when I said that all English authors were indebted to the translators, I mean several kinds of indebtedness. From histories and romances, the dramatists and poets were glad to borrow and adopt plots and even parts of the text. But there are larger debts of two kinds. First, the effort of translating into English so much literature of kinds that had not been written in English before, exercised the vocabulary as it had never been exercised before. Old words were sometimes revived, as Spenser deliberately revived them in his original poetry; new words had to be coined; popular idioms and proverbial phrases were given literary standing and preservation; meanings of words were developed. We see a similar process nowadays only when a new science is developed, and new words have been hurriedly constructed out of Greek and Latin roots, or imported from France or Germany. When it is merely a new science that is in question, we may often well wonder whether the language is not worse off than before. But the English of the sixteenth century were not merely learning new sciences, they were learning to think and to express themselves. And this leads us to the second great debt of every writer to the Tudor translators: their work with vocabulary and syntax was teaching the English mind to think in English, was maturing emotions, too. When Henry VII came to the throne, the English mind, and the civilisation that expressed it, was cruder by a century than the French mind, and still further behind the Italian. By the time of Charles II, it had caught them up. In this process, the part played by a book of the importance of Montaigne's *Essays* is incalculable. England had not yet produced a man as mature, as civilised, as Montaigne; but here he was, translated into such English that his thoughts could now be thought in English.

No one, I think, can read *Hamlet*, especially after reading the earlier plays in order, without feeling that this play represents some deep emotional and intellectual crisis in the life of the poet. Its tone is different from that of his earlier [834] plays, and is continued and transcended in the later plays. Whatever the emotional experience in Shakespeare's life may have been we shall perhaps never know, and have no business to ask; but there is very little doubt that his mind, just at this time, was fed and sustained upon the thought of Montaigne in Florio's translation. Florio appeared in good time for Shakespeare to have read the book before *Hamlet*: it was a popular, widely-read book. Hamlet in his meditations is almost a more intense projection of one aspect of the brooding inquisitiveness of Montaigne. Read especially chapter XII of the second book of Montaigne (Vol. II in the 'Everyman' Florio), that longest and most curious of all his chapters which is entitled the 'Apologie of Raimond Sebond'. One must read it all and slowly, for this is not a case of verbal borrowing, but of saturation in thought and feeling:

> When we dream, our soul liveth, worketh and exerciseth all her faculties, even and as much as, when it waketh; and if more softly, and obscurely; yet verily not so, as that it may admit so great a difference, as there is between a dark night and a clear day: Yea as between a night and a shadow: There it sleepeth, there it slumbreth: More or less, they are ever darknesses, yea, Cimmerian darknesses. We wake sleeping, and sleep waking. In my sleep I see not so clear; yet can I never find my waking clear enough, or without dimness. Sleep also in his deepest rest, doth sometimes bring dreams asleep: But our waking is never so vigilant, as it may clearly dissipate and

purge the ravings or idle phantasies, which are the dreams of the waking, and worse than dreams. Our reason and soul, receiving the phantasies and opinions, which sleeping seize on them, and authorising our dreams actions, with like approbation, as it doth the days. Why make we not a doubt, whether our thinking, and our working be another dreaming, and our waking some kind of sleeping?

You can, I think, turn to the pages of *Hamlet*, the lines of Hamlet, of which this passage rouses an echo in your minds.

I have chosen North's *Plutarch* also because of Shakespeare. Not because I think it is the best of all the translations. If comparison could be made at all, I should single out, after the Bible, Florio's *Montaigne*, Holland's translation of another work of Plutarch, the *Moralia*, and Sir Thomas Urquhart's *Rabelais*. North, like Adlington and others, made his translation from the French, but with the advantage of a very good translation in French, that of Amyot. North betters his original, and indeed his English is superior to Plutarch's Latin. But the best testimony to North's excellence is the use Shakespeare made of him: and I have taken North for this reason. You probably know quite well how heavily Shakespeare drew upon North for his Roman plays, and indeed that Shakespeare's knowledge of Greece and Rome was chiefly derived from it. But it is worth a moment, in the present context, to glance again at two brief parallel passages of North and Shakespeare in *Coriolanus*. Here is Shakespeare:

> If, Tullus,
> Not yet thou knowest me, and, seeing me, dost not
> Think me for the man I am, necessity
> Commands me name myself.

And North, in prose:

> If though knowest me not yet, Tullus, and seeing me, dost not perhaps believe me to be the man I am indeed, I must of necessity bewray myself to be that I am.

Shakespeare again:

> My name is Caius Marcius, who hath done
> To thee particularly, and to all the Volsces,
> Great hurt and mischief; thereto witness may
> My surname, Coriolanus: the painful service,
> The extreme dangers, and the drops of blood
> Shed for my thankless country, are requited

> But with that surname; a good memory,
> And witness of the malice and displeasure
> Which thou shouldst bear me; only that name remains.

And North:

> I am Caius Marcius, who hath done to thyself particularly, and to all the Volscians generally, great hurt and mischief, which I cannot deny for my surname of Coriolanus that I bear. For I never had other benefit or recompense, of all the true and painful service I have done, and the extreme dangers I have been in, but this only surname: a good memory and witness of the malice and displeasure thou shouldst bear me. Indeed, the name only remaineth with me.

My first feeling about these astonishing parallels is certainly not moral indignation against Shakespeare for robbing so openly; nor do I raise the cry of 'lack of originality'; no, I admire the self-confidence of the master, and the consummate skill of the man, who could, by altering *so little*, turn a piece of fine prose into a piece of great poetry. But, second, these verses of Shakespeare are a concentrated piece of literary criticism of the style of North. The fact that Shakespeare altered so little, is the best possible testimonial to the beauty of North's prose; and his alterations are a commentary on its limitations. Re-read the passages yourselves: Coriolanus IV. v. and North's Plutarch Coriolanus (Vol. III, p. 35, in the Temple Edition). Every change made by Shakespeare is not merely the change from prose to verse, but an absolute improvement in force, concision, and ease of syntax. The verse of Shakespeare is more mature than the prose of North; but it proves how very fine the prose of North is; and indicates one way in which the prose of the translators contributed to the development of the English language.

(From a talk on June 11)

The Elizabethan Grub Street

Listener, 1. 23 (19 June 1929), 853–4. Subheaded 'By T. S. ELIOT'. Gallup C287.

I call this 'The Elizabethan Grub Street' instead of 'Elizabethan Novelists' for two reasons. Although most of the men I shall mention wrote novels or romances, among their many other tasks, it is their whole work in all its variety, not their novels by themselves, which throws light upon their time. And I wished to omit two novels which are not in the Grub

Street class: the *Arcadia* of Sidney and the *Euphues* of Lyly. The latter is a very dull book; the former I believe to be absolutely the dullest novel in the language. Both have much higher literary pretensions than my Grub Street work; and just because they are more studied and artificial and 'literary', remain as curiosities of the literature of a period, rather than as documents of life. And furthermore, it is not out of *Arcadia* and *Euphues*, but out of the work of the hack novelists and pamphleteers that the modern novel comes; for it emerges triumphantly in the work of a man who belongs to their type but wrote a more developed language and wrote with greater genius: Daniel Defoe.

Some of the more important of these men are Greene, Dekker, Nashe, Deloney, and Lodge. Greene and Dekker are particularly known as dramatists, but any of these men would have turned his hand to anything. They belonged to a new class of men which the Tudor age produced, and to which Marlowe himself belonged. They were mostly university men who, on coming down from Oxford or Cambridge, found themselves able to earn some sort of poor living by their pen. They were sometimes a little disreputable, and often lived recklessly and in great poverty, and wrote from hand to mouth; they were the first hack and free lance journalists whose life, even in the pages of Thackeray who has immortalised their nineteenth century descendants, has been made to appear more picturesque than it really was. This humble literary type is really a product of the sixteenth century. The universities bred a race of educated men who had no inclination for the church but found that they could write; the multiplication of printing presses, and the increasing popular demand for sensational reading matter as well as for plays, gave them an opportunity. They were proud of their academic distinction, and sported their M.A.s whenever possible; but they were rather despised, especially by such university pundits as Gabriel Harvey.

Their forms of composition are several. They were ready, as in the famous Martin Marprelate case, to write controversial pamphlets to order, mostly (as was the custom of the time) highly vituperative; political or theological pamphlets – for Church affairs were as popular and as acrimonious then as they are now. Another form of their activity has its parallel in the modern world; their exposures, or pretended exposures, for they had little scruple in mixing fact and fiction, of the life of the underworld. This perennial interest is, of course, for us very competently supplied by the daily press, though we require also our volumes of confessions of criminals, accounts of famous crimes, etc. One of the most resourceful masters of this form of literature was Robert Greene, who wrote several successful pamphlets on the art of 'conny-catching', that is to say, various kinds of thieving and swindling, as practised in London.

I must add that the authors of pamphlets sometimes pretended to be reformed thieves, sometimes to be merely public-spirited citizens; but that their intention was invariably to warn the public against the dangers and temptations of London. They mingled a certain amount of truth with what may be called realistic fiction, and in this prepared the way for their greater exemplar Defoe. Robert Greene was a resourceful [854] fellow, and managed to do well with a special line of his own, which was *deathbed confessions*. Two were published in one year, his *Groats worth of Wit Bought with a million of repentance* and *The Repentance of Robert Greene*. The fact that he repented and died so often has thrown some doubt on his sincerity, and obscured the genuine literary art which gives them plausibility and interest.

The Elizabeth public liked to have its flesh creep, and the horrors of the tragic stage were supplemented by the prose writers. Dekker, far above any other of the pamphleteers as a dramatist, wrote in several forms. His *Wonderful Year* is a grisly account of the plague in London, again anticipating Defoe; and the comparison with Defoe's *Journal of the Plague Year* has great interest in showing the swift development of the English mind. Defoe still makes us shudder by his plain matter-of-fact narration; his is a style which anyone would be proud to emulate; Dekker more often makes us laugh, for in his narrative are shrieking mandrakes, gibbering ghosts, and the other properties which only the poetry of the drama can make us take seriously. Yet in the midst of all this rubbish you find here and there a straightforward paragraph, a simple tale well told. In *The Gull's Horn Book* Dekker turns his hand to satirising amusingly the pretentious young man about town; in *Lanthorn and Candle Light* he rivals Greene in exposing villainies.

When these writers turned their hand to romance, it is precisely the qualities exercised by their pamphleteering that preserves their novels, and which gave rise to a new type of novel. The old type was chivalrous or pastoral; chivalrous so far as it derived from medieval fiction and pastoral in imitation of the late Greek and Latin through the Italian renaissance. The work of Sidney and Lyly is mostly pastoral. So is much of the Grub Street fiction, and that part of it is very dull reading. But there is another kind of fiction, represented very well in Mr Saintsbury's selection in the Everyman Library by Deloney's *Jack of Newbury*, and *Thomas of Reading*, and Nashe's *Unfortunate Traveller*. Deloney has, I think, been overrated in recent years, and especially by Mr Saintsbury.

But Thomas Nashe is a very great writer indeed, in his own way; the only one of the Grub Street prose writers to show real genius. His *Unfortunate Traveller* is the first really interesting English novel. The plot is extremely crude. The hero, Jack Wilton, is a pleasing rascal who serves a nobleman; the two travel through Europe, and a tenuous narrative links together various escapades in courts, camps and cities. What really keeps the story moving, although it also interrupts it, is Nashe's marvellous gift for words. He seems always intoxicated with his own vocabulary. If he has a piece of murderous villainy to describe, he speaks as follows:

> He grasped her by the ivory throat, and shook her as a mastiff would shake a young bear, swearing and staring he would tear out her weasand if she refused. Not content with that savage constraint, he slipped his sacrilegious hand from her lily lawn skinned neck, and enscarfed it in her long silver locks, which with struggling were unrolled. Backward he dragged her even as a man backwards would pluck a tree down by the twigs, and then like a traitor that is drawn to execution on a hurdle, he traileth her up and down the chamber by those tender untwisted braids, and setting his barbarous foot on her bare snowy breast, bade her yield or have her wind stamped out. She cryed, stamp, stifle me in my hair, hang me up by it on a beam, and so let me die, rather than that I should go to heaven with a beam in my eye . . .

and so forth. After a number of scenes equally thrilling, we are rather surprised to be told by the author towards the end of the tale: 'Prepare your ears and your tears, for never till this thrust I any tragical matter upon you.'

Nashe has a genius of torrential flow of language. Mr Wyndham Lewis, in his book *Time and Western Man*, has a good paragraph about Nashe, whom he compares with James Joyce, rather to the detriment of the latter. But there is great fun, besides great stimulus to one's own freedom in the use of words, in the reading of Thomas Nashe. Of all these men he is the greatest writer. He has a facility in coining and a resourcefulness in using words which make him comparable to Rabelais. His humour is by no means rabelaisian; that is to say it has none of the geniality. He writes most often to hurt someone. Combine the garrulity of Falstaff with something of the bitterness of Swift, and you have some approximation. A large part of his time was spent in attacking or defending; in the art of vituperation he has no superior; like other of his contemporaries, he knew something of the inside of prison life. Robertson says well of his style that he could 'stamp distinction upon scurrility and compass beauty of rhythm in a treatise penned either for writing's sake or for gain.' Much of his prose work is a part of that extraordinary controversy of anonymous pamphleteers which is known as the Martin Marprelate controversy; and much is devoted to his enemy, the Cambridge scholar Gabriel Harvey. In the novel, his masterpiece is

The Unfortunate Traveller. For a thrilling pamphlet about ghosts and apparitions, the *Terrors of the Night* has real beauty; in *Lenten Stuffe* there is a jovial humour; for invective, I think that *Have With You to Saffron Walden*, one of his attacks upon Harvey, is the top of his form. Unfortunately, these are hardly to be found except in the collected edition; and Nashe's very abundance makes him little read except by those who will take the trouble to find their way about. I will therefore quote from the only book, except *The Unfortunate Traveller*; that is *Pierce Penniless his Supplication to the Devil*, which, like most of the pamphlets by other authors to which I have referred, can be had in the admirable and cheap series of Bodley Head Quartos published by John Lane. (Price 3/-).

Pierce Penniless professes to be a hack writer who has fallen upon bad times. He decides to appeal to the Devil, who for some reason is out of town. The appeal itself, when Pierce has found a messenger to deliver it, is a defence of poetry very different from Sidney's, incidental to abusing every sort of evil doer except poets. While reviewing the Seven Deadly Sins, he finds time to explain:

> With the enemies of poetry, I care not if I have a bout, and those are they that term our best writers but babbling ballad makers, holding them fantastical fools, that have wit, but cannot tell how to use it. I myself have been so censured among some dull-headed divines: who deem it no more cunning to write an exquisite poem than to preach pure Calvin, or distil the justice of a commentary in a quarter sermon. Prove it when you will, you slow-spirited Saturnists, that have nothing but the pilfries of your pen, to polish an exhortation withal: no eloquence but tautologies, to tie the ears of your auditory unto you: no invention but here is to be noted, I stole this note out of Beza or Marlorat: no wit to move, no passion to urge, but only an ordinary form of preaching, blown up by use of often hearing and speaking: and you shall find there goes more exquisite pains and purity of wit, to the writing of one such rare poem as *Rosamund*, than to a hundred of your dunsticall sermons.

But when one becomes a little used to the long breathing sentences, the torrential phrases, and the perpetual surprises of conceit, one finds something more than archaic quaintness: one finds life in this style, a life from which our language can still be renewed. We look to old prose like this for two qualities. First, it issues from something inferior and proceeds to something better: it has the quality of development. Second, if it has more than merely historical interest, it has some quality peculiar to its own stage: something which had not existed before, and which is lost in the very process of improvement by the next generation. In the invectives and absurdities of Nashe there is this quality, which is *not* quaintness but the vigour of youth with its inexperience. To call such a style quaint is to lack imagination: for it is to view something as interestingly dead which is really interestingly alive.

(From a talk on June 18*)*

The Genesis of Philosophic Prose

BACON AND HOOKER

Listener, 1. 24 (26 June 1929), 907 –8. Subheaded 'By T. S. ELIOT'. Gallup C288.

In case this sounds rather forbidding, I must say at once that I do not propose to discuss either the philosophy of Bacon or the theology of Hooker; I wish only to consider the two men as great prose writers, and indicate their contribution to the English language which we use to-day. Think first of what would be left in English prose of the last years of Elizabeth without these two men. There would be the rich and lively prose of the translators, and the skilful popular journalism of the men like Greene, Dekker and Nashe. There would be a language well fitted for historical narrative, description, and even biography; a language fitted for splendid pulpit oratory, more gorgeous with Donne, more intellectual with Andrewes. And there is another prose which I have not mentioned and shall not discuss: the great prose of the great dramatists. I do not take it up here, because dramatic prose, being the brief give and take of dialogue, is a rather special type: but I would ask you to keep it in mind. It is difficult to discuss by itself: some of it, as in the comedies of Middleton, is related to the prose of the Grub Street writers; there is the heightened style of Jonson – the most intelligent man of his time – and finally there is the unique prose of Shakespeare, who was one of the greatest prose writers of all time. And by the way, we are apt to overlook the great prose of Shakespeare because of the drama and the greater poetry: but try the experiment of reading aloud a passage of his prose, say from the *Oxford Book of English Prose*, without informing your listeners of the author's name, and see the effect. There is no finer prose than Shakespeare's.

But if you took merely the writers whom I have already mentioned, and those with whom I shall deal later, and ignored Hooker and Bacon, I think that you would find in all of it either a certain boyishness, as in the people we looked over last week, or a certain pedantry and quaint stiffness, as in Donne and Andrewes, or a kind of luxuriance of style, as in

Donne and Andrewes and later in Jeremy Taylor, and especially Browne and Burton, all of which are qualities to be enjoyed, but which seem to us antique. Of all of the writers we examine, Bacon and Hooker seem to me among the most modern. That they are the fathers of modern philosophy and theology respectively is not the point with which I have to deal: my point here is that they are the fathers of the modern abstract style. We do not all study philosophy, but we must all make use of a kind of writing which these two men made possible; make use of it, I mean, either when we write or in much that we read. Any kind of argument, legal, political, or general; any kind of scientific exposition or explanation, from the theory of relativity to how to clean a typewriter or oil a motor car, owes something to Bacon and Hooker.

About the personalities of these two men, close contemporaries, I need say little. Francis Bacon, the great Chancellor, is too important an historical figure, and too picturesque and tragic a figure; there is the great essay on him by Macaulay, and the glittering portrait of him by Mr Lytton Strachey in his recent *Elizabeth and Essex*. About Richard Hooker, you can find out all you need to know from the introduction to the 'Everyman' edition of his great work, the *Laws of Ecclesiastical Polity*. If Bacon were alive to-day, he would be a K.C., earning, as he did in his time, a very large income; he would be a cabinet minister, or a cabinet minister out of office. If Hooker were alive to-day, he might be a Lady Margaret or Regius Professor of Divinity. Bacon's name would be known to every newspaper reader, Hooker's only in university and theological circles. The two men had no more in common then than they would have now; they certainly did not know the common work in the creation of English prose in which they collaborated; but as prose masters, after three hundred years, they are now equals.

I should not advise anyone to tackle Hooker, either in his great work, the *Ecclesiastical Polity*, or in his minor works, unless he is interested in the subject. Nothing is more dreary, or more deadening to this sensibility, than to read 'for the sake of the style' some book on a subject about which you care nothing. I think myself that the subject of Hooker's book is a very interesting one, and indeed very pertinent to some modern problems. For he set himself no less a task than a justification of the Church of England as against both Romans and dissenters, a task which involved a statement of the relation of the Established Church to the Civil Government. The nature of the task implies both philosophical training and legal gifts for its execution. I will not say that Hooker settled the matter once for all; for the problem is, if anything, more difficult and complicated now than it was then: my point is that he was dealing with a problem which is as much ours as it was his, and dealing with it as a master.

Although I do not wish to incite anybody to read Hooker unless he is interested in the subject, I should like to quote a passage almost at random, to show the maturity of Hooker's prose:

> Some things are so familiar and plain, that truth from falsehood, and good from evil, is most easily discerned in them, even by men of no deep capacity. And of that nature, for the most part, are things absolutely unto all men's salvation necessary, either to be held or to be denied, either to be done or avoided. For which cause St Augustine acknowledgeth that they are not only set down, but plainly set down in Scripture; so that he which heareth or readeth may without any great difficulty understand. Other things also there are belonging (though in a lower degree of importance) unto the offices of Christian men: which, because they are more obscure, more intricate and hard to be judged of, therefore God hath appointed some to spend their whole time principally in the study of things divine, to the end that in these more doubtful cases their understanding might be a light to direct others.

Now there are obviously, in the choice and especially in the arrangement of words, a good many antiquities. Compare it with the writing of any good modern theologian, like Canon Rawlinson, or with one of the best written decisions of the Law Lords, or with the style of such modern masters of philosophical prose as Mr Bertrand Russell or the late F. H. Bradley, and it will appear obsolete. The style of Hooker, and the style of Bacon, have a stiffness due to their [908] intellectual antecedents being Latin and not English prose; and this stiffness continues in the next generation into the styles of Thomas Hobbes in his *Leviathan* and Edward Hyde, Earl of Clarendon in his *History of the Great Rebellion*. But it is the stiffness of the first exercises of the muscles and joints of English prose: you have only to read a paragraph from one of the early Tudor writers, such as Elyot or Ascham, to find it supple and subtle in comparison. And I must ask you to accept a distinction between this stiffness and what I call *immaturity*. One is a question of style, the other a question of mind. Read again something that you read in connexion with my last subject, something by Nashe or Greene or Deloney: these journalists will seem to you to have the mental development of boisterous schoolboys, but Hooker will seem quite grown up.

And the difference of mind will be still more obvious to the general reader when he takes up Bacon. The only readers for Hooker will be those who are interested in theology; but anyone who is interested in the history of the modern and the English mind must attend to Bacon. He wrote, among a great mess of work in Latin and English, two small books which anyone can buy and everyone should read: the *Essays*, and the *Advancement of Learning*, published in the Oxford World's Classics, each at two shillings.

I hope that some of you have at least looked at Florio's translation of Montaigne's *Essays*: you may even have read the 'Apologie de Raimond Sebond' and then re-read *Hamlet*. The form of thought of Montaigne's *Essays* undoubtedly supplied the inspiration to Bacon. The likeness, and still more the difference, is very interesting.

The prose of the *Essays* shows, certainly, a less mature mind than Montaigne's. Montaigne is a very highly civilised man indeed. I must confess that he is rather too civilised for me, and that I prefer cruder forms of literature: but that is an aside. But Montaigne, in his essays, is a personality: one feels that he is quite willing to give himself away, to admit his defects and peculiarities with a humorous detachment, and an entire absence of self-consciousness, vanity or pose, which is the mark of a highly civilised person. Bacon does not thus betray himself, and in this is inferior to Montaigne. And yet for England to produce the Essay at all, a highly cultivated form of thought, was a great step forward. And in his essays Bacon has a kind of polished ease which we have not met within in our previous Elizabethans, and will not meet again. He has that gift of putting what we have often thought vaguely ourselves, in a phrase which seems quite final. Here is a passage from his essay 'Of Great Place' which has application to Bacon's own life, and to the lives of any politicians of our own time:

> Men in great place are thrice servants – servants of the sovereign or state, servants of fame, and servants of business; so as they have no freedom, neither in their persons, nor in their actions, nor in their times. It is a strange desire to seek power, and to lose liberty; or to seek power over others, and to lose power over a man's self. The rising unto place is laborious, and by pains men come to greater pains; and it is sometimes base, and by indignities men come to dignities. The standing is slippery, and the regress is either a downfall, or at least an eclipse, which is a melancholy thing: *cum non sis qui fueris, non esse cur velis vivere*. Nay, retire men could not when they would, neither will they when it is reason; but are impatient of privateness even in age and sickness, which require the shadow; like old townsmen, they will be still sitting at their street door, though thereby they offer age to scorn.

This might serve as a funeral oration for a present-day politician. It serves also for the venal and corrupt politician, the great Chancellor, Francis Bacon, Earl of Verulam and Viscount St Albans, whose life twittered out at Highgate in 1626. But it was a very great thing, towards the end of the 16th century, for a writer in the English language to produce this kind of meditation; and almost every paragraph of Bacon's essays is as good as this. The writers we have examined before, and most of those we shall examine later, have, with all their virtues, the vice of long-windedness and diffuseness; often we can say of them as was said of a modern theologian, that they never use one word when four will do: but in Bacon you find the very mature virtue of concision and sparseness.

But to my mind – being, as I have said, not civilised enough to enjoy the Essay as much as some of my friends do – Bacon's most exciting book is *The Advancement of Learning.* It is not quite true that Bacon is the first modern philosopher – though Bacon is at least the compatriot of two and namesake of one, of the first modern philosophers: I mean William of Ockham and Roger Bacon. But he is the first modern English philosopher to write in English. It is true that he committed what he thought his more serious works to a rather third-rate Latin; but when he wrote in English, he wrote well. The first book of his *Advancement of Learning* is concerned with the advantages of learning in general: skip it and begin with the second book.

> The mathematics are either pure or mixed. To the pure mathematics are those sciences belonging which handle quantity determinate, merely severed from any axioms of natural philosophy; and these are two, geometry and arithmetic, the one handling quantity continued, and the other dissevered. Mixed hath for subject some axioms or parts of natural philosophy, and considereth quantity determined, as it is auxiliary and incident unto them. For many parts of nature can neither be invented with sufficient subtlety, nor demonstrated with sufficient perspicuity, nor accommodated unto use with sufficient dexterity, without the aid and intervention of the mathematics, of which sort are perspective, music, astronomy, cosmography, architecture, enginery, and divers others.

You might compare this passage with a paragraph from some good modern book explaining recent scientific theory to the general reader. Take Professor Eddington's new book *The Nature of the Physical World.* There is no living scientist of any where near Mr Eddington's eminence who can write better English, precise, spare, lucid, and free from unnecessary technicalities. But if you compare his writings with the *Advancement of Learning,* you will find certainly an immensely greater mastery of the subject than Bacon's – Bacon, even for his day, was inadequately equipped with scientific learning and practice – but no greater mastery of English. What Professor Eddington has to say could almost be said in the language of Bacon; what Bacon had to say could not have been said in the English language of a generation before Bacon.

> Bacon was no scientist; but what he had was an intuitive understanding of the future before experimental science, and a passionate faith in it.

It is not my business here to criticise Bacon's ideas: only to make two points. One, that Bacon, in the two books I have discussed, is certainly one of the authors we must read in order to understand the modern world; and two, that Bacon is with Hooker, otherwise so different from him in temper, the founder of the modern English prose style for philosophy, theology, law, science, and every form of prose in which exact reasoning, classification and exposition of ideas is the first thing; of prose which is truly prose, not merely prose aspiring after the condition of poetry. And of this kind of prose Bacon and Hooker have never been antiquated and will never be surpassed.

(*From a talk on June* 25)

A Commentary

C., 8. 33 (July 1929), 575–9. Unsigned. Gallup C289.

NATIONAL PRESERVATION

A good deal has been accomplished, during the last year or two, towards preserving monuments and places of historical interest or beauty; and much generosity, devotion and hard work have been well spent. Much has been done locally at Oxford and at Cambridge, and the danger and desecration of Stonehenge is known to everybody.

We choose this moment for expressing regret that none of the political parties found room to provide any programme of National Preservation among its mostly vague or dubious policies. For, as we have said before, our present behaviour is hardly more than hand to mouth, and should at least be supplemented by some far-sighted central direction. We say 'direction', rather than 'authority', because there are obvious demerits in replacing local zeal by central bureaucracy. Yet, while Oxford and Cambridge are comparatively able to look after themselves, there are many parts of the country, and isolated monuments, which cannot. A central Association could do much towards surveying the whole country, with an intelligent eye to necessary or inevitable developments, and calling attention in good time to those buildings and pieces [576] of countryside which may be threatened and ought to be preserved. But an organisation having government standing and government funds (to be supplemented, no doubt, by private generosity), could accomplish much more. What is needed is a working arrangement between central and local effort and between public and private responsibility.

There is all the more reason for some government responsibility, in that *any* government is (as at Lulworth) a possible offender, and a difficult one to bring to book. When reading the Liberal election pamphlet on unemployment, we reflected that this enthusiasm for construction might, in the name of making work, involve a good deal of destruction too, or at least of defacement; and some of Mr Lloyd George's phantom employees might well have been engaged on work of preservation.

We need a central organisation under government auspices and with government funds to deal with the country as a unit; if we cannot have that, there should at least be a central private association. Such a society should prepare, with the assistance of affiliated local societies, a report of the condition of every country and every village; and when any building or piece of country worth preserving is in danger, it should be ready at least to advertise the fact, and be able to arouse interest. It should be concerned with the City Churches as well as the Wye Valley; with buildings which are merely perishing from decay as well as those which are in risk of demolition. At present there is always the danger that while our attention is being directed to one menace something else will be happening of which we may not hear till too late. St Magnus Martyr was not as important as Stonehenge, but still it was not insignificant.

AN INTERNATIONAL AWARD

The *Criterion* is to co-operate with four other European reviews in presenting a new form of literary prize. [577] The five reviews – The *Criterion* representing Britain, *La Nouvelle Revue Française* representing France, *La Rivista de Occidente* representing Spain, *Nuova Antologia* representing Italy, and *Die Europaeische Revue* representing the German-speaking countries, will compose a jury to decide on the merits of unpublished fiction of suitable length submitted to it from each of the five countries in turn. As the project originated with the *Europaeische Revue*, it is right that the first competition should be for stories in German. The story chosen as the best by a majority of the jury will be published as nearly simultaneously as possible in the five reviews, but of course in translation. The intention is to follow the competition for German fiction, with awards to be made in the same way for the best stories submitted in English, French, Italian and Spanish. An announcement of the conditions will be made when the jury is ready to consider English fiction.

It is obvious that such an enterprise is sympathetic to a review like *The Criterion*, which has always tried to make known in England the best of foreign thought and literary art. We feel some pride in the fact that *The Criterion* was the first literary review in England to print work by such writers as Marcel Proust, Paul Valéry, Jacques Rivière, Ramon Fernandez, Jacques Maritain, Charles Maurras, Henri Massis, Wilhelm Worringer, Max Scheler, E. R. Curtius, and others. We welcome the opportunity of association with reviews of the same standing and of similar ideals in their respective countries. We hope to have the successful German story for publication in September.

THE DOLMETSCH FOUNDATION

A society was incorporated a year ago, under the presidency of Robert Bridges, which has not had enough notice. Arnold Dolmetsch has the gratitude and admiration of everyone who cares for music. His work in dis-[578]covering and interpreting old music, in the technique of copying the old instruments and in the technique of playing them, is known throughout the world. But it is not realised that Mr Dolmetsch has not yet communicated any share of his learning and accomplishment to more than a very few persons; and the Foundation is to serve the purpose of carrying on his work. It has already maintained one scholarship out of temporary funds and hopes to maintain such scholarships permanently, for the purpose of enabling young students to perfect themselves in Mr Dolmetsch's work. It also hopes to establish workshops for manufacturing and repairing instruments such as Mr Dolmetsch makes.

This is a society which deserves and needs the support of everyone. Full information can be had from the Secretary, at 37, Walbrook, E.C.4.

SECOND THOUGHTS ON THE BRAINLESS ELECTION

A number of kindly, tired gentlemen with hoarse voices and nothing to say, made speeches; when they found themselves forced to mention each other, their remarks were in the best of taste, if not always in the purest English. It was cricket, and extremely slow cricket. In their broadcast-oratory, they only omitted to do two things: split their infinitives, or produce a new idea.

We should not murmur a word of objection against the 'new faces' (not so new either) being provided with 'old consciences' (often quite satisfied ones), if we had any hope of their being provided with 'new ideas'. But who, inspecting photographs of the amiable Mr Macdonald,

Mr Thomas, Mr Henderson, or Mr Snowden (a lamb in economist's clothing), could still look for inventions and discoveries?

There is of course a great opportunity – for the Conservative Party; an opportunity which we are quite certain it will fail to seize. It is the opportunity of thinking in [579] leisure, and of appreciating the efforts of private persons who have committed some thinking already. The Labour Party is a capitalist party in the sense that it is living on the reputation of the thinking done by the Fabians of a generation ago (we do not know whether any Fabian veterans are still thinking or not). The names of a few men of brains (though not necessarily of sense) still lend it a sunset glory. The Conservative Party has a great opportunity, in the fact that within memory of no living man under sixty, has it acknowledged any contact with intelligence. And also it has a long, if extremely muddled tradition; or at least, it has a history which an agile mind at any time can manipulate into a tradition. It has, what no other political party at present enjoys, a complete mental vacuum: a vacancy that might be filled with anything, even with something valuable. Will it, during its holiday, be inclined to take any notice of the fancies of men who like to think, and do not want to hold office of any sort? We are ready to place a bet on the negative.

Mr Barnes and Mr Rowse

C., 8. 33 (July 1929), 682–91. Subheaded '*By* T. S. ELIOT'. Gallup C290.

I am gratified that my comments on the literature of Fascism, in *The Criterion* of December last, provided the occasion for the very able articles on Fascism and Communism by Mr J. S. Barnes and Mr A. L. Rowse respectively in the April number. My own rôle was merely to ask questions; but I find that Mr Barnes and Mr Rowse have suggested to me new, and I hope more intelligent, questions to ask. Indeed I think the interesting questions are those which can be asked of both parties or schools, for the most interesting is precisely the question of what the two political theories have in common. Between the exposition of the two causes there is one obvious superficial difference: that Mr Barnes, who is a friend of Signor Mussolini and a Director of the International Centre of Fascist Studies at Lausanne, speaks as a convinced supporter of fascism, whereas Mr Rowse, like some other intellectual students of communism, speaks rather (if I understand him) as a sympathetic critic. Yet the phrase is attributed to Mussolini that 'fascism is not for export'; whereas the protagonists of communism in Russia seem to be desirous of converting the whole world to the doctrine of Moscow. In spite of these and other contradictions I am by no means the first person to observe a family likeness between fascism and communism – Major Douglas, I believe, has called attention to it, among others: but perhaps it deserves reiteration.

One of the characteristics which the two doctrines have in common is certainly *familiarity*. They have both been already partially absorbed by the popular mind, so that, in the intellectual sense, there is nothing 'shocking' about [683] them; and as they seem to be so easily absorbed by the popular mind, one suspects that they must have a good deal in common with what was in the popular mind already. They are both, in other words, perfectly *conventional* ideas. When the ordinary man is terrified by the bogey of a fascist or communist dictatorship, it is not his *mind* that is terrified. He may be terrified by the notion that fascism may interfere with his right to 'brawl as he likes', or that communism may confiscate his savings, or merely by a vague prospect of bullets flying about the streets. If, on the other hand, you talk to him about the divine right of kings, or the advantages of an hereditary oligarchy, he will retort either with open derision and hearty giggles, or with the patient gentleness with which he treats a harmless maniac. These ideas, are, as ideas, and whether true or false, revolutionary; and a really revolutionary *idea* is often to be divined by the laughter it evokes. Fascism and communism, as ideas, seem to me to be thoroughly sterilised. A revolutionary idea is one which requires a reorganisation of the mind; fascism or communism is now the natural idea for the thoughtless person. This in itself is a hint that the two doctrines are merely variations of the same doctrine: and even that they are merely variations of the present state of things. Nothing pleases people more than to go on thinking what they have always thought, and at the same time imagine that they are thinking something new and daring: it combines the advantage of security and the delight of adventure.

Man can *believe* almost anything: his capacity for credulity is unlimited. Only, he makes one condition: that his old beliefs shall not be disturbed. (I distinguish between what he believes, and what he thinks he believes.) The wildest fancy, which does not touch his rooted beliefs, can be accepted; the strongest reasoning will be rejected with contumely if it injures one of these beliefs. It is easy to believe the proposition 'that the propositions of Einstein are true' – because they disturb nothing: the 'disturbance' [684] has all taken place in the minds of physicists. Facility of belief is of course irrelevant to the question of truth and error: I have merely made the point that neither fascism nor communism is now shocking or revolutionary to the ordinary mind.

I must hasten to declare that I have cleared my mind of any prejudice against what communists or Marxians call the 'materialist theory of history'. Marxians sometimes fear that outsiders will connect the materialist theory of history with materialism. There is an ancient and respectable philosophical doctrine called 'materialism', which is almost extinct; represented to-day by the eminent solitary figure of George Santayana. But what could this Aristotelian, neo-Thomist materialism of Mr Santayana have to do with a 'materialism' which issues almost directly from the brain of Hegel? The 'materialist interpretation of history' bears the imprint of its idealistic German origin: it might better be called the *fatalistic*, or even the *conventional* interpretation of history. For it seems to be merely a theory that things happen. I have no quarrel with Marx's 'materialistic interpretation' of past history, which is intelligent and within limits very illuminating, but this materialistic interpretation seems to be simply incompatible with *desiring* anything; or if not, then it is rather suspicious that what the communists say must come to pass should be so exactly what they desire to come to pass. Suppose that the materialistic interpretation of history had been discovered four hundred years ago by some capitalist intellectual: he might have said that 'capitalism' was something that was bound to be realised sooner or later. So the communist seems to say that communism is bound to be realised; but surely the 'materialist interpretation' of history ought to carry him further, and make him admit that communism is bound to lead to something else (if being is indeed becoming, as most people think); and that something else to something else; and finally to something that might horrify the [685] communist of to-day as much as communism might have horrified my imaginary 'capitalist' of four hundred years ago. In other words, this historical conception seems to me incompatible with *value*; for if all these things are bound to happen then there is no reason for preferring any state of things to any other, either earlier or later.

In fact, communism, so far as I can understand it, is like fascism and most political theories, in mingling science with feeling. I can see no reason why the theoretical communist should desire anything, since what he desires is bound to give place to something else. But if communism is *desirable*, then the materialistic interpretation of history does not matter a fig one way or the other.

In spite of the fact that the materialistic interpretation is not materialistic, I still fear that the word 'materialism' has some emotional charm for communists which I cannot share. I suspect, in fact, that the communist is under the spell of Victorian science. I turn for enlightenment to our refreshing contemporary *La Revue Marxiste*, and read in its manifesto the following:

> La croissance du prolétariat a contraint cette bourgeoisie à se replier vers des formes de pensée de plus en plus réactionnaires, à passer par toutes les nuances de l'idéalisme pour en arriver – en plein XX siècle – à reconnaître et à utiliser, dans son exploitation des masses opprimées, les aspects les plus grossiers de la superstition religieuse. Mais ce recul coincide avec le triomphe du matérialisme dialectique dans le mouvement. Le temps est venu d'armer le matérialisme présent et d'appeler les témoignages du matérialisme passé, inconnu en France, ou dénaturé.

This is a little hard on that large part of the French bourgeoisie which has fought the battle of anti-clericalism during fifty years, and which has not always had to employ 'the religious superstition' in order to oppress its inferiors; but what seems to me more deplorable is this flinging about of the magic word 'materialism'. If the defenders of communism reprehend its opponents for mistaking the use of the word 'materialism', then they ought to warn their own [686] friends to use it more cautiously. In the interior of the same review I found a very interesting essay by the late Nicolai Lenin, entitled '*De l'importance du matérialisme militant*'. According to Lenin, 'militant materialism' should be also 'militant atheism'. But he says further that 'militant materialism ought to make an alliance with the representatives of the natural sciences, who incline towards materialism'. It appears presently that the political materialist must try to bring in the 'natural scientists', even Einstein who 'does not attack the foundations of materialism'. The materialistic interpretation of history is of course like any other interpretation of history, an *aspect* of history. It is just as genuine an aspect as any other. Like every other interpretation of history, it asserts itself to be the 'fundamental' interpretation: and if one went into the matter thoroughly, one would question it, not from the point of view of any other interpretation, but from the point of view of an observer who believes that any interpretation of history is merely a selection of a particular abstracted series of causes and effects, and is valid only from a particular point of view. I suspect that the materialistic interpretation derives much of its cogency (like any other) from a sentimental prejudice: namely, for this interpretation, that the most important thing is that human beings should be fed and clothed and sheltered (which is not self-evident). I believe, that is, that *any* interpretation of history being a selection, is preceded by a valuation, which is a postulate and cannot be justified rationally.

I am quite ready to admit that the 'materialistic interpretation of history' is not materialistic; but quotations like the above make me suspect that the communist has also a sentimental attachment to the word 'materialism'; that he is, in fact, a French revolutionist a hundred and fifty years behind the times, as well as an Hegelian revolutionist. And to the Anglo-Saxons, accustomed to regard God with good-humoured tolerance, the 'militant atheism' is disturbingly silly.

[687] What I find in both fascism and communism is a combination of statements with unexamined enthusiasms. It may well be that in any political theory there must be this combination. But then it is the part of the political thinker to analyse these elements, and to recognise the *irrational* element in his own philosophy. But that is what political philosophers never do. Mr Barnes seems to me to confound the rational and irrational elements in fascism; and Mr Rowse seems to me to try to isolate the rational and ignore the irrational element in communism. It is true that the latter observes that the Russians 'are a great and gifted nation, and one cannot but think that a race of a hundred and thirty millions will be very important in world politics in the future'. Without denying the great gifts of the Russian races, I cannot see why a people should be important because of its numbers, except for a reason that Mr Rowse does not mention: that everybody else wants to sell them goods at a profit (and get paid.)

There is much in the essays of Mr Barnes and Mr Rowse with which I cordially agree. For instance, when Mr Rowse speaks of the 'revolutionary character of the bourgeoisie', I can only express assent: the bourgeoisie is timid in thought, and revolutionary in act. Nothing is more revolutionary than the two-seater.

> Merrily sang the monks of Cowley
> As Morris Bart. went driving by. . . .

But I want to know how much the verbal incantations count, in both these doctrines. It seems to me that any political theory ought to be analysable roughly into three parts: an economic doctrine, a wisdom (sophia) and an enthusiasm. And the political theorist ought to be quite clear in criticising his own theory, as to the distinctions; he should, so far as he can, isolate the irrational element and confess it frankly. What most do is to diffuse the emotional element through the theory, and so conceal it from themselves as from others, and become the servants, [688] not the masters, of words. By admitting to oneself the existence of the irrational nature of one's enthusiasm, it is possible to effect a kind of continuity between the enthusiasm, the wisdom, or humane knowledge of humanity, and the strict economic doctrine.

I do not mean that every political theory should be based upon an original economic doctrine: it may start from ethical or even theological premises; but it should have an economic doctrine appropriate to it.

What strikes me about the two doctrines I am criticising, and about much political theory, is the muddle of economics and enthusiasm for words. Nor do I suggest that political thought is impossible to anyone but an economist, for a glance at the world of economists would dispel this fancy. But one ought to know where things begin and where they end. The really interesting thing about fascism is its syndicalism, its organisation of workers, and its financial policy, if it has any. Order, Loyalty, realisation of the individual in the life of the State, are words of good implication and good report, which sum up the tendency of a mass of feelings in the mind of the person who uses them. But what the outsider would like to know is, first, to what the difference in economic theory between fascism and communism amounts. Mr Barnes tells us that 'Fascism would substitute for the commonly accepted contractual interpretation of the idea of the Sovereign People, the idea of the *sovereignty of the State machine*' – an idea, I should suppose, common to fascism and communism. He admits, further, that Fascism is not 'just a revolt against Communism'.

> The threat of Communism, which was the work of the non-combatants, provided merely the anarchical conditions which gave Mussolini and the ex-combatants their opportunity of sweeping away the old regime, which . . . had allowed Italian society to fall into a condition of practical anarchy.

It would seem from this that Fascism was a revolt against a *threat* only of Communism, but still more against an actual *anarchy*. No one can confuse communism with [689] anarchy. The revolt was against anarchy, but took a fascist instead of communist form: so its word became Nationalism instead of Internationalism.

Now I must confess, as an onlooker, that I cannot see very much fundamental difference between Nationalism and Internationalism: the first term can sound either more pernicious or more glorious than it is, and the second as well. The first exalts one particular group of men, the second (in theory) all mankind; and neither of these deities seems to me particularly worthy of worship. The wise man will pay due respect to both, the fanatic to one.

The test of both doctrines is of course their finances. Both doctrines are apparently anti-capitalistic. The essence of capitalism does not seem to me, as an ignorant observer, to be the division of humanity into those who live on earned and those who live on unearned income, but the concentration of power into a few hands; it is not the numbers of obscure though wealthy persons who can live on their dividends who matter – not the shareholder, but the active director. The interesting point about capitalism is its creation of economic or financial power, distinct from the political power, and in a way less responsible. If Italy or Russia wishes there to be but one power, they cannot afford, let us say, to borrow money from America. The interesting question to answer is whether Russia or Italy succeeds in concentrating all power into political hands, or whether they will merely evolve a *new* financial class.

I willingly concede to Mr Barnes that the philosophy of the *Action Française* is evolved from eighteenth century rationalism. What is important is the extent to which it has transcended its origins. I would point out too that its 'nationalism' (which was primarily a struggle against *internal* enemies, not an instrument of foreign aggression) is less nationalistic in essence than is fascism. The vital dogma is not nationalism but royalism. For it is not, as Mr Barnes thinks, a 'deification of the State', nor is it what Mr Barnes commends, 'the idea of the sovereignty [690] of the State machine'; it is the reintroduction of the idea of loyalty to a King, who incarnates the idea of the Nation. And in this idea is I think the *alternative* to Nationalism. Fascism seems to me rather (in the form in which it has succeeded up to date) to represent the Napoleonic idea. The latter, in contrast to the idea of Monarchy, is a familiar conventional modern idea: it is the doctrine of success. The feeling towards a dictator is quite other than that towards a king; it is merely the consummation of the feeling which the newspapers teach us to have towards Mr Henry Ford, or any other big business man. In the *success* of a man like Mussolini (a man of 'the people') a whole nation may feel a kind of self-flattery; and the Russian people deified itself in Lenin. Both Italy and Russia seem to me to be suffering from Napoleonism. And this does not strike one as an 'utter repudiation of materialism'.

To sum up. Both fascism and communism seem to me to be well-meaning revolts against 'capitalism', but revolts which do not appear to get to the bottom of the matter; so that they are likely to be merely transformations of the present system which will completely satisfy the materialistic interpretation of history. Their economic and political doctrines, which have much in common, are attached to enthusiasms which appear to be contradictory. Fascism supports the Church, Communism would destroy it. But neither attitude seems to me to have any necessary connection: an atheistical fascism, or a devout communism, is theoretically conceivable; but it is quite intelligible that local circumstances should determine the attitude in each place. Fascism is (begging Mr Barnes's pardon) nationalistic, and communism internationalistic: yet it is conceivable that in particular circumstances fascism might make for peace, and communism for war. The objections of fascists and communists to each other are mostly quite irrational. I confess to a preference for fascism in practice, which I dare say most of my readers share; and I will not admit [691] that this preference is itself wholly irrational. I believe that the fascist form of unreason is less remote from my own than is that of the communists, but that my form is a more reasonable form of unreason. But my chief purpose in venturing to criticise two authors immeasurably more learned and competent than myself, is to affirm my previous contention that neither fascism nor communism is new or revolutionary as *idea*.

[*Extraits d'un Journal* by Charles du Bos]

Review of *Extraits d'un Journal: 1908–1928* by Charles du Bos (1928).

C., 8 (July 1929), 762. Unsigned. Not in Gallup, but would be C290a.

Charles du Bos is a writer whose name is known to everyone who knows contemporary French literature, though he writes but little. This is a journal of a man of culture and taste and insight, who knows well several literatures, including English, and who in two volumes entitled *Approximations* has written some of the best pieces of contemporary criticism. It is, in fact, a book of some importance.

The Prose of the Preacher

THE SERMONS OF DONNE

Listener, 2. 25 (3 July 1929), 22–3. Subheaded 'By T. S. ELIOT'. Gallup C291.

In the classification of prose styles the theology of Hooker is nearer to the philosophy of Bacon than it is to the prose of Donne and other great preachers. The first represents an important step in the development of reasoning; the second represents a step in the development of oratory. However far apart in beliefs, the work of Bacon and Hooker brings us nearer to Hobbes and Berkeley and Locke and Hume; however different in subject matter and in style, the sermons of Donne bring us nearer to the speeches of Burke and other great politicians. They have a relation, on the other hand, to the more 'decorative' or 'poetic' prose in English; to Jeremy Taylor, of course, but also to De Quincey. In Hooker and Bacon we find what we may call 'reasoning in tranquillity'; in Donne we find 'reasoning in emotion'.

Up to quite recent times the sermons of Donne were hardly read except by the specialist in seventeenth-century prose; most people, if they have the prejudice that sermons must be dull, suppose that their dullness increases in direct ratio to their age. This is not true, for the best sermons of the sixteenth and seventeenth centuries are not only among the most interesting sermons in the language, but among the best prose of any kind in the language. Even to-day very few people have the courage or interest to read through the many volumes of Donne. But we had, a few years ago, the admirable selection of passages from these sermons edited by Mr Logan Pearsall Smith at the Clarendon Press. The chief defect in the introduction to this book, otherwise excellently critical, is that the editor did not appear sufficiently interested in the other preachers of the period; and the chief defect of the book is that the selections are all much too short, and give the impression that Donne in preaching was from time to time inspired to a paragraph or so of superb English between dreary wastes of antiquated theology. The truth is that Donne's sermons are brilliantly written throughout, and brilliantly constructed, with a beginning, a middle and an end. For this reason I prefer the selections, including one complete sermon, given by Mr John Hayward in his recent volume of Donne's poetry and selected prose published by the Nonesuch Press.

To put ourselves into a mood to read one of Donne's sermons, it is worth while reminding ourselves of the reasons for the popularity of preaching at that time. In the first place, theological questions were taken very seriously by everyone but the most ribald. Theology was, indeed, a very important part of politics, and politics meant serious matters of peace or strife, prosperity or persecutions. The English Church had a dangerous position to defend, and the security of Church was then one question with the security of Crown and State. With all questions of foreign politics, the relations of England with France, Spain and the Empire, was inextricably involved the question of Canterbury *versus* Rome; and a priest from Rome was regarded with as much suspicion, and was indeed in much greater danger at times, than a Russian Communist emissary is now. With all questions of domestic politics was involved the question of Canterbury *versus* Geneva and Zurich: that is to say, the struggle which culminated in the Civil Wars and the assassination of Charles I was the struggle between the Established Church and the Presbyterians, Independents, Anabaptists, Brownists, Family-of-Love and the other stern dissenting sects. A sermon, by an important preacher, in an age when there were no regular newspapers, had something of the excitement of an important political speech at a moment when people are politically excited.

The second reason for the popularity of the sermon is that it took the place now taken by many other popular Sunday amusements; the third to be remembered is the greater emotionality of the people. The beatitude of Paradise, the horror of Hell, could be painted in colours to delight or terrify the auditors. They were, I suppose, neither better nor worse than ourselves for being so easily moved; but they enjoyed themselves more thoroughly.

Donne was by no means either the first or the last of the great English preachers; I believe that his contemporary, Bishop Andrewes, is greater, and Jeremy Taylor certainly must take an equal rank. But Donne is undoubtedly the most readable. Hugh Latimer, Bishop of Worcester, was a great preacher and a great prose writer long before Donne; and you can read some of his sermons preached before Edward VI in a volume in the Everyman edition. The peculiarity of Donne is that he was not only a great prose master, but also a great poet, and in many passages in his sermons we are reminded that he is not only a theologian but a poet, and a very human poet too. And both as a poet and as a man, a very modern person. He imports into English prose two qualities for the first time – qualities which we find among his contemporaries only in the blank verse of Shakespeare and the highest passages of Shakespeare's dramatic contemporaries: a curious knowledge of the human heart, and a stateliness of phrase and image hitherto possible only in verse. As an example of the former a very well-known passage will suffice:

> I am not all here, I am here now preaching upon this text, and I am at home in my library considering whether St. Gregory, or St. Jerome, have said best of this text, before I am here speaking to you, and yet I consider by the way, in the same instant, what is likely you will say to one another, when I have done, you are not all here either; you are here now, hearing me, and yet you are thinking that you have heard a better sermon somewhere else, of this text before; you are here, and yet you think you could have heard some other doctrine of down-right Predestination, and Reprobation roundly delivered somewhere else with more edification to you; you are here, and you remember yourselves that now ye think of it: This had been the fittest time, now, when everybody else is at church, to have made such and such a private visit; and because you would be there, you are there.

Donne was in early years brought up, before deciding upon the Church of England, among Jesuit surroundings; his command of the terrors of death and damnation in other passages shows him a student of the Ignatian method; and I think he shows his training here too, in winning his auditors by sympathy and understanding, and suddenly pulling them up at the end. You would not find a passage like this in any other great contemporary preacher. He confesses later:

> I throw myself down in my chamber, and I call in, and invite God, and His Angels thither, and when they are there, I neglect God and His Angels, for the noise of a fly, for the rattling of a coach, for the whining of a door; I talk on, in the same posture of praying: eyes lifted up; knees bowed down; as though I prayed to God; and if God, or His Angels should ask me when I thought last of God in that prayer, I cannot tell: Sometimes I find that I had forgot what I was about, but when I began to forget it, I cannot tell. A memory of yesterday's pleasures, a fear of to-morrow's dangers, a straw under my knee, a noise in mine ear, a light in mine eye, an anything, a nothing, a fancy, a chimaera in my brain, troubles me in my prayer.

It is interesting to remark about Donne that although he appears first in history as a poet and aspiring worldly courtier, he betrays almost no contact with the literature of the time. [23] He never alludes to his contemporary dramatists or poets, and certainly shows no direct influence by them; yet we know that he sometimes frequented the society of Ben Jonson, who left a critical phrase and a commendation of Donne. We are apt to suppose that a poet of all people must have read a great deal of poetry, certainly that he must enjoy poetry. There are, however, poets who do not much care for reading poetry, and Donne was one of them. His poetic imagination was fed chiefly on works of theology and law. In his verse, he is a theologian and a lawyer, and in his theology, he is very much a poet. We admit that there are greater poets than Donne; we should, I think, admit that there are greater theological writers and greater preachers.

But it is this mixture that gives Donne the quality which we express by the feeble worn-out word 'fascination'. Hugh Latimer was adept in homely illustrations to drive a point home to an unlettered audience; Jeremy Taylor, in the next generation, has a sweetness and purity of tone unknown to Donne, Andrewes in his sermons, and Cranmer in his great prayer-book, rose to greater heights. But Donne could best appeal to the ordinary worldly person of his day and of our day; and being a poet, could appeal, too, to an audience educated in verbal beauty by the Shakespearian drama. In the following passage we hear, I think, in the voice of the preacher, the minor tones of Shakespearian drama. Donne is the contemporary of John Webster, John Ford, Thomas Middleton and Cyril Tourneur:

> Shall we, that are but worms, but silkworms, but glowworms at best, chide God that he hath made slowworms, and other venomous creeping things? shall we that are nothing but boxes of poison in ourselves, reprove God for making toads and spiders in the world?

shall we that are all discord, quarrel the harmony of His creation, or His providence? Can an apothecary make a sovereign triacle of vipers, and other poisons, and cannot God admit offences, and scandals into his physic?

And again, in the following, the poet speaks:

Methuselah, with all his hundreds of years, was but a mushroom of a night's growth, to this day. And all the four monarchies, with all their thousands of years, And all the powerful Kings, and all the beautiful Queens of this world, were but as a bed of flowers, some gathered at six, some at seven, some at eight, All in one morning, in respect of this day.

These are the sorts of passage to delight in first; we can then proceed to study the ingenuity with which Donne, in a long passage, will employ one simile, and develop it in immense detail. It is an old method in the sermon; it was used by the Buddha; you find it in Latimer's Sermons on the Card and on the Plough; it has been used again. But Donne has an exceptional fertility in detail. One specimen is found on p. 72 of Mr Pearsall Smith's selection 'The World is a Sea', in which he brings forth every possible interpretation of this metaphor. The Elizabethan congregation was prepared to stay a long while, to listen standing for two hours; and in a sermon of such length to such an audience it was highly desirable to hammer every point very hard indeed. And for such hammering Donne's metaphors and similes were perfectly adapted. And it is of interest that many of them, as every reader of his poems knows, were drawn from his personal experience; many are of seafaring, ships and tempests; and send us back to his early poems for reminiscences of his voyage, as an adventurous young man, long before he thought seriously of the Church, to the Azores.

And finally no one can fully appreciate the greatness of Donne's enrichment of English prose without reading carefully at least one sermon from beginning to end. His method is that of other contemporary divines, in so far as he takes his text seriously and searches for exact meanings in every word and phrase. There is invariably this process, in an age when the exactness of the biblical text was undoubted, and the verbal inspiration taken literally. The meanings of one small text may be many, but they are all based on the exact word. This way of dealing with the text of a sermon is remote from us, but it had its literary as well as its theological advantages: for in those days a text had to be something more than a *pre*text; and the reasoning from it had to be close, and the illustrations of it clear.

While insisting on the peculiar qualities of the prose of Donne, which make it unique in its own and any time, one ought to show him also in his place as one among the great divines of the English Church of that period, of whom Hooker is another, and Andrewes is another, and remark upon the extent to which not the Church only, but the whole of English civilisation, is indebted to those men. Without Hooker, the prose of the philosopher, the jurist, even of the scientist, would not have developed so rapidly; without Donne, the more ornate types of English prose, of Sir Thomas Browne and Jeremy Taylor, would not have developed so rapidly. And compare the prose of Donne with that of Thomas Nashe. Donne is of a more mature intellectual generation: not merely a greater writer, but more adult. There are 'poetic' passages in the prose of Nashe and his group: but with Donne the sensibility of the poet and dramatist is infused into a prose which is that of the man of thought.

(*From a talk on July* 1)

Elizabethan Travellers' Tales

Listener, 2. 26 (10 July 1929), 59–60. Subheaded 'By T. S. ELIOT'. Gallup C292. In the quotation from Hakluyt 'The 12 in the morning' has been emended to 'Then 12 in the morning'.

I wish to turn away for a while from the professional men of letters, to consider a type of prose which is interesting in any period, because it gives a good index of the general state of prose writing in its time. All of the men we have so far dealt with have been professional writers, each in his own line; we shall presently meet with the amateur writer, the courtier and man of action, in Sir Walter Raleigh and Fulke Greville. But there are also men who, in the exercise of some other business, have occasion to set down plain accounts of their affairs. Among such people are travellers and explorers – except, of course, those who merely travel for the sake of writing up their adventures afterwards – and especially sea-captains, who are obliged to keep log-books. Often such writing, when simple and sincere, has a beauty of its own. For a famous modern specimen I will refer you, not to Doughty's *Arabia Deserta*, which is the work of a very highly sophisticated professional writer, but to Captain Scott's account of the death of Oates on the Antarctic Expedition, as moving a story of heroism as any I know, which is quoted in *The Oxford Book of English Prose*. Not only was there a good deal of such writing in Tudor times, but there was a good deal of public interest in it; and I do not think that I should give you a fair view of the types of Tudor prose unless I lingered a little over this one.

It was natural that the English reading public, in the later days of Elizabeth, should take a lively interest in accounts of foreign countries. The exploits of their own navigators, before and after the Armada, filled them with exultation and curiosity. So there was a large consumption of books purporting to describe foreign parts and the Antipodes; and any account, from the most fraudulently fabulous to that of the genuine eye-witness, was eagerly received. Most of these books have no literary merit, but to Richard Hakluyt we owe a great debt. I have not recommended you to read Hakluyt yourselves, and you will understand the difficulty when I explain the nature of his book. It is called *Principal Navigations, Voyages and Discoveries of the English Nation*, and is designed to be nothing less than an encyclopedia of travels, voyages and explorations of Englishmen. It is in many volumes. Hakluyt was solely an editor, for the book is a compilation from many sources ancient and contemporary; it is, in fact, a source book. Many, perhaps most, of the inclusions are of little interest except to the historian; the literary merit varies indefinitely between one piece and the next. What are of interest to us are the narratives written by Elizabethan voyagers, often obscure or anonymous, about what they have themselves witnessed, and without pretence to literary style. If I knew of a good book of selections from Hakluyt, made with a view to illustrating the prose of Tudor navigators, I should recommend it to you; but so far as I know, there is no way with Hakluyt but to plough straight through the many volumes, or to look in each volume for what may be of interest.

I will quote a passage which I have chosen because it is nothing out of the ordinary, but typical of the way these men write. It is from an account of the Last Voyage of Sir Francis Drake and Sir John Hawkins in the West Indies.

> The 4th of November we began to unlade the Richard, one of our victuallers, which was by the next day unladen, unrigged and then sunken. Then we stood North-west and then North; and the next morning saw the islands of Monserrata, Redonda, Estazia, St. Christopher and Saba. The biggest of these islands is not past 8 leagues long. There is good anchorage in 8, 7 and 5 fathoms water, fair white sand. Then we stood away south west, and on the 8 in the morning came to an anchor some 7 or 8 leagues off within certain broken islands called Las Virgines, which have been accounted dangerous: but we found there a very good road, had it been for a thousand sails of ships in 14, 12 and 8 fathoms fair sand

and good anchorage, high islands on either side, but no fresh water that we could find: here is much fish to be taken with hooks and nets: also we stayed on shore and fowled. Here Sir John Hawkins was extreme sick; which his sickness began upon news of the taking of the Francis . . . Then 12 in the morning we weighed and set sail into the sea due south through a small straight but without danger, and then stood West and by North for St. Juan de Puerto Rico, and in the afternoon left the three small islands called 'The Passages' to the Southward of us, and that night came up to the Easternmost end of St. John, where Sir John Hawkins departed this life.

It ought to strike you as curious how like this anonymous entry in an Elizabethan log-book is to any entry in any seaman's log-book to-day. Somehow this passage strikes on my ear as more modern than anything I have quoted before. One reason for giving it is to point out to you that the skeleton, so to speak, of English prose was almost the same in Elizabethan times as it is to-day. When you find an Elizabethan with a plain tale to tell – and for plain tales one should go to log-books – he told it much as a master mariner of our own time would tell it; and told it, I think, very well. I get more of the sensation of reality in Elizabethan voyages out of reports like that than out of, let us say, Kingsley's *Westward Ho!* This is not the romance of Drake and Hawkins fabricated in London; it is the reality.

Here is an account of another adventure, the taking of Cartagena, by Sir Francis Drake:

Our Lieutenant-General, taking the advantage of the dark (the daylight as yet not broken out) approached by the lowest ground, according to the express direction which himself had formerly given, the same being the sea-wash shore, where the water was somewhat fallen, so as most of all their shot was in vain. Our Lieutenant-General commanded our shot to forbear shooting until we were come to the wallside, and so with pikes roundly together we approached the place, where we soon found out the barricades of pipes or buts, to be the meetest place for our assault, which, notwithstanding it was well furnished with pikes and shot, was without staying attempted by us: down went the buts of earth, and pell mell came our swords and pikes together, after our shot had first given their volley, even at the enemies nose. Our pikes were somewhat longer than theirs, and our bodies better armed; for very few of them were armed; with which advantage our swords and pikes grew too hard for them, and they driven to give place. In this furious entry the Lieutenant-General slew with his own hands the chief Ensign Bearer of the Spaniards, who fought very manfully to his life's end.

This sort of narrative not only seems to me very good workmanlike prose, but brings me nearer to the reality of Elizabethan adventure than any modern romancing, or any contemporary romancing, such as the boisterous patriotism of Heywood in his play *The Fair Maid of the West*. In that play the Spanish captain, baffled by the stolid fortitude of his English prisoner, exclaims:

These English! Can *nothing* daunt 'em?

In the paragraph above the unknown narrator remarks modestly 'our pikes were somewhat longer than theirs, and our bodies better armed'. He seems to me all the more a hero for that modest statement.

I hope that a comparison of these passages with what I have quoted previously, and what you have read, will help to give you a wider view of the accomplishments of Tudor prose than you had before. I must pass now to a writer by no means anonymous, who has much in common with these [60] writers, but whose varied interests united several kinds of prose in his writings, just as they brought together several kinds of activity in his life. It is Sir Walter Raleigh.

Now Raleigh is remarkable as a prose writer by the fact that, belonging to several worlds, the world of the court, the world of literature, the world of the quarterdeck, the world of the camp, he can combine several styles of prose. I might remind you as well of the still obscure and little-known club of atheists which is supposed to have met at his house, of which Thomas Kyd and Marlowe, the dramatists, are supposed to have been members. There is hardly a side of Elizabethan life which this Devonshire soldier of fortune did not touch. His account of the end of the *Revenge*, the fight off the Azores, is, I think, his masterpiece. There are many bits I should like to quote: his picture of the sailors falling off the deck of a Spanish galley stuck on a mudbank, like sacks of coals poured out. But I cannot find anything better or more typical than the passage already quoted by Mr Robertson and by Sir Arthur Quiller-Couch.

All the powder of the 'Revenge' to the last barrel was now spent, all her pikes broken, forty of her best men slain, and the most part of the rest hurt. In the beginning of the fight she had but one hundredth free from sickness, and fourscore and ten sick, laid in hold upon the ballast. A small troop of men to such a ship, and a weak garrison to resist so mighty an army. By those hundred all was sustained, the volleys, boardings, and entrings of fifteen ships of war, besides those which beat her at large. On the contrary, the Spanish were always supplied with soldiers brought from every squadron; all manner of arms, and powder at will. Unto ours there remained no comfort at all, no hope, no supply either of ships, men or weapons; the masts all beaten overboard, all her tackle cut asunder, her upper work altogether razed; and in effect evened she was with the water – but the very foundation or bottom of a ship, nothing being left overhead either for flight or defence.

The same man could write a dithyrambic address to Death which reminds us of Donne, Taylor, or Thomas Browne; but the style of the paragraph I have just quoted he learned in the same school as the humble authors of log-books such as I have mentioned. In his account of the discovery of Guiana he could give a fair plain narrative, with observations upon the geography, flora and fauna, and the customs of the inhabitants. Not the least interesting part of that book is the report of recommendations which Raleigh drew up for the Queen, including a practical scheme for discrediting the Spaniards among the natives:

De las Casas book of the Spanish cruelties with fair pictures, or at least a large table of pictures expressing the particularities of the cruelties there specified (neatly wrought for the better credit of our workmanship, and their easier understanding) would be sent to the Inca, and his Caciques by some interpreters, that they may publish them among their vassals, and to all the estates of the confining countries round about that they may be all (as much as is possible) conjointly linked, and exasperated against the Spaniards. And by informing them that the Spaniards do hold their religion of the Pope, the great enchanter or cousener, and troubler of the world, who sent them first to invade those countries, who teacheth them to break all faith, promises, oaths, covenants with all such as be not of their own religion, so far forth as may serve his turn, who giveth his followers dispensation to steal, rob, rebel and murder; and likewise pardoneth for money whatsoever wrongs or villainies, are by them committed.

I am not able, in the space that I have, to describe the rise of historical writing in Tudor England, or to deal with it as a special type. I have had to make rather simple divisions; and to deal with history by itself. I should have to bring in the work of translators, and particularly Berners' translation of Froissart's *Chronicles*; and I should have had to touch upon it in discussing Bacon, whose *History of the Reign of Henry VII* is one of the first modern English histories. Modern history had begun in France and Italy before it was practised in England. From Machiavelli and

Guicciardini, Bacon and others learned something of the art of scholarly and reflective history; from Froissart and Commines they learned that the Chronicle can be a living memoir of events in which the author took part. I would point out especially that I believe the writing of history in English was very much aided by the work of men like Raleigh and the various navigators who recounted their own experiences. Gradually the sense of fact asserts itself, gradually the English mind becomes more critical of hearsay and old myths and records. Holinshed, to whom Shakespeare owed so much, is still a medieval chronicler; Bacon and Raleigh are modern historians. We must still wait for Lord Clarendon, writing after the accession of Charles II, for the first great historical work in English by an Englishman. But the sense of history was greatly developed by men writing about their own experiences with a feeling that they were a part of history, not merely personal adventures.

Raleigh's *History of the World* is an important historical work in another way. It is not important for its information, because he began with the Creation of the World and left it unfinished before he had reached A.D., but because of his conception of there being such a thing as a history of the world. Bacon, in his history of Henry VII's reign, shows a perception of history as not merely a chronicle of events, but as an illustration of character, and as material for the study of the theory of government. Raleigh, in his history of the world, is the first person to show a perception of the unity of history, of the relation of the history of one race and nation to that of another; and though he does not use the modern word, he is the first to have some grasp of the concept of civilisation in general, of a process and development in the history of people after people. It is, I think, a very remarkable thing that the man who was primarily a soldier and sailor and courtier, incidentally a minor poet, could both set down in such fine English the images of actions in which he had taken part, such curiosity about the countries and strange peoples which he visited, and, at the same time, have such a view of the meaning of history as a whole.

(*From a talk on July* 9)

The Tudor Biographers

Listener, 2. 27 (17 July 1929), 94–5. Subheaded 'By T. S. ELIOT'.
In the penultimate para. 'Stewart' has been corrected to 'Stuart'. Gallup C293.

The three specimens of the art of biography, with which I shall close my review of Tudor types, all come rather late in history. Fulke Greville's life of his friend Sir Philip Sidney was not published until 1652, twenty-four years after the author's death. Lord Herbert of Cherbury, the brother of the more famous George Herbert, is really a Caroline, born in 1583. Sir Thomas Urquhart, whose translation of Rabelais I have already mentioned, is a true anachronism, for his little biography of Crichtoun was published in 1652. Yet he is an Elizabethan in spirit, and in those days his native seat of Cromartie was a long way from London; and as Mr Charles Whibley, in his essay on Urquhart reprinted in his *Studies in Frankness*, has vindicated his inclusion of Urquhart as a Tudor translator, I need not supply a fresh vindication of my inclusion of him as a Tudor biographer. And the recent appearance of an edition of *The Admirable Crichtoun*, by Harpers, edited by Mr Hamish Miles – a book of which my only complaint is that it costs a guinea – makes Urquhart's inclusion all the more desirable.

And when we have considered the biography, I hope and believe that I shall have covered all the important types of late Tudor prose. I do not suggest that other types of prose have not been discovered later. Pepys's Diary, for instance, represents a later stage of civilisation; for perfect specimens of letter-writing we must wait at least for Dorothy Temple; good parliamentary oratory is hardly possible before the eighteenth century. But nearly all the major possibilities of English prose were first exploited by Elizabethans.

The informal biography is very popular at the present time, both here and abroad; witness the work of Mr Lytton Strachey and of his semi-disciple M. André Maurois, whose lectures, called *Aspects of Biography*, have lately been published in England. It represents, of course, a reaction against the official two-volume biography – not necessarily against only the biographies of statesmen published by authority of their executors. The Elizabethans knew nothing of the official biography. Fulke Greville writes with passionate enthusiasm of a friend, Urquhart with equal enthusiasm, though not as a personal friend, of his countryman.

Fulke Greville, Lord Brooke, whose proud tomb you can see at Warwick, was a man of Sir Philip Sidney's own type, and one of the set of courtly poets associated with the name of Sidney's sister, the Countess of Pembroke. He was the author of several plays in which there is much really fine poetry; he was one of those called 'Senecals' who tried unsuccessfully to impose the classical or Senecan form upon modern English tragedy. He followed much the same career as Philip Sidney, with less distinction and with less romance. He had, I think, a profounder mind, a better intellect, than Sidney, yet he survives more as the biographer of Sidney than for any other of his accomplishments. It is not wholly unjust; for Greville was not a great enough thinker or great enough poet to stand out in an age of so many great men. Neither was Sidney; but Sidney remains as the typical figure of the literary courtier and soldier of the age; and Greville as his biographer.

Greville does not follow any method that the reader of any modern biography might expect. He gives no dates, says nothing of Sidney's marriage or domestic life; and on the other hand includes, even in quite a short book, a good deal that we should not expect: reflections on the policy of Queen Elizabeth and the situation abroad; and critical remarks about his own dramatic works. Yet his enthusiastic admiration for his friend does, in the end, give us something like a portrait.

There is one story of Sir Philip Sidney which every child has read, but not every adult has read it in the words in which Greville tells it. At the battle of Zutphen Sidney was mortally wounded:

> Howsoever, by this stand, an unfortunate hand out of those forespoken trenches, brake the bone of Sir Philip's thigh with a musket shot. The horse he rode upon, was rather furiously choleric, than bravely proud, and so forced him to forsake the field, but not his back, as the noblest, and fittest bier to carry a martial commander to his grave. In which sad progress, passing along by the rest of the Army, where his uncle the general was, and being thirsty with excess of bleeding, he called for drink, which was presently brought him; but as he was putting the bottle to his mouth, he saw a poor soldier carried along, who had eaten his last at the same feast, ghastly casting up his eyes at the bottle. Which Sir Philip perceiving, took it from his head, before he drank, and delivered it to the poor man, with these words, 'Thy necessity is greater than mine.' And when he had pledged this poor soldier, he was presently carried to Arnheim.

Greville is not, I admit, a great prose writer; it is seldom that he writes even as well as this; he is at his best in verse, and verse of a solemn declamatory sort. Yet his little *Life of Sidney*, with all the tiresome irrelevancies he includes, and all the interesting detail he leaves out, remains a biography of permanent enjoyment; and an important step towards modern biographical writing.

Urquhart is a very different figure, a great if extravagant prose writer, and a real eccentric. He was a Scot of very long lineage, which he made still longer, by compiling a family tree tracing the descent of the Urquharts from Adam, and bringing in on the way the best mythological families of Greece, as well as the Queen of Sheba. With such a descent, it is not surprising that he stood by his King, and hated Presbyterians, against whom he employed the resources of his enormous vocabulary. It is also not surprising, though deplorable, that some of the Roundhead troops retaliated by destroying many of his manuscripts. But out of what were left he himself survived to make some compilations: the little *Life of Crichtoun* is really an incident in a greater work, but complete in itself. It is not, like Greville's Sidney, a memorial to a friend or acquaintance; The Admirable Crichtoun, a Scottish adventurer at Italian courts, was merely a personage who excited Urquhart's imagination, as another Scot who was his model in the arts and practices of manhood, warfare, scholarship, gallantry and courtesy. His story is therefore a kind of fantasia, yet a more straightforward and lucid narrative than that of Greville. While Greville's prose hobbles, that of Urquhart's sports like a dancing horse – I was going to say a dancing elephant, but that would not be quite [95] fair. Here is his account of a duel in which the Scot, the 'matchless Crichtoun', of course vanquished his Italian adversary:

> The sweetness of Crichtoun's countenance, in the hottest of the assault, like a glance of lightning on the hearts of the spectators, brought all the Italian ladies on a sudden to be enamoured of him; whilst the sternness of the other's aspect, he looking like an enraged bear, would have struck terror into wolves, and affrighted an English mastiff. Though they were both in their linens (to wit, shirts and drawers, without any other apparel) and in all outward conveniences equally adjusted; the Italian, with redoubling his strokes, foamed at the mouth with a choleric heart, and fetched a pantling breath: the Scot, in sustaining his charge, kept himself in a pleasant temper, without passion, and made void his designs: he alters his wards from tierce to quart; he primes and seconds it, now high, now low, and casts his body (like another Proteus) into all the shapes he can, to spy an open on his adversary, and lay hold of an advantage; but all in vain: for the invincible Crichtoun, whom no cunning was able to surprise, contrepostures his respective wards, and with an incredible nimbleness of both hand and foot, evades his intent, and frustrates the invasion.

I admit that Urquhart, in this passage, is not altogether orderly with his pronouns; so that you probably were not sure at every moment whether he was speaking of the Scot or of his Italian antagonist; but there is life and beauty in the style. Urquhart has a verbal vitality similar to that of Nashe; but I think he is a finer and more mature writer. You say at every page: 'he can never keep this up', but he does keep it up, and the lyrical strain never flags to the end. He has, of course, a fine theme to end on, in Crichtoun's death. Crichtoun is waylaid by the ungrateful and jealous Italian princeling whom he had loyally tutored, with a band of ruffians. Crichtoun, single-handed, routs the band utterly, and is about to despatch the prince himself, who was masked, when he is made aware of the prince's identity. Then, as the flower of courtesy, he kneels and humbly offers his sword to the prince, who, I am sorry to say, runs Crichtoun through the body with it. 'In the interim of which accident', as Urquhart puts it, the beautiful Italian lady who was enamoured of Crichtoun:

> having slipped herself into a cloth of gold petticoat, in the anterior scente whereof was an asterisk pouch, wherein were enchased fifteen several diamonds, representative of the constellation of the primest stars in the sign of Virgo . . .

(the rest of her dress and the beauty of her person are described in a sentence three pages long) appears upon the scene, and

> All this from their imagination being conveyed into the penitissim corners of their souls in that short space which I have already told, she, rending her garments, and tearing her hair, like one of the graces possessed with a fury, spoke thus: 'O villains! what have you done? you vipers of men, that have thus basely slain the valiant Crichtoun, the sword of his own sex, and buckler of ours, the glory of his age, and restorer of the lost honour of the court of Mantua: O Crichtoun, Crichtoun!'

Greville's *Life of Sidney*, and Urquhart's *Life of Crichtoun* still more so, are delightful books to read, or I should not have dealt with them. But we must recognise also that in spite of the prolix inconsequence of the first, and the amazing extravaganza of the second, there is in them the beginning of modern biography. Any earlier works which may look like biography belong more nearly to the beginning of modern history.

Lord Herbert of Cherbury, a great member of a great family, was one of those curious mixed natures – philosopher, scholar, poet, courtier, and not wholly admirable politician – who belong to a type not so purely Elizabethan and Stuart as we like to suppose. He wrote the story of his own life, as he says and no doubt believed, for usefulness to posterity: its usefulness has been not quite that aimed at. He was extremely conceited, and rather thick-skinned; somewhat vainglorious, and he sometimes twists the facts to suit his vanity. The first and dullest part of the book takes its origins in such works as *The Courtier* and *The Gouvernor*, which deal with the proper education for young gentlemen. We learn, what is not very interesting, that Lord Herbert approved of swimming, except for those who are subject to convulsions and cramps, and disapproved of horse-racing and dicing. The story only begins to be interesting when he decides, after an inconclusive argument with his wife about the settlements they should make for their children to travel abroad, taking with him as secretary, by the way, one of the most charming minor poets of the time, Aurelian Townshend.

The book was written by a tiresome and not altogether honest-minded man, yet an able philosopher and poet. It is interesting in the story of English prose, because the beginning of autobiography marks a further stage beyond the beginning of biography, in the development of the English mind. What information Herbert gives us about himself is not quite what he intended to convey; but although he is not, we feel, really frank about himself, yet he professed and pretended to be, and that is already something. And when we read some of the greater biographies in English, such as that of Gibbon or that of John Stuart Mill, we shall appreciate them all the better for knowing something about the beginnings of this type of prose.

(*From a talk on July* 16)

The Early Novel

Review of *The History of the English Novel: The Elizabethan Age and After* by Ernest A. Baker (1929), and *John Lyly and the Italian Renaissance* by Violet A. Jeffery (1929).

TLS, 1434 (25 July 1929), 589. Unsigned. Not in Gallup, but would be C293a.

Professor Baker's book succeeds in fulfilling two functions: by itself, it summarises usefully all the information about the forms of fiction in Elizabethan times; and it also takes its place as one volume in his history of the novel of which several volumes remain to be written. It covers, we believe, the most difficult period of the history of the novel; and the task was difficult because the 'novel' at that period must be a somewhat arbitrary distinction. Few of the writers of the time were solely or even primarily novelists; and with the exception of Deloney, they are all more interesting for their miscellaneous work than for their novels or romances. Dr Baker has made the book, rightly, as comprehensive as possible; nothing is omitted which could be fitted in; and he has made a useful book of reference as well as one section of a history.

Only a study of this kind can impress upon us how very slow the development of the modern novel was, how long it had to wait for the propitious moment to emerge as a distinct form of writing. As Dr Baker says, if the Elizabethans had evolved the novel, it would have been of a very different type from that of Richardson and Fielding. The needs which the novel came to satisfy were not existent; for the major needs of literature were all satisfied by the drama. Therefore the Elizabethan 'novel' takes two forms: the artificial and sterile form of Sidney and Lyly; and the popular journalism of Deloney and the pamphleteers: it is the latter which provides the real origins. Elizabethan fiction, in Dr Baker's words, is 'an obscure, slight and unsatisfactory affair'. He points out admirably the two chief obstacles to its being anything else:

> One vital need – one, however, of which no writer saw the real bearings – was the want of a suitable prose. Most of the current prose – all of it indeed that was employed in works to be read for enjoyment – was a much more artificial mode of expression than the diction of contemporary verse. Denied the charms of rhyme and metre, the prose writer did not reflect that poetic licence was also disallowed; on the contrary, he tried to make up for the deficiency by an exhausting strain after point and epigram, trope and metaphor, and such artificial effects of assonance, alliteration, and iterating cadence as in verse would have been intolerable.

The other reason was that

> writers had the vaguest and most confused apprehension of the problem to be solved; whether the main object was the story or the moral, the incidents or the picture of life; truth, insight, life-likeness, or strangeness, ingenuity, surprise.

And Dr Baker concludes that 'fiction does not normally arise and flourish in times of intense creative energy', but rather 'in the quiet intervals when writers are less imaginative and more critical'.

Concerning the individual writers – Sidney, Lyly, Greene, Lodge, Nashe, Deloney, Dekker and others, there is little new to be said; but the reader will find an accurate account, with specimens. Dr Baker's inclusion of the writers of 'characters' may seem a little superfluous, but it is vindicated by its issue in the imaginary portraits of Addison. The inclusion of Addison remains to be vindicated by the next volume of the work. Our only question of Dr Baker's method is one which cannot be answered until these volumes appear: we wonder whether his method is to take the modern novel, the developed type, and trace the causes which led up to it, or whether he is merely chronicling the various writings which look something like the novel. We do not see how his work can be more than a chronicle unless he has made up his mind as to what a novel is. But the acuteness of some of his comments lends us to hope that he has done so.

Miss Jeffery's book is a thesis on a special subject. Some modern scholars have asserted that Lyly owes no direct debt to Italian authors. The common reader would suppose the contrary; and the researches of other scholars, such as Professor Schoell, show more and more the indebtedness of Elizabethan writers to Continental contemporaries. Miss Jeffery has not quite as clear a case as Dr Schoell had in tracing the borrowings of Chapman, but her accumulation of probabilities, powerful and concurrent, lends to conviction. We often suppose that if a writer borrows he must borrow from those of his contemporaries who are still remembered and important. Lyly was probably influenced in some general tricks of story-telling by such writers as Boccaccio and Bandello; but Miss Jeffery's evidence goes to show that a huge mass of now forgotten Italian literature was in circulation in England, and that Lyly took more from forgotten authors than from remembered.

The extent to which Lyly 'borrowed' does not, however, impugn his originality. He does nothing that any modern author would be ashamed to do. Miss Jeffery's dissertation does help us to a more critical appraisal of that strange genius. Lyly issues from her hands still one of the most inventive and original of authors. He is one of those unfortunate writers who illustrate the truth that originality is not enough. His inventions left so little mark – he did no more than invent a fashion which better men adopted and worked their way out of – because they were so superficial. They did not represent any serious development of mind or sensibility; yet Lyly helped other men to develop. Investigations like Miss Jeffery's are of the greatest value to anyone who wishes to understand the Elizabethan mind. When we have studied it for many years we come to recognise that it is different from ours in many ways in which we had taken it to be similar; and similar to ours in many ways in which we had taken it to be different.

Second Thoughts about Humanism

'Second Thoughts about Humanism' was publ. in *New Adelphi*, 2. 4 (June/Aug. 1929), [304]–10, and revised in *Hound and Horn*, 2. 4 (July/Sept. 1929), 339–50: Gallup C285. Further revised in *SE. See below*, pp. 604–13.

Preface

Dante was publ. by Faber & Faber as 'The Poets on The Poets – No. 2' on 27 Sept. 1929: Gallup A13. Revised in *SE. See below*, pp. 448–83.

Eliot's Preface (pp. 11–13) is printed here.

If my task had been to produce another brief 'introduction to the study of Dante' I should have been incompetent to perform it. But in a series of essays of 'Poets on Poets' the undertaking, as I understand it, is quite a different one. A contemporary writer of verse, in writing a pamphlet of this description, is required only to give a faithful account of his acquaintance with the poet of whom he writes. This, and no more, I can do; and this is the only way in which I can treat an author of whom so much has been written, that can make any pretence to novelty. I have found no other poet than Dante to whom I could apply continually, for many purposes, and with much profit, during a familiarity of twenty years. I am not a Dante scholar; my Italian is chiefly self-taught, and learnt primarily in order to read Dante; I need still to make constant reference to translations. Yet it has occurred to me that by relating the process of my own gradual and still very imperfect knowledge of Dante, I might give some help to persons who must begin where I began – with a public school knowledge of Latin, a traveller's smattering of Italian, and a literal translation beside the text. For this reason my order, in the [12] following chapters, is the order of my own initiation. I begin with detail, and approach the general scheme. I began myself with passages of the *Inferno* which I could understand, passed on to the *Purgatorio* in the same way, and only after years of experience began to appreciate the *Paradiso*; from which I reverted to the other parts of the poem and slowly realised the unity of the whole. I believe that it is quite natural and right to tackle the *Vita Nuova* afterwards. For an English reader who reads the *Vita Nuova* too soon is in danger of reading it under Pre-Raphaelite influence.

My purpose has been to persuade the reader first of the importance of Dante as a master – I may even say, *the* master – for a poet writing to-day in any language. And there ensues from that, the importance of Dante to anyone who would appreciate modern poetry, in any language. I should not trust the opinion of anyone who pretended to judge modern verse without knowing Homer, Dante, and Shakespeare. It does not in the least follow that a *poet* is negligible because he does not know these three.

Having thus excused this book, I do not feel called upon to give any bibliography. Anyone can easily discover more Dante bibliography than anyone can use. But I should like to mention one book which has been of use to me: the *Dante* of Professor Charles Grandgent of Harvard. I owe something to an essay by Mr Ezra Pound in his *Spirit of Romance*, but more to his table-talk; and [13] I owe something to Mr Santayana's essay in *Three Philosophical Poets*. And one should at least glance at the *Readings* of W. W. Vernon in order to see how far into medieval philosophy, theology, science, and literature a thorough study of Dante must go.

The reader whom I have kept in mind, in writing this essay, is the reader who commences his reading of Dante with Messrs Dent's invaluable *Temple Classics* edition (3 volumes at 2s. each). For this reason I have in quotations followed the *Temple Classics* edition text, and have followed pretty closely the translation in the same volumes. It is hardly necessary to say that where my version varies it nowhere pretends to greater accuracy than that excellent translation. Anyone who reads my essay before attempting Dante at all will be likely to turn next to the *Temple Classics* edition, with its text and translation on opposite pages. There is something to be said for Longfellow's, and something for Norton's translation; but for anyone who can follow the Italian even gropingly the Temple translation is the best.

A Commentary

C., 9. 34 (Oct. 1929), 1–6. Unsigned. Gallup C295.

LORD BRENTFORD'S APOLOGY

In the *Nineteenth Century* for August is published a very interesting article by the late Conservative Home Secretary over his new name. It confirms the opinion that we have always held; that the late Sir William Joynson-Hicks is a very honest, conscientious, public-spirited and bewildered man. The article is entitled '"Censorship" of Books.' As the inverted commas suggest, Lord Brentford reminds us of what we already knew, that there is no 'censorship' of books in Britain. Lord Brentford answers, with perfect honesty and almost 'disarming ingenuousness' some of his critics; he does not answer the criticisms, or respond to the proposals, made in *The Criterion*, of which we are sure he has never heard. It is for this reason that we venture to comment on his apology.

Lord Brentford's defence of his action in the case of *The Well of Loneliness* is conducted against those opponents whom it is easiest to attack; those who believe that the book is a 'work of art'. It has therefore no force against the comments previously made in this review. We have held, throughout, the view that the question of whether a work *is* a 'work of art' is a red herring. It would mean [2] in practice that we should be judged by pundits of art (Bereson or Duveen) or pundits of literary criticism instead of by Mr Mead – and we had as soon deal with Mr Mead. It is not a question of 'art' but of public liberties. We should like to point out to Lord Brentford that we did not consider *The Well of Loneliness* to be a work of art, but merely a dull, badly written, hysterical book with an unpleasant strain of religiosity; and that judging it thus we still insisted that it should have been allowed to circulate.

A large part of Lord Brentford's defence may be summed up in the plaintive cry: 'what else is a Home Secretary to do – *in the actual circumstances*?' It is indeed very difficult to say what else a Home Secretary should do. A daily newspaper, or a Sunday newspaper informs its readers that a certain book, of which the vast majority would not otherwise have heard, is frightfully shocking. Its readers, no doubt, flock to be shocked. And the matter is 'brought to the notice' of the Home Secretary. And a Home Secretary has to think of the interests of the nation, and of the interests of his party, and so matters take their course. And the Home Secretary, being a Home Secretary, has no time to think what he, as an individual, thinks about it, or how his opinion, as an individual's, weighs against that of other individuals who are distinguished not by being cabinet ministers but because of what they have done as individuals; he is in the unfortunate position of being a Home Secretary, as there have been, are and will be.

It is interesting to note from Lord Brentford's article that 'the Home Secretary never moved against other than admittedly pornographic productions of his own volition.' He admits that there *are* 'pornographic productions' which even a Home Secretary can detect without prompting! and neither we nor anyone else has ever objected to his 'movements' against such. But there are apparently other productions, in the case of which the Home Secretary cannot move because he does not trust his own opinion, [3] but only moves because he takes the opinion of the penny press, or of any busybody who chooses to protest, and finally of Mr Mead. But the late Home Secretary has admitted that there are 'admittedly' pornographic productions; which is what we have contended; so we suggest that Home Secretaries should confine themselves to 'moving' against what is 'admitted.'

Lord Brentford concedes that 'there is already a far greater freedom in literature now than there was when the act of 1857 was passed'. But he fails to say whether this freedom is commendable or deplorable. It must be one or the other. If it is good, then perhaps a little more freedom would be better. If it is bad, then Lord Brentford ought to have the courage to say that we have too much freedom. He seems to say at this point; be patient, and before long you will be able to publish anything you like.

We fear that Lord Brentford, like many other people, has ceased to be a human being – that is to say, has ceased to think independently – because he has been a Statesman. The views he has expressed in this article are of no more value than those of the humblest Police Officer – like Lord Brentford, a servant of the public. When Lord Brentford provides us with his frank opinion of what public morals really *are*, when he shows us that he has thought out for himself what public morals ought to be; when he convinces us that he really knows what the words mean when he talks glibly of books 'debauching the young,' or 'corrupting,' we may be inclined to give him the attention that we would give to any serious undergraduate. Has he really spent much time considering *how* the young are debauched or *how* human souls are corrupted, and how much *books* have to do with it? Has he, in his busy life, ever had time to think deeply about the relation of art and morals, and morals and religion? Some men have found these problems so difficult that they have had no time for anything else.

[4] MR MEAD, AND THE BISHOP OF NATAL

Mr Mead the magistrate, has meanwhile exhibited the British sense of fair play, by ordaining that Mr D. H. Lawrence's paintings shall no longer be exhibited, but need not be destroyed. Some reproductions of these paintings are to be destroyed, but not the paintings themselves. Here again, we are not interested to decide whether Mr Lawrence's paintings are masterpieces or daubs. We learn that features of these paintings were 'unnecessarily developed', and we must accept the Marlborough Street Theory of Necessity. But one of the interesting points in the inquest is shown by the following quotation from the conversation at the hearing, which we take from a newspaper of August 9th, 1929:

Mr Hutchinson: Were the proceedings started by a private individual or the authorities?

Mr Mead (to Inspector Hester): You need not answer that.

Inspector Hester did not need to answer that, but it is a question which the public would very much like to hear answered; and the public has a right to know the answer. Because, the same news-sheet which first informed us that there was an exhibition of shocking paintings by Mr Lawrence had previously informed us of another shocking exhibition by a famous foreign painter of whom we had never heard, so shocking that the Ambassador of the country to which that painter belonged (we were told) did not visit the show until the most shocking of these passionate canvasses had been removed. Yet neither Mr Mead nor Mr Muskett was called upon to judge these paintings. We have not seen either these or Mr Lawrence's. Mr Lawrence is a British subject, one of half a dozen writers whose work commands respect in foreign countries. We are reminded of three sentences of Matthew Arnold:

> Occasionally, the uncritical spirit of our race determines to perform a great public act of self-humiliation. Such an act it has recently accomplished. It has just [5] sent forth as its scape-goat into the wilderness, amidst a titter from educated Europe, the Bishop of Natal.

FURTHER REFLECTIONS

But what we should like to be able to gauge, is the extent to which public action is *hustled* by a certain section of the daily press. We have lately seen the daily press, which offers to its readers a small amount of news and an extensive space of bathing beauties, direct its readers to 'obscene' books and 'obscene' picture shows, and then exult in their condemnation. We also see the daily press providing 'policies' for political parties. Now we have not concealed our opinion that the party upon which these benefactions have most liberally been showered is remarkably destitute of ideas. But we must add that the method in question is the last one which we should recommend for injection of energy. We conjure any members of that party who have any incipient tendency towards thought, to think themselves and to welcome thinking, but to remain hostile to any programme which shows no evidence of having germinated from the solitary thought of a disinterested individual. The first requisite of any political movement which may hope to influence the future, should be *indifference to success* and loyalty to slowly formed conviction.

OF YOUR CHARITY

Pray for the soul of Hugo von Hofmannsthal. We mention him particularly because he supported and contributed to the *Criterion*. Hofmannsthal, who is not long dead, was a fine poet and a fine prose writer. He was, during his lifetime, the leading man of letters in Vienna. Not only by his own work, but by his patronage, his influence, and the periodicals which he affected, one of the great European men of letters. Most English readers know him only as the author of the librettos of Strauss's operas, especially *Elektra*. Those who know German recognise the poet and prose writer. Hofmannsthal was a man of European culture. In some [6] of his verse plays, such as *Sobeidens Hochzeit*, he showed himself to be saturated in Elizabethan and Jacobean drama, which he knew intimately; in some of his later work, he showed an equal intimacy with Spanish drama, with Lope and Calderón. Yet his work was never pastiche. He is one of the writers in German whose work appears as fine after the War as it did before, and whose tendency and influence may be described as 'classical.' And he was a man of great charm and great culture.

Experiment in Criticism

'Experiment in Criticism' was publ. in *Bookman*, 70. 3 (Nov. 1929), 225–33. Subheaded *by T. S. Eliot*. Gallup C296. Revised as *Tradition and Experiment in Present-Day Literature* (publ. 25 Nov. 1929): Gallup B11. See next item.

Tradition and Experiment in Present-Day Literature

Tradition and Experiment in Present-Day Literature: Addresses Delivered at the City Literary Institute (publ. 25 Nov. 1929), [198]–215. Subheaded *'By* T. S. ELIOT'. Gallup B11. Revised from *Bookman*, 70. 3 (Nov. 1929), 225–33: Gallup C296.
On p. 202 'exasperating books' has been corrected to 'exasperating book'.

1 There is no department of literature in which it is more difficult to establish a distinction between 'traditional' and 'experimental' work than literary criticism. For here both words may be taken in two senses. By traditional criticism we may mean that which follows the same methods, aims at the same ends, and expresses much the same state of mind as the criticism of the preceding generation. Or we may mean something quite different: a criticism which has a definite theory of the meaning and value of the term 'tradition', and which may be experimental in reverting to masters who have been forgotten. And as for 'experiment' one may mean the more original work of the present generation, or else the work of critics who are pushing into new fields of inquiry, or enlarging

the scope of criticism with other kinds of knowledge. To use the word 'experimental' in the first sense would be invidious, for it would cover all the critical work of our time which one considers to have merit. For it is obvious that every generation has a new point of view, and is self-conscious in the critic; his work is twofold, to interpret the past to the present, and to judge the present in the light of the past. We have to see literature through our own temperament in order to see it at all, though our vision is always partial and our judgement always prejudiced; no generation, and no individual, can appreciate *every* dead author and every past period; universal good taste is never realised. In this way, all criticism is experimental, just as the mode of life of every generation is an experiment. It is [199] only in my second sense, therefore, that it is worth while to talk of experimental criticism; only by considering what critics to-day may be *deliberately* attempting some kind of critical work which has not been deliberately attempted before.

2 In order to make clear exactly what there is that is new in contemporary critical writing I shall have to go back a hundred years. We may say, roughly, that modern criticism begins with the work of the French critic Sainte-Beuve, that is to say about the year 1826. Before him, Coleridge had attempted a new type of criticism, a type which is in some respects more allied to what is now called aesthetics than to literary criticism. But from the Renaissance through the eighteenth century literary criticism had been confined to two narrow and closely related types. One was a type which has always existed and I hope always will; for it can always have very great value: it may be called practical notes on the art of writing by practitioners, parallel to the treatises on painting which have been left us by Leonardo da Vinci and others. Such notes are of the greatest value to other artists, particularly when studied in conjunction with the author's own work. Two classical examples in English are the Elizabethan treatises on rhymed and unrhymed verse written by Thomas Campion and Samuel Daniel. The prefaces and essays of Dryden, the prefaces of Corneille, are of the same type but on a larger scale and engage wider issues. But at the same time there is a large body of criticism, a considerable quantity in English and still more in French, written by men who were professionally critics rather than creative writers: the most famous critic of this sort is of course Boileau. This type of critic was primarily the [200] *arbiter of taste*, and his task was to praise and condemn the work of his contemporaries, and especially to lay down the laws of good writing. These laws were supposed to be drawn from the practice, but still more from the theory, of the ancients. Aristotle was highly respected; but in practice this type of criticism was usually far

from following the profound insight of Aristotle, and confined itself to translating, imitating, and plagiarising Horace's *Art of Poetry*. At its best, it confirmed and maintained permanent standards of good writing; at its worst it was a mere sequence of precepts. In general, French criticism was more theoretic, and as in La Harpe, more desiccated; the normal English type was nearer to plain good sense, as in Johnson's *Lives of the Poets*; though interesting theory, usually on specific literary types such as the drama, is found in authors like Thomas Rymer and Daniel Webb in the seventeenth and eighteenth centuries.

3 It is worth delaying for a moment to point out one of the qualities of seventeenth- and eighteenth-century literary criticism, which gives it enduring value and at the same time marks it off from more modern criticism. We are apt to think of this older criticism as dry and formal, and as setting up classical moulds in which no living literature could be shaped. But we should remember in its favour that this criticism recognised literature as literature, and not another thing. Literature was something distinct from philosophy and psychology and every other study; and its purpose was to give a refined pleasure to persons of sufficient leisure and breeding. If the older critics had not taken for granted that literature was something primarily to be enjoyed, they could not have occupied themselves so sedulously with laying [201] down rules of what was right to enjoy. This seems a very commonplace remark, and no distinction; but if you compare the criticism of those two centuries with that of the nineteenth, you will see that the latter does not take this simple truth wholly for granted. Literature is often treated by the critic rather as a means for eliciting truth or acquiring knowledge. If the critic is of a more philosophic or religious mind, he will look for the expression of philosophic or religious intuition in the work of the author criticised; if he is of a more realistic turn, he will look to literature as material for the discovery of psychological truths, or as documents illustrating social history. Even in the mouths of Walter Pater and his disciples, the phrase 'art for art's sake' means something very different from the sense in which literature was for literature's sake up to the latter part of the eighteenth century. If you read carefully the famous epilogue to Pater's *Studies in the Renaissance* you will see that 'art for art's sake' means nothing less than art as a substitute for everything else, and as a purveyor of emotions and sensations which belong to life rather than to art. To distinguish clearly between these two attitudes, that of art for art's sake and that of the eighteenth century, does require a strong effort of imagination. But the former doctrine would have been unintelligible to the earlier age. For the earlier period, art and literature were not substitutes for religion

or philosophy or morals or politics, any more than for duelling or love-making: they were special and limited adornments of life. On each side there is a profit and a loss. We have gained perhaps a deeper insight, now and then; whether we enjoy literature any more keenly than our ancestors I do not know; but I think we should [202] return again and again to the critical writings of the seventeenth and eighteenth centuries, to remind ourselves of that simple truth that literature is primarily literature, a means of refined and intellectual pleasure.

4 How, we ask immediately, did human beings ever come to abandon so simple and satisfying a limitation of criticism? The change comes about incidentally to a larger change, which may be described as the growth of the *historical* attitude. But this change – to which I shall return in a moment – is preceded, so far as literary criticism is concerned – by a freakish phenomenon, by a book written by one of the wisest and most foolish men of his time and perhaps the most extraordinary; a book which is itself one of the wisest and silliest, the most exciting and most exasperating book of criticism ever written – the *Biographia Literaria* of Coleridge. There, if you like, was 'experiment in criticism', everything in fact except the power of sticking to the point – a power noticeably absent from Coleridge's ill-regulated life. Coleridge was one of the most learned men of his time, and no man of his time had wider interests except Goethe; and one of the first things that strikes us about his book, besides its uncommon diffuseness, is the novel variety of knowledge which he brings to bear on literary criticism. Much of his knowledge, as of the romantic German philosophers, does not seem to us to-day particularly worth having, but it was held to be valuable then; and we owe to Coleridge as much as to anybody our enjoyment of the doubtful benefits of German Idealism. His book naturally contains specimens of several types of criticism; its impulse, of course, was a defence of the new – or as the newspapers of our time would say, 'modernist' poetry of Wordsworth; and as [203] such belongs to the type of technical notes of a craftsman; but when Coleridge started on anything, it could lead to almost everything else. He had not the historical point of view, but by the catholicity of his literary lore, and his ability for sudden and illuminating comparisons drawn from poetry of different ages and different languages, he anticipated some of the most useful accomplishments of the historical method. But one thing that Coleridge did effect for literary criticism is this. He brought out clearly the relation of literary criticism to that branch of philosophy which has flourished amazingly under the name of aesthetics; and, following German writers whom he had studied, he puts the criticism of literature in its place as merely one

department of the theoretic study of the Fine Arts in general. His fine discrimination of Fancy and Imagination cannot be held as permanent, for terms and relations change; but it remains one of the important texts for all who would consider the nature of poetic imagination. And he establishes literary criticism as a part of philosophy: or, to put it more moderately, he made it necessary for the 'literary critic' to acquaint himself with general philosophy and metaphysics.

5 *Biographia Literaria* appeared in 1817; the activities of Charles Augustin Sainte-Beuve may be said to begin about 1826. Coleridge and Sainte-Beuve have very little in common, as little, that is, as two men who were both great critics could have in common. And Sainte-Beuve would not have been a great critic solely on the ground of what is new and experimental in his work. He had a very French intelligence and good taste which enabled him to share the ideals and sympathies of the great French writers of every time; there was much in [204] him of the eighteenth century, a good deal even of the seventeenth. There were many gaps, certainly, in his appreciations, both of his contemporaries and of his predecessors; but he had that essential critical quality of imagination which made it possible for him to grasp literature as a whole. Where he differed from previous French critics was in his implicit conception of literature, not only as a body of writings to be enjoyed, but as a process of change in history, and as a part of the study of history. The notion that literary values are relative to literary periods, that the literature of a period is primarily an expression and a symptom of the time, is so natural to us now that we can hardly detach our minds from it. We can hardly conceive that the degree and kind of self-consciousness which we have could ever not have been. How much criticism of contemporary literature is taken up with discussing whether, and in what degree, this book or novel or poem is expressive of *our* mentality, of the personality of *our* age; and how often our critics seem to be interested rather in inquiring what *we* (including themselves) are like, than with the book, novel, or poem as a work of art! This is an extreme, but the extreme of a tendency which began, in criticism, a good hundred years ago. Sainte-Beuve was not, like Coleridge, a metaphysician; he is indeed more modern and more sceptical; but he was the first interesting historian in criticism. And it is by no means irrelevant that he began his career with the study of medicine; he is not only an historian but a biologist in criticism.

6 It is, I think, interesting to turn to some good recent piece of literary criticism, and underline some of the assumptions of knowledge and theory which you would [205] not find in criticism of two hundred years

ago. Mr Herbert Read's lucid little primer, *Phases of English Poetry*, will do for our purpose. On the second page he tells us that his is an inquiry into the *evolution* of poetry, and speaks presently of English poetry as a 'living and developing organism'. Even these few words should give a hint of the extent to which the critical apparatus has changed with the general changes in scientific and historical conceptions, when a literary critic can treat his audience to terms like 'evolution' and 'living organism' with the assurance of their being immediately apprehended. He is taking for granted certain vague but universal biological ideas. A little later he informs us that 'the beginning of this study belongs to anthropology'. Now, a great deal of work has had to be done by a great many people, and already more or less popularised, before a critic of literature can talk in this way. The work of Bastian, Tylor, Mannhardt, Durkheim, Lévy-Bruhl, Frazer, Miss Harrison, and many others has gone before. And a great deal of purely literary investigation has been made too, before anyone can talk of the evolution of poetry. Mr Read begins by studying the origins of ballad poetry. It would not have been possible for him to do so without a great deal of work done in the later nineteenth century and the early twentieth; for example, by Professor Child of Harvard, Professor Gommere of Haverford, Professor Gaston Paris of the Sorbonne, and Professor W. P. Ker of London. Such studies in ballad poetry, and in all the heretofore unexplored ages of literature, have fostered in us the sense of flux and evolution, the sense of the relation of the poetry of each period to the civilisation of the period, and also have tended slightly [206] to *level* literary values. It was W. P. Ker, who perhaps knew the whole history of European poetry better than any man of his time, who said that in literature there were no Dark Ages. And in the next paragraph to the one which I have just quoted, Mr Read observes that in theories of the origin of poetry we 'go right back to the origin of speech'. Even to make so simple a remark as this requires the work of another group of scientists: the philologists. The modern critic must have some acquaintance with them too – with the work of such contemporary philologists as Professor Jespersen of Copenhagen.

7 There are other branches of knowledge (or at least of science) some acquaintance with which you take for granted in any applicant whom you may employ as literary critic. Especially of course psychology, particularly analytical psychology. All of the studies I have mentioned, and more, do themselves touch the edges, and handle some of the problems, of criticism; so conversely the critic has to know something about them. The modern critic is distinguished first by the current notions which he shares with all educated or half-educated persons, such as the notion of

evolution, and by the number and variety of sciences of which he has to know a little. And he has to know them, not in order to do their work for them, but to collaborate – and also, in order that he may know where to stop. We require much general knowledge in order to see the limits of our particular ignorance.

8 Now although Sainte-Beuve did not have the equipment which we expect of our contemporaries, he had a great deal of the method, and very typically the state of mind which results from such a method at our stage [207] of history. The awareness of the process of time has obscured the frontiers between literature and everything else. If you read the earlier critics, such as Dryden, you find the problems of literature comparatively simple ones. For Dryden and his contemporaries there were the Greek and Latin classics, a solid block of accepted canon, and there were their contemporaries, that is to say, English literature from Shakespeare and French literature from Malherbe; and they spent a good deal of their time in discussing whether the moderns, as they called themselves, had any literary values not surpassed by the ancients. Their estimate of the classics was not complicated by worrying about serpent and mistletoe cults, or the finances of the Athenian government. And between the ancients and Shakespeare and Malherbe there was nothing much to think about. They had really a great deal more faith in themselves than we have. They were certainly not bothered about 'the future'. It often seems to me that all our concern about the future, and even the most optimistic visions of it which Mr Shaw and Mr Wells used to enjoy, are tokens of a profound pessimism. We hardly have time to get any fun out of what is being written now, so concerned are we about the quality of what may be written fifty years hence. Even Mr Read's chapter on 'Modern Poetry' seems to be as much engrossed by the puzzle of what poetry will be as by the puzzle of what it is. This kind of doubt seems to me to continue the doubt of Sainte-Beuve and Renan. Sainte-Beuve wrote a book of seven volumes on that remarkable French religious movement of the seventeenth century known as *Port Royal*, and on that remarkable group of religious people of whom the most famous is Pascal. It is the [208] masterpiece on that subject. It comes to no conclusion. It ends with the words:

> He who had it most at heart to know his object, whose ambition was most engaged in seizing it, whose pride was most alert to paint it – how powerless he feels, and how far beneath his task, on the day when, seeing it almost finished and the result obtained, he feels his exaltation sink, feels himself overcome by faintness and inevitable

disgust, and perceives in his turn that he too is only a fleeting illusion in the midst of the infinite illusory flux!

Sainte-Beuve was a modern critic for this reason: he was a man of restless curiosity about life, society, civilisation, and all the problems which the study of history arouses. He studied these things *through* literature, because that was the centre of his interests; and he never lost his literary sensibility in his investigation of problems reaching far beyond literature. But he was an historian, a sociologist (in the best sense of that word) and a moralist. He is a typical modern critic in that he found himself obliged to brood over the larger and darker problems which, in the modern world, lie behind the specific problems of literature.

9 The criticism of literature has by no means been absorbed in something else, as alchemy into chemistry. The core of the matter is still there, though the ramifications are endless, and the task of the critic is indeed hard. But there is still a valid distinction to be drawn between those modern critics who would make literature a *substitute* for a definite philosophy and theology, and thus promulgate, in an inverted form, the old gospel of art for art's sake, and those who would try to keep the distinctions clear, while admitting that the study of the one leads to the other, and that the posses-[209]sion of clear literary standards must imply the possession of clear moral standards. The various attempts to find the fundamental axioms behind both good literature and good life are among the most interesting 'experiments' of criticism in our time.

10 The most considerable of such attempts so far is that which is known under the name of Humanism, and which owes its origin chiefly to the work of Professor Babbitt of Harvard. Mr Babbitt, who is one of the most learned men of our time, is to some extent a disciple of Sainte-Beuve. There is no one living who knows more intimately (among many other things) the whole history of literary criticism. In his own writings, still more positively than in those of Sainte-Beuve, the criticism of literature has been a means of criticising every aspect of modern society. He is a scholar of classical education and classical tastes. He is keenly aware of the fact that the weaknesses of modern literature are symptoms of the weaknesses of modern civilisation, and he has set himself with immense patience and perseverance to analyse these weaknesses. His conclusions may be read in his two most recent books, *Rousseau and Romanticism*, an account and a theory of the deterioration of taste since the early eighteenth century, and a book of still wider scope, *Democracy and Leadership*. As a moralist and as an Anglo-Saxon, he has on one

side more in common with Matthew Arnold than with Sainte-Beuve. The tendency of the 'humanist' in France is rather to diagnose without prescribing a remedy; witness two recent books of brilliant literary and social criticism by M. Julien Benda, *Belphégor* and *La Trahison des Clercs*; the Anglo-Saxon finds it intolerable to diagnose a disease without prescribing a remedy. [210] Mr Babbitt, like Arnold and Sainte-Beuve, finds that the decay of religious dogma has inflicted grave injury on society; like Arnold and Sainte-Beuve, he refuses to accept the remedy of returning to religious dogma; like Arnold and unlike Sainte-Beuve, he proposes another remedy, a theory of positive ethics based on human experiment, on the needs and capacities of the human as human, without reference to revelation or to supernatural authority or aid.

11 I do not propose, in this brief account, to discuss Mr Babbitt's positive contribution, or the points at which I agree or disagree. I only want to call attention to a most important movement which is primarily, or in its inception, a movement within literary criticism, and of which a great deal more will be heard. It is significant because it shows that the modern literary critic must be an 'experimenter' outside of what you might at first consider his own province; and as evidence that nowadays there is no literary problem which does not lead us irresistibly to larger problems. There is one weakness, or rather danger, of literary criticism which perceives the inevitable continuation of literary questions into general questions, which I might as well point out, because otherwise you will see it for yourselves and attach too much importance to it. The danger is that when a critic has grasped these vital moral problems which rise out of literary criticism, he may lose his detachment and submerge his sensibility. He may become too much a servant of his mind and conscience; he may be too impatient with contemporary literature, having pigeonholed it under one or another of the modern social maladies; and may demand edification at once, when appreciation of genius and accomplish-[211]ment should come first. When he upholds 'classicism' and denounces 'romanticism' he is likely to give the impression that we should write like Sophocles or Racine: that everything contemporary is 'romantic' and therefore not worth talking about. He makes us suspect that if a truly great, original classical work of imagination were to be written to-day, no one would like it. There will always be romantic people to admire romantic work; but we wonder whether the classicists would certainly know a classical work when it came. But these qualifications should not lead us to reject the humanist's theories: they should only lead us to apply them for ourselves.

12 Mr Ramon Fernandez is a younger critic, who has also taken the word Humanism for his device, though his humanism, arrived at independently in France, is of a rather different brand from that which has arisen in America. His humanism has this in common: that it is also a development from literary criticism, and that it is also an attempt to arrive at a positive system of ethics while rejecting any revealed religion or supernatural authority. His first volume of essays, *Messages*, has been translated into English (Cape): it is important, I think, not so much by its achievement – for indeed the author has still a great many tangled knots in his style, which is cumbered by a good deal of philosophical and psychological terminology – as by its new attempt. Mr Fernandez is less encyclopedic, less concerned with the past. He pores steadily over contemporaries and over the nineteenth century, and is more devoted to the study of special individuals, such as Montaigne, than to the study of the general course of literary history. Like the American humanists, he ponders over 'classicism' [212] and 'romanticism'; but he wishes to be flexible, and is anxious to distinguish the essentials of classicism (which he finds, for instance, in George Eliot) from its appearances at any particular time. His theory is one which I do not wholly understand, and which has not yet been fully expounded, and probably not yet fully developed: but he illustrates, as clearly as the American humanists, the new experimental method of dealing with literary problems as moral problems, and the attempt to find guidance in conduct out of statement in literature – especially from the great novelists, and particularly, for he is a close student of English literature, from George Eliot and George Meredith. (In any case, his essay on Marcel Proust, the French novelist, in the volume mentioned, is a masterpiece of his particular method.) He is, in general, less the sociologist and more the individual psychologist. And from the best of his essays on novelists one draws this conclusion: that if we should exclude from literary criticism all but purely literary considerations, there would not only be very little to talk about, but actually we should be left without even literary appreciation. This is true of our appreciation of ancient authors, but still more obviously of our appreciation of modern authors. For the same expansion of interest which has been imposed upon the modern critic has been imposed, or at least has been assumed, by the modern imaginative writer. We cannot write a purely literary criticism of George Eliot, for instance, unless it is admittedly a very imperfect criticism: for as the interests of the author were wide, so must be those of the critic.

13 I have tried to show that the tendency throughout a whole epoch to the present moment has been to widen [213] the scope of criticism and

increase the demands made upon the critic. This development might be traced in terms of the development of human self-consciousness, but that is a general philosophical question beyond the margin of this lecture. There is along with this expansion a compensating tendency. As the number of sciences multiply, of sciences that is which have a bearing upon criticism, so we ask ourselves first whether there is still any justification for literary criticism at all, or whether we should not merely allow the subject to be absorbed gently into exacter sciences which will each annex some side of criticism. Just as in the history of philosophy, we find many subjects surrendered from time to time by philosophy, now to mathematics and physics, now to biology and psychology; until there seems to be nothing left to philosophise about. I think that the answer is clear: that so long as literature is literature, so long will there be a place for criticism of it, for criticism, that is, on the same basis as that on which the literature itself is made. For so long as poetry and fiction and such things are written, its first purpose must always be what it always has been – to give a peculiar kind of pleasure which has something constant in it throughout the ages, however different and various our explanations of that pleasure may be. The task of criticism will be, accordingly, not only to expand its borders but to clarify its centre, and the insistency of the latter need grows with that of the former. Two hundred years ago, when it was taken for granted that one knew well enough what literature was, and it was not the number of other things which it is always now seeming to be, terms could be used more freely and carelessly without close definition. Now, there is an urgent need [214] for experiment in criticism of a new kind, which will consist largely in a logical and dialectical study of the terms used. My own interest in these problems has been fostered partly by dissatisfaction with the *meaning* of my own statements in criticism, and partly by dissatisfaction with the terminology of the Humanists. In literary criticism we are constantly using terms which we cannot define, and defining other things by them. We are constantly using terms which have an *in*tension and an *ex*tension which do not quite fit; theoretically they ought to be made to fit; but if they cannot, then some other way must be found of dealing with them so that we may know at every moment what we mean. I will take a very simple example with which I have been dealing myself: the possibility of defining 'metaphysical poetry'. Here is a term which has a whole history of meanings down to the present time, all of which must be recognised, although it cannot have all of them at once. The term means, on the one hand, a certain group of English poets in the seventeenth century. On the other hand, it must have an intensive meaning, must stand for a peculiar whole of qualities which is exemplified by the several poets. The ordinary critical method would be to define what 'metaphysical poetry' means to you in the abstract, fit as many poets to it as well you can, and reject the rest. Or else, you take the poets who have been held to be 'metaphysical', and find out what they have in common. The odd thing is that by doing the sum, so to speak, in two different ways, you get two different results. A larger problem in the same kind of definition is that of Classicism and Romanticism. Every one who writes about these two abstractions believes that he knows what the words mean; actually they [215] mean something a little different for each observer, and merely mean to mean the same things. In this way you have material for endless wrangling with no conclusion, which is not satisfactory. Such problems involve, of course, both logic and the theory of knowledge and psychology; there is no one, perhaps, more concerned with them than Mr I. A. Richards, the author of *Principles of Literary Criticism* and *Practical Criticism*.

14 There is good cause for believing – apart from the obvious assertion that every generation must criticise for itself – that literary criticism, far from being exhausted, has hardly begun its work. On the other hand, I am more than sceptical of the old superstition that criticism and 'creative writing' never flourish in the same age: that is a generalisation drawn from a superficial inspection of some past ages. 'Creative writing' can look after itself; and certainly it will be none the better for suppressing the critical curiosity. And in any case, the times which we have lived in seem to me, on the false antithesis mentioned, rather 'creative' than 'critical'. (The current superstition that our epoch is Alexandrine, decadent, or 'disillusioned' is parallel; there are no 'disillusioned ages', only disillusioned individuals; and our time is just as deluded as any other.) The present age has been, rather, uncritical, and partly for economic causes. The 'critic' has been chiefly the reviewer, that is to say, the hurried amateur wage-slave. I am aware of the danger that the types of criticism in which I am interested may become too professional and technical. What I hope for is the collaboration of critics of various special training, and perhaps the pooling and sorting of their contributions by men who will be neither specialists nor amateurs.

Variants from *Bookman* (1929):

Title Experiment in Criticism

1 *every* dead author] every dead author
  deliberately] deliberately

2 at its worst] at its worst,
  theoretic, and] theoretic and,

4 'modernist'] 'modernist' –

TRADITION AND EXPERIMENT IN PRESENT-DAY LITERATURE · 83

5 common, as little] common – as little
our mentality] our mentality
our age] our age
we] we

6 *evolution*] evolution
Levy-Bruhl] Lévy-Brühl
Gommere] Gummere
level] level

7 so conversely the critic has to know something about them. The modern critic is distinguished] so conversely the critic is distinguished
and also,] and also

8 values] virtues
concern about the future, and even the most optimistic visions of it which Mr Shaw] concern of it, which Mr Shaw
through] through

9 *substitute*] substitute

10 In his own writings, still more positively than in those of Sainte-Beuve, the criticism] in his own writings, criticism
classical education and] classical education, and
rather to diagnose without] rather to diagnose, without

12 system of ethics] ethics
English (Cape): it] English. It
important, I think,] important I think
upon the modern critic] upon the modern critic,

13 lecture] paper
any justification] still any justification
criticism of it, for] criticism of it – for
meaning] meaning
, on the one hand,] on the one hand
other hand,] other hand

1930

A Commentary

C., 9. 35 (Jan. 1930), 181–4. Unsigned. Gallup C297.
In para. 1 'Hoffmansthal' has been corrected to 'Hofmannsthal'.

THE FIVE REVIEWS' AWARD

In our July number we announced a new form of literary award to be conferred by five reviews: *The Criterion*, the *Europaeische Revue* of Berlin, the *Nouvelle Revue Française* of Paris, the *Revista de Occidente* of Madrid and the *Nuova Antologia* of Milan. Our project, it will be remembered, was to make the award in five successive years: first for the best short story submitted in German, then for short stories in English, French, Italian and Spanish in that order; the winning piece of fiction to be printed as nearly simultaneously as possible in the five reviews. As the scheme originated with the *Europaeische Revue*, it is right that the German story should be chosen first. In this number we print *The Centurion (Der Hauptmann von Kaparneum)* by Mr Ernst Wiechert. This story was selected unanimously by the German committee, which consisted of Dr Max Clauss, the Editor of the *Europaeische Revue*, Professor E. R. Curtius, who is very well known to readers of *The Criterion*, and Thomas Mann the novelist, who replaces the late Hugo von Hofmannsthal on the committee; it was then approved by the editors of the other four reviews. We hope to be able to announce, [182] early next year the conditions of submitting manuscripts of English fiction: the manuscripts to be read first by a similar committee of three English critics, and subsequently referred to the editors of the four European reviews.

We take particular pleasure in the inception of this form of international activity (though we cannot take any credit for the idea itself). It is not merely a means of bringing to notice new prose writers in five languages, or a means of comparing the methods and views of the writers of five peoples. We remark upon it still more as visible evidence of a community of interest, and a desire for co-operation, between literary and general reviews of different nations, which has been growing steadily since 1918, and which is now so much more pronounced than at any time before the war as to be almost a new phenomenon. All of these periodicals, and others, have endeavoured to keep the intellectual blood of Europe circulating throughout the whole of Europe; and perhaps at no time during the nineteenth century was this circulation so healthy as it is now. It is of vital importance that the best thought and feeling of each country of high civilisation should be contributed to the others while it is still fresh. Only so can there be any direction towards that higher community which existed in some ways throughout the middle ages, which persisted into the eighteenth century, and which was only dissolved finally after the Napoleonic wars. And without such intellectual community and co-operation of different organs in one body all peace pacts, world congresses, disarmament discussions, and reform leagues appear merely to be concerned with the body and not with the soul.

NATIONALISM, DISARMAMENT, AND PEACE

We hope, next year, to publish in *The Criterion*, some discussions from various points of view and by critics of several nationalities, on the subjects of Nationalism and International Relations. Half a dozen serious books, and many more less serious ones, have [183] lately been written; Mr Macdonald, we all know, has lately been to America; every successful politician has views on international amity. On the other hand, a push – not so far under very good omens – has been made for 'Empire Free Trade'; and we have heard something of a new 'war' between Europe and America in which the munitions are to be cheaper and cheaper motor cars. We are given to believe that the Conservative Party is defunct, which indeed it looks to be, but also that it can only be revived (or 'gingered') by elements which do not appear to be either Conservative, Liberal, or Radical, but merely Irresponsible. The only merit of the Labour Party, from the same point of view, appears to be that it is at the moment quite inert: one party being approved for that for which the other is condemned. These are unpleasant symptoms. But we can hardly believe that there are not, scattered over the continents of Europe and America, a few men of thought and observation, who are concerned with the Theory of Politics. And we are very badly in need of that; and half a dozen Aristotles working together would be only enough to supply the need. All that we have is confusion of voices in popular discussion, exaggerating the importance of various details. Perhaps the most significant thing about the War is its *insignificance*; and it is this insignificance which makes it so acutely tragic. Perhaps *fear* of war is now rather an incentive, than a preventive, of war. It is easy to convince people of the horrors, and of the harm that war does; but it is at least as important to convince them that it does no good, and has no grandeur, and that 'the sense of glory' has other, and only other, means of expression.

A NOTE ON THE PRESS

It is, or was for several years, a commonplace of dignified political observation that the 'popular press' has now no influence on opinion. It may be true that certain potentates of the press have not the influence that they think they have; [184] it may be true that when they set out to divert public opinion in one direction it flies in another. But stupidity and vanity do not always mean powerlessness; they only make power more dangerous. It is true that the common newspaper reader no longer consciously asks his paper to provide his opinions for him; but that would be a superior state of consciousness to what actually exists. What the reader allows his paper to do for him is to select what is important and to suppress what is unimportant, to divert his mind with shallow discussions of serious topics, to destroy his wits with murders and weddings and curates' confessions, and to reduce him to a condition in which he is less capable of voting with any discrimination at the smallest municipal election, than if he could neither read nor write. To amuse people is to have power over them; and power is power, even if its possessors have not the slightest notion what they are doing with it.

A NOTE ON OUR REVIEWS

The fact that the bulk of book publication takes place twice a year, in the autumn and the spring, occasions some trouble to the editor of any quarterly review. In this number, for instance, we have been obliged to omit some important reviews; and other important books, such as Dr Bridges's poem, have appeared too late for review. In apology, we remind our readers that it is the function of a quarterly review to review at leisure, and to allow its reviewers ample time to present their mature views upon any book worth reviewing. There have appeared recently a number of books which our readers might expect to find reviewed in this number. Some of those absent will be reviewed in the spring number. When some important books are ignored altogether, the reader must remember that we aim to review adequately those books which we do review, rather than to give a complete survey of the best of the season. For such a survey, one must turn to periodicals which appear at more frequent intervals.

A Humanist Theory of Value
By Ramon Fernandez

C., 9. 35 (Jan. 1930), 228–45. Gallup C298.

The opponents of humanism have it all their own way. They judge and condemn a doctrine which is not yet self-conscious, or conscious of its tendency or of its exact place in the universe of discourse. They make haste to stifle an embryo of thought, the future of which is still unpredictable. A few pages of William James, the essays of Schiller and of Hulme, the synthesis of Max Scheler – these views are still very incomplete, very tentative under their appearance of boldness. The American humanists, with whom *The Criterion* has lately concerned itself, are essayists rather than philosophers. They do not seem to have tested their notions by a rigorous critique, and are easily entrapped in their own pretensions.

I should like here to outline a preliminary examination, which seems to me of the first importance, and without which every discussion of humanism must inevitably be a wild-goose chase. Before defining humanism, I should like to describe the *humanist adventure*, to try to show the conditions under which it happens, and finally, how the humanist problem is proposed in the concrete life of humanity.

Partisans and adversaries of humanism seem to me to commit the same error in method. They prattle of 'naturalism', (or 'naturism'), of morals, of religion in connexion with humanism, as if humanism was a coherent doctrine, an established Wisdom or Gnosis whose adepts were to spread its evangel. If they were right, the logician and the historian would be justified in challenging the origin and in denouncing the capriciousness of a choice which falls here and there according to fancy and temperament; and in demonstrating that a system built up in [229] this way is always in need of that with which it professes to dispense. But to set the problem in this way is to set it wrong. Humanism is not a body of Doctrine; and if its champions present it as such, so much the worse for it and them. Humanism, at least in its origin, is still less a body of Wisdom. Humanism is first of all, a *resultant situation*.

Humanism appears, or at least is taken notice of when the divorce between the *law* (natural or supernatural) which rules over men at a particular moment of history, and the human *custom*, the way in which men *really* think, feel, will, act – becomes too extreme. Beneath the law a habit of living has been formed, a sort of freemasonry of admitted, though unhallowed rites. The divorce has become so great the law, such as it persists in being, not only can no longer correspond to the reality of man, but can no longer express its own ideal. If humanism were nothing more than expression of a will-to-live, it could easily be reintegrated, at least dialectically, in the established order. But it embraces an ethics in process of formation which is at least in partial opposition to orthodox ethics. The rules, transformed by repeated variations in application, have given rise to a jurisprudence in which the representations of good and evil have become more or less deeply modified. And the humanist question is raised whenever the need for decision becomes urgent – whether to re-adjust custom to law or law to custom. But at that point it exists only as a question, and not at all as a doctrine. Now, in human custom we find a chaotic criss-crossing of the tendencies which dogmas and theories abstract, separate, oppose and purify. So it is natural enough that humanistic thought should offer at first a considerable vagueness and even confusion; and that it should show itself, for instance, incapable of drawing a frontier between naturalism and religion.

Considered as an historical movement, humanism is always trying to make the law both flexible and complete – for the sound reason that it has discovered in custom, in human jurisprudence, values which the law has not yet [230] assimilated. Mr Santayana says well, concerning Christian humanism of the Renaissance:

> So it became necessary to reform something: either the world of joy to adapt it to the austerity and the primitive asceticism of the Church, or else the Church to adapt it to the inclusive profane interests of the world. The latter task was undertaken, more or less consciously by the humanists, who would have liked to reduce the wealth of the clergy and to weaken its irrational authority, to advance polite culture, and, while preserving Christianity – for why should we change an inherited religion? – would have preserved it as a form of paganism, as an ornament and a poetic expression of human life.[1]

To-day, after the attempt of the natural law of science in the nineteenth century to obliterate the supernatural law of the Church, we see the American humanists striving to make flexible and complete the law of science by considering realities such as intuition, ethical imagination, etc. They incline towards the supernatural just as the humanists of the Renaissance inclined towards the natural, under the pressure of the same need of bringing back everything human that has been ignored in the constitution of a spiritual doctrine and an art of living.

But these rectifications in one direction or the other must not be allowed to distract us. The greatest mistake, in these matters, consists in

---

1. This is merely my own re-translation from the French, as I did not have the original text by me. I apologise to Mr Santayana. – TRANSLATOR.

taking too seriously the term 'naturalist' or the term 'Christian' which we apply to humanism by turns. The real question concerns a 'naturalism' or a 'Christianity' so transmogrified by human custom, by the course of life and culture, by all sorts of associations which modify beliefs and instincts, that the same word has no longer the same meaning. The opponents of humanism, when, for instance, they classify Montaigne as a naturalist, are skilfully exploiting an ambiguity; for Montaigne's 'nature' was highly cultivated, positively ethical; because it preserved, beneath a lively homely form, the riches of a long [231] complex tradition in which Christian and pagan sources are mingled. All that he perceived more clearly in himself than in the injunctions of heaven and of society, and it was through his own self that he found contact with the whole form of human nature.

But humanism is not merely a collective movement, an enterprise of learned and refined culture. It is moreover – and I am tempted to say especially – a private drama, echoes of which are reflected into the public life, an effort to save oneself without the support of the law, or, in case of need, against the law. Take an example as simple and homely as possible: the extra-conjugal union of a man and a woman who are already married or who are prevented from marriage by some ineluctable circumstance. They do not give themselves up to licentiousness, but physical love is a beneficent source of energy to them; they have no greed for the coarse art of 'living one's life'; but their liaison makes possible for them, in their appropriate sphere, the realisation of a human *maximum* which they could not reach without it. They are Christian by inheritance and education: and they are outlawed by their Church. Religion imposes sacrifice upon them; and I have no doubt that sacrifice, in many cases, is capable of producing a spiritual *maximum* equal or superior to that realised by the two lovers; but that is, by hypothesis, impossible in the case I have put, and it is such a case, precisely, that we are trying to understand. Certainly, these will have to bear the reproach of playing ducks and drakes with the tables of the law, with no better authority than their own caprice. The reproach will even go so far as to denounce in their case an amorous willingness-to-oblige themselves with the hypocrisy of the sublime. That is only to change ground without answering the question. These lovers have only the choice of two divergent courses: either to continue in the way of Christianity, either as sinners or as sacrifice, or to blaze bravely for themselves a human way and assert frankly the *value* of their decision.

In fields of discourse very different from this, things hap-[232]pen in the same way. It is easy to imagine a man who after having accepted the laws of 'science' – I do not say science – and feeling himself to be impoverished, desiccated and so to speak qualified thereby, should decide to ignore no longer those mysterious powers such as imagination, intuition, sense of destiny, etc., which he has been taught to despise and which have become indispensable to him. In either case, in order to resume contact with human fulness, there is a rupture, more or less violent, with a law imposed from without, there is the establishment of a custom by virtue of man's private judgement, and there is a progress beyond doctrine to a point at which the obedience to oneself replaces the other servitudes.

There is a close relation – which is sometimes relation of cause and effect – between these private adventures and the collective movements of humanism. It occurs when the individual can no longer set himself in order without arraigning the law, or without taking liberties with the law which become conscious in the effort of transformation and regeneration. In this sense, we may say that the law is never seriously threatened except by the best people. To take oneself in hand and to free oneself are often two aspects of one and the same adventure. *'C'est une vie exquise (rare), celle qui se maintient en ordre jusques en son privé.'* This prayer of Montaigne rounds off his principles of free thought. Is there need to insist upon the importance, in the formation of the humanist jurisprudence of the nineteenth century, of those crises of nonconformity, themselves provoked by the need of saving one's soul without losing values deemed to be precious and judged to be indispensable?

This slipping, this dislocation of the spiritual centre of gravity from commandment to custom, from law to jurisprudence, is precipitated not at all by a relaxation of the moral tone (a moral atony) but on the contrary by the necessity of reassembling human values, of preventing, even by a compromise, their dissipation and shipwreck. He who fails to perceive this condemns himself to judging [233] humanism without understanding it. Sometimes it issues as an attempt, primarily, to accommodate the law to the richness of life in process of formation by the concurrence of all human potencies; sometimes it issues primarily as an individual refusal to accept judgement, to admit oneself condemned: a refusal which brings a man to challenging the orthodox notions of good and evil. Under both aspects, its essential traits reveal themselves, one principle of which, resulting evidently in what has been observed above, is the assimilation – at least provisional – of the real and the ideal. By recognising in his own experience, individual or collective, more truth than in the law, the humanist reduces to the kernel of reality that enveloping ideal structure which he knows to be crumbling away. Hence the moderating, the simplifying character of the great humanist experiments. There is no genuine humanism without a certain heroic modesty. To the law itself, humanism brings the benefits of those attenuations to which a vigorous scepticism has submitted the law's pretensions. And for the same reason which has made it assimilate the ideal and the reality, it assigns to this reality a new importance, by the fact that the reality alone is placed in a position to assure the possibility of a persistence of the ideal.

Reduction of the ideal, reduction of human pretensions and pretences, heroism of modesty and responsibility for the capital of humanity, such are the characteristics of humanism as it constitutes them and spontaneously proposes them to itself. So it cannot confine itself for long to these reactions of custom and circumstance. The actual tends to become the *right*. After having asserted itself, humanism finds itself charged with the task of self-justification.

II. DIFFICULTIES OF HUMANISM

At this point we must acknowledge that humanism is up against serious troubles, of various kinds: some provoked by the reactions that it arouses, others by the very nature of [234] its attempt. These difficulties, the most important of which we must examine, unite in preventing humanism from definition and delimitation, and in leaving it only the appearance of a skeleton-key-word referring to any fancy you please.

Humanism, groping tentatively toward some rearrangement of human forces, jostles first of all the *dogmatic instinct*, which is very deeply rooted in all of us. The doctrinal structure of dogma operates upon thought with an extraordinary efficacy. The formation of logic, in so far as it is in existence previous to the actual effort of thought, manipulates this effort and affirms it in paths already marked out. We know to what extent memory, or rather apperception-mass, reinforces the reality of an impression. The minimal sensation, if it but evoke a memory similar to itself, finds therein a facile confirmation. A doctrine is nothing but a total of ideas conceived and repeated again and again. Being familiar, it reinforces every idea that we conceive, with memories similar to the new idea – similar but stronger and clearer, and which have an irresistible attraction for it. It does more than that: the idea is not only polished off, revealed and so to speak baptised by the reminiscences of ideas that it evokes – it is at the same time *judged* – for the memories impose their own associations upon it. Its relations are settled in advance, its place is fixed in advance. To put it in another way, the idea, hardly formed, is thought introduced into a judgement which is not derivative from it but is prior to it. Now, to judge in advance is exactly what humanism refuses to do, because it feels that its idea in formation may be big with a *new* judgement. Dogmatists present humanism with a *fait accompli* – that of a thought which has nothing to do but to repeat itself to itself, which by virtue of this mere repetition accumulates mighty force of persuasion. Consequently it is natural for the humanist, when stood up against the wall by the dogmatist, to look as if he was refusing to think, when actually he is trying to save the life of his real thought. But when [235] the law is put into the dock it appears in the same sharp relief. In the light of debate the law is seen more clearly, its seductiveness is more evident. So that on the way the law picks up new adepts, sharper-witted and better armed.

Thus is formed the religion of authority, the basis of all powerful religions. The principle of authority amounts to this: that every thought has already been thought before it exists, and that order consists in finding the *mot d'ordre*. Therein is the origin of realism, according to which our thoughts do no more than rejoin, outside and beyond themselves, their perfect pre-existent models. Every form of realism is fundamentally dogmatic, and the tendency of the mind towards realism is the same thing as its craving for authority. By a striking peculiarity, the recourse to authority, which is psychologically an evasion in face of the unknown element in the nascent thought, assumes the appearance of being the real right kind of thought – for the following reason. Any thought, however modest, tends to self-completion as a kind of profound justification. But it cannot come to completion without completing all the rest, without embracing the whole mental universe. And as this undertaking exceeds the powers of a particular thought, the understanding, to satisfy itself, makes a short cut across dogma: re-discovers instead of inventing, reconstructs instead of constructing. The art of fitting in ideas in process of formation to a finished system is subtle and difficult. It naturally gives its practitioner the illusion of thinking. And at the same time the awareness of the goal assures the dogmatist of the presence of that intelligible whole which seems to be the supreme guarantee of thought. How can we make head against the intimate alliance of these two great inclinations: the need of reaching an end, and the need of security? The two get on so well together that the latter does not need to make itself known. Its interests are loyally defenced by the former. And the precautions inspired by uncertainty or fear are presented as the austere principles of truth.

[236] The pundits of authority represent to humanism what political journalists call the 'menace from the extreme right'. Humanism is exposed to a 'menace from the left' which is just as serious, and against which it has just as much trouble in protecting itself. Any doctrine or dogma or conformity whatever rests on the assumption that its edicts correspond to realities. As soon as we query one of these edicts we query implicitly the reality which corresponds. That is to say that we offer more or less clearly, whether we want to or not, a symbolic interpretation of the law.

At the same time we introduce new realities in order to justify the liberties we have taken. For instance: you assert that Good and Evil are roughly as religion conceives them to be; but that their concrete representations, in that particular religion, are no more than symbols, variable, modifiable, according to one age or another. Time is accordingly the new function the emergence of which is enough to transform the law. But what happens then? The most temperate humanism, if only by the fact that it professes an alliance of custom and doctrine, admits, consciously or unconsciously, that values are variables: values, that is to say, these things which men deem worthy of respect and desire. And it admits that these values vary according to the function of time, that is to say History, that is to say in fine the men who make it and live it. But if men alter values, how shall humanism succeed in salvaging the dualism upon which it professes to base its ethics? And how shall humanism be distinguished from the revolutionism which conceives History as the successive destruction of values by other values?

The notion of value comprises two different notions. Subjectively: what we desire, what we wish to happen, what we esteem, these things have value. Objectively: that only has value which is founded by the law as valuable, whatever be our personal desires. Obviously, no system of ethics is possible without the distinction between the subjective and the objective values. In its effort to assimilate the ideal and the real – the objective value and the subjective value – [237] humanism must pull up before it reaches the point of complete identification, under the penalty of destroying itself in destroying the possibility of a truly human life. But where does it stop? and what sort of brake is it that humanism throws on? The revolutionist, for his part, has no trouble in demonstrating that the humanist stops just where he pleases; that he is restrained in his demolition of values by illegitimate motives such as a sentimental attachment to the past, or the caprices of his ego, or the interests of his class. And just as the revolutionist himself is induced – as we shall see later – to establish objectively his destruction of values, so humanism finds itself condemned by both parties as a formless, tentative, incoherent and contemptible experiment.

The objection which I anticipated at the beginning of this essay, that is, the objection that humanism is not a doctrine but a condition of fact, a status, should now cease to be tenable. I have followed the humanist adventure from its birth to the moment of its justification, that is to say to the moment when humanism, no longer satisfied to impose itself as a fact, offers itself as a system of ethics. Now the weakness of humanism reveals itself as soon as the question of value is raised; because it shakes the very foundation of the value on which it depends. If value must be founded in law, if it is measured by the divergence between its subjective and objective aspects, then the pretences of a doctrine which subordinates desires to values and at the same time makes values depend upon human custom, contain a manifest contradiction.

To take a precise example: a Catholic and a Marxist will raise objections against a humanist which will be of the same nature and for the same reasons. The Marxist furthermore will have the advantage of being able to say: 'I believe, as you do, in the evolution of values. But for me this evolution has an objective foundation, witness the dialectic of historical materialism. My doctrine accordingly takes notice of this division between value and individual [238] appreciation which you cannot maintain.' In this way we are brought to the following alternative: either humanism is no more than a more or less accidental and more or less negligible transition between two objective doctrines of value; or else the idea of value is itself misunderstood and must be investigated afresh. From every point of view, the problem of humanism is identical with the problem of value.

III. VALUE OF HUMANISM

Let us revert to the contradiction which humanism, in its current form, has been unable to avoid. On the one hand it professes to be more or less emancipated, to be in a position to modify the interpretation of the law; on the other hand it recognises the objective nature of value, which precisely is founded on the law. We notice about humanists that they do not want to change values or to suppress them, in the revolutionary fashion. They profess to respect the same values as the dogmatists whom they oppose, but not at all in the same way. They are like those young people who refuse to obey but who do not understand by that the rejection of the education they have received. They deem themselves to be freed from their bonds, but not from the values which formed them.

Their only chance of escaping their dilemma is to establish the principle, that although value is really objective, it is nevertheless not its objectivity which constitutes it *qua* value.

Beyond doubt, value must be independent of the will to be really valid. The man who resists his personal appreciations must be aware of that; the man who resists the appreciations which insurge according to his passions and caprices. And as the coercive influence of value is one of its essential tokens, principally during moral crises, we are led to associate the value with the acts themselves, to see in the objectivity of the injunction not only the sign, but the very reality of the value. From that point to believing that good and evil, for [239] example, are part of the tissue of things, are presented to our consciousness in forms determined once for all, there is only one step, which is always taken. If we say that Peter has done the right thing, we mean it to be understood that the action of Peter is good in itself, and that Peter's merit resides in the effort he has made to choose this action rather than another. If we admit that one action is better than another, we mean by that that it has a greater infusion of good, just as one cachet contains a bigger dose of quinine than another cachet. The man who is grappling with moral difficulties, according to this system, is rather like the weaver who sorts out a heap of tufts in order to pick the colours he wants; or like the chemist who doses different bodies according to the quantities of the same acid that they contain.

But there is another way of conceiving value, which does not modify its essential structure, and which on the contrary aims at restoring it in its purity. It rests upon the analysis of the act of evaluation. The more we reflect upon the significance of this act, the more we become convinced that the doctrines which assign value to injunction, which connect value with determinate representations, imply the postulate that value causes valuing – which is absurd, for obviously it is the valuing which gives rise to the value. The dogmatists themselves admit that conscious evaluation or intention creates the value of an act. But the intention is meaningless unless it bestows value, otherwise basis, because an enjoined intention derives its knowledge of the value from its knowledge of the injunction – and, *a fortiori*, its value itself. From this point of view, we should not say that the intention bestows the value upon the act, but that once the value is defined, the value of the intention consists in the recognition of that value. Or else we must have the courage to restore to 'evaluation' its real meaning, and put the intention *before* the injunction. According to this way of conceiving value, the injunction is only the fixation, and so to speak the solidification of our normative [240] tendencies, in formulas which express them roughly and very generally. But these tendencies precede the formulas. 'Thou shalt not kill': this looks of course like a command, but it does not found the value of the actions which I shall perform or which I shall not perform in order to obey it. For, far from being the principle from which issue my judgements of value, I take it to be the summary, the projection, the dynamic scheme of a great number of similar actions which will be enjoined, not by the order, but by my rating (*estimation*) of that order. What appears to me at first, under the pressure of time and of society, to be an injunction, is only the formula and so to speak the mnemonic help of my normative tendencies, a way of recognising my craving for the good, through the boobytraps and the mists of passion. According to this notion of value, when we say that Peter has done well, we do not mean that he has found a certain quantity of good in his action, but that he has willed to express, by acting in this way, some certain craving for the good which he has, and upon which are founded the injunctions which he obeys, as well as this or that particular act.

The implications of this notion of value must be frankly disclosed. Man, individually or collectively, is the source of all values. Our normative tendencies spring from our physical and moral structure. These are categories, if you like, *a priori* forms of will, or instincts, or intentions: call it what you choose. As the principles are only approximate general expressions, our acts are not the clumsy imitations of some illustrious and perfect models or other. On the contrary, each of our acts realises a little of the good of which our tendencies only translate the craving, the appetite, for which the realisation of this good is needed. The least of our acts is infinitely important, for it adds or subtracts a part of the real values of the world. There is more value in the concrete particular act than in the principle or in the law. This is the essential ethic of humanism and the heroic significance of its modesty.

[241] But the analysis of evaluation would still be incomplete if we overlooked another aspect. We have seen that evaluation has no meaning unless it implies the priority of the internal act which evaluates, which constitutes the value of the object; and that the injunction, in spite of appearances, itself relies upon evaluation. But the injunction is not merely a formula; it is an undertaking, and this undertaking distinguishes evaluation from every other form of appreciation. To rate something is precisely to preserve it, in a way by decree, from the caprices of personal appreciation; it is to give it a right over oneself, and thereby the cogency of law. Value is nothing else than the legalisation of a wish (*souhait*). If I judge it proper to act always in such a way as to respect a certain principle, my judgement can be analysed as follows: I have first given consent to the principle which seems to me to sum up and define my craving for the good; then, in the same movement, I have made this principle into a law, in order to guarantee me against myself. But what I have sworn fealty to is not the law, but the vow which gave rise to the law; and the very nature of this vow makes it my duty not to associate good and evil with this or that particular act, with this or that determinate form. Perhaps it is now possible to see the causes of the error of the dogmatists. The definitive association of good with certain forms to the exclusion of others is the evidence of a materialisation of value; and this materialisation is mistaken, by a veritable inversion, for its objectivity. The particular forms of good and evil depend upon circumstances, upon the degree of spiritual and social maturity. The tendency toward the good remains the same. Loyalty (*loyalisme*) to the

sovereign, loyalty to the fatherland, loyalty to humanity are forms which can be reciprocally destructive without destroying the moral energy which has successively created them. The evolution of values is the history of forsaken loves and illegitimate fidelities. But the gift of self, the power of loving and of making contracts, these survive the betrayals. And it is this power which [242] forms the objective element in value, not the objects upon which it concentrates itself in turn.

Thus are preserved both the objectivity of value, and the right which humanism, ingenuously enough, has always arrogated to itself, of modifying the particular forms of value. Humanism is in fact man's resumption of possession of that which is his right: that is, the origin, the very foundation of value. This re-possession does not take place without disasters. That is because life is taught to us before it is lived. Values are communicated to us in the particular actions to which they are provisionally attached. And injunctions serve us for a long time as our spiritual ceiling. Our nurse teaches us 'good' as our drawing-master teaches us 'beauty'. When our own experiences reveal to us the genuine good and the genuine beautiful, we feel as if the world was swaying under our feet like a rocking boat. Values appear to us like fulgurant inventions, like apocalyptic caprices. The revelation of the true source of values turns us into revolutionaries. Because the act of evaluating strikes us of a sudden as primordial, we think ourselves called upon to create something altogether new. And those of us who have given the signal for the change, but who feel keenly, although confusedly, that there is something eternal in man, take refuge, not altogether comfortably, in what we call 'custom' and 'nature'.

But the spirit of catastrophe is a defect of education. Our education it is which makes us see the world upside down, offering us effects for causes and causes for effects. It is not the moral world which is to be changed, but the perspective in which we see it. Here, the dogmatists will no doubt bring up an objection which they must consider formidable. They will call to my attention that if it is true that principles rest finally upon evaluation, then the moral tendencies of man, when they come to change these principles, will themselves change, thus abolishing the objective coherence of values. Honestly, I think we must oppose this objection with an exception. I do not believe that man [243] wishes to put good in the place of evil or evil in the place of good, and I do not believe that he *can* do it. The attempts of which we have been notified, with a great burst of trumpets, have turned out silly and impotent. The confusion of public and private ends, in the catastrophic years which we have endured, has not made us forget what proper behaviour is. I do not believe that the physical and moral organism of man has much chance of great modification, certainly not to such a point that man will some day be endowed with a different physical and moral structure.

All we can say is that to-day the conflict between the really vital moral life and the petrified forms of morality is manifest with such violence as to authorise, at least in appearance, illegitimate hopes.

If the foregoing is correct, humanism must become an ethic based upon a certain conception of value. I have especially wished to establish that the humanist attitude implies pretensions and undertakings. I may be allowed to sum them up and define them in conclusion.

1. Man, individually or collectively, is the source of all values. Values are based upon evaluation, which is ordained by tendencies which translate the physical and moral structure of man. These tendencies express themselves, in a wholly general way, by principles, rules and injunctions. As it is highly probable that our physical and moral structure is fixed, these principles may pass for practically unchangeable. But value is not founded upon these principles. They are only dynamic schemata to remind man of the objectivity and the permanence of his normative tendencies. In fact, it is an essential character evaluation that it strives to objectify itself, and thereby differs from other modes of appreciation.

2. As the normative principles are very general, we have only to adapt them to the concrete events of life. Hence the formation of a moral and political legislation which tends to fix itself in dogmas, in definitive injunctions. But hence also the formation of a jurisprudence which [244] distinguishes itself more and more from the law. The history of humanism is the history of the struggle between custom and law. And as custom becomes law in its turn and becomes fixed, humanism keeps up a constant criticism of values, reminding us at once of the true source of values and of the permanence of the moral activity which founds them. Its critique consists essentially (*a*) in denouncing the errors of dogmatism, and (*b*) in keeping abreast with the human custom of its time, and (*c*) in dissociating the judgement of value from the concrete representations which express it provisionally, and to which we wrongly assign an absolute value.

3. Humanism, once conscious of its own principles and of its method, appears as an ideal higher than those proposed by dogmatism of any kind. This ideal consists in firmly denying any explanation of man which shall be transcendent of man. It is legitimate to speak at this point of the heroism of modesty: modesty, because the directive principles of the moral life are measured to the height and the nature of man; heroism, because, in compliance to this ideal, we renounce supports and consolations, as well as certitudes – which mankind finds difficult to do without. Thus humanism corresponds to the maturity of the human spirit. It admits that neither all men nor all social classes can yet claim possession of this

maturity, and that the era of dogmatism is not yet concluded. But it sees no reason why the most emancipated men should not constitute an inner circle of wisdom, and it sees with regret a great number of the elect of our generation fail in their mission, either from attachment to the past of the spirit, or from personal weakness, or from sentimental attraction towards those of mankind who are still disinherited.

4. The principles and the method of humanism must not be taken for an aristocratic doctrine. One can live in the inner circle without necessarily forgetting the periphery. An aristocratic doctrine establishes a difference of nature between the values of some and the values of others. [245] Humanism on the other hand changes nothing but our *point of view* towards value, not value itself. In other words, it cultivates the same values as the common run of mortals, but interprets them in a way that the crowd can neither understand nor tolerate. On the contrary, humanism is a democratic wisdom, for it recognises more value in the act which realises a value, than in the principle which enjoins that act, and thus it elevates every genuine effort to a high rank of dignity. Humanism thus is led to the advance liberation of all men, in order to advance the creation of the greatest possible quantity of real values.

(Translated by T. S. Eliot.)

[*God* by J. Middleton Murry]

Review of *God: Being an Introduction to the Science of Metabiology* by J. Middleton Murry (1929).

C., 9. 35 (Jan. 1930), 333–6. Signed 'T. S. Eliot'. Gallup C299.

This book is a natural sequel to the author's *Life of Jesus*. It is a more important book than its predecessor in that it not only generalises the same problem into a form in which its relevancy to the modern world will be more easily recognised, but also has a more sustained clarity of expression than we are accustomed to expect from Mr [334] Murry. He has evidently worked hard not only to arrive at conclusions for himself, but to make them apprehensible to the reader.

The question at issue may be simply stated: Mr Murry rejects 'Humanism' in all of its forms. It is true that the philosophy or the philosophies of Humanism have not yet been fully developed; argument which may have force against Mr Babbitt may not be applicable to Mr Fernandez, or vice versa. Nevertheless, I believe that there is a fundamental separation between Mr Murry and anyone who would ever call himself a humanist;

that is, the framework of Mr Murry's construction is and must be definitely religious, the quality and the arrangement of his sensibility are and must be religious. Mr Murry's search therefore, is for a view of life which shall reject rationalism, or ordinary materialistic naturalism, and supernaturalism as well. It is by no means the first attempt to find a third view. Bergsonism was another. We must make clear that whereas Humanism is a *compromise* between imperfectly joined elements of the natural and the supernatural, a faith like Mr Murry's will probably turn out, if it is not a success, to be wholly a naturalism, or a supernaturalism, in disguise.

The first part of the book is autobiographical. It seems to have served for the author the purpose of working his mind up to the proper point at which he was able to say what he wanted to say; and it will probably have the same use for many readers. For the purpose of a review which must limit itself, the first part may be disregarded. Its chief relevance to the central idea of the book is its repudiation, from the author's experience, of the 'mystical experience' by itself as religious evidence. But as every student of mysticism should agree with that conclusion, and should feel no surprise at Mr Murry's experience, and as I am quite in accord that no mystical experience in and by itself can be for human beings the guarantee of anything, as it must itself be verified in daily life, I do not need to dwell upon this point.

The interpretation of the life of Jesus is substantially the same as that put forward in the earlier book, and is open to the same objections. It involves a theory of Illusion which is to me impossible as a theory of knowledge, and which I believe can be assimilated to several varieties of pragmatism.

The chief development of this book over its predecessor is the theory of metabiology, which is nothing less than what Mr Murry calls a *complete* naturalism which at the same time preserves all [335] spiritual values. Mr Murry would, I suppose, call the naturalism of Bergson incomplete, and the naturalism of Mr Russell more rationalism.

One's first enquiry about a theory of 'metabiology' should not be whether it is false or true – for that is merely to jump for our prejudices – but whether it has any meaning, and why. At any epoch there will be a number of terms which tend to command popular assent. To find meaning in Mr Murry's terminology involves a modicum of what can only be called faith in certain current diction. If we are out of tune with our generation we cannot assent, not because we find the philosophy unreasonable or out of joint with the facts, but because it is meaningless to us. I find this difficulty with Mr Murry. In order to swallow his philosophy, I suspect that I should have had to swallow a number of other things first, so as to accept a number of terms *without requiring definition* of them. Words like *emergent, organism, biological unity of life*, simply do not rouse the right 'response' in my breast. They are terms which may have definite meanings within the restricted field of discourse of biology; but a philosophy based upon biological knowledge is a different thing from biology. To call it *metabiology* seems to me a verbal trick; playing on the useful pun of 'physics' and 'metaphysics.' When we proceed from words to phrases, and from phrases to sentences, the difficulties multiply. Mr Murry says:

> 'Value' is creative newness in the organic process of the universe; more than this, it is creative newness which maintains itself.

In this sentence value is defined in terms which to me need more explication than the term 'value'. What is the difference between newness which is creative and plain newness? Perhaps 'creative newness' is 'organic newness', but that does not help me much. In any case creation is hardly creation unless it creates something new. But why creative newness, or organic novelty as we might call it, should *be* Value I cannot puzzle out. We are told that the value of a poem or a temple (p. 183) consists simply in its power to maintain itself as an object of response. But surely it must consist in its power to maintain itself as the object of the particular response which assigns to it value. And is its 'power' anything more than a metaphorical way of saying that people have continued to respond to it in ways which have a common element? Metabiology seems to me to be a philosophy which employs terms which appeal to the biological [336] imagination. And I cannot believe that the biological imagination is as permanent as the religious one, or that Mr Murry's philosophy is more than a variant of that philosophy of our time of which we have other 'significant variations' in Bergson, Driesch, Whitehead or Eddington or Lloyd Morgan.

On page 184 I find the word 'organic' five times; 'metabiological' three times; 'variation' twice.

In this short note I have merely tried to express my own fundamental difficulty with the book: it may be no difficulty to others. From my point of view, the book has also a very important merit: though Mr Murry seems to me in the end to offer only a variation of biological naturalism, yet he has seen far more clearly than others the real issue; the choice that one must make, the fact that you must either take the whole of revealed religion or none of it. And he shows a really remarkable understanding of Catholicism; it may even seem that he understands Catholicism better than he understands his own beliefs.

[*Baudelaire and the Symbolists* by Peter Quennell]

Review of *Baudelaire and the Symbolists. Five Essays* by Peter Quennell (1929).
C., 9. 35 (Jan. 1930), 357–9. Signed 'T. S. Eliot'. Gallup C300.

Mr Quennell has done for his generation what Arthur Symons did many years ago with his *Symbolist Movement in Literature*. I am not disposed to disparage Mr Symons's book; it was a very good book for its time; it did make the reader want to read the poets Mr Symons wrote about. I myself owe Mr Symons a great debt: but for having read his book, I should not, in the year 1908, have heard of Laforgue or Rimbaud; I should probably not have begun to read Verlaine; and but for reading Verlaine, I should not have heard of Corbière. So the Symons book is one of those which have affected the course of my life. Nevertheless, it was time that a new book on the same subject should be written, omitting, as does Mr Quennell very rightly, Maeterlinck. Whoever reads the one book ought to read the other, certainly; but we are no longer in a flush of discovery: the poets of whom Mr Quennell treats are now as much in our bones as Shakespeare or Donne: the need is for what is called appraisal.

The chief fault I have to find with Mr Quennell's book is the form, *five essays*. One anticipates – five essays, essays as Mr Symons wrote them, starting afresh and with fresh enthusiasm on each author. But these are not really five essays; they are five chapters in one whole essay on a part of the great subject of Post-Romanticism. I found Mr Quennell's first essay, that on Baudelaire (the key poet not included in Mr Symons's volume, and a poet whom Mr Symons has fumbled more badly than the minor successors) the least satisfactory on first reading. For there is a great deal more to be said about Baudelaire than Mr Quennell has said. On the other hand, Baudelaire is so much greater a man than all of his successors, that he cannot be confined, as can they, within one essay. Therefore the difficulty of a scheme such as Mr Quennell has adopted, is that a master like Baudelaire must be reduced to those aspects in which the least among his significant disciples can be profitably compared with him.

With this reservation, – or making on Mr Quennell's behalf a statement which I feel he should have made for himself, – the essay on Baudelaire is an admirable study, and except for the studies of Laforgue and Mallarmé, really the best in the book. It is the first of a sequence of studies in the post-mortem of Romanticism, and in the insurgence of something which can hardly be called classicism, but which may decently be called Counter-Romanticism. The [358] difficulty is that the minor men can be wholly, and even more than generously, confined within what can beyond question be called literary criticism; whereas any adequate criticism of Baudelaire must inevitably lead the critic outside of *literary* criticism. For it will not do to label Baudelaire; he is not merely, or in my opinion even primarily, the *artist*; and if I compared him with anyone in his own century, it would be to Goethe and to Keats – that is to say, I should place him with men who are important first because they are human prototypes of new experience, and only second because they are poets. I think that Mr Quennell is not unaware of this, for in one of his best sentences on Baudelaire he says (p. 64):

> He had enjoyed a *sense of his own age*, had recognized its pattern when the pattern was yet incomplete, and – because it is only our misapprehension of the present which prevents our looking into the immediate future, our ignorance of to-day and of its real as apart from its spurious tendencies and requirements – had anticipated many problems, both on the aesthetic and on the moral plane, in which the fate of modern poetry is still concerned.

This affirmation is, I believe, certainly true: it is this 'sense of the age' that is important about Baudelaire, and is what he imparted, in varying fractions, to his minor successors. And a 'sense of one's age' implies some sense of other ages; so that Baudelaire's sense of Racine is integral with his sense of his own age.

Of course, the short period in which Baudelaire lived was a muddled one. Although *literary* criticism compels us to consider Villiers and Gerard de Nerval when we consider the whole movement after Baudelaire, we must remember that Villiers and Gerard (and Huysmans, a sort of Zola crossed capriciously with all that is least important about Baudelaire) are distractions from the main issue, I complain against Mr Quennell that he ought to have ignored Villiers, except as a footnote upon others; for Villiers at this moment is a mere period piece, a curiosity of the fashions of popular philosophy, more dignified only by being longer dead, than a Maeterlinck. Even Mr Quennell's industry cannot make Villiers interesting, any more interesting than a reproduction of a photograph of a lady on a bicycle in 1897. The only important successors of Baudelaire are Laforgue, Corbière and Mallarmé.

One difference between Baudelaire and the later poets – Laforgue, Verlaine, Corbière, Rimbaud, Mallarmé – is that Baudelaire not [359] only reveals the troubles of his own age and predicts those of the age to come, but also foreshadows some issue from these difficulties. When we get to Laforgue, we find a poet who seems to express more clearly even than Baudelaire the difficulties of his own age: he speaks to us, or spoke to my generation, more intimately than Baudelaire seemed to do. Only later we conclude that Laforgue's 'present' is a narrower present than Baudelaire's, and that Baudelaire's present extends to more of the past and more of the future.

Mr Quennell might, I think, have made more of the influences of English literature; he might have made more of the German influences upon Laforgue, particularly the influence of Schopenhauer and Hartmann; and of the generally 'nordic' cast of Symbolism, with its contrast in the meridional construction of Valéry. In his actual writing, he indulges himself in metaphor and simile; he has an exuberance of style which often confuses, but sometimes rewards with a striking remarkable phrase. But his book is a good book on what is the most important part of the history of the poetry of the nineteenth century. I look back to the dead year 1908; and I observe with satisfaction that it is now taken for granted that the current of French poetry which sprang from Baudelaire is one which has, in these twenty-one years, affected all English poetry that matters. Mr Symons's book is one milestone, and Mr Quennell's will be another.

A Game at Chesse

Review of *A Game at Chesse* by Thomas Middleton, ed. R. C. Bald (1929).

TLS, 1460 (23 Jan. 1930), 56. Unsigned. Not in Gallup, but would be C300a.

Thomas Middleton is conspicuously an Elizabethan dramatist who has been highly praised, but who has never yet received his due. That is not altogether the fault of the critics. The work of Webster, for instance, even with the perplexingly inferior later plays, is comparatively easy to grasp as a whole; so is that of Ford, or that of Tourneur – if he be Tourneur; even Chapman has received in recent years an amount of scholarly attention which makes him easier for the critic to appraise. But the work of Middleton is more various than that of any other Elizabethan except Shakespeare himself; and being so much inferior to Shakespeare, with therefore so much the less coherent pattern in his carpet, he is more difficult to place justly than Shakespeare. Of Shakespeare, superlatives may not always be illuminating, but they can never be quite wrong; but with Middleton we must confine ourselves to the more hazardous vocabulary of comparatives. And with Middleton, more perhaps than with any other Elizabethan dramatist, criticism waits upon scholarship. No one collaborated more freely; and his own variety is complicated by his readiness to work with almost anybody.

It is all the more remarkable that one of the finest plays of Middleton, one which has never been attributed, even in part, to anyone else, *A Game at Chesse*, should have remained so long unedited. It is, of course, in the edition of Dyce, and in that of Bullen, who, in editing this play, cannot be said to have improved upon Dyce; but until the appearance of this text by Mr R. C. Bald, it has not received adequate scholarly attention. Swinburne, to be sure, speaks highly of it; but among Swinburne's many encomiums his praise of *A Game at Chesse* is hardly noticeable. Swinburne called it 'complete and exquisite', and 'the only work of English poetry which may properly be called Aristophanic'. We must take 'Aristophanic', of course, in a Swinburnian sense; but even so this is high and deserved praise. But as most people will have read Swinburne's eulogy in the introduction to the 'Mermaid' Middleton, and as *A Game at Chesse* is not included in the 'Mermaid' collection, Swinburne's applause will have fallen upon deaf as well as deafened ears. Yet one of the few conjectures which we may safely make about this personage named Middleton is that he must have been a chess player, and that he was a poet who was fascinated by the dramatic element in the game; and we feel safe in asserting that the brilliant and ironic chess scene in *Women Beware Women* is by the same hand as *A Game at Chesse*. And that it was the interest in, and the constraint of, the same game that produced the particularly orderly play by this exceedingly disorderly and even slovenly dramatist.

We should be very grateful to Mr Bald for editing separately a text of this fine play, even though Mr Bald is not interested primarily in either the poetry or the drama. Mr Bald's purpose is first to exhibit a general method of textual criticism of Elizabethan plays, and secondly to make some interesting and plausible conjectures about the political background and allusions. The play has, perhaps, suffered as literature from its notoriety as a daring political satire of the day; nevertheless, this aspect is important. Mr Bald sums up all the agreed interpretation of the political satire, and adds some intelligent guesses of his own. His introduction is the best introduction to the play from the point of view of the historian. He gives full credit to the importance of the Spanish Ambassador Gondomar; and, in a few pages, a sufficient description of that curious figure De Dominis, who is certainly the original of the Fat Bishop in the play. Most of the attributions of originals to the pieces in *A Game at Chesse* have, of course, been settled. We think that Mr Bald is quite right in agreeing with Fleay, against some other scholars, that the two Queens are not the wives of the two Kings in actual life, but that they represent the Churches of England and Rome. The whole dialogue is much more comprehensible on this assumption. An interesting attribution of Mr Bald's is the conjecture that the White King's Pawn is

Lionel Cranfield, Earl of Middlesex, rather than Sir Toby Matthew. And Mr Bald's assertion that the underplot of the play cannot be interpreted so exactly as the main plot has much to justify it; although it is still possible that this underplot contains references, not thoroughly worked out, to the Thirty Years' War. Yet it is likely that for the contemporary audience, as for ourselves, the Black Knight (the Spanish Ambassador) and the Fat Bishop (De Dominis, sometime Dean of Windsor) were of such extreme importance that the consistency of the underplot hardly mattered. It would be a parallel in our time if some dramatist satirised in the same way, let us say, the Foreign Secretary of the moment and the representative in London of some suspected foreign Power: were these two figures recognisable enough, the audience would hardly bother about the minor plot. And the interest of the Jacobean public in *A Game at Chesse* was comparable to that of the modern public in any book or play which is expected, from hour to hour, to be 'withdrawn' from circulation or from the stage under pressure from public authorities.

Mr Bald's introduction and his critical apparatus will interest students of Elizabethan texts still more than students of Elizabethan and Jacobean history and intrigue. It is impossible, in a general review of the book, to do more than summarise Mr Bald's arguments and conclusions. There are actually five manuscripts of the play; two presumably in the hand of a well-known scrivener named Ralph Crane; one has a note, another a page of dedicatory verses, apparently in the hand of Middleton himself. There are three quartos, all possibly of the year 1625. Mr Bald believes that one manuscript (that of Trinity College, Cambridge) is in Middleton's hand, and that another (that of the Huntington collection) was completed and corrected by Middleton. Mr Bald asks: If (as there is good reason to believe) the theatrical prompt-copy of the play had been confiscated, on what materials can the numerous surviving texts have been based? He then contests the theory offered by Mr Crompton Rhodes and Professor Dover Wilson, that a play was often 'assembled' out of the individual players' parts. He infers that there were loose sheets ('foul papers') in the author's handwriting, of which use was made. Of the Huntington manuscript he says:

> At II., ii., l. 13 the scribe found that there was a gap in the papers that he was transcribing; he left a page blank and began the next page where his papers went on. But what he copied out there was the beginning of III., i., and a quarto page could not possibly contain the 250 lines he had left out. Accordingly, when Middleton was looking over and completing the manuscript, he tried deftly to bridge over the gap by adding a few of the following lines (II. 13–19 and 48–60),

altered the stage-direction *Enter Fat Bishop* at the beginning of III., i. to a speech-heading, and inserted 1. 78 between ll. 56 and 57 in order to make the events of III., i. comprehensible.

Enough has been quoted to show that Shakespeare scholars will find much interesting and controversial matter in the book, and that ordinary readers will find much that is above their heads. But though the textual theories are for experts, the historical attributions are for everybody. As for the literary and dramatic merit of the piece, that is still to be studied; but the literary critic and even the mere reader of Middleton may be grateful to Mr Bald for having provided a critical text of one of Middleton's finest plays, a play which is unique even in the great variety of the Elizabethan and Jacobean stage.

Poetry and Propaganda

Bookman, 70 (Feb. 1930), 595–602. Subheaded *'By T. S. Eliot'*. Gallup C301.
Originally entitled 'Poetry and Philosophy'.

The text for this paper is taken from Whitehead's *Science and the Modern World*, page 127:

> The literature of the nineteenth century, especially its English poetic literature, is a witness to the discord between the esthetic intuitions and the mechanism of science. Shelley brings vividly before us the elusiveness of the eternal objects of sense as they haunt the change which infects underlying organisms. Wordsworth is the poet of nature as being the field of enduring permanences carrying within themselves a message of tremendous significance. The eternal objects are also there for him,
> 'The light that never was, on sea or land.'
> Both Shelley and Wordsworth emphatically bear witness that nature cannot be divorced from its esthetic values; and that these values arise from the cumulation, in some sense, of the brooding presence of the whole onto its various parts. Thus we gain from the poets the doctrine that a philosophy of nature must concern itself at least with these six notions: change, value, eternal objects, endurance, organism, interfusion.

So far Professor Whitehead. Now I must insist clearly at the beginning that what I have to say has nothing to do with this book as a whole, or with Mr Whitehead's theory as a whole: I am not here judging or valuing his theory or his method or his results. I am concerned only with this one chapter, which is called 'The Romantic Reaction', and only with this one passage in that chapter. And only, therefore with two specific questions: can poetry be cited to *prove* anything? and to what extent can it even be cited to *illustrate* anything?

It appears to me that Mr Whitehead is here summoning Shelley and Wordsworth to *prove* something in connection with what he calls a 'philosophy of nature'; that is what his words *thus we gain from the poets the doctrine that*, seem to me to mean; even if the author did not mean that, it is at least what many of his readers must have taken it to mean.

When so distinguished a scientist and philosopher makes this use of poetry, a great many people will follow him, in the belief that anyone who can understand symbolic logic must certainly understand anything so simple as poetry. And indeed I must say that in the earlier part of his book Mr Whitehead does prepare us to consent to any use of literature he may choose to make: his knowledge and appreciation of history and literature are so great, and his summaries and reviews of historic processes and periods so very skilful, his allusions so apt, that we are charmed into assent. Nevertheless, I believe that the passage I have just read is nonsense, and dangerous nonsense at that. Consider first how really remarkable it is that we should

> gain from the poets the doctrine that a philosophy of nature must concern itself at least with these six notions: change, value, eternal objects, endurance, organism, interfusion.

[596] There are, to begin with, two steps in Whitehead's legerdemain. He has quoted, and discussed generally, two poets of one period, Shelley and Wordsworth. These two then become 'the poets'; would any beginner in scientific enquiry ever exhibit such a perfect example of imperfect induction? And then the poets are said to demonstrate that a philosophy of nature must be concerned at least with the six concepts mentioned.

Let us take the first sentence:

> The literature of the nineteenth century, especially its English poetic literature, is a witness to the discord between the esthetic intuitions of mankind and the mechanism of science.

To call the whole of English poetry of the nineteenth century to witness such a generality is certainly rash, and the meaning of the sentence is not clear. It might mean that the great English poets were all *aware* of this discord between intuition and mechanism. In this form the statement might be true of the author of *In Memoriam*. But how far is it true of Browning or Swinburne, and as far as it may be true how significant is it in their respective views of life? But perhaps Mr Whitehead means merely that poets, by affirming the reality of values, are denying by implication the sufficiency of a mechanistic philosophy. But in this form the statement is too comprehensive, for it applies to all artists at every time, as they all have affirmed the validity of esthetic intuitions. And in the proposition there are two terms to be examined, 'esthetic intuitions', and 'the mechanism of science'; and we must then consider in what way there can be any 'discord' between terms so disparate.

That poor old creature, 'mechanistic philosophy' or 'materialism' has been in our time thoroughly repudiated by its old friends the scientists, and receives no kindness from anyone but a few liberal theologians. It is not of course quite the same thing as 'the mechanism of science': the latter is strictly merely the corpus of pre-Einstein and pre-Rutherford physical theory, which has been rejected more or less by physicists on the good ground that it does not account for all the facts – not on the doubtful ground that it offends poetic intuitions. The mechanism of science is not the same thing as a *philosophy* based on that science, which would assert that physical science would explain the whole universe, and that what would not be explained in this way was unworthy of notice. But in any case, I find myself in the curious position of having to defend the 'mechanism of science', which is no friend of mine, against an eminent scientist.

Are we to suppose that a mechanistic philosophy is fundamentally antagonistic to the esthetic intuitions of mankind? That is certainly surprising, as some works of literary art seem to have been built upon it. The philosophy, such as it is, of Thomas Hardy's novels, seems to be based upon the mechanism of science. I think it is a very bad philosophy indeed, and I think that Hardy's work would be better for a better philosophy, or none at all; but there it is: has he not exploited determinism to extract his esthetic values from the contemplation of a world in which values do not count? There is a more important poet than Hardy, who is Lucretius. We cannot deny 'esthetic intuitions' to Lucretius. His world was mechanical enough, in all conscience; and just because it was, Lucretius gets the particular emotional values that he does get. We may admit therefore a discord between the mechanism of science and *some* esthetic intuitions; but then we shall have to say that *every* philosophy is discordant with *some* intuitions. The new philosophy of Professor Eddington, for instance, is discordant with some of the intuitions of all Christians except members of the Society of Friends; the philosophy of Dante is not the ideal ground on which to reap the intuitions of Wordsworth.

So far I have not questioned the term 'esthetic intuitions'; but this term is beset with ambiguity and vagueness. I suppose that Mr [597] Whitehead means such intuitions as are more or less common to mankind, but of which the artist is the most sensitive receiver, and without which he would not have the material for great art. But however we define the term, there is a gulf, and I think an impassable one, between the intuitions of poets *as such*, and any particular philosophy, or even any philosophical direction rather than any other. The existence of art certainly implies the reality of values, but that does not take us anywhere, and certainly points to no philosophic theory of value.

If I examined each of the sentences I should quickly grow tedious, so I will pass now to the last of them:

> Thus we gain from the poets the doctrine that a philosophy of nature must concern itself at least with these six notions: change, value, eternal objects, endurance, organism, interfusion.

The first question is, if we get all this from the poets, where do the poets get it? Take *change* and *endurance*, for which Mr Whitehead is so obliged to Shelley. Shelley, I suspect, got them where everybody else has got them in the end – that is, from Plato. The reality of eternal objects sounds to me much more like Plato than a discovery of Shelley, or all the romantic poets together. I do not deny the possibility that Shelley may have had a fresh intuition of these things, but Plato did get there first. And also it is very difficult to spot these intuitions: Shelley must have had an esthetic intuition that there is no God, and that the Christian religion is an odious lie; for he could hardly have reached such passionate conviction on the subject from mere reasoning. (Of course it is possible that he read Rousseau and Voltaire, or even Godwin.) Even if we gain the doctrine in question from *the poets*, we hardly needed to have gone to the poets for that. And in passing, I wonder whether the concept of *organism* is so fundamental to a philosophy of nature as Mr Whitehead supposes. We may get a better term some day, or we may even return to Aristotle, who knew as much about what this term represents as anybody.

At the very best, Mr Whitehead is I think confusing the *persuasive* power of poetry with evidence of truth. He is transferring to poetry, as a scientist, that credulity which previous generations, including some poets, are said to have bestowed upon science.

Professor Whitehead may serve as a warning that a man may be one of the greatest living exponents of formal logic, and yet be quite helpless in a field with which he is not familiar. I should not however have devoted this space merely to the churlish pleasure of attacking a famous man; but because I believe that the theory of poetry implicit in Whitehead's chapter is dangerous, because we could prove by it, choosing our examples judiciously, almost anything we like. I also believe, what is a related point which I cannot deal with here, that Mr Whitehead errs by his ignorance of theology just as he errs by his not having thought seriously enough about poetry.

Now among those persons who have thought directly about poetry – and indeed some of them are greatly indebted to Mr Whitehead and Mr Russell for their logical training – there have arisen lately two interesting views. One is that of Mr Montgomery Belgion, in one chapter of his recent book *Our Present Philosophy of Life*. His theory is that the *literary* artist – he is not concerned with the other arts – is what he calls an 'irresponsible propagandist'. That is to say, every writer adopts a view or theory of life; his choice may have been more or less justified or capricious, may be more or less right, may be true or false: it happens to be the view which suits *him*; he makes use of it as material for his literary art. The effect of the work of literary art is always to *persuade* the reader to accept that view or theory. This persuasion is always illicit. That is to say, that the reader is always led to believe something, and that assent is hypnotic – the art of the presentation seduces the reader: [598] even if what he is led to believe is right to believe, the reader has been *mis*led into believing it. This theory is, as you see, rather depressing, and is remotely similar to that of Plato, who ejected the poets from his ideal republic; but it is neither fantastic nor easy to overthrow.

The other theory is that of Mr I. A. Richards, as expressed particularly in his recent book *Practical Criticism*. Mr Richards holds that while it is probably necessary for the poet to believe something, in order to write his poetry – although he inclines to think that a further step will be made when the poet believes nothing – the ideal reader will appreciate the poetry in a state of mind which is not belief, but rather a temporary suspension of disbelief. The one critic would say, you see, that you will value Dante more highly if you are a Catholic; or alternatively, that if you are enchanted by the poetry of Dante you will probably become a Catholic. Mr Richards would say, I think, that the more you know about what Dante believed or more exactly the more you know about the philosophy of life on which Dante's poem is based – leaving out of account the question of what and how Dante himself believed – the better: but that when you are enjoying Dante's poem to the full as poetry, you cannot be said either to believe, or to doubt, or to disbelieve, its scholastic philosophy. So you *ought* to be able to appreciate, as literature, *all* literature, of whatever place, race or time.

These two theories are not so antithetical as they at first seem. Mr Belgion is more concerned with what actually does happen; he says that, whether you know it or not, you tend to believe, you are *influenced*, by any author whose form of expression you admire. Mr Richards is less concerned with the actual than with the ideal reader: he says, in effect, this may happen, but in so far as it does happen your reaction is impure; you *ought not* to be affected in this way: it is possible and it is right to enjoy poetry as poetry and you merely use in the reading the philosophy of the author; just as the author was using, unconsciously, that philosophy in order to write the poetry.

In a note to a recent essay which I have published on Dante, I made a first attempt to criticise both views, and to find some way of mediation between the truth of both. I am now making a fresh start.

First of all no art, and particularly and especially no literary art, can exist in a vacuum. We are, in practice, creatures of divers interests, and in many of our ordinary interests there is no obvious coherence. Read, for instance, the information given by those personages in *Who's Who* who condescend to fill that space of the form marked *Recreations*. There is no apparent relation, to fabricate a specimen, between breeding prize Persian cats and racing toy yachts. This is one extreme of the scale. At the other end, we do tend, I am sure, to unify our interests. To suppose that anyone likes only the *best* poetry, and that he likes all of the best poetry equally, and that he likes all of the second-best poetry in a second-best liking, and so on until he detests all of the worst poetry equally, is to suppose a monster. I do not suppose that there ever has been, or ever will be, a critic of any art, whose appreciation was a separate faculty, quite judicious and wholly isolated from his other interests and his private passions: if there was, is or will be, he was, is or will be a bore with nothing at all to say. And yet, on the other hand, there is no worse bore, and no more futile critic, than the one who renounces all objective standards in order to recount his own reactions. 'A voyage among masterpieces' is I believe the phrase that Anatole France used to describe his own criticism, implying that it was merely an account of his own feelings – yet the phrase itself admits that the masterpieces were there as masterpieces, before the voyage began.

But this apparent paradox – this need of aiming at one thing in order to do another – this apparent gospel of hypocrisy or self-[599]deception, is right, because it is in the nature of the human soul and embodies its need and craving for perfection and unity. We do tend, I think, to organise our tastes in various arts into a whole; we aim in the end at a theory of life, or a view of life, and so far as we are conscious, to terminate our enjoyment of the arts in a philosophy, and our philosophy in a religion – in such a way that the personal to oneself is fused and completed in the personal and general, not extinguished, but enriched, expanded, developed, and more itself by becoming more something not itself.

There is, according to my view, not *one*, but a *series*, of appreciators of poetry. One of the errors, I think, of critical theory, is to conceive one hypothetical poet on the one hand, and one hypothetical reader on the other. It is perhaps a less dangerous error than to have no hypotheses at all. My point is that the legitimate motives of the poet, and also the legitimate responses of the reader, vary very widely, but that there is a possible order in the variations. In my series let us put Mr Belgion at one end of the scale and Mr Richards at the other. The one extreme is to like poetry merely for what it has to say: that is, to like it merely because it voices our own beliefs or prejudices – which is of course to be quite indifferent to the *poetry* of the poetry. The other extreme is to like the poetry because the poet has manipulated his material into perfect art, which is to be indifferent to the material, and to isolate our enjoyment of poetry from life. The one extreme is not enjoyment of poetry at all, the other is enjoyment of an abstraction which is merely *called* poetry. But between these extremes occurs a continuous range of appreciations, each of which has its limited validity.

The validity of this range of appreciations is confirmed by our examination of the impulses of different poets. We may for convenience contrast three different types. There is the philosophic poet like Lucretius and Dante, who accepts one philosophy of life so to speak in advance, and who constructs his poem on one idea. There is the poet like Shakespeare, or possibly Sophocles, who accepts current ideas and makes use of them, but in whose work the question of Belief is much more baffling and evasive. There is finally another type, of which we might take Goethe as an example, who neither quite accepts a particular view of the whole, nor merely sees views of life to make poetry out of, but who in himself more or less combines the functions of philosopher and poet – or perhaps Blake; poets who have their own ideas and definitely believe them.

Some poets are of so mixed a type that it is impossible to say how far they write their poetry because of what they believe, and how far they believe a thing merely because they see that they can make poetry out of it. And if I am justified in allowing this range of possible motives to the true poet (and an analogous range to the true reader of poetry) then Mr Belgion's and Mr Richards's theories must be considerably modified. For the 'irresponsible propaganda' is sometimes less irresponsible, and sometimes less propaganda. Lucretius and Dante, for instance, are what Mr Belgion would call propagandists, certainly, but they are particularly conscious and responsible ones: you have only to read what Dante says in the *Convivio* and in his letter to Can Grande to understand what his purpose was.

Milton was also a deliberate propagandist; but here we must allow for another difference. The philosophies of Lucretius and Dante, different as they are from each other, are still potent to influence mankind. I cannot imagine any reader today being affected in his theological views by Milton. The reason is, I think, that Lucretius and Dante are each summing up and restating in great poetry two views which are central to the history of the mind of western man; whereas Milton is merely restating in great poetry a view which was very largely his own invention or his own concoction, and which repre-[600]sents an eccentric heresy revived in his own mind. In Milton it is much easier to separate the greatness of the poetry from the thought, serious as it is, behind that poetry. Milton, therefore, is much more apprehensible from the Richards point of view; because in reading Milton we are I think rapt by the splendid verse without being tempted to believe the philosophy or theology. In considering whether a literary artist is an irresponsible propagandist or not, we have therefore to take into account both varieties of intention, and varieties of effect in time. Milton may, I feel, have had this powerful influence at one time which I feel that Lucretius and Dante can have at any time; but I do not believe that he has it now. And in general, the element of propaganda in the actual effect of any piece of literature upon us will depend either upon the permanence of the doctrine, or upon its nearness to us in time. The effect of a book like *The Way of All Flesh* was, I am sure, for the generation immediately following Butler much what he intended; for the next generation it is not at all the same.

You will infer, perhaps, that we must come to the conclusion that it is impossible to enjoy (or judge) a work of art as such, until sufficient time has elapsed for its doctrines to be quite out of date: so that we merely inspect and accept them, as Mr Richards would have us do: wait a few hundred years, and we shall know how good any piece of literature is. There are several reasons why this simple solution will not do. One is that when an author is so remote from us, in time or in race, that we know nothing of his material and cannot at all understand his beliefs, we cannot appreciate his work as poetry. To enjoy Homer as poetry, we need a good deal more than Greek vocabulary and Greek accidence and syntax; and the more we saturate ourselves in the life of the ancient Greeks, the more we attempt to recreate imaginatively their world, the better we understand and enjoy the poetry of that world. Another reason is that time, alas, does not necessarily bring detachment. It may merely substitute for a set of prejudices favourable to the poet, another set unfavourable to him. It is interesting to read the comments of Mr Richards's students, as set forth in *Practical Criticism*, on Donne's great sonnet 'At the round world's imagined corners . . .' Some of the misunderstanding is due, I believe, not so much to ignorance of the theology of Donne's time, as to these students' more or less conscious acceptance of another set of beliefs current in our own time.

I have called Lucretius and Dante *responsible propagandists*. But there are some poets whom it is a strain to think of as propagandists at all. Take Shakespeare. He is never, like the former, expounding one definite philosophical system. I am aware that many attempts have been made, and will be made, to expound in clear prose the theory of life which Shakespeare is supposed to have held; and that any number of views of life have been extracted from Shakespeare. I do not say that such attempts are illegitimate or altogether futile; it is a natural tendency to philosophise on Shakespeare just as it is to philosophise on the world itself. Only, the philosophy of Shakespeare is quite a different thing from that of Dante; it really has more in common with, let us say, the philosophy of Beethoven. That is to say, those of us who love Beethoven find in his music something that we call its meaning, though we cannot confine it in words; but it is this meaning which fits it in, somehow, to our whole life; which makes it an emotional exercise and discipline, and not merely an appreciation of virtuosity. Shakespeare does certainly influence us; but as he influences each man according to his own education, temperament and sensibility, and as we have no clue to the relation of his influence upon any one mind with what Shakespeare actually meant, it is almost fantastic to call it propaganda.

When we come to Mr Whitehead's men-[601]tors, Shelley and Wordsworth, the situation is again different. Judging from their effect upon Mr Whitehead, we should certainly call them irresponsible propagandists. But I suspect that their influence upon such a mind as Mr Whitehead's is in direct ratio to the vagueness of their ideas, or to the fact that they take certain things for granted, instead of expounding them. The orthodox Christian, for example, is hardly likely to take Dante as proving Christianity; the orthodox materialist is hardly likely to adduce Lucretius as evidence of materialism or atomism. What he will find in Dante or in Lucretius is the *esthetic* sanction: that is, the partial justification of these views of life by the art to which they give rise. And there is no doubt that we are all of us powerfully influenced by the esthetic sanction; and that any way or view of life which gives rise to great art is for us more plausible than one which gives rise to inferior art or to none. And on the other hand I do not believe that a Christian can fully appreciate Buddhist art, or vice versa.

But Mr Whitehead was not, I suspect, making this use, which I consider legitimate, of the esthetic sanction. You do not get this by going to the poets for maxims or gnomic sayings, or by attributing to them some inspiration as of the Delphic oracle. You can only say: this or that poet has used these ideas to make poetry, and has accordingly shown that these ideas can and do give rise to certain values. These ideas consequently are valid not merely in a theory, but can be integrated into life through art. But in order to do this we are obliged to value first the art of a Shelley or a Wordsworth. How complete, how intelligent, how well understood, is the philosophy used by the poet, how completely does he realise it poetically; where does he get it from, how much of life does it cover? Such questions we must ask first. And what poetry proves about any philosophy is merely its possibility for being lived – for life includes both philosophy and art.

But we may ask, is the greatness, the comprehensiveness of the philosophy in any actual or theoretical relation to the greatness of the poetry? Actually, we may find a poet giving greater validity to an inferior philosophy, by realising it more fully and masterfully in literary art, and another employing a better philosophy and realising it less satisfactorily. Yet we can hardly doubt that the 'truest' philosophy is the best material for the greatest poet; so that the poet must be rated in the end both by the philosophy he realises in poetry and by the fullness and adequacy of the realisation. For poetry – here and so far I am in accord with Mr Richards – is not the assertion that something is true, but the making that truth more fully real to us; it is the creation of a sensuous embodiment. It is the making the Word Flesh, if we remember that for poetry there are various qualities of Word and various qualities of Flesh. Of course, as I said above, for some kinds of poetry it is necessary that the poet himself should believe the philosophy of which he is making use. I do not wish however to overemphasise the importance of the philosophy, or to speak of it as if it was the exclusive material. What we find when we read Lucretius or Dante is that the poet has effected a fusion between that philosophy and his natural feelings, so that the philosophy becomes real, and the feelings become elevated, intensified and dignified.

And we must remember that part of the *use* of poetry for human beings is similar to their use for philosophy. When we study philosophy as a humane discipline we do not do so merely in order to pick out one which we shall adopt as 'true', or either to confect a philosophy of our own out of all philosophies. We do so largely for the exercise in assumption or entertaining ideas; for the enlargement and exercise of mind we get by trying to penetrate a man's thought and think it after him, and then passing out of that experience to another. Only by the exercise of understanding without believing, so far as that is possible, can we come in full con-[602]sciousness to some point where we believe and understand. Similarly with the experience of poetry. We aim ideally to come to rest in some poetry which shall realise poetically what we ourselves believe; but we have no contact with poetry unless we can pass in and out freely, among the various worlds of poetic creation. In practice, our literary judgement is always fallible, because we inevitably tend to overestimate a poetry which embodies a view of life which we can understand and which we accept; but we are not really entitled to prize such poetry so highly unless we also make the effort to enter those worlds of poetry in which we are alien. Poetry cannot prove that anything is *true*; it can only create a variety of wholes composed of intellectual and emotional constituents, justifying the emotion by the thought and the thought by the emotion: it proves successively, or fails to prove, that certain worlds of thought and feeling are *possible*. It provides intellectual sanction for feeling, and esthetic sanction for thought.

Religion without Humanism

Publ. 21 Feb. 1930 in *Humanism and America: Essays on the Outlook of Modern Civilisation*, ed. Norman Foerster, 105–12. Subheaded 'T. S. ELIOT'. Gallup B12.

I must rely, in these few pages, upon a brief summary of the limitations within which I believe humanism must work, which I published in the *Hound and Horn*, June, 1929. In that paper I stated my belief that humanism is in the end futile without religion. Here I wish to put forward briefly a view which seems to me equally important, the counterpart of the other, and one which ought to be more welcome to humanists. Having called attention to what I believe to be a danger, I am bound to call attention to the danger of the other extreme: the danger, a very real one, of *religion without humanism*.

I believe that the sceptic, even the pyrrhonist, but particularly the humanist-sceptic, is a very useful ingredient in a world which is no better than it is. In saying this I do not think that I am committing myself to any theological heresy. The ideal world would be the ideal Church. But very little knowledge of human nature is needed to convince us that hierarchy is liable to corruption, and certainly to stupidity; that religious belief, when unquestioned and uncriticised, is liable to degeneration into superstition; that the human mind is much lazier than the human body; and that the communion of saints in Tibet is of a very low order. If we cannot rely, and it seems that we can never rely, upon adequate criticism from within, it is better that there should be criticism from without. But here I wish to make a capital distinction:

criticism, infidelity and agnosticism must, to be of value, be *original* and not inherited. Orthodoxy must be [106] traditional, heterodoxy must be original. The attitude of Voltaire has value, because of its place in time; the attitude of Renan has value, in its historical perspective; Anatole France I can only consider as a man who came at the most unfortunate date for his own reputation – too late to be a great sceptic, and too soon to be a great sceptic. There must be more orthodoxy before there can be another Voltaire. And precisely I fear lest humanism should make a tradition of dissent and agnosticism, and so cut itself off from the sphere of influence in which it is most needed.

For there is no doubt in my mind that contemporary religious institutions are in danger from themselves; that they have with few exceptions lost the 'intellectual', except that pernicious kind of intellectual who adopts dogma merely because doubt is out of date. Nowhere is this more obvious than in America. All the religious forms which have some ancestry, and many which have none, flourish there; but among persons whom I have known, there is hardly one who had any connection (not to say conviction) with any of them.

But America is not isolated in this respect; it merely shows us under a magnifying glass what occurs everywhere. The two dangers to which religion is exposed are apparent everywhere – and they are both cases for which 'humanism' or 'culture' might be called in: *petrified ecclesiasticism*, and *modernism*.

The great merit of the Catholic Church, from the worldly point of view, is its catholicity. That is to say, it is obvious that every religion is effectively limited by the racial characters of the people who practise it, and that a strictly racial or national religion is certain to hold many irrelevances and impurities, from lack of an outside standard of criticism. When the Catholic Faith is really catholic, the aberrations of one race will be corrected by those of another. But it is [107] obviously very difficult even for the Roman Church, nowadays, to be truly catholic. The embarrassment of temporal powers, the virulence of racial and national enthusiasms, are enormous centrifugal forces. The great majority of English speaking people, or at least the vast majority of persons of British descent; half of France, half of Germany, the whole of Scandinavia, are outside of the Roman communion: that is to say, the Roman Church has lost some organic parts of the body of modern civilisation. It is a recognition of this fact which makes some persons of British extraction hesitate to embrace the Roman communion; and which makes them feel that those of their race who have embraced it have done so only by the surrender of some essential part of their inheritance and by cutting themselves off from their family.

But if one feels that the culture of the Roman Catholic Church to-day is imperfect – and also in danger of splitting up into various local and national bigotries and political factions which will retain only the name and the observances of catholicism – one cannot get any satisfaction from what happens outside of that church either. The Roman Church in America has little contact with some of the most valuable elements in American culture; it not only lacks humanism, but is in danger of adding vulgarity. In England it is negligible. But both in England and America, Protestantism is in still worse case. It can be, and usually is, equally vulgar; it can be equally narrow and bigoted; with the alternative that when it is not narrow and bigoted it is liberal, sloppy, hypocritical and humanitarian. The Roman Church is dangerous in one direction; the Protestant Churches are dangerous in two directions.

I have already said what I think of humanism without religion; I respect it, but believe it to be sterile. Religion without humanism produces the vulgarities and the political compromises of Roman Catholicism; the vulgarities and the [108] fanaticism of Tennessee; it produces Mrs MacPherson; and it produces liberal uplift; and it produces the Bishop of Birmingham. For it is the chief point of this short paper, that religion without humanism produces the opposite and conflicting types of religious bigotry (liberalism in religion is a form of bigotry). We have Cardinal O'Connell; the late W. J. Bryan; and we have the cultivated divines of the most radical wing of Unitarianism. The sum of *disjecta membra* is completed by the humanists.

I have examined several popular theological works by Anglican clergy of the liberal school.[1] It would I am sure be difficult to convince any of these worthy people that they were humanitarian without being humanist. Humanitarians (and among them we must include anti-humanitarians like Dean Inge, a sentimentalist *à rebours*) are often highly cultivated people who have read many books; some of them, in England at least, can read Latin and Greek; the Bishop of Birmingham took honours in mathematics. Yet in surrendering dogmatic faith they are at the same time surrendering their humanism. It is from such people that we hear most about 'science and religion'; it is such people who pay, and lead the flock to pay, exaggerated devotion to 'science' which the true humanist deplores.

It is curious that whilst on the one hand the liberal theologian tends to pay homage to an illusory divinity called 'science' the advanced scientist tends to pay homage to an equally vague 'religion'. People seem to

---

1. E.g., *Should Such a Faith Offend?*, by the Bishop of Birmingham; *I Believe in God*, by Maude Royden; *The Impatience of a Parson*, by H. R. L. Sheppard.

suppose that by science yielding points to religion, and religion yielding points to science, we shall quite soon arrive at a position of comfortable equilibrium. What will be 'real' will be the technical progress of science, and the material organisation [109] of the churches: we shall still have professors of physics and we shall still have clergy, and nobody will lose his job. Scientists and clergy alike seem to speak nowadays as if they were in terror of the spectre of unemployment: 'I will not make exaggerated claims,' they both seem to say, 'lest I may be discovered to be superfluous.'

But this apparent approximation of science and religion, which we discover in such theological works as those I have mentioned, and in such popular scientific works as those of Whitehead and Eddington, is a delusion. The meeting is a mere cancellation to zero. Nothing positive is attained by reciprocal surrender. The theologian says 'of course dogma is not truth', and the scientist says 'of course science is not truth'. Every one is happy together; and possibly both parties turn to *poetry* (about which neither scientist nor theologian knows anything) and say '*there is truth, in the inspiration of the poet.*' The poet himself, who perhaps knows more about his inspiration than a psycho-analyst does, is not allowed to reply that poetry is poetry, and not science or religion – unless he or some of his mistaken friends produce a theory that Poetry is Pure Poetry, Pure Poetry turning out to be something else than poetry and thereby securing respect.

Both parties, the liberal theologian and the scientist, are deficient in humanism. But what is more serious, to my mind, is that the humanist is deficient in humanism too, and must take his responsibility with the others. What happens, in the general confusion, is not only that each party abdicates his proper part, but that he interferes with the proper part of the others. The theologian is terrified of science, and the scientist is becoming terrified of religion; whilst the humanist, endeavouring to pay proper, but not excessive due to both, reels from side to side. And the world reels with him.

On the following point I speak with diffidence, recognis-[110]ing my lack of qualification where qualification is severe and exact. Humanism has much to say of Discipline and Order and Control; and I have parroted these terms myself. I found no discipline in humanism; only a little intellectual discipline from a little study of philosophy. But the difficult discipline is the discipline and training of emotion; this the modern world has great need of; so great need that it hardly understands what the word means; and this I have found is only attainable through dogmatic religion. I do not say that dogmatic religion is justified because it supplies this need – that is just the psychologism and the anthropocentrism that I wish to avoid – but merely state my belief that in no other way can the need be supplied. There is much chatter about mysticism: for the modern world the word means some spattering indulgence of emotion, instead of the most terrible concentration and akesis. But it takes a lifetime merely to realise that men like the forest sages, and the desert sages, and finally the Victorines and John of the Cross and (in his fashion) Ignatius really *mean what they say*. Only those have the right to talk of discipline who have looked into the Abyss. The need of the modern world is the discipline and training of the emotions; which neither the intellectual training of philosophy or science, nor the wisdom of humanism, nor the negative instruction of psychology can give.

In short, we can use the term Humanism in two ways. In the narrower sense, which tends always under emphasis to become narrower still, it is an important part in a larger whole; and humanists, by offering this part as a substitute for the whole, are lessening, instead of increasing, its importance; they offer an excuse to the modern theologian and the modern scientist (only too ready to grasp it) for *not* being humanistic themselves, and for leaving humanism to its own specialists. Humanism can offer neither the intel-[111]lectual discipline of philosophy or of science (two different disciplines), nor the emotional discipline of religion. On the other hand, these other activities depend upon humanism to preserve their sanity. Without it, religion tends to become either a sentimental tune, or an emotional debauch; or in theology, a skeleton dance of fleshless dogmas, or in ecclesiasticism, a soulless political club. Without it, science can be merely a process of technical research, bursting out from time to time, and especially in our time, into sentimental monstrosities like the Life Force, or Professor Whitehead's God.

But in the full and complete sense of the word, Humanism is something quite different from a part trying to pretend to be a whole, and something quite different from a 'parasite' of religion. It can only be quite actual in the full realisation and balance of the disciplined intellectual and emotional life of man. For, as I have said, without humanism both religion and science tend to become other than themselves, and without religion and science – without emotional and intellectual discipline – humanism tends to shrink into an atrophied caricature of itself. It is the spirit of humanism which has operated to reconcile the mystic and the ecclesiastic in one church; having done this in the past, humanism should not set itself up now as another sect, but strive to continue and enlarge its task, labouring to unite all the parts into a whole. It is the humanist who could point out to the theologian the absurdities of his repudiation, acceptance, or exploitation of 'science', and to the scientist the absurdities of his repudiation, acceptance, or exploitation of religion. For when I say 'reconcile', I mean something very different from the dangerous and essentially anti-humanistic adventures of the Bishop of Birmingham or Professor Whitehead. And let us leave Einstein alone, who has his own business to attend to.

[112] As I believe I am writing chiefly for those who know or think they know, what 'humanism' means, I have not in this paper attempted any definition of it. I take it that the reader thinks he knows what it means, and that he will understand that I am putting before him the difference between what I think he thinks it means and what I think I think it means.

I have just one note to add, which is the preface to an extensive sequel. I believe that at the present time the problem of the unification of the world and the problem of the unification of the individual, are in the end one and the same problem; and that the solution of one is the solution of the other. Analytical psychology (even if accepted far more enthusiastically than I can accept it) can do little except produce monsters; for it is attempting to produce unified individuals in a world without unity; the social, political, and economic sciences can do little, for they are attempting to produce the great society with an aggregation of human beings who are not units but merely bundles of incoherent impulses and beliefs. The problem of nationalism and the problem of dissociated personalities may turn out to be the same. The relevance of this paragraph to what precedes it will, I hope, appear upon examination.

Thinking in Verse

A SURVEY OF EARLY SEVENTEENTH-CENTURY POETRY

Listener, 3. 61 (12 Mar. 1930), [441]–3. Subheaded 'By T. S. ELIOT'. Gallup C302.

The first thing that strikes us about the poetry of the first half of the century, say, from the accession of James to the death of Charles I, is its great difference in form and content from that of the Elizabethan period. Some of our greatest plays were written during the reign of James I; yet towards the end of his reign a weakening of dramatic inspiration becomes evident. The causes of such changes are always in the end obscure. But the point is that during the reign of Elizabeth the finest poetry that was written was written in plays. For the most part, the other poetry is in comparison thin, artificial and immature. The very best of Shakespeare's sonnets are the great exception; and here and there in the innumerable other sonnets of the time occurs a line or two of deeper feeling than usual. *The Faerie Queene* is a great poem, and Spenser's technical accomplishment is beyond praise; yet with all Spenser's gifts we cannot discharge him of a certain insipidity throughout. Now and then there is fine poetry in the verse translations of the period; and Marlowe's *Hero and Leander* is a magnificent poem. And the reader who is saturated in the period can read with enjoyment some of Chapman's occasional poems, and parts of *Polyolbion*, etc. But on the whole I do not think it is too sweeping a generalisation to say that the profoundest thought and feeling of the age went into its dramatic blank verse, and it is from this, rather than from the Elizabethan lyric, which was genuinely a song, that the most interesting of the poetry we are to discuss derives. One of the most obvious parallels in thoughtfulness and richness of feeling is George Chapman; and Chapman, a true Elizabethan, is at his best in his drama, not in his other verse, interesting as it is. Mr Herbert finds an anticipation of the thought-loaded verse of Donne in such lines of Chapman as this fragment of a monologue from the play *Bussy d'Ambois*:

> That in this one thing all the discipline
> Of manners and of manhood is contained;
> A man to join himself with the Universe
> In his main sway, and make in all things fit
> One with the All, and go on, round as it;
> Not plucking from the whole his wretched part,
> And into straits, or into nought revert,
> Wishing the complete Universe might be
> Subject to such a rag of it as he;
> But to consider great Necessity,
> All things as well refract as voluntary
> Reduceth to the prime celestial cause,
> Which he that yields to with a man's applause,
> And cheek by cheek goes, crossing it no breath,
> But like God's image, follows to the death,
> That man is truly wise. . . .

I agree, in so far as it is a characteristic of the poets I shall discuss, that they *think* in verse, rather than *sing* in verse; that this is a good specimen of what preceded 'metaphysical poetry'. But it is didactic, expressing the conventional stoical philosophy of the time; and my seventeenth-century poets are not philosophers in this way. How they were, we shall see. Meanwhile, it is as well to keep such lines in mind for comparison. But it is not only in [442] passages like this that the Elizabethans in their drama are forerunners of the Jacobean and Caroline poets in their lyrical verse. To be more convincing, I will take two more passages of Elizabethan dramatic blank verse, both from the same author, Chapman:

> Guise, O my lord, how shall I cast from me
> The bands and coverts hindering me from thee?
> The garment or the cover of the mind
> The humane soul is; of the soul, the spirit
> The proper robe is; of the spirit, the blood;
> And of the blood, the body is the shroud.

This passage is not unlike the former, and, on the other hand, is, I think, still more like Donne's poetry than the former. But take a piece like this, also from one of Chapman's plays:

> ... take thy wings
> And haste thee where the grey-eyed morn perfumes
> Her rosy chariot with Sabaean spices,
> Fly, where the evening from the Iberian vales
> Takes on her swarthy shoulders Hecate,
> Crowned with a grove of oaks: fly where men feel
> The cunning axletree: and those that suffer
> Beneath the chariot of the snowy Bear.

A passage like this differs from most of the poetry of the sixteenth century, other than the dramatic. It is not a simple melody, but a complicated harmony of feeling; and this again we find in Donne. Yet, on the other hand, it is partly a paraphrase of a passage in one of Seneca's Latin plays, but with a complex richness unknown to Seneca.

The contrast of the Elizabethan lyric with the Caroline lyric is particularly enlightening. The summit of the Elizabethan lyric is, of course, the songs in Shakespeare's plays; but his songs, though ever so much better than other men's, are of the same type. They are essentially poems to be sung to a musical instrument; and the men who wrote them were not primarily trying to express any profound emotion, any subtle or ingenious idea, but to provide something lovely and tuneable. The lyrics of Shakespeare, more than anyone's, demand a tune. Now there are two kinds of 'music' in verse. One is that of the lyrics of Shakespeare or Campion, which *demand* the kindred music of the lute or other instrument; a few songs of Shelley's, such as 'Music, when soft voices die', and many songs of Burns and Heine make the same demand. Here is a song by Campion. Thomas Campion was one of the most excellent of Elizabethan song-writers, and evidently a man who knew much of music.

> Shall I come, if I swim? wide are the waves, you see:
> Shall I come, if I fly, my dear Love, to thee?
> Streams Venus will appease; Cupid gives me wings;

> All the powers assist my desire
> Save you alone, that set my woful heart on fire!

Here is the first stanza of a poem of Donne:

> If yet I have not all thy love,
> Deare, I shall never have it all,
> I cannot breathe one other sigh, to move,
> Nor can intreat one other teare to fall,
> And all my treasure, which should purchase thee,
> Sighs, teares, and oathes, and letters I have spent.
> Yet no more can be due to mee,
> Then at the bargaine made was ment,
> If then thy gift of love were partiall,
> That some to mee, some should to others fall,
>   Deare, I shall never have thee all.

The song of Campion is as simple in content as possible; its merit lies in its delicate, irregular metre responsive to the music. Donne's lyric has a similarly skilful irregularity; but the metrical beauty is so closely associated with the thought, that if it were sung, the sense would be lost. And Donne's is the second kind of musical verse: the verse which suggests music; but which, so to speak, contains in itself all its possible music; for if set to music, the play of ideas could not be followed. His poems are poems to be read aloud, *not* sung. And with the exception of some few of the lighter 'Cavalier lyrics', this is a characteristic of the poetry we shall examine. The lyric has to do more and different work from that of the Elizabethan lyric. The complications of thought and feeling which in the Elizabethan time are found chiefly in dramatic blank verse pass over, with Donne, into the shorter and semi-lyrical poem.

As most of the poets we shall study either wrote religious verse, or were engaged on one side or another in the religious struggles of the Caroline time, it is pertinent to look at both these problems. In its religious sensibility the seventeenth century seems to me the third most interesting period in the history of Christianity, the others being the early period which saw the development of dogma in the Greek and Latin churches, and the thirteenth century. (I must add that when I say the seventeenth century I am thinking primarily of England; for the sixteenth century, so far as Spain and Italy are concerned, is equally important and is part of the same movement.) But between the thirteenth and the seventeenth century there is this important difference. In the thirteenth century such science as existed could be fitted into the theological scheme; the world of thought had an impressive unity; so that one might say that the distinction between philosophers and theologians hardly existed. St Thomas Aquinas, St Bonaventura, and even Duns Scotus were philosophers and theologians at once and as one thing. During the sixteenth century two important things happened which are quite distinct. The important point about the Copernican revolution in astronomy is not that it controverted the official astronomy of the Church. It is rather that it affirmed the standing of a separate science in which the laity might be more competent, because more specialised, than the Church. The result would have been equally important in the end, though less sensational, had the astronomers confirmed the accepted astronomy of the Ptolemaic system, by scientific demonstration. For it would equally have tended to limit the sphere of theology. The coincidence of the Protestant Reformation has naturally confirmed the supposition that the scientists and the Protestants were fighting the same battle. They were two quite different battles; and Martin Luther was not more enlightened or more tolerant of the scientific spirit than those who condemned Galileo.

Now, during the sixteenth and seventeenth centuries the study of theology was very highly developed. An incredible mass of now-forgotten theological literature was turned out; perhaps not more than in our time, but the books were much bigger and much harder reading. But it was distinctly theology, and not philosophy; and highly controversial theology at that; some of the controversialists on all sides were men of the greatest ability. And one of the points worth remembering about the seventeenth century is that for a moment a kind of equilibrium and parity was arrived at; the age produced great theologians, great men of devotion, and also great scientists. In England, it produced the Royal Society and also the finest devotional verse in the language. In Europe in general, theology, religious practice, science, lay philosophy, art and music are all recorded by great names.

During the reign of James and still more during the reign of Charles I, the nation was divided in three parts, the Roman Catholic, the Anglican, and the Presbyterian and Independent, what we call vaguely the Puritan. In literature, all of these elements more or less reacted on each other. Now the Continent of Europe at that time, with the exception of Northern Germany, part of the Netherlands and Scandinavia, was under the influence of that most interesting movement called the Counter-Reformation, which is represented to us most vividly by the Society of Jesus, and by baroque art. The Society of Jesus, best known to us merely as the Jesuits, had taken upon itself, as part of its task of winning divided Europe back to the Faith, the defence and cultivation of Catholic literature and Catholic art; it aimed to win over what we should now call the intelligentsia to the Church, [443] by espousing the cause of art and letters. We are only now beginning to understand how painstaking was the labour of this attempt to unite the humanities to the Church. The result was that the poetry of Europe in the seventeenth century, such as that of Marino in Italy and, I believe, Vondel in Holland, is very largely coloured by the Spanish imagination, and the Spanish imagination is represented by two very great people indeed: St Theresa, and St Ignatius Loyola, the founder of the Society of Jesus.

Neither influence is visible in England during the lifetime of either saint; they both lived in the sixteenth century. It is only apparent at the beginning of the next century; or first in the work of that curious poet Robert Southwell. When I say neither influence, I anticipate a necessary distinction. During the sixteenth century, Spain experienced an extraordinary outburst of mysticism: in other words, she produced at least three great mystics and saints, and probably several hundred pathological ecstatics. The greatest were St Theresa, and St John of the Cross, both Carmelites. I think that St John was the greater, or rather that his writings are very much more important than St Theresa's; but probably Theresa had the greater influence. At the same time, Spain produced Ignatius, a man of a very different type, a great saint and a very great man indeed. For force of character, there is only one man in contemporary Europe to whom I can compare him, and I do so without the slightest disrespect to the saint: I can only compare him to Lenin. He had a similar intense ruthlessness, though in a better cause. And I make the comparison to Lenin chiefly to emphasise his difference from St Theresa and St John. He was no mystic; he was an administrator, a warrior, a born ruler of men; with that fanaticism which brings small men to perdition, and great men to immortality. In the ordinary acceptance of chancelleries and cabinets he was no politician; and, therefore, he was one of the greatest politicians of all.

Now, if you read and study the *Spiritual Exercises*, you will find a stock of images which reminds you, and by no mere coincidence, of Donne. Donne, as I shall try to show, was no mystic. And neither was St Ignatius. Mysticism is a gift of grace; you will never become a mystic unless you have the gift. The *Exercises* are not aimed at making mystics; they are not mystical Pelmanism. They are a very practical handbook, like the late Lieut. Muller's handbook of physical exercises, to enable anybody to extend the intellectual conviction of the Faith to imaginative conviction. A similar method might be used by an historian, so steeped in Greek history as to see Thermopylae as he has seen events in his own life, in order to make his readers realise those events. So St Ignatius works on the imagination, to make us realise the Passion as he realised it. But this is not mysticism; it is merely confirmation of Christian faith. And we shall find the visual imagery of St Ignatius in Donne, whose childhood was passed under Jesuit influence.

I spoke earlier of the difference between the thirteenth and the seventeenth century. Here is another difference: in the quality of its mysticism. The mysticism of the thirteenth and twelfth centuries was intellectual and international: two of the greatest medieval mystics, as is not generally observed, were Scots: Richard and Hugh of St Victor. The mystical treatises of Richard of St Victor are as dry and abstract as those of the great Indian expositors of mysticism. They use imagery, certainly, but always clearly as analogy. They separate positively the human from the divine. But in the Spanish mystics there is a strong vein of what would now be called eroticism. I am not in the least disposed to belittle them; but their mode of expression does render them liable to the indignities of Freudian analysis. At any rate, this Spanish mysticism is definitely sensuous or erotic in its mode of expression; and this sensuousness pervades the poetry affected by it, as it pervades baroque art. I wish, however, to keep two things separate. Donne is more affected by Ignatius; Crashaw more by Theresa. We shall see later how this Spanish influence works in with the peculiar figure of speech called the *conceit*, characteristic of much of the poetry of the time.

(From a talk on March 7)

Rhyme and Reason

THE POETRY OF JOHN DONNE

Listener, 3. 62 (19 Mar. 1930), 502–3. Subheaded 'By T. S. ELIOT'. Gallup C303.

Donne was born in 1573, of a good prosperous middle-class family probably of Welsh origin, in London. His domestic associations were favourable; in fact, he may be said to have belonged to the aristocracy of intellect. His mother was a Heywood, of a family closely associated with Sir Thomas More, that is to say with the most cultured society of Tudor times; and the Heywoods had shown literary ability for several generations. One was an early dramatist; another translated some of Seneca's plays, became a Jesuit father, and suffered considerable hardship in that capacity. The domestic atmosphere was both literary and theological, and largely Roman Catholic (I say largely, because in these times people occasionally changed to and fro from one religious allegiance to another). Izaak Walton tells us that John Donne was both an indefatigable student and a man of pleasure. His studies certainly were very wide; but he applied himself particularly to theology and still more to law, both canon and civil. As for his pleasures, he may have been a man about town in a small way.

There are five beliefs about Donne's poetry which I contest. The first is that Donne was a philosopher, and consequently a philosophical poet. Metaphysics is, of course, a part of philosophy; so you will say, if Donne is not a philosophical poet, how can he be a metaphysical poet? The answer is that when we speak of philosophical poets, we mean what we say: we are using a term which belongs to our own time and to our own point of view. When we speak of metaphysical poets, we are using a convenient term used first by Dryden, and confirmed by Dr Samuel Johnson. It is only a few years ago that a brilliant philosopher and man of letters, Mr George Santayana, in his book, *Three Philosophical Poets* (Lucretius, Dante, Goethe), fixed for us the meaning of 'philosophical poetry'. Philosophical poetry is poetry in which the poet has done one of two things. He has either written a poem to express in verse a particular theory of the universe which he has taken over from some philosopher – Lucretius wrote his poem to expound the philosophy of Epicurus and Democritus in verse, and Dante expounded substantially the philosophy of St Thomas Aquinas in verse – or else he makes his own system of philosophy and expresses that in verse; and the latter is more what Goethe did. But in philosophical poetry the poet *believes* in some theory about life and the universe and makes poetry of it. Metaphysical poetry, on the other hand, does not imply belief; it has come to mean poetry in which the poet *makes use* of metaphysical ideas and theories. He may believe some theory, or he may believe none; but he must be a poet who experiences emotion through thought, as well as one who thinks about emotion. Of metaphysical poetry in general we may say that it gets its effects by suddenly producing an emotional equivalent for what seemed merely a dry idea, and by finding the idea of a vivid emotion. It moves between abstract thought and concrete feeling; and strikes us largely by contrast and continuity, by the curious ways in which it shows thought and feeling as different aspects of one reality.

Donne was a learned student of philosophy. But his poetry is not that of a man who believes any philosophy. He enjoys his learning, and enjoys using a philosophical idea in poetry. His poetry expresses no settled belief in anything. Read all the poems given in Grierson's anthology and you will find that it is the poetry of a man of strong feelings and of powerful and learned mind. A poet like Lucretius or Dante uses one whole system of thought and philosophy, and presumably believes it. A poet like Donne has read vastly of many philosophers of many schools: he borrows notions, concepts, terms and verbal methods. Take a poem like 'The Prohibition'.[1] It is neatly constructed. The first stanza is a development of its first line, 'Take heed of loving me'. The second develops the opposite thought, 'Take heed of hating me'. The third combines the two, 'Yet, love and hate me too'. The whole is a good example of what Dryden and Johnson call 'wit': it develops two ideas and [503] unites them in a paradox. Now, you may ask, this is very amusing and clever, but is it poetry, and, if so, why? Is it serious enough to be poetry? Well, it gives the emotional equivalent of a state of mind. This borderland where an emotion turns into a thought and a thought turns into an emotion is Donne's special province. This leads us to observe that Donne is not interested so much in expounding an idea because he believes it, as in picking out ideas because he is interested in the feeling they give. Take that very beautiful poem 'The Ecstasy'. It expresses by means of ideas the feeling of spiritual union of two lovers; but it is not a definitely held Platonic theory of spiritual union. It contains some very difficult stanzas; for instance,

> But as all several souls contain
>   Mixture of things, they know not what,
> Love, these mixt souls, doth mix again,
>   And makes both one, each this and that.

and, a few lines later,

> When love, with one another so
>   Interinanimates two souls,
> That abler soul, which thence doth flow,
>   Defects of loneliness controls.

This poem has been taken as a statement of a mystical philosophy of love; and even Professor Grierson, whose opinion I must respect, speaks of it as important because of being Donne's 'metaphysic of love', referring quite rightly to obvious origins in neo-Platonic philosophy. Well, it is perhaps a little reckless of me to ask you to take Donne's philosophy less seriously than Professor Grierson does, but I cannot see that Donne held this philosophy except for the purpose of this particular poem. Dante, for example, held, I believe, a more or less consistent theory of love which informs all of his poetry. But the conviction has more and more grown on me in reading Donne that he was interested in philosophy, but very little in the discovery of truth through philosophy; and from a mind stored with wide and curious reading he drew material as he wanted

---

1. See page 22 of Grierson's *Metaphysical Lyrics and Poems of the Seventeenth Century from Donne to Butler*.

it for a particular purpose. And, in this poem, you cannot look at the experience – the sense or illusion of perfect spiritual unity between two persons – and the explanation of the experience as two separate things. It is not a philosopher explaining a feeling, for the explanation is itself felt. The feeling is transmuted by being thought about in this way; and it is feeling transformed by thought, and thought transformed by feeling, that interests Donne, not the question whether the thought forms a consistent theory.

Nor is there any evidence for saying that Donne had a 'medieval mind', or that his merit is to have expressed a dualism of medieval and modern in his work. He had read a good deal of scholastic philosophy, but not more than any other theologian of his time; and the list of his reading which has been compiled shows that he was at least equally conversant with the theological writers of his own time and the generation before. On the contrary, his serious play with ideas seems to be peculiarly modern, and to make him at least as modern as Montaigne; his delight in ideas as ideas, in theories as theories, is anything but medieval. Nor is the contention that Donne is a 'mystical poet', based chiefly on this poem 'The Ecstasy', any better founded. Had he had a mystical turn of mind, one would expect to find some trace of it in his later work, his sermons and devotional writings. He was a great preacher, a great master of a particular form of prose, a fine psychologist; and I believe his religion was quite sincere. But there he was rather the theologian, or rather the student of theology, and the preacher, than the mystic. In all of his religious writings there is little sign of that privacy so characteristic of the mystic, that assurance of experience incommunicable: he was a man of public life.

Now if we can miss the point of Donne's love poems, his songs and sonnets, by taking the philosophy too seriously: so we may miss the point also by taking the personal emotions in them too seriously. This does not mean that the poems themselves are to be taken as frivolous; it merely means that we may look for the seriousness in the wrong place. The seriousness, I will say again, is in the peculiar fusion of the thought and the feeling. Many people, taking some of his remarks about himself literally, believe that Donne led a passionate and dissolute youth, and regard his poems as outbursts of unrestrained amorousness. In many of his poems I feel myself that the original ingredient of personal experience is a rather thin fluid. 'Twicknam Garden' is an exercise on a quite conventional theme, the deserted lover. What matters is what Donne does with it.

> Blasted with sighs, and surrounded with tears,
> Hither I come to seek the spring,

> And at mine eyes, and at mine ears,
> Receive such balms, as else cure everything;
> But, O, self traitor, I do bring
> The spider love, which transubstantiates all,
> And can convert manna to gall,
> And that this place may thoroughly be thought
> True Paradise, I have the serpent brought.

The real point about this protestation, which differentiates it from the conventional exclamations of the deserted Elizabethan lover, is its complication by curious ideas. He makes what is almost a kind of pun upon the theological notion of transubstantiation, then a witty reference to the Garden of Eden. Similarly in 'The Relic' he begins with a rather grisly cynicism, suddenly strikes out a line which would distinguish the finest of Elizabethan tragedies, and proceeds to play solemnly upon a notion of religious relic-worship.

> When my grave is broke up again
> Some second guest to entertain
> (For graves have learnt that woman-head
> To be to more than one a bed),
> And he that digs it spies
> A bracelet of bright hair about the bone,
> Will he not let us alone,
> And think that there a loving couple lies,
> Who thought that this device might be some way
> To make their souls, at the last busy day,
> Meet at this grave, and make a little stay?

Then read the second stanza. You may think that Donne is letting you down, or having a joke at your expense. But what gives the particular emotional tone to this kind of poetry is just these odd changes of key, these sudden changes and strange juxtapositions which combine to make a unique emotional whole.

I have referred to the quality of Donne's thought, and its relation to his sensibility. I have not spoken of a kind of conversational tone in his poetry, which is a matter of choice and arrangement of words; and it is a rare and precious quality. It makes one feel that Donne is himself speaking to you personally and familiarly, although speaking great poetry. It is closely allied to what we call 'sincerity' in poetry; though we are not to believe that sincerity in poetry is the same as, or is due to, sincerity about the facts of the poet's life. I have not the space to explain this further; you will certainly feel it yourselves in reading him. I can only mention one more important quality of his verse: its metrical skill and variety. The eighteenth century found his verse rough and unpolished; that is because the eighteenth century had got far away from the sung poem, had so far forgotten the musical foundation of verse, that it could not understand him. I am not depreciating the very great virtues of eighteenth-century verse; but its virtues were not the virtues of song; it approximated rather to those of a really first-rate parliamentary oration. Now Donne occurs just at the turn of time when musical metre was still alive – indeed, some of his songs were set to music – and when dramatic metre was still alive; and what the eighteenth century declared to be crude irregularities in his verse we now admire and imitate. Turn again to the first stanza of 'Twicknam Garden', and you will find that it has the irregularity of the finest Elizabethan blank verse, and at the same time a singing quality which is not far removed from the Elizabethan song.

(From a talk on March 14. Mr Eliot recommends for reading the volume of Donne's complete verse and selected prose published by the Nonesuch Press at 7s. 6d.)

The Devotional Poets of the Seventeenth Century

DONNE, HERBERT, CRASHAW

Listener, 3. 63 (26 Mar. 1930), 552–3. Subheaded 'By T. S. ELIOT'. Gallup C304.

Donne's great innovation in his choice of language is his replacement of the stock vocabulary of Elizabethan poetry, what we may call its mythology, by a new mythology drawn from philosophical, theological, legal and scientific terminology. A similar attempt at renovation appears in some of the poetry being written to-day. One effect of such originality is to give a direct conversational quality – a quality sometimes called 'sincerity' in poetry. I do not like the term 'sincerity' for this purpose, because it suggests the direct expression of a 'sincere' feeling, which is a different thing; and it is this quality miscalled sincerity which makes people think they get so much closer to the 'personality' of Donne than they do, let us say, to Edmund Spenser. There is another, and a simpler, reason, for the conversational quality of Donne's verse, and that is that much of it is cast in the form developed by Browning: the dramatic monologue, in which we imagine a scene and the other person addressed. And there is a third reason. Besides the choice of vocabulary, Donne's great inventiveness is shown in his choice and variation of metres: and we may say that in metric he hovers between the singing and the spoken word, in content between thought and feeling, and in vocabulary between the technical word and the dramatic speech.

Ben Jonson, Dryden and Samuel Johnson all spoke hard words of Donne's irregularities in versification. This seems very odd to us, because the art of his versification is for us one of his greatest accomplishments. They may have formed their opinion partly upon the *Satires*, which are written in five-foot couplets; and the satires certainly are less polished than his best work. But there is every reason to believe that Donne worked very hard over the form of his poems. As a master of the long stanza of many lines, varying the length of line and number of syllables and the rhyme pattern, he is second in his time only to Spenser. Nearly every poem among his *Songs and Sonnets* is an experiment with a new arrangement: not all are completely successful, but the number of successes is very high. Here is the first stanza of 'The Funeral' (p. 18)[1]:

> Whoever comes to shroud me, do not harm
>   Nor question much
> That subtle wreath of hair, which crowns my arm;
> The mystery, the sign, you must not touch,
>   For 'tis my outward soul,
> Viceroy to that, which then to heaven being gone,
>   Will leave this to control,
> And keep these limbs, her provinces, from dissolution.

Here is another form of stanza (the second, in the middle of p. 14):

> But I am none; nor will my sun renew.
> You lovers for whose sake the lesser sun
>   At this time to the Goat is run
>   To fetch new lust, and give it you,
> Enjoy your summer all;
> Since she enjoys her long night's festival,
> Let me prepare towards her, and let me call
> This hour her vigil, and her eve, since this
> Both the year's, and the day's deep midnight is.

These are, I think, the two great creative acts of Donne: his introduction of a new vocabulary in verse, and his introduction of new metres. And a great poet, even when he uses a simple common metre, always gives it a personal stamp of sound; your ear, just as much as your perception of

---

[1]. The references are to Grierson's *Metaphysical Lyrics and Poems of the Seventeenth Century from Donne to Butler*. Oxford University Press.

THE DEVOTIONAL POETS OF THE SEVENTEENTH CENTURY • 135

the meaning, tells you who wrote it. Take a stanza from 'A Valediction' (p. 14):

> So let us melt, and make no noise.
>   No tear-floods, nor sigh-tempests move.
> 'Twere profanation of our joys
>   To tell the laity our love.

I must at least mention the finest of Donne's long poems, because you will not find them in any anthology, and must read them in one of the complete editions I have mentioned.[1] They are all worth reading, but there is none so fine, in my opinion, as one called *The Anatomy of the World, otherwise the two Anniversaries*. It is a strange poem, strange in its occasion; it is two funeral panegyrics written to please a rich patron, the subject being the patron's daughter, whom Donne had never even seen. Not a promising subject for inspiration, you would think, and the praise he lavished cannot be what we call 'sincere'. But he made a magnificent thing of it.

The next three poets whom I have to mention, George Herbert, Crashaw and Vaughan are chiefly known for their religious and devotional poems. That is a convenient distinction between 'religious' and 'devotional': I call 'religious' what is inspired by religious feeling of some kind; and 'devotional' that which is directly about some subject connected with revealed religion. The latter term is, therefore, the more restricted. Vaughan might be called rather a religious poet; Herbert, an Anglican Priest, and Crashaw, a convert to Rome who died in Italy, are positively devotional. Now, what is impressive about the religious poetry of this time is its variety; all of these men are very different from each other, and from Donne; so I shall first quote one famous sonnet of Donne's later years, to show what *his* best religious poetry was like (p. 86):

> At the round earth's imagined corners, blow
> Your trumpets, angels, and arise, arise
> From death, you numberless infinities
> Of souls, and to your scattered bodies go,
> All whom the flood did, and fire shall o'erthrow,
> All whom war, dearth, age, agues, tyrannies,
> Despair, law, chance, hath slain, and you whose eyes
> Shall behold God, and never taste death's woe.
> But let them sleep, Lord, and me mourn a space,
> [553] For if, above all these, my sins abound,

---

1. *The Complete Verse and Selected Prose of John Donne*. Nonesuch Press. *The Poems of John Donne*, edited by Professor Grierson. Oxford University Press.

> 'Tis late to ask abundance of thy grace,
> When we are there; here on this lowly ground,
> Teach me how to repent; for that's as good
> As if thou hadst sealed my pardon, with thy blood.

The thought is more complicated and difficult, but I think that you can catch an anticipation here of the magnificent style of Milton's religious sonnets. Donne's devotional poems have the same quality of verbal grandeur that we find in his sermons, and the tone is quite different from that of either Herbert or Crashaw.

Donne was born about 1573; Herbert was born in 1593, and died in 1633; Crashaw was born in 1613. Herbert then was twenty years younger than Donne; and Crashaw was forty years younger. So, as Donne is Elizabethan and Jacobean; these two are Jacobean and Caroline. George Herbert was one of the famous Welsh family of Herberts, and brother to the Lord Herbert who was a brilliant courtier, some of whose verse is worthily included in the Grierson anthology. George Herbert also began life as a courtier; and, like Donne, owed his entry into holy orders to the discrimination of King James. But there is this difference between Donne and Herbert, that whereas most of the poems by which Donne is remembered were written before he took orders, and are distinctly *not* religious verse, the poems by which we remember Herbert were probably all written after he took orders, and are all religious verse. It may be partly a consequence of this that Herbert gained the reputation of great saintliness; Isaac Walton, in his *Life of Mr George Herbert*, perhaps overdoes it. But we must remember that in those times a pleasure-loving man about town could become a devout clergyman without being either a case of Pauline conversion or a case of hypocrisy. Herbert, at any rate, was an exemplary Vicar of Bemerton for the last years of his short life, and there composed most of his poems. He enjoyed likewise a reputation of learning and scholarship.

I think the best way to introduce Herbert's poetry is to quote a poem which I regret is not in the Grierson anthology. It is a good poem, but I choose it particularly because it suggests very strongly the influence of Donne. It is called 'Prayer'.

> Prayer, the Church's banquet, Angel's age,
>   God's breath in man returning to his birth,
> The soul in paraphrase, heart in pilgrimage,
>   The Christian plummet sounding heaven and earth;
>
> Engine against the Almighty, sinner's tower,
>   Reversed thunder, Christ-side-piercing spear,

> The six-days-world transposing in an hour,
>   A kind of tune which all things hear and fear;
>
> Softness, and peace, and joy, and love, and bliss,
>   Exalted manna, gladness of the best,
> Heaven in ordinary, man well drest,
>   The milky way, the bird of Paradise,
>
> Church bells beyond the stars heard, the soul's blood,
> The land of spices, something understood.

I hope you remember what I said about the *conceit*, as a figure of speech used by Donne, in comparison with the strictly useful similes and metaphors used by poets like Dante and Shakespeare. The conceit is used for its own sake, and for the intellectual pleasure of far-fetched comparisons. The intellectual pleasure in this ingenuity is what was called 'wit', and in the second-rate poets of this school, some of whom I shall quote later, it remains merely wit, and seldom becomes poetry. In the real poets, on the other hand, what happens is not simply that poetry is added to wit, but the wit turns into poetry. Now, let us look at the poem I have just quoted by Herbert. It is a succession of brief conceits. We may observe that by Donne alone, with his superior mental power and dialectic skill, is one conceit ever developed successfully at length, as in 'A Valediction'. The other poets incline to pass quickly from one conceit to another. In Herbert's poem we find a very rapid succession indeed, some of which when isolated sound like wit but not like poetry: 'the soul in paraphrase', 'reversed thunder', 'heaven in ordinary', figures which I think suggest Donne strongly. Yet the poem as a whole *is* a poem, and the last two lines are so fine as to reflect a glory on what precedes:

> Church bells beyond the stars heard, the soul's blood,
> The land of spices, something understood.

lines which have some of the magic of Keats's magic casements. But Herbert is by no means merely a minor follower of Donne. He inherits and practises Donne's skill in conversational tone, and the effect of simplicity which he gives is evidence rather of a personal genius for simplification. And if I set myself to imitate either, I think that Herbert might be the more difficult model of the two. There remains his personal quality, and the necessity for saturating oneself in his verse to get it.

Crashaw is in appearance the greatest contrast to Herbert. Where Herbert seems simple and austere, Crashaw seems almost vulgarly opulent and decorated. Yet the difference is not so great as might appear. The great difference is this: that Crashaw absorbed many more, and more direct, continental influences than Herbert: he is definitely baroque. The strange thing is that the finest baroque poetry should have been written by an Englishman in English, in a country outside of the direct current.

Crashaw is more complicated than Herbert. Donne had undergone foreign influences, Herbert only through Donne. But Crashaw had the experience of Donne, and at the same time was exposed, more directly than Donne himself, to foreign literary influences. However complicated Herbert's poetic technique is, his type of religious feeling is easy for the English mind, whether Anglican or Dissenting. But in Crashaw we encounter a fine English poet who is at the same time a little alien. Herbert's plain moralising, or direct address to Our Lord, is very different from Crashaw's elaborate invocation of the saints. Crashaw is soaked in the Counter-Reformation. Let us plunge in and take him first at his worst. This is from a poem called 'The Tear' – that is, a tear in the eye of Our Lady:

> What bright soft thing is this?
>   Sweet Mary, thy fair eyes' expense?
> A moist spark it is,
>   A watery diamond; from whence
> The very term, I think, was found
> The water of a diamond.

A kind of pun, you see, in the first stanza. He develops antithesis, in the manner of Donne: Stanza II begins 'O 'tis not a tear . . .' Stanza III: 'O 'tis a tear . . .' and the climax of absurdity is the sixth:

> Fair drop, why quakst thou so?
>   Cause thou straight must lay thy head
> In the dust? O no;
>   The dust shall never be thy bed:
> A pillow for thee will I bring,
> Stuffed with down of angel's wing.

This is the very extremity of the conceit; Crashaw not only outdoes Donne, but even his Italian and Latin models: who else would provide a pillow stuffed with angel's down for the head of a tear? But now take a poem called 'The Weeper' (p. 130), on St Mary Magdalen, a subject who fascinated the poets, and some of the painters of the baroque period. Here, wit and tortuous ingenuity becomes poetry. Crashaw is a difficult poet for my purpose, because all his best poems are too long to read in full; but I can pick out a few stanzas of 'The Weeper':

> Not in the evening's eyes
> When they red with weeping are
> For the sun that dies,
> Sits sorrow with a face so fair,
> Nowhere but here did ever meet
> Sweetness so sad, sadness so sweet.
>
> The dew no more will weep
> The primrose's pale cheek to deck,
> The dew no more will sleep
> Nuzzled in the lily's neck;
> Much rather would it be thy Tear,
> And leave them both to tremble here.
>
> Golden though he be,
> Golden Tagus murmurs though;
> Were his way by thee,
> Content and quiet he would go.
> So much more rich would he esteem
> Thy silver, than his golden stream.

If you read the whole poem through, it must remind you of Shelley's 'Skylark', in its melody, and apparently in its succession of images. But if you look at the 'Skylark' you will see that Shelley's images are a straight succession of plain similes, with none of the delight in intellectual ingenuity – such as the figure of the evening's eyes being red with weeping for the dying sun – which, when combined with emotional intensity, gives the peculiar character of this poetry of the first half of the seventeenth century.

(From a talk on March 21)

A Commentary

C., 9. 36 (Apr. 1930), 381–5. Unsigned. Gallup C305.

A NATIONAL THEATRE

Matthew Arnold, in one of the most popular of his essays, expounded with great skill and persuasion the advantage of the French in the possession of an Academy of Letters, but concluded that the English would never get such an institution, and perhaps ought not to wish for it. The persistent project of a National Theatre in England suggests somewhat similar reflections. If we get it, will it be anything like the Comédie Française; and even if it is, ought we to want it?

The time to express a positive opinion has not yet arrived. A great deal more discussion is desirable first. Mr Bernard Shaw's contributions to the subject have been rather frothy, Mr Granville Barker's more serious. But so far we have not seen any detailed discussion by anyone who does *not* want a National Theatre; only a few hints from persons who believe that such a venture would be too costly; and that consideration is only likely to fire the zeal of the enthusiasts. In such an affair there are ordinarily only two classes of people: the few who are enthusiastic for it and the vast majority who are quite indifferent. If it is a pity that such a grand scheme should fail through public indifference, it would be equally a pity if it succeeded for the [382] same reason: the caprice of a few millionaires might suddenly saddle us with an expensive public luxury worth exactly nothing.

We should like to see a tentative repertoire proposed by some qualified supporter of the scheme. Will the National Theatre give us more or better Shakespeare than the Old Vic? Will it produce *Troilus* or *Pericles*? Will it take up again the work of the Phoenix Society, and will it do any of the work of the Stage Society? If it is useful, will it not be unpopular, and if it is popular will it not be useless? A periodic rotation of Shaw, Galsworthy, Barrie, the more popular plays of Shakespeare and an occasional performance of *The Way of the World*, with *Peter Pan* and *The Second Shepherds' Play* at Christmas. Will all the plays be Empire Produce, or on the other hand shall we be deluged with the accomplished drama of Central Europe?

It is not too difficult to conceive an interesting National Theatre, but it is much more easy to conceive a hopelessly dull one. The difficulty of selecting a repertoire out of the great number of fine but mostly imperfect plays of the English seventeenth century is much greater than the task of selection of French plays for the French stage; particularly if public opinion has to be reckoned with. We should not expect the National Theatre to sink quite to the level of the Royal Academy, because the British can recognise their good dramatists more readily than they can detect their good artists; but Mr Shaw will have much ado to convince us that a National Theatre will be any more useful for the advancement of British drama than the Academy for the advancement of British painting.

CENSORSHIP AND BLASPHEMY

On the subject of the 'censorship' of literature – we must continue to employ this useful word, although, as Lord Brentford has reminded us, there is no 'censorship' – *The Criterion* has pursued the middle path.

We have no wish to see the Home Office powers in relation to genuine porno-[383]graphy abolished; and unless these powers were a little too wide, in black and white, they would probably be no power at all. We only object, and shall continue to object, to the inclusion of particular works in this category; and we were and are alarmed by the ability of the popular press to draw attention to books in such a way that the Home Office is obliged to take action. We should like it to be impossible for an editor or a writer to use the public press to call attention to any work which he professes to consider to be deserving of suppression.

The recent discussions about the law of blasphemy illustrate some similar errors of fanaticism in the errors of both sides in the previous censorship discussions. Nowadays the real Puritans, or their lineal descendants, are mostly desirous that this law should be abolished. In the reports that we have read of the debates in the Commons, we have not seen much reference to the question whether the actual law had, within living memory, been grossly abused. The attacks upon it were mostly made from the assumption that the law is obsolete. They ignore the obvious practical distinction between allowing a law to be a dead letter – and repealing it. To repeal is not merely to erase: it is to put a new idea into people's heads. To abolish all restrictions on pornographic literature would be in effect to encourage pornography rather than to encourage literature. And in committing ourselves to this statement we have not forgotten one great work of English literature which Englishmen are prevented from importing into England, and for the circulation of which we have stood out from the beginning. Similarly, to repeal the law of blasphemy would be to encourage blasphemy.

No doubt, many of the persons who have fought against the censorship of books are enlisted against the blasphemy law; but no doubt there are enrolled also against the blasphemy law many people who are either indifferent to literary censorship or who positively approve the present state of things. The former group of people are at least [384] consistent; but the others should be made to understand that if there are to be no restrictions upon blasphemy, then the case for any censorship or police supervision of 'obscenity' is very much weakened.

CENSORSHIP AND THE FILMS

A cognate question is raised by a letter from Bernard Shaw in *The Times* of February 17th. If the facts about the suppression of the film in question are exactly as Mr Shaw states – and we have no ground for doubting them, and in *The Times* of the next few days saw no adequate rejoinder – then we feel as strongly about this particular instance as Mr Shaw does. But it is not clear from Mr Shaw's letter whether his objection is to the actual working of the film censorship, or to the existence of *any* film censorship. He points out that some films have been publicly advertised and exhibited to which he himself takes strong objection on moral grounds; and we do not doubt that we should be impressed by the same films in the same way. But he ought to agree that an intelligent censorship would be a good thing. And this is precisely the question which has never been thoroughly discussed: whether an intelligent censorship is possible; and, if not, whether the effects of a stupid censorship are any worse than those of no censorship at all. On the one side are ranged all the old English Radicals – sometimes 'Socialists' in name, but more Radicals in spirit – for whom Freedom, for anything and from anything, is an innate idea; and on the other side the timorous folk who defend, or accept, the actual state of things because the only alternative generally presented to them seems very much worse.

OF FREEDOM IN GENERAL

To revert to the first paragraph of this commentary, the people who are anxious to repeal every law which appears obsolete, may not always turn out to be the intimate friends of Freedom that they appear to be. Freedom can only exist [385] in a kind of balance; it is always threatened, not from one side but from both sides. The advocates of liberty, and of what in popular jargon is called the New Morality, who are so anxious that theory should be brought to square with practice, and that all humbug and hypocrisy should be swept clean away, are always likely to erect a new theory founded upon their own practice, which may be decidedly more restrictive of freedom than the old one. Freedom does not flourish in an ambiance of fanaticism. Nor is it always furthered by the passion, popular among some of the community at the present time, for *legalising* everything, which is merely tearing down old fences which had happily some holes in them, and building new barriers topped with broken glass and charged with electricity. The most conspicuous and most monstrous recent example of humanitarian tyranny is the Canal Boat Bill, a measure which in the name of health and education would destroy the family life of its victims. Such are the fruits of Liberty.

In Memoriam

C. 9. 36 (Apr. 1930). Loose leaf insert. Unsigned. Not in Gallup, but would be C305a.

At the last moment of preparation for press, we learn almost simultaneously of the death of three distinguished contributors to *The Criterion*: C. K. SCOTT-MONCRIEFF, D. H. LAWRENCE, and CHARLES WHIBLEY. There is neither time nor space to commemorate them further in this number. Editorial comment must be impersonal. We can only say for the moment, now, that each of these men represented something for which *The Criterion* stands; and that each in his kind and degree and way helped *The Criterion*; and that the loss to this periodical is very grievous.

Mystic and Politician as Poet

VAUGHAN, TRAHERNE, MARVELL, MILTON

Listener, 3. 64 (2 Apr. 1930), 590–1. Subheaded 'By T. S. ELIOT'. Gallup C306.

Henry Vaughan is in some ways the most original and difficult of all the followers of Donne. Younger than any of the men I have yet mentioned, he was still old enough to have served in the King's army during the Civil Wars. He was a Welsh country gentleman of good family, but no courtier. His biography is a little vague, but he seems to have been distinguished by a passion for learned and curious studies, and by a passionate devotion to his native valleys. In fact, the odd title which he gave himself, 'The Silurist', indicates a desire to identify himself as closely as possible with his native part of Wales.

His sensibility seems at times much nearer to that of the twentieth century; he has a curious brooding love of nature which makes us think of Wordsworth, and a rather closer observation of wild nature. Donne is a poet of the town; Herbert is a poet of the vicarage; Crashaw is a poet of Rome; but Vaughan, with all his learning and culture, is a poet of the rugged countryside. The other peculiarity of Vaughan is that he comes much nearer than any of these men to being what we may call a mystic. Much of his poetry is religious, but is not of the Church; and here and there we seem to catch flashes of an original and unique vision; of personal mystical experience – perhaps not of the highest order, but still authentic. And on this side he suggests very faintly, William Blake; but without any of Blake's arrogant theorising.

Let us look at once at the poem which has perhaps done the most to distort our view of Vaughan into that of a mere precursor of Wordsworth, 'The Retreat' (p. 145);[1]

> Happy those early days! when I
> Shined in my Angel-infancy.
> Before I understood this place
> Appointed for my second race,
> Or taught my soul to fancy ought
> But a white, celestial thought,
> When yet I had not walked above
> A mile or two, from my first love,
> And looking back (at that short space)
> Could see a glimpse of that bright face;
> When on some gilded cloud, or flower
> My gazing soul would dwell an hour,
> And in those weaker glories spy
> Some shadows of eternity . . .

This does suggest, of course, both Wordsworth's 'Ode on Intimations of Immortality' and his primrose by the river's brim, his daffodils, etc. but I think it represents something both different and more specific. It is not a general sense of what Whitehead would call 'pattern' in the life of nature, nor a love of nature for its own sake: I think it is a reference to some particular experience or experiences at some early period; just as I think that very different work, the *New Life* of Dante, also refers to a particular experience of childhood. And remark also that although Vaughan uses Christian dogma very little, he was a pious Christian of the seventeenth century with definite unquestioned beliefs: the eternal life dimly revealed through nature is still the eternal life of Christianity; therefore, he never runs the risk of deifying nature itself; and there is no trace of the pantheism to which Wordsworth is exposed.

I think we must see the love of nature and the trace of mysticism in Vaughan as one thing, remembering that his mysticism, so far as it goes, is Christian mysticism, and not the warm fog which passes for mysticism nowadays. His early poems are echoes of Donne; and to Donne he owes his start in life; but in his more mature work he develops a much more original imagery than does George Herbert. One of the frequent characteristics of Christian mysticism has been a use of various imageries of light and darkness, sometimes indeed of a light which is at the same

---

1. The references are to Grierson's *Metaphysical Lyrics and Poems of the Seventeenth Century from Donne to Butler.*

time darkness; such imagery is used by John of the Cross, perhaps the greatest psychologist of all European mystics; it is used by Meister Eckhart and the German mystics. I do not know whether it has been remarked how many of Vaughan's images are light images. He certainly did not borrow these from Donne. And very often Vaughan's are images of transient light; he is struck by the spark, the meteor, the glow-worm and the firefly:

> stars nod and sleep,
> And through the dark air spin a fiery thread,
> Such as doth gild the lazy glow-worm's bed.

> What emanations,
> Quick vibrations.
> And bright stars are there!

> One twinkling ray,
> Shot o'er some cloud,
> May clear much way . . .

Vaughan is really the most various of all our metaphysical poets. The late W. P. Ker, who probably knew the whole of European poetry better than any man of his time, loved to produce a verse or stanza by one poet which might have been written by some other poet whom we have always thought utterly unlike. I remember his quoting a stanza of Crashaw which sounded like the very best Byron. Vaughan is a capital source for this very salutary exercise:

> And still a new succession sings and flies;
> Fresh groves grow up, and their green branches shoot
> Towards the old and still enduring skies,
> While the low violet thrives at their root.

Might you not think that this was by some eminent modern Georgian poet?

I could give you other quotations, however, which you would swear were by Donne, and others exactly like George Herbert. But Vaughan is no mimic. I only mention these likenesses in order to isolate his essential originality. And I believe myself that in the following lines Vaughan is not merely making verses or boasting, but speaking of some insight in which he believes:

> I summoned Nature, pierced through all her store;
> Broke up some seals, which none had touched before;
> Her womb, her bosom, and her head,
> Where all her secrets lay abed,

>   I rifled quite; and having past
>   Through all the creatures, came at last
>   To search myself . . .

There is no stranger case of literary reputation than that of Thomas Traherne. His publisher, the late Bertram Dobell, tells us how the manuscript was seen by chance exposed on a bookstall and purchased in 1897. So after 300 years this poet was first established; and to Mr Dobell we owe both the poems and the companion volume of prose called *Centuries of Meditations*. If you read one of his poems after another, straight ahead, you will get probably an impression of monotony, that he has little to say. I think that the real trouble is that he has too much to say; or, rather, that he has one thing to say which is all-important to him. He is more mystic than poet; Vaughan just preserves the balance where Traherne upsets it. He has not the richness and variety of imagery which poetry needs; and in his prose the matter and expression are much better adapted to each other. His chief inspiration is the same curious mystical experience of the world in childhood which had also touched Vaughan; he read deeply, but the rest of his life was a prolonged meditation over his experience. At his best, he has a flash of that inspired simplicity which we find in Blake:

>   The streets were paved with golden stones,
>   The boys and girls were mine,
>   Oh how did all their lovely faces shine!
>   The sons of men were holy ones,
>   In joy and beauty they appeared to me,
>   And everything which here I found,
>   While like an angel I did see,
>   Adorned the ground.

But Blake was, first, before he succumbed to the temptations of his own philosophising, a literary artist; and he never really loses his mastery over language. Blake's early verse shows an interesting, deliberate and masterly gradual adaptation of the diction of the eighteenth century to his own purposes. Tra-[591]herne seems to me to remain a remarkable curiosity, an isolated specimen.

There could be no greater contrast within the varied unity of Caroline poetry than that of Andrew Marvell with Henry Vaughan. Herbert, Crashaw, Vaughan were all Royalists, though not all courtiers; the transition between Donne and Marvell represents the whole social and political revolution. Marvell was a Parliamentarian, a politician rather than a courtier. He was anything but a fanatical revolutionary or religious zealot, however; he was a man of culture and social position; and there is evidence that when the struggle came to a head, between King Charles and his Parliament, Marvell took sides unwillingly. Like Milton, he was for many years a hard-working servant of the public, and a member of the House of Commons. The town of Hull, which commemorated his tercentenary a few years ago, was blessed amongst constituencies by being represented by a man who was both a fine poet and an able, conscientious Parliamentarian.

Marvell stands, to my mind, half-way between the more serious disciples of Donne, such as Herbert, Crashaw and Vaughan, and the lighter 'courtly' poets. Grace, felicity of expression, and skill with the octosyllabic rhymed couplet are his distinctions; with now and then a tone of greater seriousness which is all the more striking because of the general lightness of touch. He is nothing if not sophisticated; learned and allusive. The best known of his poems is, of course, the 'Coy Mistress' (p. 73), a poem which is in every anthology, and which is too well known to quote. I should like to call attention, however, to the skilful form in which the poem is cast. The eight-syllable rhymed couplet is one of the most difficult of forms to use without monotony; and the 'Coy Mistress' is, for its length, one of the finest specimens in the language. It has, you observe, three divisions. The first (p. 73) is almost wholly, a rapid and bewilderingly clever succession of conceits; it is almost pure *wit*. The second section, beginning

> But at my back I always hear
> Time's winged chariot hurrying near;

is a sudden transition to intense seriousness; the third section, beginning

> Now therefore, while the youthful hue

is a sort of coda; or it is like the conclusion of a syllogism of which the other two are the premises.

Look at the graceful ingenuity of 'The Definition of Love': if anything, it is too clever an imitation of Donne. Marvell, the moderate Puritan, outrages the conceit as ruthlessly as does Crashaw. In his lines on Appleton House, in order to pay a compliment to its owner, Lord Fairfax, he pictures the house as adapting itself to its owner:

> Yet thus the laden house does sweat
> And scarce endures the master great:
> But where he comes, the swelling hall
> Stirs, and the square grows spherical. . . .

Not a very happy conceit, because it suggests that Lord Fairfax was a very fat man rather than a very great man.

A light grace and classical dignity which reminds of one of his masters – Horace – is Marvell's chief distinction. But he is a very interesting subject of study. He is so close to Donne, and so near to the courtly poets, such as Lovelace and Suckling, and yet on the other hand he has a kind of Latin quality which reminds me of Milton.

My chief reason for speaking of Milton at all is to explain why I do not say more about him. He is too great, and too individual, to fit into a series which aims to trace the transition between Donne and Dryden. Milton is no disciple of Donne. He is a solitary figure. He looks over the heads of all of these men, even of Donne; and his affinities are chiefly, I think, with Spenser and Marlowe: with Spenser chiefly as a master of metrical form in very long poems; and with Marlowe as a master of magniloquence in blank verse. I think the blank verse of Milton is much closer to that of Marlowe – with its use, even abuse, of high-sounding names and allusions – than to that of Shakespeare. *Comus* is perhaps the best example among his shorter poems to illustrate Milton's separate or collateral descent from the Elizabethan dramatists, Marlowe and the masques of Ben Jonson. The nearest he comes to the metaphysical poets is in a rather bad sonnet on the Cambridge carrier; and in the 'Hymn of the Nativity' which Professor Grierson has chosen rightly to include (p. 95). Some of the figures of speech are very near to the conceit in their elaboration:

> That glorious form, that light insufferable.
> And that far beaming blaze of majesty,
> Wherewith he wont at heaven's high council table,
> To sit the midst of trinal unity,
> He laid aside; and here with us to be,
> > Forsook the courts of everlasting day,
> > And chose with us a darksome house of mortal clay.

There is a similar parade of learning; but even here, you notice a kind of individual distortion of the language:

> Wherewith he wont at heaven's high council table
> To sit the midst of trinal unity

which is pure Milton. The syntax of Donne and his followers is generally pretty simple and straightforward: it is only their images which are complicated and difficult; but Milton – and it is one of his great merits and great dangers – is almost a contortionist of grammar. Yet in this Ode Milton is often near to the continental style which I mentioned in connection with Crashaw, to what is called Gongorism, after the Spanish poet Gongora. I can best express my own feeling about the poem by saying that if anyone but Milton had written it it would not be a great or even a readable poem. Milton is a very great poet indeed; but when we read a poem like this, and when we pass to a minor artist like Cowley, we may well be thankful that Dryden appeared to put the English language straight again.

(*From a talk on March* 28)

The Minor Metaphysicals

FROM COWLEY TO DRYDEN

Listener, 3. 65 (9 Apr. 1930), 641–2. Subheaded 'By T. S. ELIOT'. Gallup C307. At the beginning of the discussion of *Cooper's Hill*, 'meditation on various matters' has been emended to 'meditating on various matters'.

In an age of rich poetic accomplishment we may expect to find a swarm of minor poets each of whom is the author of one or two noteworthy pieces of verse. Donne invented an idiom, a language which less original men could learn to talk, and which they went on talking until they talked it out, and Dryden imposed a new way of speech on the next hundred years. Herbert, Crashaw, Vaughan and Marvell, all made valuable variations on this idiom. Then come a third and a fourth class of poets: those who wrote a few good short poems without altering the idiom in any interesting way; and those who achieved originality certainly, but only at the price of eccentricity. Of those who wrote a few good poems, I recommend, besides Bishop King, whose 'Exequy' I have posted, Carew, Suckling, Lovelace.

In a poet like Lovelace you observe an insensible and unconscious transition. There was a different type of poet who encouraged the change of idiom merely by his abuse of the prevailing one. These are careful professionals, not charming amateurs. Of such, the most notorious is John Cleveland, because he was chosen as the bad example by Dr Johnson in his *Life of Cowley*; and another man who passed with little notice in his own day, but who has been rescued from oblivion by Dr Saintsbury in his collection of Caroline poets. That is Benlowes. Remember that almost everyone, even in his own day, despised his verses; one satirist asserted that someone had been made ill merely by wearing a hat lined with pages of Benlowes's poems. He wrote with equal fluency and obscurity in English and Latin, sometimes in the same poem. I confess myself to a mild partiality to this man's verse – which is perhaps more likely to do my reputation harm than to do Benlowes's good. His most considerable poem is called *Pneumato-Sarco-Machia*: otherwise *Theophila's Spiritual Warfare*; and, so far as one can make out, has something to do with theology, and the struggles of the human soul.

I have spoken of Benlowes, not merely because of my fondness for this inglorious but by no means mute Browning; but in order to show how a versifier of much above the ordinary level, a man of original and ingenious fancy, better than half the poets who were well reviewed yesterday and will be well reviewed to-morrow, can bring a good idiom to such a point that a drastic reform of language is needed. Our language, or any civilised language, is like the phoenix: it springs anew from its own ashes. And correct language *is* civilisation.

Abraham Cowley was born in 1618: he was only six years younger than Crashaw, yet he belongs to another generation, in fact he almost himself created this new generation; and that is what is interesting about him. Cowley, as a biographical figure, is definitely a William-and-Mary or late Stuart museum piece rather than an early Caroline. The fervent spirituality of the early seventeenth century has gone; Cowley is a busy little enquiring mind of a rationalistic cast. He was a man of scientific tastes. He had known the great Hobbes, and, in Paris, during the exile – for he, too, was a royalist – had probably known the scientists there. His particular science was botany. He was an enthusiastic gardener. He was always drawing up schemes for founding institutions for scientific research. He had almost as many ideas as Mr H. G. Wells. He had a remarkable plan for the organisation of a modern college; and he was, so far as I know, the first man to advocate the foundation of a college for teaching agriculture as a science. He was active in the royalist cause, went to Paris during part of the Commonwealth government, and probably did a little honest secret service work for the exiled Stuarts. And he was an accomplished poet who admired John Donne.

Cowley's love poems are certainly imitations of Donne, and in these he misses what every imitator misses: the union of original language with original metric. But when Cowley turns to a really congenial subject, he becomes a different man.

Cowley has none of the religious feeling of the seventeenth century; he is a celibate epicurean churchman of eighteenth-century type, paraphrasing Horace on the virtues of the country life, and complaining that he can get no money from his tenants, and that his meadows are eaten up by cattle put in by his neighbours. He imitates the form of Donne, and yet in his content anticipates another age. Let me quote one of his finest Odes – that to Mr Hobbes the philosopher:

> Vast bodies of philosophy
> I oft have seen, and read,
> But all are bodies, dead,
> Or bodies by art fashioned;
> I never yet the living soul could see,
> But in thy books and tree.
> 'Tis only God can know
> Whether the fair Idea thou dost show
> Agree entirely with his own, or no.
> This I dare boldly tell,
> 'Tis so like truth 'twill serve our turn as well,
> Just as in nature thy proportions be,
> As full of concord thy variety,
> As firm the parts upon their centre rest,
> And all so solid are that they at least
> As much as nature, emptiness detest.

This is a transition between the style of Donne and the style of Dryden; in metric it is much more eighteenth than seventeenth century. But in feeling also it is more eighteenth century. Cowley, the admirer of Mr Hobbes the philosopher, Cowley who had probably met and conversed with the great sceptic St Evremond, in Paris, is an eighteenth-century rationalist in spirit, although to Dr Johnson he is a seventeenth-century metaphysical in form.

And with Cowley's 'Ode on Wit', and his 'Ode to Mr Hobbes', the passing of one age is marked, and the birth of another. Something has gone from English poetry which has never been recovered; and something else has begun which was itself to last only for a limited time. The Elizabethan Age had, even in its smallest writers, the sense of tragedy and of comedy, the attitude of a kind of inspired recklessness. The Jacobean-Caroline period has a more civilised grace, and a background of religious belief which casts seriousness and dignity over their lightest lines. It is not insignificant that the monarch who gives his name to the age is dignified with the style of Martyr. On all sides, it was an age of lost causes, and unpopular names, and forsaken beliefs, and impossible loyalties, as Matthew Arnold would have said; the beauty of life and the shadow of martyrdom are the background. In our own time there is a chasm of isolation between living men and women who belong to the pre-War and the post-War period; but no greater difference than that between the writers of the time of Charles I and the Commonwealth and the writers of Charles II and William and Mary and Queen Anne. When I speak of the particular seriousness of the pre-Restoration I am not thinking of one side rather than another: I include Milton, and Bunyan and Baxter as of that age, as men who knew the beauty of life and the possibility of martyrdom and sacrifice for a cause. And I sometimes wonder whether the generation succeeding my own may not be also a generation which has lost faith in lost causes.

The reasons for such changes are too numerous and concurrent, and too various, ever to be assembled finally. The court which had been formed in exile was of course directly submitted to French influences. The alteration of English poetry is nothing sudden. As I have tried to show, on the one hand a man like Cowley imitates Donne consciously and anticipates Dryden unconsciously: compare his two odes mentioned with Dryden's 'Alexander's Feast' or his 'Ode on St Cecilia's Day'. On the other hand, some of the minor original poets of the earlier period push the style to such excesses that any change is welcome. But, of course, there were men writing verse who belong chronologically to the earlier generation, and who have acquired importance largely because their way of writing was the foundation of the new way. The three most important are Denham, Waller and Oldham; all of them specialists in the heroic or ten-syllable iambic couplet.

Neither the ten-syllable couplet nor the genre of satire was [642] the invention of Dryden. In Elizabethan times, this combination has an honourable history, with the names of Hall and Marston and, of course, the satires of Donne. But it was then only a minor mode of verse. Browne of Tavistock, and Drummond of Hawthornden, used the same couplet in more or less pastoral verse. The first poet to accomplish anything in what may be called definitely the new style was an insignificant and rather ignominious figure, Sir John Denham. Denham belonged to a good middle class family of civil service type. He was born in Dublin in 1615 – almost the same age as Crashaw, but of another generation in spirit. He was a royalist who took some part in the wars, though without distinction, and in the court of the restoration was not a wholly dignified figure. Indeed, a man of no great distinction.

But in a poem composed before the wars, though revised after, he shows himself as the precursor of Dryden and Pope. It is *Cooper's Hill*, a poem describing the prospect from a certain position near Windsor, depicting the country charms, and meditating on various matters. I will quote a few of the best-known lines; and remember that this man is a contemporary of Crashaw and the younger disciples of Donne.

> My eye, descending from the hill, surveys
> Where Thames among the wanton valleys strays.
> Thames, the most loved of all the ocean's sons

> By his old sire, to his embraces runs;
> Hasting to pay his tribute to the sea,
> Like mortal life to meet eternity.
> Though with those streams he no resemblance holds,
> Whose foam is amber, and whose gravel gold . . .
> Oh could I flow like thee, and make thy stream
> My great example, as it is my theme!
> Though deep, yet clear; though gentle, yet not dull;
> Strong without rage, without o'erflowing full. . . .

The last two lines, with their prim antitheses, were particularly admired by the eighteenth century. And now, in order to point the difference of workmanship, I will go back and quote a few lines in the same form by Donne, not from one of his satires, but from a 'verse letter':

> Our storm is past, and that storm's tyrannous rage
> A stupid calm, but nothing it, doth 'suage.
> The fable is inverted, and far more
> A block afflicts, now, than a stork before. . . .
>
> The fighting place now seamen's rags supply;
> And all the tackling is a frippery.
> No use of lanthorns; and in one place lay
> Feathers and dust, to-day and yesterday. . . .

It is no use my analysing the difference between these two exercises in the same form of verse, unless you feel it; and if you feel all the difference, there is no need for me to analyse it. But remember that if you like Donne better than Denham, that does not mean that Denham is not likeable.

John Donne, using his special equipment and developing in his own way the language already developed by the dramatists, created, as I have said, an idiom which was capable of exploitation by a number of other poets. To us, Donne's way of speech seems more 'natural' than that of Dryden; and in general we incline, I believe, to think of the poetry of the eighteenth century as more 'artificial' than that of the seventeenth. But we must remember that what is artificial in one perspective is not so in another; and that the poets of the second period of the seventeenth century, the poets who built up the idiom which was still grandly spoken by Dr Johnson in his poems, believed, and believed rightly, that they were making a reform in the direction of naturalness and simplicity. Every generation of us, as we revolt from the preceding, believes the same thing, and is usually right. What was natural and right for Donne became something highly affected when written by minor followers. The reaction was towards good sense, sobriety and the speech of a cultivated gentleman. These do not seem to us the very highest qualities of poetry; but the point to keep in mind is that they are important qualities, and that poetry cannot afford for very long to do without them. They are as vital to verse as they are to prose; and the greatest possible mistake would be to label the poetry of Dryden and his successors as *prosaic*. The infusion of the prosaic into verse is an accomplishment of the greatest masters of verse. One of the reasons why Donne is a great poet is that he was able to use in verse, thought, vocabulary, and language which men of less inspiration would have excluded as prosaic. On the contrary, if there is a reproach to be levelled against the poetry of the age inaugurated by Dryden, it is that this poetry is not prosaic enough; it is from our point of view often much too poetical. But so was much of their prose; and the prose and verse of a period should be considered in relation to each other.

(From a talk on April 4)

John Dryden

Listener, 3. 66 (16 Apr. 1930), 688–9. Subheaded 'By T. S. ELIOT'. Gallup C308.

In an essay on Dryden written eight or nine years ago, I conjectured that our time might see some rehabilitation of the reputation of Dryden and of some of his followers. My guess was inspired by a brilliant and useful critical book, *John Dryden*, by Mark Van Doren, published in New York, but I believe never republished in London. Within the last year we have the *Restoration Tragedy* of Mr Bonamy Dobrée; and the recent book by Miss Sitwell on a not unrelated subject, Alexander Pope, tends to confirm my opinion. We have at least, I think, adjusted our view of Dryden by taking account of two very important parts of his work, neglected during the last century: his plays and his literary criticism. And I think we have a higher opinion of satire in verse, and a better understanding of its varieties, than our grandfathers did. But it is a mistake to think of Dryden as solely, or even as first and foremost, a satirist: *Mac Flecknoe*, *Absalom and Achitophel*, and *The Hind and the Panther* form but a small part of his total work. He was primarily a dramatist, secondly a translator; but it is as an artisan of the English language, helping to give us the modern language for verse – and indeed for prose too – that I want to discuss him.

And Dryden is one of the most remarkable masters in this respect, that no great English poet ever began with less promise. His *Heroic Stanzas* to the memory of Oliver Cromwell, and his *Annus Mirabilis*, a paean over a naval victory of the Duke of York, are assuredly amongst the worst poems in their form that exist. The metre is monotonous, the choice of words dull, his images so heavily weighted with expiring conceits that the sense is insensible and not worth getting at.

In his beginnings, Dryden is merely a dull ape of the inferior metaphysical fashion, without really having his heart in it: therefore Shakerley Marmion and Chamberlayne, two of the most long-winded, are more readable than the early Dryden. But now let me remind you of Cowley's two odes, that on 'Wit' and that on 'Mr Hobbes', which I quoted last week; and turn, not at once to Dryden's best odes, but to an inferior one, the *Threnodia Augustalis*, not an early work, because it was written to dignify the death of Charles II. It is an irregular ode in the true Pindaric style of Cowley. Even one stanza of this elaborate work is too long to quote in full. Here, however, are a few lines descriptive of the effect of the news of the death of Charles II upon his brother, who became James II:

> His pious brother, sure the best
>   Who ever bore that name.
> Was newly risen from his rest,
>   And with a fervent flame,
> His usual morning vows had just addressed
>   For his dear sovereign's health;
>   And hoped to have 'em heard,
>   In long increase of years,
>   In honour, fame, and wealth:
> Guiltless of greatness, thus he always prayed,
>   Nor knew nor wished those vows he made
>   On his own head should be repayed.
> Soon as the ill-omened rumour reached his ear.
>   (Ill news is winged with fate and flies apace),
>   Who can describe the amazement in his face!

This is very bad verse. But it is not the badness of bad eighteenth-century verse: it is bad in a way that verse written *before* Dryden himself had written his best could be bad; bad verse written *after* Dryden had to be bad in a different way. The curse of the minor poets who succeeded Pope was not so much pomposity as sentimentality.

But Dryden had the true gift of poetry: the capacity for indefinite improvement. Look at the 'Song for St Cecilia's Day', really an irregular ode, and at *Alexander's Feast*, written respectively more than twenty and thirty years after the piece I have just quoted. He has now arrived at both freedom and originality of rhythm, and at precision and dignity of language.

>   From harmony, from heavenly harmony,
>   This universal frame began:
>   When nature underneath a heap
>   Of jarring atoms lay,
>   And could not heave her head,
>   The tuneful voice was heard from high,
>   Arise, ye more than dead.
>   Then cold and hot and moist and dry
>   In order to their stations leap,
>   And music's power obey.
>   From harmony, from heavenly harmony
>   This universal frame began:
>   From harmony to harmony
>   Through all the compass of the notes it ran,
>   The diapason closing full in Man.

This is the work of a man who knows that he knows how to do what he wants. Observe the skillful repetitions, the just arrangement of rhymes placed far apart; the adroit irregularities in assonance in *lay* and *obey* so close to *dry* and *harmony*: the preservation of vocabulary and tone of speech in all the magniloquence. It is very different from the lost music of Donne, who already seems a long way behind us, yet it comes from Cowley.

Of Dryden's three great satires, all written in the perfection of his language, I think *The Hind and the Panther* is the most brilliant, though not the most amusing. *Mac Flecknoe* the most amusing, but the least impressive; and, on the whole, *Absalom and Achitophel* the most successful. Now, satire is one of the most difficult forms of poetry. A satire must be sustained, and it must be varied; and, like everything else, it must as far as possible be coherent. It must deal with contemporary matter and yet be permanent. It must deal with matter which is by hypothesis unpoetic, and it must make that matter into poetry. And in this way satire is one of the most abstract branches of poetry; it is when successful a triumph of form; is as near to that abstraction called pure poetry as any poetry can be.

You cannot satirise, in verse, one object very long. Satire as portraiture or caricature, must be brief, or the mind of the reader wearies and feels that what began as satire continues merely as abuse. So the best satirical verse sketches of character are introduced into a long poem as passages, like Pope's portrait of Addison, and like the various portraits in *Absalom and Achitophel*. The caricature satire of the poet Shadwell in *Mac Flecknoe* is, I feel, slightly overdone; though I admit that the merit of the poem as poetry consists in the very slightness of the subject; the employment of such magnificent verse upon so mean a figure. His other caricature of Shadwell and that of the poet Settle, as Og and Doeg in *Absalom and Achitophel*, are also more amusing than poetic. There is no essential connection between writing bad verse, being a contemptible person, and eating and drinking too much: therefore Dryden's lines about Og and Doeg are more vituperative than universal. But some of the political portraiture in *Absalom and Achitophel* is masterly. It is not the particular statesman, but a permanent type of statesman that is satirised.

The following lines are applicable to some set of people at any time:

> A numerous host of dreaming saints succeed,
> Of the true old enthusiastic breed:
> 'Gainst form and order they their power employ.
> Nothing to build, and all things to destroy.

Or the better known portrait of Zimri (the Duke of Buckingham):

> A man so various, that he seemed to be
> Not one, but all mankind's epitome.
> Stiff in opinions, always in the wrong;
> Was everything by starts, and nothing long.
> But, in the course of one revolving moon,
> Was chymist, fiddler, statesman, and buffoon.
> Then all for women, painting, rhyming, drinking,
> Besides ten thousand freaks that died in thinking.
> Blest madman, who could every hour employ,
> With something new to wish, or to enjoy!
> Railing and praising were his usual themes;
> And both (to show his judgment) in extremes.
>   *   *   *   *   *
> In squandering wealth was his peculiar art;
> Nothing went unrewarded, but desert.
> Beggared by fools, whom still he found too late:
> He had his jest, and they had his estate . . .

[689] Or the still better known lines on Achitophel (Lord Shaftesbury):

> Restless, unfixed in principles and place,
> In power unpleased, impatient of disgrace;
> A fiery soul, which working out its way,
> Fretted the pygmy body to decay;
> And o'er informed the tenement of clay.
> A daring pilot in extremity,

> Pleased with the danger, when the waves went high
> He sought the storms; but for a calm unfit,
> Would steer too nigh the sands to show his wit . . .

For my present purpose such verses are only incidentally *satire*. A great poet is a poet who extends the uses of verse; who makes poetry out of what we took for granted to be only matter for prose, written or often only spoken prose, or thoughts and feelings hardly expressible at all. The small poet is the poet who can only use whatever is currently accepted in his time as the poetic material – I say 'in his time', because much of the so-called sordid and realistic matter of much contemporary verse is merely the poetic convention of our time, as pure a convention as the sighing swains of another age. And, looked at purely as poetry, the lines of Dryden I have been reading are as astounding a vivification of the language as anything of Donne. Like Donne, he is elevating ordinary speech to the dignity of poetry.

In my own experience, and I trust in that of many students of poetry, I have found that poetry fell into two classes: that which was a natural, and that which was an acquired taste. What I mean is not, you will observe, an objective classification; for other readers will have a natural taste for that which I have acquired, and may have to acquire a taste for that which I like at once. And again there is a division of natural taste. There are poets for whom one may have a strong personal feeling, who seem to be speaking privately to oneself: and sometimes these are all the dearer if they are rather small people. And there are others so great and so profound that one's feeling towards them seems to have nothing to do with one's personal and private experience. 'Seems,' I say; because actually there is no sharp division; I probably have personal reasons also for liking Shakespeare; and on the other hand there is very good impersonal reason for admiring Jules Laforgue or Cyril Tourneur, if one does admire them.

But our acquired tastes in poetry are not to be despised. It is indeed in our acquired tastes that we may be surest of liking poetry as poetry; although in the study of poetry we must always begin by surrendering ourselves entirely to our natural likings, and steeping our minds in the poetry we like. But a person who only loves one poet does not love poetry; and only when we have come to enjoy as many and as various poets as we are capable of enjoying, have we the right to believe that we have a glimmering of what poetry is. Now Dryden is not a natural taste for our time; and here he is different from Donne; so you cannot approach him in the same way. It would be easy to think that one enjoyed Dryden or Pope, merely because one liked to feel that one had different tastes from the generation that admired Tennyson. But Tennyson himself is already so remote that to recognise his greatness requires as much perception of poetry as to recognise the greatness of Dryden. We are apt to enjoy the poetry of our own time largely because we find the poets to be like ourselves – and that is as natural and right as liking our family and friends – only we ought to be conscious of the fact. And we are apt to dislike the poets of an earlier generation because they represent to us much that we dislike: and *that* we cannot always help. And we may underrate Dryden because we belong to a generation which admired Tennyson; or we may over-rate him – or rather, we may delude ourselves into thinking we appreciate him – merely in a spirit of anti-Victorian revolt. And finally we can come to a genuine and pure enjoyment of him. I once said something to the effect that no person of our time can be said to know what poetry is unless he enjoys the poetry of Pope as poetry; and I would say the same of Dryden. For what is poetic about poetry is just the invention or discovery or elaboration of a new idiom in verse: and from this point of view Marlowe, and Donne, and Dryden, and Wordsworth, and Browning, are all equal in Heaven. Their differences in rank are not poetic differences, but spiritual degrees: and I am not here concerned with the Spirit which giveth life, but with the Letter which giveth life.

It seems a very long way, indeed, from the age of Donne to the age of Dryden. In literature, as in politics, revolutions never change anything, but gradual transition changes everything. The age of Queen Anne is very alien to the age of Queen Elizabeth. If it is an inferior age, that does not diminish the greatness of the writers who expressed it and who represent it: Dryden, Congreve, Swift, Pope. The arrival of Dryden was no sudden avatar. His way was prepared by Cowley in the odes, by Denham and Waller in the style of the rhymed couplet, in ease and fluidity; by Oldham in his occasional vigorous lines in satire; and by Davenant in drama, and by Hobbes in prose writing. But Dryden's greatness consists in his success in taking all these hints; in his sensitiveness to the time, that helped him to create his time; and in his perfecting the various imperfect attempts of others, and making the English language a vehicle for the thought and feeling of a generation. Dryden is, indeed, not unworthy of one of his masters – Virgil; as when he wrote his splendid elegy upon his friend Oldham:

> Farewell, too little and too lately known,
> Whom I began to think and call my own;
> For sure our souls were near allied, and thine
> Cast in the same poetic mould as mine.

> One common note on either lyre did strike
> And knaves and fools we both abhorred alike.
>
> *   *   *   *   *
>
> Thy generous fruits, though gathered ere their prime,
> Still showed a quickness; and maturing time
> But mellows what we write to the dull fruits of rhyme.
> Once more, hail and farewell! farewell, thou young
> But ah! too short, Marcellus of our tongue!
> Thy brows with ivy and with laurels bound,
> But fate and gloomy night encompass thee around.

(*From a talk on April* 11)

Message to the Anglo-Catholic Congress in London

The Sunday Referee, 29 June 1930, Special Supplement. Unsigned.
Not in Gallup, but would be C308a.

There is no doubt a large public which is indifferent, there is a much smaller public which is hostile, and there is another public which is rejoiced, when the Anglo-Catholic Congress takes place. To my mind the value of these congresses will prove to be, in time, still more for the first two categories than for the third: the first will learn that there is something to think about, the second that there is something which it has thought mistakenly about. The third, we need to remember, consists not only of those who take part in the worship and in the instruction, but of a great many others, scattered about the country, who cannot take part, but who must be helped and encouraged in their missionary work of example and steadfastness, by knowing that such a congress is taking place.

Second Message to the Anglo-Catholic Congress

The Congress Daily Chronicle, 30 June 1930, 8. Signed 'T. S. ELIOT'.
Not in Gallup, but would be C308b.

I should like to mention, as a layman – and I think it is a suggestion which can be made most forcibly by a layman – that there is one way in which these Congresses are very valuable, which appeals to me particularly.

I am thinking of the numbers of Catholics scattered about the land who have not the benefit of a Catholic parish, or of a church in which they can find their own form of worship, or of a priest who can give them guidance and counsel. There are not only those who have known these advantages, and have then been obliged to move away to more isolated parts of England, but also those who have never had them; and even those who have never had the opportunity wholly to discover their own true thought and feeling. Such people – how many or how few of them there are, I have no means of knowing – can do as much for the dissemination of the Faith as any of us among the laity, and should be the object of particular concern. No doubt many of them are helped by the publications of the Catholic Literature Association, and I trust that many more will come to know these publications. But an annual event like the Congress should have a special significance for these people, whether they are able to attend it or not; even to read about it, and know that it is taking place, should support them in their loneliness and sustain their efforts in their immediate environment.

It has, I believe, sometimes been an objection that the contributions to past Congresses have been too difficult and intellectual. For my part, I hope that they may never be less so. The Christian Faith is a difficult subject: a man can acquire intellectual comprehension only to the limit of his own capacities; but all of us should face the necessity of effort – effort both of mental and spiritual discipline. We are opposed, surely, to a modern laxity in religion which is determined to ask as little of its adherents, both of their minds and of their souls and of their practical conduct, as it can; and I believe that the more the Church asks of the faithful, in every way, the more it will receive.

I started out to send a message to the Congress. But I find that my 'message', such as it is, is rather to those who cannot attend the Congress or any part of it: a message that nevertheless they have reason to be thankful that the Congress is taking place.

A Commentary

C., 9. 37 (July 1930), 587–90. Unsigned. Gallup C309.

THE PLACE OF ROBERT BRIDGES

Whatever nomination be made to the Laureateship, which at our moment of writing is still vacant, the discussions in the press about the 'logical' successor to Dr Bridges imply a very positive tribute to the late Laureate.

The journalistic flutter of curiosity over his successor owes its interest largely to the fact that Bridges, in his very different way, raised the Laureateship to a dignity which it had not had since the most triumphant days of Tennyson. Even Wordsworth, by the time he attained that honour, hardly added to its lustre. After Tennyson, Dr Bridges did more than any incumbent to increase the distinction conferred upon him. And it is no disparagement of any possible successor, but merely a recognition of the late Laureate's particular gifts and even limitations, to say that there is no one living who can occupy that office with so much grace as its late tenant.

For indeed, his combination of gifts were exactly the right ones; and in this context the memory of the late Earl of Oxford and Asquith who nominated him, must also be honoured. There could have been no reason for Bridges's nomination except that he was a poet. When he became [588] Laureate he not only increased the eminence of the post, but at the same time raised and maintained the estimation of poetry as a dignified occupation even in the modern world. One feeling which we are sure all other practitioners of verse had for Bridges is the feeling of respect; and when so unanimous, that is a very fine feeling to inspire. There are living poets of every generation who are more popular; there are probably living poets who will be more read a century hence; but there is no poet of any generation who could so well have represented the dignity and difficulty of poetry. Some readers prefer his earlier lyrical verse to most of his later and more ambitious experimentation; but whether this taste is later confirmed or not, it is certain that his 'experimentation' has served a valuable purpose. It has helped to accustom readers of verse to a more liberal conception of verse technique, and to the notion that the development of technique is a serious and unceasing subject of study among verse writers; it has helped to protect other versifiers of less prestige, against the charge of being just 'rebels' or 'freaks'; or as a writer in *The Morning Post* some years ago nicely named them, 'literary bolsheviks'. Dr Bridges, to his honour and to our benefit, was as much of a 'crank' as anyone; even in his archaicisms he was an innovator; the *Yattendon Hymnal* must not be forgotten, nor his interest in old music, in language reform, in younger poets, in many things that the ordinary Briton regards with suspicion; and even those poets who feel that they owe nothing to him directly, and who cannot join the chorus of praise over *The Testament of Beauty*, have reason to bless his memory.

REFLEXIONS ON OUR CAPITALIST PRESS:
INSURANCE AND CIRCUSES

A recent event in the newspaper world seems to express a need much more urgent than that of a Poet Laureate: the need for a new newspaper peer. When the *Daily Mail* and the *Daily Express* are represented in the higher [589] house, can a Labour Government justly allow the *Daily Herald* no voice in that over populated and never filled Chamber? We do not suggest Viscount Lansbury; some more Zeus-like figure may be found than that jovial frequenter of swings, roundabouts and sand piles. But the circulation, now so proudly advertised, of the *Herald*, demands instantly at least a Baron. Possibly one solution would be the creation – for which the present government could take the whole credit – of a third chamber of super-peers, such peers to be elevated or degraded in rank according to the fluctuation of relative circulation; such provisional dignity being an additional incitement to give the people what it wants in the way of insurance, competitions, divorces, society weddings, aviation, football, serials, and interviews of Mr Bernard Shaw with juvenile Hollywood stars.

FATE OF THE LABOUR PARTY

The complicity of all parties in the race to give the people what it wants, and to compromise on everything, has become a comedy not yet fully enjoyed. Thus Mr Lansbury, hastily summoned from East London to visit the Roman Wall, has the warmest sympathy both with the National Preservation Trust and with Mr Wake whose aim is to reduce unemployment by quarrying in a capitalist way. Thus we are to treat various headstrong murmuring childish peoples with the greatest respect for their sovereign independence and liberty, and at the same time to do our best to protect our mill owners, mill workers and traders, as well as to prevent these equal peoples, equal to ourselves, from oppressing and murdering each other and sundry minor peoples and untouchables not yet equal to themselves and to us. Thus we must at one and the same time tax 'those who can best afford it' and keep the City in a good humour. Thus we must give everybody the vote and at the same time provide against anybody having a mind of his own. We must be conservative about obscenity and liberal about blasphemy. We must marry according to the [590] prescriptions of the Church, but we may divorce in contradiction to them. We must wheedle and coax the Dominions to accept our goods which are almost as good as those provided by Germany and the United States; and we must, in the name of economy, decline to help the Crown Colonies to go on producing sugar if we can get it more cheaply elsewhere (vide Lord

Olivier's report and correspondence). We must support the maximum population by the dole but we must not encourage them to make lace. We profess Free Trade but protect the Motor Car Industry. And this is what is complacently worshipped as the great British instinct for Compromise. If that is the test, then the present government is certainly as true blue as any government Britain has ever had.

The danger of such a policy is that everyone who believes in principles rather than compromise will be driven in spite of himself into extremity, either of Toryism or Communism. It will soon be evident that there are only two classes: those who have in common the spirit of 'compromise', those who have in common the spirit of principle, in other words, Tories and Communists. We dislike using the term 'Tory', because such public men as Mr Churchill and Lord Birkenhead are called Tories; and we dislike using the term Communist, because such public men as Mr Lansbury have been called Communists. But our present danger is that our public men will be divided into trimmers and men of principle; that men of principle, men who refuse to listen to that siren song that the true spirit of Britain is 'the spirit of compromise', must become either extreme Tories or extreme Communists, with (no doubt) a respect for each other that they cannot feel for the trimmers, and perhaps in consequence a sense of moral relief at having something positive to fight. There is a very practical sense in which it is possible to 'love one's enemies'; and the Tory of to-morrow and the Communist of to-morrow will perhaps love each other better than they can love the politicians.

Introduction

Introduction (xi–xix) to *The Wheel of Fire: Essays in Interpretation of Shakespeare's Sombre Tragedies* by G. Wilson Knight. Publ. on 25 July 1930. Gallup B13.

It has taken me a long time to recognise the justification of what Mr Wilson Knight calls 'interpretation'. In my previous scepticism I am quite ready to admit the presence of elements of pure prejudice, as well as of some which I defend. I have always maintained, not only that Shakespeare was not a philosophical poet in the sense of Dante and Lucretius; but also, what may be more easily overlooked, that 'philosophical poets' like Dante and Lucretius are not really philosophers at all. They are poets who have presented us with the emotional and sense equivalent for a definite philosophical system constructed by a philosopher – even though they may sometimes take little liberties with the system. To say that Shakespeare is not a philosophical poet like these is not to say anything very striking or important. It is more worth while to point out that my notion of Dante or Lucretius as providing the 'emotional equivalent' for a philosophical system expressed by some one else, is not to be pressed to a literal point for point parallelism, as in the old theory of mind and body. The poet has something to say which is not even necessarily implicit in the system, something which is also over and above the verbal beauty. In other words, the pattern of Cyrene or that of the Schools is not the whole of the pattern of the carpet of Lucretius or of Dante. This other part of the pattern is something to be found in the work of other great poets than those who are 'philosophical' – I say of other, not of all – for that would exclude Horace or Dryden or Malherbe. It is also to be found in the work of some (again, not of all) of the greatest novelists: certainly of George Eliot, and of Henry James who gave the phrase its currency. And of this sort of 'pattern' the most elaborate, the most extensive, and probably the most inscrutable is that of the plays of Shakespeare. For one thing, in Dante the pattern is interwoven chiefly with the systematic pattern which he set [xii] himself, and the mystery and excitement lies in trying to trace its relations and differences – the relation, and the personal variations in another mode, between for example the Thomist doctrine of Love, the poetic provençal tradition, and the direct experience of Dante with its modifications under philosophical and literary influences. But the philosophic pattern is far more a help than a hindrance, it is indeed *a priori* a help. Furthermore, Dante in his kind of poetry was doing exactly what he liked with his own material; and the practical exigences of a badly paid playwright, popular entertainer, sometimes actor, and sometimes busy producer, can only confuse us in our study of Shakespeare. Then again, with Dante the philosophic system gives us a kind of criterion of *consciousness*, and the letter to Can Grande confirms it; just as of a lesser writer, but no less genuine a pattern-maker, Henry James, we have some gauge of consciousness in his very nearness to us in time and civilisation, in the authors he studied and the constant play of his criticism upon his own work. But with Shakespeare we seem to be moving in an air of Cimmerian darkness. The conditions of his life, the conditions under which dramatic art was then possible, seem even more remote from us than those of Dante. We dare not treat him as completely isolated from his contemporary dramatists, as we can largely isolate Dante. We see his contemporaries for the most part as busy hack writers of untidy genius, sharing a particular sense of the tragic mood: this sense, such as it is, merging into the mere sense of what the public wanted. They confuse us by the fact that what at first appears to be their 'philosophy of life' sometimes turns out to be only a felicitous but shameless lifting of a passage from almost any author, as those of Chapman from Erasmus. This, indeed, is a habit which Shakespeare shares; he has his Montaigne, his Seneca, and his Machiavelli or his Anti-Machiavel like the others. And they adapted, collaborated, and overlaid each other to the limits of confusion.

Nevertheless, they do seem, the best of Shakespeare's [xiii] contemporaries, to have more or less faint or distinct patterns. (I was tempted to use the word 'secret' as an alternative to 'pattern', but that I remembered the unlucky example of Matthew Arnold, who said much about the 'secret of Jesus', a secret which having been revealed only and finally to Arnold himself, turned out to be a pretty poor secret after all.) In Marlowe, surely, we feel the search for one; in Chapman a kind of blundering upon one; in Jonson the one clear and distinct, slight but much more serious than it looks, pattern. There is something in the *Revenger's Tragedy*, but one play does not make a pattern; and Middleton completely baffles me; and as for Ford and Shirley, I suspect them of belonging to that class of poets not unknown to any age, which has all of the superficial qualities, and none of the internal organs, of poetry. But a study of these dramatists only renders our study of Shakespeare more difficult. The danger of studying him alone is the danger of working into the essence of Shakespeare what is just convention and the dodges of an overworked and underpaid writer; the danger of studying him together with his contemporaries is the danger of reducing a unique vision to a mode.

I once affirmed that Dante made great poetry out of a great philosophy of life; and that Shakespeare made equally great poetry out of an inferior and muddled philosophy of life. I see no reason to retract that assertion: but I ought to elucidate it. When I say 'great poetry' I do not suggest that there is a pure element in poetry, the right use of words and cadences, which the real amateur of poetry can wholly isolate to enjoy. The real amateur of poetry, certainly, enjoys, is thrilled by, uses of words which to the untrained reader seem prosaic. I would say that *only* the real amateur of poetry, perhaps, if this is not too presumptuous, only the real practitioner, can enjoy a great deal of poetry which the untrained reader dismisses as clever paraphrase of prose; certainly, to enjoy Pope, to have an analytic enough mind to enjoy even *second* rate [xiv] eighteenth-century poetry, is a better test of 'love of poetry' than to like Shakespeare, which is no test at all: I can tell nothing from the fact that you enjoy Shakespeare, unless I know exactly *how* you enjoy him. But 'the greatest poetry', like the greatest prose, has a doubleness; the poet is talking to you on two planes at once. So I mean not merely that Shakespeare had as refined a sense for words as Dante; but that he also has this doubleness of speech.

Now it is only a personal prejudice of mine, that I prefer poetry with a clear philosophical pattern, if it has the other pattern as well, to poetry like Shakespeare's. But this preference means merely a satisfaction of more of my own needs, not a judgement of superiority or even a statement that I *enjoy* it more as poetry. I like a definite and dogmatic philosophy, preferably a Christian and Catholic one, but alternatively that of Epicurus or of the Forest Philosophers of India; and it does not seem to me to obstruct or diminish either the 'poetry' or the other pattern. Among readers, probably both types, that of Dante and that of Shakespeare, suffer equal transformation. Dante will be taken as a mere paraphraser of Aquinas, occasionally bursting through his rigid frame into such scenes as Paolo and Francesca, but neither by his admirers nor by his detractors credited with anything like the freedom of Shakespeare. Shakespeare will be still worse traduced, in being attributed with some patent system of philosophy of his own, esoteric guide to conduct, yoga-breathing or key to the scriptures. Thus are the planes of order and pattern confounded.

It is also the prejudice or preference of any one who practises, though humbly, the art of verse, to be sceptical of all 'interpretations' of poetry, even his own interpretations; and to rely upon his sense of power and accomplishment in language to guide him. And certainly people ordinarily incline to suppose that in order to enjoy a poem it is necessary to 'discover its meaning'; so that their minds toil to discover a meaning, a meaning which they can [xv] expound to any one who will listen, in order to prove that they enjoy it. But for one thing the possibilities of meaning of 'meaning' in poetry are so extensive, that one is quite aware that one's knowledge of the meaning even of what oneself has written is extremely limited, and that its meaning to others, at least so far as there is some consensus of interpretation among persons apparently qualified to interpret, is quite as much a part of it as what it means to oneself. But when the meaning assigned is too clearly formulated, then one reader who has grasped *a* meaning of a poem may happen to appreciate it less exactly, enjoy it less intensely, than another person who has the discretion not to inquire too insistently. So, finally, the sceptical practitioner of verse tends to limit his criticism of poetry to the appreciation of vocabulary and syntax, the analysis of line, metric and cadence; to stick as closely to the more trustworthy senses as possible.

Or rather, tends to *try* to do this. For this exact and humble appreciation is only one ideal never quite arrived at or even so far as approximated consistently maintained. The restless demon in us drives us also to 'interpret' whether we will or not; and the question of the meaning of 'interpretation' is a very pretty problem for Mr I. A. Richards, with which neither Mr Wilson Knight nor myself in this context can afford to be too narrowly concerned. But our impulse to interpret a work of art (by 'work of art' I mean here rather the work of one artist as a whole) is exactly as imperative and fundamental as our impulse to interpret the universe by metaphysics. Though we are never satisfied by any metaphysic, yet those who insist dogmatically upon the impossibility of knowledge of the universe, or those who essay to prove to us that the term 'universe' is meaningless, meet, I think, with a singularly unanimous rejection by those who are curious about the universe; and their counsels fall more flat than the flimsiest constructions of metaphysics. And Bradley's apothegm that 'metaphysics is the finding of bad reasons for what we believe upon instinct; but to find these reasons [xvi] is no less an instinct,' applies as precisely to the interpretation of poetry.

To interpret, then, or to seek to pounce upon the secret, to elucidate the pattern and pluck out the mystery, of a poet's work, is 'no less an instinct'. Nor is the effort altogether vain; for as the study of philosophy, and indeed the surrendering ourselves, with adequate knowledge of other systems, to some system of our own or of some one else, is as needful part of a man's life as falling in love or making any contract, so is it necessary to surrender ourselves to some interpretation of the poetry we like. (In my own experience, a writer needs less to 'interpret' the work of some minor poet who has influenced him, and whom he has assimilated, than the work of those poets who are too big for any one wholly to assimilate. But I dare say that if one was as great a poet as Shakespeare, and was also his 'spiritual heir', one would feel no need to interpret him; interpretation is necessary perhaps only in so far as one is passive, not creative oneself.)

And I do not mean that *nothing* solid and enduring can be arrived at in interpretation: but to me it seems that there must be, as a matter of fact, in every effort of interpretation, some part which can be accepted and necessarily also some part which other readers can reject. I believe that there is a good deal in the interpretation of Shakespeare by Mr Wilson Knight which can stand indefinitely for other people; and it would be a waste of time for me to pronounce judicially on the two elements in Mr Knight's work. For that would be merely a reinterpretation of my own; and the reader will have to perform that operation for himself anyway. But I confess that reading his essays seems to me to have enlarged my understanding of the Shakespeare pattern; which, after all, is quite the main thing. It happened, fortunately for myself, that when I read some of his papers I was mulling over some of the later plays, particularly *Pericles*, *Cymbeline*, and the *Winter's Tale*; and reading the later plays for the first time in my life as a separate group, I was impressed [xvii] by what seemed to me important and very serious recurrences of mood and theme. The old theory, current in my youth, of a Shakespeare altering and deteriorating his form and style to suit a new romantic taste, would not do; or if Shakespeare did this, then it became a remarkable coincidence that he should be able in middle life to turn about and give the public what it wanted – if these strange plays could conceivably be what any public would want – and at the same time remain steadfast in such integrity of exploration. And the mastery of language, I was sure, was quite undiminished.

To take Shakespeare's work as a whole, no longer to single out several plays as the greatest, and mark the others only as apprenticeship or decline – is I think an important and positive step in modern Shakespeare interpretation. More particularly, I think that Mr Wilson Knight has shown insight in pursuing his search for the pattern below the level of 'plot' and 'character'. There are plots and there are characters: the question of 'sources' has its rights, and we must, if we go into the matter at all, inform ourselves of the exact proportion of invention, borrowing, and adaptation in the plot; and so far as possible we must separate the lines written by Shakespeare from those written by collaborators, or taken over from an earlier hand or interpolated by a later. This sort of work must be done to prepare for the search for the real pattern. But I think that Mr Knight, among other things, has insisted upon the right way to interpret poetic drama. The writer of poetic drama is not merely a man skilled in two arts and skilful to weave them in together; he is not a writer who can decorate a play with poetic language and metre. His task is different from that of the 'dramatist' or that of the 'poet', for his pattern is more complex and more dimensional; and with the subtraction which I have noted above, that Dante's pattern is the richer by a serious philosophy, and Shakespeare's the poorer by a rag-bag philosophy, I should say that Shakespeare's pattern was more complex, and his problem more difficult, than [xviii] Dante's. The genuine poetic drama must, at its best, observe all the regulations of the plain drama, but will weave them *organically* (to mix a metaphor and to borrow for the occasion a modern word) into a much richer design. But our first duty as either critics or 'interpreters', surely, must be to try to grasp the whole design, and read *character* and *plot* in the understanding of this subterrene or submarine music. Here I say Mr Knight has pursued the right line for his own plane of investigation, not hypostasising 'character' and 'plot'. For Shakespeare is one of the rarest of dramatic poets, in that each of his characters is most nearly adequate both to the requirements of the real world and to those of the poet's world. If we can apprehend this balance in *Pericles*, we can come to apprehend it even in Goneril and

Regan. And here Mr Knight seems to me to be very helpful, in expressing the results of the passive, and more critical, poetic understanding.

My fear is, that both what I say in this prefatory way, and what Mr Wilson Knight has to say, may be misunderstood. It is a little irony that when a poet, like Dante, sets out with a definite philosophy and a sincere determination to guide conduct, his philosophical and ethical pattern is discounted, and our interpreters insist upon the pure poetry which is to be disassociated from this reprehensible effort to do us good. And that when a poet like Shakespeare, who has no 'philosophy' and apparently no design upon the amelioration of our behaviour, sets forth his experience and reading of life, he is forthwith saddled with a 'philosophy' of his own and some esoteric hints towards conduct. So we kick against those who wish to guide us, and insist on being guided by those who only aim to show us a vision, a dream if you like, which is beyond good and evil in the common sense. It is all a question of our willingness to pursue any path to the end. For the very Catholic philosophy of Dante, with its stern judgement of morals, leads us to the same point beyond good and evil as the pattern of Shakespeare. [xix] Morality, we need to be told again and again, is not itself to be judged by moral standards: its laws are as 'natural' as any discovered by Einstein or Planck: which is expounded by, among others, Piccarda. Well: we must settle these problems for ourselves, provisionally, as well as we can.

Without pursuing that curious and obscure problem of the meaning of interpretation farther, it occurs to me as possible that there may be an essential part of error in all interpretation, without which it would not be interpretation at all: but this line of thought may be persevered in by students of *Appearance and Reality.* Another point, more immediately relevant, is that in a work of art, as truly as anywhere, reality only exists in and through appearances. I do not think that Mr Wilson Knight himself, or Mr Colin Still in his interesting book on *The Tempest* called *Shakespeare's Mystery Play*, has fallen into the error of presenting the work of Shakespeare as a series of mystical treatises in cryptogram, to be filed away once the cipher is read; poetry is poetry, and the surface is as marvellous as the core. A mystical treatise is at best a poor substitute for the original experience of its author; and a poem, or the life's work of a poet, is a very different document from that. The work of Shakespeare is like life itself something to be lived through. If we lived it completely we should need no interpretation; but on our plane of appearances our interpretations themselves are a part of our living.

T. S. ELIOT.

Introductory Essay

Introductory Essay to *London: A Poem* and *The Vanity of Human Wishes*
by Samuel Johnson, the Haslewood Books series, [9]–17.
Publ. Autumn 1930, and signed 'T. S. Eliot'. Gallup B15.
On p. 11 *'Defense'* has been corrected to *'Defence'*.

Repr. in *English Critical Essays: Twentieth Century* selected by Phyllis M. Jones (1933), 301–10, as 'Johnson's London' and 'The Vanity of Human Wishes', and in *From Dryden to Johnson*, vol. 4 of *The Pelican Guide to English Literature*, ed. Boris Ford (1957), 271–7, with the title 'Poetry in the Eighteenth Century'. The former title is taken from the title page of the 1930 printing, and there is no evidence that the latter title was Eliot's.

There is an essay to be written on the quotations which Sir Walter Scott used for the chapter headings of his novels, to illustrate the wide reading and critical good taste of that novelist. It is a great many years ago – about thirty years ago – that I was struck by a quotation of four lines; I cannot now remember at what chapter of which of Scott's novels it is placed:

> His fall was destin'd to a barren strand,
> A petty fortress, and a dubious hand;
> He left the name, at which the world grew pale,
> To point a moral, or adorn a tale.

It was not for a good many years after, that I read *The Vanity of Human Wishes*, but the impression which the whole poem made upon me was only a confirmation of the impression which the four lines had made upon me long before. These lines, especially the first two, with their just inevitable sequence of *barren*, *petty*, and *dubious*, still seem to me among the finest that have ever been written in that particular idiom.

It is dangerous to generalise about the poetry of the eighteenth century as about that of any other age; for it was, like any other age, an age of transition. We are accustomed to make a rough tripartite division between the poetry of the age of Pope, the poetry of sentimental philosophising – Thomson, Young, Cowper – and the early Romantic movement. What really happened [10] is that after Pope there was no one who thought and felt nearly enough like Pope to be able to use his language quite successfully; but a good many second-rate writers tried to write something like it, unaware of the fact that the change of sensibility demanded a change of idiom. Sensibility alters from generation to generation in everybody, whether we will or no; but expression is only altered by a man of genius. A great many second-rate poets, in fact, are second rate just for this reason, that they have not the sensitiveness and consciousness to perceive that they feel differently from the preceding generation, and therefore must use words differently. In the eighteenth century there are a good many second-rate poets: and mostly they are second rate because they were incompetent to find a style of writing for themselves, suited to the matter they wanted to talk about and the way in which they apprehended this matter.

In such a period the poets who are still worth reading may be of two kinds: those who, however imperfectly, attempted innovations in idiom, and those who were just conservative enough in sensibility to be able to devise an interesting variation on the old idiom. The originality of Gray and Collins consists in their adaptation of an Augustan style to an eighteenth-century sensibility. The originality of Goldsmith consists in his having the old and the new in such just proportion that there is no conflict; he is Augustan and also sentimental and rural without discordance. Of all the eighteenth-century poets, Johnson is the nearest [11] to a die-hard. And of all the eighteenth-century poets, Goldsmith and Johnson deserve fame because they used the form of Pope beautifully, without ever being mere imitators. And from the point of view of the artisan of verse, their kind of originality is as remarkable as any other: indeed, to be original with the *minimum* of alteration, is sometimes more distinguished than to be original with the *maximum* of alteration.

Certain qualities are to be expected of any type of good verse at any time; we may say the qualities which good verse shares with good prose. Hardly any good poet in English has written *bad* prose; and some English poets have been among the greatest of English prose writers. The finest prose writer of Shakespeare's time was, I think, Shakespeare himself; Milton and Dryden were among the greatest prose writers of their times. Wordsworth and Coleridge may be cited, and Keats; and Shelley – not I think in his correspondence, but certainly in his *Defence of Poetry*. This is not a sign of versatility but of unity. For there are qualities essential to good prose which are essential to good verse as well; and we may say positively with Mr Ezra Pound, that verse must be at least as well written as prose. We may even say that the originality of some poets has consisted in their finding a way of saying in verse what no one else had been able to say except in prose written or spoken. Such is the originality of Donne, who, though employing an elaborate metric and uncommon vocabulary, yet manages to maintain a tone of direct informal address. [12] The talent of Dryden is exactly the same: the difference is only that the speech which he uses is that of a more formal age. Donne makes poetry out of a learned but colloquial dialogue speech, Dryden out of the prose of political oratory; and Pope out of the most polished drawing-room manner. And of Goldsmith and

Johnson we can say the same; their verse is poetry partly because it has the virtues of good prose.

Those who condemn or ignore *en bloc* the poetry of the eighteenth century on the ground that it is 'prosaic' are stumbling over an uncertainty of meaning of the word 'prosaic' to arrive at exactly the wrong conclusion. One does not need to examine a great deal of the inferior verse of the eighteenth century to realise that the trouble with it is that it is not prosaic enough. We are inclined to use 'prosaic' as meaning not only 'like prose', but as 'lacking poetic beauty' – and the Oxford and every other dictionary give us warrant for such use. Only, we ought to distinguish between poetry which is like *good* prose, and poetry which is like *bad* prose. And even so, I believe more prose is bad because it is like bad poetry, than poetry is bad because it is like bad prose. And to have the virtues of good prose is the first and minimum requirement of good poetry.

If you look at the bad verse of any age, you will find most of it lacking in the virtues of prose. When there is a period of good verse, it has often been preceded by a period in which verse was bad because it was too poetic, too artificial; and it is very commonly followed by such another period. [13] The development of blank verse in the hands of Shakespeare and some of his contemporaries was the work of adapting a medium which to begin with was almost intractably poetic, so that it could carry the burdens and exhibit the subtleties of prose; and they accomplished this before prose itself was highly developed. The work of Donne, in a lesser form, was the same. It has prose virtues, and the heavy toil of his minor imitators was wholly to degrade the idiom of Donne into a lifeless verse convention. Speech meanwhile was changing, and Dryden appeared to cleanse the language of verse and once more bring it back to the prose order. For this reason he is a great poet.

The idiom of the Augustan age could not last, for the age itself could not last. But so positive was the culture of that age, that for many years the ablest writers were still naturally in sympathy with it; and it crushed a number of smaller men who felt differently but did not dare to face the fact, and who poured their new wine – always thin, but sometimes of good flavour – into the old bottles. Yet the influence of Dryden and Pope over the middle of the eighteenth century is by no means so great, or so noxious, as has been supposed. A good part of the dreariest verse of the time is written under the shadow of Milton.

> Far in the watery waste, where his broad wave
> From world to world the vast Atlantic rolls,
> On from the piny shores of Labrador

> To frozen Thule east, her airy height
> Aloft to heaven remotest Kilda lifts.
> >   Mallet: *Amyntor and Theodora*

> [14] Thus far of beauty and the pleasing forms
> Which man's untutored fancy, from the scenes
> Imperfect of this ever changing world
> Creates; and views, enamoured.
> >   Akenside: *Pleasures of the Imagination*

But besides this Miltonic stuff, which is respectable only because Cowper, Thomson, and Young made this line the vehicle for reflection and for observation of nature which prepared the way for Wordsworth; and besides the innumerable Odes, of which none but Gray's and Collins's are remembered, there was a considerable output of five foot couplets of which one can only say that this form of verse is hardly more suitable for what the man had to say than any other would have been. Of such is the *Botanic Garden* and its competitors.

> Who that beholds the summer's glistening swarms,
> Ten thousand gaily gilded forms,
> In violent dance of mixed rotation play,
> Bask in the beam, and beautify the day. . . .
> >   Brooke: *Universal Beauty.*

This is decadence. The eighteenth century in English verse is not, after Pope, Swift, Prior, and Gay, an age of courtly verse. It seems more like an age of retired country gentlemen and schoolmasters. It is cursed with a Pastoral convention – Collins's Eclogues are bad enough, and those of Shenstone consummately dull – and a ruminative mind. And it is intolerably poetic. Instead of working out the proper form for its matter, when it has any, and informing verse with prose virtues, it merely applies the magniloquence of Milton or [15] the neatness of Pope to matter which is wholly unprepared for it; so that what the writers have to say always appears surprised at the way in which they choose to say it.

In this rural, pastoral, meditative age Johnson is the most alien figure. Goldsmith is more a poet of his time, with his melting sentiment just saved by the precision of his language. But Johnson remains a townsman, if certainly not a courtier; a student of mankind not of natural history; a great prose writer; with no tolerance of swains and milkmaids. He has more in common in spirit with Crabbe than with any of his contemporaries; at the same time he is the last Augustan. He is in no way an imitator of Dryden or Pope; very close to them in idiom, he gives his verse a wholly personal stamp.

The two Satires which follow are Johnson's only exercises in this genre. *London* appeared in 1738; *The Vanity of Human Wishes* in 1749. To my mind the latter is the finer poem; but both of them seem to me among the greatest verse Satires of the English or any other language; and so far as comparison is justifiable, I do not think that Juvenal, his model, is any better. They are *purer* satire than anything of Dryden or Pope, nearer in spirit to the Latin. For the satirist is in theory a stern moralist castigating the vices of his time or place; and Johnson has a better claim to this seriousness than either Pope or Dryden. In the hands of Dryden the satire becomes almost the lampoon; and Dryden had a special gift for farce. Pope also is more personal than the true [16] satirist. In one way, Johnson goes back to an earlier tradition; however inferior as satires Marston's or even Hall's may be to Johnson's, they are surely much nearer to the spirit and intention of Juvenal than are those of Dryden or Pope. Dryden is, in the modern sense, humorous and witty; Pope is in the modern sense witty though not humorous; Johnson, neither humorous nor witty in this sense, has yet 'the proper wit of poetry' as the seventeenth century and the Augustan age had it also. I can better expose this by a few quotations than by a definition.

> There mark what ills the scholar's life assail,
> Toil, envy, want, the patron and the jail.

> Condemned a needy supplicant to wait,
> While ladies interpose, and slaves debate.

> Fate never wounds more deep the generous heart,
> Than when a blockhead's insult points the dart.

> Some fiery fop, with new commission vain,
> Who sleeps on brambles till he kills his man;
> Some frolick drunkard, reeling from a feast,
> Provokes a broil, and stabs you for a jest.

The precision of such verse gives, I think, an immense satisfaction to the reader: he has said what he wanted to say, with that urbanity which contemporary verse would do well to study; and the satisfaction I get from such lines is what I call the *minimal* quality of poetry. There is much greater poetry than Johnson's; but after all, how little, how very little, good poetry there is any-[17]way. And the kind of satisfaction these lines give me is something that I must have, at least, from any poetry in order to like it. It is the certainty, the ease with which he hits the bull's-eye every time, that makes Johnson a poet. The blundering assaults of his contemporary Churchill – a man of by no means poor abilities – do not make poetry; Churchill gives us an occasional right line, but never a right poem.

And the verse of Johnson has the good qualities of his own best prose, and of the best prose of his time. Bolingbroke, for instance, at his best, has some of the same merit.

Those who demand of poetry a day dream, or a metamorphosis of their own feeble desires and lusts, or what they believe to be 'intensity' of passion, will not find much in Johnson. He is like Pope and Dryden, Crabbe and Landor, a poet for those who want poetry and not something else, some stay for their own vanity. I sometimes think that our own time, with its elaborate equipment of science and psychological analysis, is even less fitted than the Victorian age to appreciate poetry as poetry. But if lines 189–220 of *The Vanity of Human Wishes* are not poetry, I do not know what is.

Arnold and Pater

'Arnold and Pater' was publ. in *Bookman*, 72. 1 (Sept. 1930), 1–7. Signed 'T. S. Eliot'. Gallup C310.

Revised in *The Eighteen-Eighties: Essays by Fellows of the Royal Society of Literature*, ed. Walter de la Mare (Dec. 1930) as 'The Place of Pater': Gallup B16. Further revised in *SE* as 'Arnold and Pater'. *See below*, pp. 564–75.

Introduction

Charles Baudelaire: Intimate Journals, translated by Ch. Isherwood and with an Introduction by T. S. Eliot, was publ. on 30 Sept. 1930. Gallup B14.

Revised in *SE*, with the title 'Baudelaire'. *See below*, pp. 554–64.

A Commentary

C., 10. 38 (Oct. 1930), 1–4. Unsigned. Gallup C311.

THE END OF A SESSION

The summer of Parliament ended in public depression and apathy, and we look towards the autumn resumption with still less hopefulness. Until recent years Parliamentary Government meant that one section of voters wanted to keep the Government in, to carry on its good work; and another section of voters wanted to turn it out, and substitute a really good one. So everyone, satisfied or not, had something to hope; and a General Election could be the occasion of excitement and festivity. But now no one wants the present government in, and no one wants it out. Mr Snowden becomes more unpopular, and his policies more obviously ruinous; yet one shudders at the disturbance and expense of an Election which might merely instate Mr Churchill in his place. Meanwhile Parliament has been occupied chiefly with matters such as finance which very few persons, either in it or out of it, can possibly understand; and has had very little time to give to such matters as its average education and intelligence should enable it to comprehend. Such persons within that body as have strong convictions are frequently more embarrassing than their own party than to any other. In short, the distinction of M.P. is not what it once was; [2] and we may hear at any moment from the more inflammable daily press that Parliamentary Government is an 'anachronism'.

It is true that the present Government has acquitted itself moderately well in Foreign Affairs. That is to say, it has done very much as its predecessor did; in foreign affairs the Labour Government has not deviated from the Liberal policy of the previous Conservative Government. We doubt whether the Conservative Government would have done a jot better: though when a Conservative Government does it we call it a failure; and the same policy pursued by a Labour Government is called a success. It is the same old policy after all: that of presenting premature 'self-government', such self-government to be, of course, invariably on an English model; and it involves the same old fallacies. One is that the *absolute* difference between governments is not between good and bad simply, but between being governed by people of one's own race and language and being governed by people of an alien race and language: the former is invariably better and a sovereign recipe for happiness. Another is that peoples can and must be 'educated' up to our own forms of government: even if these do not work always quite so well at home as they once seemed to, they are certain to work better abroad than any other. And another is that 'self-government' or 'responsible self-government' is the one true hall-mark of a high civilisation; and that no other contributions to culture can avail to make a people hold up its head, unless it is also 'responsibly governing itself'. So we cannot congratulate the Labour Government on any wisdom or originality in its foreign policy; but merely on demonstrating that the Conservative Government was no better.

It would however be not only unfair, but dangerous self-deception, if we blamed the weak heads of contemporary ministers, ex-ministers, and Parliamentarians in general for the present depressing state of affairs at home and abroad. The rot in Parliament is only a symptom of the [3] rot without; and outside also mediocrity of mind and spirit is to be found conspicuous. The need is for causes for which sacrifices can be made: one might cheerfully submit to even higher taxes were there reason to believe that the money thus squeezed would be anything but squandered. The pathetic desire for a cause, for something simple to believe in, is shown by the partial acclamation of Lord Beaverbrook's flimsy proposals. On one page of his sixpenny pamphlet he commends the 'empire free trade' of the United States; and on another he shows us how clever the Germans are to prohibit the export of potatoes from East Prussia into the rest of Germany, with the result that they are dumped into England. Such a pinchbeck policy could only command attention in default of anything at all serious and, we might add, of more intense spiritual appeal as well as greater practical utility.

THE STANDARD OF LIVING

'Self-determination' or 'responsible self-government' is a catchword; 'the standard of living' is another. It is freely used by Protectionists and by Trade Unionists (two divisions of interest only temporarily put asunder by Mr Snowden). One would suppose, at every flourish of this unctuous phrase, that the British working man was up to this moment in a privileged position in the world; that he was far better off than any other working man; and that he had not only the privilege but the duty of supporting civilisation, a weary Atlas, by his so-called 'standard'. The phrase may be questioned from two sides: an answer to both may be found by pointing to the working class family of six (which does exist) living in four rooms with a wireless set. What *is* our standard of living? Is it overcrowding in a small and unsanitary house, or overcrowding in large and sanitary and cheerless workmen's dwellings? Is it shrimps for tea, or a gramophone or a wireless set? Is it the dole, or thirty-five shillings a week on the land? Is the British working man, in other words, very much better off than the French [4] or German or Italian working man; and if so, are the ways in which he is better off ways in which it is *good* to be better off? We only ask these questions; suggesting that they are not so simple as they may appear; for the true 'standard of living', at all events, raises moral and spiritual, as well as economic questions; and suggests also the more humble answer that the British standard of living would be higher if the British working woman knew a little more about cooking, and the British working man and woman a little more about eating; and if simple natural pleasures, such as fresh air and country walks in fine weather, could be more usual, even if cinemas and wireless sets were more costly. As for the 'standard of living' of the more affluent class, it seems at present to involve long week-ends, and golf, tennis, and motoring on Sunday. The Roman empire left behind it at least a few ruined temples, aqueducts, and walls; one is sometimes inclined to wonder whether the British will leave, for the future archaeologist, anything better than the traces of innumerable golf courses, and a number of corroded fowling-pieces, scattered like primitive arrow-heads, over the desolate wastes of Scottish moors.

On Reading Einstein

By Charles Mauron

C., 10. 38 (Oct. 1930), 23–31. Gallup C312.

I hope that it is no longer fashionable to talk about Einstein. It was a rather sad, even rather shameful comedy, during some years past, to see, swarming about the lecturers and the popularisers, a crowd which I shall not call 'incompetent' – for incompetence is not ignominious – but in reality hardly even interested in the Truth, the revelation of which it called for so vociferously. People who would never have taken notice of the reflections of Poincaré, of the work of Lorentz or of the experiments of Michelson, if by chance they had heard of them: why should they suddenly pretend to give so much importance to a theory directly derivative from these enquiries? Now that this hubbub of snobbism has died away, I imagine that there are still a few individuals here and there who read Einstein and his sources and his commentators, simply because they are directly interested: the scientists, as a guide or as a reference in their own work; others, to appease that strange craving which we call the need to understand. They read Einstein, as they would read God knows what, when that odd hunger grips them: and when they meet, they talk contentedly of the velocity of light or of non-Euclidean space, with the simplicity of peasants discussing the weather. In that spirit I wish to set down here, as briefly as possible, a few ideas which have struck me in re-reading the little book into which the famous German scientist has condensed his essential conceptions.

I have no ingenuous presumption here to establish the truth or falsity of the theories of relativity: that must be left to experiment and to physicists. What I wish to remark are the modifications of our theories of knowledge, and consequently of all our philosophy which these theories, provisionally taken to be true, must bring.

[24] Can man understand the world? To this vague and extensive question, religion and philosophies have replied with an equally extensive and vague series of attempts in every direction. And as it happens in every branch of enquiry – the behaviourists know this well enough – the first result of these attempts has been, not to resolve the question but to define it. What does 'understand' mean? Little by little, two types of opinion have been formed: the first holds that any profound knowledge of any reality, implies an intimate fusion of the mind with that reality: we only understand a thing in becoming it, in living it. In this way St Theresa believed that she knew God; in this way a Bergsonian believes that he knows at the same time his self and the world. The second type of opinion, on the contrary, holds that this mystical knowledge is meaningless, that to try to reach a reality in itself is vain, inasmuch as our mind can conceive clearly nothing but relations and systems of relations. Those who adhere to the first view recognise truth by internal evidence, by the intensity of their sensation, and, in fine, by the degree of their ecstasy: these are the mystics. Those who maintain the second demonstrate the truth of their theories by their powers of prediction: for them, to understand is to be able to predict; knowledge which fails or which merely is incapable of predicting, must be set aside: such are the men of science.

These types of knowledge coexist still; it is even possible that they will always coexist. Their fields are indeed so distinct that theoretically neither can overstep the other. But in the practice of thought – and in practice absolutely – the case is quite altered; these transgressions are incessant. They swarm in our everyday thinking, which as a matter of fact is nothing but a muddle of the two kinds of knowledge. When I say, 'I know this path well', that evidently means that I know ahead all its twists and turnings, that, if asked, I can even sketch a map more or less in detail. But after sketching this map, I am well [25] aware that I have not told all I know about that path: within myself I have my own impression, personal, useless, and incommunicable; and this impression also went to the making of my phrase, 'I know this path well.' Possibly I deplore this confusion of language, but in the end that is a small matter. Languages are not perfect, and what matters is to understand each other; and if I can keep these two modes of knowledge side by side but distinct, everything will go smoothly. But there are men who, because they have had a strong impression of the path, fancy that they will never lose their way; or who because they are keenly aware of the original character of a particular human soul, fancy that they can foresee all its reactions; such people confuse, often to their cost, the two modes of knowledge. The Bergsonians commit the same confusion, in my opinion, when they affirm that scientific psychology is *a priori* impossible, because the reality of the soul is *quality*; they merely confess the incapacity of prediction of their own kind of knowledge. It is as if a tree should say: 'it is impossible to measure my growth because I feel it to be purely qualitative.' But the men who look at the tree from the outside measure it without worrying about its quality.

We seem to be a long way from Einstein, and yet we are very close to the subject; for it is confusion of this sort upon which limited relativity throws light. But before tackling this matter, let me venture the following remark: this profound sense that we have of the reality of things is rooted in the first kind of knowledge, which I have called *mystical*. A man of science who has dreams at night and who spends his days in writing out chemical equations will tell you that the equations are *true* and the dreams illusory, and on that point he will be wholly in accord with his doctrine; but he will admit nevertheless, that the dreams give him a much stronger impression of reality than the formulae; for the latter are relations which may well serve for prediction, but have not, like dreams or any other [26] sensation, the flavour of immediate experience. From this remark we may draw the conclusion: that wherever this sense of an absolute reality intervenes, this sense of a reality 'in itself', we must suspect the presence – intrusion, sometimes – of mystical knowledge.

Now, it is difficult to believe what a place, not only in everyday life, but in science itself of the purest and most abstract kind, is occupied by this mystical knowledge and the sense of absolute reality that goes with it. It is only in recent times that a physicist dares to say that he knows the laws of 'something' which he calls electrical current, but that he is and always will be completely ignorant as to what an electrical current is 'in itself' – because the question has no meaning for him. That is, however, the only correct attitude; only, it is very difficult to adopt in a thoroughgoing manner, because it shocks most of our everyday habits (and in particular those habits of language in which a substantive designates an object, a thing, as what we call 'real'). In this correction of attitude there is a whole adaptation, a whole evolution of the mind which is nothing else than that great attempt, remarked at the beginning of this note, which is pursued from age to age, toward fixing the meaning of the word 'know'. Qualitative knowledge, for its part, is incapable of evolution, because it is individual and in consequence untransmissible; and for the same reason, it cannot be contradicted, because it cannot be verified. But scientific knowledge can be refined from generation to generation; one of these processes of refining has been precisely that of eliminating as much as possible of qualitative knowledge to the point of no longer admitting it except as the foundation, in the crude fact, the crude sensation, the point of departure and the point of arrival of its speculations. So that its reply to the question set, 'can man understand the world?' is to-day more or less the following: 'Our sensations are given. By systematising them, and by only admitting the relations which they verify, we may hope that the system of relations [27] thus constructed will be a kind of reflection, or image of that which gives them to us. As to knowing *that* which gives them to us, that is impossible. If immediate knowledge had any value, it would be able to predict.'

A proposition like this is far from being explicit on every scientific head. Not all the things-in-themselves are dead. How many may still be discovered, for example, in biology? *Life* in particular, that 'reality' of which we have so lively a conviction: can it not be resolved, in the end, into a system of physico-chemical relations? But I wander from the subject. What I wanted to say here is that before the first relativists (Lorentz, Poincaré) two vast things-in-themselves dwelt quietly at the very heart of abstract science: Space and Time. We have a very distinct sense of our personal time; we distinguish quite well, qualitatively, our present from our past and our future. From that we inferred quite naturally that there was a time-in-itself, an immense unique time in which all the phenomena of the universe took place in succession and in a determined order. This time, the time of common sense, was also the time of the physicists. When it was said that this phenomenon took place after that, or at the same time as that, no one questioned that this phrase had a universal and absolute sense. In the same way, no one doubted the existence of a limitless Space, the same for all observers. 'The trajectory of a body in space' was an expression which appeared precise. All that was admitted rather than demonstrated, but the conviction was none the less profound for being implicit, because it was the conviction of our daily life, in which everyone always believes in things-in-themselves. When Pascal wrote 'the eternal silence of these infinite spaces terrifies me', he was thinking of this Time and this Space; and of them we are thinking every time we try to imagine the Universe. I am not going to set forth the relativist theories; I shall only remind you of a few of their consequences. Space and Time cannot be defined absolutely but only in relation to a particular observer, so that there [28] is an infinity of possibles. To be more precise: the shape of objects, the movement of clocks, vary according to the velocity with which they are endowed – not their velocity-in-itself, but their velocity in relation to a particular observer. And as a body may have one velocity in relation to one observer and another velocity in relation to another observer, so it will have for them two different shapes. And as there is no one observer-elect, we shall never know what may be the 'real' shape of the body. Similarly, two events which are simultaneous for one observer, will not be so for another, and we shall never know whether they were 'really' simultaneous or not. In short, Time and Space in themselves vanish, to yield place to a multitude of particular systems which have no meaning except in relation to each other.

It has been said that this shocks our *bon sens moyen* of which Descartes thought so highly. No; it shocks nothing but our habits – unless we agree that our common sense is simply our habits, which is quite possible. Was not our common sense once shocked by a man in the antipodes walking 'upside down'? I should be gratified if, after the reading of this note, the relativist theories seemed a little less strange. They are in the direct line of scientific evolution: they are only a stage in the vast process of elimination of things-in-themselves which is going on every day in human minds. And why do we want to eliminate them? To remain loyal to the primitive definition: that knowledge is prediction. Thanks to the precision of our means of measurement, the idea of an absolute Space and Time, acceptable in the day by day world, had come into contradiction with experiment. Science could no longer predict: thanks to the salutary operation of relativity it has been able to take up business again. We are a bit shaken up by this; but the fact is that the organisations of the intellect have a sensibility as do those of life; the extraction of a 'thing-in-itself' is always painful.

Qualitative and mystical knowledge has also its relativity, [29] as has long been known, a relativity which we must take care not to confuse with the other. It is what the individual expresses when he states: 'my sensation is not yours, nor is my taste yours, nor my universe.' It is a probable truth about which there is nothing to say. The God revealed in ecstasy to St Theresa was probably not the God who revealed Himself to St Francis. Shall we say that the true God was what these two had in common? That would be to argue like a scientist who sets about at once to establish relations. The only correct attitude for a mystic is this: 'You will not know God (or the world, or one thing or another) by comparing two ecstasies from without, but only by having your own ecstasy.' The attitude of a relativist in science is the contrary; when Einstein dissipates absolute Space and Time to replace them with an infinity of particular little systems, we must understand that at the same time he is giving us the formulae which allow us to pass from one system to another. Shall we revert now to the reply which we put in the mouth of the scientist when asked the question, 'can man understand the world?' If we set the question 'can man understand Space and Time?' he would, thanks to the relativist theories, give us a parallel reply: 'Our measurements are given to us. By systematising them allowing only such relations as they verify, we may hope that the system of relations thus constructed will be a kind of image of that which gives them to us.' Otherwise: if there exist somewhere an absolute space and time, the only scientific image which we can have of them is at present to be found in the relativist formulae of transition.

And that is logical: it is, if I may say so, in the scientific tradition which is only a huge sublimation of the world into mathematical equations. Shall we say that these equations have nothing real left to them? Doubtless, they have no longer that bouquet of reality which belongs to immediate experience. But how should they have lost all reality, when they predict phenomena, that is to say our [30] sensations? They are even the only conceivable reality.

In every event, returning to the precise purpose of this note, it seems to me difficult (and after the theory of relativity more difficult than it was before) to build up a theory of knowledge, and consequently any philosophy whatever, without taking account of the following essential fact: the progressive necessary elimination of every reality-in-itself is the obligation of any knowledge conscientious to remain in harmony with experience. This affirmation does not ruin immediate mystical knowledge; it merely digs more abruptly than ever the trench which separates it from scientific knowledge, and prohibits all confusion.

I would add one more observation. To the question, 'can man understand the world?' is balanced another: 'can man know himself?' The mystic replies: 'Yes, in awareness of his own life.' Any other answer belongs to the other domain, and tends more or less blindly towards a scientific psychology. But I want to show how science in its current developments comes to reveal automatically to us an image of our intellect. A student of the relativist theory cannot fail to be struck by the bounds which it suddenly sets to our thought; for example, a velocity greater than that of light becomes inconceivable, and the universe (space-time) is probably finite. These limitations are not the first; long before Einstein, we know that temperature cannot fall below 273 degrees Centigrade, and that certain equations representing phenomena quite real between exact numerical units lose their meaning outside these limits. But we must admit that more lately these examples have multiplied. And then we are led to enquire the exact meaning of this expression: 'such and such an equation loses its meaning beyond that limit' – 'that limit cannot be exceeded'. The mind has no trouble with a descent to 274 degrees or in outstripping the velocity of light. But experiment does not follow the mind, and our expression above evidently signifies that with these figures we take leave of the zone of observable facts. To come [31] out where? Evidently to enter the domain of the mathematicians, the kingdom of the mind. It is as if the zone of abstract speculation was more comprehensive than that of real facts, and as if, by the very progress of science, we were brought to define more and more precisely this strange frontier. That can be understood by conceding that we can think several possibles, and that out of these possibles the universe has only realised one. But we can imagine also that many possibles are realised in the universe which we shall never be able to think; and this second proposition would slightly rectify the fatuity of the first. However that may be, we have been spectators, for the last century, of a veritable outburst of unrealised worlds, of two or n dimensions, or otherwise non-Euclidean. None is completely unrelated to our sensible experience, but all exceed it. And after a time the mind feels itself at ease among them; it is at home. Around this solid system of relations which constitutes science and which is doubtless a reflection of the real are displayed these mathematical fantasies, airy plumes which are reflections of possibles. The ensemble is not without beauty. I am convinced for my part that we shall acquire in these researches clearer notions of what our intellect really is. A scientific psychology will have to take the closest notice of these constructions in the unreal. But furthermore, who knows whether our successors will not see matter as invested with a new magic, more correct but stranger than the phantasmagoria of old? 'There are more things in heaven and earth, Horatio . . .'

(*Translated by* T. S. ELIOT.)

Cyril Tourneur

Review, unsigned, of *The Works of Cyril Tourneur, Edited by Allardyce Nicoll*, was publ. in *TLS*, 1502 (13 Nov. 1930), [925]–6: Gallup C314.

Revised in *SE. See below*, pp. 417–25.

1931

A Commentary

C., 10. 39 (Jan. 1931), 307–14. Signed 'T. S. E.' Gallup C315.

The Times informed us not long ago in a leading article (October 2nd), that 'never in our history has there been such a period of popular education as the last year and a half'. It further rebuked Sir Martin Conway, who had been grumbling in epistolary form about the state of the Conservative Party, for regretting the extension of the franchise, by putting forward the 'irresistible contention that the framework of democracy would not be complete without' – without what? – without the young women of twenty-one.

There are here two interesting problems to examine. One is the nature and value of this 'popular education' so vastly and rapidly extended; the other is, what, now that this tasteful piece of joinery, the 'framework of democracy', is completed, is the character of the canvas to be found within it?

What *The Times* means by 'popular education' is not in this place clear; but we all know what the Press means by political education in general. It means that if we keep the Socialist Party in office until by practical experience, which means getting into plenty of hot water, and running heads against stone walls, and generally by having their minds addled by overwork and worry, the wretched Ministers are reduced to complete incompetence and harmlessness, then the Government will be wiser and sadder and exactly like any other Government. And it also means that during this period we shall keep pointing out all the Government's mistakes to the People; so that the People, also sadder and wiser, will instal by acclamation a really good sound Government. Both assumptions appear to me to be wholly wrong, wrong both as principles and predictions. As principle, they imply that there is no principle except Caution; they deny that there are any fundamental moral divisions in politics, on which men are willing to fight to the end and to suffer and make others suffer. The ideal is the [308] ideal of two parties, or even three, so far as all parties are exactly of the same practice in regard to everything that matters; they must however differ completely on a number of showy points that don't matter; otherwise the newspapers would have nothing to write leading articles about, and the public would lose the fun of that most costly of sports – the Sport of Democrats – the General Election. It implies, in the end, a theory of politics which is by no means patented by *The Times*; which is nowadays the common property of most papers and most politicians of every stripe; which is indeed, by democratic blessing, the common property of every common subject and citizen; the view that politics has nothing whatever to do with private morals, and that national prosperity and the greatest happiness of the greatest number depend entirely upon the difference between good and bad economic theories. It is further more and more the opinion of the common man that his private morals, except when they infringe criminal law, are nobody's business but his own – unless they bring him within the clutches of the scandal press. Private morals are not only private, but wholly negative. And on the other hand, so far as they are not private, they are made contingent upon economic conditions: so that we may conceivably have, in time, legislation framed to enforce limitation of families (by the usual methods) upon certain parts of the population, and to enforce progenitiveness upon others. With the applause of some of the clergy.

It is not often that I find myself in anything but diametrical opposition to Mr Middleton Murry; for which reason, when I find myself in accord with him, now and then, I attach some importance to the fact. It is true that when we agree upon principles, we usually find ourselves again in diametrical opposition as to their application: but this again is merely a confirmation of the principle. In the October number of *The Adelphi*, in an essay on 'Northcliffe as Symbol', Mr Murry says that the social disease is so radical 'that there is only one real remedy – the slow regeneration of the [309] individual man'. And he adds 'the need of a new asceticism is upon us'. I do not like to read of things being 'upon us' – so many things, we are told, are always 'upon us'; but on this I am in perfect accord with Mr Murry. Surely, Mr Murry and I will disagree again about what form this askesis should take; but that, for the moment, is irrelevant.

And this brings us roundabout back to the point of departure: the catchword of 'popular education'. Unless popular education is also moral education, it is merely putting firearms into the hands of children. For education in History is vain, unless it teaches us to extract moral and spiritual values from History; and education in Political Economy is vain, an 'unearthly ballet of bloodless categories', so long as it is offered as a pure science unfettered by moral principles. I am not depreciating the importance of Economics, but on the contrary elevating it. We need more and better Economics. We need another Ruskin. The trouble with the Science of Economics of to-day is that it appears in a form in which very few people, if any, can understand it. And in a democracy, it is essential that people understand the matters upon which they are exhorted to make decisions, and that they should not be called upon to decide upon matters which they do not understand. When I read, say, an economic article in *The Referee*, or any of the numerous productions of Major Douglas and his disciples, I am confirmed in my suspicion that conventional economic practice is all wrong, but I can never understand enough to form any opinion as to whether the particular prescription or nostrum proffered is right. I cannot but believe that there are a few simple ideas at bottom, upon which I and the rest of the unlearned are competent to decide according to our several complexions; but I cannot for the life of me ever get to the bottom. I cannot, for instance, believe in over-population so long as there is room in the world for everyone to move about without suffocation; I cannot understand the concurrence of over-production with destitution and I cannot help feeling that this has something to do with people wanting – [310] so far as they are in a position to want anything more than food and shelter – the wrong things, and cultivating the wrong passions. So that we need Economists who will not merely demand of us enough wit to appreciate their own intellectual brilliance, who will not aim to dazzle us by their technical accomplishments, but who can descend to show us the relation between the financial cures that they advocate and our simple human principles and convictions.

I am not even convinced that the accomplished economic specialists of the Harley Street of finance always know what they are about themselves. I have served my own apprenticeship in the City; endeavoured to master the 'classics' of the subject; have written (or compiled) articles on Foreign Exchange which occasionally met with approval from my superiors; and I was never convinced that the authorities upon whom I drew, or the expert public which I addressed, understood the matter any better than I did myself – which is not at all. I concluded that there are some gracious natures, which have an instinct for making money (not necessarily for themselves) as the bee makes honey; that there are other sound conscientious natures which can faithfully carry out the innumerable details of an elaborate machine; but how the machine came to be, or what it was ultimately called into the world to accomplish – of that no one seemed to know more than I did, and they differed from myself chiefly in their unquestioning loyalty to it.

I concluded, finally, that a large part of our difficulty arises from a prejudiced notion of what constitutes 'science'. I do not call into question the obviously respectable sciences of mathematics, physics and chemistry, which do no harm to anybody, but the prejudice that certain 'sciences' are more scientific than they are, and that others are not scientific at all. Theology (as an exact study, not as the seven-and-sixpenny Lenten effusions of popular preachers) is conceded to be a science on the same footing as the science of Heraldry – a little lower, that is, than Palmistry and Phrenology. Ethics is a *champ libre* for [311] sentimental essayists, or a *champ clos* for supposedly useless but ornamental university pundits, but has no 'scientific' standing whatever. Meanwhile, Political Economy boasts itself as a science as Physics is a science; and Physics is too busy with its own job to stop to repudiate the claims of Economics. And in fact Economics *is* a science, in the humane sense; but it will never take its due place until it recognises the superior 'scientific' authority of Ethics.

The possibility of a relation between politics and morals is admitted even by Mr Edgar Mowrer, who has written an extremely agreeable, if depressing, little book in the *To-day and To-morrow* series entitled *Sinon: or the Future of Politics* (Kegan Paul, 2s. 6d.). Mr Mowrer is able to say, as late as page 73 of this book, that 'the price' (of preserving our nations and Occidental civilisation) is 'the recognition and application to politics of scientific principles'; but by the conclusion on page 91 he has come to believe that 'better individuals are the only steps to better politics'. But perhaps one of our troubles is that we are now offered so many different prescriptions for the individual Good Life. One of the most satisfactory (to me) of recent formulae is that of Mr F. McEachran (*The Civilized Man*: Faber, 7s. 6d.), but perhaps it is satisfactory to me partly because it does not point to anything novel, but to something highly traditional. I have just read with interest *The Modern Dilemma* by Hugh l'Anson Fausset (Dent, 2s. 6d.), but have not been altogether successful in understanding Mr Fausset's particular askesis. I cannot feel that Mr Fausset, who apparently is nearer to Mr Murry than to anyone else, is in a very strong position for criticising Mr Irving Babbitt. Mr Babbitt is a lucid writer; and my chief difficulty with his philosophy is in understanding and accepting certain recurrent words and phrases. But with Mr Fausset the difficulty is diffused over each of his pages. These wide generalisations about the 'cult of medievalism', 'The Church', 'The Renaissance' (p. 8) are of a kind that always kindles my distrust; and when I read that the 'system (of the Church) with its graded [312] hierarchy could not withstand the rebel forces of the Renaissance', I am about as convinced as if I were told that the system of the Soviets, with its graded hierarchy, could not withstand the rebel forces of Denekin. Nor am I helped very much by being instructed (p. 14) that 'if we are to obey the creative purpose of life we must progress'. Progress whither? But when my eye lights on the phrase, a couple of pages later, *true inwardness*, I begin to feel more at home: for I am breathing the same old stuffy atmosphere of Matthew Arnold's Cloud Cuckoo Land.

But if one sniffs the air of Arnold in Mr Fausset's book, one is almost suffocated by it in Mr Julian Huxley's Conway lecture. (*Science, Religion and Human Nature*: Watts, 2s.) Sir Arthur Keith, who appears to be one of the less intelligent of our eminent savants, is so unlucky as to have his introductory remarks reproduced too. Sir Arthur makes one comment which is worth quoting:

> In the genetic 'make-up' of Professor Julian Huxley there are blended, Mendelianwise or otherwise, a complex derived from two main sources – a Huxley source and an Arnold source. Now, to my way of thinking, his paternal grandfather was an extreme realist; he insisted on stripping all gloss from the world of humanity, laying its inwards bare to a fearless analysis. The Arnolds were of an opposite strain; they preferred to clothe humanity with idealism; they would rather not see the naked flesh beneath.

Sir Arthur has certainly put his finger on the spot: though he forgot to add the words *thou ailest here, and here*. For that is just the misfortune of Mr Julian Huxley: that the Arnold strain is dominant, and the Huxley strain suppressed. In all his lucubrations on Religion, a subject to which he has devoted considerable attention, Mr Huxley succeeds in averting his eyes from the naked flesh beneath (to use Sir Arthur's slightly indelicate phrase). When we turn from the first professor to the second, we immediately encounter such refreshing phrases as 'inspirationism had to be broken down before the free spirit of religion could emerge'. Here is sweetness for you! Here is artificial light! 'The growth of [313] Anglo-Catholicism' indicates 'a tendency to think less of dogma'! And when we learn, very quickly, that religion should be 'a function of human nature', that we must study it 'not as a problem of theology . . . but as an organic function'; then we are really and truly back in the '70's of the last century.

In our search for that new asceticism, we seem to get into some strange streets. To the hereditary solemnities of Mr Julian Huxley I much prefer the innocent pranks of Dr Freud (*Civilization and its Discontents*: Hogarth Press, 8s. 6d.) and Mr Bertrand Russell (*The Conquest of Happiness*: Allen and Unwin, 7s. 6d.). Here, we feel, are two sound realists, not abashed by the sight of the naked flesh beneath, but really exulting in the contemplation of it. Yet even here we must be prepared for some disappointment. It is not so much that both books are odd mixtures of shrewdness and commonplace. It is rather that mankind is so constituted that many of us can never hope to rise to that level of mediocrity which these authors exhort us to reach. With more psychology, but therefore less art and a less delicate knowledge of the world, these writers can only echo the words of Rémy de Gourmont about contenting ourselves with the *menus plaisirs* of life: *quant aux grands, ils n'existent guère*. It is strange, nevertheless, that in a world which Mr Russell knows as well as we do, is in a rickety condition, he should be content in his book to preach a gospel of Main Street to the converted.

Leaving, now, these and other of *the strange children*, who *have gone whoring with their own inventions*, let us revert to the isolated dicta of Mr Murry and Mr Mowrer. 'The need of a new asceticism is upon us', indeed; but a cloistered or solitary asceticism is not enough to save us at the present juncture, unless the world is wholly (and well) lost; so that few are left *redeeming the time, because the days are evil*, yet perpetually pestered with Income Tax Applications. I am afraid that the new asceticism should not only be practised by the few, but imposed upon the many; else new asceticism [314] will be merely, as it is already for some, old necessity writ large. In other words, whilst the new economists hope to improve the new world for the old Adam, the new psychologists hope to improve the old Adam for the new world; where an impulse capable of disciplining the individual and at the same time increasing his possibilities of development as an independent member of society is needed. Instead of liberty, which most people can hardly appreciate anyway, we are offered licence; instead of order, we are offered mass-production of everything; including art and religion. I do not quite like Mr Mowrer's 'application to politics of scientific principles', because the word *scientific* can be just a comprehensive cloak for quackery; but if we alter the phrase slightly, I find no real contradiction between it and his cry for 'better individuals'. But it will not do merely to call for better individuals; the asceticism must first, certainly, be practised by the few, and it must be definite enough to be explained to, and ultimately imposed upon, the many; imposed in the name of something in which they must be made to believe. It is not the asceticism urged by the *journaux de gros tirage*, to eat more Dominion fruit and prosper. When it comes to asceticism, I prefer to make some concrete suggestion not beyond the strength of any of our readers. As an abstinence for next Lent, I suggest refraining during forty days from reading any newspaper published at a penny. *Par tous les moyens, même légaux.*

Thoughts After Lambeth

'Thoughts After Lambeth' was publ. as Criterion Miscellany No. 30, on 5 Mar. 1931. Unsigned. Gallup A18.

Revised in *SE. See below*, pp. 535-54.

A Commentary

C., 10. 40 (Apr. 1931), 481-90. Signed 'T. S. E.' Gallup C316.

The social and political situation in England is such that we now hear from the most orthodox editorial pulpits in the country that something must be done – something, that is, better than merely turning the present Government out and putting the last one back again. For example, in *The Observer* of February 22nd, Mr Garvin had come to the opinion that a new National Government should be formed, to deal with the actual emergency. We do not dispute the historical knowledge and political acumen of Mr Garvin, when we suggest that a National Government, which seems to be a phrase covering a coalition of all three parties, might arouse somewhat less than one third of the mild enthusiasm which any of the three parties is now able to excite by itself, unless something more permanent is proposed to succeed it. If the country is to revert to the present system of government after the 'emergency' has been dealt with, we can hardly expect the present system of government to issue from its hibernation as youthful and virile as ever. It will have suffered a diminishment: for we shall be forced to think of it as a friendly three-handed game which is all very well when things are going well, and while it does not matter much who is in power, but which must always be stowed away as soon as any serious business is afoot. And we shall hardly be persuaded that serious business is not preparing while the game is going forward.

If on the other hand, it be admitted that the present system not only does not work well now but probably will never work well again, then something more stable than an emergency government must be envisaged, before we proceed to so serious a step as the formation of an emergency or coalition government at all. For our part, we think that a coalition government, at the present juncture, would be only one kind of deathblow, and that the most reckless, [482] to the party system. It would mean that a number of eminent politicians of three parties would weaken their prestige by surrendering some of their convictions, or else weaken it still more by admitting tacitly that their convictions were only prejudices or party creeds. It is too much to expect that men whose careers have been made by opposing each other should suddenly and openly fall into each other's arms, and kick away the ladders on which they have mounted while they are still on the top rung. We are not convinced that a combination of old gangsters will be a great improvement on the old gangs separately. And it is irrelevant to point to the coalition government of wartime. The present time may well be as critical, or more critical, than the war; it does not follow that a crisis which is primarily domestic can be overcome by the same methods as a crisis which was primarily foreign.

Even, however, should the coalition thrive for a time, it would probably not thrive as long as the 'emergency', and its disruption would probably leave the country in worse case than before. For there is no question of 'tiding over' or 'weathering' or 'stemming' anything; the matter of it is not even merely to adapt the country to world conditions which have changed, but to adapt it to world conditions which are going on changing. It is very depressing to find that the Labour Party in office has proved not only conservative but reactionary. The one most rational form of representation in the House of Commons, the representation of the Universities, is, if the Labour Party has its way, to be destroyed. It is amazing stupidity, for the sake of perhaps a slight temporary numerical advantage, to remove just those men who do actually represent something. Far from abolishing this form of representation, we ought to increase it; and to have more members responsible to genuine interests with which they are acquainted rather than to mixed constituencies which they may hardly know. But for such intelligence we can hardly look to an official Labour Party which seems merely to be a compost of the [483] most outworn beliefs and practices of the Conservative and Liberal parties together.

The Mosley programme (Macmillan: 6d.), though in some respects vague or feeble, contains at least some germs of intelligence; and a pronouncement by men who have had the courage to disassociate themselves from any party must be read with respect. It recognises that the nineteenth century is over, and that a thorough reorganisation of industry and of agriculture is essential. The fundamental objection to it, of course, is that it is not fundamental enough. The changes are propounded in the same old cautious and sensible, and at the same time catchy, phrasing, as any other political manifesto. That word of prudence, 'emergency', occurs again and again; the reader feels coaxed and reassured that there is nothing really revolutionary about all this; whoever the reader is, it is all for his good. What is lacking, perhaps, and what is essential for enthusiasm, is the evidence of profound moral conviction. We do not expect, in a popular political pamphlet, to find explicit any philosophical insight; but we should like to feel that something of the sort was agitating the minds of the framers and signatories; if the present pamphlet arose out of such depths, the emotion has been too carefully dissimulated. *Politique d' abord*, certainly; but *politique* means more than prosperity and comfort, if it is to mean even that; it means the social aspect of the Good Life.

I have recently read a book from America (*I'll Take My Stand: The South and the Agrarian Tradition*, Harper's, $3.00) which is hardly likely to have much notice in England, because the situation discussed will be considered very local even in America. It is a symposium by 'twelve southerners', and suffers from the defects common to symposia, of repetition, unevenness and incompleteness. But there is a general problem which concerns the whole world; though probably it will not be perceived to concern even the whole of America. The question of the Good Life is raised; and how far it is possible for mankind to accept [484] industrialisation without spiritual harm. The complaint not merely that the South was ruined and subjected by the Civil War, but that it is now well on the way towards being northernised; that coal, oil, iron and factories have altered the relation of man to his world, and that the Good and Happy Life is becoming less possible. The old Southern society, with all its defects, vices and limitations, was still in its way a spiritual entity; and now the organisation of society is wholly materialistic.

The writers are somewhat unfair to some other parts of their country, and they tend to exaggerate the blessings of England and Scotland in contrast to their own depression. For instance, the contrast in America is no longer, as it seemed in the '60s, a conflict between North and South. It is a conflict between all of the local and spiritually living districts or *enclaves* and the dominant uniform mode of existence which is New York and the monotony of the Middle West. A New Englander cannot read the book without admitting that his own country was ruined as the South is ruined, and that New England was ruined first. Anyone who reads Professor Morison's interesting and authoritative *Builders of the Bay Colony* (Milford: 21s.) cannot but feel that in that isolated, cantankerous, often narrow, bigoted and heretical society there was more intellectual and spiritual flowering, more beauty of manners, architecture, painting and decorative art – and a local and peculiar beauty at that – than is possible in New England to-day, when Boston is five hours from New York by train, and no distance at all by air. And the contrast and sometimes conflict, between the different and complementary types of New England and Virginia, give the late Colonial and the early Republican history of America (to 1829) an interest and an urbanity which American history has not had since. The American intellectual of to-day has almost no chance of continuous development upon his own soil and in the environment which his ancestors, however humble, helped to form. He must be an expatriate: either [485] to languish in a provincial university, or abroad, or, the most complete expatriation of all, in New York. And he is merely a more manifest example of what *tends* to happen in all countries.

Unrestrained industrialism, then (with its attendant evils of overproduction, excessive 'wealth', an irrelevance and lack of relation of production to consumption which it attempts vainly to overcome by the nightmare expedient of 'advertisement'), destroys the upper classes first. You cannot make an aristocrat out of a company chairman, though you can make him a peer; and in a thoroughly industrial society the only artist left will be the international film producer. France, of course, has resisted better than any other country. Provincial French life is dull enough, but not without grace and the beauty of family union; and the population of Paris lives entirely in flats; yet I have hardly known a French intellectual in Paris – with the exception of M. Cocteau the 'Parisian', which perhaps helps to prove the rule – who did not keep up a proud and affectionate contact with *son pays*, be it only a farmhouse in central France. 'Regionalism' may of course be carried to the point of absurdity. But it is a sound and right reaction which impelled Mr Allen Tate and his eleven Southerners to write their book; and which impels Mr George Malcolm Thomson and his Scottish friends to affirm that Scotland ought to be something more than a Suburb of Greater London, or a confined industrial district populated by lower class Irish immigrants. And it is something of which politicians ought to take thought, if they are capable of thinking in any terms except 'emergencies'.

The *Sunday Times* of February 22nd is apprehensive about the future of Oxford. Under the pressure of the Chancellor of the Exchequer, it appears, the enrolment is falling off, and something must be done to keep up the numbers of students. It would seem that Oxford is another of our big industries in a bad way. Here is overproduction again, and [486] under-consumption; a great plant of buildings, tutors and foundations going to waste for lack of undergraduates. Well then, something must be done to stimulate consumption; in other words, to attract more students, whoever they are and whatever they want to study. The *Sunday Times* is particularly disturbed by the pernicious ideas of Dr Phelps. This misguided reactionary had the temerity to suggest that some of the professional and practical studies should be dropped (the word of course is 'jettisoned') and that the Classics should remain the centre of University Study, 'with a modicum of pure science'. So the *Sunday Times* is horrified; and asserts roundly that Oxford must be made more 'up to date'; 'less exclusively a pleasant backwater of the humanities and more a place where men and women can get a practical and efficient training for life in all its branches'.

For life in all its branches! Not, you observe, for 'life'; the industrial society recognises nothing so unpractical as 'life'; 'life' is only for 'pleasant backwaters'. But for 'life in all its branches': that means training in 'efficiency', for one branch then only. It does not mean training in adaptability; but often training for an occupation which the victim may find already overoccupied by the time he is trained into readiness to occupy it. It does not mean training for the Good Life, it does not mean any training in the use of leisure, in appreciation and enjoyment; for not everybody is capable of profiting by such training. It means more and bigger and more modern buildings, Graduate Schools of Business Administration on the American model, and something for everybody except those who want an education. But it would be a national disaster if the enrolment fell off; for Oxford and Cambridge are two of our biggest industries, known the world over; and what is manufactured in them matters less than that the looms of youth should be kept running at full time; rationalisation and mass production must be applied; for it would be undemocratic to apply modern methods to motor cars and not apply them to men.

[487] It is ignored that the Universities were far more democratic in the seventeenth century than they are to-day; but they were democratic in the way of levelling up and not in the way of levelling down. Andrewes and Laud, to take the two names that first occur to my mind, were of humble origin; the Ministry of Education under the Tudors was hardly the perfect engine of culture that it is to-day; yet the system was good enough to help these two men to make their way up from almost nothing, the one to become a translator of the Bible and one of the greatest masters of devotion that England can boast (if England ever *did* boast of such eccentrics), and the other to become one of the greatest ecclesiastical statesmen that England has ever known. I dare say that they were 'traitors to their class', and that they did wrong to accept educational advantages denied to the children of their parents' neighbours; nowadays they might have risen to fame and power by the stage of being Trades' Union Officials. But though educated in 'pleasant backwaters' they left their mark on history; nor do I suppose that they, and men like them, would have governed England any better had they had diplomas from the London School of Economics.

The complaint is sometimes raised that the British do not take enough interest in their Art. If, however, they took no interest at all, everything might be managed skilfully to impose works of art upon them; a nation wholly without interest in art might be perfectly contented even if the streets of its capital were lined with masterpieces of architecture and sculpture. But the British public, unfortunately, does take a kind of muddling interest in art; that is probably due to its having too much schooling; and I am not thinking at this point of the 'lower classes', but of the over- and badly-educated middle and upper classes. The first recent instance in my mind is the case of the unfortunate Mr Hardiman, and his model for a statue of the late Earl Haig. I had never heard of Mr Hardiman until the crisis was [488] precipitated; he may be, for aught I know, an excellent sculptor; I have nothing by which to judge except the photographs in *The Times*. But whatever the merit or demerit of Mr Hardiman's work as a sculptor, he has been declared to be ignorant of horseflesh ('conformation' I believe is the word) and ignorant of the dress and demeanour of a Field Marshal sitting [on] his horse. I have only seen photographs of Mr Hardiman's first proposal and of his second. Of the two, the first seemed the more attractive, and suggested that the sculptor was not merely competing with Court Photographers, but zealously trying, to the best of his ability, to make a plastic composition of some grace. And it set me to wondering what the friends of Charles King and Martyr, had the columns of *The Times* been open to them, and supposing that they were good military and hunting people, would have said of his statue in Whitehall. But the chief point of the bitter controversy, which no one seems to have observed, is the question: what should be the relation between Art and Public Monuments? Because, if a sculptor of exceptional merit, such as Mr Epstein, or even Mr Dobson, to say nothing of Mr Brancusi (whom no one in England has ever heard of, as he is not even an American) had competed and got the lucky dip, would the correspondence in *The Times* have been any less violent than that directed against the luckless Mr Hardiman? I think not. The question is this: when we wish to show our gratitude to a noble and gallant servant of the Crown and the public, do we wish to do so by a Work of Art or an exact likeness? And if there is to be a clear distinction between the Work of Art and the Public Monument, it would be well to impress this distinction upon the minds of artists, and not mislead persons like Mr Hardiman, whose chief error seems to have been the delusion that he could produce something which might be both. As things are, we are beaten all round by the French; they can produce works of art, and they also know how to produce public monuments, which [489] are definitely ugly, but definitely public monuments. Once you are used to the convention, the Place Victor-Hugo is not intolerable, and if you are going in for monuments, there is much to be said for surrounding a portrait bust with sylphs, nymphs, pagan goddesses and muses offering wreaths, and the other allegorical female companionship with which the French are accustomed to provide the effigies of their great men. Were I a great man myself, I think I should prefer to be commemorated by sculpture which could give delight to a posterity indifferent to my name, than by sculpture which perpetuated my photograph. That perhaps is a matter of choice. But so long as we pretend that the motives of the work of Art and the Public Monument can be wholly reconciled, our streets will merely be encumbered.

If the public wants a portrait of Lord Haig it can have it; the main thing is that it should keep the distinction clear. The vocal public mind about Mr Epstein seems to be as confused as it is about Mr Hardiman. Mr Epstein has also created a new work. It may be good, as sculpture, or bad. But it is not a public monument; it has been on exhibition in a private gallery; those who do not like it need not see it; but those persons who dislike the subject have raised objections that they might be better entitled to raise, were it a Monument in the centre of Piccadilly Circus. It is not a monument; it is not a portrait of an eminent British Lady in an interesting condition, but a study of primitive gestation; and if it is good sculpture, it is more than that: if it is good sculpture it has that transition from representative meaning to a composition of masses and planes, lights and shadows, to a design; from the human to the abstractly sensuous, the transition which only art and religion can make.

We mention with deep regret the death of Mr Clere Parsons, who had recently become a contributor to *The Criterion*. Parsons had a brilliant undergraduate career [490] at Oxford, and was well known to recent Oxford generations for his editorship of the Oxford *Outlook*. Only delicate health prevented him from obtaining easily an appointment at the British Museum; at the time of his death he had just taken up his duties in a post in the Bodleian Library. Those who knew him know that he was both a poet and a critic of great promise, who lived not long enough to leave much more than that impression upon his friends and acquaintance.

John Dryden I, II and III

'John Dryden – I. The Poet who Gave the English Speech', 'John Dryden – II. Dryden the Dramatist', and 'John Dryden – III. Dryden the Critic, Defender of Sanity' were publ. respectively in *Listener*, 5. 118 (15 Apr. 1931), 621–2; 5. 119 (22 Apr. 1931), 681–2; and 5. 120 (29 Apr. 1931), 724–5. All subheaded 'By T. S. ELIOT'. Gallup C 317, 318, 319.

All three were revised in *John Dryden The Poet the Dramatist the Critic: Three Essays by T. S. Eliot*, publ. on 18 Oct. 1932: Gallup A 22.
See below, pp. 624–49.

If I Were a Dean

Chichester Diocesan Gazette, 12 (May 1931), 188–91. Headed 'B. By Mr. T. S. Eliot': it is preceded by a piece by the Dean of Minsterwell. The necessary word 'deal' has been added to the unidiomatic 'a great more' on page 189.
Not in Gallup, but would be C319a.

My first thought of 'If I were a Dean' is not of what I should want to do, but of what I should want *not* to do: and I make no apology. I have nothing but admiration and pity for those Deans who have toiled unceasingly, made appeals and collected subscriptions year after year, for – what? Merely to keep their minsters from tumbling about their ears. To me a cathedral is primarily a place of worship, the focus of devotion of its diocese, and not a National Monument: but I think – the State being already so far Socialised, and the position of the Church in the State being what it is – that the structural repair of cathedrals, and perhaps also of all those churches which have historic and architectural importance, ought to be at the cost of the State. We hear a good deal, in the Press, about the necessity of attracting American [189] tourists, or of inducing them to spend more time and money in Britain, in proportion to what they spend on the Continent – even the new Park Lane ogles the American tourist. Well, cathedrals are a valuable asset to a country, particularly if a dignified urban and rural amenity is preserved around them; they are an asset, that is, to steamship lines, railways, motor-bus services, local tradesmen, postcard makers and tourist agencies. The nation as a whole, I contend, should be made to pay for their mere *preservation*, rather than that part of the nation for which they are primarily places of worship and devotion.

I am quite well aware of all the difficulties involved in carrying out such a drastic proposal; and if I were a Dean under the settlement I suggest, I dare say I might in the end prefer to be buried by the collapse of the roof of my own cathedral, rather than buried under a mass of correspondence, memoranda and instructions from the Office of Works, to say nothing of the visits of committees and inquisitory officials. To my irresponsible vision, however, these difficulties are details to be settled by ingenious compromise; the point is that in my Utopian deanery there will be no anxiety about the framework of the cathedral.

I should thus hope to be free to collect, and to use, funds not for the mere preservation of the bones of my cathedral, but for the interior beautification of its living body. And I should try to avoid the fault of making my interior a period piece, of being overawed by the designs of its remote builders. I have seen old and beautiful churches which modern hands seemed afraid to touch, and which therefore remained mere remains; and I have also seen modern churches in which the decorators seemed fearful of departing by a decade, in the least ornament or altar cloth, from the period style in which the church was built. I prefer rather a church which shows the loving attempts of generation after generation, each according to its own notions of beauty, to leave visible testimony of its devotion. I should like to be able to encourage the best contemporary artists in stone, metal, paint and wood, to apply themselves to the decoration of my cathedral; and the best musicians to make music for its offices. As for music, if I were to be the ideal dean for my ideal deanery, I should have to know a great [deal] more about it than I do. I have, however, one heretical notion. I admit that the organ is considered indispensable everywhere, but I should like at least to supplement it, sometimes, [190] by a small orchestra, of strings and woodwind, assembled from local talent (and I am sure there is plenty of musical talent in rural England). There would be two advantages. Anyone who has heard instrumental music in certain continental churches knows that the organ is by no means the only medium for church music. And everything that engages more individuals in the responsibility and pride of beautifying the church service, is an encouragement to the communal life.

My cathedral, then, would be richly decorated inside: with tapestries (as, for example, they hang round the bases of columns in the cathedral of Toulouse), with modern religious paintings, with memorial tablets (but only to good churchmen), with chapels and church furniture. Should not the resources of art be devoted to God, instead of merely to the palaces of the rich and finally to museums? I hold also the theory, that it is chiefly in the life of such a centre as a cathedral that art can vitally affect us. Who, except the technical expert, can wholly enjoy a visit to an art museum or an evening in a concert room? I might enlarge upon this, but I must stick to my points and keep within my space: a cathedral where art – not merely archaeology – is dedicated to God, seems to me the best place in which art can flourish.

All my notions of decoration and of music, however, are ancillary to one main purpose: to make the cathedral the centre of religious and artistic activity in its diocese. In the Anglican Church, parishioners (and I think this is equally true, so far as it is true, of every division within the Church) tend to grow an excessive attachment to their own particular parish church, or the particular church of their election (and even to a particular vicar or rector). The best way to offset this particularism, would be to encourage in them the same sort of affection towards the Cathedral of their diocese. I realise that for the immediate future such an ideal is impossible in many dioceses – but my ideal deanery is not for the immediate future either.

I should devise as many cathedral ceremonies as possible beyond those which take place at times when the faithful are usually in attendance at their own churches, and with special relation to the seasons of the church year. I am sure that I should pay particular attention to the performance of religious drama. I do not underrate the beauty of our medieval religious drama, and I should try, not I hope, to 'revive' it, but to keep it alive; but at the same [191] time I should still more encourage the composition and the performance of plays by contemporary authors. Some people maintain that a good religious play cannot be written nowadays; I believe, as I believe of religious painting and sculpture, that if the opportunity is given, the work will be done. We must expect that the early attempts will be imperfect but I am sure that in time poets and dramatists, as well as painters and sculptors and artisans, will not be lacking.

But in no two cathedrals would or should conditions be quite the same; and, wherever my deanery was situated, I should wish to encourage and stimulate first the local spirit of that part of England. I should not wish my cathedral celebrations to be like getting Moisevitch or Jelly d'Arányi to entertain the guests at a country house party. And for such activities as religious drama, I should want to have them performed, as far as possible, *within* the cathedral itself.

But besides all these interests and duties, and besides all the functions of a Dean which I know nothing about, I maintain that a Dean should have sufficient continuous leisure to be able to apply himself to some considerable work of scholarship or of original theological and philosophical writing. If his other duties make this impossible, then his other duties should be reduced.

And lastly, I should want, for myself, a little more leisure still. There is a book which I have never been able to buy, and which I have never had room to accommodate even if I could buy it and house it. If I were a

Dean, I should hope that I might be able to have it, and to have shelves for it, and to read as much of it as one man can reasonably expect to be able to read in a lifetime: it is Migne's *Patrologia Latina et Graeca*.

[*The Prospects of Humanism* by Lawrence Hyde]

Review of *The Prospects of Humanism* by Lawrence Hyde (1931).

ER, 53. 1 (June 1931), 118, 120. Signed 'T. S. Eliot'. Gallup C320.

This is the second of a series of three volumes, the first of which was *The Learned Knife*; for the third we are promised a discussion of 'modern religious tendencies'. In this book, which is clearly thought out and well written, Mr Hyde establishes himself as a brilliant and thoroughgoing critic of critics; he might be described as a potential leader of the second, or perhaps the third, generation of humanists; and in these days of dog-eat-dog in the criticism of literature and life, that is no small promise. He is concerned with such writers as Benda and Fernandez in France; E. R. Curtius in Germany; Babbitt and More in America; and Wyndham Lewis, Fausset, Murry, Read, McEachren and myself in England; but chiefly, and quite rightly, with the ideas of Mr Babbitt and Mr Middleton Murry.

The book falls into three parts. In the first, Mr Hyde analyses the positive doctrine of Mr Irving Babbitt. He is quite right to ignore, for his purpose, both Mr More, who cannot be classified as a 'pure' humanist, and the young disciples of Mr Babbitt, most of whom have succeeded only in ossifying the more vital and flexible ideas of their master. The first and third parts of the book are closely parallel; and to my mind the author makes a very good job of demonstrating the inconsistency and inadequacy of both doctrines, the purely human, and the more ambitious 'naturalism' of Mr Murry: their inconsistency with themselves, and their inadequacy to the religious instincts of humanity. Mr Hyde's double success is all the more remarkable for his genuine sympathy with both of two writers so opposite in sensibility, and for his admirable temperateness and indifference to mere debating points. He is the first critic, so far as I know, to point out the affinity of Mr Murry with Mr Santayana.

It is, however, the second part of the book which seems to me the most original. The author is partly occupied with Mr Clive [120] Bell, as a typical 'high-brow' and aesthete; but the section is more important for the author's general observations than for his critique of the aesthetics of Mr Bell. It is really Mr Aldous Huxley who should be the most conspicuous figure in this part of the book, for, as Mr Hyde is quite well aware, it is Mr Huxley who has made the clearest and most conscious statements of the disease of intellectualism which Mr Huxley himself exhibits. What Mr Hyde gives is really a diagnosis of the meaning of *culture* in modern life, of its limitations and of its spiritual dangers; it is accordingly an account which every cultivated or 'civilised' person ought to read and ponder.

> The man of to-day, although highly *cultured* – in the sense that he has a very full knowledge of what happens – is at the same time conspicuously untutored in the art of conducting his life. People to-day are aware to a remarkable degree of what it is that has to be dealt with, of what facts must be faced, but they are no less distinguished by their restlessness and impotence. Never, surely, has a generation been so incredibly well informed, and yet so fatally lacking in wisdom . . .
>
> The effect which great beauty has upon us to-day is in a large measure that of exasperating our nerves, of making us restless and ultimately miserable.

We must await the third volume with alert curiosity if with some scepticism. For Mr Hyde, who so convincingly shows the religious inadequacy of modern winds of doctrine, can yet say 'the religion of the Churches is a dead religion; on that point we must remain firm.' Many people have had that thought; what is Mr Hyde's 'life'? I have yet to hear of anything more living than the word of Christ in His Church.

A Commentary

C., 10. 41 (July 1931), 709–16. Signed 'T. S. E.' Gallup C321.

Something happened at the Fishmongers' Hall not long ago which deserves some further record than the short and simple annals of *The Financial Times*. It was the dinner of the British Bankers' Association. The presiding sprite was Mr J. Beaumont Pease,[1] and the ghost of the evening was the Lord Chancellor. Mr Pease, after the toast of 'His

---

1. Mr Beaumont Pease has recently been elected to the captaincy of the Royal & Ancient Golf Club of St Andrews. He is also captain of the Royal St George's Golf Club, and therefore will hold the two offices concurrently, a distinction only achieved previously, I believe, by Lord Forster and Captain Angus V. Hambro. Mr Pease is also, I believe, distantly connected with Andrew Marvell.

Majesty's Government', took the opportunity of conveying to His Majesty's Government, through the Lord Chancellor, the following message:

> We believe that the financial and commercial condition of this country is in a *very serious state*. We do *not* believe that the condition can be met by *merely* marking time and *hoping* for better things. The position must be faced and faced *squarely*. *If* we as a nation are spending more than we can afford, it must stop. Bankers and business men know that there is only one end to such a course if pursued *sufficiently* far.

(The italics are mine, but the words are Mr Pease's.) Then, after pease porridge hot, came pease porridge cold. Mr Pease remembered that 'this type of gathering' had recently been described as an assembly of money barons and frigid penguins. This moved him to report the description of the penguin which he had read in a book of eighteenth century travels. It was a friendly bird, etc. The rest of his speech may be abbreviated as follows:

> There are many bonds of sympathy between bankers and Government.... Unemployment is said to be the fault of the Government: in my own personal opinion it is not in the power of any Government [710] to cure this evil, whatever its power may be to increase it.... Another reason why bankers and the Government should feel sympathetic towards each other is that we are both accused of extravagance.... Another bond of sympathy between us both is that we both depend for our prosperity, and even our existence, upon the prosperity and goodwill of the country.... Finally, we are both exposed to the same temptations....

Lord Sankey, in responding, was in 'humorous vein', we are told, as well he might be after this exhibition of penguin frigidity. Having, in any case, been put into a jovial mood – shall we say a Sankey Mood – he had the happy thought to remember the Royal & Ancient. 'It is a matter of proud satisfaction to all of us (1) that at any rate an Englishman will shortly play himself in at St Andrews.' (Laughter.) (2) 'Permit me, sir, as the worst golfer on any course within twenty miles of Charing Cross to offer my respectful felicitations.' (Laughter.) (3):

> We took office upon 8th June, 1929. It will very soon be June of 1931, and therefore, sir, your golfing experience will at once point out to you that the position is this: we are two up and three to go. (Laughter) ... I spend half of my time on the golf links in bunkers. (Laughter). Certainly my best club and I think the best club of

the Labour Party is a niblick. (Laughter). It makes us sympathise with that oppressed and hard-working individual the agricultural labourer. (4) ... We live in an age of great social unrest. ... Let me tell you at once that after forty years of weary waiting and unswerving loyalty what a pleasure it is to me to-night to sit next to the Chairman of Lloyds Bank. ... Plenty of work will come. Of that I have no fear. But my anxiety is, and your anxiety is, while many are waiting for work they may be losing the will to work. That is the real danger of England. ... I am sometimes astonished at the disasters which it is said will come over this country should we remain much longer in power.

Comment: (1) What! Were there no *Scottish* bankers at the dinner of this *British* Association? Bravo, Scotland. (2) There seem to have been a few Scots present after all. (3) More Scots. (4) What! No laughter?

[711] Rather surprisingly, *The Financial Times* gives as a caption to its report of this dinner 'COMMERCE AND FINANCE IN A VERY SERIOUS STATE'.

Under the form of eternity, of course, such a gathering as that reported differs little from the annual feast of the humblest cricket club in the country; to a human eye it differs in this respect, that such wit and humour, when they irradiate, as they often do, the reunions of local athletic societies, are more in place there, and in better taste.

Let Mr André Siegfried[1] wag his head over all this. Mr Siegfried has written a good book, as was to be expected from the author of *Les États-Unis d'aujourd'hui*; it will have a large sale and library demand; it will confirm many intelligent opinions; but I fear that it will leave the majority of readers with the reassuring afterthought that after all, Mr Siegfried is a Frenchman, and no foreigner can really understand British politics. And the trouble with the book is that it is too much economics and statistics – what, as Mr Siegfried admits and emphasises, has already been pointed out by blue-book after blue-book. No blue-book ever led to a change of heart; and we are so habituated now to a mood of economic pessimism that another dose of it merely cheers us up. The fact is, that Mr Siegfried, though brilliant and very readable, is superficial. It is pleasant to be told that everything is wrong, when it is all put so generally that clearly there is nothing I myself can do about it. But how much Mr Siegfried leaves out! and how much of what he puts in is only the common ammunition of the more intellectual writers in the opposition press of the moment. Mr Siegfried has hardly mentioned the public schools and the whole educational system; he says nothing about the family life, the religious

1. *England's Crisis*. By André Siegfried.

and the moral beliefs of the ordinary Briton. He is right enough so far as he goes – but that is only a little way; the real drastic criticism of England of to-day could probably only be written by an Englishman; and the book would hardly be a popular one.

[712] The man to write it is certainly not Mr Bernard Shaw. Yet we ought to examine the latest flowering of that hardy decennial, the *Fabian Essays in Socialism* (with a preface [1930] by G. B. Shaw. Fifth edition. Allen & Unwin. 2s. 6d.). The succession of prefaces runs from 1889 to 1930: an attractive title for the new edition would be *From William Morris to Sir William Morris*. For the first edition, Mr Sidney Webb told us in 1919: 'Walter Crane kindly designed for us a striking cover, and Miss May Morris a decorative back.' The fifth edition is as like a blue-book as possible, except that it is green. That is evidence of success. The authors, 'journalists and junior Civil Servants', set out to make it (in Mr Shaw's words) 'as easy and matter-of-course for the ordinary respectable Englishman to be a Socialist as to be a Liberal or a Conservative'. And even by 1908 Mr Shaw could boast that 'membership of the Fabian Society, though it involves an express avowal of Socialism, excites no more comment than membership of the Society of Friends, or even of the Church of England'; perhaps even Mr Shaw hardly anticipated that in twenty years thence a *genuine* member of the Society of Friends or of the Church of England might become far more of a drawing-room rarity than a Socialist. 'To-day (in 1908) we neither respect our opponents nor confute them.' What was it to be by 1931!

And yet, gratifying as is this triumph, success is still incomplete. 'As I write,' says Mr Shaw in 1930, 'a Fabian Socialist is Prime Minister of Britain. Two of our essayists are in the House of Lords: one of them a Cabinet minister and the other an ex-Cabinet minister' (i.e., Sidney and Sydney, who do not see quite eye to eye on matters connected with the Sugar Industry). 'Parliament swarms with Fabians,' etc. 'Our airs of democratic advance are equally imposing' (and this even before the Spanish revolution). And yet *'there is more threat of bankruptcy in it than promise of the millennium'*! So here is Mr Shaw just as alarmed as Mr Pease. Even Mr Shaw is muttering 'bread and circuses'; [713] but the trouble of course is: Not Enough Socialism; we are trying to 'gain the benefits of Socialism under Capitalism and at its expense', and therefore

> ... our old Plan of Campaign for Labour, which has now been carried out only to land us in a no-thoroughfare, must be replaced by a new plan for the political reconstruction of British Society, eligible also as a model for the reconstitution of all modern societies.

This new plan – a Ten Year Plan, perhaps – seems a pretty ambitious one. But Mr Shaw says that 'changeability is one of the recognized qualities of human nature' (p. xiii), although he acknowledges (p. xxxvi) that human nature has not changed since 1871. But the latter statement was made in 1908, so perhaps human nature has changed between 1908 and 1930; or perhaps it is merely Mr Shaw's nature that has not changed since 1871. But the programme for change for 1931–41 comprises a drastic alteration of the Parliamentary system – an abolition of the Party system altogether; a smaller and more efficient Cabinet; and 'devolution' – which is something similar to what Maurras and his friends have been advocating in France for many years now – not, I believe, under the influence of Beatrice and Sidney Webb. It is odd that the hints for the 'new plan' should include so much that many people not Socialists had been approaching of themselves – such as home rule for Scotland and England; but no doubt the Fabians can take the credit for this, under the all-comprehensive theory of 'Permeation'.

Nevertheless, whether human nature in general changes or not, the human opinions of Socialists seem to vary a good deal. Since Mr Shaw penned the preface upon which I have been commenting, he has been haranguing a gathering of librarians at Letchworth – it *would* be librarians at Letchworth – and in the course of an address on the English language, he is reported to have said 'I will remain a Communist until I die' (not I *shall*, you observe, but I *will*). In his preface indeed he remarked that the Russian revolu-[714]tion was 'a most beneficent event' (though he still boasts of the 'resolute constitutionalism' of the Fabians). What does His Holiness the Pope think of that? But Mr Lansbury (who may or may not be a good Fabian) is annoyed with the Pope for his disapproval of Socialism – Mr Lansbury was not speaking at Letchworth but at Bromley – and repeats the familiar assertion: 'it is Capitalism, and not Socialism, that is on trial. . . . *If the Pope would come to England he would see the folly of trying to stop the progress of Socialism.*' Will Mr Lansbury invite him? Let him see with his own eyes; let him come over this summer and have a bathe with Mr Lansbury in the Serpentine, and a romp with him in the sand piles, and let him meet Mr Lansbury's pals in Poplar, and he will soon recant and apologise! Yet I am not so sure. The present Lord Olivier, in his contribution to these *Fabian Essays* in 1889, was rather patronising to the Catholic Church.

> The oldest socialistic institution of considerable importance and extent is the now decrepit Catholic Church. . . . The Catholic Church developed, relatively to the enlightenment of its age (*query: what age?*), the widest and freest system of education the world

has ever seen before this century.[1] ... Out of the wreckage of the Catholic Church, and amid the dissolution of the Protestant religion, there successively emerged, at an interval of some three hundred years, the two great socialistic institutions of the Poor Law and the People's Schools.

It must be admitted that Lord Olivier, if he patronises the Catholic Church, is downright disrespectful to Protestantism. What *is* the religion of a Fabian, anyway?

What Mr Shaw and his friends do not seem to understand, in spite of the highly cultivated changeability of their human nature, is that the old contrast between Capitalism and Socialism is hardly going to suffice for the next forty years. It is not true that everyone will be born into the world either a little Capitalist or a little Socialist; and some persons even suspect that Socialism is merely a variant of Capitalism, or vice versa; and that the combat of Tweedledum and Tweedledee is not likely to lead to any millennium. Certainly, there are many people, and there will be more, who are seeking some alternative to both. There are many who suspect that Socialism is not radical enough, in the sense that its roots penetrate no deeper than the blue-book stratum of human nature. It seems to have moral enthusiasm without moral profundity. Mr Shaw might know more about the changeability of human nature if he knew more about its permanence. And there are a great many hungry sheep who look up, and down, and all around them, and are not fed by the orations of Mr Shaw, or Mr Lansbury, any more satisfyingly than by those of Mr Pease and Lord Sankey.

Whether human nature changes or not, certainly everything about it changes. One cannot but be affected by a sense of change in reading the Hon. Evan Charteris's admirable biography of the late Sir Edmund Gosse.[2] The book, I say, is an admirable piece of work; and whether or no we read the writing of Gosse, the book is well worth reading as a document upon an age that is past. The place that Sir Edmund Gosse filled in the literary and social life of London is one that no one can ever fill again, because it is, so to speak, an office that has been abolished. Mr Charteris seems to me – who have no outside means of judging – to be very just and fair, neither ignoring faults nor diminishing virtues. I will not say that Sir Edmund's activity was not a very useful activity, in a social-literary world which is rapidly receding into memory. He was,

1. Lord Olivier seems to imply that the 'age' of the Catholic Church came to an end somewhere in the early part of the nineteenth century.
2. *Life and Letters of Sir Edmund Gosse*: by the Hon. Evan Charteris.

indeed, an amenity; but not quite any sort of amenity for which I can see any great need in our time. Mr Charteris compares him to Sainte-Beuve; but I cannot see any solid ground for the [716] comparison. Sainte-Beuve was not merely a 'man of letters', he was not merely concerned to exploit and appraise and enjoy the riches of French literature of the past; he had a devouring and insatiable interest in human nature in books, and was forever brooding over problems which are perhaps insoluble. The permanent and the changing in humanity; the problems of religious faith and doubt; the problems of the mind, the flesh and the spirit. Sir Edmund could not have written a masterpiece like *Port-Royal*, because he was not interested enough; he could not even have written a book comparable to *Chateaubriand*. He was interested in literature for literature's sake; and I think that people whose interests are so strictly limited, people who are not gifted with any restless curiosity and not tormented by the demon of thought, somehow miss the keener emotions which literature can give. And, in our time, both temporary and eternal problems press themselves upon the intelligent mind with an insistence which they did not seem to have in the reign of King Edward VII.

[*Son of Woman* by John Middleton Murry]

Review of *Son of Woman: The Story of D. H. Lawrence* by John Middleton Murry (1931).

C., 10. 41 (July 1931), 768–74. Signed 'T. S. ELIOT'. Gallup C322.

Mr Murry has written a brilliant book. It seems to me the best piece of sustained writing that Mr Murry has done. At any rate, I think that I understand it better than most of his recent writings. [769] It is a definitive work of critical biography, or biographical criticism. It is so well done that it gives me the creeps: probably these matters matter no longer to Lawrence himself; but any author still living might shudder to think of the possibility of such a book of destructive criticism being written about him after he is dead. But no one but Mr Murry could have done it; and I doubt whether Mr Murry could do it about anyone but Lawrence. The victim and the sacrificial knife are perfectly adapted to each other.

Near the beginning Mr Murry says:

> If Lawrence is to be judged as the 'pure artist', then it is true that he never surpassed, and barely equalled, this rich and moving record of a life (*Sons and Lovers*). But Lawrence is not to be judged as a pure artist; if ever a writer had 'an axe to grind', it was he. Set in

the perspective – the only relevant perspective – of his own revealed intentions, *Sons and Lovers* appears as the gesture of a man who makes the heroic effort to liberate himself from the matrix of his own past.

This is true. But I am doubtful what the term 'pure artist' means to Mr Murry; and I am doubtful whether this criticism is praise or condemnation. I agree that Lawrence was not a 'pure artist', in that he never succeeded in making a work of art; but then, that is just relative failure, that is all. And if he was not trying to make a work of art, then he should have been: the less artist, the less prophet; Isaiah succeeded in being both. And to be a 'pure artist' is by no means incompatible with having 'an axe to grind'; Virgil and Dante had plenty of axes on the grindstone; Dickens and George Eliot are often at their best as artists when they are grinding axes; and Flaubert is no exception. Unless there was grinding of axes, there would be very little to write about. Mr Murry quotes a sentence of Gourmont which I have quoted myself: *ériger en lois ses impressions personelles, c'est le grand effort d'un homme s'il est sincére*. Well, Lawrence tried to do that, certainly, but to my mind he failed completely, and this book is the history of his failure. Lawrence simply did not know how. He had plenty of sensations, undoubtedly; no man of his time was more sensitive; but he could neither leave his sensations alone and accept them simply as they came, nor could he generalise them correctly. The false prophet kills the true artist.

Lawrence had the making of an artist, more than one might suppose from reading this book. Mr Murry quotes with astonishing accuracy and justice – I do not believe that there is a single quotation in the book which is mutilated or unfair to the subject, and such justice is very rare in criticism – but it is not part of his intention to insist upon Lawrence's successes as a writer at those moments when Lawrence was not occupied with the fatal task of self-justification. Not only are there magnificent descriptions here and there, everywhere, throughout Lawrence's work, but there are marvellous passages – in nearly every book, I believe – of dialogue or narrative, in which Lawrence really gets out of himself and inside other people. There is a fine episode in the life of an elementary schoolmistress in *The Rainbow*; there are one or two remarkable dialogues in *Aaron's Rod*; and there is a short story called *Two Blue Birds* which has no relation to Lawrence's own emotional disease, and in which he states a situation which no one else has ever put. Mr Murry is fully able to appreciate these achievements, but he is fairly enough not concerned with them in this book. But to me they indicate that Lawrence ought to have been a 'pure artist', but was impure. And I wonder also whether, had Lawrence been a success in this sense instead of a failure, Mr Murry would have been so interested in him.

What Mr Murry shows, and demonstrates with a terrible pertinacity throughout Lawrence's work, is the emotional dislocation of a 'mother-complex'. (It should show also how inappropriate is the common designation of 'Oedipus complex'.) And he makes clear that Lawrence was pretty well aware of what was wrong; and that Lawrence, throughout the rest of his life, was a strange mixture of sincerity or *clairvoyance* with self-deception – or rather with the effort towards self-deception. Lawrence's subsequent history, and the history of his novels, is accordingly a record of his various attempts to kid himself into believing that he was right to be as he was, and that the rest of the world was wrong. It is an appalling narrative of spiritual pride, nourished by ignorance, and possibly also by the consciousness of great powers and humble birth. Now, the 'mother-complex' of Lawrence does not seem to me in itself a sign of the times. I find it difficult to believe that a family life like that of Lawrence's parents is peculiar either to a particular class or to a particular age. Such family life, with such consequences to a sensitive child, can hardly have taken place only in the latter part of the nineteenth century. What is peculiar to the time is the way in which Lawrence tried to deal with his peculiarity. That is what is modern, and it seems to me to spring from ignorance.

[771] When I use the word ignorance I am not contrasting it with something which is popularly called 'education'. Had Lawrence been sent to a public school and taken honours at a university he would not have been a jot the less ignorant; had he become a don at Cambridge his ignorance might have had frightful consequences for himself and for the world, 'rotten and rotting others'. What true education should do – and true education would include the suitable education for every class of society – is to develop a wise and large capacity for orthodoxy, to preserve the individual from the solely centrifugal impulse of heresy, to make him capable of judging for himself and at the same time capable of judging and understanding the judgements of the experience of the race. I do not think that the unfortunate initial experience of Lawrence's life led *necessarily* to the consequences that came. He would probably have been always an unhappy man in this world; there is nothing unusual about that; many people have to be unhappy in this world, to do without things which seem essential and a matter of course to the majority; and some learn not to make a fuss about it, and to gain, or at least to strive towards, a kind of peace which Lawrence never knew. He is to be grieved over and his faults are to be extenuated; but we can hardly praise a man for his failure. It is by the adoption of a crazy theory to deal with the facts, that Lawrence seems modern, and what I mean by 'ignorant'.

I may make this clearer by instancing a peculiarity which to me is both objectionable and unintelligible. It is using the terminology of Christian faith to set forth some philosophy or religion which is fundamentally non-Christian or anti-Christian. It is a habit towards which Mr Lawrence has inclined his two principal disciples, Mr Murry himself and Mr Aldous Huxley. The variety of costumes into which these three talented artists have huddled the Father, the Son, and the Holy Ghost, in their various charades, is curious and to me offensive. Perhaps if I had been brought up in the shadowy Protestant underworld within which they all seem gracefully to move, I might have more sympathy and understanding; I was brought up outside the Christian Fold, in Unitarianism; and in the form of Unitarianism in which I was instructed, things were either black or white. The Son and the Holy Ghost were not believed in, certainly; but they were entitled to respect as entities in which many other people believed, and they were not to be employed as convenient phrases to embody any cloudy private religion. I mention this autobiographical detail simply to indicate that it is possible for unbelievers [772] as well as believers to consider this sort of loose talk to be, at the best, in bad taste. The Holy Ghost does not figure in Mr Murry's index of fictitious personages at the end of the book, but that surely is an oversight.

A better illustration of Lawrence's 'ignorance', and a fault which corrupts his whole philosophy of human relations – which is hardly anything *but* a philosophy of human relations and unrelations – is his hopeless attempt to find some mode in which two persons – of the opposite sex, and then as a venture of despair, of the same sex – may be spiritually united. As Mr Murry spares no pains to show, the whole history of Lawrence's life and of Lawrence's writings (Mr Murry tells us that it is the same history) is the history of his craving for greater intimacy than is possible between human beings, a craving irritated to the point of frenzy by his unusual incapacity for being intimate at all. His struggle against over-intellectualised life is the history of his own over-intellectualised nature. Even in his travel to more primitive lands, he could never take the crude peoples simply for what they are; he must needs always be expecting something of them that they could not give, something peculiarly medicinal for himself. He was looking for it there, just as he looked within the men and women he knew, without finding it. There is a passage from *Lady Chatterley's Lover* (one of the novels which I have not read) which Mr Murry quotes very much to the point:

> I held forth with rapture to her, positively with rapture. I simply went up in smoke. And she adored me. The serpent in the grass was sex. She somehow didn't have any; at least, not where it's supposed

to be. I got thinner and thinner. Then I said we'd got to be lovers, I talked her into it. So she let me. I was excited, and she never wanted it. She adored me, she loved me to talk to her and kiss her: in that way she had a passion for me. Bu the other she just didn't want. And there are lots of women like her. And it was just the other that I *did* want. So there we split. I was cruel and left her.

Mr Murry has analysed this passage so shrewdly that it is an impertinence to say much more; but I should like to be sure that it shocked Mr Murry, as a confession, as deeply as it shocks me. Such complacent egotism can only come from a very sick soul, and, I should say, from a man who was totally incapable of intimacy. The girl was [773] obviously in love with him, in the way appropriate to her youth and inexperience; and it was not good enough for Lawrence. What a pity that he did not understand the simple truth that of any two human beings each has privacies which the other cannot penetrate, and boundaries which the other must not transgress, and that yet human intimacy can be wonderful and life-giving: a truth well known to Christian thought, though we do not need to be Christians to understand it. And that the love of two human beings is only made perfect in the love of God.[1] These are very old and simple truths indeed. But Lawrence, as I believe Mr Murry says, remembered the second injunction of the Summary of the Law and hoped to practise it without recognising the first. And is not this same sad burden of the unsatisfactoriness of human relations wailed thinly by the corrupt characters in Mr Murry's novels, as well as some of Mr Huxley's? It is the old story that you cannot get a quart out of a pint pot; and the astonishing fact that you cannot even get a pint out of it unless you fill it. As if human love could possibly be an end in itself! And all these sad young men try to believe in a spectral abstraction called Life; yet the occasional whiffs of sepulchral high spirits wafted from their limbo are chillier than the gloom.

There remains, however, one book, which I have not read, but which I judge from Mr Murry's account to be worthy of the importance which Mr Murry assigns to it: *Fantasia of the Unconscious*. It would appear that in this book Lawrence reached his culmination, and that his subsequent work marks chiefly decline and collapse.

As Lawrence says, there is a great fascination in a completely effected 'idealism', that is, a completely achieved mental consciousness of our own natures. To this fascination the modern world is succumbing;

---

1. To many human pairs, of course, common tastes, or a common interest, as in Tariff Reform or the enfranchisement of African natives, may appear an excellent substitute.

this is, indeed, the distinguishing mark of the modern world – that which makes it modern.

Lawrence was more deeply involved in this process than any other man. It is quite wrong, totally mistaken, to conceive of him as a sort of primitive emergence. He belonged, completely, to the modern world and its 'idealism'; the intensity of his revulsion against it is the index of the completeness of his identification with it. Where he [774] differed from the vast majority of intellectuals and 'idealists' was that his ultra-sensitive organism was early aware of the fearful perils that lay along this seemingly inevitable road of complete mentality.

This seems to me important, sound and well put. Yet it would seem that Lawrence only differed from the 'vast majority of intellectuals' in his greater intellectual vision; in a fluctuating ability of diagnosis, without further and total ability of prescription and régime. That, in my view, is only to be found – and only in our time with great difficulty if at all – in Christian discipline and asceticism. To this Lawrence could not and would not come; hence his relapse into pride and hatred.

One must, in considering a writer like Lawrence, confess what will be called one's prejudices, and leave the rest to the reader. I agree with Mr Murry that there must have been a great deformed capacity for love in the man; he hungered and thirsted for love though he could not give it and could not take it. Mr Murry's comparison and contrast of Lawrence with Jesus strikes cold upon my imagination, though I could have understood a comparison with Rousseau. Unwillingly in part, I admit that this is a great tragic figure, a waste of great powers of understanding and tenderness. We may feel poisoned by the atmosphere of his world, and quit it with relief; but we cannot deny our homage as we retire. A fateful influence he must have been upon those who experienced his power; I cannot help wondering whether Mr Murry was not compelled to write his book in order to expel the demon from himself; and if so, I wonder whether Mr Murry has succeeded.

[*Essays of a Catholic Layman in England* by Hilaire Belloc]

Review of *Essays of a Catholic Layman in England* by Hilaire Belloc (1931).
ER, 53. 2 (July 1931), 245–6. Signed 'T. S. Eliot'. Gallup C323.

Perhaps the most painful criticism one has to make of Mr Belloc's polemical essays is that he has suffered through devoting much labour to combating very stupid people. He could reasonably reply that he found the stupidity there; and that when it is the stupidity of such intelligent, ignorant, and extremely active men as Mr Wells and Mr Shaw, it is a very serious matter, and must be met on its own ground, with its own weapons, and before its own audience. And looking at the situation from another point of view, the spectacle of Mr Belloc now whirling his longsword, and thundering his denunciations, over an almost deserted battlefield, is quite agreeable to watch. Yet the two weakest among this collection of essays are those in which he goes direct at Mr Haldane and the Dean of St Paul's. The trouble is perhaps that one ought to take infinite pains in attacking even the meanest antagonist; and if Mr Haldane and Dean Inge are worth so much attention – which need not be assumed – they are worth a little more. When Mr Belloc attached himself tenaciously to Mr Wells's *Outline*, he provided good sport and did good service; but here his hand is a bit heavy, and his weapon rather blunt.

But if few of Mr Belloc's individual enemies are as powerful as they seemed thirty years ago, the issues with which he is concerned are as perilous as ever. His peculiar function is to attack, not arguments, but *prejudices*; and prejudices are attacked, not with arguments, but with *convictions*. Those readers who are in sympathy with him – at least, on what seem to them the vital issues – will not be wholly satisfied. For instance, one of the most important subjects in the book, at the present time, is the secularisation of the school system of England, and this essay on 'The Schools' is to be commended. Those who already share Mr Belloc's apprehensions are prepared for a more advanced discussion. But such an essay, and most of the essays, are for the direction of those readers, an important number, who have an open mind, but have not yet begun to think.

It would be pleasant to the reviewer if the convictions which he shared with Mr Belloc were so generally accepted that he could afford to devote his time to those points where he finds himself in disagreement; it is unhappily not so. Among the good points which Mr Belloc makes, which will have to be made again and again, are particularly two. One is that *religious* differences are at least as important as racial, linguistic or geographical. It is a misfortune that Britain and some of the most important parts of Europe have been governed largely by men without strong religious convictions; because it is precisely such men who [246] are most likely to make errors in foreign and colonial policy by underrating, or by being unable to sympathise with, the religious convictions of others. And the other point is that the accepted antithesis between Capitalism and Socialism is no more the ultimate division of political philosophies than the superannuated antithesis between Conservatism and Liberalism. It is the Fabians who have apotheosised 'Capitalism'. Mr Belloc cannot remind us too often that there are older, as well as newer, political philosophies; or that there is a science more fundamental than the sciences of psychology and economics, and without which they are vain: the science of ethics.

Thomas Heywood

Review, unsigned, of *Thomas Heywood: Playwright and Miscellanist* by Arthur Melville Clark (1931) was publ. in *TLS*, 1539 (30 July 1931), [589]–90. Revised in *SE. See below*, pp. 408–17.

Introduction

Eliot's 'Introduction' to *Pascal's Pensées* (translated for the Everyman's Library series by W. F. Trotter) was publ. on 19 Sept. 1931: Gallup B17. Revised as 'The *Pensées* of Pascal', in *EAAM. See* Vol. 3, pp. 94–106, in the present edition.

A Commentary

C., 11. 42 (Oct. 1931), 65–72. Signed 'T. S. E.' Gallup C325.

Being willing to improve my scant knowledge of the theory of politics, I welcomed the appearance lately of two small books, both of which, to judge from their titles, were elementary enough for my needs. One was *An Introduction to Politics*, by Mr Harold J. Laski (Unwin: 2s. 6d.), and the other *Ich Dien: The Tory Path*, by Lord Lymington (Constable:

4s. 6d.). Mr Laski is more than well known as an exponent of moderate Socialism; Lord Lymington, as the title of his essay indicates, is a Conservative M.P. Surely, by combining and contrasting such points of view, one could arrive at some conclusion. The conclusions were indeed interesting to myself, though hardly what I expected.

Professor Laski begins with comfortable words. 'The state, so to say,' he says, 'is the crowning-point of the social edifice'; and this is reassuring; the phrase 'social edifice' has a pleasant sound to the timid-hearted. 'Its subjects desire, for instance, security for their persons and property.' Indeed we do. It is true that we may be a little disconcerted, a page or two further on, by a sentence in Mr Laski's best style:

> Yet it may be taken as a general rule that the character of any particular state will be, broadly speaking, a function of the economic system which obtains in the society it controls.

This was a little puzzling. For one was encouraged by the author's prefatory statement that he intended to set out the *basic problems* of politics: yet if the 'character of any particular state' is the 'function' of an economic system, then we may suppose that the character of politics is a function of economics: and therefore it seems that there are basic problems more basic than the political ones. This is rather disheartening to the beginner. Is it possible that I ought to have consulted some primer on the 'basic problems' of economics – the basic problems of which [66] Oustric, Madame Hanau, Teapot Dome and Marconi Shares were particular manifestations – before reading Mr Laski? And so far as Mr Laski's politics is concerned, its function seems to be merely to be a function of that economic variable, for he says:

> Not a little of the malaise of modern civilisation is due to the fact that the institutions of the state have not kept pace with other changes, particularly economic, in the society it attempts to control.

So if the business of 'institutions' of the state is merely to keep pace with economic changes, not to control them, the detached enquirer must begin to lose heart about politics, and to reflect that a more important subject of study might be these economic changes, and how to control *them*.

Finally, however, I began to suspect that Mr Laski's 'introduction to politics' was perhaps only an introduction to one kind of politics; and that kind simply a development of the old-fashioned American conception of Democracy. This view is assumed, not defended. For he says straight out:

> ... no state will realise the end for which it exists unless it is a democracy based upon universal suffrage in which there are not

only freedom of speech and association, but also a recognition that neither race nor creed, birth nor property, shall be a barrier against the exercise of civic rights.

Such a sentence merely provokes a fresh explosion of questions. For what end *does* the state exist? And why should *not* race, creed, birth and property, any one or more of them, be a desirable barrier? And what are *civic rights*? It is just these questions which we want answered in an 'introduction to politics'; and we must admit that there is more than one possible answer to all of them. And some such assumption is apt to turn up just when needed, throughout Mr Laski's essay. 'Historical research,' he says, 'has shattered all systems which claim to operate under theological sanctions': not practice, you observe, but 'historical research' – this bombshell against theocracy was flung from a window of the [67] London School of Economics. 'The power of the state is justified to the degree that it secures, at the least possible sacrifice, the maximum satisfaction of human wants.' But does *wants* here mean *needs*? Or does it include all the fluctuating capricious or undesirable desires of men? Later, Mr Laski speaks of a man's right to attain 'significance' for himself, of 'fulfilment of personality', of 'self-realization'; but the problems concealed by these words, and not the problems discussed in the pamphlet, are the real 'basic problems' of politics. He tells us unctuously that 'the right to education is therefore fundamental to citizenship.' But is citizenship itself fundamental? – and even so, what is education? Unless we mean by education that very modest amount of knowledge which can be imparted by mass-instruction, we have no more a right to education than we have to happiness, genius or beauty. So far as we have 'rights', every man or woman has the right to be educated to *some* useful function in the community; but what is meant by education must differ greatly in kind. But Mr Laski speaks as if education varied only in degree, and as if it was all directed towards one end: voting for the best candidate. He says 'the uneducated man among the complexities of modern civilization is like a blind man who cannot relate cause and effect.' I do not quite understand Mr Laski's theory of the causal relation between blindness and an inability to appreciate causality, but that is a small matter. I only hope that Mr Laski's education has enabled him to understand the complexities of modern civilisation. My own education was very defective; but I have known much better educated men than I to be completely baffled by the complexities of modern civilisation. And here again a question seems to be begged. Might it not be well to consider these complexities and to try to simplify some of them, so that simple people like myself should not be crushed by the burden of the right to so much education? For otherwise the complexities may become more complex still, and then we shall need more and more education; and then we shall have brain fever, all but Profes-[68]sor Laski. And I suspect that the complexities are already much more complex than the *Introduction to Politics* gives us to understand. At the American University at which I was partly 'educated' there used to be a course of lectures called 'Government I': and this 'course' gave one just such a view of how governments were meant to work, if they worked at all, as Mr Laski's essay.

Finding, then, Mr Laski's account as useful as a catalogue of spare parts for a motor car which is no longer manufactured, I turned hopefully in the direction of Lord Lymington. *Ich Dien: The Tory Path* – here, surely I should find not merely an abstract scheme, but something to which my human emotions could respond. And, amongst the details there is much to which 'the True Tory, however inarticulate and instinctive his action', as Lord Lymington says, can indeed respond. Perhaps the weakness is that Lord Lymington seems to think of Toryism as something to be revived, instead of something to be invented. There are, and have been, Tories; but it is doubtful whether there has ever been any continuous Tory party of which individual Tories have much reason to be proud. The author says 'Toryism is often gibed at as a relic of feudalism.' If that is so, it goes to show a widespread ignorance of feudalism. The great feudal nobles might just as genuinely be assimilated to Whiggism. I wonder whether the Bigods and the Bohuns, or the members of any of the great twelfth-century families who put their names to Magna Charta – the Clares or the Mowbrays, De Roos or Albini – could have been made to understand the patriotic devotion to King and Country which Lord Lymington would inculcate: I fear that their attitude would have been moderately cynical. The romance of Toryism begins with the Stuarts; even with the political theories of a pedantic foreign monarch and the devotion of a number of modest county families to a foreign house.

This is not to say that there is no thread of continuity in Toryism; but the thread runs through the 'inarticulate and instinctive'; and Toryism is never quite justly represented by [69] Bolingbroke, or by the Conservative philosophy of Burke, or by the daring innovations of Disraeli. And if there is one idea, however vague, by which Toryism may be tried, it is the idea, however vague, represented by the phrase 'Church and State'. Lord Hugh Cecil, in his little exposition of 'Conservatism' (published some years ago in the Home University Library), was not altogether clear or satisfactory; but his was the voice of orthodoxy compared to Lord Lymington. This is not a minor test, for Toryism. Unless Toryism maintains a definite and uncompromising theory of Church and State, Toryism is merely a fasces of expedients. And we hear from Lord Lymington that:

The Church should be represented as it is to-day, but the Church of England, because it has ceased to be the religion of the people as it was four hundred years ago, should share its representation with those great bodies of religion whose leaders will take the oath to the Crown.

There is a metaphor of 'selling the pass'; we should have a new one, for Lord Lymington's benefit, of (to vary a phrase of Bolingbroke's) 'sueing for subserviency at the doors of every sect in the world'. I have never encountered a more satisfying example of misunderstanding. To begin with, the Church is not 'represented' in the House of Lords, as various interests might be. Lord Lymington conceives of the upper house as an ideal syndicalist assembly: in which the Church should be represented, just as Big Business is represented – the bankers (blowing into their keys), the brewers, the newspaper magnates, and last come the bishops. The bankers represent so many millions who have bank accounts; the bakers represent so many millions who buy bread and crumpets; the brewers so many millions who drink beer; then the press; then the distillers; and finally the bishops represent so many thousand communicants. But as the Church of England has ceased to be the religion of the people, we must have, in our perfect Tory Democracy, amongst the bankers, newsagents and brewers and distillers who represent popular interests, representatives of the Bapt-[70]ist, Seventh Day Adventist, and Christian Science interests. And again, I feel rather abashed, after examining Lord Lymington's conception of the House of Lords, to find that I, as an individual, am there over-represented. The bankers represent me, because I have a bank account; the brewers represent me, because I drink beer; the distillers, because I drink whisky; the newsagents, because I take in *The Times*; the steamship magnates, because I occasionally travel (not, surely, because I may own shares or debentures of their lines). Surely I ought to be content to share my religious representation 'with those great bodies of religion whose leaders will take the oath to the Crown'. And should the Crown take no oath to religion?

This is not a small matter, or a debating point. Lord Lymington, like Mr Laski, wants a state in which government shall be designed for the happiness of the governed; but as alternatives to Communism, both outlines seem to me drearily incapable of arousing enthusiasm. Within limits, a political ideal ought to be made to appear desirable whether it actually *succeeds* or not. Far too much of our current criticism of Russia has been founded on nothing more secure than this criterion of success: year in year out, our newspapers were wont to sneer at Bolshevism by little pieces of information and statistics aimed to persuade us that the

Russian system was incompetent to handle the problem of production and distribution even well enough to keep the mass of the population from starving. But perhaps the present government of Russia *will* succeed, and what then? We shall have to fall back ignominiously, rather late in the day, upon our moral convictions. So long as the Bolsheviks appear to be making a mess of material things, our newspapers concentrate on statistics; but if they should succeed in running their country efficiently and attending to the people's bodies, we should begin to hear a great deal more about the harm they are doing to the people's souls. What matters is not whether they have carried out the programme of Marx, or whether they have betrayed it, or whether they [71] have improved upon it; the point is that their philosophy is equally repugnant whether it fails or succeeds. And we can only oppose it with another which shall be correspondingly dear to us whether it succeeds or fails. The Bolsheviks at any rate believe in something which has what is equivalent for them to a supernatural sanction; and it is only with a genuine supernatural sanction that we can oppose it. So I regret that Mr Laski and Lord Lymington (the latter of whom, at least, should have known better) should pay such scant respect both to religious establishments and to the theological foundations of political philosophy. The theory of nationalism, as advanced in Italy, is not good enough; it becomes both artificial and ridiculous. Mr Bernard Shaw, with his clear but quite irresponsible mind, and his humorous appreciation of Italy and Russia, has been doing his best to bring the old-fashioned William Morris and Fabian Socialism into disrepute.[1] The only hope is in a Toryism which, though not necessarily distinct for Parliamentary purposes, should refuse to identify itself philosophically with that 'Conservatism' which has been overrun first by deserters from Whiggism and later by business men. And for such a Toryism not only a doctrine of the relation of the temporal and spiritual in matters of Church and State is essential, but even a religious foundation for the whole of its political philosophy.[2] Nothing less can engage enough respect to be a worthy adversary for Communism.

[72] And even in certain details, Lord Lymington's Toryism seems to be inverted. Like all good conservatives he is solicitous, and rightly, about

---

1. The best criticism that I have seen of Mr Shaw's recent drollings about Russia, is a letter by Canon Oliver Quick, in *The Times* of August 17th.

2. See an admirable essay on 'The State and Freedom', by the Rev. Charles Smyth, in *Christendom*, June, 1931: 'The Royal Supremacy is not Erastian in its implications, because the King is a *persona mixta*, something less than a priest, but something more than a layman; he is both a secular and an ecclesiastical person; and it is the orthodox theory of the Church of England that it is his office to administer the State through his secular officers, and the Church through his spiritual officers (not excluding laymen, for they also are *viri ecclesiastici*, churchmen).'

the future of the Land of Britain. But too often the problem has been put before us as primarily an economic or even a military one; and in even a short essay like this – which is not, after all, merely a memorandum of measures for the moment – one would like to see the situation put another way about. The essential point is that agriculture ought to be saved and revived because agriculture is the foundation for the Good Life in any society; it is in fact the normal life. What matters is not that we should grow the bulk of our own wheat, even if that were possible, in pursuit of the chimera of independence; but that the land of the country should be used and dwelt upon by a stable community engaged in its cultivation. If tariffs will help, let us have tariffs, but that is a question of means. No one would pretend that life on the land is a very good one for a man with a family, whose wage is only a few shillings more than the dole; but agricultural life is capable of being the best life for the majority of any people. And it is hardly too much to say that only in a primarily agricultural society, in which people have local attachments to their small domains and small communities, and remain, generation after generation, in the same place, is genuine patriotism possible: not the artificial patriotism of the press, of political combinations and unnatural frontiers and the League of Nations. The contrast is admirably stated in a small book recently published, the title of which, after these reflections on the state of Britain, is distinctly cheering: *Décadence de la Nation Française*, by R. Aron and A. Dandieu (Reider: Paris).

[*Fashion in Literature* by E. E. Kellett]

Review of *Fashion in Literature: A Study of Changing Taste* by E. E. Kellett (1931).
ER, 53. 5 (Oct. 1931), 634–6. Signed 'T. S. Eliot.' Gallup C326.

Mr Kellett is writing on a subject on which he has already shown himself something of an authority. In this book of 369 pages he seems to me to have missed a most interesting opportunity, or both of two opportunities. He might have written a philosophical and psychological treatise on the enjoyment of art and literary art in particular: for such an investigation Mr Kellett is perhaps not fully qualified. But for a detailed historical account of the major changes of literary taste in England no one is better equipped. He has a great variety of surprising and pertinent learning; and he knows how to apply it without pedantry, in such a way as to illuminate the matter and enliven the style of his discourse. Neither of these interesting lines of investigation is that which Mr Kellett has chosen to take. We cannot blame the author for not performing what he has not undertaken; yet we may regret that Mr Kellett has provided merely a superior Guide to literary Self-Culture, of a much more advanced grade than the primers of Arnold Bennett and such exponents.

After a preliminary chapter on Taste in general, which displays much etymological knowledge without, I feel, getting us very far in any direction, Mr Kellett discusses Literary Taste in particular, Criticism, and the Rise of Conscious Art. He then, in successive chapters, considers the several chief excesses into which literary fashions may fall: e.g. preciosity, ingeniosity, allegory, the grotesque, and so on. On all these matters he usually says the right thing, or at least one of the right things to be said. This is the book to put in the hands of those defective lovers of literature [635] – and they form a numerous class – who do not understand why it might be worth their while to enlarge their appreciation of literature, and those others who desire to do so but do not know how to go about it.

Accepting the scope and design of the book for what they are, I find still two points on which I wish Mr Kellett had expatiated. He perorates

> Let us then endeavour to cultivate a catholic and generous taste; to read widely if not voraciously, and to welcome works of all kinds and of almost every rank: to find room in our sympathies not merely for the great but for the little, not merely for the exquisite but for the rough – nay, not merely for the good but for an occasional experience of the bad.

It is true that Mr Kellett has warned the reader not to strain at studying literature from which he extracts no pleasure whatever, but on the contrary to hold fast to what he really enjoys, and to seek to enlarge his enjoyment from this centre. I wish, nevertheless that he had asserted that for each one of us there must be a limit of enjoyment; that although some persons can have a much greater field of taste than others, complete catholicity is a chimera. If we try to enlarge our appreciation too much, we may diminish the intensity of enjoyment. If we were born with a catholic taste, it would be indistinguishable from no taste at all. In our enjoyment of literature much else must enter besides pure literary [636] enjoyment; and our preference of subject matter, our affinity with particular personalities, and other such limitations must condition not only our enjoyment but our appreciation – for though enjoyment and appreciation are not the same thing, they must tend to concur. This consideration might have led Mr Kellett to give some fuller account of why taste *must* change from age to age; and why each generation must be attracted to some past periods of literature and repelled from others.

Preface

Preface (i–ix) to *Transit of Venus: Poems by Harry Crosby* (1931). Publ. Nov. 1931 at The Black Sun Press, Paris, as *Collected Poems of Harry Crosby*, vol. II, for sale only with vols I, III, and IV. Signed 'T. S. ELIOT'. Gallup B18.

I doubt whether we can ever understand the poetry of a contemporary; especially if we are engaged in writing ourselves. This remark will not seem surprising, or anything more than commonplace, if we stop to try to understand the limited and peculiar sense in which we may be said to 'understand' poetry at all. In the senses in which we 'understand' a mathematical demonstration, a philosophical reasoning, a legal argument, a variety of scientific demonstrations, an historical account – and I do not say that this is all one kind of understanding either – poetry may have a greater or less understandable element, according to its particular types. The [ii] more there is to understand, in this sense, the more easily is the poetry 'understood'; which is why the poetry of Pope, let us say, appears easier to understand than that of Rimbaud. What the public wants, on the whole, is something safely between two extremes. Whatever contains a considerable rational element, as the poetry of Pope and Dryden, of Lucretius, or Sir John Davies – to take a few names at random – is rejected as 'prosaic'; whatever consists of too concentrated and exact a sequence and arrangement of image and rhythm is rejected as 'obscure'. The majority of people can get no emotional excitement, but only fatigue, from intellectual effort; the majority is unable to apprehend any exact emotion economically recorded. These observations, if true, may help to explain why a certain public enjoys the works of Mrs Wilcox, which give it the pleasure of which it is capable without the comparatively immense mental effort needed to enjoy the work of her masters, [iii] Tennyson, Browning and Swinburne.

Harry Crosby's verse was consistently, I think, the result of an effort to record as exactly as possible to his own satisfaction a particular way of apprehending life. When I first read some of his poems I concluded merely that he was a young man in a hurry; but I must add now that of being in a hurry there are two distinct kinds. To be in a hurry to get to a clearly conceived destination, a destination which is only clearly conceived because others have already arrived there and charted the country, usually results in a short journey, in the secondhand rhythms and imagery of the facile half-successes which are common in our and perhaps every time. But Crosby was in a hurry, I think, because he was aware of a direction, and ignorant of the destination, only conscious that time was short and the terminus a long way off. Incidentally, he was, it seems to me, unlike most of his contemporaries, indifferent, in his exploring interest, to whether [iv] what he wrote on the way should be poetry or not; and I do not see how anyone can go very far in poetry who is not ready to risk complete failure, or, for the most part, who does not in fact commit a great deal of failure on the way. The poet of the greatest possibilities, I believe, is disgusted always with what he has already done: or rather, relatively disgusted, for we must turn even our greatest failures to great account. I cannot admit any easy distinction between *promise* and *achievement*; for the admission of promise is a recognition of something already there; and every real achievement, in spite of the brevity of life, should be a promise of something further. Not, of course, that this continuing promise is anything but disconcerting to the majority even of the most sympathetic readers; we must all be ready to risk the imputation of having gone too far.

Poets arrive at originality by different routes. Some, by progressive imitation; [v] though the word *imitation* is truly applicable only to the successes of the negligible; for those who have something in them, the process is rather towards a finding of themselves by a progressive absorption in, and absorption of, and rejection (but never a total rejection) of other writers. Others, like Crosby, have little of this absorptive and rejective faculty; they feel from the beginning, however immaturely and with however many false expectations and misunderstandings, what they are out for. It would be, I think, premature to speak of Crosby as having had a 'philosophy' or even a definite point of view; the theories, or partial theories, which seem to have been implements for him, may only mislead us; and we must be patient to be able to read a man's writing, to perceive a new vitality in it, to recognise that real vitality is never aimless, yet not to speculate upon the aim itself. In this case, we need only admit that there was an aim, a direction. And in such a case we [vi] should expect to find, as I think we do find in Crosby's writings, that we do not pick out single poems for enjoyment: if any of it is worth reading, then it all is.

I am far from asserting, it follows naturally, that I understand in the least what Crosby was up to, or that I am sure I should like it if I did. I doubt whether anyone himself engaged in the pursuit of poetry can 'like', any more than he can 'understand', the work of his contemporaries; if it is wholly unrelated to one's own efforts it is irrelevant, and if it has some relation it is merely disturbing. But 'liking' is itself irrelevant in a serious matter like poetry; though it be appropriate enough in such international amenities as Mr Hugh Walpole's chairmanly introductions of American novelists to the British public. The testimony is the more valuable, I maintain, for the absence of this gentlemanly motive. What I do like, in a serious sense, is the fact that Crosby was definitely going his own way, whether I [vii] like the way or not. And in spite of occasional conventional phrases – so conventional as perhaps to be deliberate – I am more interested in his work because of its imperfections, its particular way of being imperfect. What interests me the most, I find, is his search for a personal symbolism of imagery. Not that the scheme of imagery which he was using was necessarily exact, or corresponded finally to what his mind was reaching for; he might, I dare say, in time have scrapped it all in favour of some other. But here, I am sure, is a right and difficult method. A final intelligibility is necessary; but that is only the fruit of much experiment and of mature synthesis; but Crosby was right, very right, in looking for a set of symbols which should relate each of his poems to the others, to himself, rather than using in each poem symbols which should merely relate it to other poems by other people. Even to speak of a 'set of symbols' is clumsy; for such a phrase [viii] suggests a lifeless, not a living and developing scheme.

And the word '*symbolism*' is unfortunately one which must be safeguarded. It suggests, I fear inevitably, (as does the word *metaphysical*) a particular group of poets; and even does these poets, the best of them, an injustice by isolating them from poetry in general. It almost intimates that there is a particular recipe; or that this is merely one way of writing among others; or that poets can be distinguished clearly as symbolist and non-symbolist. Symbolism is that to which the word tends both in religion and in poetry; the incarnation of meaning in fact; and in poetry it is the tendency of the word to mean as much as possible. To find the word and give it the utmost meaning, in its place; to mean as many things as possible; to make it both exact and comprehensive, and really to *unite* the disparate and remote, to give them a fusion and a pattern with the word, surely this is the mastery at which the [ix] poet aims; and the poet is distinguished by making the word do more *work* than it does for other writers. Of course one can 'go too far' and except in directions in which we can go too far there is no interest in going at all; and only those who will risk going too far can possibly find out just how far one can go. Not to go far enough is to remain 'in the vague' as surely and less creditably than to succeed. Indeed, the mentors of pseudo-classicism should consistently content themselves with agnosticism, or at most with the simple faith of Islam; for no extravagance of a genuine poet can go so far over the borderline of ordinary intellect as the Creeds of the Church. And the poet who fears to take the risk that what he writes may turn out not to be poetry at all, is a man who has surely failed, who ought to have adopted some less adventurous vocation.

Donne in our Time

A Garland for John Donne 1631–1931, ed. Theodore Spencer (publ. 1 Dec. 1931), [1]–19. Gallup B19. In the passage from Descartes on p. 11 'idee' has been corrected to 'idée'.

It is, I know, a tercentenary 1631–1931; but for my own experience within the terms of this paper, our time is roughly 1906–1931. I mean that Professor Briggs used to read, with great persuasiveness and charm, verses of Donne to the Freshmen at Harvard assembled in what was called, as I remember, 'English A'. I confess that I have now forgotten what Professor Briggs told us about the poet; but I know that whatever he said, his own words and his quotations were enough to attract to private reading at least one Freshman who had already absorbed some of the Elizabethan dramatists, but who had not yet approached the metaphysicals. I can from that point trace uncertainly the progress of my own relations with Donne, but I cannot account for his general emergence towards tercentenary fame. I know that when I came to London I heard more of Donne, in social conversation, than I had heard before. It was partly because Desmond MacCarthy talked enthusiastically about Donne; and everyone knew that MacCarthy had for years been designing to write a book about him. MacCarthy's book, I am sorry to say, has not yet been written – no one really expected that it would be. But however, through however many influences, for whatever reasons, Donne came to be a poet with whom every intellectual undergraduate in English-speaking countries had at least to profess familiarity. I know that by 1926, when I gave some lectures on Donne, the subject was already popular, almost topical; and I know that by 1931 the subject had been so fully treated that there appears to me no possible justification of turning my lectures into a book.

It is not exactly that anyone has actually written a definitive book. True, there are books so good that there is little pretext at present for writing another. Miss Ramsay's French dissertation is extraordinarily informative, though it promulgates opinions about Donne which I think we have outgrown; Professor Grierson, in his introduction to his anthology of metaphysical poets as well as in his introduction and notes to his great edition of the poems, combines to an uncommon degree fine scholarship with sensitive perception; Mr Mario Praz, in one long essay, joins the latter gift to a unique knowledge of the whole of European poetry contemporary with Donne; Mr John Hayward has brought out a volume which contains the whole of the verse and excellent selection from the prose; Mr George Williamson has written a book admirably relating the poetry of Donne to that of his followers and to some of the poetry of recent times; and M. Pierre Legouis has said for us nearly all that we want to say about Donne's metric. Yet, admirably and thoroughly as the subject has been handled, there might still be place for another book [5] on Donne: except that, as I believe, Donne's poetry is a concern of the present and the recent past, rather than of the future.

I by no means wish to affirm that the importance of a particular poet, or of a particular type of poetry, is merely a matter of capricious fashion. I wish simply to distinguish between the absolute and the relative in popularity, and to recognise in the relative (both when a poet is unduly preferred and when he is unduly ignored) an element of the reasonable, the just and the significant. And a study of the popularity of Donne, and the various theories held about him, can illustrate this distinction very nicely.

We must assume, if we are to talk about poetry at all, that there is some absolute poetic hierarchy; we keep at the back of our minds the reminder of some end of the world, some final Judgement Day, on which the poets will be assembled in their ranks and orders. In the long run, there is an ultimate greater and less. But at any particular time, and we exist only in particular moments of time, good taste consists, not in attaining to the vision of Judgement Day, and still less in assuming that what happens to be important for us now is certainly what will be important in the same way on that occasion, but in approximating to some analysis of the absolute and the relative in our own appreciation. The principle, if valid, must apply of course to all art; but it is convenient, and an aid to precision, if one limits the field to that department of art which one knows best.

That there was an element of fashion in our enjoy-[6]ment and exploitation of Donne it would be vain to deny; but there was nothing capricious about the fashion. For at any particular moment it may happen that the poets who are beginning to write find a particular poet, or a particular type or school of poetry, such as Donne and the school of Donne – and for our time Laforgue and some other French poets as well – with whom or which they have close sympathy, and through whom or which they elicit their own talents. The next generation of analytical literary historians may dispute indefinitely as to *why* we were like that. And it is impossible for us or for anyone else ever to disentangle how much was genuine affinity, genuine appreciation, and how much was just a *reading into* poets like Donne our own sensibility, how much was 'subjective'. However many grains of subjectivity may have gone to the prescription does not exactly matter, for the reason that there must always be such an ingredient at any time when any past poet is especially enjoyed. We may even say with some confidence that we probably understand sympathetically Donne to-day better than poets and critics fifty years hence will understand him; it is equally probable that they of fifty years hence will understand somebody else, possibly Milton, or Victor Hugo, much better than we do. I allow for the chance of complete self-deception: if we have written nothing that will stand 'the test of time', then it is likely that the reputation of Donne will sink relatively as ours sinks. And all this, it should be superfluous to add, has nothing whatever to do with literary Pyrrhonism. Width of [7] literary appreciation extends between two theoretical poles, neither of which we quite reach in practice: the enjoyment of writers whom we love without admiring, and the enjoyment of writers whom we admire without loving. The discipline of the critic is to learn on what grounds *not* to admire the poets whom he primarily loves, and to learn to love a little those poets whom he only frigidly admires. We must only finally exclude those who, like the late Miss Wilcox, can be enjoyed only if we delude ourselves into believing that they give us genuinely that which they are merely imitating.

The progress of the reputation of Donne in the last twenty years or so is a curious chapter in the history of reputations. First he was supposed to be 'medieval'; and our notions of 'medieval' have themselves undergone change. This adjective was forcibly propelled at Donne by Miss Ramsay. Fortunately, however, Miss Ramsay has provided in the body of her book a mass of information which enables us to question the conclusions set out in her foreword. That Donne was well read in scholastic philosophy is undoubted; but there is no reason to suppose that he was any better read than Hooker, or that he was so deeply influenced by medieval thought as Hooker. Donne had also read or consulted all the principal theological writers up to date; he had also read the Protestant authorities and had read pretty widely in still more heretical authors; it is pertinent to remember that his great grandmother was a sister of Sir Thomas More, who translated Pico della Mirandola. [8] In short, he had read just what any omnivorous theological and philosophical scholar of his time might have been expected to read. His mind was decidedly the mind of a man of his own time: but it was legal and controversial rather than philosophical and theological. In our time, he might even have been a very great company lawyer.

In his whole temper, indeed, Donne is the antithesis of the scholastic, of the mystic and of the philosophical system maker. The encyclopedic ambitions of the schoolmen were directed always towards unification: a *summa* was the end to be attained, and every branch of knowledge and practice was to have its relation to the whole. In Donne, there is a manifest fissure between thought and sensibility, a chasm which in his poetry he bridged in his own way, which was not the way of medieval poetry. His learning is just information suffused with emotion, or combined with emotion not essentially relevant to it. In the poetry of Dante, and even of Guido Cavalcanti, there is always the assumption of an ideal unity in experience, the faith in an ultimate rationalisation and harmonisation of experience, the subsumption of the lower under the higher, an ordering of the world more or less Aristotelian. But perhaps one reason why Donne has appealed so powerfully to the recent time is that there is in his poetry hardly any attempt at organisation; rather a puzzled and humorous shuffling of the pieces; and we are inclined to read our own more conscious awareness of the apparent irrelevance and unrelatedness of things into the mind of Donne.

[9] But to suggest that Donne was not a believer, in the sense in which it was a category of medieval thought that there was a unity in existence, a relation of real to ideal, which was not beyond the mind of man to trace in its outlines, is not to imply that he was, in the modern sense, a sceptic. To say that his cast of mind was such as made it impossible for him to be a constructive philosopher or a mystic is not to say that he knew *doubt* as the modern world has known it. The metaphysician and the mystic work differently and with different tools; but alike for metaphysics and for mysticism a unification is required which was alien to Donne. On the other hand, it was still possible for Donne to be, and I am sure that he was, genuinely *devout*. But he was a sincere churchman not because he had passed through the doubt which his type of mind finds congenial (I say his *type* of mind), but because in theology he had not yet arrived there. In short, his kind of religious belief differs both from that of the thirteenth century and that of the nineteenth and twentieth; it was sincere, but represents a period of transition.

The question of the nature of Donne's religious faith determines our solution of the 'problem' of his conversion. Nobody now, I suppose, divides Donne's life into two periods, one dissolute and irreligious, the other a revulsion to intense and austere piety, a division so complete as to suggest an alternation of personality. We agree that it is one and the same man in both early and later life. But some of the best informed critics are still inclined to take [10] for granted a period of debauchery and to emphasise it. Thus a very competent scholar, Mr John Sparrow (writing in *Theology*, March, 1931) says: 'We need only look at one of his earliest poems to see that even in his most dissolute days religion was to Donne something more than a merely intellectual interest.' Well, I suppose that this sentence needed saying; and yet I do not think that we have sufficient evidence that Donne was so *very* dissipated; we are in danger of making an attractive romance about him. The able pamphlet of M. Legouis convinces me that we can easily exaggerate the mystical element in such a poem as 'The Ecstasy'; but I suspect that we can easily exaggerate the erotic element as well. No one now is likely to follow Sir Edmund Gosse in reading Donne's *Elegies* as exact autobiography. My intention here is not to whitewash the evidence of a dissipated or immoral youth; but merely to affirm that we have no satisfactory evidence, and that it is a point of the very slightest interest anyhow. The courtly cynicism was a poetic convention of the time; Donne's sometimes scoffing attitude towards the fickleness of women may be hardly more than immature bravado; it comes to me with none of the terrible sincerity of Swift's vituperation of the human race. Nor can I take very seriously Donne's later remorse or repentance. It is pleasant in youth to think that one is a gay dog, and it is pleasant in age to think that one *was* a gay dog; because as we grow old we all like to think that we have changed, developed and improved; people shrink from acknowledging that they are exactly the [11] same at fifty as they were at twenty-five – sometimes, indeed, men alter in order to congratulate themselves that they have altered, and not out of inner necessity. If Donne in youth was a rake, then I suspect that he was a conventional rake; if Donne in age was devout, then I suspect that he was conventionally devout. An observation which, even if true, is not necessarily destructive.

The kind of religious faith expressed in Donne's religious writings is wholly consistent with the employment in his poetry of the many scraps of various philosophies which appear there. His attitude towards philosophic notions in his poetry may be put by saying that he was more interested in *ideas* themselves as objects than in the *truth* of ideas. In an odd way, he almost anticipates the philosopher of the coming age, Descartes, in his sixth Meditation:

> Je conçois donc, aisément, que l'imagination se peut faire de cette sorte, s'il est vrai qu'il y ait des corps; et parce que je ne puis rencontrer aucune autre voie pour expliquer comment elle se fait, je conjecture de là probablement qu'il y en a; mais ce n'est que probablement; et quoique j'examine soigneusement toutes choses, je ne trouve pas néanmoins que, de cette idée distincte de la nature corporelle que j'ai en mon imagination, je puisse tirer aucun argument qui conclue avec nécessité l'existence de quelque corps.

I do not mean to suggest that this is a theory to which Donne would immediately have subscribed. But it is a curious parallel: to be interested in philosophies for their own sake, apart from their degree of truth, is not a medieval attitude. Donne was, I insist, no [12] sceptic: it is only that he is interested in and amused by ideas in themselves, and interested in the way in which he *feels* an idea; almost as if it were something that he could touch and stroke. To turn the attention to the mind in this way is a kind of creation, because the objects alter by being observed so curiously. To contemplate an idea, because it is present for the moment in my own mind, to observe my emotion colour it, and to observe it colour my emotions, to play with it, instead of using it as a plain and simple meaning, brings often odd or beautiful objects to light, as a deep sea diver inspects the darting and crawling life of the depths; though it may lend itself, this petting and teasing of one's mental objects, to extremities of torturing of language. With Donne it is not, as it is with the Elizabethans in their worst excesses, the word, the vocabulary that is tormented – it is the thought itself. In the poem

> I wonder by my troth, what thou, and I . . .

the *idea* is thoroughly teased and tousled. The choice and arrangement of words is simple and direct and felicitous. There is a startling directness (as often at the beginning of Donne's poems) about the idea, which must have occurred to many lovers, of the abrupt break and alteration of the new life. These *trouvailles* themselves are enough to set Donne apart from some of his imitators: Cowley never found anything so good. But the usual course for Donne is not to pursue the meaning of the idea, but to arrest it, to play catlike with it, to develop it dialectically, to ex-[13]tract every minim of the emotion suspended in it. And as to the poetic justification of this method of dialectic I have no doubts; on this point Mr Praz sees much more clearly than M. Legouis.

M. Legouis, however, has come as near as anyone to stripping the criticism of Donne's lyrical verse of irrelevant attributes, and getting to the heart of the matter. As long as we thought of Donne as a medieval, as a mystic, as a philosopher, as a rake turned devout, or a convert, we did not see his poetry as it is. Donne is not even an absolutely first-rate devotional poet: fine as some of his religious verse is, Crashaw, Herbert and Vaughan each in his limited scope surpasses Donne; and yet Donne is absolutely a greater poet, a greater master of language, than any of them.

And detaching Donne from his relation to a particular generation, our own, a relation which may never be repeated at any subsequent time, this I think we can say at least. Donne will remain permanently in a higher place than he has occupied before. For he was a great reformer of the English language, of English verse. We may continue always to find him more of a poet, of deeper knowledge and more intense and moving expression, than Dryden; but here we can compare him favourably to Dryden in the very matter in which Dryden deserves our warmest gratitude and admiration. The verse of Dryden was once thought artificial, pedestrian and prosaic; just as in a previous century the verse of Donne was thought to be artificial, pedestrian and prosaic, as well as uncouth. But in truth Dryden and [14] Donne are both highly natural; and the merit of both is to have established a natural conversational diction instead of a conventional one. Each effected a revolution of the kind which has to occur from time to time, which will have to occur again in nearly measurable time, if the English language is to retain its vigour.

The revolutionary activity of Donne is not so immediately apparent as that of Dryden, because it began before the previous revolution, that of dramatic blank verse, was exhausted. For the age of Shakespeare, blank verse was the perfect vehicle for impassioned thought, and indeed Shakespeare himself succeeded in getting more thought expressed in great verse than any English poet before or after him. But lyric verse, under these conditions, remained subordinate to the musical instrument and to the dramatic setting – I do not know whether it has been enough remarked that the effect of the lyrics of Shakespeare (and to a less degree, those of some of his contemporaries and followers) is immensely heightened and weighted with meaning by their exact relevance to the dramatic situation which to a thoughtless ear they might seem at times merely to interrupt.

It is hardly too much to say that Donne enlarged the possibilities of lyric verse as no other English poet has done. M. Legouis has pointed out very pertinently how largely his lyrics are dramatic, in monologue and dialogue. The possibilities of this kind of verse, however, were not considerably developed by any of Donne's immediate successors; and however [15] closely they depended upon him for their language, and however they excelled him in various departments of devotional verse, none could follow so delicately the movements of the human mind or the comedy and tragedy of human behaviour and feeling. The path of exploration started by Donne ended in the blind alley of the Pindaric ode of Cowley, and the lyric ran on into tender sentiment, *vers de société* and satire. We must accordingly dissociate Donne from the 'school of Donne'; so far as these followers enjoy any particular vogue in our time, it is a popularity reflected from that of Donne, or partly one arising from a new interest in devotional verse. From one point of view, George Herbert is far more to the taste of an admirer of Christina Rossetti than necessarily to the taste of an admirer of Donne. For the technique of verse, and for its adaptability to purposes, Donne has closer affinity to Browning, to Laforgue and to Corbière. The place of Browning in this group is obscured by several accidents: by the fact that he is often tediously long-winded, that he is far less a wit and ironist, and perhaps more than anything by the fact that his knowledge of the particular human heart is adulterated by an optimism that has proved offensive to our time, though a later age may succeed in ignoring it. Browning moreover, is perhaps *too* objective, without having that large and intricate pattern which objectivity requires: Donne, Corbière, Laforgue begin with their own feelings and their limitation is that they do not always get much outside or beyond; Shakespeare, one feels, arrives at [16] an objective world by a process from himself, whoever he was, as the centre and starting point; but too often, one thinks with Browning, here is a world with no particular interesting man in it, no consistent point of view. But the verse method, in all these four men, is similar: either dramatic monologue or dramatic dialogue; and with Donne and the French poets, the pattern is given by what goes on within the mind, rather than by the exterior events which provoke the mental activity and play of thought and feeling.

But Donne effected not only a development, but a reform, of the language, just as Dryden, in his turn, reformed the language from the excesses of the minor followers of Donne. The minor Elizabethan dramatists sometimes tormented the language; where the content is often quite simple, the expression is perverse. In the verse of Donne the thought is sometimes overingenious and perverse, but the language is always pure and simple. The conceit itself is primarily an eccentricity of imagery, the far-fetched association of the dissimilar, or the overelaboration of one metaphor or simile; only with such writers as Cleveland or Benlowes it tends to corrupt the language itself – because with them, the content of thought and feeling is seldom subtle enough to justify such obscure expression. Donne introduced the natural or conversational style, which the Elizabethans at their best had excelled in producing in a highly sophisticated metric of blank verse, into the lyric; he first made it possible to think in lyric verse, and in a [17] variety of rhythms and stanza schemes which forms an inexhaustible subject of study; and at the same time retained a quality of song and the suggestion of the instrumental accompaniment of the earlier lyric. No poet has excelled him in this peculiar combination of qualities.

The eighteenth-century ear was more attuned to Cowley's verse than to Donne's; hence Cowley was taken as the master and type of this school of verse; attention was concentrated on the abuses, and distracted from the original innovation of Donne; and Donne's character as literary reformer was quite overlooked. Similarly the nineteenth century, though it admitted some grudging praise to Dryden as 'reformer', tended to think of this reform as a lamentable necessity which reduced poetry to the low estate of prose; tended to think of it as the substitution of a wild artificiality by a rational one; and laid emphasis on the Romantic Movement as the one great reform of English verse. But Donne and

Dryden were *equally* reformers of the language; both brought in a vital and energetic simplicity, and natural conversational speech in verse. And as for this 'naturalness' and 'conversational' quality in verse – or indeed in prose – it must be remembered that there is not one permanent and impersonal kind of naturalness and one of artificiality. What is natural in one man is artificial in another; for a style is natural or artificial, just as it may be vigorous or insipid, according to whether it is the right expression of, whether it is in intimate union with, a sincere, because integrated, [18] personality. What is a natural style when written by one man is artificial by another; and the artificial occurs when a man is trying to be, or trying to pretend to be, that which he is not and cannot be. There will always be more of the artificial than the natural in writing; and what is natural to-day is artificial to-morrow.

Such, I believe, are some of the conclusions of praise which another generation, not enjoying that fulness of satisfaction in Donne that we have felt, will be able to confer upon him. The fascination of the 'personality' of an author is an undependable and fluctuating influence upon posterity; the affinity which we find or invent for ourselves and various authors of various periods is uncertain, variable but partly relevant to their greatness. Yet certainly that of Donne is as definite, and as impressive, as that of Montaigne; and we are not wholly fanciful in believing that he has, in the old sense of the word, 'prevented' us. The last stage in the discovery and rehabilitation of Donne – if that can be called a rehabilitation which is really an habilitation – is the current applause of his works of divinity. I feel, myself (it is perhaps to-day an heretical sensation), that the essential originality of Donne is rather in the *Songs and Sonets*, in the *Elegies*, and in the *Satires*, than in the *Sermons*. We find in the gorgeous prose of the last something more than what is there, for we find now and then what is not to be expected, the knowledge of the weaknesses of the human soul, the frankness of admission as of Montaigne, which is not [19] in the view of the greater Jacobean and Caroline divines. But actually (I for one have always been convinced) in the history of English Theology it is not Donne, but Cranmer and Latimer and Andrewes, who are the great prose masters; and for the theologian even the high-sounding Bramhall and the depressive Thorndike are more important names than Donne's. His sermons will disappear as suddenly as they have appeared. For one age or another his personality may be no more interesting than has been, for the last seventy-five years or so (I am not at the moment careful to answer in respect of that reputation), the personality of Byron. But at any time Donne ought always to be recognised as one of the few great reformers and preservers of the English tongue.

1932

A Commentary

C., 11. 43 (Jan. 1932), 268-75. Signed 'T. S. E.' Gallup C328.

For the last few months we have been peppered with a succession of little books on financial and economic problems; little books aimed at that large part of the 'reading public' which normally is not only ignorant of such matters, but prefers to remain so. I myself am normally ignorant as anybody, with the normal disinclination to take up any subject which I did not study in my youth. But the repeated impact of these small books upon the eye cannot fail to make an impression upon the conscience. Of old it seemed that the economists preferred to discuss their mysteries among themselves, and in two-volume works priced from fifteen to thirty shillings; and that was a happy age for the man who desired to know nothing of their subject. But now economists issue into the market-place to harangue and convert the people; they almost buttonhole you, by publishing these modest volumes which seem to say 'it is now *your* duty to learn what's what in these deep matters; I am just the book to make it all clear even to your intelligence, written down exactly to your level; and the urgency is so great, that you cannot pretend that the price is beyond your means.' But the conscience which forces us to read one, compels us to go on and read the rest; and in the end the voice of conscience seems to me almost a Siren voice, coaxing one to be fair-minded and 'hear the other side'. And there are not two sides, but a great many.

Having entered upon such a course of education, however, we can only go on; and from time to time draw up a balance of convictions and doubts. Among the literature of the subject which I have examined lately are *Can Governments Cure Unemployment?* by Sir Norman Angell and Harold Wright (Dent: 3s. 6d.); *Poverty in Plenty* by J. A. Hobson (Allen & Unwin: 2s. 6d.); *Money and Prices* by Augustus Baker (Dent: 6s.); and *This Unemployment* by the Revd V. A. Demant (Student Christian Movement: 4s.). [269] None of these books would, I believe, be considered quite orthodox, but they differ among themselves in kind and degree of unorthodoxy. Among these, Sir Norman Angell and Mr Wright appear to be, if not wholly orthodox, at least, in the present state of affairs, the most conservative. For the first conviction that the beginner acquires is that the troubles from which we suffer are very deep-seated indeed, and of very long heredity; and such opinions are held even by some who could not be called 'medievalists'. We are not interested in anything that appears to promise merely temporary alleviation, however reasonable in themselves for the moment may be the measures suggested.

> The remedy which we suggest for this condition (say Sir Norman and Mr Wright) is a governmental control of marketing operations; the adaptation and co-ordination of industry under the direction of the State; a National Plan, involving co-operation between a series of interlocking industries to supply the ascertainable needs of the community, scientific marketing, the education of the consumer by advertisement, and the better organization of labour.

Perhaps it is a phrase like 'National Plan' which first arouses the suspicion of the ignoramus; but the whole sentence is as disappointing as the Mosley Plan or any of the nostrums of the moment offered by any of the politicians, whether in office or out. We have seen so many Boards, Commissions and Conferences already; and the authors of this book seem to hope much from the 'co-operation of Capitalism and Socialism', whilst we suspect that it is partly because of this 'co-operation between Capitalism and Socialism' which has been going on for a generation, that we are in the present pass. Sir Norman Angell and Mr Wright, one suspects sadly, are merely Mensheviks of the London School of Economics pattern.

It is already a relief to turn to Mr J. A. Hobson. For Mr Hobson, whatever we may think of his proposals, writes with a warmth of feeling appropriate to the subject, and without which any writing on this subject is apt to appear [270] complacent. I know the name of Mr Hobson as the author of serious economic works; I have no knowledge of his standing in academic circles. But I liked this book; and though it has a Fabian flavour, it seemed to have some of the virtue of solitary, rather than group thought. No one would say that Mr Hobson does not see the seriousness of the situation, and the profundity of the trouble. 'My thesis is,' says he, 'that our main economic troubles are of a distinctively moral origin'; and this is good; yet the beginner cannot help wondering whether his account of the relation of the moral to the economic malady is the right one. Thus he says 'the workers as a whole are wronged by the economic forces which accord too large a share of the product to non-workers'; and I cannot but feel that underlying this statement is the old fallacy of the absolute righteousness of *work*. It would seem to be more and more the fact that the workers are 'wronged' (if that is the best word) by the economic forces which prevent the non-workers from consuming what the workers produce. And Mr Hobson seems to me to hope for too much from a simple redistribution of the 'money' in existence. He wastes several pages of indignation on monopolists of talent or reputation, such as cinema stars and eminent surgeons and barristers, who are 'over-paid'. But does it really matter so much to the world at large whether a handful of people are over-paid or not? Does it matter, fundamentally, whether unskilled workers in some trades are better paid than the skilled workers in others? These are wrongs, certainly, for denouncing which we must have every sympathy with Mr Hobson. He seems to me nearer the root of the matter when he says, in speaking of the 'surpluses' of income accumulated by individuals or companies

> Their low utility for purposes of consumption or enjoyment leads to their accumulation as savings for investment in excess of the requirements and possible uses of the economic system as a whole.

One might add that if these accumulations reached a point [271] at which they could not be reinvested or lent, because the opportunities for expansion of businesses had come to an end, then they would cease to be money at all – or so it would seem. But is not the real moral error the general assumption that money is most virtuously used when it is used 'profitably' – to produce more money? We consider it virtuous to work – to work full time (whatever that may be); and we consider virtuous, and load with honours, the man who builds up a business which gives work to a great number of men; and such an employer is admired as a benefactor whether the actual produce of his industry is or is not such as it is morally good for the public to have at all, or to have in such profusion. But when Mr Hobson says that

> . . . the consumer for whose enjoyments the whole of this economic system is supposed to have been created is unable to perform his necessary part of withdrawing goods from the productive system as fast as they can be produced.

I think that I understand and agree with what he says. Yet is this failure, I wonder, merely due to an unjust *distribution* of money incomes? I do not suppose that Mr Hobson *means* that there is a definite amount of money in the world, and that all that we have to do is to reapportion it; for I suppose that such simple remedies are hardly hawked even in Hyde Park. And I cannot willingly agree to the pessimism of his later remarks:

> The conscious ordering of world industry and commerce as the organic whole it is, can alone serve to give peace, prosperity and progress to the economic life of the several parts of that organic whole.

Certainly this is the desirable end, but it is not socialism or anything else in our time. Would it not be better at present for each people to concentrate attention on what it can do at home?

The avenue from which Fr Demant approaches the social problem is sympathetic to me, which is probably why from time to time a ray of understanding seemed to penetrate the [272] twilight of my mind. I applaud, for instance, such a remark as:

> Christianity repudiates a position which allows an *economic system* to be a form of government, i.e., to determine what human desires should or should not be satisfied.

And his whole attitude toward the 'unemployment' problem seems to me to be very near the truth; possibly because my knowledge is limited; but it is the only type of explanation of that problem which seems to me to explain at all. For to me the unemployment problem seems to be one which we have had always with us. And here again, the ordinary attitude towards unemployment is vitiated by the moral error of 'the dignity of labour'. Formerly the unemployed consisted largely of women, numbers of whom, at least above a certain social status, did very little 'work' in the capitalist or socialist sense; there were also numbers of lightly employed domestics. During the earlier part of the capitalist era the unemployed consisted also of people living on the income from capital accumulated by their parents and grandparents; and it was the fashion for radical-minded persons who had to earn their livings to denounce such people as drones and parasites. That the *rentier* should disappear was considered natural justice; that women should earn their livings was hailed as a triumph for feminism – that they should 'work' in the modern sense was an assertion of their dignity, of their moral equality with men; it was almost good enough evidence to convince a Moslem that women have souls. The same moral prejudice which was once directed against women and *rentiers* is now transferred by many persons to the 'unemployed'. We hear often of the minor defects of the dole system; and if the dole system is to be continued I do not object to these defects being remedied, if possible. I believe that the great majority of unemployed men of the older generations, those who were brought up to a life occupied by work, genuinely prefer to work, would work if they could; and we have no reason for surprise if [273] young men who have never had the opportunity to work or who have entered life on a dole scale of living, have no desire to work. There is little difference between a young man brought up on the dole, and a young man brought up as a *rentier*; except that the latter, having had a better education, and larger means, has possibly been trained to a sense of responsibility and a knowledge of how to employ leisure. I do not suppose that most unemployed workmen know how, or are able, to make the best use of their leisure; but it seems to me that an unemployed man who wants 'work' is justified only for one of two reasons: (1) he desires to keep himself and his family more decently than he can on his weekly allowance, to give himself and them more advantages of comfort, education, recreation; or (2) he is aware of his miserable inability to fill his time unless he is working to make money for himself or an employer. I should think better of communism if I learned that there existed in Russia a decent leisure class; but when the defenders of Bolshevism tell us that Russia is a beehive of industrial activity, I am only the more convinced, with Mr Hobson, that the Soviet system is simply the culmination of capitalism.

The pleasant feeling that I was able to understand parts of *This Unemployment* was enhanced by finding that Fr Demant made criticisms of Mr Hobson's book which were pertinent to the doubts which Mr Hobson had raised in my own mind. And, as I may have suggested above, the thought had already occurred to me, that 'work for all', in the industrial sense of the word 'work', would never again be possible in human history so long as there exist the natural resources for making and using machinery. The unemployment can only disappear, it seems, when mankind returns to a condition of barbarism, and this it is hardly likely to do of its own accord. But meanwhile, what are we to do with people, even if we have the most efficient 'credit-reform'? This is the question which Fr Demant does not seem quite to get round to answering; nor, for my purposes, does Mr Baker. I say for my purposes, because *Money and* [274] *Prices* is a piece of more abstruse credit reform argument; and like the late F. H. Bradley, I have no capacity for the abstruse. The answer may be there, for the book is impressive and persuasive enough, and I mean to read it again; but the answer so far I have simply failed to find. I still believe that such words as *work* and *thrift* have potent moral significance, though their real moral value has been distorted by the capitalist system, a distortion which seems unlikely to be straightened out in any merely socialist system. *Property* is another such word. As for work, I find for myself that I am glad to be able to earn the greater part of my income by my personal exertions, rather than depend entirely on a dole either from my parents or the State. I prefer also a condition of affairs in which I have a daily routine of work or business the greater part of which for the greater part of the time I find boring. I am aware that if my work were as monotonous as that of an unskilled labourer in a mass-production factory, I should feel otherwise. But a certain amount of routine, of dullness and of necessity seems inseparable from work; and for myself, I am too sceptical of my own abilities to be able to make a whole-time job of writing poetry, even if I had the means. Such dependence upon work may certainly be due to some defect of character or vitality; but if so I imagine that it is a defect from which a large part of humanity suffers. And supposing that the attempt were made to solve the problem of work (for after all there will always be *some* work to be done) by shortening hours to make the work go round? You cannot subdivide labour-time to infinitesimals, and long before you reached infinitesimals you would find that the shortness of the individual's working time hampered efficiency as much as a reversion to primitive methods; and no one would be able to think of his work as anything but an irritating and unnecessary interruption of his leisure.

So that humanity would be called upon (if it is worth while 'calling upon' humanity to do anything) to invent new and I hope pleasant kinds of work beyond what is recognised at present as productive labour; indeed, to civilise itself [275] much more. It would not matter whether you called this new work by the name of work or play. A professional football player, for instance, seems to me to be engaged in useful work. But the people cannot spend all their time watching football matches, bathing in the Serpentine, visiting cinemas, listening to educative wireless talks, playing the gramophone, motoring, or reading profound philosophical works. The man who watches the football match needs to be able to feel as *useful* as the footballer. If the various parts of football audiences were themselves engaged, for a reasonable part of their time, in reciprocally entertaining the football players and each other for a similar cash consideration, that I should call a fair division of labour. I say 'for a reasonable part of their time', because I think that under the present system the majority of those who have work at all, have to work too long or too hard. If, for instance, my position is such that I can only afford one servant, and accordingly must find a very strong and hard-working servant who will do all the work I require, that may be in the circumstances commendable thrift – in view of other responsibilities which I may have for my spare cash. But I do not like the situation; and I should prefer to employ a large staff of servants, each doing much lighter work but profiting by the benefits of the cultured and devout atmosphere of the home in which they lived. That aspiration, as it stands, is no doubt 'medievalism'; but we want a modern equivalent for such a paradise.

These problems seem to me so serious that it is worth while even for the simpleton to explore them; for it is possible that his blunderings may be of some help to the simplicity of others: people often avoid thinking about matters because they are afraid of making fools of themselves; but if they see another person ready to run the risk of looking foolish, they may take heart. Likewise, the feeble stutterings of the questioner may assist the expert to explain himself more clearly still.

Charles Whibley: A Memoir

'Charles Whibley: A Memoir' was publ.as The English Association pamphlet No. 80, on 14 Jan. 1932: Gallup A20. It had been distributed to the members of the Association in Dec. 1931.
Revised in *SE. See below*, pp. 613–24.

Preface

Preface to *Bubu of Montparnasse* by Charles-Louis Philippe, translated by Laurence Vail (1932). Publ. Mar. 1932 as 'Modern Masterpieces in English, No. 4', vii–xiv. Signed 'T. S. Eliot'. Gallup B20.

It is a good many years ago, it was in the year 1910, that I first read *Bubu de Montparnasse*, when I came first to Paris. Read at an impressionable age, and under the impressive conditions, the book has always been for me, not merely the best of Charles-Louis Philippe's books, but a symbol of the Paris of that time. Little known even now outside of France, Philippe was then none too well known even within it, though he was already dead, and this book had been published ten years before. I imagine that the Paris of 1910 was more like the Paris [viii] of 1900 than like the Paris of 1932: certainly Montparnasse has changed more in these twenty-two years than it could have changed in the preceding ten. In a very much smaller way, to me *Bubu* stood for Paris as some of Dickens's novels stand for London.

The comparison suggested is between a very great novelist and a very limited one, but is not, I think, unprofitable. Had Dickens confined himself to the districts of Tom-all-alone's and Fagin's kitchen the comparison would be closer. Philippe is almost without humour, except such grim humour as is inherent in the behaviour of his characters, as when, at the end of this book, Big Jules says 'permit me to roll a cigarette'. But he has an intense pity for the humble and oppressed, a pity still more akin to that of Dickens's Russian disciple Dostoievski; and a pathos which as in Dickens and Dostoievski both, trembles on the edge of the maudlin. He differs from both of the greater men by the absence of any religious or humanitarian [ix] zeal: he is not explicitly concerned with altering things. And in that he is perhaps the most faithful to the point of view of the humble and oppressed themselves, is more their spokesman than their champion. You can look towards Christianity or towards communism, according to your predisposition, but Philippe is himself no propagandist.

It is not the sort of people that Philippe knew best who become Christian zealots or revolutionists; they simply toil and suffer, or take the easiest way out. I remember some years ago, though not so long ago as 1910 – it was indeed after the War – asking my way, in a town of southern France, of a passing workman. He gave me my direction civilly enough, though with a glance of curiosity at the foreigner; and in parting slapped himself on the chest, and added quite gratuitously, *Moi, je suis de la classe ouvrière: exploitée par les capitalistes*. When human beings awake to such a state of consciousness as that, they are far above [x] the stratum which is Philippe's proper material. Whether he is concerned, as in this book, with the prostitutes and mackerels of the Boulevard Sébastopol, or, as in more of his books, with the poorest class of decent-living provincial peasantry, it is with the inarticulate and underfed, those who are too depressed to be rebellious.

His work, like that of many minor writers, is largely autobiographical. Knowing no more of his biography than I do, I find it easy to believe that he himself is the original of Pierre Hardy. The family of Pierre Hardy, toiling humbly and decently in their village in eastern France, that their son might become a Civil Servant in Paris, is very like the family that he depicts more autobiographically in *Charles Blanchard* and *La Mère et l'Enfant*. His great quality is not imagination: it is a sincerity which makes him a faithful recorder of things as they are, and of events as they happened, without irrelevant and disturbing comment. He had [xi] a gift which is rare enough: the ability not to think, not to generalise. To be able to select, out of personal experience, what is really significant, to be able not to corrupt it by afterthoughts, is as rare as imaginative invention. I am always impressed, in Philippe, by his fidelity to the powers that were given him: nearly always, even in his worst and most lachrymose moments, he is saying what he has to say, not writing a book. He was not *un homme de lettres*.

I have never thought that any other of his books equals *Bubu*. The pathetic, even when wholly sincere, is a dangerous specialty; and that which, to the author, is the most pathetic, is not always so to the reader. Dickens may himself have wept copiously over little Nell and little Em'ly; they are not nearly so moving to me as the Chancery prisoner in *Pickwick*, of whom it is said finally, *He has got his discharge, by God!* Yet in *Charles Blanchard*, *Le Père Perdrix*, and *La Mère et l'Enfant*, the love and the pity [xii] are so obviously towards real people, so obviously real emotions and not literary confections, that they elicit love and pity from us though we may feel that this is rather Philippe himself, than the world in which he lived. *Marie Donadieu*, which some have thought his greatest book, has always left me a little cold; as if he had been trying to do something for which he was not quite fitted, something larger and more impersonal, *roman dans le genre*. It has its reality, it has its final phrases, as at the end (I quote from memory): *tu peux chercher un autre homme, Marie. Elle répondit: il faut déjà beaucoup de foi pour chercher.* But in attempting something more like a novel, more impersonal, he seems to me to give less of himself, and instead of pity, we are aware rather of an atmosphere of moral putrefaction.

Bubu de Montparnasse, then, seems to me to be the one book in which Philippe struck the most that he could do perfectly. In the books in which he is more purely [xiii] personal we find ourselves being engulfed in a morass of sentiment; in *Marie Donadieu*, the most 'ambitious', in a morass of corruption. What preserves *Bubu* from either extreme, I think, is the precise reality of two figures, Le Grand Jules and Bubu himself. Every word that they say, and every word that Philippe says about them, are absolutely veridical; have that authenticity to convince readers who have no knowledge of real *souteneurs* with whom to compare them. They are both perfectly French and universally human: you say 'given that a man of that class and that way of existence, and a Frenchman in particular, he *would* be like that.' Berthe, or Pierre Hardy, presented by themselves, would very likely appear as the sentimental harlot or the sentimental young man of artificial fiction; but set against the obduracy of Jules and Bubu, Berthe's softness and pliancy is not a sentimental version of reality, but the real thing.

[xiv] There have been many novels of low life, of metropolitan vice and degradation. Novels of sentimentality, novels of satire, novels of indignation, novels of social reform, novels of prurience. *Bubu de Montparnasse* succeeds in being none of these: emphatically not the last. Philippe certainly disturbs any lingering complacency that we may feel towards the world as it is; but he has no cure to advocate. He is both compassionate and dispassionate; in his book we *blame* no one, we blame not even a 'social system'; and even the most virtuous, in reading it, may feel: I have sinned exceedingly in thought, word and deed.

Studies in Sanctity. VIII. George Herbert

Spectator, 148. 5411 (12 Mar. 1932), 360-1. Subheaded 'By T. S. Eliot.' Gallup C329.

In *The Oxford Book of English Verse*, George Herbert is allotted five pages, the same number as Bishop King and many less than Robert Herrick. This does, I imagine, gauge pretty accurately the measure of Herbert's reputation: he is known as the author of a few fine devotional poems suitable for anthologies, which serve to illustrate his debt to Donne; and his figure is preserved, chiefly by Walton's *Life*, as one of genuine though rather conventional piety. For poetic range he is compared unfavourably with Donne, and for religious intensity he is compared unfavourably with Crashaw. This latter opinion, it may be suspected, is supported by those who choose to take a view of the Church of England into which a very temperate and 'reasonable' kind of personal devoutness will best fit. The author of the Introduction to the little 'World's Classics' edition seems to me representative of this attitude. 'The strength and support of that branch of the Catholic Church militant in our own country,' he says, 'has always lain upon the middle way; it has never been her method either to "waste in passionate dreams" or to protest overmuch with the voices of prophecy or denunciation.' But he adds, with true British tolerance, 'to say this is not to presume to depreciate the excellence of those kinds of enthusiasm which are congenitally foreign to the English character.' He completes his picture of the Church of England in the spirit of Tennysonian pastoral: 'There, as the cattle wind homeward in the evening light, the benign, whitehaired parson stands at his gate to greet the cowherd, and the village chime calls the labourers to evensong.'

In our time such a happy picture of a social fabric of [361] moderate and complacent piety – a picture which at once idealises society and travesties the Church – may provoke a smile; yet it does represent the false setting in which we still place the figure of George Herbert. We know but little of his life, it is true; but what we do know, and the very much more that we know about his period, concur to demonstrate the falsity. Whatever Herbert was, he was not the prototype of the clergyman of Dickens's Christmas at Dingley Dell. Walton's portrait is certainly formalised and starched, but probably true so far as it goes; suggesting, as it does, that he was not himself imaginative or spiritually minded enough to appreciate, though he could respect.

Of all the 'metaphysical' poets, Herbert has suffered the most from being read only in anthologies. Even in Professor Grierson's admirable specialised anthology of metaphysical verse, he is at a disadvantage compared with several writers of less importance. The usual opinion, I believe, is as I have already said in other words, that we go to Donne for poetry and to Crashaw for religious poetry: but that Herbert deserves to be remembered as the representative lyrist of a mild and tepid Church.

Yet when we take Herbert's collected poems and read industriously through the volume we cannot help being astonished both at the considerable number of pieces which are as fine as those in any anthology, and at what we may call the spiritual stamina of the work. Throughout there is brain work, and a very high level of intensity; his poetry is definitely an *oeuvre*, to be studied entire. And our gradual appreciation of the poetry gives us a new impression of the man.

All poetry is difficult, almost impossible, to write: and one of the great permanent causes of error in writing poetry is the difficulty of distinguishing between what one really feels and what one would like to feel, and between the moments of genuine feeling and the moments of falsity. This is a danger in all poetry: but it is a peculiarly grave danger in the writing of devotional verse. Above that level of attainment of the spiritual life, below which there is no desire to write religious verse, it becomes extremely difficult not to confuse accomplishment with intention, a condition at which one merely aims with the condition in which one actually lives, what one would be with what one is: and verse which represents only good intentions is worthless – on that plane, indeed, a betrayal. The greater the elevation, the finer becomes the difference between sincerity and insincerity, between the reality and the unattained aspiration.

And in this George Herbert seems to me to be as secure, as habitually sure, as any poet who has written in English. With the religious verse of Donne, as with that of Milton, one is aware of a prodigious mastery of the language employed upon religious subjects; with that of Crashaw, of a passionate fancy and a metrical ability which might also have employed themselves upon other than religious themes; and even with Gerard Hopkins, I find myself wondering whether there is an essential relation between his contribution to poetry and his religious vocation. Of George Herbert, as of St John of the Cross, I feel that no lower theme could have evoked his genius. This, no doubt, sounds like excessive praise; but I am not for a moment comparing the accomplishment of Herbert with that of the Spaniard. I am only putting forward the suggestion that it is very rare to find a poet of whom one may say, that his poetic gift would have remained dormant or unfulfilled but for his religious vocation. Crashaw (or so I believe)[,] had he remained in the world, might still have been the great poet that he is; Herbert, had he remained in the world, would (I think) at most have produced a few elegant anthology pieces like those of Herbert of Cherbury. But you will not get much satisfaction from George Herbert unless you can take seriously the things which he took seriously himself and which made him what he was.

That age of violent religious dissensions, a time in which even the most retired clergyman might find himself called upon to suffer extremely for his faith, was an age of strong passions, including religious passions; in which those who, like the Herbert family, had the best opportunity of enjoying the pleasures and glories of this world, were also sometimes the most aware of the other. Of all devotional poets, certainly of all Anglican poets, George Herbert seems nearest in feeling to Christina Rossetti – who, indeed, in a humble way, found herself obliged to make as great, and perhaps a greater, sacrifice of this world than did Herbert. But a certain resemblance of temperament immediately suggests also profound differences. Christina's religious verse suffers, when we read much of it together, from a monotony due to a narrower range of emotion and an inferior intellectual gift. Herbert is an anatomist of feeling and a trained theologian too; his mind is working continually both on the mysteries of faith and the motives of the heart.

> I know the ways of Learning; both the head
> And pipes that feed the press, and make it run . . .
>
> I know the ways of Honour, what maintains
> The quick returns of courtesy and wit . . .
>
> I know the ways of Pleasure, the sweet strains,
> The lullings and the relishings of it;
> The propositions of hot blood and brains . . .

He knew all these various motions far better than Christina Rossetti did; and his poetry expresses the slow, sometimes almost despairing and always agonising toil of the proud and passionate man of the world towards spiritual life; a toil and agony which must always be the same, for the similar temperament, to the end of the world. I never feel that the great Dean of St Paul's, with his mastery of the spoken word, his success and applause to the end, quite conquered his natural pride of mind; Herbert, the vicar of Bemerton, in his shorter life went much farther on the road of humility.

Christianity and Communism

Listener, 7. 166 (16 Mar. 1932), 382–3. Subheaded 'By T. S. ELIOT'. Gallup C330.
At head of title: 'The Modern Dilemma'.

In the first of his four contributions to this series, Mr Eliot defines the modern dilemma as essentially a religious one, a choice between Christianity and the religion of Communism

I have been tempted to begin my contribution to this discussion with the words of Trinculo in *The Tempest*: 'The folly of this island! They say there's but five upon this isle: we are three of them; if th' other two be brained like us, the state totters.' I must add that I do not use this quotation in any invidious sense. But it had some relevance to my first thought when I began to prepare my talks: why should a person like myself, whose only reasonable notoriety is due to the composition of verses and jingles, in which I have some skill, be talking on this subject? I am not educated for anything else than verses, and I have little other competence. Why should I be invited to talk to you upon a subject which comprehends everything under the sun? I am neither an historian like Mr Dawson nor a philosopher like Professor Macmurray. And also, why, except under some mad delusion of vanity, should I have the temerity to accept? If this were merely a personal query, I should not bother you with it; but it seems to me to have a direct bearing upon what we call the 'modern dilemma'. Lord Russell, speaking in another series of these talks a couple of months ago, warned us against the tyranny of the expert. This is certainly an injunction to be taken to heart; but I may add that the present is also very conspicuously an age of the amateur (at least in the field of discussion) and of popular expositions in book form. After all, Lord Russell himself is an expert in a department as confined, if perhaps more important, than my own; and on the subject on which he was talking he also is a kind of amateur. It seems to me that the reason why we care to listen to amateurs, and to read popular books of science and culture and history, and the reason why the amateurs like to talk and write, is that we are all in dumb revolt against the expert. I do not mean that we wish to remove him from his proper place, or that we wish to replace expert knowledge by mere enthusiasm – God forbid! But we feel that there is an art as well as a science of life; that the specialist is apt to exceed his terms of reference; that he can teach us how to put into effect a particular purpose, but not what purposes are worth having. We feel the need for a point of view from which we can see the world as at least potentially orderly; a point of view wider than the expert's can be, and a world in which we may accept our own tiny lives as having a justifiable place in an intelligible whole.

WHAT IS THE USE?

Here, surely, is a form in which the 'dilemma', if we call it that, comes home to roost with everybody – with everybody, I mean, who is sufficiently sensitive and conscious. There are many people, I am sure, in every walk of life, who are perfectly satisfied with themselves and with what they are doing. Happy the man, but perhaps not always enviable, to whom never comes the thought, in a sudden if momentary paralysis, 'Of what use is my work'. It is a thought which might come to the most brilliant or to the most necessary member of the community: to the speculative scientist, the inventor, the financier, the manufacturer and the unskilled labourer; it can come, I testify, to the man of letters. Of what use is this experimenting with rhythms and words, this effort to find the precise metric and the exact image to set down feelings which, if communicable at all, can be communicated to so few that the result seems insignificant compared to the labour? Such thoughts have come to men at every period of civilised history, I make no doubt; but they are especially natural in our own day. We have been told by many philosophers that the world has no design and no purpose; we have seen the revolution of peoples and the downfall of monarchies with very little apparent good coming of it; we see vast machinery for production, and destitution in the midst of it; we hear vulgarisation of taste applauded under the name of education; profligacy of manners acclaimed as an advance of civilisation; trifling amusements and unnecessary luxuries heralded as a rise in the 'standard of living'; and there are at least two million among us who have every excuse for thinking that they are not wanted at all. We have better chances of health than our predecessors, we have immense opportunities for leisure, we are better informed, and I think we have just as good brains and just as much good will; yet we seem at times to be labouring to perfect small parts – or at least to keep them going – of a vast machine which works very badly in performing some function which is unknown to us, if it have any function at all.

ULTIMATELY A RELIGIOUS PROBLEM

I believe that all our problems turn out ultimately to be a religious problem. Its most pressing form, probably, is the economic problem; but economic questions depend finally upon moral questions, as morals depend upon religion. Theology is, of course, the one fundamental science. But in putting the matter so bluntly I by no means suggest that the problem is simple, or its solution only a matter of godliness. I shall not say much directly about Christianity; but in all that I say I shall speak from the point of view of orthodox Christianity. At least, I *aim* at orthodoxy. For heresy, which consists in emphasising one aspect of the mystery to the exclusion of the other, is a natural tendency of the mind; a complete living orthodoxy is (except through the infusion of exceptional grace) almost impossible to the frail human being at every moment of his life; which is one reason why the Church is necessary. My point of view will be implicit throughout, but I am not addressing only those who share it, or those who might be converted to it. I feel, however, that my only slight hope of saying anything worth listening to is to present myself as a churchman, a writer of verses, and a literary critic; and to set the problems before you as they have affected me in my own narrow experience of living.

If you have any doubt that your problems and their solution must bring you to matters of religion, you have only to turn east-[383]ward – towards Russia. I know very little about Russia; I do not know whether the experiment being made there will turn out to be, in the worldly sense, a failure or a success. If the system can be made to work, and if the Russians can be adapted to it, or bred into the sort of being who can flourish under it, that is their affair. But I should not like it any the better for that: for Russian communism is a religion, and a religion which is not mine. Of course, other and better qualified critics – among them Mr Maynard Keynes – have remarked this fact before; and it is indeed patent enough; but the full implications do not seem to me to have yet come home to all. If you *like* the Russian religion, I cannot expect to make any impression upon you. But if you do not like it, then you must keep in mind that you can never fight a religion except with another religion. That is not a very novel thought either, but again, people do not seem to be very eager to act upon it. If we are incapable of a faith at least as strong as that which appears to animate the ruling class of Russia, if we are incapable of dying for a cause, then Western Europe and the Americans might as well be reorganised on the Moscow model at once. And you cannot hope to conquer merely with election cockades; merely with British Conservatism or British Liberalism or British Socialism. Nor will you succeed in inventing another brand new religion to compete with communism. There can only be the two, Christianity and communism: and there, if you like, is your dilemma. For dilemma is defined in the *Concise Oxford Dictionary* as 'a position which leaves only a choice between equal evils', and I fear that the majority of us do not want to choose either; at least, we do not want to go very far in either direction.

In speaking of Russian communism in this way I have one fear at the back of my mind, which I think I may as well utter frankly. I am afraid of exciting the approval of people whose approval I do not especially want. For those to whom communism means primarily inconvenience, discomfort, poverty and privation, and the absence of social seasons and fixtures, I have nothing of interest to say. To those to whom communism means barricades and machine guns, I can only say that the ends to be achieved by violence are what matter more than violence itself. With those to whom communism means forced labour and timber camps, I can sympathise; but must add that if we are to criticise conditions abroad we must first look well to conditions at home.

THE CHRISTIAN ORGANISATION OF SOCIETY

I have thought it best to put the problem from the very start as a religious problem, instead of leaving that to develop later. For I knew that some of you would foresee what I was coming to, and say to yourselves: 'This solution is merely that we should go to church regularly, and communicate at least once a year, and repeat the creeds and respect the bishops.' And this criticism I wished to forestall: that is not what I mean at all. I am not here concerned with the conversion of the world to Christianity, but with the organisation of the world in a Christian way, which is quite another aspect. The former would no doubt, when complete in the individual as well as in the mass, bring about the latter; but that is a state of affairs which has never yet been known; whereas during a long period of time Europe was, in fact, organised in a Christian way. It was certainly a very imperfect way of being imperfectly Christian. I do not want to be classified as a 'medievalist'. To erect a Christian state, a state among Christian states, we should need now a very different temper from that either of medievalism or of ordinary conservatism. We are in many ways in a position of advantage over our medieval ancestors: we are more humane, cleaner and have better table manners; we may be less saintly than some, but we are less beastly than others; we have material comforts, hygiene, machinery and invention, which we do not wish to dispense with but to manipulate wisely. The forms of social organisation in Christian states in the Middle Ages provide much from which we may learn, but little that we can exactly reproduce. We are more civilised than our ancestors, though we ought to be a great deal more civilised than we are, and they have perhaps more reason to be proud of what they did with their talent than we have. Because, instead of preserving, affirming and refining their spiritual organisation of society we have progressively secularised it, until our values are at war with each other and with life itself.

MORE OPPORTUNITY FOR TRUE FREEDOM

Now the Christian organisation of society is an ideal towards the realisation of which non-Christians can co-operate. What must no doubt deter many people of goodwill at the outset, when they hear such a phrase as 'the Christian organisation of a society', is the fear of losing their liberty; the bogey of domination by some ecclesiastical hierarchy either fanatically sincere or hypocritically self-seeking. They are repelled by the harsh necessity, which they fear may be imposed upon them whether they *see* its necessity or no, of the Christian doctrine of marriage; their imaginations may even begin to play about history-book memories like 'pardons and indulgences'. It is possible that in some respects we have now too much liberty – or, I would say, too much license; it is possible that very few people have a true notion of what true liberty is; but the kind of organisation I have in mind should give more liberty than we have now; more freedom of choice, more opportunity for all to obtain the real *goods* of life. I have no expectation and no desire to enforce the non-Christian to obey rules of life in which he cannot believe; I should only wish to persuade him, by practical results, that that rule of life is better than his own, if he has any.

For, indeed, we live in a world in which true liberty declines. Life becomes more precarious, too, without the freedom which makes precariousness tolerable: I mean the freedom and opportunity for adventure. If we have an income above the barest subsistence, we must give a fourth or a fifth to the State. A shift in the exchanges, and those of us who should travel can no longer afford to travel; at any moment, in a modern State, your food may cost you more or your wages may be worth less. The man with a job is in terror of losing it; and of those without a job he is the least unhappy who can most readily resign himself to apathy. We have comfort without grandeur, and amusement without recreation (remember what the word 'recreation' means!). If we have liberty, what is it that we have liberty to do? The Russian must resign his liberty in favour of the Russian State, or in favour of a phantom world-State; and in return, I understand, he is assigned a certain extent of licence. I should prefer to resign my liberty, if I must, in favour of something better than that; but the Russian at least resigns his liberty in favour of *something*.

To the baser minded, in the modern world, liberty, as I have suggested, tends to be tantamount to mere licence. The more intellectual experience more refined temptations; some of them are those, sometimes among the most gifted and the most conspicuous, who value so highly what seems to them intellectual liberty that they refuse to believe in anything. For that is a definite refusal. And in their own interest, being what they are, they are right, for to have a passionate conviction about anything is like falling in love: it is not merely to risk being ridiculous (and such people are afraid of being ridiculous, though nothing makes a man more ridiculous really than the fear of ridicule); it is to surrender oneself to something, to surrender liberty, the liberty of thinking irresponsibly. The chief liberty of man, however, is the liberty to choose what master he shall serve. '*Know ye not, that to whom ye yield yourselves servants to obey, his servants ye are to whom ye obey; whether of sin unto death, or of obedience unto righteousness.*'

THE CHRISTIAN SCHEME CAN NEVER WORK PERFECTLY

Towards any profound conviction one is borne gradually, perhaps insensibly over a long period of time, by what Newman called 'powerful and concurrent reasons'. Some of these reasons may appear to the outside world irrelevant; some are purely personal; and each individual, perhaps, has some reasons which could concern, some influences which could have influenced, no one but himself. At some moment or other, a kind of crystallisation occurs, in which appears an element of *faith* not strictly definable from any reason or combination of reasons. I am not speaking, mind you, of conversion to Christian faith only, but of conversion in general; there are some interesting remarks on the subject of conversion in a book by the great French novelist Stendhal entitled *On the Subject of Love*. In my own case, I believe that one of the reasons was that the Christian scheme seemed to me the only one which would work. I hasten to add that this is not a reason for believing; it is a tenable hypothesis to maintain that there is *no* scheme which will work. That was simply the removal of any reason for believing in anything else, the erasure of a prejudice, the arrival at the scepticism which is the preface to conversion. And when I say 'work', I am quite aware that I had my own notion of what the 'working' of a scheme comprehends. Among other things, the Christian scheme seemed the only possible scheme which found a place for values which I must maintain or perish (and belief comes first and practice second), the belief, for instance, in holy living and holy dying, in sanctity, chastity, humility, austerity. And it is in favour of the Christian scheme, from the Christian point of view, that it never has, and never will, work perfectly. No perfect scheme can work perfectly with imperfect men; if the Russian scheme ever comes to 'work' perfectly with what *I* call imperfect men, then to me the Russian system will be condemned by its very efficiency. You can eliminate the difficulties of the individual by eliminating individuality; original sin, by eliminating sinners. But no system that continues to repeat, and must repeat, the words '*be ye perfect*' can be expected to work perfectly. Nor can a system which respects free will, the right of the human being to choose whether to serve sin unto death, or obedience unto righteousness.

Mr Harold Monro: A Poet and his Ideal

The Times, 46084 (17 Mar. 1932), 16. Unsigned. Not in Gallup, but would be C330a.

Mr Harold Monro, a distinguished poet and man of letters, died on Tuesday, the day after his fifty-third birthday, at a nursing home at Broadstairs. His death will be mourned not only by admirers of his own verse, but by all England who have cared seriously, during the last 30 years, for serious poetry.

Both his father and his maternal grandfather were engineers. He was born at Brussels, and was educated partly abroad, so that he spoke French, German, and Italian fluently, and at Radley, whence he went up to Caius. After taking his degree at Cambridge he spent much time on the Continent for several years. One of the results was *The Chronicle of a Pilgrimage* (1909), the prose account of a walking tour from Paris to Milan; but he had already published a volume of poems in 1906 and two in 1907. His importance in the literary life of London dates from 1911, when he founded, in conjunction with the Poetry Society, the *Poetry Review*, in the first number of which (January, 1912) he affirmed that 'Poetry should be, once more, seriously and reverently discussed in its relation to life, and the same tests and criteria applied to it as to the other arts.' Difficulties arose, and Monro retired at the end of a year. In March, 1913, Monro issued the first number of another periodical to be entirely under his own direction entitled *Poetry and Drama*, which survived with distinction until December, 1914. In the first number are contributions by Rupert Brooke, Edward Thomas, Sir Henry Newbolt, Maurice Hewlett, James Elroy Flecker, and Lascelles Abercrombie; and in other numbers there was hardly any young poet or man of letters of any talent who was not a contributor.

Monro's enthusiasm next led him to found the Poetry Bookshop, for which he took an old house in a small street off Theobald's-lane. It was discovered by most readers of poetry in London, and became a place of pilgrimage for American visitors; and its removal to the more commonplace neighbourhood of Willoughby-street, Great Russell-street, was regretted. Monro then started the series of Poetry Readings which have continued almost without interruption. Of the poets who were well known when the Readings began, and of those who have become known since, there can be few who have not given readings of their own poetry, or of their favourite poets, either at the first or the present dwelling of the Bookshop. Monro's own taste was sympathetic both to the 'Georgian' poetry, which flourished just before the War, and to the more modern poetry which has risen since. His own verse had something of this mediating character. He had – what is none too common among verse writers – a steady capacity for improvement; and his latest poems are considered by good judges to be his best. The development is already evident in *Strange Meetings* (1917); it continues in *Real Property* (1922), and in *The Earth for Sale* (1928) and a poem published recently in the *Criterion* indicates that his development had not reached a climax. Throughout, however, there is a quality peculiar to himself; a way of giving to the familiar and commonplace a dreamlike and sometimes nightmarish character which is unlike the mode of either his earlier or his later colleagues.

While his poetry will remain to justify itself, his importance in the literary life of London in his time may be overlooked. As editor, as publisher, and as the proprietor of the Poetry Bookshop his efforts were wholly disinterested, and indeed meant much sacrifice of his private means. He was more concerned that other people should write poetry, that able writers in difficulties should be helped to write, and that a larger public should read and enjoy poetry, than he was concerned with what he wrote himself. One of the causes dearest to his heart was the instigation of sociability among men of letters, and to this he devoted his own social gifts. In the few years before the War he was active in keeping poets of diverse gifts in friendly contact; among them the group – including Ezra Pound, F. S. Flint, Richard Aldington, and H. D. – who produced *The Imagist Anthology*, and in his circle was included T. E. Hulme, who, after his death in action in 1917, has had a great influence upon the philosophical and critical theory of the present time. After the War he resumed his efforts, with what was left of his own generation, and with recruits from the younger generation. He had a great gift of hospitality, and was happiest when providing a fireside at which writers with common sympathies could sit and talk until late hours of the night. Such devotion to such an ideal as his – the ideal of poetry and of fraternity among poets – is rare always, and nowadays difficult to pursue. Even in the last year or two, when crippled by increasing ill-health and pain, Monro never lost faith in his ideal. He was twice married, and had one son by his first marriage. His second wife was Miss Alida Klemantaski.

The funeral will be at Golders Green on Saturday at 11.30.

Religion and Science: A Phantom Dilemma

Listener, 7. 167 (23 Mar. 1932), 428–9. Subheaded 'By T. S. ELIOT.' Gallup C331.
At head of title: 'The Modern Dilemma'.

'It is not science that has destroyed religious belief', suggests
Mr Eliot, 'but our preference of unbelief that has made
illegitimate use of science.'

Last week I was concerned chiefly, in a general way, with the 'dilemma' of Christianity and Communism. But the dilemma which presents itself to more people is the supposed dilemma of Religion *versus* Science. If my first dilemma, Christianity and Communism, is real – as I firmly believe it is – then it follows that the second dilemma, Religion and Science, is a phantom. For if the real dilemma is between one religion and another, we can hardly have, on top of that, another dilemma between religion and science. Too many dilemmas would certainly spoil my broth, and I hope at least to raise the question in your minds, whether the conundrum 'Religion or Science?' has any more meaning than the famous riddle which vexed Alice: 'Why is a raven like a writing desk?' The immediate response will be, I dare say: 'You are juggling with words. The sense in which you call Communism a religion, if justifiable at all, is not the sense in which Christianity is a religion. Science is only in conflict with the traditional religions such as Christianity, Judaism, Buddhism, Islam and the sects of India; it is perfectly in accord with a religion (if you call it that) which denies the "supernatural". That is to say, it is perfectly in accord with Communism.'

SCIENCE AT DISCORD WITH ITSELF

Well, to begin with – in the hope that I have put this reply to myself fairly – science can hardly be in accord with Communism until it is in accord with itself. Not only the various Christian divisions, but all of the great religions I have named, are in accord on something: they all accept what we call the supernatural. But nowadays science, by which we must mean various eminent scientists, does not seem to be in accord on any religious question. Two or three eminent mathematicians and physicists whom I have in mind hold widely divergent views; two or three psychologists, equally eminent in their own profession, differ just as widely from each other; and there is no manner of concord between the conclusions of physicists and psychologists.

And secondly, if you say: 'But if you call Communism a religion, it is a scientific religion in that it denies the supernatural and is solidly based upon what is observable in this world', then I must say that the term 'scientific religion' is just nonsense: the moment the emotions are engaged upon a goal to be reached, an entity to be adored, we have leapt a chasm separating religion from science. What, for instance, is 'propaganda' – something highly developed, I understand, in Soviet Russia, and also highly developed, though often for less creditable purposes, in Western Europe and America? It is merely the art of manipulating what we might call, in 'scientific' terminology, the 'lower religious centres'. Once everybody has had a thorough grounding in 'science', it will become impossible to wheedle anybody into any course of action: for science can never tell us what is ultimately [429] desirable. 'The dictatorship of the proletariat' is a fine politico-religious phrase. It seduces the multitude, because it persuades each, *qua* individual, that he or she will get something out of it. That is not a religious sentiment. It seduces the few to genuine sacrifice, by giving them religious satisfaction; for the proletariat becomes then a synonym for God. To sum up: anything which requires genuine self-sacrifice tends toward a religion.

WHAT REALLY INFLUENCES BELIEF

We have yet to attack the subject of the destructive influence of scientific enquiry upon religious belief. The influence of scientific advance upon the popular mind, in the last few hundred years, has undoubtedly been very great; but why and how this influence has been exerted is by no means a simple problem. A tendency towards belief in a mechanistic, as contrasted with a religious universe, is present in the work of two men who were certainly not aware of this implication of their thought. Francis Bacon and René Descartes in the seventeenth century were pious men, or at least assumed the appearance of piety; and they would have shrunk from the conclusion that they were preparing a world with no God in it. It was not as scientists, but as philosophers theorising about science, that they influenced belief. And here is what I think you will find everywhere: that no scientific discovery influences people either for or against revealed religion, except in so far as there already exists an atmosphere either favourable or unfavourable to religion. In the case of the individual scientist there are two influences: first, he may find that an acceptance of revealed religion, or, as the case may be, a rejection of it, is for himself at his moment of time the most convenient state of mind for the pursuit of his investigations; second, he may employ his scientific knowledge in support of an emotional state which he probably shares with many other people. My old master, Josiah Royce, now mostly forgotten but a great philosopher in his day, wrote a paper which I wish I might read again, in which he instanced the frequent occasions on which philosophical theory anticipated and prepared the way for scientific discovery. My own contention is, that mankind is usually prepared to interpret any scientific discovery that may come in one way rather than another. It is generally assumed that any scientific discovery *must* have some important bearing upon our conception of the universe – not merely the physical universe but the spiritual universe as well – and ultimately upon our conduct and our emotional life. It very often does, but chiefly because we take it for granted that it will. The assumption is very rarely challenged; nevertheless, I see no reason for accepting it.

'A PROGRESSIVE SPIRITUAL DETERIORATION'

How then has it come about that religious faith has altered and weakened since the Middle Ages, until it is no longer the rule and standard of social as well as individual life, but a mere extra, like French and Music, which a minority of people treat themselves to? To answer this question satisfactorily I should need not only a great deal more space than I have, but infinitely more detailed knowledge. I can only call it dogmatically a progressive spiritual deterioration. Yet it seems a deterioration which in some unfathomable way – for here we touch on the deepest mysteries of suffering and sin – was necessary: necessary at times that humanity should worship false gods and demi-gods, though how to square that with the salvation of individual souls I do not know. Better to say, perhaps, that even the wisest of human beings is so muddleheaded, without God, that he cannot destroy an evil without destroying some good, or grasp at some good without grasping at some evil; the wheat never grows without the tares. We needed free enquiry; we needed an atmosphere in which the several sciences could flourish and develop: we needed invention and machinery. Had we – I mean our ancestors for twelve or fifteen generations, and we must bear the responsibility for our ancestors, for we are of them and they are in us – been better men, we could have got all these advantages without giving up the good things that we have given up: I say, as I said last week, the belief in holy living and holy dying, in sanctity, chastity, humility, austerity, asceticism, the belief in Tragedy – not pagan Tragedy, but Christian Tragedy. If we (using 'we' as I have just used it) had been good enough, we could have had the benefits of science, invention, medicine, and hygiene, and all the good things that the last three hundred years have brought us, without giving up any goods. But there seem to be times when the bath water gets so bad that if we are not clever enough to remove the baby first, then the baby really has to go too. The actual question is: now we have gained these benefits, are we worthy to use them?

NEITHER OBSTACLE, NOR SUPPORT

If what I suggest is true, that it is not science that has destroyed religious belief, but our preference of unbelief that has made illegitimate use of science, then it clearly follows that we should be ready to decline politely any support which a more modern science may offer to religion. This is the peril of our own brief moment. The sort of people who are swayed now to believe that 'after all, there is a something' are exactly the same mob which was swayed to believe that, after all, there is not anything. Please understand that I am not criticising the attitudes of the eminent scientists themselves; nor am I criticising their more popular books, which even I can understand in part, and some of which I have read with pleasure and I hope profit. I instance Sir James Jeans's *The Mysterious Universe* and Professor Eddington's *Science and the Unseen World*. I am only criticising an uncritical attitude of the public towards these writers and their books, an attitude shared, I am sorry to say, sometimes by theological writers who ought to know better. What are we to make of the sympathy with religion avowed by several distinguished scientists? As autobiography of interesting men, such work is itself of great interest; as an admission of the limitation of science it is invaluable. It goes to show that outside of their special field men of science are just ignorant men like ourselves, with no better clue to the mystery than we have. And that makes them all the more likeable. If they proceed to erect some positive theological scheme of their own, they are indulging an eccentricity, and become a little comic, though not so comic as I should be if I tried to improve upon the quantum theory in physics.

But it is clear that the popular attitude of hailing modern physical science as a *support* of religion is very misguided. To remove an obstacle is not the same thing as to raise a support. It is just the same old superstition of science: you are continuing to make the natural sciences the key to ultimate truth, though the key now unlocks a different door. For to most of us science is at best a faith, and at worst a superstition; most of us do not *know* any more science than we should have done had we lived three thousand years ago. We do not understand Einstein's views any better than we understand those of St Augustine or St Athanasius. I dare say that we are impressed by the certainly impressive practical results of scientific enquiry; but engineering and plant-breeding are no clue to ultimate truth; and the genius and ingenuity which have gone to build up the machinery by which I am speaking to you are no guarantee that what I am saying is worth listening to.

The history of the last two hundred years does, I think, bear out my contention that the movement away from Christianity came before scientific discovery, and merely made use of it; so that what we want to do now is not to make use of it for another purpose, in the same way, but to see that we must dispense with it. And that would be a great benefit. For if we understand that religion has nothing to lose and nothing to gain by the progress of science, then we are at every moment prepared to give up some cherished belief, such as the belief in the movement of the sun around the earth, which we had previously thought belonged to religion and now find belongs only to science. There are certain dogmas which cannot be given up; it is possible that we still hold some beliefs as part of our faith which really belong only to immature science. We have had superstition in religion and we have had superstition in science; we can do without both.

A QUESTION OF DESIRE

What I wish to insist upon is not so much that speculative science cannot cure our maladies of thought and will, but the other aspect: that the advance of scientific knowledge is *not* the cause of them – not, at any rate, the rational cause. It may, incidentally, have disturbed our scale of values and often made us mistake the means for the end; but in my opinion mechanical invention has affected our inner as well as our outer lives far more than the free enquiry of natural science. But even mechanical invention – though its unrestrained exploitation by the human race which has not yet proved itself adult enough to be trusted with the control of such engines is perhaps the immediate cause of our actual difficulties – is secondary. What really makes the difference is not reason at all, but desire.

It is very difficult at this point to avoid obscurity and misunderstanding. I do not mean that either belief or scepticism is essentially irrational. The intellectual case for Christianity is very strong indeed, and one which demands a great deal of study; and to be quite fair, there is a good case to be made out for atheism as well. But it is not hard thinking which causes such a thing as the gradual drift away from Christianity during the last few centuries, but rather following a line of least resistance. Many people assume that, if the Christian faith had been true, Europe would have stuck to it; and the reason why the majority of people, in the most civilised countries, have drifted away from it, must be that it is not true. But this belief goes together with another crude faith, the faith that progress in enlightenment and civilisation is something automatic, that to improve from generation to generation is natural to man; and when doubt is cast on this belief that things will get better just of themselves, people are apt to fall back into despair. But civilisation is a much more complicated thing than that. We know perfectly well that at various times and in various places civilisation has been more highly developed, in some of its most essential values, than it is now. At nearly every stage in history we can discern that something is being gained, and something being lost. As the world goes on, therefore, the word 'civilisation' comes to mean more and more: because it means all the things that we have gained, and want to keep, and also all the good things that we have lost, and want to regain.

The Search for Moral Sanction

Listener, 7. 168 (30 Mar. 1932), [445]–6, 480. Subheaded 'By T. S. ELIOT' Gallup C332. At head of title: 'The Moral Dilemma'. In the paragraph headed 'Limitations of Eugenics' 'force of the results' has been emended to 'force or the results'.

> *'Men and women must seek for moral sanction for their behaviour; and when they no longer seek to act in accordance with a divine will, they must seek to act in accordance at least with some scientific law.'*

I want this week to touch upon the effect of the progress of biological and psychological science upon conduct, and upon the effect of scientific invention upon social life. First of all, I do not propose to say anything sensational, or to indulge in any rhetoric of denunciation of modern morals; that attitude has already been well exploited in the press. I see no reason for supposing that morals are much worse than they used to be, or that young people are less virtuous than the old were. Manners certainly have improved; and manners are a part of morals. There seems to me no reason for worrying about actual conduct or misconduct: what is interesting, for our purpose, is the search for moral sanction, for *reasons* for behaving in one way rather than another, by earnest people who have given up Christian faith, and also by Christians who feel that traditional morality must be in some ways altered by the advance of knowledge. And this is why I wish to touch upon psychology.

ASSERTIONS OF PSYCHOLOGY

Modern psychology or psycho-analysis received its impulse from work at the French school for mental disorders at Nancy, and from the great French psychiatrists Charcot and Ribot and Janet; but French psychology has for the most part confined itself prudently to the cure of cases, and left the more surprising developments to take place elsewhere. With the successes or failures of the several types of psychology in curing advanced cases of disorder, I am not here concerned. It is only when the psychologists tend to persuade us, first that we are all ill in mind, next that we all need to acquire something of their science in order to understand each other and ourselves, and finally that psychology will supply that guide and rule of conduct which the Christian faith used to give, and still does give to some; it is only when these three assertions appear that the modern dilemma is engaged.

To begin with, I do not deny any of these assertions out and out. Almost none of us, if any, is so 'well' as he might be. That is a perfectly Christian truth. There are, I know and believe, unexplored possibilities of physical, mental, and particularly spiritual, development. And therefore psychology, which is interested and which awakens interest in these possibilities, is helpful. And I recognise further, that if you have not the Christian faith, if you are not prepared to live by it to the best of your ability and to study it throughout your life, and if you are serious enough minded to want something to live by, then you must pin your hopes on psychology. For in one aspect, psychology represents a protest against the mere 'outwardness' of some modern dilutions of Christianity, especially in Protestant countries. To maintain certain periodic observances, to attend church regularly on Sundays, taking a 'sitting' as it is called, or if prosperous enough a whole pew, to give reasonably to a selected number of trustworthy charities, and to obey some decalogue of prohibitions; that used to represent, in English-speaking countries, the whole duty of a Christian, except to be industrious and make as much money as possible. Now the [446] human spirit does rebel against anything so arid, and forgets, or does not know, that that against which it is rebelling is only a mutilated part of true Christianity. It is right and important that people should investigate their own minds; that they should be fearless in searching out, and confessing (if only to themselves) their hidden desires and motives, and that they should use this knowledge for self-improvement.

HANDMAID TO THEOLOGY

Psychology, in short, has very great utility in two ways. It can revive, and has already to some extent revived, truths long since known to Christianity, but mostly forgotten and ignored, and it can put them in a form and a language understandable by modern people to whom the language of Christianity is not only dead but undecipherable. (It is a mistake to suppose that people understand ideas best when they are put most simply; they understand them best when they are put in the language they are familiar with, even if it is the language of Hollywood.) But I must add that I think psychology can do more than this, in discovering more about the human soul still; for I do not pretend that there is nothing more to know; the possibilities of knowledge are practically endless. Psychology is an indispensable handmaid to theology; but, I think, a very poor housekeeper. And it is unfortunate that so many eminent psychologists of our day have been either indifferent or hostile to Christianity, and in either case not very well acquainted with it; and that they have deliberately tried to do without it.

DANGERS OF DETERMINISM

I will mention two bad effects of psychology at its present stage. For the first, I can give a concrete example. A priest of my acquaintance, who was for a time chaplain in a prison, told me of a woman there who reappeared again and again, a few months after serving her sentence, for odds and ends of petty thefts and misdeeds, all of a trifling nature. When he tried to reason with her and show her that this line of conduct was wasteful and unprofitable, she replied with complacency and even pride, that she had been carefully examined by a doctor, who told her that she had a 'complex' which made her do these things. She spoke of a 'complex' as if it had been a guardian angel; and indeed it did more for her than a guardian angel, because it absolved her from all responsibility and gave her a sense of dignity and importance. This is an extreme case, and may sound like a parody. But it does indicate the danger of the 'deterministic' tendency of some psychology. Determinism means here simply: 'I am not responsible for being what I am; when I was a small child something happened to me which caused all the trouble; my parents were the guilty parties then, and society in general is the guilty party now'.

Now 'determinism' is all very well as a guiding principle for the scientist in his researches; but beyond a point it won't work – like most other non-Christian principles. And this encouragement of irresponsibility is related to another menace of modern psychology: a tendency to accept as the most real emotions those which are, or which may be, the most primitive. One school emphasises, or did at one time, sexual desire; and with its Oedipus complex introduced Original Sin in an original form. (To have to deal with Original Sin when you don't believe that there is such a thing as sin is rather a problem.) Now so far as it went, this was a good thing. To know oneself, that is good, and it is a lesson in humility to learn how primitive we are. 'Liberation', so far as it means complete self-knowledge, is a good thing; but it does not follow that all of our suppressed desires should be satisfied, and to talk of sublimating them is to put things upside down. 'Sublimation' in effect means, I think, just substitution; and there is no substitute for anything. It means, in simple language, something like this: Suppose that my trouble is diagnosed as a suppressed craving for caviare. Well, that's something, to know what the cause of the trouble is. But I have not the money to buy enough caviare to satisfy the craving. I can, however, cultivate a taste for playing the flute or cross-country running. But in my own experience I have never been able to deal with any of my low appetites or vulgar tastes in this way. I have perceived their transience, their unsatisfactoriness, and the horror of satiety which is far beyond the famine of deprivation; but I have never known a desire to be expelled by anything but another desire. And psychology seems to me for the most part to ignore the more intense, profound and satisfying emotions of religion. It must ignore their value, because its function is merely to describe and not to express preference. But if this is true, it can never take the place of religion, though it can be an important accessory.

LIMITATIONS OF EUGENICS

With certain psychological theories I am strongly in sympathy, because they seem to me to be fundamentally Christian; but for anything but religion – supernatural religion – to take the place of religion is highly dangerous. It is the same tendency as we have found in communism (and in the political field there is more excuse for it) and we find it also in the science of eugenics: the pursuit of the mirage of the Earthly Paradise – the illusion that we can be made happy and perfect by the application of legislation or force or the results of scientific discovery. Now eugenics, we must all agree, has already done a great deal for our material well-being: it has helped to provide us with a number of perfect animals and plants for various purposes, it has made wheat grow in climates where no wheat grew before, and so forth. Furthermore, it will have, we hope, when more highly developed, much to teach us about the breeding of human beings. It can help us deal better with those unfortunate members of the community who ought not to breed at all. But I think the hopes of some eugenists have been set too high, and some have advocated what many of us regard as very dubious short cuts to the improvement of the race. A few remarks will suffice. When we breed animals we know exactly what we want; the specialist in such matters has a pretty clear notion of his 'perfect' bull or pig or ear of corn; but what *is* our idea of the perfect human being? We can at best hope to arrest the propagation of characters universally recognised as undesirable. And even so, at least one eminent biologist holds that the propagation of feeble-minded persons who are the offspring of feeble-minded parents is very small indeed, and that every one of us has, so to speak, elements of imbecility in us, as well as of other undesirable characters, which may combine with similar elements in the other parent. But what is most obvious is the danger of the methods of improving the race advocated by some of those who are wholly emancipated from Christian morality.

WHERE SCIENCE LETS YOU DOWN

It is, however, not only natural, but right, that when people have ceased to hold any Christian faith they should begin to question Christian morality; and I think it extremely difficult, if not rationally impossible, for any unbeliever who can think intelligently and independently for himself to remain attached to Christian morals. I am sure that I could not. But the mind does really abhor disorder; men and women must seek for some sanction for their behavior; and when they no longer seek to act in accordance with a divine will, they must seek to act in accordance at least with some scientific law. It is so easy, too, to believe that the restrictions of Christianity are merely a barrier to happiness and a cause of misery; so easy, so natural, when we have some particular case of such misery before our eyes. And in the end society has given up some greater good, which it could not appreciate while it had it, for some lesser good which turns out, when divorced from the greater, to be no good at all. Without [480] the love of God there is no love at all. And so, finally, science lets you down.

WE NEED A NEW ECONOMIC THEORY

There is certainly one department of science which most people will agree has let us down. I mean that of mechanical invention. It has even become a bogey employed to make our flesh creep: witness Mr Aldous Huxley's latest novel *Brave New World* and some of the gloomy predictions of Lord Russell. Time was when every important invention was hailed almost like the arrival of a Messiah; when we could be cheerfully assured that all the workmen displaced by machines could be found work again by the very machinery which was taking their place. The obvious menaces of scientific invention are two. One is the social danger of machinery of comfort and pleasure to the consumer. There is the danger of mechanised pleasure – pleasure which gives the enjoyer less and less trouble to procure, and which requires less and less co-operation on his part, pleasure which can be enjoyed passively and stupidly. I do not know how much pleasure is enjoyed by the man who drives a car the machinery of which he understands no better than he does his own stomach, in a stream of similar cars along a monotonous road on a Sunday afternoon. But one effect of the motor-car has been to facilitate a tendency already discernible. Just as the centre of human life is the family, so the social unit is the village. One characteristic of London which makes it, to me, preferable to any other metropolis in the world that I know, is that it is still to a great extent, a collection of villages the borders of which touch, each retaining a local character of its own. Do not reply that a number of the London villages I have in mind are scandalously filthy and ought to be torn down; I know that quite well, and I am not simply indulging a taste for the picturesque slum. But when I see the tendency for the village to be replaced, not by the suburb, for which there is much to be said, but by an endless line of houses along a ribbon road over which passes a ceaseless stream of cars, I wonder what sort of organic unity can be left, what sort of local patriotism and activity fostered.

But from the point of view of the producer the situation is still more pernicious. It is now a commonplace of economics, apprehensible by the dullest of us, that the more machines you have, the more destitution you will get. The more easily and cheaply goods can be produced, the less manual labour required, the fewer people there are who can buy them, because they have not the money which can only be got by working. But the weavers who wanted to destroy the looms were right only in a wrong condition of society. I do not want to see machinery destroyed, but only to repeat that a machine age requires a fresh economic theory, and a fresh economic theory requires a fresh viewpoint in morals, and a fresh viewpoint in morals must get back to the foundations of morals. The old law said that those who *will* not work shall not eat; but it has no application to those who cannot, who have not the opportunity to work. Note that the very word 'work' has altered its meaning in an industrial society. Truly, for me, 'work' means work primarily for the benefit of others and for the community as a whole; and such work includes giving pleasure or amusement to others. Nowadays 'work' means rather making money; either a little money by tending a machine, or more money by manipulating money. With such a doctrine of work, you will have, as the chief alternative, idleness; where the alternative should be *leisure*. And in the present state of society, we have an extraordinary muddle of social and moral values. There are those who still feel socially, and therefore morally, superior because they do not have to work: that is, because they are on a dole provided for them by the work or by the good luck of their fathers and grandfathers. There are others who denounce such members of society, with great moral indignation, as parasites. Both points of view are wrong: there is no difference whatever between those who live on the income provided by their ancestors and those who live on the income provided by the State. They are all useful members of the community in so far as they can consume what the workers produce; the trouble is that they cannot, among the lot of them, consume enough, because they have not the money to pay for it; and as things are, the money is not there to give them.

WHAT IS MACHINERY FOR?

One effect of industrialisation is that many of those who have work must work too hard or too long, and most of those who have no work must be idle. It is obvious that the machine must be neither abolished nor prevented from further development and improvement, but controlled. I do not say that there is too much machinery; and perhaps before we reach that point we shall be too poor to build more. But we need to ask the question: What is machinery for? Perhaps we have too much for some purposes and too little for others. In some ways machinery degrades taste and sets up unnatural values. Of the majority of people who could afford either a motor-car or a really fine painting (I assume that neither is a necessity), how many would choose the painting? A motor-car is a greater help in keeping up appearances with one's neighbors than an oil painting is. And machine-making is an industry with which art cannot compete: for the maker of machinery finds himself obliged to make as many machines as possible, not because they are needed, but to keep the factory going. Thus we make machines to sell abroad to people who will use them in order to make for themselves things which they used to import from us!

Such instances could be accumulated indefinitely. Do not suppose that I think I have made any discovery, or that I pretend to be saying anything new: I am merely repeating what cannot be repeated too often. We have to-day a system, or lack of a system, which Christianity cannot possibly accept. And we need a kind of economics which will ask the question: Why? What is it good to do? And to answer this question we must find out what is the meaning of 'Good'.

A Commentary

C., 11. 44 (Apr. 1932), 467–73. Signed 'T. S. E.' Gallup C333.

I have again been reading a number of small books, pamphlets and articles of a 'revolutionary' nature; I find that younger people with whom I talk have, not exactly revolutionary ideas, but rather a yearning towards revolutionary ideas of some kind. Indeed, those who prefer things to be much as they are, including practising politicians in and out of power, and Fabians, may take comfort from the multiplicity of revolutions which seem to cancel each other. But what chiefly interests me at the moment is the general interest, not so much in economics, as in what Péguy would have called *la mystique* of economics; the mixture, which may easily be a muddle, of economic theory, humanitarian enthusiasm, and religious fervour. That is the subject of the present note.

Sympathy with communism seems to me to have three important elements: observed facts, respect for what appears to be the most or even the only 'scientific' theory about them, and pleasurable emotions of a religious type. These elements fortify each other to a very high degree, and are with difficulty distinguished. About certain very serious facts no one can dissent. The present system does not work properly, and more and more people are inclined to believe both that it never did and that it never will; and it is obviously neither scientific nor religious. It is imperfectly adapted to every purpose except that of making money; and even for money-making it does not work very well, for its rewards are neither conducive to social justice nor even proportioned to intellectual ability. It is well adapted to speculation and usury, which are the lowest forms of mental activity; and it rewards well those who can cozen and corrupt the crowd. Dislike of disorder unites with humanitarian zeal to inflame discontent: and humanitarian zeal when uncontrolled by the discipline of an exact religious faith, is always dangerous and sometimes pernicious. Secondly, no one who is seriously concerned can [468] fail to be impressed by the work of Karl Marx. He is, of course, much more cited than read; but his power is so great, and his analysis so profound, that it must be very difficult for anyone who reads him without prejudice on the one hand, or without any definite religious faith on the other, to avoid accepting his conclusions.

But those who are in this way converted to Marxism must also become converts to the religion to which it has given rise; it is the absence of the religious fervour, the complete gentility, which makes the Fabians look to-day so antique. And it is exactly in its religious development that Communism seems to me to collapse and to become something both ludicrous and repulsive. The Theology (so to speak) of Communism is still, I suppose, but imperfectly expounded; and so I am happy to see as a recruit so accomplished a theologian as Mr Middleton Murry. Anyone who has followed attentively the progress of Mr Murry's theological writings cannot fail to be struck by the inevitability of his present position. It was Mr Murry who first perceived the extraordinary resemblance between Jesus Christ and D. H. Lawrence; and it was Mr Murry who first assigned to Judas Iscariot, with sympathy and comprehension, his proper rôle in the drama. It was obvious from Mr Murry's next book that God Himself was under notice to quit; and it is only with relief that we observe that He has finally vacated Mr Murry's premises. And at least as early as January of 1929 Mr Murry showed himself warmly in sympathy with other developments necessary for the emergence of the

New Humanity. Writing in *The Forum* in that month, with his colleague, Dr James Carruthers Young, Mr Murry exclaims:

> It is, indeed, simply untrue that a greater freedom in 'experimental' relations would cheapen marriage. On the contrary, it would help to make marriage more precious, more satisfying, and more permanent. The dogma of original sin still warps our sense of psychological realities. The realities are, first, that men and women do, very ardently, desire to find a companion for life. . . .

[469] And so on. One must admire the skill with which Mr Murry, here, as elsewhere, envelops every utterance with his familiar odour of sanctity; not even the dearest of old ladies could be upset by such sentiments, Mr Murry puts things so nicely. But 'men and women do, very ardently, desire to find a companion for life': I wonder. Don't a good many of them sow an ardent desire for variety? But Mr Murry perhaps knows human nature better than I do; or if human nature isn't like that, Communism will teach us how to change it.

I am not yet quite convinced that Mr Murry can be accepted as an accredited exponent of the Communist religion. He is, to my mind, suspiciously patronising towards his comrades in the faith; and Leninism is all very well in Russia, but won't do in England; and Lenin did not understand Marx so well as Mr Murry does, anyway. I quite agree with Mr Murry about the profound differences between the Russian and the Western European situation; but to me Russian Communism seems merely an attempt to catch up with Western Capitalism, and to imitate some of what are to me its most objectionable habits. In any case, I doubt whether Mr Murry, with his taste for summary evictions, will find Lenin and Stalin as easy to turn out as God the Father.

According to not only Mr Murry, but other exponents, Communism is going, in some way, to tap an inexhaustible reservoir of human emotion upon which we have never before drawn. In Mr Murry's poetic diction – again modulated to the old ladies' ears – 'the love of man for man need beat itself against the bars no more'. A hundred and fifty years ago this love would have aroused a frenzy of enthusiasm under the name of *fraternité*; but our palates have become so jaded, partly from our seeing that word so often on French public buildings, that we need more elaborate food. And at this juncture it is always the goddess Psychology who comes to the aid of new-fledged religions. To be convinced, we must now be told that we are suffering from a [470] collective neurosis: a disease from which we all suffer together, though individually we may remain in apparent health.

The mystical belief in herd-feeling, which had been elevated to a pseudo-science under such names as 'social psychology', is one of the most disquieting superstitions of the day. To the honest freethinker, the heir of eighteenth-century enlightenment, it must seem a deliberate repudiation of civilisation and its responsibilities; to the Christian it must appear a travesty of all that in which he believes. It is apparent in extreme Nationalism, as well as in Communism; and indeed the two do not seem very far apart; even Mr Murry's variety tends to assume a form of British Jingoism. It is a symptom of weakness, but the weakness is only in part pathological; for the rest it is just the essential feebleness and impotence of the individual man which Christianity has always recognised. And being a symptom of weakness, it is also a source of strength; both the fugitive strength of a violent stimulant and the permanent strength of true communion. The craving for some passionate *conviction*, and for a living organic society, assumes odd and often extremely dangerous forms. Man must have something to which he is ready to sacrifice himself; he must, if necessary, sacrifice himself, but he must not be sacrificed. I question whether Communism would leave the individual in possession of enough of himself to sacrifice. Where the willingness towards self-sacrifice is deficient, as in any large indifference to 'patriotism', it is usually that men as individuals do not feel that they are being called upon to sacrifice themselves for anything in which they have an essential interest, but are merely being sacrificed to alien interests: and when I say 'interests', I do not mean only material interests, but ideal interests without which the man feels that he would be less himself. But what, I wonder, is this mass-identity into which our individual consciousnesses are to be merged? Admitted that the ordinary mediocre man maintains his petty and not wholly real individuality by subterfuges and expedients: by [471] money, social position, public distinctions, skill at games and other irrelevances that distinguishes him from his neighbour. The Buddhist may become merged in nirvana; but that is a voluntary extinction, accomplished by the most arduous self-discipline, not a salvation from individuality imposed upon him by society.

One great test of a society is the kind of art it produces. Art in its highest development, both in Europe and in Asia, can hardly exist without a sense of individuality, a sense of tragedy, for which Communism does not seem to leave room. There must be many people like myself, who can be more quickly and completely convinced of the justification of Communism, or of any new form of society, when we are convinced by art instead of philosophising. It is perhaps premature to judge of Russia until a generation has grown to maturity which has never known any condition but settled Bolshevism. I am, unfortunately, incapable of being convinced by the arts of the cinema; though I am willing to admit that a comparison of Russian films with American films somewhat favours the former. In Britain, certainly, Communist art is in a bad way. This is not merely my own view, but that of Comrade James Heslop, expressed at the Second International Conference of the Revolutionary Writers. Here are his words, taken from a most interesting periodical, *Literature of the World Revolution* (Kniga, Ltd, Bush House: one shilling):

> It must be recognised that proletarian art in Great Britain is in a very backward condition – and is, in fact, hardly begun. In order to illustrate this, allow me to say that, during the five years of life of the proletarian Sunday newspaper – the *Sunday Worker* – the scarcity of short stories from the pens of proletarian writers was most pronounced.

There is, however, another side to the picture, to which we must draw attention in fairness and with warm sympathy:

> Modern British bourgeois literature has sunk to a depth that is truly astonishing. It has reached a level of rottenness that can only be described as positively nauseating. It is the literature of dead people. [472] It betokens the final phase of dying capitalism. Perhaps it would be better not to weary the comrades with any lengthy analysis.

Those sentences are well worth pondering. But again:

> Of recent years other writers have sprung up among the proletariat. Of these James C. Welsh, John S. Clarke, and Joe Corrie might be cited as examples. . . . The great disappointment is Joe Corrie.

But for himself Comrade Heslop has hope:

> I make bold to say that my association with you, my stay in Soviet Russia (and) my friendship with my critical friend Ellis have put me on the path towards the creation of real proletarian art.

It is a relief to turn from Mr Murry and Mr Heslop to Mr W. T. Symonds, whose book *The Coming of Community* (Daniel: 7s. 6d. net) has not long been published. The book itself is rather a disappointment, because it is a miscellaneous collection of short papers previously published, chiefly in *The New Age*. But at the expense of considerable picking and choosing one can find much matter which is very well worth the trouble. In part, the book is simply a restatement of economic theories of Major Douglas, with an extra dose of enthusiasm; in part it expresses the more emotional, or even religious conclusions of the author himself; at times the style strikes me as a little too corybantic. And I doubt whether I should draw so much sustenance from Adler's psychology, if I knew it as well as Mr Symonds, as he seems to do. But the chief use of psychology (apart from curing people, if it does) seems to me to be to restate old truths in modern jargon which people can understand; and if psychology helps people towards truth which they cannot apprehend when put in simple theological language, so much the better. Mr Symonds believes that the reforms which he advocates

> ... would inaugurate an altogether new type of society, which would give fullest scope, both to the individual – thus securing the utmost variety in human affairs, and to the social whole – thus stimulating the rich, collective activities, which would surely come to life in [473] a society free to express its invention, its mechanical skill, its sense of the earth in agriculture and crafts, its delightful capacity for play, and its unknown psychic gifts.

I dispute the '*altogether* new type of society': but perhaps Mr Symonds does not intend such a complete severance from the past as his words might imply; and as he is not a Communist, I give him the benefit of the doubt. And I should keep a wary eye on the exploitation of 'unknown psychic gifts'; though there are psychic gifts (if one likes that phrase) once known and now mostly neglected. But otherwise, his sentence can surely not be questioned.

Building up the Christian World

Listener, 7. 169 (6 Apr. 1932), 501–2. Subheaded 'By T. S. ELIOT'. Gallup C334.
At head of title: 'The Moral Dilemma'.
In the paragraph headed 'Critics of Imperfect Christianity' 'on which they are intensely interested' has been emended to 'in which they are intensely interested'.

I have already made it quite clear that I do not propose to cure the world merely by individual conversions. In a plague epidemic, it is good that doctors should save every individual life that they can, but the epidemic is not going to be stopped in that way. In the end it is the individual soul that is the unit of value – and in that, I think, we differ radically from Communism and any other religion of Humanity. Those, by the way, who hold the religion of Communism might do well to study the attempt of a brilliant French freethinker of the nineteenth century, Auguste Comte, to establish a religion of Humanity, and take warning from his ingenious follies. It is the mass of individuals with which we are concerned: not the 'mass of humanity', or 'the masses', but the mass of individuals, each with his own precious differentiations, his eccentricities and hobbies, his own peculiar way of making the best of life; innumerable individuals, for no two of whom life has quite the same meaning; and no two or more of whom can be really united except in the love of God. The Christian view of society is, if you like, a paradox, for it is an organism in which each part has an equal value to the whole; but out of this paradox you can escape only into anarchism on the one hand, or the opposite heresy, communism, on the other. And that gives you a further paradox; for anarchism and communism respectively, in suppressing half of the value of life, suppress the whole.

I conceive then, not of conversions one by one to the faith, but of a kind of mass-conversion – by which I mean just the opposite of what is meant by a revival or a mass-meeting. In this mass-conversion you start at the other end, because you do not hope to convert the world to complete Christianity, but cherish the more modest hope that every individual will be a Christian so far as he is anything. Only a Moses could lead the people the whole way, and even to him they cried out, as you would cry too: '*Would to God we had died by the hand of the Lord in the land of Egypt, when we sat by the flesh-pots, and when we did eat bread to the full; for ye have brought us forth into this wilderness, to kill this whole assembly with hunger.*' No, the world I have in mind would merely be Christian so far as it was anything. And when I say 'the World', I mean the individuals who compose it, and I mean their social life, their economic life, their science, their values in this world. The last thing I want, however, is to revert to any medieval or early Christian society. For one thing it is impossible, with all our machinery and all our knowledge; for the other, it is undesirable. Yet I admit that our aim is almost more difficult than the impossible; for it is to try to realise the state of affairs which we should have attained had we gained all the good things we have gained and at the same time kept all the spiritual good that we have lost. And this means that we cannot simply pick and choose, by historical study, the good things out of the dustbin of the past and polish them up as fresh as new. For if we had kept them then, they would have been living in us; in, that is, our ancestors for all the generations between any period we call 'the past', and ourselves; they would not be quite the same as what we inspect through the telescope of history. Our task, then, is not antiquarianism; it is just the permanent task of making the permanent truths live in us in our own brief and particular moment of time.

I would have the consequences of Christian thinking – thinking by genuine Christians – in the practical departments of life pursued courageously and offered to the public on their merits. You may be indifferent to Christian belief and dogma, but you do at least want sound economics, sound politics, sound biology and psychology; and as for education, you ought to want either a wholly secular education, or the alternative of sound Christian training, not the poor substitute offered to so many schoolboys. Do not think that I am proposing that clergymen should necessarily be detailed to occupy themselves with these subjects, or that free scientific enquiry should be hindered, or the results mutilated to fit in with orthodoxy. But the Christian – seeing how every science, when there is no religion, tends to become a little religion itself, and feeling, as he must if he is really sincere in his faith, that Christian theology is the science which relates and gives meaning to the several sciences – must try to follow his religion out to the bitter end.

CRITICS OF IMPERFECT CHRISTIANITY

In nothing more than in constitutional theory, or the theory of politics, and in economics, is this need greater. There is a common complaint and one of long standing – I have heard it from the young and recently from correspondents; I even heard it and considered it when I was young myself – the complaint that a Church – or, I should say, Churches – for the grievance includes not only the Church of England, but Rome, Presbyterianism and most sects – which have proved so pliant to various forms of government, and so indifferent to the root causes of social injustice and oppression, are unworthy to speak in the [502] Name of Christ, or, if they are worthy, then Christianity is condemned. And the craving, which exists in nearly all of us, for some religion which shall demand a better society on earth, drives many towards Communism. For even as a perfect organisation of society, without a religion to transfigure it, is destitute of energy, hope and ecstasy; so a perfect religion which has no relation to the affairs of this world, lacks reality. The first thing to do, to convert people in the mass to being 'Christians so far as they are anything', is to convince them that the Christian faith really has something to say on these matters in which they are intensely interested; and that at least a few Christians would be prepared to take their stand for a Christian world, however different from actual society that world may turn out to be! To remove, in short, the ancient prejudice that Christianity is, or has become, merely the parasitic supporter of things as they are. I want to quote at this point from a private letter from a young man, who I think has put on paper what many feel:

> It has always seemed to me that the objection to religion is that it provides people with an escape from the organisation of society and from all materialistic problems, and that it also offers them an unreal consolation for material injustices that could be altered, and often, too, for injustices to other people and to the lower classes of

society which would seem intolerable if it were not for this escape into a sentimental dreamland.

He is wrong, of course, in confounding 'religion' with the history of the Churches during the last two or three centuries; in assuming that the consolation is unreal; and in refusing to recognise that for the individual, when *he* can do nothing about the injustices to himself or to others, this 'escape', as he calls it, is right and proper. I quote him because I think many others feel the same way. He continues:

> All the words you use, 'chastity, humility, austerity', convey to me (and hundreds of other people like me, I think) the feeling of staying in an old school-room chapel, unheated by a metal stove and doing nothing but be as consciously miserable as possible. All these words are associated too deeply with our education and our childhood.

There, I think, we are up against something very serious: the power of association. It is so difficult to talk to people about things of which they have no knowledge, when they have been made sordidly familiar with the *names* for the things: when they have heard repeated so many words belonging to Christian theology, and have never heard anything of Christian theology itself! I am not nearly so frightened of communism as I am of the 'Christianity' that many Englishmen have learnt at school; that Christianity which is merely one of the finishing processes of that over-produced commodity, the gentleman.

JUDGING FROM INSUFFICIENT KNOWLEDGE

So I always want to say to such people: 'Because you have never seen real Christianity in theory or in operation, because your early years were enveloped in a Christianity which I can hardly describe as much better than an imposture, an imposture associated with all that was most unpleasant in your early youth – and I am quite well aware how unpleasant early youth can be or how few sensitive men were happy in it – do not suppose that you are in a position to judge the Christian faith. I have more right to judge Marxism on insufficient knowledge than you have to judge Christianity on insufficient knowledge. For I can judge Marxism because I know, from its own evidence, that it is incompatible with that in which I already believe; but you, I am sure, became a Marxist because you previously did not believe in anything. I sympathise with your desire to believe something; but unless you are content to be a mere creature of environment, you are not yet in a position to deny the truths of Christianity. We are all partly creatures of environment, for good or bad, and of heredity and hereditary environment. But consider this. Suppose yourself existing a hundred, or two hundred, or any number of years ahead, and suppose that by that time communism had long since become the established religion, the established government and the established society. Is it not quite likely that if you were to be born into such a period you would be brought up in the same imposture, the same claptrap, the same diluted, adulterated and standardised sentiment, the same parroting of words which have lost their meaning, as afflicted the childhood you remember? The words would be different, because they would come out of communist theology and not out of Christian; but they would give you the same nausea and aversion from communism that you now have for Christianity. I should not like to think that then you would become a Christian, or anything else, simply by reacting from communism as you knew it. I am perfectly aware, in these matters, that we have not to do simply with intellectual conviction, but with the whole man and his desires. I dare say that you, and people like you, have no desires, no aspirations, which cannot be fulfilled in a communist society. You will have no doubt your own 'chastity', your own 'humility' and your own 'austerity', for which you will use different words, and which will give you different rules of behaviour than mine. If you are in the majority, well for you. But in that event, I only hope that I, and my like, may be allowed to expiate our intransigence quickly with our blood; and in any case I and my like shall expect little sympathy, either from the pagan society into which we and you were born, or from the communist society which you hope to construct. Mr Middleton Murry, in a little book *The Necessity of Communism*, pictures a gentle advance into communism which, like every programme offered to British voters, involves no violence or great discomfort – 'the inevitability of gradualness' again. We are to leave Egypt, but he assures us that the route will not take us through the desert. The Church – by which I think he has in mind not only our Anglican Church, but all Churches – is to be tolerated, as the persons of retarded development who will continue to patronise the Church will be tolerated. But for my part, I prefer to hope that I shall be untolerated, intolerant and intolerable.

That ends my little piece of parenthetical oratory. But I must add and repeat, for your own benefit, first that I do not wish to be named among the usual antagonists of communism. I have tried to make clear, throughout, that I and any who agree with me are in what is called a 'hopeless minority'; we loathe communism and we loathe the world as it is, and if this is the dilemma, if these are the only alternatives, then our strongest objection to communism is that it is a waste of time, of brains, of resources, and a great provocation to still more humbug, to change over from one bad system to another.

NO EASY RECIPES

At this point you must be prepared for a disappointment. My advantage is that I was prepared from the first for your disappointment, and can perhaps tell you why you must be disappointed. Many of those who have had the patience to hear me out must have been expecting me to produce some nice little recipe for setting things right; and I suspect that half of you have anticipated eagerly the moment when you could say: 'So *that's* all it comes to! as if we didn't know that that particular scheme hadn't been refuted long ago!' Of course, I have my own preferences, in the economic and other plans which are offered, but I am not going to tell you what they are.

I have avoided any expression of my views on the importance and significance of the kingship, on the merits of aristocracy and democracy, and many other matters. For I did not wish to complicate and distract my main line of thought by anything not quite vital to the present issue. For you might say: 'I object firmly to some of the things in which he believes, and I am therefore inclined to believe that he is wrong in his main thesis.' If, for instance, I had been giving elementary instruction in the Christian faith, it would have been a mistake for me to have tied it up with an exposition of the philosophy of the greatest philosophical teacher of the Church, St Thomas Aquinas. For it might have led you to believe that the whole truth of Christianity depended upon the validity of the philosophy of St Thomas Aquinas – an impression which, I suspect, some of his modern apologists have sometimes given. Similarly, I am not going to commit my belief in the possibility of a Christian society to any practical scheme put forward at the moment, and still less to any of my own invention. If you want schemes for the nationalisation of the Bank of England, for a currency supported by securities instead of gold, for bi-metallism, for the regulation of imports, for Empire Free Trade, for an Anglo-American or Anglo-Scandinavian hegemony, for the distribution of token money, for the revival of folk-dancing or craftsmanship, for the four-hour day, for the United States of Europe, for community singing, for autarchy, for marketing boards, for purchasing committees, for scout movements or pilgrimages, you will not get them now. My whole purpose has been to stimulate the belief that a Christian organisation of society is possible, that it is perhaps now more than at any previous time possible; to encourage the search for it and the testing of all offers of reform and revolution by its standards.

If I have left you unsatisfied, I can only say that I have expressed convictions only where really convinced, have expressed only the thoughts which were already in my own mind, have discussed with you only what

I had already discussed with myself. I know that many will say, with the leper: '*Are not Abana and Pharpar, rivers of Damascus, better than all the waters of Israel? may I not wash in them and be clean? – So he turned and went away in a rage*'. I think also of the words of Pascal, to be recalled even, and perhaps especially, on the day of the Resurrection: 'The Christ will be in agony even to the end of the world.' For sin and evil-doing we cannot abolish; but we can surely labour towards a social justice in this world which will prepare more souls to share not only here but in the Resurrection.

John Ford

'John Ford', an unsigned review of *Materials for the Study of the Old English Drama*, New Series, First Volume: *John Ford's Dramatic Works, Vol. II*, ed. H. De Vocht, was publ. in *TLS*, 1579 (5 May 1932), 317–18: Gallup C335.

Revised in *SE. See below*, pp. 426–35.

A Commentary

C., 11. 45 (July 1932), 676–83. Signed 'T. S. E.' Gallup C336.

In *Fiction and the Reading Public*[1] Mrs Q. D. Leavis has written a useful book: that is, a book which provides information so presented as to allow us to make our own generalisations. Those who read the book intelligently will be likely to engage in speculations further than those of the author. Mrs Leavis has attempted, not a history of the novel, but a history of the best-seller; a history, therefore, of the changes, and (as one would expect) the decline of taste in the last three hundred years. Her text may be taken as the two passages from Mr Richards's *Principles of Literary Criticism*, which she quotes:

> There is some evidence, uncertain and slight, no doubt, that such things as 'best-sellers' (compare *Tarzan* with *She*), magazine verse, mantelpiece pottery, Academy pictures, Music Hall songs, County Council buildings, War Memorials . . . are decreasing in merit.
>
> Best-sellers in all the arts, exemplifying as they do the most

[1]. Chatto, 12s. 6d. net.

general levels of attitude development, are worthy of very close study. No theory of criticism is satisfactory which is not able to explain their wide appeal and to give clear reasons why those who disdain them are not necessarily snobs.

She describes her method as 'anthropological'; and if she means by this term, as I suppose she does, that not only individual and social psychology, but also economics and sociology, are no longer to be ignored by literary criticism, then I am wholly in agreement. The book will no doubt be soon superseded, and we should hope that it will, whether by its author or by someone else; for, as the first of its kind, its business is to stimulate more comprehensive investigation than this book can pretend to make. Her information about what is published, what is sold, and how it is sold, may not be very surprising to those who have been connected with publishing houses, with periodicals, with certain branches of education, and with criticism and reviewing [677] of books; but to them the documentation should be useful, and to them and to the larger less-informed literate public, it should give much matter for meditation.

As for Mrs Leavis's conclusions, I can agree up to a certain point. I fear that to many cultivated readers she may give merely the impression that the development of modern society has inevitably brought about a deterioration of literary values, and that this is all there is to it; that in consequence, the only possible behaviour for those few who really appreciate art is a kind of monastic tenacity to values which the world has repudiated. I am not acquainted with the situation in British Honduras (see p. 272); I cannot but feel that Mrs Leavis's 'armed and conscious minority' determined to 'preserve' what can be preserved gives the effect of a gallant but hopeless rearguard action. I should be doing Mrs Leavis an injustice in suggesting that she is defending, or supposing that what she defends is a 'lost cause'. I have myself no great taste for lost causes. I mean that if I believe in a cause I find it impossible to believe that the cause is lost. If it really appears to me to be lost, then I must stop and examine, whether I have really cared purely for its essence, or whether I have attached myself as much to an impermanent form.

It may be said, of course, that the prevalence of bad taste, the pernicious habit of novel-reading, and the vast success of the fourth-rate in our time are matters of no importance so long as a small public survives to appreciate the best. We may say that it was only to be expected that when the whole public had been taught to read, it would choose to read very poor stuff; that the taste of the mob can never be much elevated, because of its invincible mental laziness; and that the Athenian crowd would never have applauded Aristophanes if it had experienced the pleasure of Mr Noel Coward and the cinema. But there is a great deal more to it than this. An *élite* which is only recognised by itself is in a bad way. And, as Mrs Leavis shows by some of her quotations from popular novels and from letters written to [678] her by popular novelists, our *élite*, such as it is, is hardly respected by the second- and third-rate writers: its rôle is to be sneered at and sometimes to be pilfered from. One of the most interesting phenomena to which she calls attention is the increasing stratification of literature into classes, each of which prefers to ignore the others. Thus the labour of the few at the top, their labour in developing human sensibility, their labour in inventing new forms of expression and new critical views of life and society, is largely in vain. A society which does not recognise the existence of art is barbaric. But a society which pretends that it recognises art, by tolerating the Royal Academy and patronising such novelists as Mr Thornton Wilder, Mr Hemingway and Mr Priestley (at best) is decidedly decadent.

There is a modern theory of art, applied with especial pertinence to literary art, of which, no doubt a great deal will be heard. It is (to put it crudely) that art is entirely a form of social expression, that it is determined in its forms by social and economic conditions, that it is wholly relative to these conditions and has no meaning beyond them.[1] I cannot, of course, hold this view myself: it seems to me that this would reduce all art, once the society which produced it had passed away, to mere archeological remains or at best, object-lessons or obscure prophecies. And anyone who is committed to religious dogma must also be committed to a theory of art which insists upon the permanent as well as the changing, and which cares as much, let us say, about the resemblances between the draughtsmanship of Hokusai and Pollaiuolo as it does about the differences. But the relation of the forms of art to the social background is a very important part of criticism which has not been adequately [679] explored, and is a problem which becomes more acute in a society which is more dissatisfied with itself, more and more conscious of change and decay.

It is certainly not the artist's business to be wholly aware of the 'elements' of permanent and transitory in his own work or deliberately to set out a composition of the permanently human with the local in time and place. It is not even altogether the critic's business; for not the purest critical sensibility can isolate the permanent 'beauty' of the work of art

---

1. See some interesting articles on the Marxian theory of literature by Mr Edmund Wilson in recent numbers of *The New Republic*; an essay by Prince D. S. Mirsky in *Échanges* (Dec.): Eliot et la fin de la poésie bourgeoise (which considerably exceeds the importance of the nominal subject); and a brilliant essay on Goethe in a recent number of the *Times Literary Supplement*.

from its time and place. But upon everything but the best the social kind of literary criticism must fall mercilessly; the more degraded a society becomes, the more clearly it will expose itself in its reading-matter; and I am inclined to wonder whether to-day Britain and America have not fallen lower than any other Western countries. And the function of fiction such as that dealt with by Mrs Leavis in her last chapter, 'Living at the Novelist's Expense', is apparently to soothe the minds of people who are not even alive enough to have anything to dream about. Just as we exclaim of readers of the tabloid press: 'these people ought to have something else to do!' so we recognise that the existence of the 'novel-reader' indicates a bad organisation of society. In a properly organised world the vast majority of novels such as are published to-day would not be published, because there would be no market; the people who read them would have something better to do than to read. And they would not be written, because their authors would have something better to do than to write. For the great majority of novels do only as the great majority of films: their purpose is to provide day-dreams. We know well enough what day-dreaming means, and what it can lead to, in individual psychology. But it is now a disease of society.

It seems to me unlikely that any social changes, whether sudden or gradual, could lead to a state of things in which the major forms of literature could long be dispensed with.[1] [680] I conceive it possible that the secondary types of literature will alter a good deal; and that some sorts of book produced to-day will no longer be required; and that some types of 'men of letters' still extant will disappear. I cannot conceive of a future society in which Sir Edmund Gosse would be possible; and there will be many other popular entertainers for whom there will be no demand. So far as literature is a trade, or even a career, it will be subject to as great changes as other trades and careers. The popular novels will very likely disappear, as both writers and readers find other occupations; and the finest living novelists are those whose work demands of the reader far more of an attention akin to poetic appreciation than any previous novelists have asked.[2] But poetry, in one form or another, will always be wanted, and there will always be a few people who will feel compelled to write it; and the need for the theatre,

---

1. In his book, *The Literary Mind* (Scribners'), Mr Max Eastman has some interesting remarks about the future of literature. He is relating it, however, to a future age which shall be generally 'scientific', and is not concerned specifically with social changes. As the book will be reviewed later, I shall not comment further upon it.

2. I am not supposing a sudden mutation, though *Ulysses* is a landmark. The tendency was discernible in the work of novelists now dead. Henry James and Conrad display it here and there, and James's precursor, Hawthorne, may be mentioned.

in one form or another, will never, unless civilisation not merely alters but disappears, be supplied by the cinema. The drama, perhaps, is one form which might gain new life in a new age, and at the same time provide a fresh, and much-needed, vehicle for poetry.[1]

But although various kinds of social change might incinerate a vast quantity of rubbish, and clear fields for fresh planting, I cannot see any likelihood that either revolution or reform will, in itself, improve the quality of the produce. Just as no constitution of society can be devised in which [68] the arts of the place-seeker will not in the end be more cultivated than those of the governor, in which the chief aim of the politician will not still be to gain power and to keep it; so also no social millennium can be conceived which will ensure the continued propagation of the highest forms of art. The simplest alternative would be the establishment of a static, uniform society in which mankind would be such that it would reject all genuine art as a superannuated superfluity. In arriving at this consummation, communism is liable to achieve what capitalism has begun.

Hitherto, periods of great art (and in that very restricted sense, great civilisation) seem always to have arisen as the unintentional and unpredictable by-products of processes of social crystallisation, in which some fortunate relation (not always, by any means, the same) appears between the individual and the community. To-day there is no community (for the Russian and the Italian seem to me mechanical rather than spiritual communities) and therefore only imperfect individuals; it is when society is really united that eccentricity is possible. Now, with the formation of a period of civilisation 'historical materialism' or 'economic determinism' seems to me to have very little to do; not because it is determinism, but because it is *incomplete* determinism.[2] Even Mr Maurice Dobb (whose pamphlet *On Marxism To-day*,[3] is the most lucid and persuasive brief account that I have read, and is calculated to dispel some errors) does not enlighten me. I can quite understand that during one brief period of time, the last two hundred years or so, conditions have been particularly favourable to prophecy. That is, life has become increasingly mechanised; and as men have been gradually discovering

---

1. The greatest deficiency in most of the contemporary verse which comes to my eye is the lack of any dramatic intent, which might help to correct its imperfectly conceived philosophies and its imperfectly objectified emotions.

2. Incomplete, that is, with reference to such experiences as that of St Peter when the cock crew. This kind of determinism is essential to Buddhism as well as to Christianity; but whether 'determinism' is the right word for it, I leave unsettled. See *Jones's Karma*, by May Sinclair, in *The Criterion* for October, 1923, p. 43.

3. Hogarth Press. 1s. 6d.

what they could [682] do with the machine, it was not impossible for one man of genius to predict with accuracy some of the things that the machine was to do with men. Man thus learns to predict his own actions, by making himself into the likeness of those creations whose actions he has determined. Economic determinism, like any other kind of determinism within the scope of the human mind, is possible, and has its legitimate application, only by a rigorous selection of elements within a restricted limit of time. And this selection is also a selection of values, and any narrow adherence to one set of values tends to be a menace. If your values are religious, then you may say that it is better that a million bodies should burn rather than one soul; if they are aesthetic, you may say that it is better that a million lives should be lost rather than one cathedral; if your values are humanitarian, that it is better that art and religion should perish rather than one man die of hunger.

It may be only my own prejudice which makes me believe that a communist régime might merely perfect the work of the capitalist régime in stamping out any vestiges of art, until finally mankind outgrew its primitive desire for that kind of enjoyment. But it is surely rational to maintain that we cannot expect any merely political or social change to raise the artistic sensibility of the public, to stimulate the flowering of artistic talent or to inaugurate a world of beauty. Things may well be much as before: 'old consciences and new faces'. Fiction, not religion (according to Marx's silliest epigram), is the opium of the people to-day, and some other form of opium will be provided to-morrow, for some sort of opium they must have, until you can give them either religion, or to each man a job in which he can be passionately interested, or both. For the present, no doubt commercial literature will continue to flourish and to pander, more and more severed from real literature. The latter will be produced by those who will not merely be content not to make a living by it, not merely content to have no career; but who will be resigned to a very small audience – for we [683] all should like to think that our poetry might be read and declaimed in the public-house, the forecastle and the shipyard. What is required for the production of great art seems to be any one of many possible situations in which the ingredients are liberty, individuality, and community.

Selected Essays 1917–1932

Selected Essays 1917-1932 was publ. on 15 Sept. 1932: Gallup A21.

Contents: I 'Tradition and the Individual Talent' (1917 [i.e. 1919]); 'The Function of Criticism' (1923); II '"Rhetoric" And Poetic Drama' (1919); 'A Dialogue on Dramatic Poetry' (1928); 'Euripides and Professor Murray' (1918 [i.e. 1920]); 'Seneca in Elizabethan Translation' (1927); III 'Four Elizabethan Dramatists' (1924); 'Christopher Marlowe' (1918 [i.e. 1919]); 'Shakespeare and the Stoicism of Seneca' (1927); 'Hamlet' (1919); 'Ben Jonson' (1919); 'Thomas Middleton' (1927); 'Thomas Heywood' (1931); 'Cyril Tourneur' (1931 [i.e. 1930]); 'John Ford' (1932); 'Philip Massinger' (1920); IV 'Dante' (1929); V 'The Metaphysical Poets' (1921); 'Andrew Marvell' (1921); 'John Dryden' (1922 [i.e. 1921]); 'William Blake' (1920); 'Swinburne as Poet' (1920); VI 'Lancelot Andrewes' (1926); 'John Bramhall' (1927); 'Thoughts after Lambeth' (1931); VII 'Baudelaire' (1930); 'Arnold and Pater' (1930); 'Francis Herbert Bradley' (1926 [i.e. 1927]); 'Marie Lloyd' (1923); 'Wilkie Collins and Dickens' (1927); 'The Humanism of Irving Babbitt' (1927 [i.e. 1928]); 'Second Thoughts about Humanism' (1929); 'Charles Whibley' (1931).

[5] To
Harriet Shaw Weaver
In Gratitude, and in Recognition
Of Her Services to English Letters

[7] Preface

My acknowledgements are due to Messrs Methuen & Co. Ltd (for the parts of *The Sacred Wood* reprinted); to the Hogarth Press (*Homage to John Dryden*); to the Haslewood Press (for *A Dialogue on Dramatic Poetry*); to Messrs Constable & Co. Ltd (for *Seneca in Elizabethan Translation*, originally printed as Introduction to the Tudor Translations Series edition of the *Tenne Tragedies*); to the Shakespeare Association (*Shakespeare and the Senecan Tradition*); to Mr Walter de la Mare and the Royal Society of Literature (*Arnold and Pater*); to the Blackamore Press (*Baudelaire*); to the English Association (*Charles Whibley*). Also to *The Egoist, The Athenaeum, The Times Literary Supplement, Art and Letters, The Forum, The Bookman* (N.Y.), *The Hound and Horn, Theology*, and *The Criterion*, in which most of these pages originally appeared.

My thanks are also due to Mr B. L. Richmond, without whose suggestions and encouragement the essays on Elizabethan dramatists would not have been written; and to Mr F. V. Morley for his assistance in selecting the essays and in reading the proofs, and for his pertinacity in harrying me to do what work I have myself done in preparation of this volume.

T. S. E.
London: April 1932.

I Tradition and the Individual Talent

SE, 13–22.

Revised from *Egoist*, 6. 4 (Sept. 1919), 54–5,
and 6. 5 ([Nov./] Dec. 1919), 72–3, both signed 'T. S. Eliot', and from *SW*.

1 In English writing we seldom speak of tradition, though we occasionally apply its name in deploring its absence. We cannot refer to 'the tradition' or to 'a tradition'; at most, we employ the adjective in saying that the poetry of So-and-so is 'traditional' or even 'too traditional'. Seldom, perhaps, does the word appear except in a phrase of censure. If otherwise, it is vaguely approbative, with the implication, as to the work approved, of some pleasing archeological reconstruction. You can hardly make the word agreeable to English ears without this comfortable reference to the reassuring science of archeology.

2 Certainly the word is not likely to appear in our appreciations of living or dead writers. Every nation, every race, has not only its own creative, but its own critical turn of mind; and is even more oblivious of the shortcomings and limitations of its critical habits than of those of its creative genius. We know, or think we know, from the enormous mass of critical writing that has appeared in the French language the critical method or habit of the French; we only conclude (we are such unconscious people) that the French are 'more critical' than we, and sometimes even plume ourselves a little with the fact, as if the French were the less spontaneous. Perhaps they are; but we might remind ourselves that criticism is as inevitable as breathing, and that we should be none the worse for articulating what passes in our minds when we read a book and feel an emotion about it, for criticising our own minds in their [14] work of criticism. One of the facts that might come to light in this process is our tendency to insist, when we praise a poet, upon those aspects of his work in which he least resembles any one else. In these aspects or parts of his work we pretend to find what is individual, what is the peculiar essence of the man. We dwell with satisfaction upon the poet's difference from his predecessors, especially his immediate predecessors; we endeavour to find something that can be isolated in order to be enjoyed. Whereas if we approach a

poet without this prejudice we shall often find that not only the best, but the most individual parts of his work may be those in which the dead poets, his ancestors, assert their immortality most vigorously. And I do not mean the impressionable period of adolescence, but the period of full maturity.

3 Yet if the only form of tradition, of handing down, consisted in following the ways of the immediate generation before us in a blind or timid adherence to its successes, 'tradition' should positively be discouraged. We have seen many such simple currents soon lost in the sand; and novelty is better than repetition. Tradition is a matter of much wider significance. It cannot be inherited, and if you want it you must obtain it by great labour. It involves, in the first place, the historical sense, which we may call nearly indispensable to any one who would continue to be a poet beyond his twenty-fifth year; and the historical sense involves a perception, not only of the pastness of the past, but of its presence; the historical sense compels a man to write not merely with his own generation in his bones, but with a feeling that the whole of the literature of Europe from Homer and within it the whole of the literature of his own country has a simultaneous existence and composes a simultaneous order. This historical sense, which is a sense of the timeless as well as of the temporal and of the timeless and of the temporal together, is what makes a writer traditional. And it is at the same time what makes a writer most acutely conscious of his place in time, of his own contemporaneity.

[15] 4 No poet, no artist of any art, has his complete meaning alone. His significance, his appreciation is the appreciation of his relation to the dead poets and artists. You cannot value him alone; you must set him, for contrast and comparison, among the dead. I mean this as a principle of aesthetic, not merely historical, criticism. The necessity that he shall conform, that he shall cohere, is not onesided; what happens when a new work of art is created is something that happens simultaneously to all the works of art which preceded it. The existing monuments form an ideal order among themselves, which is modified by the introduction of the new (the really new) work of art among them. The existing order is complete before the new work arrives; for order to persist after the supervention of novelty, the *whole* existing order must be, if ever so slightly, altered; and so the relations, proportions, values of each work of art toward the whole are readjusted; and this is conformity between the old and the new. Whoever has approved this idea of order, of the form of European, of English literature will not find it preposterous that the past should be altered by the present as much as the present is directed by the

past. And the poet who is aware of this will be aware of great difficulties and responsibilities.

5 In a peculiar sense he will be aware also that he must inevitably be judged by the standards of the past. I say judged, not amputated, by them; not judged to be as good as, or worse or better than, the dead; and certainly not judged by the canons of dead critics. It is a judgement, a comparison, in which two things are measured by each other. To conform merely would be for the new work not really to conform at all; it would not be new, and would therefore not be a work of art. And we do not quite say that the new is more valuable because it fits in; but its fitting in is a test of its value – a test, it is true, which can only be slowly and cautiously applied, for we are none of us infallible judges of conformity. We say: it appears to conform, and is perhaps individual, or it appears individual, and may con-[16]form; but we are hardly likely to find that it is one and not the other.

6 To proceed to a more intelligible exposition of the relation of the poet to the past: he can neither take the past as a lump, an indiscriminate bolus, nor can he form himself wholly on one or two private admirations, nor can he form himself wholly upon one preferred period. The first course is inadmissible, the second is an important experience of youth, and the third is a pleasant and highly desirable supplement. The poet must be very conscious of the main current, which does not at all flow invariably through the most distinguished reputations. He must be quite aware of the obvious fact that art never improves, but that the material of art is never quite the same. He must be aware that the mind of Europe – the mind of his own country – a mind which he learns in time to be much more important than his own private mind – is a mind which changes, and that this change is a development which abandons nothing *en route*, which does not superannuate either Shakespeare, or Homer, or the rock drawing of the Magdalenian draughtsmen. That this development, refinement perhaps, complication certainly, is not, from the point of view of the artist, any improvement. Perhaps not even an improvement from the point of view of the psychologist or not to the extent which we imagine; perhaps only in the end based upon a complication in economics and machinery. But the difference between the present and the past is that the conscious present is an awareness of the past in a way and to an extent which the past's awareness of itself cannot show.

7 Someone said: 'The dead writers are remote from us because we *know* so much more than they did.' Precisely, and they are that which we know.

8 I am alive to a usual objection to what is clearly part of my programme for the *métier* of poetry. The objection is that the doctrine requires a ridiculous amount of erudition (pedantry), a claim which can be rejected by appeal to the [17] lives of poets in any pantheon. It will even be affirmed that much learning deadens or perverts poetic sensibility. While, however, we persist in believing that a poet ought to know as much as will not encroach on his necessary receptivity and necessary laziness, it is not desirable to confine knowledge to whatever can be put into a useful shape for examinations, drawing-rooms, or the still more pretentious modes of publicity. Some can absorb knowledge, the more tardy must sweat for it. Shakespeare acquired more essential history from Plutarch than most men could from the whole British Museum. What is to be insisted upon is that the poet must develop or procure the consciousness of the past and that he should continue to develop this consciousness throughout his career.

9 What happens is a continual surrender of himself as he is at the moment to something which is more valuable. The progress of an artist is a continual self-sacrifice, a continual extinction of personality.

10 There remains to define this process of depersonalisation and its relation to the sense of tradition. It is in this depersonalisation that art may be said to approach the condition of science. I, therefore, invite you to consider, as a suggestive analogy, the action which takes place when a bit of finely filiated platinum is introduced into a chamber containing oxygen and sulphur dioxide.

II

11 Honest criticism and sensitive appreciation is directed not upon the poet but upon the poetry. If we attend to the confused cries of the newspaper critics and the susurrus of popular repetition that follows, we shall hear the names of poets in great numbers; if we seek not Blue-book knowledge but the enjoyment of poetry, and ask for a poem, we shall seldom find it. I have tried to point out the importance of the relation of the poem to other poems by other authors, and suggested the conception of poetry as a living whole of all the poetry that has ever been written. The other aspect [18] of this Impersonal theory of poetry is the relation of the poem to its author. And I hinted, by an analogy, that the mind of the mature poet differs from that of the immature one not precisely in any valuation of 'personality', not being necessarily more interesting, or having 'more to say', but rather by being a more finely perfected medium

in which special, or very varied, feelings are at liberty to enter into new combinations.

12 The analogy was that of the catalyst. When the two gases previously mentioned are mixed in the presence of a filament of platinum, they form sulphurous acid. This combination takes place only if the platinum is present; nevertheless the newly formed acid contains no trace of platinum, and the platinum itself is apparently unaffected: has remained inert, neutral, and unchanged. The mind of the poet is the shred of platinum. It may partly or exclusively operate upon the experience of the man himself; but, the more perfect the artist, the more completely separate in him will be the man who suffers and the mind which creates; the more perfectly will the mind digest and transmute the passions which are its material.

13 The experience, you will notice, the elements which enter the presence of the transforming catalyst, are of two kinds: emotions and feelings. The effect of a work of art upon the person who enjoys it is an experience different in kind from any experience not of art. It may be formed out of one emotion, or may be a combination of several; and various feelings, inhering for the writer in particular words or phrases or images, may be added to compose the final result. Or great poetry may be made without the direct use of any emotion whatever: composed out of feelings solely. Canto XV of the *Inferno* (Brunetto Latini) is a working up of the emotion evident in the situation; but the effect, though single as that of any work of art, is obtained by considerable complexity of detail. The last quatrain gives an image, a feeling attaching to an image, which 'came', which did not develop simply out of what pre-[19]cedes, but which was probably in suspension in the poet's mind until the proper combination arrived for it to add itself to. The poet's mind is in fact a receptacle for seizing and storing up numberless feelings, phrases, images, which remain there until all the particles which can unite to form a new compound are present together.

14 If you compare several representative passages of the greatest poetry you see how great is the variety of types of combination, and also how completely any semi-ethical criterion of 'sublimity' misses the mark. For it is not the 'greatness', the intensity, of the emotions, the components, but the intensity of the artistic process, the pressure, so to speak, under which the fusion takes place, that counts. The episode of Paolo and Francesca employs a definite emotion, but the intensity of the poetry is something quite different from whatever intensity in the supposed experience it may give the impression of. It is no more intense, furthermore, than Canto

XXVI, the voyage of Ulysses, which has not the direct dependence upon an emotion. Great variety is possible in the process of transmutation of emotion: the murder of Agamemnon, or the agony of Othello, gives an artistic effect apparently closer to a possible original than the scenes from Dante. In the *Agamemnon*, the artistic emotion approximates to the emotion of an actual spectator; in *Othello* to the emotion of the protagonist himself. But the difference between art and the event is always absolute; the combination which is the murder of Agamemnon is probably as complex as that which is the voyage of Ulysses. In either case there has been a fusion of elements. The ode of Keats contains a number of feelings which have nothing particular to do with the nightingale, but which the nightingale, partly perhaps because of its attractive name, and partly because of its reputation, served to bring together.

15 The point of view which I am struggling to attack is perhaps related to the metaphysical theory of the substantial unity of the soul: for my meaning is, that the poet has, [20] not a 'personality' to express, but a particular medium, which is only a medium and not a personality, in which impressions and experiences combine in peculiar and unexpected ways. Impressions and experiences which are important for the man may take no place in the poetry, and those which become important in the poetry may play quite a negligible part in the man, the personality.

16 I will quote a passage which is unfamiliar enough to be regarded with fresh attention in the light – or darkness – of these observations:

> And now methinks I could e'en chide myself
> For doating on her beauty, though her death
> Shall be revenged after no common action.
> Does the silkworm expend her yellow labours
> For thee? For thee does she undo herself?
> Are lordships sold to maintain ladyships
> For the poor benefit of a bewildering minute?
> Why does yon fellow falsify highways,
> And put his life between the judge's lips,
> To refine such a thing – keeps horse and men
> To beat their valours for her? . . .

In this passage (as is evident if it is taken in its context) there is a combination of positive and negative emotions: an intensely strong attraction toward beauty and an equally intense fascination by the ugliness which is contrasted with it and which destroys it. This balance of contrasted emotion is in the dramatic situation to which the speech is pertinent, but that situation alone is inadequate to it. This is, so to speak, the structural emotion, provided by the drama. But the whole effect, the dominant tone, is due to the fact that a number of floating feelings, having an affinity to this emotion by no means superficially evident, have combined with it to give us a new art emotion.

17 It is not in his personal emotions, the emotions provoked by particular events in his life, that the poet is in any way remarkable or interesting. His particular emotions may be [21] simple, or crude, or flat. The emotion in his poetry will be a very complex thing, but not with the complexity of the emotions of people who have very complex or unusual emotions in life. One error, in fact, of eccentricity in poetry is to seek for new human emotions to express; and in this search for novelty in the wrong place it discovers the perverse. The business of the poet is not to find new emotions, but to use the ordinary ones and, in working them up into poetry, to express feelings which are not in actual emotions at all. And emotions which he has never experienced will serve his turn as well as those familiar to him. Consequently, we must believe that 'emotion recollected in tranquillity' is an inexact formula. For it is neither emotion, nor recollection, nor, without distortion of meaning, tranquillity. It is a concentration, and a new thing resulting from the concentration, of a very great number of experiences which to the practical and active person would not seem to be experiences at all; it is a concentration which does not happen consciously or of deliberation. These experiences are not 'recollected', and they finally unite in an atmosphere which is 'tranquil' only in that it is a passive attending on the event. Of course this is not quite the whole story. There is a great deal, in the writing of poetry, which must be conscious and deliberate. In fact, the bad poet is usually unconscious where he ought to be conscious, and conscious where he ought to be unconscious. Both errors tend to make him 'personal'. Poetry is not a turning loose of emotion, but an escape from emotion; it is not the expression of personality, but an escape from personality. But, of course, only those who have personality and emotions know what it means to want to escape from these things.

III

ὁ δὲ νοῦς ἴσως θειότερόν τι καὶ ἀπαθές ἐστιν

18 This essay proposes to halt at the frontier of metaphysics or mysticism, and confine itself to such practical conclu-[22]sions as can be applied by the responsible person interested in poetry. To divert interest from the poet to the poetry is a laudable aim: for it would conduce to a juster

estimation of actual poetry, good and bad. There are many people who appreciate the expression of sincere emotion in verse, and there is a smaller number of people who can appreciate technical excellence. But very few know when there is an expression of *significant* emotion, emotion which has its life in the poem and not in the history of the poet. The emotion of art is impersonal. And the poet cannot reach this impersonality without surrendering himself wholly to the work to be done. And he is not likely to know what is to be done unless he lives in what is not merely the present, but the present moment of the past, unless he is conscious, not of what is dead, but of what is already living.

Variants:

2   mean] intend *Egoist* (1919)
3   his own contemporaneity] his contemporaneity *SW*
5   judged, not] judged by, not *Egoist* (1919)
11 Honest criticism] The upshot of this article and the article which preceded it is this: that honest criticism *Egoist* (1919)
    numbers] number *Egoist* (1919)
    I have tried] In the last article I tried *Egoist* (1919) [Nov./Dec.], *SW*
12 unaffected:] unaffected; *Egoist* (1919, *SW*
    neutral] passive *Egoist* (1919)
14 partly perhaps] partly, perhaps, *Egoist* (1919), *SW*

The Function of Criticism

SE, 23-34.

Revised from *C.*, 2. 5 (Oct. 1923), 31–42, subheaded '*By* T. S. Eliot':
Gallup C144. In para. 6 of the earlier text 'section' read 'capital'.
This is treated as a misprint.

I

1 Writing several years ago on the subject of the relation of the new to the old in art, I formulated a view to which I still adhere, in sentences which I take the liberty of quoting, because the present paper is an application of the principle they express:

> The existing monuments form an ideal order among themselves, which is modified by the introduction of the new (the really new) work of art among them. The existing order is complete before the new work arrives; for order to persist after the supervention of novelty, the *whole* existing order must be, if ever so slightly, altered; and so the relations, proportions, values of each work of art toward the whole are readjusted; and this is conformity between the old

and the new. Whoever has approved this idea of order, of the form of European, of English literature, will not find it preposterous that the past should be altered by the present as much as the present is directed by the past.

2 I was dealing then with the artist, and the sense of tradition which, it seemed to me, the artist should have; but it was generally a problem of order; and the function of criticism seems to be essentially a problem of order too. I thought of literature then, as I think of it now, of the literature of the world, of the literature of Europe, of the literature of a single country, not as a collection of the writings of individuals, but as 'organic wholes', as systems in relation to which, and only in relation to which, individual [24] works of literary art, and the works of individual artists, have their significance. There is accordingly something outside of the artist to which he owes allegiance, a devotion to which he must surrender and sacrifice himself in order to earn and to obtain his unique position. A common inheritance and a common cause unite artists consciously or unconsciously: it must be admitted that the union is mostly unconscious. Between the true artists of any time there is, I believe, an unconscious community. And, as our instincts of tidiness imperatively command us not to leave to the haphazard of unconsciousness what we can attempt to do consciously, we are forced to conclude that what happens unconsciously we could bring about, and form into a purpose, if we made a conscious attempt. The second-rate artist, of course, cannot afford to surrender himself to any common action; for his chief task is the assertion of all the trifling differences which are his distinction: only the man who has so much to give that he can forget himself in his work can afford to collaborate, to exchange, to contribute.

3 If such views are held about art, it follows that *a fortiori* whoever holds them must hold similar views about criticism. When I say criticism, I mean of course in this place the commentation and exposition of works of art by means of written words; for the general use of the word 'criticism' to mean such writings, as Matthew Arnold uses it in his essay, I shall presently make several qualifications. No exponent of criticism (in this limited sense) has, I presume, ever made the preposterous assumption that criticism is an autotelic activity. I do not deny that art may be affirmed to serve ends beyond itself; but art is not required to be aware of these ends, and indeed performs its function, whatever that may be, according to various theories of value, much better by indifference to them. Criticism, on the other hand, must always profess an end in view, which, roughly speaking, appears to be the elucidation of works of art

and the correction of taste. The critic's task, therefore, appears to be quite clearly cut out for him; and it [25] ought to be comparatively easy to decide whether he performs it satisfactorily, and in general, what kinds of criticism are useful and what are otiose. But on giving the matter a little attention, we perceive that criticism, far from being a simple and orderly field of beneficent activity, from which impostors can be readily ejected, is no better than a Sunday park of contending and contentious orators, who have not even arrived at the articulation of their differences. Here, one would suppose, was a place for quiet co-operative labour. The critic, one would suppose, if he is to justify his existence, should endeavour to discipline his personal prejudices and cranks – tares to which we are all subject – and compose his differences with as many of his fellows as possible, in the common pursuit of true judgement. When we find that quite the contrary prevails, we begin to suspect that the critic owes his livelihood to the violence and extremity of his opposition to other critics, or else to some trifling oddities of his own with which he contrives to season the opinions which men already hold, and which out of vanity or sloth they prefer to maintain. We are tempted to expel the lot.

4 Immediately after such an eviction, or as soon as relief has abated our rage, we are compelled to admit that there remain certain books, certain essays, certain sentences, certain men, who have been 'useful' to us. And our next step is to attempt to classify these, and find out whether we establish any principles for deciding what kinds of book should be preserved, and what aims and methods of criticism should be followed.

II

5 The view of the relation of the work of art to art, of the work of literature to literature, of 'criticism' to criticism, which I have outlined above, seemed to me natural and self-evident. I owe to Mr Middleton Murry my perception of the contentious character of the problem; or rather, my perception that there is a definite and final choice involved. [26] To Mr Murry I feel an increasing debt of gratitude. Most of our critics are occupied in labour of obnubilation; in reconciling, in hushing up, in patting down, in squeezing in, in glozing over, in concocting pleasant sedatives, in pretending that the only difference between themselves and others is that they are nice men and the others of very doubtful repute. Mr Murry is not one of these. He is aware that there are definite positions to be taken, and that now and then one must actually reject something and select something else. He is not the anonymous writer who in a literary paper several years ago asserted that Romanticism and Classicism are much the same thing, and that the true Classical Age in France was the

age which produced the Gothic cathedrals and – Jeanne d'Arc. With Mr Murry's recent formulation of Classicism and Romanticism I cannot agree; the difference seems to me rather the difference between the complete and the fragmentary, the adult and the immature, the orderly and the chaotic. But what Mr Murry does show is that there are at least two attitudes toward literature and toward everything, and that you cannot hold both. And the attitude which he professes appears to imply that the other has no standing in England whatever. For it is made a national, a racial issue.

6 Mr Murry makes his issue perfectly clear. 'Catholicism,' he says, 'stands for the principle of unquestioned spiritual authority outside the individual; that is also the principle of Classicism in literature.' Within the orbit within which Mr Murry's discussion moves, this seems to me an unimpeachable definition, though it is of course not all that there is to be said about either Catholicism or Classicism. Those of us who find ourselves supporting what Mr Murry calls Classicism believe that men cannot get on without giving allegiance to something outside themselves. I am aware that 'outside' and 'inside' are terms which provide unlimited opportunity for quibbling, and that no psychologist would tolerate a discussion which shuffled such base coinage; but I will presume that Mr Murry and myself [27] can agree that for our purpose these counters are adequate, and concur in disregarding the admonitions of our psychological friends. If you find that you have to imagine it as outside, then it is outside. If, then, a man's interest is political, he must, I presume, profess an allegiance to principles, or to a form of government, or to a monarch; and if he is interested in religion, and has one, to a Church; and if he happens to be interested in literature, he must acknowledge, it seems to me, just that sort of allegiance which I endeavoured to put forth in the preceding section. There is, nevertheless, an alternative, which Mr Murry has expressed. 'The English writer, the English divine, the English statesman, inherit no rules from their forebears; they inherit only this: a sense that in the last resort they must depend upon the inner voice.' This statement does, I admit, appear to cover certain cases; it throws a flood of light upon Mr Lloyd George. But why *in the last resort*? Do they, then, avoid the dictates of the inner voice up to the last extremity? My belief is that those who possess this inner voice are ready enough to hearken to it, and will hear no other. The inner voice, in fact, sounds remarkably like an old principle which has been formulated by an elder critic in the now familiar phrase of 'doing as one likes'. The possessors of the inner voice ride ten in a compartment to a football match at Swansea, listening to the inner voice, which breathes the eternal message of vanity, fear, and lust.

7 Mr Murry will say, with some show of justice, that this is a wilful representation. He says: 'If they (the English writer, divine, statesman) dig *deep enough* in their pursuit of self-knowledge – a piece of mining done not with the intellect alone, but with the whole man – they will come upon a self that is universal' – an exercise far beyond the strength of our football enthusiasts. It is an exercise, however, which I believe was of enough interest to Catholicism for several handbooks to be written on its practice. But the Catholic practitioners were, I believe, with the exception of certain heretics, not palpitating Narcissi; the [28] Catholic did not believe that God and himself were identical. 'The man who truly interrogates himself will ultimately hear the voice of God,' Mr Murry says. In theory, this leads to a form of pantheism which I maintain is not European – just as Mr Murry maintains that 'Classicism' is not English. For its practical results, one may refer to the verses of *Hudibras*.

8 I did not realise that Mr Murry was the spokesman for a considerable sect, until I read in the editorial columns of a dignified daily that 'magnificent as the representatives of the classical genius have been in England, they are not the sole expressions of the English character, which remains at bottom obstinately "humorous" and nonconformist'. This writer is moderate in using the qualification *sole*, and brutally frank in attributing this 'humorousness' to 'the unreclaimed Teutonic element in us'. But it strikes me that Mr Murry, and this other voice, are either too obstinate or too tolerant. The question is, the first question, *not* what comes natural or what comes *easy* to us, but what is right? Either one attitude is better than the other, or else it is indifferent. But how can such a choice be indifferent? Surely the reference to racial origins, or the mere statement that the French are thus, and the English otherwise, is not expected to settle the question: which, of two antithetical views, is *right*? And I cannot understand why the opposition between Classicism and Romanticism should be profound enough in Latin countries (Mr Murry says it is) and yet of no significance among ourselves. For if the French are *naturally* classical, why should there be any 'opposition' in France, any more than there is here? And if Classicism is not natural to them, but something acquired, why not acquire it here? Were the French in the year 1600 classical, and the English in the same year romantic? A more important difference, to my mind, is that the French in the year 1600 *had already a more mature prose.*

[29] III

9 This discussion may seem to have led us a long way from the subject of this paper. But it was worth my while to follow Mr Murry's comparison

of Outside Authority with the Inner Voice. For to those who obey the inner voice (perhaps 'obey' is not the word) nothing that I can say about criticism will have the slightest value. For they will not be interested in the attempt to find any common principles for the pursuit of criticism. Why have principles, when one has the inner voice? If I like a thing, that is all I want; and if enough of us, shouting all together, like it, that should be all that *you* (who don't like it) ought to want. The law of art, said Mr Clutton Brock, is all case law. And we can not only like whatever we like to like but we can like it for any reason we choose. We are not, in fact, concerned with literary *perfection* at all – the search for perfection is a sign of pettiness, for it shows that the writer has admitted the existence of an unquestioned spiritual authority outside himself, to which he has attempted to *conform*. We are not in fact interested in art. We will not worship Baal. 'The principle of classical leadership is that obeisance is made to the office or to the tradition, never to the man.' And we want, not principles, but men.

10 Thus speaks the Inner Voice. It is a voice to which, for convenience, we may give a name: and the name I suggest is Whiggery.

IV

11 Leaving, then, those whose calling and election are sure and returning to those who shamefully depend upon tradition and the accumulated wisdom of time, and restricting the discussion to those who sympathise with each other in this frailty, we may comment upon the use of the terms 'critical' and 'creative' by one whose place, on the whole, is with the weaker brethren. Matthew Arnold [30] distinguishes far too bluntly, it seems to me, between the two activities: he overlooks the capital importance of criticism in the work of creation itself. Probably, indeed, the larger part of the labour of an author in composing his work is critical labour; the labour of sifting, combining, constructing, expunging, correcting, testing: this frightful toil is as much critical as creative. I maintain even that the criticism employed by a trained and skilled writer upon his own work is the most vital, the highest kind of criticism; and (as I think I have said before) that some creative writers are superior to others solely because their critical faculty is superior. There is a tendency, and I think it is a whiggery tendency, to decry this critical toil of the artist; to propound the thesis that the great artist is an unconscious artist, unconsciously inscribing on his banner the words Muddle Through. Those of us who are Inner Deaf Mutes are, however, sometimes compensated by a humble conscience, which, though without oracular expertness, counsels us to do the best we can, reminds us that

our compositions ought to be as free from defects as possible (to atone for their lack of inspiration), and, in short, makes us waste a good deal of time. We are aware, too, that the critical discrimination which comes so hardly to us has in more fortunate men flashed in the very heat of creation; and we do not assume that because works have been composed without apparent critical labour, no critical labour has been done. We do not know what previous labours have prepared, or what goes on, in the way of criticism, all the time in the minds of the creators.

12 But this affirmation recoils upon us. If so large a part of creation is really criticism, is not a large part of what is called 'critical writing' really creative? If so, is there not creative criticism in the ordinary sense? The answer seems to be, that there is no equation. I have assumed as axiomatic that a creation, a work of art, is autotelic; and that criticism, by definition, is *about* something other than itself. Hence you cannot fuse creation with criticism as you [31] can fuse criticism with creation. The critical activity finds its highest, its true fulfilment in a kind of union with creation in the labour of the artist.

13 But no writer is completely self-sufficient, and many creative writers have a critical activity which is not all discharged into their work. Some seem to require to keep their critical powers in condition for the real work by exercising them miscellaneously; others, on completing a work, need to continue the critical activity by commenting on it. There is no general rule. And as men can learn from each other, so some of these treatises have been useful to other writers. And some of them have been useful to those who were not writers.

14 At one time I was inclined to take the extreme position that the *only* critics worth reading were the critics who practised, and practised well, the art of which they wrote. But I had to stretch this frame to make some important inclusions; and I have since been in search of a formula which should cover everything I wished to include, even if it included more than I wanted. And the most important qualification which I have been able to find, which accounts for the peculiar importance of the criticism of practitioners, is that a critic must have a very highly developed sense of fact. This is by no means a trifling or frequent gift. And it is not one which easily wins popular commendations. The sense of fact is something very slow to develop, and its complete development means perhaps the very pinnacle of civilisation. For there are so many spheres of fact to be mastered, and our outermost sphere of fact, of knowledge, of control, will be ringed with narcotic fancies in the sphere beyond. To the member

of the Browning Study Circle, the discussion of poets about poetry may seem arid, technical, and limited. It is merely that the practitioners have clarified and reduced to a state of fact all the feelings that the member can only enjoy in the most nebulous form; the dry technique implies, for those who have mastered it, all that the member thrills to; only that has been made into some-[32]thing precise, tractable, under control. That, at all events, is one reason for the value of the practitioner's criticism – he is dealing with his facts, and he can help us to do the same.

15 And at every level of criticism I find the same necessity regnant. There is a large part of critical writing which consists in 'interpreting' an author, a work. This is not on the level of the Study Circle either; it occasionally happens that one person obtains an understanding of another, or a creative writer, which he can partially communicate, and which we feel to be true and illuminating. It is difficult to confirm the 'interpretation' by external evidence. To anyone who is skilled in fact on this level there will be evidence enough. But who is to prove his own skill? And for every success in this type of writing there are thousands of impostures. Instead of insight, you get a fiction. Your test is to apply it again and again to the original, with your view of the original to guide you. But there is no one to guarantee your competence, and once again we find ourselves in a dilemma.

16 We must ourselves decide what is useful to us and what is not; and it is quite likely that we are not competent to decide. But it is fairly certain that 'interpretation' (I am not touching upon the acrostic element in literature) is only legitimate when it is not interpretation at all, but merely putting the reader in possession of facts which he would otherwise have missed. I have had some experience of Extension lecturing, and I found only two ways of leading any pupils to like anything with the right liking: to present them with a selection of the simpler kinds of facts about a work – its conditions, its setting, its genesis – or else to spring the work on them in such a way that they were not prepared to be prejudiced against it. There were many facts to help them with Elizabethan drama: the poems of T. E. Hulme only needed to be read aloud to have immediate effect.

17 Comparison and analysis, I have said before, and Rémy de Gourmont has said it before me (a real master of fact [33] – sometimes, I am afraid, when he moved outside of literature, a master illusionist of fact), are the chief tools of the critic. It is obvious indeed that they *are* tools, to be handled with care, and not employed in an inquiry into the number of times giraffes are mentioned in the English novel. They are not used with

conspicuous success by many contemporary writers. You must know what to compare and what to analyse. The late Professor Ker had skill in the use of these tools. Comparison and analysis need only the cadavers on the table; but interpretation is always producing parts of the body from its pockets, and fixing them in place. And any book, any essay, any note in *Notes and Queries*, which produces a fact even of the lowest order about a work of art is a better piece of work than nine-tenths of the most pretentious critical journalism, in journals or in books. We assume, of course, that we are masters and not servants of facts, and that we know that the discovery of Shakespeare's laundry bills would not be of much use to us; but we must always reserve final judgement as to the futility of the research which has discovered them, in the possibility that some genius will appear who will know of a use to which to put them. Scholarship, even in its humblest forms, has its rights; we assume that we know how to use it, and how to neglect it. Of course the multiplication of critical books and essays may create, and I have seen it create, a vicious taste for reading about works of art instead of reading the works themselves, it may supply opinion instead of educating taste. But *fact* cannot corrupt taste; it can at worst gratify one taste – a taste for history, let us say, or antiquities, or biography – under the illusion that it is assisting another. The real corruptors are those who supply opinion or fancy; and Goethe and Coleridge are not guiltless – for what is Coleridge's *Hamlet*: is it an honest inquiry as far as the data permit, or is it an attempt to present Coleridge in an attractive costume?

18 We have not succeeded in finding such a test as anyone can apply; we have been forced to allow ingress into in-[34]numerable dull and tedious books; but we have, I think, found a test which, for those who are able to apply it, will dispose of the really vicious ones. And with this test we may return to the preliminary statement of the polity of literature and of criticism. For the kinds of critical work which we have admitted, there is the possibility of co-operative activity, with the further possibility of arriving at something outside of ourselves, which may provisionally be called truth. But if anyone complains that I have not defined truth, or fact, or reality, I can only say apologetically that it was no part of my purpose to do so, but only to find a scheme into which, whatever they are, they will fit, if they exist.

Variants from C. (1923):

3 autotelic] autonomous

5 and self-evident] and (I am afraid) self-evident
   formulation] recent formulation

7 certain heretics] heretical experts who were often Teutonic
English. For its practical] English; but for its practical
 9 said Mr Clutton Brock, is all case law.] says Mr Clutton Brock (I do not pretend to quote exactly, being separated from his book) is all case law.
11 sure] sure,
12 autotelic] autonomous
13 [Between 'commenting on it.' and 'There is no general rule.':] Coleridge (if you like) had to write about others; Dryden had to write about his own occupations. I do not suppose Mr Joyce has to do either.
14 [Between 'popular commendations' and 'The sense of fact':] So important it seems to me, that I am inclined to make one distinction between Classicism and Romanticism of this, that the romantic is deficient or undeveloped in his ability to distinguish between fact and fancy, whereas the classicist, or adult mind, is thoroughly realist – without illusions, without day-dreams, without hope, without bitterness, and with an abundant resignation. But this would be really a digression. At all events, the sense
[Between 'pinnacle' and 'of civilisation':] or (as American newspapers say) 'peak quotation'

II 'Rhetoric' And Poetic Drama

SE, 37–42.

Revised from *SW*, 78–85, which was radically revised from
'Whether Rostand Had Something About Him', *A.*, 4656 (25 July 1919), 665–6:
a review, signed 'T.S.E.', of *Le Vol de la Marseillaise* by Edmond Rostand.

The revisions in *SW* are so pervasive, with more of the text changed than not, sometimes in whole stretches, but sometimes also in local detail, that it has been thought best to give the original periodical text in full rather than to record variants in an apparatus that would probably confuse more than enlighten.

1 The death of Rostand was the disappearance of the poet whom, more than any other in France, we treated as the exponent of 'rhetoric', thinking of rhetoric as something recently out of fashion. And as we find ourselves looking back rather tenderly upon the author of *Cyrano* we wonder what this vice or quality is that is associated as plainly with Rostand's merits as with his defects. His rhetoric, at least, suited him at times so well, and so much better than it suited a much greater poet, Baudelaire, who is at times as rhetorical as Rostand. And we begin to suspect that the word is merely a vague term of abuse for any style that is bad, that is so evidently bad or second-rate that we do not recognise the necessity for greater precision in the phrases we apply to it.

2 Our own Elizabethan and Jacobean poetry – in so nice a problem it is much safer to stick to one's own language – is repeatedly called 'rhetorical'. It had this and that notable quality, but, when we wish to admit that it had defects, it is rhetorical. It had serious defects, even gross faults, but we cannot be considered to have erased them from our language when we are so unclear in our perception of what they are. The fact is that both Elizabethan prose and Elizabethan poetry are written in a variety of styles with a variety of vices. Is the style of Lyly, is Euphuism, rhetorical? In contrast to the elder style of Ascham and Elyot which it assaults, it is a clear, flowing, orderly and relatively pure style, with a systematic if monotonous formula of antitheses and similes. Is the style of Nashe? A tumid, [38] flatulent, vigorous style very different from Lyly's. Or it is perhaps the strained and the mixed figures of speech in which Shakespeare indulged himself. Or it is perhaps the careful declamation of Jonson. The word simply cannot be used as synonymous with bad writing. The meanings which it has been obliged to shoulder have been mostly opprobrious; but if a precise meaning can be found for it this meaning may occasionally represent a virtue. It is one of those words which it is the business of criticism to dissect and reassemble. Let us avoid the assumption that rhetoric is a vice of manner, and endeavour to find a rhetoric of substance also, which is right because it issues from what it has to express.

3 At the present time there is a manifest preference for the 'conversational' in poetry – the style of 'direct speech', opposed to the 'oratorical' and the rhetorical; but if rhetoric is any convention of writing inappropriately applied, this conversational style can and does become a rhetoric – or what is supposed to be a conversational style, for it is often as remote from polite discourse as well could be. Much of the second and third rate in American *vers libre* is of this sort; and much of the second and third rate in English Wordsworthianism. There is in fact no conversational or other form which can be applied indiscriminately; if a writer wishes to give the effect of speech he must positively give the effect of himself talking in his own person or in one of his rôles; and if we are to express ourselves, our variety of thoughts and feelings, on a variety of subjects with inevitable rightness, we must adapt our manner to the moment with infinite variations. Examination of the development of Elizabethan drama shows this progress in adaptation, a development from monotony to variety, a progressive refinement in the perception of the variations of feeling, and a progressive elaboration of the means of expressing these variations. This drama is admitted to have grown away from the rhetorical expression, the bombast speeches, of Kyd and Marlowe to

the subtle and dispersed utterance [39] of Shakespeare and Webster. But this apparent abandonment or outgrowth of rhetoric is two things: it is partly an improvement in language and it is partly progressive variation in feeling. There is, of course, a long distance separating the furibund fluency of old Hieronimo and the broken words of Lear. There is also a difference between the famous

> Oh eyes no eyes, but fountains full of tears!
> Oh life no life, but lively form of death!

and the superb 'additions to Hieronimo.'[1]

4 We think of Shakespeare perhaps as the dramatist who concentrates everything into a sentence, 'Pray you undo this button', or 'Honest honest Iago'; we forget that there is a rhetoric proper to Shakespeare at his best period which is quite free from the genuine Shakespearian vices either of the early period or the late. These passages are comparable to the best bombast of Kyd or Marlowe, with a greater command of language and a greater control of the emotion. *The Spanish Tragedy* is bombastic when it descends to language which was only the trick of its age; *Tamburlaine* is bombastic because it is monotonous, inflexible to the alterations of emotion. The really fine rhetoric of Shakespeare occurs in situations where a character in the play *sees himself* in a dramatic light:

> OTHELLO. And say, besides, – that in Aleppo once . . .
> CORIOLANUS. If you have writ your annals true, 'tis there,
> That like an eagle in a dovecote, I
> Fluttered your Volscians in Corioli.
> Alone I did it. Boy! . . .
> TIMON. Come not to me again; but say to Athens,
> Timon hath made his everlasting mansion
> Upon the beachèd verge of the salt flood . . .

It occurs also once in *Antony and Cleopatra*, when Enobarbus is inspired to see Cleopatra in this dramatic light:

> The barge she sat in . . .

[40] Shakespeare made fun of Marston, and Jonson made fun of Kyd. But in Marston's play the words were expressive of nothing; and Jonson was criticising the feeble and conceited language, not the emotion, not the 'oratory'. Jonson is as oratorical himself, and the moments when his

---

1. Of the authorship it can only be said that the lines are by some admirer of Marlowe. This might well be Jonson.

oratory succeeds are, I believe, the moments that conform to our formula. Notably the speech of Sylla's ghost in the induction to *Catiline*, and the speech of Envy at the beginning of *The Poetaster*. These two figures are contemplating their own dramatic importance, and quite properly. But in the Senate speeches in *Catiline*, how tedious, how dusty! Here we are spectators not of a play of characters, but of a play of forensic, exactly as if we had been forced to attend the sitting itself. A speech in a play should never be intended to move us as it might conceivably move other characters in the play, for it is essential that we should preserve our position of spectators, and observe always from the outside though with complete understanding. The scene in *Julius Caesar* is right because the object of our attention is not the speech of Antony (*Bedeutung*) but the effect of his speech upon the mob, and Antony's intention, his preparation and consciousness of the effect. And, in the rhetorical speeches from Shakespeare which have been cited, we have this necessary advantage of a new clue to the character, in noting the angle from which he views himself. But when a character *in* a play makes a direct appeal to us, we are either the victims of our own sentiment, or we are in the presence of a vicious rhetoric.

5 These references ought to supply some evidence of the propriety of Cyrano on Noses. Is not Cyrano exactly in this position of contemplating himself as a romantic, a dramatic figure? This dramatic sense on the part of the characters themselves is rare in modern drama. In sentimental drama it appears in a degraded form, when we are evidently intended to accept the character's sentimental interpretation of himself. In plays of realism we often find parts which are never allowed to be consciously dramatic, [41] for fear, perhaps, of their appearing less real. But in actual life, in many of those situations in actual life which we enjoy consciously and keenly, we are at times aware of ourselves in this way, and these moments are of very great usefulness to dramatic verse. A very small part of acting is that which takes place on the stage! Rostand had – whether he had anything else or not – this dramatic sense, and it is what gives life to Cyrano. It is a sense which is almost a sense of humour (for when anyone is conscious of himself as acting, something like a sense of humour is present). It gives Rostand's characters – Cyrano at least – a gusto which is uncommon on the modern stage. No doubt Rostand's people play up to this too steadily. We recognise that in the love scenes of Cyrano in the garden, for in *Romeo and Juliet* the profounder dramatist shows his lovers melting into unconsciousness of their isolated selves, shows the human soul in the process of forgetting itself. Rostand could not do that; but in the particular case of Cyrano on Noses, the character,

the situation, the occasion were perfectly suited and combined. The tirade generated by this combination is not only genuinely and highly dramatic: it is possibly poetry also. If a writer is incapable of composing such a scene as this, so much the worse for his poetic drama.

6 *Cyrano* satisfies, as far as scenes like this can satisfy, the requirements of poetic drama. It must take genuine and substantial human emotions, such emotions as observation can confirm, typical emotions, and give them artistic form; the degree of abstraction is a question for the method of each author. In Shakespeare the form is determined in the unity of the whole, as well as single scenes; it is something to attain this unity, as Rostand does, in scenes if not the whole play. Not only as a dramatist, but as a poet, he is superior to Maeterlinck, whose drama, in failing to be dramatic, fails also to be poetic. Maeterlinck has a literary perception of the dramatic and a literary perception of the poetic, and he joins the two; the two are not, as sometimes [42] they are in the work of Rostand, fused. His characters take no conscious delight in their rôle – they are sentimental. With Rostand the centre of gravity is in the expression of the emotion, not as with Maeterlinck in the emotion which cannot be expressed. Some writers appear to believe that emotions gain in intensity through being inarticulate. Perhaps the emotions are not significant enough to endure full daylight.

7 In any case, we may take our choice: we may apply the term 'rhetoric' to the type of dramatic speech which I have instanced, and then we must admit that it covers good as well as bad. Or we may choose to except this type of speech from rhetoric. In that case we must say that rhetoric is any adornment or inflation of speech which is *not done for a particular effect* but for a general impressiveness. And in this case, too, we cannot allow the term to cover all bad writing.

Text from *A.* (1919)

WHETHER ROSTAND HAD SOMETHING ABOUT HIM

M. Rostand had, as there was never much doubt, some force, or at least some power, whether of the theatre, or of the drama, or of poetry, the most analytical had not troubled to decide by analysis. The question whether M. Rostand produced any permanent work of art cannot even now be seriously entertained; the conviction grows that what was important was not any literary perfection, but M. Rostand himself. When *l'Oiseau bleu* appeared, it was nearly enough contemporary with

Chantecler to recall the latter to mind. The recollection brought a feeling of assurance, of security; it was enough for Rostand to be present; and later, among unfamiliar and not reassuring figures, Claudel or Suarez, it became terrifying that he should be absent.

To review the present book of war verse, the last writings of Rostand, would be ungenerous to its author. The quality which saved his drama is visible here working in a matter which would be likely to render it ridiculous. It is too late to subscribe our sympathy to the emotions expressed; it is too soon to regard the book tenderly as a keepsake. If we respect the memory of Rostand, and would feel kindly toward this book, we must extract the essence of its merit from the work of earlier years.

We have heard said of Rostand, 'rhetorician'. The word is used – it is used a good deal in our time – often by people who have not stopped to consider whether 'rhetoric' is an epithet of praise or reproach, whether it is or is not synonymous with bad writing, or whether it bears any index of valuation at all. The word means a good many things in writing, and in our time mostly opprobrious; but among the many meanings that it comprehends it is possible that there may be one which is a positive virtue, and that this meaning may be applied to the rhetoric of Rostand. For the word is one of those words which it is a part of the business of criticism to dissolve, finding a variety of particular meanings, each of which is in the end a cluster of particular facts. Instead of seeking, therefore, a definition (definition is a labour of creation rather than of criticism), we might do to find a 'rhetorical' period of rhetoric similar to Rostand's, within that period to find writers who are rhetorical, and to inquire whether there is not some positive virtue in their rhetoric which may have a counterpart in the work of Rostand. Let us avoid the assumption that rhetoric is in the manner only, that it is merely bad writing, and endeavour to find a rhetoric of the stuff itself. We may distinguish also between rhetoric as the formed style of a period, and as the individual habit of a writer.

The important rhetoric, for my purpose, is the rhetoric of content, not the rhetoric of language. The distinction becomes evident and evidently capital when we examine the work of contemporary poets. At the present time there is a visible preference for the 'conversational', the style of 'direct speech', opposed to the 'oratorical'; but this conversational style may and does become a fixed convention applied to any matter, not invariably issuing out of the matter treated but imposed upon it. Certain writers have indeed succeeded in obtaining, at times, the effect of direct or simple speech desired; but the avoidance of the rhetorical expression of older writers has become a form, or has separated into a variety of forms or rhetorics which impede, as often as they assist, the expression of feeling. What is overlooked is the fact that there is no 'conversational' or other form which can be applied indiscriminately; and that if we are to express ourselves, our variety of thoughts and feelings, on a variety of subjects with inevitable rightness, we must adapt our manner to the moment with infinite variations. Examination of the development of Elizabethan drama shows this progress in adaptation, a development from monotony to variety, a progressive refinement in the perception of the variations of feeling and a progressive elaboration of the means for expressing these variations. This drama is supposed to have grown away from rhetorical expression, from the bombast speeches of Kyd and Marlowe to the subtle and dispersed utterance of the mature Shakespeare and Webster. But this apparent abandonment of outgrowth of rhetoric is two things: it is partly an improvement in language and it is partly progressive variation in feeling. There is, of course, a long distance between the furibund fluency of old Hieronimo and the broken words of Lear. We think of Shakespeare, perhaps, as the dramatist of sentences, of 'Prithee undo this button' or 'Honest honest Iago'; we forget that at the proper moments Shakespeare is as rhetorical, but with a greater command of language and a greater control of the emotion, as Kyd or Marlowe. *The Spanish Tragedy* is bombastic because the language is inferior; *Tamburlaine* is bombastic because it is monotonous, inflexible to the alterations of emotion. Shakespeare when he chooses, when the situation requires it, is as 'rhetorical' as either Kyd or Marlowe. The moments occur when a character in the play *sees himself* in a dramatic light:

> OTHELLO: And likewise say that at Aleppo once . . .
> CORIOLANUS: If you have writ your annals true, 'tis there,
> That like an eagle in a dovecote, I
> Fluttered your Volscians in Corioli . . .
> TIMON: Come not to me again; but say to Athens,
> Timon has built his everlasting mansion
> Beyond the beachèd verge of the salt flood . . .

and in *Antony and Cleopatra*, when the old captain is inspired to see Cleopatra in this dramatic light:

> The barge she sat in . . .

Shakespeare made fun of Marston, and Jonson made fun of Kyd. But in Marston's play the words were expressive of nothing; and Jonson was criticising the feeble and conceited language, not the emotion, not the 'oratory'. Jonson is as oratorical himself:

> Dost thou not feel me, Rome, not yet? lies night
> So heavy on thee, and my shade so light?

These references ought to supply some evidence of the propriety of Cyrano on Noses. What is rare in modern drama, either verse or prose, is the dramatic sense on the part of the characters in the play themselves. We are given plays of realism in which the parts are never allowed to be consciously dramatic, for perhaps, of their appearing less real. But in actual life, or in those situations in our actual life which we enjoy consciously and keenly, we are, at times, aware of ourselves in this way, and these moments are of very great usefulness to dramatic verse. The employment of this dramatic self-consciousness on the part of the figures in the play is an important cause of the success, and of the merit, of Rostand as a dramatist. It gives his characters a vitality, a gusto in living, which is very uncommon on the modern stage. No doubt they play up to this public rôle too steadily; they often fail of any other existence than this in which they are aware of their own rôle. One is conscious of that in the love scenes of Cyrano in the garden, while in *Romeo and Juliet* the profounder or intenser poet shows his lovers melting into incoherent unconsciousness of their isolated selves, shows the human soul in the process of forgetting itself. Rostand could not do that; but the thing he could do he could do very well, and in the peculiar case of Cyrano on Noses, the character, the situation, the occasion, were perfectly suited and combined. The tirade generated by this combination is not only genuinely and highly dramatic; it is possibly poetry also. If a writer is incapable of composing such a scene as this, he is probably incapable of composing a poetic drama.

Cyrano satisfies, at least as far as scenes like this can satisfy, the requirements for poetic drama. Poetic drama must take genuine and substantial human emotions, such emotions as observation can verify, typical emotions, and give them aesthetic form; the degree of abstraction reached is a question for the method of each writer separately. In Shakespeare the aesthetic form is determined in the unity of the whole, as well as in isolated scenes; it is something to attain this unity, as Rostand does, in scenes if not in the whole play. Not only as a dramatist, but as a writer of poetic drama, he is superior to Maeterlinck, whose drama, in failing to be dramatic, fails also to be poetic. Maeterlinck has a literary perception of the dramatic, and a literary perception of the poetic, and he joins the two components; but they are not, as sometimes in the work of Rostand, fused. His characters take no conscious delight in their dramatic-poetic rôle – they are sentimental; while Rostand's characters, enjoying awareness, are thereby preserved from sentimentality. The centre of gravity is in the expression of the emotion, not, as with Maeterlinck, in the emotion which cannot be expressed. Rostand is not afraid to be 'rhetorical', because he believes that emotion can be expressed; unlike many modern writers, who sometimes disingenuously hide their emotions behind obscure simplicities, because they believe that they will gain in intensity by suppression. Perhaps the emotions are not significant enough to endure full daylight. Whatever the value of anything Rostand had to expose, at least he did not shrink from exposure.

Variants from *SW* (1920):
1   was the disappearance] is the disappearance
4   And, in the rhetorical speeches] And in the rhetorical speeches
5   unconsciousness] incoherent unconsciousness

A Dialogue on Dramatic Poetry

SE, 43–58.

Publ. with a Preface, signed 'T. S. Eliot', in an edn of Dryden's *Of Dramatick Poesie* (1928), pp. xi–xxvii: Gallup B7. Revised in *SE*. On p. 45 'how much their audiences would like to behave' has been corrected to 'how their audiences would like to behave' (the earlier version) and on p.56 'Meierhold' has been corrected to 'Meyerhold'.

1 E: You were saying, *B*, that it was all very well for the older dramatic critics – you instanced Aristotle and Corneille and Dryden at random – to discuss the laws of drama as they did; that the problem is altogether different and infinitely more complicated for us. That fits in with a notion of my own, which I will expound in a moment; but first I should like to know what differences you find.

2 B: I need not go into the matter very deeply to persuade you of my contention. Take Aristotle first. He had only one type of drama to consider; he could work entirely within the 'categories' of that drama; he did not have to consider or criticise the religious, ethical or artistic prejudices of his race. He did not have to like so many things as we have to like, merely because he did not know so many things. And the less you know and like, the easier to frame aesthetic laws. He did not have to consider either what is universal or what is necessary for the time. Hence he had a better chance of hitting on some of the universals and of knowing what was right for the time. And as for Dryden. I take Dryden because there is an obvious, a too obvious, hiatus between the Tudor-Jacobean drama and that of the Restoration. We know about the closing of the theatres, and so on; and we are apt to magnify the differences and difficulties. But the differences between Dryden and Jonson are nothing to the differences between ourselves, who are sitting here to discuss

poetic drama, and Mr Shaw and Mr Galsworthy and Sir Arthur Pinero and [44] Mr Jones and Mr Arlen and Mr Coward: all of whom are almost contemporary with us. For the world of Dryden on the one hand and the world of Shakespeare and Jonson on the other were much the same world, with similar religious, ethical and artistic presuppositions. But what have we in common with the distinguished playwrights whom I have just mentioned?

3 And, to return to Aristotle for a moment, consider how much more we know (unfortunately) about Greek drama than he did. Aristotle did not have to worry about the relation of drama to religion, about the traditional morality of the Hellenes, about the relation of art to politics; he did not have to struggle with German or Italian aesthetics; he did not have to read the (extremely interesting) works of Miss Harrison or Mr Cornford, or the translations of Professor Murray, or wrinkle his brow over the antics of the Todas and the Veddahs. Nor did he have to reckon with the theatre as a paying proposition.

4 Similarly, neither Dryden, nor Corneille from whom he learned so much, was bothered by excessive knowledge about Greek civilisation. They had the Greek and Latin classics to read, and were not aware of *all* the differences between Greek and Roman civilisation and their own. As for us, we know too much, and are convinced of too little. Our literature is a substitute for religion, and so is our religion. We should do better if, instead of worrying about the place of drama in society, we simply decided what amused us. What is the purpose of the theatre except to amuse?

5 *E*: It is all very well to reduce the drama to 'amusement'. But it seems to me that that is just what has happened. I believe that the drama has something else to do except to divert us. What else does it do at the moment?

6 *B*: I have just given a list of dramatists. I admit that their intentions vary. Pinero, for instance, was concerned with setting, or, as is said in the barbarous jargon of our day, 'posing' the problems of his generation. He was much [45] more concerned with 'posing' than with answering. Shaw, on the other hand, was much more concerned with answering than with 'posing'. Both of these accomplished writers had a strong ethical motive. This ethical motive is not apparent in Mr Arlen or Mr Coward. Their drama is pure 'amusement'. The two excesses go together. The whole question is, whom does the drama amuse? and what is the quality of the amusement?

7 C: I should not for my part admit that any of these people are concerned to amuse. There is no such thing as mere amusement. They are concerned with flattering the prejudices of the mob. And their own. I do not suppose for a moment that either Shaw, or Pinero, or Mr Coward has ever spent one hour in the study of ethics. Their cleverness lies in finding out how their audiences would like to behave, and encouraging them to do it by exhibiting personages behaving in that way.

8 D: But why should a dramatist be expected to spend even five minutes in the study of ethics?

9 B: I consent. But they need to assume some moral attitude in common with their audience. Aeschylus and Sophocles, the Elizabethans, and the Restoration dramatists had this. But this must be already given; it is not the job of the dramatist to impose it.

10 E: What is the moral attitude of Dryden's *Mr Limberham*?

11 B: Impeccable. The morality of our Restoration drama cannot be impugned. It assumes orthodox Christian morality, and laughs (in its comedy) at human nature for not living up to it. It retains its respect for the divine by showing the failure of the human. The attitude of Restoration drama towards morality is like the attitude of the Blasphemer towards Religion. It is only the irreligious who are shocked by blasphemy. Blasphemy is a sign of Faith. Imagine Mr Shaw blaspheming! He could not. Our Restoration drama is all virtue. It depends upon virtue for its existence. The author of *The Queen was in the Parlour* does not depend upon virtue.

[46] 12 E: You are talking as if the drama was merely a matter of established morals. Let me for a moment transfer the discussion to the question of form. I speak as one who is satisfied neither by Elizabethan drama nor by Pinero or Barrie. A few years ago I – and you B and you C and A – was delighted by the Russian ballet. Here seemed to be everything that we wanted in drama, except the poetry. It did not teach any 'lesson', but it had form. It seemed to revive the more formal element in drama for which we craved. I concede that the more recent ballets have not given me the same pleasure. But for that I blame Mr Diaghilev, not the ballet in principle. If there is a future for drama, and particularly for poetic drama, will it not be in the direction indicated by the ballet? Is it not a question of form rather than ethics? And is not the question of verse drama versus prose drama a question of degree of form?

13 A: There I am inclined to support you. People have tended to think of verse as a restriction upon drama. They think that the emotional range, and the realistic truth, of drama is limited and circumscribed by verse. People were once content with verse in drama, they say, because they were content with a restricted and artificial range of emotion. Only prose can give the whole gamut of modern feeling, can correspond to actuality. But is not every dramatic representation artificial? And are we not merely deceiving ourselves when we aim at greater and greater realism? Are we not contenting ourselves with appearances, instead of insisting upon fundamentals? Has human feeling altered much from Aeschylus to ourselves? I maintain the contrary. I say that prose drama is merely a slight by-product of verse drama. The human soul, in intense emotion, strives to express itself in verse. It is not for me, but for the neurologists, to discover why this is so, and why and how feeling and rhythm are related. The tendency, at any rate, of prose drama is to emphasise the ephemeral and superficial; if we want to get at the permanent and universal we tend to express ourselves in verse.

[47] 14 D: But – to return to the point – can you hang all this on the ballet? How is the ballet concerned with the permanent and universal?

15 B: The ballet is valuable because it has, unconsciously, concerned itself with a permanent form; it is futile because it has concerned itself with the ephemeral in content. Apart from Stravinski, who is a real musician, and from Cocteau, who is a real playwright, what is the strength of the ballet? It is in a tradition, a training, an askesis, which, to be fair, is not of Russian but of Italian origin, and which ascends for several centuries. Sufficient to say that any efficient dancer has undergone a training which is like a moral training. Has any successful actor of our time undergone anything similar?

16 E: This seems to me the opening for which I have been waiting. You all approve of the ballet because it is a system of physical training, of traditional, symbolical and highly skilled movements. It is a liturgy of very wide adaptability, and you seem to laud the liturgy rather than the variations. Very well. B has spoken of our knowledge of Greek antecedents to Greek drama, and has implied that we know more about that than Dryden, or Aristotle, or the Greek dramatists themselves. I say that the consummation of the drama, the perfect and ideal drama, is to be found in the ceremony of the Mass. I say, with the support of the scholars whom B mentions (and others), that drama springs from religious liturgy, and that it cannot afford to depart far from religious liturgy. I agree with

B that the problem of drama was simpler for Aristotle and for Dryden and for Corneille than for us. They had only to take things as they found them. But when drama has ranged as far as it has in our own day, is not the only solution to return to religious liturgy? And the only dramatic satisfaction that I find now is in a High Mass well performed. Have you not there everything necessary? And indeed, if you consider the ritual of the Church during the cycle of the year, you have the complete drama represented. The Mass [48] is a small drama, having all the unities; but in the Church year you have represented the full drama of creation.

17 *B*: The question is not, whether the Mass is dramatic, but what is the relation of the drama to the Mass? We must take things as we find them. Are we to say that our cravings for drama are fulfilled by the Mass? I believe that a cursory examination is enough for us to reply, No. For I once knew a man who held the same views that you appear to hold, *E*. He went to High Mass every Sunday, and was particular to find a church where he considered the Mass efficiently performed. And as I sometimes accompanied him, I can testify that the Mass gave him extreme, I may even say immoderate satisfaction. It was almost orgiastic. But when I came to consider his conduct, I realised that he was guilty of a *confusion des genres*. His attention was not on the meaning of the Mass, for he was not a believer but a Bergsonian; it was on the Art of the Mass. His dramatic desires were satisfied by the Mass, precisely because he was not interested in the Mass, but in the drama of it. Now what I maintain is, that you have no business to care about the Mass unless you are a believer. And even if you are a believer you will have dramatic desires which crave fulfilment otherwise. For man lives in various degrees. We need (as I believe, but you need not believe this for the purpose of my argument) religious faith. And we also need amusement (the quality of the amusement will, of course, not be unrelated to the quality of our religious belief). Literature can be no substitute for religion, not merely because we need religion, but because we need literature as well as religion. And religion is no more a substitute for drama than drama is a substitute for religion. If we can do without religion, then let us have the theatre without pretending that it *is* religion; and if we can do without drama, then let us not pretend that religion is drama.

18 For there is a difference in attention. If we are religious, then we shall only be aware of the Mass as art, in so far as it is badly done and interferes with our devotion consequently. [49] A devout person, in assisting at Mass, is not in the frame of mind of a person attending a drama, for he is *participating* – and that makes all the difference. In participating we

are supremely conscious of certain realities, and unconscious of others. But we are human beings, and crave representations in which we are conscious, and critical, of these other realities. We cannot be aware solely of divine realities. We must be aware also of human realities. And we crave some liturgy less divine, something in respect of which we shall be more spectators and less participants. Hence we want the human drama, related to the divine drama, but not the same, as well as the Mass.

19 E: You have admitted all that I expected, and more. That is the essential relation of drama to religious liturgy.

20 D: I have a suggestion to put forward. It is this: can we not take it that the form of the drama must vary from age to age in accordance with religious assumptions of the age? That is, that drama represents a relation of the human needs and satisfactions which the age provides. When the age has a set religious practice and belief, then the drama can and should tend towards realism, I say *towards*, I do not say arrive at. The more definite the religious and ethical principles, the more freely the drama can move towards what is now called photography. The more fluid, the more chaotic the religious and ethical beliefs, the more the drama must tend in the direction of liturgy. Thus there would be some constant relation between drama and the religion of the time. The movement, in the time of Dryden and indeed of Corneille, and indeed of Aristotle, was towards freedom. Perhaps our movement should be towards what we called, in touching upon the ballet, form?

21 E: An interesting theory, with no historical backing whatever, but concluding in exactly what I said myself. But if you want form, you must go deeper than dramatic technique.

22 C: I should like to make an interruption. If I do not make [50] it now I shall probably forget to make it at all. You are all talking of form and content, of freedom and restriction, as if everything was infinitely variable. You are not, like myself, students of the popular drama of the *faubourgs*. And what I there remark is the fixity of morality. The suburban drama has to-day fundamentally the same morality as it had in the days of *Arden of Feversham* and *The Yorkshire Tragedy*. I agree with B about Restoration comedy. It is a great tribute to Christian morality. Take the humour of our great British comedian, Ernie Lotinga. It is (if you like) bawdy. But such bawdiness is a tribute to, an acknowledgement of conventional British morality. I am a member of the Labour Party. I believe in the King and the Islington Empire. I do not believe in the

plutocratic St Moritzers for whom our popular dramatists cater. But what I was saying is that our suburban drama is morally sound, and out of such soundness poetry may come. Human nature does not change. Another port, please.

23 *B*: I suggest that I agree with the late William Archer about Elizabethan drama.

24 *A*, *E*, *C*, and *D*: What!

25 *B*: Yes. William Archer was a very honest man. As a dramatic critic he had one fault: he knew nothing about poetry. Furthermore, he made the egregious error of supposing that the dramatic merit of a dramatic work could be estimated without reference to its poetic merit. Henrik Ibsen certainly had more dramatic ability than Cyril Tourneur. But as Archer did not realise that dramatic and poetic ability are less different than chalk and cheese, he made the mistake of supposing that Ibsen was a greater dramatist than Tourneur. Greater if you like, but he will not last as long. For the greatest drama is poetic drama, and dramatic defects *can* be compensated by poetic excellence. Let us ignore Tourneur. We can cite Shakespeare.

26 *C*: Do you mean that Shakespeare is a greater dramatist than Ibsen, not by being a greater dramatist, but by being a greater poet?

[51] 27 *B*: That is precisely what I mean. For, on the other hand, what great poetry is not dramatic? Even the minor writers of the *Greek Anthology*, even Martial, are dramatic. Who is more dramatic than Homer or Dante? We are human beings, and in what are we more interested than in human action and human attitudes? Even when he assaults, and with supreme mastery, the divine mystery, does not Dante engage us in the question of the human attitude towards this mystery – which is dramatic? Shakespeare was a great dramatist and a great poet. But if you isolate poetry from drama completely, have you the right to say that Shakespeare was a greater dramatist than Ibsen, or than Shaw? Shaw is right about Shakespeare, for Shaw is no poet. I am not quite right there neither, for Shaw *was* a poet – until he was born, and the poet in Shaw was stillborn. Shaw has a great deal of poetry, but all stillborn; Shaw is dramatically precocious, and poetically less than immature. The best you can say for Shaw is that he seems not to have read all the popular handbooks on science that Mr Wells and Bishop Barnes have read.

28 *E*: Yes, Shakespeare fails us, and Mr Archer is right. William Archer is only wrong in having attacked the minor figures of Elizabethan drama and not having understood that he was obliged to attack Shakespeare as well. He was wrong, as you said, in thinking that drama and poetry are two different things. If he had seen that they are the same thing he would have had to admit that Cyril Tourneur is a great dramatist, that Jonson is a great dramatist, that Marlowe is a very great dramatist, that Webster is a great dramatist, and that Shakespeare is so great a dramatist, so great a poet, that even Mr Archer should have removed his shoes, instead of evading the question, rather than ask Shakespeare to abide it. Shakespeare would have abidden it if Mr William Archer had chosen to ask it. But he did not choose.

29 *D*: I think both *B* and *E* are rather muddled about the relation of poetry and drama, but especially *B*. Just as [52] Archer made a mechanical separation, so *B* makes a mechanical reunion. Let us make it clearer by putting it about the other way, and taking up a point that *B* let slip. If drama tends to poetic drama, not by adding an embellishment and still less by limiting its scale, we should expect a dramatic poet like Shakespeare to write his finest poetry in his most dramatic scenes. And this is just what we do find: what makes it most dramatic is what makes it most poetic. No one ever points to certain plays by Shakespeare as being the most poetic, and to *other* plays as being the most dramatic. The same plays are the most poetic and the most dramatic, and this is not by a concurrence of two activities, but by the full expansion of one and the same activity. I agree that the dramatist who is not a poet is so much the less a dramatist.

30 *C*: The odd thing about William Archer's book is that he did, to some extent, recognise poetry when he saw it; but at any rate when he was dealing with an Elizabethan like Chapman, whenever he comes across a passage of poetry, he refuses to believe that it is dramatic. If this is poetry, he seems to say, that proves that it is not drama. I remember that when I read the book I noticed that Archer could certainly have picked out un-dramatic or defectively dramatic passages from Chapman's plays: instead he selects that splendidly dramatic speech of Clermont on seeing the ghosts – as an example of 'mild surprise'!

31 *B*: Perhaps the ghosts put him off.

32 *E*: Yet nothing is more dramatic than a ghost.

33 *C*: To sum up: there is no 'relation' between poetry and drama. All poetry tends towards drama, and all drama towards poetry.

34 *F*: A neat and dangerous generalisation. For you would admit that you enjoy a great deal of poetry in which hardly even your own practised eye could detect the 'tendency' towards drama; and consequently you ought surely to be able to enjoy a great deal of drama which is unquestionably written in prose.

35 *B*: Of course he does. And some of the Elizabethan plays of which Mr Archer disapproved are, in fact, bad plays. And a great many were also, as Mr Shaw has observed, bad verse. Shaw points out that it is easier to write bad verse than good prose – which nobody ever denied; but it is easy for Shaw to write good prose and quite impossible for him to write good verse.

36 *E*: Running off on this wild-goose chase after William Archer, whom you might just as well have left alone, you have forgotten to tell us why Shakespeare fails us.

37 *B*: I mean that Archer's objections to Elizabethan drama were partly based upon a right instinct. He used some deplorable terms, such as 'humanitarianism', in expressing his dislike. But had he observed that his fundamental objection applied as much to Shakespeare as to anybody, as much to the best as to the worst, he might have admitted an obligation to find another and profounder explanation for it.

38 *A*: Are we to infer that you criticise Shakespeare on the ground that his plays are not morally edifying?

39 *B*: In a sense, yes.

40 *A*: But a little while ago you were defending Restoration comedy against the charge of immorality and indecency.

41 *B*: Not against indecency, that was unnecessary. We all like its indecency when it is really witty, as it sometimes is. But the question of Wycherley and the question of Shakespeare are not on the same plane. Restoration comedy is a comedy of social manners. It presupposes the existence of a society, therefore of social and moral laws. (It owes much to Jonson, but little to Shakespeare – anyway, Shakespeare was too great to have much influence.) It laughs at the members of society who transgress

its laws. The tragedy of Shakespeare goes much deeper and yet it tells us only that weakness of character leads to disaster. There is no background of social order such as you perceive behind Corneille and Sophocles.

[54] 42 C: Why should there be? You can't deduce from that that Shakespeare is inferior to Sophocles and Corneille.

43 B: No, I can't. All I know is that something is lacking, I am left dissatisfied and disturbed. I think there are other people who feel the same thing. So far as I can isolate Shakespeare, I prefer him to all other dramatists of every time. But I can not do that altogether; and I find the age of Shakespeare moved in a steady current, with back-eddies certainly, towards anarchy and chaos.

44 C: But that has nothing to do with the question.

45 B: Possibly not.

46 E: Surely the dramatic poet, being when and where he is, has no business with his own background. He can't help that, and his business is with the audience. The Elizabethan drama, or at any rate Shakespeare, was good enough to justify artistically its own background. But it does not seem to me that it is as much the lack of moral and social conventions as the lack of artistic conventions that stands in the way of poetic drama to-day. Shaw is our greatest stage moralist, and his conventions are only negative: they consist in all the things he doesn't believe. But there again, Shaw cannot help that.

47 A: This sort of moralising censorship would leave us nothing. Are you prepared to say that you are the worse for having read Shakespeare and seen him played?

48 B: No.

49 A: Are you prepared to maintain that you are none the better, none the wiser, and none the happier for it?

50 B: No.

51 A: Very well. I have also heard you railing at Wagner as 'pernicious'. But you would not willingly resign your experience of Wagner either. Which seems to show that a world in which there was no art that was not

morally edifying would be a very poor world indeed.

52 B: So it would. I would not suppress anything that is good measured by artistic standards. For there is always [55] something to be learned from it. I would not have Shakespeare any different from what he is. But it is like life in general. There are heaps of things in the world which I should like to see changed; but in a world without Evil life would not be worth living.

53 E: Well, you have taken a long time to leave us just where we were before.

54 B: Not quite. You can never draw the line between aesthetic criticism and moral and social criticism; you cannot draw a line between criticism and metaphysics; you start with literary criticism, and however rigorous an aesthete you may be, you are over the frontier into something else sooner or later. The best you can do is to accept these conditions and know what you are doing when you do it. And, on the other hand, you must know how and when to retrace your steps. You must be very nimble. I may begin by moral criticism of Shakespeare and pass over into aesthetic criticism, or vice versa.

55 E: And all you do is to lead the discussion astray.

56 C: I cannot agree with that wild generalisation about the anarchy of Elizabethan drama. In fact it would only make the present-day situation more puzzling. We seem to agree that the modern world is chaotic, and we are inclined to agree that its lack of social and moral conventions makes the task of the dramatic poet more difficult, if not impossible. But if the Elizabethan and Jacobean period was also a period of chaos, and yet produced great poetic drama, why cannot we?

57 B: I don't know.

58 C: You will have to qualify your statement about Elizabethan drama. You would have had to do that in any case, for there are a great many more things to take account of than this simple idea of decay. To begin with, there is no precedent for a nation having *two* great periods of drama. And its great period is always short, and is great because of a very small number of great dramatists. And a very great period of any kind of poetry is never repeated. Per-[56]haps each great race has just strength enough for one period of literary supremacy.

59 D: If C is not side-tracked he will lead us presently into politics.

60 A: All this is true and perfectly commonplace. But it does not help. When it comes to the present age, we are not going to be deterred by a fatalistic philosophy of history from wanting a poetic drama, and from believing that there must be some way of getting it. Besides, the craving for poetic drama is permanent in human nature. At this point I suspect that F is waiting to let off on us what he calls the economic factors; and the state of the public, and the producers, and the cost of theatres; and the competition of cheap cinemas, et cetera. I believe that if you want a thing you can get it, and hang the economic factors.

61 F: And your way of getting it is to talk about it.

62 A: I like talking about things; it helps me to think.

63 C: I agree with A, whether he has thought about it or not. All this talk about periods of art is interesting and sometimes useful when we are occupied with the past, but is quite futile when we come to consider the present in relation to the future. Let us begin by observing the several kinds of way in which contemporary drama fails. There are the plays written by poets who have no knowledge of the stage: this kind has been sufficiently abused. There are the plays written by men who know the stage and are not poets. Of these two extremes I will only remark that experience proves that neither is of any pertinence to our present subject.

64 A: But what is our present subject?

65 C: The possibility of poetic drama.

66 G: You seem to have covered nearly the whole field of discussion of contemporary drama, except for the topics of Gordon Craig, Reinhardt, Meyerhold, Sir Barry Jackson, the Old Vic, Eugene O'Neill, Pirandello and Toller. And we are not here concerned with methods of production – which rules out the first four of these names – but with the [57] production of something to produce. I have only one suggestion to offer, but it will be the only practical suggestion that has been made. We should hire a barn or studio, and produce plays of our own, or even disjected scenes of plays and produce them by ourselves and only for ourselves, no friends to be admitted. We might learn at least by practice first whether we have anything in common, and second what forms of versification are possible.

We must find a new form of verse which shall be as satisfactory a vehicle for us as blank verse was for the Elizabethans.

67 *F*: And I know what will happen. We shall start selling tickets in order to pay the costs, we shall then have to import plays in order to supply the demand, and we shall end with a perfectly conventional cosmopolitan little-theatre or Sunday-society performance.

68 *B*: What is much more likely is that nothing will be done at all. We are all too busy; we have to earn our living in other ways. It is even doubtful whether we are sufficiently interested. We cannot make the plays unless we think there is a demand, and there will be no demand until we have made it. There is not one of us who has not a dozen things to do, within the next six months, which he knows to be more important for himself than to prance about in a stable-theatre.

69 *C*: One thing has struck me in this conversation. We started by speaking of Dryden, then passed to poetic drama in general; and we have not taken up one of the subjects that Dryden thought it worth while to discuss, and all of the subjects raised have been subjects that Dryden would never have thought of.

70 *B*: It is one thing to discuss the rules of an art when that art is alive, and quite another when it is dead. When there is a contemporary practice, the critic must start from that point, and all his criticism must return to it. Observe how confident Dryden is! Even the difference between the drama of his age and that of the Elizabethans, when the tumults and disorders of the Great Rebellion had hardly [58] been subdued, seemed to him less important than they seem to us. He admits that his age is inferior, essentially in the respects in which we find it inferior, to the preceding: yet he thought of his generation – and at bottom he must have been thinking, with justifiable pride, of himself – as improving and polishing the earlier drama in many ways. He is quite right: the relation of his drama to that of the Elizabethans should be conceived as he conceived it; the chasm is not so vast as it is usually taken to be; and the French influence was far less than it was supposed to be. But the questions which he discussed are not out of date.

71 *E*: The Unities of Time and Place, for instance. Dryden gives what is the soundest and most commonsense view possible for his time and place. But the Unities have for me, at least, a perpetual fascination. I believe they will be found highly desirable for the drama of the future. For one

thing, we want more concentration. All plays are now much too long. I never go to the theatre, because I hate to hurry over my dinner, and I dislike to dine early. A continuous hour and a half of *intense* interest is what we need. No intervals, no chocolate-sellers, or ignoble trays. The Unities do make for intensity, as does verse rhythm.

72 *A*: You think that we need stronger stimulants, in a shorter space of time, to get the same exaltation out of the theatre that a sensitive contemporary may be supposed to have gotten out of a tragedy by Shakespeare or even out of one by Dryden.

73 *E*: And meanwhile let us drink another glass of port to the memory of John Dryden.

Variants from 1928:
Preface: To compete with the late W. P. Ker and Mr Nichol Smith and other scholars by attempting a learned introduction to Dryden's essay would be merely to commit a presumption and a superfluity. The following method occurred to me as hitherto untried and as challenging no comparisons. Dryden composed his essay in the form of a dialogue, which might by some stretch of imagination have taken place between cultivated critics of his time. I have therefore composed a dialogue which may, with less stretch of imagination, for my language is less elegant and my periods shorter-breathed, be supposed to have taken place between half a dozen fairly intelligent men of our time. And as the topics discussed in Dryden's party were issues of his day, so are mine issues of our day. If I cannot add to the knowledge and understanding of Dryden, I can perhaps add to his glory by the contrast. But my purpose is, if possible, to throw the dialogue of Dryden into a rather new light, by the great contrast between the topics, and between the attitudes towards them. For this the centuries are responsible. My dialogue represents the scraps of many actual conversations and divers times and in divers circumstances; and is intended to collect some representative topics amongst those which arise in any such conversation to-day. Dryden and his friends could discuss a 'dramatic poetry' which actually existed, which was still being written; and their aim was therefore to construct its critical laws. We, on the other hand, are always discussing something which does not exist but which we should like to have brought into existence; so we are not occupied with critical laws; and so we range [x] over a wide field of speculation, asking many questions and answering none.

    The dialogue is a form even more convenient for my purpose than it was for Dryden's. Dryden had written great plays; but the contemporary critic has not written a great play, so is in a weak position for laying down the law about plays. If he dogmatised, he would expose himself to the adjuration to go and write the poetic drama of the future instead of talking about it. But the dialogue form enables me to discuss the subject without pretending to come to any conclusion. Furthermore, Dryden's own opinions issue quite clearly from his dialogue; I have no clear opinions on this subject. Hence I have distributed my own theories quite indiscriminately among the speakers; and the reader must not try to identify the persons in the dialogue with myself or anyone else. They are not even fictions; they are merely voices; a half-dozen men who may be imagined sitting in a tavern after lunch, lingering over port and conversation at an hour when they should all be doing something else.

Title A Dialogue on Poetic Drama

22 suburban] suburban
   suburban] suburban
   port] double port

43 disturbed] disturbed, and not in a state of Aristotelian purgation.

Euripides and Professor Murray

SE, 59–64.

Publ. in *A&L*, 3. 2 (Spring 1920), 36–43. Unsigned. Gallup C107.
Repr. with a change of title in *SW*, and further revised in *SE*.

1 The appearance of Miss Sybil Thorndike some years ago as Medea at the Holborn Empire was an event which has a bearing upon three subjects of considerable interest: the drama, the present standing of Greek literature; and the importance of good contemporary translation. On the occasion on which I was present the performance was certainly a success; the audience was large, it was attentive, and its applause was long. Whether the success was due to Euripides is uncertain; whether it was due to Professor Murray is not proved; but that it was in considerable measure due to Miss Thorndike there is no doubt. To have held the centre of the stage for two hours in a rôle which requires both extreme violence and restraint, a rôle which requires simple force and subtle variation; to have sustained so difficult a rôle almost without support; this was a legitimate success. The audience, or what could be seen of it from one of the cheaper seats, was serious and respectful and perhaps inclined to self-approval at having attended the performance of a Greek play; but Miss Thorndike's acting might have held almost any audience. It employed all the conventions, the theatricalities, of the modern stage; yet her personality triumphed over not only Professor Murray's verse but her own training.

2 The question remains whether the production was a 'work of art'. The rest of the cast appeared slightly ill at ease; the nurse was quite a tolerable nurse of the crone type; Jason was negative; the messenger was uncomfortable at having to make such a long speech; and the refined [60] Dalcroze chorus had mellifluous voices which rendered their lyrics

happily inaudible. All this contributed toward the highbrow effect which is so depressing; and we imagine that the actors of Athens, who had to speak clearly enough for 20,000 auditors to be able to criticise the versification, would have been pelted with figs and olives had they mumbled so unintelligibly as most of this troupe. But the Greek actor spoke in his own language, and our actors were forced to speak in the language of Professor Gilbert Murray.

3 I do not believe, however, that such performances will do very much to rehabilitate Greek literature or our own, unless they stimulate a desire for better translations. The serious auditors, many of whom I observed to be like myself provided with Professor Murray's eighteenpenny translation, were probably not aware that Miss Thorndike, in order to succeed as well as she did, was really engaged in a struggle against the translator's verse. She triumphed over it by attracting our attention to her expression and tone and making us neglect her words; and this, of course, was not the dramatic method of Greek acting at its best. The English and Greek languages remained where they were. But few persons realise that the Greek language and the Latin language, and *therefore*, we say, the English language, are within our lifetime passing through a critical period. The Classics have, during the latter part of the nineteenth century and up to the present moment, lost their place as a pillar of the social and political system – such as the Established Church still is. If they are to survive, to justify themselves as literature, as an element in the European mind, as the foundation for the literature we hope to create, they are very badly in need of persons capable of expounding them. We need someone – not a member of the Church of Rome, and perhaps preferably not a member of the Church of England – to explain how vital a matter it is, if Aristotle may be said to have been a moral pilot of Europe, whether we shall or shall not drop that [61] pilot. And we need a number of educated poets who shall at least have opinions about Greek drama, and whether it is or is not of any use to us. And it must be said that Professor Gilbert Murray is not the man for this. Greek poetry will never have the slightest vitalising effect upon English poetry if it can only appear masquerading as a vulgar debasement of the eminently personal idiom of Swinburne. These are strong words to use against the most popular Hellenist of his time; but we must witness of Professor Murray ere we die that these things are not otherwise but thus.

4 This is really a point of capital importance. That the most conspicuous Greek propagandist of the day should almost habitually use two words where the Greek language will provide him with one; that he should

render σκιάν by '*grey* shadow'; and that he should stretch the Greek brevity to fit the loose frame of William Morris, and blur the Greek lyric to the fluid haze of Swinburne; these are not faults of infinitesimal significance. The first great speech of Medea Mr Murray begins with:

> Women of Corinth, I am come to show
> My face, lest ye despise me. . . .

We find in the Greek ἐζῆλθον δόμον. 'Show my face', therefore is Mr Murray's gift.

> This thing undreamed of, sudden from on high,
> Hath sapped my soul: I dazzle where I stand,
> The cup of all life shattered in my hand. . .

Again, we find that the Greek is:

> ἐμοὶ δ᾽ἄελπτον πρᾶγμα προσπεσόν τόδε
> ψυχὴν διέφθαρκ᾽. οἴχομαι δὲ καὶ βίου
> χάριν μεθεῖσα κατθανεῖν χρῄζω, φίλαι.

So, here are two striking phrases which we owe to Mr Murray; it is he who has sapped our soul and shattered the cup of all life for Euripides. And these are only random examples.

[62] οὐκ ἔστιν ἄλλη φρὴν μιαιφονωτέρα

becomes 'no bloodier spirit between heaven and hell'! Surely we know that Professor Murray is acquainted with *Sister Helen*? Professor Murray has simply interposed between Euripides and ourselves a barrier more impenetrable than the Greek language. We do not reproach him for preferring, apparently, Euripides to Aeschylus. But if he does, he should at least appreciate Euripides. And it is inconceivable that any one with a genuine feeling for the sound of Greek verse should deliberately elect the William Morris couplet, the Swinburne lyric, as an equivalent.

5 As a poet, Mr Murray is merely a very insignificant follower of the pre-Raphaelite movement. As a Hellenist, he is very much of the present day, and a very important figure in the day. This day began, in a sense, with Tylor and a few German anthropologists; since then we have acquired sociology and social psychology, we have watched the clinics of Ribot and Janet, we have read books from Vienna and heard a discourse of Bergson; a philosophy arose at Cambridge; social emancipation crawled abroad; our historical knowledge has of course increased; and we have a curious Freudian-social-mystical-rationalistic-higher-critical interpretation of the Classics and what used to be called the Scriptures. I do not deny the

very great value of all work by scientists in their own departments, the great interest also of this work in detail and in its consequences. Few books are more fascinating than those of Miss Harrison, Mr Cornford, or Mr Cooke, when they burrow in the origins of Greek myths and rites; M. Durkheim, with his social consciousness, and M. Lévy-Bruhl, with his Bororo Indians who convince themselves that they are parroquets, are delightful writers. A number of sciences have sprung up in an almost tropical exuberance which undoubtedly excites our imagination, and the garden, not unnaturally, has come to resemble a jungle. Such men as Tylor, and Robertson Smith, and Wilhelm Wundt, who [63] early fertilised the soil, would hardly recognise the resulting vegetation; and indeed poor Wundt's *Völkerpsychologie* was a musty relic before it was translated.

6 All these events are useful and important in their phase, and they have sensibly affected our attitude towards the Classics; and it is this phase of classical study that Professor Murray – the friend and inspirer of Jane Harrison – represents. The Greek is no longer the awe-inspiring Belvedere of Winckelmann, Goethe, and Schopenhauer, the figure of which Walter Pater and Oscar Wilde offered us a slightly debased re-edition. And we realise better how different – not how much more Olympian – were the conditions of the Greek civilisation from ours; and at the same time Mr Zimmern has shown us how the Greek dealt with analogous problems. Incidentally we do not believe that a good English prose style can be modeled upon Cicero, or Tacitus, or Thucydides. If Pindar bores us, we admit it; we are not certain that Sappho was *very* much greater than Catullus; we hold various opinions about Virgil; and we think more highly of Petronius than our grandfathers did.

7 It is to be hoped that we may be grateful to Professor Murray and his friends for what they have done, while we endeavour to neutralise Professor Murray's influence upon Greek literature and English language in his translations by making better translations. The choruses from Euripides by H. D. are, allowing for errors and even occasional omissions of difficult passages, much nearer to both Greek and English than Mr Murray's. But H. D. and the other poets of the 'Poets' Translation Series' have so far done no more than pick up some of the more romantic crumbs of Greek literature; none of them has yet shown himself competent to attack the *Agamemnon*. If we are to digest the heavy food of historical and scientific knowledge that we have eaten we must be prepared for much greater exertions. We need a digestion that can assimilate both Homer and Flaubert. We need a careful study of Renaissance Humanists

and [64] Translators, such as Mr Pound has begun. We need an eye which can see the past in its place with its definite differences from the present, and yet so lively that it shall be as present to us as the present. This is the creative eye; and it is because Professor Murray has no creative instinct that he leaves Euripides quite dead.

Variants:

Title Euripides and Gilbert Murray: A Performance at the Holborn Empire *A&L* (1920)

1 appearance] recent appearance *A&L* (1920), *SW*
   some years ago] [Not in *A&L* (1920), *SW.*]
   was an event] is an event *A&L* (1920), *SW*

2 [After 'Gilbert Murray'.] So that on the whole we may say that the performance was an interesting one. *A&L* (1920), *SW*

Seneca in Elizabethan Translation

SE, 65–105.

Revised from the Introduction to *Seneca His Tenne Tragedies Translated into English Edited by Thomas Newton Anno 1581* (publ. Sept. 1927), v–liv: Gallup B5. On p. 71 the punctuation of 'Latin historian, with Thucydides' has been corrected to 'Latin historian with Thucydides,'.

1 No author exercised a wider or deeper influence upon the Elizabethan mind or upon the Elizabethan form of tragedy than did Seneca. To present the Elizabethan translations of the tragedies in their proper setting, it is necessary to deal with three problems which at first may appear to be but slightly connected: (1) the character, virtues and vices of the Latin tragedies themselves; (2) the directions in which these tragedies influenced our Elizabethan drama; (3) the history of these translations, the part they played in extending the influence of Seneca, and their actual merit as translation and as poetry. There are here several questions which, with the greater number of important Tudor translations, do not arise. Most of the better-known translations are of authors whose intrinsic merit is unquestioned, and the translations derive some of their prestige from the merit and fame of the author translated; and most of the better-known prose translations have an easy beauty of style which arrests even the least prepared reader. But with the translations of the *Tenne Tragedies* (for they are by several hands) we are concerned first of all with a Latin poet whose reputation would deter any reader but the most curious; with translations of unequal merit, because by different scholars; and with translation into a metre – the 'fourteener' – which is superficially a mere archaism, and which repels readers who have not the patience

to accustom their ears and nerves to its beat. The translations have, as I hope to show, considerable poetic charm and quite adequate accuracy, with occa-[66]sional flashes of real beauty; their literary value remains greater than that of any later translations of Seneca's tragedies that I have examined, either in English or French. But the appreciation of the literary value of these translations is inseparably engaged with the appreciation of the original and of its historical importance; so that although at first sight a consideration of the historical problems may appear irrelevant, it should in the end enhance our enjoyment of the translations as literature.

I

2 In the Renaissance, no Latin author was more highly esteemed than Seneca; in modern times, few Latin authors have been more consistently damned. The prose Seneca, the 'Seneca morale' of Dante, still enjoys a measure of tepid praise, though he has no influence; but the poet and tragedian receives from the historians and critics of Latin literature the most universal reprobation. Latin literature provides poets for several tastes, but there is no taste for Seneca. Mackail, for instance, whose taste in Latin literature is almost catholic, dismisses Seneca with half a page of his *Short History of Latin Literature*, and a few of the usual adjectives such as 'rhetorical'. Professor Mackail is inclined by his training to enjoy the purer and more classical authors, and is inclined by his temperament to enjoy the most romantic: like Shenstone or some other eighteenth-century poets, Seneca falls between. Nisard, in his *Poètes Latins de la décadence*, devotes many pages and much patience to the difference of conditions which produced great tragedy in Athens, and only rhetorical declamation in Rome. Butler, after a more detailed and more tolerant examination from a more literary point of view (*Post-Augustan Poetry*), commits himself to the damaging statement that 'to Seneca more than to any other man is due the excessive predominance of declamatory rhetoric, which has characterised the drama throughout Western Europe [67] from the Renaissance down to the latter half of the nineteenth century'. The most recent critic, Mr F. L. Lucas, (*Seneca and Elizabethan Tragedy*) admits 'the exasperatingly false rhetoric of the Seneca stage, with its far-fetched and frigid epigrams'. Yet this is a dramatist whom Scaliger preferred to Euripides, and whom the whole of Europe in the Renaissance delighted to honour. It is obviously a task of some difficulty to disentangle him from his reputation.

3 We must admit, first, that the tragedies of Seneca deserve the censure that has been directed upon them. On the other hand, it may be true – I think it is true – that the critics, especially the English critics, have

been often biased by Seneca's real and supposed bad influence upon the Renaissance, that they have included the demerits of his admirers in his own faults. But before we proceed to what redemption of his fame is possible, it is expedient to resume those universally admitted strictures and limitations which have become commonplaces of Senecan criticism. First, it is pretty generally agreed that the plays of Seneca were composed, not for stage performance, but for private declamation.[1] This theory attenuates the supposed 'horrors' of the tragedies, many of which could hardly have been represented on a stage, even with the most ingenious machinery, without being merely ridiculous; the Renaissance assumption to the contrary gave licence to a taste which would probably have been indulged even without Seneca's authority. And if the plays were written to be declaimed, probably by a single speaker ('elocutionist' is really the word), we can account for other singularities. I say 'account for', I do not say without qualification that this peculiar form was the 'cause'; for the ultimate cause was probably the same Latin temper which made such an unacted drama possible. The cause lies in the Latin sensibility which is expressed by the Latin language. But if we [68] imagine this unacted drama, we see at once that it is at one remove from reality, compared with the Greek. Behind the dialogue of Greek drama we are always conscious of a concrete visual actuality, and behind that of a specific emotional actuality. Behind the drama of words is the drama of action, the timbre of voice and voice, the uplifted hand or tense muscle, and the particular emotion. The spoken play, the words which we read, are symbols, a shorthand, and often, as in the best of Shakespeare, a very abbreviated shorthand indeed, for the acted and felt play, which is always the real thing. The phrase, beautiful as it may be, stands for a greater beauty still. This is merely a particular case of the amazing unity of Greek, the unity of concrete and abstract in philosophy, the unity of thought and feeling, action and speculation, in life. In the plays of Seneca, the drama is all in the word, and the word has no further reality behind it. His characters all seem to speak with the same voice, and at the top of it; they recite in turn.

4 I do not mean to suggest that the method of delivery of a play of Seneca was essentially different from that of Greek tragedy. It was probably nearer to the declamation of Greek tragedy than was the delivery of Latin comedy. The latter was acted by professional actors. I imagine that Seneca's plays were declaimed by himself and other amateurs, and it is likely that the Athenian tragedies were performed by amateurs.

---

1. I must admit, however, that this view has recently been contested with great force by Léon Herrmann: *Le Théâtre de Sénèque* (Paris, 1924). See p. 195 of that book.

I mean that the beauty of phrase in Greek tragedy is the shadow of a greater beauty – the beauty of thought and emotion. In the tragedies of Seneca the centre of value is shifted from what the personage says to the way in which he says it. Very often the value comes near to being mere smartness. Nevertheless, we must remember that 'verbal' beauty is still a kind of beauty.

5 The plays are admirably adapted for declamation before an imperial highbrow audience of crude sensibility but considerable sophistication in the ingenuities of language. They would have been as unactable on the Greek stage as they are on the English. Superficially neat and trim, they are, [69] for the stage, models of formlessness. The Athenians were accustomed to long speeches from Messengers, speeches which embarrass both the modern actor and the modern audience; this was a convention with practical advantages; their other long speeches usually have some dramatic point, some place in the whole scheme of the play. But the characters in a play by Seneca behave more like members of a minstrel troupe sitting in a semicircle, rising in turn each to do his 'number', or varying their recitations by a song or a little back-chat. I do not suppose that a Greek audience would have sat through the first three hundred lines of the *Hercules Furens*. Only at the 523rd line does Amphitryon detect the sound of Hercules' tread, ascending from Hell, at which inopportune moment the chorus interrupt for two or three pages. When Hercules finally appears, he seems to be leading Cerberus, who presently evaporates, for he is not on the stage a few minutes later. After Amphitryon has in a rather roundabout way, but more briefly than might have been expected, explained to Hercules the pressing danger to his family and country, Hercules makes off to kill Lycus. While Hercules is thus engaged in a duel on the result of which everybody's life depends, the family sit down calmly and listen to a long description by Theseus of the Tartarean regions. The account is not a straight monologue, as Amphitryon from time to time puts leading questions about the fauna, and the administration and system of justice, of the world below. Meanwhile, Hercules has (contrary to the usual belief that Seneca murders all his victims in full view of the audience) despatched Lycus off-stage. At the end of the play, when Juno has stricken Hercules with madness, it is not at all clear whether he destroys his family on-stage or off. The slaughter is accompanied by a running commentary by Amphitryon, whose business it is to tell the audience what is going forward. If the children are slain in sight of the audience, this commentary is superfluous. Amphitryon also reports the collapse of Hercules; but presently Hercules comes to, cer-[70]tainly on-stage, and spies his dead wife and children. The

whole situation is inconceivable unless we assume the play to have been composed solely for recitation; like other of Seneca's plays, it is full of statements useful only to an audience which sees nothing. Seneca's plays might, in fact, be practical models for the modern 'broadcasted drama'.

6 We need not look too closely into the conditions of the age which produced no genuine drama, but which allowed this curious freak of non-theatrical drama. The theatre is a gift which has not been vouchsafed to every race, even of the highest culture. It has been given to the Hindus, the Japanese, the Greeks, the English, the French, and the Spanish, at moments; in less measure to the Teutons and Scandinavians. It was not given to the Romans, or generously to their successors the Italians. The Romans had some success in low comedy, itself an adaptation of Greek models, but their instinct turned to shows and circuses, as does that of the later race which created the Commedia dell' Arte, which still provides the best puppet shows, and which gives a home to Mr Gordon Craig. No cause can be assigned, for every cause demands a further cause. It is handy to speak of 'the genius of the language', and we shall continue to do so, but why did the language adopt that particular genius? At any rate, we should discourage any criticism which, in accounting for the defects and faults of the plays of Seneca, made much of the 'decadence' of the age of Nero. In the verse, yes, Seneca is unquestionably 'silver age', or more exactly he is not a poet of the *first* rank in Latin. He is far inferior to Virgil. But for tragic drama, it would be a gross error to suppose that an earlier and more heroic age of Rome could have produced anything better. Many of the faults of Seneca which appear 'decadent' are, after all, merely Roman and (in the narrower sense) Latin.

7 It is so with the characterisation. The characters of Seneca's plays have no subtlety and no 'private life'. But it would be an error to imagine that they are merely cruder and coarser versions of the Greek orig-[71]inals. They belong to a different race. Their crudity is that which was of the Roman, as compared with the Greek, in real life. The Roman was much the simpler creature. At best, his training was that of devotion to the State, his virtues were public virtues. The Greek knew well enough the idea of the State, but he had also a strong traditional morality which constituted, so to speak, a direct relation between him and the gods, without the mediation of the State, and he had furthermore a sceptical and heterodox intelligence. Hence the greater efficiency of the Roman, and the greater interest of the Greek. Hence the difference between Greek Stoicism and Roman Stoicism – the latter being the form through which Stoicism influenced greater Europe. We must think of the characters of

Seneca as offspring of Rome, more than we think of them as offspring of their age.

8 The drama of Antigone – which Seneca did not attempt – could hardly have been transposed for Roman sentiment. In the drama of Seneca there are no conflicts, except the conflict of passion, temper, or appetite with the external duties. The literary consequence, therefore, is the tendency which persists in modern Italy; the tendency to 'rhetoric'; and which, on such a large scale, may be attributed to a development of language exceeding the development of sensibility of the people. If you compare Catullus with Sappho, or Cicero with Demosthenes, or a Latin historian with Thucydides, you find that the genius is the genius of a different language, and what is lost is a gift of sensibility. So with Seneca and the Greek dramatists. Hence we should think of the long ranting speeches of Seneca, the beautiful but irrelevant descriptions, the smart stichomythia, rather as peculiarities of Latin than as the bad taste of the dramatist.

9 The congeniality of Stoicism to the Roman mind is no part of my duty to analyse; and it would be futile to decide what, in the dialogue, and characterisation of Seneca's plays, is due to Stoicism, what due to the [72] Roman mind, and what due to the peculiar form which Seneca elected. What is certain is the existence of a large element of Stoicism in the plays, enough to justify the belief that the plays and the prose are by the hand of the same Seneca. In the plays, indeed, the Stoicism is present in a form more quickly to catch the fancy of the Renaissance than in the prose epistles and essays. Half of the commonplaces of the Elizabethans – and the more commonplace half – are of Senecan origin. This ethic of sententious maxims was, as we shall see, much more sympathetic to the temper of the Renaissance than would have been the morals of the elder Greek dramatists; the Renaissance itself was much more Latin than Greek. In the Greek tragedy, as Nisard and others have pointed out, the moralising is not the expression of a conscious 'system' of philosophy; the Greek dramatists moralise only because morals are woven through and through the texture of their tragic idea. Their morals are a matter of feeling trained for generations; they are hereditary and religious, just as their dramatic forms themselves are the development of their early liturgies. Their ethics of thought are one with their ethics of behaviour. As the dramatic form of Seneca is no growth, but a construction, so is his moral philosophy and that of Roman Stoicism in general. Whether the Roman scepticism was, as Nisard suggests, the result of a too rapid and great expansion and mixture of races cancelling each other's beliefs, rather than the product of a lively inquiring intelligence, the 'beliefs' of

Stoicism are a consequence of scepticism; and the ethic of Seneca's plays is that of an age which supplied the lack of moral habits by a system of moral attitudes and poses. To this the natural public temper of Rome contributed. The ethic of Seneca is a matter of postures. The posture which gives the greatest opportunity for effect, hence for the Senecan morality, is the posture of dying: death gives his characters the opportunity for their most sententious aphorisms – a hint which Elizabethan dramatists were only too ready to follow.

[73] 10 When all reserves have been made, there is still much to be said for Seneca as a dramatist. And I am convinced that the proper approach to his appreciation and enjoyment is not by comparison and contrast – to which, in his case, criticism is violently tempted – but by isolation. I made a careful comparison of the *Medea* and the *Hippolytus* of Seneca – perhaps his two best plays – with the *Medea* of Euripides and the *Phèdre* of Racine respectively; but I do not think that any advantage would be gained by reporting the results of this inquiry, by contrasting either the dramatic structure or the treatment of the title figures. Such comparisons have already been made; they magnify the defects and obscure the merits of the Senecan tragedy. If Seneca is to be compared, he should rather be compared for versification, descriptive and narrative power, and taste, with the earlier Roman poets. The comparison is fair, though Seneca comes off rather ill. His prosody is monotonous; in spite of a mastery of several metres, his choruses fall heavily on the ear. Sometimes his chorus rhythms seem to hover between the more flexible measures of his predecessors and the stiffer but more impressive beat of the medieval hymn.[1] But within the limits of his declamatory purpose, Seneca obtains, time after time, magnificent effects. In the verbal *coup de théâtre* no one has ever excelled him. The final cry of Jason to Medea departing in her car is unique; I can think of no other play which reserves such a shock for the last word:

> Per alta vada spatia sublimi aethere;
> testare nullos esse, qua veheris, deos.[2]

---

1. E.g. O mors amoris una sedamen mali,
    O mors pudoris maximum laesi decus. – (Hippolytus, 1188–89.)
2. Here the translator seems to me to have hit on the sense:

    Bear witness, grace of God is none in place of thy repayre.

    A modern translator (Professor Miller, editing the Loeb Translation text) gives 'bear witness, where thou ridest, that there are no gods'. It seems to me more effective if we take the meaning to be that there are no gods *where (ever) Medea is*, instead of a mere outburst of atheism. But the old Farnaby edition observes 'testimonium contra decorum justitiam, vel argumento nullos esse in caelo deos'.

[74] Again and again the epigrammatic observation on life or death is put in the most telling way at the most telling moment. It is not only in his brief ejaculations that Sencea triumphs. The sixteen lines addressed by the chorus to the dead sons of Hercules (*Hercules Furens*, I. 1135 ff.), which are exquisitely rendered by the Elizabethan translator, seem to me highly pathetic. The descriptive passages are often of great charm, with phrases which haunt us more than we should expect. The lines of Hercules,

> ubi sum? sub ortu solis, an sub cardine
> glacialis ursae?

must have lain long in the memory of Chapman before they came out in *Bussy d'Ambois* as

> fly where men feel
> The cunning axle-tree, or those that suffer
> Under the chariot of the snowy Bear.

Though Seneca is long-winded, he is not diffuse; he is capable of great concision; there is even a monotony of forcefulness; but many of his short phrases have for us as much oratorical impressiveness as they had for the Elizabethans. As (to take an unworn example) the bitter words of Hecuba as the Greeks depart:

> concidit virgo ac puer;
> bellum peractum est.

Even the most sentarious sayings of stoical commonplace preserve their solemnity in that Latin language which carries such thoughts more grandly than could any other:

> Fatis agimur; cedite fatis.
> non sollicitae possunt curae
> mutare rati stamina fusi.
> quidquid patimur mortale genus,
> quidquid facimus venit ex alto,
> servatque suae decreta colus
> Lachesis nulla revoluta manu,
> omnia secto tramite vadunt
> primusque dies dedit extremum. – (*Oedipus*, 980 ff.)

[75] II But to quote Seneca is not criticism; it is merely to offer baits to a possible reader; it would indeed be bad criticism if we left the impression that these and such as these are moments in which Seneca excels himself,

and which he could not sustain. An essential point to make about Seneca is the consistency of his writing, its maintenance on one level, below which he seldom falls and above which he never mounts. Seneca is not one of those poets who are to be remembered because they now and then rise to the tone and vocabulary of greater poets. Seneca is wholly himself; what he attempted he executed, he created his own genre. And this leads us to a consideration which we must keep in mind in considering his later influence: whether we can treat him seriously as a *dramatist*. Critics are inclined to treat his drama as a bastard form. But this is an error which critics of the drama are in general apt to make; the forms of drama are so various that few critics are able to hold more than one or two in mind in pronouncing judgement of 'dramatic' and 'undramatic'. What is 'dramatic'? If one were saturated in the Japanese Noh, in Bhasa and Kalidasa, in Aeschylus, Sophocles and Euripides, Aristophanes and Menander, in the popular medieval plays of Europe, in Lope de Vega and Calderón, as well as the great English and French drama, and if one were (which is impossible) equally sensitive to them all, would one not hesitate to decide that one form is more dramatic than another? And Seneca's is definitely a 'form'. It does not fall within either of the categories of the defectively dramatic. There are the 'closet dramas' which are mostly simply inferior dramas: the plays of Tennyson, Browning, and Swinburne. (Whether a writer expected his play to be played or not is irrelevant, the point is whether it is playable.) And there is another, more interesting type, where the writer is trying to do something more or something different from what the stage can do, but yet with an implication of performance, where there is a mixture of dramatic and extra-dramatic elements. This is a modern [76] and sophisticated form: it contains *The Dynasts*, Goethe's *Faust*, and possibly (not having seen it played I cannot speak with confidence) *Peer Gynt*. Seneca's plays do not belong to either of these types. If, as I believe, they are intended for *recitation*, they have a form of their own; and I believe that they were intended for recitation because they are perfectly adapted for recitation – they are better recited than read. And I have no doubt – though there is no external evidence – that Seneca must have had considerable practice himself in reciting the plays. He would have been, therefore, a playwright of as practical experience as Shakespeare or Molière. His form is a practical form; it is even, I suggest, a form which might be interesting to attempt in our own time, when the revival of the theatre is obstructed by some of the difficulties which made the stage an impossibility in the age of Seneca.

12 What lessons the Elizabethans learnt from Seneca, and whether they were the same as those which we might learn ourselves, is the next

subject to consider. But whether they profited by the study, or whether they admired him and pillaged him to their own detriment, we must remember that we cannot justly estimate his influence unless we form our own opinion of Seneca first, without being influenced by his influence.

II

13 The influence of Seneca upon Elizabethan drama has received much more attention from scholars than from literary critics. The historical treatment has been very thorough. The admirable edition of the works of Sir William Alexander, Earl of Stirling, by Kastner and Charlton (Manchester University Press, vol. i. 1921), has a full account of this influence both direct and through Italy and France; in this introduction will also be found the best bibliography of the subject. Dr F. S. Boas, especially in his edition of Kyd's plays, has treated the matter at length. Professor J. W. Cunliffe's *Influence of Seneca on Elizabethan Tragedy* (1893) [77] remains, within its limits, the most useful of all books, and Mr Cunliffe has handled the question in a more general way in his *Early English Classical Tragedies*. Indirect Senecan influences have also been studied in detail, as in Professor A. M. Witherspoon's *Influence of Robert Garnier on Elizabethan Drama*. And work which is now being done on the earlier drama (see Dr A. W. Reed's recent *Early Tudor Drama*, 1926) will enable us to understand better the junction of the Senecan influence with the native tradition. It is not fitting that a literary critic should retrace all this labour of scholarship, where either his dissent or his approval would be an impertinence; but we may benefit by this scholarship to draw certain general conclusions.

14 The plays of Seneca exerted their influence in certain ways and to several results. The results are of three main types: (1) the popular Elizabethan tragedy; (2) the 'Senecal' drama, pseudo-classical, composed by and for a small and select body of persons not closely in touch with or in sympathy with the popular drama of the day, and composed largely in protest against the defects and monstrosities of that drama; (3) the two Roman tragedies of Ben Jonson, which appear to belong between the two opposed classes, to constitute an attempt, by an active practising playwright, to improve the form of popular drama by the example of Seneca; not by slavish imitation but by adaptation, to make of popular drama a finished work of art. As for the ways in which Seneca influenced the Elizabethans, it must be remembered that these were never simple, and became more complicated. The Italian and the French drama of the day was already penetrated by Seneca. Seneca was a regular part of the school curriculum, while Greek drama was unknown to all but a few

great scholars. Every schoolboy with a smattering of Latin had a verse or two of Seneca in his memory; probably a good part of the audiences could recognise the origin of the occasional bits of Seneca which are quoted in Latin in some of the popular plays (e.g. several times by Marston). And by the time that *The* [78] *Spanish Tragedy* and the old *Hamlet* had made their success, the English playwright was under the influence of Seneca by being under the influence of his own predecessors. Here the influence of Kyd is of the greatest importance: if Senecan Kyd had such a vogue, that was surely the path to facile success for any hard-working and underpaid writer.

15 All that I wish to do is to consider certain misconceptions of the Senecan influence, which I believe are still current in our opinions of Elizabethan drama, although they do not appear in works of scholarship. For such a purpose the contemporary translations possess a particular value: whether they greatly affected the conception of Seneca, or greatly extended his influence, they give a reflection of the appearance of Seneca to the Englishman of the time. I do not suggest that the influence of Seneca has been exaggerated or diminished in modern criticism; but I believe that too much importance has been attached to his influence in some directions, and too little to his influence in others. There is one point on which everyone is agreed, and hardly more than one: the five-act division of the modern European play is due to Seneca. What I chiefly wish to consider are, first, his responsibility for what has been called since Symonds's day the Tragedy of Blood – how far Seneca is the author of the horrors which disfigure Elizabethan drama; second, his responsibility for *bombast* in Elizabethan diction; and third, his influence upon the *thought*, or what passes for thought, in the drama of Shakespeare and his contemporaries. It is the first which I think has been overestimated, the second misconstrued, the third undervalued.

16 Certainly, among all national dramas, the Elizabethan tragedies are remarkable for the extent to which they employ the horrible and revolting. It is true that but for this taste and practice we should never have had *King Lear* or *The Duchess of Malfy*; so impossible is it to isolate the vices from the virtues, the failures from the masterpieces of Elizabethan tragedy. We cannot reprehend a custom [79] but for which one great experiment of the human spirit must have been left unmade, even if we cannot like it; nor can we wholly deplore anything which brings with it some information about the soul. And even leaving Shakespeare apart, the genius of no other race could have manipulated the tragedy of horror into the magnificent farce of Marlowe, or the magnificent nightmare of

Webster. We must therefore reserve two measures of comparison: one, that between the baser tragedy of the time and the best tragedy of the time, the other (which is perhaps a moral measure, the application of which would lead us too far for the present discussion) between the tragedy of the time as a whole and another tragedy of horror – we think of Dante's Ugolino and the Oedipus of Sophocles – in which, in the end, the mind seems to triumph. Here, the question of Seneca's influence is capital. If the taste for horror was a result of being trained on Seneca, then it has neither justification nor interest; if it was something inherent in the people and in the age, and Seneca merely the excuse and precedent, then it is a phenomenon of interest. Even to speak of Seneca as offering a precedent and excuse is probably to falsify; for it implies that the Elizabethans would otherwise have been a little uneasy in conscience at indulging such tastes – which is ridiculous to suppose. They merely assumed that Seneca's taste was like their own – which is not *wholly* untrue; and that Seneca represented the whole of classical antiquity – which is quite false. Where Seneca took part is in affecting the type of plot; he supported one tendency against another. But for Seneca, we might have had more plays in the *Yorkshire Tragedy* mould; that is to say, the equivalent of the *News of the World* murder report; Seneca, and particularly the Italianised Seneca, encouraged the taste for the foreign, remote, or exotic. No doubt *The Jew of Malta* or *Titus Andronicus* would have made the living Seneca shudder with genuine aesthetic horror; but his influence helped to recommend work with which he had little in common.

[80] 17 When we examine the plays of Seneca, the actual horrors are not so heinous or so many as are supposed. The most unpleasantly sanguinary is the *Thyestes*, a subject which so far as I know, was not attempted by a Greek dramatist. Even here, if the view that the tragedies were intended only for recitation is true, the cultivated Roman audience were listening to a story which was part of their Hellenic culture, and which is in fact a common property of folklore. The story was sanctified by time. The plots of Elizabethan tragedy were, so far as the audience were concerned, novelties. This plot of *Thyestes* is not employed by any Elizabethan, but the play has undoubtedly more in common with the Tragedy of Blood, especially in its early form, than any other of Seneca's. It has a particularly tedious Ghost. It has, more emphatically than any other, the motive of Revenge, unregulated by any divine control or justice. Yet even in the *Thyestes* the performance of the horrors is managed with conventional tact; the only visible horror is perhaps the unavoidable presentation of the evidence – the children's heads in a dish.

18 The most significant popular play under Senecan influence is of course *The Spanish Tragedy*, and the further responsibility of Kyd for the translation of the pseudo-Senecan *Cornelia* of Garnier has marked him as the disciple of Seneca. But in *The Spanish Tragedy* there is another element, not always sufficiently distinguished from the Senecan, which (though it may have relations among the Italian Renaissance progeny of Seneca) allies it to something more indigenous. The Senecan apparatus, it is true, is impressive. The Ghost, and Revenge, who replace the Tantalus and the Fury of the *Thyestes*, use all the infernal allusions – Acheron, Charon, and the rest – so dear to Seneca. Temporary insanity is an expedient well known to Seneca. But in the type of plot there is nothing classical or pseudo-classical at all. 'Plot' in the sense in which we find plot in *The Spanish Tragedy* does not exist for Seneca. He took a story perfectly well known to everybody, and [81] interested his auditors entirely by his embellishments of description and narrative and by smartness and pungency of dialogue; suspense and surprise attached solely to verbal effects. *The Spanish Tragedy*, like the series of Hamlet plays, including Shakespeare's, has an affinity to our contemporary detective drama.[1] The plot of Hieronymo to compass his revenge by the play allies it with a small but interesting class of drama which certainly owes nothing essential to Seneca: that which includes *Arden of Faversham*[2] and *The Yorkshire Tragedy*. These two remarkable plays are both based on contemporary or recent crimes committed in England. Unless it be the hint of divine retribution in the epilogue to *Arden*, there is no token of foreign or classical influence in these two plays. Yet they are bloody enough. The husband in *The Yorkshire Tragedy* kills his two young sons, throws the servant downstairs and breaks her neck, and nearly succeeds in killing his wife. In *Arden of Faversham* the wife and her conspirators stab the husband to death upon the stage – the rest of the play being occupied by a primitive but effective police inquiry. It is only surprising that there are not more examples of this type of play, since there is evidence of as lively a public interest in police court horrors as there is to-day. One of the pieces of evidence is associated with Kyd; it is a curious little account of a poisoning case, *The Murder of John Brewen*. (A little later, Dekker was to supply the deficiency of penny journalism with his plague Pamphlets.) In Kyd, whether *Arden* be by him or by an imitator, we find the union of Senecan with native elements, to the advantage of both. For the Senecan

---

1. I suggest also that besides *Hamlet*, *Macbeth* and to some extent *Othello* among Shakespeare's major tragedies have this 'thriller' interest, whilst it is not introduced into *King Lear*, *Antony and Cleopatra*, or *Coriolanus*. It is present in *Oedipus Tyrannus*.
2. I dissent from Dr Boas, and agree with that body of opinion which attributes *Arden* to Kyd, e.g. Fleay, Robertson, Crawford, Dugdale Sykes, Oliphant.

influence is felt in the structure of the play – the structure of *The Spanish Tragedy* is more drama-[82]tic than that of *Arden* or *The Yorkshire Tragedy*; whilst the material of *The Spanish Tragedy*, like that of the other two plays, is quite different from the Senecan material, and much more satisfying to an unlettered audience.

19 The worst that can be urged against Seneca, in the matter of responsibility for what is disgusting in Elizabethan drama, is that he may have provided the dramatist with a pretext or justification for horrors which were not Senecan at all, for which there was certainly a taste, and the taste for which would certainly have been gratified at that time whether Seneca had ever written or not. Against my use of *The Yorkshire Tragedy*, it may be said that this play (the crime in question was committed only in 1603) and *Arden* also were written after the success of *The Spanish Tragedy*, and that the taste for horrors developed only after it had received Senecan licence. I cannot *prove* the contrary. But it must be admitted that the greater number of the horrors are such as Seneca himself would not have tolerated. In one of the worst offenders – indeed one of the stupidest and most uninspired plays ever written, a play in which it is incredible that Shakespeare had any hand at all, a play in which the best passages would be too highly honoured by the signature of Peele – in *Titus Andronicus*[1] – there is nothing really Senecan at all. There is a wantonness, an irrelevance, about the crimes of which Seneca would never have been guilty. Seneca's Oedipus has the traditional justification for blinding himself; and the blinding itself is far less offensive than that in *Lear*. In *Titus*, the hero cuts off his own hand in view of the audience, who can also testify to the mutilation of the hands and the tongue of Lavinia. In *The Spanish Tragedy* Hieronymo bites off his own tongue. There is nothing like this in Seneca.

20 But if this is very unlike Seneca, it is very like the contemporary drama of Italy. Nothing could better illustrate the accidental character of literary 'influence' – accidental, [83] that is, with reference to the work exercising the influence – than the difference between Senecan drama in Italy and in France. The French drama is from the beginning restrained and decorous; to the French drama, especially to Garnier, the Senecan drama of Greville, Daniel and Alexander is allied. The Italian is bloodthirsty in the extreme. Kyd knew both; but it was to the Italian that he and Peele yielded themselves with sympathetic delight. We must remember, too, that Italy had developed stagecraft and stage machinery

---

1. See J. M. Robertson: *An Introduction to the Study of the Shakespeare Canon*.

to the highest point – for the most sumptuous masques in England, Italian managers, engineers and artists were brought over; that the plastic arts were much more important in Italy than elsewhere, and that consequently the spectacular and sensational elements of drama were insisted upon; that Italian civilisation had, in short, everything to dazzle the imagination of unsophisticated northerners emerging into a period of prosperity and luxury. I have no first-hand acquaintance with Italian plays of this epoch; it is a library which few readers would penetrate in pursuit of pleasure; but its character, and influence in England, are well attested. It is possible to say that Seneca hardly influenced this Italian drama at all; he was made use of by it and adopted into it; and for Kyd and Peele he was thoroughly Italianised.

21 The Tragedy of Blood is very little Senecan, in short, though it made much use of Senecan machinery; it is very largely Italian; and it added an ingenuity of plot which is native.

22 If we wished to find the reason for the sanguinary character of much Elizabethan drama – which persists to its end – we should have to allow ourselves some daring generalisations concerning the temper of the epoch. When we consider it, and reflect how much more refined, how much more *classical* in the profounder sense, is that earlier popular drama which reached its highest point in *Everyman*, I cannot but think that the change is due to some fundamental release of restraint. The tastes gratified are always [84] latent: they were then gratified by the drama, as they are now gratified by crime reports in the daily press. It is no more reasonable to make Seneca responsible for this aspect of Elizabethan drama than it is to connect Aeschylus or Sophocles with *Jude the Obscure*. I am not sure that the latter association has not been made, though no one supposes that Hardy prepared himself by close application to the study of Greek drama.

23 It is pertinent to inquire, in this context, what was the influence of Seneca, in the way of horrors, upon the small body of 'Senecal' dramatists who professedly imitated him. But this collation is relevant also to the question of Seneca's influence upon language; so that before making the comparison we may consider this latter question next. Here, the great influence of Seneca is unquestionable. Quotation after quotation, parallel after parallel, may be adduced; the most conspicuous are given in Cunliffe's *Influence of Seneca*, others in Lucas's *Seneca and Elizabethan Tragedy*. So great is this influence that we can say neither that it was good nor that it was bad; for we cannot imagine what Elizabethan dramatic

verse would have been without it. The direct influence is restricted to the group of Marlowe and to Marston; Jonson and Chapman are, each in his own way, more sophisticated and independent; the later or Jacobean dramatists, Middleton, Webster, Tourneur, Ford, Beaumont and Fletcher, found their language upon their own predecessors, and chiefly upon Shakespeare. But none of these authors hesitated to draw upon Seneca when occasion served, and Chapman owes much, both good and bad, of his dramatic style to his admiration for Seneca. No better examples can be found, however, of plays which, while not Senecan in form, are yet deeply influenced by Seneca in language, than the *True Tragedy of Richard Duke of York*, and the Shakespearian *Richard II* and *Richard III*. These, with the work of Kyd and that of Marlowe and of Peele, and several of the plays included in the Shakespeare Apocrypha, have a great deal in common.

[85] 24 The precise pilferings and paraphrases have been thoroughly catalogued by the scholars I have mentioned, and others; hardly a dramatist, between Kyd and Massinger, is not many times indebted to Seneca. Instead of repeating this labour, I prefer to call attention to his general influence. Not only the evolution of the dramatic structure, but the evolution of the blank verse cadence, took place under the shadow of Seneca; it is hardly too much to say that Shakespeare could not have formed the verse instrument which he left to his successors, Webster, Massinger, Tourneur, Ford, and Fletcher, unless he had received an instrument already highly developed by the genius of Marlowe and the influence of Seneca. Blank verse before 1600, or thereabouts, is a crude form of music compared to blank verse after that date; but its progress in fifteen years had been astonishing. In the first place, I believe that the establishment of blank verse as the vehicle of drama, instead of the old fourteener, or the heroic couplet, or (what might have happened) a particular form of prose rhythm, received considerable support from its being obviously the nearest equivalent to the solemnity and weight of the Senecan iambic. A comparison of the trotting metre of our translations with Surrey's translation of Virgil will show, I think, that while the former has undeniable poetic charms of its own, the latter would reveal more resources to the ear of the dramatist. The pre-Marlowe versification is competent, but extremely monotonous; it is literally a *monotone*, containing none of the musical counter-rhythms which Marlowe introduced, nor the rhythms of individual speech which were later added.

> When this eternal substance of my soul
> Did live imprison'd in my wanton flesh,

Each in their function serving other's need,
I was a courtier in the Spanish court:
(Prologue, *Spanish Tragedy*, xxx.)

But to illustrate the early use of this metre under Senecan influence, a worse play serves our purpose better; the [86] Senecan content justifies our quoting at some length from *Locrine*, an early play[1] of no merit whatever. Here is the Revival of Learning in the brain of a fourth rate playwright:

HUMBER.

> Where may I find some desert wilderness,
> Where I may breathe out curses as I would,
> And scare the earth with my condemning voice;
> Where every echo's repercussion
> May help me to bewail mine overthrow,
> And aid me in my sorrowful laments?
> Where I may find some hollow uncouth rock,
> Where I may damn, condemn, and ban my fill
> The heavens, the hell, the earth, the air, the fire,
> And utter curses to the concave sky,
> Which may infect the airy regions,
> And light upon the Brittain Locrine's head?
> You ugly sprites that in Cocytus mourn,
> And gnash your teeth with dolorous laments:
> You fearful dogs that in black Lethe howl,
> And scare the ghosts with your wide open throats:
> You ugly ghosts that, flying from these dogs,
> Do plunge yourselves in Puryflegiton:
> Come, all of you, and with your shriking notes
> Accompany the Brittain's conquering host.
> Come, fierce Erynnys, horrible with snakes;
> Come, ugly Furies, armed with your whips;
> You threefold judges of black Tartarus,
> And all the army of you hellish fiends,
> With new-found torments rack proud Locrine's bones!
> O gods, and stars! damned be the gods and stars
> That did not drown me in fair Thetis' plains!
> Curst be the sea, that with outrageous waves,

---

1. Usually attributed to Greene, and dated about 1585 (see Brooke, *Shakespeare Apocrypha*). Neither authorship nor date is important for my purpose: the play was obviously written by someone who had not yet experienced the influence of Marlowe.

[87] With surging billows did not rive my ships
       Against the rocks of high Cerannia,
       Or swallow me into her wat'ry gulf!
       Would God we had arriv'd upon the shore
       Where Polyphemus and the Cyclops dwell,
       Or where the bloody Anthropophagi
       With greedy jaws devour the wandering wights!

             Enter the ghost of ALBANACT

       But why comes Albanact's bloody ghost,
       To bring a corsive to our miseries?
       Is't not enough to suffer shameful flight,
       But we must be tormented now with ghosts,
       With apparitions fearful to behold?

GHOST.
       Revenge! revenge for blood!

HUMBER.
       So nought will satisfy your wand'ring ghost
       But dire revenge, nothing but Humber's fall,
       Because he conquered you in Albany.
       Now, by my soul, Humber would be condemned
       To Tantal's hunger or Ixion's wheel,
       Or to the vulture of Prometheus,
       Rather than that this murther were undone.
       When as I die I'll drag thy cursed ghost
       Through all the rivers of foul Erebus,
       Through burning sulphur of the Limbo-lake,
       To allay the burning fury of that heat
       That rageth in mine everlasting soul.

GHOST.
       Vindicta, vindicta.   [Exeunt.]

This is the proper Ercles bombast, ridiculed by Shakespeare, Jonson, and Nashe. From this, even to *Tamburlaine*, is a long way; it is too absurdly distorted to serve even as a burlesque of Seneca; but the metre has some-[88]thing Senecan about it. From such verse there is a long distance to the melodies of

       Now comes my lover tripping like a roe,
       And brings my longings tangled in her hair.

or

> Welcome, my son: who are the violets now
> That strew the green lap of the new-come spring?

or

> But look, the morn, in russet mantle clad,
> Walks o'er the dew of yon high eastern hill:

that is to say, to the *lyrical* phase of blank verse, before Shakespeare had analysed it into true dramatic differentiation; it belongs to the first or *declamatory* phase. But this declamation is in its impulse, if not in its achievement, Senecan; and progress was made, not by rejection, but by dissociating this type of verse into products with special properties.

25 The next stage also was reached with the help of a hint from Seneca. Several scholars, Butler in particular, have called attention to a trick of Seneca of repeating one word of a phrase in the next phrase, especially in stichomythia, where the sentence of one speaker is caught up and twisted by the next. This was an effective stage trick, but it is something more; it is the crossing of one rhythm pattern with another.

> – Sceptrone nostro *famulus* est potior tibi?
> – Quot iste *famulus* tradidit *reges* neci.
> – Cum ergo *regi* servit et patitur iugum?
> (*Hercules*.)

Seneca also gets a kind of double pattern by breaking up lines into minimum antiphonal units:

> Rex est timendus.
>   Rex meus fuerat pater.
> Non metuis arma?
>   Sint licet terra edita.
> [89] Moriere.
>   Cupio.
>   Profuge.
>   Paenituit fugae.
> Medea,
>   Fiam.
>   Mater es.
>   Cui sim vides.
>   (*Medea*, 168 ff.)

A man like Marlowe, or even men with less scholarship or less genius for the use of words than he, could hardly have failed to learn something from this. At any rate, I believe that the study of Seneca had its part in the formation of verse like the following:

– Wrong not her birth, she is of royal blood.
– To save her life, I'll say she is not so.
– Her life is safest only in her birth.
– And only in that safety died her brothers.

It is only a step (and a few lines farther) to the pun:

Cousins, indeed; and by their uncle cozen'd.

Some of the effects in such plays as *Richard II* and *Richard III* are indeed of pre-Marlowe origin, as:

I had an Edward, till a Richard kill'd him;
I had a Henry, till a Richard kill'd him;
Thou hadst an Edward, till a Richard kill'd him;
Thou hadst a Richard, till a Richard kill'd him.

which is already even in *Locrine*, as:

The boisterous Boreas thundreth forth Revenge,
The stony rocks cry out on sharp revenge,
The thorny bush pronounceth dire revenge,

but in the following lines from Clarence's Dream we see an immense advance over *Locrine* in the use of infernal machinery:

[90] I pass'd, methought, the melancholy flood,
With that grim ferryman which poets write of,
Unto the kingdom of perpetual night.
The first that there did greet my stranger soul,
Was my great father-in-law, renowned Warwick;
Who cried aloud, 'What scourge for perjury
Can this dark monarchy afford false Clarence?'[1]

The 'kingdom of perpetual night' and the last two lines are an approximation in English to the magnificence of Senecan Latin at its best; they are far from being a mere burlesque. The best of Seneca has here been absorbed into English.

---

1. I once expressed the opinion that these lines must be by Shakespeare. I am not so confident now. See J. M. Robertson: *The Shakespeare Canon*, Part II.

26 In *Richard II*, which is usually dated a little earlier than *Richard III*, I find such interesting variations of versification that I am convinced that it is a slightly later play,[1] or else that there is more of Shakespeare in it. There is the same play of words:

Give Richard leave to live till Richard die.

A brittle glory shineth in his face;
As brittle as the glory is the face.

but there is less stichomythia, less mere repetition, and a dexterity in retaining and developing the same rhythm with greater freedom and less obvious calculation. (See the long speeches of Richard in Act III, sc. ii. and sc. iii, and compare with the more gracefully balanced verses of Queen Margaret's tirade in *Richard III*, Act IV, sc. iv.)

27 When blank verse has reached this point, and passed into the hands of its greatest master, there is no need to look for fresh infusions of Seneca. He has done his work, and the one influence on later blank verse is the influence of Shakespeare. Not that later dramatists do not make great use of Seneca's plays. Chapman uses him, and employs the old machinery; but Seneca's influence on Chapman was chiefly on Chapman's 'thought'. Jonson uses Seneca deliberately; the superb prologues of 'Envy' and 'Sylla's Ghost' are adaptations of the Senecan ghost-prologue form, not an inheritance from Kyd. Massinger, a most accomplished dramatist and versifier, sometimes falls back most lamentably upon ghosts and spectacles, but the verse is formed, and Seneca no further responsible for its vices or virtues.

28 Certainly, Elizabethan bombast can be traced to Seneca; Elizabethans themselves ridiculed the Senecan imitation. But if we reflect, not on the more grotesque exaggerations, but on the dramatic poetry of the first half of the period, as a whole, we see that Seneca had as much to do with its merits and its progress as with its faults and its delays. Certainly it is all 'rhetorical', but if it had not been rhetorical, would it have been anything? Certainly it is a relief to turn back to the austere, close language of *Everyman*, the simplicity of the mysteries; but if new influences had not entered, old orders decayed, would the language not have left some of its greatest resources unexplored? Without bombast, we should not have had *King Lear*. The art of dramatic language, we must remember,

---

1. I do not deny that some parts, or some lines, of *Richard III* are later than *Richard II*. Both plays may have undergone revision from time to time, and in any case must be dated near together.

is as near to oratory as to ordinary speech or to other poetry. We are not entitled to try fine effects unless we achieve the coarse ones. If the Elizabethans distorted and travestied Seneca in some ways, if they learned from him tricks and devices which they applied with inexpert hands, they also learned from him the essentials of declaimed verse. Their subsequent progress is a process of splitting up the primitive rhetoric, developing out of it subtler poetry and subtler tones of conversation, eventually mingling, as no other school of dramatists has done, the oratorical, the conversational, the elaborate and the simple, the direct and the indirect; so that they were able to write plays which can still be viewed as plays, with any plays, and which can still be read as poetry, with any poetry.

[92] 29 It is improper to pass from the questions of Seneca's influence upon the Tragedy of Blood and upon the language of the Elizabethans without mentioning the group of 'Senecal' plays, largely produced under the aegis of the Countess of Pembroke. The history of this type of play belongs rather to the history of scholarship and culture than to the history of the Drama; it begins in a sense with the household of Sir Thomas More, and therefore is doubly allied to the present subject by Jasper Heywood; it is continued in the conversations at Cambridge of Mr Ascham, Mr Watson, and Mr (later Sir John) Cheke. The first to attack openly the common stage was Sir Philip Sidney, whose words are well known:

> Our Tragedies and Comedies (not without cause cried out against), observing rules neither of honest civility nor of skilful Poetry, excepting *Gorboduc* (againe, I say, of those that I have seen), which notwithstanding, as it is full of stately speeches and well sounding Phrases, climbing to the height of Seneca his style, and as full of notable morality, which it doth most delightfully teach, and so obtain the very end of Poesie, yet in troth it is very defectious in the circumstances, which grieveth me, because it might not remain as an exact model of all Tragedies. For it is faulty both in place and time, the two necessary companions of all corporal actions. . . . But if it be so in *Gorboduc*, how much more in all the rest, where you shall have Asia of the one side, and Afric of the other, and so many other under-kingdoms, that the Player, when he cometh in, must ever begin with telling where he is: or else the tale will not be conceived? Now ye shall have three Ladies walk to gather flowers, and then we must believe the stage to be a Garden. By and by, we hear news of shipwrack in the same place, and then we are to blame if we accept it not for a Rock.

30 It was after Sidney's death that his sister, the Countess of Pembroke, tried to assemble a body of wits to compose drama in the proper Senecan style, to make head against the popular melodrama of the time. Great poetry should [93] be both an art and a diversion; in a large and cultivated public like the Athenian it can be both; the shy recluses of Lady Pembroke's circle were bound to fail. But we must not draw too sharp a line of separation between the careful workman who laboured to create a classical drama in England and the hurried purveyors of playhouse successes: the two worlds were not without communication, and the work of the earlier Senecals was not without fruit.

31 With the part played by the *Tenne Tragedies* in this Senecan tradition I shall deal in the next section of this essay. Here, I wish only to call attention to certain characteristics of Senecal Tragedy in its final form, in the work of Greville, Daniel and Alexander. I would only remind the reader that these final Senecal plays were written after any real hope of altering or reforming the English stage had disappeared. In the early Elizabethan years appeared a succession of tragedies, mostly performed by the Inns of Court, and therefore not popular productions, which might in favourable circumstances have led to a living Senecan drama. Notably, *Gorboduc* (mentioned by Sidney above), *Jocasta*, and *Gismond of Salerne* (three of the four plays contained in Cunliffe's *Early English Classical Tragedies*). When *The Spanish Tragedy* appeared (with, as I have suggested, its particularly non-classical element) these feeble lights were snuffed out. I pass on to the finished Senecal product, because I am only concerned to elicit the effect of Seneca upon his sedulous admirers and imitators who professed to be, and were, men of taste and culture.

32 The Monarchic Tragedies of Alexander, Earl of Stirling, are the last on our list, composed under the auspices of the scholarly King James I. They are poor stuff: I imagine that they are more important in the history of the Union than in the history of the Drama, since they represent the choice, by a Scotsman of accidental eminence, to write verse in English instead of in Scots. Their faults are the faults of the other plays of the group; but they have not the virtues of the others. The two plays of Fulke Greville, Lord Brooke [94] the friend and biographer of Sidney, have some magnificent passages, especially in the choruses; Greville had a true gift for sententious declamation. But they have much dullness also; and they do not imitate Seneca nearly so faithfully as either those of Alexander or those of Daniel. Greville not only cannot stick to one chorus, but will introduce, on one occasion, a chorus of 'Bashas or Caddies', and after the next act, a chorus of 'Mahometan Priests'; he introduces the still more

doubtful practice of supernatural figures, a 'dialogue of Good and Evil Spirits', or even a chorus of two allegorical figures, 'Time and Eternity' (ending indeed with the fine line spoken by Eternity: *I am the measure of felicity*). The best, the best sustained, the most poetic and the most lyrical, are two tragedies of Samuel Daniel: *Cleopatra* and *Philotas*. They contain many lovely passages, they are readable all through, and they are well built.

33 Now, in comparison with the supposed influence of Seneca on the barbarity of Elizabethan tragedy, and his supposed bad influence upon the language, what do we find in the plays of those who took him as their model in their attack upon the popular stage, in that attack in which Daniel, in his dedication of *Cleopatra* to the Countess of Pembroke, declared himself the foe of 'Gross Barbarism'? Deaths there are, of course, but there is none of these tragedies that is not far more restrained, far more discreet and sober, not only than the Tragedy of Blood, but than Seneca himself. Characters die so decently, so remote from the stage, and the report of their deaths is wrapped up in such long speeches by messengers stuffed with so many moral maxims, that we may read on unaware that anyone concerned in the play has died at all. Where the popular playwrights travestied Seneca's melodrama and his fury, the Senecals travesty his reserve and his decorum. And as for the language, that, too, is a different interpretation of Seneca. How vague are our notions of bombast and rhetoric when they must include styles and vocabularies so [95] different as those of Kyd and Daniel! It is by opposite excesses that Senecals and popular dramatists attract the same reproach. The language of Daniel is pure and restrained; the vocabulary choice, the expression clear; there is nothing far-fetched, conceited, or perverse:

CLEOPATRA.

> What, hath my face yet power to win a Lover?
>   Can this torne remnant serve to grace me so,
> That it can Caesar's secret plots discover,
>   What he intends with me and mine to do?
> Why then, poor beauty, thou hast done thy last,
>   And best good service thou could'st do unto me;
> For now the time of death reveal'd thou hast,
>   Which in my life did'st serve but to undo me.

The first two lines are admirable; the rest are good serviceable lines; almost any passage from *Cleopatra* is as good, and some are far better. The whole thing is in excellent taste. Yet we may ponder the fact that it would not have made the slightest difference, to the formation of our Augustan poetry, if Daniel and his friends had never written a line; that Dryden and Pope are nearer allied to – Cowley; and that they owe more to Marlowe than to the purest taste of the sixteenth century. Daniel and Greville are good poets, and there is something to be learned from them; but they, and Sir John Davies who somewhat resembles them, had no influence. The only one of Lady Pembroke's heroes who had any influence is Edmund Spenser.

34 Within the limits of an essay it is impossible to do more than touch on the influence of Seneca upon the 'thought' of the Elizabethans, or more exactly, upon their attitude toward life so far as it can be formulated in words. I would only say enough, at this point, to remind the reader that Seneca's influence upon dramatic form, upon versification and language, upon sensibility, and upon thought, must in the end be all estimated together; they cannot be divided. How the influence of Seneca is related, in the Elizabethan mind, with [96] other influences, perhaps those of Montaigne and Machiavelli, I do not know; and I think it is a subject still to be investigated. But the frequency with which a quotation from Seneca, or a thought or figure ultimately derived from Seneca, is employed in Elizabethan plays whenever a moral reflection is required, is too remarkable to be ignored; and when an Elizabethan hero or villain dies, he usually dies in the odour of Seneca. These facts are known to scholars; but if known, they are usually ignored by literary critics. In a comparison of Shakespeare with Dante, for instance, it is assumed that Dante leant upon a system of philosophy which he accepted whole, whereas Shakespeare created his own: or that Shakespeare had acquired some extra- or ultra-intellectual knowledge superior to a philosophy. This occult kind of information is sometimes called 'spiritual knowledge' or 'insight'. Shakespeare and Dante were both merely poets (and Shakespeare a dramatist as well); our estimate of the intellectual material they absorbed does not affect our estimate of their poetry, either absolutely or relatively to each other. But it must affect our vision of them and the use we make of them, the fact that Dante, for instance, had behind him an Aquinas, and Shakespeare behind him a Seneca. Perhaps it was Shakespeare's special rôle in history to have effected this peculiar union – perhaps it is a part of his special eminence to have expressed an inferior philosophy in the greatest poetry. It is certainly one cause of the terror and awe with which he inspires us.

> Omnia certo tramite vadunt
> primusque dies dedit extremum.

> non illa deo vertisse licet
> quae nexa suis currunt causis.
> it cuique ratus prece non ulla
> mobilis ordo.
> multis ipsum timuisse nocet.
> multi ad fatum venere suum
> dum fata timent.

[97] Compare with *Edward III*, Act IV, sc. iv (see Cunliffe, *Influence of Seneca*, p. 87), and with *Measure for Measure*, Act III, sc. i. And

> Men must endure
> Their going hence, even as their coming hither,
> Ripeness is all.[1]

III

35 The *Tenne Tragedies* were translated and printed separately over a space of about eight years, with the exception of the *Thebais*, which was translated by Newton in 1581 to complete his work for his edition of the whole. The order and dates of the several translations are of interest. The first and best of the translators was Jasper Heywood:[2] his *Troas* was printed in 1559, his *Thyestes* in 1560, his *Hercules Furens* in 1561. The *Oedipus* by Alexander Nevyle (translated 1560) was printed in 1563. In 1566 appeared the *Octavia* of Nuce, the *Agamemnon*, *Medea*, and *Hercules Oetaeus* of Studley in 1566, and the *Hippolytus* of Studley probably in 1567. About fourteen years then elapse before Newton produced his complete edition, and it may [98] be presumed that he translated the *Thebais* for that purpose.[3]

---

1. Mr F. L. Lucas, in his *Seneca and Elizabethan Tragedy*, says (p. 122): 'But it must be said once for all about the bulk of Shakespeare's supposed borrowings from Seneca, that one grows more and more sceptical.' What has been said once for all is not for me to dispute, but I would point out that I am not here concerned with Shakespeare's 'borrowings' (where I am inclined to agree) but with Shakespeare as the voice of his time, and this voice in poetry is, in the most serious matters of life and death, most often the voice of Seneca. I subscribe to the observation of Cunliffe (op. cit., p. 85): 'We have (in *King Lear*) Seneca's hopeless fatalism, not only in the catastrophe, but repeatedly brought forward in the course of the play'.

> As flies to wanton boys are we to the gods;
> They kill us for their sport.

2. Sometime Fellow of All Souls College, and later an eminent Jesuit; but chiefly remembered as the uncle of John Donne. Much information about Heywood and his family is contained in A. W. Reed's *Early Tudor Drama*.

3. These facts are given succinctly in Cunliffe's *Influence of Seneca*. The slight textual differences between the early editions and that of 1581 are given by E. M. Spearing: *The Elizabethan Translations of Seneca's Tragedies*.

36 It has never been supposed, in spite of the acid taunt of Nashe, that any of the Elizabethan dramatists owe any great debt to these translations.[1] Most of the playwrights, as I have intimated before, may be supposed to have had a smattering of Seneca at school; two of the popular dramatists who exercised a decisive influence at an important moment – Kyd and Peele – were acquainted with several languages, and therefore themselves subjected to several influences. But if we look at the dates we cannot overlook the probability that these translations helped to direct the course of events. They (all but one) appeared between 1559 and 1566. The first plays of Senecan form which could be called popular were Sackville and Norton's *Gorboduc*, which appeared in 1561, Gascoyne's *Jocasta* in 1566, and *Gismond of Salerne* in 1567. We must also take account, of course, of the fact that plays of Seneca, and plays in imitation of Seneca, were being produced in Latin at the Universities.[2] The *Troades* was performed in Latin at Trinity College, Cambridge, in 1551. Trinity resumed its enterprise in 1559 – the year of Heywood's *Troas* – and between 1559 and 1561 the College produced in Latin four plays of Seneca. And during the 'sixties the two Universities first, and the Inns of Court subsequently, composed and performed a number of Latin plays on the Senecan model. This would have occurred, no doubt, even had Heywood never translated Seneca at all. But there can be little doubt that his translations indicate a nascent interest in a new vernacular drama to vie with classical drama, and [99] that they in turn stimulated the beginning of this drama. At the same busy moment took place another event of capital importance, which combined with this Senecan work to produce English tragedy. In 1557 came the publication of Surrey's translation of Book II of the *Aeneid*, in the new 'blank verse', the instrument without which the Elizabethan drama would have been impossible. The first-fruits, *Gorboduc*, are inconsiderable; but this play marks a new epoch; there is no clearer division in the whole of English literature.

37 We have, in fact, within a period of about forty years, three distinct phases in the development of English tragedy: the first, from 1559 to some time in the early 'eighties, is announced by Heywood's translations; the second is the period in which flourished Kyd and Peele, both of whom came to be influenced by the sudden and soon extinguished genius of

---

1. See E. M. Spearing: op. cit.
2. For a convenient summary of the Senecan movement throughout Europe, and particularly in England, see Kastner and Charlton's edition of Alexander, above mentioned.

Marlowe; the third is the period of Shakespeare up to his culminating tragedies. Then follows a period of Jacobean drama which belongs not so much to Shakespeare, although Shakespeare's last plays fall within the first years of it, as to Beaumont and Fletcher: it is the period, not typically of tragedy, but of tragi-comic romance.

38 In the preceding section I insisted upon the difference between Seneca's influence upon popular drama and his influence upon those fastidious spirits, the Senecals, who tried to observe his dramatic laws. But this difference of tendency is hardly apparent in the first period, or until the appearance of Kyd and Peele. During this period the fashions set at the Universities were followed at the Inns of Court. The plays produced by the legal wits were sometimes acted at the Queen's Court, with which, indeed, the Inns had a kind of formal connection. And in turn the plays produced at the Royal Court affected the more popular drama.[1] *Gorboduc* is followed by *Gismond of Salerne*, and [100] *Gismond* later by the popular and atrocious *Locrine* (in which Peele almost certainly had a heavy hand); *The Misfortunes of Arthur* was probably too tardy to play much part in the transition. Another play of importance, which shows the persistence of the influence from the Universities upon popular drama, is Legge's *Richardus Tertius*, a Latin chronicle play acted at St John's College, Cambridge, in 1573, and apparently repeated in 1579 and 1582. This play is the parent of *The True Tragedy of Richard III*, and consequently of the entire brood of chronicle plays.

39 Another point which I have already considered, but which must be mentioned here in a different context, is the relation of Seneca to *Italian* Seneca, and of both to the native tendencies of the time. Italian Seneca is not conspicuous until the period of Kyd and Peele; but even among the translations of Heywood we can find evidence that he was to be by no means unwelcome. Besides other peculiarities of these translations which we must examine, there is an interesting addition made by Heywood to the *Troas*. In the play of Seneca Achilles' Ghost makes no appearance; it is merely mentioned as having been seen. The play was the first to be translated, and there is some reason for believing that the translation was intended to be played. The 'divers and sundrye' additions which Heywood invents render this supposition all the more plausible; for they are such as a translator would be much more likely to make if he had a performance in view, than if his translation were intended only for

---

1. See J. M. Manly's introduction (p. v) to F. S. Miller's translation of *The Tragedies of Seneca* (1907).

reading; in the latter event he might be expected to stick pretty closely to the text. Between the second and third acts of the *Troas* Heywood allows himself the liberty of interpolating a new scene of his own invention, which is a long soliloquy in thirteen stanzas by the Ghost of Achilles. And this independent 'Sprite' rants in a tone which hardly Peele could outdo:

> From burning lakes the furies wrath I threate,
> And fire that nought but streames of bloud may slake
> [101] The rage of wind and seas their shippes shall beat,
> And Ditis deepe on you shall vengeance take,
> The sprites crye out, the earth and seas do quake,
> The poole of Styx ungratefull Greekes it seath,
> With slaughtred bloud revenge Achilles death.

It is to be observed that Nevyle and Studley both joined Inns of Court; that Nevyle came there to know Gascoyne, the author of *Jocasta*; and that Heywood knew, or at least knew of, Sackville and Norton before they had written *Gorboduc*. The impulse toward the Tragedy of Blood is already present in these translators, and they do not hesitate to add or to alter; the distortion of Seneca begins in his translation.

40 It is not only as an embryonic form of Elizabethan tragedy that these translations have documentary interest. They represent the transformation of the older form of versification into the new – consequently the transformation of language and sensibility as well. Few things that can happen to a nation are more important than the invention of a new form of verse. And at no other time, and to no other country than England at that time, has such an achievement as that of Henry Howard, Earl of Surrey, had greater consequences. To the French or to the Italians it could not have mattered so much. Their sensibility had already learned to express itself in large part in prose: Boccaccio and Machiavelli in one country, and the chroniclers – Froissart, Joinville, Commines – in the other, had already done a great work in forming the local mind. But the Elizabethan mind, far more than the contemporary mind in any other country, grew and matured through its verse rather than through its prose. The development of prose between Elyot and Bacon is certainly remarkable; but a comparison of styles between, say, Latimer and Andrewes shows a slower rate of change than the same space of time in verse, or the same space of time in prose in the next century. On the other hand, a study of the [102] styles, the syntax, and the cadences of blank verse from *Gorboduc* to Shakespeare, and even after Shakespeare in the work of Webster and Tourneur, brings to light a process which is wholly astonishing.

41 The *Tenne Tragedies* must have shown conclusively to the most sensitive contemporary ears that the fourteener had had its day; it was certain that the verse of Surrey's *Aeneid* was in every way the verse in which to render the dignity and pomposity of the Senecan rhythm. And the slower iambic pentameter brought with it an alteration in vocabulary. The fourteener had served very well in rough comedy; it runs jollily in *Roister Doister* and *Gammer Gurton*. It is no vehicle for solemn tragedy, and the miracle is that Heywood and Studley made as good a job with it as they did. The fourteener, and the kindred loose metres of the interlude, are not adapted to a highly Latinised vocabulary; they are adapted to a vocabulary containing a large proportion of short words and monosyllables of Germanic origin; a vocabulary which must have come to seem, as it seems to us, naïf and 'countrified', if fresh and vigorous. The language of early Tudor times is indeed in some ways a deterioration from the language of Chaucer. One reason for this is no doubt the change in pronunciation, the suppression of syllables; the melody of the older tongue had gone, and with this melody much of its dignity; new rhythms, and new infusions from abroad, were very much needed. At first, in fact, the innovations overpowered the language; the Elizabethan bombast was a verbal even more than an emotional debauch; it was not until the prose of Dryden and Hobbes that English settled down to something like sobriety.

42 In the *Iliad* of Chapman we see new wine bursting old bottles; the poem is a magnificent *tour de force* in which Chapman sometimes succeeds in fitting the new vocabulary to the old 'stretched' metre. But it is, consequently, a poem of brilliant passages rather than sustained success. Heywood and Studley – particularly Studley – make no [103] such attempt: their fourteener is early, not late Tudor; it is a different thing from Chapman's. Only in the pentameter rhymed choruses does their sensibility become more modern; the contrast between their dialogue and their chorus verse is interesting. Here is a random bit of Studley:

> O *wanny* jaws of Blacke Averne, *eake* Tartar dungeon *grim*,
> O Lethes Lake of woful Soules the joy that therein swimme,
> And *eake* ye *glummy* Gulphes destroy, destroy me wicked
>   wight
> And still in *pit of pangues* let me be plunged by day and
>   night.
> Now, now, come up ye Goblins grim from water *creekes*
>   alow ...

The majority of the rhyme words are monosyllables. The most sonorous and canorous Latin names are truncated (it remained for Marlowe to discover, and Milton to perfect, the musical possibilities of classical names almost to the point of *incantation*). Alliteration, in as primitive a form as that of *Piers Plowman*, is constant. For instance, Heywood has

> shal *S*isyphus his *s*tone
> That *s*lipper *r*estles *r*ollyng payse uppon my *b*acke be *b*orne,
> Or shall my lymmes with *s*wifter *s*winge of *w*hirling *w*hele be torne?
> Or shall my *p*aynes be Tytius *p*anges th' encreasing liver still,
> Whose *g*rowing *g*uttes the *g*nawing *g*ripes and *f*ylthy *f*oules
> do *f*yll?

To examine such lines under the microscope is not to do them justice; the vigorous vocabulary and swinging metre appear at their best when we read through a long descriptive or narrative passage: in the same play (the *Thyestes*) the messenger's account of the crime of Atreus (Act IV) is admirably rendered.

43 In their handling of the choruses the translators are less scrupulous. When they translate the dialogue they are literal to the best of their ability – occasional inaccuracies or mistranslations being admitted – but in the choruses they [104] will sometimes lengthen or shorten, sometimes omit altogether, or substitute an invention of their own. On the whole, their alterations tend to make the play more dramatic; sometimes they may be suspected of adding a political innuendo to the Senecan moralising on the vanity of place and power. And it is especially in the choruses that we find, now and then, flashes of that felicity which is present in Tudor translation more perhaps than in the translations of any period into any language. For example, the whole of the chorus at the end of Act IV of Heywood's *Hercules Furens* is very fine, but the last six lines seem to me of singular beauty; and as the original, too, is a lovely passage, it is both fair and interesting to quote original and translation. The persons addressed are the dead children of Hercules, whom he has just slain in his madness:

> ite ad Stygios, umbrae, portus
> ite, innocues, quas in primo
> limine vitae scelus oppressit
> patriusque furor;
> ite, iratos visite reges.

And Heywood:

> Goe hurtles soules, whom mischiefe hath opprest
> Even in the first porch of life but lately had,
> And fathers fury goe unhappy kind
> O little children, by the way ful sad
> > Of journey knowen.
> > Goe see the angry kynges.

Nothing can be said of such a translation except that it is perfect. It is a last echo of the earlier tongue, the language of Chaucer, with an overtone of that Christian piety and pity which disappears with Elizabethan verse. The greater part of the chorus work has not this purity: one feels a curious strain on the old vocabulary to say new things; the fluctuation, the shades of variation between the old world and the new deserve inquisitive study; the ambiguity probably contributes to give these translations a unique mood, [105] which is only to be extracted and enjoyed after patient perusals. They are not translations to be read in a hurry; they do not yield their charm easily.

> Such friendship finde wyth Gods yet no man myght,
> That he the morowe might be sure to lyve.
> The God our things all tost and turned quight
> > Rolles with a whyrle wynde.

Variants from 1927:

Title Introduction

1 the Elizabethan translations of the *Tenne Tragedies*] the present translations
2 most romantic] more romantic
5 are admirably] were admirably
6 the Japanese,] the Japanese (if anything so alien can be included), to Virgil. But] Virgil, but
7 and no 'private life'] and, strictly speaking, no 'private life'
8 a Latin historian with Thucydides] Thucydides with a Latin historian
9 they are hereditary] it is hereditary
10 **(fn.2)** the translator] our translator (vol. ii p. 98)
   the Elizabethan translator] our translator
15 wish to do] wish do to in this Introduction
17 so far as I know] so far as we know
18 exist for Seneca] exist for Seneca at all
   police inquiry] police inquiry into evidence
19 bites off] bites out
23 [Between 'Senecan in form,' and 'are yet deeply influenced':] and not containing anything of the more obvious Senecan apparatus such as Ghosts,
24 general influence] universal influence

28 [Between 'or to other poetry.' and 'We are not entitled':] On the stage, M. Jean Cocteau reminds us, we must weave a pattern of coarse rope that can be apprehended from the back of the pit, not a pattern of lace that can only be apprehended from the printed page.

30 [New para.]

31 the *Tenne Tragedies*] our *Tenne Tragedies*

34 the limits of an essay] our limits
coming hither,] coming hither:

35 [Between 'his edition of the whole.' and 'The order and dates':] Copies of most of the first editions exist in the British Museum; the text which is here presented is that of the collected *Tenne Tragedies* produced by Newton.

36 taunt] taunts

37 Heywood's translations] our translations of Heywood's

38 had a heavy hand] had at least a heavy hand

41 naïf] *naif*

43 the translators] our translators
original and translation] both original and translation

III Four Elizabethan Dramatists

A PREFACE TO AN UNWRITTEN BOOK

SE, 109–17.

Revised from *C.*, 2. 6 (Feb. 1924), 115–23: Gallup C152.

1 To attempt to supplement the criticism of Lamb, Coleridge, and Swinburne on these four Elizabethan dramatists – Webster, Tourneur, Middleton, and Chapman – is a task for which I now believe the time has gone by. What I wish to do is to define and illustrate a point of view toward the Elizabethan drama, which is different from that of the nineteenth-century tradition. There are two accepted and apparently opposed critical attitudes toward Elizabethan drama, and what I shall endeavour to show is that these attitudes are identical, and that another attitude is possible. Furthermore, I believe that this alternative critical attitude is not merely a possible difference of personal bias, but that it is the inevitable attitude for our time. The statement and explication of a conviction about such an important body of dramatic literature, toward what is in fact the only distinct form of dramatic literature that England has produced, should be something more than an exercise in mental ingenuity or in refinement of taste: it should be something of revolutionary influence on the future of drama. Contemporary literature, like contemporary politics, is confused by the moment-to-moment struggle for existence; but the time arrives when an examination of

principles is necessary. I believe that the theatre has reached a point at which a revolution in principles should take place.

2 The accepted attitude toward Elizabethan drama was established on the publication of Charles Lamb's *Specimens*. By publishing these selections, Lamb set in motion the [110] enthusiasm for poetic drama which still persists, and at the same time encouraged the formation of a distinction which is, I believe, the ruin of modern drama – the distinction between drama and literature. For the *Specimens* made it possible to read the plays as poetry while neglecting their function on the stage. It is for this reason that all modern opinion of the Elizabethans seems to spring from Lamb, for all modern opinion rests upon the admission that poetry and drama are two separate things, which can only be *combined* by a writer of exceptional genius. The difference between the people who prefer Elizabethan drama, in spite of what they admit to be its dramatic defects, and the people who prefer modern drama although acknowledging that it is never good poetry, is comparatively unimportant. For in either case, you are committed to the opinion that a play can be good literature but a bad play and that it may be a good play and bad literature – or else that it may be outside of literature altogether.

3 On the one hand we have Swinburne, representative of the opinion that plays exist as literature, and on the other hand Mr William Archer, who with great lucidity and consistency maintains the view that a play need not be literature at all. No two critics of Elizabethan literature could appear to be more opposed than Swinburne and Mr William Archer; yet their assumptions are fundamentally the same, for the distinction between poetry and drama, which Mr Archer makes explicit, is implicit in the view of Swinburne; and Swinburne as well as Mr Archer allows us to entertain the belief that the difference between modern drama and Elizabethan drama is represented by a gain of dramatic technique and the loss of poetry.

4 Mr Archer in his brilliant and stimulating book,[1] succeeded in making quite clear all of the dramatic faults of Elizabethan drama. What vitiates his analysis is his failure to see why these faults are faults, and not simply different conventions. And he gains his apparent victory over [111] the Elizabethans for this reason, that the Elizabethans themselves admit the same criteria of realism that Mr Archer asserts. The great vice of English drama from Kyd to Galsworthy has been that its aim of realism was

---

1. *The Old Drama and the New* (Heinemann, 1923).

unlimited. In one play, *Everyman*, and perhaps in that one play only, we have a drama within the limitations of art; since Kyd, since *Arden of Feversham*, since *The Yorkshire Tragedy*, there has been no form to arrest, so to speak, the flow of spirit at any particular point before it expands and ends its course in the desert of exact likeness to the reality which is perceived by the most commonplace mind. Mr Archer confuses faults with conventions; the Elizabethans committed faults and muddled their conventions. In their plays there are faults of inconsistency, faults of incoherency, faults of taste, there are nearly everywhere faults of carelessness. But their great weakness is the same weakness as that of modern drama, it is the lack of a convention. Mr Archer facilitates his own task of destruction, and avoids offending popular opinion, by making an exception of Shakespeare: but Shakespeare, like all his contemporaries, was aiming in more than one direction. In a play of Aeschylus, we do not find that certain passages are literature and other passages drama; every style of utterance in the play bears a relation to the whole and because of this relation is dramatic in itself. The imitation of life is circumscribed, and the approaches to ordinary speech and withdrawals from ordinary speech are not without relation and effect upon each other. It is essential that a work of art should be self-consistent, that an artist should consciously or unconsciously draw a circle beyond which he does not trespass: on the one hand actual life is always the material, and on the other hand an abstraction from actual life is a necessary condition to the creation of the work of art.

5 Let us try to conceive how the Elizabethan drama would appear to us if we had in existence what has never existed in the English language: a drama formed within a conventional scheme – the convention of an individual dramatist, [112] or of a number of dramatists working in the same form at the same time. And when I say convention, I do not necessarily mean any particular convention of subject matter, of treatment, of verse or of dramatic form, of general philosophy of life or any other convention which has already been used. It may be some quite new selection or structure or distortion in subject matter or technique; any form or rhythm imposed upon the world of action. We will take the point of view of persons accustomed to this convention and finding the expression of their dramatic impulses in it. From this point of view such performances as were those of the Phoenix Society are most illuminating. For the drama, the existence of which I suppose, will have its special conventions of the stage and the actor as well as of the play itself. An actor in an Elizabethan play is either too realistic or too abstract in his treatment, whatever system of speech, of expression and of

movement he adopts. The play is for ever betraying him. An Elizabethan play was in some ways as different from a modern play, its performance is almost as much a lost art, as if it were a drama of Aeschylus or Sophocles. And in some ways it is more difficult to reproduce. For it is easier to present the effect of something in a firm convention, than the effect of something which was aiming, blindly enough, at something else. The difficulty of presenting Elizabethan plays is that they are liable to be made too modern, or falsely archaic. Why are the asides ridiculous, which Mr Archer reprehends in *A Woman Killed with Kindness*? Because they are not a convention, but a subterfuge; it is not Heywood who assumes that asides are inaudible, it is Mrs Frankford who *pretends* not to hear Wendoll. A convention is not ridiculous: a subterfuge makes us extremely uncomfortable. The weakness of the Elizabethan drama is not its defect of realism, but its attempt at realism; not its conventions, but its lack of conventions.

6 In order to make an Elizabethan drama give a satisfactory effect as a work of art, we should have to find a [113] method of acting different from that of contemporary social drama, and at the same time to attempt to express all the emotions of actual life in the way in which they actually would be expressed: the result would be something like a performance of *Agamemnon* by the Guitrys. The effect upon actors who attempt to specialise in Shakespearean or other seventeenth-century revivals is unfortunate. The actor is called upon for a great deal that is not his business, and is left to his own devices for things in which he should be trained. His stage personality has to be supplied from and confounded with his real personality. Anyone who has observed one of the great dancers of the Russian school will have observed that the man or woman whom we admire is a being who exists only during the performances, that it is a personality, a vital flame which appears from nowhere, disappears into nothing and is complete and sufficient in its appearance. It is a conventional being, a being which exists only in and for the work of art which is the ballet. A great actor on the ordinary stage is a person who also exists off it and who supplies the rôle which he performs with the person which he is. A ballet is apparently a thing which exists only as acted and would appear to be a creation much more of the dancer than of the choreographer. This is not quite true. It is a development of several centuries into a strict form. In the ballet only that is left to the actor which is properly the actor's part. The general movements are set for him. There are only limited movements that he can make, only a limited degree of emotion that he can express. He is not called upon for his personality. The differences between a great dancer

and a merely competent dancer is in the vital flame, that impersonal, and, if you like, inhuman force which transpires between each of the great dancer's movements. So it would be in a strict form of drama; but in realistic drama, which is drama striving steadily to escape the conditions of art, the human being intrudes. Without the human being and without this intrusion, the drama [114] cannot be performed, and this is as true of Shakespeare as it is of Henry Arthur Jones. A play of Shakespeare's and a play of Henry Arthur Jones's are essentially of the same type, the difference being that Shakespeare is very much greater and Mr Jones very much more skilful. They are both dramatists to be read rather than seen because it is precisely in that drama which depends upon the interpretation of an actor of genius, that we ought to be on our guard against the actor. The difference is, of course, that without the actor of genius the plays of Mr Jones are nothing and the plays of Shakespeare are still to be read. But a true acting play is surely a play which does not depend on the actor for anything but acting, in the sense in which a ballet depends upon the dancer for dancing. Lest anyone should fall into a contrary misunderstanding, I will explain that I do not by any means intend the actor to be an automaton, nor would I admit that the human actor can be replaced by a marionette. A great dancer, whose attention is set upon carrying out an appointed task, provides the life of the ballet through his movements; in the same way the drama would depend upon a great trained actor. The advantages of convention for the actor are precisely similar to its advantages for the author. No artist produces great art by a deliberate attempt to express his personality. He expresses his personality indirectly through concentrating upon a task which is a task in the same sense as the making of an efficient engine or the turning of a jug or a table-leg.

7 The art of the Elizabethans is an impure art. If it be objected that this is a prejudice of the case, I can only reply that one must criticise from some point of view and that it is better to know what one's point of view is. I know that I rebel against most[1] performances of Shakespeare's plays because I want a direct relationship between the work [115] of art and myself, and I want the performance to be such as will not interrupt or alter this relationship any more than it is an alteration or interruption for me to superpose a second inspection of a picture or building upon the first. I object, in other words, to the interpretation, and I would have a work of art such that it needs only to be completed and cannot be altered

---

1. A really good performance of Shakespeare, such as the very best productions of the Old Vic and Sadler's Wells, may add much to our understanding.

by each interpretation. Now it is obvious that in realistic drama you become more and more dependent upon the actor. And this is another reason why the drama which Mr Archer desires, as the photographic and gramophonic record of its time, can never exist. The closer a play is built upon real life, the more the performance by one actor will differ from another, and the more the performances of one generation of actors will differ from those of the next. It is furthermore obvious that what we ask involves a considerable sacrifice of a certain kind of interest. A character in the conventional play can never be as real as is the character in a realistic play while the rôle is being enacted by a great actor who has made the part his own. I can only say that wherever you have a form you make some sacrifice against some gain.

8 If we examine the faults which Mr Archer finds in Elizabethan drama, it is possible to come to the conclusion (already indicated) that these faults are due to its tendencies rather than what are ordinarily called its conventions. I mean that no single convention of Elizabethan drama, however ridiculous it may be made to appear, is essentially bad. Neither the soliloquy, nor the aside, nor the ghost, nor the blood-and-thunder, nor absurdity of place or time is in itself absurd. There are, of course, definite faults of bad writing, careless writing, and bad taste. A line-by-line examination of almost any Elizabethan play, including those of Shakespeare, would be a fruitful exercise. But these are not the faults which weaken the foundations. What is fundamentally objectionable is that in the Elizabethan drama there has been no firm principle of what is to be postulated as a convention and what is not. The fault [116] is not with the ghost but with the presentation of a ghost on a plane on which he is inappropriate, and with the confusion between one type of ghost and another. The three witches in *Macbeth* are a distinguished example of correct supernaturalism amongst a race of ghosts who are too frequently equivocations. It seems to me strictly an error, although an error which is condoned by the success of each passage in itself, that Shakespeare should have introduced into the same play ghosts belonging to such different categories as the three sisters and the ghost of Banquo.[1] The aim of the Elizabethans was to attain complete realism without any of the advantages which as artists they observed in unrealistic conventions.

9 We shall take up the work of four Elizabethan dramatists and attempt to subject them to an analysis from the point of view which I have

---

1. This will appear to be an objection as pedantic as that of Thomas Rymer to *Othello*. But Rymer makes out a very good case.

indicated. We shall take the objections of Mr Archer to each one of these dramatists and see if the difficulty does not reside in this confusion of convention and realism, and we must make some attempt also to illustrate the faults as distinguished from the conventions. There were, of course, tendencies toward form. There was a general philosophy of life, if it may be called such, based on Seneca and other influences which we find in Shakespeare as in the others. It is a philosophy which, as Mr Santayana observed in an essay which passed almost unheeded, may be summarised in the statement that Duncan is in his grave. Even the philosophical basis, the general attitude toward life of the Elizabethans, is one of anarchism, of dissolution, of decay. It is in fact exactly parallel and indeed one and the same thing with their artistic greediness, their desire for every sort of effect together, their unwillingness to accept any limitation and abide by it. The Elizabethans are in fact a part of the movement of progress or deterioration which has culminated [117] in Sir Arthur Pinero and in the present regiment of Europe.[1]

10 The case of John Webster, and in particular *The Duchess of Malfy*, will provide an interesting example of a very great literary and dramatic genius directed toward chaos. The case of Middleton is an interesting one, because we have from the same hand plays so different as *The Changeling, Women beware Women, The Roaring Girl*, and *A Game at Chess*.[2] In the one great play of Tourneur's, the discord is less apparent, but not less real. Chapman appears to have been potentially perhaps the greatest artist of all these men: his was the mind which was the most classical, his was the drama which is the most independent in its tendency toward a dramatic form – although it may seem the most formless and the most indifferent to dramatic necessities. If we can establish the same consequence independently by an examination of the Elizabethan philosophy, the Elizabethan dramatic form, and the variations in the rhythms of Elizabethan blank verse as employed by several of the greatest dramatists, we may come to conclusions which will enable us to understand why Mr Archer, who is the opponent of the Elizabethans, should also be unconsciously their last champion, and why he should be a believer in progress, in the growth

---

1. Mr Archer calls it progress. He has certain predispositions. 'Shakespeare,' he says, 'was not alive to the great idea which differentiates the present age from all that have gone before – the idea of progress.' And he admits, speaking of Elizabethan drama in general, that 'here and there a certain glimmer of humanitarian feeling is perceptible'.

2. I agree with Mr Dugdale Sykes, to whose acute observations I am under a great debt, that certain work attributed to Middleton is not Middleton's, but there appears to be no reason for questioning the authorship of the plays I have just mentioned.

of humanitarian feeling, and in the superiority and efficiency of the present age.

Variants from C. (1924):
Subtitle I. A Preface

2   *Specimens*] Selections
    Specimens] Selections

2   seems to spring] springs

4   succeeded] has succeeded

5   as were those] as those
    [Between 'the play itself.' and 'An actor':] It is impossible for any Elizabethan drama to be performed in a satisfactory way.
    treatment,] treatment;

6   transpires between] transpires through

7   most performances] performances
    [No fn. in 1924.]

8   confusion] constant confusion
    witches in *Macbeth*] witches

10 *Malfy*] Malfi
    at Chess] of Chess

Christopher Marlowe

SE, 118–25.

Publ. in A&L, 2. 4 (Autumn 1919), 194–9. Headed 'T. S. ELIOT.' Gallup C89. Revised in *SW*, and in *SE* (1932) as 'Christopher Marlowe', in later edns 'Marlowe'. The *SE* text was repr. in *EE* and *ED*.

1 Swinburne observes of Marlowe that 'the father of English tragedy and the creator of English blank verse was therefore also the teacher and the guide of Shakespeare'. In this sentence there are two misleading assumptions and two misleading conclusions. Kyd has as good a title to the first honour as Marlowe; Surrey has a better title to the second; and Shakespeare was not taught or guided by one of his predecessors or contemporaries alone. The less questionable judgement is, that Marlowe exercised a strong influence over later drama, though not himself as great a dramatist as Kyd; that he introduced several new tones into blank verse, and commenced the dissociative process which drew it farther and farther away from the rhythms of rhymed verse; and that when Shakespeare borrowed from him, which was pretty often at the beginning, Shakespeare either made something inferior or something different.

2 The comparative study of English versification at various periods is a large tract of unwritten history. To make a study of blank verse alone would be to elicit some curious conclusions. It would show, I believe, that blank verse within Shakespeare's lifetime was more highly developed, that it became the vehicle of more varied and more intense feeling than it has ever conveyed since; and that after the erection of the Chinese Wall of Milton, blank verse has suffered not only arrest but retrogression. That the blank verse of Tennyson, for example, a consummate master of this form in certain applications, is cruder (*not* 'rougher' or less perfect in technique) than that of half [119] a dozen contemporaries of Shakespeare; cruder, because less capable of expressing complicated, subtle, and surprising emotions.

3 Every writer who has written any blank verse worth saving has produced particular tones which his verse and no other's is capable of rendering; and we should keep this in mind when we talk about 'influences' and 'indebtedness'. Shakespeare is 'universal' because he has more of these tones than anyone else; but they are all out of the one man; one man cannot be more than one man; there might have been six Shakespeares at once without conflicting frontiers; and to say that Shakespeare expressed nearly all human emotions, implying that he left very little for anyone else, is a radical misunderstanding of art and the artist – a misunderstanding which, even when explicitly rejected, may lead to our neglecting the effort of attention necessary to discover the specific properties of the verse of Shakespeare's contemporaries. The development of blank verse may be likened to the analysis of that astonishing industrial product coal-tar. Marlowe's verse is one of the earlier derivatives, but it possesses properties which are not repeated in any of the analytic or synthetic blank-verses discovered somewhat later.

4 The 'vices of style' of Marlowe's and Shakespeare's age is a convenient name for a number of vices, no one of which, perhaps, was shared by all of the writers. It is pertinent, at least, to remark that Marlowe's 'rhetoric' is not, or not characteristically, Shakespeare's rhetoric; that Marlowe's rhetoric consists in a pretty simple huffe-snuffe bombast, while Shakespeare's is more exactly a vice of style, a tortured perverse ingenuity of images which dissipates instead of concentrating the imagination, and which may be due in part to influences by which Marlowe was untouched. Next, we find that Marlowe's vice is one which he was gradually attenuating, and even, what is more miraculous, turning into a virtue. And we find that this poet of torrential imagination recognised many of his best bits (and [120] those of one or two others), saved them, and

reproduced them more than once, almost invariably improving them in the process.

5 It is worth while noticing a few of these versions, because they indicate, somewhat contrary to usual opinion, that Marlowe was a deliberate and conscious workman. Mr J. M. Robertson has spotted an interesting theft of Marlowe's from Spenser. Here is Spenser (*Faery Queen*, I. vii. 32):

> Like to an almond tree y-mounted high
>   On top of green Selinis all alone,
> With blossoms brave bedeckèd daintily;
>   Whose tender locks do tremble every one
> At every little breath that under heaven is blown.

And here Marlowe (*Tamburlaine*, Part II. Act IV. Sc. iii.):

> Like to an almond tree y-mounted high
> Upon the lofty and celestial mount
> Of evergreen Selinus, quaintly deck'd
> With blossoms more white than Erycina's brows,
> Whose tender blossoms tremble every one
> At every little breath that thorough heaven is blown.

6 This is interesting, not only as showing that Marlowe's talent, like that of most poets, was partly synthetic, but also because it seems to give a clue to some particularly 'lyric' effects found in *Tamburlaine*, not in Marlowe's other plays, and not, I believe, anywhere else. For example, the praise of Zenocrate in Part II. Act II. Sc. iv:

> Now walk the angels on the walls of heaven,
> As sentinels to warn th'immortal souls
> To entertain divine Zenocrate.

7 This is not Spenser's movement, but the influence of Spenser must be present. There had been no great blank verse before Marlowe; but there was the powerful presence of this great master of melody immediately precedent; and [121] the combination produced results which could not be repeated. I do not think that it can be claimed that Peele had any influence here.

8 The passage quoted from Spenser has a further interest. It will be noted that the fourth line:

> With blooms more white than Erycina's brows,

is Marlowe's contribution. Compare this with these other lines of Marlowe's:

> So looks my love, shadowing in her brows
> (*Tamburlaine*)

> Like to the shadows of Pyramides
> (*Tamburlaine*)

and the final and best version:

> Shadowing more beauty in their airy brows
> Than have the white breasts of the queen of love.
> (*Doctor Faustus*).

and compare the whole set with Spenser again (F. Q.):

> Upon her eyelids many graces sate
> Under the shadow of her even brows,

a passage which Mr Robertson says Spenser himself used in three other places.

9 This economy is frequent in Marlowe. Within *Tamburlaine* it occurs in the form of monotony, especially in the facile use of resonant names (e.g. the recurrence of 'Caspia' or 'Caspian' with the same tone effect), a practice in which Marlowe was followed by Milton, but which Marlowe himself outgrew. Again,

> Zenocrate, lovlier than the love of Jove,
> Brighter than is the silver Rhodope,

is paralleled later by

> Zenocrate, the lovliest maid alive,
> Fairer than rocks of pearl and precious stone.

[122] One line Marlowe remodels with triumphant success:

> And set black streamers in the firmament
> (*Tamburlaine*).

becomes

> See, see, where Christ's blood streams in the firmament!
> (*Doctor Faustus*).

10 The verse accomplishments of *Tamburlaine* are notably two: Marlowe gets into blank verse the melody of Spenser, and he gets a new driving power by reinforcing the sentence period against the line period. The rapid long sentence, running line into line, as in the famous soliloquies 'Nature compounded of four elements' and 'What is beauty, saith my sufferings, then?' marks the certain escape of blank verse from the rhymed couplet, and from the elegiac or rather pastoral note of Surrey, to which Tennyson returned. If you contrast these two soliloquies with the verse of Marlowe's greatest contemporary, Kyd – by no means a despicable versifier – you see the importance of the innovation:

> The one took sanctuary, and, being sent for out,
> Was murdered in Southwark as he passed
> To Greenwich, where the Lord Protector lay.
> Black Will was burned in Flushing on a stage;
> Greene was hanged at Osbridge in Kent ...

which is not really inferior to:

> So these four abode
> Within one house together; and as years
> Went forward, Mary took another mate;
> But Dora lived unmarried till her death.
> (Tennyson, *Dora*.)

11 In *Faustus* Marlowe went further: he broke up the line, to a gain in intensity, in the last soliloquy; and he developed a new and important conversational tone in the dialogues [123] of Faustus with the devil. *Edward II* has never lacked consideration: it is more desirable, in brief space, to remark upon two plays, one of which has been misunderstood and the other underrated. These are the *Jew of Malta* and *Dido Queen of Carthage*. On the first of these, it has always been said that the end, even the last two acts, are unworthy of the first three. If one takes the *Jew of Malta* not as a tragedy, or as a 'tragedy of blood', but as a farce, the concluding act becomes intelligible; and if we attend with a careful ear to the versification, we find that Marlowe develops a tone to suit this farce, and even perhaps that this tone is his most powerful and mature tone. I say farce, but with the enfeebled humour of our times the word is a misnomer; it is the farce of the old English humour, the terribly serious, even savage comic humour, the humour which spent its last breath in the decadent genius of Dickens. It has nothing in common with J. M. Barrie,

Captain Bairnsfather, or *Punch*. It is the humour of that very serious (but very different) play, *Volpone*.

> First, be thou void of these affections,
> Compassion, love, vain hope, and heartless fear;
> Be moved at nothing, see thou pity none . . .
> As for myself, I walk abroad o' nights,
> And kill sick people groaning under walls:
> Sometimes I go about and poison wells . . .

and the last words of Barabas complete this prodigious caricature:

> But now begins th' extremity of heat
> To pinch me with intolerable pangs,
> Die, life! fly, soul! tongue, curse thy fill, and die!

It is something which Shakespeare could not do, and which he did not want to do.

12 *Dido* appears to be a hurried play, perhaps done to order with the *Aeneid* in front of him. But even here there is progress. The account of the sack of Troy is in this newer style [124] of Marlowe's, this style which secures its emphasis by always hesitating on the edge of caricature at the right moment:

> The Grecian soldiers, tir'd with ten years war,
> Began to cry, 'Let us unto our ships,
> Troy is invincible, why stay we here?' . . .
>
> By this, the camp was come unto the walls,
> And through the breach did march into the streets,
> Where, meeting with the rest, 'Kill, kill!' they cried. . .
>
> And after him, his band of Myrmidons,
> With balls of wild-fire in their murdering paws . . .
>
> At last, the soldiers pull'd her by the heels,
> And swung her howling in the empty air. . . .
>
> We saw Cassandra sprawling in the streets . . .

13 This is not Virgil, or Shakespeare; it is pure Marlowe. By comparing the whole speech with Clarence's dream, in *Richard III*, one acquires a little insight into the difference between Marlowe and Shakespeare:

> What scourge for perjury
> Can this dark monarchy afford false Clarence?

14 There, on the other hand, is what Marlowe's style could not do; the phrase has a concision which is almost classical, certainly Dantesque. Again, as often with the Elizabethan dramatists, there are lines in Marlowe, besides the many lines that Shakespeare adapted, that might have been written by either:

> If thou wilt stay,
> Leap in mine arms; mine arms are open wide;
> If not, turn from me, and I'll turn from thee;
> For though thou hast the heart to say farewell,
> I have not power to stay thee.

[125] **15** But the direction in which Marlowe's verse might have moved, had he not 'dyed swearing', is quite un-Shakespearian, is toward this intense and serious and indubitably great poetry, which, like some great painting and sculpture, attains its effects by something not unlike caricature.

Variants:

Title 'Some Notes on the Blank Verse of Christopher Marlowe' *A&L* (1919); 'Notes on the Blank Verse of Christopher Marlowe' *SW*

Subheading 'Marloe was stabd with a dagger, and dyed swearing.' *A&L* (1919), *SW*

1. Swinburne observes of Marlowe] A more friendly critic, Mr A. C. Swinburne, observes of this poet *A&L* (1919), *SW*
2. feeling] art-emotions *A&L* (1919), *SW*
3. 'universal'] 'universal' (if you like) *A&L* (1919), *SW*
   artist – a misunderstanding] artist. A misunderstanding *A&L* (1919)
4. poet of torrential] bard of torrential *A&L* (1919), *SW*
5. J. M. Robertson] J. G. Robertson *A&L* (1919)
   Act IV sc. IV] Act II sc.3 *A&L* (1919)), *SW*
6. not, I believe,] not I believe *A&L* (1919)
   divine Zenocrate] divine Zenocrate: etc. *A&L* (1919), *SW*
8. brows,] brows *A&L* (1919), *SW*
11. further] farther *A&L* (1919), *SW*
    in the decadent] on the decadent *A&L* (1919), *SW*
    did not want to do] could not have understood *A&L* (1919), *SW*
13. Virgil] Vergil *A&L* (1919), *SW*
15. 'dyed swearing'] dyed swearing *A&L* (1919)

Shakespeare and the Stoicism of Seneca

SE, 126–40.
Publ. by The Shakespeare Association on 22 Sept. 1927: Gallup A10.

In the 1927 text 'In any case, so important as that of Shakespeare,' was printed, and this was carried over into para. 1 of *SE*. This has been emended to 'In any case so important as Shakespeare's'. The editor is grateful to Christopher Ricks for drawing his attention to this.

1 The last few years have witnessed a number of recrudescences of Shakespeare. There is the fatigued Shakespeare, a retired Anglo-Indian, presented by Mr Lytton Strachey; there is the messianic Shakespeare, bringing a new philosophy and a new system of yoga, presented by Mr Middleton Murry; and there is the ferocious Shakespeare, a furious Samson, presented by Mr Wyndham Lewis in his interesting book, *The Lion and the Fox*. On the whole, we may all agree that these manifestations are beneficial. In any case so important as Shakespeare's, it is good that we should from time to time change our minds. The last conventional Shakespeare is banished from the scene, and a variety of unconventional Shakespeares takes his place. About anyone so great as Shakespeare, it is probable that we can never be right; and if we can never be right, it is better that we should from time to time change our way of being wrong. Whether Truth ultimately prevails is doubtful and has never been proved; but it is certain that nothing is more effective in driving out error than a new error. Whether Mr Strachey, or Mr Murry, or Mr Lewis, is any nearer to the truth of Shakespeare than Rymer, or Morgann, or Webster, or Johnson, is uncertain; they are all certainly more sympathetic in this year 1927 than Coleridge, or Swinburne, or Dowden. If they do not give us the real Shakespeare – if there is one – they at least give us several up-to-date Shakespeares. If the only way to prove that Shakespeare did not feel and think exactly as people felt [127] and thought in 1815, or in 1860, or in 1880, is to show that he felt and thought as we felt and thought in 1927, then we must accept gratefully that alternative.

2 But these recent interpreters of Shakespeare suggest a number of reflections on literary criticism and its limits, on general aesthetics, and on the limitations of the human understanding.

3 There are, of course, a number of other current interpretations of Shakespeare: that is, of the *conscious opinions* of Shakespeare: interpretations of category, so to speak: which made him either a Tory journalist or a Liberal journalist, or a Socialist journalist (though Mr Shaw has

done something to ward off his co-religionists from claiming Shakespeare, or from finding anything uplifting in his work); we have also a Protestant Shakespeare, and a sceptical Shakespeare, and some case may be made out for an Anglo-Catholic, or even a Papist Shakespeare. My own frivolous opinion is that Shakespeare may have held in private life very different views from what we extract from his extremely varied published works; that there is no clue in his writings to the way in which he would have voted in the last or would vote in the next election; and that we are completely in the dark as to his attitude about prayer-book revision. I admit that my own experience, as a minor poet, may have jaundiced my outlook; that I am used to having cosmic significances, which I never suspected, extracted from my work (such as it is) by enthusiastic persons at a distance; and to being informed that something which I meant seriously is *vers de société*; and to having my personal biography reconstructed from passages which I got out of books, or which I invented out of nothing because they sounded well; and to having my biography invariably ignored in what I *did* write from personal experience; so that in consequence I am inclined to believe that people are mistaken about Shakespeare just in proportion to the relative superiority of Shakespeare to myself.

[128] 4 One more personal 'note': I believe that I have as high an estimate of the greatness of Shakespeare as poet and dramatist as anyone living; I certainly believe that there is nothing greater. And I would say that my only qualification for venturing to talk about him is, that I am *not* under the delusion that Shakespeare in the least resembles myself, either as I am or as I should like to imagine myself. It seems to me that one of the chief reasons for questioning Mr Strachey's Shakespeare, and Mr Murry's, and Mr Lewis's, is the remarkable resemblance which they bear to Mr Strachey, and Mr Murry, and Mr Lewis respectively. I have not a very clear idea of what Shakespeare was like. But I do not conceive him as very like either Mr Strachey, or Mr Murry, and Mr Wyndham Lewis, or myself.

5 We have had Shakespeare explained by a variety of influences. He is explained by Montaigne, and by Machiavelli. I imagine that Mr Strachey would explain Shakespeare by Montaigne, though this would also be Mr Strachey's Montaigne (for all of Mr Strachey's favourite figures have a strong Strachey physiognomy) and not Mr Robertson's. I think that Mr Lewis, in the intensely interesting book mentioned, has done a real service in calling attention to the importance of Machiavelli in Elizabethan England, though this Machiavelli be only the Machiavelli

of the *Contre-Machiavel*, and not in the least the real Machiavelli, a person whom Elizabethan England was as incapable of understanding as Georgian England, or any England, is. I think, however, that Mr Lewis has gone quite wrong if he thinks (I am not sure what he thinks) that Shakespeare, and Elizabethan England in general, was 'influenced' by the thought of Machiavelli. I think that Shakespeare, and other dramatists, used the popular Machiavellian idea, for stage purposes; but this idea was no more like Machiavelli, who was an Italian and a Roman Christian, than Mr Shaw's idea of Nietzsche – whatever that is – is like the real Nietzsche.

6 I propose a Shakespeare under the influence of the stoic-[129]ism of Seneca. But I do not believe that Shakespeare was under the influence of Seneca. I propose it largely because I believe that after the Montaigne Shakespeare (not that Montaigne had any philosophy whatever) and after the Machiavelli Shakespeare, a stoical or Senecan Shakespeare is almost certain to be produced. I wish merely to disinfect the Senecan Shakespeare before he appears. My ambitions would be realised if I could prevent him, in so doing, from appearing at all.

7 I want to be quite definite in my notion of the possible influence of Seneca on Shakespeare. I think it is quite likely that Shakespeare read some of Seneca's tragedies at school. I think it quite unlikely that Shakespeare knew anything of that extraordinarily dull and uninteresting body of Seneca's prose, which was translated by Lodge and printed in 1612. So far as Shakespeare was influenced by Seneca, it was by his memories of school conning and through the influence of the Senecan tragedy of the day, through Kyd and Peele, but chiefly Kyd. That Shakespeare deliberately took a 'view of life' from Seneca there seems to be no evidence whatever.

8 Nevertheless, there is, in some of the great tragedies of Shakespeare, a new attitude. It is not the attitude of Seneca, but is derived from Seneca; it is slightly different from anything that can be found in French tragedy, in Corneille or in Racine; it is modern, and it culminates, if there is ever any culmination, in the attitude of Nietzsche. I cannot say that it is Shakespeare's 'philosophy'. Yet many people have lived by it; though it may only have been Shakespeare's instinctive recognition of something of theatrical utility. It is the attitude of self-dramatisation assumed by some of Shakespeare's heroes at moments of tragic intensity. It is not peculiar to Shakespeare; it is conspicuous in Chapman: Bussy, Clermont and Biron, all die in this way. Marston – one of the most interesting and least

explored of all the Elizabethans – uses it; and Marston and Chapman were particularly Senecan. But Shakespeare, of course, does it [130] very much better than any of the others, and makes it somehow more integral with the human nature of his characters. It is less verbal, more real. I have always felt that I have never read a more terrible exposure of human weakness – of universal human weakness – than the last great speech of Othello. I am ignorant whether anyone else has ever adopted this view, and it may appear subjective and fantastic in the extreme. It is usually taken on its face value, as expressing the greatness in defeat of a noble but erring nature:

> Soft you; a word or two before you go.
> I have done the state some service, and they know't.
> No more of that. I pray you, in your letters,
> When you shall these unlucky deeds relate,
> Speak of me as I am; nothing extenuate,
> Nor set down aught in malice: then must you speak
> Of one that loved not wisely but too well;
> Of one not easily jealous, but, being wrought,
> Perplex'd in the extreme; of one whose hand,
> Like the base Indian, threw a pearl away
> Richer than all his tribe; of one whose subdued eyes,
> Albeit unused to the melting mood,
> Drop tears as fast as the Arabian trees
> Their medicinal gum. Set you down this;
> And say, besides, that in Aleppo once,
> Where a malignant and a turban'd Turk
> Beat a Venetian and traduced the state,
> I took by the throat the circumcised dog,
> And smote him, thus.

What Othello seems to me to be doing in making this speech is *cheering himself up*. He is endeavouring to escape reality, he has ceased to think about Desdemona, and is thinking about himself. Humility is the most difficult of all virtues to achieve; nothing dies harder than the desire to think well of oneself. Othello succeeds in turning himself into a pathetic figure, by adopting an *aesthetic* rather than [131] a moral attitude, dramatising himself against his environment. He takes in the spectator, but the human motive is primarily to take in himself. I do not believe that any writer has ever exposed this *bovarysme*, the human will to see things as they are not, more clearly than Shakespeare.

9 If you compare the deaths of several of Shakespeare's heroes – I do not say *all*, for there are very few generalisations that can be applied to the whole of Shakespeare's work – but notably Othello, Coriolanus and Antony – with the deaths of heroes of dramatists such as Marston and Chapman, consciously under Senecan influence, you will find a strong similarity – except only that Shakespeare does it both more poetically and more lifelike.

10 You may say that Shakespeare is merely illustrating, consciously or unconsciously, human nature, not Seneca. But I am not so much concerned with the influence of Seneca on Shakespeare as with Shakespeare's illustration of Senecan and stoical principles. Much of Chapman's Senecanism has lately been shown by Professor Schoell to be directly borrowed from Erasmus and other sources. I am concerned with the fact that Seneca is the *literary* representative of Roman stoicism, and that Roman stoicism is an important ingredient in Elizabethan drama. It was natural that in a time like that of Elizabeth stoicism should appear. The original stoicism, and especially the Roman stoicism, was of course a philosophy suited to slaves: hence its absorption into early Christianity.

> A man to join himself with the Universe
> In his main sway, and make in all things fit –

A man does not join himself with the Universe so long as he has anything else to join himself with; men who could take part in the life of a thriving Greek city-state had something better to join themselves to; and Christians have had something better. Stoicism is the refuge for the individual in an indifferent or hostile world too big for him; it is the permanent substratum of a number of versions of cheering [132] oneself up. Nietzsche is the most conspicuous modern instance of cheering oneself up. The stoical attitude is the reverse of Christian humility.

11 In Elizabethan England we have conditions apparently utterly different from those of imperial Rome. But it was a period of dissolution and chaos; and in such a period any emotional attitude which seems to give a man something firm, even if it be only the attitude of 'I am myself alone', is eagerly taken up. I hardly need – and it is beyond my present scope – to point out how readily, in a period like the Elizabethan, the Senecan attitude of Pride, the Montaigne attitude of Scepticism, and the Machiavelli attitude[1] of Cynicism, arrived at a kind of fusion in the Elizabethan individualism.

---

1. I do not mean the attitude of Machiavelli, which is not cynical. I mean the attitude of Englishmen who had heard of Machiavelli.

12 This individualism, this vice of Pride, was, of course, exploited largely because of its dramatic possibilities. But other drama had before existed without depending on this human failing. You do not find it in *Polyeucte*, or in *Phèdre* either. But even Hamlet, who has made a pretty considerable mess of things, and occasioned the death of at least three innocent people, and two more insignificant ones, dies fairly well pleased with himself –

> Horatio, I am dead;
> Thou liv'st; report me and my cause aright
> To the unsatisfied. . . .
> O good Horatio, what a wounded name,
> Things standing thus unknown, shall live behind me!

Antony says, 'I am Antony still', and the Duchess, 'I am Duchess of Malfy still'; would either of them have said that unless Medea had said *Medea superest*?

13 I do not wish to appear to maintain that the Elizabethan hero and the Senecan hero are identical. The influence of Seneca is much more apparent in the Elizabethan drama than it is in the plays of Seneca. The influence of any man [133] is a different thing from himself. The Elizabethan hero is much more stoical and Senecan, in this way, than the Senecan hero. For Seneca was following the Greek tradition, which was not stoical; he developed familiar themes and imitated great models; so that the vast difference between his emotional attitude and that of the Greeks is rather latent in his work, and more apparent in the work of the Renaissance. And the Elizabethan hero, the hero of Shakespeare, was not invariable even in Elizabethan England. A notable exception is Faustus. Marlowe – not excepting Shakespeare or Chapman, the most *thoughtful* and philosophic mind, though immature, among the Elizabethan dramatists – could conceive the proud hero, as Tamburlaine, but also the hero who has reached that point of horror at which even pride is abandoned. In a recent book on Marlowe, Miss Ellis-Fermor has put very well this peculiarity of Faustus, from another point of view than mine, but in words from which I take support:

> Marlowe follows Faustus further across the borderline between consciousness and dissolution than do any of his contemporaries. With Shakespeare, with Webster, death is a sudden severing of life; their men die, conscious to the last of some part at least of their surroundings, influenced, even upheld, by that consciousness and preserving the personality and characteristics they have possessed

through life.... In Marlowe's Faustus alone all this is set aside. He penetrates deeply into the experience of a mind isolated from the past, absorbed in the realization of its own destruction.

14 But Marlowe, the most thoughtful, the most blasphemous (and therefore, probably, the most Christian) of his contemporaries, is always an exception. Shakespeare is exceptional primarily by his immense superiority.

15 Of all of Shakespeare's plays, *King Lear* is often taken as the most Senecan in spirit. Cunliffe finds it to be imbued with a Senecan fatalism. Here, again, we must distinguish between a man and his influence. The differences between [134] the fatalism of Greek tragedy, and the fatalism of Seneca's tragedies, and the fatalism of the Elizabethans, proceed by delicate shades; there is a continuity, and there is also a violent contrast, when we look at them from far off. In Seneca, the Greek ethics is visible underneath the Renaissance stoicism. In the Elizabethans, the Roman stoicism is visible beneath the Renaissance anarchism. In *King Lear* there are several significant phrases, such as those which caught the attention of Professor Cunliffe, and there is a tone of Senecan fatalism: *fatis agimur*. But there is much less and much more. And this is the point at which I must part company with Mr Wyndham Lewis. Mr Lewis proposes a Shakespeare who is a *positive* nihilist, and intellectual force *willing* destruction. I cannot see in Shakespeare either a deliberate scepticism, as of Montaigne, or a deliberate cynicism, as of Machiavelli, or a deliberate resignation, as of Seneca. I can see that he *used* all of these things, for dramatic ends; you get perhaps more Montaigne in *Hamlet*, and more Machiavelli in *Othello*, and more Seneca in *Lear*. But I cannot agree with the following paragraph:

> With the exception of Chapman, Shakespeare is the only thinker we meet with among the Elizabethan dramatists. By this is meant, of course, that his work contained, apart from poetry, phantasy, rhetoric or observation of manners, a body of matter representing explicit processes of the intellect which would have furnished a moral philosopher like Montaigne with the natural material for his essays. But the quality of this thinking – as it can be surprised springing naturally in the midst of the consummate movements of his art – is, as must be the case with such a man, of startling force sometimes. And if it is not systematic, at least a recognizable physiognomy is there.

16 It is this general notion of 'thinking' that I would challenge. One has the difficulty of having to use the same words for different things. We say, in a vague way, that Shakespeare, or Dante, or Lucretius, is a poet who thinks, and that Swinburne is a poet who does not think, even [135] that Tennyson is a poet who does not think. But what we really mean is not a difference in quality of thought, but a difference in quality of emotion. The poet who 'thinks' is merely the poet who can express the emotional equivalent of thought. But he is not necessarily interested in the thought itself. We talk as if thought was precise and emotion was vague. In reality there is precise emotion and there is vague emotion. To express precise emotion requires as great intellectual power as to express precise thought. But by 'thinking' I mean something very different from anything that I find in Shakespeare. Mr Lewis, and other champions of Shakespeare as a great philosopher, have a great deal to say about Shakespeare's power of thought, but they fail to show that he thought to any purpose; that he had any coherent view of life, or that he recommended any procedure to follow. 'We possess a great deal of evidence,' says Mr Lewis, 'as to what Shakespeare thought of military glory and martial events.' Do we? Or rather, did Shakespeare think anything at all? He was occupied with turning human actions into poetry.

17 I would suggest that none of the plays of Shakespeare has a 'meaning', although it would be equally false to say that a play of Shakespeare is meaningless. All great poetry gives the illusion of a view of life. When we enter into the world of Homer, or Sophocles, or Virgil, or Dante, or Shakespeare, we incline to believe that we are apprehending something that can be expressed intellectually; for every precise emotion tends towards intellectual formulation.

18 We are apt to be deluded by the example of Dante. Here, we think, is a poem which represents an exact intellectual system; Dante has a 'philosophy', therefore every poet as great as Dante has a philosophy too. Dante had behind him the system of St Thomas, to which his poem corresponds point to point. There Shakespeare had behind him Seneca, or Montaigne, or Machiavelli; and if his work does not correspond point to point with any or a [136] composition of these, then it must be that he did a little quiet thinking on his own, and was better than any of these people at their own job. I can see no reason for believing that either Dante or Shakespeare did any thinking on his own. The people who think that Shakespeare thought, are always people who are not engaged in writing poetry, but who are engaged in thinking, and we all like to think that great men were like ourselves. The difference between Shakespeare and

Dante is that Dante had one coherent system of thought behind him; but that was just his luck, and from the point of view of poetry is an irrelevant accident. It happened that at Dante's time thought was orderly and strong and beautiful, and that it was concentrated in one man of the greatest genius; Dante's poetry receives a boost in a sense it does not merit, from the fact that the thought behind it is the thought of a man as great and lovely as Dante himself: St Thomas. The thought behind Shakespeare is of men far inferior to Shakespeare himself: hence to alternative errors, first, that as Shakespeare was as great a poet as Dante, he must have supplied, out of his own thinking, the difference in quality between a St Thomas and a Montaigne or a Machiavelli or a Seneca, or second, that Shakespeare is inferior to Dante. In truth neither Shakespeare nor Dante did any real thinking – that was not their job; and the relative value of the thought current at their time, the material enforced upon each to use as the vehicle of his feeling, is of no importance. It does not make Dante a greater poet, or mean that we can learn more from Dante than from Shakespeare. We can certainly learn more from Aquinas than from Seneca, but that is quite a different matter. When Dante says

> la sua voluntade è nostra pace

it is great poetry, and there is a philosophy behind it. When Shakespeare says

> As flies to wanton boys, are we to the gods;
> They kill us for their sport.

[137] it is *equally* great poetry, though the philosophy behind it is not great. But the essential is that each expresses, in perfect language, some permanent human impulse. Emotionally, the latter is just as strong, just as true, and just as informative – just as useful and beneficial in the sense in which poetry is useful and beneficial, as the former.

19 What every poet starts from is his own emotions. And when we get down to these, there is not much to choose between Shakespeare and Dante. Dante's railings, his personal spleen – sometimes thinly disguised under Old Testamental prophetic denunciations – his nostalgia, his bitter regrets for past happiness – or for what seems happiness when it is past – and his brave attempts to fabricate something permanent and holy out of his personal animal feelings – as in the *Vita Nuova* – can all be matched out of Shakespeare. Shakespeare, too, was occupied with the struggle – which alone constitutes life for a poet – to translate his personal and private agonies into something rich and strange, something universal and impersonal. The rage of Dante against Florence, or Pistoia, or what not,

the deep surge of Shakespeare's general cynicism and disillusionment, are merely gigantic attempts to metamorphose private failures and disappointments. The great poet, in writing himself, writes his time.[1] Thus Dante, hardly knowing it, became the voice of the thirteenth century; Shakespeare, hardly knowing it, became the representative of the end of the sixteenth century, of a turning point in history. But you can hardly say that Dante believed, or did not believe, the Thomist philosophy; you can hardly say that Shakespeare believed, or did not believe, the mixed and muddled scepticism of the Renaissance. If Shakespeare had written according to a better philosophy, he would have written worse poetry; it was his business to express the greatest emotional intensity of his time, based on whatever his time happened to think. Poetry is not a substitute for philosophy or theology or religion, as Mr [138] Lewis and Mr Murry sometimes seem to think; it has its own function. But this function is not intellectual but emotional, it cannot be defined adequately in intellectual terms. We can say that it provides 'consolation': strange consolation, which is provided by writers so different as Shakespeare and Dante.

20 What I have said could be expressed more exactly, but at much greater length, in philosophical language: it would enter into the department of philosophy which might be called the Theory of Belief (which is not psychology but philosophy, or phenomenology proper) – the department in which Meinong and Husserl have made some pioneer investigation; the different meanings which belief has in different minds according to the activity for which they are oriented. I doubt whether belief proper enters into the activity of a great poet, *qua* poet. That is, Dante, *qua* poet, did not believe or disbelieve the Thomist cosmology or theory of the soul: he merely made use of it, or a fusion took place between his initial emotional impulses and a theory, for the purpose of making poetry. The poet makes poetry, the metaphysician makes metaphysics, the bee makes honey, the spider secretes a filament; you can hardly say that any of these agents believes; he merely does.

21 The problem of belief is very complicated and probably quite insoluble. We must make allowances for differences in the emotional quality of believing not only between persons of different occupation, such as the philosopher and the poet, but between different periods of time. The end of the sixteenth century is an epoch when it is particularly difficult to associate poetry with systems of thought or reasoned views of life. In making some very commonplace investigations of the 'thought' of

---

1. Rémy de Gourmont said much the same thing, in speaking of Flaubert.

Donne, I found it quite impossible to come to the conclusion that Donne believed anything. It seemed as if, at that time, the world was filled with broken fragments of systems, and that a man like Donne merely picked up, like a magpie, various [139] shining fragments of ideas as they struck his eye, and stuck them about here and there in his verse. Miss Ramsay, in her learned and exhaustive study of Donne's sources, came to the conclusion that he was a 'mediaeval thinker'; I could not find either any 'mediaevalism' or any thinking, but only a vast jumble of incoherent erudition on which he drew for purely poetic effects. The recent work of Professor Schoell on the sources of Chapman seems to show Chapman engaged in the same task; and suggests that the 'profundity' and 'obscurity' of Chapman's dark thinking are largely due to his lifting long passages from the works of writers like Ficino and incorporating them in his poems completely out of their context.

22 I do not for a moment suggest that the method of Shakespeare was anything like this. Shakespeare was a much finer instrument for transformations than any of his contemporaries, finer perhaps even than Dante. He also needed less contact in order to be able to absorb all that he required. The element of Seneca is the most completely absorbed and transmogrified, because it was already the most diffused throughout Shakespeare's world. The element of Machiavelli is probably the most indirect, the element of Montaigne the most immediate. It has been said that Shakespeare lacks unity; it might, I think, be said equally that it is Shakespeare chiefly that *is* the unity, that unifies so far as they could be unified all the tendencies of a time that certainly lacked unity. Unity, in Shakespeare, but not universality; no one can be universal; Shakespeare would not have found much in common with his contemporary St Theresa. What influence the work of Seneca and Machiavelli and Montaigne seems to me to exert in common on that time, and most conspicuously through Shakespeare, is an influence toward a kind of self-consciousness that is new; the self-consciousness and self-dramatisation of the Shakespearian hero, of whom Hamlet is only one. It seems to mark a stage, even if not a very agreeable one, in human history, or progress, or deterioration, or [140] change. Roman stoicism was in its own time a development in self-consciousness; taken up into Christianity, it broke loose again in the dissolution of the Renaissance. Nietzsche, as I suggested, is a late variant: his attitude is a kind of stoicism upside-down: for there is not much difference between identifying oneself with the Universe and identifying the Universe with oneself. The influence of Seneca on Elizabethan drama has been exhaustively studied in its formal aspect, and in the borrowing and adaptation of phrases and situations;

the penetration of Senecan sensibility would be much more difficult to trace.

Variants from 1927:

[Before para. 1:] Desiring to make the most of the opportunity which had been given me of addressing the inmost circle of Shakespeare experts, I cast about, as any other mere journalist would do in the circumstances, for some subject in treating which I could best display my agility and conceal my ignorance of all the knowledge of which everyone present is master. I abandoned several interesting topics on which I might hope to impress almost any other audience – such as the development of dramatic blank verse or the relation of Shakespeare to Marlowe – in favour of one which, if I am in disagreement with anybody, I shall be in disagreement with persons whose opinions will be regarded as suspiciously by the Shakespeare Association as are my own. I am a timid person, easily overawed by authority; in what I have to say I hope that authority is at least as likely to be of my opinion as not.

1 interesting book] recent and most interesting book
felt and thought in] feel and think in
3 varied] various
8 is derived] it derived
know't.] know't; –
of that.] of that. –
say, besides,] say, besides, –
smote him, thus] smote him – thus
14 [No new para. in 1927.]
15 must part company] part company
16 not necessarily interested] not interested
20 some pioneer] a little pioneer

Hamlet

SE, 141–6.

Revised from *A.*, 4665 (26 Sept. 1919), 940–1, signed 'T. S. E.' (Gallup C92), and from *SW*.

1 Few critics have ever admitted that *Hamlet* the play is the primary problem, and Hamlet the character only secondary. And Hamlet the character has had an especial temptation for that most dangerous type of critic: the critic with a mind which is naturally of the creative order, but which through some weakness in creative power exercises itself in criticism instead. These minds often find in Hamlet a vicarious existence for their own artistic realisation. Such a mind had Goethe, who made of Hamlet a Werther; and such had Coleridge, who made of Hamlet a Coleridge; and probably neither of these men in writing about Hamlet remembered that his first business was to study a work of art. The

kind of criticism that Goethe and Coleridge produced, in writing of Hamlet, is the most misleading kind possible. For they both possessed unquestionable critical insight, and both make their critical aberrations the more plausible by the substitution – of their own Hamlet for Shakespeare's – which their creative gift effects. We should be thankful that Walter Pater did not fix his attention on this play.

2 Two writers of our own time, J. M. Robertson and Professor Stoll of the University of Minnesota, have issued small books which can be praised for moving in the other direction. Mr Stoll performs a service in recalling to our attention the labours of the critics of the seventeenth and eighteenth centuries,[1] observing that

> they knew less about psychology than more recent Hamlet [142] critics, but they were nearer in spirit to Shakespeare's art; and as they insisted on the importance of the effect of the whole rather than on the importance of the leading character, they were nearer, in their old-fashioned way, to the secret of dramatic art in general.

3 *Qua* work of art, the work of art cannot be interpreted; there is nothing to interpret; we can only criticise it according to standards, in comparison to other works of art; and for 'interpretation' the chief task is the presentation of relevant historical facts which the reader is not assumed to know. Mr Robertson points out, very pertinently, how critics have failed in their 'interpretation' of *Hamlet* by ignoring what ought to be very obvious; that *Hamlet* is a stratification, that it represents the efforts of a series of men, each making what he could out of the work of his predecessors. The *Hamlet* of Shakespeare will appear to us very differently if, instead of treating the whole action of the play as due to Shakespeare's design, we perceive his *Hamlet* to be superposed upon much cruder material which persists even in the final form.

4 We know that there was an older play by Thomas Kyd, that extraordinary dramatic (if not poetic) genius who was in all probability the author of two plays so dissimilar as the *Spanish Tragedy* and *Arden of Feversham*; and what this play was like we can guess from three clues: from the *Spanish Tragedy* itself, from the tale of Belleforest upon which Kyd's *Hamlet* must have been based, and from a version acted in Germany in Shakespeare's lifetime which bears strong evidence of having been adapted from the earlier, not from the later, play. From these three

---

[1]. I have never, by the way, seen a cogent refutation of Thomas Rymer's objections to *Othello*.

sources it is clear that in the earlier play the motive was a revenge motive simply; that the action or delay is caused, as in the *Spanish Tragedy*, solely by the difficulty of assassinating a monarch surrounded by guards; and that the 'madness' of Hamlet was feigned in order to escape suspicion, and successfully. In the final play of Shakespeare, on the other [143] hand, there is a motive which is more important than that of revenge, and which explicitly 'blunts' the latter; the delay in revenge is unexplained on grounds of necessity or expediency; and the effect of the 'madness' is not to lull but to arouse the king's suspicion. The alteration is not complete enough, however, to be convincing. Furthermore, there are verbal parallels so close to the *Spanish Tragedy* as to leave no doubt that in places Shakespeare was merely *revising* the text of Kyd. And finally there are unexplained scenes – the Polonius-Laertes and the Polonius-Reynaldo scenes – for which there is little excuse; these scenes are not in the verse style of Kyd, and not beyond doubt in the style of Shakespeare. These Mr Robertson believes to be scenes in the original play of Kyd reworked by a third hand, perhaps Chapman, before Shakespeare touched the play. And he concludes, with very strong show of reason, that the original play of Kyd was, like certain other revenge plays, in two parts of five acts each. The upshot of Mr Robertson's examination is, we believe, irrefragable: that Shakespeare's *Hamlet*, so far as it is Shakespeare's, is a play dealing with the effect of a mother's guilt upon her son, and that Shakespeare was unable to impose this motive successfully upon the 'intractable' material of the old play.

5 Of the intractability there can be no doubt. So far from being Shakespeare's masterpiece, the play is most certainly an artistic failure. In several ways the play is puzzling, and disquieting as is none of the others. Of all the plays it is the longest and is possibly the one on which Shakespeare spent most pains; and yet he has left in it superfluous and inconsistent scenes which even hasty revision should have noticed. The versification is variable. Lines like

> Look, the morn, in russet mantle clad,
> Walks o'er the dew of yon high eastern hill,

are of the Shakespeare of *Romeo and Juliet*. The lines in Act V, Sc. ii,

[144] Sir, in my heart there was a kind of fighting
> That would not let me sleep . . .
> Up from my cabin,
> My sea-gown scarf'd about me, in the dark
> Grop'd I to find out them: had my desire;
> Finger'd their packet;

are of his quite mature. Both workmanship and thought are in an unstable position. We are surely justified in attributing the play, with that other profoundly interesting play of 'intractable' material and astonishing versification, *Measure for Measure*, to a period of crisis, after which follow the tragic successes which culminate in *Coriolanus*. *Coriolanus* may not be as 'interesting' as *Hamlet*, but it is, with *Antony and Cleopatra*, Shakespeare's most assured artistic success. And probably more people have thought *Hamlet* a work of art because they found it interesting, than have found it interesting because it is a work of art. It is the 'Mona Lisa' of literature.

6 The grounds of *Hamlet*'s failure are not immediately obvious. Mr Robertson is undoubtedly correct in concluding that the essential emotion of the play is the feeling of a son towards a guilty mother:

> [Hamlet's] tone is that of one who has suffered tortures on the score of his mother's degradation.... The guilt of a mother is an almost intolerable motive for drama, but it had to be maintained and emphasized to supply a psychological solution or rather a hint of one.

7 This, however, is by no means the whole story. It is not merely the 'guilt of a mother' that cannot be handled as Shakespeare handled the suspicion of Othello, the infatuation of Antony, or the pride of Coriolanus. The subject might conceivably have expanded into a tragedy like these, intelligible, self-complete, in the sunlight. *Hamlet*, like the sonnets, is full of some stuff that the writer could not drag to light, contemplate, or manipulate into art. And when we search for this feeling, we find it, as in the sonnets, very difficult to localise. You cannot point to it in the speeches; [145] indeed, if you examine the two famous soliloquies you see the versification of Shakespeare, but a content which might be claimed by another, perhaps by the author of the *Revenge of Bussy d'Ambois*, Act V, Sc. i. We find Shakespeare's *Hamlet* not in the action, not in any quotations we might select, so much as in an unmistakable tone which is unmistakably not in the earlier play.

8 The only way of expressing emotion in the form of art is by finding an 'objective correlative'; in other words, a set of objects, a situation, a chain of events which shall be the formula of that *particular* emotion; such that when the external facts, which must terminate in sensory experience, are given, the emotion is immediately evoked. If you examine any of Shakespeare's more successful tragedies, you will find this exact equivalence;

you will find that the state of mind of Lady Macbeth walking in her sleep has been communicated to you by a skilful accumulation of imagined sensory impressions; the words of Macbeth on hearing of his wife's death strike us as if, given the sequence of events, these words were automatically released by the last event in the series. The artistic 'inevitability' lies in this complete adequacy of the external to the emotion; and this is precisely what is deficient in *Hamlet*. Hamlet (the man) is dominated by an emotion which is inexpressible, because it is in *excess* of the facts as they appear. And the supposed identity of Hamlet with his author is genuine to this point: that Hamlet's bafflement at the absence of objective equivalent to his feelings is a prolongation of the bafflement of his creator in the face of his artistic problem. Hamlet is up against the difficulty that his disgust is occasioned by his mother, but that his mother is not an adequate equivalent for it; his disgust envelops and exceeds her. It is thus a feeling which he cannot understand; he cannot objectify it, and it therefore remains to poison life and obstruct action. None of the possible actions can satisfy it; and nothing that Shakespeare can do with the plot can express Hamlet for him. And it must be noticed that the very nature of the [146] *données* of the problem precludes objective equivalence. To have heightened the criminality of Gertrude would have been to provide the formula for a totally different emotion in Hamlet; it is just *because* her character is so negative and insignificant that she arouses in Hamlet the feeling which she is incapable of representing.

9 The 'madness' of Hamlet lay to Shakespeare's hand; in the earlier play a simple ruse, and to the end, we may presume, understood as a ruse by the audience. For Shakespeare it is less than madness and more than feigned. The levity of Hamlet, his repetition of phrase, his puns, are not part of a deliberate plan of dissimulation, but a form of emotional relief. In the character Hamlet it is the buffoonery of an emotion which can find no outlet in action; in the dramatist it is the buffoonery of an emotion which he cannot express in art. The intense feeling, ecstatic or terrible, without an object or exceeding its object, is something which every person of sensibility has known; it is doubtless a subject of study for pathologists. It often occurs in adolescence: the ordinary person puts these feelings to sleep, or trims down his feelings to fit the business world; the artist keeps them alive by his ability to intensify the world to his emotions. The Hamlet of Laforgue is an adolescent; the Hamlet of Shakespeare is not, he has not that explanation and excuse. We must simply admit that here Shakespeare tackled a problem which proved too much for him. Why he attempted it at all is an insoluble puzzle; under compulsion of what experience he attempted to express the inexpressibly horrible, we

cannot ever know. We need a great many facts in his biography; and we should like to know whether, and when, and after or at the same time as what personal experience, he read Montaigne, II. xii, *Apologie de Raimond Sebond*. We should have, finally, to know something which is by hypothesis unknowable, for we assume it to be an experience which, in the manner indicated, exceeded the facts. We should have to understand things which Shakespeare did not understand himself.

Variants:

Title Hamlet and his Problems *A*. (1919), *SW*

1 We are very glad to find Hamlet in the hands of so learned and scrupulous a critic as Mr Robertson. [Opening sentence, *A*. (1919), not represented in *SE*.]
ever admitted] even admitted *A*. (1919), *SW*

2 [Para. not represented in *A*. (1919).]
writers of our own time] recent writers *SW*

4 the later, play] the later play *A*. (1919), *SW*

5 clad,] clad, – *A*. (1919)

9 subject of study for] study to *A*. (1919), *SW*
feelings to fit] feeling to fit *A*. (1919), *SW*
keeps them] keeps it *A*. (1919), *SW*
[After 'understand himself.' at the end:] In the Storm in 'Lear', and in the last scene of 'Othello', Shakespeare triumphed in tearing art from the impossible: 'Hamlet' is a failure. The material proved intractable in a deeper sense than that intended by Mr Robertson in his admirable essay. *A*. (1919)

Ben Jonson

SE, 147–60.

Publ. in *TLS*, 930 (13 Nov. 1919), [637]–8, as an unsigned review of *Ben Jonson* by G. Gregory Smith (Gallup C99). Revised in *SW*, and further revised in *SE*. The *SW* text incorporated paras from 'The Comedy of Humours', *A*., 4672 (14 Nov. 1919), and these are noted below. On p. 150 'as determined beat as if' has been emended to 'a determined beat as if'.

1 The reputation of Jonson has been of the most deadly kind that can be compelled upon the memory of a great poet. To be universally accepted; to be damned by the praise that quenches all desire to read the book; to be afflicted by the imputation of the virtues which excite the least pleasure; and to be read only by historians and antiquaries – this is the most perfect conspiracy of approval. For some generations the reputation of Jonson has been carried rather as a liability than as an asset in the balance-sheet of English literature. No critic has succeeded in making him appear pleasurable or even interesting. Swinburne's book on Jonson

satisfies no curiosity and stimulates no thought. For the critical study in the 'Men of Letters Series' by Mr Gregory Smith there is a place; it satisfies curiosity, it supplies many just observations, it provides valuable matter on the neglected masques; it only fails to remodel the image of Jonson which is settled in our minds. Probably the fault lies with several generations of our poets. It is not that the value of poetry is only its value to living poets for their own work; but appreciation is akin to creation, and true enjoyment of poetry is related to the stirring of suggestion, the stimulus that a poet feels in his enjoyment of other poetry. Jonson has provided no creative stimulus for a very long time; consequently we must look back as far as Dryden – precisely, a poetic practitioner who learned from Jonson – before we find a living criticism of Jonson's work.

2 Yet there are possibilities for Jonson even now. We have no difficulty in seeing what brought him to this pass; how, [148] in contrast, not with Shakespeare, but with Marlowe, Webster, Donne, Beaumont and Fletcher, he has been paid out with reputation instead of enjoyment. He is no less a poet than these men, but his poetry is of the surface. Poetry of the surface cannot be understood without study, for to deal with the surface of life, as Jonson dealt with it, is to deal so deliberately that we too must be deliberate, in order to understand. Shakespeare, and smaller men also, are in the end more difficult, but they offer something at the start to encourage the student or to satisfy those who want nothing more; they are suggestive, evocative, a phrase, a voice; they offer poetry in detail as well as in design. So does Dante offer something, a phrase everywhere (*tu se' ombra ed ombra vedi*) even to readers who have no Italian; and Dante and Shakespeare have poetry of design as well as of detail. But the polished veneer of Jonson only reflects the lazy reader's fatuity; unconscious does not respond to unconscious; no swarms of inarticulate feelings are aroused. The immediate appeal of Jonson is to the mind; his emotional tone is not in the single verse, but in the design of the whole. But not many people are capable of discovering for themselves the beauty which is only found after labour; and Jonson's industrious readers have been those whose interest was historical and curious, and those who have thought that in discovering the historical and curious interest they had discovered the artistic value as well. When we say that Jonson requires study, we do not mean study of his classical scholarship or of seventeenth-century manners. We mean intelligent saturation in his work as a whole; we mean that, in order to enjoy him at all, we must get to the centre of his work and his temperament, and that we must see him unbiased by time, as a contemporary. And to see him as a contemporary does not so much require the power of putting

ourselves into seventeenth-century London as it requires the power of setting Jonson in our London.

3 It is generally conceded that Jonson failed as a tragic [149] dramatist; and it is usually agreed that he failed because his genius was for satiric comedy and because of the weight of pedantic learning with which he burdened his two tragic failures. The second point marks an obvious error of detail; the first is too crude a statement to be accepted; to say that he failed because his genius was unsuited to tragedy is to tell us nothing at all. Jonson did not write a good tragedy, but we can see no reason why he should not have written one. If two plays so different as *The Tempest* and *The Silent Woman* are both comedies, surely the category of tragedy could be made wide enough to include something possible for Jonson to have done. But the classification of tragedy and comedy, while it may be sufficient to mark the distinction in a dramatic literature of more rigid form and treatment – it may distinguish Aristophanes from Euripides – is not adequate to a drama of such variations as the Elizabethans. Tragedy is a crude classification for plays so different in their tone as *Macbeth*, *The Jew of Malta*, and *The Witch of Edmonton*; and it does not help us much to say that *The Merchant of Venice* and *The Alchemist* are comedies. Jonson had his own scale, his own instrument. The merit which *Catiline* possesses is the same merit that is exhibited more triumphantly in *Volpone*; *Catiline* fails, not because it is too laboured and conscious, but because it is not conscious enough; because Jonson in this play was not alert to his own idiom, not clear in his mind as to what his temperament wanted him to do. In *Catiline* Jonson conforms, or attempts to conform, to conventions; not to the conventions of antiquity, which he had exquisitely under control, but to the conventions of tragico-historical drama of his time. It is not the Latin erudition that sinks *Catiline*, but the application of that erudition to a form which was not the proper vehicle for the mind which had amassed the erudition.

4 If you look at *Catiline* – that dreary Pyrrhic victory of tragedy – you find two passages to be successful: Act II. Sc. i, the dialogue of the political ladies, and the Prologue [150] of Sylla's ghost. These two passages are genial. The soliloquy of the ghost is a characteristic Jonson success in content and in versification –

> Dost thou not feel me, Rome? not yet! is night
> So heavy on thee, and my weight so light?
> Can Sylla's ghost arise within thy walls,

> Less threatening than an earthquake, the quick falls
> Of thee and thine? Shake not the frighted heads
> Of thy steep towers, or shrink to their first beds?
> Or as their ruin the large Tyber fills,
> Make that swell up, and drown thy seven proud hills? . . .

This is the learned, but also the creative, Jonson. Without concerning himself with the character of Sulla, and in lines of invective, Jonson makes Sylla's ghost, while the words are spoken, a living and terrible force. The words fall with a determined beat as if they were the will of the morose Dictator himself. You may say: merely invective; but mere invective, even if as superior to the clumsy fisticuffs of Marston and Hall as Jonson's verse is superior to theirs, would not create a living figure as Jonson has done in this long tirade. And you may say: rhetoric; but if we are to call it 'rhetoric' we must subject that term to a closer dissection than any to which it is accustomed. What Jonson has done here is not merely a fine speech. It is the careful, precise filling in of a strong and simple outline, and at no point does it overflow the outline; it is far more careful and precise in its obedience to this outline than are many of the speeches in *Tamburlaine*. The outline is not Sulla, for Sulla has nothing to do with it, but 'Sylla's ghost'. The words may not be suitable to an historical Sulla, or to anybody in history, but they are a perfect expression for 'Sylla's ghost'. You cannot say they are rhetorical 'because people do not talk like that', you cannot call them 'verbiage'; they do not exhibit prolixity or redundancy or the other vices in the rhetoric books; there is a definite artistic emotion which demands expression at that length. The [151] words themselves are mostly simple words, the syntax is natural, the language austere rather than adorned. Turning then to the induction of *The Poetaster*, we find another success of the same kind –

> Light, I salute thee, but with wounded nerves . . .

Men may not talk in that way, but the Spirit of Envy does, and in the words of Jonson Envy is a real and living person. It is not human life that informs Envy and Sylla's ghost, but it is energy of which human life is only another variety.

5 Returning to *Catiline*, we find that the best scene in the body of the play is one which cannot be squeezed into a tragic frame, and which appears to belong to satiric comedy. The scene between Fulvia and Galla and Sempronia is a living scene in a wilderness of oratory. And as it recalls other scenes – there is a suggestion of the college of ladies in *The Silent Woman* – it looks like a comedy scene. And it appears to be satire.

> They shall all give and pay well, that come here,
> If they will have it; and that, jewels, pearl,
> Plate, or round sums to buy these. I'm not taken
> With a cob-swan or a high-mounting bull,
> As foolish Leda and Europa were;
> But the bright gold, with Danaë. For such price
> I would endure a rough, harsh Jupiter,
> Or ten such thundering gamesters, and refrain
> To laugh at 'em, till they are gone, with my much suffering.

This scene is no more comedy than it is tragedy, and the 'satire' is merely a medium for the essential emotion. Jonson's drama is only incidentally satire, because it is only incidentally a criticism upon the actual world. It is not satire in the way in which the work of Swift or the work of Molière may be called satire: that is, it does not find its source in any precise emotional attitude or precise intellectual criticism of the actual world. It is satire perhaps as the work of Rabelais is satire; certainly not more so. The important thing is that if fiction can be divided into crea-[152]tive fiction and critical fiction, Jonson's is creative. That he was a great critic, our first great critic, does not affect this assertion. Every creator is also a critic; Jonson was a conscious critic, but he was also conscious in his creations. Certainly, one sense in which the term 'critical' may be applied to fiction is a sense in which the term might be used of a method antithetical to Jonson's. It is the method of *Education Sentimentale*. The characters of Jonson, of Shakespeare, perhaps of all the greatest drama, are drawn in positive and simple outlines. They may be filled in, and by Shakespeare they are filled in, by much detail or many shifting aspects; but a clear and sharp and simple form remains through these – though it would be hard to say in what the clarity and sharpness and simplicity of Hamlet consists. But Frédéric Moreau is not made in that way. He is constructed partly by negative definition, built up by a great number of observations. We cannot isolate him from the environment in which we find him; it may be an environment which is or can be universalised; nevertheless it, and the figure in it, consist of very many observed particular facts, the actual world. Without this world the figure dissolves. The ruling faculty is a critical perception, a commentary upon experienced feeling and sensation. If this is true of Flaubert, it is true in a higher degree of Molière than of Jonson. The broad farcical lines of Molière may seem to be the same drawing as Jonson's. But Molière – say in Alceste or Monsieur Jourdain – is criticising the actual; the reference to the actual world is more direct. And having a more tenuous reference, the work of Jonson is much less directly satirical.

6 This leads us to the question of Humours. Largely on the evidence of the two Humour plays, it is sometimes assumed that Jonson is occupied with types; typical exaggerations, or exaggerations of type. The Humour definition, the expressed intention of Jonson, may be satisfactory for these two plays. *Every Man in his Humour* is the first mature work of Jonson, and the student of Jonson must [153] study it; but it is not the play in which Jonson found his genius: it is the last of his plays to read first. If one reads *Volpone*, and after that re-reads the *Jew of Malta*; then returns to Jonson and reads *Bartholomew Fair*, *The Alchemist*, *Epicoene* and *The Devil is an Ass*, and finally *Catiline*, it is possible to arrive at a fair opinion of the poet and the dramatist.

7 The Humour, even at the beginning, is not a type, as in Marston's satire, but a simplified and somewhat distorted individual with a typical mania. In the later work, the Humour definition quite fails to account for the total effect produced. The characters of Shakespeare are such as might exist in different circumstances than those in which Shakespeare sets them. The latter appear to be those which extract from the characters the most intense and interesting realisation; but that realisation has not exhausted their possibilities. Volpone's life, on the other hand, is bounded by the scene in which it is played; in fact, the life is the life of the scene and is derivatively the life of Volpone; the life of the character is inseparable from the life of the drama. This is not dependence upon a background, or upon a substratum of fact. The emotional effect is single and simple. Whereas in Shakespeare the effect is due to the way in which the characters *act upon* one another, in Jonson it is given by the way in which the characters *fit in* with each other. The artistic result of *Volpone* is not due to any effect that Volpone, Mosca, Corvino, Corbaccio, Voltore have upon each other, but simply to their combination into a whole. And these figures are not personifications of passions; separately, they have not even that reality, they are constituents. It is a similar indication of Jonson's method that you can hardly pick out a line of Jonson's and say confidently that it is great poetry; but there are many extended passages to which you cannot deny that honour.

> I will have all my beds blown up, not stuft;
> Down is too hard; and then, mine oval room
> [154] Fill'd with such pictures as Tiberius took
> From Elephantis, and dull Aretine
> But coldly imitated. Then, my glasses
> Cut in more subtle angles, to disperse
> And multiply the figures, as I walk . . .

Jonson is the legitimate heir of Marlowe. The man who wrote, in *Volpone*:

> for thy love,
> In varying figures, I would have contended
> With the blue Proteus, or the hornèd flood. . . .

and

> See, a carbuncle
> May put out both the eyes of our Saint Mark;
> A diamond would have bought Lollia Paulina,
> When she came in like star-light, hid with jewels. . . .

is related to Marlowe as a poet; and if Marlowe is a poet, Jonson is also. And, if Jonson's comedy is a comedy of humours, then Marlowe's tragedy, a large part of it, is a tragedy of humours. But Jonson has too exclusively been considered as the typical representative of a point of view towards comedy. He has suffered from his great reputation as a critic and theorist, from the effects of his intelligence. We have been taught to think of him as the man, the dictator (confusedly in our minds with his later namesake), as the literary politician impressing his views upon a generation; we are offended by the constant reminder of his scholarship. We forget the comedy in the humours, and the serious artist in the scholar. Jonson has suffered in public opinion, as anyone must suffer who is forced to talk about his art.

8 If you examine the first hundred lines or more of *Volpone* the verse appears to be in the manner of Marlowe, more deliberate, more mature, but without Marlowe's inspiration. It looks like mere 'rhetoric', certainly not 'deeds and language such as men do use.' It appears to us, in fact, forced and flagitious bombast. That it is not 'rhetoric', or at [155] least not vicious rhetoric, we do not know until we are able to review the whole play. For the consistent maintenance of this manner conveys in the end an effect not of verbosity but of bold, even shocking and terrifying directness. We have difficulty in saying exactly what produces this simple and single effect. It is not in any ordinary way due to management of intrigue. Jonson employs immense dramatic constructive skill: it is not so much skill in plot as skill in doing without a plot. He never manipulates as complicated a plot as that of *The Merchant of Venice*; he has in his best plays nothing like the intrigue of Restoration comedy. In *Bartholomew Fair* it is hardly a plot at all; the marvel of the play is the bewildering rapid chaotic action of the fair; it is the fair itself, not anything that happens in the fair. In *Volpone*, or *The Alchemist*, or *The Silent Woman*, the plot is enough to keep the players in motion; it is rather an 'action' than a plot.

The plot does not hold the play together; what holds the play together is a unity of inspiration that radiates into plot and personages alike.

9 We have attempted to make more precise the sense in which it was said that Jonson's work is 'of the surface'; carefully avoiding the word 'superficial'. For there is work contemporary with Jonson's which is superficial in a pejorative sense in which the word cannot be applied to Jonson – the work of Beaumont and Fletcher. If we look at the work of Jonson's great contemporaries, Shakespeare, and also Donne and Webster and Tourneur (and sometimes Middleton), they have a depth, a third dimension, as Mr Gregory Smith rightly calls it, which Jonson's work has not. Their words have often a network of tentacular roots reaching down to the deepest terrors and desires. Jonson's most certainly have not; but in Beaumont and Fletcher we may think that at times we find it. Looking closer, we discover that the blossoms of Beaumont and Fletcher's imagination draw no sustenance from the soil, but are cut and slightly withered flowers stuck into sand.

> [156] Wilt thou, hereafter, when they talk of me,
> As thou shalt hear nothing but infamy,
> Remember some of these things? . . .
> I pray thee, do; for thou shalt never see me so again.
>
> Hair woven in many a curious warp,
> Able in endless error to enfold
> The wandering soul; . . .

Detached from its context, this looks like the verse of the greater poets; just as lines of Jonson, detached from their context, look like inflated or empty fustian. But the evocative quality of the verse of Beaumont and Fletcher depends upon a clever appeal to emotions and associations which they have not themselves grasped; it is hollow. It is superficial with a vacuum behind it; the superficies of Jonson is solid. It is what it is; it does not pretend to be another thing. But it is so very conscious and deliberate that we must look with eyes alert to the whole before we apprehend the significance of any part. We cannot call a man's work superficial when it is the creation of a world; a man cannot be accused of dealing superficially with the world which he himself has created; the superficies *is* the world. Jonson's characters conform to the logic of the emotions of their world. They are not fancy, because they have a logic of their own; and this logic illuminates the actual world, because it gives us a new point of view from which to inspect it.

10 A writer of power and intelligence, Jonson endeavored to promulgate, as a formula and programme of reform, what he chose to do himself; and he not unnaturally laid down in abstract theory what is in reality a personal point of view. And it is in the end of no value to discuss Jonson's theory and practice unless we recognise and seize this point of view, which escapes the formulae, and which is what makes his plays worth reading. Jonson behaved as the great creative mind that he was: he created his own world, a world from which his followers, as well as the dramatists [157] who were trying to do something wholly different, are excluded. Remembering this, we turn to Mr Gregory Smith's objection – that Jonson's characters lack the third dimension, have no life out of the theatrical existence in which they appear – and demand an inquest. The objection implies that the characters are purely the work of intellect, or the result of superficial observation of a world which is faded or mildewed. It implies that the characters are lifeless. But if we dig beneath the theory, beneath the observation, beneath the deliberate drawing and the theatrical and dramatic elaboration, there is discovered a kind of power, animating Volpone, Busy, Fitzdottrel, the literary ladies of *Epicoene*, even Bobadil, which comes from below the intellect, and for which no theory of humours will account. And it is the same kind of power which vivifies Trimalchio, and Panurge, and some but not all of the 'comic' characters of Dickens. The fictive life of this kind is not to be circumscribed by a reference to 'comedy' or to 'farce'; it is not exactly the kind of life which informs the characters of Molière or that which informs those of Marivaux – two writers who were, besides, doing something quite different the one from the other. But it is something which distinguishes Barabas from Shylock, Epicure Mammon from Falstaff, Faustus from – if you will – Macbeth; Marlowe and Jonson from Shakespeare and the Shakespearians, Webster, and Tourneur. It is not merely Humours: for neither Volpone nor Mosca is a humour. No theory of humours could account for Jonson's best plays or the best characters in them. We want to know at what point the comedy of humours passes into a work of art, and why Jonson is not Brome.

11 The creation of a work of art, we will say the creation of a character in a drama, consists in the process of transfusion of the personality, or, in a deeper sense, the life, of the author into the character. This is a very different matter from the orthodox creation in one's own image. The ways in which the passions and desires of the creator may be [158] satisfied in the work of art are complex and devious. In a painter they may take the form of a predilection for certain colours, tones, or lightings; in a writer

the original impulse may be even more strangely transmuted. Now, we may say with Mr Gregory Smith that Falstaff or a score of Shakespeare's characters have a 'third dimension' that Jonson's have not. This will mean, not that Shakespeare's spring from the feelings or imagination and Jonson's from the intellect or invention; they have equally an emotional source; but that Shakespeare's represent a more complex tissue of feelings and desires, as well as a more supple, a more susceptible temperament. Falstaff is not only the roast Manningtree ox with the pudding in his belly; he also 'grows old', and, finally, his nose is as sharp as a pen. He was perhaps the *satisfaction* of more, and of more complicated feelings; and perhaps he was, as the great tragic characters must have been, the offspring of deeper, less apprehensible feelings: deeper, but not necessarily stronger or more intense, than those of Jonson. It is obvious that the spring of the difference is not the difference between feeling and thought, or superior insight, superior perception, on the part of Shakespeare, but his susceptibility to a greater range of emotion, and emotion deeper and more obscure. But his characters are no more 'alive' than are the characters of Jonson.

12 The world they live in is a larger one. But small worlds – the worlds which artists create – do not differ only in magnitude; if they are complete worlds, drawn to scale in every part, they differ in kind also. And Jonson's world has this scale. His type of personality found its relief in something falling under the category of burlesque or farce – though when you are dealing with a *unique* world, like his, these terms fail to appease the desire for definition. It is not, at all events, the farce of Molière: the latter is more analytic, more an intellectual redistribution. It is not defined by the word 'satire'. Jonson poses as a satirist. But satire like Jonson's is great in the end not by hitting off its object, but by [159] creating it; the satire is merely the means which leads to the aesthetic result, the impulse which projects a new world into a new orbit. In *Every Man in his Humour* there is a neat, a very neat comedy of humours. In discovering and proclaiming in this play the new genre Jonson was simply recognising, unconsciously, the route which opened out in the proper direction for his instincts. His characters are and remain, like Marlowe's, simplified characters; but the simplification does not consist in the dominance of a particular humour or monomania. That is a very superficial account of it. The simplification consists largely in reduction of detail, in the seizing of aspects relevant to the relief of an emotional impulse which remains the same for that character, in making the character conform to a particular setting. This stripping is essential to the art, to which is also essential a flat distortion in the drawing; it is

an art of caricature, of great caricature, like Marlowe's. It is a great caricature, which is beautiful; and a great humour, which is serious. The 'world' of Jonson is sufficiently large; it is a world of poetic imagination; it is sombre. He did not get the third dimension, but he was not trying to get it.

13 If we approach Jonson with less frozen awe of his learning, with a clearer understanding of his 'rhetoric' and its applications, if we grasp the fact that the knowledge required of the reader is not archaeology but knowledge of Jonson, we can derive not only instruction in two-dimensional life – but enjoyment. We can even apply him, be aware of him as a part of our literary inheritance craving further expression. Of all the dramatists of his time, Jonson is probably the one whom the present age would find the most sympathetic, if it knew him. There is a brutality, a lack of sentiment, a polished surface, a handling of large bold designs in brilliant colours, which ought to attract about three thousand people in London and elsewhere. At least, if we had a contemporary Shakespeare and a contemporary Jonson, it might be the Jonson who would arouse the enthusiasm of the intelligentsia. Though he is [160] saturated in literature, he never sacrifices the theatrical qualities – theatrical in the most favourable sense – to literature or to the study of character. His work is a titanic show. Jonson's masques, an important part of his work, are neglected; our flaccid culture lets shows and literature fade, but prefers faded literature to faded shows. There are hundreds of people who have read *Comus* to ten who have read the *Masque of Blackness*. *Comus* contains fine poetry, and poetry exemplifying some merits to which Jonson's masque poetry cannot pretend. Nevertheless, *Comus* is the death of the masque; it is the transition of a form of art – even of a form which existed for but a short generation – into 'literature', literature cast in a form which has lost its application. Even though *Comus* was a masque at Ludlow Castle, Jonson had, what Milton came perhaps too late to have, a sense for the living art; his art was applied. The masques can still be read, and with pleasure, by anyone who will take the trouble – a trouble which in this part of Jonson is, indeed, a study of antiquities – to imagine them in action, displayed with the music, costumes, dances, and the scenery of Inigo Jones. They are additional evidence that Jonson had a fine sense of form, of the purpose for which a particular form is intended; evidence that he was a literary artist even more than he was a man of letters.

Variants:
1 by Mr Gregory Smith] which Mr Gregory Smith has just produced *TLS* (1919)
 the fault lies with several generations of our poets] the fault lies not with

conscientious critics like Mr. Gregory Smith but with several generations of our poets. *TLS* (1919)

2 se'] sei *TLS* (1919)
only reflects] reflects only *TLS* (1919), *SW*
our London.] our London: a more difficult triumph of divination. *TLS* (1919), *SW*

4 Spirit of Envy] spirit of envy *TLS* (1919)
Envy] envy *TLS* (1919)
Envy] envy *TLS* (1919)

5 other scenes] other scenes there *TLS* (1919)
That he was a great critic] That he was, as Mr. Gregory Smith points out, a great critic *TLS* (1919)
Frédéric] Frederic *TLS* (1919)
be universalised] be much universalized *TLS* (1919), *SW*

6–7 [Between 'these two plays.' and 'The Humour, even at the beginning':] But though we are very glad to have at last a scholarly edition of *Every Man in his Humour* [fn.: *Every Man in his Humour*. By Ben Jonson. Edited by Percy Simpson. (Oxford: The Clarendon Press. London: Milford. 6s. net.)] this play is only the beginning of Jonson's good work, and his work reached a much higher development. *TLS* [Not represented in *SW*, and replaced, as in *SE*, with '"Every Man in His Humour" . . . the poet and the dramatist' from para. 2 of *A*.]

7–8 [Between 'as I walk . . .' and 'If you examine':] [Not represented in *TLS* (1919). It is the first para. in A., inserted in *SW*.]

8 men do use.'] men do use'. *TLS* (1919), *SW*

9 [Between 'emotions of their world.' and 'They are not fancy':] It is a world like Lobatchevsky's; the worlds created by artists like Jonson are like systems of non-Euclidean geometry. *TLS* (1919)), *SW*

9–13 [Between 'to inspect it.' and 'If we approach Jonson':] [Not represented in *TLS* (1919). The paras. were inserted in *SW* from *A*.]

11 Manningtree] Malmesbury *A.*, *SW*

13 two-dimensional life] non-Euclidean humanity *TLS* (1919), *SW*
intelligentsia.] intelligentsia! *TLS* (1919), *SW*
Jonson's masques] But Jonson's masques *TLS* (1919), *SW*
the living art] living art *TLS* (1919), *SW*

Thomas Middleton

SE, 161–70.

Revised from *TLS*, 1326 (30 June 1927), [445]–6 (Gallup C212) and from *FLA*.

1 Thomas Middleton, the dramatic writer, was not very highly thought of in his own time; the date of his death is not known; we know only that he was buried on July 4, 1627. He was one of the most voluminous, and one of the best, dramatic writers of his time. But it is easy to understand

why he is not better known or more popular. It is difficult to imagine his 'personality'. Several new personalities have recently been fitted to the name of Shakespeare; Jonson is a real figure – our imagination plays about him discoursing at the Mermaid, or laying down the law to Drummond of Hawthornden; Chapman has become a breezy British character as firm as Nelson or Wellington; Webster and Donne are real people for the more intellectual; even Tourneur (Churton Collins having said the last word about him) is a 'personality'. But Middleton, who collaborated shamelessly, who is hardly separated from Rowley, Middleton, who wrote plays so diverse as *Women Beware Women* and *A Game at Chess* and *The Roaring Girl*, Middleton remains merely a collective name for a number of plays – some of which, like *The Spanish Gypsy*, are patently by other people.[1]

2 If we write about Middleton's plays we must write about Middleton's plays, and not about Middleton's personality. Many of these plays are still in doubt. Of all the Elizabethan dramatists Middleton seems the most impersonal, the most indifferent to personal fame or perpetuity, the readiest, except Rowley, to accept collaboration. Also he [162] is the most various. His greatest tragedies and his greatest comedies are as if written by two different men. Yet there seems no doubt that Middleton was both a great comic writer and a great tragic writer. There are a sufficient number of plays, both tragedies and comedies, in which his hand is so far unquestioned, to establish his greatness. His greatness is not that of a peculiar personality, but of a great artist or artisan of the Elizabethan epoch. We have among others *The Changeling*, *Women Beware Women*, and *A Game at Chess*; and we have *The Roaring Girl* and *A Trick to Catch the Old One*. And that is enough. Between the tragedies and comedies of Shakespeare, and certainly between the tragedies and comedies of Jonson, we can establish a relation; we can see, for Shakespeare or Jonson, that each had in the end a personal point of view which can be called neither comic nor tragic. But with Middleton we can establish no such relation. He remains merely a name, a voice, the author of certain plays, which are all of them great plays. He has no point of view, is neither sentimental nor cynical; he is neither resigned, nor disillusioned, nor romantic; he has no message. He is merely the name which associates six or seven great plays.

3 For there is no doubt about *The Changeling*. Like all of the plays attributed to Middleton, it is long-winded and tiresome; the characters talk too

---

1. Mr Dugdale Sykes has written authoritatively on this subject.

much, and then suddenly stop talking and act; they are real and impelled irresistibly by the fundamental motions of humanity to good or evil. This mixture of tedious discourse and sudden reality is everywhere in the work of Middleton, in his comedy also. In *The Roaring Girl* we read with toil through a mass of cheap conventional intrigue, and suddenly realise that we are, and have been for some time without knowing it, observing a real and unique human being. In reading *The Changeling* we may think, till almost the end of the play, that we have been concerned merely with a fantastic Elizabethan morality, and then discover that we are looking on at a dispassionate exposure of fundamental passions of [163] any time and any place. The usual opinion remains the just judgement: *The Changeling* is Middleton's greatest play. The morality of the convention seems to us absurd. To many intelligent readers this play has only an historical interest, and serves only to illustrate the moral taboos of the Elizabethans. The heroine is a young woman who, in order to dispose of a fiancé to whom she is indifferent, so that she may marry the man she loves, accepts the offer of an adventurer to murder the affianced, at the price (as she finds in due course) of becoming the murderer's mistress. Such a plot is, to a modern mind, absurd; and the consequent tragedy seems a fuss about nothing. But *The Changeling* is not merely contingent for its effect upon our acceptance of Elizabethan good form or convention; it is, in fact, no more dependent upon the convention of its epoch than a play like *A Doll's House*. Underneath the convention there is the stratum of truth permanent in human nature. The tragedy of *The Changeling* is an eternal tragedy, as permanent as *Oedipus* or *Antony and Cleopatra*; it is the tragedy of the not naturally bad but irresponsible and undeveloped nature, caught in the consequences of its own action. In every age and in every civilisation there are instances of the same thing: the unmoral nature, suddenly trapped in the inexorable toils of morality – of morality not made by man but by Nature – and forced to take the consequences of an act which it had planned light-heartedly. Beatrice is not a moral creature; she becomes moral only by becoming damned. Our conventions are not the same as those which Middleton assumed for his play. But the possibility of that frightful discovery of morality remains permanent.

4 The words in which Middleton expresses his tragedy are as great as the tragedy. The process through which Beatrice, having decided that De Flores is the instrument for her purpose, passes from aversion to habituation, remains a permanent commentary on human nature. The directness and precision of De Flores are masterly, as is also the virtuousness of Beatrice on first realising his motives –

[164] Why, 'tis impossible thou canst be so wicked,
Or shelter such a cunning cruelty,
To make his death the murderer of my honour!
Thy language is so bold and vicious,
I cannot see which way I can forgive it
With any modesty.

– a passage which ends with the really great lines of De Flores, lines of which Shakespeare or Sophocles might have been proud:

Can you weep Fate from its determined purpose?
So soon may you weep me.

But what constitutes the essence of the tragedy is something which has not been sufficiently remarked; it is the *habituation* of Beatrice to her sin; it becomes no longer sin but merely custom. Such is the essence of the tragedy of *Macbeth* – the habituation to crime. And in the end Beatrice, having been so long the enforced conspirator of De Flores, becomes (and this is permanently true to human nature) more *his* partner, *his* mate, than the mate and partner of the man for the love of whom she consented to the crime. Her lover disappears not only from the scene but from her own imagination. When she says of De Flores,

A wondrous necessary man, my lord,

her praise is more than half sincere; and at the end she belongs far more to De Flores – towards whom, at the beginning, she felt strong physical repulsion – than to her lover Alsemero. It is De Flores, in the end, to whom she belongs as Francesca to Paolo:

Beneath the stars, upon yon meteor
Ever hung my fate, 'mongst things corruptible;
I ne'er could pluck it from him; my loathing
Was prophet to the rest, but ne'er believed.

And De Flores's cry is perfectly sincere and in character:

I loved this woman in spite of her heart;
Her love I earned out of Piracquo's murder . . .
[165] Yes, and her honour's prize
Was my reward; I thank life for nothing
But that pleasure; it was so sweet to me,
That I have drunk up all, left none behind
For any man to pledge me.

The tragedy of Beatrice is not that she has lost Alsemero, for whose possession she played; it is that she has won De Flores. Such tragedies are not limited to Elizabethan times: they happen every day and perpetually. The greatest tragedies are occupied with great and permanent moral conflicts; the great tragedies of Aeschylus, of Sophocles, of Corneille, of Racine, of Shakespeare, have the same burden. In poetry, in dramatic technique, *The Changeling* is inferior to the best plays of Webster. But in the moral essence of tragedy it is safe to say that in this play Middleton is surpassed by one Elizabethan alone, and that is Shakespeare. In some respects in which Elizabethan tragedy can be compared to French or to Greek tragedy *The Changeling* stands above every tragic play of its time, except those of Shakespeare.

5 The genius which blazed in *The Changeling* was fitful but not accidental. The best tragedy after *The Changeling* is *Women Beware Women*. The thesis of the play, as the title indicates, is more arbitrary and less fundamental. The play itself, although less disfigured by ribaldry or clowning, is more tedious. Middleton sinks himself in conventional moralising of the epoch, so that, if we are impatient, we decide that he gives merely a document of Elizabethan humbug – and then suddenly a personage will blaze out in genuine fire of vituperation. The wickedness of the personages in *Women Beware Women* is conventional wickedness of the stage of the time; yet slowly the exasperation of Bianca, the wife who married beneath her, beneath the ambitions to which she was entitled, emerges from the negative; slowly the real human passions emerge from the mesh of interest in which they begin. And here again Middleton, in writing what appears on the surface a con-[166]ventional picture-palace Italian melodrama of the time, has caught permanent human feelings. And in this play Middleton shows his interest – more than any of his contemporaries – in innuendo and double meanings; and makes use of that game of chess, which he was to use more openly for satire in that perfect piece of literary political art, *A Game at Chess*. The irony could not be improved upon:

> Did I not say my duke would fetch you o'er, Widow?
> I think you spoke in earnest when you said it, madam,
> And my black king makes all haste he can too.
> Well, madam, we may meet with him in time yet.
> I've given thee blind mate twice.

There is hardly anything truer or more impressive in Elizabethan drama than Bianca's gradual self-will and self-importance in consequence of her courtship by the Duke:

> Troth, you speak wondrous well for your old house here;
> 'Twill shortly fall down at your feet to thank you,
> Or stoop, when you go to bed, like a good child,
> To ask you blessing.

In spite of all the long-winded speeches, in spite of all the conventional Italianate horrors, Bianca remains, like Beatrice in *The Changeling*, a real woman; as real, indeed, as any woman of Elizabethan tragedy. Bianca is a type of the woman who is purely moved by vanity.

6 But if Middleton understood woman in tragedy better than any of the Elizabethans – better than the creator of the Duchess of Malfy, better than Marlowe, better than Tourneur, or Shirley, or Fletcher, better than any of them except Shakespeare alone – he was also able, in his comedy, to present a finer woman than any of them. *The Roaring Girl* has no apparent relation to Middleton's tragedies, yet it is agreed to be primarily the work of Middleton. It is typical of the comedies of Middleton, and it is the best. In his tragedies Middleton employs [167] all the Italianate horrors of his time, and obviously for the purpose of pleasing the taste of his time; yet underneath we feel always a quiet and undisturbed vision of things as they are and not 'another thing'. So in his comedies. The comedies are long-winded; the fathers are heavy fathers, and rant as heavy fathers should; the sons are wild and wanton sons, and perform all the pranks to be expected of them; the machinery is the usual Elizabethan machinery; Middleton is solicitous to please his audience with what they expect; but there is underneath the same steady impersonal passionless observation of human nature. *The Roaring Girl* is as artificial as any comedy of the time; its plot creaks loudly; yet the Girl herself is always real. She may rant, she may behave preposterously, but she remains a type of the sort of woman who has renounced all happiness for herself and who lives only for a principle. Nowhere more clearly than in *The Roaring Girl* can the hand of Middleton be distinguished from the hand of Dekker. Dekker is all sentiment; and, indeed, in the so admired passages of *A Fair Quarrel*, exploited by Lamb, the mood if not the hand of Dekker seems to the unexpert critic to be more present than Middleton's. *A Fair Quarrel* seems as much, if not more, Dekker's than Middleton's. Similarly with *The Spanish Gypsy*, which can with difficulty be attributed to Middleton. But the feeling about Moll Cut-Purse of *The Roaring Girl* is Middleton's rather than anybody's. In Middleton's tragedy there is a strain of realism underneath, which is one with the poetry; and in his comedy we find the same thing.

7 In her recent book on *The Social Mode of Restoration Comedy*, Miss Kathleen Lynch calls attention to the gradual transition from Elizabethan-Jacobean to Restoration comedy. She observes, what is certainly true, that Middleton is the greatest 'realist' in Jacobean comedy. Miss Lynch's extremely suggestive thesis is that the transition from Elizabethan-Jacobean to later Caroline comedy is primarily economic: that the interest changes from the citizen [168] aping gentry to the citizen become gentry and accepting that code of manners. In the comedy of Middleton certainly there is as yet no code of manners; but the merchant of Cheapside is *aiming* at becoming a member of the county gentry. Miss Lynch remarks: 'Middleton's keen concentration on the spectacle of the interplay of different social classes marks an important development in realistic comedy.' She calls attention to this aspect of Middleton's comedy, that it marks, better than the romantic comedy of Shakespeare, or the comedy of Jonson, occupied with what Jonson thought to be permanent and not transient aspects of human nature, the transition between the aristocratic world which preceded the Tudors and the plutocratic modern world which the Tudors initiated and encouraged. By the time of the return of Charles II, as Miss Lynch points out, society had been re-organised and formed, and social conventions had been created. In the Tudor times birth still counted (though nearly all the great families were extinct); by the time of Charles II only breeding counted. The comedy of Middleton, and the comedy of Brome, and the comedy of Shirley, is intermediate, as Miss Lynch remarks. Middleton, she observes, marks the transitional stage in which the London tradesman was anxious to cease to be a tradesman and to become a country gentleman. The words of his City Magnate in *Michaelmas Terme* have not yet lost their point:

> A fine journey in the Whitsun holydays, i'faith, to ride with a number of citizens and their wives, some upon pillions, some upon side-saddles, I and little Thomasine i' the middle, our son and heir, Sim Quomodo, in a peach-colour taffeta jacket, some horse length, or a long yard before us – there will be a fine show on's I can tell you.

8 But Middleton's comedy is not, like the comedy of Congreve, the comedy of a set social behaviour; it is still, like the later comedy of Dickens, the comedy of individuals, in spite of the continual motions of city merchants towards [169] county gentility. In the comedy of the Restoration a figure such as that of Moll Cut-Purse would have been impossible. As a social document the comedy of Middleton illustrates the transition from government by a landed aristocracy to government

by a city aristocracy gradually engrossing the land. As such it is of the greatest interest. But as literature, as a dispassionate picture of human nature, Middleton's comedy deserves to be remembered chiefly by its real – perpetually real – and human figure of Moll the Roaring Girl. That Middleton's comedy was 'photographic', that it introduces us to the low life of the time far better than anything in the comedy of Shakespeare or the comedy of Jonson, better than anything except the pamphlets of Dekker and Greene and Nashe, there is little doubt. But it produced one great play – *The Roaring Girl* – a great play in spite of the tedious long speeches of some of the principal characters, in spite of the clumsy machinery of the plot: for the reason that Middleton was a great observer of human nature, without fear, without sentiment, without prejudice.

9 And Middleton in the end – after criticism has subtracted all that Rowley, all that Dekker, all that others contributed – is a great example of great English drama. He has no message; he is merely a great recorder. Incidentally, in flashes and when the dramatic need comes, he is a great poet, a great master of versification:

> I that am of your blood was taken from you
> For your better health; look no more upon't,
> But cast it to the ground regardlessly,
> Let the common sewer take it from distinction:
> Beneath the stars, upon yon meteor
> Ever hung my fate, 'mongst things corruptible;
> I ne'er could pluck it from him; my loathing
> Was prophet to the rest, but ne'er believed.

The man who wrote these lines remains inscrutable, solitary, unadmired; welcoming collaboration, indifferent to [170] fame; dying no one knows when and no one knows how; attracting, in three hundred years, no personal admiration. Yet he wrote one tragedy which more than any play except those of Shakespeare has a profound and permanent moral value and horror; and one comedy which more than any Elizabethan comedy realises a free and noble womanhood.

Variants:
1 most voluminous] more voluminous *TLS* (1927), *FLA*
  [No fn. in *TLS* (1927).]
3 dispassionate] impassionate *TLS* (1927)
  usual] conventional *TLS* (1927)
  (as she finds in due course)] [Not in *TLS* (1927), *FLA*.]
  truth permanent in] permanent truth to *TLS* (1927), *FLA*

caught] suddenly caught *TLS* (1927)
trapped] caught *TLS* (1927)

4   [Between 'habituation to crime.' and 'And in the end':] , the deadening of all moral sense. *TLS* (1927), *FLA*
strong physical] such physical *TLS* (1927)
It is De Flores] And it is De Flores *TLS* (1927)
belongs] belongs, *TLS* (1927)
[Between 'won De Flores.' and 'Such tragedies':] , that she thereafter belongs to him and he to her. *The Changeling* is one of the great tragedies of character originally neither good nor bad deflected by circumstance (a character neither good nor bad may always be) towards evil. *TLS* (1927)
[Between 'of Webster.' and 'But in the moral essence':] , even of Tourneur. *TLS* (1927)
some respects] every essential respect *TLS* (1927)

6   [Between 'Middleton' and 'understood':] , this obscure and uninteresting person, *TLS* (1927)
[Between 'anybody's' and 'In Middleton's tragedy':] , and after Miranda, and Dante's Beatrice, there is hardly any heroine of fiction who does more honour to her sex than Moll. *TLS* (1927)
underneath,] underneath *TLS* (1927)

7   [Between '*Restoration Comedy*,' and 'Miss Kathleen Lynch':] (reviewed here on February 24) *TLS* (1927)
citizen] bourgeois *TLS* (1927)
citizen] bourgeois *TLS* (1927)

8   [No para. indent in *FLA*.]
[After 'prejudice':] , without personality *TLS* (1927), *FLA*

9   [Before 'has no message':] He means nothing, he *TLS* (1927)
[Between 'unadmired;' and 'welcoming':] purely an Elizabeth and not himself; *TLS* (1927)
[Between 'knows how' and 'attracting':] , or with what thoughts, if any, *TLS* (1927)
[After 'womanhood':] ; and he remains, inscrutable, unphilosophical, interesting only to those few who care for such things. *TLS* (1927)

Thomas Heywood

SE, 171–81.

Publ. in *TLS*, 1539 (30 July 1931), [589]–90 (Gallup C324), and revised in *SE*.

1   There are a few of the Elizabethan dramatists, notably Marlowe and Ben Jonson, who always return to our minds with the reality of personal acquaintances. We know them unmistakably through their own writings – Jonson partly through his conversations with Drummond – and by a few anecdotes of the kind which, even when apocryphal, remain as evidence of the personal impression that such men must have made upon their contemporaries. There are others whom we can remember only by

the association of their names with a play, or a group of plays. Of all these men Thomas Heywood is one of the dimmest figures; and it is interesting to remark how very dim he still remains even after Dr Clark's exhaustive industry.[1] Dr Clark appears to have discovered and assembled all the information that we can ever expect to have; and it is certainly not his fault that Heywood makes still but a faint impression; in fact, Dr Clark's book can help us considerably to understand why this is so. The book is solidly documentary; it is not, like some biographical essays with scanty material, stuffed out with appreciation and conjecture. It is, in fact, an admirable account of the life of a typical literary Jack of all trades of the epoch; the summary of Heywood's activities as a pamphleteer, with his works of what may be termed popular theology in the Puritan cause, is full of interest for anyone who cares about this lively and, in some respects, very remote age. And the book confirms the impression that Heywood – whom Dr [172] Clark shows convincingly to have been a Heywood of Mottram, in Cheshire, and not of the family of Heywood of Lincolnshire, the county of his birth – was a facile and sometimes felicitous purveyor of goods to the popular taste.

2 Heywood's reputation, which we owe primarily to Lamb and Hazlitt, is founded on *A Woman Killed with Kindness*; but *The English Traveller* and *The Wise Woman of Hogsdon* are not far below it; and the first part of *The Fair Maid of the West*, when it has been performed – twice, we believe, in recent years – was revealed as a rollicking piece of popular patriotic sentiment. Before considering whether this output has enough coherence to be treated with the dignity of an *oeuvre*, there are several interesting attributions of Dr Clark's which demand attention. The first and most important is *Appius and Virginia*.

3 The date of this play, which has long been a difficulty to students of Webster – a play far below Webster's best work, and in some respects dissimilar to it – forms one of Dr Clark's reasons for attributing the play primarily to Heywood. This was, of course, the guess of Rupert Brooke; but, given the initial doubt which strikes any admirer of Webster, the opinion, when it comes from a close student of Heywood, has much stronger authority. Dr Clark, however, is not content to take issue only with Mr Sykes (who gives the whole play to Webster), though that is a serious task in itself. He dismisses, with hardly more attention than a few footnotes, the moderate and so far, we believe, impregnable view of

---

1. *Thomas Heywood: Playwright and Miscellanist*, by A. M. Clark. Oxford: Blackwell. 1931.

Mr F. L. Lucas. He refers, certainly, to Mr Lucas's 'attempt to depreciate Heywood' as 'uncritical'; because Mr Lucas, in his introduction to the play in his complete edition of Webster, doubts whether Heywood

> could have produced unaided so well-planned and reasonable a play. For there is a peculiar oafish simplicity about him which made him unable ever to create a single piece, [173] except perhaps *Edward IV*, which is not deformed by pages of utter drivel.

Mr Lucas has perhaps written with a heat uncommon among Elizabethan scholars, though refreshing; yet his doubt whether Heywood could have planned the play is one likely to strike anyone who reads both Webster and Heywood without prejudices. To such a reader, the fact that Heywood is the author of *The Rape of Lucrece* strains credulity to the breaking point. But this, indeed, is the whole issue between Dr Clark and Mr Lucas. Neither doubts that both Heywood and Webster had a hand in the play; neither makes a claim for any third author. Dr Clark concludes that Heywood wrote the play and that 'at an unknown date Webster revised the play somewhat carelessly'. Mr Lucas can more easily believe that Webster wrote, or designed and partly wrote, the play, and that Heywood either revised or completed it. We are left with a narrow choice and a fine distinction; in fact, we are left to our personal impressions. The feeling of the present reviewer, at least, is that the structure of the play is more creditably assignable to Webster, as well as the good lines which nobody denies him.

4 Our inclination to this conclusion is confirmed, if anything, by Dr Clark's theory of Heywood's hand in *The Jew of Malta*. It seems to us that here Dr Clark's scholarly theory is really founded upon a critical presupposition. He holds a not uncommon view that 'so far as [Marlowe's] conception of Barabas is concerned, the play might finish with the second act'. But he adds, 'so far as we know Marlowe invented the plot', which is a considerable concession; and also admits that there is very little in Acts III, IV and V which Marlowe may have written. He says, 'in the play we probably still have the main incidents as originally determined, but now crowded mostly into V to make room for certain ribaldry and gruesome farce'. There is perhaps a little ribaldry which we should prefer not to attribute to [174] Marlowe, and of a kind of which Heywood was certainly capable; but the most 'gruesome farce' is found in Act IV, Scenes i and ii; which the mere critic may maintain to be farce of a gruesomeness a cut above Heywood, and by no means unworthy of Marlowe. That the latter part of the play is garbled, few would doubt; that the writer who filled in the remains of Marlowe's play was Heywood, Dr Clark makes

out a good case; but mutilated and patched as the play probably is, we may still see in it a conception of Barabas which is by no means finished with the second act.

5 The third of Dr Clark's interesting ascriptions concerns *A Yorkshire Tragedy*. This abrupt little play has been somewhat overrated, singularly so by Swinburne. Dr Clark's association of it with *The Miseries of Enforced Marriage*, and his explanation of its inconsistencies through this association, is an excellent piece of reasoning. So far as the verse is concerned, the most if it is not too bad to be Heywood's, and the best line and a half –

> But you are playing in the angels' laps
> And will not look on me –

strike us as a *trouvaille* which might have been possible to Heywood. The best of the play is the part of the 'little son':

> What, ail you, father? are you not well? I cannot scourge my top as long as you stand so: you take up all the room with your wide legs. Puh, you cannot make me afeard with this; I fear no vizards, nor bugbears –

and as we cannot allege any other minor dramatist as more competent to have written this touching dialogue than Heywood, we are hardly in a strong position to refuse it to him. This then, we think, is the most valuable of Dr Clark's ascriptions.

6 None of these attributions, interesting as is the last of them in itself, can make very much difference to our estimate of Heywood as a dramatist and a poet; and it is upon [175] the indisputable plays that we found our opinion of him. These indisputable plays exhibit what may be called the minimum degree of unity. Similar subject-matter and treatment appear in several; the same stage skill, the same versifying ability. The sensibility is merely that of ordinary people in ordinary life – which is the reason, perhaps, why Heywood is misleadingly called a 'realist'. Behind the motions of his personages, the shadows of the human world, there is no reality of moral synthesis; to inform the verse there is no vision, none of the artist's power to give undefinable unity to the most various material. In the work of nearly all of those of his contemporaries who are as well known as he there is at least some inchoate pattern; there is, as it would often be called, personality. Of those of Heywood's plays which are worth reading, each is worth reading for itself, but none throws any illumination upon any other.

7 Heywood's versification is never on a very high poetic level, but at its best is often on a high dramatic level. This can be illustrated by one of the best known of quotations from *A Woman Killed with Kindness*:

> O speak no more!
> For more than this I know, and have recorded
> Within the red-leaved table of my heart.
> Fair, and of all beloved, I was not fearful
> Bluntly to give my life into your hand,
> And at one hazard all my earthly means.
> Go, tell your husband; he will turn me off,
> And I am then undone. I care not, I;
> 'Twas for your sake. Perchance in rage he'll kill me,
> I care not, 'twas for you. Say I incur
> The general name of villain through the world,
> Of traitor to my friend; I care not, I.
> Beggary, shame, death, scandal, and reproach,
> For you I'll hazard all: why, what care I?
> For you I'll live, and in your love I'll die.

[176] The image at the beginning of this passage does not, it is true, deserve its fame. 'Table of my heart' is a legitimate, though hardly striking, metaphor; but to call it *red-leaved* is to press the anatomical aspect into a ridiculous figure. It is not a conceit, as when Crashaw deliberately telescopes one image into another, but merely the irreflective grasping after a fine trope. But in the lines that follow the most skilful use is made of regular blank verse to emphasise the argument; and it is, even to the judicious couplet at the end, a speech which any actor should be happy to declaim. The speech is perfect for the situation; the most persuasive that Wendoll could have made to Mrs Frankford; and it persuades us into accepting her surrender. And this instance of verse which is only moderately poetical but very highly dramatic is by no means singular in Heywood's work.

8 And undeniably Heywood was not without skill in the construction of plays. It is unreasonable to complain of *A Woman Killed with Kindness* that it is improbable that a woman who has lived very happily with her husband and borne children should suddenly and easily be seduced by a man who had been living in the house the whole time; we consider that the seduction is made extremely plausible. What is perhaps clumsy is the beginning superfluously by a scene directly after the marriage of the Frankfords, instead of by a scene marking the happiness of the pair up to the moment of Wendoll's declaration. Sufficient verisimilitude is main-

tained to the end; we accept the Elizabethan convention of very quick death from heartbreak; and the last scene is really affecting. It is true that Mistress Frankford's words:

Out of my zeal to Heaven, whither now I'm bound,

seem to rely upon some curiously unorthodox theology; and even if death from broken heart secures the remission of sins, it hardly became Mrs Frankford to be so certain of it. But such a moral sentiment is perhaps not unique in the ethics of Elizabethan drama; and other small touches in [177] the play, such as the finding of the guitar, well deserve the praise they have received. It is in the underplot, as in some other plays, that Heywood is least skilful. This theme – a man ready to prostitute his sister as payment for a debt of honour – is too grotesque even to horrify us; but it is too obviously there merely because an underplot is required to fill out the play for us to feel anything but boredom when it recurs. Middleton's *The Changeling*, in every other respect a far finer play, must share with *A Woman Killed with Kindness* the discredit of having the weakest underplot of any important play in the whole Elizabethan repertory.

9 Indeed, Heywood suffers from one great handicap in attempting to write underplots at all – he was gifted with very little sense of humour, and therefore could not fall back upon the comic for the purpose. In attempting to be amusing he sometimes has recourse, as other men than harried playwrights have been known to do, to the lowest bawdiness, which leaves us less with a sense of repugnance for the man who could write it than with a sense of pity for the man who could think of nothing better. Here and there, in *The Wise Woman of Hogsdon* for instance, he succeeds with something not too far below Jonson to be comparable to that master's work; the wise woman herself, and her scenes with her clientèle, are capitally done, and earn for Heywood the title of 'realist' if any part of his work can. The scene of the unmasking of Young Chartley must be excellent fun when played. The underplot of *The English Traveller*, on the other hand, is a clumsy failure to do that in which only Jonson could have succeeded. But Heywood has no imaginative humour; and as he has so often been spoken of in the same breath with Dekker, that is a comparison which may justly be made. Just as Bess, the Fair Maid of the West, is a purely melodramatic figure beside the heroine of *The Roaring Girl*, so Heywood could no more have created the character of Cuddie Banks, in *The Witch*, than he could have written the magnificent tirade (a tirade which, if anything can, goes to prove that Middle-[178]ton wrote *The Revenger's Tragedy*) which Middleton puts into the mouth

of the chief character in the same play. Cuddie Banks, loving the dog whom he knows to be a devil, but loving him as dog while reproving him as devil, is worthy to rank with clowns of Shakespeare; he is not 'realistic', he is true.

10 It was in *The English Traveller* that Heywood found his best plot. Possibly the elder critics disapproved of the heroine's plighting herself to marry her admirer as soon as her elderly husband should die; but it is far less offensive to modern taste than many other situations in Elizabethan drama, and it is one which a modern novelist – not perhaps a quite modern novelist, but a Stendhal – might have made the most of. It is indeed a plot especially modern among Elizabethan plots; for the refinement of agony of the virtuous lover who has controlled his passion and then discovers that his lady has deceived both her husband, who is his friend, and himself, is really more poignant than the torment of the betrayed husband Frankford. The strange situation *à quatre*, Master Wincott and his wife, young Geraldine and his faithless companion Delavil – and old Geraldine neatly worked into the pattern as well – is not only well thought of but well thought out; and it is delicately phrased:

Y. GER.
> Your husband's old, to whom my soul doth wish
> A Nestor's age, so much he merits from me;
> Yet if (as proof and Nature daily teach
> Men cannot always live, especially
> Such as are old and crazed) he be called hence,
> Fairly, in full maturity of time,
> And we two be reserved to after life,
> Will you confer your widowhood on me?

WIFE.
> You ask the thing I was about to beg;
> Your tongue hath spoke mine own thoughts. . . .

[179] WIFE.
> Till that day come, you shall reserve yourself
> A single man; converse nor company
> With any woman, contract nor combine
> With maid or widow; which expected hour
> As I do wish not haste, so when it happens
> It shall not come unwelcome. You hear all;
> Vow this.

Y. GER.
> By all that you have said, I swear,
> And by this kiss confirm.

WIFE.
> You're now my brother;
> But then, my second husband.

It could not have been done better. As in the passage from *A Woman Killed with Kindness* quoted above, the verse, which nowhere bursts into a flame of poetry, is yet economical and tidy, and formed to extract all the dramatic value possible from the situation. And it is by his refinement of sentiment, by his sympathetic delicacy in these two plays that Heywood deserves, and well deserves, to be remembered; for here he has accomplished what none of his contemporaries have succeeded in accomplishing.

11 Yet we must concede that the interest is always sentimental, and never ethical. One has seen plays in our time which are just the sort of thing that Heywood would have written had he been our contemporary. It is usual for inferior authors at any time to accept whatever morality is current, because they are interested not to analyse the ethics but to exploit the sentiment. Mrs Frankford yields to her seducer with hardly a struggle, and her decline and death are a tribute to popular sentiment; not, certainly, a vindication of inexorable moral law. She is in the sentimental tradition which peopled a period of nineteenth-century fiction with Little Em'lys; and which, if it now [180] produces a generation of rather robuster heroines, has yet made no moral advance, because it has no vital relation to morals at all. For a Corneille or a Racine, the centre of interest in the situation of Mrs Frankford or Mrs Wincott would have been the moral conflict leading up to the fall; and even the absence of conflict, as in the seduction of Mathilde (if seduction it can be called) in *Le Rouge et le Noir*, can be treated by a moralist. The capital distinction is that between representation of human actions which have moral reality and representation of such as have only sentimental reality; and beside this, any distinction between 'healthy' and 'morbid' sentiment is trivial. It is well enough to speak of Heywood, as does Dr Clark, as 'a man of tender charity . . . ever kindly to the fallen and with a gift of homely pathos and simple poetry' though it does less than justice to Heywood to describe his pathos as 'homely' (for the famous pathos of 'Nan, Nan!' is no homelier than Lear's 'Never, never, never, never, never', though far below it.) What matters is not whether Heywood was inspired by tender charity, but whether his actual productions are any

more edifying, any more moral, than what Dr Clark would call 'the slippery ethics' of Fletcher, Massinger and Ford.

12 The ethics of most of the greater Elizabethan dramatists is only intelligible as leading up to, or deriving from, that of Shakespeare: it has its significance, we mean, only in the light of Shakespeare's fuller revelation. There is another type of ethics, that of the satirist. In Shakespeare's work it is represented most nearly by *Timon* and *Troilus*, but in a mind with such prodigious capacity of development as Shakespeare's, the snarling vein could not endure. The kind of satire which is approached in *The Jew of Malta* reaches perhaps its highest point with *Volpone*; but it is a kind to which also approximates much of the work of Middleton and Tourneur, men who as writers must be counted morally higher than Fletcher or Ford or Heywood.

[181] These by enchantments can whole lordships change
       To trunks of rich attire, turn ploughs and teams
       To Flanders mares and coaches, and huge trains
       Of servitors to a French butterfly.
       Have you not city-witches who can turn
       Their husbands' wares, whole standing shops of wares,
       To sumptuous tables, gardens of stolen sin;
       In one year wasting what scarce twenty win?
       Are not these witches?

That dolorous aspect of human nature which in comedy is best portrayed by Molière, though Jonson and even Wycherley have the same burden, appears again and again in the tragic drama of Middleton and Tourneur. Without denying to Heywood what Dr Clark attributes to him, a sense of 'the pity of it', we can find a profounder sense of the 'pity of it', in the lines quoted above which Middleton gives to the Witch of Edmonton. Heywood's sense of pity is genuine enough, but it is only the kind of pity that the ordinary playgoer, of any time, can appreciate. Heywood's is a drama of common life, not, in the highest sense, tragedy at all; there is no supernatural music from behind the wings. He would in any age have been a successful playwright; he is eminent in the pathetic, rather than the tragic. His nearest approach to those deeper emotions which shake the veil of Time is in that fine speech of Frankford which surely no men or women past their youth can read without a twinge of personal feeling:

   O God! O God! that it were possible
   To undo things done; to call back yesterday....

Variants from *TLS* (1931):
1 [No fn. in *TLS*.]
7 kill me,] kill me:
8 bound,] bound
10 especially] uniquely
11 Fletcher, Massinger and Ford] Fletcher and Massinger, and of Ford
12 men or women] man or woman

Cyril Tourneur

SE, 182–92.

Revised from an unsigned review of *The Works of Cyril Tourneur*,
ed. Allardyce Nicoll, in *TLS*, 1502 (13 Nov. 1930), [925]–6: Gallup C314.

1 Although the tragedies which make immortal the name of Cyril Tourneur are accessible to every one in the Mermaid edition, it is still an event to have a new edition of the 'work' of this strange poet. Fifty-two years have passed since the edition in two volumes by Churton Collins. And this sumptuous critical edition of Professor Nicoll's[1] reminds us that it is time to revalue the work of Tourneur.

2 None of the Elizabethan dramatists is more puzzling; none offers less foothold for the scholarly investigator; and none is more dangerous for the literary critic. We know almost nothing of his life; we trace his hand in no collaboration. He has left only two plays; and it has been doubted even whether the same man wrote both; and if he did, as most scholars agree, there is still some doubt as to which he wrote first. Yet in no plays by any minor Elizabethan is a more positive personality revealed than in *The Revenger's Tragedy*. No Elizabethan dramatist offers greater temptation: to the scholar, to hazard conjecture of fact; and to the critic, to hazard conjecture of significance. We may be sure that what Mr Nicoll does not know is unknown to anybody; and it is no disrespect to his scholarship and diligence to remark how little, in the fifty-two years of Elizabethan research since Collins, has been added to our knowledge of the singular poet with the delightful name. Churton Collins, in his admirable introduction, really knows nothing at all about the man's life; and all [183] that later students have been able to do is to piece together several probable shreds. That there was a family of Tourneurs is certain; the precise place in it of Cyril is, as Mr Nicoll freely admits, a matter

---

1. *The Works of Cyril Tourneur*. Edited by Allardyce Nicoll. With decorations by Frederick Carter. London: The Fanfrolico Press.

of speculation. And, with all the plausible guesses possible, Mr Nicoll tells us that Tourneur's 'whole early life is a complete blank'. What he does is give us good reason for believing that Tourneur, with perhaps other members of the family, was a servant of the Cecils; and he adds to our knowledge of a prose piece, *The Character of Robert Earl of Salisbury*. Besides the two tragedies, he also gives 'The Transformed Metamorphosis', the 'Funeral Poem upon the Death of Sir Francis Vere', and the Elegy on the death of Prince Henry, already canonically attributed to Tourneur; and *Laugh and Lie Down*, a satirical pamphlet, no better and no worse than dozens of others, which is probably Tourneur's – at least, it is attributed to him, and there is no particular reason why he should not be the author.

3 The information of fifty years is meagre, and probably will never be improved. It is astonishingly incongruous with what we feel we know about Tourneur after reading the two plays: two plays as different from all plays by known Elizabethans as they are from each other. In Elizabethan drama, the critic is rash who will assert boldly that any play is by a single hand. But with each of these, *The Atheist's Tragedy* and *The Revenger's Tragedy*, the literary critic feels that, even were there some collaboration, one mind guided the whole work; and feels that the mind was not that of one of the other well-known dramatic writers. Certainly, Tourneur has made a very deep impression upon the minds of those critics who have admired him. It is to be regretted, however, that Professor Nicoll, at the beginning of his otherwise sober and just introduction, has quoted the hysterical phrase of Marcel Schwob's *vie imaginaire* of Tourneur. To say that Tourneur *naquit de l'union d'un dieu inconnu avec une prostituée* is a pardonable excess of a romantic period, a pardonable excess on the part of a [184] poet discovering a foreign poet. But this is not criticism; and it is a misleading introduction to the work of a man who was a great English poet; and it produces an impression which is increased by the excellent but too *macabre* decorations of Mr Carter. What matters is the beauty of the verse and the unity of the dramatic pattern in the two plays.

4 The author of *The Atheist's Tragedy* and *The Revenger's Tragedy* belongs critically among the earlier of the followers of Shakespeare. If Ford and Shirley and Fletcher represent the decadence, and Webster the last ripeness, then Tourneur belongs a little earlier than Webster. He is nearer to Middleton, and has some affinity to that curious and still underestimated poet Marston. The difference between his mind and that of Webster is very great; if we assigned his plays to any other

known dramatist, Webster would be the last choice. For Webster is a slow, deliberate, careful writer, very much the conscious artist. He was incapable of writing so badly or so tastelessly as Tourneur sometimes did, but he is never quite so surprising as Tourneur sometimes is. Moreover, Webster, in his greatest tragedies, has a kind of pity for *all* of his characters, an attitude towards good and bad alike which helps to unify the Webster pattern. Tourneur has no such feeling for any of his characters; and in this respect is nearer, as Professor Stoll has pointed out and Professor Nicoll has reminded us, to the author of *Antonio and Mellida*. Of all his other contemporaries, Middleton is the nearest. But Mr Nicoll, we think quite rightly, rejects Mr E. H. C. Oliphant's theory that Middleton is the author of *The Revenger's Tragedy*, and with Mr Dugdale Sykes restores the play to Tourneur. And, in spite of Mr Oliphant's weight of probabilities, there is one quality of Middleton which we do not find in the two plays attributed to Tourneur. The finest of the tragic characters of Middleton live in a way which differs from Tourneur's, not in degree but kind; and they have flashes of a kind of satiric wit unknown to Tourneur, in whom wit is supplied [185] by a fierce grotesquerie. In reading one play of Middleton, either *The Changeling* or *Women Beware Women*, for instance, we can recognise an author capable of considerable variety in his dramatic work; in reading either of Tourneur's plays we recognise a narrow mind, capable at most of the limited range of Marston.

5 Indeed, none of the characters of Tourneur, even the notable Vindice, the protagonist of *The Revenger's Tragedy*, is by himself invested with much humanity either for good or evil. But dramatic characters may live in more than one way; and a dramatist like Tourneur can compensate his defects by the intensity of his virtues. Characters should be real in relation to our own life, certainly, as even a very minor character of Shakespeare may be real; but they must also be real in relation to each other; and the closeness of emotional pattern in the latter way is an important part of dramatic merit. The personages of Tourneur have, like those of Marston, and perhaps in a higher degree, this togetherness. They may be distortions, grotesques, almost childish caricatures of humanity, but they are all distorted to scale. Hence the whole action, from their appearance to their ending, 'no common action' indeed, has its own self-subsistent reality. For closeness of texture, in fact, there are no plays beyond Shakespeare's, and the best of Marlowe and Jonson, that can surpass *The Revenger's Tragedy*. Tourneur excels in three virtues of the dramatist: he knew how, in his own way, to construct a plot, he was cunning in his manipulation of stage effects, and he was a master of

versification and choice of language. *The Revenger's Tragedy* starts off at top speed, as every critic has observed; and never slackens to the end. We are told everything we need to know before the first scene is half over; Tourneur employs his torrent of words with the greatest economy. The opening scene, and the famous Scene v of Act III, are remarkable feats of melodrama; and the suddenness of the end of the final scene of Act V matches the sudden explosiveness of the beginning.

[186] 6 Before considering the detail of the two plays, we must face two problems which have never been solved and probably never will be: whether the two plays are by the same hand and, if so, in which order they were written. For the first point, the consensus of scholarship, with the exception of Mr Oliphant's brilliant ascription of *The Revenger's Tragedy* to Middleton – an ascription which leaves the other play more of a mystery than before – assigns the two plays to Tourneur. For the second point, the consensus of scholarship is counter to the first impressions of sensibility; for all existing evidence points to the priority of *The Revenger's Tragedy* in time. The records of Stationers' Hall cannot be lightly disregarded; and Mr Dugdale Sykes, who is perhaps our greatest authority on the texts of Tourneur and Middleton, finds stylistic evidence also. Professor Nicoll accepts the evidence, although pointing out clearly enough the anomaly. Certainly, any testimony drawn from the analogy of a modern poet's experience would urge that *The Atheist's Tragedy* was immature work, and that *The Revenger's Tragedy* represented a period of full mastery of blank verse. It is not merely that the latter play is in every way the better; but that it shows a highly original development of vocabulary and metric, unlike that of every other play and every other dramatist. The versification of *The Revenger's Tragedy* is of a very high order indeed. And yet, with the evidence before us, summed up briefly in Mr Nicoll's preface, we cannot affirm that this is the later play. Among all the curiosities of that curious period, when dramatic poets worked and developed in ways alien to the modern mind, this is one of the most curious. But it is quite possible. We may conjecture either that *The Atheist's Tragedy* was composed, or partly composed, and laid by until after *The Revenger's Tragedy* was written and entered. Or that after exhausting his best inspiration on the latter play – which certainly bears every internal evidence of having been written straight off in one sudden heat – Tourneur, years after, in [187] colder blood, with more attention to successful models – not only Shakespeare but perhaps also Chapman – produced *The Atheist's Tragedy*, with more regular verse, more conventional moralising, more conventional scenes, but with here and there flashes of the old fire. Not that the scenes of *The

Atheist's Tragedy are altogether conventional; or, at least, he trespasses beyond the convention in a personal way. There was nothing remarkable in setting a graveyard scene at midnight; but we feel that to set it for the action of a low assignation and an attempted rape at the same time seems more to be expected of the author of *The Revenger's Tragedy* than of anyone else; while the low comedy, more low than comic, does not seem of the taste of either Webster or Middleton. Webster's farcical prose is harmonious with his tragic verse; and in this respect Webster is a worthy follower of the tradition of the Porter in *Macbeth*. Middleton again, in his tragedies, has a different feel of the relation of the tragic and the comic; whereas the transitions in the two tragedies of Tourneur – and especially in *The Atheist's Tragedy* – are exactly what one would expect from a follower of Marston; especially in *The Atheist's Tragedy* they have that offensive tastelessness which is so positive as to be itself a kind of taste, which we find in the work of Marston.

7 *The Atheist's Tragedy* is indeed a peculiar brew of styles. It has well-known passages like the following:[1]

> Walking next day upon the fatal shore,
> Among the slaughtered bodies of their men,
> Which the full-stomached sea had cast upon
> The sands, it was my unhappy chance to light
> Upon a face, whose favour when it lived
> My astonished mind informed me I had seen.
> He lay in his armour, as if that had been
> [188] His coffin; and the weeping sea (like one
> Whose milder temper doth lament the death
> Of him whom in his rage he slew) runs up
> The shore, embraces him, kisses his cheek;
> Goes back again, and forces up the sands
> To bury him, and every time it parts
> Sheds tears upon him, till, at last (as if
> It could no longer endure to see the man
> Whom it had slain, yet loth to leave him) with
> A kind of unresolved unwilling pace,
> Winding her waves one in another, (like
> A man that folds his arms, or wrings his hands
> For grief) ebbed from the body, and descends;

---

1. The text used in the following quotations is the critical text of Professor Nicoll; but for convenience and familiarity the modernised spelling and punctuation of the 'Mermaid' text is used.

> As if it would sink down into the earth
> And hide itself for shame of such a deed.

The present writer was once convinced that *The Atheist's Tragedy* was the earlier play. But lines like these, masterly but artificial, might well belong to a later period; the regularity of the versification, the elaboration of the long suspended sentences, with three similes expressed in brackets, remind us even of Massinger. It is true that Charles Lamb, commenting on this passage, refers this parenthetical style to Sir Philip Sidney, who 'seems to have set the example to Shakespeare'; but these lines have closer syntactical parallels in Massinger than in Shakespeare. But lines like

> To spend our substance on a minute's pleasure

remind one of *The Revenger's Tragedy*, and lines like

> Your gravity becomes your perished soul
> As hoary mouldiness does rotten fruit

of *The Revenger's Tragedy* where it is likest Middleton.

8 As a parallel for admitting the possibility of *The Atheist's Tragedy* being the later play, Professor Nicoll cites the fact that *Cymbeline* is later than *Hamlet*. This strikes us as about the most unsuitable parallel that could be found. Even though some critics may still consider *Cymbeline* as evidence of 'declining powers', it has no less a mastery of [189] words than *Hamlet*, and possibly more; and, like every one of Shakespeare's plays, it adds something or develops something not explicit in any previous play; it has its place in an orderly sequence. Now accepting the canonical order of Tourneur's two plays, *The Atheist's Tragedy* adds nothing at all to what the other play has given us; there is no development, no fresh inspiration; only the skilful but uninspired use of a greater metrical variety. Cases are not altogether wanting, among poets, of a precocious maturity exceeding the limits of the poet's experience – in contrast to the very slow and very long development of Shakespeare – a maturity to which the poet is never again able to catch up. Tourneur's genius, in any case, is in *The Revenger's Tragedy*; his talent only in *The Atheist's Tragedy*.

9 Indeed, *The Revenger's Tragedy* might well be a specimen of such isolated masterpieces. It does express – and this, chiefly, is what gives it its amazing unity – an intense and unique and horrible vision of life; but is such a vision as might come, as the result of few or slender experiences, to a highly sensitive adolescent with a gift for words. We are apt to expect of youth only a fragmentary view of life; we incline to see youth as

exaggerating the importance of its narrow experience and imagining the world as did Chicken Licken. But occasionally the intensity of the vision of its own ecstasies or horrors, combined with a mastery of word and rhythm, may give to a juvenile work a universality which is beyond the author's knowledge of life to give, and to which mature men and women can respond. Churton Collins's introduction to the works is by far the most penetrating interpretation of Tourneur that has been written; and this introduction, though Collins believed *The Revenger's Tragedy* to be the later play, and though he thinks of Tourneur as a man of mature experience, does not invalidate this theory. 'Tourneur's great defect as a dramatic poet,' says Collins, 'is undoubtedly the narrowness of his range of vision': and this narrowness of range might be that of a young man. The cynicism, the loathing [190] and disgust of humanity, expressed consummately in *The Revenger's Tragedy*, are immature in the respect that they exceed the object. Their objective equivalents are characters practising the grossest vices; characters which seem merely to be spectres projected from the poet's inner world of nightmare, some horror beyond words. So the play is a document on humanity chiefly because it is a document on one human being, Tourneur; its motive is truly the death-motive, for it is the loathing and horror of life itself. To have realised this motive so well is a triumph; for the hatred of life is an important phase – even, if you like, a mystical experience – in life itself.

10 *The Revenger's Tragedy*, then, is in this respect quite different from any play by any minor Elizabethan; it can, in this respect, be compared only to *Hamlet*. Perhaps, however, its quality would be better marked by contrasting it with a later work of cynicism and loathing, *Gulliver's Travels*. No two compositions could be more dissimilar. Tourneur's 'suffering, cynicism and despair', to use Collins's words, are static; they might be prior to experience, or be the fruit of but little; Swift's is the progressive cynicism of the mature and disappointed man of the world. As an objective comment on the world, Swift's is by far the more terrible. For Swift had enough pettiness, as well as enough sin of pride, and lust of dominion, to be able to expose and condemn mankind by its universal pettiness and pride and vanity and ambition; and his poetry, as well as his prose, attests that he hated the very smell of the human animal. We may think as we read Swift, 'how loathsome human beings are'; in reading Tourneur we can only think, 'how terrible to loathe human beings so much as that'. For you cannot make humanity horrible merely by presenting human beings as consistent and monotonous maniacs of gluttony and lust.

11 Collins, we think, tended to read into the plays of Tourneur too much, or more than is necessary, of a lifetime's experience. Some of his phrases, however, are memorable [191] and just. But what still remains to be praised, after Swinburne and Collins and Mr Nicoll, is Tourneur's unique style in blank verse. His occasional verses are mediocre at best; he left no lyric verse at all; but it is hardly too much to say that, after Marlowe, Shakespeare and Webster, Tourneur is the most remarkable technical innovator – an innovator who found no imitators. The style of *The Revenger's Tragedy* is consistent throughout; there is little variation, but the rapidity escapes monotony.

> Faith, if the truth were known, I was begot
> After some gluttonous dinner; some stirring dish
> Was my first father, when deep healths went round
> And ladies' cheeks were painted red with wine,
> Their tongues, as short and nimble as their heels,
> Uttering words sweet and thick; and when they rose,
> Were merrily disposed to fall again.
> In such a whispering and withdrawing hour . . .
>   . . . and, in the morning
> When they are up and drest, and their mask on,
> Who can perceive this, save that eternal eye
> That sees through flesh and all? Well, if anything be damned,
> It will be twelve o' clock at night. . . .

His verse hurries:

> O think upon the pleasure of the palace!
> Secured ease and state! the stirring meats,
> Ready to move out of the dishes, that e'en now
> Quicken when they are eaten!
> Banquets abroad by torchlight! music! sports!
> Bareheaded vassals, that had ne'er the fortune
> To keep on their own hats, but let horns wear 'em!
> Nine coaches waiting – hurry, hurry, hurry –

His phrases seem to contract the images in his effort to say everything in the least space, the shortest time:

> Age and bare bone
> Are e'er allied in action . . .

[192] To suffer wet damnation to run through 'em . . .

> The poor benefit of a bewildering minute . . .

(*Bewildering* is the reading of the 'Mermaid' text; but Churton Collins and Mr Nicoll give *bewitching* without mentioning any alternative reading: it is a pity if they be right, for *bewildering* is much the richer word here.)

> forgetful feasts . . .
> falsify highways . . .

And the peculiar abruptness, the frequent change of tempo, characteristic of *The Revenger's Tragedy*, is nowhere better shown than by the closing lines:

> This murder might have slept in tongueless brass,
> But for ourselves, and the world died an ass.
> Now I remember too, here was Piato
> Brought forth a knavish sentence once;
> No doubt (said he), but time
> Will make the murderer bring forth himself.
> 'Tis well he died; he was a witch.
> And now, my lord, since we are in for ever,
> This work was ours, which else might have been slipped!
> And if we list, we could have nobles clipped,
> And go for less than beggars; but we hate
> To bleed so cowardly, we have enough,
> I' faith, we're well, our mother turned, our sister true,
> We die after a nest of dukes. Adieu!

12 The versification, as indeed the whole style of *The Revenger's Tragedy*, is not that of the last period of the great drama. Although so peculiar, the metric of Tourneur is earlier in style than that of the later Shakespeare, or Fletcher, or Webster; to say nothing of Massinger, or Shirley, or Ford. It seems to derive, as much as from anyone's, from that of Marston. What gives Tourneur his place as a great poet is this one play, in which a horror of life, singular in his own or any age, finds exactly the right words and the right rhythms.

Variants from *TLS* (1930):
2   And, with all the plausible] And with all the plausible
4   And, in spite] And in spite
9   Chicken Licken] Chicken Little
11 contract the images] telescope the images
    could have nobles] might have nobles
    cowardly,] cowardly:

John Ford

SE, 193–204.

Revised from 'John Ford', an unsigned review of *Materials for the Study of Old English Drama*, New Series, First Volume: *John Ford's Dramatic Works*, vol. II, ed. H. De Vocht, *TLS*, 1579 (5 May 1932), [317]–18: Gallup C335.
In para. 5 *'Tristran'* has been corrected to *'Tristan'*.

1 Among other possible classifications, we might divide the Elizabethan and Jacobean dramatists into those who would have been great even had Shakespeare never lived, those who are positive enough to have brought some positive contribution after Shakespeare, and those whose merit consists merely in having exploited successfully a few Shakespearian devices or echoed here and there the Shakespearian verse. In the first class would fall Marlowe, Jonson and Chapman; in the second, Middleton, Webster and Tourneur; in the third, Beaumont and Fletcher and Shirley as tragedian. This kind of division could not support very close question, especially in its distinction between the second and the third class; but it is of some use at the beginning, in helping us to assign a provisional place to John Ford.

2 The standard set by Shakespeare is that of a continuous development from first to last, a development in which the choice both of theme and of dramatic and verse technique in each play seems to be determined increasingly by Shakespeare's state of feeling, by the particular stage of his emotional maturity at the time. What is 'the whole man' is not simply his greatest or maturest achievement, but the whole pattern formed by the sequence of plays; so that we may say confidently that the full meaning of any one of his plays is not in itself alone, but in that play in the order in which it was written, in its relation to all of Shakespeare's other plays, earlier and later: we must know all of Shakespeare's work in order to know any of it. No other dramatist of the time approaches anywhere near to this perfec-[194]tion of pattern, of pattern superficial and profound; but the measure in which dramatists and poets approximate to this unity in a lifetime's work is one of the measures of major poetry and drama. We feel a similar interest, in less degree, in the work of Jonson and Chapman, and certainly in the unfinished work of Marlowe; in less degree still, the interest is in the work of Webster, baffling as the chronological order of Webster's plays makes it. Even without an *oeuvre*, some dramatists can effect a satisfying unity and significance of pattern in single plays, a unity springing from the depth and coherence of a number of emotions and feelings, and not only from dramatic and poetic skill. The *Maid's*

Tragedy, or *A King and No King*, is better constructed, and has as many poetic lines, as *The Changeling*, but is far inferior in the degree of inner necessity in the feeling: something more profound and more complex than what is ordinarily called 'sincerity'.

3 It is significant that the first of Ford's important plays to be performed, so far as we have knowledge, is one which depends very patently upon some of the devices, and still more upon the feeling tone, of Shakespeare's last period. *The Lover's Melancholy* was licensed for the stage in 1628; it could hardly have been written but for *Cymbeline*, *The Winter's Tale*, *Pericles*, and *The Tempest*. Except for the comic passages, which are, as in all of Ford's plays, quite atrocious, it is a pleasant, dreamlike play without violence or exaggeration. As in other of his plays, there are verbal echoes of Shakespeare numerous enough; but what is more interesting is the use of the Recognition Scene, so important in Shakespeare's later plays, to the significance of which as a Shakespeare symbol Mr Wilson Knight has drawn attention. In Shakespeare's plays, this is primarily the recognition of a long-lost daughter, secondarily of a wife; and we can hardly read the later plays attentively without admitting that the father-and-daughter theme was one of very deep symbolic value to him in his last productive years; Perdita, Marina and Miranda share some beauty of which his earlier heroines do not possess the secret. Now Ford is struck by the dramatic and poetic effectiveness of the situation, and uses it on a level hardly higher than that of the device of twins in comedy; so in *The Lover's Melancholy* he introduces two such scenes, one the recognition of Eroclea in the guise of Parthenophil by her lover Palador, the second her recognition (accompanied, as in *Pericles*, by soft music) by her aged father Meleander. Both of these scenes are very well carried out, and in the first we have a passage in that slow solemn rhythm which is Ford's distinct contribution to the blank verse of the period.

> Minutes are numbered by the fall of sands,
> As by an hourglass; the span of time
> Doth waste us to our graves, and we look on it:
> An age of pleasure, revelled out, comes home
> At last, and ends in sorrow; but the life,
> Weary of riot, numbers every sand,
> Wailing in sighs, until the last drop down;
> So to conclude calamity in rest.

The tone and movement are so positive that when in a dull masque by Ford and Dekker, called *The Sun's Darling*, we come across such a passage as

> Winter at last draws on the Night of Age;
> Yet still a humour of some novel fancy
> Untasted or untried, puts off the minute
> Of resolution, which should bid farewell
> To a vain world of weariness and sorrows. . . .

we can hardly doubt the identity of the author. The scenes, as said above, are well planned and well written, and are even moving; but it is in such scenes as these that we are convinced of the incommensurability of writers like Ford (and Beaumont and Fletcher) with Shakespeare. It is not merely that they fail where he succeeds; it is that they had no conception of what he was trying to do; they speak another and cruder language. In their poetry there is no symbolic value; theirs is good poetry and good drama, but [196] it is poetry and drama of the surface. And in a play like *The Revenger's Tragedy*, or *Women Beware Women*, or *The White Devil*, there is some of that inner significance which becomes the stronger and stronger undertone of Shakespeare's plays to the end. You do not find that in Ford.

4 It is suggested, then, that a dramatic poet cannot create characters of the greatest intensity of life unless his personages, in their reciprocal actions and behaviour in their story, are somehow dramatising, but in no obvious form, an action or struggle for harmony in the soul of the poet. In this sense Ford's most famous, though not necessarily best, play may be called 'meaningless'; and in so far as we may be justified in disliking its horrors, we are justified by its lack of meaning. *'Tis Pity She's a Whore* is surely one of the most read of minor Jacobean plays, and the only one of Ford's which has been lately revived upon the stage. It is the best constructed, with the exception of *Perkin Warbeck*, and the latter play is somewhat lacking in action. To the use of incest between brother and sister for a tragic plot there should be no objection of principle: the test is, however, whether the dramatic poet is able to give universal significance to a perversion of nature which, unlike some other aberrations, is defended by no one. The fact that it is defended by no one might, indeed, lend some colour of inoffensiveness to its dramatic use. Certainly, it is to Ford's credit that, having chosen this subject – which was suggested by an Italian tale – he went in for it thoroughly. There is none of the prurient flirting with impropriety which makes Beaumont and Fletcher's *King and No King* meretricious, and which is most evident and nauseous in the worst play which Ford himself ever wrote, *The Fancies Chaste and Noble*; a kind of prurience from which the comedy of Wycherley is absolutely free. Furthermore, Ford handles the theme with all the

seriousness of which he is capable, and he can hardly be accused here of wanton sensationalism. It is not the sort of play which an age wholly corrupt would produce; and the signs of decay in Ford's age are more clearly visible in the plays of Beaumont and Fletcher than in his own. Ford does not make the unpleasant appear pleasant; and when, at the moment of avowed love, he makes Annabella say

> Brother, even by our mother's dust, I charge you,
> Do not betray me to your mirth or hate . . .

he is certainly double-stressing the horror, which from that moment he will never allow you to forget; but if he did not stress the horror he would be the more culpable. There is nothing in the play to which could be applied the term appropriately used in the advertisements of some films: the 'peppy situation'.

5 We must admit, too, that the versification and poetry, for example the fine speech of Annabella in Act V, Sc. v, are of a very high order:

> Brother, dear brother, know what I have been,
> And know that now there's but a dining-time
> 'Twixt us and our confusion. . . .
> Be not deceived, my brother;
> This banquet is an harbinger of death
> To you and me; resolve yourself it is,
> And be prepared to welcome it.

Finally, the low comedy, bad as it is, is more restrained in space, and more relevant to the plot, than is usual with Ford; and the death of Bergetto ('is all this mine own blood?') is almost pathetic. When all is said, however, there are serious shortcomings to render account of. The subplot of Hippolita is tedious, and her death superfluous. More important, the passion of Giovanni and Annabella is not shown as an affinity of temperament due to identity of blood; it hardly rises above the purely carnal infatuation. In *Antony and Cleopatra* (which is no more an apology for adultery than *'Tis Pity* is an apology for incest) we are made to feel convinced of an overpowering attraction towards each other of two persons, not only in defiance of conventional morality, but against self-interest: an attrac-[198]tion as fatal as that indicated by the love-potion motif in *Tristan und Isolde*. We see clearly why Antony and Cleopatra find each other congenial, and we see their relation, during the course of the play, become increasingly serious. But Giovanni is merely selfish and self-willed, of a temperament to want a thing the more because it is forbidden; Annabella is pliant, vacillating and negative: the one almost a monster of egotism, the other virtually a moral defective. Her rebellious taunting of her violent husband has an effect of naturalness and arouses some sympathy; but the fact that Soranzo is himself a bad lot does not extenuate her willingness to ruin him. In short, the play has not the general significance and emotional depth (for the two go together) without which no such action can be justified; and this defect separates it completely from the best plays of Webster, Middleton and Tourneur.

6 There are two other plays, however, which are superior to *'Tis a Pity She's a Whore*. The first is *The Broken Heart*, in which, with *'Tis a Pity* and *The Lover's Melancholy*, we find some of the best 'poetical' passages. Some of the best lines in *The Broken Heart* are given to the distraught Penthea; and being reminded of another fine passage given to a crazed woman in *Venice Preserved*, we might be tempted to generalise, and suggest that it is easier for an inferior dramatic poet to write poetry when he has a lunatic character to speak it, because in such passages he is less tied down to relevance and ordinary sense. The quite irrelevant and apparently meaningless lines

> Remember,
> When we last gathered roses in the garden,
> I found my wits; but truly you lost yours.

are perhaps the purest poetry to be found in the whole of Ford's writings; but the longer and better known passage preceding them is also on a very high level:

> Sure, if we were all Sirens, we should sing pitifully,
> And 'twere a comely music, when in parts
> One sung another's knell: the turtle sighs
> When he hath lost his mate; and yet some say
> He must be dead first: 'tis a fine deceit
> To pass away in a dream; indeed, I've slept
> With mine eyes open a great while. No falsehood
> Equals a broken faith; there's not a hair
> Sticks on my head but, like a leaden plummet,
> It sinks me to the grave: I must creep thither;
> The journey is not long.

[199]

Between the first and the second of these passages there is, however, a difference of kind rather than degree: the first is real poetry, the second is the echo of a mood which other dramatic poets had caught and realised with greater mastery. Yet it exhibits that which gives Ford his most certain claim to perpetuity: the distinct personal rhythm in blank verse which could be no one's but his alone.

7 As for the play itself, the plot is somewhat overloaded and distracted by the affairs of unfortunate personages, all of whom have an equal claim on our attention; Ford overstrains our pity and terror by calling upon us to sympathise now with Penthea, now with Calantha, now with Orgilus, now with Ithocles; and the recipe by which good and evil are mixed in the characters of Orgilus and Ithocles is one which renders them less sympathetic, rather than more human. The scene in which Calantha, during the revels, is told successively the news of the death of her father, of Penthea and of her betrothed, and the scene in the temple which follows, must have been very effective on the stage; and the style is elevated and well sustained. The end of the play almost deserves the extravagant commendation of Charles Lamb; but to a later critic it appears rather as a recrudescence of the Senecan mood:

> They are the silent griefs which cut the heart-strings,
> Let me die smiling.

than as a profound searching of the human heart. The best of the play, and it is Ford at his best, is the character and [200] the action of Penthea, the lady who, after having been betrothed to the man she loves, is taken from him and given to a rival to gratify the ambitions of her brother. Even here, Ford misses an opportunity, and lapses in taste, by making the unloved husband, Bassanes, the vulgar jealous elderly husband of comedy: Penthea is a character which deserved, and indeed required, a more dignified and interesting foil. We are also diverted from her woes by the selfish revengefulness of her lost lover, who having been robbed of happiness himself, is determined to contrive that no one else shall be happy. Penthea, on the other hand, commands all our sympathy when she pleads the cause of her brother Ithocles, the brother who has ruined her life, with the Princess Calantha whom he loves. She is throughout a dignified, consistent and admirable figure; Penthea, and the Lady Katherine Gordon in *Perkin Warbeck*, are the most memorable of all Ford's characters.

8 *Perkin Warbeck* is little read, and does not contain any lines and passages such as those which remain in the memory after reading the other plays; but it is unquestionably Ford's highest achievement, and is one of the very best historical plays outside of the works of Shakespeare in the whole of Elizabethan and Jacobean drama. To make this base-born pretender to the throne of England into a dignified and heroic

figure was no light task, and is not one which we should, after reading the other plays, have thought Ford competent to perform; but here for once there is no lapse of taste or judgement. Warbeck is made to appear as quite convinced that he is the lawful heir to the throne of England. We ourselves are left almost believing that he was; in the right state of uncertainty, wondering whether his kingly and steadfast behaviour is due to his royal blood, or merely due to his passionate conviction that he is of royal blood. What is more remarkable still, is that Ford has succeeded, not merely, as with Penthea, in creating one real person among shadows, but in fixing the right fitness and the right contrast between characters. [201] Even at the end, when the earlier pretender, Lambert Simnel, who contentedly serves the King (Henry VII) in the humble capacity of falconer, is brought forward to plead with Perkin to accept a similar destiny, the scene is not degrading, but simply serves to emphasise the nobility and constancy of the hero. But to make a man, who went down to history as an impostor, into a heroic figure was not Ford's only difficulty and success. The King of Scotland, in order to demonstrate his faith, and emphasise his support, of Perkin Warbeck's claim to the English throne, gives him to wife his own niece, the Lady Katherine Gordon, very much against her father's wishes. To make a lady, so abruptly given away to a stranger and dedicated to such very doubtful fortunes, into not only a loyal but a devoted wife, is not easy; but Ford succeeds. The introduction of her admirer, her countryman Lord Dalyell, does not disturb the effect, for Katherine is not shown as having already reciprocated his affection. Dalyell is merely present as a reminder of the kind of happy and suitable marriage which Katherine would have made in her own country but for the appearance of Warbeck and the caprice of the King; and his touching devotion to her cause throughout the action only exhibits more beautifully her own devotion to her husband. Ford for once succeeded in a most difficult attempt; and the play of *Perkin Warbeck* is almost flawless.

9 Of Ford's other plays, *Love's Sacrifice* is reprinted in the 'Mermaid' selection. It has a few fine scenes, but is disfigured by all the faults of which Ford was capable. In the complete editions – the Moxon edition with introduction (to Ford and Massinger) by Hartley Coleridge is obtainable, and there is also the edition of the Quarto texts published at the University of Louvain, the first volume edited by the late Professor Bang, and the second (1927) by Professor De Vocht – there are no other plays solely by Ford which retain any interest. It is difficult now to assent to Lamb's words, 'Ford was of the first order of poets', or [202] to Mr Havelock Ellis's attempt (in his excellent introduction to the 'Mermaid'

volume) to present Ford as a modern man and a psychologist. Mr Ellis makes the assertion that Ford is nearer to Stendhal and Flaubert than he is to Shakespeare. Ford, nevertheless, depended upon Shakespeare; but it would be truer to say that Shakespeare is nearer to Stendhal and Flaubert than he is to Ford. There is a very important distinction to be drawn at this point. Stendhal and Flaubert, and to them might be added Balzac, are analysts of the individual soul as it is found in a particular phase of society; and in their work is found as much sociology as individual psychology. Indeed, the two are aspects of one thing; and the greater French novelists, from Stendhal to Proust, chronicle the rise, the regime, and the decay of the upper bourgeoisie in France. In Elizabethan and Jacobean drama, and even in the comedy of Congreve and Wycherley, there is almost no analysis of the particular society of the times, except in so far as it records the rise of the city families, and their ambition to ally themselves with needy peerages and to acquire country estates. Even that rise of the City, in *Eastward Hoe* and *Michaelmas Term*, is treated lightly as a foible of the age, and not as a symptom of social decay and change. It is indeed in the lack of this sense of a 'changing world', of corruptions and abuses peculiar to their own time, that the Elizabethan and Jacobean dramatists are blessed. We feel that they believed in their own age, in a way in which no nineteenth- or twentieth-century writer of the greatest seriousness has been able to believe in his age. And accepting their age, they were in a position to concentrate their attention, to their respective abilities, upon the common characteristics of humanity in all ages, rather than upon the differences. We can partly criticise their age through our study of them, but they did not so criticise it themselves. In the work of Shakespeare as a whole, there is to be read the profoundest and indeed one of the most sombre studies of humanity that has ever been made in poetry; though it is in fact so comprehensive [203] that we cannot qualify it as a whole as either glad or sorry. We recognise the same assumption of permanence in his minor fellows. Dante held it also, and the great Greek dramatists. In periods of unsettlement and change we do not observe this: it was a changing world which met the eyes of Lucian or of Petronius. But in the kind of analysis in which Shakespeare was supreme the other Elizabethan and Jacobean dramatists differed only in degree and comprehensiveness.

10 Such observations are not made in order to cast doubt upon the ultimate value or the permanence of the greatest nineteenth-century fiction. But for the age in which Shakespeare lived and the age into which his influence extended after his death, it must be his work, and his work as a whole, that is our criterion. The whole of Shakespeare's work is *one*

poem; and it is the poetry of it in this sense, not the poetry of isolated lines and passages or the poetry of the single figures which he created, that matters most. A man might, hypothetically, compose any number of fine passages or even of whole poems which would each give satisfaction, and yet not be a great poet, unless we felt them to be united by one significant, consistent, and developing personality. Shakespeare is the one, among all his contemporaries, who fulfils these conditions; and the nearest to him is Marlowe. Jonson and Chapman have the consistency, but a far lower degree of significant development; Middleton and Webster take a lower place than these; the author of *The Revenger's Tragedy*, whether we call him Tourneur or Middleton or another, accomplishes all that can be accomplished within the limits of a single play. But in all these dramatists there is the essential, as well as the superficies, of poetry; they give the pattern, or we may say the undertone, of the personal emotion, the personal drama and struggle, which no biography, however full and intimate, could give us; which nothing can give us but our experience of the plays themselves. Ford, as well as Fletcher, wrote enough plays for us to see the [204] absence of essential poetry. Ford's poetry, as well as Beaumont and Fletcher's, is of the surface: that is to say, it is the result of the stock of expressions of feeling accumulated by the greater men. It is the absence of purpose – if we may use the word 'purpose' for something more profound than any formulable purpose can be – in such dramatists as Ford, Beaumont, Fletcher, Shirley, and later Otway, and still later Shelley, which makes their drama tend towards mere sensationalism. Many reasons might be found, according to the particular historical aspect from which we consider the problem. But Ford, as dramatic poet, as writer of dramatic blank verse, has one quality which assures him of a higher place than even Beaumont and Fletcher; and that is a quality which any poet may envy him. The varieties of cadence and tone in blank verse are none too many, in the history of English verse; and Ford, though intermittently, was able to manipulate sequences of words in blank verse in a manner which is quite his own.

Variants from *TLS* (1932):

[Between paras 2 and 3, additional para.:] There are two accessible complete editions of Ford. There is the Moxon edition of Massinger and Ford together, with an Introduction by Hartley Coleridge (1840). And we have now the second volume (1927) of the edition begun by Bang in his *Materielen zur Kunde des Aelteren Englischen Dramas*, completed by Professor de Vocht. The latter is an edition primarily for scholars and is a reproduction of the Quarto texts: we are promised a third volume, with variants and textual notes, and an essay by Mr Bertram Lloyd, who is preparing a critical edition of Ford's works.

3 father-and-daughter] father and daughter
    well written, and] well written and
    it is in such scenes that] in such scenes
4 necessarily best] necessarily, best
    its horrors,] its horrors
    Certainly,] Certainly
5 are of a very high] is of a very high
6 blank verse which could be no one's but his alone.] blank verse.
7 husband, Bassanes, the vulgar jealous] husband Bassanes the vulgar, jealous
8 royal blood] Royal blood
    royal blood] Royal blood
    a man, who went down] a man who went down
    impostor,] impostor
    doubtful fortunes,] doubtful fortunes
    wife, is not easy] wife is not easy
9 [Text between 'was capable.' and 'It is difficult':] [Not represented (but see variant above between paras 2 and 3).]
    City families,] city families
    And accepting] And, accepting
    Shakespeare as a whole,] Shakespeare as a whole
10 after his death,] after his death
    too many, in the history] too many in the history

Philip Massinger

SE, 205–20.

Part I publ. in *TLS*, 958 (27 May 1920), [325]–6, as an unsigned review of *Philip Massinger* by A. H. Cruickshank (Gallup C111). It was revised for *SW*, and revised again very slightly for *SE*. When he quotes the same passage from Cruickshank a second time in *SE*, Eliot misquotes 'culture' as 'more culture': this error has been corrected. Part II publ. in *A.*, 4702 (11 June 1920), 760–1, as a review, signed 'T. S. E.', of Cruickshank entitled 'The Old Comedy' (Gallup C112). It was repr. in *SW* with the first para. cut, and repr. without further revision in *SE*.

1 Massinger has been more fortunately and more fairly judged than several of his greater contemporaries. Three critics have done their best by him: the notes of Coleridge exemplify Coleridge's fine and fragmentary perceptions; the essay of Leslie Stephen is a piece of formidable destructive analysis; and the essay of Swinburne is Swinburne's criticism at its best. None of these, probably, has put Massinger finally and irrefutably into a place.

2 English criticism is inclined to argue or persuade rather than to state; and, instead of forcing the subject to expose himself, these critics have left in their work an undissolved residuum of their own good taste, which, however impeccable, is something that requires our faith. The principles which animate this taste remain unexplained. Canon Cruickshank's book[1] is a work of scholarship; and the advantage of good scholarship is that it presents us with evidence which is an invitation to the critical faculty of the reader: it bestows a method, rather than a judgement.

3 It is difficult – it is perhaps the supreme difficulty of criticism – to make the facts generalise themselves; but Mr Cruickshank at least presents us with facts which are capable of generalisation. This is a service of value; and it is therefore wholly a compliment to the author to say that his appendices are as valuable as the essay itself.

4 The sort of labour to which Mr Cruickshank has devoted himself is one that professed critics ought more willingly to undertake. It is an important part of criticism, [206] more important than any mere expression of opinion. To understand Elizabethan drama it is necessary to study a dozen playwrights at once, to dissect with all care the complex growth, to ponder collaboration to the utmost line. Reading Shakespeare and several of his contemporaries is pleasure enough, perhaps all the pleasure possible, for most. But if we wish to consummate and refine this pleasure by understanding it, to distil the last drop of it, to press and press the essence of each author, to apply exact measurement to our own sensations, then we must compare; and we cannot compare without parcelling the threads of authorship and influence. We must employ Mr Cruickshank's judgements; and perhaps the most important judgement to which he has committed himself is this:

> Massinger, in his grasp of stagecraft, his flexible metre, his desire in the field of ethics to exploit both vice and virtue, is typical of an age which had much culture, but which, without being exactly corrupt, lacked moral fibre.

5 Here, in fact, is our text: to elucidate this sentence would be to account for Massinger. We begin vaguely with good taste, by a recognition that Massinger is inferior: can we trace this inferiority, dissolve it, and have left any element of merit?

---

1. *Philip Massinger.* By A. H. Cruickshank. Oxford: Blackwell. 1920.

6 We turn first to the parallel quotations from Massinger and Shakespeare collocated by Mr Cruickshank to make manifest Massinger's indebtedness. One of the surest of tests is the way in which a poet borrows. Immature poets imitate; mature poets steal; bad poets deface what they take, and good poets make it into something better, or at least something different. The good poet welds his theft into a whole of feeling which is unique, utterly different from that from which it was torn; the bad poet throws it into something which has no cohesion. A good poet will usually borrow from authors remote in time, or alien in language, or diverse in interest. Chapman borrowed from Seneca; Shakespeare and Webster from Montaigne. The two great followers of Shakespeare, Webster and Tour-[207]neur, in their mature work do not borrow from him; he is too close to them to be of use to them in this way. Massinger, as Mr Cruickshank shows, borrows from Shakespeare a good deal. Let us profit by some of the quotations with which he has provided us –

MASSINGER:
    Can I call back yesterday, with all their aids
    That bow unto my sceptre? or restore
    My mind to that tranquillity and peace
    It then enjoyed?

SHAKESPEARE:
    Not poppy, nor mandragora,
    Nor all the drowsy syrops of the world
    Shall ever medicine thee to that sweet sleep
    Which thou owedst yesterday.

Massinger's is a general rhetorical question, the language just and pure, but colourless. Shakespeare's has particular significance; and the adjective 'drowsy' and the verb 'medicine' infuse a precise vigour. This is, on Massinger's part, an echo, rather than an imitation or a plagiarism – the basest, because least conscious form of borrowing. 'Drowsy syrop' is a condensation of meaning frequent in Shakespeare, but rare in Massinger.

MASSINGER:
    Thou didst not borrow of Vice her indirect,
    Crooked, and abject means.

SHAKESPEARE:
    God knows, my son,
    By what by-paths and indirect crook'd ways
    I met this crown.

Here, again, Massinger gives the general forensic statement, Shakespeare the particular image. 'Indirect crook'd' is forceful in Shakespeare; a mere pleonasm in Massinger. [208] 'Crook'd ways' is a metaphor; Massinger's phrase only the ghost of a metaphor.

MASSINGER:
    And now, in the evening,
    When thou shoud'st pass with honour to thy rest,
    Wilt thou fall like a meteor?

SHAKESPEARE:
    I shall fall
    Like a bright exhalation in the evening,
    And no man see me more.

Here the lines of Massinger have their own beauty. Still, a 'bright exhalation' appears to the eye and makes us catch our breath in the evening; 'meteor' is a dim simile; the word is worn.

MASSINGER:
    What you deliver to me shall be lock'd up
    In a strong cabinet, of which you yourself
    Shall keep the key.

SHAKESPEARE:
    'Tis in my memory locked,
    And you yourself shall keep the key of it.

In the preceding passage Massinger has squeezed his simile to death, here he drags it round the city at his heels; and how swift Shakespeare's figure is! We may add two more passages, not given by our commentator; here the model is Webster. They occur on the same page, an artless confession.

                Here he comes,
  His nose held up; he hath something in the wind,

is hardly comparable to 'the Cardinal lifts up his nose like a foul porpoise before a storm', and when we come upon

                as tann'd galley-slaves
  Pay such as do redeem them from the oar

[209] it is unnecessary to turn up the great lines in the *Duchess of Malfy*. Massinger fancied this galley-slave; for he comes with his oar again in the *Bondman* –

> Never did galley-slave shake off his chains,
> Or looked on his redemption from the oar. . . .

Now these are mature plays; and the *Roman Actor* (from which we have drawn the two previous extracts) is said to have been the preferred play of its author.

7 We may conclude directly from these quotations that Massinger's feeling for language had outstripped his feeling for things; that his eye and his vocabulary were not in co-operation. One of the greatest distinctions of several of his elder contemporaries – we name Middleton, Webster, Tourneur – is a gift for combining, for fusing into a single phrase, two or more diverse impressions.

> . . . in her strong toil of grace

of Shakespeare is such a fusion; the metaphor identifies itself with what suggests it; the resultant is one and is unique –

> Does the silk worm *expend* her yellow labours? . . .
> Why does yon fellow *falsify highways*
> And lays his life between the judge's lips
> To *refine* such a one? keeps horse and men
> To *beat their valours* for her?

> Let the common sewer take it from distinction. . . .
> Lust and forgetfulness have been amongst us. . . .

These lines of Tourneur and Middleton exhibit that perpetual slight alteration of language, words perpetually juxtaposed in new and sudden combinations, meanings perpetually *eingeschachtelt* into meanings, which evidences a very high development of the senses, a development of the English language which we have perhaps never equalled. And, indeed, with the end of Chapman, Middleton, Webster, Tourneur, Donne we end a period when the [210] intellect was immediately at the tips of the senses. Sensation became word and word was sensation. The next period is the period of Milton (though still with a Marvell in it); and this period is initiated by Massinger.

8 It is not that the word becomes less exact. Massinger is, in a wholly eulogistic sense, choice and correct. And the decay of the senses is not inconsistent with a greater sophistication of language. But every vital development in language is a development of feeling as well. The verse of Shakespeare and the major Shakespearian dramatists is an innovation of this kind, a true mutation of species. The verse practised by Massinger

is a different verse from that of his predecessors; but it is not a development based on, or resulting from, a new way of feeling. On the contrary, it seems to lead us away from feeling altogether.

9 We mean that Massinger must be placed as much at the beginning of one period as at the end of another. A certain Boyle, quoted by Mr Cruickshank, says that Milton's blank verse owes much to the study of Massinger's:

> In the indefinable touches which make up the music of a verse [says Boyle], in the artistic distribution of pauses, and in the unerring choice and grouping of just those words which strike the ear as the perfection of harmony, there are, if we leave Cyril Tourneur's *Atheist's Tragedy* out of the question, only two masters in the drama, Shakespeare in his latest period and Massinger.

10 This Boyle must have had a singular ear to have preferred Tourneur's secondary work to his *Revenger's Tragedy*, and one must think that he had never glanced at Ford. But though the appraisal be ludicrous, the praise is not undeserved. Mr Cruickshank has given us an excellent example of Massinger's syntax –

> What though my father
> Writ man before he was so, and confirm'd it,
> By numbering that day no part of his life
> In which he did not service to his country;
> [211] Was he to be free therefore from the laws
> And ceremonious form in your decrees?
> Or else because he did as much as man
> In those three memorable overthrows,
> At Granson, Morat, Nancy, where his master,
> The warlike Charalois, with whose misfortunes
> I bear his name, lost treasure, men, and life,
> To be excused from payment of those sums
> Which (his own patrimony spent) his zeal
> To serve his country forced him to take up?

It is impossible to deny the masterly construction of this passage; perhaps there is not one living poet who could do the like. It is impossible to deny the originality. The language is pure and correct, free from muddiness or turbidity. Massinger does not confuse metaphors, or heap them one upon another. He is lucid, though not easy. But if Massinger's age, 'without being exactly corrupt, lacks moral fibre', Massinger's verse, without being exactly corrupt, suffers from cerebral anemia. To say that an involved style is necessarily a bad style would be preposterous. But such a style should follow the involutions of a mode of perceiving, registering, and digesting impressions which is also involved. It is to be feared that the feeling of Massinger is simple and overlaid with received ideas. Had Massinger had a nervous system as refined as that of Middleton, Tourneur, Webster, or Ford, his style would be a triumph. But such a nature was not at hand, and Massinger precedes, not another Shakespeare, but Milton.

11 Massinger is, in fact, at a further remove from Shakespeare than that other precursor of Milton – John Fletcher. Fletcher was above all an opportunist, in his verse, in his momentary effects, never quite a pastiche; in his structure ready to sacrifice everything to the single scene. To Fletcher, because he was more intelligent, less will be forgiven. Fletcher had a cunning guess at feelings, and betrayed them; Massinger was unconscious and innocent. As an artisan of the theatre he is not inferior to Fletcher, and [212] his best tragedies have an honester unity than *Bonduca*. But the unity is superficial. In the *Roman Actor* the development of parts is out of all proportion to the central theme; in the *Unnatural Combat*, in spite of the deft handling of suspense and the quick shift from climax to a new suspense, the first part of the play is the hatred of Malefort for his son and the second part is his passion for his daughter. It is theatrical skill, not an artistic conscience arranging emotions, that holds the two parts together. In the *Duke of Milan* the appearance of Sforza at the Court of his conqueror only delays the action, or rather breaks the emotional rhythm. And we have named three of Massinger's best.

12 A dramatist who so skilfully welds parts together which have no reason for being together, who fabricates plays so well knit and so remote from unity, we should expect to exhibit the same stylistic cunning in character. Mr Cruickshank, Coleridge, and Leslie Stephen are pretty well agreed that Massinger is no master of characterisation. You can, in fact, put together heterogeneous parts to form a lively play; but a character, to be living, must be conceived from some emotional unity. A character is not to be composed of scattered observations of human nature, but of parts which are felt together. Hence it is that although Massinger's failure to draw a moving character is no greater than his failure to make a whole play, and probably springs from the same defective sensitiveness, yet the failure in character is more conspicuous and more disastrous. A 'living' character is not necessarily 'true to life'. It is a person whom we can see and hear, whether he be true or false to human nature as we

know it. What the creator of character needs is not so much knowledge of motives as keen sensibility; the dramatist need not understand people; but he must be exceptionally aware of them. This awareness was not given to Massinger. He inherits the traditions of conduct, female chastity, hymeneal sanctity, the fashion of honour, without either criticising or inform-[213]ing them from his own experience. In the earlier drama these conventions are merely a framework, or an alloy necessary for working the metal; the metal itself consisted of unique emotions resulting inevitably from the circumstances, resulting or inhering as inevitably as the properties of a chemical compound. Middleton's heroine, for instance, in *The Changeling*, exclaims in the well-known words –

> Why, 'tis impossible thou canst be so wicked,
> To shelter such a cunning cruelty
> To make his death the murderer of my honour!

The word 'honour' in such a situation is out of date, but the emotion of Beatrice at that moment, given the conditions, is as permanent and substantial as anything in human nature. The emotion of Othello in Act V is the emotion of a man who discovers that the worst part of his own soul has been exploited by someone more clever than he; it is this emotion carried by the writer to a very high degree of intensity. Even in so late and so decayed a drama as that of Ford, the framework of emotions and morals of the time is only the vehicle for statements of feeling which are unique and imperishable: Ford's and Ford's only.

13 What may be considered corrupt or decadent in the morals of Massinger is not an alteration or diminution in morals; it is simply the disappearance of all the personal and real emotions which this morality supported and into which it introduced a kind of order. As soon as the emotions disappear the morality which ordered it appears hideous. Puritanism itself became repulsive only when it appeared as the survival of a restraint after the feelings which it restrained had gone. When Massinger's ladies resist temptation they do not appear to undergo any important emotion; they merely know what is expected of them; they manifest themselves to us as lubricious prudes. Any age has its conventions; and any age might appear absurd when its conventions get into the hands of a man like Massinger – a man, we mean, of so exceptionally superior [214] a literary talent as Massinger's, and so paltry an imagination. The Elizabethan morality was an important convention; important, because it was not consciously of one social class alone, because it provided a framework for emotions to which all classes could respond, and it hindered no feeling. It was not hypocritical, and it did not suppress; its dark corners are haunted

by the ghost of Mary Fitton and perhaps greater. It is a subject which has not been sufficiently investigated. Fletcher and Massinger rendered it ridiculous; not by not believing it, but because they were men of great talents who could not vivify it; because they could not fit into it passionate, complete human characters.

14 The tragedy of Massinger is interesting chiefly according to the definition given before; the highest degree of verbal excellence compatible with the most rudimentary development of the senses. Massinger succeeds better in something which is not tragedy; in the romantic comedy. *A Very Woman* deserves all the praise that Swinburne, with his almost unerring gift of selection, has bestowed upon it. The probable collaboration of Fletcher had the happiest result; for certainly that admirable comic personage, the tipsy Borachia, is handled with more humour than we expect of Massinger. It is a play which would be enjoyable on the stage. The form, however, of romantic comedy is itself inferior and decadent. There is an inflexibility about the poetic drama which is by no means a matter of classical, or neoclassical, or pseudo-classical law. The poetic drama might develop forms highly different from those of Greece or England, India or Japan. Conceded the utmost freedom, the romantic drama would yet remain inferior. The poetic drama must have an emotional unity, let the emotion be whatever you like. It must have a dominant tone; and if this be strong enough, the most heterogeneous emotions may be made to reinforce it. The romantic comedy is a skilful concoction of inconsistent emotion, a *revue* of emotion. *A Very Woman* is surpassingly well plotted. The [215] debility of romantic drama does not depend upon extravagant setting, or preposterous events, or inconceivable coincidences: all these might be found in a serious tragedy or comedy. It consists in an internal incoherence of feelings, a concatenation of emotions which signifies nothing.

15 From this type of play, so eloquent of emotional disorder, there was no swing back of the pendulum. Changes never come by a simple reinfusion into the form which the life has just left. The romantic drama was not a new form. Massinger dealt not with emotions so much as with the social abstractions of emotions, more generalised and therefore more quickly and easily interchangeable within the confines of a single action. He was not guided by direct communications through the nerves. Romantic drama tended, accordingly, toward what is sometimes called the 'typical', but which is not the truly typical; for the *typical* figure in a drama is always particularised – an individual. The tendency of the romantic drama was towards a form which continued it in removing

its more conspicuous vices, was towards a more severe external order. This form was the Heroic Drama. We look into Dryden's 'Essay on Heroic Plays', and we find that 'love and valour ought to be the subject of an heroic poem'. Massinger, in his destruction of the old drama, had prepared the way for Dryden. The intellect had perhaps exhausted the old conventions. It was not able to supply the impoverishment of feeling.

16 Such are the reflections aroused by an examination of some of Massinger's plays in the light of Mr Cruickshank's statement that Massinger's age 'had much culture, but, without being exactly corrupt, lacked moral fibre'. The statement may be supported. In order to fit into our estimate of Massinger the two admirable comedies – *A New Way to Pay Old Debts* and *The City Madam* – a more extensive research would be required than is possible within our limits.

[216] II

17 Massinger's tragedy may be summarised for the unprepared reader as being very dreary. It is dreary, unless one is prepared by a somewhat extensive knowledge of his livelier contemporaries to grasp without fatigue precisely the elements in it which are capable of giving pleasure; or unless one is incited by a curious interest in versification. In comedy, however, Massinger was one of the few masters in the language. He was a master in a comedy which is serious, even sombre; and in one aspect of it there are only two names to mention with his: those of Marlowe and Jonson. In comedy, as a matter of fact, a greater variety of methods were discovered and employed than in tragedy. The method of Kyd, as developed by Shakespeare, was the standard for English tragedy down to Otway and to Shelley. But both individual temperament, and varying epochs, made more play with comedy. The comedy of Lyly is one thing; that of Shakespeare, followed by Beaumont and Fletcher, is another; and that of Middleton is a third. And Massinger, while he has his own comedy, is nearer to Marlowe and Jonson than to any of these.

18 Massinger was, in fact, as a comic writer, fortunate in the moment at which he wrote. His comedy is transitional; but it happens to be one of those transitions which contain some merit not anticipated by predecessors or refined upon by later writers. The comedy of Jonson is nearer to caricature; that of Middleton a more photographic delineation of low life. Massinger is nearer to Restoration comedy, and more like his contemporary, Shirley, in assuming a certain social level, certain distinctions of class, as a postulate of his comedy. The resemblance to later comedy is also the important point of difference between Massinger

and earlier comedy. But Massinger's comedy differs just as widely from the comedy of manners proper; he is closer to that in his romantic drama – in *A Very Woman* – than in *A New Way to Pay Old Debts*; in his comedy his interest is [217] not in the follies of love-making or the absurdities of social pretence, but in the unmasking of villainy. Just as the Old Comedy of Molière differs in principle from the New Comedy of Marivaux, so the Old Comedy of Massinger differs from the New Comedy of his contemporary Shirley. And as in France, so in England, the more farcical comedy was the more serious. Massinger's great comic rogues, Sir Giles Overreach and Luke Frugal, are members of the large English family which includes Barabas and Sir Epicure Mammon, and from which Sir Tunbelly Clumsy claims descent.

19 What distinguishes Massinger from Marlowe and Jonson is in the main an inferiority. The greatest comic characters of these two dramatists are slight work in comparison with Shakespeare's best – Falstaff has a third dimension and Epicure Mammon has only two. But this slightness is part of the nature of the art which Jonson practised, a smaller art than Shakespeare's. The inferiority of Massinger to Jonson is an inferiority, not of one type of art to another, but within Jonson's type. It is a simple deficiency. Marlowe's and Jonson's comedies were a view of life; they were, as great literature is, the transformation of a personality into a personal work of art, their lifetime's work, long or short. Massinger is not simply a smaller personality; his personality hardly exists. He did not, out of his own personality, build a world of art, as Shakespeare and Marlowe and Jonson built.

20 In the fine pages which Rémy de Gourmont devotes to Flaubert in his *Problème du Style*, the great critic declares:

> La vie est un dépouillement. Le but de l'activité propre de l'homme est de nettoyer sa personnalité, de la laver de toutes les souillures qu'y déposa l'éducation, de la dégager de toutes les empreintes qu'y laissèrent nos admirations adolescentes;

and again:

> Flaubert incorporait toute sa sensibilité à ses oeuvres.... [218] Hors de ses livres, où il se transvasait goutte à goutte, jusqu'à la lie, Flaubert est fort peu intéressant.

Of Shakespeare notably, of Jonson less, of Marlowe (and of Keats to the term of life allowed him), one can say that they *se transvasaient goutte à goutte*; and in England, which has produced a prodigious number of men of genius and comparatively few works of art, there are not many writers of whom one can say it. Certainly not of Massinger. A brilliant master of technique, he was not, in this profound sense, an artist. And so we come to inquire how, if this is so, he could have written two great comedies. We shall probably be obliged to conclude that a large part of their excellence is, in some way which should be defined, fortuitous; and that therefore they are, however remarkable, not works of perfect art.

21 The objection raised by Leslie Stephen to Massinger's method of revealing a villain has great cogency; but I am inclined to believe that the cogency is due to a somewhat different reason from that which Leslie Stephen assigns. His statement is too *apriorist* to be quite trustworthy. There is no reason why a comedy or a tragedy villain should not declare himself, and in as long a period as the author likes; but the sort of villain who may run on in this way is a simple villain (simple, not *simpliste*). Barabas and Volpone can declare their character, because they have no inside; appearance and reality are coincident; they are forces in particular directions. Massinger's two villains are not simple. Giles Overreach is essentially a great force directed upon small objects; a great force, a small mind; the terror of a dozen parishes instead of the conqueror of a world. The force is misapplied, attenuated, thwarted, by the man's vulgarity; he is a great man of the City, without fear, but with the most abject awe of the aristocracy. He is accordingly not simple, but a product of a certain civilisation, and he is not wholly conscious. His monologues are meant to be not what he thinks he is, but what he really is: and yet they are not the truth about him, and he himself cer-[219]tainly does not know the truth. To declare himself, therefore, is impossible.

> Nay, when my ears are pierced with widows' cries,
> And undone orphans wash with tears my threshold,
> I only think what 'tis to have my daughter
> Right honourable; and 'tis a powerful charm
> Makes me insensible of remorse, or pity,
> Or the least sting of conscience.

This is the wrong note. Elsewhere we have the right:

> Thou art a fool;
> In being out of office, I am out of danger;
> Where, if I were a justice, besides the trouble,
> I might or out of wilfulness, or error,
> Run myself finely into a praemunire,
> And so become a prey to the informer,

> No, I'll have none of 't; 'tis enough I keep
> Greedy at my devotion: so he serve
> My purposes, let him hang, or damn, I care not . . .

And how well tuned, well modulated, here, the diction! The man is audible and visible. But from passages like the first we may be permitted to infer that Massinger was unconscious of trying to develop a different kind of character from any that Marlowe or Jonson had invented.

22 Luke Frugal, in *The City Madam*, is not so great a character as Sir Giles Overreach. But Luke Frugal just misses being almost the greatest of all hypocrites. His humility in the first act of the play is more than half real. The error in his portraiture is not the extravagant hocus-pocus of supposed Indian necromancers by which he is so easily duped, but the premature disclosure of villainy in his temptation of the two apprentices of his brother. But for this, he would be a perfect chameleon of circumstance. Here, again, we feel that Massinger was conscious only of inventing a rascal of the old simple farce type. But the play is not a farce, in the sense in which *The Jew of Malta*, *The Alchemist*, [220] *Bartholomew Fair* are farces. Massinger had not the personality to create great farce, and he was too serious to invent trivial farce. The ability to perform that slight distortion of *all* the elements in the world of a play or a story, so that this world is complete in itself, which was given to Marlowe and Jonson (and to Rabelais) and which is prerequisite to great farce, was denied to Massinger. On the other hand, his temperament was more closely related to theirs than to that of Shirley or the Restoration wits. His two comedies therefore occupy a place by themselves. His ways of thinking and feeling isolate him from both the Elizabethan and the later Caroline mind. He might almost have been a great realist; he is killed by conventions which were suitable for the preceding literary generation, but not for his. Had Massinger been a greater man, a man of more intellectual courage, the current of English literature immediately after him might have taken a different course. The defect is precisely a defect of personality. He is not, however, the only man of letters who, at the moment when a new view of life is wanted, has looked at life through the eyes of his predecessors, and only at manners through his own.

Variants:
1 fine and fragmentary] fragmentary and fine *TLS* (1920), *SW*
[Between 'into a' and 'English criticism':] place; and if we still aspire to settle this distinguished and unread playwright, we shall find Professor Cruickshank's book more useful, perhaps, than any of them. *TLS* (1920)

2 [No new para. in *TLS* (1920).]
Canon Cruickshank's book] Mr. Cruickshank's book *TLS* (1920), *SW*
[Fn.: after 'Cruickshank':] M.A., Professor of Greek in the University of Durham. Blackwell, Oxford. 15s. net. *TLS* (1920) [No fn. in *SW*.]
[Between 'rather than a judgement.' and 'It is difficult':] Mr Cruickshank, like most scholars, feels obliged to offer some undeveloped generalizations which do not attach themselves at once to his evidence. *TLS* (1920)

3 [No new para. in *TLS* (1920).]

5 [No new para. in *SW*.]

6 *Malfy*] *Malfi TLS* (1920), *SW*

7 co-operation] close co-operation *TLS* (1920)

10 take up?] take up! *TLS* (1920), *SW*

14 of selection] for selection *TLS* (1920)), *SW*

[Part II] Title The Old Comedy *A.* (1920)

17 [Before 'Massinger's tragedy may be summarised':] In this country the co-operation between scholarship and criticism has never been so efficient as it has in France. Mr Cruickshank modestly hopes that his book on Massinger will stimulate the production of similar books on other writers of the period. The ignorance of English Literature is very great; and we search our breasts in vain for an echo to his hope; the most we can expect is that the subsequent writers on Massinger will be forced to recognise the existence of Mr Cruickshank's book. For it is a conscientious work, which contains, we suppose, all the information, and nearly all the serious speculations possible, about its subject. In expression of judgement and comparison, it is useful; for if any opinion is to be expressed of Mr Cruickshank's criticism, it is deficient rather than aberrant. It will lead no one astray and it ought to provoke reflection. *A. (1920)*

IV Dante

SE, 223–63.

Originally publ. in book form by Faber & Faber in 1929: Gallup A13.

It looks as if Eliot corrected some of the Italian from 1929 in *SE* (see the variants below). Eliot's quotations are often inaccurate.

I

THE *INFERNO*

1 In my own experience of the appreciation of poetry I have always found that the less I knew about the poet and his work, before I began to read it, the better. A quotation, a critical remark, an enthusiastic essay, may well be the accident that sets one to reading a particular author; but an elaborate preparation of historical and biographical knowledge has always been to me a barrier. I am not defending poor scholarship; and I admit that such experience, solidified into a maxim, would be very

difficult to apply in the study of Latin and Greek. But with authors of one's own speech, and even with some of those of other modern languages, the procedure is possible. At least, it is better to be spurred to acquire scholarship because you enjoy the poetry, than to suppose that you enjoy the poetry because you have acquired the scholarship. I was passionately fond of certain French poetry long before I could have translated two verses of it correctly. With Dante the discrepancy between enjoyment and understanding was still wider.

2 I do not counsel anyone to postpone the study of Italian grammar until he has read Dante, but certainly there is an immense amount of knowledge which, until one has read some of his poetry with intense pleasure – that is, with as keen pleasure as one is capable of getting from any poetry – is positively undesirable. In saying this I am avoiding two possible extremes of criticism. One might say that understanding of the scheme, the philosophy, the con-[224]cealed meanings, of Dante's verse was *essential* to appreciation; and on the other hand one might say that these things were quite irrelevant, that the poetry in his poems was one thing, which could be enjoyed by itself without studying a framework which had served the author in producing the poetry but could not serve the reader in enjoying it. The latter error is the more prevalent, and is probably the reason why many people's knowledge of the *Comedy* is limited to the *Inferno*, or even to certain passages in it. The enjoyment of the *Divine Comedy* is a continuous process. If you get nothing out of it at first, you probably never will; but if from your first deciphering of it there comes now and then some direct shock of poetic intensity, nothing but laziness can deaden the desire for fuller and fuller knowledge.

3 What is surprising about the poetry of Dante is that it is, in one sense, extremely easy to read. It is a test (a positive test, I do not assert that it is always valid negatively), that genuine poetry can communicate before it is understood. The impression can be verified on fuller knowledge; I have found with Dante and with several other poets in languages in which I was unskilled, that about such impressions there was nothing fanciful. They were not due, that is, to *mis*understanding the passage, or to reading into it something not there, or to accidental sentimental evocations out of my own past. The impression was new, and of, I believe, the objective 'poetic emotion'. There are more detailed reasons for this experience on the first reading of Dante, and for my saying that he is easy to read. I do not mean that he writes very simple Italian, for he does not; or that his content is simple or always simply expressed. It is often expressed with such a force of compression that the elucidation of

three lines needs a paragraph, and their allusions a page of commentary. What I have in mind is that Dante is, in a sense to be defined (for the word means little by itself), the most *universal* of poets in the modern languages. That does not mean that he is 'the greatest', or that [225] he is the most comprehensive – there is greater variety and detail in Shakespeare. Dante's universality is not solely a personal matter. The Italian language, and especially the Italian language in Dante's age, gains much by being the product of universal Latin. There is something much more *local* about the languages in which Shakespeare and Racine had to express themselves. This is not to say, either, that English and French are inferior, as vehicles of poetry, to Italian. But the Italian vernacular of the late Middle Ages was still very close to Latin, as literary expression, for the reason that the men, like Dante, who used it, were trained, in philosophy and all abstract subjects, in medieval Latin. Now medieval Latin is a very fine language; fine prose and fine verse were written in it; and it had the quality of a highly developed and literary Esperanto. When you read modern philosophy, in English, French, German, and Italian, you must be struck by national or racial differences of thought: modern languages *tend* to separate abstract thought (mathematics is now the only universal language); but medieval Latin tended to concentrate on what men of various races and lands could think together. Some of the character of this universal language seems to me to inhere in Dante's Florentine speech; and the localisation ('Florentine' speech) seems if anything to emphasise the universality, because it cuts across the modern division of nationality. To enjoy any French or German poetry, I think one needs to have some sympathy with the French or German mind; Dante, none the less an Italian and a patriot, is first a European.

4 This difference, which is one of the reasons why Dante is 'easy to read', may be discussed in more particular manifestations. The style of Dante has a peculiar lucidity – a *poetic* as distinguished from an *intellectual* lucidity. The thought may be obscure, but the word is lucid, or rather translucent. In English poetry words have a kind of opacity which is part of their beauty. I do not mean that the beauty of English poetry is what is called mere 'verbal beauty'. It [226] is rather that words have associations, and the groups of words *in* association have associations, which is a kind of local self-consciousness, because they are the growth of a *particular* civilisation; and the same thing is true of other modern languages. The Italian of Dante, though essentially the Italian of to-day, is not in this way a modern language. The culture of Dante was not of one European country but of Europe. I am aware, of course, of a directness of speech which Dante shares with other great poets of pre-

Reformation and pre-Renaissance times, notably Chaucer and Villon. Undoubtedly there is something in common between the three, so much that I should expect an admirer of any one of them to be an admirer of the others; and undoubtedly there is an opacity, or inspissation of poetic style throughout Europe after the Renaissance. But the lucidity and universality of Dante are far beyond those qualities in Villon and Chaucer, though they are akin.

5 Dante is 'easier to read', for a foreigner who does not know Italian very well, for other reasons: but all related to this central reason, that in Dante's time Europe, with all its dissensions and dirtiness, was mentally more united than we can now conceive. It is not particularly the Treaty of Versailles that has separated nation from nation; nationalism was born long before; and the process of disintegration which for our generation culminates in that treaty began soon after Dante's time. One of the reasons for Dante's 'easiness' is the following – but first I must make a digression.

6 I must explain why I have said that Dante is 'easy to read', instead of talking about his 'universality'. The latter word would have been much easier to use. But I do not wish to be thought to claim a universality for Dante which I deny to Shakespeare or Molière or Sophocles. Dante is no more 'universal' than Shakespeare: though I feel that we can come nearer to understanding Dante than a foreigner can come to understanding those others. Shakespeare, or even Sophocles, or even Racine and Molière, are deal-[227]ing with what is as universally human as the material of Dante; but they had no choice but to deal with it in a more local way. As I have said, the Italian of Dante is very near in feeling to medieval Latin: and of the medieval philosophers whom Dante read, and who were read by learned men of his time, there were, for instance, St Thomas who was an Italian, St Thomas's predecessor Albertus, who was a German, Abelard who was French, and Hugh and Richard of St Victor who were Scots. For the *medium* that Dante had to use compare the opening of the *Inferno*

> Nel mezzo del cammin di nostra vita
> > mi ritrovai per una selva oscura,
> > che la diritta via era smarrita.
>
> In the middle of the journey of our life I found myself in a dark wood, having lost the straight path.

with the lines with which Duncan is introduced to Macbeth's castle:

> This castle hath a pleasant seat; the air
> Nimbly and sweetly recommends itself
> Unto our gentle senses.
>   This guest of summer,
> The temple-haunting martlet, does approve
> By his loved masonry that the heaven's breath
> Smells wooingly here: no jutty, frieze,
> Buttress, nor coign of vantage, but this bird
> Hath made his pendant bed and procreant cradle:
> Where they most breed and haunt, I have observed
> The air is delicate.

   I do not at all pretend that we appreciate everything, even in one single line of Dante, that a cultivated Italian can appreciate. But I do maintain that more is lost in translating Shakespeare into Italian than in translating Dante into English. How can a foreigner find words to convey in his own language just that combination of intelligibility and remoteness that we get in many phrases of Shakespeare?

[228] 7 I am not considering whether the language of Dante or Shakespeare is superior, for I cannot admit the question: I merely affirm that the differences are such as make Dante easier for a foreigner. Dante's advantages are not due to greater genius, but to the fact that he wrote when Europe was still more or less one. And even had Chaucer or Villon been exact contemporaries of Dante, they would still have been farther, linguistically as well as geographically, from the centre of Europe than Dante.

8 But the simplicity of Dante has another detailed reason. He not only thought in a way in which every man of his culture in the whole of Europe then thought, but he employed a method which was common and commonly understood throughout Europe. I do not intend, in this essay, to go into questions of disputed interpretations of Dante's allegory. What is important for my purpose is the fact that the allegorical method was a definite method not confined to Italy; and the fact, apparently paradoxical, that the allegorical method makes for simplicity and intelligibility. We incline to think of allegory as a tiresome cross-word puzzle. We incline to associate it with dull poems (at best, *The Romance of the Rose*), and in a great poem to ignore it as irrelevant. What we ignore is, in a case like Dante's, its particular effect towards lucidity of style.

9 I do not recommend, in first reading the first canto of the *Inferno*, worrying about the identity of the Leopard, the Lion, or the She-Wolf. It is really better, at the start, not to know or care what they do mean. What we should consider is not so much the meaning of the images, but the reverse process, that which led a man having an idea to express it in images. We have to consider the type of mind which by nature and *practice* tended to express itself in allegory: and for a competent poet, allegory means *clear visual images*. And clear visual images are given much more intensity by having a meaning – we do not need to know what that meaning is, but in our awareness of the image we [229] must be aware that the meaning is there too. Allegory is only one poetic method, but it is a method which has very great advantages.

10 Dante's is a *visual* imagination. It is a visual imagination in a different sense from that of a modern painter of still life: it is visual in the sense that he lived in an age in which men still saw visions. It was a psychological habit, the trick of which we have forgotten, but as good as any of our own. We have nothing but dreams, and we have forgotten that seeing visions – a practice now relegated to the aberrant and uneducated – was once a more significant, interesting, and disciplined kind of dreaming. We take it for granted that our dreams spring from below: possibly the quality of our dreams suffers in consequence.

11 All that I ask of the reader, at this point, is to clear his mind, if he can, of every prejudice against allegory, and to admit at least that it was not a device to enable the uninspired to write verses, but really a mental habit, which when raised to the point of genius can make a great poet as well as a great mystic or saint. And it is the allegory which makes it possible for the reader who is not even a good Italian scholar to enjoy Dante. Speech varies, but our eyes are all the same. And allegory was not a local Italian custom, but a universal European method.

12 Dante's attempt is to make us see what he saw. He therefore employs very simple language, and very few metaphors, for allegory and metaphor do not get on well together. And there is a peculiarity about his *comparisons* which is worth noticing in passing.

13 There is a well-known comparison or simile in the great XVth canto of the *Inferno*, which Matthew Arnold singled out, rightly, for high praise; which is characteristic of the way in which Dante employs these figures. He is speaking of the crowd in Hell who peered at him and his guide under a dim light:

> e sì ver noi aguzzevan le ciglia,
> come vecchio sartor fa nella cruna

[230] and sharpened their vision (knitted their brows) at us, like an old tailor peering at the eye of his needle.

The purpose of this type of simile is solely to make us *see more definitely* the scene which Dante has put before us in the preceding lines.

> she looks like sleep,
> As she would catch another Antony
> In her strong toil of grace.

The image of Shakespeare's is much more complicated than Dante's, and more complicated than it looks. It has the grammatical form of a kind of simile (the 'as if' form), but of course 'catch in her toil' is a metaphor. But whereas the simile of Dante is merely to make you see more clearly how the people looked, and is explanatory, the figure of Shakespeare is expansive rather than intensive; its purpose is to *add* what you see (either on the stage or in your imagination) a reminder of that fascination of Cleopatra which shaped her history and that of the world, and of that fascination being so strong that it prevails even in death. It is more elusive, and it is less possible to convey without close knowledge of the English language. Between men who could make such inventions as these there can be no question of greater or less. But as the whole poem of Dante is, if you like, one vast metaphor, there is hardly any place for metaphor in the detail of it.

14 There is all the more reason to acquaint oneself well with Dante's poem first part by part, even dwelling specially on the parts that one likes most at first, because we cannot extract the full significance of any part without knowing the whole. We cannot understand the inscription at Hell Gate:

> Giustizia mosse il mio alto Fattore;
>   fecemi la divina Potestate,
>   la somma Sapienza e il primo Amore.

> Justice moved my high Maker; what made me were the divine Power, the supreme Wisdom, and the primal Love.

[231] until we have ascended to the highest Heaven and returned. But we can understand the first Episode that strikes most readers, that of Paolo and Francesca, enough to be moved by it as much as by any poetry, on

the first reading. It is introduced by two similes of the same explanatory nature as that which I have just quoted:

> E come gli stornei ne portan l'ali,
>> nel freddo tempo, a schiera larga e piena,
>> così quel fiato gli spiriti mali;

> And as their wings bear along the starlings, at the cold season, in large full troop.

> E come i gru van cantando lor lai
>> facendo in aer di sè lunga riga;
>> cosi vid' io venir, traendo guai,
> ombre portate dalla detta briga;

> And as the cranes go chanting their lays, making themselves a long streak in the air, so I saw the wailing shadows come, wailing, carried on the striving wind.

We can see and feel the situation of the two lost lovers, though we do not yet understand the meaning which Dante gives it. Taking such an episode by itself, we can get as much out of it as we get from the reading of a whole single play of Shakespeare. We do not understand Shakespeare from a single reading, and certainly not from a single play. There is a relation between the various plays of Shakespeare, taken in order; and it is a work of years to venture even one individual interpretation of the pattern in Shakespeare's carpet. It is not certain that Shakespeare himself knew what it was. It is perhaps a larger pattern than Dante's, but the pattern is less distinct. We can read with full comprehension the lines:

> Noi leggevamo un giorno per diletto
>> di Lancillotto, come amor lo strinse;
>> soli eravamo e senza alcun sospetto.
> [232] Per più fiate gli occhi ci sospinse
>> quella lettura, e scolorocci il viso;
>> ma solo un punto fu quel che ci vinse.
> Quando leggemmo il disiato riso
>> esser baciato da cotanto amante,
>> questi, che mai da me non fia diviso,
> La bocca mi baciò tutto tremante:

> One day, for pastime, we read of Lancelot, how love constrained him; we were alone, and without all suspicion. Several times that reading urged our eyes to meet, and changed the colour of our faces; but one moment alone it was that overcame us. When we

read how the fond smile was kissed by such a lover, he, who shall never be divided from me, kissed my mouth all trembling.

When we come to fit the episode into its place in the whole *Comedy*, and see how this punishment is related to all other punishments and to purgations and rewards, we can appreciate better the subtle psychology of the simple line of Francesca:

> se fosse amico il re dell' universo

> if the King of the Universe were our friend. . . .

or of the line

> Amor, che a nullo amato amar perdona

> Love, which to no loved one permits excuse for loving. . . .

or indeed of the line already quoted:

> questi, che mai da me non fia diviso
> he, who shall never be divided from me. . . .

Proceeding through the *Inferno* on a first reading, we get a succession of phantasmagoric but clear images, of images which are coherent, in that each reinforces the last; of glimpses of individuals made memorable by a perfect phrase, like that of the proud Farinata degli Uberti:

> ed ei s'ergea col petto e colla fronte,
> come avesse lo inferno in gran dispitto.

> [233] He rose upright with breast and countenance, as though he entertained great scorn of Hell.

and of particular longer episodes, which remain separately in the memory. I think that among those which impress themselves most at the first reading are the episode of Brunetto Latini (Canto XV), Ulysses (Canto XXVI), Bertrand de Born (Canto XXVIII), Adamo di Brescia (Canto XXX), and Ugolino (Canto XXXIII).

15 Although I think it would be a mistake to skip, and find it much better to await these episodes until we come to them in due course, they certainly remain in my memory as the parts of the *Inferno* which first convinced me, and especially the Brunetto and the Ulysses episodes, for which I was unprepared by quotation or allusion. And the two may well be put together: for the first is Dante's testimony of a loved master of arts, the second his reconstruction of a legendary figure of ancient epic; yet both have the quality of *surprise* which Poe declared to be essential to

poetry. This *surprise*, at its highest, could by nothing be better illustrated than by the final lines with which Dante dismisses the damned master whom he loves and respects:

> Poi si rivolse, e parve di coloro
> che coronno a Verona il drappo verde
> per la campagna; e parve di costoro
> quegli che vince e non colui che perde.
>
> Then he turned back, and seemed like one of those who run for the green cloth at Verona through the open field; and of them he seemed like him who wins, and not like him who loses.

One does not need to know anything about the race for the roll of green cloth, to be *hit* by these lines; and in making Brunetto, so fallen, *run like the winner*, a quality is given to the punishment which belongs only to the greatest poetry. So Ulysses, unseen in the hornèd wave of flame,

> Lo maggior corno della fiamma antica
> cominciò a crollarsi mormorando,
> pur come quella cui vento affatica.
> [234] Indi la cima qua e là menando,
> come fosse la lingua che parlasse,
> gittò voce di fuori e disse: 'Quando
> mi diparti' da Circe, che sottrasse
> me più d'un anno la presso a Gaeta....'
>
> The greater horn of the ancient flame began to shake itself, murmuring, like a flame struggling against the wind. Then moving to and fro the peak, as though it were the tongue that spoke, threw forth a voice and said: 'When I left Circe, who kept me more than a year there near Gaeta....'

is a creature of the pure poetic imagination, apprehensible apart from place and time and the scheme of the poem. The Ulysses episode may strike us first as a kind of excursion, an irrelevance, a self-indulgence on the part of Dante taking a holiday from his Christian scheme. But when we know the whole poem, we recognise how cunningly and convincingly Dante has made to fit in real men, his contemporaries, friends, and enemies, recent historical personages, legendary and Biblical figures, and figures of ancient fiction. He has been reproved or smiled at for satisfying personal grudges by putting in Hell men whom he knew and hated; but these, as well as Ulysses, are transformed in the whole; for the real and the unreal are all representative of types of sin, suffering, fault, and merit, and all become of the same reality and contemporary.

The Ulysses episode is particularly 'readable', I think, because of its continuous straightforward narrative, and because to an English reader the comparison with Tennyson's poem – a perfect poem at that – is very instructive. It is worth while noticing the greatly superior degree of *simplification* of Dante's version. Tennyson, like most poets, like most even of those whom we can call great poets, has to get his effect with a certain amount of *forcing*. Thus the line about the sea which

> moans round with many voices,

a true specimen of Tennyson-Virgilianism, is too *poetical* in comparison with Dante, to be the highest poetry. (Only [235] Shakespeare can be so 'poetical' without giving any effect of overloading, or distracting us from the main issue:

> Put up your bright swords or the dew will rust them.)

Ulysses and his shipmates pass through the pillars of Hercules, that 'narrow pass' where

> ov' Ercole segnò li suoi riguardi
> acciocchè l'uom più oltre non si metta.

Hercules set his marks, so that man should pass no farther.

> 'O frati,' dissi, 'che per cento milia
>   perigli siete giunti all'occidente,
>   a questa tanto picciola vigilia
> de' vostri sensi, ch'è del rimanente,
>   non vogliate negar l'esperienza
>   di retro al sol, del mondo senza gente.
> Considerate la vostra semenza,
>   fatti non foste a viver come bruti
>   ma per seguir virtute e conoscenza.'

'O brothers!' I said, who through a hundred thousand dangers have reached the West, deny not, to this so brief vigil of your senses that remains, experience of the world without men that lies behind the sun. Consider your nature, you were made not to live like beasts, but to pursue virtue and knowledge.

They fare forth until suddenly

> n'apparve una montagna bruna
> per la distanza, e parvemi alta tanto
> quanto veduta non n'aveva alcuna.

> Noi ci allegrammo, e tosto tornò in pianto,
> > chè dalla nuova terra un turbo nacque,
> > e percosse del legno il primo canto.
> Tre volte il fe' girar con tutte l'acque,
> > alla quarta levar la poppa in suso,
> > e la prora ire in giù, com' altrui piacque,
> infin che il mar fu sopra noi richiuso.

[236] there appeared a mountain brown in the distance, and it seemed to me the highest that I had ever seen. We rejoiced, but soon our joy was turned to lamentation: for a storm came up from the new land, and caught the stem of our ship. Three times it whirled her round with all the waters; the fourth time it heaved up the stern and drove her down at the head, as pleased Another; until the sea closed over us.

The story of Ulysses, as told by Dante, reads like a straightforward piece of romance, a well-told seaman's yarn; Tennyson's Ulysses is primarily a very self-conscious poet. But Tennyson's poem is flat, it has only two dimensions; there is nothing more in it than what the average Englishman, with a feeling for verbal beauty, can see. We do not need, at first, to know what mountain the mountain was, or what the words mean *as pleased Another*, to feel that Dante's sense has further depths.

16 It is worth pointing out again how very right was Dante to introduce among his historical characters at least one character who even to him could hardly have been more than a fiction. For the *Inferno* is relieved from any question of pettiness or arbitrariness in Dante's selection of damned. It reminds us that Hell is not a place but a *state*; that man is damned or blessed in the creatures of his imagination as well as in men who have actually lived; and that Hell, though a state, is a state which can only be thought of, and perhaps only experienced, by the projection of sensory images; and that the resurrection of the body has perhaps a deeper meaning than we understand. But these are such thoughts as come only after many readings; they are not necessary for the first poetic enjoyment.

17 The experience of a poem is the experience both of a moment and of a lifetime. It is very much like our intenser experiences of other human beings. There is a first, or an early moment which is unique, of shock and surprise, even of terror (*Ego dominus tuus*); a moment which can never be forgotten, but which is never repeated integrally; and yet which would become destitute of significance if it did not [237] survive in a larger

whole of experience; which survives inside a deeper and a calmer feeling. The majority of poems one outgrows and outlives, as one outgrows and outlives the majority of human passions; Dante's is one of those which one can only just hope to grow up to at the end of life.

17 The last canto (XXXIV) is probably the most difficult on first reading. The vision of Satan may seem grotesque, especially if we have fixed in our minds the curly-haired Byronic hero of Milton; it is too like a Satan in a fresco in Siena. Certainly no more than the Divine Spirit can the Essence of Evil be confined in one form and place; and I confess that I tend to get from Dante the impression of a Devil suffering like the human damned souls; whereas I feel that the *kind* of suffering experienced by the Spirit of Evil should be represented as utterly different. I can only say that Dante made the best of a bad job. In putting Brutus, the noble Brutus, and Cassius with Judas Iscariot he will also disturb at first the English reader, for whom Brutus and Cassius must always be the Brutus and Cassius of Shakespeare: but if my justification of Ulysses is valid, then the presence of Brutus and Cassius is also. If any one is repelled by the last canto of the *Inferno*, I can only ask him to wait until he has read and lived for years with the last canto of the *Paradiso*, which is to my thinking the highest point that poetry has ever reached or ever can reach, and in which Dante amply repairs any failure of Canto XXXIV of the *Inferno*; but perhaps it is better, on our first reading of the *Inferno*, to omit the last canto and return to the beginning:

> Per me si va nella città dolente;
>> per me si va nell' eterno dolore;
>> per me si va tra la perduta gente.
> Giustizia mosse il mio alto Fattore;
>> fecemi la divina Potestate,
>> la somma Sapienza e il primo Amore.

[238] II

THE *PURGATORIO* AND THE *PARADISO*

18 For the science or art of writing verse, one has learned from the *Inferno* that the greatest poetry can be written with the greatest economy of words, and with the greatest austerity in the use of metaphor, simile, verbal beauty, and elegance. When I affirm that more can be learned about how to write poetry from Dante than from any English poet, I do not at all mean that Dante's way is the only right way, or that Dante is thereby *greater* than Shakespeare or, indeed, any other English poet. I put my meaning into other words by saying that Dante can do less

harm to any one trying to learn to write verse, than can Shakespeare. Most great English poets are *inimitable* in a way in which Dante was not. If you try to imitate Shakespeare you will certainly produce a series of stilted, forced, and violent distortions of language. The language of each great English poet is his own language; the language of Dante is the perfection of a common language. In a sense, it is more pedestrian than that of Dryden or Pope. If you follow Dante without talent, you will at worst be pedestrian and flat; if you follow Shakespeare or Pope without talent, you will make an utter fool of yourself.

19 But if one has learned this much from the *Inferno*, there are other things to be learnt from the two successive divisions of the poem. From the *Purgatorio* one learns that a straightforward philosophical statement can be great poetry; from the *Paradiso*, that more and more rarefied and remote *states of beatitude* can be the material for great poetry. And gradually we come to admit that Shakespeare understands a greater extent and variety of human life than Dante; but that Dante understands deeper degrees of degradation and higher degrees of exaltation. And a further wisdom is reached when we see clearly that this indicates the equality of the two men.

20 On the one hand, the *Purgatorio* and the *Paradiso* belong, [239] in the way of understanding, together. It is apparently easier to accept damnation as poetic material than purgation or beatitude; less is involved that is strange to the modern mind. I insist that the full meaning of the *Inferno* can only be extracted after appreciation of the two later parts, yet it has sufficient meaning in and by itself for the first few readings. Indeed, the *Purgatorio* is, I think, the most difficult of the three parts. It cannot be enjoyed by itself like the *Inferno*, nor can it be enjoyed merely as a sequel to the *Inferno*; it requires appreciation of the *Paradiso* as well; which means that its first reading is arduous and apparently unremunerative. Only when we have read straight through to the end of the *Paradiso*, and re-read the *Inferno*, does the *Purgatorio* begin to yield its beauty. Damnation and even blessedness are more exciting than purgation.

21 By compensation, the *Purgatorio* has a few episodes which, so to speak, 'let us up' (as the counterpart to letting down) more easily than the rest, from the *Inferno*. We must not stop to orient ourselves in the new astronomy of the Mount of Purgatory. We must linger first with the shades of Casella and Manfred slain, and especially Buonconte and La Pia, those whose souls were saved from Hell only at the last moment.

'Io fui di Montefeltro, io son Buonconte;
    Giovanna o altri non ha di me cura;
    per ch'io vo tra costor con bassa fronte.'
Ed io a lui: 'Qual forza o qual ventura
    ti traviò si fuor di Campaldino
    che non si seppe mai tua sepoltura?'
'Oh,' rispos' egli, 'a piè del Casentino
    traversa un' acqua che ha nome l'Archiano,
    che sopra l'Ermo nasce in Apennino.
Dove il vocabol suo diventa vano
    arriva' io forate nella gola,
    fuggendo a piede e sanguinando il piano.
[240] Quivi perdei la vista, e la parola
    nel nome di Maria finii: e quivi
    caddi, e rimase la mia carne sola.'

'I was of Montefeltro, I am Buoncone; neither Giovanna nor any other has care of me, wherefore I go with these, with lowered brow.' I said to him: 'What force or chance led you so far away from Campaldino that your place of sepulture has always been unknown?' 'Oh,' said he, 'at the foot of Casentino a stream crosses, which is called Archiano, and rises in the Apennines above the Hermitage. There, where its name is lost, came I, jabbed in the throat, fleeing on foot, dripping blood over the plain. There my sight left me, and I ended speech with (crying on) the name of Mary. There I fell, and my flesh alone remained.'

When Buonconte ends his story, the third spirit speaks:

'Deh, quando tu sarai tornato al mondo,
    e riposato della lunga via,'
seguitò il terzo spirito al secondo,
'ricorditi di me, che son la Pia;
    Siena mi fe', disfecemi Maremma:
    salsi colui che innanellata, pria
    disposando, m'avea con la sua gemma.'

'O pray, when you return to the world, and are rested from your long journey,' followed the third spirit after the second, 'remember me, who am La Pia. Siena made me, Maremma unmade me: this is known to him who after due engagement wedded me with his ring.'

22 The next episode that impresses the reader coming fresh from the *Inferno* is the meeting with Sordello the poet (Canto VI), the soul who appeared

> altera e disdegnosa
> e nel mover degli occhi onesta e tarda!

proud and disdainful, superb and slow in the movement of his eyes!

> E il dolce duca incominciava:
> 'Mantova' . . . e l'ombra, tutta in sè romita,
> [241] surse ver lui del loco ove pria stava,
> dicendo: 'O Mantovano, io son Sordello
> della tua terra.' E l'un l'altro abbracciava.

The gentle guide (Virgil) began: 'Mantua' . . . and the shade, suddenly rapt, leapt towards him from the place where first it was, saying, 'O Mantuan, I am Sordello of thy very soil.' And the one embraced the other.

23 The meeting with Sordello *a guisa di leon quando si posa*, like a couchant lion, is no more affecting than that with the poet Statius, in Canto XXI. Statius, when he recognises his master Virgil, stoops to clasp his feet, but Virgil answers – the lost soul speaking to the saved:

> 'Frate,
> non far, chè tu se' ombra, ed ombra vedi.'
> Ed ei surgendo: 'Or puoi la quantitate
> comprender dell' amor ch'a te mi scalda,
> quando dismento nostra vanitate,
> trattando l'ombre come cosa salda.'

'Brother! refrain, for you are but a shadow, and a shadow is but what you see.' Then the other, rising: 'Now can you understand the quantity of love that warms me towards you, so that I forget our vanity, and treat the shadows like the solid thing.'

The last 'episode' at all comparable to those of the *Inferno* is the meeting with Dante's predecessors, Guido Guinicelli and Arnaut Daniel (Canto XXVI). In this canto the Lustful are purged in flame, yet we see clearly how the flame of purgatory differs from that of hell. In hell, the torment issues from the very nature of the damned themselves, expresses their essence; they writhe in the torment of their own perpetually perverted nature. In purgatory the torment of flame is deliberately and consciously accepted by the penitent. When Dante approaches with Virgil these souls in purgatory flame, they crowd towards him:

> Poi verso me, quanto potevan farsi,
> > certi si feron, sempre con riguardo
> > di non uscir dove non fossero arsi.

> [242] Then certain of them made towards me, so far as they could, but ever watchful not to come so far that they should not be in the fire.

The souls in purgatory suffer because they *wish to suffer*, for purgation. And observe that they suffer more actively and keenly, being souls preparing for blessedness, than Virgil suffers in eternal limbo. In their suffering is hope, in the anaesthesia of Virgil is hopelessness; that is the difference. The canto ends with the superb verses of Arnaut Daniel in his Provençal tongue:

> 'Ieu sui Arnaut, que plor e vau cantan;
> > consiros vei la passada folor,
> > e vei jausen lo jorn, qu' esper, denan.
> Ara vos prec, per aquella valor
> > que vos guida al som de l'escalina,
> > sovegna vos a temps de ma dolor.'
> POI S'ASCOSE NEL FOCO CHE GLI AFFINA.

> 'I am Arnold, who weeps and goes singing. I see in thought all the past folly. And I see with joy the day for which I hope, before me. And so I pray you, by that Virtue which leads you to the topmost of the stair – be mindful in due time of my pain.' Then dived he back into that fire which refines them.

24 These are the high episodes, to which the reader initiated by the *Inferno* must first cling, until he reaches the shore of Lethe, and Matilda, and the first sight of Beatrice. In the last cantos (XXIX–XXXIII) of the *Purgatorio* we are already in the world of the *Paradiso*.

25 But in between these episodes is the narrative of the ascent of the Mount, with meetings, visions, and philosophical expositions, all important, and all difficult for the uninstructed reader who finds it less exciting than the continuous phantasmagoria of the *Inferno*. The allegory in the *Inferno* was easy to swallow or ignore, because we could, so to speak, grasp the concrete end of it, its solidification into imagery; but as we ascend from Hell to Heaven we [243] are more and more required to grasp the whole from idea to image.

26 Here I must make a diversion, before tackling a specifically philosophical passage of the *Purgatorio*, concerning the nature of Belief. I wish merely to indicate certain tentative conclusions of my own, which might affect one's reading of the *Purgatorio*.

27 Dante's debt to St Thomas Aquinas, like his debt (a much smaller one) to Virgil, can be easily exaggerated; for it must not be forgotten that Dante read and made use of other great medieval philosophers as well. Nevertheless, the question of how much Dante took from Aquinas and how much from elsewhere is one which has been settled by others and is not relevant to my present essay. But the question what Dante 'believed' is always relevant. It would not matter, if the world were divided between those persons who are capable of taking poetry simply for what it is and those who cannot take it at all; if so, there would be no need to talk about this question to the former and no use in talking about it to the latter. But most of us are somewhat impure and apt to confuse issues: hence the justification of writing books about books, in the hope of straightening things out.

28 My point is that you cannot afford to *ignore* Dante's philosophical and theological beliefs, or to skip the passages which express them most clearly; but that on the other hand you are not called upon to believe them yourself. It is wrong to think that there are parts of the *Divine Comedy* which are of interest only to Catholics or to medievalists. For there is a difference (which here I hardly do more than assert) between philosophical *belief* and poetic *assent*. I am not sure that there is not as great a difference between philosophical belief and scientific belief; but that is a difference only now beginning to appear, and certainly inapposite to the thirteenth century. In reading Dante you must enter the world of thirteenth-century Catholicism: which is not the world of modern Catholicism, as his [244] world of physics is not the world of modern physics. You are not called upon to believe what Dante believed, for your belief will not give you a groat's worth more of understanding and appreciation; but you are called upon more and more to understand it. If you can read poetry as poetry, you will 'believe' in Dante's theology exactly as you believe in the physical reality of his journey; that is, you suspend both belief and disbelief. I will not deny that it may be in practice easier for a Catholic to grasp the meaning, in many places, than for the ordinary agnostic; but that is not because the Catholic believes, but because he has been instructed. It is a matter of knowledge and ignorance, not of belief or scepticism. The vital matter is that Dante's poem is a whole; that you must in the end come to understand every part in order to understand any part.

29 Furthermore, we can make a distinction between what Dante believes as a poet and what he believed as a man. Practically, it is hardly likely that even so great a poet as Dante could have composed the *Comedy* merely with understanding and without belief; but his private belief becomes a different thing in becoming poetry. It is interesting to hazard the suggestion that this is truer of Dante than of any other philosophical poet. With Goethe, for instance, I often feel too acutely 'this is what Goethe the man believed', instead of merely entering into a world which Goethe has created; with Lucretius also; less with the *Bhagavad-Gita*, which is the next greatest philosophical poem to the *Divine Comedy* within my experience. That is the advantage of a coherent traditional system of dogma and morals like the Catholic: it stands apart, for understanding and assent even without belief, from the single individual who propounds it. Goethe always arouses in me a strong sentiment of disbelief in what he believes: Dante does not. I believe that this is because Dante is the purer poet, not because I have more sympathy with Dante the man than Goethe the man.

[245] 30 We are not to take Dante for Aquinas or Aquinas for Dante. It would be a grievous error in psychology. The *belief attitude* of a man reading the *Summa* must be different from that of a man reading Dante, even when it is the same man, and that man a Catholic.

31 It is not necessary to have read the *Summa* (which usually means, in practice, reading some handbook) in order to understand Dante. But it is necessary to read the philosophical passages of Dante with the humility of a person visiting a new world, who admits that every part is essential to the whole. What is necessary to appreciate the poetry of the *Purgatorio* is not belief, but suspension of belief. Just as much effort is required of any modern person to accept Dante's allegorical method, as is required of the agnostic to accept his theology.

32 When I speak of understanding, I do not mean merely knowledge of books or words, any more than I mean belief: I mean a state of mind in which one sees certain beliefs, as the order of the deadly sins, in which treachery and pride are greater than lust, and despair the greatest, as *possible*, so that we suspend our judgement altogether.

33 In the XVIth Canto of the *Purgatorio* we meet Marco Lombardo, who discourses at some length on the Freedom of the Will, and on the Soul:

> Esce di mano a lui, che la vagheggia
>> prima che sia, a guisa di fanciulla
>> che piangendo e ridendo pargoleggia,
> l'anima semplicetta, che sa nulla,
>> salvo che, mossa da lieto fattore,
>> volentier torna a ciò che la trastulla.
> Di picciol bene in pria sente sapore;
>> quivi s'inganna, e retro ad esso corre,
>> se guida o fren non torce suo amore.
> Onde convenne legge per fren porre;
>> convenne regge aver, che discernesse
>> della vera cittade almen la torre.

[246] From the hands of Him who loves her before she is, there issues like a little child that plays, with weeping and laughing, the simple soul, that knows nothing except that, come from the hands of a glad creator, she turns willingly to everything that delights her. First she tastes the flavour of a trifling good; then is beguiled, and pursues it, if neither guide nor check withhold her. Therefore laws were needed as a curb; a ruler was needed, who should at least see afar the tower of the true City.

Later (Canto XVII) it is Virgil himself who instructs Dante in the nature of Love:

> 'Nè creator nè creatura mai,'
>> cominciò ei, 'figiuol, fu senza amore,
>> o naturale o d'animo; e tu il sai.
> Lo natural è sempre senza errore,
>> ma l'altro puote errar per malo obbietto,
>> o per poco o per troppo di vigore.
> Mentre ch'egli è ne' primi ben diretto,
>> e ne' secondi sè stesso misura,
>> esser non può cagion di mal diletto;
> ma, quando al mal si torce, o con più cura
>> o con men che non dee corre nel bene,
>> contra il fattore adopra sua fattura.
> Quinci comprender puoi ch'esser conviene
>> amor sementa in voi d'ogni virtute,
>> e d'ogni operazion che merta pene.'

He began: 'neither Creator, nor creature, my son, was ever without love, either natural or rational: and you know it. The natural is always without error; but the other may err through mistaking the object, or through excess or deficiency of force. While it is directed towards the primal goods, and in the secondary moderates itself, it cannot be the cause of delight of sin; but when it turns to evil, or hurries towards the good with more or less solicitude than is right, then the creature works against the Creator. Accordingly you may understand how Love must be the seed in you both of every virtue and of every act that merits punishment.'

I have quoted these two passages at some length, because [247] they are of the sort that a reader might be inclined to skip, thinking that they are only for scholars, not for readers of poetry, or thinking that it is necessary to have studied the philosophy underlying them. It is not necessary to have traced the descent of this theory of the soul from Aristotle's *De Anima* in order to appreciate it as poetry. Indeed, if we worry too much about it at first as philosophy we are likely to prevent ourselves from receiving the poetic beauty. It is the philosophy of that world of poetry which we have entered.

34 But with the XXVIIth canto we have left behind the stage of punishment and the stage of dialectic, and approach the state of Paradise. The last cantos have the quality of the *Paradiso* and prepare us for it; they move straight forward, with no detour or delay. The three poets, Virgil, Statius, and Dante, pass through the wall of flame which separates Purgatory from the Earthly Paradise. Virgil dismisses Dante, who henceforth shall proceed with a higher guide, saying:

> Non aspettar mio dir più, nè mio cenno.
> > Libero, dritto e sano è tuo arbitrio,
> > e fallo fora non fare a suo senno:
> per ch'io te sopra te corono e mitrio.

> No more expect my word, or sign. Your Will is free, straight and whole, and not to follow its direction would be sin: wherefore I crown and mitre you (king and bishop) over yourself.

I.e. Dante has now arrived at a condition, for the purposes of the rest of his journey, which is that of the blessed: for political and ecclesiastical organisation are only required because of the imperfections of the human will. In the Earthly Paradise Dante encounters a lady named Matilda, whose identity need not at first bother us,

> una donna soletta, che si già
> > cantando ed iscegliendo fior da fiore,
> > ond' era pinta tutta la sua via.

[248] A lady alone, who went singing and plucking flower after
flower, wherewith her path was pied.

After some conversation, and explanation by Matilda of the reason and nature of the place, there follows a 'Divine Pageant'. To those who dislike – not what are popularly called pageants – but the serious pageants of royalty, of the Church, of military funerals – the 'pageantry' which we find here and in the *Paradiso* will be tedious; and still more to those, if there be any, who are unmoved by the splendour of the Revelation of St John. It belongs to the world of what I call the *high dream*, and the modern world seems capable only of the *low dream*. I arrived at accepting it, myself, only with some difficulty. There were at least two prejudices, one against pre-Raphaelite imagery, which was natural to one of my generation, and perhaps affects generations younger than mine. The other prejudice – which affects this end of the *Purgatorio* and the whole of the *Paradiso* – is the prejudice that poetry not only must be found *through* suffering but can find its material only *in* suffering. Everything else was cheerfulness, optimism, and hopefulness; and these words stood for a great deal of what one hated in the nineteenth century. It took me many years to recognise that the states of improvement and beatitude which Dante describes are still further from what the modern world can conceive as cheerfulness, than are his states of damnation. And little things put one off: Rossetti's 'Blessed Damozel', first by my rapture and next by my revolt, held up my appreciation of Beatrice by many years.

35 We cannot understand fully Canto XXX of the *Purgatorio* until we know the *Vita Nuova*, which in my opinion should be read after the *Divine Comedy*. But at least we can begin to understand how skilfully Dante express the recrudescence of an ancient passion in a new emotion, in a new situation, which comprehends, enlarges, and gives a meaning to it.

[249] sopra candido vel cinta d'oliva
  donna m'apparve, sotto verde manto,
   vestita di color di fiamma viva.
 E lo spirito mio, che già cotanto
  tempo era stato che alla sua presenza
   non era di stupor, tremando, affranto,
 senza degli occhi aver più conoscenza,
  per occulta virtù che da lei mosse,
   d'antico amor sentì la gran potenza.
 Tosto che nella vista mi percosse
  l'alta virtù, che già m'avea trafitto

>   primo ch'io fuor di puerizia fosse,
> volsimi alla sinistra col rispitto
>   col quale il fantolin corre alla mamma,
>   quando ha paura o quando egli è afflitto,
> per dicere a Virgilio: 'Men che dramma
>   di sangue m' è rimaso, che non tremi;
>   conosco i segni dell' antica fiamma.'

> Olive-crowned over a white veil, a lady appeared to me, clad, under a green mantle, in colour of living flame. And my spirit, after so many years since trembling in her presence it had been broken with awe, without further knowledge by my eyes, felt, through hidden power which went out from her, the great strength of the old love. As soon as that lofty power struck my sense, which already had transfixed me before my adolescence, I turned leftwards with the trust of the little child who runs to his mama when he is frightened or distressed, to say to Virgil: 'Hardly a drop of blood in my body does not shudder: I know the tokens of the ancient flame.'

And in the dialogue that follows we see the passionate conflict of the old feelings with the new; the effort and triumph of a new renunciation, greater than renunciation at the grave, because a renunciation of feelings that persist beyond the grave. In a way, these cantos are those of the greatest *personal* intensity in the whole poem. In the *Paradiso* Dante himself, save for the Cacciaguida episode, be-[250]comes de- or super-personalised; and it is in these last cantos of the *Purgatorio*, rather than in the *Paradiso*, that Beatrice appears most clearly. But the Beatrice theme is essential to the understanding of the whole, *not* because we need to know Dante's biography – not, for instance, as the Wesendonck history is supposed to cast light upon *Tristan* – but because of Dante's *philosophy* of it. This, however, concerns more our examination of the *Vita Nuova*.

36 The *Purgatorio* is the most difficult because it is the *transitional* canto: the *Inferno* is one thing, comparatively easy; the *Paradiso* is another thing, more difficult as a whole than the *Purgatorio*, because more a whole. Once we have got the hang of the kind of feeling in it no one part is difficult. The *Purgatorio*, here and there, might be called 'dry': the *Paradiso* is never dry, it is either incomprehensible or intensely exciting. With the exception of the episode of Cacciaguida – a pardonable exhibition of family and personal pride, because it provides splendid poetry – it is not episodic. All the other characters have the best credentials. At first, they seem less distinct than the earlier unblessed people; they seem ingeniously varied but fundamentally monotonous variations of insipid blessedness. It is a matter of gradual adjustment of our vision. We have (whether we know it or not) a prejudice against beatitude as material for poetry. The eighteenth and nineteenth centuries knew nothing of it; even Shelley, who knew Dante well and who towards the end of his life was beginning to profit by it, the one English poet of the nineteenth century who could even have begun to follow those footsteps, was able to enounce the proposition that our sweetest songs are those which tell of saddest thought. The early work of Dante might confirm Shelley; the *Paradiso* provides the counterpart, though a different counterpart from the philosophy of Browning.

37 The *Paradiso* is not monotonous. It is as various as any poem. And take the *Comedy* as a whole, you can compare it to nothing but the *entire* dramatic work of Shakespeare. [251] The comparison of the *Vita Nuova* with the *Sonnets* is another, and interesting, occupation. Dante and Shakespeare divide the modern world between them; there is no third.

38 We should begin by thinking of Dante fixing his gaze on Beatrice:

> Nel suo aspetto tal dentro mi fei,
>   qual si fe' Glauco nel gustar dell' erba,
>   che il fe' consorto in mar degli altri dei,
> Trasumanar significar per verba
>   non si poria; pero l'esemplo basti
>   a cui esperienza grazia serba.

> Gazing on her, so I became within, as did Glaucus, on tasting of the grass which made him sea-fellow of the other gods. To transcend humanity may not be told in words, wherefore let the instance suffice for him for whom that experience is reserved by Grace.

And as Beatrice says to Dante: '*You make yourself dull with false fancy*'; warns him, that here there are divers sorts of blessedness, as settled by Providence.

39 If this is not enough, Dante is informed by Piccarda (Canto III) in words which even those who know no Dante know:

> la sua voluntade è nostra pace.

> His will is our peace.

It is the mystery of the inequality, and of the indifference of that inequality, in blessedness, of the blessed. It is all the same, and yet each degree differs.

40 Shakespeare gives the greatest *width* of human passion; Dante the greatest altitude and greatest depth. They complement each other. It is futile to ask which undertook the more difficult job. But certainly the 'difficult passages' in the *Paradiso* are Dante's difficulties rather than ours: his difficulty in making us apprehend sensuously the various states and stages of blessedness. Thus the long oration of Beatrice about the Will (Canto IV) is really directed at [252] making us *feel* the reality of the condition of Piccarda; Dante has to educate our senses as he goes along. The insistence throughout is upon states of feeling; the reasoning takes only its proper place as a means of reaching these states. We get constantly verses like

> Beatrice mi guardò con gli occhi pieni
> di faville d'amor così divini,
> che, vinta, mia virtù diedi le reni,
> e quasi mi perdei con gli occhi chini.
>
> Beatrice looked on me with eyes so divine filled with sparks of love, that my vanquished power turned away, and I became as lost, with downcast eyes.

The whole difficulty is in admitting that this is something that we are meant to feel, not merely decorative verbiage. Dante gives us every aid of images, as when

> Come in peschiera, ch' è tranquilla e pura,
> traggonsi i pesci a ciò che vien di fuori
> per modo che lo stimin lor pastura;
> sì vid' io ben più di mille splendori
> trarsi ver noi, ed in ciascun s'udia:
> *Ecco chi crescerà li nostri amori.*
>
> As in a fishpond still and clear, the fishes draw near to anything that falls from without in such a way as to make them think it something to eat, so I saw more than a thousand splendours draw towards us, and in each was heard: *Lo! here is one that shall increase our loves.*

About the persons whom Dante meets in the several spheres, we need only to enquire enough to consider why Dante placed them where he did.

41 When we have grasped the strict *utility* of the minor images, such as the one given above, or even the simple comparison admired by Landor:

> Quale allodetta che in aere si spazia
> > prima cantando, e poi tace contenta
> > dell' ultima dolcezza che la sazia,
>
> [253] Like the lark which soars in the air, first singing, and then ceases, content with the last sweetness that sates her,

we may study with respect the more elaborate imagery, such as that of the figure of the Eagle composed by the spirits of the just, which extends from Canto XVIII onwards for some space. Such figures are not merely antiquated rhetorical devices, but serious and practical means of making the spiritual visible. An understanding of the rightness of such imagery is a preparation for apprehending the last and greatest canto, the most tenuous and most intense. Nowhere in poetry has experience so remote from ordinary experience been expressed so concretely, by a masterly use of that imagery of *light* which is the form of certain types of mystical experience.

> Nel suo profondo vidi che s'interna,
> > legato con amore in un volume,
> > ciò che per l'universo si squaderna;
> sustanzia ed accidenti, e lor costume,
> > quasi conflati insieme per tal modo,
> > che ciò ch' io dico è un semplice lume.
> La forma universal di questo nodo
> > credo ch' io vidi, perchè più di largo,
> > dicendo questo, mi sent ch' io godo.
> Un punto solo m'è maggior letargo,
> > che venticinque secoli alla impresa,
> > che fe' Nettuno ammirar l'ombra d'Argo.

> Within its depths I saw ingathered, bound by love in one mass, the scattered leaves of the universe: substance and accidents and their relations, as though together fused, so that what I speak of is one simple flame. The universal form of this complex I think I saw, because, as I say this, more largely I feel myself rejoice. One single moment to me is more lethargy than twenty-five centuries upon the enterprise which made Neptune wonder at the shadow of the Argo (passing over him).

One can feel only awe at the power of the master who could thus at every moment realise the inapprehensible in [254] visual images. And I do not know anywhere in poetry a more authentic sign of greatness than the power of association which could in the last line, when the poet is speaking of the Divine vision, yet introduce the Argo passing over the head of wondering Neptune. Such association is utterly different from that of Marino speaking in one breath of the beauty of the Magdalen and the opulence of Cleopatra (so that you are not quite sure what adjectives apply to which). It is the real right thing, the power of establishing relations between beauty of the most diverse sorts; it is the utmost power of the poet.

> O quanto è corto il dire, e come fioco
> al mio concetto!

> How scant the speech, and how faint, for my conception!

42 In writing of the *Divine Comedy* I have tried to keep to a few very simple points of which I am convinced. First that the poetry of Dante is the one universal school of style for the writing of poetry in any language. There is much, naturally, which can profit only those who write Dante's own Tuscan language; but there is no poet in any tongue – not even in Latin or Greek – who stands so firmly as a model for all poets. I tried to illustrate his universal mastery in the use of images. In the actual writing I went so far as to say that he is safer to follow, even for us, than any English poet, including Shakespeare. My second point is that Dante's 'allegorical' method has great advantages for the writing of *poetry*: it simplifies the diction, and makes clear and precise the images. That in good allegory, like Dante's, it is not necessary to understand the meaning first to enjoy the poetry, but that our enjoyment of the poetry makes us want to understand the meaning. And the third point is that the *Divine Comedy* is a complete scale of the *depths* and *heights* of human emotion; that the *Purgatorio* and *Paradiso* are to be read as extensions of the ordinarily very limited human range. Every degree of the feeling of humanity, from lowest to highest, has, moreover, an intimate relation [255] to the next above and below, and all fit together according to the logic of sensibility.

43 I have only now to make certain observations on the *Vita Nuova*, which may also amplify what I have suggested about the medieval mind expressed in allegory.

NOTE TO SECTION II

44 The theory of poetic belief and understanding here employed for a particular study is similar to that maintained by Mr I. A. Richards (see his *Practical Criticism*, pp. 179 ff. and pp. 271 ff.). I say 'similar,' because my own *general* theory is still embryonic, and Mr Richards's also is capable of much further development. I cannot therefore tell how far the similarity extends; but for those who are interested in the subject, I should point out one respect in which my view differs from that of Mr Richards; and then proceed to qualify my own tentative conclusions.

45 I am in agreement with Mr Richards's statement on p. 271 (*op. cit.*). I agree for the reason that if you hold any contradictory theory you deny, I believe, the existence of 'literature' as well as of 'literary criticism'. We may raise the question whether 'literature' exists; but for certain purposes, such as the purpose of this essay on Dante, we must assume that there is a literature and literary appreciation; we must assume that the reader can obtain the full 'literary' or (if you will) 'aesthetic' enjoyment without sharing the beliefs of the author. *If* there is 'literature', *if* there is 'poetry', then it must be possible to have full literary or poetic appreciation without sharing the beliefs of the poet. That is as far as my thesis goes in the present essay. It may be argued whether there is literature, whether there is poetry, and whether there is any meaning in the term 'full appreciation'. But I have assumed for this essay that these things exist and that these terms are understood.

46 I deny, in short, that the reader must share the beliefs of the poet in order to enjoy the poetry fully. I have also asserted that we can distinguish between Dante's beliefs as a man and his beliefs as a poet. But we are forced to believe that there is a particular relation between the two, and that the poet 'means what he says'. If we learned, for instance, that *De Rerum Natura* was a Latin exercise which Dante had composed for relaxation after completing the *Divine Comedy*, and published under the name of one Lucretius, I am sure that our capacity for enjoying either poem would be mutilated. Mr Richards's statement (*Science and Poetry*, p. 76 footnote) that a certain writer has effected 'a complete severance between his poetry and *all* beliefs' is to me incomprehensible.

47 If you deny the theory that full poetic appreciation is possible without belief in what the poet believed, you deny the existence of 'poetry' as well as 'criticism'; and if you push this denial to its conclusion, you will be [256] forced to admit that there is very little poetry that you can appreciate, and that your appreciation of it will be a function of your philosophy or theology or something else. If, on the other hand, I push *my* theory to the extreme, I find myself in as great a difficulty. I am quite aware of the ambiguity of the

word 'understand'. In one sense, it means to understand without believing, for unless you can understand a view of life (let us say) without believing in it, the word 'understand' loses all meaning, and the act of choice between one view and another is reduced to caprice. But if you yourself are convinced of a certain view of life, then you irresistibly and inevitably believe that if anyone else comes to 'understand' it fully, his understanding *must* terminate in belief. It is possible, and sometimes necessary, to argue that full understanding must identify itself with full belief. A good deal, it thus turns out, hangs on the meaning, if any, of this short word *full*.

48 In short, both the view I have taken in this essay, and the view which contradicts it, are, if pushed to the end, what I call heresies (not, of course, in the theological, but in a more general sense). Each is true only within a limited field of discourse, but unless you limit fields of discourse, you can have no discourse at all. Orthodoxy can only be found in such contradictions, though it must be remembered that a pair of contradictions may *both* be false, and that not all pairs of contradictions make up a truth.

49 And I confess to considerable difficulty in analysing my own feelings, a difficulty which makes me hesitate to accept Mr Richards's theory of 'pseudo-statements'. On reading the line which he uses,

> Beauty is truth, truth beauty. . .

I am at first inclined to agree with him, because this statement of equivalence means nothing to me. But on re-reading the whole Ode, this line strikes me as a serious blemish on a beautiful poem; and the reason must be either that I fail to understand it, or that it is a statement which is untrue. And I suppose that Keats meant something by it, however remote his truth and his beauty may have been from these words in ordinary use. And I am sure that he would have repudiated any explanation of the line which called it a pseudo-statement. On the other hand the line I have often quoted of Shakespeare,

> Ripeness is all,

or the line I have quoted of Dante,

> la sua voluntade è nostra pace,

strikes very differently on my ear. I observe that the propositions in these words are very different in kind, not only from that of Keats, but from each other. The statement of Keats seems to me meaningless: or perhaps, the fact that it is grammatically meaningless conceals another meaning from me. The statement of Shakespeare seems to me to have profound emotional meaning, with, at least, no literal fallacy. And the statement of Dante seems to me *literally true*. And I confess that it has more beauty for [257] me now, when my own experience has deepened its meaning, than it did when I first read it. So I can only conclude that I cannot, in practice, wholly separate my poetic appreciation from my personal beliefs. Also that the distinction between a statement and a pseudo-statement is not always, in particular instances, possible to establish. The theory of Mr Richards is, I believe, incomplete until he defines the species of religious, philosophical, scientific, and other beliefs, as well as that of 'everyday' belief.

50 I have tried to make clear some of the difficulties inhering in my own theory. Actually, one probably has more pleasure in the poetry when one shares the beliefs of the poet. On the other hand there is a distinct pleasure in enjoying poetry as poetry when one does *not* share the beliefs, analogous to the pleasure of 'mastering' other men's philosophical systems. It would appear that 'literary appreciation' is an abstraction, and pure poetry a phantom; and that both in creation and enjoyment much always enters which is, from the point of view of 'Art', irrelevant.

III
THE *VITA NUOVA*

51 All of Dante's 'minor works' are important, because they are works of Dante; but the *Vita Nuova* has a special importance, because it does more than any of the others help us to a fuller understanding of the *Divine Comedy*. I do not suggest that the others may be neglected; the *Convivio* is important, and also the *De Volgari Eloquio*: and every part of Dante's writings can give us some light on other parts. But the *Vita Nuova* is a youthful work, in which some of the method and design, and explicitly the intention, of the *Divine Comedy* are shown. Because it is an immature work, it requires some knowledge of the masterpiece to understand; and at the same time helps particularly towards understanding of the *Comedy*.

52 A great deal of scholarship has been directed upon examination of the early life of Dante, in connexion with the *Vita Nuova*. Critics may be roughly divided into those who regard it as primarily biographical, and those who regard it as primarily allegorical. It is much easier for the second group to make a good case than for the first. If this curious medley of verse and prose is biographical, then the bio-graphy has unquestionably been manipulated almost out of recognition to fit into conventional forms of allegory. The imagery of much of it is certainly in a very ancient tradition of vision literature: just as the scheme of the *Divine Comedy* has been shown to be closely similar to similar supernatural peregrination stories in Arabic and in old Persian literature – to say nothing of the descents of Ulysses and Aeneas – so there are parallels to

the visions of the *Vita Nuova* such as the *Shepherd of Hermas* in Greek. And as the book is obviously not a literal statement, whether of vision or delusion, it is easy to make out a case for its being an entire allegory: for asserting, that is, that Beatrice is merely a personification of an abstract virtue, intellectual or moral.

53 I wish to make clear that my own opinions are opinions founded only upon reading the text. I do not think that they are such as can either be verified or refuted by scholars; I mean to restrict my comments to the unprovable and the irrefutable.

54 It appears likely, to any one who reads the *Vita Nuova* without prejudice, that it is a mixture of biography and allegory; but a mixture according to a recipe not available to the modern mind. When I say the 'modern mind', I mean the minds of those who have read or could have read such a document as Rousseau's *Confessions*. The modern mind can understand the 'confession', that is, the literal account of oneself, varying only in degree of sincerity and self-understanding, and it can understand 'allegory' in the abstract. Nowadays 'confessions', of an insignificant sort, pour from the press; every one *met son coeur à nu*, or pretends to; 'personalities' succeed one another in interest. It is difficult to conceive of an age (of many ages) when human beings cared somewhat about the salvation of the 'soul', but not about each other as 'personalities'. Now Dante, I believe, had experiences which seemed to him of some importance; not of importance because they had happened to him and because he, Dante Alighieri, was an [259] important person who kept press-cutting bureaux busy; but important in themselves; and therefore they seemed to him to have some philosophical and impersonal value. I find in it an account of a particular kind of experience: that is, of something which had actual experience (the experience of the 'confession' in the modern sense) *and* intellectual and imaginative experience (the experience of thought and the experience of dream) as its materials; and which became a third kind. It seems to be of importance to grasp the simple fact that the *Vita Nuova* is neither a 'confession' nor an 'indiscretion' in the modern sense, nor is it a piece of Pre-Raphaelite tapestry. If you have that sense of intellectual and spiritual realities that Dante had, then a form of expression like the *Vita Nuova* cannot be classed either as 'truth or 'fiction'.

55 In the first place, the type of sexual experience which Dante describes as occurring to him at the age of nine years is by no means impossible or unique. My only doubt (in which I found myself confirmed by a

distinguished psychologist) is whether it could have taken place so *late* in life as the age of nine years. The psychologist agreed with me that it is more likely to occur at about five or six years of age. It is possible that Dante developed rather late, and it is also possible that he altered the dates to employ some other significance of the number nine. But to me it appears obvious that the *Vita Nuova* could only have been written around a personal experience. If so, the details do not matter: whether the lady was the Portinari or not, I do not care; it is quite as likely that she is a blind for some one else, even for a person whose name Dante may have forgotten or never known. But I cannot find it incredible that what has happened to others should have happened to Dante with much greater intensity.

56 The same experience, described in Freudian terms, would be instantly accepted as fact by the modern public. It is merely that Dante, quite reasonably, drew other conclusions and used another mode of expression, which [260] arouses incredulity. And we are inclined to think – as Rémy de Gourmont, for once misled by his prejudices into the pedantic attitude, thought – that if an author like Dante follows closely a form of vision that has a long history, it proves that the story is mere allegory (in the modern sense) or fake. I find a much greater difference in sensibility between the *Vita Nuova* and the *Shepherd of Hermas* than Gourmont did. It is not at all the simple difference between the genuine and the fraud; it is a difference in mind between the humble author of early Christian times and the poet of the thirteenth century, perhaps as great as that between the latter and ourselves. The similarities might prove that a certain *habit* in dream-imagery can persist throughout many changes of civilisation. Gourmont would say that Dante borrowed; but that is imputing our own mind to the thirteenth century. I merely suggest that possibly Dante, in his place and time, was following something more essential than merely a 'literary' tradition.

57 The attitude of Dante to the fundamental experience of the *Vita Nuova* can only be understood by accustoming ourselves to find meaning in *final causes* rather than in origins. It is not, I believe, meant as a description of what he *consciously* felt on his meeting with Beatrice, but rather as a description of what that meant on mature reflection upon it. The final cause is the attraction towards God. A great deal of sentiment has been spilt, especially in the eighteenth and nineteenth centuries, upon idealising the reciprocal feelings of man and woman towards each other, which various realists have been irritated to denounce: this sentiment ignoring the fact that the love of man and woman (or for that matter of

man and man) is only explained and made reasonable by the higher love, or else is simply the coupling of animals.

58 Let us entertain the theory that Dante, meditating on the astonishment of an experience at such an age, which no subsequent experience abolished or exceeded, found mean-[261]ings in it which we should not be likely to find ourselves. His account is then just as reasonable as our own; and he is simply prolonging the experience in a different direction from that which we, with different mental habits and prejudices, are likely to take.

59 We cannot, as a matter of fact, understand the *Vita Nuova* without some saturation in the poetry of Dante's Italian contemporaries, or even in the poetry of his Provençal predecessors. Literary parallels are most important, but we must be on guard not to take them in a purely literary and literal way. Dante wrote more or less, at first, like other poets, not simply because he had read their works, but because his modes of feeling and thought were much like theirs. As for the Provençal poets, I have not the knowledge to read them at first hand. That mysterious people had a religion of their own which was thoroughly and painfully extinguished by the Inquisition; so that we hardly know more about them than about the Sumerians. I suspect that the difference between this unknown, and possibly maligned, Albigensianism and Catholicism has some correspondence with the difference between the poetry of the Provençal school and the Tuscan. The system of Dante's organisation of sensibility – the contrast between higher and lower carnal love, the transition from Beatrice living to Beatrice dead, rising to the Cult of the Virgin, seems to me to be his own.

60 At any rate, the *Vita Nuova*, besides being a sequence of beautiful poems connected by a curious vision-literature prose, is, I believe, a very sound psychological treatise on something related to what is now called 'sublimation'. There is also a practical sense of realities behind it, which is anti-romantic: not to expect more from *life* than it can give or more from *human* beings than they can give; to look to *death* for what life cannot give. The *Vita Nuova* belongs to 'vision literature'; but its philosophy is the Catholic philosophy of disillusion.

61 Understanding of the book is greatly advanced by [262] acquaintance with Guido Guinicelli, Cavalcanti, Cino, and others. One ought, indeed, to study the development of the art of love from the Provençal poets onwards, paying just attention to both resemblances and differences in spirit; as well as the development of verse form and stanza form and

vocabulary. But such study is vain unless we have first made the conscious attempt, as difficult and hard as re-birth, to pass through the looking-glass into a world which is just as reasonable as our own. When we have done that, we begin to wonder whether the world of Dante is not both larger and more solid than our own. When we repeat

> Tutti li miei penser parlan d'Amore

we must stop to think what *amore* means – something different from its Latin original, its French equivalent, or its definition in a modern Italian dictionary.

62 It is, I repeat, for several reasons necessary to read the *Divine Comedy* first. The first reading of the *Vita Nuova* gives nothing but Pre-Raphaelite quaintness. The *Comedy* initiates us into the world of medieval imagery, in the *Inferno* most apprehensible, in the *Paradiso* most rarefied. It initiates us also into the world of medieval thought and dogma: far easier for those who have had the college discipline of Plato and Aristotle, but possible even without that. The *Vita Nuova* plunges us direct into medieval sensibility. It is not, for Dante, a masterpiece, so that it is safer for us to read it, the first time, for the light it can throw on the *Comedy* than for itself.

63 Read in this way, it can be more useful than a dozen commentaries. The effect of many books about Dante is to give the impression that it is more necessary to read about him than to read what he has written. But the next step after reading Dante again and again should be to read some of the books that he read, rather than modern books about his work and life and times, however good. We may easily be distracted by following up the histories of Emperors and Popes. With a poet like Shakespeare, we are [263] less likely to ignore the text for the commentary. With Dante there is just as much need for concentrating on the text, and all the more because Dante's mind is more remote from the ways of thinking and feeling in which we have been brought up. What we need is not information but knowledge: the first step to knowledge is to recognise the differences between his form of thought and feeling and ours. Even to attach great importance to Thomism, or to Catholicism, may lead us astray, in attracting us too much to such differences as are entirely capable of intellectual formulation. The English reader needs to remember that even had Dante not been a good Catholic, even had he treated Aristotle or Thomas with sceptical indifference, his mind would still be no easier to understand; the forms of imagination, phantasmagoria, and sensibility would be just as strange to us. We have to learn to accept these forms:

and this *acceptance* is more important than anything that can be called belief. There is almost a definite moment of acceptance at which the New Life begins.

64 What I have written is, as I promised, not an 'introduction' to the study but a brief account of my own introduction to it. In extenuation, it may be observed that to write in this way of men like Dante or Shakespeare is really less presumptuous than to write of smaller men. The very vastness of the subject leaves a possibility that one may have something to say worth saying; whereas with smaller men, only minute and special study is likely to justify writing about them at all.

Variants from 1929:

[11] PREFACE

If my task had been to produce another brief 'introduction to the study of Dante' I should have been incompetent to perform it. But in a series of essays of 'Poets on Poets' the undertaking, as I understand it, is quite a different one. A contemporary writer of verse, in writing a pamphlet of this description, is required only to give a faithful account of his acquaintance with the poet of whom he writes. This, and no more, I can do; and this is the only way in which I can treat an author of whom so much has been written, that can make any pretence to novelty. I have found no other poet than Dante to whom I could apply continually, for many purposes, and with much profit, during a familiarity of twenty years. I am not a Dante scholar; my Italian is chiefly self-taught, and learnt primarily in order to read Dante; I need still to make constant reference to translations. Yet it has occurred to me that by relating the process of my own gradual and still very imperfect knowledge of Dante, I might give some help to persons who must begin where I began – with a public school knowledge of Latin, a traveller's smattering of Italian, and a literal translation beside the text. For this reason my order, in the [12] following chapters, is the order of my own initiation. I begin with detail, and approach the general scheme. I began myself with passages of the *Inferno* which I could understand, passed on to the *Purgatorio* in the same way, and only after years of experience began to appreciate the *Paradiso*; from which I reverted to the other parts of the poem and slowly realized the unity of the whole. I believe that it is quite natural and right to tackle the *Vita Nuova* afterwards. For an English reader who reads the *Vita Nuova* too soon is in danger of reading it under pre-Raphaelite influence.

    My purpose has been to persuade the reader first of the importance of Dante as a master – I may even say, *the* master – for a poet writing to-day in any language. And there ensues from that, the importance of Dante to anyone who would appreciate modern poetry, in any language. I should not trust the opinion of anyone who pretended to judge modern verse without knowing Homer, Dante, and Shakespeare. It does not in the least follow that a *poet* is negligible because he does not know these three.

    Having thus excused this book, I do not feel called upon to give any bibliography. Anyone can easily discover more Dante bibliography than anyone can use. But I should like to mention one book which has been of use to me: the *Dante* of Professor Charles Grandgent of Harvard. I owe something to an essay by Mr Ezra Pound in his *Spirit of Romance*, but more to his table-talk; and [13] I owe something to Mr Santayana's essay in *Three Philosophical Poets*. And one should at least glance at the *Readings* of W. W. Vernon in order to see how far into medieval philosophy, theology, science, and literature a thorough study of Dante must go.

   The reader whom I have kept in mind, in writing this essay, is the reader who commences his reading of Dante with Messrs Dent's invaluable *Temple Classics* edition (3 volumes at 2s. each). For this reason I have in quotations followed the *Temple Classics* edition text, and have followed pretty closely the translation in the same volumes. It is hardly necessary to say that where my version varies it nowhere pretends to greater accuracy than that excellent translation. Anyone who reads my essay before attempting Dante at all will be likely to turn next to the *Temple Classics* edition, with its text and translation on opposite pages. There is something to be said for Longfellow's, and something for Norton's translation; but for anyone who can follow Italian even gropingly the Temple translation is the best.

5   soon after] soon enough after

18–19 [Between 'utter fool of yourself.' and 'But if one has learned']: Nevertheless, the *simple* style of which Dante is the greatest master is a very difficult style. In twenty years I have written about a dozen lines in that style successfully; and compared to the dullest passage in the *Divine Comedy*, they are 'as straw'. So I believe that it is difficult.

21 seguitò] seguito

27 to Virgil,] to Virgil (for he owes more to Ovid than to Virgil),

31 usually means] means

34 Church] church
    through suffering] only *through* suffering

35 volsimi] volsemi

40 stimin] stiman

41 allodetta] alledetta
    the Magdalen] Our Lady

Heading SECTION] CHAPTER

59 Provençal school and the Tuscan] Tuscan school and that of Provence

62 , the first time,] first

V The Metaphysical Poets

SE, 267-77.

Publ. in *TLS*, 1031 (20 Oct. 1921), [669]-70, as an unsigned review of
Metaphysical Lyrics and Poems of the Seventeenth Century: Donne to Butler,
selected and edited by Herbert J. C. Grierson (Gallup C128).
Repr. in *HJD*, and slightly revised in *SE*.

1 By collecting these poems[1] from the work of a generation more often named than read, and more often read than profitably studied, Professor Grierson has rendered a service of some importance. Certainly the reader will meet with many poems already preserved in other anthologies, at the same time that he discovers poems such as those of Aurelian Townshend or Lord Herbert of Cherbury here included. But the function of such an anthology as this is neither that of Professor Saintsbury's admirable edition of the Caroline poets nor that of the *Oxford Book of English Verse*. Mr Grierson's book is in itself a piece of criticism, and a provocation of criticism; and we think that he was right in including so many poems of Donne, elsewhere (though not in many editions) accessible, as documents in the case of 'metaphysical poetry'. The phrase has long done duty as a term of abuse, or as the label of a quaint and pleasant taste. The question is to what extent the so-called metaphysicals formed a school (in our own time we should say a 'movement'), and how far this so-called school or movement is a digression from the main current.

2 Not only is it extremely difficult to define metaphysical poetry, but difficult to decide what poets practise it and in which of their verses. The poetry of Donne (to whom Marvell and Bishop King are sometimes nearer than any of the other authors) is late Elizabethan, its feeling often [268] very close to that of Chapman. The 'courtly' poetry is derivative from Jonson, who borrowed liberally from the Latin; it expires in the next century with the sentiment and witticism of Prior. There is finally the devotional verse of Herbert, Vaughan, and Crashaw (echoed long after by Christina Rossetti and Francis Thompson); Crashaw, sometimes more profound and less sectarian than the others, has a quality which returns through the Elizabethan period to the early Italians. It is difficult to find any precise use of metaphor, simile, or other conceit, which is common to all the poets and at the same time important enough as an element of style to isolate these poets as a group. Donne, and often Cowley, employ

---

1. *Metaphysical Lyrics and Poems of the Seventeenth Century: Donne to Butler.* Selected and edited, with an Essay, by Herbert J. C. Grierson (Oxford: Clarendon Press. London: Milford).

a device which is sometimes considered characteristically 'metaphysical': the elaboration (contrasted with the condensation) of a figure of speech to the furthest stage to which ingenuity can carry it. Thus Cowley develops the commonplace comparison of the world to a chess-board through long stanzas ('To Destiny'), and Donne, with more grace, in 'A Valediction', the comparison of two lovers to a pair of compasses. But elsewhere we find, instead of the mere explication of the content of a comparison, a development by rapid association of thought which requires considerable agility on the part of the reader.

> On a round ball
> A workeman that hath copies by, can lay
> An Europe, Afrique, and an Asia,
> And quickly make that, which was nothing, All,
> So doth each teare,
> Which thee doth weare,
> A globe, yea world by that impression grow,
> Till thy tears mixt with mine doe overflow
> This world, by waters sent from thee, my heaven dissolved so.

Here we find at least two connexions which are not implicit in the first figure, but are forced upon it by the poet: from the geographer's globe to the tear, and the tear to [269] the deluge. On the other hand, some of Donne's most successful and characteristic effects are secured by brief words and sudden contrasts –

> A bracelet of bright hair about the bone,

where the most powerful effect is produced by the sudden contrast of associations of 'bright hair' and of 'bone'. This telescoping of images and multiplied associations is characteristic of the phrase of some of the dramatists of the period which Donne knew: not to mention Shakespeare, it is frequent in Middleton, Webster, and Tourneur, and is one of the sources of the vitality of their language.

3 Johnson, who employed the term 'metaphysical poets', apparently having Donne, Cleveland, and Cowley chiefly in mind, remarks of them that 'the most heterogeneous ideas are yoked by violence together'. The force of this impeachment lies in the failure of the conjunction, the fact that often the ideas are yoked but not united; and if we are to judge of styles of poetry by their abuse, enough examples may be found in Cleveland to justify Johnson's condemnation. But a degree of heterogeneity of material compelled into unity by the operation of the poet's mind is omnipresent in poetry. We need not select for illustration such a line as:

> Notre âme est un trois-mâts cherchant son Icarie;

we may find it in some of the best lines of Johnson himself (*The Vanity of Human Wishes*):

> His fate was destined to a barren strand,
> A petty fortress, and a dubious hand;
> He left a name at which the world grew pale,
> To point a moral, or adorn a tale,

where the effect is due to a contrast of ideas, different in degree but the same in principle, as that which Johnson mildly reprehended. And in one of the finest poems of the age (a poem which could not have been written in any other age), the 'Exequy' of Bishop King, the extended comparison is used with perfect success: the idea and the simile become one, in the passage in which the Bishop illustrates his impatience to see his dead wife, under the figure of a journey:

> Stay for me there; I will not faile
> To meet thee in that hollow Vale.
> And think not much of my delay;
> I am already on the way,
> And follow thee with all the speed
> Desire can make, or sorrows breed.
> Each minute is a short degree,
> And ev'ry houre a step towards thee.
> At night when I betake to rest,
> Next morn I rise nearer my West
> Of life, almost by eight houres sail,
> Than when sleep breath'd his drowsy gale. . . .
> But heark! My Pulse, like a soft Drum
> Beats my approach, tells *Thee* I come;
> And slow howere my marches be,
> I shall at last sit down by *Thee*.

(In the last few lines there is that effect of terror which is several times attained by one of Bishop King's admirers, Edgar Poe.) Again, we may justly take these quatrains from Lord Herbert's Ode, stanzas which would, we think, be immediately pronounced to be of the metaphysical school:

> So when from hence we shall be gone,
>   And be no more, nor you, nor I,
>   As one another's mystery,
> Each shall be both, yet both but one.

> This said, in her up-lifted face,
>> Her eyes, which did that beauty crown,
>> Were like two starrs, that having faln down,
> Look up again to find their place:
>
> While such a moveless silent peace
>> Did seize on their becalmed sense,
>> One would have thought some influence
> Their ravished spirits did possess.

[271]

There is nothing in these lines (with the possible exception of the stars, a simile not at once grasped, but lovely and justified) which fits Johnson's general observations on the metaphysical poets in his essay on Cowley. A good deal resides in the richness of association which is at the same time borrowed from and given to the word 'becalmed'; but the meaning is clear, the language simple and elegant. It is to be observed that the language of these poets is as a rule simple and pure; in the verse of George Herbert this simplicity is carried as far as it can go – a simplicity emulated without success by numerous modern poets. The *structure* of the sentences, on the other hand, is sometimes far from simple, but this is not a vice; it is a fidelity to thought and feeling. The effect, at its best, is far less artificial than that of an ode by Gray. And as this fidelity induces variety of thought and feeling, so it induces variety of music. We doubt whether, in the eighteenth century, could be found two poems in nominally the same metre, so dissimilar as Marvell's 'Coy Mistress' and Crashaw's 'Saint Teresa'; the one producing an effect of great speed by the use of short syllables, and the other an ecclesiastical solemnity by the use of long ones:

> Love, thou art absolute sole lord
> Of life and death.

4 If so shrewd and sensitive (though so limited) a critic as Johnson failed to define metaphysical poetry by its faults, it is worth while to inquire whether we may not have more success by adopting the opposite method: by assuming that the poets of the seventeenth century (up to the Revolution) were the direct and normal development of the precedent age; and, without prejudicing their case by the adjective 'metaphysical', consider whether their virtue was not something permanently valuable, which subsequently disappeared, but ought not to have disappeared. [272] Johnson has hit, perhaps by accident, on one of their peculiarities, when he observes that 'their attempts were always analytic'; he would not agree that, after the dissociation, they put the material together again in a new unity.

5 It is certain that the dramatic verse of the later Elizabethan and early Jacobean poets expresses a degree of development of sensibility which is not found in any of the prose, good as it often is. If we except Marlowe, a man of prodigious intelligence, these dramatists were directly or indirectly (it is at least a tenable theory) affected by Montaigne. Even if we except also Jonson and Chapman, these two were notably erudite, and were notably men who incorporated their erudition into their sensibility: their mode of feeling was directly and freshly altered by their reading and thought. In Chapman especially there is a direct sensuous apprehension of thought, or a recreation of thought into feeling, which is exactly what we find in Donne:

> in this one thing, all the discipline
> Of manners and of manhood is contained;
> A man to join himself with th' Universe
> In his main sway, and make in all things fit
> One with that All, and go on, round as it;
> Not plucking from the whole his wretched part,
> And into straits, or into nought revert,
> Wishing the complete Universe might be
> Subject to such a rag of it as he;
> But to consider great Necessity.

We compare this with some modern passage:

> No, when the fight begins within himself,
> A man's worth something. God stoops o'er his head,
> Satan looks up between his feet – both tug –
> He's left, himself, i' the middle; the soul wakes
> And grows. Prolong that battle through his life!

[273] It is perhaps somewhat less fair, though very tempting (as both poets are concerned with the perpetuation of love by offspring), to compare with the stanzas already quoted from Lord Herbert's Ode the following from Tennyson:

> One walked between his wife and child,
> With measured footfall firm and mild,
> And now and then he gravely smiled.
>   The prudent partner of his blood
>   Leaned on him, faithful, gentle, good,
>   Wearing the rose of womanhood.
> And in their double love secure,
> The little maiden walked demure,

> Pacing with downward eyelids pure.
>> These three made unity so sweet,
>> My frozen heart began to beat,
>> Remembering its ancient heat.

The difference is not a simple difference of degree between poets. It is something which had happened to the mind of England between the time of Donne or Lord Herbert of Cherbury and the time of Tennyson and Browning; it is the difference between the intellectual poet and the reflective poet. Tennyson and Browning are poets, and they think; but they do not feel their thought as immediately as the odour of a rose. A thought to Donne was an experience; it modified his sensibility. When a poet's mind is perfectly equipped for its work, it is constantly amalgamating disparate experience; the ordinary man's experience is chaotic, irregular, fragmentary. The latter falls in love, or reads Spinoza, and these experiences have nothing to do with each other, or with the noise of the typewriter or the smell of cooking; in the mind of the poet these experiences are always forming new wholes.

6 We may express the difference by the following theory: The poets of the seventeenth century, the successors of the dramatists of the sixteenth, possessed a mechanism of sensibility which could devour any kind of experience. They are simple, artificial, difficult, or fantastic, as their pre-[274]decessors were; no less nor more than Dante, Guido Cavalcanti, Guinicelli, or Cino. In the seventeenth century a dissociation of sensibility set in, from which we have never recovered; and this dissociation, as is natural, was aggravated by the influence of the two most powerful poets of the century, Milton and Dryden. Each of these men performed certain poetic functions so magnificently well that the magnitude of the effect concealed the absence of others. The language went on and in some respects improved; the best verse of Collins, Gray, Johnson, and even Goldsmith satisfies some of our fastidious demands better than that of Donne or Marvell or King. But while the language became more refined, the feeling became more crude. The feeling, the sensibility, expressed in the *Country Churchyard* (to say nothing of Tennyson and Browning) is cruder than that in the 'Coy Mistress'.

7 The second effect of the influence of Milton and Dryden followed from the first, and was therefore slow in manifestation. The sentimental age began early in the eighteenth century, and continued. The poets revolted against the ratiocinative, the descriptive; they thought and felt by fits, unbalanced; they reflected. In one or two passages of Shelley's *Triumph*

of Life, in the second *Hyperion*, there are traces of a struggle toward unification of sensibility. But Keats and Shelley died, and Tennyson and Browning ruminated.

8 After this brief exposition of a theory – too brief, perhaps, to carry conviction – we may ask, what would have been the fate of the 'metaphysical' had the current of poetry descended in a direct line from them, as it descended in a direct line to them? They would not, certainly, be classified as metaphysical. The possible interests of a poet are unlimited; the more intelligent he is the better; the more intelligent he is the more likely that he will have interests: our only condition is that he turn them into poetry, and not merely meditate on them poetically. A philosophical theory which has entered into poetry is established, for its [275] truth or falsity in one sense ceases to matter, and its truth in another sense is proved. The poets in question have, like other poets, various faults. But they were, at best, engaged in the task of trying to find the verbal equivalent for states of mind and feeling. And this means both that they are more mature, and that they wear better, than later poets of certainly not less literary ability.

9 It is not a permanent necessity that poets should be interested in philosophy, or in any other subject. We can only say that it appears likely that poets in our civilisation, as it exists at present, must be *difficult*. Our civilisation comprehends great variety and complexity, and this variety and complexity, playing upon a refined sensibility, must produce various and complex results. The poet must become more and more comprehensive, more allusive, more indirect, in order to force, to dislocate if necessary, language into his meaning. (A brilliant and extreme statement of this view, with which it is not requisite to associate oneself, is that of M. Jean Epstein, *La Poésie d'aujourd'hui*.) Hence we get something which looks very much like the conceit – we get, in fact, a method curiously similar to that of the 'metaphysical poets', similar also in its use of obscure words and of simple phrasing.

> O géraniums diaphanes, geurroyeurs sortilèges,
> Sacrilèges monomanes!
> Emballages, dévergondages, douches! O pressoirs
> Des vendanges des grands soirs!
> Layettes aux obois,
> Thyrses au fond des bois!
> Transfusions, représailles,
> Relevailles, compresses et l'éternal potion,

> Angélus! n'en pouvoir plus
> De débâcles nuptiales! de débâcles nuptiales!

The same poet could write also simply:

> Elle est bien loin, elle pleure,
> Le grand vent se lamente aussi . . .

[276] Jules Laforgue, and Tristan Corbière in many of his poems, are nearer to the 'school of Donne' than any modern English poet. But poets more classical than they have the same essential quality of transmuting ideas into sensations, of transforming an observation into a state of mind.

> Pour l'enfant, amoureux de cartes et d'estampes,
> L'univers est égal à son vaste appétit.
> Ah, que le monde est grand à la clarté des lampes!
> Aux yeux du souvenir que le monde est petit!

In French literature the great master of the seventeenth century – Racine – and the great master of the nineteenth – Baudelaire – are in some ways more like each other than they are like anyone else. The greatest two masters of diction are also the greatest two psychologists, the most curious explorers of the soul. It is interesting to speculate whether it is not a misfortune that two of the greatest masters of diction in our language, Milton and Dryden, triumph with a dazzling disregard of the soul. If we continued to produce Miltons and Drydens it might not so much matter, but as things are it is a pity that English poetry has remained so incomplete. Those who object to the 'artificiality' of Milton or Dryden sometimes tell us to 'look into our hearts and write'. But that is not looking deep enough; Racine or Donne looked into a good deal more than the heart. One must look into the cerebral cortex, the nervous system, and the digestive tracts.

10 May we not conclude, then, that Donne, Crashaw, Vaughan, Herbert and Lord Herbert, Marvell, King, Cowley at his best, are in the direct current of English poetry, and that their faults should be reprimanded by this standard rather than coddled by antiquarian affection? They have been enough praised in terms which are implicit limitations because they are 'metaphysical' or 'witty', 'quaint' or 'obscure', though at their best they have not these attributes more than other serious poets. On the other hand, we must not reject the criticism of Johnson (a dan-[277]gerous person to disagree with) without having mastered it, without having assimilated the Johnsonian canons of taste. In reading the celebrated passage in his essay on Cowley we must remember that

by wit he clearly means something more serious than we usually mean to-day; in his criticism of their versification we must remember in what a narrow discipline he was trained, but also how well trained; we must remember that Johnson tortures chiefly the chief offenders, Cowley and Cleveland. It would be a fruitful work, and one requiring a substantial book, to break up the classification of Johnson (for there has been none since) and exhibit these poets in all their difference of kind and of degree, from the massive music of Donne to the faint, pleasing tinkle of Aurelian Townshend – whose 'Dialogue between a Pilgrim and Time' is one of the few regrettable omissions from the excellent anthology of Professor Grierson.

Variants:

2 furthest] farthest *TLS* (1921), *HJD*
multiplied associations] multiplied association *TLS* (1921), *HJD*
6 difficult,] difficult *TLS* (1921)
Guinicelli] Guinizelli *TLS* (1921), *HJD*
aggravated by] due to *TLS* (1921), *HJD*
10 the excellent anthology of Professor Grierson.] this excellent anthology. *TLS* (1921), *HJD*

Andrew Marvell

SE, 278–90.

Publ. in *TLS*, 1002 (31 Mar. 1921), [201]–2: Gallup C121. Repr. in *Andrew Marvell 1621–1678 Tercentenary Tributes*, ed. Wm. H. Bagguley (1922), 63–78. Revised in *HJD*, and further revised in *SE*.

1 The tercentenary of the former member for Hull deserves not only the celebration proposed by that favoured borough, but a little serious reflection upon his writing. That is an act of piety, which is very different from the resurrection of a diseased reputation. Marvell has stood high for some years; his best poems are not very many, and not only must be well known, from the *Golden Treasury* and the *Oxford Book of English Verse*, but must also have been enjoyed by numerous readers. His grave needs neither rose nor rue nor laurel; there is no imaginary justice to be done; we may think about him, if there be need for thinking, for our own benefit, not his. To bring the poet back to life – the great, the perennial, task of criticism – is in this case to squeeze the drops of the essence of two or three poems; even confining ourselves to these, we may find some precious liquor unknown to the present age. Not to determine rank, but to isolate this quality, is the critical labour. The fact that of all Marvell's

verse, which is itself not a great quantity, the really valuable part consists of a very few poems indicates that the unknown quality of which we speak is probably a literary rather than a personal quality; or, more truly, that it is a quality of a civilisation, of a traditional habit of life. A poet like Donne, or like Baudelaire or Laforgue, may almost be considered the inventor of an attitude, a system of feeling or of morals. Donne is difficult to analyse: what appears at one time a curious personal point of view may at another time appear rather the precise concentration of a kind of feeling diffused in the air about him. Donne and his shroud, [279] the shroud and his motive for wearing it, are inseparable, but they are not the same thing. The seventeenth century sometimes seems for more than a moment to gather up and to digest into its art all the experience of the human mind which (from the same point of view) the later centuries seem to have been partly engaged in repudiating. But Donne would have been an individual at any time and place; Marvell's best verse is the product of European, that is to say Latin, culture.

2 Out of that high style developed from Marlowe through Jonson (for Shakespeare does not lend himself to these genealogies) the seventeenth century separated two qualities: wit and magniloquence. Neither is as simple or as apprehensible as its name seems to imply, and the two are not in practice antithetical; both are conscious and cultivated, and the mind which cultivates one may cultivate the other. The actual poetry, of Marvell, of Cowley, of Milton, and of others, is a blend in varying proportions. And we must be on guard not to employ the terms with too wide a comprehension; for like the other fluid terms with which literary criticism deals, the meaning alters with the age, and for precision we must rely to some degree upon the literacy and good taste of the reader. The wit of the Caroline poets is not the wit of Shakespeare, and it is not the wit of Dryden, the great master of contempt, or of Pope, the great master of hatred, or of Swift, the great master of disgust. What is meant is some quality which is common to the songs in *Comus* and Cowley's *Anacreontics* and Marvell's 'Horatian Ode'. It is more than a technical accomplishment, or the vocabulary and syntax of an epoch; it is, what we have designated tentatively as wit, a tough reasonableness beneath the slight lyric grace. You cannot find it in Shelley or Keats or Wordsworth; you cannot find more than an echo of it in Landor; still less in Tennyson or Browning; and among contemporaries Mr Yeats is an Irishman and Mr Hardy is a modern Englishman – that is to say, Mr Hardy is without it and [280] Mr Yeats is outside of the tradition altogether. On the other hand, as it certainly exists in Lafontaine, there is a large part of it in Gautier. And of the magniloquence, the deliberate exploitation of the

possibilities of magnificence in language which Milton used and abused, there is also use and even abuse in the poetry of Baudelaire.

3 Wit is not a quality that we are accustomed to associate with 'Puritan' literature, with Milton or with Marvell. But if so, we are at fault partly in our conception of wit and partly in our generalisations about the Puritans. And if the wit of Dryden or of Pope is not the only kind of wit in the language, the rest is not merely a little merriment or a little levity or a little impropriety or a little epigram. And, on the other hand, the sense in which a man like Marvell is a 'Puritan' is restricted. The persons who opposed Charles I and the persons who supported the Commonwealth were not all of the flock of Zeal-of-the-land Busy or the United Grand Junction Ebenezer Temperance Association. Many of them were gentlemen of the time who merely believed, with considerable show of reason, that government by a Parliament of gentlemen was better than government by a Stuart; though they were, to that extent, Liberal Practitioners, they could hardly foresee the tea-meeting and the Dissidence of Dissent. Being men of education and culture, even of travel, some of them were exposed to that spirit of the age which was coming to be the French spirit of the age. This spirit, curiously enough, was quite opposed to the tendencies latent or the forces active in Puritanism; the contest does great damage to the poetry of Milton; Marvell, an active servant of the public, but a lukewarm partisan, and a poet on a smaller scale, is far less injured by it. His line on the statue of Charles II, 'It is such a King as no chisel can mend', may be set off against his criticism of the Great Rebellion: 'Men . . . ought and might have trusted the King.' Marvell, therefore, more a man of the century than a Puritan, speaks more clearly and unequivocally with the voice of his literary age than does Milton.

[281] 4 This voice speaks out uncommonly strong in the 'Coy Mistress'. The theme is one of the great traditional commonplaces of European literature. It is the theme of 'O mistress mine', of 'Gather ye rosebuds', of 'Go, lovely rose'; it is in the savage austerity of Lucretius and the intense levity of Catullus. Where the wit of Marvell renews the theme is in the variety and order of the images. In the first of the three paragraphs Marvell plays with a fancy which begins by pleasing and leads to astonishment.

> Had we but world enough and time,
> This coyness, lady, were no crime,
> . . . I would
> Love you ten years before the Flood,

> And you should, if you please, refuse
> Till the conversion of the Jews;
> My vegetable love should grow
> Vaster than empires and more slow. . . .

We notice the high speed, the succession of concentrated images, each magnifying the original fancy. When this process has been carried to the end and summed up, the poem turns suddenly with that surprise which has been one of the most important means of poetic effect since Homer:

> But at my back I always hear
> Time's wingèd chariot hurrying near,
> And yonder all before us lie
> Deserts of vast eternity.

A whole civilisation resides in these lines:

> Pallida Mors aequo pulsat pede pauperum tabernas,
> Regumque turris. . . .

And not only Horace but Catullus himself:

> Nobis, cum semel occidit brevis lux,
> Nox est perpetua una dormienda.

The verse of Marvell has not the grand reverberation of Catullus's Latin; but the image of Marvell is certainly [282] more comprehensive and penetrates greater depths than Horace's.

5 A modern poet, had he reached the height, would very likely have closed on this moral reflection. But the three strophes of Marvell's poem have something like a syllogistic relation to each other. After a close approach to the mood of Donne,

> then worms shall try
> That long-preserved virginity . . .
> The grave's a fine and private place,
> But none, I think, do there embrace,

the conclusion,

> Let us roll all our strength and all
> Our sweetness up into one ball,
> And tear our pleasures with rough strife.
> Through the iron gates of life.

6 It will hardly be denied that this poem contains wit; but it may not be evident that this wit forms the crescendo and diminuendo of a scale of great imaginative power. The wit is not only combined with, but fused into, the imagination. We can easily recognise a witty fancy in the successive images ('my *vegetable* love', 'till the conversion of the Jews'), but this fancy is not indulged, as it sometimes is by Cowley or Cleveland, for its own sake. It is structural decoration of a serious idea. In this it is superior to the fancy of *L'Allegro* or *Il Penseroso*, or the lighter and less successful poems of Keats. In fact, this alliance of levity and seriousness (by which the seriousness is intensified) is a characteristic of the sort of wit we are trying to identify. It is found in

> Le squelette était invisible
> Au temps heureux de l'art païen!

of Gautier, and in the *dandysme* of Baudelaire and Laforgue. It is in the poem of Catullus which has been quoted, and in the variation by Ben Jonson:

> Cannot we deceive the eyes
> Of a few poor household spies?
> 'Tis no sin love's fruits to steal,
> But that sweet sin to reveal,
> To be taken, to be seen,
> These have sins accounted been.

It is in Propertius and Ovid. It is a quality of a sophisticated literature; a quality which expands in English literature just at the moment before the English mind altered; it is not a quality which we should expect Puritanism to encourage. When we come to Gray and Collins, the sophistication remains only in the language, and has disappeared from the feeling. Gray and Collins were masters, but they had lost that hold on human values, that firm grasp of human experience, which is a formidable achievement of the Elizabethan and Jacobean poets. This wisdom, cynical perhaps but untired (in Shakespeare, a terrifying clairvoyance) leads toward, and is only completed by, the religious comprehension; it leads to the point of the *Ainsi tout leur a craqué dans la main* of Bouvard and Pécuchet.

7 The difference between imagination and fancy, in view of this poetry of wit, is a very narrow one. Obviously, an image which is immediately and unintentionally ridiculous is merely a fancy. In the poem *Upon Appleton House*, Marvell falls in with one of these undesirable images, describing the attitude of the house toward its master:

> Yet thus the leaden house does sweat,
> And scarce endures the master great;
> But, where he comes, the swelling hall
> Stirs, and the square grows spherical;

which, whatever its intention, is more absurd than it was intended to be. Marvell also falls into the even commoner error of images which are over-developed or distracting; which support nothing but their own misshapen bodies:

> And now the salmon-fishers moist
> Their leathern boats begin to hoist;
> And, like Antipodes in shoes,
> Have shod their heads in their canoes.

[284] Of this sort of image a choice collection may be found in Johnson's *Life of Cowley*. But the images in the 'Coy Mistress' are not only witty, but satisfy the elucidation of Imagination given by Coleridge:

> This power ... reveals itself in the balance or reconcilement of opposite or discordant qualities: of sameness, with difference; of the general, with the concrete; the idea with the image; the individual with the representative; the sense of novelty and freshness with old and familiar objects; a more than usual state of emotion with more than usual order; judgment ever awake and steady self-possession with enthusiasm and feeling profound or vehement. . . .

Coleridge's statement applies also to the following verses, which are selected because of their similarity, and because they illustrate the marked caesura which Marvell often introduces in a short line:

> The tawny mowers enter next,
> Who seem like Israelites to be
> Walking on foot through a green sea . . .

> And now the meadows fresher dyed,
> Whose grass, with moister colour dashed,
> Seems as green silks but newly washed . . .

> He hangs in shades the orange bright,
> Like golden lamps in a green night. . . .

> Annihilating all that's made
> To a green thought in a green shade. . . .

> Had it lived long, it would have been
> Lilies without, roses within.

The whole poem, from which the last of these quotations is drawn ('The Nymph and the Fawn'), is built upon a very slight foundation, and we can imagine what some of our modern practitioners of slight themes would have made [285] of it. But we need not descend to an invidious contemporaneity to point out the difference. Here are six lines from 'The Nymph and the Fawn':

> I have a garden of my own,
> But so with roses overgrown
> And lilies, that you would it guess
> To be a little wilderness;
> And all the spring-time of the year
> It only lovèd to be there.

And here are five lines from 'The Nymph's Song to Hylas' in the *Life and Death of Jason*, by William Morris:

> I know a little garden close
> Set thick with lily and red rose.
> Where I would wander if I might
> From dewy dawn to dewy night,
> And have one with me wandering.

So far the resemblance is more striking than the difference, although we might just notice the vagueness of allusion in the last line to some indefinite person, form, or phantom, compared with the more explicit reference of emotion to object which we should expect from Marvell. But in the latter part of the poem Morris divaricates widely:

> Yet tottering as I am, and weak,
> Still have I left a little breath
> To seek within the jaws of death
> An entrance to that happy place;
> To seek the unforgotten face
> Once seen, once kissed, once reft from me
> Anigh the murmuring of the sea.

Here the resemblance, if there is any, is to the latter part of 'The Coy Mistress'. As for the difference, it could not be more pronounced. The effect of Morris's charming poem depends upon the mistiness of the feeling and the vagueness of its object; the effect of Marvell's upon its bright, hard precision. And this precision is not due to the fact that [286] Marvell is concerned with cruder or simpler or more carnal emotions. The emotion of Morris is not more refined or more spiritual; it is merely more vague: if any one doubts whether the more refined or spiritual emotion can be precise, he should study the treatment of the varieties of discarnate emotion in the *Paradiso*. A curious result of the comparison of Morris's poem with Marvell's is that the former, though it appears to be more serious, is found to be the slighter; and Marvell's *Nymph and the Fawn*, appearing more slight, is the more serious.

> So weeps the wounded balsam; so
> The holy frankincense doth flow;
> The brotherless Heliades
> Melt in such amber tears as these.

These verses have the suggestiveness of true poetry; and the verses of Morris, which are nothing if not an attempt to suggest, really suggest nothing; and we are inclined to infer that the suggestiveness is the aura around a bright clear centre, that you cannot have the aura alone. The day-dreamy feeling of Morris is essentially a slight thing; Marvell takes a slight affair, the feeling of a girl for her pet, and gives it a connexion with that inexhaustible and terrible nebula of emotion which surrounds all our exact and practical passions and mingles with them. Again, Marvell does this in a poem which, because of its formal pastoral machinery, may appear a trifling object:

> CLORINDA. Near this, a fountain's liquid bell
> Tinkles within the concave shell.
>
> DAMON. Might a soul bathe there and be clean,
> Or slake its drought?

where we find that a metaphor has suddenly rapt us to the image of spiritual purgation. There is here the element of *surprise*, as when Villon says:

> Necessité faict gens mesprendre
> Et faim saillir le loup des boys,

[287] the surprise which Poe considered of the highest importance, and also the restraint and quietness of tone which make the surprise possible. And in the verses of Marvell which have been quoted there is the making the familiar strange, and the strange familiar, which Coleridge attributed to good poetry.

8 The effort to construct a dream-world, which alters English poetry so greatly in the nineteenth century, a dream-world utterly different from the visionary realities of the *Vita Nuova* or of the poetry of Dante's contemporaries, is a problem of which various explanations may no doubt be

found; in any case, the result makes a poet of the nineteenth century, of the same size as Marvell, a more trivial and less serious figure. Marvell is no greater personality than William Morris, but he had something much more solid behind him: he had the vast and penetrating influence of Ben Jonson. Jonson never wrote anything purer than Marvell's 'Horatian Ode'; this ode has that same quality of wit which was diffused over the whole Elizabethan product and concentrated in the work of Jonson. And, as was said before, this wit which pervades the poetry of Marvell is more Latin, more refined, than anything that succeeded it. The great danger, as well as the great interest and excitement, of English prose and verse, compared with French, is that it permits and justifies an exaggeration of particular qualities to the exclusion of others. Dryden was great in wit, as Milton in magniloquence; but the former, by isolating this quality and making it by itself into great poetry, and the latter, by coming to dispense with it altogether, may perhaps have injured the language. In Dryden wit becomes almost fun, and thereby loses some contact with reality; becomes pure fun, which French wit almost never is.

> The midwife placed her hand on his thick skull,
> With this prophetic blessing: *Be thou dull.*
>
> A numerous host of dreaming saints succeed,
> Of the true old enthusiastic breed.

[288] This is audacious and splendid; it belongs to satire besides which Marvell's Satires are random babbling, but it is perhaps as exaggerated as:

> Oft he seems to hide his face,
> But unexpectedly returns,
> And to his faithful champion hath in place
> Bore witness gloriously; whence Gaza mourns,
> And all that band them to resist
> His uncontrollable intent.

How oddly the sharp Dantesque phrase 'whence Gaza mourns' springs out from the brilliant contortions of Milton's sentence!

> Who from his private gardens, where
> He lived reservèd and austere,
>   (As if his highest plot
>   To plant the bergamot)
>
> Could by industrious valour climb
> To ruin the great work of Time,

> And cast the kingdoms old
> Into another mold;
>
>   .   .   .   .
>
> The Pict no shelter now shall find
> Within his parti-coloured mind,
>   But, from this valour sad,
>   Shrink underneath the plaid:

There is here an equipoise, a balance and proportion of tones, which, while it cannot raise Marvell to the level of Dryden or Milton, extorts an approval which these poets do not receive from us, and bestows a pleasure at least different in kind from any they can often give. It is what makes Marvell a classic; or classic in a sense in which Gray and Collins are not; for the latter, with all their accredited purity, are comparatively poor in shades of feeling to contrast and unite.

[289] 9 We are baffled in the attempt to translate the quality indicated by the dim and antiquated term wit into the equally unsatisfactory nomenclature of our own time. Even Cowley is only able to define it by negatives:

> Comely in thousand shapes appears;
>   Yonder we saw it plain; and here 'tis now,
>   Like spirits in a place, we know not how.

It has passed out of our critical coinage altogether, and no new term has been struck to replace it; the quality seldom exists, and is never recognised.

> In a true piece of Wit all things must be
>   Yet all things there agree;
> As in the Ark, join'd without force or strife,
> All creatures dwelt, all creatures that had life.
>   Or as the primitive forms of all
>   (If we compare great things with small)
> Which, without discord or confusion, lie
> In that strange mirror of the Deity.

So far Cowley has spoken well. But if we are to attempt even no more than Cowley, we, placed in a retrospective attitude, must risk much more anxious generalisations. With our eye still on Marvell, we can say that wit is not erudition; it is sometimes stifled by erudition, as in much of Milton. It is not cynicism, though it has a kind of toughness which may be confused with cynicism by the tender-minded. It is confused with erudition because it belongs to an educated mind, rich in generations of experience; and it is confused with cynicism because it implies a constant inspection and criticism of experience. It involves, probably, a recognition, implicit in the expression of every experience, of other kinds of experience which are possible, which we find as clearly in the greatest as in poets like Marvell. Such a statement may seem to take us a long way from *The Nymph and the Fawn*, or even from the *Horatian Ode*; but it is perhaps justified by the desire to [290] account for that precise taste of Marvell's which finds for him the proper degree of seriousness for every subject which he treats. His errors of taste, when he trespasses, are not sins against this virtue; they are conceits, distended metaphors and similes, but they never consist in taking a subject too seriously or too lightly. This virtue of wit is not a peculiar quality of minor poets, or of the minor poets of one age or of one school; it is an intellectual quality which perhaps only becomes noticeable by itself, in the work of lesser poets. Furthermore, it is absent from the work of Wordsworth, Shelley, and Keats, on whose poetry nineteenth-century criticism has unconsciously been based. To the best of their poetry wit is irrelevant:

> Art thou pale for weariness
> Of climbing heaven and gazing on the earth,
> Wandering companionless
> Among the stars that have a different birth,
> And ever changing, like a joyless eye,
> That finds no object worth its constancy?

We should find it difficult to draw any useful comparison between these lines of Shelley and anything by Marvell. But later poets, who would have been the better for Marvell's quality, were without it; even Browning seems oddly immature, in some way, beside Marvell. And nowadays we find occasionally good irony, or satire, which lack wit's internal equilibrium, because their voices are essentially protests against some outside sentimentality or stupidity; or we find serious poets who are afraid of acquiring wit, lest they lose intensity. The quality which Marvell had, this modest and certainly impersonal virtue – whether we call it wit or reason, or even urbanity – we have patently failed to define. By whatever name we call it, and however we define that name, it is something precious and needed and apparently extinct; it is what should preserve the reputation of Marvell. *C'était une belle âme, comme on ne fait plus à Londres.*

Variants:

2   some quality which is common] something which is a common quality *TLS* (1921), *HJD*
3   Zeal] Rabbi Zeal *TLS* (1921) *HJD*
4   aequo] aequa *TLS* (1921), *HJD*
    [Between 'Regumque turris' and 'And not only Horace':]
        Eheu fugaces, Postume, Postume,
        Labuntur anni. . . .
        Post equitem sedet atra Cura *TLS* (1921)
    Horace's] any of those quoted from Horace *TLS* (1921)
7   leaden] laden *TLS* (1921), *HJD*
8   purer than] so pure as *TLS* (1921), *HJD*
    brilliant] brilliant but ridiculous *TLS* (1921) *HJD*
    Marvell a classic; or classic] Marvell, in the best sense, a classic: classic *TLS* (1921)

John Dryden

SE, 291–302.

Publ. in *TLS*, 1012 (9 June 1921), [361]–2, as a review of *John Dryden*
by Mark Van Doren: Gallup C125. Revised in *HJD*, and further revised in *SE*.
In para. 4 '*Testaments*' has been corrected to '*Testament*'.

1 If the prospect of delight be wanting (which alone justifies the perusal of poetry) we may let the reputation of Dryden sleep in the manuals of literature. To those who are genuinely insensible of his genius (and these are probably the majority of living readers of poetry) we can only oppose illustrations of the following proposition: that their insensibility does not merely signify indifference to satire and wit, but lack of perception of qualities not confined to satire and wit and present in the work of other poets whom these persons feel that they understand. To those whose taste in poetry is formed entirely upon the English poetry of the nineteenth century – to the majority – it is difficult to explain or excuse Dryden: the twentieth century is still the nineteenth, although it may in time acquire its own character. The nineteenth century had, like every other, limited tastes and peculiar fashions; and, like every other, it was unaware of its own limitations. Its tastes and fashions had no place for Dryden; yet Dryden is one of the tests of a catholic appreciation of poetry.

2 He is a successor of Jonson, and therefore the descendant of Marlowe; he is the ancestor of nearly all that is best in the poetry of the eighteenth century. Once we have mastered Dryden – and by mastery is meant a full and essential enjoyment, not the enjoyment of a private whimsical fashion – we can extract whatever enjoyment and edification there is in

his contemporaries – Oldham, Denham, or the less remunerative Waller; and still more his successors – not only Pope, but Phillips, Churchill, Gray, Johnson, Cowper, Goldsmith. His inspiration is prolonged in Crabbe and [292] Byron; it even extends, as Mr Van Doren cleverly points out, to Poe. Even the poets responsible for the revolt were well acquainted with him: Wordsworth knew his work, and Keats invoked his aid. We cannot fully enjoy or rightly estimate a hundred years of English poetry unless we fully enjoy Dryden; and to enjoy Dryden means to pass beyond the limitations of the nineteenth century into a new freedom.

> All, all of a piece throughout!
> Thy Chase had a Beast in View;
> Thy Wars brought nothing about;
> Thy Lovers were all untrue.
> 'Tis well an Old Age is out,
> And time to begin a New.
>
> . . . .
>
> The world's great age begins anew,
> The golden years return,
> The earth doth like a snake renew
> Her winter weeds outworn:
> Heaven smiles, and faiths and empires gleam
> Like wrecks of a dissolving dream.

The first of these passages is by Dryden, the second by Shelley; the second is found in the *Oxford Book of English Verse*, the first is not; yet we might defy anyone to show that the second is superior on intrinsically poetic merit. It is easy to see why the second should appeal more readily to the nineteenth, and what is left of the nineteenth under the name of the twentieth, century. It is not so easy to see propriety in an image which divests a snake of 'winter weeds'; and this is a sort of blemish which would have been noticed more quickly by a contemporary of Dryden than by a contemporary of Shelley.

3 These reflections are occasioned by an admirable book on Dryden which has appeared at this very turn of time, when taste is becoming perhaps more fluid and ready for a new mould.[1] It is a book which every practitioner of [293] English verse should study. The consideration is so thorough, the matter so compact, the appreciation so just, temperate, and enthusiastic, and supplied with such copious and well-chosen extracts from the poetry, the suggestion of astutely placed facts leads our thought

---

1. *John Dryden*. By Mark Van Doren. (New York: Harcourt, Brace & Howe.)

so far, that there only remain to mention, as defects which do not detract from its value, two omissions: the prose is not dealt with, and the plays are somewhat slighted. What is especially impressive is the exhibition of the very wide range of Dryden's work, shown by the quotations of every species. Everyone knows *MacFlecknoe*, and parts of *Absalom and Achitophel*; in consequence, Dryden has sunk by the persons he has elevated to distinction – Shadwell and Settle, Shaftesbury and Buckingham. Dryden was much more than a satirist; to dispose of him as a satirist is to place an obstacle in the way of our understanding. At all events, we must satisfy ourselves of our definition of the term satire; we must not allow our familiarity with the word to blind us to differences and refinements; we must not assume that satire is a fixed type, and fixed to the prosaic, suited only to prose; we must acknowledge that satire is not the same thing in the hands of two different writers of genius. The connotations of 'satire' and of 'wit', in short, may be only prejudices of nineteenth-century taste. Perhaps, we think, after reading Mr Van Doren's book, a juster view of Dryden may be given by beginning with some other portion of his work than his celebrated satires; but even here there is much more present, and much more that is poetry, than is usually supposed.

4 The piece of Dryden's which is the most fun, which is the most sustained display of surprise after surprise of wit from line to line, is *MacFlecknoe*. Dryden's method here is something very near to parody; he applies vocabulary, images, and ceremony which arouse epic associations of grandeur, to make an enemy helplessly ridiculous. But the effect, though disastrous for the enemy, is very different from that of the humour which merely belittles, such as [294] the satire of Mark Twain. Dryden continually enhances: he makes his object great, in a way contrary to expectation; and the total effect is due to the transformation of the ridiculous into poetry. As an example may be taken a fine passage plagiarised from Cowley, from lines which Dryden must have marked well, for he quotes them directly in one of his prefaces. Here is Cowley:

> Where their vast courts the mother-waters keep,
> And undisturbed by moons in silence sleep. . . .
> Beneath the dens where unfledged tempests lie,
> And infant winds their tender voices try.

In *MacFlecknoe* this becomes:

> Where their vast courts the mother-strumpets keep,
> And undisturbed by watch, in silence sleep.

> Near these, a nursery erects its head,
> Where queens are formed, and future heroes bred;
> Where unfledged actors learn to laugh and cry,
> Where infant punks their tender voices try,
> And little Maximins the gods defy.

The passage from Cowley is by no means despicable verse. But it is a commonplace description of commonly poetic objects; it has not the element of *surprise* so essential to poetry, and this Dryden provides. A clever versifier might have written Cowley's lines; only a poet could have made what Dryden made of them. It is impossible to dismiss his verses as 'prosaic'; turn them into prose and they are transmuted, the fragrance is gone. The reproach of the prosaic, levelled at Dryden, rests upon a confusion between the emotions considered to be poetic – which is a matter allowing considerable latitude of fashion – and the *result* of personal emotion in poetry; and also, there is the emotion *depicted* by the poet in some kinds of poetry, of which the *Testament* of Villon is an example. Again, there is the intellect, the originality and independence and clarity of what we vaguely call the poet's 'point of view'. Our [295] valuation of poetry, in short, depends upon several considerations, upon the permanent and upon the mutable and transitory. When we try to isolate the essentially poetic, we bring our pursuit in the end to something insignificant; our standards vary with every poet whom we consider. All we can hope to do, in the attempt to introduce some order into our preferences, is to clarify our reasons for finding pleasure in the poetry that we like.

5 With regard to Dryden, therefore, we can say this much. Our taste in English poetry has been largely founded upon a partial perception of the value of Shakespeare and Milton, a perception which dwells upon sublimity of theme and action. Shakespeare had a great deal more; he had nearly everything to satisfy our various desires for poetry. The point is that the depreciation or neglect of Dryden is not due to the fact that his work is not poetry, but to a prejudice that the material, the feelings, out of which he built is not poetic. Thus Matthew Arnold observes, in mentioning Dryden and Pope together, that 'their poetry is conceived and composed in their wits, genuine poetry is conceived in the soul'. Arnold was, perhaps, not altogether the detached critic when he wrote this line; he may have been stirred to a defence of his own poetry, conceived and composed in the soul of a mid-century Oxford graduate. Pater remarks that Dryden:

Loved to emphasize the distinction between poetry and prose, the protest against their confusion coming with somewhat diminished effect from one whose poetry was so prosaic.

But Dryden was right, and the sentence of Pater is cheap journalism. Hazlitt, who had perhaps the most uninteresting mind of all our distinguished critics, says:

> Dryden and Pope are the great masters of the artificial style of poetry in our language, as the poets of whom I have already treated – Chaucer, Spenser, Shakespeare, and Milton – were of the natural.

[296] In one sentence Hazlitt has committed at least four crimes against taste. It is bad enough to lump Chaucer, Spenser, Shakespeare, and Milton together under the denomination of 'natural'; it is bad to commit Shakespeare to one style only; it is bad to join Dryden and Pope together; but the last absurdity is the contrast of Milton, our greatest master of the *artificial* style, with Dryden, whose *style* (vocabulary, syntax, and order of thought) is in a high degree natural. And what all these objections come to, we repeat, is a repugnance for the material out of which Dryden's poetry is built.

6 It would be truer to say, indeed, even in the form of the unpersuasive paradox, that Dryden is distinguished principally by his *poetic* ability. We prize him, as we do Mallarmé, for what he made of his material. Our estimation is only in part the appreciation of ingenuity: in the end the result *is* poetry. Much of Dryden's unique merit consists in his ability to make the small into the great, the prosaic into the poetic, the trivial into the magnificent. In this he differs not only from Milton, who required a canvas of the largest size, but from Pope, who required one of the smallest. If you compare any satiric 'character' of Pope with one of Dryden, you will see that the method and intention are widely divergent. When Pope alters, he diminishes; he is a master of miniature. The singular skill of his portrait of Addison, for example, in the *Epistle to Arbuthnot*, depends upon the justice and reserve, the apparent determination not to exaggerate. The genius of Pope is not for caricature. But the effect of the portraits of Dryden is to transform the object into something greater, as were transformed the verses of Cowley quoted above.

> A fiery soul, which working out its way,
> Fretted the pigmy body to decay:
> And o'er informed the tenement of clay.

These lines are not merely a magnificent tribute. They create the object which they contemplate. Dryden is, in [297] fact, much nearer to the master of comic creation than to Pope. As in Jonson, the effect is far from laughter; the comic is the material, the result is poetry. The Civic Guards of Rhodes:

> The country rings around with loud alarms,
> And raw in fields the rude militia swarms;
> Mouths without hands; maintained at vast expense,
> In peace a charge, in war a weak defence;
> Stout once a month they march, a blust'ring band,
> And ever, but in times of need, at hand;
> This was the morn, when issuing on the guard,
> Drawn up in rank and file they stood prepared
> Of seeming arms to make a short essay,
> Then hasten to be drunk, the business of the day.

Sometimes the wit appears as a delicate flavour to the magnificence, as in *Alexander's Feast*:

> Sooth'd with the sound the king grew vain;
> Fought all his battles o'er again;
> And thrice he routed all his foes, and thrice he slew the slain.

7 The great advantage of Dryden over Milton is that while the former is always in control of his ascent, and can rise or fall at will (and how masterfully, like his own Timotheus, he directs the transitions!), the latter has elected a perch from which he cannot afford to fall, and from which he is in danger of slipping.

>   food alike those pure
> Intelligential substances require
> As doth your Rational; and both contain
> Within them every lower faculty
> Of sense, whereby they hear, see, smell, touch, taste,
> Tasting concoct, digest, assimilate,
> And corporeal into incorporeal turn.

Dryden might have made poetry out of that; his translation from Lucretius is poetry. But we have an ingenious example, on which to test our contrast of Dryden and [298] Milton: it is Dryden's 'Opera', called *The State of Innocence and Fall of Man*, of which Nathaniel Lee neatly says in his preface:

> For Milton did the wealthy mine disclose,
> And rudely cast what you could well dispose:
> He roughly drew, on an old-fashioned ground,
> A chaos, for no perfect world were found,
> Till through the heap, your mighty genius shined.

In the author's preface Dryden acknowledges his debt generously enough:

> The original being undoubtedly, one of the greatest, most noble, and most sublime poems, which either this age or nation has produced.

The poem begins auspiciously:

> LUCIFER.
>   Is this the seat our conqueror has given?
>   And this the climate we must change for Heaven?
>   These regions and this realm my wars have got;
>   This mournful empire is the loser's lot:
>   In liquid burnings, or on dry to dwell,
>   Is all the sad variety of Hell.

It is an early work; it is on the whole a feeble work; it is not deserving of sustained comparison with *Paradise Lost*. But 'all the sad variety of Hell'! Dryden is already stirring; he has assimilated what he could from Milton; and he has shown himself capable of producing as splendid verse.

8 The capacity for assimilation, and the consequent extent of range, are conspicuous qualities of Dryden. He advanced and exhibited his variety by constant translation; and his translations of Horace, of Ovid, of Lucretius, are admirable. His gravest defects are supposed to be displayed in his dramas, but if these were more read they might be more praised. From the point of view of either the Elizabethan or the French drama they are obviously inferior; but the charge of inferiority loses part of its force if we [299] admit that Dryden was not quite trying to compete with either, but was pursuing a direction of his own. He created no character; and although his arrangements of plot manifest exceptional ingenuity, it is the pure magnificence of diction, of poetic diction, that keeps his plays alive:

>   How I loved
> Witness ye days and nights, and all ye hours,
> That danced away with down upon your feet,
> As all your business were to count my passion.
> One day passed by, and nothing saw but love;
> Another came, and still 'twas only love:

> The suns were wearied out with looking on,
> And I untired with loving.
> I saw you every day and all the day;
> And every day was still but as the first:
> So eager was I still to see you more . . .
>
> > While within your arms I lay,
> > The world fell mould'ring from my hands each hour.

Such language is pure Dryden: it sounds, in Mr Van Doren's phrase, 'like a gong'. *All for Love*, from which the lines are taken, is Dryden's best play, and this is perhaps the highest reach. In general, he is best in his plays when dealing with situations which do not demand great emotional concentration; when his situation is more trivial, and he can practise his art of making the small great. The back-talk between the Emperor and his Empress Nourmahal, in *Aurungzebe*, is admirable purple comedy:

EMPEROR.

> Such virtue is the plague of human life:
> A virtuous woman, but a cursèd wife.
> In vain of pompous chastity y'are proud:
> Virtue's adultery of the tongue, when loud.
> I, with less pain, a prostitute could bear,
> [300] Than the shrill sound of virtue, virtue hear.
> In unchaste wives –
> There's yet a kind of recompensing ease:
> Vice keeps 'em humble, gives 'em care to please:
> But against clamorous virtue, what defence?
> It stops our mouths, and gives your noise pretence. . . .
>
> What can be sweeter than our native home?
> Thither for ease, and soft repose, we come;
> Home is the sacred refuge of our life:
> Secure from all approaches but a wife.
> If thence we fly, the cause admits no doubt:
> None but an inmate foe could force us out.
> Clamours, our privacies uneasy make:
> Birds leave their nests disturbed, and beasts their haunts
>   forsake.

But drama is a mixed form; pure magnificence will not carry it through. The poet who attempts to achieve a play by the single force of the word provokes comparison, however strictly he confine himself to his capacity, with poets of other gifts. Corneille and Racine do not attain their triumphs by magnificence of this sort; they have concentration also, and, in the midst of their phrases, an undisturbed attention to the human soul as they knew it.

9 Nor is Dryden unchallenged by his supreme ability to make the ridiculous, or the trivial, great.

> Avez-vous observé que maints cercueils de vieilles
> Sont presque aussi petits que celui d'un enfant?

Those lines are the work of a man whose verse is as magnificent as Dryden's, and who could see profounder possibilities in wit, and in violently joined images, than ever were in Dryden's mind. For Dryden, with all his intellect, had a commonplace mind. His powers were, we believe, wider, but no greater, than Milton's; he was confined by boundaries as impassable, though less strait. He bears a curious antithetical resemblance to Swinburne. Swinburne was also a master of words, but Swinburne's words are all [301] suggestions and no denotation; if they suggest nothing, it is because they suggest too much. Dryden's words, on the other hand, are precise, they state immensely, but their suggestiveness is often nothing.

> That short dark passage to a future state;
> That melancholy riddle of a breath,
> That something, or that nothing, after death,

is a riddle, but not melancholy enough, in Dryden's splendid verse. The question, which has certainly been waiting, may justly be asked: whether without this which Dryden lacks, verse can be poetry? What is man to decide what poetry is? Dryden's use of language is not, like that of Swinburne, weakening and demoralising. Let us take as a final test his elegy upon Oldham, which deserves not to be mutilated:

> Farewell, too little and too lately known,
> Whom I began to think and call my own;
> For sure our souls were near allied, and thine
> Cast in the same poetic mould with mine.
> One common note on either lyre did strike,
> And knaves and fools we both abhorred alike.
> To the same goal did both our studies drive;
> The last set out the soonest did arrive.
> Thus Nisus fell upon the slippery place,
> Whilst his young friend performed and won the race.
> O early ripe! To thy abundant store

What could advancing age have added more?
It might (what nature never gives the young)
Have taught the numbers of thy native tongue.
But satire needs not those, and wit will shine
Through the harsh cadence of a rugged line.
A noble error, and but seldom made,
When poets are by too much force betrayed.
Thy generous fruits, though gathered ere their prime,
Still showed a quickness; and maturing time
But mellows what we write to the dull sweets of rhyme.
[302] Once more, hail and farewell; farewell, thou young,
But ah! too short, Marcellus of our tongue!
Thy brows with ivy and with laurels bound;
But fate and gloomy night encompass thee around.

From the perfection of such an elegy we cannot detract; the lack of suggestiveness is compensated by the satisfying completeness of the statement. Dryden lacked what his master Jonson possessed, a large and unique view of life; he lacked insight, he lacked profundity. But where Dryden fails to satisfy, the nineteenth century does not satisfy us either; and where that century has condemned him, it is itself condemned. In the next revolution of taste it is possible that poets may turn to the study of Dryden. He remains one of those who have set standards for English verse which it is desperate to ignore.

Variants:

3   the term satire] the term "satire" *HJD*

4   poetic – which is a matter] poetic, which is a matter *HJD*
    fashion – and] fashion, and *HJD*
    result] result *TLS* (1921)
    and also there is] and, in the third place, there is *TLS* (1921), *HJD*
    depicted] depicted *TLS* (1921)
    there is the intellect] there are the intellect *HJD*
    and transitory] upon the transitory *TLS* (1921), *HJD*

6   [Between 'create the object which they [contemplate.]' and 'Dryden is, in fact':] contemplate; the poetry is purer than anything in Pope except the last two lines of the "Dunciad." *TLS* (1921), *HJD*

9   often nothing] almost nothing *HJD*
    verse can be poetry] poetry can exist *TLS* (1921)
    suggestiveness] nebula *TLS* (1921), *HJD*

William Blake

SE, 303–8.

Publ. in A., 4685 (13 Feb. 1920), 208–9, as a review, signed 'T. S. E.', of *William Blake the Man* by Charles Gardner: Gallup C105. Revised in *SW*, and further revised in *SE*.

1 If one follows Blake's mind through the several stages of his poetic development it is impossible to regard him as a naïf, a wild man, a wild pet for the supercultivated. The strangeness is evaporated, the peculiarity is seen to be the peculiarity of all great poetry: something which is found (not everywhere) in Homer and Aeschylus and Dante and Villon, and profound and concealed in the work of Shakespeare – and also in another form in Montaigne and in Spinoza. It is merely a peculiar honesty, which, in a world too frightened to be honest, is peculiarly terrifying. It is an honesty against which the whole world conspires, because it is unpleasant. Blake's poetry has the unpleasantness of great poetry. Nothing that can be called morbid or abnormal or perverse, none of the things which exemplify the sickness of an epoch or a fashion, have this quality; only those things which, by some extraordinary labour of simplification, exhibit the essential sickness or strength of the human soul. And this honesty never exists without great technical accomplishment. The question about Blake the man is the question of the circumstances that concurred to permit this honesty in his work, and what circumstances define its limitations. The favouring conditions probably include these two: that, being early apprenticed to a manual occupation, he was not compelled to acquire any other education in literature than he wanted, or to acquire it for any other reason than that he wanted it; and that, being a humble engraver, he had no journalistic-social career open to him.

[304] 2 There was, that is to say, nothing to distract him from his interests or to corrupt these interests: neither the ambitions of parents or wife, nor the standards of society, nor the temptations of success; nor was he exposed to imitation of himself or of anyone else. These circumstances – not his supposed inspired and untaught spontaneity – are what make him innocent. His early poems show what the poems of a boy of genius ought to show, immense power of assimilation. Such early poems are not, as usually supposed, crude attempts to do something beyond the boy's capacity; they are, in the case of a boy of real promise, more likely to be quite mature and successful attempts to do something small. So with Blake, his early poems are technically admirable, and their originality is in an occasional rhythm. The verse of 'Edward III' deserves study. But his affection for certain Elizabethans is not so surprising as his affinity

with the very best work of his own century. He is very like Collins, he is very eighteenth century. The poem 'Whether on Ida's shady brow' is eighteenth-century work; the movement, the weight of it, the syntax, the choice of words:

> The *languid* strings do scarcely move!
> The sound is *forc'd*, the notes are few!

this is contemporary with Gray and Collins, it is the poetry of a language which has undergone the discipline of prose. Blake up to twenty is decidedly a traditional.

3 Blake's beginnings as a poet, then, are as normal as the beginnings of Shakespeare. His method of composition, in his mature work, is exactly like that of other poets. He has an idea (a feeling, an image), he develops it by accretion or expansion, alters his verse often, and hesitates often over the final choice.[1] The idea, of course, simply comes, but upon arrival it is subjected to prolonged manipulation. In [305] the first phase Blake is concerned with verbal beauty; in the second he becomes the apparent naïf, really the mature intelligence. It is only when the ideas become more automatic, come more freely and are less manipulated, that we begin to suspect their origin, to suspect that they spring from a shallower source.

4 The *Songs of Innocence and of Experience*, and the poems from the Rossetti manuscript, are the poems of a man with a profound interest in human emotions, and a profound knowledge of them. The emotions are presented in an extremely simplified, abstract form. The form is one illustration of the eternal struggle of art against education, of the literary artist against the continuous deterioration of language.

5 It is important that the artist should be highly educated in his own art; but his education is one that is hindered rather than helped by the ordinary processes of society which constitute education for the ordinary man. For these processes consist largely in the acquisition of impersonal ideas which obscure what we really are and feel, what we really want, and what really excites our interest. It is of course not the actual information

---

1. I do not know why M. Berger should say, without qualification, in his *William Blake: mysticisme et poésie*, that 'son respect pour l'esprit qui soufflait en lui et qui dictait ses paroles l'empêchait de les corriger jamais.' Dr Sampson, in his Oxford edition of Blake, gives us to understand that Blake believed much of his writing to be automatic, but observes that Blake's 'meticulous care in composition is everywhere apparent in the poems preserved in rough draft . . . alteration on alteration, rearrangement after rearrangement, deletions, additions, and inversions . . .'

acquired, but the conformity which the accumulation of knowledge is apt to impose, that is harmful. Tennyson is a very fair example of a poet almost wholly encrusted with opinion, almost wholly merged into his environment. Blake, on the other hand, knew what interested him, and he therefore presents only the essential, only, in fact, what can be presented, and need not be explained. And because he was not distracted, or frightened, or occupied in anything but exact statements, he understood. He was naked, and saw man naked, and from the centre of his own crystal. To him there was no more reason why Swedenborg should [306] be absurd than Locke. He accepted Swedenborg, and eventually rejected him, for reasons of his own. He approached everything with a mind unclouded by current opinions. There was nothing of the superior person about him. This makes him terrifying.

II

6 But if there was nothing to distract him from sincerity there were, on the other hand, the dangers to which the naked man is exposed. His philosophy, like his visions, like his insight, like his technique, was his own. And accordingly he was inclined to attach more importance to it than an artist should; this is what makes him eccentric, and makes him inclined to formlessness.

> But most through midnight streets I hear
> How the youthful harlot's curse
> Blasts the new-born infant's tear,
> And blights with plagues the marriage hearse,

is the naked vision;

> Love seeketh only self to please,
> To bind another to its delight,
> Joys in another's loss of ease,
> And builds a Hell in Heaven's despite,

is the naked observation; and *The Marriage of Heaven and Hell* is naked philosophy, presented. But Blake's occasional marriages of poetry and philosophy are not so felicitous.

> He who would do good to another must do it in Minute
>   Particulars.
> General Good is the plea of the scoundrel, hypocrite, and
>   flatterer;
> For Art and Science cannot exist but in minutely organized
>   particulars. . . .

One feels that the form is not well chosen. The borrowed philosophy of Dante and Lucretius is perhaps not so interesting, but it injures their form less. Blake did not have [307] that more Mediterranean gift of form which knows how to borrow as Dante borrowed his theory of the soul; he must needs create a philosophy as well as a poetry. A similar formlessness attacks his draughtsmanship. The fault is most evident, of course, in the longer poems – or rather, the poems in which structure is important. You cannot create a very large poem without introducing a more impersonal point of view, or splitting it up into various personalities. But the weakness of the long poems is certainly not that they are too visionary, too remote from the world. It is that Blake did not see enough, became too much occupied with ideas.

7 We have the same respect for Blake's philosophy (and perhaps for that of Samuel Butler) that we have for an ingenious piece of home-made furniture: we admire the man who has put it together out of the odds and ends about the house. England has produced a fair number of these resourceful Robinson Crusoes; but we are not really so remote from the Continent, or from our own past, as to be deprived of the advantages of culture if we wish them.

8 We may speculate, for amusement, whether it would not have been beneficial to the north of Europe generally, and to Britain in particular, to have had a more continuous religious history. The local divinities of Italy were not wholly exterminated by Christianity, and they were not reduced to the dwarfish state which fell upon our trolls and pixies. The latter, with the major Saxon deities, were perhaps no great loss in themselves, but they left an empty place; and perhaps our mythology was further impoverished by the divorce from Rome. Milton's celestial and infernal regions are large but insufficiently furnished apartments filled by heavy conversation; and one remarks about the Puritan mythology its thinness. And about Blake's supernatural territories, as about the supposed ideas that dwell there, we cannot help commenting on a certain meanness of culture. They illustrate the crankiness, the eccentricity, which frequently affects writers outside of the Latin [308] traditions, and which such a critic as Arnold should certainly have rebuked. And they are not essential to Blake's inspiration.

9 Blake was endowed with a capacity for considerable understanding of human nature, with a remarkable and original sense of language and the music of language, and a gift of hallucinated vision. Had these been controlled by a respect for impersonal reason, for common sense, for the

objectivity of science, it would have been better for him. What his genius required, and what it sadly lacked, was a framework of accepted and traditional ideas which would have prevented him from indulging in a philosophy of his own, and concentrated his attention upon the problems of the poet. Confusion of thought, emotion, and vision is what we find in such a work as *Also Sprach Zarathustra*; it is eminently not a Latin virtue. The concentration resulting from a framework of mythology and theology and philosophy is one of the reasons why Dante is a classic, and Blake only a poet of genius. The fault is perhaps not with Blake himself, but with the environment which failed to provide what such a poet needed; perhaps the circumstances compelled him to fabricate, perhaps the poet required the philosopher and mythologist; although the conscious Blake may have been quite unconscious of the motives.

Variants:

Title The Naked Man *A.* (1920); Blake *SW*

1 [Before 'If one follows':] This book is not well written, and it is not a complete success in the attempt implied by the title. It is a readable short biography, not a critique; it is an honest, and not, indeed, a useless book. There is very little to which exception need be taken, and at least it does not set us on the wrong tack. We are not led to believe that Blake was abnormal or hallucinated; we are not encouraged to take too seriously the fact that the infant Blake saw angels in the foliage of Peckham Rye, or to believe that his method of composition was automatic writing. We are left unsatisfied; the book displays no profound analytic ability. But it allows the important fact to appear: that Blake's mind was a perfectly sane mind of abnormal intensity and strong passions, occupied with intelligible objects, and appearing under peculiar conditions, and conditions is some ways peculiarly favourable. [New para.] The conception of Blake extracted from Mr. Gardner's book or from any tolerable biography is confirmed by re-reading Blake's poems from beginning to end. *A.* (1920)
follows] follow *SW*
against which the whole world conspires] which the whole world conspires against *A.* (1920)
that, being] that being *A.* (1920)

2 [Between 'discipline of' and 'Blake up to twenty':] prose, it is not remote from Landor *A.* (1920)

3 [No fn. in *A.* (1920)]
edition] Edition *SW*

5 opinion] parasitic opinion *A.* (1920), *SW*
statements] statement *A.* (1920), *SW*

7 [After 'occupied with ideas':] But even these poems evince an intelligence more powerful, in its way, than that of, let us say, Tennyson or Browning. [The rest not represented.] *A.* (1920)

8 its thinness] an historical thinness *SW*

Swinburne as Poet

SE, 309–13.
Repr., from *SW. See* Vol. 1, pp. 340–4, in the present edition.

VI Lancelot Andrewes

SE, 317–29.
Originally published in *TLS*, 1286 (23 Sept. 1926), [621]–2: Gallup C182.
Revised in *FLA*, and further revised in *SE*. Repr. from *SE* in *EAAM*.
In para. 8 'Griffin Farran Okeden and Welsh' has been corrected to 'Griffin, Farran, Okeden and Welsh': it was thus in *TLS*, and in *FLA* and *EAAM*.

1 The Right Reverend Father in God, Lancelot Bishop of Winchester, died on September 25, 1626. During his lifetime he enjoyed a distinguished reputation for the excellence of his sermons, for the conduct of his diocese, for his ability in controversy displayed against Cardinal Bellarmine, and for the decorum and devotion of his private life. Some years after Andrewes's death Lord Clarendon, in his *History of the Rebellion*, expressed regret that Andrewes had not been chosen instead of Abbott to the Archbishopric of Canterbury, for thus affairs in England might have taken a different course. By authorities on the history of the English Church Andrewes is still accorded a high, perhaps the highest, place; among persons interested in devotion his *Private Prayers* are not unknown. But among those persons who read sermons, if they read them at all, as specimens of English prose, Andrewes is little known. His sermons are too well built to be readily quotable; they stick too closely to the point to be entertaining. Yet they rank with the finest English prose of their time, of any time. Before attempting to remove the remains of his reputation to a last resting place in the dreary cemetery of literature, it is desirable to remind the reader of Andrewes's position in history.

2 The Church of England is the creation not of the reign of Henry VIII or of the reign of Edward VI, but of the reign of Elizabeth. The *via media* which is the spirit of Anglicanism was the spirit of Elizabeth in all things; the last of the humble Welsh family of Tudor was the first and most complete incarnation of English policy. The taste or [318] sensibility of Elizabeth, developed by her intuitive knowledge of the right policy for the hour and her ability to choose the right men to carry out that policy, determined the future of the English Church. In its persistence in finding a mean between Papacy and Presbytery the English Church under

Elizabeth became something representative of the finest spirit of England of the time. It came to reflect not only the personality of Elizabeth herself, but the best community of her subjects of every rank. Other religious impulses, of varying degrees of spiritual value, were to assert themselves with greater vehemence during the next two reigns. But the Church at the end of the reign of Elizabeth, and as developed in certain directions under the next reign, was a masterpiece of ecclesiastical statesmanship. The same authority that made use of Gresham, and of Walsingham, and of Cecil, appointed Parker to the Archbishopric of Canterbury; the same authority was later to appoint Whitgift to the same office.

3 To the ordinary cultivated student of civilisation the genesis of a Church is of little interest, and at all events we must not confound the history of a Church with its spiritual meaning. To the ordinary observer the English Church in history means Hooker and Jeremy Taylor – and should mean Andrewes also: it means George Herbert, and it means the churches of Christopher Wren. This is not an error: a Church is to be judged by its intellectual fruits, by its influence on the sensibility of the most sensitive and on the intellect of the most intelligent, and it must be made real to the eye by monuments of artistic merit. The English Church has no literary monument equal to that of Dante, no intellectual monument equal to that of St Thomas, no devotional monument equal to that of St John of the Cross, no building so beautiful as the Cathedral of Modena or the basilica of St Zeno in Verona. But there are those for whom the City churches are as precious as any of the four hundred odd churches in Rome which are in no danger of demolition, and for [319] whom St Paul's, in comparison with St Peter's, is not lacking in decency; and the English devotional verse of the seventeenth century – admitting the one difficult case of conversion, that of Crashaw – finer than that of any other country or religious communion at the time.

4 The intellectual achievement and the prose style of Hooker and Andrewes came to complete the structure of the English Church as the philosophy of the thirteenth century crowns the Catholic Church. To make this statement is not to compare the *Laws of Ecclesiastical Polity* with the *Summa*. The seventeenth century was not an age in which the Churches occupied themselves with metaphysics, and none of the writings of the fathers of the English Church belongs to the category of speculative philosophy. But the achievement of Hooker and Andrewes was to make the English Church more worthy of intellectual assent. No religion can survive the judgement of history unless the best minds of its time have collaborated in its construction; if the Church of Elizabeth is worthy of

the age of Shakespeare and Jonson, that is because of the work of Hooker and Andrewes.

5 The writings of both Hooker and Andrewes illustrate that determination to stick to essentials, that awareness of the needs of the time, the desire for clarity and precision on matters of importance, and the indifference to matters indifferent, which was the general policy of Elizabeth. These characteristics are illustrated in the definition of the Church in the second book of the *Ecclesiastical Polity*. ('The Church of Christ which was from the beginning is and continueth until the end.') And in both Hooker and Andrewes – the latter the friend and intimate of Isaac Casaubon – we find also that breadth of culture, an ease with humanism and Renaissance learning, which helped to put them on terms of equality with their Continental antagonists and to elevate their Church above the position of a local heretical sect. They were fathers of a national Church and they were Europeans. Compare a sermon of Andrewes [320] with a sermon by another earlier master, Latimer. It is not merely that Andrewes knew Greek, or that Latimer was addressing a far less cultivated public, or that the sermons of Andrewes are peppered with allusion and quotation. It is rather that Latimer, the preacher of Henry VIII and Edward VI, is merely a Protestant; but the voice of Andrewes is the voice of a man who has a formed visible Church behind him, who speaks with the old authority and the new culture. It is the difference of negative and positive. Andrewes is the first great preacher of the English Catholic Church.

6 The sermons of Andrewes are not easy reading. They are only for the reader who can elevate himself to the subject. The most conspicuous qualities of the style are three: ordonnance, or arrangement and structure, precision in the use of words, and relevant intensity. The last remains to be defined. All of them are best elucidated by comparison with a prose which is much more widely known, but to which I believe that we must assign a lower place – that of Donne. Donne's sermons, or fragments from Donne's sermons, are certainly known to hundreds who have hardly heard of Andrewes; and they are known precisely for the reasons because of which they are inferior to those of Andrewes. In the introduction to an admirable selection of passages from Donne's sermons, which was published a few years ago by the Oxford Press, Mr Logan Pearsall Smith, after 'trying to explain Donne's sermons and account for them in a satisfactory manner', observes:

> And yet in these, as in his poems, there remains something baffling and enigmatic which still eludes our last analysis. Reading these

old hortatory and dogmatic pages, the thought suggests itself that Donne is often saying something else, something poignant and personal, and yet, in the end, incommunicable to us.

We may cavil at the word 'incommunicable', and pause to ask whether the incommunicable is not often the vague [321] and unformed; but the statement is essentially right. About Donne there hangs the shadow of the impure motive; and impure motives lend their aid to a facile success. He is a little of the religious spellbinder, the Reverend Billy Sunday of his time, the flesh-creeper, the sorcerer of emotional orgy. We emphasise this aspect to the point of the grotesque. Donne had a trained mind; but without belittling the intensity or the profundity of his experience, we can suggest that this experience was not perfectly controlled, and that he lacked spiritual discipline.

7 But Bishop Andrewes is one of the community of the born spiritual, one

> che in questo mondo,
> contemplando, gustò di quella pace.

Intellect and sensibility were in harmony; and hence arise the particular qualities of his style. Those who would prove his harmony would do well to examine, before proceeding to the sermons, the volume of *Preces Privatae*. This book, composed by him for his private devotions, was printed only after his death; a few manuscript copies may have been given away during his lifetime – one bears the name of William Laud. It appears to have been written in Latin and translated by him into Greek; some of it is in Hebrew; it has been several times translated into English. The most recent edition is the translation of the late F. E. Brightman, with an interesting introduction (Methuen, 1903). They are almost wholly an arrangement of Biblical texts, and of texts from elsewhere in Andrewes's immense theological reading. Dr Brightman has a paragraph of admirable criticism of these prayers which deserves to be quoted in full:

> But the structure is not merely an external scheme or framework: the internal structure is as close as the external. Andrewes develops an idea he has in his mind: every line tells and adds something. He does not expatiate, but moves forward: if he reports, it is because the repetition has a real [322] force of expression; if he accumulates, each new word or phrase represents a new development, a substantive addition to what he is saying. He assimilates his material and advances by means of it. His quotation is not decoration or irrelevance,

but the matter in which he expresses what he wants to say. His single thoughts are no doubt often suggested by the words he borrows, but the thoughts are made his own, and the constructive force, the fire that fuses them, is his own. And this internal, progressive, often poetic structure is marked outwardly. The editions have not always reproduced this feature of the *Preces*, nor perhaps is it possible in any ordinary page to represent the structure adequately; but in the manuscript the intention is clear enough. The prayers are arranged, not merely in paragraphs, but in lines advanced and recessed, so as in a measure to mark the inner structure and the steps and stages of the movement. Both in form and in matter Andrewes's prayers may often be described rather as hymns.

The first part of this excellent piece of criticism may be applied equally well to the prose of Andrewes's sermons. The prayers themselves, which, as Canon Brightman seems to hint, should take for Anglicans a place beside the Exercises of St Ignatius and the works of St François de Sales, illustrate the devotion to private prayer (Andrewes is said to have passed nearly five hours a day in prayer) and to public ritual which Andrewes bequeathed to William Laud; and his passion for order in religion is reflected in his passion for order in prose.

8 Readers who hesitate before the five large volumes of Andrewes's sermons in *The Library of Anglo-Catholic Theology* may find their introduction more easy through the *Seventeen Sermons on the Nativity*, which were published separately in a small volume by Griffith, Farran, Okeden and Welsh, in *The Ancient and Modern Library of Theological Literature*, and which can still be picked up here and there. It is an additional advantage that these sermons are all on the same subject, the Incarnation; they are the Christmas [323] Day sermons preached before King James between 1605 and 1624. And in the sermons preached before King James, himself a theologian, Andrewes was not hampered as he sometimes was in addressing more popular audiences. His erudition had full play, and his erudition is essential to his originality.

9 Bishop Andrewes, as was hinted above, tried to confine himself in his sermons to the elucidation of what he considered essential in dogma; he said himself that in sixteen years he had never alluded to the question of predestination, to which the Puritans, following their continental brethren, attached so much importance. The Incarnation was to him an essential dogma, and we are able to compare seventeen developments of the same idea. Reading Andrewes on such a theme is like listening to a

great Hellenist expounding a text of the *Posterior Analytics*: altering the punctuation, inserting or removing a comma or a semicolon to make an obscure passage suddenly luminous, dwelling on a single word, comparing its use in its nearer and in its most remote contexts, purifying a disturbed or cryptic lecture-note into lucid profundity. To persons whose minds are habituated to feed on the vague jargon of our time, when we have a vocabulary for everything and exact ideas about nothing – when a word half-understood, torn from its place in some alien or half-formed science, as of psychology, conceals from both writer and reader the meaninglessness of a statement, when all dogma is in doubt except the dogmas of sciences of which we have read in the newspapers, when the language of theology itself, under the influence of an undisciplined mysticism of popular philosophy, tends to become a language of tergiversation – Andrewes may seem pedantic and verbal. It is only when we have saturated ourselves in his prose, followed the movement of his thought, that we find his examination of words terminating in the ecstasy of assent. Andrewes takes a word and derives the world from it; squeezing and squeezing the word until it yields a [324] full juice of meaning which we should never have supposed any word to possess. In this process the qualities we have mentioned, of ordonnance and precision, are exercised.

10 Take, almost at random, a passage from Andrewes's exposition of the text, 'For unto you is born this day in the city of David a Saviour, which is Christ the Lord' (Luke ii. 11). Any passage that we can choose must be torn violently from its context.

> Who is it? Three things are said of this Child by the Angel. (1) He is 'a Saviour'. (2) 'Which is Christ'. (3) 'Christ the Lord'. Three of his titles, well and orderly inferred one of another by good consequence. We cannot miss one of them; they be necessary all. Our method on earth is to begin with great; in heaven they begin with good first.
>
> First, then, 'a Saviour'; that is His name, Jesus, *Soter*; and in that Name His benefit, *Salus*, 'saving health or salvation'. Such a name as the great Orator himself saith of it, *Soter, hoc quantum est? Ita magnum est ut latino uno verbo exprimi non possit*. 'This name Saviour is so great as no one word can express the force of it.'
>
> But we are not so much to regard the *ecce* how great it is, as *gaudium* what joy is in it; that is the point we are to speak to. And for that, men may talk what they will, but sure there is no joy in the world to the joy of a man saved; no joy so great, no news so welcome, as to one ready to perish, in case of a lost man, to hear of one that will save him. In danger of perishing by sickness, to hear

of one will make him well again; by sentence of the law, of one with a pardon to save his life; by enemies, of one that will rescue and set him in safety. Tell any of these, assure them but of a Saviour, it is the best news he ever heard in his life. There is joy in the name of a Saviour. And even this way, this Child is a Saviour too. *Potest hoc facere, sed hoc non est opus Ejus.* 'This He can do, but this is not His work'; a farther matter there is, a greater salvation He [325] came for. And it may be we need not any of these; we are not presently sick, in no fear of the law, in no danger of enemies. And it may be, if we were, we fancy to ourselves to be relieved some other way. But that which He came for, that saving we need all; and none but He can help us to it. We have therefore all cause to be glad for the Birth of this Saviour.

And then, after this succession of short sentences – no one is more master of the short sentence than Andrewes – in which the effort is to find the exact meaning and make that meaning live, he slightly but sufficiently alters the rhythm in proceeding more at large:

I know not how, but when we hear of saving or mention of a Saviour, presently our mind is carried to the saving of our skin, of our temporal state, of our bodily life, and farther saving we think not of. But there is another life not to be forgotten, and greater the dangers, and the destruction more to be feared than of this here, and it would be well sometimes we were remembered of it. Besides our skin and flesh a soul we have, and it is our better part by far, that also hath need of a Saviour; that hath her destruction out of which, that hath her destroyer from which she would be saved, and those would be thought on. Indeed our chief thought and care would be for that; how to escape the wrath, how to be saved from the destruction to come, whither our sins will certainly bring us. Sin it is will destroy us all.

In this extraordinary prose, which appears to repeat, to stand still, but is nevertheless proceeding in the most deliberate and orderly manner, there are often flashing phrases which never desert the memory. In an age of adventure and experiment in language, Andrewes is one of the most resourceful of authors in his devices for seizing the attention and impressing the memory. Phrases such as 'Christ is no wild-cat. What talk ye of twelve days?' or 'the word within a word, unable to speak a word' do not [326] desert us; nor do the sentences in which, before extracting all the spiritual meaning of a text, Andrewes forces a concrete presence upon us.

Of the wise men come from the East:

> It was no summer progress. A cold coming they had of it at this time of the year, just the worst time of the year to take a journey, and specially a long journey in. The ways deep, the weather sharp, the days short, the sun farthest off, *in solstitio brumali*, 'the very dead of winter'.

Of 'the Word made flesh' again:

> I add yet farther; what flesh? The flesh of an infant. What, *Verbum infans*, the Word of an infant? The Word, and not be able to speak a word? How evil agreeth this! This He put up. How born, how entertained? In a stately palace, cradle of ivory, robes of estate? No; but a stable for His palace, a manger for His cradle, poor clouts for His array.

He will not hesitate to hammer, to inflect, even to play upon a word for the sake of driving home its meaning:

> Let us then make this so accepted a time in itself twice acceptable by our accepting, which He will acceptably take at our hands.

We can now better estimate what is this that we have called relevant intensity, for we have had enough of passages from Andrewes to recognise the extremity of his difference from Donne.

11 Everyone knows a passage from a sermon of Donne's, which is given by Mr Pearsall Smith under the title of 'I am Not all Here.'

> I am here speaking to you, and yet I consider by the way, in the same instant, what it is likely you will say to one another, when I have done, you are not all here neither; you are here now, hearing me, and yet you are thinking that you have heard a better sermon somewhere [327] else of this text before; you are here, and yet you think you could have heard some other doctrine of downright *Predestination* and *Reprobation* roundly delivered somewhere else with more edification to you; you are here, and you remember yourselves that now yee think of it: This had been the fittest time, now, when everybody else is at church, to have made such and such a private visit; and because you would bee there, you are there,

after which Mr Pearsall Smith very happily places the paragraph on 'Imperfect Prayers':

> A memory of yesterday's pleasures, a feare of tomorrow's dangers, a straw under my knee, a noise in mine eare, a light in mine eye,

an anything[,] a nothing, a fancy, a Chimera in my braine, troubles me in my prayer. So certainly is there nothing, nothing in spirituall things, perfect in this world.

These are thoughts which would never have come to Andrewes. When Andrewes begins his sermon, from beginning to end you are sure that he is wholly in his subject, unaware of anything else, that his emotion grows as he penetrates more deeply into his subject, that he is finally 'alone with the Alone', with the mystery which he is seeking to grasp more and more firmly. One is reminded of the words of Arnold about the preaching of Newman. Andrewes's emotion is purely contemplative; it is not personal, it is wholly evoked by the object of contemplation, to which it is adequate; his emotions wholly contained in and explained by its object. But with Donne there is always the something else, the 'baffling' of which Mr Pearsall Smith speaks in his introduction. Donne is a 'personality' in a sense in which Andrewes is not: his sermons, one feels, are a 'means of self-expression.' He is constantly finding an object which shall be adequate to his feelings; Andrewes is wholly absorbed in the object and therefore responds with the adequate emotion. Andrewes has the *goût pour la vie spirituelle*, which is not native to Donne. [328] On the other hand, it would be a great mistake to remember only that Donne was called to the priesthood by King James against his will, and that he accepted a benefice because he had no other way of making a living. Donne had a genuine taste both for theology and for religious emotion; but he belonged to that class of persons, of which there are always one or two examples in the modern world, who seek refuge in religion from the tumults of a strong emotional temperament which can find no complete satisfaction elsewhere. He is not wholly without kinship to Huysmans.

12 But Donne is not the less valuable, though he is the more dangerous for this reason. Of the two men, it may be said that Andrewes is the more medieval, because he is the more pure, and because his bond was with the Church, with tradition. His intellect was satisfied by theology and his sensibility by prayer and liturgy. Donne is the more modern – if we are careful to take this word exactly, without any implication of value, or any suggestion that we must have more sympathy with Donne than with Andrewes. Donne is much less the mystic; he is primarily interested in man. He is much less traditional. In his thought Donne has, on the one hand, much more in common with the Jesuits, and, on the other hand, much more in common with the Calvinists, than has Andrewes. Donne many times betrays the consequences of early Jesuit influence

and of his later studies in Jesuit literature; in his cunning knowledge of the weaknesses of the human heart, his understanding of human sin, his skill in coaxing and persuading the attention of the variable human mind to Divine objects, and in a kind of smiling tolerance among his menaces of damnation. He is dangerous only for those who find in his sermons an indulgence of their sensibility, or for those who, fascinated by 'personality' in the romantic sense of the word – for those who find in 'personality' an ultimate value – forget that in the spiritual hierarchy there are places higher than that of Donne. Donne will certainly have al-[329]ways more readers than Andrewes, for the reason that his sermons can be read in detached passages and for the reason that they can be read by those who have no interest in the subject. He has many means of appeal, and appeals to many temperaments and minds, and, among others, to those capable of a certain wantonness of the spirit. Andrewes will never have many readers in any one generation, and his will never be the immortality of anthologies. Yet his prose is not inferior to that of any sermons in the language, unless it be some of Newman's. And even the larger public which does not read him may do well to remember his greatness in history – a place second to none in the history of the formation of the English Church.

Variants:

3   decency] decorum *TLS* (1926)
6   I believe] we believe *TLS* (1926)
7   the late F. E. Brightman] F. E. Brightman *TLS* (1926)
    introduction (Methuen, 1903)] introduction, in 1903 (Methuen) *TLS* (1926)
    Dr Brightman] Canon Brightman *TLS* (1926)
    should take for Anglicans ... illustrate] might take the same place for Anglicans which the Exercises of St. Ignatius and St. François de Sales take for Roman Catholics, illustrate *TLS* (1926)
9   when a word] when a word, a concrete statement, *TLS* (1926)
10 'For unto you is born ... (Luke ii. 11)'] 'That there is born unto you this day a Saviour, Which is Christ the Lord, in the City of David' (Luke ii. 10, 11) *TLS* (1926), *FLA*

John Bramhall[1]

SE, 330–8.

Publ. in *Theology*, 15. 85 (July 1927), 11–17: Gallup C215. Revised in *FLA*, and further revised in *SE*. In para. 8 'tactful' has been corrected to 'tactical'.
Repr. from *SE* in *EAAM*.

1 John Bramhall, Bishop of Derry under Charles I and Primate of Ireland under Charles II, is not at all an easy subject for biography. He was a great man; but either by defect of genius or by ill-luck he is not known as he should be known, and his works are not read as they should be read. Indeed, it is largely ill luck. Not only were his immense energy and ability divided among a number of important actions, so that he has never become the symbolical representative of anything; but some of his most important activity was exerted upon causes which are now forgotten. As Bishop of Derry, as the lieutenant of Wentworth and Laud, he did much to reform and establish the Irish Church and to bring it into conformity with the English Church; he saw his work largely undone by Cromwell; as Primate of Ireland during the first years of Charles II, and in his old age, he set to work to build it up again. Had his labours been in England instead of Ireland he might now be better remembered. His middle years were spent in exile; and perhaps it is the work he performed during these years, often in illness, danger, and vicissitudes, that should earn him particular gratitude from his Church. This is a chapter of Church history which is too little known; few people realise how near in those years the English Church came to perishing utterly, or realise that had the Commonwealth survived a few years longer the Church would have fallen into a disorder from which it might never have recovered. During the exile Bramhall was the stoutest inheritor of the tradition of Andrewes and Laud.

[331] 2 Canon Sparrow-Simpson has treated the history of Bramhall's career in Ireland and his activities abroad during the Commonwealth fully, but with a proper sense of proportion. He leaves himself space to devote several chapters to Bramhall's controversial writings; he is specially to be praised for the skill with which he has digested these writings and condensed and organised so much various information into two hundred and fifty-one pages. With the purely historical matter I am not competent to deal; Bramhall's life includes an important part of the history of the Church and the history of England. But there is still much

---

1. *Archbishop Bramhall*, by W. J. Sparrow-Simpson, D.D. (In the English Theologians Series.) S.P.C.K.

interest to be found in Bramhall's writings, and some of them are very much to the point at the present day. One part of his work that is of particular importance is his controversy with Hobbes. It is sometimes cited by historians of philosophy, but has never received the attention it deserves. Bramhall, as Dr Sparrow-Simpson points out, had by no means the worst of the argument, and the whole debate, with the two striking and opposed personalities engaged in it, throws light upon the condition of philosophy and theology at that time. The most important of the questions at issue are two: the freedom of the will and the relation between Church and State.

3 Thomas Hobbes was one of those extraordinary little upstarts whom the chaotic motions of the Renaissance tossed into an eminence which they hardly deserved and have never lost. When I say the Renaissance I mean for this purpose the period between the decay of scholastic philosophy and the rise of modern science. There was nothing particularly new about the determinism of Hobbes; but he gave to his determinism and theory of sense perception a new point and piquancy by applying it, so to speak, almost to topical questions; and by his metaphor of Leviathan he provided an ingenious framework on which there was some peg or other to hang every question of philosophy, psychology, government, and economics.

4 Hobbes shows considerable ingenuity and determina-[332]tion in his attempt to carry out his theory of the Will rigorously to explain the whole and every aspect of human behaviour. It is certain that in the end he lands himself in sophistries. But at the time of Hobbes and Bramhall, and indeed ever since until recently, it was unlikely that a controversy on this subject would keep to the point. For a philosopher like Hobbes has already a mixed attitude, partly philosophic and partly scientific; the philosophy being in decay and the science immature. Hobbes's philosophy is not so much a philosophy as it is an adumbration of the universe of material atoms regulated by laws of motion which formed the scientific view of the world from Newton to Einstein. Hence there is quite naturally no place in Hobbes's universe for the human will; what he failed to see is that there was no place in it for consciousness either, or for human beings. So his only philosophical theory is a theory of sense perception, and his psychology leaves no place in the world for his theory of government. His theory of government has no philosophic basis: it is merely a collection of discrete opinions, prejudices, and genuine reflections upon experience which are given a spurious unity by a shadowy metaphysic.

5 The attitude of Hobbes toward moral philosophy has by no means disappeared from human thought; nor has the confusion between moral philosophy and a mechanistic psychology. There is a modern theory, closely akin to that of Hobbes, which would make value reside entirely in the degree of organisation of natural impulses. I cite the following passage from an important book by one of the most acute of younger psychologists:

> Anything is valuable which will satisfy an appetency without involving the frustration of some equal or more important appetency; in other words, the only reason which can be given for not satisfying a desire is that more important desires will thereby be thwarted. Thus morals become purely prudential, and ethical codes merely the [333] expression of the most general schemes of expediency to which an individual or a race has attained.[1]

6 And Mr Bertrand Russell, in his book, *What I Believe*, p. 43, sings the same tune:

> The practical need of morals arises from the conflict of desires, whether of different people or of the same person at different times or even at one time. A man desires to drink, and also to be fit for his work next morning. We think him immoral if he adopts the course which gives him the smaller total satisfaction of desire.

7 The difficulty with such theories[2] is that they merely remove the inherently valuable a further degree; just as Hobbes's Theory of Will removes freedom from the individual considered as the object of psychology, but really implies the reality of freewill in society. It will be remembered that Hobbes wished to maintain the activity of human legislation in his deterministic universe; so he considered that law acts as a deterrent force. He did not consider that if human laws themselves are created by the same necessity under which human beings act when encouraged or deterred by the laws, then the whole system ceases to have any meaning, and all values, including his own value of good government, disappear.

8 It is not to be expected that the arguments advanced by Bramhall against this position should appear very powerful when opposed to the reasonings of modern disciples of Hobbes. But in their own time and

---

1. Richards, *Principles of Literary Criticism*, p. 48.
2. A thoroughgoing 'Behaviourism', as of Professor Watson, is a different affair.

place they were excellent. I disregard that part of Bramhall's reasoning which consists in showing that Hobbes's system was incompatible with Christianity. Hobbes was here in a very weak position of which the Bishop with praiseworthy slyness took full advantage. Hobbes was undoubtedly an atheist and [334] could hardly have been unconscious of the fact; but he was no Spinoza, and would hardly have been willing to sacrifice his worldly prospects for the sake of establishing consistency in his argument. Therefore he has always the worst of the debate. But this is a minor point. Bramhall was able to meet Hobbes also on his own ground. His method of attack illustrates very clearly his type of mind. It was not a subtle mind: it had not the refinement necessary to make a scholastic metaphysician, nor was it the mind of a doctor of the Church who could develop and explicate the meaning of a dogma. It was essentially common sense and right instinct, a mind not gifted to discover truth but tenacious to hold it. It was typical of the best theological minds of that age. Hobbes suffers from not only a tactical but a real disadvantage in his confusion of the spheres of psychology and ethics. Bramhall is single-minded; he does not penetrate the real philosophical incoherence of Hobbes's position; but he touches the point of practical importance and implies the profounder objection to Hobbes when he says simply that Hobbes makes praise and blame meaningless. 'If a man be born blind or with one eye, we do not blame him for it; but if a man have lost his sight by his intemperance, we blame him justly.' This objection is finally unanswerable.

9 I have asserted that Hobbes's psychological analysis of the human mind has no rational connection with his theory of the State. But it has, of course, an emotional connection; one can say that both doctrines belong naturally to the same temperament. Materialistic determinism and absolutist government fit into the same scheme of life. And this theory of the State shows the same lack of balance which is a general characteristic of philosophers after the Renaissance. Hobbes merely exaggerates one aspect of the good State. In doing so he developed a particularly lamentable theory of the relation between Church and State.

10 There is no question to which a man like Hobbes can give a less satisfactory answer than that of Church and [335] State. For Hobbes thought in extremes, and in this problem the extreme is always wrong. In the relation of Church and State, a doctrine when pushed to the extreme may even be transformed to the opposite of itself. Hobbes has something in common with Suarez.

11 Bramhall's position on this subject is characteristic of his sense of realities and his ability to grasp what was expedient. He had also what Hobbes lacked, the historical sense, which is a gift not only of the historian, but of the efficient lawyer, statesman, or theologian. His account of the relations of the English kings with the Papacy, from the earliest times, and his selection of parallels from the history of continental Europe, show both wide knowledge and great skill in argument. His thinking is a perfect example of the pursuit of the *via media*, and the *via media* is of all ways the most difficult to follow. It requires discipline and self-control, it requires both imagination and hold on reality. In a period of debility like our own, few men have the energy to follow the middle way in government; for lazy or tired minds there is only extremity or apathy: dictatorship or communism, with enthusiasm or with indifference. An able Conservative writer, Mr Keith Feiling, in his *England under the Tudors and Stuarts*, refers to Hobbes as 'the acutest thinker of the age'. It would be equally true to say that he is the most eminent example in his age of a particularly lazy type of thinker. At any rate, the age owes a very great part of its distinction, both in England and in France, to thinkers of wholly the opposite type to Hobbes.

12 The French Church in the time of Louis XIV (*'il fut gallican, ce siècle, et janséniste'*) resembled the English Church under the Stuarts in several respects. In both countries a strong and autocratic civil Government controlled and worked with a strongly national Church. In each country there was a certain balance of power; in France between the throne and the Papacy; in England an internal balance of power between strong personalities. [336] There was much in common between Bramhall and Bossuet. But between Bramhall and Hobbes there is no sympathy whatever. Superficially their theories of the kingship bear some resemblance to each other. Both men were violently hostile to democracy in any form or degree. Both men believed that the monarch should have absolute power. Bramhall affirmed the divine right of kings: Hobbes rejected this noble faith, and asserted in effect the divine right of power, however come by. But Bramhall's view is not so absurdly romantic, or Hobbes's so soundly reasonable, as might seem. To Bramhall the king himself was a kind of symbol, and his assertion of divine right was a way of laying upon the king a double responsibility. It meant that the king had not merely a civil but a religious obligation toward his people. And the kingship of Bramhall is less absolute than the kingship of Hobbes. For Hobbes the Church was merely a department of the State, to be run exactly as the king thought best. Bramhall does not tell us clearly what would be the duties of a private citizen if the king should violate or

overturn the Christian religion, but he obviously leaves a wide expedient margin for resistance or justified rebellion. It is curious that the system of Hobbes, as Dr Sparrow-Simpson has observed, not only insists on autocracy but tolerates *unjustified* revolution. Hobbes's theory is in some ways very near to that of Machiavelli, with this important exception, that he has none of Machiavelli's profound observation and none of Machiavelli's limiting wisdom. The sole test and justification for Hobbes is in the end merely material success. For Hobbes all standards of good and evil are frankly relative.

13 It is extraordinary that a philosophy so essentially revolutionary as that of Hobbes, and so similar to that of contemporary Russia, should ever have been supposed to give any support to Toryism. But its ambiguity is largely responsible for its success. Hobbes was a revolutionary in thought and a timid conservative in action; and his theory of government is congenial to that type of person who is [337] conservative from prudence but revolutionary in his dreams. This type of person is not altogether uncommon. In Hobbes there are symptoms of the same mentality as Nietzsche: his belief in violence is a confession of weakness. Hobbes's violence is of a type that often appeals to gentle people. His specious effect of unity between a very simple theory of sense perception and an equally simple theory of government is of a kind that will always be popular because it appears to be intellectual but is really emotional, and therefore very soothing to lazy minds.

14 Bramhall's abilities of thought and language are nowhere better displayed than in his *Just Vindication of the English Church*. As for the language of Bramhall, I think that Dr Sparrow-Simpson does him less than justice. It is true that he employs in his vocabulary the most extraordinary confections of Latinity, but the catalogue of some of these expressions which Dr Sparrow-Simpson gives would lead one to believe that they occur in every sentence. And although Bramhall is not an easy writer, his phrases are lucid and direct and occasionally have real beauty and rhythm. A theologian of his powers, at that period of English prose, a man trained on the theology and the style of Bishop Andrewes, could hardly fail to write prose of distinction.

> Every sudden passionate heat or misunderstanding or shaking of charity amongst Christians, though it were even between the principal pastors of the Church, is not presently schism. As that between Saint Paul and Barnabas in the Acts of the Apostles – who dare say that either of them were schismatic? or that between Saint

Hierome and Ruffinus, who charged one another mutually with heresy; or that between Saint Chrysostom and Epiphanius, who refused to join in prayers; Saint Chrysostom wishing that Epiphanius might never return home alive, and Epiphanius wishing that Saint Chrysostom might not die a Bishop; both which things, by the just disposition of Almighty God, fell out according to the passionate and un-[338]charitable desires of these holy persons; who had Christian charity still radicated in their hearts, though the violent torrent of sudden passion did for a time beat down all other respects before it.

15 This is rather heavy going, and the word 'radicated' is one of those blemishes to which Dr Sparrow-Simpson calls attention; but the style has distinction. In prose style, as well as in theology, Bramhall is a link between the generation of Andrewes and the generation of Jeremy Taylor. The prose of Bramhall is great prose only in the sense that it is good prose of a great epoch. I cannot believe that Bramhall was a great preacher. Andrewes and Donne and Taylor had a poetic sensibility; that is to say, they had the sensitiveness necessary to record and to bring to convergence on a theological point a multitude of fleeting but universal human feelings. Their words linger and echo in the mind as Bramhall's never do; we forget Bramhall's phrases the moment we turn away from Bramhall's subject.

16 But for ordonnance, logical arrangement, for mastery of every fact relevant to a thesis, Bramhall is surpassed only by Hooker; and I am not sure that in the structure of the *Just Vindication of the English Church* he does not surpass even Hooker. And this book is no antiquity; it is a work which ought to be studied by anyone to whom the relation of Church and State is an actual and importunate problem. There could hardly be a greater difference than that between the situation during the first half of the seventeenth century and the situation to-day. Yet the differences are such as to make the work of Bramhall the more pertinent to our problems. For they are differences in relation to a fundamental unity of thought between Bramhall, and what he represents, and ourselves.

Variants:

Title Archbishop Bramhall *Theology* (1927)

1 biography] a biography *Theology* (1927), *FLA*
 near] nearly *Theology* (1927)

2 Canon] Dr *Theology* (1927), *FLA*

3 [Between 'rise of modern science.' and 'There was nothing particularly new':] The thirteenth century had the gift of philosophy, or reason; the later seventeenth

century had the gift of mathematics, or science; but the period between had ceased to be rational without having learned to be scientific. Three men who are typical of this interim epoch are Machiavelli, Montaigne, and Hobbes. Machiavelli is so much the greatest of these three (and in some ways so much more medieval) that it is a pity that he must be included with the others; but he is guilty of the same type of error. It is characteristic of all these men that their ideas are often right and sometimes profound; but that they are always one-sided and imperfect. They are therefore typical heresiarchs; for the essence of heresy is not so much the presentation of new and false notions, as the isolation and exaggeration of ideas which are true in themselves but which require completion and compensation. Hobbes, like Machiavelli and Montaigne, did not invent errors; he merely forced certain ideas as far as they can be made to go; his great weakness was lack of balance. Such men have an historical justification, for they show us the points at which we shall arrive if we go far enough in directions in which it is not desirable to go. *Theology* (1927); The thirteenth century had the gift of philosophy, of reason; the later seventeenth century had the gift of mathematics, or science; but the period between had ceased to be rational without having learned to be scientific. *FLA*

4 unlikely] impossible *Theology* (1927), *FLA*
would] should *Theology* (1927), *FLA*
8 opposed to the reasonings] contrasted with those *Theology* (1927)
9 scheme of life] *Weltanschauung Theology* (1927)
is a general] I affirmed to be a general *Theology* (1927)
philosophers after] the philosophers of *Theology* (1927)
11 Stuarts] Stewarts *FLA*
12 *janséniste*] janseniste *FLA*
noble] noble but untenable *Theology* (1927)
16 ordonnance] *ordonnance FLA*

Thoughts after Lambeth

SE, 339–63.

Publ. on 5 Mar. 1931 as Criterion Miscellany No. 30: Gallup A18. Revised in *SE*. In para. 10 'Schroedinger' has been corrected to 'Schrödinger'. In fn. 1 'C. Hace Tollman' has been corrected to 'Chace Tolman', and 'Tillman' and 'Tollman' to 'Tolman'

1 The Church of England washes its dirty linen in public. It is convenient and brief to begin with this metaphorical statement. In contrast to some other institutions both civil and ecclesiastical, the linen does get washed. To have linen to wash is something; and to assert that one's linen never needed washing would be a suspicious boast. Without some understanding of these habits of the Church, the reader of the Report of the Lambeth Conference (1930) will find it a difficult and in some directions a misleading document. The Report needs to be read in the light of

previous Reports; with some knowledge, and with some sympathy for that oddest of institutions, the Church of England.

2 The Conference is certainly more important than any report of it can be. I mean that each Conference has its place in the history of Lambeth Conferences, and that directions and tendencies are more significant than the precise formulation of the results obtained at any particular moment. To say that a significant direction can be traced, is not to applaud any aimless flux. But I suspect that many readers of the Report, especially those outside of the Anglican communion, are prepared to find (or prepared to condemn because they know they will not find) the clear hard and fast distinctions and decisions of a Papal Encyclical. Of such is Mr George Malcolm Thomson, whose lively pamphlet in this series[1] has given me food for thought. Between a Lambeth Conference Report and a [340] Papal Encyclical there is little similarity; there is a fundamental difference of intent. Perhaps the term 'encyclical letter' for the archiepiscopal communication heading the Report is itself misleading, because it suggests to many minds the voice of final authority *de fide et moribus*; and to those who hope for the voice of absoluteness and the words of hard precision, the recommendations and pious hopes will be disappointing. Many, like Mr Thomson, will exclaim that they find only platitudes, commonplaces, tergiversations and ambiguities. The Report of the Conference is not intended to be an absolute decree on questions of faith and morals; for the matter of that, the opinions expressed have no compulsion until ratified by Convocation. The Report, as a whole, is rather the expression of the ways in which the Church is moving, than an instruction to the faithful on belief and conduct.

3 Another consideration which we must keep in mind, before venturing to criticise the Report, is the manner of its composition. Some of the Report is to me, I admit at once, mere verbiage; some parts seem to me evasive; some parts seem to me to be badly expressed, at least if the ordinary uninstructed reader is acknowledged; one or two recommendations I deplore. But it ought not to be an occasion to us for mirth that three hundred bishops together assembled should, on pooling their views on most momentous matters, come out with a certain proportion of nonsense. I should not enjoy having to commit myself on any subject to any opinion which should also be that of any two hundred and ninety-nine of my acquaintance. Let us consider the quantity of nonsense that some of our most eminent scientists, professors and men of letters are

1. *The Lambeth Conference*, by George Malcolm Thomson. Criterion Miscellany.

able, each for himself, to turn out during every publishing season. Let us imagine (if we can imagine such persons agreeing to that extent) the fatuity of an encyclical letter produced by the joint efforts of Mr H. G. Wells, Mr Bernard Shaw and Mr Russell; or Professors Whitehead, Eddington and Jeans; or Dr Freud, Dr Jung and Dr [341] Adler; or Mr Murry, Mr Fausset, the Huxley Brothers and the Reverend Dr Potter of America.

4 With this comparison in mind, it is, I think, profitable to dispose first of those sections of the Report which are most insipid, and of that which has received most popular notice. I regret that what seem to me some of the best parts of the Report, such as the section on *The Christian Doctrine of God*, have been neglected in favour of those sections about which readers of the penny press are most ready to excite themselves. But if one is writing about the Report, one must be willing to offer one's own comment on these already over-commented sections. The report on 'Youth and its Vocation' suggests that the bishops had been listening to ordinary popular drivel on the subject, or ordinary popular drivel about what the bishops themselves are supposed to believe. They begin with a protest which for any intelligent reader should be unnecessary. 'We desire at the outset to protest emphatically against the contention that the Youth of to-day are, as a whole, less moral or less religious than youth of previous generations.' It ought to be obvious that the Youth of to-day are not 'as a whole' more or less anything than the youth of previous generations. The statement, not having much meaning, need not occupy much attention. 'There are signs of a great intellectual stirring among the rising generation.' One could wish that this journalistic hyperbole had been avoided. There can hardly be a great intellectual stirring among a whole generation, because the number of persons in any generation capable of being greatly stirred intellectually is always and everywhere very very small. What the bishops might have said, I think, with justice, is this: that one does find here and there among educated young men a respect for the Church springing from a recognition of the intellectual ability which during two thousand years has gone to its formation. The number of persons interested in philosophy is always small; but whereas twenty years ago a young man attracted by metaphysical speculation [342] was usually indifferent to theology, I believe that to-day a similar young man is more ready to believe that theology is a masculine discipline, than were those of my generation. If the capacity for faith be no greater, the prejudice against it is less; though one must remember to congratulate youth on finding themselves in this situation, before admiring them for taking advantage of it. I hope at this point that of the fifty bishops who

committed themselves to the dismal trope that 'youth of this generation . . . has admittedly struck its tents and is on the march', there was a large minority of dissentients. That is one of the troubles of the time: not only Youth but Middle Age is on the march; everybody, at least according to Fleet Street, is on the march; it does not matter what the destination is, the one thing contemptible is to sit still.

5 Youth, of course, is from one point of view merely a symptom of the results of what the middle-aged have been thinking and saying. I notice that the same fifty bishops refer guardedly to 'the published works of certain authors whose recognised ability and position give undue weight to views on the relations of the sexes which are in direct conflict with Christian principles.' I wish that they had mentioned names. For unfortunately the only two authors, of 'recognized ability and position', officially disapproved in England, are Mr James Joyce and D. H. Lawrence; so that the fifty bishops have missed an opportunity of dissociating themselves from the condemnation of these two extremely serious and improving writers.[1] If, however, the fifty were thinking of Mr Bertrand Russell or even of Mr Aldous Huxley, then they are being apprehensive about what to me is a reason for cheerfulness; for if Youth has the spirit of a tomtit or the brain of a goose, it can hardly rally with enthusiasm to these two depressing [343] life-forcers. (Not that Mr Huxley, who has no philosophy that I can discover, and who succeeds to some extent in elucidating how sordid a world without any philosophy can be, has much in common with Mr Russell.) I cannot regret that such views as Mr Russell's, or what we may call the enervate *gospel of happiness*, are openly expounded and defended. They help to make clear, what the nineteenth century had been largely occupied in obscuring, that there is no such thing as just Morality; but that for any man who thinks clearly, as his Faith is so will his Morals be. Were my religion that of Mr Russell, my views of conduct would very likely be his also; and I am sure in my own mind that I have not adopted my faith in order to defend my views of conduct, but have modified my views of conduct to conform with what seem to me the implications of my beliefs. The real conflict is not between one set of moral prejudices and another, but between the theistic and the atheistic faith; and it is all for the best that the division should be sharply drawn. Emancipation had some interest for venturous spirits when I was young, and must have been quite exciting to the previous generation;

---

1. Some time ago, during the consulship of Lord Brentford, I suggested that if we were to have a Censorship at all, it ought to be at Lambeth Palace; but I suppose that the few persons who read my words thought that I was trying to be witty.

but the Youth to which the bishops' words apply is grey-haired now. Emancipation loses some of its charm in becoming respectable. Indeed, the gospel of happiness in the form preached by Mr Russell in middle age is such as I cannot conceive as capable of making any appeal to Mr Russell in youth, so mediocre and respectable is it. It has nothing to offer to those born into the world which Mr Russell and others helped to create. The elders have had the satisfaction of throwing off prejudices; that is, of persuading themselves that the way they want to behave is the only moral way to behave; but there is not much in it for those who have no prejudices to reject. Christian morals gain immeasurably in richness and freedom by being seen as the consequence of Christian faith, and not as the imposition of tyrannical and irrational habit. What chiefly remains of the new freedom is its meagre impoverished [344] emotional life; in the end it is the Christian who can have the more varied, refined and intense enjoyment of life; which time will demonstrate.

6 Before leaving the not very remunerative subject of Youth, I must mention another respect, not unrelated, in which Youth of to-day has some advantage over an earlier generation. (I dislike the word 'generation', which has been a talisman for the last ten years; when I wrote a poem called *The Waste Land* some of the more approving critics said that I had expressed the 'disillusionment of a generation', which is nonsense. I may have expressed for them their own illusion of being disillusioned, but that did not form part of my intention.) One of the most deadening influences upon the Church in the past, ever since the eighteenth century, was its acceptance, by the upper, upper-middle and aspiring classes, as a political necessity and as a requirement of respectability. There are signs that the situation to-day is quite different. When, for instance, I brought out a small book of essays, several years ago, called *For Lancelot Andrewes*, the anonymous reviewer in the *Times Literary Supplement* made it the occasion for what I can only describe as a flattering obituary notice. In words of great seriousness and manifest sincerity, he pointed out that I had suddenly arrested my progress – whither he had supposed me to be moving I do not know – and that to his distress I was unmistakably making off in the wrong direction. Somehow I had failed, and had admitted my failure; if not a lost leader, at least a lost sheep; what is more, I was a kind of traitor; and those who were to find their way to the promised land beyond the waste might drop a tear at my absence from the roll-call of the new saints. I suppose that the curiosity of this point of view will be apparent to only a few people. But its appearance in what is not only the best but the most respected and most respectable of our literary periodicals, came home to me as a hopeful sign of the times. For

it meant that the orthodox faith of England is at last relieved from its burden of respect-[345]ability. A new respectability has arisen to assume the burden; and those who would once have been considered intellectual vagrants are now pious pilgrims, cheerfully plodding the road from nowhere to nowhere, trolling their hymns, satisfied so long as they may be 'on the march'.

7 These changed conditions are so prevalent that any one who has been moving among intellectual circles and comes to the Church, may experience an odd and rather exhilarating feeling of isolation. The new orthodoxy, of course, has many forms, and the sectaries of one form sometimes speak hard words of others, but the outline of respectability is fairly clear. Mr Middleton Murry, whose highly respectable new religion is continually heard to be 'on the march' round the corner, though it has not reached us yet,[1] is able to say of his own version: 'the words do not matter. If we can recreate the meaning – all the words of all the religions will be free to us, and we shall not want to use them.' One is tempted to suggest that Mr Murry has so many words in his employ already, including some of his own creation, that he has no need to summon others. A writer still more respectable than Mr Murry, because he is a Professor at an American University, is Mr Norman Foerster, the fugleman of Humanism. Mr Foerster, who has the honest simplicity to admit that he has very little acquaintance with Christianity beyond a narrow Protestantism which he repudiates, offers Humanism because it appeals to those 'who can find in themselves no vocation for spiritual humility'! without perceiving at all that this is an exact parallel to saying that Companionate Marriage 'appeals to those who can find in themselves no vocation for spiritual continence'. It is true that to judge from his next paragraph he has at the back of his mind some foggy distinction between 'spiritual humility' and 'humility' plain, but the distinction, if present, is not developed. One can now be a distinguished professor, and a professional moralist to boot, without understanding the devotional sense of the word [346] *vocation* or the theological sense of the virtue *humility*; a virtue, indeed, not conspicuous among modern men of letters. We have as many, as solemn, and as splendidly robed prophets to-day as in any decade of the last century; and it is now the fashion to rebuke the Christian in the name of some higher 'religion' – or more often, in the name of something higher called 'religion' plain.

---

1. *i.e., in 1931.*

8 However low an opinion I held of Youth, I could not believe that it can long be deceived by that vacuous word 'religion'. The Press may continue for a time, for the Press is always behind the times, to organise battues of popular notables, with the religion of a this and of a that; and to excite such persons to talk nonsense about the revival or decay of 'religion'. Religion can hardly revive, because it cannot decay. To put the matter bluntly on the lowest level, it is not to anybody's interest that religion should disappear. If it did, many compositors would be thrown out of work; the audiences of our best-selling scientists would shrink to almost nothing; and the typewriters of the Huxley Brothers would cease from tapping. Without religion the whole human race would die, as according to W. H. R. Rivers, some Melanesian tribes have died, solely of boredom. Everyone would be affected: the man who regularly has a run in his car and a round of golf on Sunday, quite as much as the punctilious churchgoer. Dr Sigmund Freud, with characteristic delicacy of feeling, has reminded us that we should 'leave Heaven to the angels and the sparrows'; following his hint, we may safely leave 'religion' to Mr Julian Huxley and Dr Freud.

9 At this point I may make a transition from Youth to another point in the Report, at which I feel that the bishops also had their eyes on Youth. On page 19 we read:

> Perhaps most noteworthy of all, there is much in the scientific and philosophic thinking of our time which provides a climate more favorable to faith in God than has existed for generations.

[347] I cannot help wishing that the bishops had consulted some of the able theologians and philosophers within the Church (such as Professor A. E. Taylor, who published an excellent article on the God of Whitehead, in *Theology*) before they had bestowed this benediction on our latest popular ramp of best-sellers. I do not disagree with the literal sense of the pronouncement which I have just quoted. Perhaps it is rather the tone of excessive amiability that I deprecate. I feel that the scientists should be received as penitents for the sins of an earlier scientific generation, rather than acclaimed as new friends and allies. And it may be an exceptional austerity or insensitiveness on my part, but I cannot consent to take climatic conditions so seriously as the phrase above seems to allow us to do. I do not wish to disparage the possible usefulness of the views set forth by Whitehead and Eddington and others. But it ought to be made quite clear that these writers cannot confirm anyone in the faith; they can merely have the practical value of removing prejudices from the minds of those who have not the faith but who might possibly come to it: the distinction seems to me of capital importance.

10 One characteristic which increased my suspicion of the scientific paladins of religion is that they are all Englishmen, or at least all Anglo-Saxons. I have seen a few reported remarks on religion and philosophy from the lips of such men as Einstein, Schrödinger and Planck; but they had the excuse of being interviewed by Mr Sullivan; and the remarks were chiefly interesting, as I imagine Mr Sullivan intended them to be, for the light they threw on the minds of these interesting scientists; none of these men has so far written a popular book of peeps into the fairyland of Reality. I suspect that there is some taint of Original H. G. Wells about most of us in English-speaking countries; and that we enjoy drawing general conclusions from particular disciplines, using our accomplishment in one field as the justification for theorising about the world in general. It is also a weakness of Anglo-Saxons to like to [348] hold personal and private religions and to promulgate them. And when a scientist gets loose into the field of religion, all that he can do is to give us the impression which his scientific knowledge and thought has produced upon his everyday, and usually commonplace, personal and private imagination.[1]

11 Even, however, in the section on Youth, we may find some wise and true sayings, if we have the patience to look for them. 'The best of the younger generation in every section of the community,' we are told, 'and in every country of the world, are not seeking a religion that is watered down or robbed of the severity of its demands, but a religion that will

---

1. Under the heading *Nature of Space: Professor Einstein's Change of Mind*, I read in *The Times* of 6th February, 1931, the following news from New York:

'At the close of a 90-minute talk on his unified field theory to a group of physicists and astronomers in the Carnegie Institution at Pasadena yesterday, Professor Einstein startled his hearers by smilingly declaring, "Space can never be anything similar to the old symmetrical spherical space theory."

That theory, he said, was not possible under the new equations. Thus he swept aside both his own former hypothesis that the universe and the space it occupied were both static and uniform, and the concept of his friend the Dutch astronomer, de Sitter, that though the universe was static it was non-uniform, which de Sitter had based upon the hypothesis that instead of matter determining space it was space that determined matter, and hence also the size of the universe.

Astronomers who heard Professor Einstein make his declaration said it was an indication that he had accepted the work of two American scientists, Dr Edwin P. Hubble, an astronomer in the Mount Wilson Observatory, and Dr Richard Chace Tolman, a physicist of the California Institute of Technology, who hold that the universe is non-static, although uniformly distributed in space. In the belief of Dr Hubble and Dr Tolman the universe is constantly expanding and matter is constantly being converted into energy.'

Our next revelation about the attitude of Science to Religion will issue, I trust, from Dr Hubble and Dr Tolman.

not only give them a sure basis and an ultimate sanction for morals, but also a power to persevere in reaching out after the ideal which in their heart of hearts they recognize as the finest and best.' I wish that [349] this might have been said in fewer words, but the meaning is sound, and cannot be repeated too often. There is no good in making Christianity easy and pleasant; 'Youth', or the better part of it, is more likely to come to a difficult religion than to an easy one. For some, the intellectual way of approach must be emphasised; there is need of a more intellectual laity. For them and for others, the way of discipline and asceticism must be emphasised; for even the humblest Christian layman can and must live what, in the modern world, is comparatively an ascetic life. Discipline of the emotions is even rarer, and in the modern world still more difficult, than discipline of the mind; some eminent lay preachers of 'discipline' are men who know only the latter. Thought, study, mortification, sacrifice: it is such notions as these that should be impressed upon the young – who differ from the young of other times merely in having a different middle-aged generation behind them. You will never attract the young by making Christianity easy; but a good many can be attracted by finding it difficult: difficult both to the disorderly mind and to the unruly passions.

12 I refer with some reluctance, but with positive conviction, to the much-discussed Resolution 15 on marriage and birth control. On one part of the problem there is an admirable analytical study by the Master of Corpus in *Theology* for December, 1930. I can only add one suggestion to that statement, without attempting the problems of casuistry which the Master of Corpus discusses with great skill. I feel that the Conference was not only right and courageous to express a view on the subject of procreation radically different from that of Rome; but that the attitude adopted is more important than this particular question, important as it may be, and indicates a radical difference between the Anglican and the Roman views on other matters. I regret, however, that the bishops have placed so much reliance upon the Individual Conscience; and by so doing jeopardised the benefits of their independ-[350]ence. Certainly, anyone who is wholly sincere and pure in heart may seek for guidance from the Holy Spirit; but who of us is always wholly sincere, especially where the most imperative of instincts may be strong enough to simulate to perfection the voice of the Holy Spirit?

13 The Resolution shows pretty clearly both the strength and the weakness of the Report, and the strength and weakness of the Anglican Church. The recognition of contraception is, I feel sure, something quite different from a concession to 'modern' opinion. It was a courageous facing of

facts of life; and was the only way of dealing with the question possible within the Anglican organisation. But before asserting the distinct character of the Anglican Church in this way, the bishops must have taken a good deal of thought about it; all the more astonishing that they did not take a little more thought, and not proceed to a statement which seems to me almost suicidal. For to allow that 'each couple' should take counsel only *if perplexed in mind* is almost to surrender the whole citadel of the Church. It is ten to one, considering the extreme disingenuity of humanity, which ought to be patent to all after so many thousand years, that only a very small minority will be 'perplexed'; and in view of the words of the bishops it is ten to one that the honest minority which takes 'competent advice' (and I observe that the order of words is '*medical* and spiritual') will have to appeal to a clergy just as perplexed as itself, or else be stung into an obstinacy, greater than that of any Roman clergy, by the futility of this sentence.

14 In short, the whole resolution shows the admirable English devotion to common sense, but also the deplorable Anglican habit of standing things on their heads in the name of common sense. It is exactly this matter of 'spiritual advice' which should have been examined and analysed if necessary for years, before making any pronouncement. But the principle is simple, though the successful application might require time. I do not suggest that the full [351] Sacrament of Confession and Penance should be imposed upon every communicant of the Church; but the Church ought to be able to enjoin upon all its communicants that they should take spiritual advice upon specified problems of life; and both clergy and parishioners should recognise the full seriousness and responsibility of such consultation. I am not unaware that as opinions and theories vary at present, those seeking direction can always find the direction they seek, if they know where to apply; but that is inevitable. But here, if anywhere, is definitely a matter upon which the Individual Conscience is no reliable guide; spiritual guidance should be imperative; and it should be clearly placed above medical advice – where also, opinions and theories vary indefinitely. In short, a general principle of the greatest importance, exceeding the application to this particular issue alone, might have been laid down; and its enunciation was evaded.

15 To put it frankly, but I hope not offensively, the Roman view in general seems to me to be that a principle must be affirmed without exception; and that thereafter exceptions can be dealt with, without modifying the principle. The view natural to the English mind, I believe, is rather that a principle must be framed in such a way as to include all allowable

exceptions. It follows inevitably that the Roman Church must profess to be fixed, while the Anglican Church must profess to take account of changed conditions. I hope that it is unnecessary to give the assurance that I do not consider the Roman way of thought dishonest, and that I would not endorse any cheap and facile gibes about the duplicity and dissimulation of that Church; it is another conception of human nature and of the means by which, on the whole, the greatest number of souls can be saved; but the difference goes deep. *Prudenti dissimulatione uti*[1] [352] is not a precept which appeals to Anglo-Saxon theology; and here again, the Anglican Church can admit national (I do not mean nationalistic) differences in theory and practice which the more formal organisation of Rome cannot recognise. What in England is the right balance between individual liberty and discipline? – between individual responsibility and obedience? – active co-operation and passive reception? And to what extremity are divergences of belief and practice permissible? These are questions which the English mind must always ask; and the answers can only be found, if with hesitation and difficulty, through the English Church. The admission of inconsistencies, sometimes ridiculed as indifference to logic and coherence, of which the English mind is often accused, may be largely the admission of inconsistencies inherent in life itself, and of the impossibility of overcoming them by the imposition of a uniformity greater than life will bear.

16 Even, however, if the Anglican Church affirmed, as I think it should affirm, the necessity for spiritual direction in admitting the exceptions, the Episcopate still has the responsibility of giving direction to the directors. I cannot but suspect that here the Roman doctrine, so far as I have seen it expounded, leaves us uncertain as does the Anglican. For example: according to the Roman doctrine, which is more commendable – prudent continence in marriage, or unlimited procreation up to the limit of the mother's strength? If the latter, the Church seems to me obliged to offer some solution to the economic questions raised by such a practice: for surely, if you lay down a moral law which leads, in practice, to unfortunate social consequences – such as over-population or destitution – you make yourself responsible for providing some resolution of these consequences. If the former, what motives are right motives? The latest Papal Encyclical appears to be completely decisive about the question of Resolution 15 – at the cost of solving no individual's problems. And the

---

1. See *Theology*, December, 1930, p. 307. It has been pointed out to me that here *dissimulatio* should perhaps be translated as 'tactfulness' rather than 'dissimulation'; but a tactfulness which consists primarily in not asking awkward questions seems to me to be pretty close to simulation and dissimulation.

Resolution is equally, though perhaps no more, unsatis-[353]factory. The Roman statement leaves unanswered the questions: When is it right to limit the family? and: When is it wrong not to limit it? And the Anglican statement leaves unanswered the questions: When is it right to limit the family and right to limit it only by continence? and When is it right to limit the family by contraception?

17   On the other hand, the fact that Resolution 15, as I take it, is wrong *primarily* in isolating and treating as independent a question which should be considered as a detail subsumed under the more general question which should have been treated first – that of Spiritual Direction and Authority; this fact does I think indicate one recurrent cause of weakness. When the episcopal mind sees that something is self-evidently desirable in itself, it seems inclined to turn first to consider the means for bringing it into being, rather than to find the theological grounds upon which it can be justified; and there are traces of this zeal here and there in the suggestions towards Reunion and fraternisation. For instance (p. 117 of the Report), it is suggested that a bishop might authorise and encourage baptised communicant members of churches not in communion with our own, to communicate in his diocese with Anglicans 'when the ministrations of their own Church are not available'. It is true that this is to be done only under special and temporary local conditions; and it does not form part of my purpose to doubt that under the conditions which the bishops must have had in mind, such intercommunion is most desirable. But what does the suggestion imply? Surely, *if* dissenters should never communicate in Anglican churches, or *if* in certain circumstances they should be encouraged to do so, two very different theories of the Sacrament of the Altar are implied. For the innovation proposed, theological justification is required. What is required is some theory of degrees of reception of the Blessed Sacrament, as well as the validity of the ministration of a celebrant not episcopally ordained. My objection therefore is not to the admission of dissenters [354] to the Altar – and I do not wish to attack what has not yet been defended – but to the propagation of this practice before theological justification has been expounded. Possibly theology is what Bradley said philosophy was: 'the finding of bad reasons for what we believe upon instinct'; I think it may be the finding of good reasons for what we believe upon instinct; but if the Church of England cannot find these reasons, and make them intelligible to the more philosophically trained among the faithful, what can it do?

18   A similar danger seems to me to inhere in the statement about the Historic Episcopate. Mr Malcolm Thomson, looking, as I suspect, for

the Roman view, or for one of the tenable Roman views (as an outsider naturally would), and not finding it, extracts and exaggerates one possible perversion; on the other hand he does point to a danger of which we should be aware. He quotes the words of the Report:

> While we thus stand for the Historic Episcopate as a necessary element in any union in which the Anglican Church can take part ... we do not require of others acceptance of those reasons, or of any particular theory or interpretation of the Episcopate as a condition of reunion.

What the bishops had in mind committing themselves to this serious statement, I am sure, is the fact that the Church has never held one rigid theory of the nature of the Episcopate. Even in the Roman Church I understand that there are still at least two theories tenable. But such theological subtleties pass beyond the ordinary lay mind; and the greatest value of Mr Thomson's interesting pamphlet, to me, is its exposure of the possibilities of misunderstanding in the wording of some of the Report. And I agree with him to this extent, that the words *we do not require of others acceptance of those reasons* might be taken to mean 'we do not require of others acceptance of *any* reasons except expediency': in other words, we beg that [355] Nonconformists should accept the Episcopate as a harmless formality, for the sake of a phantom unity.

19 I do not imagine for a moment that the 'conversations' of the Church of England with the Free Churches will bear any fruit whatever in our time; and I rather hope they will not; for any fruit of this harvest would be unripe and bitter fruit, untimely nipped. But at the same time I cannot cat-call with those who accuse the Church of facing-both-ways, and making one profession to the innocent Levantines and Swedes, and another to the implacable Methodists. It would be very poor statesmanship indeed to envisage any reunion which should not fall ultimately within a scheme for complete reunion; and in spite of mirth, 'reunion all round' is the only ideal tenable. To the Methodists, certainly, the Church of England owes a heavy responsibility, somewhat similar to that of the Church of Rome towards ourselves; and it would be almost effrontery for Anglican bishops to seek an alliance with Uppsala and Constantinople without seeking some way of repatriating those descended from men who would (I am sure) never have left the Church of England had it been in the eighteenth century what it is now in the second quarter of the twentieth. In such difficult negotiations the Church is quite properly and conscientiously facing-both-ways: which only goes to show that the Church of England is at the present juncture the one church upon which the duty of working

towards reunion most devolves. There are possible risks, which have been seized upon as actualities when they have been merely potentialities; the risk of feeling more orthodox when transacting with the Eastern and Baltic Churches, and more Evangelical when transacting with the Nonconformists. But I do not believe that the bishops have, according to the Report, conceded to the Nonconformists in England anything that the Eastern authorities could reasonably abhor. On the contrary, the attitude of eminent dissenters, in their objections still more than in their approval, seems to me to [356] indicate that the bishops have stopped at the right point. The points of difference with the other orthodox churches are simple and direct, and in a near way of being settled. It is easier to agree with a man who differs from you in blood but less in faith, than to agree with one who is of your own blood but has different ideas: because the irrelevant differences between those of the same blood are less superable than the relevant differences between those of different blood. The problems of dissent between Anglicans and Free Churchmen are (we might just as well admit it) much more complicated than the problems between the Anglicans and the Swedish. Our doctrinal difficulties with Free Churchmen are complicated by divisions social, local and political; by traditions of prejudice on both sides; and it is likely that several generations must pass before the problems of theology and hierarchy can be fairly detached and faced. The Lambeth Conference of 1930 has accomplished in this direction this much: that it has determined the limits beyond which the Church cannot go in commending itself to Free Churchmen; further concession would be abandonment of the Church itself, and mere incorporation, as possibly the most important member, in a loose federation of autonomous sects without stability and without significance.

20 The actuality of the approximation towards intercommunion with the Eastern Churches, however, has very much more than picturesque value. It brings with it the hope of a greater stability, instead of the old stability, real or apparent, which seemed to characterise an Establishment. On matters of doctrine, the summary of discussions between Anglican bishops and orthodox representatives (p. 138 ff.) is of great importance, especially paragraph 11:

> It was stated by the Anglican bishops that in the Sacrament of the Eucharist 'the Body and Blood of Christ are verily and indeed taken and received by the faithful in the Lord's Supper', and that 'the Body of Christ is given, taken and eaten in the Supper only after an heavenly and [357] spiritual manner', and that after Communion

the consecrated elements remaining are regarded sacramentally as the Body and Blood of Christ; further, that the Anglican Church teaches the doctrine of Eucharistic sacrifice as explained in the Answer of the Archbishops of Canterbury and York to Pope Leo XIII on Anglican Ordinations; and also that in the offering of the Eucharistic Sacrifice the Anglican Church prays that 'by the merits and death of Thy Son Jesus Christ, and through faith in His blood, we and all Thy whole Church may obtain remission of our sins, and all other benefits of His passion', as including the whole company of faithful people, living and departed.

Reunion with the East is of the greatest significance for a Church the position of which in the national life is inevitably changing. We still think, and rightly, of the Church of England as the 'National Church'; but the word *national* in this context can no longer mean what it once meant. I entirely sympathise with Mr Malcolm Thomson, and with any other Scot, Irishman or Methodist, in his objection to the vapid phrase about St Paul's, 'the parish church of the British Empire'. An 'imperial' Church, perhaps under the patronage of the four evangelists of imperialism, Lords Rothermere, Beaverbrook, Riddell and Camrose, would be something more odious, because far more vulgar, than the Erastian Church of the eighteenth century. I prefer to think of the Church as what I believe it is more and more coming to be, not the 'English Church', but national as 'the Catholic Church in England'.

21 For the last three hundred years the relation of Church to State has been constantly undergoing change. I do not propose in this essay to enter upon the difficult question of Disestablishment. I am not here concerned with the practical difficulties and anomalies which have made the problem of Church and State more acute in the last few years; I am not concerned with prognosticating their future relations, or with offering any facile solution for so complex a problem, or with discussing the future discipline [358] within the Church itself. I wish to say nothing about Disestablishment, first because I have not made up my own mind, and second because it does not seem to me fitting at this time that one layman, with no special erudition in that subject, should publicly express his views. I am considering only the political and social changes within the last three hundred years. A National Church in the early Caroline sense depended upon the precarious harmony of the King, a strong Archbishop and a strong First Minister; and perhaps the Laudian Church came just too late to be more for us than the type of one form of order. The political-social Erastianism of the eighteenth century has gone its

way too; there can be no more Hoadleys; there is not much financial or social advantage in holy orders; nowadays the smaller folk, who seek security, find their way if they can into the Civil Service, and the larger and more predatory seek success in the City. Less and less is there any reason for taking orders, but just vocation. I suspect that the rule by Prime Ministers is dwindling, too; no possible Prime Minister (except perhaps Lord Rothermere's sometime nominee, Lord Brentford, which God forfend) would now, I trust, venture to impose his own choice upon the Church in the way of episcopal preferment, or would do anything except consult the safest authorities. And the House of Commons, which has seemed to cling to the Church as the last reality in England over which it has any control, must eventually relinquish that tardy shadow of power too. The only powers left are those with which we must all reckon, the Chancellor of the Exchequer and the Bank of England.

22 Whether established or disestablished, the Church of England can never be reduced to the condition of a Sect, unless by some irrational act of suicide; even in the sense in which, with all due respect, the Roman Church is in England a sect. It is easier for the Church of England to become Catholic, than for the Church of Rome in England to become English; and if the Church of England was [359] mutilated by separation from Rome, the Church of Rome was mutilated by separation from England. If England is ever to be in any appreciable degree converted to Christianity, it can only be through the Church of England.

23 To revert to the sense of the first paragraph of this essay, the Church of England may easily be made to appear in a better way, or in a worse way, than she is. The sudden heat of the Prayer Book controversy, the vivaciousness of Lord Brentford and Lord Cushendun, the 'brawl' at St Paul's, the unpleasantness in the diocese of Birmingham, the awareness of the Press that there is sometimes good copy in ecclesiastical affairs, the journalism of Dean Inge, and the large sales of popular theological literature; all these things together would seem to suggest that never was there such a lively interest in the Church as to-day. And the same dissensions, when interpreted to mean that opinion in the Church is divided to the point of disruption; the lack of ordinands and lack of funds, the anomalous and often humiliating relation of Church to State, the insurrection of what is popularly called the new morality, and the patent fact that the majority of Englishmen and women are wholly indifferent to the obligations of their faith, even when they have not quite repudiated it: such signs may seem to point towards collapse or superannuation.

24 I take such phenomena to be, for the most part, merely symptoms of the changing place, not only of the Anglican Church in the State, but of the Universal Church in the World. As I have said already, the Church of England can no longer be, and must no longer be, a National Church in the old nationalistic or in the old Erastian way. The high power it may seem to have lost was either a bad power, or an obsolete power, or the shadow of a power. The political pressure from without, a force of cohesion in the sixteenth and seventeenth centuries, no longer exists except as the spectral dread of Popery; the fear of the social con-[360]sequences of disruption within no longer exists, for the disruption and secession have long since taken place, and the dread has been succeeded by the faint hope of construction. The problem of the relation of Church and State – and I am not thinking here only of the Anglican Church, but of any body of believers in any country, and of the manifold and perplexing problems of the Holy See – is as acute as ever it was; but it takes ever new forms. I believe that in spite of the apparently insoluble problems with which it has to deal, the Church of England is strengthening its position as a branch of the Catholic Church, the Catholic Church in England. I am not thinking of the deliberate struggles of one party within the Church, but of an inevitable course of events which has not been directed by human hands.

25 At this point I must turn aside for a moment to protest against certain assumptions of Mr Malcolm Thomson which are not peculiar to himself, but are probably shared by most of those who are only interested in church affairs as they read of them in the newspapers. When Mr Thomson wrote his spirited pamphlet *Will the Scottish Church Survive?*[1] he was full of praise for the animation manifested in the English Church in the dissensions of Catholics, Evangelicals and Modernists. He may have slightly caricatured these differences for the sake of picturesqueness, if only as a stick to beat his Presbyterian victim. I think that his chief error in treating the Lambeth Conference is that he discusses the Report without reference to the history and development of the English Church, and treats it as if it were the creation of one individual intelligence, instead of considering what must be the composite production of three hundred minds. But on some matters he not only lacks perspective, but is definitely misleading. Mr Thomson is a metaphor-addict and his mind is ridden by images of underground passages (very short ones), ferries, wher-[361]ries, and other figures of easy transport from Canterbury to Rome. He remarks for instance:

1. The Porpoise Press, Edinburgh.

> And the careers of several prominent Anglo-Catholics served to strengthen the general suspicion. For they had a habit of using the Church of England as a junction and not as a terminus.

I cannot see how *several* can form a habit; unless Mr Thomson wishes to suggest that Father Knox and Father Vernon have formed the 'habit' of leaving the English Church. I should like to know the names of the 'few well-known authors' who have been converted: I doubt whether Mr Thomson's list would contain many names that I do not know – one or two of his converts may even have started life as Presbyterians; and by the sum of the names which I know, I am not greatly impressed. And here again, I suspect that more capital is made of the transit of an Anglo-Catholic to Rome, than of that of a plain Low Churchman. For some souls, I admit, there is no satisfaction outside of Rome; and if Anglo-Catholicism has helped a few such to find their way to where they belong, I am very glad; but if Anglo-Catholicism has assisted a few persons to leave the Church of England who could never have rested in that uneasy bed anyway, on the other hand it has helped many more, I believe – one cannot quote statistics in the negative – to remain within the Anglican Church. Why, for instance, has Lord Halifax not saved himself a deal of trouble, of generous toil and disappointment, by becoming a convert out of hand? And why are not Lord Brentford and Lord Cushendun taken by the neck and dropped respectively into Methodism and Presbyterianism? The Anglican Church is supposed to be divided, by newspaper verdict, either into Catholics and Modernists, or into Catholics and Evangelicals, or sometimes into Catholics, Modernists *and* Evangelicals. If the divisions were so clear as all that, there might be something to be said for a voluntary liquidation. To those for whom [362] the English Church means Lord Brentford, the Bishop of Birmingham and *The Church Times*, it may well seem that nothing keeps it together but inertia, and the unwillingness, for various motives, to scrap an extensive plant of machinery.

26 To detached observers like Mr Malcolm Thomson, entering England from the comparative calm of Edinburgh, Lhassa or Rome, the disorder of the Church of England may seem fatal. When clergymen hasten to reply with severity if a Bishop writes a letter to *The Times*[1] and when even plain people like myself can make use of such eminences as Lord Brentford and the Bishop of Birmingham for comic relief,[2] there is at

---

1. See *a* remarkable letter from the Bishop of Durham in *The Times* of 2nd December, 1930, and the poverty of the replies.

2. When I say 'comic', I am considering their *essence*, not their *operation*.

least the opportunity for misunderstanding. For such freedom of speech and such diversity of opinion there is, however, something to be said: within limits – which, I grant, have been transgressed; but what matters is not so much uniformity of liturgy as fixity of dogma. There are, of course, differences of opinion which are fundamental and permanent; but I am not at all sure that it is not a very good thing for the intellectual life of the Church that there should be. When they come to light in the public press, they usually appear to be the clear and irreconcilable views of two or more well-regimented and hostile forces. But in practice, each division is itself divided, and the lines of sectional division are far from clear. You cannot point to one group of 'Modernists': there are Catholics who may be called modernist, and Evangelicals who may call themselves modernist, as well as a few persons in whom Modernism seems to signify merely confused thinking. I have known Evangelicals to whom the name of Dr Barnes was more displeasing than that of Lord Halifax. There are persons who do not *always* agree with the Editor of *The Church Times*; and I sometimes am moved to admire an article in *The Modern Church*-[363]*man*. To a large degree accordingly the differences within the Church are healthy differences within a living body, and to the same degree their existence qualifies the Church of England for assuming the initiative toward Reunion.

27 And the Conference of 1930 has marked an important stage in that direction. It has affirmed, beyond previous conferences, the Catholicity of the Church; and in spite of defects and dubious statements in detail, the Report will have strengthened the Church both within and without. It has made clearer the limits beyond which the Church cannot go towards meeting Nonconformity, and the extent to which it is prepared to go to meet the Eastern and Baltic Churches. This advance is of no small importance in a world which will obviously divide itself more and more sharply into Christians and non-Christians. The Universal Church is to-day, it seems to me, more definitely set against the World than at any time since pagan Rome. I do not mean that our times are particularly corrupt; all times are corrupt. I mean that Christianity, in spite of certain local appearances, is not, and cannot be within measurable time, 'official'. The World is trying the experience of attempting to form a civilised but non-Christian mentality. The experiment will fail; but we must be very patient in awaiting its collapse; meanwhile redeeming the time: so that the Faith may be preserved alive through the dark ages before us; to renew and rebuild civilisation, and save the World from suicide.

Variants from 1931:

1 Conference (1930)] *Conference*
2 [No fn.]
5 unfortunately] unfortunately,
  authors,] authors
  position',] position'
  dissociating] disassociating
6 waste] waste one
7 [No fn.]
10 fn. 6th February] February 6th
14 communicant] part
   can always] could always
15 Anglo-Saxon theology] Anglo-Saxon mind

VII Baudelaire

SE, 367–78.

Previously publ. as the Introduction, signed 'T. S. Eliot', to *Charles Baudelaire: Intimate Journals*, ed. Ch. Isherwood (1930): Gallup B14. Revised in *SE*.

1 Anything like a just appreciation of Baudelaire has been slow to arrive in England, and still is defective or partial even in France. There are, I think, special reasons for the difficulty in estimating his worth and finding his place. For one thing, Baudelaire was in some ways far in advance of the point of view of his own time, and yet was very much of it, very largely partook of its limited merits, faults, and fashions. For another thing, he had a great part in forming a generation of poets after him; and in England he had what is in a way the misfortune to be first and extravagantly advertised by Swinburne, and taken up by the followers of Swinburne. He was universal, and at the same time confined by a fashion which he himself did most to create. To dissociate the permanent from the temporary, to distinguish the man from his influence, and finally to detach him from the associations of those English poets who first admired him, is no small task. His comprehensiveness itself makes difficulty, for it tempts the partisan critic, even now, to adopt Baudelaire as the patron of his own beliefs.

2 It is the purpose of this essay to affirm the importance of Baudelaire's prose works, a purpose justified by the translation of one of those works

which is indispensable for any student of his poetry.[1] This is to see Baudelaire as something more than the author of the *Fleurs du Mal*, and consequently to revise somewhat our estimate of that book. Baudelaire came into vogue at a time when 'Art for Art's [368] sake' was a dogma. The care which he took over his poems and the fact that, contrary to the fluency of his time, both in France and England he restricted himself to this one volume, encouraged the opinion that Baudelaire was an artist exclusively for art's sake. The doctrine does not, of course, really apply to anybody; no one applied it less than Pater, who spent many years, not so much in illustrating it, as in expounding it as a *theory of life*, which is not the same thing at all. But it was a doctrine which did affect criticism and appreciation, and which did obstruct a proper judgement of Baudelaire. He is in fact a greater man than was imagined, though perhaps not such a perfect poet.

3 Baudelaire has, I believe, been called a fragmentary Dante, for what that description is worth. It is true that many people who enjoy Dante enjoy Baudelaire; but the differences are as important as the similarities. Baudelaire's inferno is very different in quality and significance from that of Dante. Truer, I think, would be the description of Baudelaire as a later and more limited Goethe. As we begin to see him now, he represents his own age in somewhat the same way as that in which Goethe represents an earlier age. As a critic of the present generation, Mr Peter Quennell has recently said in his book, *Baudelaire and the Symbolists*:

> He had enjoyed *a sense of his own age*, had recognized its pattern while the pattern was yet incomplete, and – because it is only our misapprehension of the present which prevents our looking into the immediate future, our ignorance of to-day and of its real as apart from its spurious tendencies and requirements – had anticipated many problems, both on the aesthetic and on the moral plane, in which the fate of modern poetry is still concerned.

Now the man who has this sense of his age is hard to analyse. He is exposed to its follies as well as sensitive to its inventions; and in Baudelaire, as well as in Goethe, is some of the out-moded nonsense of his time. The parallel between the German poet who has always been the symbol [369] of perfect 'health' in every sense, as well as of universal curiosity, and the French poet who has been the symbol of morbidity in mind and concentrated interests in work, may seem paradoxical. But after this lapse

---

1. *Journeaux Intimes*, translated by Christopher Isherwood, and published by the Blackamore Press.

of time the difference between 'health' and 'morbidity' in the two men becomes more negligible; there is something artificial and even priggish about Goethe's healthiness, as there is about Baudelaire's unhealthiness; we have passed beyond both fashions, of health or malady, and they are both merely men with restless, critical, curious minds and the 'sense of the age'; both men who understood and foresaw a great deal. Goethe, it is true, was interested in many subjects which Baudelaire left alone; but by Baudelaire's time it was no longer necessary for a man to embrace such varied interests in order to have the sense of the age; and in retrospect some of Goethe's studies seem to us (not altogether justly) to have been merely dilettante hobbies. The most of Baudelaire's prose writings (with the exception of the translations from Poe, which are of less interest to an English reader) are as important as the most of Goethe. They throw light on the *Fleurs du Mal* certainly, but they also expand immensely our appreciation of their author.

4 It was once the mode to take Baudelaire's Satanism seriously, as it is now the tendency to present Baudelaire as a serious and Catholic Christian. Especially as a prelude to the *Journeaux Intimes* this diversity of opinion needs some discussion. I think that the latter view – that Baudelaire is essentially Christian – is nearer the truth than the former, but it needs considerable reservation. When Baudelaire's Satanism is dissociated from its less creditable paraphernalia, it amounts to a dim intuition of a part, but a very important part, of Christianity. Satanism itself, so far as not merely an affectation, was an attempt to get into Christianity by the back door. Genuine blasphemy, genuine in spirit and not purely verbal, is the product of partial belief, and is as impossible to the complete atheist as to the perfect Christian. It is a way of affirming belief. This state of partial [370] belief is manifest throughout the *Journeaux Intimes*. What is significant about Baudelaire is his theological innocence. He is discovering Christianity for himself; he is not assuming it as a fashion or weighing social or political reasons, or any other accidents. He is beginning, in a way, at the beginning; and, being a discoverer, is not altogether certain what he is exploring and to what it leads; he might almost be said to be making again, as one man, the effort of scores of generations. His Christianity is rudimentary or embryonic; at best, he has the excesses of a Tertullian (and even Tertullian is not considered wholly orthodox and well balanced). His business was not to practise Christianity, but – what was much more important for his time – to assert its *necessity*.

5 Baudelaire's morbidity of temperament cannot, of course, be ignored: and no one who has looked at the work of Crépet or the recent small

biographical study of François Porché can forget it. We should be misguided if we treated it as an unfortunate ailment which can be discounted or attempted to detach the sound from the unsound in his work. Without the morbidity none of his work would be possible or significant; his weaknesses can be composed into a larger whole of strength, and this is implied in my assertion that neither the health of Goethe nor the malady of Baudelaire matters in itself: it is what both men made of their endowments that matters. To the eye of the world, and quite properly for all questions of private life, Baudelaire was thoroughly perverse and insufferable: a man with a talent for ingratitude and unsociability, intolerably irritable, and with a mulish determination to make the worst of everything; if he had money, to squander it; if he had friends, to alienate them; if he had any good fortune, to disdain it. He had the pride of the man who feels in himself great weakness and great strength. Having great genius, he had neither the patience nor the inclination, had he had the power, to overcome his weakness; on the contrary, he exploited it for theoretical pur-[371]poses. The morality of such a course may be a matter for endless dispute; for Baudelaire, it was the way to liberate his mind and give us the legacy and lesson that he has left.

6 He was one of those who have great strength, but strength merely to *suffer*. He could not escape suffering and could not transcend it, so he *attracted* pain to himself. But what he could do, with that immense passive strength and sensibilities which no pain could impair, was to study his suffering. And in this limitation he is wholly unlike Dante, not even like any character in Dante's Hell. But, on the other hand, such suffering as Baudelaire's implies the possibility of a positive state of beatitude. Indeed, in his way of suffering is already a kind of presence of the supernatural and of the superhuman. He rejects always the purely natural and the purely human; in other words, he is neither 'naturalist' nor 'humanist'. Either because he cannot adjust himself to the actual world he has to reject it in favour of Heaven and Hell, or because he has the perception of Heaven and Hell he rejects the present world: both ways of putting it are tenable. There is in his statements a good deal of romantic detritus; *ses ailes de géant l'empêchent de marcher*, he says of the Poet and the Albatross, but not convincingly; but there is also truth about himself and about the world. His *ennui* may of course be explained, as everything can be explained in psychological or pathological terms; but it is also, from the opposite point of view, a true form of *acedia*, arising from the unsuccessful struggle towards the spiritual life.

II

7 From the poems alone, I venture to think, we are not likely to grasp what seems to me the true sense and significance of Baudelaire's mind. Their excellence of form, their perfection of phrasing, and their superficial coherence, may give them the appearance of presenting a definite and final state of mind. In reality, they seem to me to have the [372] external but not the internal form of classic art. One might even hazard the conjecture that the care for perfection of form, among some of the romantic poets of the nineteenth century, was an effort to support, or to conceal from view, an inner disorder. Now the true claim of Baudelaire as an artist is not that he found a superficial form, but that he was searching for a form of life. In minor form he never indeed equalled Théophile Gautier, to whom he significantly dedicated his poems: in the best of the slight verse of Gautier there is a satisfaction, a balance of inwards and form, which we do not find in Baudelaire. He had a greater technical ability than Gautier, and yet the content of feeling is constantly bursting the receptacle. His apparatus, by which I do not mean his command of words and rhythms, but his stock of imagery (and every poet's stock of imagery is circumscribed somewhere), is not wholly perdurable or adequate. His prostitutes, mulattoes, Jewesses, serpents, cats, corpses form a machinery which has not worn very well; his Poet, or his Don Juan, has a romantic ancestry which is too clearly traceable. Compare with the costumery of Baudelaire the stock of imagery of the *Vita Nuova*, or of Cavalcanti, and you find that Baudelaire's does not everywhere wear as well as that of several centuries earlier; compare him with Dante or Shakespeare, for what such a comparison is worth, and he is found not only a much smaller poet, but one in whose work much more that is perishable has entered.

8 To say this is only to say that Baudelaire belongs to a definite place in time. Inevitably the offspring of romanticism, and by his nature the first counter-romantic in poetry, he could, like anyone else, only work with the materials which were there. It must not be forgotten that a poet in a romantic age cannot be a 'classical' poet except in tendency. If he is sincere, he must express with individual differences the general state of mind – not as a *duty*, but simply because he cannot help participating in it. For such poets, we may expect often to get much help from [373] reading their prose works and even notes and diaries; help in deciphering the discrepancies between head and heart, means and end, material and ideals.

9 What preserves Baudelaire's poetry from the fate of most French poetry of the nineteenth century up to his time, and has made him, as M. Valéry has said in a recent introduction to the *Fleurs du Mal*, the one modern French poet to be widely read abroad, is not quite easy to conclude. It is partly that technical mastery which can hardly be overpraised, and which has made his verse an inexhaustible study for later poets, not only in his own language. When we read

> Maint joyau dort enseveli
> Dans les ténèbres et l'oubli
> Bien loin des pioches et des sondes;
> Mainte fleur épanche à regret
> Son parfum doux comme un secret
> Dans les solitudes profondes,

we might for a moment think it a more lucid bit of Mallarmé; and so original is the arrangement of words that we might easily overlook its borrowing from Gray's *Elegy*. When we read

> Valse mélancolique et langoureux vertige!

we are already in the Paris of Laforgue. Baudelaire gave to French poets as generously as he borrowed from English and American poets. The renovation of the versification of Racine has been mentioned often enough; quite genuine, but might be overemphasised, as it sometimes comes near to being a trick. But even without this, Baudelaire's variety and resourcefulness would still be immense.

10 Furthermore, besides the stock of images which he used that seems already second-hand, he gave new possibilities to poetry in a new stock of imagery of contemporary life.

> ... Au coeur d'un vieux faubourg, labyrinthe fangeux
> Où l'humanité grouille en ferments orageux,

[374] On voit un vieux chiffonnier qui vient, hochant la tête,
> Buttant, et se cognant aux murs comme un poète.

This introduces something new, and something universal in modern life. (The last line quoted, which in ironic terseness anticipates Corbière, might be contrasted with the whole poem 'Bénédiction' which begins the volume.) It is not merely in the use of imagery of common life, not merely in the use of imagery of the sordid life of a great metropolis, but in the elevation of such imagery to the *first intensity* – presenting it as it is, and yet making it represent something much more than itself –

that Baudelaire has created a mode of release and expression for other men.

11 This invention of language, at a moment when French poetry in particular was famishing for such invention, is enough to make Baudelaire a great poet, a great landmark in poetry. Baudelaire is indeed the greatest exemplar in *modern* poetry in any language, for his verse and language is the nearest thing to a complete renovation that we have experienced. But his renovation of an attitude towards life is no less radical and no less important. In his verse, he is now less a model to be imitated or a source to be drained than a reminder of the duty, the consecrated task, of sincerity. From a fundamental sincerity he could not deviate. The superficies of sincerity (as I think has not always been remarked) is not always there. As I have suggested, many of his poems are insufficiently removed from their romantic origins, from Byronic paternity and Satanic fraternity. The 'satanism' of the Black Mass was very much in the air; in exhibiting it Baudelaire is the voice of his time; but I would observe that in Baudelaire, as in no one else, it is redeemed by *meaning something else*. He uses the same paraphernalia, but cannot limit its symbolism even to all that of which he is conscious. Compare him with Huysmans in *À rebours, En route,* and *Là-bas.* Huysmans, who is a first-rate realist of his time, only succeeds in making his diabolism interesting when he treats it externally, when he is [375] merely describing a manifestation of his period (if such it was). His own interest in such matters is, like his interest in Christianity, a petty affair. Huysmans merely provides a document. Baudelaire would not even provide that, if he had been really absorbed in that ridiculous hocus-pocus. But actually Baudelaire is concerned, not with demons, black masses, and romantic blasphemy, but with the real problem of good and evil. It is hardly more than an accident of time that he uses the current imagery and vocabulary of blasphemy. In the middle nineteenth century, the age which (at its best) Goethe had prefigured, an age of bustle, programmes, platforms, scientific progress, humanitarianism and revolutions which improved nothing, an age of progressive degradation, Baudelaire perceived that what really matters is Sin and Redemption. It is a proof of his honesty that he went as far as he could honestly go and no further. To a mind observant of the post-Voltaire France (*Voltaire . . . le prédicateur des concierges*), a mind which saw the world of *Napoléon le petit* more lucidly than did that of Victor Hugo, a mind which at the same time had no affinity for the *Saint-Sulpicerie* of the day, the recognition of the reality of Sin is a New Life; and the possibility of damnation is so immense a relief in a world of electoral reform, plebiscites, sex reform and dress reform, that damnation is itself

an immediate form of salvation – of salvation from the ennui of modern life, because it at last gives some significance to living. It is this, I believe, that Baudelaire is trying to express; and it is this which separates him from the modernist Protestantism of Byron and Shelley. It is apparently Sin in the Swinburnian sense, but really Sin in the permanent Christian sense, that occupies the mind of Baudelaire.

12 Yet, as I said, the sense of Evil implies the sense of good. Here too, as Baudelaire apparently confuses, and perhaps did confuse, Evil with its theatrical representations, Baudelaire is not always certain in his notion of the Good. The romantic idea of Love is never quite exorcised, but never [376] quite surrendered to. In 'Le Balcon', which M. Valéry considers, and I think rightly, one of Baudelaire's most beautiful poems, there is all the romantic idea, but something more: the reaching out towards something which cannot be had *in*, but which may be had partly *through*, personal relations. Indeed, in much romantic poetry the sadness is due to the exploitation of the fact that no human relations are adequate to human desires, but also to the disbelief in any further object for human desires than that which, being human, fails to satisfy them. One of the unhappy necessities of human existence is that we have to 'find things out for ourselves'. If it were not so, the statement of Dante would, at least for poets, have done once for all. Baudelaire has all the romantic sorrow, but invents a new kind of romantic nostalgia – a derivative of his nostalgia being the *poésie des départs*, the *poésie des salles d'attente*. In a beautiful paragraph of the volume in question, *Mon coeur mis à nu*, he imagines the vessels lying in harbour as saying: *Quand partons-nous vers le bonheur?* and his minor successor Laforgue exclaims: *Comme ils sont beaux, les trains manqués*. The poetry of flight – which, in contemporary France, owes a great debt to the poems of the A. O. Barnabooth of Valery Larbaud – is, in its origin in this paragraph of Baudelaire, a dim recognition of the direction of beatitude.

13 But in the adjustment of the natural to the spiritual, of the bestial to the human and the human to the supernatural, Baudelaire is a bungler compared with Dante; the best that can be said, and that is a very great deal, is that what he knew he found out for himself. In his book, the *Journeaux Intimes*, and especially in *Mon coeur mis à nu*, he has a great deal to say of the love of man and woman. One aphorism which has been especially noticed is the following: *la volupté unique et suprême de l'amour gît dans la certitude de faire le mal*. That means, I think, that Baudelaire has perceived that what distinguishes the relations of man and woman from the copulation of beasts is the knowledge of [377]

Good and Evil (or *moral* Good and Evil which are not natural Good and Bad or Puritan Right and Wrong). Having an imperfect, vague romantic conception of Good, he was at least able to understand that the sexual act as evil is more dignified, less boring, than as the natural 'life-giving', cheery automatism of the modern world. For Baudelaire, sexual operation is at least something not analogous to Kruschen Salts.

14 So far as we are human, what we do must be either evil or good;[1] so far as we do evil or good, we are human; and it is better, in a paradoxical way, to do evil than to do nothing: at least, we exist. It is true to say that the glory of man is his capacity for salvation; it is also true to say that his glory is his capacity for damnation. The worst that can be said of most of our malefactors, from statesmen to thieves, is that they are not men enough to be damned. Baudelaire was man enough for damnation: whether he *is* damned is, of course, another question, and we are not prevented from praying for his repose. In all his humiliating traffic with other beings, he walked secure in this high vocation, that he was capable of a damnation denied to the politicians and the newspaper editors of Paris.

III

15 Baudelaire's notion of beatitude certainly tended to the wishy-washy; and even in one of the most beautiful of his poems, 'L'invitation au voyage', he hardly exceeds the *poésie des départs*. And because his vision is here so restricted, there is for him a gap between human love and divine love. His human love is definite and positive, his divine love vague and uncertain: hence his insistence upon the evil of love, hence his constant vituperations of the female. In this there is no need to pry for psychopathological causes, which would [378] be irrelevant at best; for his attitude towards women is consistent with the point of view which he had reached. Had he been a woman he would, no doubt, have held the same views about men. He has arrived at the perception that a woman must be to some extent a symbol; he did not arrive at the point of harmonising his experience with his ideal needs. The complement, and the correction to the *Journeaux Intimes*, so far as they deal with the relations of man and woman, is the *Vita Nuova* and the *Divine Comedy*. But – I cannot assert it too strongly – Baudelaire's view of life, such as it is, is objectively apprehensible, that is to say, his idiosyncrasies can partly explain his view of life, but they cannot explain it away. And this view

---

1. 'Know ye not, that to whom ye yield yourselves servants to obey, his servants ye are to whom ye obey; whether of sin unto death, or of obedience unto righteousness?' – Romans vi.16.

of life is one which has grandeur and which exhibits heroism; it was an evangel to his time and to ours. *La vraie civilisation*, he wrote, *n'est pas dans le gaz, ni dans la vapeur, ni dans les tables tournantes. Elle est dans la diminution des traces du péché originel.* It is not quite clear what *diminution* here implies, but the tendency of his thought is clear, and the message is still accepted by but few. More than half a century later T. E. Hulme left behind him a paragraph which Baudelaire would have approved:

> In the light of these absolute values, man himself is judged to be essentially limited and imperfect. He is endowed with Original Sin. While he can occasionally accomplish acts which partake of perfection, he can never himself *be* perfect. Certain secondary results in regard to ordinary human action in society follow from this. A man is essentially bad, he can only accomplish anything of value by discipline – ethical and political. Order is thus not merely negative, but creative and liberating. Institutions are necessary.

Variants from 1930:

Title INTRODUCTION

2 [No. fn.]
  that, contrary] that contrary

3 somewhat] something
  way as that in] way in
  is hard] is apt to be very hard

4 scores] hundreds

5 We should be misguided if we treated] It would be quite misguided to treat
  attempted] to attempt
  dispute] disputation

7 his poems] his book
  mulattoes] Mulattoes

11 realist] realist-novelist
  revolutions] sanguine revolutions
  prédicateur] *predicateur*
  Napoléon] Napoleon

12 Valéry] Valery
  which, being human,] which
  nostalgia –] nostalgia,
  volume in question] present volume

13 Puritan] puritan
  understand that] see that to conceive of
  than] than to think of it

14 [No. fn.]
  also true] equally true

Additional paragraph at end:

IV

To translate successfully an imperfect series of notes and jottings like the *Journeaux Intimes* is a more difficult task than the whole of Baudelaire's formal prose. There are repetitions (of thoughts which are probably all the more important to the author because of being repeated); there are short phrases and single words which seem to be memoranda for thoughts, unknown to us, to be developed later; and there are many references to Baudelaire's familiars and to personages of the day. There is the opportunity for vast annotation by some French student who can devote much time to the subject. Pending the appearance of a definitive text of this book in one or other of the two large French editions which are in process of publication, it would be absurd to make such an attempt in an English translation. The reader need not, however, be deterred. The most important passages are also the most comprehensible. We need not stop to guess at meanings in cryptogram, or to enquire the identity of all the persons mentioned. There is enough to be done in pondering the passages which are fully expressed. And the more we study it, the more coherence appears, the more sane and severe and clear-sighted we find a view of life which is, I believe, much more modern for us than are most philosophies between Baudelaire's time and our own.

Arnold and Pater

SE, 379–91.

Publ. in *Bookman*, 72. 1 (Sept. 1930), 1–7: Gallup C310; then, revised, in *The Eighteen-Eighties: Essays by Fellows of the Royal Society of Literature*, ed. Walter de la Mare (Dec. 1930), Gallup B16; then, further revised, in *SE*.

1 Although Pater is as appropriate to the 'seventies as to the 'eighties, because of the appearance of *Studies in the History of the Renaissance* in 1873, I have chosen to discuss him in this volume[1] because of the date 1885, the middle of the decade, which marks the publication of *Marius the Epicurean*. The first may certainly be counted the more 'influential' book; but *Marius* illustrates another, but related aspect of Pater's work. His writing of course extended well into the 'nineties; but I doubt whether anyone would consider the later books and essays of anything like the importance, in social history or in literary history, of the two I have mentioned.

2 The purpose of the present paper is to indicate a direction from Arnold, through Pater, to the 'nineties, with, of course, the solitary figure of Newman in the background.

---

1. A volume entitled *The Eighteen-Eighties*. Edited by Walter de la Mare for the Royal Society of Literature. Cambridge.

3 It is necessary first of all to estimate the aesthetic and religious views of Arnold: in each of which, to borrow his own phrase against him, there is an element of *literature* and an element of *dogma*. As Mr J. M. Robertson has well pointed out in his *Modern Humanists Reconsidered*, Arnold had little gift for consistency or for definition. Nor had he the power of connected reasoning at any length: his flights are either short flights or circular flights. Nothing in his prose work, therefore, will stand very close analysis, and we may well feel that the positive content of many words is very small. Culture and Conduct are the first things, we are told; but what Culture and Conduct are, I feel that I [380] know less well on every reading. Yet Arnold does still hold us, at least with *Culture and Anarchy* and *Friendship's Garland*. To my generation, I am sure, he is a more sympathetic prose writer than Carlyle or Ruskin; yet he holds his position and achieves his effects exactly on the same plane, by the power of his rhetoric and by representing a point of view which is particular though it cannot be wholly defined.

4 But the revival of interest in Arnold in our time – and I believe he is more admired and read not only more than Carlyle and Ruskin, but than Pater – is a very different thing from the influence he exerted in his own time. We go to him for refreshment and for the companionship of a kindred point of view to our own, but not as disciples. And therefore it is the two books I have mentioned that are most readable. Even the *Essays in Criticism* cannot be read very often; *Literature and Dogma*, *God and the Bible*, and *Last Essays on Church and Religion*, have served their turn and can hardly be read through. In these books, he attempts something which must be austerely impersonal; in them reasoning power matters, and it fails him; furthermore, we have now our modern solvers of the same problem Arnold there set himself, and they, or some of them, are more accomplished and ingenious in this sort of rationalising than Arnold was. Accordingly, and this is my first point, his Culture survives better than his Conduct, because it can better survive vagueness of definition. But both Culture and Conduct were important for his own time.

5 Culture has three aspects, according as we look at it in *Culture and Anarchy*, in *Essays in Criticism*, or in the abstract. It is in the first of these two books that Culture shows to best advantage. And the reason is clear: Culture there stands out against a background to which it is contrasted, a background of definite items of ignorance, vulgarity and prejudice. As an invective against the crudities of the industrialism of his time, the book is perfect of its kind. Compared with Carlyle, it looks like

clear thinking, and is certainly clearer expression; and compared with Arnold, [381] Ruskin often appears long-winded and peevish. Arnold taught English expository and critical prose a restraint and urbanity it needed. And hardly, in this book, do we question the meaning of Culture; for the good reason that we do not need to. Even when we read that Culture 'is a study of perfection', we do not at that point raise an eyebrow to admire how much Culture appears to have arrogated from Religion. For we have shortly before been hearing something about 'the will of God'; or of a joint firm called 'reason and the will of God'; and soon after we are presented with Mr Bright and Mr Frederic Harrison as foils to Culture; and appearing in this way between the will of God and Mr Bright, Culture is here sufficiently outlined to be recognisable. *Culture and Anarchy* is on the same side as *Past and Present* or *Unto this Last*. Its ideas are really no clearer – one reason why Arnold, Carlyle and Ruskin were so influential, for precision and completeness of thought do not always make for influence. (Arnold, it is true, gave something else: he produced a kind of illusion of precision and clarity; that is, maintained these qualities as ideals of style.)

6 Certainly, the prophets of the period just before that of which I am supposed to be writing excelled in denunciation (each in his own way) rather than in construction; and each in his own fashion lays himself open to the charge of tedious querulousness. And an idea, such as that of Culture, is apt to lead to consequences which its author cannot foresee and probably will not like. Already, in the *Essays*, Culture begins to seem a little more priggish – I do not say 'begins' in a chronological sense – and a little more anaemic. Where Sir Charles Adderley and Mr Roebuck appear, there is more life than in the more literary criticism. Arnold is in the end, I believe, at his best in satire and in apologetics for literature, in his defence and enunciation of a needed attitude.

7 To us, as I have said, Arnold is rather a friend than a leader. He was a champion of 'ideas' most of whose ideas we no [382] longer take seriously. His Culture is powerless to aid or to harm. But he is at least a forerunner of what is now called Humanism, of which I must here say something, if only to contrast it and compare it with the Aestheticism of Pater. How far Arnold is responsible for the birth of Humanism would be difficult to say; we can at least say that it issues very naturally from his doctrine, that Charles Eliot Norton is largely responsible for its American form, and that therefore Arnold is another likely ancestor. But the resemblances are too patent to be ignored. The difference is that Arnold could father something apparently quite different – the view of life of Walter Pater.

The resemblance is that literature, or Culture, tended with Arnold to usurp the place of Religion. From one point of view, Arnold's theory of Art and his theory of Religion are quite harmonious, and Humanism is merely the more coherent structure. Arnold's prose writings fall into two parts; those on Culture and those on Religion; and the books about Christianity seem only to say again and again – merely that the Christian faith is of course impossible to the man of culture. They are tediously negative. But they are negative in a peculiar fashion: their aim is to affirm that the emotions of Christianity can and must be preserved without the belief. From this proposition two different types of man can extract two different types of conclusion: (1) that Religion is Morals, (2) that Religion is Art. The effect of Arnold's religious campaign is to divorce Religion from thought.

8 In Arnold himself there was a powerful element of Puritan morality, as in most of his contemporaries, however diverse. And the strength of his moral feeling – we might add its blindness also – prevented him from seeing how very odd might look the fragments of the fabric which he knocked about so recklessly. 'The power of Christianity has been in the immense emotion which it has excited,' he says: not realising at all that this is a counsel to get all the emotional kick out of Christianity one can, without the bother of believing it, without reading the future [383] to foresee *Marius the Epicurean*, and finally *De Profundis*. Furthermore, in his books dealing with Christianity he seems bent upon illustrating in himself the provincialisms which he rebuked in others. 'M. de Lavelaye,' he says in the preface to *God and the Bible*, with as deferential a manner as if he were citing M. Renan himself, 'is struck, as any judicious Catholic may well be struck, with the superior freedom, order, stability, and religious earnestness, of the Protestant Nations as compared with the Catholic.' He goes on complacently, 'their religion has made them what they are'. I am not here concerned with the genuine differences between Catholic and Protestant; only with the tone which Arnold adopts in this preface and throughout this book; and which is in no wise more liberal than that of Sir Charles Adderley or Mr Roebuck or 'Mr Tennyson's great broad-shouldered Englishman'. He girds at (apparently) Herbert Spencer for substituting *Unknowable* for *God*; quite unaware that his own Eternal not ourselves comes to exactly the same thing as the Unknowable. And when we read Arnold's discourses on Religion, we return to scrutinise his Culture with some suspicion.

9 For Arnold's Culture, at first sight so enlightened, moderate and reasonable, walks so decorously in the company of the will of God, that

we may overlook the fact that it tends to develop its own stringent rules and restrictions.

> Certainly, culture will never make us think it an essential of religion whether we have in our Church discipline 'a popular authority of elders', as Hooker calls it, or whether we have Episcopal jurisdiction.

Certainly, 'culture' in itself can never make us think so, any more than it can make us think that the quantum theory is an essential of physical science: but such people as are interested in this question at all, however cultured they be, hold one or the other opinion pretty strongly; and Arnold is really affirming that to Culture all theological and ecclesiastical differences are indifferent. But this [384] is a rather positive dogma for Culture to hold. When we take *Culture and Anarchy* in one hand, and *Literature and Dogma* in the other, our minds are gradually darkened by the suspicion that Arnold's objection to Dissenters is partly that they do hold strongly to that which they believe, and partly that they are not Masters of Arts of Oxford. Arnold, as Master of Arts, should have had some scruple about the use of words. But in the very preface to the second edition of *Literature and Dogma* he says:

> The *Guardian* proclaims 'the miracle of the incarnation' to be the 'fundamental truth' for Christians. How strange that on me should devolve the office of instructing the *Guardian* that the fundamental thing for Christians is not the Incarnation but the imitation of Christ!

While wondering whether Arnold's own 'imitation' is even a good piece of mimicry, we notice that he employs *truth* and *thing* as interchangeable: and a very slight knowledge of the field in which he was skirmishing should have told him that a 'fundamental truth' in theology and a 'fundamental thing' in his own loose jargon have nothing comparable about them. The total effect of Arnold's philosophy is to set up Culture in the place of Religion, and to leave Religion to be laid waste by the anarchy of feeling. And Culture is a term which each man not only may interpret as he pleases, but must indeed interpret as he can. So the gospel of Pater follows naturally upon the prophecy of Arnold.

10 Even before the 'seventies began Pater seems to have written, though not published, the words,

> The theory, or idea, or system, which requires of us the sacrifice of any part of this experience, in consideration of some interest into which we cannot enter, or some abstract morality we have not

identified with ourselves, or what is only conventional, has no real claim upon us.[1]

[385] Although more outspoken in repudiating any measure than man for all things, Pater is not really uttering anything more subversive than the following words of Arnold:

> Culture, disinterestedly seeking in its aim at perfection to see things as they really are, shows how worthy and divine a thing is the religious side in man, though it is not the whole of man. But while recognizing the grandeur of the religious side in man, culture yet makes us eschew an inadequate conception of man's totality.

Religion, accordingly, is merely a '"side" in (sic) man'; a side which so to speak must be kept in its place. But when we go to Arnold to enquire what is 'man's totality', that we may ourselves aim at so attractive a consummation, we learn nothing; any more than we learn about the 'secret' of Jesus of which he has so much to say.

11 The degradation of philosophy and religion, skilfully initiated by Arnold, is competently continued by Pater. 'The service of philosophy, and of religion and culture as well, to the human spirit,' he says in the 1873 conclusion to *The Renaissance*, 'is to startle it into a sharp and eager observation.' 'We shall hardly have time,' he says, 'to make theories about the things we see and touch.' Yet we have to be 'curiously testing new opinions'; so it must be – if opinions have anything to do with theories, and unless wholly capricious and unreasoning they must have – that the opinions we test can only be those provided for our enjoyment by an inferior sort of drudges who are incapable of enjoying our own free life, because all their time is spent (and '*we* hardly have time') in making theories. And this again is only a development of the intellectual Epicureanism of Arnold.

12 Had Pater not had one gift denied to Arnold, his permutation of Arnold's view of life would have little interest. He had a taste for painting and the plastic arts, and particularly for Italian painting, a subject to which Ruskin had introduced the nation. He had a visual imagination; [386] he had also come into contact with another generation of French writers than that which Arnold knew; the zealous Puritanism of Arnold was in him considerably mitigated, but the zeal for culture was equally virulent. So his peculiar appropriation of religion into culture was from

---

1. In quoting from *The Renaissance* I use the first edition throughout.

another side: that of emotion, and indeed of sensation; but in making this appropriation he was only doing what Arnold had given licence to do.

13 *Marius the Epicurean* marks indeed one of the phases of the fluctuating relations between religion and culture in England since the Reformation; and for this reason the year 1885 is an important one. Newman, in leaving the Anglican Church, had turned his back upon Oxford. Ruskin, with a genuine sensibility for certain types of art and architecture, succeeded in satisfying his nature by translating everything immediately into terms of morals. The vague religious vapourings of Carlyle, and the sharper, more literate social fury of Ruskin yield before the persuasive sweetness of Arnold. Pater is a new variation.

14 We are liable to confusion if we call this new variation the 'aesthete'. Pater was, like the other writers I have just mentioned (except Newman), a moralist. If as the *Oxford Dictionary* tells us, an aesthete is a 'professed appreciator of the beautiful', then there are at least two varieties: those whose profession is most vocal, and those whose appreciation is most professional. If we wish to understand painting, we do not go to Oscar Wilde for help. We have specialists, such as Mr Berenson, or Mr Roger Fry. Even in that part of his work which can only be called literary criticism, Pater is always primarily the moralist. In his essay on Wordsworth he says,

> To treat life in the spirit of art, is to make life a thing in which means and ends are identified: to encourage such treatment, the true moral significance of art and poetry.

That was his notion: to find the 'true moral significance of art and poetry'. Certainly, a writer may be, none the less [387] classified as a moralist if his moralising is suspect or perverse. We have to-day a witness in the person of M. André Gide. As always in his imaginary portraits, so frequently in his choice of other writers as the subjects of critical studies, Pater is inclined to emphasise whatever is morbid or associated with physical malady. His admirable study of Coleridge is charged with this attraction.

> More than Childe Harold (he says of Coleridge), more than Werther, more than René himself, Coleridge, by what he did, what he was, and what he failed to do, represents that inexhaustible discontent, languor, and home-sickness, that endless regret, the chords of which ring all through our modern literature.

Thus again in Pascal he emphasises the malady, with its consequences upon the thought; but we feel that somehow what is important about

Pascal has been missed. But it is not that he treats philosophers 'in the spirit of art', exactly; for when we read him on Leonardo or Giorgione, we feel that there is the same preoccupation, coming between him and the object as it really is. He is, in his own fashion, moralising upon Leonardo or Giorgione, on Greek art or on modern poetry. His famous dictum: 'Of this wisdom, the poetic passion, the desire of beauty, the love of art for art's sake has most: for art comes to you professing frankly to give nothing but the highest quality to your moments as they pass, and simply for those moments' sake', is itself a theory of ethics; it is concerned not with art but with life. The second half of the sentence is of course demonstrably untrue, or else being true of everything else besides art is meaningless; but it is a serious statement of morals. And the disapproval which greeted this first version of the conclusion to *The Renaissance* is implicitly a just recognition of that fact. 'Art for art's sake' is the offspring of Arnold's Culture: and we can hardly venture to say that it is even a perversion of Arnold's doctrine, considering how very vague and ambiguous that doctrine is.

[388] 15 When religion is in a flourishing state, when the whole mind of society is moderately healthy and in order, there is an easy and natural association between religion and art. Only when religion has been partly retired and confined, when an Arnold can sternly remind us that Culture is wider than Religion, do we get 'religious art' and in due course 'aesthetic religion'. Pater undoubtedly had from childhood a religious bent, naturally to all that was liturgical and ceremonious. Certainly this is a real and important part of religion; and Pater cannot thereby be accused of insincerity and 'aestheticism'. His attitude must be considered both in relation to his own mental powers and to his moment of time. There were other men like him, but without his gift of style, and such men were among his friends. In the pages of Thomas Wright, Pater, more than most of his devout friends, appears a little absurd. His High Churchmanship is undoubtedly very different from that of Newman, Pusey and the Tractarians, who, passionate about dogmatic essentials, were singularly indifferent to the sensuous expressions of orthodoxy. It was also dissimilar to that of the priest working in a slum parish. He was 'naturally Christian' – but within very narrow limitations: the rest of him was just the cultivated Oxford don and disciple of Arnold, for whom religion was a matter of feeling, and metaphysics not much more. Being incapable of sustained reasoning, he could not take philosophy or theology seriously; just as, being primarily a moralist, he was incapable of seeing any work of art simply as it is.

16 *Marius the Epicurean* represents the point of English history at which the repudiation of revealed religion by men of culture and intellectual leadership coincides with a renewed interest in the visual arts. It is Pater's most arduous attempt at a work of literature; for *Plato and Platonism* can be almost dissolved into a series of essays. *Marius* itself is incoherent; its method is a number of fresh starts; its content is a hodge-podge of the learning of the classical don, [389] the impressions of the sensitive holiday visitor to Italy, and a prolonged flirtation with the liturgy. Even A. C. Benson, who makes as much of the book as anyone can, observes in a passage of excellent criticism:

> But the weakness of the case is, that instead of emphasizing the power of sympathy, the Christian conception of Love, which differentiates Christianity from all other religious systems, Marius is after all converted, or brought near to the threshold of the faith, more by its sensuous appeal, its liturgical solemnities; the element, that is to say, which Christianity has in common with all religions, and which is essentially human in character. And more than that, even the very peace which Marius discerns in Christianity is the old philosophical peace over again.

This is sound criticism. But – a point with which Dr Benson was not there concerned – it is surely a merit, on the part of Pater, and one which deserves recognition, to have clarified the issues. Matthew Arnold's religion is the more confused, because he conceals, under the smoke of strong and irrational moral prejudice, just the same, or no better, Stoicism and Cyrenaicism of the amateur classical scholar. Arnold Hellenises and Hebraicises by turns; it is something to Pater's credit to have Hellenised purely.

17 Of the essence of the Christian Faith, as Dr Benson frankly admits, Pater knew almost nothing. One might say also that his intellect was not powerful enough to grasp – I mean, to grasp as firmly as many classical scholars whose names will never be so renowned as that of Pater – the essence of Platonism or Aristotelianism or Neo-Platonism. He therefore, or his Marius, moves quite unconcerned with the intellectual activity which was then amalgamating Greek metaphysics with the tradition of Christ; just as he is equally unconcerned with the realities of Roman life as we catch a glimpse of them in Petronius, or even in such a book as Dill's on the reign of Marcus Aurelius. Marius merely *drifts* towards the Christian [390] Church, if he can be said to have any motion at all; nor does he or his author seem to have any realisation of the chasm to be leapt between the meditations of Aurelius and the Gospel. To the

end, Marius remains only a half-awakened soul. Even at his death, in the midst of the ceremonies of which he is given the benefit, his author reflects 'often had he fancied of old that not to die on a dark or rainy day might itself have a little alleviating grace or favour about it', recalling to our minds the 'springing of violets from the grave' in the Conclusion to *The Renaissance*, and the death of Flavian.

18 I have spoken of the book as of some importance. I do not mean that its importance is due to any influence it may have exerted. I do not believe that Pater, in this book, has influenced a single first-rate mind of a later generation. His view of art, as expressed in *The Renaissance*, impressed itself upon a number of writers in the 'nineties, and propagated some confusion between life and art which is not wholly irresponsible for some untidy lives. The theory (if it can be called a theory) of 'art for art's sake' is still valid in so far as it can be taken as an exhortation to the artist to stick to his job; it never was and never can be valid for the spectator, reader or auditor. How far *Marius the Epicurean* may have assisted a few 'conversions' in the following decade I do not know: I only feel sure that with the direct current of religious development it has had nothing to do at all. So far as that current – or one important current – is concerned, *Marius* is much nearer to being merely due to Pater's contact – a contact no more intimate than that of Marius himself – with something which was happening and would have happened without him.

19 The true importance of the book, I think, is as a document of one moment in the history of thought and sensibility in the nineteenth century. The dissolution of thought in that age, the isolation of art, philosophy, religion, ethics and literature, is interrupted by various chimerical attempts to effect imperfect syntheses. Religion became [391] morals, religion became art, religion became science or philosophy; various blundering attempts were made at alliances between various branches of thought. Each half-prophet believed that he had the whole truth. The alliances were as detrimental all round as the separations. The right practice of 'art for art's sake' was the devotion of Flaubert or Henry James; Pater is not with these men, but rather with Carlyle and Ruskin and Arnold, if some distance below them. *Marius* is significant chiefly as a reminder that the religion of Carlyle or that of Ruskin or that of Arnold or that of Tennyson or that of Browning, is not enough. It represents, and Pater represents more positively than Coleridge of whom he wrote the words, 'that inexhaustible discontent, languor, and home-sickness . . . the chords of which ring all through our modern literature'.

Variants:

Title The Place of Pater *The Eighteen-Eighties* (Dec. 1930)

1. because of the date 1885 . . . publication] The middle of the eighties, 1885, marked the publication [Opening sentence of para. 2 in *Bookman* (Sep. 1930).]
   The first] *Studies in the History of the Renaissance Bookman* (Sep. 1930)
   the more] a more *Bookman* (Sep. 1930)

2. [Para. 1 in *Bookman* (Sep. 1930).]
   a direction] the direction taken by taste and thought *Bookman* (Sep. 1930)

3. *dogma*] dogma *Bookman* (Sep. 1930)
   Culture and Conduct are the first] That Culture and Conduct are first *Bookman* (Sep. 1930)

4. for his own time.] for his own time, and they were wrong. *Bookman* (Sep. 1930)

5. Culture has] But Culture has *Bookman* (Sep. 1930), *The Eighteen-Eighties* (Dec. 1930)
   clear] perfectly clear *Bookman* (Sep. 1930), *The Eighteen-Eighties* (Dec. 1930)
   background to] background against *Bookman* (Sep. 1930)
   definite] perfectly definite *Bookman* (Sep. 1930), *The Eighteen-Eighties* (Dec. 1930)
   the book] it *Bookman* (Sep. 1930)
   meaning of Culture] meaning of "culture" *Bookman* (Sep. 1930)
   read that Culture] read that culture *Bookman* (Sep. 1930)
   Culture [throughout the para.]] culture *Bookman* (Sep. 1930)
   no clearer –] no clearer; – *The Eighteen-Eighties* (Dec. 1930)
   do not always make] do not make *Bookman* (Sep. 1930)
   influence] great influence *Bookman* (Sep. 1930)

6. cannot foresee] could not have foreseen *Bookman* (Sep. 1930)

7. than a leader.] than a leader, or if a leader, only as a stimulus to proceed *Bookman* (Sep. 1930), *The Eighteen-Eighties* (Dec. 1930)
   Humanism] humanism [throughout the para.] *Bookman* (Sep. 1930)
   are quite harmonious] fit perfectly *Bookman* (Sep. 1930)
   Religion] religion [throughout the para.] *Bookman* (Sep. 1930)
   and the books] and for such a man as Pater the books *Bookman* (Sep. 1930)
   seem only to say again and again] could have said *Bookman* (Sep. 1930)
   Art] art *Bookman* (Sep. 1930)

8. contemporaries,] contemporaries *Bookman* (Sep. 1930)
   might look the fragments] the fragments might look *Bookman*, *The Eighteen-Eighties* (Dec. 1930)
   reading] reading into *Bookman* (Sep. 1930)
   Unknowable] Unknowable *Bookman* (Sep. 1930)
   God] God *Bookman* (Sep. 1930)
   Eternal not ourselves] Eternal-not-ourselves *Bookman* (Sep. 1930)

9. to Culture] to culture *Bookman* (Sep. 1930)
   for Culture] for culture *Bookman* (Sep. 1930)
   in one hand] on one hand *Bookman* (Sep. 1930)
   in the other] , on the other *Bookman* (Sep. 1930)
   as Master][as such a Master *Bookman* (Sep. 1930)
   Arts, should] Arts should *Bookman* (Sep. 1930)

10 [Section 'II' begins here in *Bookman* (Sep. 1930).]
[No fn. in *Bookman* (Sep. 1930).]
than man for all things] for all things than man *Bookman* (Sep. 1930), *The Eighteen-Eighties* (Dec. 1930)
'"side" in (*sic*) man'] "side" in (sic) man *Bookman* (Sep. 1930)

13 sweetness of Arnold.] sweetness of Arnold, who at least made a statement for a generation *The Eighteen-Eighties* (Dec. 1930)

14 We are liable] But we are liable *Bookman* (Sep. 1930), *The Eighteen-Eighties* (Dec. 1930)
painting,] painting, or architecture, or poetry, *Bookman* (Sep. 1930)
his moralising] the morality he finds *Bookman*, *The Eighteen-Eighties* (Dec. 1930)
dictum:] dictum – *Bookman* (Sep. 1930)
sake',] sake" – *Bookman* (Sep. 1930)

16 Dr Benson] Mr. Benson *Bookman* (Sep. 1930)

17 Dr Benson] Mr. Benson *Bookman* (Sep. 1930)

Francis Herbert Bradley

SE, 392–403.

Originally a review of F. H. Bradley's *Ethical Studies* (2nd edn) in *TLS*, 1352 (29 Dec. 1927), [981]–2: Gallup C239. Revised in *FLA* and again in *SE*. Repr. from *SE* in *EAAM*.

1 It is unusual that a book so famous and so influential should remain out of print so long as Bradley's *Ethical Studies*.[1] The one edition appeared in 1876: Bradley's refusal to reprint it never wavered. In 1893, in a footnote in *Appearance and Reality*, and in words characteristic of the man, he wrote: 'I feel that the appearance of other books, as well as the decay of those superstitions against which largely it was directed, has left me free to consult my own pleasure in the matter.' The dates of his three books, the *Ethical Studies* in 1876, the *Principles of Logic* in 1883, and *Appearance and Reality* in 1893, leave us in no doubt that his pleasure was the singular one of thinking rather than the common one of writing books. And Bradley always assumed, with what will remain for those who did not know him a curious blend of humility and irony, an attitude of extreme diffidence about his own work. His *Ethical Studies*, he told us (or told our fathers), did not aim at 'the construction of a system of Moral Philosophy'. The first words of the preface to his *Principles of Logic* are: 'The following work makes no claim to supply any systematic treatment of logic.' He begins the preface to *Appearance and Reality* with the words: 'I have described the following work as an essay in metaphysics. Neither in form nor extent does it carry out the idea of a system.' The phrase for each book is almost the same. And many readers,

---

1. *Ethical Studies*, by F. H. Bradley, O.M., LL.D. Second Edition. (Oxford: Clarendon Press. London: Milford.)

having in mind Bradley's polemical irony and his obvious zest in using it, his habit of discomfiting an op-[393]ponent with a sudden profession of ignorance, of inability to understand, or of incapacity for abstruse thought, have concluded that this is all a mere pose – and even a somewhat unscrupulous one. But deeper study of Bradley's mind convinces us that the modesty is real, and his irony the weapon of a modest and highly sensitive man. Indeed, if this had been a pose it would never have worn so well as it has. We have to consider, then, what is the nature of Bradley's influence, and why his writings and his personality fascinate those whom they do fascinate; and what are his claims to permanence.

2 Certainly one of the reasons for the power he still exerts, as well as an indubitable claim to permanence, is his great gift of style. It is for his purposes – and his purposes are more varied than is usually supposed – a perfect style. Its perfection has prevented it from cutting any great figure in prose anthologies and literature manuals, for it is perfectly welded with the matter. Ruskin's works are extremely readable in snippets even for many who take not a particle of interest in the things in which Ruskin was so passionately interested. Hence he survives in anthologies, while his books have fallen into undue neglect. Bradley's books can never fall into this neglect because they will never rise to this notoriety; they come to the hands only of those who are qualified to treat them with respect. But perhaps a profounder difference between a style like Bradley's and a style like Ruskin's is a greater purity and concentration of purpose. One feels that the emotional intensity of Ruskin is partly a deflection of something that was baffled in life, whereas Bradley, like Newman, is directly and wholly that which he is. For the secret of Bradley's style, like that of Bergson – whom he resembles in this if in nothing else – is the intense addiction to an intellectual passion.

3 The nearest resemblance in style, however, is not Ruskin but Matthew Arnold. It has not been sufficiently observed that Bradley makes use of the same means as Arnold, and [394] for similar ends. To take first the most patent resemblance, we find in Bradley the same type of fun as that which Arnold has with his young friend Arminius. In *The Principles of Logic* there is a celebrated passage in which Bradley is attacking the theory of the association of ideas according to Professor Bain, and explains how on this principle an infant comes to recognise a lump of sugar:

> A young child, or one of the lower animals, is given on Monday a round piece of sugar, eats it and finds it sweet. On Tuesday it sees a square piece of sugar, and proceeds to eat it. . . . Tuesday's

sensation and Monday's image are not only separate facts, which, because alike, are therefore *not* the same; but they differ perceptibly both in quality and environment. What is to lead the mind to take one for the other?

Sudden at this crisis, and in pity at distress, there leaves the heaven with rapid wing a goddess Primitive Credulity. Breathing in the ear of the bewildered infant she whispers, The thing which has happened will happen once more. Sugar was sweet and sugar will be sweet. And Primitive Credulity is accepted forthwith as the mistress of our life. She leads our steps on the path of experience, until her fallacies, which cannot always be pleasant, at length become suspect. We wake up indignant at the kindly fraud by which the goddess so long has deceived us. So she shakes her wings, and flying to the stars, where there are no philosophers, leaves us here to the guidance of – I cannot think what.

This sort of solemn banter is exactly what an admirer of Arnold is ready to enjoy. But it is not only in his fun, or in his middle style, that Bradley is like Arnold; they are alike in their purple passages. The two following may be compared. By Arnold:

And yet, steeped in sentiment as she lies, spreading her gardens to the moonlight, and whispering from her towers the last enchantments of the Middle Age, who will deny [395] that Oxford, by her ineffable charm, keeps ever calling us nearer to the true goal of all of us, to the ideal, to perfection – to beauty, in a word, which is only truth seen from another side – nearer, perhaps, than all the science of Tübingen. Adorable dreamer, whose heart has been so romantic! who hast given thyself so prodigally, given thyself to sides and to heroes not mine, only never to the Philistines! home of lost causes, and forsaken beliefs, and unpopular names, and impossible loyalties! what example could ever so inspire us to keep down the Philistine in ourselves, what teacher could ever so save us from that bondage to which we are all prone, that bondage which Goethe, in his incomparable lines on the death of Schiller, makes it his friend's highest praise (and nobly did Schiller deserve the praise) to have left miles out of sight behind him – the bondage of 'was uns alle bändigt, *das Gemeine*!'

The passage from *The Principles of Logic* is not so well known:

It may come from a failure in my metaphysics, or from a weakness of the flesh which continues to blind me, but the notion that existence could be the same as understanding strikes as cold and ghost-like as the dreariest materialism. That the glory of this world in the end is appearance leaves the world more glorious, if we feel it is a show of some fuller splendour; but the sensuous curtain is a deception and a cheat, if it hides some colourless movement of atoms, some spectral woof of impalpable abstractions, or unearthly ballet of bloodless categories. Though dragged to such conclusions we cannot embrace them. Our principles may be true, but they are not reality. They no more *make* that Whole which commands our devotion than some shredded dissection of human tatters *is* that warm and breathing beauty of flesh which our hearts found delightful.

Any one who is at all sensitive to style will recognise the similarity of tone and tension and beat. It is not altogether [396] certain that the passage from Bradley is not the better; at any rate such a phrase as Arnold's 'ineffable charm' has not worn at all well.

4 But if the two men fought with the same weapons – and fundamentally, in spite of Bradley's assault upon Arnold, for the same causes – the weapons of Bradley had behind them a heavier force and a closer precision. Exactly what Bradley fought for and exactly what he fought against have not been quite understood; understanding has been obscured by the dust of Bradley's logical battles. People are inclined to believe that what Bradley did was to demolish the logic of Mill and the psychology of Bain. If he had done that, it would have been a lesser service than what he has done; and if he had done that it would have been less of a service than people think, for there is much that is good in the logic of Mill and the psychology of Bain. But Bradley did not attempt to destroy Mill's logic. Any one who reads his own *Principles* will see that his force is directed not against Mill's logic as a whole but only against certain limitations, imperfections and abuses. He left the structure of Mill's logic standing, and never meant to do anything else. On the other hand, the *Ethical Studies* are not merely a demolition of the Utilitarian theory of conduct but an attack upon the whole Utilitarian mind. For Utilitarianism was, as every reader of Arnold knows, a great temple in Philistia. And of this temple Arnold hacked at the ornaments and cast down the images, and his best phrases remain for ever gibing and scolding in our memory. But Bradley, in his philosophical critique of Utilitarianism, undermined the foundations. The spiritual descendants of Bentham have built anew, as they always will; but at least, in building another temple for the same worship, they have had to apply a different style of architecture. And this is the social basis of Bradley's distinction, and the social basis is even more his claim to our gratitude than the

logical basis: he replaced a philosophy which was crude and raw and provincial by one which was, in comparison, catholic, civi-[397]lised, and universal. True, he was influenced by Kant and Hegel and Lotze. But Kant and Hegel and Lotze are not so despicable as some enthusiastic medievalists would have us believe, and they are, in comparison with the school of Bentham, catholic and civilised and universal. In fighting the battles that he fought in the 'seventies and 'eighties Bradley was fighting for a European and ripened and wise philosophy, against an insular and immature and cranky one; the same battle that Arnold was fighting against the *British Banner*, Judge Edmonds, Newman Weeks, Deborah Butler, Elderess Polly, Brother Noyes, Mr Murphy, the Licensed Victuallers and the Commercial Travellers.

5 It is not to say that Arnold's work was vain if we say that it is to be done again; for we must know in advance, if we are prepared for that conflict, that the combat may have truces but never a peace. If we take the widest and wisest view of a Cause, there is no such thing as a Lost Cause because there is no such thing as a Gained Cause. We fight for lost causes because we know that our defeat and dismay may be the preface to our successors' victory, though that victory itself will be temporary; we fight rather to keep something alive than in the expectation that anything will triumph. If Bradley's philosophy is to-day a little out of fashion, we must remark that what has superseded it, what is now in favour, is, for the most part, crude and raw and provincial (though infinitely more technical and scientific) and must perish in its turn. Arnold turned from mid-century Radicalism with the reflection 'A new power has suddenly appeared.' There is always a new power; but the new power destined to supersede the philosophy which has superseded Bradley will probably be something at the same time older, more patient, more supple and more wise. The chief characteristics of much contemporary philosophy are newness and crudeness, impatience, inflexibility in one respect and fluidity in another, and irresponsibility and lack of wisdom. Of wisdom Bradley had a large share; wisdom consists largely of scepticism [398] and uncynical disillusion; and of these Bradley had a large share. And scepticism and disillusion are a useful equipment for religious understanding; and of that Bradley had a share too.

6 Those who have read the *Ethical Studies* will be ready with the remark that it was Bradley, in this book and in the year 1876, who knocked the bottom out of *Literature and Dogma*. But that does not mean that the two men were not on the same side; it means only that *Literature and Dogma* is irrelevant to Arnold's main position as given in the Essays and

in *Culture and Anarchy*, that the greatest weakness of Arnold's culture was his weakness in philosophical training, and that in philosophical criticism Bradley exhibits the same type of culture that Arnold exhibited in political and social criticism. Arnold had made an excursion into a field for which he was not armed. Bradley's attack upon Arnold does not take up much space, but Bradley was economical of words; it is all in a few paragraphs and a few footnotes to the 'Concluding Remarks':

> But here once more 'culture' has come to our aid, and has shown us how here, as everywhere, the study of polite literature, which makes for meekness, makes needless also all further education; and we felt already as if the clouds that metaphysic had wrapped about the matter were dissolving in the light of a fresh and sweet intelligence. And, as we turned towards the dawn, we sighed over poor Hegel, who had read neither Goethe nor Homer, nor the Old and New Testaments, nor any of the literature which has gone to form 'culture', but, knowing no facts, and reading no books, nor ever asking himself 'such a tyro's question as what being really was', sat spinning out of his head those foolish logomachies which impose on no person of refinement.

Here is the identical weapon of Arnold, sharpened to a razor edge and turned against Arnold.

> But the 'stream' and the 'tendency' having served [399] their turn, like last week's placards, now fall into the background, and we learn at last that 'the Eternal' is not eternal at all, unless we give that name to whatever a generation sees happen, and believes both has happened and will happen – just as the habit of washing ourselves might be termed 'the Eternal not ourselves that makes for cleanliness', or 'Early to bed and early to rise' the 'Eternal not ourselves that makes for longevity', and so on – that 'the Eternal', in short, is nothing in the world but a piece of literary clap-trap. The consequence is that all we are left with is the assertion that 'righteousness' is 'salvation' or welfare, and that there is a 'law' and a 'Power' which has something to do with this fact; and here again we must not be ashamed to say that we fail to understand what any one of these phrases means, and suspect ourselves once more to be on the scent of clap-trap.

A footnote continues the Arnold-baiting in a livelier style:

> 'Is there a God?' asks the reader. 'Oh yes,' replies Mr. Arnold, 'and I can verify him in experience.' 'And what is he then?' cries the reader.

'Be virtuous, and as a rule you will be happy,' is the answer. 'Well, and God?' 'That is God,' says Mr. Arnold; 'there is no deception, and what more do you want?' I suppose we do want a good deal more. Most of us, certainly the public which Mr. Arnold addresses, want something they can worship; and they will not find that in an hypostasized copy-book heading, which is not much more adorable than 'Honesty is the best policy', or 'Handsome is that handsome does', or various other edifying maxims, which have not yet come to an apotheosis.

Such criticism is final. It is patently a great triumph of wit and a great delight to watch when a man's methods, almost his tricks of speech, are thus turned against himself. But if we look more closely into these words and into the whole chapter from which they are taken, we find Bradley to have been not only triumphant in polemic but right in [400] reason. Arnold, with all his great virtues, was not always patient enough, or solicitous enough of any but immediate effect, to avoid inconsistency – as has been painstakingly shown by Mr J. M. Robertson. In *Culture and Anarchy*, which is probably his greatest book, we hear something said about 'the will of God'; but the 'will of God' seems to become superseded in importance by 'our best self, or right reason, to which we want to give authority'; and this best self looks very much like Matthew Arnold slightly disguised. In our own time one of the most remarkable of our critics, one who is fundamentally on most questions in the right, and very often right quite alone, Professor Irving Babbitt, has said again and again that the old curbs of class, of authoritative government, and of religion must be supplied in our time by something he calls the 'inner check'. The inner check looks very much like the 'best self' of Matthew Arnold; and though supported by wider erudition and closer reasoning, is perhaps open to the same objections. There are words of Bradley's, and in the chapter from which we have already quoted, that might seem at first sight to support these two eminent doctrines:

> How can the human-divine ideal ever be my will? The answer is, Your will never can be as the will of your private self, so that your private self should become wholly good. To that self you must die, and by faith be made one with that ideal. You must resolve to give up your will, as the mere will of this or that man, and you must put your whole self, your entire will, into the will of the divine. That must be your one self, as it is your true self; that you must hold to both with thought and will, and all other you must renounce.

There is one direction in which these words – and, indeed, Bradley's philosophy as a whole – might be pushed, which would be dangerous; the direction of diminishing the value and dignity of the individual, of sacrificing him to a Church or a State. But, in any event, the words cannot be [401] interpreted in the sense of Arnold. The distinction is not between a 'private self' and a 'public self' or a 'higher self', it is between the individual as himself and no more, a mere numbered atom, and the individual in communion with God. The distinction is clearly drawn between man's 'mere will' and 'the will of the Divine'. It may be noted also that Bradley is careful, in indicating the process, not to exaggerate either will or intellect at the expense of the other. And in all events it is a process which neither Arnold nor Professor Babbitt could accept. But *if* there is a 'will of God', as Arnold, in a hasty moment, admits, then some doctrine of Grace must be admitted too; or else the 'will of God' is just the same inoperative benevolence which we have all now and then received – and resented – from our fellow human beings. In the end it is a disappointment and a cheat.

7 Those who return to the reading of *Ethical Studies*, and those who now, after reading the other works of Bradley, read it for the first time, will be struck by the unity of Bradley's thought in the three books and in the collected Essays. But this unity is not the unity of mere fixity. In the *Ethical Studies*, for instance, he speaks of the awareness of the self, the knowledge of one's own existence as indubitable and identical. In *Appearance and Reality*, seventeen years later, he had seen much deeper into the matter; and had seen that no one 'fact' of experience in isolation is real or is evidence of anything. The unity of Bradley's thought is not the unity attained by a man who never changes his mind. If he had so little occasion to change it, that is because he usually saw his problems from the beginning in all their complexity and connexions – saw them, in other words, with wisdom – and because he could never be deceived by his own metaphors – which, indeed, he used most sparingly – and was never tempted to make use of current nostrums.

8 If all of Bradley's writings are in some sense merely 'essays', that is not solely a matter of modesty, or caution, [402] and certainly not of indifference, or even of ill health. It is that he perceived the contiguity and continuity of the various provinces of thought. 'Reflection on morality,' he says, 'leads us beyond it. It leads us, in short, to see the necessity of a religious point of view.' Morality and religion are not the same thing, but they cannot beyond a certain point be treated separately. A system of ethics, if thorough, is explicitly or implicitly a system of theology;

and to attempt to erect a complete theory of ethics without a religion is none the less to adopt some particular attitude toward religion. In this book, as in others, Bradley is thoroughly empirical, much more empirical than the philosophies that he opposed. He wished only to determine how much of morality could be founded securely without entering into the religious questions at all. As in *Appearance and Reality* he assumes that our common everyday knowledge is on the whole true so far as it goes, but that we do not know how far it does go; so in the *Ethical Studies* he starts always with the assumption that our common attitude towards duty, pleasure, or self-sacrifice is correct so far as it goes – but we do not know how far it does go. And in this he is all in the Greek tradition. It is fundamentally a philosophy of common sense.

9 Philosophy without wisdom is vain; and in the greater philosophers we are usually aware of that wisdom which for the sake of emphasis and in the most accurate and profound sense could be called even worldly wisdom. Common sense does not mean, of course, either the opinion of the majority or the opinion of the moment; it is not a thing to be got at without maturity and study and thought. The lack of it produces those unbalanced philosophies, such as Behaviourism, of which we hear a great deal. A purely 'scientific' philosophy ends by denying what we know to be true; and, on the other hand, the great weakness of Pragmatism is that it ends by being of no *use* to anybody. Again, it is easy to underestimate Hegel, but it is easy to overestimate Bradley's debt to Hegel; in a philosophy like [403] Bradley's the points at which he *stops* are always important points. In an unbalanced or uncultured philosophy words have a way of changing their meaning – as sometimes with Hegel; or else they are made, in a most ruthless and piratical manner, to walk the plank: such as the words which Professor J. B. Watson drops overboard, and which we know to have meaning and value. But Bradley, like Aristotle, is distinguished by his scrupulous respect for words, that their meaning should be neither vague nor exaggerated; and the tendency of his labours is to bring British philosophy closer to the great Greek tradition.

Variants:
Title Bradley's 'Ethical Studies' *TLS* (1927)
1 systematic] systemic *TLS* (1927)
3 become suspect] becomes suspect *FLA*
4 On the other hand] Similarly *TLS* (1927)
9 such as the words] the words *FLA*
   meaning and value.] meaning and value, are almost innumerable. *FLA*

Marie Lloyd

SE, 404-7.

Publ. in *Dial*, 73. 6 (Dec. 1922) [659]-63, signed 'T. S. Eliot',
and revised in *C.*, 1. 2 (Jan. 1923), 192-5: Gallup C136. Further revised in *SE*.

1 It requires some effort to understand why one person, among many who do a thing with accomplished skill, should be greater than the others; and it is not always easy to distinguish superiority from great popularity, when the two go together. Although I have always admired the genius of Marie Lloyd I do not think that I always appreciated its uniqueness; I certainly did not realise that her death would strike me as the important event that it was. Marie Lloyd was the greatest music-hall artist of her time in England: she was also the most popular. And popularity in her case was not merely evidence of her accomplishment; it was something more than success. It is evidence of the extent to which she represented and expressed that part of the English nation which has perhaps the greatest vitality and interest.

2 Among all of that small number of music-hall performers, whose names are familiar to what is called the lower class, Marie Lloyd had far the strongest hold on popular affection. The attitude of audiences toward Marie Lloyd was different from their attitude toward any other of their favourites of that day, and this difference represents the difference in her art. Marie Lloyd's audiences were invariably sympathetic, and it was through this sympathy that she controlled them. Among living music-hall artists none can better control an audience than Nellie Wallace. I have seen Nellie Wallace interrupted by jeering or hostile comment from a boxful of Eastenders; I have seen her, hardly pausing in her act, make some quick retort that [405] silenced her tormenters for the rest of the evening. But I have never known Marie Lloyd to be confronted by this kind of hostility; in any case, the feeling of the vast majority of the audience was so manifestly on her side, that no objector would have dared to lift his voice. And the difference is this: that whereas other comedians amuse their audiences as much [as] and sometimes more than Marie Lloyd, no other comedian succeeded so well in giving expression to the life of that audience, in raising it to a kind of art. It was, I think, this capacity for expressing the soul of the people that made Marie Lloyd unique, and that made her audiences, even when they joined in the chorus, not so much hilarious as happy.

3 In the details of acting Marie Lloyd was perhaps the most perfect, in her own style, of British actresses. There are no cinema records of her; she never descended to this form of money-making; it is to be regretted, however, that there is no film of her to preserve for the recollection of her admirers the perfect expressiveness of her smallest gestures. But it is less in the accomplishment of her act than in what she made it, that she differed from other comedians. There was nothing about her of the grotesque; none of her comic appeal was due to exaggeration; it was all a matter of selection and concentration. The most remarkable of the survivors of the music-hall stage, to my mind, are Nellie Wallace and Little Tich;[1] but each of these is a kind of grotesque; their acts are an orgy of parody of the human race. For this reason, the appreciation of these artists requires less knowledge of the environment. To appreciate, for instance, the last turn in which Marie Lloyd appeared, one ought to know what objects a middle-aged woman of the charwoman class would carry in her bag; exactly how she would go through her bag in search of something; and exactly the tone of voice in which she would enumerate the objects she found in it. This was only part of the acting [406] in Marie Lloyd's last song, 'One of the Ruins That Cromwell Knocked Abaht a Bit'.

4 Marie Lloyd's art will, I hope, be discussed by more competent critics of the theatre than I. My own chief point is that I consider her superiority over other performers to be in a way a moral superiority: it was her understanding of the people and sympathy with them, and the people's recognition of the fact that she embodied the virtues which they genuinely most respected in private life, that raised her to the position she occupied at her death. And her death is itself a significant moment in English history. I have called her the expressive figure of the lower classes. There is no such expressive figure for any other class. The middle classes have no such idol: the middle classes are morally corrupt. That is to say, their own life fails to find a Marie Lloyd to express it; nor have they any independent virtues as a class which might give them as a conscious class any dignity. The middle classes, in England as elsewhere, under democracy, are morally dependent upon the aristocracy, and the aristocracy are subordinate to the middle class, which is gradually absorbing and destroying them. The lower class still exists; but perhaps it will not exist for long. In the music-hall comedians they find the expression and dignity of their own lives; and this is not found in the most elaborate and expensive revue. In England, at any rate, the revue expresses almost nothing. With the decay of the music-

---

1. Without prejudice to the younger generation.

hall, by the encroachment of the cheap and rapid-breeding cinema, the lower classes will tend to drop into the same state of protoplasm as the bourgeoisie. The working man who went to the music-hall and saw Marie Lloyd and joined in the chorus was himself performing part of the act; he was engaged in that collaboration of the audience with the artist which is necessary in all art and most obviously in dramatic art. He will now go to the cinema, where his mind is lulled by continuous senseless music and continuous action too rapid for the brain to act upon, and will receive, without giving, in that same listless [407] apathy with which the middle and upper classes regard any entertainment of the nature of art. He will also have lost some of his interest in life. Perhaps this will be the only solution. In a most interesting essay in the recent volume of *Essays on the Depopulation of Melanesia*, the psychologist W. H. R. Rivers adduced evidence which has led him to believe that the natives of that unfortunate archipelago are dying out principally for the reason that the 'Civilisation' forced upon them has deprived them of all interest in life. They are dying from pure boredom. When every theatre has been replaced by 100 cinemas, when every musical instrument has been replaced by 100 gramophones, when every horse has been replaced by 100 cheap motor-cars, when electrical ingenuity has made it possible for every child to hear its bedtime stories through a loudspeaker, when applied science has done everything possible with the materials on this earth to make life as interesting as possible, it will not be surprising if the population of the entire civilised world rapidly follows the fate of the Melanesians.[1]

Variants:
Title London Letter *Dial (1922)*; In Memoriam: Marie Lloyd C. (1923)
1   effort] effort of analysis *Dial* (1922)
    and it is not] nor is it *Dial* (1922)
    [Between 'go together.' and 'Although I':] I am thinking of Marie Lloyd, who has died only a short time before the writing of this letter.
    the genius of Marie Lloyd] her genius *Dial* (1922)
    important event that it was] most important event which I have had to chronicle in these pages *Dial* (1922)
    artist of her time] artist *Dial* (1922)
[**Between paras 1 and 2:**] Marie Lloyd's funeral became a ceremony which surprised even her warmest admirers:
    The scenes from an early hour yesterday, had been eloquent of the supreme place which Marie Lloyd held in the affection of the people. Wreaths had poured into the house in Woodstock Road from all parts of the country. There were hundreds of them from people whose names are almost household words on

1. These lines were written nine years ago.

the variety stage, and from such people as 'a flower boy' in Piccadilly Circus: the taxi-drivers of Punter's Garage: and the Costermongers' Union of Farringdon Road. . . . Bombardier Wells sent a wreath. It was a white cushion, and across it in violets were the words 'At Rest: With deepest sympathy from Mrs and Billie Wells.' . . . Tributes were also sent by Hetty King, Clarice Mayne, Clara Mayne, Little Tich, Arthur Prince, George Mozart, Harry Weldon, Charles Austin, Gertie Gitana, the Brothers Egbert, Zetta Mare, Julia Neilson, and Fred Terry, Mr and Mrs Frank Curzon, Marie Loftus, many of the provincial music-halls, the Gulliver halls, and dressers from most of the theatres, and many of Miss Lloyd's old school chums. . . . A favourite song of Miss Lloyd's was recalled by a wreath fashioned like a bird's cage. The cage was open, but the old cock linnet had flown. . . . A large floral horseshoe, with whip, cap, and stirrups, was from 'Her Jockey Pals' – Donoghue, Archibald, and other men famous in the racing world. . . . There were other wreaths from the National Sporting Club, the Eccentric Club, the Ladies' Theatrical Guild, the Variety Artists' Federation, Albert and Mrs Whelan, Lorna and Toots Pound, Kate Carney, Nellie Wallace, the Ring at Blackfriars, Connie Ediss (who sent red roses), the Camberwell Palace (a white arch with two golden gates), Lew Lake, Major J. Arnold Wilson, and innumerable other people. *Dial* (1922)

2   [Between 'popular affection.' and 'The attitude':] She is known to many audiences in America. I have never seen her perform in America, but I cannot imagine that she would be seen there at her best; she was only seen at her best under the stimulus of those audiences in England, and especially in Cockney London, who had crowded to hear her for thirty years. *Dial* (1922)
    The attitude . . . favourites of that day] The attitude of these audiences was different, toward Marie Lloyd, from what it was toward any other of their favourites *Dial* (1922)
    favourites of that day] favourites *C.* (1923)
    better] so well *Dial* (1922), *C.* (1923)
    than Nellie] as Nellie *Dial* (1922), *C.* (1923)

3   In the details] It is true than in the details *Dial* (1922), *C.* (1923)
    style] line *Dial* (1922)
    are no] are – thank God – no *Dial* (1922), *C.* (1923)
    less in . . . what she made it] more in the thing that she made it, than in the accomplishment of her act *Dial* (1922)
    Tich;] [No fn. in *Dial* (1922), *C.* (1923).]
    orgy] inconceivable orgy *Dial* (1922), *C.* (1923)
    what objects] already exactly what objects *Dial* (1922), *C.* (1923)
    middle-aged] middle-age *C.* (1923)
    One of the] I'm One of the *Dial* (1922)

[**Between paras. 3 and 4:**] Marie Lloyd was of London – in fact of Hoxton – and on the stage from her earliest years. It is pleasing to know that her first act was for a Hoxton audience, when at the age of ten she organised the Fairy Bell Minstrels for the Nile Street Mission of the Band of Hope; at which she sang and acted a song entitled 'Throw Down the Bottle and Never Drink Again', which is said to have converted at least one member of the audience to the cause now enforced by law in America. It was similar audiences to her first audience that supported her to the last. *Dial* (1922)

4 sympathy with] sympathy for *Dial* (1922), *C.* (1923)
  There is no] There has been no *Dial* (1922)
  their own life ... express it] it is themselves and their own life which find no expression in such a person as Marie Lloyd *Dial* (1922)
  subordinate to] morally in fear of *Dial* (1922), *C.* (1923)
  lower ... perhaps it] lower classes still exist; but perhaps they *Dial* (1922)
  expression] artistic expression *Dial* (1922)
  found in] found for any life in *Dial* (1922)
  decay] dwindling *Dial* (1922)
  protoplasm] amorphous protoplasm *Dial* (1922)
  the act] the work of acting *Dial* (1922)
  will receive] he will receive *Dial* (1922)
  an interesting] a most interesting *Dial* (1922)
  psychologist] great psychologist *Dial* (1922), *C.* (1923)
  adduced] adduces *Dial* (1922)
  loudspeaker] wireless receiver attached to both ears *Dial (1922)*; wireless receiver attached to its ears *C.* (1923)
  Melanesians. [No fn. in *Dial* (1922), *C.* (1923).]
  [After 'Melanesians.':] You will see that the death of Marie Lloyd has had a depressing effect, and that I am quite incapable of taking any interest in any literary events in England in the last two months, if any have taken place. *Dial* (1922)

Wilkie Collins and Dickens

SE, 408–18.

Revised from *TLS*, 1331 (4 Aug. 1927), [525]–6: Gallup C220.
In para. 7 '*The Tale of Two Cities*' has been corrected to '*A Tale of Two Cities*'.

1 It is to be hoped that some scholarly and philosophic critic of the present generation may be inspired to write a book on the history and aesthetic of melodrama. The golden age of melodrama passed, it is true, before any person living was aware of its existence: in the very middle of the last century. But there are many living who are not too young to remember the melodramatic stage before the cinema replaced it; who have sat entranced, in the front stalls of local or provincial theatres, before some representation of *East Lynne*, or *The White Slave*, or *No Mother to Guide Her*; and who are not too old to have observed with curious interest the replacement of dramatic melodrama by cinematographic melodrama, and the dissociation of the elements of the old three-volume melodramatic novel into the various types of the modern 300-page novel. Those who have lived before such terms as 'high-brow fiction', 'thrillers' and 'detective fiction' were invented realise that melodrama is perennial and that the craving for it is perennial and must be satisfied. If we cannot

get this satisfaction out of what the publishers present as 'literature', then we will read – with less and less pretence of concealment – what we call 'thrillers'. But in the golden age of melodramatic fiction there was no such distinction. The best novels *were* thrilling; the distinction of genre between such-and-such a profound psychological novel of to-day and such-and-such a masterly 'detective' novel of to-day is greater than the distinction of genre between *Wuthering Heights*, or even *The Mill on the Floss*, and *East Lynne*, the [409] last of which 'achieved an enormous and instantaneous success, and was translated into every known language, including Parsee and Hindustani'. We believe that several contemporary novels have been 'translated into every known language'; but we are sure that they have less in common with *The Golden Bowl*, or *Ulysses*, or even *Beauchamp's Career*, than *East Lynne* has in common with *Bleak House*.

2 In order to enjoy and to appreciate the work of Wilkie Collins, we ought to be able to reassemble the elements which have been dissociated in the modern novel. Collins is the contemporary of Dickens, Thackeray, George Eliot; of Charles Reade and almost of Captain Marryat. He has something in common with all of these novelists; but particularly and significantly with Dickens. Collins was the friend and sometimes the collaborator of Dickens; and the work of the two men ought to be studied side by side. There is, unhappily for the literary critic, no full biography of Wilkie Collins; and Forster's *Life of Dickens* is, from this point of view, most unsatisfactory. Forster was a notable biographer; but as a critic of the work of Dickens his view was a very narrow view. To any one who knows the bare facts of Dickens's acquaintance with Collins, and who has studied the work of the two men, their relationship and their influence upon one another is an important subject of study. And a comparative study of their novels can do much to illuminate the question of the difference between the dramatic and the melodramatic in fiction.

3 Dickens's 'best novel' is probably *Bleak House*; that is Mr Chesterton's opinion, and there is no better critic of Dickens living than Mr Chesterton. Collins's best novel – or, at any rate, the only one of Collins's novels which every one knows – is *The Woman in White*. Now *Bleak House* is the novel in which Dickens most closely approaches Collins (and after *Bleak House*, *Little Dorrit* and parts of *Martin Chuzzlewit*); and the *Woman in White* is the novel in which Collins most closely approaches Dickens. Dickens [410] excelled in character; in the creation of characters of greater intensity than human beings. Collins was not usually strong in the creation of character; but he was a master of plot and situation,

of those elements of drama which are most essential to melodrama. *Bleak House* is Dickens's finest piece of construction; and *The Woman in White* contains Collins's most real characterisation. Every one knows Count Fosco and Marion Halcombe intimately; only the most perfect Collins reader can remember even half a dozen of his other characters by name.

4 Count Fosco and Marion are indeed real personages to us; as 'real' as much greater characters are, as real as Becky Sharp or Emma Bovary. In comparison with the characters of Dickens they lack only that kind of reality which is almost supernatural, which hardly seems to belong to the character by natural right, but seems rather to descend upon him by a kind of inspiration or grace. Collins's best characters are fabricated, with consummate skill, before our eyes; in Dickens's greatest figures we see no process or calculation. Dickens's figures belong to poetry, like figures of Dante or Shakespeare, in that a single phrase, either by them or about them, may be enough to set them wholly before us. Collins has no phrases. Dickens can with a phrase make a character as real as flesh and blood – 'What a life young Bailey's was!' – like Farinata

> Chi fur gli maggior tui?

or like Cleopatra,

> I saw her once
> Hop forty paces through the public street.

Dickens's characters are real because there is no one like them; Collins's because they are so painstakingly coherent and lifelike. Whereas Dickens often introduces a great character carelessly, so that we do not realise, until the story is far advanced, with what a powerful personage we have to do, Collins, at least in these two figures in *The Woman in White*, employs every advantage of dramatic effect. Much [411] of our impression of Marion is due to the words in which she is first presented:

> The instant my eyes rested on her I was struck by the rare beauty of her form, and by the unaffected grace of her attitude. Her figure was tall, yet not too tall; comely and well developed, yet not fat; her head set on her shoulders with an easy, pliant firmness; her waist, perfection in the eyes of a man, for it occupied its natural place, it filled out its natural circle, it was visibly and delightfully undeformed by stays. She had not heard my entrance into the room, and I allowed myself the luxury of admiring her for a few moments before I moved one of the chairs near me as the least

embarrassing means of attracting her attention. She turned towards me immediately. The easy elegance of every movement of her limbs and body, as soon as she began to advance from the far end of the room, set me in a flutter of expectation to see her face clearly. She left the window – and I said to myself, The lady is dark. She moved forward a few steps – and I said to myself, The lady is young. She approached nearer, and I said to myself (with a sense of surprise which words fail me to express), The lady is ugly!

The introduction of Count Fosco – too long to quote in full – requires many more small strokes; but we should observe, Marion Halcombe being already given, that our impression of the Count is made very much stronger by being given to us as Marion's impression of him:

There are peculiarities in his personal appearance, his habits, and his amusements, which I should blame in the boldest terms, or ridicule in the most merciless manner, if I had seen them in another man. What is it that makes me unable to blame them, or to ridicule them in *him*?

After this who can forget the white mice or the canaries, or the way in which Count Fosco treated Sir Percival's sulky bloodhound? If *The Woman in White* is the greatest of [412] Collins's novels, it is so because of these two characters. If we examine the book apart from Marion and Fosco, we must admit that it is not Collins's finest work of construction, and that certain of his peculiar melodramatic gifts are better displayed in other books. The book is dramatic because of two characters; it is dramatic in the way in which the dramatic differs from the melodramatic. Sir Percival Glyde is a figure of pasteboard, and the mystery and the plot of which he is the centre are almost grotesque. The one of Collins's books which is the most perfect piece of construction, and the best balanced between plot and character, is *The Moonstone*; the one which reaches the greatest melodramatic intensity is *Armadale*.

5 *The Moonstone* is the first and greatest of English detective novels. We say *English* detective novels, because there is also the work of Poe, which has a *pure* detective interest. The detective story, as created by Poe, is something as specialised and as intellectual as a chess problem; whereas the best English detective fiction has relied less on the beauty of the mathematical problem and much more on the intangible human element. In detective fiction England probably excels other countries; but in a genre invented by Collins and not by Poe. In *The Moonstone* the mystery is finally solved, not altogether by human ingenuity, but

largely by accident. Since Collins, the best heroes of English detective fiction have been, like Sergeant Cuff, fallible; they play their part, but never the sole part, in the unraveling. Sherlock Holmes, not altogether a typical English sleuth, is a partial exception; but even Holmes exists, not solely because of his prowess, but largely because he is, in the Jonsonian sense, a humorous character, with his needle, his boxing, and his violin. But Sergeant Cuff, far more than Holmes, is the ancestor of the healthy generation of amiable, efficient, professional but fallible inspectors of fiction among whom we live to-day. And *The Moonstone*, a book twice the length of the 'thrillers' that our contemporary masters write, maintains its interest [413] and suspense at every moment. It does this by devices of a Dickensian type; for Collins, in addition to his particular merits, was a Dickens without genius. The book is a comedy of humours. The eccentricities of Mr Franklin Blake, the satire on false philanthropy in the character of Mr Godfrey Ablewhite (to say nothing of the Life, Letters and Labours of Miss Jane Ann Stamper), Betteridge with his *Robinson Crusoe*, and his daughter Penelope, support the narrative. In other of Collins's novels, the trick of passing the narration from one hand to another, and employing every device of letters and diaries, becomes tedious and even unplausible (for instance, in *Armadale*, the terrific villain, Miss Gwilt, commits herself to paper far too often and far too frankly); but in *The Moonstone* these devices succeed, every time, in stimulating our interest afresh just at the moment when it was about to flag.

6 And in *The Moonstone* Collins succeeds in bringing into play those aids of 'atmosphere' in which Dickens (and the Brontës) exhibited such genius, and in which Collins has everything except their genius. For his purpose, he does not come off badly. Compare the description of the discovery of Rosanna's death in the Shivering Sands – and notice how carefully, beforehand, the *mise-en-scène* of the Shivering Sands is prepared for us – with the shipwreck of Steerforth in *David Copperfield*. We may say, 'There is no comparison!' but there *is* a comparison; and however unfavourable to Collins, it must increase our estimation of his skill.

7 There is another characteristic of Wilkie Collins which also brings him closer to Dickens, and it is a characteristic which has very great melodramatic value: compare the work of Collins with the work of Mrs Henry Wood, already mentioned, and one sees how important for melodrama is the presence or absence of this. Forster, in his *Life of Dickens*, observes:

On the coincidences, resemblances and surprises of life Dickens liked especially to dwell, and few things moved [414] his fancy so pleasantly. The world, he would say, was so much smaller than we thought it; we were all connected by fate without knowing it; people supposed to be far apart were so constantly elbowing each other; and tomorrow bore so close a resemblance to nothing half so much as to yesterday.

Forster mentions this peculiarity early in the life of Dickens, long before Dickens became acquainted with Collins. We may take it that this feeling was common to Dickens and Collins, and that it may have been one of the causes of their being drawn so sympathetically together, once they had become acquainted. The two men had obviously in common a passionate feeling for the drama. Each had qualities which the other lacked, and they had certain qualities in common. It is perfectly reasonable to believe that the relations of the two men – of which Forster gives us only the barest and most unsatisfactory hints – affected profoundly the later work of each. We seem to find traces of it in *Little Dorrit* and in *A Tale of Two Cities*. Collins could never have invented Durdles and Deputy; but Durdles and Deputy were obviously to play their part in a whole, *bien charpenté* as Collins's work is, and as the work of Dickens prior to *Bleak House* is not.

8 One of the minor works of Collins which illustrates especially this insistence upon the 'coincidences, resemblances and surprises of life' is *The Frozen Deep*. The story, as we read it, was patched up from the melodrama which Collins wrote first; which was privately performed with great success on several occasions, and in which Dickens took the leading part. Collins was cleverer at writing stage pieces; but we may imagine that Dickens was the cleverer at acting them; and Dickens may have given to the rôle of Richard Wardour, in acting it, an individuality which it certainly lacks in the story. This story, we may add for the benefit of those who have not read it, depends upon coincidence with a remarkably long arm; for the two men [415] who ought not to meet – the accepted and the rejected lover – do meet, and under the most unlikely conditions they join, without knowing each other's identity, the same Polar Expedition.

9 In *The Frozen Deep* Collins wrote a piece of pure melodrama. That is to say, it is nothing but melodrama. We are asked to accept an improbability, simply for the sake of seeing the thrilling situation which arises in consequence. But the frontier of drama and melodrama is vague; the difference is largely a matter of emphasis; perhaps no drama has ever

been greatly and permanently successful without a large melodramatic element. What is the difference between *The Frozen Deep* and *Oedipus the King*? It is the difference between coincidence, set without shame or pretence, and fate – which merges into character. It is not necessary, for high drama, that accident should be eliminated; you cannot formulate the proportion of accident that is permissible. But in great drama character is always felt to be – not more important than plot – but somehow integral with plot. At least, one is left with the conviction that if circumstances had not arranged the events to fall out in such and such a way, the personages were, after all, such that they would have ended just as badly, or just as well, and more or less similarly. And sometimes the melodramatic – the accidental – becomes for Collins the dramatic – the fatal. There is one short tale, not one of his best known, and far from being his best – a tale with an extremely improbable ghost – which nevertheless is almost dramatic. It is called *The Haunted Hotel*; what makes it better than a mere readable second-rate ghost story is the fact that fatality in this story is no longer merely a wire jerking the figures. The principal character, the fatal woman, is herself obsessed by the idea of fatality; her motives are melodramatic; she therefore compels the coincidences to occur, feeling that she is compelled to compel them. In this story, as the chief character is internally melodramatic, the story itself ceases to be merely melodramatic, and partakes of true drama.

[416] 10 There is another characteristic of certain tales of Collins's, which may be said to belong to melodrama, or to the melodramatic part of drama. It consists in delaying, longer than one would conceive it possible to delay, a conclusion which is inevitable and wholly foreseen. A story like *The New Magdalen* is from a certain moment merely a study in stage suspense; the *dénouement* is postponed, again and again, by every possible ingenuity; the situations are in the most effective sense theatrical, without being in the profounder sense dramatic. They are seldom, as in *The Woman in White*, situations of conflict between significant personalities; they are more often conflicts between chessmen which merely occupy hostile positions on the board. Such, for instance, is the prolonged battle between Captain Wragge and Mrs Lecomte at Aldburgh, in *No Name*.

11 The one of Collins's novels which we would choose as the most typical, or as the best of the more typical, and which we should recommend as a specimen of the melodramatic fiction of the epoch, is *Armadale*. It has no merit beyond melodrama, and it has every merit that melodrama can have. If Miss Gwilt did not have to bear such a large part of the burden

of revealing her own villainy, the construction would be almost perfect. Like most of Collins's novels, it has the immense – and nowadays more and more rare – merit of being never dull. It has, to a very high degree, the peculiar Collins merit above mentioned, which we might call the air of spurious fatality. The machinery of the book is operated by the Dream. The mind of the reader is very carefully prepared for acceptance of the Dream; first by the elaborately staged coincidence of the two cousins getting marooned on the wreck of the ship on which the father of the one had long before entrapped the father of the other; secondly by the way in which the Dream is explained away by the doctor. The doctor's explanation is so reasonable that the reader immediately reacts in favour of the Dream. Then, the character of the dreamer himself is made plausibly intuitive; and the stages [417] by which the various parts of the Dream are realised are perfectly managed. Particularly is this true of the scene in which, after some excellent comedy of humours on the boating party, Miss Gwilt arrives at sunset on the desolate shore of the Norfolk Broads. By means of the Dream, we are kept in a state of tension which makes it possible to believe in characters which otherwise we should find preposterous.

12 The greatest novels have something in them which will ensure their being read, at least by a small number of people, even if the novel, as a literary form, ceases to be written. It is not pretended that the novels of Wilkie Collins have this permanence. They are interesting only if we enjoy 'reading novels'. But novels are still being written; and there is no contemporary novelist who could not learn something from Collins in the art of interesting and exciting the reader. So long as novels are written, the possibilities of melodrama must from time to time be re-explored. The contemporary 'thriller' is in danger of becoming stereotyped; the conventional murder is discovered in the first chapter by the conventional butler, and the murderer is discovered in the last chapter by the conventional inspector – after having been already discovered by the reader. The resources of Wilkie Collins are, in comparison, inexhaustible.

13 And even if we refused to take Collins very seriously by himself, we can hardly fail to treat him with seriousness if we recognise that the art of which he was a master was an art which neither Charles Reade nor Dickens despised. You cannot define Drama and Melodrama so that they shall be reciprocally exclusive; great drama has something melodramatic about it, and the best melodrama partakes of the greatness of drama. *The Moonstone* is very near to *Bleak House*. The theft of a diamond has some of the same blighting effect on the lives about it as the suit

in Chancery; Rosanna Spearman is destroyed by the diamond as Miss Flite is destroyed by Chancery. Collins's novels suggest [418] questions which no student of 'the art of fiction' can afford to neglect. It is possible that the artist can be too conscious of his 'art'. Perhaps Henry James – who in his own practice could be not only 'interesting', but had a very cunning mastery of the finer melodrama – may have had as a critic a bad influence. We cannot afford to forget that the first – and not one of the least difficult – requirements of either prose or verse is that it should be interesting.

Variants from *TLS* (1927):
1   page novel] page 7s. 6d. novel
2   almost of Captain] Captain
4   blood – 'What a Life Young Bailey's Was!' – like Farinata] blood: like Farinata
5   England probably excels other countries] we are inclined to assert that England at present 'whips the universe'
    twice the length] three times the length

The Humanism of Irving Babbitt

SE, 419–28.

Publ. as 'The Humanism of Irving Babbitt in *Forum* 80. 1 (July 1928), [37]–44: Gallup C261. Revised in *FLA*, and again in *SE*. Repr. from *SE* in *EAAM*.

1 It is proverbially easier to destroy than to construct; and, as a corollary of this proverb, it is easier for readers to apprehend the destructive than the constructive side of an author's thought. More than this: when a writer is skilful in destructive criticism, the public is satisfied with that. If he has no constructive philosophy, it is not demanded; if he has, it is overlooked. This is especially true when we are concerned with critics of society, from Arnold to the present day. All such critics are criticised from one common standard, and that the lowest: the standard of brilliant attack upon aspects of contemporary society which we know and dislike. It is the easiest standard to take. For the criticism deals with concrete things in our world which we know, and the writer may be merely echoing, in neater phrasing, our own thoughts; whereas construction deals with things hard and unfamiliar. Hence the popularity of Mr Mencken.

2 But there are more serious critics than Mr Mencken, and of these we must ask in the end what they have to offer in place of what they denounce. M. Julien Benda, for instance, makes it a part of his deliberate programme to offer nothing; he has a romantic view of critical detachment which limits his interest. Mr Wyndham Lewis is obviously

striving courageously toward a positive theory, but in his published work he has not yet reached that point. But in Professor Babbitt's latest book, *Democracy and Leadership*, the criticism is related to a positive theory and dependent upon it. This theory is not altogether expounded, but is [420] partly assumed. What I wish to do in the present essay is to ask a few questions about Mr Babbitt's constructive theory.

3 The centre of Mr Babbitt's philosophy is the doctrine of humanism. In his earlier books we were able to accept this idea without analysis; but in *Democracy and Leadership* – which I take to be at this point the summary of his theory – we are tempted to question it. The problem of humanism is undoubtedly related to the problem of religion. Mr Babbitt makes it very clear, here and there throughout the book, that he is unable to take the religious view – that is to say he cannot accept any dogma or revelation; and that humanism is the *alternative* to religion. And this brings up the question: is this alternative any more than a *substitute*? and, if a substitute, does it not bear the same relation to religion that 'humanitarianism' bears to humanism? Is it, in the end, a view of life that will work by itself, or is it a derivative of religion which will work only for a short time in history, and only for a few highly cultivated persons like Mr Babbitt – whose ancestral traditions, furthermore, are Christian, and who is, like many people, at the distance of a generation or so from definite Christian belief? Is it, in other words, durable beyond one or two generations?

4 Mr Babbitt says, of the 'representatives of the humanitarian movement', that

> they wish to live on the naturalistic level, and at the same time to enjoy the benefits that the past had hoped to achieve as a result of some humanistic or religious discipline.

The definition is admirable, but provokes us to ask whether, by altering a few words, we cannot arrive at the following statement about humanists:

> they wish to live on the humanistic level, and at the same time to enjoy the benefits that the past had hoped to achieve as a result of some religious discipline.

[421] If this transposition is justified, it means that the difference is only of one step: the humanitarian has suppressed the properly human, and is left with the animal; the humanist has suppressed the divine, and is left with a human element which may quickly descend again to the animal from which he has sought to raise it.

5 Mr Babbitt is a stout upholder of tradition and continuity, and he knows, with his immense and encyclopedic information, that the Christian religion is an essential part of the history of our race. Humanism and religion are thus, as historical facts, by no means parallel; humanism has been sporadic, but Christianity continuous. It is quite irrelevant to conjecture the possible development of the European races without Christianity – to imagine, that is, a tradition of Christian humanism equivalent to the actual tradition of Christianity. For all we can say is that we should have been very different creatures, whether better or worse. Our problem being to form the future, we can only form it on the materials of the past; we must *use* our heredity, instead of denying it. The religious habits of the people are still very strong, in all places, at all times, and for all people. There is no humanistic habit: humanism is, I think, merely the state of mind of a few persons in a few places at a few times. To exist at all, it is dependent upon some other attitude, for it is essentially critical – I would even say parasitical. It has been, and can still be, of great value; but it will never provide showers of partridges or abundance of manna for the chosen peoples.

6 It is a little difficult to define humanism in Mr Babbitt's terms, for he is very apt to line it up in battle order *with* religion *against* humanitarianism and naturalism; and what I am trying to do is to *contrast* it with religion. Mr Babbitt is very apt to use phrases like 'tradition humanistic and religious' which suggest that you could say also 'tradition humanistic *or* religious'. So I must make shift to define humanism as I can from a few examples that Mr Babbitt seems to hold up to us.

[422] 7 I should say that he regarded Confucius, Buddha, Socrates, and Erasmus as humanists (I do not know whether he would include Montaigne). It may surprise some to see Confucius and Buddha, who are popularly regarded as founders of religions, in this list. But it is always the human reason, not the revelation of the supernatural, upon which Mr Babbitt insists. Confucius and Buddha are not in the same boat, to begin with. Mr Babbitt of course knows infinitely more about these men than I do; but even people who know even less about them than I do, know that Confucianism endured by fitting in with popular religion, and that Buddhism endured by becoming[1] as distinctly a *religion* as Christianity – recognising a dependence of the human upon the divine.

---

1. I wrote *becoming*, but it seems to me that Buddhism is as truly a religion from the beginning as is Christianity.

8 And finally, the attitude of Socrates and that of Erasmus toward the religion of their place and time were very different from what I take to be the attitude of Professor Babbitt. How much Socrates believed, and whether his legendary request of the sacrifice of a cock was merely gentlemanly behaviour or even irony, we cannot tell; but the equivalent would be Mr Babbitt receiving Extreme Unction, and that I cannot at present conceive. But both Socrates and Erasmus were content to remain critics, and to leave the religious fabric untouched. So that I find Mr Babbitt's humanism to be very different from that of any of the humanists above mentioned.

9 This is no small point, but the question is a difficult one. It is not at all that Mr Babbitt has *misunderstood* any of these persons, or that he is not fully acquainted with the civilisations out of which they sprang. On the contrary, he knows all about them. It is rather, I think, that in his interest in the messages of individuals – messages conveyed in books – he has tended merely to neglect the conditions. The great men whom he holds up for our admiration and example are torn from their contexts of race, place, and [423] time. And in consequence, Mr Babbitt seems to me to tear himself from his own context. His humanism is really something quite different from that of his exemplars, but (to my mind) alarmingly like very liberal Protestant theology of the nineteenth century: it is, in fact, a product – a by-product – of Protestant theology in its last agonies.

10 I admit that all humanists – as humanists – have been individualists. As humanists, they have had nothing to offer to the mob. But they have usually left a place, not only for the mob, but (what is important) for the mob part of the mind in themselves. Mr Babbitt is too rigorous and conscientious a Protestant to do that: hence there seems to be a gap between his own individualism (and indeed intellectualism, beyond a certain point, must be individualistic) and his genuine desire to offer something which will be useful to the American nation primarily and to civilisation itself. But the historical humanist, as I understand him, halts at a certain point and admits that the reason will go no further, and that it cannot feed on honey and locusts.

11 Humanism is either an alternative to religion, or is ancillary to it. To my mind, it always flourishes most when religion has been strong; and if you find examples of humanism which are anti-religious, or at least in opposition to the religious faith of the place and time, then such humanism is purely destructive, for it has never found anything to replace what it destroyed. And religion, of course, is for ever in danger

of petrifaction into mere ritual and habit, though ritual and habit be essential to religion. It is only renewed and refreshed by an awakening of feeling and fresh devotion, or by the critical reason. The latter may be the part of the humanist. But if so, then the function of humanism, though necessary, is secondary. You cannot make humanism itself into a religion.

12 What Mr Babbitt, on one side, seems to me to be trying to do is to make humanism – his own form of humanism – work without religion. For otherwise, I cannot see the significance of his doctrine of self-control. This doctrine [424] runs throughout his work, and sometimes appears as the 'inner check'. It appears as an alternative to both political and religious anarchy. In the political form it is more easily acceptable. As forms of government become more democratic, as the outer restraints of kingship, aristocracy, and class disappear, so it becomes more and more necessary that the individual no longer controlled by authority or habitual respect should control himself. So far, the doctrine is obviously true and impregnable. But Mr Babbitt seems to think also that the 'outer' restraints of an orthodox religion, as they weaken, can be supplied by the inner restraint of the individual over himself. If I have interpreted him correctly, he is thus trying to build a Catholic platform out of Protestant planks. By tradition an individualist, and jealous of the independence of individual thought, he is struggling to make something that will be valid for the nation, the race, the world.

13 The sum of a population of individuals, all ideally and efficiently checking and controlling themselves, will never make a whole. And if you distinguish so sharply between 'outer' and 'inner' checks as Mr Babbitt does, then there is nothing left for the individual to check himself by but his own private notions and his judgement, which is pretty precarious. As a matter of fact, when you leave the political field for the theological, the distinction between outer and inner becomes far from clear. Given the most highly organised and temporally powerful hierarchy with all the powers of inquisition and punishment imaginable, still the idea of the religion is the *inner* control – the appeal not to a man's behaviour but to his soul. If a religion cannot touch a man's self, so that in the end he is controlling himself instead of being merely controlled by priests as he might be by policemen, then it has failed in its professed task. I suspect Mr Babbitt at times of an instinctive dread of organised religion, a dread that it should cramp and deform the free operations of his own mind. If so, he is surely under a misapprehension.

[425] 14 And what, one asks, are all these millions, even these thousands, or the remnant of a few intelligent hundreds, going to control themselves *for*? Mr Babbitt's critical judgement is exceptionally sound, and there is hardly one of his several remarks that is not, by itself, acceptable. It is the joints of his edifice, not the materials, that sometimes seem a bit weak. He says truly:

> It has been a constant experience of man in all ages that mere rationalism leaves him unsatisfied. Man craves in some sense or other of the word an enthusiasm that will lift him out of his merely rational self.

15 But it is not clear that Mr Babbitt has any other enthusiasm to offer except the enthusiasm for being lifted out of one's merely rational self by some enthusiasm. Indeed, if he can infect people with getting even up to the level of their rational selves, he will accomplish a good deal.

16 But this seems to me just the point at which 'humanistic control' ends, if it gets that far. He speaks of the basis 'of religion and humanistic control' in Burke, but what we should like to know is the respective parts played by religion and humanism in this basis. And with all the references that Mr Babbitt makes to the rôle of religion in the past, and all the connexions that he perceives between the decline of theology and the growth of the modern errors that he detests, he reveals himself as uncompromisingly detached from any religious belief, even the most purely 'personal':

> To be modern has meant practically to be increasingly positive and critical, to refuse to receive anything on an authority 'anterior, exterior, and superior' to the individual. With those who still cling to the principle of outer authority I have no quarrel. I am not primarily concerned with them. I am myself a thoroughgoing individualist, writing for those who are, like myself, irrevocably committed to the modern experiment. In fact, so far as I object [426] to the moderns at all, it is because they have not been sufficiently modern, or, what amounts to the same thing, have not been sufficiently experimental.

17 Those of us who lay no claim to being modern may not be involved in the objection, but, as bystanders, we may be allowed to inquire whither all this modernity and experimenting is going to lead. Is everybody to spend his time experimenting? And on what, and to what end? And if the experimenting merely leads to the conclusion that self-control is good, that seems a very frosty termination to our hunt for 'enthusiasm'. What

is the higher will to *will*, if there is nothing either 'anterior, exterior, or superior' to the individual? If this will is to have anything on which to operate, it must be in relation to external objects and to objective values. Mr Babbitt says:

> To give the first place to the higher will is only another way of declaring that life is an act of faith. One may discover on positive grounds a deep meaning in the old Christian tenet that we do not know in order that we may believe, but we believe in order that we may know.

18 This is quite true; but if life is an act of faith, in what is it an act of faith? The Life-Forcers, with Mr Bernard Shaw at their head, would say I suppose 'in Life itself'; but I should not accuse Mr Babbitt of anything so silly as that. However, a few pages farther on he gives something more definite to will: it is civilisation.

19 The next idea, accordingly, to be examined is that of civilisation. It seems, on the face of it, to mean something definite; it is, in fact, merely a frame to be filled with definite objects, not a definite object itself. I do not believe that I can sit down for three minutes to will civilisation without my mind's wandering to something else. I do not mean that civilisation is a mere word; the word means something quite real. But the minds of the individuals who can be said to 'have willed civilisation' are minds filled with a great variety of objects of will, according to [427] place, time, and individual constitution; what they have in common is rather a habit in the same direction than a will to civilisation. And unless by civilisation you mean material progress, cleanliness, etc. – which is not what Mr Babbitt means; if you mean a spiritual and intellectual co-ordination on a high level, then it is doubtful whether civilisation can endure without religion, and religion without a church.

20 I am not here concerned with the question whether such a 'humanistic' civilisation as aimed at by Professor Babbitt is or is not *desirable*; only with the question whether it is *feasible*. From this point of view the danger of such theories is, I think, the danger of collapse. For those who had not followed Mr Babbitt very far, or who had felt his influence more remotely, the collapse would be back again into humanitarianism thinly disguised. For others who had followed him hungrily to the end and had found no hay in the stable, the collapse might well be into a Catholicism *without* the element of humanism and criticism, which would be a Catholicism of despair. There is a hint of this in Mr Babbitt's own words:

The choice to which the modern man will finally be reduced, it has been said, is that of being a Bolshevist or a Jesuit. In that case (assuming that by Jesuit is meant the ultramontane Catholic) there does not seem to be much room for hesitation. Ultramontane Catholicism does not, like Bolshevism, strike at the very root of civilisation. In fact, under certain conditions that are already partly in sight, the Catholic Church may perhaps be the only institution left in the Occident that can be counted upon to uphold civilised standards. It may also be possible, however, to be a thoroughgoing modern and at the same time civilised . . .

21 The last sentence somehow seems to me to die away a little faintly. But the point is that Mr Babbitt seems to be giving away to the Church in anticipation more than [428] would many who are more concerned with it in the present than he. Mr Babbitt is much more ultramontane than I am. One may feel a very deep respect and even love for the Catholic Church (by which I understand Mr Babbitt means the hierarchy in communion with the Holy See); but if one studies its history and vicissitudes, its difficulties and problems past and present, one is struck with admiration and awe certainly, but is not the more tempted to place all the hopes of humanity on one institution.

22 But my purpose has been, not to predict a bad end for Mr Babbitt's philosophy, but to point out the direction which I think it should follow if the obscurities of 'humanism' were cleared up. It should lead, I think, to the conclusion that the humanistic point of view is auxiliary to and dependent upon the religious point of view. For us, religion is Christianity; and Christianity implies, I think, the conception of the Church. It would be not only interesting but invaluable if Professor Babbitt, with his learning, his great ability, his influence, and his interest in the most important questions of the time, could reach this point. His influence might thus join with that of another philosopher – Charles Maurras – and might, indeed, correct some of the extravagances of that writer.

23 Such a consummation is impossible. Professor Babbitt knows too much; and by that I do not mean merely erudition or information or scholarship. I mean that he knows too many religions and philosophies, has assimilated their spirit too thoroughly (there is probably no one in England or America who understands early Buddhism better than he) to be able to give himself to any. The result is humanism. I believe that it is better to recognise the weaknesses of humanism at once, and allow for them, so that the structure may not crash beneath an excessive weight;

and so that we may arrive at an enduring recognition of its value for us, and of our obligation to its author.

Variants:

1 and, as a corollary] and as a corollary *Forum* (1928), *FLA*
in destructive] at destructive *Forum* (1928), *FLA*
if he has] and if he has *Forum* (1928), *FLA*
construction] the construction *Forum* (1928), *FLA*
2 questions about] questions of *Forum* (1928), *FLA*
3 ancestral traditions, furthermore,] ancestral traditions *Forum* (1928)
7 Confucius and Buddha are not] But Confucius and Buddha are not *Forum* (1928)
[No fn. in *Forum* (1928), *FLA*.]
8 Extreme Unction] extreme unction *Forum* (1928), *FLA*
10 further] farther *Forum* (1928), *FLA*
15 one's merely rational self by some enthusiasm] one's merely rational self – by some enthusiasm *Forum* (1928)
17 the objection] this scuffle *Forum* (1928)
whither] where *Forum* (1928), *FLA*
18 farther on] further on *Forum* (1928), *FLA*
22 religion is Christianity] religion is of course Christianity *Forum* (1928), *FLA*
the Church] the church *Forum* (1928)
another philosopher] another philosopher of the same rank *Forum* (1928), *FLA*

Second Thoughts about Humanism

SE, 429–39.

Publ. in *New Adelphi*, 2. 4 (June/Aug. 1929), [304]–10, subheaded '*By* T. S. Eliot', and slightly revised in *Hound & Horn*, 2. 4 (July/Sept. 1929), 339–50: Gallup C285. (Gallup gives the original title wrongly as 'Second Thoughts on Humanism'.) Further revised in *SE*. In para. 13 of the *SE* text 'world' has been emended to 'word' (the reading in the previous versions).

1 In July, 1928, I published in *The Forum* a note on the Humanism of Irving Babbitt, which appears on the foregoing pages. I understand that Professor Babbitt considers that I misstated his views: but as I have not yet received detailed correction from any Humanist, I am still in the dark. It is quite likely that I am at fault, because I have meanwhile heard comments, from sympathetic friends, which indicate that they have misunderstood me. The present essay is therefore inspired rather by desire to make my own position clearer, than by desire towards aggression. Here, I shall find it more useful to refer to Mr Norman Foerster's brilliant book, *American Criticism*, than to Mr Babbitt's works. Mr Foerster's book, as the work of a disciple, seems to give clearer hints of what Humanism is likely to

become and do, than the work of Mr Babbitt, which is more personal to himself.

2 My previous note has been interpreted, I am afraid, as an 'attack' on humanism from a narrow sectarian point of view. It was not intended to be an attack. Having myself begun as a disciple of Mr Babbitt, and feeling, as I do, that I have rejected nothing that seems to me positive in his teaching, I was hardly qualified to 'attack' humanism. I was concerned rather to point out the weak points in its defences, before some genuine enemy took advantage of them. It can be – indeed is already – of immense value: but it must be subjected to criticism while there is still time.

3 One of the criticisms which I have heard of my criticism [430] is this: that my criticism is all very well from the point of view of those who 'believe'; but if I succeed in proving that humanism is insufficient without religion, what is left for those who cannot believe? Now I have no desire to undermine the humanist position. But I fear that it may take on more and more of the character of a positive philosophy – and any philosophy, in our time, is likely to take on the character of a substitute for religious dogma. It is Humanism's positivistic tendencies that are alarming. In the work of the master, and still more in that of the disciples, there is a tendency towards a positive and exclusive dogma. Conceive a Comtism from which all the absurdities had been removed – and they form, I admit, a very important part of the Comtist scheme – and you have something like what I imagine Humanism might become.

4 In the actual Humanist position there is, as I have tried to show, on the one hand an admission that in the past Humanism has been allied with religion, and on the other hand a faith that it can in the future afford to ignore positive religion. This curious trick of identifying humanism and religion in one context, and contrasting them in another, plays a very large part in the Humanist formulation. Mr Foerster says (p. 244):

> This centre to which humanism refers everything, this centripetal energy which counteracts the multifarious centrifugal impulses, this magnetic will which draws the flux of our sensations toward it while itself remaining at rest, is the reality which gives rise to religion. Pure humanism is content to describe it thus in physical terms, as an observed fact of experience; it hesitates to pass beyond its experimental knowledge to the dogmatic affirmations of any of the great religions. It cannot bring itself to accept a formal theology

(any more than it can accept a romantic idealism) that has been set up in defiance of reason, for it holds that the value of supernatural intuition must be tested by the intellect. Again, it fears the asceticism to which [431] religion tends in consequence of a too harsh dualism of the flesh and the spirit, for, as we have said, humanism calls for completeness, wishing to use and not annihilate dangerous forces. Unlike religion, it assigns an important place to the instruments of both science and art. Nevertheless it agrees with religion in its perception of the ethical will as a power above the ordinary self, an impersonal reality in which all men may share despite the diversity of personal temperament and towards which their attitude must be one of subjection. This perception, immensely strengthened for us by Christianity, was already present in the humanism of the Greeks, who saw that the unpardonable sin is insolence or presumption, an overweening pride of passion or reason, a failure to be mindful of the Nemesis that lies in wait for disproportionate self-assertion. Humanism, no less than religion, enjoins the virtue of *humility*.

With all respect to Mr Foerster's sound literary criticism, and his usual brilliance of statement which one cannot fail to admire, the passage I have just quoted seems to me a composition of ignorance, prejudice, confused thinking and bad writing. His first sentence, for the meaning of which I am at a loss, is a cloudy pseudo-scientific metaphor; and his remark that 'pure humanism is content to describe it thus in physical terms' seems to give his hand away completely to what he calls 'naturism'. Either his first sentence is, as I think, merely a metaphor drawn from nineteenth-century physics; in which case it is not a 'description', and no one can be content with it; or else the author is surrendering to the mechanistic ethics based upon old-fashioned physics. 'The reality which gives rise to religion' is a phrase which suggests the older school of anthropology; it is a guarded hint that religion is merely a state of feeling produced by certain physical or quasi-physical 'realities' and 'facts'. Mr Foerster's 'hesitates' and 'cannot bring itself' conceal dogmatism behind apparent prudence. Here he confuses, I think, the Humanist with Humanism. If an [432] individual humanist hesitates or cannot bring himself, that is a perfectly natural human attitude, with which one has sympathy; but if the humanist affirms that *Humanism* hesitates and cannot bring itself, then he is making the hesitation, and the inability to bring itself, into a *dogma*: the humanist *Credo* is then a *Dubito*. He is asserting that there is a 'pure Humanism' which is *incompatible* with religious faith. When he proceeds to distinguish Humanism from religion by saying that Humanism 'holds that the value of supernatural intuition must be tested by the intellect', one wonders with what sort of religion he is contrasting it: for this kind of test was held by the Church long before the word Humanism was coined. Next, the 'fear or asceticism' is characteristic, not only of Humanism, but of liberal Protestantism, from which Humanism sometimes seems to descend. The typical humanist, I agree, is not conceived as a cenobite; but *Humanism*, if it goes so far as to include in its Creed 'I fear asceticism', is merely committing itself to another anti-religious dogma. Humanism, Mr Foerster says, 'wishes to use and not annihilate dangerous forces'; but does he really believe that the Christian religion, except in several heretical varieties, has ever tried to *annihilate* those dangerous forces? And if he thinks that religion depreciates science and art, I can only suppose that his religious training took place in the mountains of Tennessee. Humanism, he says, agrees with religion in only one point: in believing in the ethical will. There was once an organisation called the Ethical Culture Society, which held Sunday morning services: that seems to be the kind of liberal religion to which Mr Foerster's Humanism comes down.

5 Mr Foerster's Humanism, in fact, is too ethical to be true. Where do all these morals come from? The advantage of an orthodox religion, to my mind, is that it puts morals in their proper place. In spite of all the hard (and I consider just) things that Mr Babbitt and Mr More have said about Kant, the second generation of humanism seems to found its ethics on a similar basis to Kant's. Mr Foerster finds that [433] 'the essential reality of experience is ethical'. For the person with a definite religious faith, such a statement has one meaning: for the positivistic humanist, who repudiates religion, it must have another. And that meaning seems to rest upon obscurities and confusions. I can understand, though I do not approve, the naturalistic systems of morals founded upon biology and analytical psychology (what is valid in these consists largely of things that were always known); but I cannot understand a system of morals which seems to be founded on nothing but itself – which exists, I suspect, only by illicit relations with either psychology or religion or both, according to the bias of mind of the individual humanist.

6 Humanism depends very heavily, I believe, upon the tergiversations of the word 'human'; and in general, upon implying clear and distinct philosophic ideas which are never there. My objection is that the humanist makes use, in his separation of the 'human' from the 'natural', of that 'supernatural' which he denies. For I am convinced that if this 'supernatural' is suppressed (I avoid the word 'spiritual' because it can mean almost anything), the *dualism* of man and nature collapses at

once. Man is man because he can recognise supernatural realities, not because he can invent them. Either everything in man can be traced as a development from below, or something must come from above. There is no avoiding that dilemma: you must be either a naturalist or a supernaturalist. If you remove from the word 'human' all that the belief in the supernatural has given to man, you can view him finally as no more than an extremely clever, adaptable, and mischievous little animal. Mr Foerster's ethics would be much more 'reasonable' if they were those of Mr Bertrand Russell; as they are, they are a form which is quite untenable and meaningless without a religious foundation.[1]

[434] 7 The real trouble, of course, is one of simple human fallibility. Mr Foerster, like most humanists, was I believe trained as a man of letters; and Humanism bears the imprint of the academic man of letters. His approach to every other field of study is through literature. This is a perfectly proper approach; for we must all approach what we do not know with a limited equipment of the things that we do know. The trouble is that, for a modern humanist, literature thus becomes itself merely a means of approach to something else. If we try to make something do for something else, it is likely to become merely an amateur substitute for that other thing. Mr Foerster and I would probably agree about the prevalent desiccation of the study of philosophy in universities.[2] Nevertheless, there is a philosophic training, and it is not the literary training; there are rules of the philosophic game about the use and definition of terms, and they are not the literary rules. One may consider the study of philosophy vain, but then one should not philosophise. What one is likely to do is to philosophise badly, because unconsciously. My objection is not to Humanism, but to Mr Foerster for not being humanistic enough; and for playing the games of philosophy and theology without knowing the rules.

---

1. Mr Foerster's 'reason' seems to me to differ from any Greek equivalent (λόγος) by being exclusively human; whereas to the Greek there was something inexplicable about λόγος so that it was a participation of man in the Divine. See the late Max Scheler's *Mensch und Geschichte* (Neue Schweizer Rundschau), p. 21.

2. Not, however, primarily the fault of the teachers, but of the whole educational system of which this teaching is a part. The teaching of philosophy to young men who have no background of humanistic education, the teaching of Plato and Aristotle to youths who know no Greek and are completely ignorant of ancient history, is one of the tragic farces of American education. We reap the whirlwind of pragmatists, behaviourists, etc. Incidentally, it is a public misfortune that Mr Bertrand Russell did not have a classical education.

Humanism has done no greater service than in its criticism of modern education. See Mr Babbitt's admirable essay on President Eliot in a recent number of *The Forum*.

8 There is another aspect to Mr Foerster's position which might earn him the title of 'The Newest Laocoön': the interesting consideration that this trick of making literature do the work of philosophy, ethics and theology tends to vitiate one's judgement and sensibility in literature; but this [435] aspect has been so well exposed in an essay (not yet published) by Mr Allen Tate, that I shall not linger over it here. But I should like to mention that Mr Foerster, in seeking, as he says, 'an ethos which has never existed', looks for guidance to:

> Greek sculpture (*of what period?*) Homer, Sophocles, Plato, Aristotle, Virgil, Horace, Jesus, Paul, Augustine, Francis of Assisi, Buddha, Confucius, Shakespeare, Milton and Goethe. (p. 242).

Mr Foerster is not quite so silly as this list makes him seem, perilously as he does approach towards Five Foot Shelf Culture; he is merely confusing two points of view. For *culture* (and Mr Foerster's culture is a propagation of Arnold's), these are the sorts of authority to which we may properly look; and the man who has frequented them all will so far as that goes be a better, in the sense of being a *more cultured* man, than the man who has not. This is the best possible background. But the search for an 'ethos' is a very much more serious and risky business than Mr Foerster imagines; and Mr Foerster is more likely to end in respectability than in perfection. Those who hunger and thirst after righteousness, and are not satisfied with a snack-at-the-bar, will want a great deal more; and if they follow any one of these leaders, will not be able to follow all the rest. Boil down Horace, the Elgin Marbles, St Francis and Goethe, and the result will be pretty thin soup. Culture, after all, is not enough, even though nothing is enough without culture.

9 With these odd mixed motives, Mr Foerster does not make very much of Shakespeare, though he gives him a patronising word or two. Shakespeare is not a humanist. Mr Foerster's judgement of Shakespeare is neither a literary nor a moral judgement. He seems to me to depreciate Shakespeare for the wrong reasons, just as, with all respect, Mr Middleton Murry seems to me to extol him for the wrong reasons. If, as he says, Shakespeare was concerned 'rather with mirroring life than with interpreting it', and with submitting 'to actuality rather than transcending it', [436] I should say that such a good mirror, if you call that a mirror, is worth a great many interpretations, and that such submission is worth more than most transcendence. If you stick to a literary judgement, you cannot say that Shakespeare is inferior to any poet who has ever written, even if you are prepared to substantiate your opinion by detailed analysis; and if

you depreciate Shakespeare for his lower view of life, then you have issued out of literary criticism into social criticism; you are criticising not so much the man but the age. I prefer the culture which produced Dante to the culture which produced Shakespeare; but I would not say that Dante was the greater poet, or even that he had the profounder mind; and if humanism chooses Goethe and leaves Shakespeare, then humanism is incapable of distinguishing between the chaff and the wheat.

10 Mr Foerster is what I call a Heretic: that is, a person who seizes upon a truth and pushes it to the point at which it becomes a falsehood. In his hands, Humanism becomes something else, something more dangerous, because much more seductive to the best minds, than let us say Behaviourism. I wish to try to distinguish the functions of true Humanism from those imposed upon it by zealots.

I. The function of Humanism is not to provide dogmas, or philosophical theories. Humanism, because it is general culture, is not concerned with philosophical foundations; it is concerned less with 'reason' than with common sense. When it proceeds to exact definitions it becomes something other than itself.

II. Humanism makes for breadth, tolerance, equilibrium and sanity. It operates against fanaticism.

III. The world cannot get on without breadth, tolerance and sanity; any more than it can get on without narrowness, bigotry and fanaticism.

IV. It is not the business of Humanism to refute anything. Its business is to *persuade*, according to its unformulable axioms of culture and good sense. It does not, for instance, [437] overthrow the *arguments* of fallacies like Behaviourism: it operates by taste, by sensibility trained by culture. It is critical rather than constructive. It is necessary for the criticism of social life and social theories, political life and political theories.

11 Without humanism we could not cope with Mr Shaw, Mr Wells, Mr Russell, Mr Mencken, Mr Sandburg, M. Claudel, Herr Ludwig, Mrs Macpherson, or the governments of America and Europe.

V. Humanism can have no positive theories about philosophy or theology. All that it can ask, in the most tolerant spirit, is: Is this particular philosophy or religion civilised or is it not?

VI. There is a type of person whom we call the Humanist, for whom humanism is enough. This type is valuable.

VII. Humanism is valuable (*a*) by itself, in the 'pure humanist', who will not set up humanism as a substitute for philosophy and religion, and (*b*) as a mediating and corrective ingredient in a positive civilisation founded on definite belief.[1]

VIII. Humanism, finally, is valid for a very small minority of *individuals*. But it is culture, not any subscription to a common programme or platform, which binds these individuals together. Such an 'intellectual aristocracy' has not the economic bonds which unite the individuals of an 'aristocracy of birth'.

12 Such a modest limitation of Humanism as I have tried to indicate above (the list is not exhaustive or defining but consists merely of the qualifications which occur immediately to my mind) will seem more than unsatisfactory to the more hopeful and ambitious devotees of the word. I wish to distinguish sharply, however, between what seems to me the correct and *necessarily* vague Humanism, and what T. E. Hulme means by Humanism in his notes in [438] *Speculations*. I agree with what Hulme says; and I am afraid that many modern Humanists are explicitly or implicitly committed to the view which Hulme denounces; and that they are, in consequence, men of the Renaissance rather than men of our time. For instance, Hulme gives as one characteristic of the Humanist (in his sense) the 'refusal to believe any longer in the radical imperfection of either Man or Nature'. I cannot help feeling that Mr Foerster and even Mr Babbitt are nearer to the view of Rousseau than they are to the religious view. For it is not enough to chastise the romantic visions of perfectibility, as they do; the modern humanistic view implies that man is either perfectible, or capable of indefinite improvement, because from that point of view the only difference is a difference of degree – so that there is always hope of a higher degree. It is to the immense credit of Hulme that he found out for himself that there is an *absolute* to which Man can *never* attain. For the modern humanist, as for the romantic, 'the problem of evil disappears, the conception of sin disappears'. This is illustrated in Mr Foerster's illusion of the *normally or typically human* (p. 241). (If Mr Foerster met Jesus, Buddha, St Francis or anyone in the least like them, I question whether they would strike him as conforming to this ideal of 100 per cent. normalcy.) Hulme put the matter into one paragraph:

> I hold the religious conception of ultimate values to be right, the humanist wrong. From the nature of things, these categories are not inevitable, like the categories of time and space, but are *equally*

---

1. An interesting infusion of Humanism in a remarkable religious personality is shown in the late Baron von Hügel's *Letters to a Niece*.

objective. In speaking of religion, it is to this level of abstraction that I wish to refer. I have none of the feelings of *nostalgia*, the reverence of tradition, the desire to recapture the sentiment of Fra Angelico, which seems to animate most modern defenders of religion. All that seems to me to be bosh. What is important, is what nobody seems to realise – the dogmas like that of Original Sin, which are the closest expression of the categories of [439] the religious attitude. That man is in no sense perfect, but a wretched creature, who can yet apprehend perfection. It is not, then, that I put up with the dogma for the sake of the sentiment, but that I may possibly swallow the sentiment for the sake of the dogma.

This is a statement which Mr Foerster, and all liberal theologians, would do well to ponder. Most people suppose that some people, because they enjoy the luxury of Christian sentiments and the excitement of Christian ritual, swallow or pretend to swallow incredible dogma. For some the process is exactly opposite. Rational assent may arrive late, intellectual conviction may come slowly, but they come inevitably without violence to honesty and nature. To put the sentiments in order is a later, and an immensely difficult task: intellectual freedom is earlier and easier than complete spiritual freedom.

13 There is no opposition between the religious and the *pure* humanistic attitude: they are necessary to each other. It is because Mr Foerster's brand of humanism seems to me *impure*, that I fear the ultimate discredit of all humanism.

Variants from *New Adelphi* (1929), *Hound & Horn* (1929):

Title 'Second Thoughts about Humanism', *New Adelphi*, *Hound & Horn*

1 the note] a note *New Adelphi*, *Hound & Horn*
which appears on the foregoing pages] which I reprinted in a small volume of essays entitled *For Lancelot Andrewes New Adelphi*, *Hound & Horn*
[Eliot alternates between 'humanism' and 'Humanism', and 'humanist' and 'Humanist' throughout the essay. The alternation does not seem to carry significance.]

2 and is already] indeed is already *New Adelphi*

4 ['With all respect' begins a new para. in *New Adelphi*.]
Church] church *Hound & Horn*
comes down] boils down *New Adelphi*, *Hound & Horn*

5 and just] and I consider just *New Adelphi*

6 supernatural realities] spiritual realities *New Adelphi*, *Hound & Horn*

7 , for a modern humanist,] for a modern humanist *New Adelphi*

8 Laocoön] Laocoon *New Adelphi*
  essay] essay (not yet published) *New Adelphi, Hound & Horn*
  a propagation] merely a propagation *New Adelphi, Hound & Horn*
  a better] a better man *New Adelphi*
10 than let us say] than, let us say, *New Adelphi*
12 sharply, however,] sharply however *Hound & Horn*
  (If Mr Foerster met Jesus . . . normalcy.): [Not represented in *New Adelphi* or *Hound & Horn*.]

Charles Whibley

SE, 440–54.
Originally publ. as *Charles Whibley: A Memoir*, The English Association pamphlet No. 80, distributed to members of the Association in Dec. 1931 and publ. on 14 Jan. 1932: Gallup A20. Revised in *SE*.

1 There is a peculiar difficulty, which I experience for the first time, in attempting an estimate of the literary work of a writer whom one remembers primarily as a friend. It is not so much that from a kind of reticence and fear of being uncritical one is inclined to reserve praise: it is rather that one's judgement is inevitably an amalgam of impressions of the work and impressions of the man. Anyone who knew Charles Whibley, and had frequent opportunities of enjoying his conversation, will recognise the strength of the impression which his personality could produce in such intercourse, and the difficulty of valuing the writings which remain, apart from the man who is gone.

2 What adds to the difficulty is the fact that his true place in history is not altogether to be deduced by posterity merely from the writings he has left; and the fact that a great deal of the work into which he threw himself most zealously is of the kind which will be called ephemeral, or only to be consulted, in future, by some scholarly ferret into a past age. It was largely what is called journalism; so that I hope I shall be tolerated in a digression, which is really a preamble, on the nature of the activity which that word loosely denotes. The distinction between 'journalism' and 'literature' is quite futile, unless we are drawing such violent contrast as that between Gibbon's *History* and to-night's evening paper; and such a contrast is too violent to have meaning. You cannot, that is, draw any useful distinction between journalism and literature merely in a scale of literary values, as a difference between the well [441] written and the supremely well written: a second-rate novel is not journalism, but it certainly is not literature. The term 'journalism' has deteriorated in the

last thirty years; and it is particularly fitting, in the present essay, to try to recall it to its more permanent sense. To my thinking, the most accurate as well as most comprehensive definition of the term is to be obtained through considering the state of mind, and the type of mind, concerned in writing what all would concede to be the *best* journalism. There is a type of mind, and I have a very close sympathy with it, which can only turn to writing, or only produce its best writing, under the pressure of an immediate occasion; and it is this type of mind which I propose to treat as the journalist's. The underlying causes may differ: the cause may be an ardent preoccupation with affairs of the day, or it may be (as with myself) inertia or laziness requiring an immediate stimulus, or a habit formed by early necessity of earning small sums quickly. It is not so much that the journalist works on different material from that of other writers, as that he works from a different, no less and often more honourable, motive.

3 The indignity commonly thrown at the journalist is this, that his work is said to be of only passing interest, intended to make an immediate strong impression, and destined to eternal oblivion after that instant effect has been produced. To say merely this, however, is to overlook the reasons for which writing may be 'ephemeral', and the loose application of that adjective itself, as well as the curious accidents which protect a piece of writing from oblivion. Those persons who are drawn by the powerful attraction of Jonathan Swift read and re-read with enchanted delight *The Drapier's Letters*; and these letters are journalism according to my hint of a definition, if anything is. But *The Drapier's Letters* are such an important item now in English letters, so essential to anyone who would be well read in the literature of England, that we ignore the accident by which we still read them. If Swift had never written [442] *Gulliver's Travels*, and if he had not played a striking and dramatic part in political life, and if this amazing madman had not supplemented these claims to permanence by a most interesting private life, what would be the place of *The Drapier's Letters* now? They would be praised now and then by some student of Anglo-Irish history of the epoch who happened by some odd coincidence to have also an exceptional degree of literary acumen; and they would be read by nobody else. The same fate would have overcome the pamphleteering of Defoe, were he not the author of *Robison Crusoe* and *Moll Flanders*; or the pamphleteering of Samuel Johnson, were he not the hero of Boswell. To turn to another great English writer of quite a different kind, let us suppose that John Henry Newman had not been also the great leader of the English Church whose defection Gladstone described as a 'catastrophe'; that he had not played the prominent rôle in the nineteenth century that he did play; supposing also that the material

of his *Apologia* was as defunct as the subject of Wood's halfpence in Ireland, who but a few discerning connoisseurs of style would ever read that book now or a century hence? And the *Apologia* of Newman is as surely journalism as is the journalism of Swift, Defoe, or Johnson.

4 To quote an example on the opposite side: the *Martin Marprelate* tracts are not, certainly, as fine prose as the best of Swift, Defoe, Johnson, or Newman. They belong to a cruder period. But still they contain some very fine passages indeed, and the whole controversy is on a high literary level. Who reads them now? except a very small number of people, those who interest themselves in the religious squabbles of that epoch, and those who interest themselves in the prose styles of that epoch. They are not considered a part of the necessary education of the cultivated English-speaking person. Literary style is sometimes assigned almost magical qualities, or is credited with being a mysterious preservative for subject-matter which no longer interests. This is far from being absolutely true. [443] Style alone cannot preserve; only good style in conjunction with permanently interesting content can preserve. All other preservation, such as that of Swift's or Defoe's journalism, is due to a happy accident. Even poetry is not immune, though poetry usually concerns itself with simpler and more external matters than anything else; for who, except scholars, and except the eccentric few who are born with a sympathy for such work, or others who have deliberately studied themselves into the right appreciation, can now read through the whole of *The Faerie Queene* with delight?

5 Charles Whibley, then, was a journalist in that he wrote chiefly for occasion, either in his monthly commentary on men, events, and current books; or in his essays and prefaces, or sometimes in a lecture; with the one apparent exception of that charming biographical work, *Lord John Manners and his Friends*. Had he been exactly of my generation, when the typewriter has become the direct means of transmitting even poetry to the page, I am sure that he would have employed that now indispensable engine; as it was, he used suitably a quill pen, but composed rapidly in a fine hand and made very few *ratures* or corrections. Here again, I may remark, speed and ease are no test of writing, one way or the other; and some may hold that the pains of Pater produced less fine prose than the speed of Newman. As for the type of Whibley's style of writing, I think we must look, as we must always look where possible, towards the great writers of the same language in the past with whom the writer has most sympathy, and on whose thoughts his mind has been nourished. His style was fed on the great historical and political writers. Whibley's

mind was not an abstract mind; rather, he saw the principle through the act. There is a paragraph beginning his essay 'The Trimmer' – an essay on the Marquess of Halifax – which reveals his interest in politics, the angle from which he looked on politics, and the antecedents of his own style:

> [444] Politics is a profession of the second-rate. The man of genius strays into it by accident. We do not need the fingers of both hands to count the statesmen who have served England since the seventeenth century. The Ministers who have served themselves are like the sands for number. And from this mob of mediocrities it is not strange that very few writers have emerged. It is not an extravagant claim that they should have some mastery of literary expression. Words are the material of their craft. They know not how to use them save in the cause of rhetoric. Charles James Fox, the world was told, was an accomplished man of letters. To hear him discourse of the Classics was almost as fine an experience as to see him take the bank at faro. And then he wrote a book, and his fame was blown away like a bubble. Halifax and Bolingbroke, Burke and Disraeli – these are secure of remembrance. Where shall you find a fifth?

I regret the qualification 'since the seventeenth century', only because I should have liked a reminder of the greater name of Clarendon, with whom, however, Whibley dealt elsewhere. But the paragraph is most illuminating, both upon Whibley's own style, and upon his judgements of political men. He had a particular sympathy with – and a particular gift for explaining and making sympathetic to his readers – three classes of men of letters: statesmen, gentlemen, and ragamuffins. As for the first I think that the paragraph I have just quoted accounts for a bias of judgement sometimes discernible in his general opinions of statesmen: he may, I think, have somewhat overpraised the virtues, and too much extenuated the faults, of Bolingbroke as a statesman, because of the brilliance and vigour of Bolingbroke's style, and the great attraction of his personality. (On the other hand, he seems to me to have given justice to Manners and Smythe against the more brilliant Disraeli.) However, the relation of a statesman's statesmanship to his prose style is not negligible; we can find in-[445]teresting laboratory material in the writing of Mr MacDonald, Mr Lloyd George, and particularly Mr Winston Churchill.

6 People sometimes talk vaguely about the *conversational style* in writing. Still more often, they deplore the divorce between the language as spoken and the language as written. It is true that the spoken and the written language can drift too far apart – with the eventual consequence

of forming a new written language. But what is overlooked is that an *identical* spoken and written language would be practically intolerable. If we spoke as we write we should find no one to listen; and if we wrote as we speak we should find no one to read. The spoken and the written language must not be too near together, as they must not be too far apart. Henry James's later style, for instance, is not exactly a conversational style; it is the way in which the later James dictated to a secretary. The famous monologue at the end of *Ulysses* is not the way in which persons of either sex actually *think*: it is a very skilful attempt by a master of language to give the illusion of mental process by a different medium, that of written words. There is, however, an essential connexion between the written and the spoken word, though it is not to be produced by aiming at a 'conversational' style in writing, or a periodic style in speech; and I have found this intimate, though indefinable, connexion between the speech and the writing of every writer whom I have known personally who was a good writer – even between the speech and the most recent writing of Mr James Joyce. Now, one could not say of Whibley, any more than of anyone else, that he wrote as he talked, or that he talked as he wrote. Nevertheless, his writings have a quality which relates them more closely to his speech than to the writing of anyone else. I know that the word 'sincerity' sounds very vague; yet it represents that moral integrity which unites the prose styles of speech and writing of any good writer: however the rhythm, the syntax, the vocabulary may differ. One can-[446]not, obviously, produce negative instances; I can only repeat that whenever I have known both the man and the work of any writer of what seemed to me good prose, the printed word has always reminded me of the man speaking.

7 One of the phrases of commendation which Whibley often used, at least in conversation, about the style of another writer, was (even when he had little sympathy with the matter) that it had *life* in it; and what makes his own prose hold one's attention, in spite of, perhaps even emphasised by, its relation to remote models in the history of English literature, is that it is charged with life. He gives always the impression of a fearless sincerity, and that is more important than being always right. One always feels that he is ready to say bluntly what everyone else is afraid to say. Thus a feeling of apprehensiveness, conducive to attention, is aroused in the reader. And, in fact, he was, when he chose to be, a master of invective. Now invective is a form of writing which varies at different times and in different countries according to the customs and laws in vogue at the time and in the place. It is now the fashion to deplore the decay of abuse. Certainly, the rules of the game are altered. Many years

ago, in an open letter to Lord John Russell, Disraeli addressed Lord John as an 'insignificant insect'. I am not aware that a duel, or even a solicitor's letter followed; yet when I used the same phrase about a contemporary in a letter to a journal, my letter was rejected on the ground that it might possibly be considered libellous. Well, that does not matter; for however the rules of the game may be tightened, it is all the more stimulating to the connoisseur in controversy to do what he can according to the actual rules; and once the rules are recognised, a mild statement may carry all the force of a more violent statement under laxer rules. Indeed, I think that we, looking at the daily volleys of that great French master of vituperation, Léon Daudet – who was, incidentally, a friend of Whibley – become fatigued by the very licence which this amazing journalist permits himself, and feel that a little less [447] liberty in abuse would refine the point of sarcasm. When I add to the name of Daudet, that of a master of a very different, and much more austere style, Charles Maurras, I have named with Whibley the three best writers of invective of their time. There is a great deal of fuss nowadays about freedom of speech, but very few persons nowadays care really about genuine *plain speaking*. 'Free speech' has been narrowed down to speaking freely about sex, sexual irregularities and sexual perversions; it has become the peculiar privilege of World-Leaguers for Sexual Reform; but few, so far as I am aware, now claim the free speech to call a knave a knave or a fool a fool. *And knaves and fools we both abhorred alike*, says Dryden in his noble epitaph on Oldham; perhaps nowadays our abhorrence is blunted by habituation.

8 The 'Musings Without Method' which Whibley contributed once a month to *Blackwood's* for thirty years, excepting two months, one of which was the last, are the best sustained piece of literary journalism that I know in recent times. Daudet is sometimes tiresome and Maurras sometimes dull, and both are iterative; Mr Wyndham Lewis, the most brilliant journalist of my generation (in addition to his other gifts) often squanders his genius for invective upon objects which to everyone else but himself seem unworthy of his artillery, and arrays howitzers against card houses; but Whibley always had the tact to vary his objects of attack and to vary his methods according to the object. Whether he was opposing the act of a Government, or giving his opinion of Gladstone, or objecting to the insistent advertisements of what he held to be a debased *Encyclopedia Britannica*, or denouncing the project of a National Theatre, or speaking his mind about Mr Pinero or Mr Jones or Mr Edmund Gosse or the Omar Khayyám Club, he modulated his thunders according to the tree, shrub, or weed to be blasted. Nor did he ever hold too long to one topic. There would be a sudden transition to something else: a book of travels

that he liked, [448] or French wines and cookery. And what excites my particular admiration is the skill of these transitions. It looks artless; as if he had exhausted the subject for the moment, and had turned quite at random to another. But I have for some months been going slowly through these 'Musings', with a view to making an anthology, primarily of those paragraphs which are concerned with literature and art. It has been like trying to carve a bird with flexible bones but no joints; you remove one paragraph from a monthly 'Musing', a paragraph apparently self-contained, and unrelated to what precedes and to what follows, and something has gone out of it. The anthology will be made, but it will, I fear, have the same relation to the month's 'Musing' that a falcon skilfully stuffed in the attitude of flight has to the living flash or swoop through the air. It is because the 'Musings' were methodically 'without method' that they were so living. Whibley followed faithfully and easily the movement of his own mind; he did not, as I and most people do, have to think up half a dozen subjects to talk about and then shuffle them into the most suitable order; the transition from one subject to the next suggested itself. Critics sometimes comment upon the sudden transitions and juxtapositions of modern poetry; that is, when right and successful, an application of somewhat the same method without method. Whether the transition is cogent or not, is merely a question of whether the mind is *serré* or *délié*, whether the whole personality is involved; and certainly, the whole personality of Whibley is present in whatever he wrote, and it is the unity of a personality which gives an indissoluble unity to his variety of subject.

9 In attaining such unity, and indeed in attaining a *living* style, whether in prose or in verse, the practice of conversation is invaluable. Indeed, I believe that to write well it is necessary to converse a great deal. I say 'converse' instead of 'talk'; because I believe that there are two types of good writers: those who talk a great deal to others, and those, perhaps less fortunate, who talk a great deal to themselves. [449] It is two thousand and hundreds of years since, that the theory was propounded that thought is conversation with oneself; all literary creation certainly springs either from the habit of talking to oneself or from the habit of talking to others. Most people are unable to do either, and that is why they lead such active lives. But anyone who would write must let himself go, in one way or the other, for there are only four ways of thinking: to talk to others, or to one other, or to talk to oneself, or to talk to God.

10 Whibley had another quality, not unrelated to the preceding, which is essential for the literary critic. The first requisite of literary criticism, as of

every other literary or artistic activity, is that it shall be interesting. And the first condition of being interesting is to have the tact to choose only those subjects in which one is really interested, those which are germane to one's own temper. Universality of knowledge is a less chimerical ideal than universality of taste; but there is a kind of saturation in the text of an author, more important than erudition. Whibley had this discretion, that of the *honnête homme* as critic, to select subjects suited to his own temperament. Learning he had and scholarship. He was a good Grecian, and no Hellenist. His standards of classical scholarship were acquired from such devoted scholars as R. A. Neil, but having acquired them he wore them easily. He did not, like some more pretentious and pontifical critics, occupy himself with reviewing and bluepencilling literary reputations already well established, or adding one more superfluous essay to the bibliography of some already over-criticised author. In consequence, he has added to English criticism a number of essays on subjects which have never been so well handled (if handled at all) in the past, and to his treatment of which there will be little to add in the future; and has thereby made a secure place for himself in criticism.

11 I have said earlier that he took a particular delight in men of letters who were gentlemen or ragamuffins; perhaps his greatest enjoyment and amusement was in men of letters [450] who were something of both. His appreciation of Sir Thomas Urquhart, Christianus Presbyteromastix, descended from Adam the Protoplast, with his *Ekskubalauron* and his *Logopandekteison*, as well as his great translation of Rabelais, is the best possible introduction to that author. As in politics Whibley saw theory through men, so in literature he was at his best, and indeed most just in his criticism, when the author of an admired work was also a man after his own heart. Another essay which shows this delight in personality, even to the point of conjecture, is his essay on Petronius. Who else would have thought to remark of the author of the *Satyricon* that he 'was a great gentleman'? but the phrase, as used here by Whibley, has its proper significance. It is not, however, true that he often distorted the literary value because of his enjoyment of the author's personality; he is able to say truly that 'Petronius is as secret as Shakespeare, as impersonal as Flaubert.' On the other hand, he is able to appreciate the book even when one feels that he has some dislike of the author, as with Laurence Sterne. And in the essay on Petronius his amused and catholic delight in what he called 'the underworld of letters' is as well expressed as anywhere.

> You may meet Encolpius to-day (he says) without surprise or misunderstanding. He haunts the bars of the Strand, or hides him in the

dismal alleys of Gray's Inn Road. One there was (one of how many!) who after a brilliant career at the University, found the highway his natural home, and forthwith deserted the groves of learning for the common hedgerow of adventure. The race-course knew him, and the pavement of London; blacklegs and touts were his chosen companions; now and again he would appear among his old associates, and enjoy a taste of Trimalchio's banquet, complaining the while that the money spent on his appetite might have been better employed in the backing of horses. Though long since he forgot he was a gentle-[451]man, he always remembered that he was a scholar, and, despite his drunken blackguardism, he still took refuge in Horace from the grime and squalor of his favourite career. Not long since he was discovered in a cellar, hungry and dishevelled; a tallow candle crammed into a beer bottle was his only light; yet so reckless was his irresponsibility that he forgot his pinched belly and his ragged coat, and sat on the stone floor, reciting Virgil to another of his profession. Thus, if you doubt the essential truth of Petronius, you may see his grim comedy enacted every day. . . .

I would not give the impression, however, that Whibley's service to letters was simply to fish up from the bottom of the past its forgotten and outmoded cranks and whimsies, any more than it was to descant amusingly upon greater and well-known writers. His peculiar merit as a critic, I think, resided in the combination of this personal gusto and curiosity, with a faculty of just literary appreciation. If he talked of Lucian or Herondas otherwise than professors do, he did not see them out of scale with the greatest masterpieces of Greek literature, nor did he merely bring forth a pleasant chat. He was not a bookish critic in the style of James Russell Lowell. And if he talked of the minor writers and journalists of the sixteenth and seventeenth century, with whom he had so much sympathy and for whom he had so much charity, it was never to elevate them above their proper place. The history of literature, he might have said, is always being simplified into a Hall of Fame of dusty noble statues and a list of names such as are being used for decorating the domes of libraries. But the *honnête homme* in literary appreciation cannot be satisfied to worship a few mummified reputations; he must have the imagination and the heart to desire to feel literature as something alive; and we can touch the life of the great works of literature of any age all the better if we know something of the less.

12 As I said before, Whibley had what is perhaps the first of all critical gifts, without which others are vain: the [452] ability to detect the living

style from the dead. (And I may interject parenthetically, that though he never criticised in print any of the writers of my own generation, I found in conversation that he was able to recognise vitality even in writers with whom he had little sympathy.) It is largely owing to his insight and enthusiasm as well as to his editorial toil, that the Tudor Translators have become recognised as they deserve. In his appreciation of these humble workmen and great prose writers, he shows the recognition of the life, not merely of men, but of speech, as expressed in a note which he wrote many years ago on Henry Bradley's *The Making of English* (*Blackwood's*, Aug. 1904, p. 280):

> He, therefore, is the finest master of style who never loses hold of the past, who feels, what he can only express to minds as knowing as his own, that the words of his choice have each its own pedigree and its own life. Nor will he limit himself either to Saxon or to Latin. He will use the full resources of his speech with a justified pride, remembering that our language has as many colonies as our King, and that in this one respect at least we are the resolute conquerors of the world.

13 It is in such ways as I have indicated, not aspiring to any literary dictatorship or pontificate, or to academic or extra-academic honours, and never caring to express his mind except on what really interested him or excited his admiration or indignation, that Charles Whibley made and holds his place in literary criticism. He was too modest, and had too varied tastes and interests in life, to care to be the monumental critic; and indeed, the monumental and encyclopedic critic is to be regarded with a carefully appraising eye; for the monument is sometimes constructed either by indifference to literature or by indifference to life. Criticism, certainly, was only a part of his activity in life; and in being only a part, it is genuine in its kind. I had no intention in this paper to estimate his place in the tradition social [453] and political which is represented by his connexion with W. E. Henley and his early labours on the *Scots Observer* and the *National Observer*; that is the subject-matter of other chapters; I allude to them merely as a reminder of the place of his literary essays in his work.

14 There is a passage in one of his 'Musings without Method' celebrating the late Professor York Powell of Oxford (*Blackwood's*, June 1904, p. 860 ff.), which I may be permitted to transcribe with suitable excisions and slight alteration, as applicable by analogy to its author:

There was nothing that had happened in the past which was not of living interest to him. No man of his time had a deeper acquaintance with life, literature, and policy. . . . He was, for instance, the first or second expert (for he had a rival) in the history of the Prize Ring. We remember once that, the art of pantomime being mentioned in his presence, he was ready with a complete biography of Dubureau, together with an account of the pantomimes which Gautier and Charles Nodier wrote for him. This is but a single instance, taken at random, of his multifarious knowledge. . . . His knowledge of literature outstripped the common boundaries of this country or that . . . but his chief interest was perhaps in the French poetry of the newest school. He spoke French and understood it with an ease and a skill that is given to few Englishmen. . . . Like the late W. E. Henley, with whom he had many points of . . . sympathy, he was a keen upholder of some oppressed citizens, and at the same time a sturdy Jingo, where the interests of England were involved. . . . While the egoism of most men inspires them to the composition of a work which shall make them for ever famous, (he) lavished his gifts in talk, and made his friend a sharer, as it were, in his own talent. . . . In conversation no subject came amiss to him, because he was familiar with all; but he was so richly endowed with humour that he regarded nothing with an overserious eye. . . . The result is that, while his contemporaries will do full justice [454] to his temperament and omniscience, he may appear to posterity, which knew him not, as far less than he really was. . . . But he has lived his life; he has scattered his learning with a generous hand; he has bequeathed a memory of affection to all who knew him; he has set his mark on works of younger men. . . . And who shall say that this achievement is not greater than half a dozen volumes in octavo?

Variants from Jan. 1932:
Title *Charles Whibley: A Memoir*
2   has deteriorated] has of course deteriorated
5   a fine hand] a small fine hand
    rather, he saw the principle] he saw the principle rather
6   mental process] 'thought'
7   perhaps indeed] perhaps even
8   Khayyám] Khayyam
    to the next suggested itself] and the next was given by his own mind
11 catholic] Catholic
14 policy. . . .] policy . . .
    knowledge. . . .] knowledge . . .

Englishmen. . . .] Englishmen . . .
involved. . . .] involved . . .
talent. . . .] talent . . .
eye. . . .] eye . . .
was. . . .] was . . .
men. . . .] men . . .

John Dryden The Poet the Dramatist the Critic

THREE ESSAYS BY T. S. ELIOT

Publ. on 18 Oct. 1932: Gallup A22.

The three essays are revised versions of 'John Dryden – I. The Poet who Gave the English Speech', *Listener*, 5. 118 (15 Apr. 1931), 621–2: Gallup C317; 'John Dryden – II. Dryden the Dramatist', *Listener*, 5. 119 (22 Apr. 1931), 681–2: Gallup C318; and 'John Dryden – III. Dryden the Critic, Defender of Sanity', *Listener*, 5. 120 (29 Apr. 1931), 724–5: Gallup C319.

Dryden the Poet

JDPDC, 5–24

1 Dryden's position in English literature is unique. Far below Shakespeare, and even below Milton, as we must put him, he yet has, just by reason of his precise degree of inferiority, a kind of importance which neither Shakespeare nor Milton has – the importance of his *influence*. It is this nice question of influence that I wish to investigate first, in relation to what I may call the 'literary dictator', that is, in our history, Ben Jonson, Dryden, Samuel Johnson and in his way, Coleridge. Are we to say that poets like Shakespeare and Milton were without influence? Certainly not, but 'influence', in the sense in which we can cope with the term, is something more limited. The disproportion between Shakespeare and his immediate followers, among the dramatists, is so great that the influence of Shakespeare is a trifling [6] thing in comparison with Shakespeare himself; and as for Milton, that was so peculiar a genius that although he had plenty of mimics during the eighteenth century, he can hardly be said to have any followers. For 'influence', as Dryden had influence, a poet must not be so great as to overshadow all followers. Dryden was followed by Pope, and, a century later, by Samuel Johnson; both men of great original genius, who developed the medium left them by Dryden, in ways which cast honour both on them and on him. It should seem then no paradox to say that Dryden was the great influence

upon English verse that he was, because he was *not* too great to have any influence at all. He was neither the consummate poet of earlier times, nor the eccentric poet of later. He was happy both in his predecessors and in his successors. A hundred years is a long time for the stamp of one man to remain upon a literature; poets' influence and reputation cannot last so long in our days, and that makes Dryden a central, a typical figure [7] in English letters. He is in himself the Malherbe, the Boileau, the Corneille, and almost the Molière (almost, because Congreve refined and surpassed him in comedy) of the seventeenth century in England: and to him, as much as to any individual, we owe our civilisation.

2 As a figure, there is nothing picturesque about the man John Dryden. He came of a small county family like hundreds of others; he had, for a man of his origins, no great worldly advantages; he married a lady of superior rank, who brought him no exceptional advantage either, and apparently little domestic happiness. He was an ordinary-seeming, florid countryman, whose manners, according to the next and more refined generation, were not of the most polished. We do not know whether it was by the brilliance of his conversation that he was the great figure of Wills's Coffee House for all the hours that he passed there every day; but there he was, admired by minor men of letters, and courted by bluestocking noblemen. If not be-[8]cause of his powers of talk, in an age when men talked and drank for more hours a day than they can afford to do now, and when they wrote, wrote at higher speed than we can, then it was because they all recognised that Dryden could do everything that they would have liked to do, and because what he wrote did not exceed the scope of their comprehension. I cannot imagine Shakespeare cutting such a figure in a tavern or coffee-house; that solitary person surely had too much in his head which his tap-room companions could not understand; the predecessor of Dryden in this role is, of course, Ben Jonson. But although of Jonson we have so few personal remains, yet the notes and the anecdotes which we have give us at least the illusion of as definite a character as that of Dr Samuel Johnson. We remember the story of Ben Jonson, that when he returned to the Anglican fold after his temporary defection to Rome, he showed his enthusiasm by seizing the chalice, at his first communion, and draining [9] it to the last drop. We can never see Dryden so clearly; yet his age was in accord that he expressed each man better than any man could express himself.

3 Being so completely representative, Dryden not only formed the mould for the next, but himself derived very clearly from the last. In his work there is nothing unexpected, no new element with unknown properties. As

a poet, Dryden came to resolve the contradictions of the previous period, and select from it the styles which were capable of development. His first verse, though clever enough of its kind to earn ready commendations, is distinctly bad. It is encumbered with all the late metaphysical conceits which he was himself to destroy. Cleveland and Benlowes are lightfooted by comparison; for they traced their patterns with conviction; and of the early verses of Dryden one can only say that they are by a man doing his best to talk an idiom alien to him: but for sudden flashes of wit and sense here and there, one [10] would say that their author could never be a poet. It used to be thought that the poetic styles of Dryden and Pope were artificial. One has only to compare them with the style of Dryden's immediate predecessor, Abraham Cowley, to prove the contrary. Dryden became a great poet because he could *not* write an artificial style; because it was intolerable to him; because he had that incorruptible sincerity of word which at all times distinguishes the good writer from the bad, and at critical times such as his, distinguishes the great writer from the little one. What Dryden did, in fact, was to reform the language, and devise a natural, conversational style of speech in verse in place of an artificial and decadent one.

4 Too much can still be made, I think, of Dryden's debt to Waller and Denham, and to his contemporary Oldham. Oldham, certainly, is very near to him; Oldham is rough and unpolished, but occasionally in his 'rugged line' there breaks out a vigour not unlike Dryden's. [11] His satires are still readable. But to Waller and Denham, as practitioners of the heroic couplet, his debt can be exaggerated. As Pope says, 'Waller was smooth', indeed, but his smoothness is feebleness, compared to anything accomplished by Dryden or Pope himself: the smoothness of an ambling pad-pony compared to that of a fiery horse with an expert rider. Waller mostly, and Denham except in one passage, send us to sleep; and Dryden never allows us to do that. I think that Dryden owes more to his reaction against the artifices of the late metaphysical verse, than to any sedulous study of Waller. For the content of his couplet, the sensibility which informs it, is as different from that of Waller as well could be.

5 It is not irrelevant to compare the operation of Dryden with that of Donne. Donne likewise was a reformer of the language. This is not so immediately apparent in Donne's case, for his career is overlapped by the Elizabethan dramatists, who were still, after Shakespeare, explor-[12]ing the possibilities of dramatic blank verse. But consider that Shakespearean blank verse was soon to expire with the set phrases of Shirley and others, that it had nearly gone its course, and consider what the lyric verse of

Shakespeare's time was. It was essentially verse for music; therefore its intellectual content and its range of emotion were restricted. The songs of Shakespeare gain a great deal – perhaps this has not been enough remarked – by their dramatic position in the plays; a song like 'full fathom five' is suffused by the meaning and feeling of the passage in which it occurs; the songs of Shakespeare are not interludes or interruptions, but part of the structure of the plays in which they occur. Observing this attribute, we can say that for lyric verse there was very little future, had it not been for Donne. Donne did away with all the stage properties of the ordinary lyric verse of the Elizabethans; he introduced into lyric verse a style of conversation, of direct, natural speech; and this was a revolution compar-[13]able to the development of blank verse into a conversational medium, from Kyd to the mature Shakespeare. And by this innovation Donne gave to the Caroline Poets a vehicle which they would hardly have been able to devise for themselves.

6 By the time when Dryden began to write, the vigour of the style initiated by Donne had quite gone: the natural had become the artificial. For there is not, in verse, any wholly objective distinction between the natural and the artificial style. Whether a style is natural is whether it is natural to the man who writes it. It is harder to be natural than to be artificial; it requires a great deal more work, and is painful and unpleasant, because sincerity is always painful and unpleasant. Dryden did the work, and experienced no doubt the pain and unpleasantness, and he restored English verse to the condition of speech.

7 Now when we say 'conversational', or the quality of the spoken language in verse, we [14] are inclined to limit it to certain kinds of conversation, perhaps more particularly of an intimate nature; so it is easier for us to perceive this naturalness in Donne than in Dryden. But we have to consider what are the essentials of good speech. At no time, I know, are the written language and the spoken language identical. Obviously they cannot be: if we talked extempore exactly as we write no one would listen, and if we wrote exactly as we talk no one would read. But speech can never divorce itself, beyond some point, from the written word, without damage to itself; and writing can never beyond some point alienate itself from speech, without self-destruction. Now Dryden's couplets may not seem at first sight to echo our own way of speech. That may be partly because the standards of good English in conversation were higher then, and partly because the spoken word, in the late seventeenth and eighteenth centuries, meant much more *public* speech than it does to us: it meant oratory and eloquence. [15] True, thanks to the radio, we

more often listen to public oratory than we did a few years ago. But we hardly expect the sublime; we may prefer the chatty, and if any of our acquaintance, in private company, holds forth and harangues at length, we are apt to qualify him as a bore. But, in the time of Dryden, speech was rather speech in public than in private; and Dryden helped to form a language for generations which were prepared to speak, and to listen, in public.

8 There are, of course, three main divisions of Dryden's verse, apart from the verse of the heroic plays: the satires, the songs, and the translations. Now one of the good offices of Dryden in his satires is this: to show us that if verse should not stray too far from the customs of speech, so also it should not abandon too much the uses of prose. Everyone knows the verses of *Mac Flecknoe* and the more varied if less sustained satire of *Absalom and Achitophel*; I should like here to mention rather those two pieces [16] of sustained reasoning in verse, *Religio Laici* and *The Hind and the Panther*. Here are two poems which could no more have been written in the eighteenth century than in the nineteenth, for they are poems of religious controversy. Other poets, before Dryden, had philosophised in verse: Chapman, and Sir John Davies, and Donne, in his way, in *The Progress of the Soul*. But in *The Hind and the Panther* for the first time and for the last is political-religious controversy elevated to the condition of poetry. However one views these differences now, one cannot but appreciate the characterisation of the Church of England, under the guise of the Panther, which Dryden draws, after his conversion to Rome:

> Thus, like a creature of a double kind,
> In her own labyrinth she lives confined.
> To foreign lands no sound of her is come,
> Humbly content to be despised at home.
> Such is her faith, where good cannot be had,
[17] At least she leaves the refuse of the bad.
> Nice in her choice of ill, though not of best,
> And least deform'd, because reform'd the least . . .
> A real presence all her sons allow,
> And yet 'tis flat idolatry to bow,
> Because the Godhead's there, they know not how . . .
> What is 't those faithful then partake or leave?
> For what is signified and understood,
> Is, by her own confession, flesh and blood.
> Then, by the same acknowledgement, we know
> They take the sign, and take the substance too.

> The lit'ral sense is hard to flesh and blood.
> But nonsense never can be understood.

This is not, when analysed, convincing theological argument – Dryden was no theologian – but it is first-rate oratorical persuasion; and Dryden was the first man to raise oratory to the dignity of poetry, and to descend with poetry to teach the arts of oratory; and to do any one thing with verse better than anyone else has done it, at the same time that one is the first to attempt it, is no small achievement. But it is not only by biting passages like this that [18] a poem of Dryden's succeeds, but by a perfect lifting and lowering of his flight, in a varied unity without monotony. Take the beginning of the earlier and inferior of the two poems, *Religio Laici*, the passage attacking the principles of deism:

> Dim as the borrowed beams of moon and stars
> To lonely, weary, wandering travellers
> Is Reason to the soul; and as on high
> Those rolling fires discover but the sky,
> Not light us here, so Reason's glimmering ray
> Was lent, not to assure our doubtful way,
> But guide us upward to a better day.
> And as those nightly tapers disappear
> When day's bright lord ascends our hemisphere,
> So pale grows Reason at Religion's sight,
> So dies, and so dissolves in supernatural light.

This, if I am not greatly mistaken, is first-rate poetry not incomparable to Lucretius – of whom, by the way, Dryden by a few passages proved himself the most worthy translator into [19] English of any time. And the same vein is repeated, with still greater power, in *The Hind and the Panther*:

> But, gracious God, how well dost thou provide
> For erring judgements an unerring guide!
> Thy throne is darkness in the abyss of light,
> A blaze of glory that forbids the sight.
> O teach me to believe Thee thus concealed,
> And search no farther than Thyself revealed;
> But her alone for my director take,
> Whom Thou hast promised never to forsake!
> My thoughtless youth was winged with vain desires;
> My manhood, long misled by wandering fires,
> Followed false lights; and when their glimpse was gone,
> My pride struck out new sparkles of her own.

> Such was I, such by nature still I am;
> Be Thine the glory, and be mine the shame!

Anyone who to-day could make such an exact statement in verse of such nobility and elegance, [20] and with such originality of versification and language, might well look down upon his contemporaries. We are very far, here, from the smoothness of Waller or Denham. The surface is equally polished; but the difference is between the smooth surface of a piece of sculpture conceived and finished by a master and the smooth surface of a cake of soap.

9 I shall have occasion to refer again to Dryden's verse translations, including his translations from Chaucer, in connection with his literary criticism. I will only say here that they are more or less satisfactory, naturally, according to Dryden's sympathy with the original, and that perhaps his translations from Lucretius are the most inspired. All are of the best workmanship. Their importance, however, in considering Dryden's place then and now, is this: that it was by his translations almost as much as by his original poems; that Dryden helped to form our modern English tongue. It is no inconsiderable service to a language to dem-[21]onstrate that great poetry of other languages and times can be translated into the speech which we use daily, and remain great poetry. It might be a good thing for the language to-day if living poets would devote more attention to translating poetry from both living languages and dead; for the language at Dryden's time it was of vital assistance. Nor shall I say much about, or quote from, Dryden's lyrical verse. Whatever we think of the 'Song for St Cecilia's Day' or of 'Alexander's Feast' we must remember that in these Dryden perfected a form used with less skill by Cowley, and bequeathed it to Gray, Collins, Wordsworth, Coleridge and Tennyson; and without Dryden the 'Intimations of Immortality' could not have been written.

10 The main point, which I wish to drive home about Dryden is this: that it was Dryden who for the first time, and so far as we are concerned, for all time, established a *normal* English speech, a speech valid for both verse and prose, and imposing its laws which greater poetry than [22] Dryden's might violate, but which no poetry since has overthrown. The English language as left by Shakespeare, and within much narrower limits, by Milton, was a language like the club of Hercules, which no lesser strength could wield: so I believe that the language after Shakespeare and Milton could only have deteriorated until some genius appeared as great as they – or indeed, greater than they: for the language would have

been quickly in far worse case than that in which Shakespeare found it. It was Dryden, more than any other individual, who formed a language possible for the mediocrity, and yet possible for later great writers to do great things with.

11 And what Dryden accomplished was no by-product and no accident. Never was there a worker more conscious of what he was attempting. His theories, as we shall see, were all theories directed to what the poet could *consciously* attempt. Coleridge, in his writings on poetry, far exceeds the limited flight of Dryden, and [23] disappears in metaphysic clouds. The theory of Coleridge is partly, certainly, as was that of Wordsworth, a defence of his conscious precepts of workmanship; but with Wordsworth, and still more with Coleridge, we can say that their theory does not wholly account for the best of their poetry. In this way, Dryden was a far more *conscious* poet than either; perhaps more conscious than any poet of great eminence since. His essays are his conscious thoughts about the kinds of work he was doing; he uttered no metaphysical speculations, he was no prophet or teacher. I can think of no man in literature whose aims are so exactly fulfilled by his performance; and in the whole vineyard no labourer who more deserved his hire.

12 So I think now that we can understand a little better why John Dryden, of whose personality we know little except to know that there was little that was romantic or eccentric about it, should have dominated his time. Even if this portly country gentleman had sat hour [24] after hour at Wills's, as silent as Addison's description of himself as Mr Spectator, it is perfectly intelligible. It is hardly too much to say that Dryden found the English speechless, and he gave them speech; and they accordingly acknowledged their master; the language which we can refine, enrich, distort or corrupt as we may, but which we cannot do without. No one, in the whole history of English literature, has dominated that literature so long, or so completely. And even in the nineteenth century the language was still the language of Dryden, as it is to-day. In two hundred odd years, or exactly three hundred years from his birth, hardly a word or a phrase has become quaint and obsolete. And yet the man who accomplished so much, and accomplished it so consciously, was content to do whatever came to hand; and for twenty years of his life occupied himself exclusively in order to make his living with a form of literature to which his talent was little suited, and that form too he transformed.

Variants from 1931:

Title *John Dryden – I | The Poet who Gave the English Speech*
1   upon a literature] on a literature
2   was, admired] was admired
     than they can afford to do] than they do
     [Between 'their comprehension.' and 'Being so completely']: [Not represented.]
3   did, in fact,] did in fact
[Para. 4 not represented.]
5   were restricted] was restricted
6   experienced no doubt] experienced, no doubt,
7   the quality of the spoken language] the quality of spoken language
     divorce itself,] divorce itself
     public speech] public speech
     ['True, thanks to the radio . . . a bore.']: [Not represented.]
     But, in the time of Dryden,] In the time of Dryden
8   philosophised in verse:] philosophised in verse.
     ['Chapman . . . *the Soul*.':] [Not represented.]
     the smooth surface of a piece of sculpture conceived and finished by a master and the smooth surface of a cake of soap.] the smooth surface of a cake of soap and the smooth surface of a piece of sculpture conceived and finished by a master.
9   ['I shall have occasion . . . literary criticism.']: [Not represented.]
     I will only say] Of Dryden's verse translations I will only say
     translations almost as much] translations, almost as much
     ['It might be a good thing . . . could not have been written.']: [Not represented.]
10   drive home] drive home,
11   His theories, as we shall see,] His theories
     ['Coleridge, in his writings . . . eminence since.']: [Not represented.]
[Para. 12 not represented.]

Dryden the Dramatist

JDPDC, 27–45.
'Charmion' has been corrected to 'Charmian' in para. 3,
and in para. 7 'ethos' to *'ethos'* (as earlier in the same para.).

1 It is not such an easy matter to explain the utility to English letters and civilisation of Dryden's dramatic work, as it is to persuade of the importance of his poetry. Here are, in the edition of 1735 which I have, six volumes of miscellaneous plays, the chief product of twenty years of his life: it would be in a modern edition a fairly stout volume. The point is: are we to consider these plays as merely the by-product or waste-product of a man of genius, or as the brilliant effort to establish an impossible cause, or have they, perhaps, any important relation to the development

of English literature? Would Dryden be as important as he is, would he have accomplished just as much as he did, if he had never written these plays at all; plays, one or two of which a small number of people to-day have had the opportunity of seeing on the stage, and three or four of which a rather larger number of people have read?

[28] 2 We begin, all of us, with every prejudice against Dryden's 'heroic drama'. There is one great play in blank verse, *All for Love*, and the difficulty about that is that Shakespeare's play on the same subject, *Antony and Cleopatra*, is very much greater – though not necessarily a much finer *play*. There are several fine plays in rhymed couplets, of which there is none better than *The Conquest of Granada*, and the trouble with them is that they are not in blank verse. It is extraordinarily difficult not to apply to these plays irrelevant standards of criticism, and standards, moreover, which are not exactly of play-writing or even of verse-making. We have always at the back of our minds a comparison which is not in kind. Most of us prefer the reading, not only of Shakespeare, but of several other Elizabethan dramatists, to that of Dryden. And in our reading of Elizabethan plays we are inclined to confer upon them the dramatic virtues of the most actable (on the modern stage) of Shakespeare's plays, because they have some of the *reading* [29] virtues of these and the rest of Shakespeare's plays. I shall not venture here to investigate the nature of the *dramatic* in poetic drama, as distinguishable from the *poetic* in poetic drama; only to point out that the problem is much more of a tangle than it looks. For instance, there is *that which expressed in word and action is effective on the stage without our having read the text before*: that might be called the *theatrically dramatic*; and there is also the 'poetically dramatic', that which, when we read it, we recognise to have dramatic value, but which would not have dramatic value for us upon the stage unless we had already the perception of it from reading. *Theatrically* dramatic value in verse exists when the speech has its equivalent in, or can be projected by, the action and gesture and expression of the actor; *poetic* dramatic value is something dramatic in essence which can only be expressed by the word and by the reception of the word.

3 Shakespeare, of course, made the utmost use of each value; and therefore confuses us in our at-[30]tempt to estimate between the minor Elizabethans and Dryden, for neither they nor Dryden had such vast resources. But to make my point a little clearer I will take parallel passages from *Antony and Cleopatra* and from *All for Love*. In the former play, when the soldiers burst in after Cleopatra's death Charmian is made to say:

> It is well done, and fitting for a princess
> Descended of so many royal kings.
> Ah, soldier!   (*dies*).

Dryden's Charmian says:

> Yes, 'tis well done, and like a Queen, the last
> Of her great race. I follow her.
> (*Sinks down and dies.*)

Now, if you take these two passages by themselves, you cannot say that the two lines of Dryden are either less *poetic* than Shakespeare's, or less *dramatic*; a great actress could make just as much, I believe, of those of Dryden as of those of Shakespeare. But consider Shakespeare's re-[31]markable addition to the original text of North, the two plain words, *ah, soldier*. You cannot say that there is anything peculiarly *poetic* about these two words, and if you isolate the dramatic from the poetic you cannot say that there is anything peculiarly dramatic either, because there is nothing in them for the actress to express in action; she can at best enunciate them clearly. I could not myself put into words the difference I feel between the passage if these two words, *ah, soldier*, were omitted and with them. But I know there is a difference, and that only Shakespeare could have made it.

4 One might say that Dryden was a great poet who, by close application of a first-rate mind, made himself a great dramatist. His best plays are a happy marriage, or a happy compromise, between poetry and drama. You cannot say, when he is at his best, that he is less dramatic than Shakespeare, often he is more *purely* dramatic; nor can you say that he is less poetic. It is merely that there is a flight above, at which [32] poetry and drama become one thing; of which one is often reminded in passages of Homer or Dante. We often feel with Shakespeare, and now and then with his lesser contemporaries, that the dramatic action on the stage is the symbol and shadow of some more serious action in a world of feeling more real than ours, just as our perceptions, in dreams, are often more ominously weighted than they are in practical waking life. As Chapman says

> That all things to be done, as here we live,
> Are done before all times in the other life.

Here again is a passage, from the dying words of a hero of Chapman, which I will contrast presently with words of a hero of Dryden.

> Here like Roman statue I will stand
> Till death hath made me marble; oh, my fame,
> Live in despite of murder; take thy wings
> And haste thee where the grey-eyed morn perfumes
> Her rosy chariot with Saboean spices,
> Fly, where the evening from the Iberian vales
> [33] Takes on her swarthy shoulders Hecate
> Crowned with a grove of oaks: fly where men feel
> The cunning axle-tree: and those that suffer
> Beneath the chariot of the snowy Bear:
> And tell them all that D'Ambois now is hasting
> To the eternal dwellers.

Here is an equally well known passage from *All for Love*:

> How I loved
> Witness ye Days and nights, and all ye hours,
> That danced away with down upon your feet,
> As all your business were to count my passion.
> One day passed by, and nothing saw but love,
> Another came, and still 'twas only love,
> The suns were wearied out with looking on,
> And I untired with loving.
> I saw you every day, and all the day;
> And every day was still but as the first:
> So eager was I still to see you more . . .
>   While within your arms I lay,
> The world fell mouldering from my hands each hour
> [34] And left me scarce a grasp . . .
> . . . I knew not that I fled;
> But fled to follow you.
> – What haste she made to hoist her purple sails!

Now, you cannot say that one of these passages, that of Chapman or that of Dryden, is more purple than the other, or better poetry. Both are inferior in that each does to excess one part of what Shakespeare can do. Chapman departs too far from the direct stage action into the second world which the visual symbolises; Dryden is also excessively poetic, or rather too consciously poetic, by lavishing such fine poetry *solely* in the direct action. Chapman has only overtone; and Dryden has none. But if you consider the lines of Dryden solely as poetry, or solely as drama, you cannot find a flaw in them.

5 As for the verse of *All for Love* and the best of Dryden's blank verse in the other plays in which he used it, it is to me a miracle of revivification. I think that it has more influence than [35] it has had credit for; and that it is really the norm of blank verse for later blank verse playwrights. How Dryden could have escaped so completely the bad influence of the last followers of Shakespeare, with their dissolution of rhythm nearly into prose, and their worn-out wardrobe of imagery, is as wonderful as his superiority to, and difference from the other schools of verse, that of the Senecal poets, and D'Avenant to whom he was somewhat indebted. I will hazard here an heretical and contestable opinion; that later blank verse dramatists have written better verse when they wrote more like Dryden, and worse blank verse when they were conscious of Shakespeare. When Shelley wrote in *The Cenci*:

> My God! Can it be possible I have
> To die so suddenly? So young to go
> Under the obscure, cold, rotting, wormy ground!
> To be nailed down into a narrow place;
> To see no more sweet sunshine . . .

[36] I feel that this was not worth doing, because it is only a feeble echo of the tremendous speech of Claudio in *Measure for Measure*; but Shelley is not the only poet who has been Shakespearian by the appropriation of worms and rot and such Elizabethan stage properties. But other lines, such as

> worse than despair,
> Worse than the bitterness of death, is hope:
> It is the only ill which can find place
> Upon the giddy, sharp and narrow hour
> Tottering beneath us

are more, in their context, like Dryden – though in *The Cenci* resemblances are confused by the nature of the subject, which is more sympathetic to Ford than to either Shakespeare or Dryden. And much more obviously than in the play of Shelley – which I have chosen for mention because it is obviously of Elizabethan model – is the debt to Dryden present in the plays of Byron.

[37] 6 The skill of Dryden's blank verse is all the more admirable when one admits that it is a *tour de force*: blank verse is not natural to him. We shall see that in one of his critical essays he presents a most able defence of the rhymed couplet in heroic drama; but I always feel that here Dryden found his reasons for what he believed upon instinct. Just as he had to

defend the heroic drama because it happened to be the only form possible for the time, so I suspect that he defended the rhymed couplet because it was the form of verse which came most natural to him. There is not a line in *All for Love* which has, to my ear, the conversational tone of the best of Dryden's satires. As he adapted himself to drama, so he had, as far as possible, to adapt the drama to himself. Not that he was the first or the last to rhyme on the stage. But there is no other poet to whom the couplet came so naturally as the vehicle of speech as it did to Dryden; what he did not do with it cannot be done; and his couplet, miraculously, [38] is speech. There are two reasons for the comparative success of his rhyming in drama; first, he regularly relaxed the phrasing and made his lines run on as much as possible, so that they are technically different from his satire, and though still closely packed, less compressed; and of course he helps himself out with broken lines and triplets. The other reason is that he limits himself to those dramatic effects for which the rhymed couplet is adequate. Now the kind of play that he tried to write, and succeeded in writing, was a kind which would have been in existence, whether Dryden had written or not; and as it was there, it is wholly a merit on the part of Dryden to have written that kind of play in rhymed verse. The rhymed plays, such as *The Conquest of Granada* and *Aurung-Zebe*, would *not* have been such good plays as they are had they been written in blank verse, even blank verse as good as Dryden's. So that Dryden himself, in defending rhyme in the drama, oversimplifies the problem: for as a [39] particular type of play modifies versification, so the play is in turn modified by the versification.

7 No one still supposes that Dryden made his plays out of whole cloth on the French pattern. What there is in common, including the Spanish and Oriental themes, can be enumerated. But at the same time we do not always recognise how very different is the *ethos* of either Corneille or Racine from that of Dryden. The order of French tragedy sprang from an origin which has its parallel in the Senecal drama of the Countess of Pembroke's circle, the sort of play that Fulke Greville wrote. I do not think that Dryden's drama has any essential relation to that abortive movement. The great French tragedy is classical in the sense that it is strongly moral. Now Dryden's plays are emphatically not 'moral' in this way; they are diversified, certainly, with fine, if not very profound, moralising, but that is not at all the same thing. The Elizabethan tragedy was not moral either, as the French was; but Shakespeare's work as a [40] whole, and some of the best plays of his contemporaries, explore the possibilities of human sin and suffering so profoundly as to give us something more than morals. But with Dryden I am afraid you get something less; he is a moralist only

in speeches, not in plot; and the rest is a pageantry of humanity in heroic roles. And so I think that the true antecedent of Dryden is to be found in the plays of Beaumont and Fletcher. There is a similar exploitation of stage effect, the same dependence upon the strained situation for its immediate dramatic effectiveness. I cannot myself see any fundamental resemblance between the plays of Shakespeare's last period and the work of Beaumont and Fletcher; but the resemblance between *A King and No King* and *Don Sebastian* in their *ethos* is obvious. And if I am right in drawing this comparison, then it may be allowed that Dryden came at the right time, and that he did well to substitute for the enervated Jacobean blank verse of Beaumont and Fletcher his firm and masculine couplet.

[41] 8 We must call Dryden's plays 'heroic drama' because we certainly cannot call them tragedy. Even though he kills people off at the end, and though a dying queen raves in couplets better than one would conceive it possible for rhymed couplets to rave, what Dryden has is not the sense of tragedy at all. Indeed, it is from one point of view ironic to call these plays even 'heroic'; for though he does not introduce the comic scene, some of his most effective passages are in a tone of witty satire, and are those in which the protagonists appear least heroic. For Dryden is an observer of human nature, rather than a creator.

9 I suspect that when Dryden regretted his efforts in comedy he was not merely deploring their licentiousness, which seems pretty innocent fun nowadays, but less consciously admitting their defects. Everything else that Dryden attempted, he brought to perfection in its kind, but in comedy he is a crude precursor of Congreve, and less admirable than Wycherley at his [42] best. His is the Restoration world, certainly, not that of the simple Elizabethan humours; but his most polished figures of comedy are, compared to the finest Restoration comedy, almost bumpkins; that delightful lady of *Marriage à la Mode*, Melantha, is still too 'humorous' in her French affectations; and the fun of *Mr Limberham* is not altogether well bred. What I think is most noticeable, however, is that in his comedies Dryden was not able to bring his prose to perfection; it is a transition prose; and I doubt, anyway, whether his heart was in it. Dryden was quick enough to recognise the real right thing in prose dialogue; when young Mr Congreve came along no one extolled him more highly than the old master of English letters. Congreve's prose is truly what we ordinarily call poetic; at any rate, I believe that the only two dramatists who have ever attained perfect prose in comedy – meaning perfect prose *for* comedy – are Shakespeare and Congreve.

JOHN DRYDEN: THE DRAMATIST

10 But Dryden was not *naturally* a dramatist, [43] as Shakespeare and Congreve were natural dramatists. His direct service to English drama is – apart from the value of his plays themselves – but here I am estimating the obligation of later times to Dryden, and not Dryden himself – his direct service is largely negative: had he not developed his own form of heroic play, which was suited to, and representative of his time, it is likely that a more and more etiolated Jacobeanism, with decayed versification, would have lingered on. His great service to the drama is merely incidental to his service to English letters.

11 We are apt to think for convenience, and to forget that it is merely a convenience, of the development of prose and the development of verse as two parallel currents which never mingle. But Dryden's verse, for example, affects the history of English prose almost as much as his prose does. I have suggested that it is a bad sign when the written language and the spoken language drift too far apart. It is also bad when poetry and prose are too far apart; certainly, a poet [44] can learn essential knowledge from the study of the best prose, and a prose writer can learn from the study of the best verse; for there are problems of expression common to both. But for Dryden's verse, we might not have had the perfection of Congreve's prose: though this is not demonstrable. Prose which has *nothing* in common with verse is dead; verse which has nothing in common with prose is probably artificial, false, diffuse, and syntactically weak. We commonly find versifiers who are prosaic, and prose writers who dress out their flat writing with withered flowers of poetic rhetoric, and this is just the opposite of what I have in mind. I do not believe that in any modern civilisation prose can flourish if all the verse being written is bad, or that good verse can be written in an atmosphere choked with bad prose. If I am right, the beneficent influence of Dryden's poetry cannot be confined to those poets his disciples, but is diffused over the whole of English thought and expression.

[45] 12 I cannot, finally, pretend to demonstrate that Dryden had a beneficent influence on English tragic drama – but only for the reason that since Dryden there has been no English tragic drama to influence. I have tried to affirm a belief, at least, that Dryden's dramatic work has, besides the pleasure it can give us for its merits unique in English literature, importance in the following ways: first, I believe that it strengthened his command of his verse medium for other work, and enlarged his interests; then, because of its interest for his own time, and because of the importance of the theatre in his time, it helped to consolidate his influence upon his contemporaries and successors; and it is an essential

member of the body of his work, which must be taken as a whole; and lastly, because it gave him the knowledge and the opportunity for some of his best critical writing – which last, as I shall try to show next week, has been of enduring value.

Variants from 1931:

Title *John Dryden – II* | Dryden the Dramatist

[Para. 1 not represented.]

2   *reading* virtues] reading virtues
    the *dramatic*] the dramatic
    the *poetic*] the poetic
    that which expressed . . . the text before:] that which expressed . . . the text before.
    theatrically dramatic] theatrically dramatic
    Theatrically] Theatrically
    poetic dramatic value] poetic dramatic value

[Para. 3 headed **Shakespeare and Dryden**.]

3   less *poetic*] less poetic
    less *dramatic*] less dramatic
    ah, soldier] 'Ah, soldier'
    peculiarly *poetic*] peculiarly poetic
    ah, soldier] 'Ah, soldier'

[Para. 4 headed **Influence of his Blank Verse**.]

4   *purely* dramatic] purely dramatic
    , in dreams,] in dreams
    [Between 'As Chapman says' and 'As for the verse of *All for Love*:] [Not represented.]

[Para. 5 headed **Master of the Couplet**.]

5   superiority to, and difference from] superiority to, and difference from,
    more like Dryden,] more like Dryden (whether they were aware of it or not),
    lines, such as] lines, such as –
    beneath us] beneath us,
    than to either Shakespeare or Dryden.] than to either Shakespeare or Dryden, in the blank verse plays

6   believed upon instinct] already believed upon instinct
    rhymed couplet] couplet rhymed verse
    is speech] *is* speech
    [Between 'adequate.' and 'The rhymed plays':] [Not represented.]

[Para. 7 headed **Humanity in heroic Role**.]

8   cannot call them] cannot call it

9   *Marriage*] Mariage
    doubt, anyway,] doubt anyway
    is truly] is, truly,
    ordinarily call] ordinarily, but confusingly, call

[Para. 10 headed **Services to Drama**.]

10 *naturally*] naturally
His direct service to English drama . . . is largely negative:] His direct service to English drama is – apart from the value of his plays themselves – largely negative: representative of] representative of,

11 I have suggested] I suggested last week
nothing in common] nothing in common

[Para. 12 headed **Creator of a Dramatic Type**.]

12 as I shall try to show] as I shall try to show next week

Additional para. But possibly, if serious poetic drama is ever again written, and I believe that it will be, Dryden's plays may have another service to perform. The few civilisations which have contributed essential types of poetic drama to the world's literature have none of them succeeded in producing more than one type apiece, and that usually has been perfected within a short space of time. In England there has been the late medieval drama of which the consummate example is *Everyman*, the Elizabethan drama, and the third, so different from the Elizabethan as to be a distinct type, that of Dryden. Dryden as a dramatist has his antecedents and derivations, like everyone else; he has his limitations, narrower than those of the best of Shakespeare's contemporaries; but no dramatist has ever come nearer to creating a dramatic type by his own solitary exertions. With so much variety, why should there not still be more? And any poet who had the ambitious design of writing a verse play would do well to saturate himself in all three kinds of English drama – he will have a better chance of writing something which will be not a pastiche of any, but different from all.

Dryden the Critic

JDPDC 49–68.
In para. 12 'others in others' has been emended to 'others in other'.

1 The prose writings of Dryden, whether in the standard edition of W. P. Ker, or in the convenient 'Everyman' edition, consist entirely of prefaces to various volumes of verse or of verse plays. For the most part, they are concerned either with his views on poetic drama, or with his views on the art of translation. They are occasional, and constitute a kind of commentary on what he was doing in verse; they are the notes of a practitioner. They are obviously important in two ways: in the history of the development of English prose style, and in the history of English criticism; they are of further importance to us here, in reckoning the importance of the whole work of Dryden; for they form a part of this whole work which cannot be neglected.

2 Dryden's Essays are, first, important in the history of English prose. As I have said, Dryden's verse exercised the most vital influence [50] on English poetry for nearly a century; similarly, his prose had a temporary, and has a permanent, value for English critical prose style; but the great influence of Dryden cannot be divided into two currents: his main influence was upon the matter of thought and feeling out of which both verse and prose are made; his own verse and prose can therefore not be wholly separated, though we may say that he probably influenced prose by his verse still more than by his prose. I mean, that if we consider him as a writer of critical prose alone, we cannot say that his influence was dominant. We find similar tendencies in style in other contemporary writers on other subjects; and no one could go so far as to maintain that but for Dryden, we should have had neither the essays of Addison nor the writings of Swift at the point of perfection which these two writers reached. One can more plausibly conjecture, that but for the criticism of Dryden, we might not have had Addison's critical essays on Milton or on the ballads; for Dryden [51] was positively the first master of English criticism; and he set a good example for critics by practising what he preached.

3 In Dryden's prose style, we find no such painful development as we find in his verse. His prose seems to spring spontaneously, perfectly modelled. There is nothing surprising about this; it would be surprising if Dryden had not written good prose. Anyone who has studied his poetry, from his crude beginnings to his perfect accomplishment, must be aware that Dryden was gradually acquiring those elements of good writing which are fundamental to both verse and prose, whilst he was freeing himself from the artificial poeticality of the previous age. His training in verse was training in prose as well; so that when, in maturity, he set himself, after the example of Corneille, to writing critical introductions to his own verse, his prose style is perfectly finished – indeed, larger and more supple than the prose style of Corneille himself. I have conceded that Dryden's prose [52] is only one of the prose styles of his time that went to the formation of our form of classic English prose; but among these styles it is certainly one of the most admirable. He has all the virtues you would expect. He neither descends too low, nor attempts to fly too high; he is perfectly clear as to what he has to say; and he says it always with the right control and changes of intensity of feeling. His wit exceeds that of all his contemporaries; it contributes elegance and liveliness of figure, without ever overreaching itself into facetiousness. He has not the passion of his cousin Swift; but he everywhere convinces us of the serious, singleminded integrity of his love of truth in poetry; and his contempt for shams; and no writer in the next and more polished generation, not even Addison, has more urbanity. 'Elegance' and 'urbanity'; two words of commendation which have long been in disrepute; but which are always needed.

4 I know of no finer example of the precision and also of the range of Dryden's prose style, [53] than the essay which we usually read first: the *Essay of Dramatic Poesy*. It may seem an absurd and unjust comparison, but I can think of no essay in dialogue form in English, which on its own plane – less sublime, less profound in thought – compares more favourably with some of the dialogues of Plato: it reminds me, at the beginning particularly, of the beautiful introduction to the *Theaetetus*. 'It was that memorable day, in the first summer of the late war, when our navy engaged the Dutch.' No one who has ever read it can forget the undertone of naval cannonading above which are raised the voices of Eugenius, Crites, Neander and Lisideius as they discuss in their barge on the river the various practices of Greek, French and English drama, the merits of the several tragic writers, and the claims of blank and rhymed verse. And here, and in all his prose, Dryden is, as in his verse, in perfect training; there is nowhere an ounce of superfluous fat; he is neither anemic nor apoplectic; every blow delivered has just the right force [54] behind it. When we read such memorable phrases as these from his essay, *Examen Poeticum*:

> The same parts and applications which have made me a poet might have raised me to any honours of the gown, which are often given to men of as little learning and less honesty than myself. No Government has ever been, or ever can be, wherein timeservers and blockheads will not be uppermost. The persons are only changed, but the same jugglings in State, the same hypocrisy in religion, the same self-interest and mismanagement, will remain for ever. Blood and money will be lavished in all ages only for the preferment of new faces and old consciences.

Who, reading such passages, cannot understand at once that they should be by the author of *Absalom and Achitophel*, and who could doubt that their author, had he set himself the task, might have been one of the greatest of political orators?

5 But to turn from the manner to the matter of these prefaces, we observe first that they are [55] the first serious literary criticism in English by an English poet. We cannot quite say the first serious criticism, because there is, for instance, the contemporary criticism of Thomas Rymer – a critic of whom Dryden speaks highly, and of whom I should be tempted to speak more highly still. But Dryden was the first poet to theorise, on any large scale, about his own craft. I say on any large scale. There had been criticism in the previous age; but the only one I know, which has any precise and permanent value, is the admirable short treatise of Campion

on metre and quantity – unless one except the reply to it by Daniel, and the graceful but ineffectual skirmishing of Philip Sidney. Dryden had, certainly, the example of the prefaces of Corneille in French, to which he was clearly indebted. But Dryden has proved a more important critic for the English language than was Corneille for the French. Rapin and Bossu, to whom Dryden refers, were more important in France than their colleagues in England; it is [56] possible that France has had too many critics of poetry who could not practise it, and England too many poets who were not self-critical; but in Dryden we have, considering his limitation by his own time, an almost ideal balance between the critic and the creative poet.

6   And as for his limitations of taste by his own time – I should be glad if I could be sure that I or any critic to-day was as catholic in taste, or had such justification for his limitations. It would seem nowadays a futile pastime, for instance, to turn Chaucer into modern English. But for Dryden's time it was no more futile than it would be considered nowadays, to paraphrase such a thing as *Gawain and the Green Knight*, or even Anglo-Saxon. For one point, Chaucer was then a neglected and unappreciated author; Dryden was not, any more than most of his contemporaries, a scholarly student of middle English; and it shows great perceptiveness on his part to have recognised Chaucer and praised him as he did. Furthermore, Dryden [57] could not consider the English language, as we very foolishly and lazily are inclined to do, as finished and complete; he was in the thick of the struggle to modernise it. We must keep in mind this latter point, when we read his strictures upon the Elizabethans, and especially upon Shakespeare. Possibly, in retrospect, we are right in thinking that he somewhat exaggerates the worth of Fletcher, relative to Shakespeare. But take his comments upon Shakespeare one by one, and you will find, I believe, that most of them are just. We are so habituated to considering Shakespeare above criticism, that we cannot admit that Dryden's praise of Shakespeare is as high praise as our own; and that if we stop to apprehend the values which were rightly important for Dryden in his time, his occasional censure of Shakespeare is usually right.

7   It is natural that, with the French theory and practice in view, and with the imperfect knowledge of the Greek theatre, and of the meaning of Aristotle's comments upon it, current at the [58] time, Dryden should often have gone wrong in his dramatic criticism. Owing to thus abusing the sense of Aristotle's *Poetics*, many men have erred in trying to erect a final theory of what the theatre ought to be and must be from what it has

been. We must not look to Dryden's theories for the genesis of Dryden's practice in the theatre; rather, we find a theory which is a compromise between Aristotle, as he understood Aristotle through distorting French lenses, and his own practice which is itself a compromise between earlier English practice and French practice. Much, for which he appeals to authority, is merely, in his own practice, the result of a sense of form and order working against the disorderliness of the Elizabethan stage. And it must be admitted that the Elizabethans neglected certain very positive dramatic virtues. We are accustomed, and rightly, to look to Shakespeare for more than dramatic virtues, for a 'pattern' of feeling which Dryden could not see, because Dryden was not looking for it but for [59] something else; and, therefore, some of Dryden's criticisms of Shakespeare's later plays appear to us supercilious and shallow. But Shakespeare could play his own mighty music upon any instruments that came to hand; and he was not concerned, consciously, greatly to alter the form which he found ready. But Dryden's common sense, and sense of order, were imperative to him; and we must take his theory largely as a kind of legal justification for what he felt was right.

8 Dryden first, following the French, misunderstands the Aristotelian theory of the Unities of Time and Place; and then, disapproving of the French strictness (he is a good patriot, and never fails to speak up for English drama against French when the occasion offers), proceeds to qualify it. For instance, he reprehends the attempt to condense the history of twenty-four years into a representation of three hours (one would like to read his critique of *Back to Methuselah*), but approves the representation of [60] twenty-four hours in the same space. What is true is, I think, in practice, that more *unity of poetic feeling* (which is the only unity that matters) can be obtained *as a rule*, with a minimum of difference between times and places. I say *as a rule*, for some actions obviously cannot be represented at all without making great leaps of time or space. Dryden's view, as it stands, is literally absurd: for it would make *Coriolanus* a better play than *Antony and Cleopatra*, solely for the reason that the distance from Rome to Actium is shorter than that from Rome to Egypt. But the rigidity of Dryden's theory must not blind us to the accuracy of Dryden's common sense.

9 Here and there Dryden goes wrong in ways which it is less easy to pardon. For instance, he speaks of the comic element in Elizabethan tragedy as being employed for what we call 'comic relief'. No doubt, from the point of view of dramatic effect, this comic element was, for the great majority of the Elizabethan au-[61]dience, comic *relief*. 'Laughter

and tears' are still advertised in attractions to some American film or other; and doubtless the Elizabethans liked to sandwich their laughter and tears as much as modern audiences do. But a very little examination of Elizabethan drama, and especially of Shakespeare, will convince us that the comic is not really 'relief' at all, but on the contrary, at [its best an intensification of the sombreness. The Porter in *Macbeth*, the Gravedigger in *Hamlet*, the Fool in *Lear*, the drunkenness of Lepidus in *Antony and Cleopatra* – there is no 'relief' in these: they merely make the horror or tragedy more real by transposing it for a moment from the sublime to the common. But we were wrong if we expected Dryden to perceive this; for it is just the sort of thing he would not have perceived.

10 Dryden was not only the first great English poet to set down carefully his theories about the practice of his own art, but he is also, allowing for the limitations of his age, what we may [62] call the *normal* critic. Johnson, in his *Lives of the Poets*, adopts a more particular method; his general views of the nature of poetry, and regulations of the art, occur here and there during the course of biographical critiques of particular poets; Dryden is directly concerned with the proper art of poetry, and his remarks on particular poets occur only as illustrations. Coleridge, in his great disorderly book of criticism, is no safe model for other reasons than mere disorder, for he does not restrain himself to criticism, but runs into philosophy and aesthetics. Wordsworth is occupied, in his fine prefaces to the *Lyrical Ballads*, with defending his own practices, and is not accordingly a model for normal criticisms of poetry; and Matthew Arnold is too largely concerned with finding the moral lesson. Dryden is concerned neither with appreciation nor with aesthetics. He was fortunate in his age, when philosophical writing was practised in England with a language which had just been developed to the point of express-[63]ing adequately abstract ideas, and before writing about poetry had come to mean philosophising about it. It is also fortunate for us to have had a critic who wrote so well and with such authority about poetry, at a time when neither the fundamental nature of the poetic activity nor the social function of poetry was yet considered the subject matter of literary criticism. As testimony of the clarity of Dryden's expression, and the just sobriety of his theory, I mention an essay called *The Proper Wit of Poetry*, and particularly the third paragraph, in which he defines Wit. It will be observed that it does not occur to Dryden to distinguish to the point of isolation the reasoning from the imaginative faculty; it would not have occurred to him that there was or should be anything *irrational* in poetic imagination. He says –

The first happiness of the poet's imagination is properly invention, or finding of the thought; the second is fancy, or the variation, deriving or mould-[64]ing of that thought, as the judgment represents it proper to the subject; the third is elocution, or the art of clothing and adorning that thought so found and varied in apt, significant and sounding words: the quickness of the imagination is seen in the invention, the fertility in the fancy and the accuracy in the expression.

The distinction between the thought and the image, and the distinction between the thought and the clothing of it in elocution, are foreign to modern theory of poetry; but I think that these distinctions are safer than many that more recent writers have made; and the part of inspiration (or free association from the unconscious) and the part of conscious labour are justly kept in place.

11 A great merit of Dryden as a critic and as a critical influence is that he never transgresses the line beyond which the criticism of poetry becomes something else. In that happy age it did not occur to him to enquire what poetry was *for*, how it affected the nerves of listeners, how [65] it sublimated the wishes of the poet, whom it should satisfy, and all the other questions which really have nothing to do with poetry as poetry; and the poet was not expected to be either a sibyl or a prophet. The purpose of poetry and drama was to *amuse*; but it was to amuse properly; and the larger forms of poetry should have a moral significance; by exhibiting the thoughts and passions of man through lively image and melodious verse, to edify and to refine the reader and auditor.

12 I do not know that we have improved upon this conception of the place and function of poetry. I do not pretend that Dryden as a critic is often profound, any more than I make that claim for him as a poet; but the more I consider contemporary reflexion upon poetry, the more thankful I am for what we may call Dryden's critical orthodoxy. In his opinions there is no extravagance. Now it seems to me that there is a very widespread tendency, which takes various forms nowadays, to treat poetry as a kind of [66] religion or substitute for religion. The germ, or something more developed than the germ, of this way of thinking is to be found in the criticism of Matthew Arnold, who is to that extent an heresiarch. Arnold dismisses altogether the intellectual element in religion, and leaves only art and morals; art, and particularly literary art, inculcates morals, and truly moral art is all that Arnold leaves us in the place of religious faith. It is only a short step, if any step be necessary, to

finding in literature the satisfaction which we deny ourselves in religion. This new confusion takes several forms. I find it in the humanism of Irving Babbitt, and in the more recent theories of critics of such opposed views as Middleton Murry and I. A. Richards. Mr Murry seems to maintain that poetry *is* religion; Mr Richards rather more moderately that poetry is the best thing we can have nowadays instead of religion. I am not concerned to criticise such theories from a theological point of view; for indeed they fall beyond the reach of such criticism; I [67] am anxious rather lest they distort our enjoyment of poetry. The poet tends to be appointed, not indeed a priest of his own cult, for he is not allowed to interpret himself; but rather a Grand Llama imprisoned in princely privacy while the critical priests carry on the real business. A dead poet for this purpose is better than a living one, as he cannot be so indiscreet as to speak for himself. But criticism itself will be biassed, according to the particular oracles we consult; and as some critics will find their religion in some poetry and others in other, the judgement of poetry will become of dwindling interest.

13 Dryden, then, both as poet and as critic, seems to me a very great defender of sanity. I do not think that I have made any extravagant claims for him. For that matter, I have not said much that is original. Dryden is no discovery; there are few of his merits as a writer that have not been discovered and brought to light by one or another earlier critic. I have no desire to see his [68] works on every drawing room table, or even to see a generation of versifiers employ their talent upon political satire and theological controversy. I do not suppose that at any time he will ever be anyone's favourite poet, or engross the adolescent mind for a season as the romantic poets can do. I have purposely avoided trying to give a course in 'How to Enjoy Dryden', because the people who can really enjoy his poetry need no assistance from me or from anyone. But it is worth while to know what Dryden did for the English language in verse and in prose, because we shall understand better what the language is, and of what it is capable.

Variants from 1931:

Title *John Dryden – III.* | *Dryden the Critic, Defender of Sanity*
[Para. 1 not represented.]

2 As I have said] As I tried to hint last week
   feeling out of which] feeling, out of which
[Para. 3 not represented.]
[Para. 4 headed **The Prose of Perfect Training**.]

JOHN DRYDEN: THE CRITIC • 649

4   at the beginning particularly] at the beginning, particularly
    Lisideius, as they discuss in their barge on the river] Lisideius as they discuss, in their barge on the river,
    application] applications
    Consciences. Who] Consciences.—Who

[Para. 5 headed **Critic and Poet in Balance**.]

5   of whom I should] of whom, had I time and place, I should

[Para. 6 headed **His Literary Sympathies**.]

[Para. 7 headed **Dramatic Criticism**.]

7   concerned, consciously] concerned, consciously,

8   Dryden] For instance, Dryden
    Methuselah] Methusalah'
    unity of poetic feeling] unity of poetic feeling
    as a rule] as a rule
    as a rule] as a rule

9   *relief*] relief
    film] American film

[Para. 10 headed **The Normal Critic**.]

10   normal criticisms] normal criticism is the correct record of variants.
    in England with a language] in England, with a language
    nor the social function of poetry] , nor the social function of poetry,
    irrational] irrational
    so found and varied] , so found and varied,
    in the fancy] in the fancy,
    are foreign] is foreign
    free association] free association from the unconscious

11   *amuse*] amuse

[Para. 12 not represented.]

[Para. 13 headed **Defender of Sanity**.]

13   think that I have made] think, in reviewing what I have said in these three talks, that I have made
    of what it is capable, and of what it is still capable.] of what it is capable, and of what it can be.

A Commentary

C., 12. 46 (Oct. 1932), 73-9. Signed 'T. S. E.' Gallup C337.

It is greatly to the credit of the intellectuals of post-War Germany, living in a country which has been more politics-ridden than any other of Western Europe, and in an atmosphere which one might suppose most discouraging to dispassionate thought, that they have been able to produce so much that is first rate. It is a pity that work of this kind finds little appreciation in England; the spring comes slowly up our way, and modern Germany is only known by some of its novels and by a few books of topical interest. Writers of more permanent importance than Spengler are unknown. Such names as those of Heidegger in philosophy and Heim in theology are known to only a handful; Friedrich Gundolf and Max Scheler are slightly known to some of our readers. Ernst Robert Curtius is in a different category from any of these, and is already much more widely known, although we must admit that he is, like other important German writers, better known in Paris than in London. One justification for his being less known here – except to readers of *The Criterion* – is that he has occupied himself very largely for many years with the task of interpreting French civilisation and French literature to Germany, as a number of books: his *Balzac*, his *Proust*, his *Französischer Geist im Neuen Europa*, and the book which has been recently (and not too well) translated under the title of *The Civilization of France* (Allen & Unwin: 12s. 6d. net) all attest. But as one of those men such as Gide and Larbaud in France, Hofmannsthal in Austria and Ortega y Gasset in Spain, who have steadily laboured in the interest of the European spirit, his work deserves as much attention from us as from the French.

His recent small book, *Deutscher Geist in Gefahr* (Deutsche-Verlags-Anstalt, pp. 131) is perhaps not a book to be translated, inasmuch as it is a direct appeal to his German readers, but it is certainly a book to be read by [74] everyone who can follow a simple and lucid German style, and who can also appreciate the problems of our time as being more serious than such as can be eased by national or imperial nostrums. It consists of five essays, of which the most valuable to foreigners are perhaps the last two, 'Soziologie oder Revolution?' and 'Humanismus als Initiative'. The second of these is one of the best and most reasonable expositions of a 'humanist' attitude that I have ever read. But it was by a passage in the first that I was especially struck. Dr Curtius is concerned with the view of a contemporary sociologist named Mannheim, of whose work I am ignorant, and who has hitherto been only a name to me. 'Indeed', says Curtius, 'for many contemporary thinkers, Mannheim among them, there seems to exist a crude antithesis between Change and Value on the one side, and Permanence (*Dauer*) and Valuelessness on the other.'

The antithesis is not a new one. It is at least as old as pre-Socratic philosophy, and metaphysics has struggled with its conundrums ever since. It is the form in which it is accepted to-day, not only by technical philosophers like Mannheim, but as an unconscious assumption of popular philosophy, that makes it interesting and important for us. One might expect it, in its crudity, to have become out-dated; it seems to belong to the year 1910, with the pleasant essays of William James (as popular a writer for his time as are Eddington and Jeans in ours) and with the epidemic of Bergsonism. But the course of events has led it to take less obvious forms. We cannot deny that the words (so impressive because of their association with physics) *static* and *dynamic* are popularly used almost always, the one disparagingly, the other eulogistically. We may have forgotten the philosophy of James, we may even sneer at the idea of 'progress' (and perhaps 'progress' has only become unfashionable because we have been able to qualify it as 'Victorian'); but we are still over-valuing the changing and ignoring the permanent. As Curtius remarks, the permanent has come to mean Paralysis and Death.

[75] One of the consequences, as it seems to me, of our failure to grasp the proper relation of the Eternal and the Transient, is our *overestimation of the importance of our own time*. This is natural to an age which, whatever its professions, is still imbued with the doctrine of progress. The doctrine of progress cannot make the future seem to us more real than the present – this faith our senses bluntly deny; and a future in time, of infinite and indefinite extent, is something which we can by no means realise. But the doctrine of progress, while it can do little to make the future more real to us, has a very strong influence towards making the past less real to us. For it leads us to take for granted that the past, any part or the whole of it, has its meaning only in the present; leads us to ask of any past age, not what it has been in itself, not what the individuals composing it have made of themselves, but, what has that age done for *us*? If it has left us any inheritance that we still value, then that age is justified; and when we have ceased to value anything that the age has left us, then that age has come to appear to be just pure waste, and might as well have never existed. The values of a past age are right only so far as they serve the values of our own – whatever our values may happen to be; if our values happen to be those of an H. G. Wells, then a peculiar account of history ensues. The notion that a past age or civilisation might be great in itself, precious in the eye of God, because it succeeded in adjusting the delicate relation of the Eternal to the Transient, is completely alien to us. No age has been more egocentric, so

to speak, than our own; others have been ego-centric through ignorance, ours through complacent historical knowledge. Everything in the past was a necessary evil – evil in itself, but necessary because it led up to the present. Thus we take ourselves, and our transient affairs, too seriously.

I am here, of course, distinguishing very sharply the theoretic from the practical activity. In the practical activity, every living generation takes itself with equal seriousness; especially those members of it who have not [76] enough to eat, or those who can get no work, and feel that they are superfluous; and all of us in so far as we live to struggle for anything whatever. We must, perforce, treat our own economic crisis as more serious in this sense than the decay of the Roman Empire, or the Black Death. Those of us who do not understand technical matters must leave them to those who do; but we are at least as well entitled as the technicians to investigate to what extent our difficulties really are just technical and how far they are spiritual. And it may be that the *crise dans l'homme* is all the more serious exactly because we take ourselves, theoretically, too seriously; because we have ignored the supernatural and the eternal.

Our preference for the changing over the permanent manifests itself in various details of life. One instance is a prevalent tendency in literary criticism: the tendency to treat each work of art, especially those contemporary with ourselves, as a manifestation of the spirit of the age. The first-rate artist, the original writer, we say, is he who has most fully voiced this spirit; and when he has done this, he has done enough and has done all; our criticism consists in explaining what the spirit of the age is and how it is expressed in the writer's work. We are, in short, interested solely in ourselves, and the poet engages our attention merely by telling us about ourselves. Even as a practical instrument of valuation, this method is no very reliable one; for it will not show us how to distinguish between the great writer who has helped to create his time and the clever ape who is no more than the instantaneous mimic of its society manners. But even if it discriminated accurately, this attitude would still be mistaken. All great art is in a sense a document on its time; but great art is never merely a document, for mere documentation is not art. All great art has something permanent and universal about it, and reflects the permanent as well as the changing – a particular relation in time of the permanent and the transient. And as no great art is explicable simply by the society of its time, so it is not fully explicable simply by the personality of its author: in the greatest [77] poetry there is always a hint of something behind, something impersonal, something in relation to which the author has been no more than the passive (if not always pure) medium. A good deal of brilliant criticism seems to me wasted labour just because it ignores the enduring in favour of the topical.

The problem for our time is, I think, still more complicated than as stated by Dr Curtius. It is not simply the problem of realising an exact and delicate relation between the various pairs of opposites; it is also a problem of realising what each is. We have only to consider the communist Utopia. Here, it may be affirmed, we have a relation of 'static' and 'dynamic'. The philosophy of change is here to be enjoyed with the utmost gusto. For, not only things do change, and must change by dialectical necessity, but we want them to change and can help them to change, much as a group of small boys will ostentatiously lend their hands when a couple of burly mechanics are pushing a broken down motor car. We thus gain a great access of vitality in assisting the inevitable. But we have the satisfaction of the static too, for we look forward to the consummation of the classless and government-less society, upon which, apparently, no further change is possible or necessary. But the believer in the values only of this world can only offer himself a dilemma. If the progress of mankind is to continue as long as man survives upon this earth, then, as I have said, progress becomes merely change; for the values of man will change, and a world of changed values is valueless to *us* – just as we, being a part of the past, will be valueless to *it*. Or if the progress of mankind is to continue only until a 'perfect' state of society is reached, then this state of society will be valueless simply because of its perfection. It will be, at best, a smooth-running machine which runs without a purpose; an efficient bureaucracy with no meaning: and this it might well become. Does the bee in the efficient bee-hive find anything about it abhorrent or repulsive? No. Does it find anything to admire or aspire to? No. Of course any idea of earthly perfection must be static; to this extent the [78] communist ideal is right. I remember many years ago hearing an eminent man of letters, now deceased, remark that he had just read Plato's *Republic*, and hearing him criticise the Platonic ideal state as 'too static'. It did not occur to me until too late to mention, that an 'ideal state' *must* be an ideal of the *static*. But – apart from the fact that 'justice' meant not quite the same thing to the Greek philosophers that it seems to mean to communists – the Greek ideal state was one in which each citizen could realise, according to his capacity, the highest values of art and religion: it was, as in the Christian conception, a state in which each citizen could *become* perfect. For we cannot banish *becoming* any more than we can banish *being. Estote perfecti.*

It seems to me, accordingly, that the humane and civilised faith must comprehend all the others. We must believe, first, that the human race can, if it will, improve indefinitely; that it can improve both its material well-being and its spiritual capacities. We must also have a conception of a perfect society attainable on earth. And we must also admit the inadequacy of these ambitions and ideals. We must say that man, however he is improved by social and economic reorganisation, by eugenics, and by any other external means possible to the science of intellect, will still be only the *natural* man, at an infinite remove from perfection. And we must affirm that perfection is as nearly attainable for man here and now as it ever will be in any future in any place. That there can be no art *greater* than the art which has already been created: there will only be different and necessarily different combinations of the eternal and the changing in the forms of art. That men individually can never attain anything higher than has been already attained among the Saints; but that in any place, at any time, another Saint may be born. Such a just perception of the permanent relations of the Enduring and the Changing should on the one hand make us realise our own time in better proportion to times past and times to come: we are now inclined to think of our age and moment as hysterically as people did in the year 1000. [79] And on the other hand it should help us to think better of our time, as not isolated or unique, and remind us that fundamentally our individual problems and duties are the same as they have been for others at any time – and equally our opportunities. What we can do towards the greatest material well-being of the greatest number is indeed of the utmost importance; but important only so long as we remember that the extent of our accomplishment can be only to remove obstacles in the way of individual self-improvement: such obstacles as want, insecurity, overwork and idleness.

The death of Goldsworthy Lowes Dickinson must be commemorated in the *Criterion*, for it matters not only to his friends and colleagues and all the successive generations at King's, but to everyone who sympathised – without necessarily sharing his views – with his courageous, humane and civilised attitude towards public affairs, with which his classical scholarship was in happy combination. Death at his age is premature and painful for friends and admirers; but Dickinson always seemed – at least to one who knew him only causally over a period of some fifteen years – much younger than his age: he always was, and always would have been, so eagerly sympathetic and understanding towards young men and new writers. We hope to publish some appreciation in our next issue.

We regret to discover that the name of one of the translators of the fragment of Hermann Broch's novel published in our last issue, Mrs Willa Muir, was given incorrectly.

From T. S. Eliot

Testimony no. XII of those printed in *The Cantos of Ezra Pound: Some Testimonies by Ernest Hemingway, Ford Madox Ford, T. S. Eliot, Hugh Walpole, Archibald MacLeish, James Joyce, and Others* (Farrar & Rinehart, Inc., New York), 16–17, was. publ. early in 1933: Gallup B21. But Eliot's testimony is dated '1 Dec. 1932' at the end.

I don't think that the publication of Ezra's *Cantos* in this country needs any word from me or from anybody else. It is rather an impertinence. There was a time when it did not seem unfitting for me to write a pamphlet, *Ezra Pound, His Poetry and Metric* but Ezra was then known only to a few and I was so completely unknown that it seemed more decent that the pamphlet should appear anonymously. I owe too much to Ezra to be a critic. (I wish that the manuscript of *The Waste Land* with Ezra's criticisms and still more important, his excisions, thank God he reduced a mess of some [17] eight hundred lines to about half its size, might some day be exhumed. John Quinn had it. As a masterpiece of critical literature.) I have preached the *Cantos* for some years now to young practitioners as well as tried to tell them what I owed to Pound in London, Paris, Excideuil and Rapallo. (It shall not all be told.) One result is that – I blame no one – my copy of the *Cantos* had disappeared and I want them to be re-published so that I may have another copy. I find that, with the exception of *Mauberley*, there is no other contemporary – with disrespect for none, for I include myself – whom I ever want to re-read for pleasure.

Apology for the Countess of Pembroke

Publ. in *Harvard Graduates' Magazine*, 41. 2 (Dec. 1932),63–[75]: Gallup C338. Revised in *UPUC. See below*, pp. 700–8.

1933

A Commentary

C., 12. 47 (Jan. 1933), 244–9. Signed 'T. S. E.' Gallup C340.

Writing from a country in which communistic theories appear to have more vogue among men of letters than they have yet reached in England, I have recently looked at two books which discuss the relation of literature to social affairs. One is not very new; Trotsky's *Literature and Revolution* was first published in translation in 1925, and has since become a text-book for revolutionary *littérateurs*. The other, Mr Calverton's *Liberation of American Literature*, is pretty fresh from the mint. The former is much shorter and of course more important. It is natural, and not necessarily convincing, to find young intellectuals in New York turning to communism, and turning their communism to literary account. The literary profession is not only, in all countries, overcrowded and underpaid (the few overpaid being chiefly persons who have outlived their influence, if they ever had any); it is embarrassed by such a number of ill-trained people doing such a number of unnecessary jobs, and writing so many unnecessary books and unnecessary reviews of unnecessary books, that it has much ado to maintain its dignity as a profession at all. One is almost tempted to form the opinion that the world is at a stage at which men of letters are a superfluity. To be able therefore to envisage literature under a new aspect, to take part in the creation of a new art and new standards of literary criticism, to be provided with a whole stock of ideas and of words, that is for a writer in such circumstances to be given a new lease of life. It is not always easy, of course, in the ebullitions of a new movement, to distinguish the man who has received the living word from the man whose access of energy is the result of being relieved of the necessity of thinking for himself. Men who have stopped thinking make a powerful force. There are obvious inducements, besides that – never wholly absent – of simple conversion, to entice the man of letters into political and social theory which he then employs to revive his sinking fires and rehabilitate his profession.

[245] There is no such obvious reason why a man like Trotsky should take the trouble to pronounce upon the literature of revolution and the literature of the future; the only reason that occurs to me in reading his

book is that he may have been exasperated by the futilities of previous Russian writers upon the subject. He is certainly a man of first-rate intelligence, expressing himself in a rough and ready metaphorical style, and he utters a good deal of sound sense. Most of his book is devoted to the criticism of authors whom I have not read, and who I imagine have not been translated and never will be; but as an antidote to the false art of revolution his treatise is admirable.

The faith of Trotsky, however, in the possibilities of Marxian literature, has about it something very touching – still more touching than that of Mr Calverton. The early champions of the Christian Faith, one remembers, often adopted a very different attitude towards literature and art in general. No attempt was made to conciliate or to seduce the literary world. Eminent literary conversions were not then received with a burst of applause because of their advertisement value. Classical authors fared more hardly than any dead writers are likely to fare in reputation under the rule of Marxian criticism; and the fathers of the young Church did not feel any pressing need for literature and art as evidence of the truth of Christianity. Those manifestations followed in due course. They are never likely to reappear any more quickly than they did then. Trotsky is quite aware – more aware than his compatriots seem to have been before he wrote his book – of the difference between literature written in and for a period of revolution, and literature produced by a people which has gone through a revolution, and he seems to understand that the first is unlikely to have any permanent value; but he seems to feel, in common with other communists, an impatience for the latter to appear.

I can agree with Mr Trotsky up to a point. 'The proletarian,' he says, 'has to have in art the expression of the [246] new spiritual[1] point of view which is just beginning to be formulated within him, and to which art must help him to give form.' If we assume for the moment that the revolution is to take place, and that the final classless society will appear, then I concede the possibility that great works of art in new forms will subsequently appear too; I disbelieve, not only that the new art will be any better than the art of all the past, but that the new art will owe its life to communism. The chances for art are no better than out of any other possible development of society, and are not improved by a flood of anticipatory criticism. I certainly prefer the greatest Christian art to the greatest art of pagan times, before or since, but I do not believe that because it is Christian art it is greater art. What would happen, at best, under a wholly new dispensation, would be that the artist would have his material given him, and would be so inoculated with communism as to

---

1. One would like to penetrate Mr Trotsky's conception of 'the spiritual'.

be able to ignore it. Christian apologists have not, those who have been serious and qualified, cited Christian art as an apology for Christianity. From the point of view of art, if there is such a point of view, Christianity was merely a change, a provision of a new world with new material; from the point of view of communism as of Christianity, art and literature are strictly irrelevant.

There is a great deal more to the difference, however, than a mere change of mental categories. Both Mr Trotsky and Mr Calverton speak as if you had only to adopt the categories of communism, and after that, if you were an artist, you would be able to devote your attention to questions of 'form'. Mr Trotsky says:

> It is unquestionably true that the need for art is not created by economic conditions. But neither is the need for food created by economic conditions. On the contrary, the need for food and warmth creates economics. It is very true that one cannot always go by the principles of Marxism in deciding whether to reject or to accept a [247] work of art. A work of art should, in the first place, be judged by its own law, that is, by the law of art. But Marxism alone can explain why and how a given tendency in art has originated in a given period of history; in other words, who it was who made a demand for such an artistic form and not for another, and why. . . . Materialism does not deny the significance of form, either in logic, jurisprudence, or art.

And Mr Calverton:

> The revolutionary proletarian critic does not aim to underestimate literary craftsmanship. What he contends is simply that literary craftsmanship is not enough. The craftsmanship must be utilised to create objects of revolutionary meaning.

Now, this is all quite praiseworthy, so far as it goes, but I find it difficult to apply in comprehensive criticism of any great piece of literature of the past: what was the 'meaning' of a play of Shakespeare which corresponds to the 'revolutionary meaning' of the art of the future? the 'meaning' which it must have or must have had, if we are to regard it as anything more than the 'literary craftsmanship' which is not enough? If Marxism explains why and how a given tendency in history originated, such as the tendency for Shakespeare's plays to be written, and who it was who made a demand for such an artistic form as that of *Antony and Cleopatra*, and if everything else is 'literary craftsmanship' (an accomplishment in which Mr Calverton is not notably proficient), then there seems to me to be a good deal left to explain. Mr Calverton, in fact, does leave a great deal, for throughout his book on American literature everything is explained except the genius of the greater men of letters, who do not, on the whole, receive very much of his attention. They are 'explained' by their environment, and their genius, apparently, is just a genius for literary craftsmanship.

I should suppose it to be desirable that every country shall provide an environment in which its best minds can flourish; it also seems desirable that these best minds should come to terms with their environment; but it is possible also that some amount of maladaptation is desirable. Hawthorne was [248] apparently adapted to the past of America rather than to its future; but it is just possible that this retrospective inclination suited Hawthorne's peculiar spiritual qualities. If Mr Calverton had treated Poe as a case of maladaptation, and Emerson as a case of excessive adaptation, the results might have been interesting. But the spectacle of the individual in conflict with the dominant tendencies and prejudices of his time, and consequently that of the individual in conflict with the dominant prejudices and tendencies of the coming time, does not influence critics like Mr Calverton in favour of the individual.

There are also people who, while recognising the interest of the work of literature as a document upon the ideas and the sensibility of its epoch, and recognising even that the permanent work of literature is one which does not lack this interest, yet cannot help valuing literary work, like philosophical work, in the end by its transcendence of the limits of its age; by its breaking through the categories of thought and sensibility of its age; by its speaking, in the language of its time and in the imagery of its own tradition, the word which belongs to no time. Art, we feel, aspires to the condition of the timeless; and communist art, according to the sentence of those who would foretell what it is to be, is bound to be temporal.

> It is the decay of the whole middle class way of existence, that of the upper bourgeoisie as well as the petty bourgeoisie, which has robbed the contemporary writer in Europe as well as in America of his faith in life, and left him without beliefs or convictions.

What faith in life may be I know not; I might inform Mr Calverton that, for the Christian, faith in death is what matters. He continues:

> The sickness and sham which underlay the nature of middle-class life is no longer concealed from him.

It was no doubt the sickness and sham which underlay the nature of Pharisee and Sadducee life that, being no longer [249] concealed from the writers of the Gospels, left them without beliefs or convictions, and with a less polished prose style than that of Mr Calverton or that of Mr Murry. And yet we persist in believing that Confucius and Plato, Homer and Shakespeare, even though 'their faith was founded upon a false premise; fitting and persuasive enough in their generation', have yet something to say to every future generation if it will listen, no matter how many future generations there may be to come.

In matters of aesthetics the Christian theorist is in a position of unfair terms with the communist, of which he is not slow to take advantage. He is able to recognise an inconsistency in the affairs of his world, even to admitting the possibility that a man might be a communist, an orthodox Marxian dialectician, in our time, in this very year and month, and yet write decent English prose; even that such a one might be a great poet. He might even derive pleasure and instruction from the man's poetry. But the Marxian is compelled to scorn delights, even such moderate ecstasies as may be provoked by the reading of Emerson's *Essays*, and live laborious days in deciding what art ought to be. For this knowledge of literature he is obliged to apply himself, not to the furtive and facile pleasures of Homer and Virgil – the former a person of doubtful identity and citizenship, the latter a sycophantic supporter of a middle-class imperialist dynasty – but to the arduous study of Ernest Hemingway and John Dos Passos; and the end of his precipitous ascent will be an appreciation of the accomplishment of Sam Ornitz, Lester Cohen, and Granville Hicks.[1]

A Commentary

C., 12. 48 (Apr. 1933), 468–73. Signed 'T. S. E.' Gallup C342.

I do not know whether a book called *The Ironic Temper*, by Haakon Chevalier (whose name was previously unknown to me) has been published in London or not. It is a book worth reading, and also one that inspires the kind of reflexions appropriate to the literary form of these commentaries, if they have a form. Its primary aim is what the title affirms, a study of the ironic temper; it is, incidentally, a very sympathetic and understanding analysis of Anatole France.

The book is a study of a temper and a temperature which the author believes to belong to the past, which in Anatole France reach their

---

1. *The Liberation of American Literature*, p. 479. By V. F. Calverton, author of *Sex Expression in Literature* and *Bankruptcy of Marriage* which has been translated into eight languages and used in leading universities in London (ask Mr Laski), Berlin and Tokyo. Scribners. $3.75.

culmination. It is therefore by implication a study of the 'modern temper' as well; and Mr Chevalier makes, by the way, some shrewd and destructive criticisms of the book by Mr Joseph Wood Krutch, *The Modern Temper*, which was widely noticed a few years ago. Being at present engaged in the attempt to give a course of lectures on contemporary literature, I feel that the modern temper is something that I ought to inform myself about; and it is with this aspect of the book, rather than with Mr Chevalier's very able analysis of the ironic temper, as exemplified by Anatole France, that I am concerned. Mr Chevalier observes in his introduction:

> Anatole France's generation still lived under the spell of the past. The everywhere (*sic*) visible contrasts between the past and the present formed rich soil for the growth of Irony; and the prevailing mood of reminiscent piety allowed pity also to flourish. Hemingway's generation has lost that sense of the past. 'Irony and Pity'. Meaningless words. There is no irony, because there is no complex interplay of concepts and beliefs casting ambiguous shadows over human affairs. There is no Pity: no sense of value attaches to pain and defeat to throw them into emotional relief.
>
> Irony and Pity are foreign alike to ages of faith and to an age like our own, to which the loss of faith, if not the lack of it, is not a matter of acute concern.

To generalise about the present is a dangerous business; un-[469]safe as predicting the future. Mr Chevalier is by no means unaware of the dangers; he adds, 'when we differentiate our own generation from that of Anatole France we are drawing, possibly, a fine line of distinction of which the future will take no account'. Certainly, France is one of those writers who do represent for us the age which is past. Perhaps his remoteness from us might be expressed in terms other than that of Irony – though for Mr Chevalier, of course, Irony means the ironic temper, and not the polemic irony which is a permanent weapon for the sensitive civilised man. What we rebel against is neither the use of irony against definite men, institutions or abuses, nor is it the use (as by Jules Laforgue) to express a *dédoublement* of the personality against which the subject struggles. It is the use of irony to give the appearance of a philosophy of life, as something final and not instrumental, that leaves us now indifferent; it seems to us an evasion of the difficulty of living, where it pretends to be a kind of solution of it. And the work built upon it comes to seem merely superfluous, an encumbrance, a luxury article produced for a public that has disappeared.

Our time (but possibly when we say our time we mean ourselves and perhaps a few friends) is impatient of the superfluous and the complicated.

The international situations, the elaborate complications in which many of Henry James's problems involve themselves, now seem remote; what is not remote is his curious search, often in the oddest places, like country houses, for spiritual life. And in Anatole France we find, I think, a kind of pretentiousness which is unendurable. He appears before us, with his long row of books, as a popular entertainer, and a very good entertainer he is; but the sad thing is to find that an essential trick of the entertainment is to impress us with a profound worldly wisdom, sapping all other philosophies, and a sophistication with which he flatters us by making us feel that we share it. The flattery is turned to fraud when we realise how shallow is his philosophy, how puny and defensive is his sophistication. Like good breeding, sophistication is a quality to be [470] dissimulated; when it is paraded, it becomes childish. Nor is disillusion possible as an end in itself; for when it becomes an end, it is paraded, and that again is childish and ill bred. The man who is properly disillusioned is almost unconscious of the fact; and he knows that it is childish to let his mind dwell upon the things he no longer believes in; and that it is adult to believe in something and occupy his mind with that. And Mr Chevalier does very well elicit the fact that Anatole France was always a precocious child. Many men of great ability are inefficient in practical detail, and even weak of will; but France's mind was actually an arrested one.

Anatole France of the French Academy is not the sole example of arrested development; and since the past and the present overlap as do the present and the future, we may cite here M. André Gide. What a superb philosophy he offered to adolescents! It was more up to date than Anatole France's; it was for the time when men ten years younger than myself were young. We should learn to suspect those who, like France and M. Gide, write at their best or almost best when they write about their childhood. We should also learn that one kind of sham is offered to the public when *decadence* is in vogue, and another when *revolution* is in vogue; and that they may be at bottom the same old sham: just a defence organisation by timid and undeveloped men who have a talent for writing. I hope that Mr Aldous Huxley will not write about his infancy. M. Gide, as I say, has stepped it up. Instead of the sophistication of the man who knows all about the past, who has understood all philosophies and faiths and seen through them, infinitely learned, infinitely 'intelligent' (magic word), and infinitely weary, weary; instead of that kind of humbug he offered us the sophistication of the daring mind, freed from all prejudices and inhibitions (how that word fatigues one!), exploring all possibilities, willing to try anything – the slave, not of the past, but of the future. M. Gide, I imagine, has a smaller public than France had; but he has all the public there is; as large a public, I dare say, as France would have had if he had been the con-[471]temporary of M. Gide. The essential point is not how large a public one writes for; the essential point is whether one writes for a public at all. And M. Gide does definitely write to be read. In this he seems to me to differ from Montaigne. It is usually possible to tell the difference between the letters of people who write for their correspondent and those of people who write, not forgetting that their letters may be preserved, and after preservation, published. And after all, it is not difficult to be sophisticated. One only needs to be born a little later than some other eminent person. France is more sophisticated than Renan. Gide is more sophisticated than France. For Mr Huxley, as I suggested, the future is still open. The most lamentable case of sophistication in this island was perhaps Lytton Strachey.

In America, this pseudo – or not quite good mannered sophistication takes the form of what they call hard boiling. To each climate its own illusion; but the illusion which pervades the whole various-climated American continent is the illusion of the hard boiled. Even Mr Ernest Hemingway – that writer of tender sentiment, and true sentiment, as in *The Killers* and *A Farewell to Arms* (I am told that Mr Hemingway refused to look at the Film which was produced under the same title) has been taken as the representative of hard boiling. Hard boiling is, of course, only another defence-mechanism adopted by the world's babies; if the Chinese bandits ever discover that they are hard boiled I shall have to infer that the oldest civilisation in the world has reverted to the condition of puerility. Mr Hemingway is a writer for whom I have considerable respect; he seems to me to tell the truth about his own feelings at the moment when they exist. He does not belong in the class in which I have placed France, and Gide, and (tentatively) Mr Aldous Huxley. He has, at the moment, a popularity which I think (it is a high compliment) is largely undeserved.

To any writer, once he has attained a certain notoriety, comes temptation. Any writer, after he arrives at some success, has to discriminate between three classes of friends: [472] those who care for him, those who care for his work, and those who care only for his reputation. The first class is, of course, the smallest, yet it may overlap the second. I think that I may say, on behalf of those who write, that the distinction between the second and the third class is usually painfully evident. Any writer, who arrives at some success, discriminates between three classes of disciples: those who will go the whole way with him (number usually zero); those who will go part of the way with him; and, lastly, those who will adopt some catchword and go in the opposite direction. Ordinarily, one knows that a Leader may be defined as that one of the Gadarene Swine which runs the fastest. But the real Leader is the one who does not look back to see whether there are any followers. Perhaps D. H. Lawrence lived long enough to discover that he had none.

Communism – I mean the ideas of communism, not the reality, which would be of no use in this way – has come as a godsend (so to speak) to those young people who would like to grow up and believe in something. Once they have committed themselves, they must find (if they are honest, and really growing) that they have let themselves in for all the troubles that afflict the person who believes in something. I speak of those who are moved by the desire to be possessed by a conviction, rather than by the obvious less laudable motives which make a man believe that he has a belief. They have joined that bitter fraternity which lives on a higher level of doubt; no longer the doubting which is just play with ideas, on the level of a France or of a Gide, but that which is a daily battle. The only end to the battle, if we live to the end, is holiness; the only escape is stupidity, and stupidity, for the majority of people, is no doubt the best solution of the difficulty of thinking; it is far better to be stupid in a faith, even a stupid faith, than to be stupid and believe nothing. For the smaller number, the first step is to find the least incredible belief and live with it for some time; and that in itself is uncomfortable; but in time we come to perceive that everything else is still more uncomfortable. Everyone, [473] in a sense, believes in something; for every action involving any moral decision implies a belief; but a formulated belief is better, because more conscious, than an unformulated or informulable one. And, on the other hand, a belief which is *merely* a formulation of the way in which one acts has no validity; unless it turns and compels action of certain kinds in certain circumstances it has no status. Anatole France had his 'philosophy of life', if you like; but a philosophy of life which involves no sacrifice turns out in the end to be merely an excuse for being the sort of person that one is. I have, in consequence of these reflexions, much sympathy with communists of the type with which I am here concerned; I would even say that, as it is the faith of the day, there are only a small number of people living who have achieved the right *not* to be communists. My only objection to it is the same as my objection to the cult of the Golden Calf. It is better to worship a golden calf than to worship nothing; but that, after all, is not, in the circumstances, an adequate excuse. My objection is that it just happens to be mistaken.

Critical

Publ. in May 1933 in *The Collected Poems of Harold Monro*, ed. Alida Monro with a biographical sketch by F. S. Flint and a critical note by T. S. Eliot (xiii–xvi). Gallup B22.

If we considered the poetry of Harold Monro, as it is natural to do, from an historical point of view, we should see him isolated between the 'Georgian' poets of one decade and the more 'modern' poets of another. The historical point of view, especially when we are concerned with our immediate predecessors and our contemporaries, is largely impersonal; that is to say, it tends to emphasise what a man has in common with others, in subject matter, in manner of style and technique, in his social background and assumptions. It also judges men according to what is taken to be their influence, or their importance in the main current. Such an attitude is bound to be unfair to the reputation of such a poet as Monro. What he contributed is hardly to be considered either in close relation to the work of the earlier generation or to that of the later.

Technically, certainly, he was not an innovator. It is a poet's business to be original, in all that is comprehended by 'technique', only so far as is absolutely necessary for saying what he has to say; only so far as is dictated, not by the idea – but by the nature of that dark embryo within him which gradually takes on the form and speech of a poem. Monro's style developed and changed, of course; like that of any other writer who is of serious interest. His later manner is more like that of his younger contemporaries than like that of his elder contemporaries; but this is not due, I think, to any influence from without, but to the needs of the matter to be said. But with Georgian poetry he had little in common. Of that poetry I speak with much diffidence. What I remember of it is a small number of poems by two or three men. I supposed, long ago, that Harold Monro's poetry belonged in this category – with the poetry of writers not unfairly [xiv] representable in anthologies; and in those days I was interested only in the sort of thing I wanted to do myself, and took no interest in what diverged from my own directions. But his poetry differs from Georgian verse proper in important respects. The majority of those writers occupied themselves with subject matter which is – and not in the best sense – impersonal; which belongs to the sensibility of the ordinary sensitive person, not primarily only to that of the sensitive poet; it was not always easy to distinguish the work of one author from the work of another; the result was a considerable number of pleasing anthology pieces. Furthermore, most of it was static: it failed to show any very interesting development in the mind and experience of the author. Now Monro, with his amiable, but uncritical capacity for admiring other people's verse, gives me the impression of having tried, in some of his earlier work, but probably unconsciously, to be more like other writers than he really was. His originality, in all but his latest work, is not immediately apparent from any one poem; it was not indeed until re-reading the whole of his published work that I recognised completely how distinctly, in his whole work, the vision is the personal vision of Harold Monro.

Had Monro been a poet who could have worked out his own method in isolation, and ignored the attempts of his contemporaries, he might earlier have found a more personal idiom. It was part of the irony of his situation that, being essentially a different kind of poet, with different things to say, from any of his elder or younger contemporaries, he was yet actively and passionately interested in 'poetry', in the confraternity of poets, and in the publication and dissemination of their writings. The other poets about him were occupied with either more obvious or more recondite imaginings. And his difficulties in expression must have been considerable. He is at the same time very intimate [xv] and very reticent. He does not express the spirit of an age; he expresses the spirit of one man, but that so faithfully that his poetry will remain as one variety of the infinite number of possible expressions of tortured human consciousness.

Monro is obviously not a 'nature poet'. The attitude towards nature which we find again and again in his poems is that of the town-dweller, of the man who, as much by the bondage of temperament and habit as by that of external necessity, must pass his life among streets. Some poets, such as Baudelaire, similarly possessed by the town, turn directly to the littered streets, the squinting slums, the grime and smoke and the viscid human life within the streets, and find there the centre of intensity. Monro's poetry, so far as it is concerned with the countryside, is rather that of the perpetual week-ender, oscillating between departure and return; his city is that of the man who would flee to the country, his country that of the man who must tomorrow return to town. Now, this is not only a state of mind important enough to deserve reporting in poetry, but it also becomes, in some of Monro's poems, representative of something larger and less easily apprehensible, a *poésie des brefs départs* (as in the sonnet sequence *Weekend*).

Here a distinction may conveniently be made. There are various degrees of symbolism in imagery. A poet may have a set of imagery come whole and self-sufficient to his mind, so that his sole conscious concern is to set down that vision without concerning himself, in the act of composition, with the meaning of it, but only with the delight of the symmetry of the picture. Monro's mind did not work in this way; I feel always that the centre of his interest is never in the visible world at all, but in the spectres and the 'bad dreams' which live inside the skull, in the ceaseless question and answer of the tortured mind, or the unspoken question and answer between two human beings. To get inside his [xvi] world takes some trouble, and it is not a happy or sunny world to stay in, but it is a world which we ought to visit. The external world, as it appears in his poetry, is manifestly but the mirror of a darker world within. It takes the form sometimes of what a superficial glance might dismiss as the whimsical: talking Beds and Teapots. Inanimate objects take on animation of a kind; his old houses are not so much haunted by ghosts as they are ghosts themselves haunting the folk who briefly visit them. Under the influence of this sincere and tormented introspection, the warm reality dissolves: both that for which we hold out our arms, and at which we strike vain blows.

It takes time. There is no one poem, no few poems, which I could point to and say: this will give you the essence of Monro; the nearest approach, and the dourest excruciation, is his last *Bitter Sanctuary*. This one poem must at least demonstrate that Monro's vision of life was different from that of any of his contemporaries. But we must read the lot of them in order to understand.

There was no way out. There never is. The compensations for being a poet are grossly exaggerated; and they dwindle as one becomes older, and the shadows lengthen, and the solitude becomes harder to endure. We can only say: 'Sleep, and if life was bitter to thee, pardon.' Monro's work is so manifestly honest and bitter that we may be sure he would have cared for no praise that was not just and moderate. I have not overpraised. I think that his poetry, as a whole, is more nearly the real right thing than any of the poetry of a somewhat older generation than mine except Mr Yeats's. That is only the one way of looking at it. In the end, it will remain because, like every other good poet, he has not simply done something better than anyone else, but done something that no one else has done at all.

T. S. ELIOT

A Commentary

C., 12. 49 (July 1933), 642–7. Signed 'T. S. E.' Gallup C343.

It seems to be the necessity of the moment – at least in America – for the editor of a literary periodical to explain exactly where that periodical stands on the great political and social issues of the day. I have no intention of doing that myself on this occasion; and I have not yet framed any manifesto against manifestoes. In the new *American Review* I recognise doctrines with which I have already expressed sympathy; and it is just as well to be told again that Communism and Capitalism are only forms of the same thing; I said this myself several years ago, and the statement was already so obvious a commonplace that I have forgotten who said it last before me. In *The Symposium* is another manifesto – this one drawn up formally, perhaps too formally; for its thirteen propositions are a sad reminder of the methods of the late President Wilson. It is interesting to observe that *The American Review* and *The Symposium* agree in denouncing Communism and Capitalism; there is one interesting, and rather important point, on which they appear to differ. I say 'appear', because only *The Symposium* formulates its view in so many words; but an opposite point of view emerges from contributions to *The American Review*; and the earliest contributions to a review of this character may have something of editorial authority. The words of the editors of *The Symposium* are these: *The moral and spiritual goods should not be the direct concern of a politico-economic party at the present time.*

Here, I think, is a real issue. It appears that the word 'direct' used above is a superfluity, to judge from the sentence which follows: 'If its programme is acceptable at the level of social practice and if it does not *conflict* with these moral and spiritual goods, then that programme is just, is all that should be attempted, and all that any individual has a right to ask for.' It would appear, then, that the 'party' does not need to be concerned with moral and spiritual goods at [643] all in order to do its job, to save us on the politico-economic plane. Furthermore, I do not find it stated in any part of the manifesto, that it is necessary or desirable for the individuals composing that party to have as individuals any direct concern with the moral and spiritual goods either; possibly, indeed, the children of this world are wiser in their generation than the children of light. And this does seem to me to create a real issue between two types of reformer or revolutionist: the coming type of Liberal Reformer, which the *Symposium* strikes me as prefiguring, and the Reactionary, who at this point feels a stronger sympathy with the communist. What, in fact, is the relation of morals and politics?

It might seem at first that an ally of any sort is welcome in an emergency – and we are always in an emergency – and that the temperate economic or political reformer, the sensible revolutionist, should be on working terms with one kind of ethical reformer or revolutionist, we will say the Christian ethical reformer. But if that is to be accepted, we must be very sure about the terms, and dupe neither others nor ourselves. I remember that I was once scolded (and if my memory serves me it was by the editor of *The American Review*) for sowing discord among the ranks of the well-intentioned, for betraying the cause, by exposing my doubts about Humanism. That was only a few years ago; but where is Humanism now? In the arms of John Dewey and a committee of Unitarian clergy. She is a fallen sister; we cannot now speak of her in front of the children. A united group, we should have learned by now, acts, if we have patience, more surely than a large and miscellaneous group. There were equivocations about Humanism towards which no compromise could be extended; so there may be about some of the economic philosophies which aim at setting things right without moral discipline. Disguised as they are, veiled from common minds like mine, by the categories of their sacred science, any of them may belong in those utopias which take no account of human nature. But I believe that the study of ethics has priority over the study of [644] politics; that this priority is something immutable which not famine or war can change; and that, even when a philosopher is expressly 'not directly concerned' with ethics, yet his politics and economics will have some obscure ethical assumption, or the defect of some ethical assumption, by which, if I could find it, I could judge them. Even such demure and sedately walking revolutionists as Sir Arthur Salter and Maynard Keynes must be concerned very circumspectly from this point of view.

The great merit of Communism is the same as one merit of the Catholic Church, that there is something in it which minds on every level can grasp. Marx may not be intelligible, but Communism is. Communism has what is now called a 'myth'. It interferes with people's private lives, and therefore excites men as sensible economists never excite the inhabitants of Poplar and Hoxton. It interferes just as much by giving people licence in ways which they had been brought up not to expect, or else by telling them that the way in which they instinctively behave is the right way, as by restraining them in ways in which they were not accustomed to be restrained. People like licence, and they like restraint. They like surprise. The one thing they do not like is boredom. And Communism is successful so long as it gives people the illusion that they are not bored; so long as it can give them the illusion that they are important. For it has been shown again and again in history that people can put up with the absence of all the things that economists tell us they most need, with every rigour, every torment, so long as they are not bored. Why did the children of Israel murmur against Moses? Because they got tired of walking and seemingly arriving nowhere. *And the whole congregation of the children of Israel murmured against Moses and Aaron in the wilderness; and the children of Israel said unto them, Would to God we had died by the hand of the Lord in the land of Egypt, when we sat by the flesh pots, and when we did eat bread to the full; for ye have brought us forth into this wilderness, to kill this whole assembly with hunger.*

[645] The children of Israel saw the economic problem; the problem was simpler for them, because the quails, when they arrived, were consumed, instead of being buried; but really their trouble was lack of inspiration, in other words boredom.

The British people has been taught that it should manage its own affairs; but wrongly taught. Every man knows that he should manage his own household; every village knows that it should manage itself. Yet everything has been reversed: instead of managing our own affairs we are given a ticket entitling us to some voice in managing other people's affairs. We are led to believe that a Parliamentary election is the most important occasion on which we may exercise our Right; whereas it should matter much more to us – and we are much more competent to decide – who should manage our own village than who should manage Parliament. We are taught, in every modern nation, to worship the nation first, the district second, and the local community third, and the family last; whereas we are only capable of understanding the nation through its relation to the family.

A social system which has no explicit moral foundation, in which the church, rather than the brothels, is tolerated, in which ownership of land, except for speculative purposes, is not encouraged, may yet have moral consequences and influences upon the individual. A system based on moral presuppositions of which we disapprove may turn the individual into a kind of person whom we dislike, but he will still be a person who feels that he has a reason for existing; the result of a system which has no moral presuppositions may be nothing better than decay. I can quite understand the antipathy of the editors of the *Symposium* to the Communist ideology:

> It is, on the one hand, in its exaggerated internationalism (which is actually Slavophilism), equalitarianism, 'revolutionary optimism', in its conception of the possibilities of social development and its vision of future anarchic heaven on earth, ridiculously utopian; and, on the other, in the cluttering ideology with which it loads and impedes its [646] political activities, in its conceptions and analyses of literature, art, morality, religion, and human nature, it is barbaric.

A good many people feel the same way about it; and it is difficult to take seriously people who take themselves humourlessly, as the Russians seem to do. But I am not so sure as the editors of the *Symposium* seem to be, that this 'cluttering ideology' has actually 'impeded' the political activities of the Communists in Russia. I should have to see that proved; otherwise I am inclined to believe that the 'cluttering ideology' holds the whole thing together; and that it is this which has attracted most converts of an intellectual and pseudo-intellectual kind. We certainly do not want an ideology which is going to obstruct efficient and sensible administration. And I cannot think that the Communist ideology, however suited it may be to the contemporary Russian mind, is quite adaptable to a civilisation which is predominantly middle-class, as is the whole of western Europe, Britain and America. I am not in a position to know how closely the forms of government now in practice in Italy and Germany are adaptable to the needs of Anglo-Saxon cultures; I do not even know how far they are permanently adapted to the needs of their own; but they appear to issue from a lower middle-class movement rather than from a proletarian movement.

My affirmation of the necessity of a conception of the good life for the individual, as underlying political-economic ideas, is (I imagine) akin to Mr Douglas Jerrold's notion of the Ethical State. It needs, however, some qualifications which may bring it nearer to the *Symposium*'s thirteenth point, which is made as follows:

> The primary business of criticism is always at the critical level; but at the present time it is necessary for the critical point of view to recognise also the issues at the level of social practice, and to study the relations between the two levels; and to attempt to reconcile the just side of the politico-economic issue with values acceptable at the critical level.

[647] I am not quite sure, however, of the meaning of this sentence. It does not necessarily imply that 'the moral and spiritual goods' are the concern of criticism; and, if not, I should like to know whose concern they are. Furthermore, I should like to know in what precise ways, in the opinion of the *Symposium*, 'the present time' differs from other times, and also what historical parallels there are for our time, if any. And the term 'social practice' may comprehend almost as much or as little as we like. My qualification of my own statement is this: that the best form of politico-economic reform or revolution, which is compatible with the facts and with our ethical views, may be accepted, even if the person or persons who have devised it are not themselves animated by those views. We cannot, however, leave it at that. We cannot say that the emergency requires first a readjustment in the politico-economic world, and that when that is effected we may turn our attention to making it a world in which there is positive value. The system which the intelligent economist discovers or invents must immediately be related to a moral system.

I hold that it is ultimately the moralists and philosophers who must supply the foundations of statesmanship, even though they never appear in the forum. We are constantly being told that the economic problem cannot wait. It is equally true that the moral and spiritual problems cannot wait: they have already waited far too long.

Catholicism and International Order

'Catholicism and International Order', the Opening Address to the Anglo-Catholic Summer School of Sociology', was publ. in *Christendom*, 3. 11 (Sept. 1933), [171]–84. Unsigned. Gallup C344. Revised in *EAAM*. See Vol. 3, pp. 82–94, in the present edition.

[Letters of Mrs Gaskell and Charles Eliot Norton]

Review of *Letters of Mrs Gaskell and Charles Eliot Norton, 1855–1865*, edited with an Introduction by Jane Whitehill (1932).

New England Quarterly, 6. 3 (Sept. 1933), 627–8. Signed 'T. S. Eliot.' Gallup C345.

This is not a book for admirers of Norton so much as for admirers of Mrs Gaskell. In 1857 Mrs Gaskell took a holiday from Manchester, and paid a visit to the Storys in Rome. Her daughters, Marianne and Meta, accompanied her; in a letter some years later Meta recalls the first meeting to Norton himself:

> I can see your face and smile now (as distinctly as if I were only just turning away from them) when you caught at some confetti that Mama was dangling on a long stick from the balcony – and Mama said 'Oh look what a charming face' and Mr Story (I think it was) said 'Oh, that's Charles Norton,' and then there was a chorus of welcome and bidding you come up.

And later in life Mrs Gaskell wrote to the Storys:

> It was in those charming Roman days that my life at any rate, culminated. I shall never be so happy again. I don't think I was ever so happy before.

Neither Norton nor Mrs Gaskell, seventeen years his senior, was a European. The lady, as her admirers know, came from a parsonage in Manchester. Mr Gaskell was an earnest, conscientious, somewhat humourless Unitarian pastor, writing sermons, lectures, and hymns; he never absented himself voluntarily from Manchester; he took an annual holiday at Morecambe Bay, but even that was in the same county. Mrs Gaskell, who bore him a number of children and who devoted herself, and in the end sacrificed herself, to her husband, was entitled to take a holiday with her daughters. She could not have made a more desirable acquaintance than Charles Norton. He was a young man of the highest principles, he was engaged in learning all he could in Italy, and was ready to impart his knowledge; furthermore, he was a Unitarian. In those days sectarian differences were social differences; and Mrs Gaskell was acutely aware of living, in Manchester, in a social *enclave*. In her letters there is the solemn young Mr Bosanquet, who, but for his family's religious opinions, might possibly have proved eligible for one of her daughters; and she complains that 'here (in Manchester) the Unitarian young men are either good *and* uncultivated, or else rich *and* regardless of those higher qualities the "spiritual" qualities as it were, which those *must* appreciate who would think of my girls.' She thinks of Norton as a brother, an elder brother, to her girls. But Norton was a Unitarian of a type unfamiliar to Mrs Gaskell. He was rich, good, *and* cultivated; he had the best introductions everywhere and knew how to use them; and he had a French courier named François. There is nothing to suggest that Mrs Gaskell had ever before met a Unitarian with a French courier named François. She had a sense of humour, timid and fluttering as it was; she had an unsatisfied love of beauty, gaiety, and civilisation; she profited by her visit to Italy and by Norton's explanations of the art of Titian; her later correspondence with Norton must have been a relief from the labors of slaving to provide for the old age of Mr Gaskell.

This book, as I have said, is not an essential contribution to the biography of Norton. He seems, at thirty, rather a callow, if very estimable young man. The interesting Norton is in the later years, rising to a solitary grandeur at the time of the Spanish War. This is a book about Mrs Gaskell. She was not George Sand; but the best of her writing is perhaps more permanently readable, for she is among those English (and American) writers who have known how to make a literary virtue of provinciality – and, in her case, simple goodness.

A Commentary

C., 13. 50 (Oct. 1933), 115–20. Signed 'T. S. E.': Gallup C346
On p. 117 'are of no doubt of'has been emended to 'are no doubt of'.

In the month of July, Irving Babbitt died at his home in Cambridge, Massachusetts, at the end of an illness of some nine months. After a life of indefatigable, and for many years almost solitary intellectual struggle, he had secured for his views, if not full appreciation, at least wide recognition; he had established a great and beneficent influence, of a kind which has less show than substance, through the many pupils who left him to become teachers throughout America; and he had established a strong counter-current in education.

Those who only know Babbitt through his writings, and have had no contact with him as a teacher and friend, will probably not be able to appreciate the greatness of his work. For he was primarily and always a teacher and a talker. He combined rare charm with great force: so that those who knew him will always remember his foibles with affection, and cherish the memory of his brusqueness when other men's suavity is forgotten. Twenty-four years ago, when I first knew him, his reputation was only amongst a few. He was the author of two books, the first of which I still regard as the more important, *Literature and the American College*, and *The New Laocoon*. He was considered an interesting, eccentric and rebellious figure amongst the teaching profession; and his outspoken contempt for methods of teaching in vogue had given him a reputation for unpopularity which attracted to him some discerning graduates and undergraduates at Harvard University. Fortunately for his pupils, his classes in those days were small, and could be conducted informally round a small table. For Babbitt, I think, like some other great teachers, was at his best with a small group of pupils. Superficially, his lectures were almost without method. He would enter the room with a pile of books, papers and notes, which he shifted and shuffled throughout the hour; beginning to talk before he sat down, beginning anywhere and ending anywhere, he gave us the impression that a life-[116]time was too short for telling us all that he wanted to say. The lectures which I attended were, I believe, concerned with French Literary Criticism; but they had a great deal to do with Aristotle, Longinus and Dionysius of Halicarnassus; they touched frequently upon Buddhism, Confucius, Rousseau, and contemporary political and religious movements. Somehow or other one read a number of books, Aristotle's *Politics* or Lafontaine's *Fables*, just because Babbitt assumed that any educated man had already read them. What held the lectures or talks together was his intellectual passion, one might say intellectual fury; what made them cohere was the constant recurrence of his dominant ideas; what gave them delight was their informality, the demand which they made upon one's mental agility, and the frankness with which he discussed the things that he disliked, and which his pupils came to dislike too.

I think that the point at which Babbitt's ideas converged with the greatest force was the subject of Education. In England, where a traditional fabric of education still stands, though there are not wanting signs of the death-beetle in its timbers, it is difficult to bring home the urgency of the subject. In America, where education has for two or three generations responded to the whim of any modern theory, where a single man of character and conviction can impose his views, from time to time, upon the methods of the whole nation, and where the divergent tastes and ideals of scholars variously trained in Germany, France or England, have been a source of weakness and instability, every vagary has had its opportunity, and successive scholastic generations have only suffered from successive experiments. All this may appear irrelevant to the European, specifically to the English situation; but I believe that it has a bearing. Changes there must always be, reforms there will always be need for, because any system of education is imperfect and requires constant adaptation. But bad changes are as easily made as good; and the fact that a method has failed in one country is no guarantee that it will not be tried [117] in another; and on the other hand the success of a system in one country does not warrant its suitability to another: I should like to know, for instance, whether English models are appropriate for Scotland. The errors against which Babbitt fought are errors from which we are not immune. We insist upon 'educating' too many people; and Heaven knows what for. Thirty years ago Babbitt was a young tutor of insecure position, when he began almost single-handed (though perhaps under the approving eye of Charles Norton) to attack the system which Charles Eliot of Harvard had built up and popularised throughout the country; to the end of his life he opposed the heresies of the school of John Dewey. These facts deserve to be recorded in his honour; as particular facts they are no doubt of only local interest; but they represent moments in a consistent campaign which will have been, I think, to the benefit not only of his own country but of others. Not that American education has yet turned about. When I was a boy we began Latin at twelve or thirteen, and Greek a year later, and that seems to me late enough; now they begin Latin at fourteen or fifteen; in most schools Greek cannot, I understand, be learnt at all, and in the more expensive schools – those which correspond to the Public Schools – Greek is an optional subject, like the piano or violin, taken up by only a very few. When I asked, at a Prize Day, why no Greek prize was offered, I was told that not enough boys studied Greek to make a prize feasible. The most one can say is that Babbitt has won recognition for a different view of education than that prevailing, and has trained a devoted number of pupils who will propagate his view where they can.

In some domains, as in that of the arts, Babbitt was not in so strong a position; and here his work should be taken up and his conclusions reformed by men better qualified than he. With his evangelising spirit, and his ethical passion, I think that he rather starved his capacity for pure enjoyment; he often, I fear, gave his pupils the impression that he en-[118]joyed nothing but the *Iliad*, Sophocles, and Gray's *Elegy*; and even those, perhaps, he only allowed himself to enjoy on principle. Men who might otherwise have followed him, may have lost heart at the suspicion that if a masterpiece should be produced in our time, Babbitt (with his faculty of heresy-hunting) would probably denounce it. At any rate, he was not one of those who are ready to acclaim everything new lest their pupils should think them old fogeys. He may be accused, certainly, of reading new books voraciously in order to find out what was wrong with their philosophy; this does not alter the fact, however, that their philosophy usually *is* wrong. Babbitt certainly approached modern art of every kind without any predisposition in its favour; but I think that his natural sensibility was greater than his moral interests allowed it to appear. But it is not art with which he was directly concerned; his most important single book is *Democracy and Leadership*.

A regrettable error, for which I think Babbitt himself was partly responsible, has led, within the last ten years or so, to people looking into his doctrine for something which is not there: the search has been unfortunate both for those who thought they found it and those who have repudiated his views because they did not find it. His mind was in one sense profoundly philosophical; he had an intuitive apprehension of certain – but not all – essentials. But of philosophical technique he had none; and in his writings you will find no coherent system, but some apparently important inconsistencies. He was by temperament too extreme an individualist to be a system-builder or the founder of a school. He elaborated a way of life that served for him; other men must find their own. Any attempt to present his works as a body of canonical writings must end in failure, and worse. I have in mind the attempt, a few years ago, by a number of his devoted pupils to present 'humanism' as almost a proprietary medicine recommended for those who cannot 'believe' yet who abominate the radical materialism which is offered as an alternative. I have every sympathy, though a [119] little irritability, with people in this position. But I maintain that their 'humanism' would collapse like a house of cards the moment the support gives way; and the support which keeps humanism erect is simply the existence in the world of a body of people – however small that body may become – who are convinced of the reality of the Christian supernatural order and of the operation of the supernatural in the world. And one piece of evidence is that another 'humanism', a damnable infringement of patent, which the advocates of the first must abhor, has already been put upon the market in America by some liberal 'ministers'. We must regret deeply that Babbitt's attitude towards Christianity remained, in spite of his sometimes deceptive references to 'religion', definitely obdurate. Writing so soon after his death, however, we may be permitted to regret, more, that a certain inflexibility, or *raideur*, or almost excessive integrity of doctrine, did not allow him to recognise as disciples some who went too far for him as well as some who did not go far enough, but who acknowledge to him a very great debt, and revere his memory in affection, admiration and gratitude.

A letter from Mr Ezra Pound appears amongst the Correspondence; this would not be the place in which to refer to it, except that it animadverts upon the Commentary for last quarter. I cannot understand why Mr Pound should have bothered to write it, unless he wishes to deny outright the point which the Commentary attempted to make; but if that was his purpose, he has carried it out with unnecessary delicacy and periphrasis. He cannot suppose me to be wholly unacquainted with the person or the writings of Major Douglas, since, to give credit where due, it was Mr Pound who introduced me to both the person and the writings many years ago. Nor can Mr Pound justly suppose that I and perhaps several other contributors to the *Criterion*, are anything but friendly to the theory. Perhaps there is a more convinced acceptance of the diagnosis than the remedy; but it is easier for the lay mind to distinguish be-[120]tween diagnoses of a malady of which we are all aware, than between schemes any one of which may ignore important considerations which we have not been trained to look for. I hope that Major Douglas is right from top to bottom and copper-plated; but whether he is right or wrong does not matter a fig to my argument for the priority of ethics over politics. Indeed, if there is an economic remedy at hand, then the considerations I have put forward seem to me all the more pertinent. I may be wholly in error. Possibly the difficulty is merely that Mr Pound is interested in public affairs primarily as an artist – and with much greater solicitude, it should not be necessary to add, for other artists than for himself; and I am inclined to approach public affairs from the point of view of a moralist. As for morals, I will offer Mr Pound, if he cares to use it for admonishing me, the admirable phrase addressed by the Director of Talks to the gallant gentleman who offered to take part in a broadcast discussion of Air-Bombing: *the subject is not at the moment exercising the public mind and it would be better to wait until some turn of circumstances gives it a more topical value.*

Housman on Poetry

Review of *The Name and Nature of Poetry* by A. E. Housman (1933).

C., 13. 50 (Oct. 1933), 151–4. Signed 'T. S. Eliot'. Title from wrapper. Gallup C347.

It has long been known to the majority of those who really care about such matters, that Mr A. E. Housman is one of the few living masters of English prose; and that on those subjects on which he chooses to exercise his talents, there is no one living who can write better. We hope that he may consent to collect his scattered prose writings: the immortal Preface to Manilius is not so accessible as it ought to be. In the present short essay, which was the Leslie Stephen lecture for this year, Mr Housman is addressing himself to a larger audience, and has adapted himself perfectly to the requirements of such an occasion; and this lecture will serve admirably to introduce his prose to those who are unacquainted with it.

Mr Housman's prose owes its distinction to the power which separates all first-class prose from the merely efficient: a certain emotional intensity. I say 'a certain' merely as a reminder that you cannot abstract completely an identity recognisable in all great prose. Nor is this intensity to be confounded with explicit emotion arising from or suitably infused into the subject-matter, such as indignation, scorn or enthusiasm. It is the intensity of the artist, and is capable of informing any subject-matter, even the most abstract, the most arid, or the most impersonal, narrative, expository, or scientifically descriptive. The present subject, however, gives Mr Housman a wider range than those with which he is accustomed to deal; for he is both a nineteenth (or twentieth) century romantic poet and an eighteenth-century wit; and here, in his appreciation and his expression, he is able to expose both aspects in happy union.

We must keep in mind that this essay is a lecture; and the exigencies of a popular lecture require the author to select his points very carefully, to aim at form and proportion rather than connected profundity, and to avoid going too deeply into anything which is, for the purposes of the moment, another problem. We must not, in short, judge a lecture of Poetry as if it was a book on Aesthetics. The author may himself walk the straight line, but if he is to say anything at all in the time it is difficult for him, if not impossible, not to make assertions which, if pressed firmly and indefatigably by an unfriendly critic, will not yield a concentrated drop of heresy. I think that such a critic might be able to extract (1) the Essence of Poetry Theory, (2) the Pure Poetry Theory, (3) the Physiological Theory. None of these theories can be flatly denied without equal error; I do not believe that Mr Housman maintains any of them to a vicious degree; I mention them in the hope of sparing other critics the trouble of denouncing Mr Housman for what he does not maintain.

[153] Repeated meditations led me first to suspect, that there are surprisingly few things that can be said about Poetry; and of these few, the most turn out either to be false or to say nothing of significance. There are a great many things worth saying about one kind of poetry or another; and a good many might not have been said if their authors had not been under the impression that they were talking about all Poetry, when they were only talking about the kind of poetry they liked. Those who indulge in the Essence of Poetry fantasy are given to using 'touchstones', or test lines, which are almost always true poetry, and usually very great poetry. What none of them give us, yet what we are apt to delude ourselves into believing they give us, is an absolute dividing line between Poetry and Non-Poetry. Mr Housman does not actually say that the poetry of the eighteenth century (by which he means primarily Dryden and Pope) is not poetry, or rather he seems to say both that it is and is not; but it seems to me, with all due respect, that he is giving himself unnecessary pains. We know that there has been much greater poetry both before and since, and that is all that we need. You can assert that Pope was a poet, or you can assert that he was not a poet; if you enjoy his poetry it does not matter, and if you do not enjoy it that does not matter either. Whichever assertion you make will depend upon some definition of Poetry, explicit or implicit, which you cannot compel anyone else to accept. I feel a certain sympathy with Mr Housman's acid comments on the poetry of the seventeenth and eighteenth centuries, because I suspect that both have lately been for some amateurs a fashion rather than a taste. But when he suggests that the 'poetry' and the 'wit' in the metaphysicals can be separated as the sound and rotten parts of an apple or a banana with a knife, I am more than doubtful.

When Mr Housman asks himself: 'Am I capable of recognising poetry if I come across it?' I would unhesitatingly answer for him, so far as anyone can for any human being, in the affirmative. But there is more to it than that. You cannot divide human beings, in this respect, as you might separate compasses which are true from those which have more or less deviation. Mr Housman's quotations, in this lecture, show about as sensitive and refined a perception as any human being can aspire to.

But, in this way, is he quite fair to Dryden? and what is much more important, for here he is concerned with a poet for whom he feels almost unqualified admiration, is he quite fair to Blake? I am sure that Blake would not be happy about it, but we have not here to do with Blake's feelings, but with the Problem of Meaning. There is [154] probably no ground for taking issue with Mr Housman; and I have no space here to develop the difficulties involved in any theory; but I cannot leave the subject without at least affirming the extraordinary complexity of the problem, and the mazes of intellectual subtlety into which it is bound to lead the conscientious enquirer. 'Meaning is of the intellect, poetry is not.' I should not like to deny this, still less to assert it; I am in the same quandary as Mr Housman is with Pope. For what do we mean by meaning? and what by intellect? 'Poetry indeed seems to me more physical than intellectual.' Well, here again, is something I should not like to deny; but I am not sure that I know what 'physical' and 'intellectual' mean. But from the bottom of page 47 to the end of the lecture on page 51 Mr Housman has given us an account of his own experience in writing poetry which is important evidence. Observation leads me to believe that different poets may compose in very different ways; my experience (for what that is worth) leads me to believe that Mr Housman is recounting the authentic processes of a real poet. 'I have seldom,' he says, 'written poetry unless I was rather out of health.' I believe that I understand that sentence. If I do, it is a guarantee – if any guarantee of that nature is wanted – of the quality of Mr Housman's poetry.

The Modern Dilemma

Modified reprint of an unpublished address delivered on 3 Apr. 1933 before a gathering of Unitarian clergymen in Boston.

Christian Register, 102. 41 (19 Oct. 1933), [675]–6: Gallup C348.
Originally entitled 'Two Masters'.

Several years ago, at the end of a pamphlet on the last Lambeth Conference, I wrote the words: 'The world is trying the experiment of attempting to form a civilised but non-Christian mentality. The experiment will fail; but we must be very patient in awaiting its collapse; meanwhile redeeming the time so that the Faith may be preserved alive through the dark ages before us; to renew and rebuild civilisation, and save the world from suicide.'

It has struck me since that these words, and the paragraph from which they are taken, must have impressed a good many readers as merely a rather rhetorical flourish in concluding a rather polemical pamphlet. During the last fifteen years or so we have become so accustomed to gloomy predictions of the future of civilisation that we take them as a matter of course, or as a pleasant opiate. But my prediction differed from other predictions by being really a statement of what is already a fact. What I expect to happen in the future is merely the sort of thing that will make more evident that what I predict has already happened. It is quite possible that we are at the beginning of the Dark Ages. In the last three or four hundred years we have passed through successive stages of schism, heresy, and toleration. Possibly the age of toleration is coming to an end, and we may be again approaching a period in which Christians in Western Europe and America will be persecuted. I hardly expect so much as that: life will simply be made more and more inconvenient for them. Christians will not be persecuted until they are feared; and they will not be feared until they are powerful. They may, for the efficient regiment of the state, be segregated into ghettos; but they will probably be tolerated on the assumption that they are a dying race for some time to come.

Meanwhile, the intermediate stages between Christianity will, I believe, tend to disappear, and it is well that they should disappear. The future will be black and white. That is, however, a slow process; the humanitarians, the sentimentalists, the conservatives, and the fundamentalists are tenacious of life. But amongst the more intelligent, and in the main centers of activity, I think it is no exaggeration to say that men and women tend to be either more orthodox or else do not pretend to be Christians at all. It is still premature to conjecture on what lines the amorphous body of non-Christians will organise itself: and it is difficult to conceive what their minds will be like. Many of the most charming and congenial persons I know are atheists (they may call themselves agnostics). But they are either the children, or grandchildren, or at most the great-grandchildren, of professing Christians; their religious inheritance is involved with their social inheritance, their 'class' values, their social and financial position, their notions of correct behavior, however debased. Their agnosticism represents a transitional stage, as broadmindedness and tolerance on any large scale are transitional. Their great-grandchildren will probably find themselves with some positive belief; and this belief will either be for Christianity or against it.

I am sure that it is only in its complete form that Christianity will survive at all – though some of us may disagree at present as to what this completeness comprehends. The lingering political importance of Protestantism, in Britain, northern Europe, and America, is an importance of democratic numbers rather than of intellectual activity and leadership; and democratic numbers themselves seem to become less powerful than they were. I do not, of course, present this forecast as offering an argument in favour of Catholicism; arguments are concerned with its *truth*, not with the probable consequences of failing to support it, however disastrous those consequences may be. Nor am I manipulating the political bogey of Communism. Most people's prejudices against Communism are no better founded than other people's prejudices in its favour. Communism is, at any rate, something with which the Catholic can have a kind of sympathy. It does aim at something. To the liberal, Communism finds a mythical value in something called society or humanity, and Catholicism finds a mythical value in something called the individual soul. It is true that Communism does not make much of the Christian virtue of chastity, but I cannot see why anyone who is not a Christian should attach much importance to chastity; and Communism does not make much of a virtue of humility – but that is either a Christian virtue or it is not a virtue at all; on the other hand it exalts, in common with the monastic orders, the virtues of poverty and obedience. The actual order has merely made poverty a badge of shame, and for obedience it has substituted economic pressure. And the Catholic should be too dissatisfied with the world as it is to be afraid of change in itself, nor does he *expect* a great deal of the world at any time, though his *demands* be severe. He is not interested in degrees.

[676] I cannot draw the distinction between the Catholic and the conservative – who is usually confused as to what he wants to conserve – more easily than in the matter of morality, or sin. The conservative is concerned, not so much with moral laws as with habits and conventions; so that the morality of his own generation, or perhaps of that immediately preceding, is his criterion. To many excellent people sexual sin is the most repellent; they can hardly conceive that the sin of pride may be more deadly. They not only conceive 'morality' too narrowly, but they care more for morality than for religion; and they fear their natural appetites, but not their natural tendency towards heresy and intellectual error. They may support Christianity – in a degraded form usually – because of a prudential or purely irrational terror of immorality; but that in which they believe is often a morality of custom and prejudice rather than that which Christianity teaches. If I did not believe in something so fundamental as the Incarnation, I should find it difficult to defend the morality which I try to practice.

Accordingly, what gives me concern, in the modern world, is not so much the growth of sexual laxity, or even of financial corruption, as the disappearance of the *sense* of sin. People often talk as if the sense of sin were something invented by a peculiarly gloomy race of fanatics which sprang up suddenly in England and immediately fled to Massachusetts. But the sense of sin is absolutely essential to Christianity, and to Judaism from which it came; and as for Puritanism, there is more genuine Puritanism inside the Catholic Church than outside of it. I am not so much alarmed today at there being so many sinners as I am by there being so many people who feel virtuous. I can hardly think that there was ever a time before when so many people felt virtuous. And when people feel virtuous, civilisation totters. It is not the movie stars that are the menace: if, as I dare say is not the case, their standards of morality are unedifying, they are only filling a popular demand. The danger comes from the virtuous and well-intentioned; from the pioneers of Ethical Culture, the World-Leaguers for Sexual Reform, the Utopians, the enthusiastic, the unsophisticated, the self-appointed saints, and the people who will *not* study Latin and Greek.

The real abyss is between those who believe in the supernatural and those who do not; and amongst the latter I class all those who are liberal enough to allow a *little* place for the supernatural. To believe in the supernatural is not simply to believe that after living a successful, material, and fairly virtuous life here one will continue to exist in the best possible substitute for this world, or that after living a starved and stunted life here one will be compensated with all the good things one has gone without: it is to believe that the supernatural is the greatest reality here and now. We have to make it our source of values and the pattern of our life. It is well put in Harton's *Elements of the Spiritual Life*:

> It is clear that the Christian life is essentially supernatural. It is the ignoring or denying of this element which is the cause of most of the ineffectiveness of present-day religion. Supernatural religion is not popular, but that does not make it untrue. Protestantism dislikes it, the Reformation was largely a movement for its dethronement; Modernism dislikes it – the pathetic desire to find a purely human Christ and the condemnation of sacramental action as 'magic' attest as much; Science dislikes it because it appears to the scientist to introduce an incalculable and undemonstrable element into Nature; the Man in the Street dislikes it because it is beyond his comprehension, and it is a common weakness to fear and therefore to hate the unknown; it remains for the Catholic uncompromisingly to nail his colors to the mast and live supernaturally, confident that on that level alone will he find fully Him for whom his soul thirsts.

As the sense of sin depends upon the supernatural, so from the sense of sin issues the ascetic life. The ascetic ideal is essential to Christianity.

The modern world suffers from two great disasters: the decay of the study of Latin and Greek and the dissolution of the monasteries. These defects can be supplied. The benefit of monasticism is not only for those individuals who have the vocation for that life; it is also in the ideal of life that it sets before those whose lives are in the world. For Christian asceticism is a matter of degree; and every life, in so far as it is Christian, is ascetic: in self-abnegation, self-discipline, and the love of God. Exceptional austerities are for exceptional men; for ordinary men, the practice of prayer and meditation and the daily battle against the distractions which the world offers to the mind and the spirit. The ascetic ideal – and asceticism is of course far more than a mere *doing without* – seems to me implied in the Summary of the Law.

We like to interpret the love of our neighbours as ourselves as a vague benevolence, or as practical charity alone. We like to think that as we want to be happy, and have some 'right' to be happy, so we must remember that our neighbours have rights too and that we should try to make them happy: the love of our neighbours becomes fair play, and doing the decent thing. But the real love of our neighbour, in and for God, means transcending the bounds of love and benevolence as we know them, and reaching a plane at which what is given is not as the world gives.

In the way in which the modern world uses the terms 'human' and 'inhuman', there is undoubtedly something 'inhuman' about this. As a supernatural religion, Christianity must aim to lead its followers to something above the human – though the last thing a Christian wants to be is a 'superman', and the majority of human beings hate and fear any summons to be more than healthy natural human beings. St Paul, perhaps, was not perfectly 'integrated', or his interpretation of *estote perfecti* was not that of Freud. *For I know that in me (that is, in my flesh) dwelleth no good thing: for to will is present with me; but how to perform that which is good I know not.... O wretched man that I am! who shall deliver me from the body of this death?* We can have no ideal, for human beings, lower than that of saintliness: an ideal which the world repudiates, or reduces to the saintliness of a Santa Claus. We recognise the chasm between the divine and the human, we admit our shortcomings and wrongdoings. 'It is not true that we have never been broken: we have been broken upon the wheel.' The world insists upon being right. It insists upon being virtuous. It is right, it is virtuous, it is damned.

The Use of Poetry and the Use of Criticism
Studies in the Relation of Criticism to Poetry in England

Publ. on 2 Nov. 1933. Gallup A24.

Contents: 'Preface'; 'Introduction'; 'Apology for the Countess of Pembroke'; 'The Age of Dryden'; 'Wordsworth and Coleridge'; 'Shelley and Keats'; 'Matthew Arnold'; 'The Modern Mind'; 'Conclusion'.

[7] To the Memory of
CHARLES WHIBLEY
to whom I promised a better book

[11] Preface

These lectures, delivered at Harvard University during the winter of 1932–33, owe much to an audience only too ready to applaud merit and condone defect; but I am aware that such success as they had was largely dramatic, and that they will be still more disappointing to those who heard them than they will be to those who did not. I should much prefer to leave my auditors with whatever impression they then received; but by the terms of the Foundation by Mr Stillman the lectures must be submitted for publication, and within a fixed period. Thus I explain my commission of another unnecessary book.

I am glad, however, of the opportunity to record in print my obligation to the President and Fellows of Harvard College; to the Norton Professorship Committee; and in particular my gratitude to Professor John Livingston Lowes; to the Master of Eliot House and Mrs Merriman, with most pleasant memories of the Associates and Tutors of the House; to Dr Theodore Spencer; and to Mr and Mrs Alfred Dwight Sheffield for innumerable criticisms and suggestions.

I much regret that while I was preparing these lectures for delivery in America, Mr I. A. Richards was in England; and that while I was preparing them for publication in England, he was in America. I had hoped that they might have the benefit of his criticism.

T. S. E.
London, August 1933.

[13] Introduction

November 4th, 1932

UPUC, 13-36

'The whole country is now excited by the political campaign, and in a condition of irrational emotion. The best of the prospect is that a re-organisation of parties seems not unlikely as an indirect result of the present contest between the Republicans and the Democrats . . . But any radical change is not to be hoped for.'

These words occur in a letter written by Charles Eliot Norton on September 24th, 1876. The present lectures will have no concern with politics; I have begun with a political quotation only as a reminder of the varied interests of the scholar and humanist whom this foundation commemorates. The lecturer on such a foundation is fortunate who can feel, as I do, sympathy and admiration for the man whose memory the lectures are intended to keep living. Charles Eliot Norton had the moral and spiritual qualities, of a stoic kind, which are possible without the benefits of revealed religion; and the mental gifts which are possible without genius. To do the useful thing, to say the courageous thing, to contemplate the beautiful thing: that is enough for one man's life. Few men have known better than he how to give just place to the claims of the public and of the private life; few men have had better opportunity, few of those having the opportunity have [14] availed themselves of it better than he. The usual politician, the man of public affairs, is rarely able to go to the 'public place' without assuming the 'public face': Norton always preserved his privacy. And living as he did in a non-Christian society, and in a world which, as he saw it on both sides of the Atlantic, showed signs of decay, he maintained the standards of the humanity and humanism that he knew. He was able, even at an early age, to look upon the passing order without regret, and towards the coming order without hope. In a letter of December 1869 he speaks more strongly and more comprehensively than in that which I have quoted:

> The future is very dark in Europe, and to me it looks as if we were entering upon a period quite new in history – one in which the questions on which parties will divide, and from which outbreak after outbreak of passion and violence will arise, will no longer be political but immediately social . . . Whether our period of economic enterprise, unlimited competition, and unrestrained individualism, is the highest stage of human progress is to me very doubtful; and sometimes, when I see the existing conditions of European (to say

nothing of American) social order, bad as they are for the mass alike of upper and lower classes, I wonder whether our civilisation can maintain itself against the forces which are banding together for the destruction of many of the institutions in which it is embodied, or whether we are not to have another period of decline, fall, and ruin and revival, like that of the first thirteen hundred years of our era. It would not grieve me much to know that this were to be the case. No man who [15] knows what society at the present day really is but must agree that it is not worth preserving on its present basis.[1]

These are words to which many who approach contemporary problems with more dogmatic assumptions than Norton's can give assent. Yet for him the permanent importance of literature if not of dogma was a fixed point. The people which ceases to care for its literary inheritance becomes barbaric; the people which ceases to produce literature ceases to move in thought and sensibility. The poetry of a people takes its life from the people's speech and in turn gives life to it; and represents its highest point of consciousness, its greatest power and its most delicate sensibility.

In these lectures I have to deal as much or more with criticism of poetry as with poetry itself; and my subject is not merely the relation of criticism to poetry, if by that we assume that we know already what poetry is, and does, and is for. Indeed, a good part of criticism has consisted simply in the pursuit of answers to these questions. Let me start with the supposition that we do not know what poetry is, or what it does or ought to do, or of what use it is; and try to find out, in examining the relation of poetry and criticism, what the use of both of them is. We may even discover that we have no very clear idea of what *use* is; at any rate we had better not assume that we know.

I shall not begin with any general definition of what is and what is not poetry, or any discussion of whether poetry need be always in verse, or any consideration of the dif-[16]ference between the poetry-verse antithesis and the poetry-prose antithesis. Criticism, however, may be separated from the beginning not into two kinds, but according to two tendencies. I assume that criticism is that department of thought which either seeks to find out what poetry is, what its use is, what desires it satisfies, why it is written and why read, or recited; or which, making some conscious or unconscious assumption that we do know these things, assesses actual poetry. We may find that good criticism has other designs than these; but these are the ones which it is allowed to profess. Criticism, of course, never does find out what poetry is, in the sense of

---

1. My quotations from Norton's letters are taken from the *Life and Letters of Charles Eliot Norton* (Houghton, Mifflin: 2 vols.).

arriving at an adequate definition; but I do not know of what use such a definition would be if it were found. Nor can criticism ever arrive at any final appraisal of poetry. But there are these two theoretical limits of criticism: at one of which we attempt to answer the question 'what is poetry?' and at the other 'is this a good poem?' No theoretic ingenuity will suffice to answer the second question, because no theory can amount to much which is not founded upon a direct experience of good poetry; but on the other hand our direct experience of poetry involves a good deal of generalising activity.

The two questions, which represent the most abstract formulation of what is far from being an abstract activity, imply each other. The critic who remains worth reading has asked, if he has only imperfectly answered, both questions. Aristotle, in what we possess of his writings upon poetry, does, I think, quicken our appreciation of the Greek tragic dramatists; Coleridge, in his defence of the poetry of Wordsworth, is led into generalisations about poetry [17] which are of the greatest interest; and Wordsworth, in his explanation of his own poetry, makes assertions about the nature of poetry which, if excessive, have a wider bearing than even he may have realised. Mr I. A. Richards, who ought to know, if anyone does, what equipment the scientific critic needs, tells us that 'both a passionate knowledge of poetry and a capacity for dispassionate psychological analysis' are required. Mr Richards, like every serious critic of poetry, is a serious moralist as well. His ethics, or theory of value, is one which I cannot accept; or rather, I cannot accept any such theory which is erected upon purely individual-psychological foundations. But his psychology of the poetic experience is based upon his own experience of poetry, as truly as his theory of value arises out of his psychology. You may be dissatisfied with his philosophical conclusions but still believe (as I do) in his discriminating taste in poetry. But if on the other hand you had no faith in the critic's ability to tell a good poem from a bad one, you would put little reliance upon the validity of his theories. In order to analyse the enjoyment and appreciation of a good poem, the critic must have experienced the enjoyment, and he must convince us of his taste. For the experience of enjoying a bad poem while thinking it is a good one is very different from that of enjoying a good poem.

We do expect the critic who theorises to know a good poem when he sees it. It is not always true that a person who knows a good poem when he sees it can tell us why it is a good poem. The experience of poetry, like any other experience, is only partially translatable into words; to begin with, as Mr Richards says, 'it is never what a poem [18] *says* that matters, but what it *is*'. And we know that some people who are inarticulate, and cannot say why they like a poem, may have deeper and more discriminating sensibility than some others who can talk glibly about it; we must remember too that poetry is not written simply to provide material for conversation. Even the most accomplished of critics can, in the end, only point to the poetry which seems to him to be the real thing. Nevertheless, our talking about poetry is a part of, an extension of, our experience of it; and as a good deal of thinking has gone to the making of poetry, so a good deal may well go to the study of it. The rudiment of criticism is the ability to select a good poem and reject a bad poem; and its most severe test is of its ability to select a good *new* poem, to respond properly to a new situation. The experience of poetry, as it develops in the conscious and mature person, is not merely the sum of the experiences of good poems. Education in poetry requires an organisation of these experiences. There is not one of us who is born with, or who suddenly acquires at puberty or later, an infallible discrimination and taste. The person whose experience is limited is always liable to be taken in by the sham or the adulterate article; and we see generation after generation of untrained readers being taken in by the sham and the adulterate in its own time – indeed preferring them, for they are more easily assimilable than the genuine article. Yet a very large number of people, I believe, have the native capacity for enjoying *some* good poetry: how much, or how many degrees of capacity may profitably be distinguished, is not part of my present purpose to enquire. It is only the exceptional reader, certainly, [19] who in the course of time comes to classify and compare his experiences, to see one in the light of others; and who, as his poetic experiences multiply, will be able to understand each more accurately. The element of enjoyment is enlarged into appreciation, which brings a more intellectual addition to the original intensity of feeling. It is a second stage in our understanding of poetry, when we no longer merely select and reject, but organise. We may even speak of a third stage, one of reorganisation; a stage at which a person already educated in poetry meets with something new in his own time, and finds a new pattern of poetry arranging itself in consequence.

This pattern, which we form in our own minds out of our own reading of poetry that we have enjoyed, is a kind of answer, which we make each for himself, to the question 'what is poetry?' At the first stage we find out what poetry is by reading it and enjoying some of what we read; at a later stage our perception of the resemblances and differences between what we read for the first time and what we have already enjoyed itself contributes to our enjoyment. We learn what poetry is – if we ever learn – from reading it; but one might say that we should not be able to recognise poetry in particular unless we had an innate idea of poetry in general. At any rate, the question 'what is poetry?' issues quite naturally from our experience of poems. Even, therefore, although we may admit that few forms of intellectual activity seem to have less to show for themselves, in the course of history, in the way of books worth reading, than does criticism, it would appear that criticism, like any philosophical activity, is inevitable and [20] requires no justification. To ask 'what is poetry?' is to posit the critical function.

I suppose that to many people the thought must have occurred, that at some periods when great poetry was written there was no written criticism; and that in some periods in which much criticism has been written the quality of the poetry has been inferior. This fact has suggested an antithesis between the critical and the creative, between critical ages and creative ages; and it is sometimes thought that criticism flourishes most at times when creative vigour is in defect. It is with such a prejudice in mind that people have coupled with 'critical ages' the adjective 'Alexandrian'. Several gross assumptions underlie this prejudice, including a confusion between several different things, and between works of very different quality, included under 'criticism'. I am using the term 'criticism' throughout these lectures, as I hope you will discover, with a pretty narrow extension. I have no desire to extenuate the vices of the vast number of books which pass by that designation, or to flatter the lazy habit of substituting, for a careful study of the texts, the assimilation of other people's opinions. If people only wrote when they had something to say, and never merely because they wanted to write a book, or because they occupied a position such that the writing of books was expected of them, the mass of criticism would not be wholly out of proportion to the small number of critical books worth reading. Nevertheless, those who speak as if criticism were an occupation of decadence, and a symptom, if not a cause, of the creative impotence of a people, isolate the circumstances of litera-[21]ture, to the extent of falsification, from the circumstances of life. Such changes as that from the epic poem composed to be recited to the epic poem composed to be read, or those which put an end to the popular ballad, are inseparable from social changes on a vast scale, such changes as have always taken place and always will. W. P. Ker, in his essay on 'The Forms of English Poetry', observed that:

> The art of the Middle Ages generally is corporate and social; the sculpture, for example, as it is found on the great cathedrals. With the Renaissance the motive of poetry is changed. In the Middle Ages there is a natural likeness to the Greek conditions; after the Renaissance there is a conscious and intentional reproduction among the modern nations of the conditions which prevailed in the poetry of Rome. Greek poetry in many respects is mediaeval;

the Latin poetry of the great age is Renaissance, an imitation of types derived from Greece, with quite different circumstances and a different relation of the poet to his audience.

Not that Latin or modern poetry is unsocial. It is true . . . that the tendency of modern art, including poetry, is often contrary to the popular taste of its time; the poets are often left to themselves to find their themes and elaborate their modes of expression in solitude, with results that are often found as perplexing and offensive, and as negligible, as Browning's *Sordello* was generally found to be.

What is true of the major changes in the form of poetry is, I think, true also of the change from a pre-critical to a critical age. It is true of the change from a pre-philosophical to a philosophical age; you cannot deplore criticism unless you deprecate philosophy. You may say that the develop-[22]ment of criticism is a symptom of the development, or change, of poetry; and the development of poetry is itself a symptom of social changes. The important moment for the appearance of criticism seems to be the time when poetry ceases to be the expression of the mind of a whole people. The drama of Dryden, which furnishes the chief occasion for his critical writing, is formed by Dryden's perception that the possibilities of writing in the mode of Shakespeare were exhausted; the form persists in the tragedies of such a writer as Shirley (who is much more up to date in his comedies), after the mind and sensibility of England has altered. But Dryden was not writing plays for the whole people; he was writing in a form which had not grown out of popular tradition or popular requirements, a form the acceptance of which had therefore to come by diffusion through a small society. Something similar had been attempted by the Senecan dramatists. But the part of society to which Dryden's work, and that of the Restoration comedians, could immediately appeal constituted something like an intellectual aristocracy; when the poet finds himself in an age in which there is no intellectual aristocracy, when power is in the hands of a class so democratised that whilst still a class it represents itself to be the whole nation; when the only alternatives seem to be to talk to a coterie or to soliloquise, the difficulties of the poet and the necessity of criticism become greater. In the essay from which I have just quoted, Ker says:

> There is no doubt that in the nineteenth century poets are more left to themselves than they were in the eighteenth, and the result is unmistakable in their strength and weak-[23]ness. . . . The heroic independence of Browning, and indeed all the adventurous capricious poetry of the nineteenth century, is closely related to criticism, and to the eclectic learning which ranges over the whole

world in search of artistic beauty. . . . The themes are taken from all the ages and countries; the poets are eclectic students and critics, and they are justified, as explorers are justified; they sacrifice what explorers sacrifice when they leave their native home. . . . I shall not be misunderstood if I remark that their victories bring along with them some danger, if not for themselves, at least for the fashion, that tradition of poetry.

The gradual changes in the function of poetry, as society alters, will, I hope, emerge somewhat after we have considered several critics as representatives of several generations. During three hundred years criticism has come to modify its assumptions and its purposes, and it will surely continue to do so. There are several forms which criticism may take; there is always a large proportion of criticism which is retrograde or irrelevant; there are always many writers who are qualified neither by knowledge of the past nor by awareness of the sensibility and the problems of the present. Our earliest criticism, under the influence of classical studies and of Italian critics, made very large assumptions about the nature and function of literature. Poetry was a decorative art, an art for which sometimes extravagant claims were made, but an art in which the same principles seemed to hold good for every civilisation and for every society; it was an art deeply affected by the rise of a new social class, only loosely (at best) associated [24] with the Church, a class self-conscious in its possession of the mysteries of Latin and Greek. In England the critical force due to the new contrast between Latin and vernacular met, in the sixteenth century, with just the right degree of resistance. That is to say, for the age which is represented for us by Spenser and Shakespeare, the new forces stimulated the native genius and did not overwhelm it. The purpose of my second lecture will be to give to the criticism of this period the due which it does not seem to me to have received. In the next age, the great work of Dryden in criticism is, I think, that at the right moment he became conscious of the necessity of affirming the native element in literature. Dryden is more consciously English, in his plays, than were his predecessors; his essays on the drama and on the art of translation are conscious studies of the nature of the English theatre and the English language; and even his adaptation of Chaucer is an assertion of the native tradition – rather than, what it has sometimes been taken to be, an amusing and pathetic failure to appreciate the beauty of the Chaucerian language and metric. Where the Elizabethan critics, for the most part, were aware of something to be borrowed or adapted from abroad, Dryden was aware of something to be preserved at home. But throughout this period, and for much longer, one assumption remained the same: the assumption as to what was the use of poetry. Any reader of Sidney's *Apology for Poetry* can see that his *misomousoi* against whom he defends poetry are men of straw, that he is confident of having the sympathy of his reader with him, and that he never seriously has to ask himself the questions, what poetry is for, what it does, or [25] whether it is desirable. Sidney's assumption is that poetry gives at once delight and instruction, and is an adornment of social life and an honour to the nation.

I am very far from dissenting from these assumptions, so far as they go; my point is that for a long time they were never questioned or modified; that during that time great poetry was written, and some criticism which just because of its assumptions has permanent instruction to give. I hold indeed that in an age in which the use of poetry is something agreed upon you are more likely to get that minute and scrupulous examination of felicity and blemish, line by line, which is conspicuously absent from the criticism of our time, a criticism which seems to demand of poetry, not that it shall be well written, but that it shall be 'representative of its age'. I wish that we might dispose more attention to the correctness of expression, to the clarity or obscurity, to the grammatical precision or inaccuracy, to the choice of words whether just or improper, exalted or vulgar, of our verse: in short to the good or bad breeding of our poets. My point here is that a great change in the attitude towards poetry, in the expectations and demands made upon it, did come, we may say for convenience towards the end of the eighteenth century. Wordsworth and Coleridge are not merely demolishing a debased tradition, but revolting against a whole social order; and they begin to make claims for poetry which reach their highest point of exaggeration in Shelley's famous phrase, 'poets are the unacknowledged legislators of mankind'. Earlier laudators of poetry had said the same thing, but it did not mean the same thing: Shelley (to borrow a successful phrase from Mr Bernard [26] Shaw) was the first, in this tradition, of Nature's M.P.'s. If Wordsworth thought that he was simply occupied with reform of language, he was deceived; he was occupied with revolution of language; and his own language was as capable of artificiality, and no more capable of naturalness, than that of Pope – as Byron felt, and as Coleridge candidly pointed out. The decay of religion, and the attrition of political institutions, left dubious frontiers upon which the poet encroached; and the annexations of the poet were legitimised by the critic. For a long time the poet is the priest: there are still, I believe, people who imagine that they draw religious aliment from Browning or Meredith. But the next stage is best exemplified by Matthew Arnold. Arnold was too temperate and reasonable a man to maintain exactly that religious instruction is best conveyed by poetry, and he himself had very little to convey; but he discovered a new formula: poetry is not religion, but it is a capital substitute for religion – not invalid port, which may lend itself to hypocrisy, but coffee without caffeine, and tea without tannin. The doctrine of Arnold was extended, if also somewhat travestied, in the doctrine of 'art for art's sake'. This creed might seem a reversion to the simpler faith of an earlier time, in which the poet was like a dentist, a man with a definite job. But it was really a hopeless admission of irresponsibility. The poetry of revolt and the poetry of retreat are not of the same kind.

In our time we have moved, under various impulses, to new positions. On the one hand the study of psychology has impelled men not only to investigate the mind of the poet with a confident ease which has led to some fantastic [27] excesses and aberrant criticism, but also to investigate the mind of the reader and the problem of 'communication' – a word which perhaps begs a question. On the other hand the study of history has shown us the relation of both form and content of poetry to the conditions of its time and place. The psychological and the sociological are probably the two best advertised varieties of modern criticism; but the number of ways in which the problems of criticism are approached was never before so great or so confusing. Never were there fewer settled assumptions as to what poetry is, or why it comes about, or what it is for. Criticism seems to have separated into several diverse kinds.

I have not made this brief review of the progress of criticism in order to lead up to associating myself with any particular tendency of modern criticism, least of all the sociological. I suggest that we may learn a good deal about criticism and about poetry by examining the history of criticism, not merely as a catalogue of successive notions about poetry, but as a process of readjustment between poetry and the world in and for which it is produced. We can learn something about poetry simply by studying what people have thought about it at one period after another; without coming to the stultifying conclusion that there is nothing to be said but that opinion changes. Second, the study of criticism, not as a sequence of random conjectures, but as readaptation, may also help us to draw some conclusions as to what is permanent or eternal in poetry, and what is merely the expression of the spirit of an age; and by discovering what does change, and how, and why, we may become able to apprehend what does not change. [28] And by investigating the problems of what has seemed to one age and another to matter, by examining differences and identities, we may somewhat hope to extend our own limitations and liberate ourselves from some of our prejudices. I will quote at this point two passages which I may have occasion to quote again. The first is from Dryden's 'Preface to *Annus Mirabilis*':

The first happiness of the poet's imagination is properly invention, or the finding of the thought; the second is fancy, or the variation, deriving, or moulding of that thought, as the judgement represents it proper to the subject; the third is elocution, or the art of clothing and adorning that thought, as found and varied, in apt, significant, and sounding words; the quickness of the imagination is seen in the invention, the fertility in the fancy, and the accuracy in the expression.

The second passage is from Coleridge's *Biographia Literaria*:

Repeated meditations led me first to suspect ... that Fancy and Imagination were two distinct and widely different faculties, instead of being, according to the general belief, either two names with one meaning, or, at furthest, the lower and higher degree of one and the same power. It is not, I own, easy to conceive a more apposite translation of the Greek *phantasia* than the Latin *imaginatio*; but it is equally true that in all societies there exists an instinct of growth, a certain collective, unconscious good sense working progressively to desynonymise those words originally of the same meaning, which the conflux of dialects supplied to the more homogeneous languages, as the Greek and [29] the German.... Milton had a highly imaginative, Cowley a very fanciful mind.[1]

The way in which the expression of the two poets and critics is determined by their respective backgrounds is very marked. Evident also is the more developed state of mind of Coleridge: his greater awareness of philology, and his conscious determination to make certain words mean certain things. But what we have to consider is, whether what we have here is two radically opposed theories of Poetic Imagination, or whether the two may be reconciled after we have taken account of the many causes of difference which are found in the passage of time between Dryden's generation and Coleridge's.

It may appear that most of what I have said, while it may have some bearing on the appreciation and understanding of poetry, has very little to do with the writing of it. When the critics are themselves poets, it may be suspected that they have formed their critical statements with a

---

1. I may remark here as well as anywhere else that the statement contained in this last sentence is liable to operate an irrational persuasion upon the mind of the reader. We *agree* that Milton is a much greater poet than Cowley, and of another and superior kind. We then concede without examination that the difference may be formulated by this neat antithesis, and accept without examination the distinction between *imagination* and *fancy* which Coleridge has done no more than impose. The antithesis of *highly* against *very* is also an element of persuasion. See p. 58.

view to justifying their poetic practice. Such criticism as the two passages quoted is hardly designed to form the style of younger poets; it is rather, at its best, an account of the poet's experience of his own poetic activity, related in terms [30] of his own mind. The critical mind operating *in* poetry, the critical effort which goes to the writing of it, may always be in advance of the critical mind operating *upon* poetry, whether it be one's own or some one else's. I only affirm that there is a significant relation between the best poetry and the best criticism of the same period. The age of criticism is also the age of critical poetry. And when I speak of modern poetry as being extremely critical, I mean that the contemporary poet, who is not merely a composer of graceful verses, – is forced to ask himself such questions as 'what is poetry for?'; not merely 'what am I to say?' but rather 'how and to whom am I to say it?' We have to communicate – if it is communication, for the word may beg the question – an experience which is not an experience in the ordinary sense, for it may only exist, formed out of many personal experiences ordered in some way which may be very different from the way of valuation of practical life, in the expression of it. *If* poetry is a form of 'communication', yet that which is to be communicated is the poem itself, and only incidentally the experience and the thought which have gone into it. The poem's existence is somewhere between the writer and the reader; it has a reality which is not simply the reality of what the writer is trying to 'express', or of his experience of writing it, or of the experience of the reader or of the writer as reader. Consequently the problem of what a poem 'means' is a good deal more difficult than it at first appears. If a poem of mine entitled *Ash-Wednesday* ever goes into a second edition, I have thought of prefixing to it the lines of Byron from *Don Juan*:

[31] Some have accused me of a strange design
    Against the creed and morals of this land,
And trace it in this poem, every line.
    I don't pretend that I quite understand
My own meaning when I would be *very* fine;
    But the fact is that I have nothing planned
Except perhaps to be a moment merry . . .

There is some sound critical admonition in these lines. But a poem is not just either what the poet 'planned' or what the reader conceives, nor is its 'use' restricted wholly to what the author intended or to what it actually does for readers. Though the amount and the quality of the pleasure which any work of art has given since it came into existence is not irrelevant, still we never judge it by that; and we do not ask, after being greatly moved by the sight of a piece of architecture or the audition of a piece of music, 'what has been my benefit or profit from seeing this temple or hearing this music?' In one sense the question implied by the phrase 'the use of poetry' is nonsense. But there is another meaning to the question. Apart from the variety of ways in which poets have used their art, with greater or less success, with designs of instruction or persuasion, there is no doubt that a poet wishes to give pleasure, to entertain or divert people; and he should normally be glad to be able to feel that the entertainment or diversion is enjoyed by as large and various a number of people as possible. When a poet deliberately restricts his public by his choice of style or writing or of subject-matter, this is a special situation demanding explan-[32]ation and extenuation, but I doubt whether this ever happens. It is one thing to write in a style which is already popular, and another to hope that one's writing may eventually become popular. From one point of view, the poet aspires to the condition of the music-hall comedian. Being incapable of altering his wares to suit a prevailing taste, if there be any, he naturally desires a state of society in which they may become popular, and in which his own talents will be put to the best use. He is accordingly vitally interested in the *use* of poetry. The subsequent lectures will treat of the varying conceptions of the use of poetry during the last three centuries, as illustrated in criticism, and especially in the criticism provided by the poets themselves.

NOTE TO CHAPTER I
ON THE DEVELOPMENT OF TASTE IN POETRY

It may be not inopportune, in connexion with some of the questions touched upon in the foregoing chapter, to summarise here certain remarks which I made elsewhere upon the Development of Taste. They are, I hope, not without some bearing upon the teaching of literature in schools and colleges.

I may be generalising my own history unwarrantably, or on the other hand I may be uttering what is already a commonplace amongst teachers and psychologists, when I put forward the conjecture that the majority of children, up to say twelve or fourteen, are capable of a certain enjoyment of poetry; that at or about puberty the majority of these find little further use for it, but that a small minority [33] then find themselves possessed of a craving for poetry which is wholly different from any enjoyment experienced before. I do not know whether little girls have a different taste in poetry from little boys, but the responses of the latter I believe to be fairly uniform. *Horatius*, *The Burial of Sir John Moore*, *Bannockburn*, Tennyson's *Revenge*, some of the border ballads: a liking for martial and sanguinary poetry is no more to be discouraged than engagements with lead soldiers and pea-shooters. The only pleasure that I got from

Shakespeare was the pleasure of being commended for reading him; had I been a child of more independent mind I should have refused to read him at all. Recognising the frequent deceptions of memory, I seem to remember that my early liking for the sort of verse that small boys do like vanished at about the age of twelve, leaving me for a couple of years with no sort of interest in poetry at all. I can recall clearly enough the moment when, at the age of fourteen or so, I happened to pick up a copy of Fitzgerald's *Omar* which was lying about, and the almost overwhelming introduction to a new world of feeling which this poem was the occasion of giving me. It was like a sudden conversion; the world appeared anew, painted with bright, delicious and painful colours. Thereupon I took the usual adolescent course with Byron, Shelley, Keats, Rossetti, Swinburne.

I take this period to have persisted until about my twenty-second year. Being a period of rapid assimilation, the end may not know the beginning, so different may the taste become. Like the first period of childhood, it is one beyond which I dare say many people never advance; so that such [34] taste for poetry as they retain in later life is only a sentimental memory of the pleasures of youth, and is probably entwined with all our other sentimental retrospective feelings. It is, no doubt, a period of keen enjoyment; but we must not confuse the intensity of the poetic experience in adolescence with the intense experience of poetry. At this period, the poem, or the poetry of a single poet, invades the youthful consciousness and assumes complete possession for a time. We do not really see it as something with an existence outside ourselves; much as in our youthful experiences of love, we do not so much see the person as infer the existence of some outside object which sets in motion these new and delightful feelings in which we are absorbed. The frequent result is an outburst of scribbling which we may call imitation, so long as we are aware of the meaning of the word 'imitation' which we employ. It is not a deliberate choice of a poet to mimic, but writing under a kind of daemonic possession by one poet.

The third, or mature stage of enjoyment of poetry, comes when we cease to identify ourselves with the poet we happen to be reading; when our critical faculties remain awake; when we are aware of what one poet can be expected to give and what he cannot. The poem has its own existence, apart from us; it was there before us and will endure after us. It is only at this stage that the reader is prepared to distinguish between degrees of greatness in poetry; before that stage he can only be expected to distinguish between the genuine and the sham – the capacity to make this latter distinction must always be practised first. The poets we frequent in adolescence will not be arranged [35] in any objective order of eminence, but by the personal accidents which put them into relation with us; and this is right. I doubt whether it is possible to explain to school children or even undergraduates the differences of degree among poets, and I doubt whether it is wise to try; they have not yet had enough experience of life for these matters to have much meaning. The perception of *why* Shakespeare, or Dante, or Sophocles holds the place he has is something which comes only very slowly in the course of living. And the deliberate attempt to grapple with poetry which is not naturally congenial, and some of which never will be, should be a very mature activity indeed; an activity which well repays the effort, but which cannot be recommended to young people without grave danger of deadening their sensibility to poetry and confounding the genuine *development* of taste with the sham acquisition of it.

It should be clear that the 'development of *taste*' is an abstraction. To set before oneself the goal of being able to enjoy, and in the proper objective order of merit, all good poetry, is to pursue a phantom, the chase after which should be left to those whose ambition it is to be 'cultivated' or 'cultured', for whom art is a luxury article and its appreciation an accomplishment. For the development of genuine taste, founded on genuine feeling, is inextricable from the development of the personality and character.[1] Genuine taste is always imperfect taste – but we are all, as a matter of fact, imperfect people; and the man whose taste in poetry does not bear the stamp of his particular per-[36]sonality, so that there are differences in what he likes from what we like, as well as resemblances, and differences in the way of liking the same things, is apt to be a very uninteresting person with whom to discuss poetry. We may even say that to have better 'taste' in poetry than belongs to one's state of development, is not to 'taste' anything at all. One's taste in poetry cannot be isolated from one's other interests and passions; it affects them and is affected by them, and must be limited as one's self is limited.

This note is really introductory to a large and difficult question: whether the attempt to teach students to appreciate English literature should be made at all; and with what restrictions the teaching of English literature can rightly be included in any academic curriculum, if at all.

---

1. In making this statement I refuse to be drawn into any discussion of the definitions of 'personality' and 'character'.

Apology for the Countess of Pembroke

November 25th, 1932

UPUC, 37–52

The literary criticism of the Elizabethan period is not very great in bulk; to the account which George Saintsbury has given there cannot in its kind be very much to add, and from his critical valuation there is not much to detract. What concerns me here is the general opinion of it which students are likely to form, in relation to the poetry of the age, on account of two 'lost causes' which that criticism championed. The censure of the popular drama, and the attempt to introduce a more severe classical form illustrated by the essay of Sir Philip Sidney, and the censure of rhymed verse, and the attempt to introduce some adaptation of classical forms illustrated by the essay of Campion, might be taken, and have been taken, as striking examples of the futility of corrective criticism, and of the superiority of irreflective inspiration over calculation. If I can show that no such clear contrast is possible, and that the relation of the critical to the creative mind was not one of simple antagonism in the Elizabethan age, it will be easier for me to demonstrate the intimacy of the creative and the critical mind at a later period.

Everyone has read Campion's *Observations in the Art of English Poesie* and Daniel's *Defence of Ryme*. Campion, who except for Shakespeare was the most accomplished master of rhymed lyric of his time, was certainly in a weak posi-[38]tion for attacking rhyme, as Daniel in his reply was not slow to observe. His treatise is known to most people merely as the repository of two very beautiful pieces, *Rose-cheeked Laura come* and *Raving war begot*, and of a number of other exercises most of which by their inferiority bear witness against him. Experimentation with semi-classical metres is less derided to-day than it was before the time of Robert Bridges. I do not believe that good English verse can be written quite in the way which Campion advocates, for it is the natural genius of the language, and not ancient authority, that must decide; better scholars than I, have suspected even that Latin versification was too much influenced by Greek models; I do not even believe that the metric of *The Testament of Beauty* is successful, and I have always preferred Dr Bridges' earlier and more conventional verse to his later experiments. Ezra Pound's 'Seafarer', on the other hand, is a magnificent paraphrase exploiting the resources of a parent language; I discern its beneficent influence upon the work of some of the more interesting younger poets to-day. Some of the older forms of English versification are being revived to good purpose. But the point to dwell upon is not that Campion was altogether wrong, for he was not; or that he was completely downed by Daniel's rejoinder; and we must remember that in other matters Daniel was a member of the classicising school. The result of the controversy between Campion and Daniel is to establish, both that the Latin metres cannot be copied in English, and that rhyme is neither an essential nor a superfluity. Furthermore, no prosodic system ever invented can teach anyone to write good English verse. It is, [39] as Mr Pound has so often remarked, the musical phrase that matters.[1] The great achievement of Elizabethan versification is the development of blank verse; it is the dramatic poets, and eventually Milton, who are Spenser's true heirs. Just as Pope, who used what is nominally the same form as Dryden's couplet, bears little resemblance to Dryden, and as the writer to-day who was genuinely influenced by Pope would hardly want to use that couplet at all, so the writers who were significantly influenced by Spenser are not those who have attempted to use his stanza, which is inimitable. The second greatest accomplishment of the age was the lyric; and the lyric of Shakespeare and Campion owes its beauty not primarily to its use of rhyme or to its perfection of a 'verse form', but to the fact that it is written to musical form; it is written to be sung. Shakespeare's knowledge of music is hardly likely to have been comparable to Campion's; but in that age a writer could hardly escape knowing a little. I can hardly conceive such a song as *Come away death* being written except in collaboration with the musician.[2] But, to return to Campion and Daniel, [40] I consider the controversy important, not because either was quite right or wrong, but because it is a part of the struggle between native and foreign elements as the result of which our greatest poetry was created. Campion pushed to an extreme a theory which he did not himself often practise; but the fact that people could then think along such lines is significant.

The essay of Sidney in which occur the passages ridiculing the contemporary stage, so frequently quoted, may have been composed as early as 1580; at any rate, was composed before the great plays of the age were written. We can hardly suppose that the writer who in passing showed not only a lively appreciation of *Chevy Chase*, but also of Chaucer, singling for mention what is Chaucer's greatest poem – *Troilus* – would have been

1. When Mr. Drinkwater says (*Victorian Poetry*) 'there is now no new verse form to be discovered in English' it is his own conception of form that precludes novelty. He really means 'there can be no new verse form exactly like the old ones' – or like what he thinks the old ones are. See a curious book on the relation of poetry to music, intended for readers with no technical knowledge of music, *Magic of Melody*, by John Murray Gibbon (Dent).

2. The real superiority of Shakespeare's songs over Campion's is not to be found, so to speak, internally, but in their setting. I have elsewhere commented upon the intense dramatic value of Shakespeare's songs at the points where they occur in the plays.

imperceptive of the excellence of Shakespeare. But when we think of the multitude of bad plays, and the number of precious but imperfect plays, which Sidney did not live to read or see performed, we cannot deny that his lamentations have some application to the whole period. We are apt, in thinking of the age of Shakespeare, to imagine something like a fertile field in which tares and fine wheat luxuriated, in which the former could not have been eradicated without risk to the latter. Let both grow together until the harvest. I am not inclined to deny the exceptional number of writers of real poetic and dramatic genius; but I cannot help regretting that some of their best plays are no better than they are. 'So falleth it out,' says Sidney, 'that having indeed no right Comedy, in that comical part of our Tragedy we have nothing but scurrility, unworthy of any chaste ears, or some [41] extreme show of doltishness, indeed fit to lift up a loud laughter, and nothing else.' He is perfectly right. *The Changeling* is only a solitary example in its extreme contrast between the grandeur of the main plot and the nauseousness of the secondary plot from which it has its title. The plays of Marston and Heywood – the latter a writer of some theatrical ability, the former considerably more – are similarly disfigured. In *The Witch of Edmonton* we have the odd spectacle of a play containing comic and tragic elements, each pretty certainly contributed by a different writer, each rising at moments to great heights in its own kind, but very imperfectly welded; I find the readjustments of mood required in this play very trying. Now the desire for 'comic relief' on the part of an audience is, I believe, a permanent craving of human nature; but that does not mean that it is a craving that ought to be gratified. It springs from a lack of the capacity for concentration. Farce and love-romances, especially if seasoned with scabrousness, are the two forms of entertainment upon which the human mind can most easily, lovingly and for the longest time maintain its attention; but we like some farce as a relief from our sentiment, however salacious, and some sentiment as a relief from our farce, however broad. The audience which can keep its attention fixed upon *pure* tragedy or *pure* comedy is much more highly developed. The Athenian stage got relief through the chorus; and perhaps some of its tragedy may have held attention largely by its sensationalism. To my mind, Racine's *Bérénice* represents about the summit of civilisation in tragedy; and it is, in a way, a Christian tragedy, with devotion to the State [42] substituted for devotion to divine law. The dramatic poet who can engross the reader's or the auditor's attention during the space of a *Bérénice* is the most civilised dramatist – though not necessarily the greatest, for there are other qualities to consider.

My point is this: that the Elizabethan drama did tend to approach that *unity of feeling* which Sidney desires. From the tragedy or history in which the comic element was simply left blank to be supplied by some clown favoured by the pit (as some of the farce in *Faustus* is supposed to be an abbreviation of the gags of one comedian), the drama grew to maturity, in, for example, *Coriolanus*, *Volpone*, and in a later generation *The Way of the World*. And it did this, not because docile dramatists obeyed the wishes of Sidney, but because the improvements advocated by Sidney happened to be those which a maturing civilisation would make for itself. The doctrine of *Unity of Sentiment*, in fact, happens to be right. And I think, in passing, that simply because we have been inclined to accept the 'comic relief' notion as a kind of fixed law of Elizabethan drama, we have sometimes misunderstood the intention of the dramatist: as, for instance, in treating *The Jew of Malta* as a huffe-snuffe grand tragedy disfigured by clownish irrelevancies of doubtful taste, we have missed its point.

Some objectors may bring forward Shakespeare either as a triumphant exception to this theory or as a triumphant refutation of it. I know well how difficult it is to fit Shakespeare into any theory, especially if it be a theory about Shakespeare; and I cannot here undertake a complete justification, or enter upon all the qualifications that the [43] theory requires. But we start with 'comic relief' as a practical necessity of the time for the writer who had to make his living by writing plays. What is really interesting is what Shakespeare made of this necessity. I think that when we turn to *Henry IV* we often feel that what we want to re-read and linger over are the Falstaff episodes, rather than the political highfalutin of the King's party and its adversaries. That is an error. As we read from Part I to Part II and see Falstaff, not merely gluttonising and playing pranks indifferent to affairs of State, but leading his band of conscripts and conversing with local magnates, we find that the relief has become serious contrast, and that political satire issues from it. In *Henry V* the two elements are still more fused; so that we have not merely a chronicle of kings and queens, but a universal comedy in which all the actors take part in one event. But it is not in the histories, plays of a transient and unsatisfactory type, that we find the comic relief most nearly taken up into a higher unity of feeling. In *Twelfth Night* and *A Midsummer Night's Dream* the farcical element is an essential to a pattern more complex and elaborate than any constructed by a dramatist before or since. The Knocking On the Gate in *Macbeth* has been cited too often for me to call attention to it; less hackneyed is the scene upon Pompey's galley in *Antony and Cleopatra*. This scene is not only in itself a prodigious piece of political satire –

    A beares the third part of the world, man . . .

but is a key to everything that precedes and follows. To demonstrate this point to your satisfaction would, I know, [44] require a whole essay to itself. Here, I can only affirm that for me the violence of contrast between the tragic and the comic, the sublime and the bathetic, in the plays of Shakespeare, disappears in his maturing work; I only hope that a comparison of *The Merchant of Venice*, *Hamlet* and *The Tempest* will lead others to the same conclusion. I was once under censure for suggesting that in *Hamlet* Shakespeare was dealing with 'intractable material': my words were even interpreted as maintaining that *Coriolanus* is a greater play than *Hamlet*. I am not very much interested in deciding which play of Shakespeare is greater than which other; because I am more and more interested, not in one play or another, but in Shakespeare's work as a whole. I do not think it any derogation to suggest that Shakespeare did not always succeed: such a suggestion would imply a very narrow view of success. His success must always be reckoned in understanding of what he attempted; and I believe that to admit his partial failures is to *approach* the recognition of his real greatness more closely than to hold that he was always granted plenary inspiration. I do not pretend that I think *Measure for Measure*, or *Troilus and Cressida*, or *All's Well That Ends Well*, to be a wholly 'successful' play; but if any one of Shakespeare's plays were omitted we should not be able to understand the rest as well as we do. In such plays, we must consider not only the degree of unification of all the elements into a 'unity of sentiment', but the quality and kind of the emotions to be unified, and the elaborateness of the pattern of unification.

This consideration may appear to have carried us far away from Sidney's simple assertion about the decorum to [45] be observed in excluding extraneous matter; but we are really with him all the time. So much, for the present, for the Unity of Sentiment. But Sidney is orthodox in laws still more difficult to observe; for he says roundly, 'the stage should represent but one place, and the uttermost time presupposed in it should be, both by Aristotle's precept and common reason, but one day.' This unity of place and time is a stumbling-block so old that we think it long since worn away: a law, like some others, so universally violated, that, like the heroine of Hood,

> We thought it dying when it slept
>   And sleeping when it died.

But my point is simply that the unities differ radically from human legislation in that they are laws of nature, and a law of nature, even when it is a law of human nature, is quite another thing from a human law. The kind of literary law in which Aristotle was interested was not law that he laid down, but law that he discovered. The laws (*not* rules) of unity of place and time remain valid in that every play which observes them *in so far as its material allows* is in that respect and degree superior to plays which observe them less. I believe that in every play in which they are not observed we only put up with their violation because we feel that something is gained which we could not have if the law *were* observed. This is not to establish another law. There *is* no other law possible. It is merely to recognise that in poetry as in life our business is to make the best of a bad job. Furthermore, we must observe that the Unities are not three separate laws. They are three aspects of one law: we [46] may violate the law of Unity of Place more flagrantly if we preserve the law of Unity of Time, or vice versa; we may violate both if we observe more closely the law of Unity of Sentiment.

We start, most of us, with an unconscious prejudice against the Unities – I mean, we are unconscious of the large element in our feeling which is mere ignorance and mere prejudice. I mean that English-speaking peoples have immediate and intimate experience of great plays in which the Unities are grossly violated, and perhaps of inferior plays in which they are more nearly observed. Furthermore, we have a natural, inevitable and largely justifiable sympathy with the literature of our own country and language; and we have had the Unities so rubbed into us, when we studied Greek or French drama, that we may think it is because of the unfamiliar dramatic form that we do not care for them so much as we care for Shakespeare. But it is just as likely that we do not care for them because they represent the genius of an alien people and a foreign tongue, and hence are prejudiced against the dramatic form. I believe that those plays of Shakespeare which approximate more nearly to observation of the Unities are *in that respect* better plays; I would even go as far as to say that the King of Denmark, in sending Hamlet to England, was attempting to violate the Unity of Action: a crime far worse, for a man in his position, than attempted murder. And what I have denominated Unity of Sentiment is only a slightly larger term than Unity of Action.

Unity, says Butcher, in his edition of the *Poetics*, is manifested mainly in two ways:

> [47] First, in the casual connexion that binds together the several parts of a play – the thoughts, the emotions, the decisions of the will, the external events being inextricably interwoven. Secondly, in the fact that the whole series of events, with all the moral forces that are brought into collision, are directed to a single end. The action as it advances converges on a definite point. The thread of purpose running through it becomes more marked. All minor effects are subordinated to the sense of an ever-growing unity.

The end is linked to the beginning with inevitable certainty, and in the end we discern the meaning of the whole.

It should be obvious that the observance of this Unity must lead us, given certain dramatic material otherwise highly valuable, inevitably to violation of the Unities of Place and Time.[1] As for Time, Aristotle only remarks rather casually that the usual practice of tragedy was to confine itself, so far as possible, to the action of twenty-four hours. The only modern author who has succeeded in observing this Unity exactly is Mr. James Joyce; and he has done so with only slight deviation from the Unity of Place, as the action all takes place in or near the town of Dublin, and Dublin is a contributing cause of the unity of the whole book. But Sir Philip Sidney, with the weight of Italian criticism upon his back, and probably not having read Aristotle so deeply as he had read Latin authors and Italian critics widely, only went a little too far: he was right in principle, and he was justified in his strictures upon the [48] drama of his day. A greater critic than Sidney, the greatest critic of his time, Ben Jonson, says wisely:

> I know nothing can conduce more to letters, than to examine the writings of the Ancients, and not to rest in their sole authority, or take all upon trust from them; provided the plagues of judging, and pronouncing against them, be away; such as envy, bitterness, precipitation, impudence, and scurrile scoffing. For to all observations of the Ancients, we have our own experience; which, if we will use and apply, we have better means to pronounce. It is true they opened the gates, and made the way that went before us; but as guides, not commanders.

And further:

> Let Aristotle and others have their dues; but if we can make farther discoveries of truth and fitness than they, why are we envied?

It was natural that a member of the Countess of Pembroke's circle, writing while popular literature was still mostly barbarous, should be more fearful and intolerant than Ben Jonson, writing towards the end of his days, with a rich creative past in retrospect, and reviewing his own great work. I do not pretend that Sidney's criticism made any more impression upon the form which later poetic drama took than did, say, the example of Greville, Daniel or Alexander. The chief channel through which the Countess of Pembroke's circle may have affected the course

---

1. The authority for the Unity of Place is usually held to be Castelvetro. This is not, of course, an Aristotelian doctrine.

of English poetry is the great civilising influence of Spenser. Spenser exercised great influence upon Marlowe; Marlowe first showed what could be done with dramatic blank verse, and Marlowe's great disciple Milton showed what [49] could be done with blank verse in a long poem. So great the influence of Spenser seems to me, that I should say that without it we might not have had the finest developments of blank verse. Such a derivation in itself should be enough to rescue the Countess of Pembroke's friends and relatives from obscurity, enough to dignify their critical efforts, to raise them from the ignominy of wealthy well-born amateurs of the arts, or obscurantist supporters of a fastidious and sterile classicism.

So much for the two real problems of specific interest which occupied the attention of Elizabethan critics: the problem of dramatic form and the problem of verse technique. Of the fashion set by Sidney, the panegyric of poetry and the poet, I shall have more to say when I come to contrast it with the laudation of the Poet by Shelley, and with, so to speak, his ordination by Matthew Arnold. Puttenham and Webbe play chorus to Sidney. Poetry, we are repeatedly told, is 'making', and we are reminded that ποιεῖν means to make. Lip-service is paid to the Aristotelian 'imitation', but none of the writers of the period seems to have penetrated very deeply into the notion of mimesis. The opinions of Plato and Aristotle are garbled like a judicious advertisement selection from a book-review. Webbe would have us believe that Plato and Aristotle join in supposing 'all wisdom and knowledge to be included mystically in that divine instinction wherewith they thought their *vates* to be inspired'. The notion of divine inspiration is made the most of. The poet expresses both divine and worldly truth, and exerts moral influence – here 'imitation' is brought in again. Finally, the poet [50] gives delight, and in effect helps materially to maintain and to raise the level of culture; no court is glorious without him, and no people great which has no poets. Interspersed in the discourses of Sidney, Puttenham and Webbe are some acute observations; and Puttenham's prefatory note on Speech is most interesting. I am not concerned with these, or with the circumstances in which these essays were brought forth; though I may be allowed to offer a word of thanks, in passing, to Gosson because his *School of Abuse* provoked them. It is, however, worthy of remembrance that these critical treatises appeared just *before* the beginning of the great age; so that if they are a sign of anything, it is of growth and not of decay.

And in these simple effusions we have in embryo the critical questions which were to be discussed much later. To talk of poets as makers and as inspired does not get us very far, and this notion of inspiration need not be pressed for literalness; but it shows some perception of the question:

'how does the making of poetry come about?' To talk vaguely of poets as philosophers does not get us very far either, but it is the simplest reply to the question: 'what is the content of poetry?' Similarly with the account of poetry in its high moral purpose, the question of the relation of art and ethics appears; and finally, in the simple assertions that poetry gives high delight and adorns society is some awareness of the problem of the relation of the poem to the reader and the place of poetry in society. Once you have started you cannot stop. And these people started before Shakespeare.

I shall have spoken to no purpose if I have given the [51] impression that I wish simply to affirm the importance of a neglected, or rather belittled group of literary people whose taste is supposed to have been counter to that of the age. Had that been my intention I should have adopted a different scheme of treatment, dealt with them severally, and in particular have had something to say about the special importance of John Lyly in the development of English prose and of proper comedy. My purpose has been rather to determine the relation of the critical currents to the general stream of creative activity. In that form of historical survey which is not concerned with the total movement of literature, but with – on the lowest level – mere readability, and which aims to tell us what works we can still enjoy, which emphasises those books which men have found it worth their while to continue to read and which are valuable to us irrespective of their historical position, some of these writers are properly ignored. The works of Sir Philip Sidney, excepting a few sonnets, are not among those to which one can return for perpetual refreshment; the *Arcadia* is a monument of dulness. But I have wished to affirm that in looking at the period with an interest in the development of the critical consciousness in and towards poetry, you cannot dissociate one group of people from another; you cannot draw a line and say here is backwater, here is the main stream. In the drama, we seem to have on the one hand almost the whole body of men of letters, a crowd of scholars coming down from Oxford and Cambridge to pick a poor living in London, needy and often almost desperate men of talent; and on the other an alert, curious, semi-barbarous public, fond [52] of beer and bawdry, including much the same sort of people whom one encounters in the local outlying theatres to-day, craving cheap amusement to thrill their emotions, arouse their mirth and satisfy their curiosity; and between the entertainers and the entertained a fundamental homogeneity of race, of sense of humour and sense of right and wrong. The worst fault that poetry can commit is to be dull; and the Elizabethan dramatists were more or less frequently saved from dulness or galvanised into animation by the necessity to amuse. Their livelihood depended upon it: they had to amuse or starve.

The Age of Dryden

December 2nd, 1932

UPUC, 53-65.

In my previous lecture I was concerned with the Elizabethan critical mind expressing itself before the greater part of the great literature of the age had been written. Between them and Dryden occurs one great critical mind, that of a great poet whose critical writing appears to belong to quite the end of the period. If I treated Ben Jonson's opinions with complete respect, I should condemn myself for speaking or writing at all; for he says roundly, 'to judge of poets is only the faculty of poets; and not of all poets, but the best'. Nevertheless, though I am not a good enough poet to judge of Jonson, I have already tried to do so, and cannot now make matters worse. Between Sidney and Campion in the latter part of the sixteenth century, and Jonson writing towards the end of his life, the greatest period of English poetry is comprehended; and the maturing of the English mind in this time is well seen by reading the treatises of Sidney and his contemporaries, and then the *Discoveries* of Jonson. He called his *Discoveries* also *Timber*, and it is timber with much undergrowth and dead wood in it, but also living trees. In some places, Jonson does but express in a more adult style the same commonplaces. About poetry:

> The study of it (if we will trust Aristotle) offers to man-[54]kind a certain rule, and pattern of living well, and happily; disposing us to all civil offices of society. If we will believe Tully, it nourisheth, and instructeth, our youth; delights our age; adorns our prosperity; comforts our adversity; entertains us at home; keeps us company abroad, travails with us; watches, divides the time of our earnest, and sports; shares in our country recesses, and recreations; insomuch as the wisest and best learned have thought her the absolute mistress of manners, and nearest of kin to virtue.

This list of the merits of poetry, with its conditional references to Aristotle and Tully, has the quaintness of a generation near to Montaigne, and is no more convincing than a patent medicine circular; and it has some of the heavy sententiousness of Francis Bacon. Secondary to the serious advantages to be derived from poetry, comes the assurance that poetry gives pleasure, or, as he says, guides us by the hand of action, with a ravishing delight, and incredible sweetness. The questions implied are, as I said towards the end of my last lecture, among those fundamental to criticism: Jonson has put them in a riper style than that of the critics who wrote in his youth, but he has not advanced the enquiry. The authority of antiquity, and the assent of our prejudices, are enough. It is rather in his practical criticism – I mean here not so much his criticism of individual writers, but his advice to the practitioner – that Jonson has made progress. He requires in the poet, first, 'a goodness of natural wit'. 'To this perfection of nature in our poet, we require exercise of those parts, and frequent.' His third requisite in a poet pleases me especially: 'The third requisite in our poet, or maker, is *Imitation*, to be able [55] to convert the substances, or riches of another poet, to his own use.' When we come to a passage beginning 'In writing there is to be regarded the Invention, and the Fashion' we may, if we have already read some later critics, expect more than we get. For so far as I understand him Jonson means nothing more than that before you write you must have something to write about; which is a manifest truth frequently ignored both by those who are trying to learn to write and by some of those who endeavour to teach writing. But when we compare such passages as these from Jonson with the passage which I quoted from Dryden in my first lecture, we feel that in Dryden we meet for the first time a man who is speaking to *us*. It is from a critical essay written before Dryden had really found out how to write poetry; but it is something very different from an appeal to the ancients; it is really analytical. I will presume to quote it again for the purpose of closer examination:

> The first happiness of the poet's imagination is properly invention, or the finding of the thought; the second is fancy, or the variation, deriving, or moulding of that thought, as the judgement represents it proper to the subject; the third is elocution, or the art of clothing and adorning that thought, as found and varied, in apt, significant, and sounding words; the quickness of the imagination is seen in the invention, the fertility in the fancy, and the accuracy in the expression.

'Finding of the thought' does not mean finding a copy-book maxim, or starting with a synopsis of what we are going to put into verse, finding an 'idea' which is later to [56] be 'clothed and adorned' in a rather literal interpretation of the metaphor. It corresponds to the inception of any piece of imaginative writing. It is not casting about for a subject, upon which, when found, the 'imagination' is to be exercised; for we must remark that 'invention' is the first moment in a process only the *whole* of which Dryden calls 'imagination', and no less than the whole of which corresponds to the celebrated and admirable account of imagination given by Shakespeare in *A Midsummer Night's Dream*. 'Invention' in the sense used here by Dryden does not seem to me to be properly covered by the *New English Dictionary*, which quotes this very passage in support of the following definition: 'The devising of a subject, idea, or method of treatment, by exercise of the intellect or imagination.' The words 'intellect or imagination' strike me as a burking of the question: if there is a clear distinction between invention by exercise of intellect and invention by exercise of imagination, then two definitions are called for; and if there is no difference between intellectual and imaginative invention there can hardly be much difference between imagination and intellect. But Dryden is talking expressly about imagination, not about intellect. Furthermore, the word 'devising' suggests the deliberate putting together out of materials at hand; whereas I believe that Dryden's 'invention' includes the sudden irruption of the germ of a new poem, possibly merely as a state of feeling. His 'invention' is surely a finding, a *trouvaille*. 'Fancy' represents the conscious elaboration of the original *donnée* – I prefer not to call that which is found by invention by the name of 'idea'; and fancy, I believe, covers also the con-[57]scious and deliberate uniting of several inventions in one poem. 'Variation, deriving, or moulding of that thought', Dryden calls it. 'Variation' and 'moulding' are, I think, pretty clear; 'deriving' is more difficult. I think that the definition 3b in the *N.E.D.* comes pretty close to it: 'To extend by branches or modifications.' Fancy is an activity of the imagination rather than of the intellect, but is necessarily in part an intellectual activity, inasmuch as it is a 'moulding of the thought as judgement represents it proper'. Dryden does not, I believe, necessarily imply that the 'third happiness' of poetic imagination, 'elocution', is a third *act*; I mean, that the act of finding the proper words, 'clothing and adorning' the thought, begins only after the operation of fancy is complete. In fancy the finding of the words seems to me already to have begun; that is, fancy is partly verbal; nevertheless, the work of elocution, 'clothing and adorning in apt, significant and sounding words', is the last to be completed. Observe that 'sounding' here means what we, just as approximately, should be likely to call 'musical': the finding of the words and the order of words expressive of the underlying mood which belongs to the invention. (Shakespeare's great line in *King Lear*,

>   Never, never, never, never, never,

is just as *sounding* as Poe's line admired by Ernest Dowson,

>   The viol, the violet and the vine.)

We are liable, I think, to underrate Dryden's critical analyses, by assuming that they only apply to the kind of poetry that he writes himself; and thus we may overlook his meaning, as of the word 'invention'. Even if Dryden's [58] poetry seems to us of a peculiar, and, as it has seemed to many, a peculiarly unpoetic type, we need not conclude that his mind operated quite differently from those of poets at other periods; and we must remember his catholic and discriminating taste in poetry.

I do not need, I think, to quote again here the passage from Coleridge which I quoted in contrast to that of Dryden, because I do not propose to examine it so narrowly. You will have observed the more developed etymological sense. I am not sure that Coleridge has made as satisfactory an analysis as that of Dryden. The distinction is too simple. The last sentence, 'Milton has a highly imaginative, Cowley a very fanciful mind', should be enough to arouse suspicion. It represents a course of argument which is specious. You assert a distinction, you select two authors who illustrate it to your satisfaction, and you ignore the negative instances or difficult cases. If Coleridge had written, 'Spenser had a highly imaginative, Donne a very fanciful mind', the assumed superiority of imagination to fancy might not appear quite so immediately convincing. Not only Cowley, but all the metaphysical poets, had very fanciful minds, and if you removed the fancy and left only imagination, as Coleridge appears to use these terms, you would have no metaphysical poetry. The distinction is admittedly a distinction of value; the term 'fancy' is really made derogatory, just applicable to clever verse that you do not like.

Between Dryden, and Wordsworth and Coleridge the one great critical mind is that of Johnson. After Dryden, and before Johnson, there is much just criticism, but no [59] great critic. The inferiority of common minds to great is more painfully apparent in those modest exercises of the mind in which common sense and sensibility are needed, than in their failure to ascend to the higher flights of genius. Addison is a conspicuous example of this embarrassing mediocrity, and he is a symptom of the age which he announced. The difference between the temper of the eighteenth century and that of the seventeenth is profound. Here, for example, is Addison on the subject on which we have already heard Dryden and Coleridge, the Imagination:

> There are few words in the English language which are employed in a more loose and uncircumscribed sense than those of the fancy and the imagination. I therefore thought it necessary to fix and determine the notion of these two words, as I intend to make use of them in the thread of my following speculations, that the reader may conceive rightly what is the subject which I proceed upon.[1]

It is perhaps as well to warn you that Addison is a writer towards whom I feel something very like antipathy. It seems to me that even in these few words the smugness and priggishness of the man appear. Of an

---

1. *The Spectator*, June 21st, 1712, No. 411.

age during which the Church sank to an unloveliness unequalled before or since, Addison was one of the most apposite ornaments; he possessed the Christian virtues, and all in the wrong order: humility was the least of his attainments. It would seem, from his account of 'fancy' and 'imagination', that Addison had never read, certainly never pondered, Dryden's remarks upon the subject. I do not feel sure, however, that [60] this yoking of fancy and imagination by Addison did not strike the eye of Coleridge, and start him upon his process of differentiation. For Dryden 'imagination' was the whole process of poetic creation in which fancy was one element. Addison starts out to 'fix and determine' the notion of the two words; I cannot find any fixing or determining of the word 'fancy' in this or the following essays on the subject; he is entirely occupied with the imagination, and primarily with the visual imagination, and solely with the visual imagination according to Mr Locke. That is a debt which he hastens to acknowledge: he pays a handsome testimonial to the scientific truths which Locke has established. Alas, philosophy is not science, nor is literary criticism; and it is an elementary error to think that we have discovered as objective laws what we have merely imposed by private legislation.

It is curious to find the old notions of delight and instruction, with which the sixteenth century defended poetry, cropping up again in a form typical of the age of Addison, but hardly with any greater profundity of meaning. Addison observes that:

> A man of a polite imagination is let into a great many pleasures that the vulgar are not capable of receiving. He can converse with a picture, and find an agreeable companion in a statue. He meets with a secret refreshment in a description, and often finds a greater satisfaction in the prospect of fields and meadows, than another does in the possession.

The eighteenth-century emphases are illuminating. Instead of the courtier, we have the man of polite imagin-[61]ation. I suppose that Addison is what one would describe as a gentleman; as one might say, no better than a gentleman. His notion of recommending imagination, because it enables you to enjoy a statue or a piece of property without having to put your hand in your pocket to pay for it, is a very happy thought indeed. And gentleman as he is, he has a very low opinion of those who are not genteel:

> There are indeed but very few who know how to be idle and innocent, or have a relish of any pleasures that are not criminal.

Tell that, we might add, to the Unemployed. The particular examination of Addison may be left to Mr Saintsbury, whose *History of*

Criticism is always delightful, generally useful, and most often right. My introduction of Addison has not been, however, merely in order to poke fun at him. What is interesting and relevant to observe in Addison is not merely deterioration, a deterioration of society, but of interesting change. In the same series of papers on Imagination he says:

> It may here be worth our while to examine how it comes to pass that several readers, who are all acquainted with the same language, and know the meaning of the words they read, should nevertheless have a different relish of the same descriptions.

Addison does not succeed in following up this very important question with any very important answer, but it is suggestive as the first awareness of the problem of communication; and his whole discussion of the nature of imagination, however fruitless for the purposes of literary criticism, is a very interesting attempt at a general [62] aesthetics. Any matter which comes eventually to be the subject of detailed investigation and specialised labour may be preceded, long before any fruitful development takes place, by such random guesses as these, which though not directly productive of fruitful results indicate the direction in which the mind is moving.

Addison, although too poor a poet to be strictly comparable to the other critics whom I have mentioned and have to mention, acquires importance by being thoroughly representative of his age. The history of every branch of intellectual activity provides the same record of the diminution of England from the time of Queen Anne. It is not so much the intellect, but something superior to intellect, which went for a long time into eclipse; and this luminary, by whatever name we may call it, has not yet wholly issued from its secular obnubilation. The age of Dryden was still a great age, though beginning to suffer death of the spirit, as the coarsening of its verse-rhythms shows; by the time of Addison theology, devotion and poetry fell fast into a formalistic slumber. Addison is definitely a writer for the middle class, a bourgeois literary dictator. He was a popular lecturer. To him poetry meant delight and edification in a new way. Johnson has here, in his own language, fixed admirably the difference between Dryden and Addison as directors of taste:

> Dryden has, not many years before, scattered criticism over his prefaces with very little parsimony; but though he sometimes condescended to be somewhat familiar, his manner was in general too scholastic for those who had yet their rudiments to learn, and found it not easy to under-[63]stand their master. His observations were framed rather for those that were learning to write, than for those that read only to talk.

An instructor like Addison was now wanting, whose remarks, being superficial, might be easily understood, and being just, might prepare the mind for more attainments. Had he presented *Paradise Lost* to the public with all the pomp of system and severity of science, the criticism would perhaps have been admired, and the poem still have been neglected; but by the blandishments of gentleness and facility he has made Milton an universal favourite, with whom readers of every class think it necessary to be pleased.

It was still then, apparently, a not unlettered period, in which readers of *any* class could think it necessary to be pleased with *Paradise Lost*. But the usual classification of Dryden, Addison and Johnson together as critics of an Augustan age fails to allow adequately for two differences: the spiritual deterioration in society between the periods of the first two, and the remarkable isolation of the third. It is surely by unconscious irony that we speak of an 'age of Johnson' as we do of an 'age of Dryden' or an 'age of Addison'. Lonely in his life, Johnson seems to me still more lonely in his intellectual and moral existence. He could not even very much *like* the poetry of his age with which admirers of the eighteenth century now 'think it necessary to be pleased'; if more than just to Collins, he was no more than severe to Gray. He himself, I am convinced, is their superior as a poet, not in sensibility, not in metrical dexterity or aptness of phrase, but in a moral elevation just short of sublimity.

[64] Such writing as Johnson's *Lives of the Poets* and his essay on Shakespeare loses none of its permanence from the consideration that every generation must make its own appraisal of the poetry of the past, in the light of the performance of its contemporaries and immediate predecessors. Criticism of poetry moves between two extremes. On the one hand the critic may busy himself so much with the implications of a poem, or of one poet's work – implications moral, social, religious or other – that the poetry becomes hardly more than a text for a discourse. Such is the tendency of the moralising critics of the nineteenth century, to which Landor makes a notable exception. Or if you stick too closely to the 'poetry' and adopt no attitude towards what the poet has to say, you will tend to evacuate it of all significance. And furthermore there is a philosophic borderline, which you must not transgress too far or too often, if you wish to preserve your standing as a critic, and are not prepared to present yourself as a philosopher, metaphysician, sociologist, or psychologist instead. Johnson, in these respects, is a type of critical integrity. Within his limitations, he is one of the great critics; and he is a great critic partly because he keeps within his limitations. When you know what they are, you know where you are. Considering all the

temptations to which one is exposed in judging contemporary writing, all the prejudices which one is tempted to indulge in judging writers of the immediately preceding generation, I view Johnson's *Lives of the Poets* as a masterpiece of the judicial bench. His style is not so formally perfect as that of some other prose writers of his time. It reads often like the writing of [65] a man who is more habituated to talking than to writing; he seems to think aloud, and in short breaths, rather than in the long periods of the historian or the orator. His criticism is as salutary against the dogmatic excesses of the eighteenth century – more indulged in France than in England – as it is against excessive adulation of individual poets with their faults as well as virtues. We shall have, in the nineteenth century, several vagaries to contemplate, of critics who do not so much practise criticism as make use of it for other purposes. For Johnson poetry was still poetry, and not another thing. Had he lived a generation later, he would have been obliged to look more deeply into the foundations, and so would have been unable to leave us an example of what criticism ought to be for a civilisation which, being settled, has no need, while it lasts, to enquire into the functions of its parts.

Wordsworth and Coleridge

December 9th, 1932

UPUC, 67–85.

It is natural, and in so rapid and superficial a review as this inevitable, to consider the criticism of Wordsworth and of Coleridge together. But we must keep in mind how very different were not only the men themselves, but the circumstances and motives of the composition of their principal critical statements. Wordsworth's *Preface to Lyrical Ballads* was written while he was still in his youth, and while his poetic genius still had much to do; Coleridge wrote the *Biographia Literaria* much later in life, when poetry, except for that one brief and touching lament for lost youth, had deserted him, and when the disastrous effects of long dissipation and stupefaction of his powers in transcendental metaphysics were bringing him to a state of lethargy. With the relation of Coleridge's thought to subsequent theological and political development I am not here concerned. The *Biographia* is our principal document; and in connexion with that there is one piece of his formal verse which in its passionate self-revelation rises almost to the height of great poetry. I mean *Dejection: an Ode*.

> There was a time when, though my path was rough,
>   This joy within me dallied with distress,

>   And all misfortunes were but as the stuff
>   Whence Fancy made me dream of happiness:
> [68]   For hope grew round me, like the twining vine,
>   And fruits and foliage, not my own, seemed mine.
>   But now affliction bows me down to earth:
>   Nor care I that they rob me of my mirth;
>   But oh! each visitation
>   Suspends what nature gave me at my birth,
>   My shaping spirit of imagination.
>   For not to think of what I needs must feel,
>   But to be still and patient, all I can;
>   And haply by abstruse research to steal
>   From my own nature all the natural man –
>   This was my sole resource, my only plan:
>   Till that which suits a part infects the whole,
>   And now is almost grown the habit of my soul.

This ode was written by April 4th, 1802: the *Biographia Literaria* were not published for fifteen years after that. The lines strike my ear as one of the saddest of confessions that I have ever read. When I spoke of Coleridge as drugging himself with metaphysics I was thinking seriously of these his own words: 'haply by abstruse research to steal from my own nature all the natural man'. Coleridge was one of those unhappy persons – Donne, I suspect, was such another – of whom one might say, that if they had not been poets, they might have made something of their lives, might even have had a career; or conversely, that if they had not been interested in so many things, crossed by such diverse passions, they might have been great poets. It was better for Coleridge, as poet, to read books of travel and exploration than to read books of metaphysics and political economy. He did genuinely want [69] to read books of metaphysics and political economy, for he had a certain talent for such subjects. But for a few years he had been visited by the Muse (I know of no poet to whom this hackneyed metaphor is better applicable) and thenceforth was a haunted man; for anyone who has ever been visited by the Muse is thenceforth haunted. He had no vocation for the religious life, for there again somebody like a Muse, or a much higher being, is to be invoked; he was condemned to know that the little poetry he had written was worth more than all he could do with the rest of his life. The author of *Biographia Literaria* was already a ruined man. Sometimes, however, to be a 'ruined man' is itself a vocation.

Wordsworth, on the other hand, wrote his *Preface*, as I have said, while in the plenitude of his poetic powers and while his reputation was still only sustained by readers of discernment. And he was of an opposite poetic type to Coleridge. Whether the bulk of his genuine poetic achievement is so much greater than Coleridge's as it appears, is uncertain. Whether his power and inspiration remained with him to the end is, alas, not even doubtful. But Wordsworth had no ghastly shadows at his back, no Eumenides to pursue him; or if he did, he gave no sign and took no notice; and he went droning on the still sad music of infirmity to the verge of the grave. His inspiration never having been of that sudden, fitful and terrifying kind that visited Coleridge, he was never, apparently, troubled by the consciousness of having lost it. As André Gide's Prometheus said, in the lecture which he gave before a large audience in Paris: *Il faut avoir un aigle*. Coleridge [70] remained in contact with his eagle. Neither in detail of life and interest were the two men similar – Wordsworth indifferent to books, Coleridge the voracious reader. But they had that in common which was more important than all differences: they were the two most original poetic minds of their generation. Their influence upon each other was considerable; though probably the influence of Wordsworth upon Coleridge, during their brief period of intimate association, was greater than that of Coleridge upon Wordsworth. This reciprocal influence would hardly have been possible to such a degree without another influence which held the two men together, and affected both of them more deeply than either knew, the influence of a great woman. No woman has ever played so important a part in the lives of two poets at once – I mean their poetic lives – as did Dorothy Wordsworth.

The emphasis upon the differences of mind, temperament and character of the two men must be all the greater because their critical statements must be read together. In some respects there is of course, as would be expected, a conscious difference of opinion. Wordsworth wrote his *Preface* to defend his own manner of writing poetry, and Coleridge wrote the *Biographia* to defend Wordsworth's poetry; or in part he did. I must confine myself to two points. One is Coleridge's doctrine of fancy and imagination; the other is that on which Coleridge and Wordsworth made common cause: their new theory of poetic diction.

Let me take up the latter point first. In this matter of poetic diction, it is at first very hard to understand what all the fuss is about. Wordsworth's poems had met with no [71] worse reception than verse of such novelty is accustomed to receive. I myself can remember a time when some question of 'poetic diction' was in the air; when Ezra Pound issued his statement that 'poetry ought to be as well written as prose'; and when he and I and our colleagues were mentioned by a writer in *The Morning Post* as 'literary bolsheviks' and by Mr Arthur Waugh (with a point which has always escaped me) as 'drunken helots'. But I think that we believed that we were affirming forgotten standards, rather than setting up new idols. Wordsworth, when he said that his purpose was 'to imitate, and as far as possible, to adopt, the very language of men', was only saying in other words what Dryden had said, and fighting the battle which Dryden had fought; and Mr Garrod, in calling attention to this fact, seems to me intemperate in asserting that Dryden had never made real to himself 'two vital considerations: first, that such language must express passion, and secondly, that it must base itself in just observation'. Dryden among the shades might meditate upon Mr Garrod's conception of passion and observation. And on the other hand, as has also been pointed out, first by Coleridge himself in the *Biographia*, Wordsworth by no means worried himself to excess in observing his own principles. 'The language of the middle and lower classes of society'[1] is of course perfectly proper when you are representing dramatically the *speech* of these classes, and then no other language is proper; similarly when you are representing dramatically the language of the upper classes; but on other occasions, it is not the business of the poet to talk like *any* class of society, but like himself – rather better, we hope, than any actual class; though when any class of society happens to have the best word, phrase or expletive for anything, then the poet is entitled to it. As for the current style of writing when the *Lyrical Ballads* appeared, it was what any style of writing becomes when it falls into the hands of people who cannot even be called mediocrities. True, Gray was overrated: but then Johnson had come down on Gray with a deadlier force than Wordsworth could exert. And Donne has seemed to us, in recent years, as striking a peculiarly conversational style; but did Wordsworth or Coleridge acclaim Donne? No, when it came to Donne – and Cowley – you will find that Wordsworth and Coleridge were led by the nose by Samuel Johnson; they were just as eighteenth century as anybody; except that where the eighteenth century spoke of lack of elegance the Lake poets found lack of passion. And much of the poetry of Wordsworth and Coleridge is just as turgid and artificial and elegant as any eighteenth century die-hard could wish. What then was all the fuss about?

There really was something to make a fuss about. I do not know whether Professor Garrod has grasped it, but if so he seems to ignore it; Professor Harper,[2] however, seems to have it by the right lug. There is a remarkable letter of Wordsworth's in 1801 which he wrote to Charles James Fox in sending him a copy of the *Ballads*. You will find

---

1. What was Wordsworth's conception of the language of the upper classes of society?
2. In his Life of Wordsworth.

a long extract from this letter in Professor Harper's book. [73] I quote one sentence. In commending his poems to the fashionable politician's attention Wordsworth says:

> Recently by the spreading of manufactures through every part of the country, by the heavy taxes upon postage, by workhouses, houses of industry, and the invention of soup shops, etc., superadded to the increasing disproportion between the price of labour and that of the necessaries of life, the bonds of domestic feeling among the poor, as far as the influence of these things has extended, have been weakened, and in innumerable instances entirely destroyed.

Wordsworth then proceeds to expound a doctrine which nowadays is called distributism. And Wordsworth was not merely taking advantage of an opportunity to lecture a rather disreputable statesman and rouse him to useful activity; he was seriously explaining the content and purpose of his poems: without this preamble Mr Fox could hardly be expected to make head or tail of the Idiot Boy or the sailor's parrot. You may say that this public spirit is irrelevant to Wordsworth's greatest poems; nevertheless I believe that you will understand a great poem like *Resolution and Independence* better if you understand the purposes and social passions which animated its author; and unless you understand these you will misread Wordsworth's literary criticism entirely. Incidentally, those who speak of Wordsworth as the original Lost Leader (a reference which Browning, as I remember, denied) should make pause and consider that when a man takes politics and social affairs seriously the difference between revolution and reaction may be by the breadth of a hair, and that Wordsworth may possibly have been no renegade but a man who thought, so [74] far as he thought at all, for himself. But it is Wordsworth's social interest that inspires his own novelty of form in verse, and backs up his explicit remarks upon poetic diction; and it is really this social interest which (consciously or not) the fuss was all about. It was not so much from lack of thought as from warmth of feeling that Wordsworth originally wrote the words 'the language of conversation in middle and lower class society'. It was not from any recantation of political principles, but from having had it brought to his attention that, as a general literary principle, this would never do, that he altered them. Where he wrote 'my purpose was to imitate, and as far as possible, to adopt, the very language of men' he was saying what no serious critic could disapprove.

Except on this point of diction, and that of 'choosing incidents from common life', Wordsworth is a most orthodox critic. It is true that he uses the word 'enthusiasm' which the eighteenth century did not like, but in the matter of mimesis he is more deeply Aristotelian than some who have aimed at following Aristotle more closely. He says of the poet:

> To these qualities he has added a disposition to be affected more than other men by absent things as if they were present; an ability of conjuring up in himself passions, which are indeed far from being the same as those produced by real events, yet (especially in those parts of the general sympathy which are pleasing and delightful) do more nearly resemble the passions produced by real events, than anything which, from the motions of their own minds merely, other men are accustomed to feel in themselves.

[75] Here is the new version of Imitation, and I think that it is the best so far:

> Aristotle, I have been told, has said, that Poetry is the most philosophic of all writing; it is so: its object is truth, not individual and local, but general, and operative.

I find that 'it is so' very exhilarating. For my part, rather than be parrotted by a hundred generations, I had rather be neglected and have one man eventually come to my conclusions and say 'there is an old author who found this out before I did'.

When you find Wordsworth as the seer and prophet whose function it is to instruct and edify through pleasure, as if this were something he had found out for himself, you may begin to think that there is something in it, at least for some kinds of poetry. Some portions of this enthusiasm I believe Wordsworth communicated to Coleridge. But Wordsworth's revolutionary faith was more vital to him than it was to Coleridge. You cannot say that it inspired his revolution in poetry, but it cannot be disentangled from the motives of his poetry. Any radical change in poetic form is likely to be the symptom of some very much deeper change in society and in the individual. I doubt whether the impulse in Coleridge would have been strong enough to have worked its way out, but for the example and encouragement of Wordsworth. I would not be understood as affirming that revolutionary enthusiasm is the best parent for poetry, or as justifying revolution on the ground that it will lead to an outburst of poetry – which would be a wasteful, and hardly justifiable way of producing poetry. Nor am I indulging in sociological criticism, which has to [76] suppress so much of the data, and which is ignorant of so much of the rest. I only affirm that all human affairs are involved with each other, that consequently all history involves abstraction, and that in attempting to win a full understanding of the poetry of a period you are led to the consideration of subjects which at first sight appear to have little bearing upon poetry. These subjects have accordingly a good deal to do with the criticism of poetry; and it is such subjects which make intelligible Wordsworth's inability to appreciate Pope, and the irrelevance of the metaphysical poets to the interest which he and Coleridge had at heart.

With the foregoing observations in mind, let me turn to consider the great importance, in the *Biographia Literaria*, of the distinction between Fancy and Imagination already touched upon, and of the definition of Imagination given in a later passage. 'Repeated meditations led me first to suspect . . . that Fancy and Imagination were two distinct and widely different faculties, instead of being, according to the general belief, either two names with one meaning, or, at furthest, the lower and higher degrees of one and the same power.' In Chapter XIII he draws the following important distinctions:

> The Imagination then I consider either as primary, or secondary. The Primary Imagination I hold to be the living power and prime agent of all human perception, and as a repetition in the finite mind of the eternal act of creation in the infinite I AM. The Secondary Imagination I consider as an echo of the former, co-existing with the conscious will, yet still as identical with the primary in the *kind* of its agency, and differing only in *degree*, and in the *mode* of [77] its operation. It dissolves, diffuses, dissipates, in order to recreate; or where this process is rendered impossible, yet still at all events it struggles to idealise and to unify. It is essentially *vital*, even as all objects (*as* objects) are essentially fixed and dead.
>
> FANCY, on the other hand, has no other counters to play with, but fixities and definites. The fancy is indeed no other than a mode of memory emancipated from the order of time and space; while it is blended with, and modified by that empirical phenomenon of the will, which we express by the word Choice. But equally with the ordinary memory the Fancy must receive all its materials ready made from the law of association.

I have read some of Hegel and Fichte, as well as Hartley (who turns up at any moment with Coleridge), and forgotten it; of Schelling I am entirely ignorant at first hand, and he is one of those numerous authors whom, the longer you leave them unread, the less desire you have to read. Hence it may be that I wholly fail to appreciate this passage. My mind is too heavy and concrete for any flight of abstruse reasoning. If, as I have already suggested, the difference between imagination and fancy amounts in practice to no more than the difference between good and bad poetry, have we done more than take a turn round Robin Hood's barn? It is only if fancy can be an ingredient in good poetry, and if you can show some good poetry which is the better for it; it is only if the distinction illuminates our immediate preference of one poet over another, that it can be of use to a practical mind like mine. Fancy may be 'no other than a mode of memory emancipated from the order of space and [78] time'; but it seems unwise to talk of memory in connexion with fancy and omit it altogether from the account of imagination. As we have learnt from Dr Lowe's *Road to Xanadu* (if we did not know it already) memory plays a very great part in imagination, and of course a much larger part than can be proved by that book; Professor Lowes had only literary reminiscences to deal with, and they are the only kind of reminiscence which can be fully traced and identified: but how much more of memory enters into creation than only our reading! Mr Lowes has, I think, demonstrated the importance of instinctive and unconscious, as well as deliberate selection. Coleridge's taste, at one period of life, led him first to read voraciously in a certain type of book, and then to select and store up certain kinds of imagery from those books.[1] And I should say that the mind of any poet would be magnetised in its own way, to select automatically, in his reading (from picture papers and cheap novels, indeed, as well as serious books, and least likely from works of an abstract nature, though even these are aliment for some poetic minds) the material – an image, a phrase, a word – which may be of use to him later. And this selection probably runs through the whole of his sensitive life. There might be the experience of a child of ten, a small boy peering through sea-water in a rock-pool, [79] and finding a sea-anemone for the first time: the simple experience (not so simple, for an exceptional child, as it looks) might lie dormant in his mind for twenty years, and re-appear transformed in some verse-context charged with great imaginative pressure. There is so much memory in imagination that if you are to distinguish between imagination and fancy in Coleridge's way you must define the difference between memory in imagination and memory in fancy; and it is not enough to say that the one 'dissolves, diffuses and dissipates' the memories in order to re-create, whilst the other deals with 'fixities and definites'. This distinction, in itself, need not give you distinct imagination and fancy, but only degrees of imaginative success. It would seem from Mr Richards's note[2] that he is almost as much baffled by the passage which I have quoted, or at least

1. And by a right appreciation. The circumstances of early exploration might well stimulate the imaginations of those who endeavoured to set down precisely what they had seen in such a way as to convey an accurate impression to Europeans who had no experience of anything similar. They would often, naturally, stimulate the imagination beyond the perception, but it is usually the accurate images, the fidelity of which may still be recognised, that are the most telling.

2. *Principles of Literary Criticism*, p. 191.

by part of it, as I am. You have to forget all about Coleridge's fancy to learn anything from him about imagination – as with Addison – but from Coleridge there is a good deal to learn. I quote another passage, in the form in which Mr Richards has abbreviated it:

> That synthetic and magical power, to which we have exclusively appropriated the name of imagination ... reveals itself in the balance or reconciliation of opposite or discordant qualities ... the sense of novelty and freshness, with old and familiar objects; a more than usual state of emotion, with more than usual order; judgement ever awake and steady self-possession with enthusiasm and feeling profound or vehement.
>
> The sense of musical delight ... with the power of reducing multitude into [80] variety of effect, and modifying a series of thoughts by some one predominant thought or feeling.

What such descriptions are worth, from the point of view of psychological criticism of to-day, can best be learnt from Mr Richards's book from which I have quoted them. What is my concern here is a less profound matter, the place of Wordsworth and Coleridge in the historical process of criticism. You will have observed in the passage just quoted a richness and depth, an awareness of complication which takes it far out of the range of Dryden. This is not simply because Coleridge thought more profoundly than Dryden, though he did. Nor am I sure that Coleridge learned so much from German philosophers, or earlier from Hartley, as he thought he did; what is best in his criticism seems to come from his own delicacy and subtlety of insight as he reflected upon his own experience of writing poetry. Of the two poets as critics, it was Wordsworth who knew better what he was about: his critical insight, in this one *Preface* and the *Supplement*, is enough to give him the highest place. I do not assign him this position because he cared about the revival of agriculture and the relation of production and consumption, though such interests are symptomatic; there is, in his poetry and in his Preface, a profound spiritual revival, an inspiration communicated rather to Pusey and Newman, to Ruskin, and to the great humanitarians, than to the accredited poets of the next age. Coleridge, with his authority due to his great reading, probably did much more than Wordsworth to bring attention to the profundity of the philosophic problems into which the study of poetry may take us. And the two men [81] together need no third with them to illustrate the mind of an age of conscious change. It is not merely that they were interested in a variety of speculative subjects and of practical matters of importance for their time, but that their interests were involved in each other: and the first faint sign of such complication appeared when Addison derived his theory of imagination in the arts from the theories of Locke. In Wordsworth and Coleridge we find not merely a variety of interests, even of passionate interests; it is all one passion expressed through them all: poetry was for them the expression of a totality of unified interests.

I have tried to exhibit the criticism of Dryden and of Johnson, in this very brief review, in its appropriateness to their periods of history, periods when there was, for the purpose of literary determination, a *stasis*. And to exhibit that of Wordsworth and Coleridge as the criticism of an age of change. Even if it be true that change is always making ready, underneath, during a stable period, and that a period of change contains within itself the elements of limitation which will bring it to a halt, yet some stabilisations are more deeply founded than others. It is with Matthew Arnold that we come to a period of apparent stabilisation which was shallow and premature.

NOTE TO CHAPTER IV ON MR HERBERT READ'S
APPRAISAL OF THE POETRY OF WORDSWORTH

There is a view of English poetry, already of some antiquity, which considers the main line of English poetry [82] from Milton to Wordsworth, or from perhaps even before Milton, as an unfortunate interlude during which the English muse was, if not beside herself, at least not in possession of her faculties. I am sorry to find this view, which was largely Wordsworth's own, re-stated and confirmed by Mr Herbert Read. Mr Read is one of a few contemporaries, like Mr Richards, with whom I almost never feel quite happy in disagreeing; but when, in his admirable small essay, *Form in Modern Poetry*, he writes as follows, I can only exclaim, 'What are we coming to?':

> The main tradition of English poetry . . . begins with Chaucer and reaches its final culmination in Shakespeare. It is contradicted by most French poetry before Baudelaire, by the so-called classical phase of English poetry culminating in Alexander Pope, and by the late Poet Laureate. It was re-established in England by Wordsworth and Coleridge, developed in some degree by Browning and Gerard Manley Hopkins, and in our own day by poets like Wilfred Owen, Ezra Pound and T. S. Eliot.

To some extent I am in agreement; that is, I dare say that my valuation of the earlier poets, poet for poet, would approximate closely enough to Mr Read's; and my admiration for the late Poet Laureate is as moderate as his, though I suspect a slight wilfulness in bringing him into this context. But I observe first that Mr Read goes Wordsworth one better and excludes Milton; and when a poet has done as big a job as Milton, is it helpful to suggest that he has just been up a blind alley? And is Blake too minor a poet to count? As for French poetry, Mr Read saves the situation with the qualification 'most', so that I [83] suppose Baudelaire's master Racine just squeaks in. And is it not arbitrary to assert that the 'classical phase' of English poetry (if we are to employ that term at all) culminates in Pope? Surely Johnson belongs to it, and, with a touch of sentimentalism and even mawkishness, Gray and Collins; and where would Landor be but for the classical tradition? I hasten to add Mr Read's next remark: 'The distinction is not merely that between "classical" and "romantic". This division cuts across in a different direction.' I think that I understand this qualification, and if I understand I agree; nevertheless Mr Read seems to have been using the term 'classical' in two different meanings. Mr Read's divisions are too clear-cut to leave my mind at ease. He considers that the poetic process of a mind like Dryden's and that of a mind like Wordsworth's are essentially diverse; and he says roundly of Dryden's art, 'Such art is not poetry.' Now I cannot see why Dryden's and Wordsworth's minds should have worked any more differently from each other than those of any other two poets. I do not believe that any two poets' minds work quite in the same way, so far as we can know enough about the matter for 'working' to mean anything at all; I do not believe that even the same poet's mind need work in the same way in two different but equally good poems; but there must also be something in common in the poetic process of all poets' minds. Mr Read quotes, in support of his contention, a passage from the *Annus Mirabilis* which I have not given:

> The Composition of all poems is or ought to be of wit; and wit in the Poet, or *wit writing* (if you will give me leave to use a School distinction), is no other than the faculty of [84] imagination in the Writer; which, like a nimble Spaniel, beats over and ranges through the field of Memory, till it springs the Quarry it hunted after; or, without metaphor, which searches over all the Memory for the Species or Ideas of those things which it designs to represent. *Wit written* is that which is well defined, the happy result of Thought, or product of Imagination.

I should have thought this merely a happy description, in the language available at Dryden's time, and at a less profound level of insight than that of Coleridge or Wordsworth at their best, of the same sort of process that the latter were attempting to describe in language nearer to our own. But Mr Read says No, what Dryden is talking about is something different: it is *wit written*, not poetry. Mr Read seems to me to have fallen into the error which I mentioned in the text, of thinking that Dryden is only talking of his own kind of poetic composition, and that he was quite incapable of appreciating Chaucer and Shakespeare. Yet all that I myself have to go upon, in the end, is the kind of enjoyment that I get from Dryden's poetry.

The difference of opinion might be put in a metaphor. In reviewing English poetry, Mr Read seems to charge himself with the task of casting out devils – though less drastically than Mr Pound, who leaves nothing but a room well swept and not garnished. What I see, in the history of English poetry, is not so much daemonic possession as the splitting up of personality. If we say that one of these partial personalities which may develop in a national mind is that which manifested itself in the period between Dryden and Johnson, then what we have to do is to re-integ-[85]rate it: otherwise we are likely to get only successive alternations of personality. Surely the great poet is, among other things, one who not merely restores a tradition which has been in abeyance, but one who in his poetry re-twines as many straying strands of tradition as possible. Nor can you isolate poetry from everything else in the history of a people; and it is rather strong to suggest that the English mind has been deranged ever since the time of Shakespeare, and that only recently have a few fitful rays of reason penetrated its darkness. If the malady is as chronic as that, it is pretty well beyond cure.

Shelley and Keats

February 17th, 1933

UPUC, 87–102.

It would appear that the revolution effected by Wordsworth was very far-reaching indeed. He was not the first poet to present himself as the inspired prophet, nor indeed is this quite Wordsworth's case. Blake may have pretended, and with some claim, to have penetrated mysteries of heaven and hell, but no claim that Blake might make seems to descend upon the 'poet' in general; Blake simply had the visions, and made use of poetry to set them forth. Scott, and Byron in his more popular works, were merely society entertainers. Wordsworth is really the first, in the unsettled state of affairs in his time, to annex new authority for the poet, to meddle with social affairs, and to offer a new kind of religious sentiment which it seemed the peculiar prerogative of the poet to interpret. Since Matthew Arnold made his Selections from Wordsworth's poetry, it has become a commonplace to observe that Wordsworth's true greatness as poet is independent of his opinions, of his theory of diction or of his nature-philosophy, and that it is found in poems in which he has no ulterior motive whatever. I am not sure that this critical eclecticism cannot go too far; that we can judge and enjoy a man's poetry while leaving wholly out of account all of the things for which he cared deeply, and on behalf of which he turned his poetry to account. If we dismiss Wordsworth's interests [88] and beliefs, just how much, I wonder, remains? To retain them, or to keep them in mind instead of deliberately extruding them in preparation for enjoying his poetry, is that not necessary to appreciate how great a poet Wordsworth really is? Consider, for instance, one of the very finest poets of the first part of the nineteenth century: Landor. He is an undoubted master of verse and prose; he is the author of at least one long poem which deserves to be much more read than it is; but his reputation has never been such as to bring him into comparison with Wordsworth or with either of the younger poets with whom we have now to deal. It is not only by reason of a handful of poems or a number of isolated lines expressive of deeper emotion than that of which Landor was capable, that we give Wordsworth his place; there is something integral about such greatness, and something significant in his place in the pattern of history, with which we have to reckon. And in estimating for ourselves the greatness of a poet we have to take into account also the *history* of his greatness. Wordsworth is an essential part of history; Landor only a magnificent by-product.

Shelley both had views about poetry and made use of poetry for expressing views. With Shelley we are struck from the beginning by the number of things poetry is expected to do; from a poet who tells us, in a note on vegetarianism, that 'the orang-outang perfectly resembles man both in the order and the number of his teeth', we shall not know what not to expect. The notes to *Queen Mab* express, it is true, only the views of an intelligent and enthusiastic schoolboy, but a schoolboy who knows how to write; and throughout his work, which is of no small bulk for a [89] short life, he does not, I think, let us forget that he took his ideas seriously. The ideas of Shelley seem to me always to be ideas of adolescence – as there is every reason why they should be. And an enthusiasm for Shelley seems to me also to be an affair of adolescence: for most of us, Shelley has marked an intense period before maturity, but for how many does Shelley remain the companion of age? I confess that I never open the volume of his poems simply because I want to read poetry, but only with some special reason for reference. I find his ideas repellent; and the difficulty of separating Shelley from his ideas and beliefs is still greater than with Wordsworth. And the biographical interest which Shelley has always excited makes it difficult to read the poetry without remembering the man: and the man was humourless, pedantic, self-centred, and sometimes almost a blackguard. Except for an occasional flash of shrewd sense, when he is speaking of someone else and not concerned with his own affairs or with fine writing, his letters are insufferably dull. He makes an astonishing contrast with the attractive Keats. On the other hand, I admit that Wordsworth does not present a very pleasing personality either; yet I not only enjoy his poetry as I cannot enjoy Shelley's, but I enjoy it more than when I first read it. I can only fumble (abating my prejudices as best I can) for reasons why Shelley's abuse of poetry does me more violence than Wordsworth's.

Shelley seems to have had to a high degree the unusual faculty of passionate apprehension of abstract ideas. Whether he was not sometimes confused about his own feelings, as we may be tempted to believe when confounded [90] by the philosophy of *Epipsychidion*, is another matter. I do not mean that Shelley had a metaphysical or philosophical mind; his mind was in some ways a very confused one: he was able to be at once and with the same enthusiasm an eighteenth-century rationalist and a cloudy Platonist. But abstractions could excite in him strong emotion. His views remained pretty fixed, though his poetic gift matured. It is open to us to guess whether his mind would have matured too; certainly, in his last, and to my mind greatest though unfinished poem, *The Triumph of Life*, there is evidence not only of better writing than in any previous long poem, but of greater wisdom:

> Then what I thought was an old root that grew
> To strange distortion out of the hillside,
> Was indeed one of those (*sic*) deluded crew
> And that the grass, which methought hung so wide
> And white, was but his thin discoloured hair
> And that the holes he vainly sought to hide
> Were or had been eyes . . .

There is a precision of image and an economy here that is new to Shelley. But so far as we can judge, he never quite escaped from the tutelage of Godwin, even when he saw through the humbug as a man; and the weight of Mrs Shelley must have been pretty heavy too. And, taking his work as it is, and without vain conjectures about the future, we may ask: is it possible to ignore the 'ideas' in Shelley's poems, so as to be able to enjoy the poetry?

Mr I. A. Richards deserves the credit of having done the pioneer work in the problem of Belief in the enjoyment of [91] poetry; and any methodical pursuit of the problem I must leave to him and to those who are qualified after him. But Shelley raises the question in another form than that in which it presented itself to me in a note on the subject which I appended to an essay on Dante. There, I was concerned with two hypothetical readers, one of whom accepts the philosophy of the poet, and the other of whom rejects it; and so long as the poets in question were such as Dante and Lucretius, this seemed to cover the matter. I am not a Buddhist, but some of the early Buddhist scriptures affect me as parts of the Old Testament do; I can still enjoy Fitzgerald's *Omar*, though I do not hold that rather smart and shallow view of life. But some of Shelley's views I positively dislike, and that hampers my enjoyment of the poems in which they occur; and others seem to me so puerile that I cannot enjoy the poems in which they occur. And I do not find it possible to skip these passages and satisfy myself with the poetry in which no proposition pushes itself forward to claim assent. What complicates the problem still further is that in poetry so fluent as Shelley's there is a good deal which is just bad jingling. The following, for instance:

> On a battle-trumpet's blast
> I fled hither, fast, fast, fast,
> Mid the darkness upward cast.
> From the dust of creeds outworn,
> From the tyrant's banner torn,
> Gathering round me, onward borne,
> There was mingled many a cry–
> Freedom! Hope! Death! Victory!

[92] Walter Scott seldom fell as low as this, though Byron more often. But in such lines, harsh and untunable, one is all the more affronted by the ideas, the ideas which Shelley bolted whole and never assimilated, visible in the catchwords of creeds outworn, tyrants and priests, which Shelley employed with such reiteration. And the bad parts of a poem can contaminate the whole, so that when Shelley rises to the heights, at the end of the poem:

> To suffer woes which Hope thinks infinite;
> To forgive wrongs darker than death or night;
> To defy Power, which seems omnipotent;
> To love, and bear; to hope till Hope creates
> From its own wreck the thing it contemplates . . .

lines to the content of which belief is neither given nor denied, we are unable to enjoy them fully. One does not expect a poem to be equally sustained throughout; and in some of the most successful long poems there is a relation of the more tense to the more relaxed passages, which is itself part of the pattern of beauty. But good lines amongst bad can never give more than a regretful pleasure. In reading *Epipsychidion* I am thoroughly gravelled by lines like:

> True love in this differs from dross or clay,
> That to divide is not to take away . . .
> I never was attached to that great sect
> Whose doctrine is, that each one should select
> Out of the crowd, a mistress or a friend
> And all the rest, though fair and wise, commend
> To cold oblivion. . .

[93] so that when I come, a few lines later, upon a lovely image like:

> A vision like incarnate April, warning
> With smiles and tears, Frost the anatomy
> Into his summer grave,

I am as much shocked at finding it in such indifferent company as pleased by finding it at all. And we much admit that Shelley's finest long poems, as well as some of his worst, are those in which he took his ideas very seriously.[1] It was these ideas that blew the 'fading coal' to life; no more than with Wordsworth, can we ignore them without getting something no more Shelley's poetry than a wax effigy would be Shelley.

Shelley said that he disliked didactic poetry; but his own poetry is chiefly didactic, though (in fairness) not exactly in the sense in which he was using that word. Shelley's professed view of poetry is not dissimilar to that of Wordsworth. The language in which he clothes it in the *Defence of Poetry* is very magniloquent, and with the exception of the magnificent image which Joyce quotes somewhere in *Ulysses* ('the mind in creation is as a fading coal, which some invisible influence, like an inconstant wind, awakens to transitory brightness') it seems to me an inferior piece of writing to Wordsworth's great preface. He says other fine things too; but the following is more significant of the way in which he relates poetry to the social activity of the age:

> [94] The most unfailing herald, companion and follower of the awakening of a great people to work a beneficial change in opinion or institution, is poetry. At such periods there is an accumulation of the power of communicating and receiving intense and impassioned conceptions respecting man and nature. The persons in whom this power resides may often, so far as regards many portions of their nature, have little apparent correspondence with that spirit of good

---

1. He did not, for instance, appear to take his ideas very seriously in *The Witch of Atlas*, which, with all its charm, I think we may dismiss as a trifle.

of which they are the ministers. But even whilst they deny and abjure, they are yet compelled to serve, the power which is seated on the throne of their own soul.

I know not whether Shelley had in mind, in his reservations about 'the persons in whom this power resides', the defects of Byron or those of Wordsworth; he is hardly likely to have been contemplating his own. But this is a statement, and is either true or false. If he is suggesting that great poetry always tends to accompany a popular 'change in opinion or institution', that we know to be false. Whether at such periods the power of 'communicating and receiving intense and impassioned conceptions respecting man and nature' accumulates is doubtful; one would expect people to be too busy in other ways. Shelley does not appear, in this passage, to imply that poetry itself helps to operate these changes, and accumulate this power, nor does he assert that poetry is a usual by-product of change of these kinds; but he does affirm some relation between the two; and in consequence, a particular relation between his own poetry and the events of his own time; from which it would follow that the two throw light upon each other. This is perhaps the first appearance of the kinetic or revolu-[95]tionary theory of poetry; for Wordsworth did not generalise to this point.

We may now return to the question how far it is possible to enjoy Shelley's poetry without approving the use to which he put it; that is, without sharing his views and sympathies. Dante, of course, was about as thoroughgoing a didacticist as one could find; and I have maintained elsewhere, and still maintain, that it is not essential to share Dante's beliefs in order to enjoy his poetry.[1] If in this instance I may appear to be extending the tolerance of a biassed mind, the example of Lucretius will do as well: one may share the essential beliefs of Dante and yet enjoy Lucretius to the full. Why then should this general indemnity not extend to Wordsworth and to Shelley? Here Mr Richards comes very patly to our help:[2]

> Coleridge, when he remarked that a 'willing suspension of disbelief' accompanied much poetry, was noting an important fact, but not quite in the happiest terms, for we are neither aware of a disbelief nor voluntarily suspending it in these cases. It is better to say that the question of belief or disbelief, in the intellectual sense, never arises when we are reading well. If unfortunately it does arise, either

---

1. Mr A. E. Housman has affirmed (*The Name and Nature of Poetry*, p. 34) that 'good religious poetry, whether in Keble or Dante or Job, is likely to be most justly appreciated and most discriminatingly relished by the undevout'. There is a hard atom of truth in this, but if taken literally it would end in nonsense.
2. *Practical Criticism*, p. 277.

through the poet's fault or our own, we have for the moment ceased to be reading and have become astronomers, [96] or theologians, or moralists, persons engaged in quite a different type of activity.

We may be permitted to infer, in so far as the distaste of a person like myself for Shelley's poetry is not attributable to irrelevant prejudices or to a simple blind spot, but is due to a peculiarity in the poetry and not in the reader, that it is not the presentation of beliefs which I do not hold, or – to put the case as extremely as possible – of beliefs that excite my abhorrence, that makes the difficulty. Still less is it that Shelley is deliberately making use of his poetic gifts to propagate a doctrine; for Dante and Lucretius did the same thing. I suggest that the position is somewhat as follows. When the doctrine, theory, belief, or 'view of life' presented in a poem is one which the mind of the reader can accept as coherent, mature, and founded on the facts of experience, it interposes no obstacle to the reader's enjoyment, whether it be one that he accept or deny, approve or deprecate. When it is one which the reader rejects as childish or feeble, it may, for a reader of well-developed mind, set up an almost complete check. I observe in passing that we may distinguish, but without precision, between poets who employ their verbal, rhythmic and imaginative gift in the service of ideas which they hold passionately, and poets who employ the ideas which they hold with more or less settled conviction as material for a poem; poets may vary indefinitely between these two hypothetical extremes, and at what point we place any particular poet must remain incapable of exact calculation. And I am inclined to think that the reason why I was intoxicated by Shelley's poetry at the age of fifteen, and now find it almost unreadable, [97] is not so much that at that age I accepted his ideas, and have since come to reject them, as that at that age 'the question of belief or disbelief', as Mr Richards puts it, did not arise. It is not so much that thirty years ago I was able to read Shelley under an illusion which experience has dissipated, as that because the question of belief or disbelief did not arise I was in a much better position to enjoy the poetry. I can only regret that Shelley did not live to put his poetic gifts, which were certainly of the first order, at the service of more tenable beliefs – which need not have been, for my purposes, beliefs more acceptable to me.

There is, however, more to the problem than that. I was struck by a sentence in Mr Aldous Huxley's Introduction to D. H. Lawrence's *Letters*. 'How bitterly,' he says of Lawrence, 'he loathed the Wilhelm-Meisterish view of love as an education, as a means to culture, a Sandow-exerciser for the soul!' Precisely; Lawrence in my opinion was right; but that view runs through the work of Goethe, and if you dislike it, what are you going to do about Goethe? Does 'culture' require that we make (what Lawrence never did, and I respect him for it) a deliberate effort to put out of mind all our convictions and passionate beliefs about life when we sit down to read poetry? If so, so much the worse for culture. Nor, on the other hand, may we distinguish, as people sometimes do, between the occasions on which a particular poet is 'being a poet' and the occasions on which he is 'being a preacher'. That is too facile. If you attempt to edit Shelley, or Wordsworth or Goethe in this way, there is no point at which you must stop rather than another, and what you get in the end by this process is something [98] which is not Shelley, or Wordsworth or Goethe at all, but a mere unrelated heap of charming stanzas, the debris of poetry rather than the poetry itself. And by using, or abusing, this principle of isolation you are in danger of seeking from poetry some illusory *pure* enjoyment, of separating poetry from everything else in the world, and cheating yourself out of a great deal that poetry has to give to your development.

Some years ago I tried to make the point, in a paper on Shakespeare, that Dante possessed a 'philosophy' in a sense in which Shakespeare held none, or none of any importance. I have reason to believe that I did not succeed in making the point clear at all. Surely, people say, Shakespeare held a 'philosophy', even though it cannot be formulated; surely our reading of Shakespeare gives us a deeper and wider understanding of life and death. And although I was anxious not to give such an impression, I seem to have given some readers to think that I was thereby estimating the poetry of Shakespeare as of less value than Dante's. People tend to believe that there is just some one essence of poetry, for which we can find the formula, and that poets can be ranged according to their possession of a greater or less quantity of this essence. Dante and Lucretius expounded explicit philosophies, as Shakespeare did not. This simple distinction is very clear, but not necessarily highly important. What is important is what distinguishes all of these poets from such poets as Wordsworth, Shelley and Goethe. And here again I think that Mr Richards can throw some light on the matter.

I believe that for a poet to be also a philosopher he would [99] have to be virtually two men; I cannot think of any example of this thorough schizophrenia, nor can I see anything to be gained by it: the work is better performed inside two skulls than one. Coleridge is the apparent example, but I believe that he was only able to exercise the one activity at the expense of the other. A poet may borrow a philosophy or he may do without one. It is when he philosophises upon his own *poetic* insight that he is apt to go wrong. A great deal of the weakness of modern poetry is accounted for in a few pages of Mr Richards's short essay, *Science and*

Poetry; and although he has there D. H. Lawrence under specific examination, a good deal of what he says applies to the Romantic generation as well. 'To distinguish', he says, 'an intuition of an emotion from an intuition *by* it, is not always easy.' I believe that Wordsworth was inclined to the same error of which Mr Richards finds Lawrence guilty. The case of Shelley is rather different: he borrowed ideas – which, as I have said, is perfectly legitimate – but he borrowed shabby ones, and when he had got them he muddled them up with his own intuitions. Of Goethe perhaps it is truer to say that he dabbled in both philosophy and poetry and made no great success of either; his true role was that of the man of the world and sage – a La Rochefoucauld, a La Bruyère, a Vauvenargues.

On the other hand, I should consider it a false simplification to present any of these poets, or Lawrence of whom Mr Richards was speaking, simply as a case of *individual error*, and leave it at that. It is not a wilful paradox to assert that the greatness of each of these writers is indissolubly attached to his practice of the error, of his own specific [100] variation of the error. Their place in history, their importance for their own and subsequent generations, is involved in it; this is not a purely personal matter. They would not have been as great as they were but for the limitations which prevented them from being greater than they were. They belong with the numbers of the great heretics of all times. This gives them a significance quite other than that of Keats, a singular figure in a varied and remarkable period.

Keats seems to me also a great poet. I am not happy about *Hyperion*: it contains great lines, but I do not know whether it is a great poem. The Odes – especially perhaps the *Ode to Psyche* – are enough for his reputation. But I am not so much concerned with the degree of his greatness as with its kind; and its kind is manifested more clearly in his Letters than in his poems; and in contrast with the kinds we have been reviewing, it seems to me to be much more the kind of Shakespeare.[1] The Letters are certainly the most notable and the most important ever written by any English poet. Keats's egotism, such as it is, is that of youth which time would have redeemed. His letters are what letters ought to be; the fine things come in unexpectedly, neither introduced nor shown out, but between trifle and trifle. His observations suggested by Wordsworth's *Gypsey*, in a letter to Bailey of 1817, are of the finest quality of criticism, and the deepest penetration:

---

1. I have not read Mr Murry's *Keats and Shakespeare*: perhaps I say no more than Mr Murry has said better and more exhaustively in that book; I am sure that he has meditated the matter much more deeply than I have.

> It seems to me that if Wordsworth had thought a little [101] deeper at that moment, he would not have written the poem at all. I should judge it to have been written in one of the most comfortable moods of his life – it is a kind of sketchy intellectual landscape, not a search for truth.

And in a letter to the same correspondent a few days later he says:

> In passing, however, I must say one thing that has pressed upon me lately, and increased my Humility and capability of submission – and that is this truth – Men of Genius are great as certain ethereal chemicals operating on the Mass of neutral intellect – but they have not any individuality, any determined character – I would call the top and head of those who have a proper self Men of Power.[1]

This is the sort of remark, which, when made by a man so young as was Keats, can only be called the result of genius. There is hardly one statement of Keats about poetry, which, when considered carefully and with due allowance for the difficulties of communication, will not be found to be true; and what is more, true for greater and more mature poetry than anything that Keats ever wrote.

But I am being tempted into a descant upon the general brilliance and profundity of the observations scattered through Keats's letters, and should probably be tempted further into remarking upon their merit as models of correspondence (not that one should ever take a model in letter-writing) and their revelation of a charming personality. My design, in this very narrow frame, has been [102] only to refer to them as evidence of a very different kind of poetic mind than any of those I have just been considering. Keats's sayings about poetry, thrown out in the course of private correspondence, keep pretty close to intuition; and they have no apparent bearing upon his own times, as he himself does not appear to have taken any absorbing interest in public affairs – though when he did turn to such matters, he brought to bear a shrewd and penetrating intellect. Wordsworth had a very delicate sensibility to social life and social changes. Wordsworth and Shelley both theorise. Keats has no theory, and to have formed one was irrelevant to his interests, and alien to his mind. If we take either Wordsworth or Shelley as representative of his age, as being a voice of the age, we cannot so take Keats. But we cannot accuse Keats of any withdrawal, or refusal; he was merely about his business. He had no theories, yet in the sense appropriate to the poet, in the same sense, though to a lesser degree than Shakespeare, he

---

1. Mr Herbert Read quotes this passage in his *Form in Modern Poetry*, but pursues his speculations to a point to which I would not willingly follow him.

had a 'philosophic' mind. He was occupied only with the highest use of poetry; but that does not imply that poets of other types may not rightly and sometimes by obligation be concerned about the other uses.

Matthew Arnold

March 3rd, 1933

UPUC, 103-19
On p. 106 'oppressive' has been emended to 'oppressed'.

The rise of the democracy to power in America and Europe is not, as has been hoped, to be a safeguard of peace and civilisation. It is the rise of the uncivilised, whom no school education can suffice to provide with intelligence and reason. It looks as if the world were entering upon a new stage of experience, unlike anything heretofore, in which there must be a new discipline of suffering to fit men for the new conditions.

I have quoted the foregoing words, partly because they are by Norton[1] and partly because they are not by Arnold. The first two sentences might well be Arnold's. But the third – 'a new stage of experience, unlike anything heretofore, in which there must be a new discipline of suffering': these words are not only not Arnold's, but we know at once that they could not have been written by him. Arnold hardly looks ahead to the new stage of experience; and though he speaks to us of discipline, it is the discipline of culture, not the discipline of suffering. Arnold represents a period of stasis; of relative and precarious stability, it is true, a brief halt in the endless march of humanity in some, or in any direction. Arnold is neither a reactionary nor a revolutionary; he marks a period of time, as do Dryden and Johnson before him.

[104] Even if the delight we get from Arnold's writings, prose and verse, be moderate, yet he is in some respects the most satisfactory man of letters of his age. You remember the famous judgement which he pronounced upon the poets of the epoch which I have just been considering; a judgement which, at its time, must have appeared startlingly independent. 'The English poetry of the first quarter of this century,' he says in his essay on *The Function of Criticism*, 'with plenty of energy, plenty of creative force, did not know enough.' We should be right too, I think, if we added that Carlyle, Ruskin, Tennyson, Browning, with plenty of energy, plenty of creative force, had not enough wisdom. Their culture was not always well-rounded; their knowledge of the human soul was often partial and

---

1. Letter to Leslie Stephen, January 8th, 1896.

often shallow. Arnold was not a man of vast or exact scholarship, and he had neither walked in hell nor been rapt to heaven; but what he did know, of books and men, was in its way well-balanced and well-marshalled. After the prophetic frenzies of the end of the eighteenth and the beginning of the nineteenth century, he seems to come to us saying:

> This poetry is very fine, it is opulent and careless, it is sometimes profound, it is highly original; but you will never establish and maintain a tradition if you go on in this haphazard way. There are minor virtues which have flourished better at other times and in other countries: these you must give heed to, these you must apply, in your poetry, in your prose, in your conversation and your way of living; else you condemn yourselves to enjoy only fitful and transient bursts of literary brilliance, and you will never, as a people, a nation, a race, have a fully formed tradition and person-[105]ality.

However well-nourished we may be on previous literature and previous culture, we cannot afford to neglect Arnold.

I have elsewhere tried to point out some of Arnold's weaknesses when he ventured into departments of thought for which his mind was unsuited and ill-equipped. In philosophy and theology he was an undergraduate; in religion a Philistine. It is a pleasanter task to define a man's limitations within the field in which he is qualified; for there, the definition of limitation may be at the same time a precision of the writer's excellences. Arnold's poetry has little technical interest. It is academic poetry in the best sense; the best fruit which can issue from the promise shown by the prize-poem. When he is not simply being himself, he is most at ease in a master's gown: *Empedocles on Etna* is one of the finest academic poems ever written. He tried other robes which became him less well; I cannot but think of *Tristram and Iseult* and *The Forsaken Merman* as charades. *Sohrab and Rustum* is a fine piece, but less fine than *Gebir*; and in the classical line Landor, with a finer ear, can beat Arnold every time. But Arnold is a poet to whom one readily returns. It is a pleasure, certainly, after associating with the riff-raff of the early part of the century, to be in the company of a man *qui sait se conduire*; but Arnold is something more than an agreeable Professor of Poetry. With all his fastidiousness and superciliousness and officiality, Arnold is more intimate with us than Browning, more intimate than Tennyson ever is except at moments, as in the passionate flights in *In Memoriam*. He is the poet and critic of a period of false stability. All his writing in the [106] kind of *Literature and Dogma* seems to me a valiant attempt to dodge the issue, to mediate between Newman and Huxley; but his poetry, the best of it, is too honest to employ any but his genuine feelings of unrest, loneliness and dissatisfaction. Some of his limitations are manifest enough. In his essay on *The Study of Poetry* he has several paragraphs on Burns, and for an Englishman and an Englishman of his time, Arnold understands Burns very well. Perhaps I have a partiality for small oppressed nationalities like the Scots that makes Arnold's patronising manner irritate me; and certainly I suspect Arnold of helping to fix the wholly mistaken notion of Burns as a singular untutored English dialect poet, instead of as a decadent representative of a great alien tradition. But he says (taking occasion to rebuke the country in which Burns lived) that 'no one can deny that it is of advantage to a poet to deal with a beautiful world'; and this remark strikes me as betraying a limitation. It is an advantage to mankind in general to live in a beautiful world; that no one can doubt. But for the poet is it so important? We mean all sorts of things, I know, by Beauty. But the essential advantage for a poet is not, to have a beautiful world with which to deal: it is to be able to see beneath both beauty and ugliness; to see the boredom, and the horror, and the glory.

The vision of the horror and the glory was denied to Arnold, but he knew something of the boredom. He speaks much of the 'consolatory' power of Wordsworth's poetry, and it is in connexion with Wordsworth that he makes many of his wisest observations about poetry.

[107] But when will Europe's latter hour
Again find Wordsworth's healing power?
Others will teach us how to dare,
And against fear our breast to steel:
Others will strengthen us to bear –
But who, ah who, will make us feel?
The cloud of mortal destiny,
Others will front it fearlessly –
But who, like him, will put it by?[1]

His tone is always of regret, of loss of faith, instability, nostalgia:

And love, if love, of happier men.
Of happier men, for they, at least,
Have *dreamed* two human hearts might blend
In one, and were through faith released
From isolation without end
Prolonged, nor knew, although no less
Alone than thou, their loneliness.

---

1. I do not quote these lines as good verse. They are very carelessly written. The fourth line is particularly clumsy, the sixth has a bathetic repetition. To 'put by' the cloud of human destiny is not a felicitous expression. The dashes at the end of two lines are a symptom of weakness, like Arnold's irritating use of italicised words.

This is a familiar enough sentiment; and perhaps a more robust comment on the situation is, that if you don't like it, you can get on with it; and the verse itself is not highly distinguished. Marguerite, at best, is a shadowy figure, neither very passionately desired nor very closely observed, a mere pretext for lamentation. His personal emotion is indeed most convincing when he deals with an impersonal [108] subject. And when we know his poetry, we are not surprised that in his criticism he tells us little or nothing about his experience of writing it, and that he is so little concerned with poetry from the maker's point of view. One feels that the writing of poetry brought him little of that excitement, that joyful loss of self in the workmanship of art, that intense and transitory relief which comes at the moment of completion and is the chief reward of creative work. As we can forget, in reading his criticism, that he is a poet himself, so it is all the more necessary to remind ourselves that his creative and his critical writings are essentially the work of the same man. The same weakness, the same necessity for something to depend upon, which make him an academic poet make him an academic critic.

From time to time, every hundred years or so, it is desirable that some critic shall appear to review the past of our literature, and set the poets and the poems in a new order. This task is not one of revolution but of readjustment. What we observe is partly the same scene, but in a different and more distant perspective; there are new and strange objects in the foreground, to be drawn accurately in proportion to the more familiar ones which now approach the horizon, where all but the most eminent become invisible to the naked eye. The exhaustive critic, armed with a powerful glass, will be able to sweep the distance and gain an acquaintance with minute objects in the landscape with which to compare minute objects close at hand; he will be able to gauge nicely the position and proportion of the objects surrounding us, in the whole of the vast panorama. This metaphorical fancy only represents the ideal; but [109] Dryden, Johnson and Arnold have each performed the task as well as human frailty will allow. The majority of critics can be expected only to parrot the opinions of the last master of criticism; among more independent minds a period of destruction, of preposterous over-estimation, and of successive fashions takes place, until a new authority comes to introduce some order. And it is not merely the passage of time and accumulation of new artistic experience, nor the ineradicable tendency of the great majority of men to repeat the opinions of those few who have taken the trouble to think, nor the tendency of a nimble but myopic minority to progenerate heterodoxies, that makes new assessments necessary. It is that no generation is interested in Art in quite the same way as any other; each generation, like each individual, brings to the contemplation of art its own categories of appreciation, makes its own demands upon art, and has its own uses for art. 'Pure' artistic appreciation is to my thinking only an ideal, when not merely a figment, and must be, so long as the appreciation of art is an affair of limited and transient human beings existing in space and time. Both artist and audience are limited. There is for each time, for each artist, a kind of alloy required to make the metal workable into art; and each generation prefers its own alloy to any other. Hence each new master of criticism performs a useful service merely by the fact that his errors are of a different kind from the last; and the longer the sequence of critics we have, the greater amount of correction is possible.

It was desirable after the surprising, varied and abundant contribution of the Romantic Period that this task of [110] criticism should be undertaken again. Nothing that was done in this period was of the nature of what Arnold was able to do, because that was not the time in which it could be done. Coleridge, Lamb, Hazlitt, De Quincey, did work of great importance upon Shakespeare and the Elizabethan dramatists, and discovered new treasure which they left for others to calculate. The instruments of Arnold's time appear now, of course, very antiquated: his was the epoch of Ward's *English Poets*, and of *The Golden Treasury*, birthday albums and calendars with a poetical quotation for each day. Arnold was not Dryden or Johnson; he was an Inspector of Schools and he became Professor of Poetry. He was an educator. The valuation of the Romantic poets, in academic circles, is still very largely that which Arnold made. It was right, it was just, it was necessary for its time; and of course it had its defects. It is tinged by his own uncertainty, his own apprehensions, his own view of what it was best that his own time should believe; and it is very much influenced by his religious attitude. His taste is not comprehensive. He seems to have chosen, when he could – for much of his work is occasional – those subjects in connexion with which he could best express his views about morals and society: Wordsworth – perhaps not quite as Wordsworth would have recognised himself – Heine, Amiel, Guérin. He was capable of learning from France and from Germany. But the *use* to which he put poetry was limited; he wrote about poets when they provided a pretext for his sermon to the British public; and he was apt to think of the greatness of poetry rather than of its genuineness.

There is no poetry which Arnold experienced more [111] deeply than that of Wordsworth; the lines which I quoted above are not so much a criticism of Wordsworth as a testimonial of what Wordsworth had done for *him*. We may expect to find in the essay on Wordsworth, if anywhere, a statement of what poetry meant to Arnold. It is in his essay on Wordsworth that occurs his famous definition: 'Poetry is at bottom a criticism of life.' At bottom: that is a great way down; the bottom is the bottom. At the bottom of the abyss is what few ever see, and what those cannot bear to look at for long; and it is not a 'criticism of life'. If we mean life as a whole – not that Arnold ever saw life as a whole – from top to bottom, can anything that we can say of it ultimately, of that awful mystery, be called criticism? We bring back very little from our rare descents, and that is not criticism. Arnold might just as well have said that Christian worship is at bottom a criticism of the Trinity. We see better what Arnold's words amount to when we recognise that his own poetry is decidedly critical poetry. A poem like *Heine's Grave* is criticism, and very fine criticism too; and a kind of criticism which is justified because it could not be made in prose. Sometimes Arnold's criticism is on a lower level:

> One morn, as through Hyde Park we walked,
> My friend and I, by chance we talked,
> Of Lessing's famed Laocoon.[1]

[112] The poem about Heine is good poetry for the same reason that it is good criticism: because Heine is one of the *personae*, the masks, behind which Arnold is able to go through his performance. The reason why some criticism is good (I do not care to generalise here about all criticism) is that the critic assumes, in a way, the personality of the author whom he criticises, and through this personality is able to speak with his own voice. Arnold's Wordsworth is as much like Arnold as he is like Wordsworth. Sometimes a critic may choose an author to criticise, a role to assume, as far as possible the antithesis to himself, a personality which has actualised all that has been suppressed in himself; we can sometimes arrive at a very satisfactory intimacy with our anti-masks.

'The greatness of a poet,' Arnold goes on to say, 'lies in his powerful and beautiful application of ideas to life.' Not a happy way of putting it, as if ideas were a lotion for the inflamed skin of suffering humanity. But it seems to be what Arnold thought he was doing. He presently qualifies this assertion by pointing out that 'morals' must not be interpreted too narrowly:

> Morals are often treated in a narrow and false fashion; they are bound up with systems of thought and belief which have had their day; they are fallen into the hands of pedants and professional dealers; they grow tiresome to some of us.

---

1. It may be said of Arnold's inferior work, as was said of that of an inferior poet, that he faggoted his verses as they fel. And if they rhymed and rattled, all was well. Of course we do not judge Arnold as a poet by such effusions as this, but we cannot be blamed for forming a lower opinion of his capacity for self-criticism. He need not have printed them.

Alas! for morals as Arnold conceived them; they are grown still more tiresome. He then remarks significantly in speaking of the 'Wordsworthians':

> The Wordsworthians are apt to praise him for the wrong [113] things, and to lay far too much stress upon what they call his philosophy. His poetry is the reality, his philosophy – so far, at least, as it may put on the form and habit of a 'scientific system of thought', and the more that it puts them on – is the illusion. Perhaps we shall one day learn to make this proposition general, and to say: Poetry is the reality, philosophy the illusion.

This seems to me a striking, dangerous and subversive assertion. Poetry is at bottom a criticism of life; yet philosophy is illusion; the reality is the criticism of life. Arnold might have read Lessing's famed Laocoon with a view to disentangling his own confusions.

We must remember that for Arnold, as for everyone else, 'poetry' meant a particular selection and order of poets. It meant, as for everyone else, the poetry that he liked, that he re-read; when we come to the point of making a statement about poetry, it is the poetry that sticks in our minds that weights that statement. And at the same time we notice that Arnold has come to an opinion about poetry different from that of any of his predecessors. For Wordsworth and for Shelley poetry was a vehicle for one kind of philosophy or another, but the philosophy was something believed in. For Arnold the best poetry supersedes both religion and philosophy. I have tried to indicate the results of this conjuring trick elsewhere.[1] The most generalised form of my own view is simply this: that nothing in this world or the next is a substitute for anything else; and if you find that you must do without something, such as religious faith or philosophic belief, then you must just do without it. [114] I can persuade myself, I find, that some of the things that I can hope to get are better worth having than some of the things I cannot get; or I may hope to alter myself so as to want different things; but I cannot persuade myself that it is the same desires that are satisfied, or that I have in effect the same thing under a different name.

A French friend said of the late York Powell of Oxford: '*Il était aussi tranquille dans son manque de foi que le mystique dans sa croyance.*' You could not say that of Arnold; his charm and his interest are largely due to the painful position that he occupied between faith and disbelief. Like many people the vanishing of whose religious faith has left behind only habits, he placed an exaggerated emphasis upon morals. Such people

---

1. 'Arnold and Pater', in *Selected Essays*.

often confuse morals with their own good habits, the result of a sensible upbringing, prudence, and the absence of any very powerful temptation; but I do not speak of Arnold or of any particular person, for only God knows. Morals for the saint are only a preliminary matter; for the poet a secondary matter. How Arnold finds morals in poetry is not clear. He tells us that:

'A poetry of revolt against moral ideas is a poetry of revolt against *life*; a poetry of indifference towards moral ideas is a poetry of indifference towards *life*,' but the statement left in suspension, and without Arnold's illustrating it by examples of poetic revolt and poetic indifference, seems to have little value. A little later he tells us why Wordsworth is great:

> Wordsworth's poetry is great because of the extraordinary power with which Wordsworth feels the joy offered to us in nature, the joy offered to us in the simple [115] primary affections and duties; and because of the extraordinary power with which, in case after case, he shows us this joy, and renders it so as to make us share it.

It is not clear whether 'the simple primary affections and duties' (whatever they are, and however distinguished from the secondary and the complex) is meant to be an expansion of 'nature', or another joy superadded: I rather think the latter, and take 'nature' to mean the Lake District. I am not, furthermore, sure of the meaning of the conjunction of two quite different reasons for Wordsworth's greatness: one being the power with which Wordsworth *feels* the joy of nature, the other the power by which he makes us *share* it. In any case, it is definitely a communication theory, as any theory of the poet as teacher, leader, or priest is bound to be. One way of testing it is to ask why other poets are great. Can we say that Shakespeare's poetry is great because of the extraordinary power with which Shakespeare feels estimable feelings, and because of the extraordinary power with which he makes us share them? I enjoy Shakespeare's poetry to the full extent of my capacity for enjoying poetry; but I have not the slightest approach to certainty that I share Shakespeare's feelings; nor am I very much concerned to know whether I do or not. In short, Arnold's account seems to me to err in putting the emphasis upon the poet's feelings, instead of upon the poetry. We can say that in poetry there is communication from writer to reader, but should not proceed from this to think of the poetry as being primarily the vehicle of communication. Communication may take place, but will explain nothing. Or Arnold's statement may [116] be criticised in another way, by asking whether Wordsworth would be a less great poet, if he felt with extraordinary power the horror offered to us in nature, and the boredom and sense of restriction in the simple primary affections and duties? Arnold seems to think that because, as he says, Wordsworth 'deals with more of *life*' than Burns, Keats and Heine, he is dealing with more of moral ideas. A poetry which is concerned with moral ideas, it would appear, is concerned with life; and a poetry concerned with life is concerned with moral ideas.

This is not the place for discussing the deplorable moral and religious effects of confusing poetry and morals in the attempt to find a substitute for religious faith. What concerns me here, is the disturbance of our literary values in consequence of it. One observes this in Arnold's criticism. It is easy to see that Dryden underrated Chaucer; not so easy to see that to rate Chaucer as highly as Dryden did (in a period in which critics were not lavish of superlatives) was a triumph of objectivity for its time, as was Dryden's consistent differentiation between Shakespeare and Beaumont and Fletcher. It is easy to see that Johnson underrated Donne and overrated Cowley; it is even possible to come to understand why. But neither Johnson nor Dryden had any axe to grind; and in their errors they are more consistent than Arnold. Take, for instance, Arnold's opinion of Chaucer, a poet who, although very different from Arnold, was not altogether deficient in high seriousness. First he contrasts Chaucer with Dante: we admit the inferiority, and are almost convinced that Chaucer is not serious enough. But is Chaucer, in the end, less serious than Wordsworth, with whom Arnold does not compare him? And when Arnold puts Chaucer below François Villon, although he is in a way right, and although it was high time that somebody in England spoke up for Villon, one does not feel that the theory of 'high seriousness' is in operation. That is one of the troubles of the critic who feels called upon to set the poets in rank: if he is honest with his own sensibility he must now and again violate his own rules of rating. There are also dangers arising from being too sure that one knows what 'genuine poetry' is. Here is one very positive pronouncement:

> The difference between genuine poetry and the poetry of Dryden, Pope and all their school, is briefly this: their poetry is conceived and composed in their wits, genuine poetry is conceived in the soul. The difference between the two kinds of poetry is immense.[1]

And what, we wonder, had Arnold –

---

[1]. Practically the same distinction as that of Arnold is maintained, though with more subtlety and persuasiveness, by Mr Housman in his *Name and Nature of Poetry*. A newer and more radical classification to the same effect is that of Mr Herbert Read already quoted.

> For rigorous teachers seized his youth
> And purged its faith, and trimmed its fire,
> Showed him the high white star of Truth,
> There bade him gaze, and there aspire;
> > Even now their whispers pierce the gloom:
> > What dost thou in this living tomb?

what had a man whose youth was so rigorously seized and purged at Rugby, to do with an abstract entity like the Soul? 'The difference between the two kinds of poetry is [118] immense.' But there are not two kinds of poetry, but many kinds; and the difference here is no more immense than that between the kind of Shakespeare and the kind of Arnold. There is petulance in such a judgement, arrogance and excess of heat. It was justifiable for Coleridge and Wordsworth and Keats to depreciate Dryden and Pope, in the ardour of the changes which they were busy about; but Arnold was engaged in no revolution, and his short-sightedness can only be excused.

I do not mean to suggest that Arnold's conception of the use of poetry, an educator's view, vitiates his criticism. To ask of poetry that it give religious and philosophic satisfaction, while depreciating philosophy and dogmatic religion, is of course to embrace the shadow of a shade. But Arnold had real taste. His preoccupations, as I have said, make him too exclusively concerned with *great* poetry, and with the greatness of it. His view on Milton is for this reason unsatisfying. But you cannot read his essay on *The Study of Poetry* without being convinced by the felicity of his quotations: to be able to quote as Arnold could is the best evidence of taste. The essay is a classic in English criticism: so much is said in so little space, with such economy and with such authority. Yet he was so conscious of what, for him, poetry was *for*, that he could not altogether see it for what it is. And I am not sure that he was highly sensitive to the musical qualities of verse. His own occasional bad lapses arouse the suspicion; and so far as I can recollect he never emphasises this virtue of poetic style, this fundamental, in his criticism. What I call the 'auditory imagination' is the feeling for syllable and rhythm, pene-[119]trating far below the conscious levels of thought and feeling, invigorating every word; sinking to the most primitive and forgotten, returning to the origin and bringing something back, seeking the beginning and the end. It works through meanings, certainly, or not without meanings in the ordinary sense, and fuses the old and obliterated and the trite, the current, and the new and surprising, the most ancient and the most civilised mentality. Arnold's notion of 'life', in his account of poetry, does not perhaps go deep enough.

I feel, rather than observe, an inner uncertainty and lack of confidence and conviction in Matthew Arnold: the conservatism which springs from lack of faith, and the zeal for reform which springs from dislike of change. Perhaps, looking inward and finding how little he had to support him, looking outward on the state of society and its tendencies, he was somewhat disturbed. He had no real serenity, only an impeccable demeanour. Perhaps he cared too much for civilisation, forgetting that Heaven and Earth shall pass away, and Mr Arnold with them, and there is only one stay. He is a representative figure. A man's theory of the place of poetry is not independent of his view of life in general.

The Modern Mind
March 17th, 1933

UPUC, 121-42.

There is a sentence in Maritain's *Art and Scholasticism* which occurs to me in this context: 'Work such as Picasso's,' he says, 'shows a fearful progress in self-consciousness on the part of painting.'

So far I have drawn a few light sketches to indicate the changes in the self-consciousness of poets thinking about poetry. A thorough history of this 'progress in self-consciousness' in poetry and the criticism of poetry would have kinds of criticism to consider which do not fall within the narrow scope of these lectures: the history of Shakespeare criticism alone, in which, for instance, Morgann's essay on the character of Falstaff, and Coleridge's *Lectures on Shakespeare* would be representative moments, would have to be considered in some detail. But we have observed the notable development in self-consciousness in Dryden's Prefaces, and in the first serious attempt, which he made, at a valuation of the English poets. We have seen his work in one direction continued, and a method perfected, by Johnson in his careful estimation of a number of poets, an estimate arrived at by the application of what are on the whole admirably consistent standards. We have found a deeper insight into the nature of the poetic activity in remarks scattered through the writings of Coleridge and in [122] the *Preface* of Wordsworth and in the Letters of Keats; and a perception, still immature, of the need to elucidate the social function of poetry in Wordsworth's *Preface* and in Shelley's *Defence*. In the criticism of Arnold we find a continuation of the work of the Romantic poets with a new appraisal of the poetry of the past by a method which, lacking the precision of Johnson's, gropes towards wider and deeper connexions. I have not wished to exhibit this 'progress in self-consciousness' as being necessarily *progress* with an association of higher value. For one thing, it cannot be wholly abstracted from the general changes in the human mind in history; and that these changes have any teleological significance is not one of my assumptions.

Arnold's insistence upon order in poetry according to a moral valuation was, for better or worse, of the first importance for his age. When he is not at his best he obviously falls between two stools. Just as his poetry is too reflective, too ruminative, to rise ever to the first rank, so also is his criticism. He is not, on the one hand, quite a pure enough poet to have the sudden illuminations which we find in the criticism of Wordsworth, Coleridge and Keats; and on the other hand he lacked the mental discipline, the passion for exactness in the use of words and for consistency and continuity of reasoning, which distinguishes the philosopher. He sometimes confuses words and meanings: neither as poet nor as philosopher should he have been satisfied with such an utterance as that 'poetry is at bottom a criticism of life'. A more profound insight into poetry and a more exact use of language than Arnold's are required. The critical method of Arnold, the assumptions of [123] Arnold, remained valid for the rest of his century. In quite diverse developments, it is the criticism of Arnold that sets the tone: Walter Pater, Arthur Symons, Addington Symonds, Leslie Stephen, F. W. H. Myers, George Saintsbury – all the more eminent critical names of the time bear witness to it.

Whether we agree or not with any or all of his conclusions, whether we admit or deny that his method is adequate, we must admit that the work of Mr I. A. Richards will have been of cardinal importance in the history of literary criticism. Even if his criticism proves to be entirely on the wrong track, even if this modern 'self-consciousness' turns out to be only a blind alley, Mr Richards will have done something in accelerating the exhaustion of the possibilities. He will have helped indirectly to discredit the criticism of persons qualified neither by sensibility nor by knowledge of poetry, from which we suffer daily. There is some hope of greater clarity; we should begin to learn to distinguish the appreciation of poetry from theorising about poetry, and to know when we are not talking about poetry but about something else suggested by it. There are two elements in Richards's scheme, both of considerable importance for its ultimate standing, of which I have the gravest doubts but with which I am not here concerned: his theory of Value and his theory of Education (or rather the theory of Education assumed in or implied by his attitude in *Practical Criticism*). As for psychology and linguistics, that is his field and not mine. I am more concerned here with what seem to me to be a few unexamined assumptions that he has made. I do [124] not know whether he still adheres to certain assertions made in his early essay *Science and Poetry*; but I do not understand that he has yet made any public modification of them. Here is one that is in my mind:

> The most dangerous of the sciences is only now beginning to come into action. I am thinking less of Psychoanalysis or of Behaviourism than of the whole subject which includes them. It is very probable that the Hindenburg Line to which the defence of our traditions retired as a result of the onslaughts of the last century will be blown up in the near future. If this should happen a mental chaos such as man has never experienced may be expected. We shall then be thrown back, as Matthew Arnold foresaw, upon poetry. Poetry is capable of saving us. . . .

I should have felt completely at a loss in this passage, had not Matthew Arnold turned up; and then it seemed to me that I knew a little better what was what. I should say that an affirmation like this was highly characteristic of one type of modern mind. For one of the things that one can say about the modern mind is that it comprehends every extreme and degree of opinion. Here, from the essay, *Art and Scholasticism*, which I have already quoted is Mr Maritain:

> It is a deadly error to expect poetry to provide the super-substantial nourishment of man.

Mr Maritain is a theologian as well as a philosopher, and you may be sure that when he says 'deadly error' he is in deadly earnest. But if the author of *Anti-Moderne* is hardly to be considered a 'modern' man, we can find other varieties of opinion. In a book called *The Human Parrot*, [125] Mr Montgomery Belgion has two essays, one called *Art and Mr. Maritain* and the other *What is Criticism*, from which you will learn that neither Maritain nor Richards knows what he is talking about. Mr Richards further maintains that the experience of poetry is not a mystical revelation, and the Abbé Henri Brémond,[1] in *Prayer and Poetry*, is concerned with telling us in what kind and degree it is. On this point Mr Belgion is apparently in accord with Mr Richards. And we may be wise to keep in mind a remark of Mr Herbert Read in *Form in Modern Poetry*: 'If a literary critic happens to be also a poet . . . he is liable to suffer from dilemmas which do not trouble the philosophic calm of his more prosaic colleagues.'

Beyond a belief that poetry does something of importance, or has something of importance to do, there does not seem to be much

---

1. While preparing this book for press I learn with great regret of the Abbé Brémond's untimely death. It is a great pity that he could not have lived to complete the *Histoire du sentiment religieux en France*.

agreement. It is interesting that in our time, which has not produced any vast number of important poets, so many people – and there are many more – should be asking questions about poetry. These problems are not those which properly concern poets as poets at all; if poets plunge into the discussion, it is probably because they have interests and curiosities outside of writing poetry. We need not summon those who call themselves Humanists (for they have for the most part not been primarily occupied with the nature and function of poetry) to bear witness that we have here the problem of religious faith and its substitutes. Not all contemporary critics, of [126] course, but at least a number who appear to have little else in common, seem to consider that art, specifically poetry, has something to do with religion, though they disagree as to what this something may be. The relationship is not always envisaged so moralistically as it was by Arnold, nor so generally as in the statement by Mr Richards which I quoted. For Mr Belgion, for instance,

> An outstanding example of poetic allegory is in the final canto of the *Paradiso*, where the poet seeks to give an allegorical account of the Beatific Vision, and then declares his efforts vain. We may read this over and over again, and in the end we shall no more have had a revelation of the nature of the Vision than we had before ever we had heard of either it or Dante.

Mr Belgion seems to have taken Dante at his word. But what we experience as readers is never exactly what the poet experienced, nor would there be any point in its being, though certainly it has some relation to the poet's experience. What the poet experienced is not poetry but poetic material; the writing of the poetry is a fresh 'experience' for him, and the reading of it, by the author or anyone else, is another thing still. Mr Belgion, in denying a theory which he attributes to Mr Maritain, seems to me to make his own mistakes; but it is a religion-analogy which is in question. Mr Richards is much occupied with the religious problem simply in the attempt to avoid it. In an appendix to the second edition of *Principles of Literary Criticism* he has a note on my own verse, which, being as favourable as I could desire, seems to me very acute. But he observes that Canto XXVI of the *Purgatorio* illuminates my 'persistent [127] concern with sex, the problem of our generation, as religion was the problem of the last.' I readily admit the importance of Canto XXVI, and it was shrewd of Mr Richards to notice it; but in his contrast of sex and religion he makes a distinction which is too subtle for me to grasp. One might think that sex and religion were 'problems' like Free Trade and Imperial Preference; it seems odd that the human race should have gone on for so many thousands of years before it suddenly realised that religion and sex, one right after the other, presented problems.

It has been my view throughout – and it is only a commonplace after all – that the development and change of poetry and of the criticism of it is due to elements which enter from outside. I tried to draw attention not so much to the importance of Dryden's 'contribution' to literary criticism, as if he were merely adding to a store of quantity, as to the importance of the fact that he should *want* to articulate and expound his view on drama and translation and on the English poetry of the past; and, when we came to Johnson, to call attention to the further development of an historical consciousness which made Johnson *want* to estimate, in more detail, the English poets of his own age and of previous ages;[1] and it seemed to me that Wordsworth's theories about poetry drew their aliment from social sources. To Matthew Arnold we owe the credit of bringing the religious issue explicitly into the discussion of literature and poetry; and with due respect to Mr Richards, and with Mr Richards himself as a witness, it does not [128] seem to me that this 'issue' has been wholly put aside and replaced by that of 'sex'. My contemporaries seem to me still to be occupied with it, whether they call themselves churchmen, or agnostics, or rationalists, or social revolutionists. The contrast between the doubts that our contemporaries express, and the questions that they ask and the problems they put themselves, and the attitude of at least a part of the past, was well put by Jacques Rivière in two sentences:

> If in the seventeenth century Molière or Racine had been asked why he wrote, no doubt he would have been able to find but one answer; that he wrote 'for the entertainment of decent people' (*pour distraire les honnêtes gens*). It is only with the advent of Romanticism that the literary act came to be conceived as a sort of raid on the absolute and its result as a revelation.

Rivière's form of expression is not, to my mind, altogether happy. One might suppose that all that had happened was that a wilful perversity had taken possession of literary men, a new literary disease called Romanticism. That is one of the dangers of expressing one's meaning in terms of 'Romanticism': it is a term which is constantly changing in different contexts, and which is now limited to what appear to be purely literary and purely local problems, now expanding to cover almost the whole of the life of a time and of nearly the whole world. It has perhaps not been observed that in its more comprehensive significance 'Romanticism'

---

1. The fact that Johnson was working largely to order only indicates that this historical consciousness was already developed.

comes to include nearly everything that distinguishes the last two hundred and fifty years or so from their predecessors, and includes so much that it ceases [129] to bring with it any praise or blame. The change to which Rivière alludes is not a contrast between Molière and Racine on the one hand and more modern French writers on the other; it neither reflects credit upon the former nor implies inferiority in the latter. In the interest of clarity and simplicity I wish myself to avoid employing the terms Romanticism and Classicism, terms which inflame political passions, and tend to prejudice our conclusions. I am only concerned with my contention that the notion of what poetry is for, of what is its function to do, does change, and therefore I quoted Rivière; I am concerned further with criticism as evidence of the conception of the use of poetry in the critic's time, and assert that in order to compare the work of different critics we must investigate their assumptions as to what poetry does and ought to do. Examination of the criticism of our time leads me to believe that we are still in the Arnold period.

I speak of Mr Richards's views with some diffidence. Some of the problems he discusses are themselves very difficult, and only those are qualified to criticise who have applied themselves to the same specialised studies and have acquired proficiency in this kind of thinking. But here I limit myself to passages in which he does not seem to be speaking as a specialist, and in which I have no advantage of special knowledge either. There are two reasons why the writer of poetry must not be thought to have any great advantage. One is that a discussion of poetry such as this takes us far outside the limits within which a poet may speak with authority; the other is that the poet does many things upon instinct, for which he can give no better [130] account than anybody else. A poet can try, of course, to give an honest report of the way in which he himself writes: the result may, if he is a good observer, be illuminating. And in one sense, but a very limited one, he knows better what his poems 'mean' than can anyone else; he may know the history of their composition, the material which has gone in and come out in an unrecognisable form, and he knows what he was trying to do and what he was meaning to mean. But what a poem means is as much what it means to others as what it means to the author; and indeed, in the course of time a poet may become merely a reader in respect to his own works, forgetting his original meaning – or without forgetting, merely changing. So that, when Mr Richards asserts that *The Waste Land* effects 'a complete severance between poetry and *all* beliefs' I am no better qualified to say No! than is any other reader. I will admit that I think that either Mr Richards is wrong, or I do not understand his meaning. The statement might mean that it was the first poetry to do what all poetry in the past would have been the better for doing: I can hardly think that he intended to pay me such an unmerited compliment. It might also mean that the present situation is radically different from any in which poetry has been produced in the past: namely, that now there is nothing in which to believe, that Belief itself is dead; and that therefore my poem is the first to respond properly to the modern situation and not call upon Make-Believe. And it is in this connexion, apparently, that Mr Richards observes that 'poetry is capable of saving us'.

A discussion of Mr Richards's theories of knowledge, [131] value and meaning would be by no means irrelevant to this assertion, but it would take us far afield, and I am not the person to undertake it. We cannot of course refute the statement 'poetry is capable of saving us' without knowing which one of the multiple definitions of salvation Mr Richards has in mind.[1] (A good many people behave as if they thought so too: otherwise their interest in poetry is difficult to explain.) I am sure, from the differences of environment, of period, and of mental furniture, that salvation by poetry is not quite the same thing for Mr Richards as it was for Arnold; but so far as I am concerned these are merely different shades of blue. In *Practical Criticism*[2] Mr Richards provides a recipe which I think throws some light upon his theological ideas. He says:

> Something like a technique or ritual for heightening sincerity might well be worked out. When our response to a poem after our best efforts remains uncertain, when we are unsure whether the feelings it excites come from a deep source in our experience, whether our liking or disliking is genuine, is *ours*, or an accident of fashion, a response to surface details or to essentials, we may perhaps help ourselves by considering it in a frame of feelings whose sincerity is beyond our questioning. Sit by the fire (with eyes shut and fingers pressed firmly upon the eyeballs) and consider with as full 'realisation' as possible –

[132] five points which follow, and which I shall comment upon one by one. We may observe, in passing, the intense religious seriousness of Mr Richards's attitude towards poetry.[3] What he proposes – for he hints in

---

1. See his *Mencius on the Mind*. There is of course a locution in which we say of someone 'he is not one of *us*'; it is possible that the 'us' of Mr Richards's statement represents an equally limited and select number.
2. Second Impression, p. 290.
3. This passage is introduced by a long and important discussion of Confucius's conception of 'sincerity', which should be read attentively. In passing, it is worthy of remark that Mr Richards shares his interest in Chinese philosophy with Mr Ezra Pound and with the late Irving Babbitt. An investigation of an interest common to three apparently quite different thinkers would, I believe, repay the labour. It seems to

the passage above that his sketch might be elaborated – is nothing less than a regimen of Spiritual Exercises. Now for the points.

I. *Man's loneliness (the isolation of the human situation).*

Loneliness is known as a frequent attitude in romantic poetry, and in the form of 'lonesomeness' (as I need not remind American readers) is a frequent attitude in contemporary lyrics known as 'the blues'. But in what sense is Man in general isolated, and from what? What *is* the 'human situation'? I can understand the isolation of the human situation as Plato's Diotima expounds it, or in the Christian sense of the separation of Man from God; but not an isolation which is not a separation from anything in particular.

II. *The facts of birth and of death, in their inexplicable oddity.*

I cannot see why the facts of birth and of death should appear odd in themselves, unless we have a conception of [133] some other way of coming into the world and of leaving it, which strikes us as more natural.

III. *The inconceivable immensity of the Universe.*

It was not, we remember, the 'immense spaces' themselves but their *eternal silence* that terrified Pascal. With a definite religious background this is intelligible. But the effect of popular astronomy books (like Sir James Jeans's) upon me is only of the insignificance of vast space.

IV. *Man's place in the perspective of time.*

I confess that I do not find this especially edifying either, or stimulating to the imagination, unless I bring to its contemplation some belief that there is a sense and a meaning in the place of human history in the history of the world. I fear that in many people this subject of meditation can only stimulate the idle wonder and greed for facts which are satisfied by Mr Wells's compendia.

V. *The enormity (sc. enormousness) of man's ignorance.*

Here again, I must ask, ignorance of what? I am acutely aware, for instance, of my own ignorance of specific subjects on which I want to know more; but Mr Richards does not, surely, mean the ignorance of any individual man, but of *Man*. But 'ignorance' must be relative to the sense in which we take the term 'knowledge'; and in *Mencius on the Mind* Mr Richards has given us a useful analysis of the numerous meanings of 'knowledge'. Mr Richards, who has engaged in what I believe will be most fruitful investigations of controversy as systematised misunderstanding, [134] may justly be able to accuse me of perverting his meanings. But his modern substitute for the *Exercises* of St Ignatius is an appeal to our

---

indicate, at least, a deracination from the Christian tradition. The thought of these three men seems to me to have an interesting similarity.

feelings, and I am only trying to set down how they affect mine. To me Mr Richards's five points only express a modern emotional attitude which I cannot share, and which finds its most sentimental expression in *A Free Man's Worship*. And as the contemplation of Man's place in the Universe has led Lord Russell to write such bad prose, we may wonder whether it will lead the ordinary aspirant to understanding of good poetry. It is just as likely, I suspect, to confirm him in his taste for the second-rate.

I am willing to admit that such an approach to poetry may help some people: my point is that Mr Richards speaks as though it were good for everybody. I am perfectly ready to concede the existence of people who feel, think and believe as Mr Richards does in these matters, if he will only concede that there are some people who do not. He told us in *Science and Poetry*:

> For centuries . . . countless pseudo-statements – about God, about the universe, about human nature, the relations of mind to mind, about the soul, its rank and destiny . . . have been believed; now they are gone, irrecoverably; and the knowledge which has killed them is not of a kind upon which an equally fine organisation of the mind can be based.

I submit that this is itself a pseudo-statement, if there is such a thing. But these things are indeed gone, so far as Mr Richards is concerned, if they are no longer believed by people whose minds Mr Richards respects: we have no ground for controversy there. I only assert again that what he is trying to do is essentially the same as what Arnold [135] wanted to do: to preserve emotions without the beliefs with which their history has been involved. It would seem that Mr Richards, on his own showing, is engaged in a rear-guard religious action.[1]

Mr Maritain, with an equally strong conviction that poetry will *not* save us, is equally despondent about the world of to-day. 'Could any weakness', he asks, 'be greater than the weakness of our contemporaries?' It is no more, as I have said before, the particular business of the poet as poet to concern himself with Maritain's attempt to determine the position of poetry in a Christian world than it is to concern himself with Richards's attempt to determine the position of poetry in a pagan world: but these various ambient ideas get in through the pores, and produce an unsettled state of mind. Trotsky, whose *Literature and Revolution* is

---

1. Somewhat in the spirit of 'religion without revelation', of which a greater exponent than Mr Julian Huxley was Emmanuel Kant. On Kant's attempt (which deeply influenced later German theology) see an illuminating passage in A. E. Taylor's *The Faith of a Moralist*, vol. ii, chap. ii.

the most sensible statement of a Communist attitude that I have seen,[1] is pretty clear on the relation of the poet to his environment. He observes:

> Artistic creation is always a complicated turning inside out of old forms, under the influence of new stimuli which [136] originate outside of art. In this large sense of the word, art is a handmaiden. It is not a disembodied element feeding on itself, but a function of social man indissolubly tied to his life and environment.

There is a striking contrast between this conception of art as a handmaiden, and that which we have just observed of art as a saviour. But perhaps the two notions are not so opposed as they appear. Trotsky seems, in any case, to draw the commonsense distinction between art and propaganda, and to be dimly aware that the material of the artist is not his beliefs as *held*, but his beliefs as *felt* (so far as his beliefs are part of his material at all); and he is sensible enough to see that a period of revolution is not favourable to art, since it puts pressure upon the poet, both direct and indirect, to make him overconscious of his beliefs as *held*. He would not limit Communist poetry to the writing of panegyrics upon the Russian State, any more than I should limit Christian poetry to the composition of hymns; the poetry of Villon is just as 'Christian' in this way as that of Prudentius or Adam of St Victor – though I think it would be a long time before Soviet society could afford to approve a Villon, if one arose.[2] It is probable, however, that Russian literature will become increasingly unintelligible, increasingly meaningless, to the peoples of Western Europe unless they develop in the same direction as Russia. Even as things are, in the present chaos of opinion and belief, we [137] may expect to find quite different literatures existing in the same language and the same country. 'The unconcealed and palpable influence of the devil on an important part of contemporary literature,' says Mr Maritain, 'is one of the significant phenomena of the history of our time.' I can hardly expect most of my readers to take this remark seriously;[3] those who do will have very different criteria of criticism from those who do not. Another observation of Mr Maritain's may be less unacceptable:

---

1. There were also some interesting articles in *The New Republic* by Mr Edmund Wilson, in controversy (if I remember correctly) with Mr Michael Gold. I regret that I cannot give the exact reference. The major part of Trotsky's book is not very interesting for those who are unacquainted with the modern Russian authors: one suspects that most of Trotsky's swans are geese.

2. The Roman and Communist idea of an index of prohibited books seems to me perfectly sound in principle. It is a question (*a*) of the goodness and universality of the cause, (*b*) of the intelligence that goes to the application.

3. With the influence of the devil on contemporary literature I shall be concerned in more detail in another book.

By showing us where moral truth and the genuine supernatural are situate, religion saves poetry from the absurdity of believing itself destined to transform ethics and life: saves it from overweening arrogance.

This seems to me to be putting the finger on the great weakness of much poetry and criticism of the nineteenth and twentieth centuries. But between the motive which Rivière attributed to Molière and Racine[1] and the motive of Matthew Arnold bearing on shoulders immense what he thought to be the orb of the poet's fate, there is a serious *via media*.

As the doctrine of the moral and educational value of poetry has been elaborated in different forms by Arnold and Mr Richards, so the Abbé Brémond presented a modern equivalent for the theory of divine inspiration. [138] The task of *Prayer and Poetry* is to establish the likeness, and the difference of kind and degree, between poetry and mysticism. In his attempt to demonstrate this relation he safeguards himself by just qualifications, and makes many penetrating remarks about the nature of poetry. I will confine myself to two pieces of caution. My first qualm is over the assertion that 'the more of a poet any particular poet is, the more he is tormented by the need of communicating his experience.' This is a downright sort of statement which is very easy to accept without examination; but the matter is not so simple as all that. I should say that the poet is tormented primarily by the need to write a poem – and so, I regret to find, are a legion of people who are not poets: so that the line between 'need' to write and 'desire' to write is by no means easy to draw. And what is the experience that the poet is so bursting to communicate? By the time it has settled down into a poem it may be so different from the original experience as to be hardly recognisable. The 'experience' in question may be the result of a fusion of feelings so numerous, and ultimately so obscure in their origins, that even if there be communication of them, the poet may hardly be aware of what he is communicating; and what is there to be communicated was not in existence before the poem was completed. 'Communication' will not explain poetry. I will not say that there is not always some varying degree of communication in poetry, or that poetry could exist without any communication taking place. There is room for very great individual variation in the motives of equally good individual poets; and we have the assurance of Coleridge, [139] with the approval of Mr Housman, that 'poetry gives most pleasure when

---

1. Which does not seem to me to cover the case. Let us say that it was the primary motive (even in *Athalie*). An exact statement would need much space; for we cannot concern ourselves only with what went on inside the poet's head, but with the general state of society.

only generally and not perfectly understood'. And I think that my first objection to Brémond's theory is related to the second, in which also the question of motive and intention enters. Any theory which relates poetry very closely to a religious or a social scheme of things aims, probably, to *explain* poetry by discovering its natural laws; but it is in danger of *binding* poetry by legislation to be observed – and poetry can recognise no such laws. When the critic falls into this error he has probably done what we all do: when we generalise about poetry, as I have said before, we are generalising from the poetry which we best know and best like; not from all poetry, or even all of the poetry which we have read. What is 'all poetry'? Everything written in verse which a sufficient number of the best minds have considered to be poetry. By a sufficient number, I mean enough persons of different types, at different times and places, over a space of time, and including foreigners as well as those to whom the language is native, to cancel every personal bias and eccentricity of taste (for we must all be slightly eccentric in taste to have any taste at all). Now when an account like the Abbé Brémond's is tested by being made itself a test, it tends to reveal some narrowness and exclusiveness; at any rate, a good deal of poetry that I like would be excluded, or given some other name than poetry; just as other writers who like to include much prose as being essentially 'poetry' create confusion by including too much. That there is a relation (not necessarily noetic, perhaps merely psychological) between mysticism and some kinds of poetry, or [140] some of the kinds of state in which poetry is produced, I make no doubt. But I prefer not to define, or to test, poetry by means of speculations about its origins; you cannot find a sure test for poetry, a test by which you may distinguish between poetry and mere good verse, by reference to its putative antecedents in the mind of the poet. Brémond seems to me to introduce extra-poetic laws for poetry: such laws as have been frequently made, and constantly violated.

There is another danger in the association of poetry with mysticism besides that which I have just mentioned, and that of leading the reader to look in poetry for religious satisfactions. These were dangers for the critic and the reader; there is also a danger for the poet. No one can read Mr Yeats's *Autobiographies* and his earlier poetry without feeling that the author was trying to get as a poet something like the exaltation to be obtained, I believe, from hashisch or nitrous oxide. He was very much fascinated by self-induced trance states, calculated symbolism, mediums, theosophy, crystal-gazing, folklore and hobgoblins. Golden apples, archers, black pigs and such paraphernalia abounded. Often the verse has an hypnotic charm: but you cannot take heaven by magic, especially if you are, like Mr Yeats, a very sane person. Then, by a great triumph of development, Mr Yeats began to write and is still writing some of the most beautiful poetry in the language, some of the clearest, simplest, most direct.[1]

[141] The number of people capable of appreciating 'all poetry' is probably very small, if not merely a theoretical limit; but the number of people who can get *some* pleasure and benefit from some poetry is, I believe, very large. A perfectly satisfactory theory which applied to all poetry would do so only at the cost of being voided of all content; the more usual reason for the unsatisfactoriness of our theories and general statements about poetry is that while professing to apply to all poetry, they are really theories about, or generalisations from, a limited range of poetry. Even when two persons of taste like the same poetry, this poetry will be arranged in their minds in slightly different patterns; our individual taste in poetry bears the indelible traces of our individual lives with all their experience pleasurable and painful. We are apt either to shape a theory to cover the poetry that we find most moving, or – what is less excusable – to choose the poetry which illustrates the theory we want to hold. You do not find Matthew Arnold quoting Rochester or Sedley. And it is not merely a matter of individual caprice. Each age demands different things from poetry, though its demands are modified, from time to time, by what some new poet has given. So our criticism, from age to age, will reflect the things that the age demands; and the criticism of no one man and of no one age can be expected to embrace the whole nature of poetry or exhaust all of its uses. Our contemporary critics, like their predecessors, are making particular responses to particular situations. No two readers, perhaps, will go to poetry with quite the same demands. Amongst all these demands from poetry and responses to it there is always some permanent [142] element in common, just as there are standards of good and bad writing independent of what any one of us happens to like and dislike; but every effort to formulate the common element is limited by the limitations of particular men in particular places and at particular times; and these limitations become manifest in the perspective of history.

---

1. The best analysis of the weakness of Mr Yeats's poetry that I know is in Mr Richards's *Science and Poetry*. But I do not think that Mr Richards quite appreciated Mr Yeats's later work.

Conclusion

March 31st, 1933

UPUC, 143-56

I hope that I have not given the impression, in this cursory review of theories past and present, that I estimate the value of such theories according to their degree of approximation to some doctrine which I hold myself, and pay them off accordingly. I am too well aware of limitations of interest for which I do not apologise, and of incapacity for abstruse reasoning as well as less pardonable shortcomings. I have no general theory of my own; but on the other hand I would not appear to dismiss the views of others with the indifference which the practitioner may be supposed to feel towards those who theorise about his craft. It is reasonable, I feel, to be on guard against views which claim too much for poetry, as well as to protest against those which claim too little; to recognise a number of uses for poetry, without admitting that poetry must always and everywhere be subservient to any one of them. And while theories of poetry may be tested by their power of refining our sensibility by increasing our understanding, we must not ask that they serve even that purpose of adding to our enjoyment of poetry: any more than we ask of ethical theory that it shall have a direct application to and influence upon human behaviour. Critical speculation, like philosophical speculation and scientific research, must be free to follow its own course; and cannot be called upon to show imme-[144]diate results; and I believe that the pondering (in judicious moderation) of the questions which it raises will tend to enhance our enjoyment.

That there is an analogy between mystical experience and some of the ways in which poetry is written I do not deny; and I think that the Abbé Brémond has observed very well the differences as well as the likenesses; though, as I have said, whether the analogy is of significance for the student of religion, or only to the psychologist, I do not know. I know, for instance, that some forms of ill-health, debility or anaemia, may (if other circumstances are favourable) produce an efflux of poetry in a way approaching the condition of automatic writing – though, in contrast to the claims sometimes made for the latter, the material has obviously been incubating within the poet, and cannot be suspected of being a present from a friendly or impertinent demon. What one writes in this way may succeed in standing the examination of a more normal state of mind; it gives me the impression, as I have just said, of having undergone a long incubation, though we do not know until the shell breaks what kind of egg we have been sitting on. To me it seems that at these moments, which are characterised by the sudden lifting of the burden of anxiety and fear which presses upon our daily life so steadily that we are unaware of it, what happens is something *negative*: that is to say, not 'inspiration' as we commonly think of it, but the breaking down of strong habitual barriers – which tend to re-form very quickly.[1] [145] Some obstruction is momentarily whisked away. The accompanying feeling is less like what we know as positive pleasure, than a sudden relief from an intolerable burden. I agree with Brémond, and perhaps go even further, in finding that this disturbance of our quotidian character which results in an incantation, an outburst of words which we hardly recognise as our own (because of the effortlessness), is a very different thing from mystical illumination. The latter is a vision which may be accompanied by the realisation that you will never be able to communicate it to anyone else, or even by the realisation that when it is past you will not be able to recall it to yourself; the former is not a vision but a motion terminating in an arrangement of words on paper.

But I should add one reservation. I should hesitate to say that the experience at which I have hinted is responsible for the creation of all the most profound poetry written, or even always of the best of a single poet's work. For all I know, it may have much more significance for the psychologist's understanding of a particular poet, or of one poet in a certain phase, than it has for anyone's understanding of [146] poetry. Some finer minds, indeed, may operate very differently; I cannot think of Shakespeare or Dante as having been dependent upon such capricious releases. Perhaps this throws no light on poetry at all. I am not even sure that the poetry which I have written in this way is the best that I have written; and so far as I know, no critic has ever identified the passages I have in mind. The way in which poetry is written is not, so far as our knowledge of these obscure matters as yet extends, any clue to its value. But, as Norton wrote in a letter to Dr L. P. Jacks in 1907, 'I have no belief that such views as mine are likely within any reasonable time to be held by a considerable body of men'; for people are always ready to grasp at any guide which will help them to recognise the best

---

1. I should like to quote a confirmation of my own experience from Mr A. E. Housman's *Name and Nature of Poetry*: 'In short I think that the production of poetry, in its first stage, is less an active than a passive and involuntary process; and if I were obliged, not to define poetry, but to name the class of things to which it belongs, I should call it a secretion; whether a natural secretion, like turpentine in the fir, or a morbid secretion, like the pearl in the oyster. I think that my own case, though I may not deal with the matter so cleverly as the oyster does, is the latter; because I have seldom written poetry unless I was rather out of health, and the experience, though pleasurable, was generally agitating and exhausting.' I take added satisfaction in the fact that I only read Mr Housman's essay some time after my own lines were written.

poetry without having to depend upon their own sensibility and taste. The faith in mystical inspiration is responsible for the exaggerated repute of *Kubla Khan*. The imagery of that fragment, certainly, whatever its origins in Coleridge's reading, sank to the depths of Coleridge's feeling, was saturated, transformed there – 'those are pearls that were his eyes' – and brought up into daylight again. But it is not *used*: the poem has not been written. A single verse is not poetry unless it is a one-verse poem; and even the finest line draws its life from its context. Organisation is necessary as well as 'inspiration'. The re-creation of word and image which happens fitfully in the poetry of such a poet as Coleridge happens almost incessantly with Shakespeare. Again and again, in his use of a word, he will give a new meaning or extract a latent one; again and again the right imagery, saturated while it lay in the depths of Shakespeare's [147] memory, will rise like Anadyomene from the sea. In Shakespeare's poetry this reborn image or word will have its rational use and justification; in much good poetry the organisation will not reach to so rational a level. I will take an example which I have used elsewhere: I am glad of the opportunity to use it again, as on the previous occasion I had an inaccurate text. It is from Chapman's *Bussy D'Ambois*:

> Fly where the evening from the Iberian vales
> Takes on her swarthy shoulders Hecate
> Crowned with a grove of oaks: fly where men feel
> The burning axletree, and those that suffer
> Beneath the chariot of the snowy Bear. . . .

Chapman borrowed this, as Dr Boas points out, from Seneca's *Hercules Œteus*:

> dic sub Aurora positis Sabaeis
> dic sub occasu positis Hiberis
> quique sub plaustro patiuntur ursae
> quique ferventi quatiuntur axe

and probably also from the same author's *Hercules Furens*:

> sub ortu solis, an sub cardine
> glacialis ursae?

There is first the probability that this imagery had some personal saturation value, so to speak, for Seneca; another for Chapman, and another for myself, who have borrowed it twice from Chapman. I suggest that what gives it such intensity as it has in each case is its saturation – I will not say with 'associations', for I do not want to revert to Hartley – but with feelings too obscure for the authors [148] even to know quite what they were. And of course only a part of an author's imagery comes from his reading. It comes from the whole of his sensitive life since early childhood. Why, for all of us, out of all that we have heard, seen, felt, in a lifetime, do certain images recur, charged with emotion, rather than others? The song of one bird, the leap of one fish, at a particular place and time, the scent of one flower, an old woman on a German mountain path, six ruffians seen through an open window playing cards at night at a small French railway junction where there was a water-mill: such memories may have symbolic value, but of what we cannot tell, for they come to represent the depths of feeling into which we cannot peer. We might just as well ask why, when we try to recall visually some period in the past, we find in our memory just the few meagre arbitrarily chosen set of snapshots that we do find there, the faded poor souvenirs of passionate moments.[1]

Thus far is as far as my experience will take me in this direction. My purpose has not been to examine thoroughly any one type of theory of poetry still less to confute it; but rather to indicate the kinds of defect and excess that we must expect to find in each, and to suggest that the current tendency is to expect too much, rather than too little, of [149] poetry. No one of us, when he thinks about poetry, is without his own bias; and Abbé Brémond's preoccupation with mysticism and Mr Richards's lack of interest in theology are equally significant. One voice was raised, in our time, to express a view of a different kind; that of a man who wrote several remarkable poems himself, and who also had an aptitude for theology. It is that of T. E. Hulme:

> There is a general tendency to think that verse means little else than the expression of unsatisfied emotion. People say: 'But how can you have verse without sentiment?' You see what it is; the project alarms them. A classical revival to them would mean the prospect of an arid desert and the death of poetry as they understand it, and could only come to fill the gulf caused by that death. Exactly why this dry classical spirit should have a positive and legitimate necessity to express itself in poetry is utterly inconceivable to them. . . . The great aim is accurate, precise and definite description. The first thing is to realise how extraordinarily difficult this is. . . . Language has its own special nature, its own conventions and communal ideas.

---

1. In chapter xxii of *Principles of Literary Criticism* Mr Richards discusses these matters in his own way. As evidence that there are other approaches as well, see a very interesting article *Le symbolisme et l'âme primitive* by E. Cailliet and J. A. Bédé in the *Revue de littérature comparée* for April–June 1932. The authors, who have done field-work in Madagascar, apply the theories of Lévy-Bruhl: the pre-logical mentality persists in civilised man, but becomes available only to or through the poet.

It is only by a concentrated effort of the mind that you can hold it fixed to your own purpose.

This is, we must remark at once, not a general theory of poetry, but an assertion of the claims of a particular kind of poetry for the writer's own time. It may serve to remind us how various are the kinds of poetry, and how variously poetry may appeal to different minds and generations equally qualified to appreciate it.

The extreme of theorising about the nature of poetry, the essence of poetry if there is any, belongs to the study of [150] aesthetics and is no concern of the poet or of a critic with my limited qualifications. Whether the self-consciousness involved in aesthetics and in psychology does not risk violating the frontier of consciousness, is a question which I need not raise here; it is perhaps only my private eccentricity to believe that such researches are perilous if not guided by sound theology. The poet is much more vitally concerned with the social 'uses' of poetry, and with his own place in society; and this problem is now perhaps more importunately pressed upon his conscious attention than at any previous time. The uses of poetry certainly vary as society alters, as the public to be addressed changes. In this context something should be said about the vexed question of obscurity and unintelligibility. The difficulty of poetry (and modern poetry is supposed to be difficult) may be due to one of several reasons. First, there may be personal causes which make it impossible for a poet to express himself in any but an obscure way; while this may be regrettable, we should be glad, I think, that the man has been able to express himself at all. Or difficulty may be due just to novelty: we know the ridicule accorded in turn to Wordsworth, Shelley and Keats, Tennyson and Browning – but must remark that Browning was the first to be *called* difficult; hostile critics of the earlier poets found them difficult, but called them silly. Or difficulty may be caused by the reader's having been told, or having suggested to himself, that the poem is going to prove difficult. The ordinary reader, when warned against the obscurity of a poem, is apt to be thrown into a state of consternation very unfavourable to poetic receptivity. Instead of beginning, as [151] he should, in a state of sensitivity, he obfuscates his senses by the desire to be clever and to look very hard for something, he doesn't know what – or else by the desire not to be taken in. There is such a thing as stage fright, but what such readers have is pit or gallery fright. The more seasoned reader, he who has reached, in these matters, a state of greater *purity*, does not bother about understanding; not, at least, at first. I know that some of the poetry to which I am most devoted is poetry which I did not understand at first reading; some is poetry which I am not sure I understand yet: for instance, Shakespeare's. And finally, there is the difficulty caused by the author's having left out something which the reader is used to finding; so that the reader, bewildered, gropes about for what is absent, and puzzles his head for a kind of 'meaning' which is not there, and is not meant to be there.

The chief use of the 'meaning' of a poem, in the ordinary sense, may be (for here again I am speaking of some kinds of poetry and not all) to satisfy one habit of the reader, to keep his mind diverted and quiet, while the poem does its work upon him: much as the imaginary burglar is always provided with a bit of nice meat for the house-dog. This is a normal situation of which I approve. But the minds of all poets do not work that way; some of them, assuming that there are other minds like their own, become impatient of this 'meaning' which seems superfluous, and perceive possibilities of intensity through its elimination. I am not asserting that this situation is ideal; only that we must write our poetry as we can, and take it as we find it. It may be that for some periods of society a more relaxed form of [152] writing is right, and for others a more concentrated. I believe that there must be many people who feel, as I do, that the effect of some of the greater nineteenth-century poets is diminished by their bulk. Who now, for the pure pleasure of it, reads Wordsworth, Shelley and Keats even, certainly Browning and Swinburne and most of the French poets of the century – entire? I by no means believe that the 'long poem' is a thing of the past; but at least there must be more in it for the length than our grandparents seemed to demand; and for us, anything that can be said as well in prose can be said better in prose. And a great deal, in the way of meaning, belongs to prose rather than to poetry. The doctrine of 'art for art's sake', a mistaken one, and more advertised than practised, contained this true impulse behind it, that it is a recognition of the error of the poet's trying to do other people's work. But poetry has as much to learn from prose as from other poetry; and I think that an interaction between prose and verse, like the interaction between language and language, is a condition of vitality in literature.

To return to the question of obscurity: when all exceptions have been made, and after admitting the possible existence of minor 'difficult' poets whose public must always be small, I believe that the poet naturally prefers to write for as large and miscellaneous an audience as possible, and that it is the half-educated and ill-educated, rather than the uneducated, who stand in his way: I myself should like an audience which could neither read nor write.[1] The most [153] useful poetry, socially, would

---

1. On the subject of education, there are some helpful remarks in Lawrence's *Fantasia of the Unconscious*.

be one which could cut across all the present stratifications of public taste – stratifications which are perhaps a sign of social disintegration. The ideal medium for poetry, to my mind, and the most direct means of social 'usefulness' for poetry, is the theatre. In a play of Shakespeare you get several levels of significance. For the simplest auditors there is the plot, for the more thoughtful the character and conflict of character, for the more literary the words and phrasing, for the musically sensitive the rhythm, and for auditors of greater sensitiveness and understanding a meaning which reveals itself gradually. And I do not believe that the classification of audience is so clear-cut as this; but rather that the sensitiveness of every auditor is acted upon by all these elements at once, though in different degrees of consciousness. At none of these levels is the auditor bothered by the presence of that which he does not understand, or by the presence of that in which he is not interested. I may make my meaning a little clearer by a simple instance. I once designed, and drafted a couple of scenes, of a verse play. My intention was to have one character whose sensibility and intelligence should be on the plane of the most sensitive and intelligent members of the audience; his speeches should be addressed to them as much as to the other personages in the play – or rather, should be addressed to the latter, who were to be material, literal-minded and visionless, with the consciousness of being overheard by the former. There was to be an understanding between this protagonist and a small number of the audience, while the rest of the audience would share the responses of the other characters in the play. [154] Perhaps this is all too deliberate, but one must experiment as one can.

Every poet would like, I fancy, to be able to think that he had some direct social utility. By this, as I hope I have already made clear, I do not mean that he should meddle with the tasks of the theologian, the preacher, the economist, the sociologist or anybody else; that he should do anything but write poetry, poetry not defined in terms of something else. He would like to be something of a popular entertainer, and be able to think his own thoughts behind a tragic or a comic mask. He would like to convey the pleasures of poetry, not only to a larger audience, but to larger groups of people collectively; and the theatre is the best place in which to do it. There might, one fancies, be some fulfillment in exciting this communal pleasure, to give an immediate compensation for the pains of turning blood into ink. As things are, and as fundamentally they must always be, poetry is not a career, but a mug's game. No honest poet can ever feel quite sure of the permanent value of what he has written: he may have wasted his time and messed up his life for nothing. All the better, then, if he could have at least the satisfaction of having a part to play in society as worthy as that of the music-hall comedian. Furthermore, the theatre, by the technical exactions which it makes and limitations which it imposes upon the author, by the obligation to keep for a definite length of time the sustained interest of a large and unprepared and not wholly perceptive group of people, by its problems which have constantly to be solved, has enough to keep the poet's *conscious* mind fully occupied, as the painter's by the mani-[155]pulation of his tools. If, beyond keeping the interest of a crowd of people for that length of time, the author can make a play which is real poetry, so much the better.

I have not attempted any definition of poetry, because I can think of none which does not assume that the reader already knows what it is, or which does not falsify by leaving out much more than it can include. Poetry begins, I dare say, with a savage beating a drum in a jungle, and it retains that essential of percussion and rhythm; hyperbolically one might say that the poet is *older* than other human beings – but I do not want to be tempted to ending on this sort of flourish. I have insisted rather on the variety of poetry, variety so great that all the kinds seem to have nothing in common except the rhythm of verse instead of the rhythm of prose: and that does not tell you much about all poetry. Poetry is of course not to be defined by its uses. If it commemorates a public occasion, or celebrates a festival, or decorates a religious rite, or amuses a crowd, so much the better. It may effect revolutions in sensibility such as are periodically needed; may help to break up the conventional modes of perception and valuation which are perpetually forming, and make people see the world afresh, or some new part of it. It may make us from time to time a little more aware of the deeper, unnamed feelings which form the substratum of our being, to which we rarely penetrate; for our lives are mostly a constant evasion of ourselves, and an evasion of the visible and sensible world. But to say all this is only to say what you know already, if you have felt poetry and thought about your feelings. And I fear that I have already, throughout these [156] lectures, trespassed beyond the bounds which a little self-knowledge tells me are my proper frontier. If, as James Thomson observed, 'lips only sing when they cannot kiss', it may also be that poets only talk when they cannot sing. I am content to leave my theorising about poetry at this point. The sad ghost of Coleridge beckons to me from the shadows.

Address By T. S. Eliot, '06
To the Class of '33, June 17, 1933

Milton Graduates Bulletin, 3 (9 Nov. 1933), 5–9. Not in Gallup, but would be C578a.

Eliot wrote on Henry Ware Eliot, Jr's, printed copy after publication: 'Evidently taken down in shorthand without my knowledge. It goes wrong here and there!' (Houghton MS AC9.El464.LZ999e). Milton Academy received three pages of Eliot's MS notes (last page missing), with some parts only in outline, from the Revd John Carroll Perkins. On Henry Ware Eliot, Jr's, copy Eliot corrected 'three shipping companies' to 'Greek shipping companies' on p. 7. On p. 8 he placed an insertion mark between 'out' and 'being' in 'go out being eccentric', with a question mark in the left margin; emended here to 'go on being eccentric'.

Twenty-seven years ago I sat here with the graduating class – not in this hall, we did not seem to need so much room in those days – and somebody then got up on the platform and made the sort of speech I am supposed to make. At least, I believe some one did. I really do not remember. I have not the slightest recollection who it was or a word that he said, and it never occurred to me even to regret that fact until today. Perhaps if I had attended to his words, I should know better how to behave now, but I do not believe that any other member of my class can remember that speech any better than I can. I do not believe any graduating class ever remembers what the speaker of the day says to it. The reason of this extraordinary lapse of memory must be that none of us ever listen. There are too many other things to think about at the moment, more pressing and more interesting. The immediate future, the next day, the summer, and the next year at college are all more interesting things to think about than what you hear from some old duffer who gets up on the platform when you are anxious to get away.

That being so, the question is: Whom am I to talk to? The graduating class, if it is true to form, does not listen. Of course, I cannot condescend to anyone else. I can hear what I am saying myself, but you must remember that, differently from twenty-seven years ago, I am now on my best behaviour and have to listen. Besides, three of my old masters are present, and you will find yourselves when you come back after a long time that two things strike you about your old masters: one is that they are very much younger than you thought they were, and the other is that they inspire you with very much more awe than they ever did when you were in school.

However, it occurred to me that as I had to talk to somebody, I would take more or less a metaphorical figure and make him as real as I could – that is, it occurred to me to say a few words to the ghost of myself at the age of seventeen or thereabouts, whom we may suppose to be skulking somewhere about this hall. I have always wanted to say something to him and I have a number of grievances against that character.

I should like to face him and say: 'Now look at me. See what a mess you have made of things. What have you got to say for yourself?' So I shall begin by saying to him: 'Up to now you have contributed something to your own education, but for the most part you have been taught, and from now on you have got to contribute a good deal more to your own education and co-operate, because from now on you won't learn unless to a large extent you are teaching yourself. You have got to find out for yourself what you want to do in the next few years. You must find out what you want to do and whether you are [6] capable of doing it. The probability is assuming that you are neither a rotter nor an absolute weakling – that you belong to one of three general classes of individuals. The first always seemed to me a rather fortunate class of people. They are those who from very early time seem to have developed a very clear bent in a certain direction and, having abilities in that way, it is quite clear what they want to do and what they ought to do for the rest of their lives. A great many of these people, I think, are very often scientifically inclined. They include the fellows who are always six experiments ahead of you in the laboratory – I was always three or four behind with those; I never used to get anything to explode. Their part is not necessarily easy, but it is very plainly marked.

Then there is a large class of people who do not seem to have a particular bent for one thing rather than another, but who, with the aid of character and good nature, family, friends, influence, and so on, get on very well in the world and go on fairly smoothly in a pretty direct line to a very satisfactory career.

Then there is a third class of people who have to find a good deal more out for themselves, who do not seem destined for the straightforward, conventional sort of life. After all, it is the third class of people who are the backbone of a country and who have shown no early evidence of a career in them. Some of them become noted, some remain obscure; but they are people who have to make their own mistakes, find out for themselves, and for good or ill do their own thinking.

Now, scholarship, of course, has sonic qualities for all of these people, both in bringing out their separate types and individualities and in giving them something in common. It seems to me that one of the things which scholarship has to do is to protect us from over-specialisation, from knowing only the thing we can do better than other people, and being completely ignorant and indifferent about what other people can do and have to do to make the world. Also, on the other hand, it protects us from smattering, from knowing a little about a good many things, but not really being a master of anything; and whatever else scholarship has to give us, it seems to me that it must give us this balanced understanding of things, a mastery of one thing which we do and a sympathetic understanding of others.

Now, just here, I think my ghost, who does not like me any better than I like him, would put in a word and say: 'That is all very well, but look at you. You did a good deal of smattering and not enough concentrating, and your career, so-called, has not been a career at all, but just like nothing better than a series of accidents, some of them happy ones, but certainly nothing that you can take credit for.'

I am quite willing to admit about smattering. That is why I am such an authority on the subject. I once, very long ago, gave nearly a whole lecture on the subject of ignorance, and my own ignorance in particular. It was very serious, but the audience only laughed at me.

I am perfectly willing to admit also that I have been the victim, sometimes the happy victim, of circumstances. When I first discovered many years ago – and it came rather as a surprise to me – that one did have to earn a living and do something in the world, I first became for a time a schoolmaster. I did learn certainly one thing from trying to teach. I learned to have a great respect for my own teachers when I found out how extraordinarily difficult it was to teach anybody anything. I had to teach a variety of subjects: history – I remember that after a whole term spent with an upper form on Tudor history, nothing else, one of the boys was able to write correctly at the end the names, and in the right order, of all of Henry the Eighth's wives, but he somewhat diminished the effect by adding very conscientiously, 'These are all that I can remember'. I also taught, I think, or tried to [7] teach, Latin, French, German, arithmetic, drawing – and mental arithmetic in pounds, shillings, and pence is no joke, I can tell you, when you have been brought up on the decimal system – several other subjects, and swimming. I tried to teach some of the smaller boys – this was a school in London – baseball, and they tried to teach me rugby and cricket. I do not know which was the greater failure. Then I came to the conclusion, with a good deal of admiration for those who can do it, that teaching was not a career for me. After all, all I wanted to do was to write poetry, and teaching seemed to take up less time than anything else, but that was a delusion. I assure you it takes all your time, even when you are asleep. I was a house master for three weeks. I cannot think of anything more awful.

Well, I gave that up without a sigh and finally – to the advantage of all the boys too – I found myself, again entirely by luck and false pretences, in a bank. The first thing I had to find out was the difference between what you put on the right-hand side of the page and what you put on the left, and not get them mixed up. I made a good many mistakes there. I remember paying for the same consignment of butter and eggs from Denmark three times over by mistake. Of course, little things like that can be set straight. It is true that a few of my academic accomplishments came in play in this career; for instance, the study of Greek was very useful in banking when I had to translate annual reports and balance sheets of Greek shipping companies. In fact, I rather acquired a reputation as a linguist, but I discovered that that is not always an advantage. I was once asked by one of the really big men in the bank to translate something for him. I looked at it and said, 'I am very sorry, sir, but I do not know any Polish.' He said, 'What! And I understood that you were a linguist.'

Then I did more interesting things in time, graduating from the bank and gravitating toward journalism. In one period we produced a daily newspaper, another man and I, under the title of *Extracts from the Foreign Press*. At the beginning we even set the type ourselves. Later we had two or three typists dirty their fingers over it instead.

This may seem incredible, but to show you what you can do if you have to, without knowing anything about the subject, for a year or more I contributed monthly articles on the movements of foreign exchange. I really think that sort of thing is easier to do if you know nothing about it. I do not want to disparage any subject, but when I had to write those articles, I can tell you that I was thankful that I never studied economics in college. It would just have been a nuisance, and sometimes I guessed right.

Well, then, by another series of accidents again, merely in the interest of trying to find something which would provide a living and take as little time as possible so that I could write, I became what I am now, a publisher. I do not know whether or not that is a really reputable business to be engaged in, but I cannot help it.

If you want to write poetry, you are, perhaps, outside of all the classes that I have mentioned, because writing poetry is not a career. It is something to be avoided, and I should say to everybody very seriously: Don't write poetry if you can possibly avoid it. If you want to write poetry, keep away from pencils and paper and typewriters until you have overcome the temptation, because it will do you no good; it will only get you into trouble.

Up to this point I have been getting myself into a weaker and weaker position in dealing with this ghost of mine, whom I had wanted to cow, but I will say to him: I have learned three things in life which I wish you had learned for me. I have had to learn them by hard experience. The first is: Whatever [8] you think, be sure that it is what you think; whatever you want, be sure that it is what you want; whatever you feel, be sure that it is what you feel. It is bad enough to think and want the things that your elders want you to think and want. But it is still worse to think and want just like all your contemporaries. Of course, I do not mean that everybody should go on being eccentric or just doing things that nobody else is doing. I mean that if you think for yourself, nine times out of ten you will probably be thinking and feeling and acting just like the majority or, at any rate, like a great many other people, but if you think for yourself, there will come some time sooner or later when you have to stand quite alone, and you have to be prepared for that one time, if it is only one, and it may come early and it may come late, but I do not feel that anyone is really an educated man unless he can think for himself, without influence.

Then the second thing is that one finds out in life one has to make a good many choices. Now, most choices you can get over. I mean that if you make the wrong choice, you can rub it out and make the other one, but there are always some choices sooner or later which are irrevocable and, whether you make the right one or the wrong one, there is no going back on it. 'Whatever you do,' I wish some one had said to me then, 'don't whimper, but take the consequences.'

And the third thing which I have learned is this: Don't admire or desire success. Admire and desire the qualities, moral and mental, which go to make success. Admire the end of any successful career, if it has been a good end to pursue, but never admire the success itself. In fact, I sometimes wonder whether there is such a thing as success, except in a safe and mediocre way. It is so very difficult even to distinguish between success and failure.

That reminds me, in closing, of two illustrations of that, which also illustrate the question of courage, two of the bravest acts that I know of. One you will not have heard of, because it happened to a man I know and is not generally known. It is an almost incredible story, but it did happen. This man was in the English army during the War. He happened to have spent a good deal of his childhood and youth in Germany, so that he could talk German like a native. One night on a raid he captured a German officer who was so like him in appearance that he was struck by it himself – almost a double. He took this officer, took his uniform and papers, and he questioned him for two or three days until the man had told him practically everything about himself. Then he put on the uniform and took the papers, and the next dark night when there was a skirmish he slipped over into the German lines.

For three weeks he impersonated this German officer with the officer's mess, talked to them, made friends with them, fought with them, got all the information about the movements of that German division that he could.

In about two or three weeks he made a mistake. The officers one evening were discussing Shakespeare. They were all men of superior education. He made a slip. He quoted Shakespeare in English. Most of them did not take any notice, but one man, a young officer with whom he had made very particular friends and of whom he had become very fond, he could see was suspicious. So he thought he had done all he could; he had better get back to the English lines, if he could, as quickly as possible. The next night or so he was able to manage it – there was a raid and he scurried over – but in order to get back to the English lines he had to shoot the man with whom he had made friends.

He got back, went to his commanding officer and reported, and gave all the information which he had acquired, quite valuable information about the German movements, and then he went out and the officer had him followed and they got him in time and he was six months [9] in a hospital. He is not a man who talks very much; certainly that is one thing he does not talk about. Of course, he would not get a V.C. for that. It was flagrant disregard of discipline to have done that without permission or command, and he has been a very unhappy man in consequence. I think it is one of the bravest things I have ever heard of, incredibly brave, but from his point of view was that success or failure?

The other instance you will probably know. It is the instance of Captain Oates, who was one of Scott's expedition into the Antarctic. You will remember the party that got off, wandering about in the snow, and nearly ran out of provisions. Scott tells the story in his diary. Oates thought that if there was one less of them to eat, the provisions might hold out until they were recovered. So he said one evening, 'I am just going outside and I shall be gone some time,' and walked out until he was frozen in the snow. Now, that seems to me a very brave thing to have done, one of the finest things a man could do, but he was not successful. The party was not recovered. After all, it would not have made any difference to the lives or deaths of the others if he had stayed. Still, it was the right thing to do and he saw that one thing. It might, so far as he knew, have been successful. He was right in acting on that chance.

That, it seems to me, is all that any of us can do. It does not really matter whether we succeed or fail in life. That is as it happens, but what does matter is that we should find out the right thing to do and then do it, whether it leads to success or celebrity or obscurity or even to infamy.

1934

A Commentary
C., 13. 51 (Jan. 1934), 270–8. Signed 'T. S. E.' Gallup C350.

I am quite willing to believe that Mr Winston Churchill is an honester historian than Macaulay; that his facts are indisputable, and his judgement of motive and character sound. His *Marlborough* may, for aught I know, deserve to the full the encomiums pronounced upon it by reviewers with no uncertain voice, the roses strewn with no niggard hand. In the foregoing sentence I have endeavoured to trace a mimic miniature of the virtues of Mr Churchill's prose style. Ours is said to be an age of specialisation; and for specialised departments of thought, we find specialised kinds of second-rate prose. On this level of expression, Mr Harold J. Laski is in one department an acknowledged master; in another, we might award the palm to Mr F. L. Lucas; but in that of popular historical exposition, Mr Winston Churchill is not easily to be surpassed. A characteristic which all of these varieties of writing have in common is deadness; but death can assume various expressions. The historical style, as developed by Mr Churchill and others[,] has one quality not shared with the literary or the philosophical: it is the style of a man accustomed to public speaking – to oratory, an art largely concerned with evoking stock emotional responses. It is sometimes maintained that practice in speech is excellent preparation for writing; this may be so, but the kinds of speaking and of writing must be taken into account; and furthermore no kind of speaking is without its dangers as well as its benefits. In a style formed by oratory, we must never expect intimacy; we must never expect the author to address us as individual readers, but always as members of a mob. The mob of course may be assumed to possess every intellectual and moral virtue, as mobs addressed by orators usually do; it may even be a select mob. That addressed in the pages of *Marlborough* is a kind of Whig-Tory amalgam, men of the world of course, used to good manners and to downright plain speaking, [271] virtuous but tolerant of the morals of Restoration times; recognising the importance of good blood, but a little cynical about ancient pedigrees ('All this was very fine, but . . . we enter a rather shady phase', p. 30). What is more important, however, than the particular constitution of the audience addressed by Mr Churchill, is that characteristic of his kind of writing, which consists in constantly pitching the tone a little too high. At the end of a period we seem to observe the author pause for the invariable burst of hand-clapping. Here, for instance, is the situation of England at the beginning of Chapter IV:

> But for the storm-whipped seas which lapped the British islands, our fortunes would have followed the road upon which our neighbours had started. England had not, however, the same compulsive need for a standing army as the land Powers. She stood aloof, moving slowly and lagging behind the martial throng. In the happy nick of time her Parliament grew strong enough to curb the royal power and to control the armed forces, and she thus became the cradle, as she is still the citadel, of free institutions throughout the world.
> There she lay, small, weak, divided, and almost unarmed...

It is obvious that Mr Churchill is on the right side, the side of his readers: stout royalists except on such occasions as Charles I's oppression of wealthy landed gentry; and strong Parliamentarians except when too many of the rabble get in. There is one subject on which Mr Churchill's mind is not evenly balanced, and that is Popery; but the audience, although reasonably indifferent about such matters at the present time, is always ready for an outbreak of applause when sixteenth and seventeenth century Popery is mentioned in the right tone.

> Since the days of Queen Elizabeth and the Spanish Armada, Spain had been the bugbear of Protestant England. Many devout families, suffering all things, still adhered to the Catholic faith. But deep in the hearts of the English people from peer to peasant memories of Smithfield burned with a fierce glow which any breeze could rouse into flame. And now Spain was in decrepitude, insolvent, incoherent, tracing her genealogies and telling her beads....

[272] (Perhaps it is over-fastidious to observe that other people besides decrepit Spaniards tell their beads, and that Mr Churchill has devoted some pages to his own genealogy; but it is in his own defence that I point out that the term 'peasant' in this context is not used invidiously, but only for the sake of alliteration; I should hardly expect him to address an audience of British agricultural labourers as 'peasants' – a rank, indeed, which some of them might envy.) I am not concerned, however, with the truth of Mr Churchill's observations; but with the unreality with which his language invests them. To the ordinary man of letters, who is no historian, there is nothing better written or more moving in the book than the letters exchanged between John and Sarah. We are,

for a moment, among real human beings, not mere public figures. And after these letters, from which the descendant of the writers might have learned something about writing, what has Mr Churchill to say? He spoils it all by another appeal to the crowd:

> The facts could not be disputed. They proclaim the glory of that wedlock in which the vast majority of civilized mankind find happiness and salvation in a precarious world.

It is only fair to Mr Churchill to add, that while his historical style possesses beauties that the charm of no other personality than his could give, it is not unique. Here is a paragraph from another modern historian, a champion of Nationalism:

> Such was the state of things in France when the *émigrés* first began to conspire with feudal Europe against their own countrymen. By our modern ways of thinking, their conduct in calling in the foreigner stands heavily condemned. (*Mr. Churchill, with reminiscences of Archangel, might dissent*). But they had been bred up in a world almost without patriotic tradition, which regarded a Church and an Order as units commanding allegiance more strongly than a nation. Indeed, their 'nation' was the *noblesse* of Europe, not the French peasants and bourgeoisie. (*The author thus commits himself to opposition to international communism*). The horror that their conduct caused in France, surprised them, for it was, in fact, something new. France, in becoming democratic, had doubled her sense of nationhood. The peasant had [273] become not indeed a Jacobin, but a patriot, ready to shed his blood for '*la belle France*' who had given him his field and freedom. These traitors would bring the Teuton into our plains to rivet our chains once more! Let their blood stain our furrows! The terrible words of the Marseillaise glow with the blended passions of the furnace out of which modern France emerged.

The last sentence pronounces the author to be an historian of the same (literary) school as Mr Churchill: the quotation is from a *British History of the Nineteenth Century*, by Sir George Macaulay Trevelyan.

I suspect that the interest in Communist Russia is at the moment on the decline, and that the flood of books on the subject is for the moment exhausted. While one always welcomes a diversion from any over-exploited subject of publicity, there may be no reason to congratulate ourselves on having something else to think about. Communism is at least a respectable political theory, with its own standards of orthodoxy, in the eyes of those who agree with Joseph de Maistre that *toutes les institutions imaginables reposent sur une idée religieuse, ou ne font que passer.* It appears to recognise a primacy of intellect, rather than of hysteria; and in times like ours we need ideas, not only our own, but antagonistic ideas against which our own may keep themselves sharp: it is when ideas are absent, or when their force is exhausted, that the irresponsible political adventurer has his opportunity. Mr John Macmurray is one of our leading *philosophes* of communism, but of his recent book, *The Philosophy of Communism*, I will not speak, as it is to be reviewed in our next number. I have also read Mr H. G. Wood's *The Truth and Error of Communism* and Mr A. J. Penty's *Communism and the Alternative*, both published by the Student Christian Movement Press, which is to be commended for its enterprise. Mr Wood's book, after some praises bestowed upon it in the press, I found just not quite good enough. It is not because he takes Mr Middleton Murry seriously as the exponent of a kind of commun-[274]ism; nor is it because the fundamental religious heresies of communism have already been better exposed by Berdyaev and Waldemar Gurian; it is because the communism which he attacks is a definite thing, and the Christianity which he maintains is a rather vaporous entity. He tells us that 'three Christian principles are essential to the building up of the new order in politics and industry': what are they? The first is the 'recognition that all have sinned'. Now as Mr Wood puts it, I cannot feel that this amounts to very much more than, let us say, the admission that there were selfish, short-sighted, narrow and unscrupulous interests at work in framing the Treaty of Versailles. But to recognise such facts does not illustrate any particularly Christian principle, or anything more Christian than common sense.

The first Christian principle involved is not that 'all have sinned' – how easy and inexpensive that is to admit! – but that we are all sinners: which, with all due respect, is a very different and very much deeper truth, and one very much harder to grasp. And Mr Wood's second Christian principle is what he calls 'constructive citizenship', by which, so far as I can gather, he means that we must move cautiously, be careful in plucking tares for fear we pull up good wheat, and proceed according to the best prudential precepts. And his third Christian principle is that 'nothing can rightly be done without mutual respect' – which means, I think, the 'spirit of community'.

Now these principles are all very well, but they suffer from the fact that everyone can accept them: there is nothing specifically Christian about them. I cannot help thinking that Mr Wood has taken more pains to inform himself about communism than he has about Christianity, even though the plurality of his references be only to Mr Middleton Murry and Mr Maurice Dobb. You cannot arrive at a Christian social philosophy, any more than you can arrive at a communist one, merely by looking into your heart and writing. You need a knowledge of the whole history of Christianity up to the Reformation, and in particular some [275] acquaintance, for instance, with the views of Aquinas, to whom Mr Wood does not once refer. And with this equipment, there are two paths which may be followed. You may confine yourself to investigating and defining those social theories and practices which the Christian may not accept, or you may elaborate a theory which aims to be consonant with Christianity, though it may not be in every respect logically derivable from those beliefs which are essential to faith and morals. The orthodox Christian is likely to have certain predispositions in the temporal sphere, modified according to time, place and circumstance: it is not insignificant that the meanings of the term 'Liberalism' in theology and in politics are not, historically, to be kept wholly distinct. The danger of the former kind of theory is that it may be so negative as to be no guide at all; the danger of the latter kind is that it may implicate the universal with the individual, the eternal with the transient: the theorist must be careful to keep matters distinct. Examples of the latter kind may be found in the work of such writers as de Maistre and Bonald; of its abuse, in the condemnation (rightly or wrongly) of the *Action Française*, in 1927. But Mr Wood can be included in neither category; his Christian theory is no theory at all; and his book is hardly likely to serve any useful purpose.

Mr Penty's book shows much more precision. He does not, perhaps, add very much to the analysis of bolshevism which other Christian critics have already given; but readers who are not familiar with other books on the subject will find the Christian objections very clearly set forth. One might admit also that his book falls into two parts. One is the summary of the Christian argument against communism, the other the presentation of Mr Penty's own views. It is no disrespect to the latter to say that they have already been fully expounded in his *Means and Ends* and other volumes, for they are worth repeating. Whether Mr Penty, or Major Douglas[,] is right in their difference about the rôle of the machine is a minor question: Mr Penty asserts a principle [276] more important than that. The principle involved is that we should enquire what is *right* before we enquire what is *inevitable*. Nor is the question what form of society is a *possible* alternative to communism, but what form is *worthy* to be an alternative; for any form which engages support simply from fear of communism is doomed. And in the following paragraph Mr Penty has supplied something which Mr Wood has failed to give:

> The first requisite of such a theory is that it shall be based upon the principles of Christianity, not in the sentimental sense in which

any proposal which professes to be for the good of mankind asks for the support of the churches, but in the sense that it is the civil equivalent of Christian theology; the logical implication of its teaching. Christianity, because it takes its stand on the spiritual nature of man, is the only principle capable of challenging the root assumptions of materialist Communism. The strength of Communism finally rests on the fact that the Communist is a man of principle, persuaded of the absolute truth of the materialist philosophy and conception of history. He takes his stand upon it without equivocation, and this gives him a driving force against which the ordinary secular reformer, who because of his denial of Christianity has nothing to appeal to but common sense and expediency, fights in vain. In consequence it will not be until those who are opposed to Communism take their stand as unequivocally upon the principles of Christianity as Communists do upon those of materialism that a force will be set in motion capable of successfully challenging it and restoring the lost equilibrium between the spiritual and material sides of life.

I have suggested that the Christian social philosopher may legitimately, so long as he is careful to distinguish between that which is essential and that which is merely desirable, make use of associated ideas: there is political inspiration, not only in such writers as de Maistre, but in such as Coleridge or Newman. But the Christian social philosopher of our time can only follow such a course safely if he is equally prepared for a *dis*sociation of ideas. He must be able to consider the ideas of class, of property, of nationality not according to current or local prejudices, but according to permanent principles. The Reverend V. A. [277] Demant's *God*[,] *Man and Society* (also published by the Student Christian Movement Press) possesses, among other excellences, this merit of contributing to the dissociation of ideas. With Sir George Trevelyan's observations on the French Revolution in mind, it is well that we should be told that

> to place the redemptive work of the Christian Faith in social affairs in its proper setting, it is necessary to have clearly in mind at the outset that the consciousness of 'the nation' as *the* social unit is a very recent and contingent experience. It belongs to a limited historical period and is bound up with certain specific happenings, theories of society and attitudes to life as a whole. It is therefore not an inevitable or essential aspect of men's social consciousness.

Mr Demant is here in accord with Mr Christopher Dawson, to whom he refers us in the footnote. And here he touches what is perhaps the chief malady of the modern liberal state – a malady which, however, may not be so fatal as some of the nostrums offered for its cure:

> The modern state if it acts for the sake of all its citizens finds it therefore more and more difficult to further directly the fulfilment of what one or other section of its citizens consider to be 'the good life', in so far as citizens differ in their notions of 'the good life' or have none at all. It is simply a fact that the modern state includes people of all religions and none, and with ethical assumptions of varying quality and intensity.

But Mr Demant's book is too important to serve merely as one of the texts for a single Commentary; and I am likely to refer to it again.

While our October number was in press, and too late for mention in the Commentary of that issue, we learned with great regret of the death of Arnaud Dandieu, who in collaboration with Robert Aron had contributed the article 'Back to Flesh and Blood' to *The Criterion* a year ago. M. Dandieu, who was only thirty-five at the time of his death, had attracted attention with his first book, *Marcel Proust*, which was published by the Oxford Press as well as in [278] Paris. Of three books written in collaboration with M. Aron, the first, *Décadence de la nation française*, was the subject of some observations in this Commentary; the second, *Le cancer américain*, I have not seen; the third, *La révolution nécessaire*, has I believe been published recently by Grasset. With M. Aron, M. Dandieu was engaged also in editing a quarterly review, *L'ordre nouveau*.

I regret having had no personal acquaintance with M. Dandieu, of whose personal charm and conversational powers I had heard much. The direction and the quality of his thinking struck me as a most promising symptom among the younger generation in Paris; and his death is a loss to *The Criterion* as well as to the intellectual life of Paris.

Personality and Demonic Possession

Publ. in *Virginia Quarterly Review*, 10. 1 (Jan. 1934), [94]–103: Gallup C351. Revised as ch. III of *ASG* (publ. 25 Feb. 1934). *See below*, pp. 795–803.

After Strange Gods

A Primer of Modern Heresy
The Page-Barbour Lectures at the University Of Virginia
1933

Publ. 22 Feb. 1934. On p. [9] 'herschenden' has been corrected to 'herrschenden'.

καὶ ταῦτ' ἰὼν
εἴσω λογίζου. κἂν λάβῃς ἐψευσμένον,
φάσκειν ἔμ' ἤδη μαντικῇ μηδὲν φρονεῖν.
Oedipus Rex: 1. 460–462.

[7] To
ALFRED and ADA SHEFFIELD

[9] Das Chaos in der 'Literatur', die mit vagen Grenzen zwar, aber immer noch deutlicher ein Gebiet für sich ist; sie, die in gesunden Zeiten ein relativ reiner, gefälliger Spiegel aller herrschenden Dinge und Undinge ist, in kranken, chaotischen ein selber trüber all der trüben Dinge und Ideen, die es gibt, ist zur cloaca maxima geworden. Jegliche Unordnung im Humanen, im Menschen selber – ich sprach von dem dreifachen Gesichtspunkt, unter dem sie betrachtet werden kann, dem Primat der Lust, dem Primat der Sentimentalität, dem Primat der technischen Intelligenz – an Stelle der einzig wahren hierarchischen Ordnung, des Primates des Geistes und des Spiritualen – jegliche Unordnung findet ihr relativ klares oder meist selber noch neuerlich verzerrtes Bild in der Literatur dieser Tage.

– THEODOR HAECKER: *Was ist der Mensch?* p. 65.

Preface

ASG, 11–14.

Le monde moderne avilit. It also provincialises,
and it can also corrupt.

The three lectures which follow were not undertaken as exercises in literary criticism. If the reader insists upon considering them as such, I should like to guard against misunderstanding as far as possible. The lectures are not designed to set forth, even in the most summary form, my opinions of the work of contemporary writers: they are concerned with certain ideas in illustration of which I have drawn upon the work of some of the few modern writers whose work I know. I am not primarily concerned either with their absolute importance or their importance relatively to each other; and other writers, who in any literary survey of our time ought to be included, are unmentioned or barely mentioned, because they do not provide such felicitous illustration of my thesis, or because they are rare exceptions to it, or because I am unacquainted with their work. I am sure that those whom I have discussed are among the best; and for my purpose the second-rate were useless. The extent to which I have criticised the authors whose names find place, is accordingly some measure of my respect for them. I dare say that a detached critic could find an equally rich vein of error in my own writings. If such error is there, I am probably the last person to be able to [12] detect it; but its presence and discovery would not condemn what I say here, any more than its absence would confirm it.

There is no doubt some curiosity to know what any writer thinks of his contemporaries: a curiosity which has less to do with literary criticism than with literary gossip. I hope that a reader who takes up this essay in that expectation will be disappointed. I am uncertain of my ability to criticise my contemporaries as artists; I ascended the platform of these lectures only in the role of moralist.

I have not attempted to disguise, but rather have been pleased to remind the reader, that these are lectures; that they were composed for vocal communication to a particular audience. What the Foundation requires is that the lectures shall be published, not that a book shall subsequently be written on the same subject; and a lecture composed for the platform cannot be transformed into something else. I should be glad if the reader could keep this in mind when he finds that some ideas are put forward without a full account of their history or of their activities, and that others are set down in an absolute way without qualifications. I am aware that my assertion of the obsolescence of Blasphemy might thus be subject to stricture: but if I had developed the refinements and limitations which present themselves to the mind of the Christian enquirer, I should have needed at least the space of one whole lecture; and what I was concerned to do was merely to explain that the charge of blasphemy was *not* one of those that I wished to prefer against modern literature. It may be said that no blasphemy can be purely verbal; and it may [13] also be said that there is a profounder meaning of the term 'blasphemy', in which some modern authors (including, possibly, myself) may possibly have been gravely guilty.

In such matters, as perhaps in everything, I must depend upon some good-will on the part of the reader. I do not wish to preach only to the converted, but primarily to those who, never having applied moral principles to literature quite explicitly – perhaps even having conscientiously believed that they ought not to apply them in this way to 'works of art' – are possibly convertible. I am not arguing or reasoning, or engaging in controversy with those whose views are radically opposed to such as mine. In our time, controversy seems to me, on really fundamental matters, to be futile. It can only usefully be practised where there is common understanding. It requires common assumptions; and perhaps the assumptions that are only felt are more important than those that can be formulated. The acrimony which accompanies much debate is a symptom of differences so large that there is nothing to argue about. We experience such profound differences with some of our contemporaries, that the nearest parallel is the difference between the mentality of one epoch and another. In a society like ours, worm-eaten with Liberalism, the only thing possible for a person with strong convictions is to state a point of view and leave it at that.

I wish to express my thanks to Professor Wilbur Nelson and the Page-Barbour Lectureship Committee; to the Acting President and the members of the Faculty of the University of Virginia who helped to make my visit to [14] Virginia a very pleasant memory; to my hosts, Professor and Mrs Scott Buchanan; to Professor Buchanan for conversations and suggestions out of which these lectures arose; and to the Revd M. C. D'Arcy, S.J., and Mr F. V. Morley for their criticisms. It is a pleasure to me to think that these lectures were delivered at one of the older, smaller and most gracious of American educational institutions, one of those in which some vestiges of a traditional education seem to survive. Perhaps I am mistaken: but if not, I should wish that I might be able to encourage such institutions to maintain their communications with the past, because in so doing they will be maintaining their communications with any future worth communicating with.

T. S. E.
London, January 1934.

I

ASG, 15–30.

Part I was revised as 'Tradition and Orthodoxy' in *American Review*, 5 (Mar. 1934) 513–28: Gallup C354, where it is stated that the article was revised in *ASG*. But *ASG* was publ. on 22 Feb. 1934.

See below, pp. 809–19.

II

ASG, 31–49.

I hope that it is quite clear, both for the sake of what I have said already and for the sake of what I have still to say, that the sense in which I am using the terms *tradition* and *orthodoxy* is to be kept distinctly in mind as not identical with the use of the same terms in theology. The difference is widest with the term *tradition*, for I have wished to use the word to cover much in our lives that is accounted for by habit, breeding and environment. I should not on the other hand like to have it supposed that my meanings were arbitrarily chosen. That they bear a relation to the more exact meanings I have no wish to conceal: if they did not, my discussion of these matters would lose all significance. But the two terms have been so frequently and so subtly expounded by more philosophical writers, that I would guard against being thought to employ, in a loose and inexpert manner, terms which have already been fully and sharply defined. With the terms in their theological use I shall presume no acquaintance; and I appeal only to your common-sense: or, if that word sounds too common, to your wisdom and experience of life. That an acceptance of the validity of the two terms as I use them should lead one to dogmatic theology, I naturally believe; but I am not here concerned with pursuing investigation in that path. My enquiries take the opposite direction: let us consider [32] the denial or neglect of tradition in my mundane sense, and see what *that* leads to.

The general effect in literature of the lack of any strong tradition is twofold: extreme individualism in views, and no accepted rules or opinions as to the limitations of the literary job. I have spoken elsewhere[1] of poetry as a substitute for religion, and of kinds of criticism which assumed that the function of poetry was to replace religion. The two results are naturally concomitant. When one man's 'view of life' is as good as another's, all the more enterprising spirits will naturally evolve their own; and where there is no custom to determine what the task of literature is, every writer will determine for himself, and the more enterprising will range as far afield as possible. But at this point I should develop one distinction between the usual sense of 'orthodoxy' and that in which it is here used. I do not take orthodoxy to mean that there is a narrow path laid down for every writer to follow. Even in the stricter discipline of the Church, we hardly expect every theologian to succeed in being orthodox in every particular, for it is not a sum of theologians, but the Church itself, in which orthodoxy resides. In my sense of the

---

1. In *The Use of Poetry*.

term, perfect orthodoxy in the individual artist is not always necessary, or even desirable. In many instances it is possible that an indulgence of eccentricities is the condition of the man's saying anything at all. It is impossible to separate the 'poetry' in *Paradise Lost* from the peculiar doctrines that it enshrines; it means very little to assert that if Milton had held more normal doctrines he would have written a [33] better poem; as a work of literature, we take it as we find it: but we can certainly enjoy the poetry and yet be fully aware of the intellectual and moral aberrations of the author. It is true that the existence of a right tradition, simply by its influence upon the environment in which the poet develops, will tend to restrict eccentricity to manageable limits: but it is not even by the lack of this restraining influence that the absence of tradition is most deplorable. What is disastrous is that the writer should deliberately give rein to his 'individuality', that he should even cultivate his differences from others; and that his readers should cherish the author of genius, not in spite of his deviations from the inherited wisdom of the race, but because of them.

What happens is not, to be sure, always just what the author intends. It is fatally easy, under the conditions of the modern world, for a writer of genius to conceive of himself as a Messiah. Other writers, indeed, may have had profound insights before him; but we readily believe that everything is relative to its period of society, and that these insights have now lost their validity; a new generation is a new world, so there is always a chance, if not of delivering a wholly new gospel, of delivering one as good as new. Or the messiahship may take the form of revealing for the first time the gospel of some dead sage, which no one has understood before; which owing to the backward and confused state of men's minds has lain unknown to this very moment; or it may even go back to the lost Atlantis and the ineffable wisdom of primitive peoples. A writer who is fired with such a conviction is likely to have some devoted [34] disciples; but for posterity he is liable to become, what he will be for the majority of his contemporaries, merely one among many entertainers. And the pity is that the man *may* have had something to say of the greatest importance: but to announce, as your own discovery, some truth long known to mankind, is to secure immediate attention at the price of ultimate neglect.

The general effect upon readers – most of them quite uneducated – is quite different from what the serious messiah intends. In the first place, no modern messiah can last for more than a generation; it is tacitly assumed that the leaders of the previous generation are as useless as the soldiers who died in the first year of a hundred years' war (and alas, they mostly are); those who enjoy the normal span of life may be sure of surviving their popularity. Secondly, as the public is not very well qualified for discriminating between nostrums, it comes to enjoy sampling all, and taking none seriously. And finally, in a world that has as nearly lost all understanding of the meaning of *education* as it well can, many people act upon the assumption that the mere accumulation of 'experiences', including literary and intellectual experiences, as well as amorous and picaresque ones, is – like the accumulation of money – valuable in itself. So that a serious writer may sweat blood over his work, and be appreciated as the exponent of still one more 'point of view'.

It is too much to expect any literary artist at the present time to be a model of orthodoxy. That, as I have said, is something to demand only in a spirit of indulgent criticism at any time: it is not to be demanded now. It is a very [35] different thing to be a classical author in a classical age, and to maintain classical ideals in a romantic age. Furthermore, I ask the same compassion for myself that I would have you extend to others. What we can try to do is to develop a more critical spirit, or rather to apply to authors critical standards which are almost in desuetude. Of the contemporary authors whom I shall mention, I cannot recall having seen any criticism in which these standards have been employed.

Perhaps it will make the foregoing considerations appear more real, and exonerate me from the charge of dealing only in abstractions, offering only a kind of unredeemable paper currency, if at this point I give testimony in the form of three contemporary short stories, all of very great merit. It was almost by accident that I happened to read all of these stories in rapid succession during the course of some recent work at Harvard. One is *Bliss* by Katherine Mansfield; the second is *The Shadow in the Rose Garden* by D. H. Lawrence, and the third *The Dead* by James Joyce.[1] They are all, I believe, fairly youthful work; and all turn on the same theme of disillusion. In Miss Mansfield's story a wife is disillusioned about her relations with her husband; in the others a husband is disillusioned about his relations with his wife. Miss Mansfield's story – it is one of her best known – is brief, poignant and in the best sense, slight; Mr Joyce's is of considerable length. What is interesting in the three together is the differences of moral implication. In *Bliss*, I should say, the moral implication is negligible: [36] the centre of interest is the wife's feeling, first of ecstatic happiness, and then at the moment of revelation. We are given neither comment nor suggestion of any moral issue of good and evil, and within the setting this is quite right. The story is limited to this sudden change of feeling, and the moral and social ramifications are outside of the terms of reference. As the material is limited in this way – and indeed our satisfaction recognises the skill with which the author has handled perfectly the *minimum* material –

1. From volumes entitled *Bliss*, *The Prussian Officer*, and *Dubliners* respectively.

it is what I believe would be called feminine. In the story of Lawrence there is a great deal more than that; he is concerned with the feelings of both husband and wife; and as the tempo is much slower (no story of any considerable structure could move as rapidly as Miss Mansfield's does) there is time for thought as well as feeling, and for calculated action. An accident, trifling in itself, but important in the twist which Lawrence gives to it, leads or forces the wife to reveal to her commonplace lower middle-class husband (no writer is more conscious of class-distinctions than Lawrence) the facts of her intrigue with an army officer several years before their marriage. The disclosure is made with something nearly approaching conscious cruelty. There is cruelty, too, in the circumstances in which she had met her former lover:

> 'And I saw him to-day,' she said. 'He is not dead, he's mad.' Her husband looked at her, startled. 'Mad!' he said involuntarily. 'A lunatic,' she said.

Of this alarming strain of cruelty in some modern literature I shall have something more to say later. What I wish chiefly to notice at this point, is what strikes me in all of the [37] relations of Lawrence's men and women: the absence of any moral or social sense. It is not that the author, in that Olympian elevation and superior indifference attributed to great artists, and which I can only imperfectly understand, has detached himself from any moral attitude towards his characters; it is that the characters themselves, who are supposed to be recognisably human beings, betray no respect for, or even awareness of, moral obligations, and seem to be unfurnished with even the most commonplace kind of conscience. In Mr Joyce's story, which is very much longer and which incidentally employs a much more elaborate and interesting method, the wife is saddened by memories associated with a song sung at an evening party which has just been described in minute detail. In response to solicitous questions by her husband, she reveals the fact that the song had been sung by a boy she knew in Galway when she was a girl, and that between them was an intense romantic and spiritualised love. She had had to go away; the boy had risen from a sick bed to come to say goodbye to her; and he had in consequence died. That is all there was to it; but the husband realises that what this boy had given her was something finer than anything he had to give. And as the wife falls asleep at last:

> Generous tears filled Gabriel's eyes. He had never felt like that himself towards any woman, but he knew that such a feeling must be love. The tears gathered more thickly in his eyes and in the partial darkness he imagined he saw the form of a young man

standing under a dripping tree. Other forms were near. His soul had approached that region where dwell the vast hosts of the dead.

[38] It is impossible to produce the full value of evidence such as this without reading the stories entire; but something of what I have in mind should now be apparent. We are not concerned with the authors' *beliefs*, but with orthodoxy of sensibility and with the sense of tradition, our degree of approaching 'that region where dwell the vast hosts of the dead'. And Lawrence is for my purposes, an almost perfect example of the heretic. And the most ethically orthodox of the more eminent writers of my time is Mr Joyce. I confess that I do not know what to make of a generation which ignores these considerations.

I trust that I shall not be taken as speaking in a spirit of bigotry when I assert that the chief clue to the understanding of most contemporary Anglo-Saxon literature is to be found in the decay of Protestantism. I am not concerned with Protestantism itself: and to discuss that we should have to go back to the seventeenth century. I mean that amongst writers the rejection of Christianity – Protestant Christianity – is the rule rather than the exception; and that individual writers can be understood and classified according to the type of Protestantism which surrounded their infancy, and the precise state of decay which it had reached. I should include those authors who were reared in an 'advanced' or agnostic atmosphere, because even agnosticism – *Protestant* agnosticism – has decayed in the last two generations. It is this background, I believe, that makes much of our writing seem provincial and crude in the major intellectual centres of Europe – everywhere except northern Germany and perhaps Scandinavia; it is this which contributes the prevailing flavour of [39] immaturity. One might expect the unlovelier forms of this decline to be more deeply marked upon American authors than upon English, but there is no reason to generalise: nothing could be much drearier (so far as one can judge from his own account) than the vague hymn-singing pietism which seems to have consoled the miseries of Lawrence's mother, and which does not seem to have provided her with any firm principles by which to scrutinise the conduct of her sons. But lest I be supposed to be concerned primarily with the decay of morals (and especially sexual morals) I will mention the name of one for whose memory I have the highest respect and admiration: that of the late Irving Babbitt.

It is significant to observe that Babbitt was saturated with French culture; in his thought and in his intercourse he was thoroughly cosmopolitan. He believed in tradition; for many years he stood almost alone in maintaining against the strong tendency of the time a right theory of education; and such effects of decadence as are manifest in

Lawrence's work he held in abomination. And yet to my mind the very width of his culture, his intelligent eclecticism, are themselves symptoms of a narrowness of tradition, in their extreme reaction against that narrowness. His attitude towards Christianity seems to me that of a man who had had no *emotional* acquaintance with any but some debased and uncultured form: I judge entirely on his public pronouncements and not at all on any information about his upbringing. It would be exaggeration to say that he wore his cosmopolitanism like a man who had lost his *complet bourgeois* and had to go about in fancy dress. But he seemed [40] to be trying to compensate for the lack of living tradition by a herculean, but purely intellectual and individual effort. His addiction to the philosophy of Confucius is evidence: the popularity of Confucius among our contemporaries is significant. Just as I do not see how anyone can expect really to understand Kant and Hegel without knowing the German language and without such an understanding of the German mind as can only be acquired in the society of living Germans, so *a fortiori* I do not see how anyone can understand Confucius without some knowledge of Chinese and a long frequentation of the best Chinese society. I have the highest respect for the Chinese mind and for Chinese civilisation; and I am willing to believe that Chinese civilisation at its highest has graces and excellences which may make Europe seem crude. But I do not believe that I, for one, could ever come to understand it well enough to make Confucius a mainstay.

I am led to this conclusion partly by an analogous experience. Two years spent in the study of Sanskrit under Charles Lanman, and a year in the mazes of Patanjali's metaphysics under the guidance of James Woods, left me in a state of enlightened mystification. A good half of the effort of understanding what the Indian philosophers were after – and their subtleties make most of the great European philosophers look like schoolboys – lay in trying to erase from my mind all the categories and kinds of distinction common to European philosophy from the time of the Greeks. My previous and concomitant study of European philosophy was hardly better than an obstacle. And I came to the conclusion – seeing also that the 'influence' of Brah-[41]min and Buddhist thought upon Europe, as in Schopenhauer, Hartmann, and Deussen, had largely been through romantic misunderstanding – that my only hope of really penetrating to the heart of that mystery would lie in forgetting how to think and feel as an American or a European: which, for practical as well as sentimental reasons, I did not wish to do. And I should imagine that the same choice would hold good for Chinese thought: though I believe that the Chinese mind is very much nearer to the Anglo-Saxon than is the Indian. China is – or was until the missionaries initiated her into

Western thought, and so blazed a path for John Dewey – a country of tradition; Confucius was not born into a vacuum; and a network of rites and customs, even if regarded by philosophers in a spirit of benignant scepticism, make a world of difference. But Confucius has become the philosopher of the rebellious Protestant. And I cannot but feel that in some respects Irving Babbitt, with the noblest intentions, has merely made matters worse instead of better.

The name of Irving Babbitt instantly suggests that of Ezra Pound (his peer in cosmopolitanism) and that of I. A. Richards: it would seem that Confucius is the spiritual adviser of the highly educated and fastidious, in contrast to the dark gods of Mexico. Mr Pound presents the closest counterpart to Irving Babbitt. Extremely quick-witted and very learned, he is attracted to the Middle Ages, apparently, by everything except that which gives them their significance. His powerful and narrow post-Protestant prejudice peeps out from the most unexpected places: one can hardly read the erudite notes and commentary to his edition of [42] Guido Cavalcanti without suspecting that he finds Guido much more sympathetic than Dante, and on grounds which have little to do with their respective merits as poets: namely, that Guido was very likely a heretic, if not a sceptic – as evidenced partly by his possibly having held some pneumatic philosophy and theory of corpuscular action which I am unable to understand. Mr Pound, like Babbitt, is an individualist, and still more a libertarian.

Mr Pound's theological twist appears both in his poetry and his prose; but as there are other vigorous prose writers, and as Mr Pound is probably the most important living poet in our language, a reference to his poetry will carry more weight. At this point I shall venture to generalise, and suggest that with the disappearance of the idea of Original Sin, with the disappearance of the idea of intense moral struggle, the human beings presented to us both in poetry and in prose fiction to-day, and more patently among the serious writers than in the underworld of letters, tend to become less and less real. It is in fact in moments of moral and spiritual struggle depending upon spiritual sanctions, rather than in those 'bewildering minutes' in which we are all very much alike, that men and women come nearest to being real. If you do away with this struggle, and maintain that by tolerance, benevolence, inoffensiveness and a redistribution or increase of purchasing power, combined with a devotion, on the part of an élite, to Art, the world will be as good as anyone could require, then you must expect human beings to become more and more vaporous. This is exactly what we find of the society which Mr. Pound puts in Hell, in his *Draft of XXX Cantos*. It consists (I may have [43] overlooked one or two species) of politicians, profiteers, financiers, newspaper proprietors and their hired men, *agents provocateurs*, Calvin, St Clement of Alexandria, the English, vice-crusaders, liars, the stupid, pedants, preachers, those who do not believe in Social Credit, bishops, lady golfers, Fabians, conservatives and imperialists; and all 'those who have set money-lust before the pleasures of the senses'. It is, in its way, an admirable Hell, 'without dignity, without tragedy'. At first sight the variety of types – for these are types, and not individuals – may be a little confusing; but I think it becomes a little more intelligible if we see at work three principles, (1) the aesthetic, (2) the humanitarian, (3) the Protestant. And I find one considerable objection to a Hell of this sort: that a Hell altogether without dignity implies a Heaven without dignity also. If you do not distinguish between individual responsibility and circumstances in Hell, between essential Evil and social accidents, then the Heaven (if any) implied will be equally trivial and accidental. Mr Pound's Hell, for all its horrors, is a perfectly comfortable one for the modern mind to contemplate, and disturbing to no one's complacency: it is a Hell for the *other people*, the people we read about in the newspapers, not for oneself and one's friends.[1]

An equally interesting example of the modern mind is that of the other important poet of our time, Mr William Butler Yeats. Few poets have told us more about themselves – more, I mean, of what is relevant and of what we are entitled to know – than Mr Yeats in his *Autobiographies*, a document of great and permanent interest. Mr [44] Yeats had still greater difficulties to contend with, I should say, than Mr Pound. He was born of Irish Protestant stock, and was brought up in London; Ireland was for his childhood rather a holiday country, to which his sentiment attached itself; his father adhered to mid-century Rationalism, but otherwise the household atmosphere was Pre-Raphaelite. In *The Trembling of the Veil* he says significantly:

> I was unlike others of my generation in one thing only. I am very religious, and deprived by Huxley and Tyndall, whom I detested, of the simple-minded religion of my childhood, I had made a new religion, almost an infallible church of poetic tradition, of a fardel of stories, and of personages, and of emotions, inseparable from their first expression, passed on from generation to generation by poets and painters with some help from philosophers and theologians.

Thus, in Yeats at the age of sixteen (or at least, as in retrospect he seems to himself to have been at sixteen) is operative the doctrine of Arnold, that Poetry can replace Religion, and also the tendency to fabricate an

---

1. Consult *Time and Western Man* by Wyndham Lewis.

individual religion. The rationalistic background, the Pre-Raphaelite imagery, the interest in the occult, the equally early interest in Irish nationalism, the association with minor poets in London and Paris, make a curious mixture. Mr Yeats was in search of a tradition, a little too consciously perhaps – like all of us. He sought for it in the conception of Ireland as an autonomous political and social unity, purged from the Anglo-Saxon pollution. He wished also to find access to the religious sources of poetry, as, a little later, did another restless seeker for myths, D. H. Lawrence. The result, for a long period, is a somewhat artificially induced poeticality. Just [45] as much of Swinburne's verse has the effect of repeated doses of gin and water, so much of Mr Yeats's verse is stimulated by folklore, occultism, mythology and symbolism, crystal-gazing and hermetic writings.

> Who will go drive with Fergus now,
> And pierce the deep wood's woven shade,
> And dance upon the level shore?
> Young man, lift up your russet brow,
> And lift your tender eyelids, maid,
> And brood on hopes and fears no more.

This is to me very beautiful but highly artificial. There is a deliberate evocation of trance, as he virtually confesses in his essay on *The Symbolism of Poetry*:

> The purpose of rhythm, it has always seemed to me, is to prolong the moment of contemplation, the moment when we are both asleep and awake, which is the one moment of creation, by hushing us with an alluring monotony, while it holds us waking by its variety, to keep us in that state of perhaps real trance, in which the mind liberated from the pressure of the will is unfolded in symbols.

There is a good deal of truth in this theory, but not quite enough, and its practice exposes Mr Yeats to the just criticism of Mr I. A. Richards, as follows:

> After a drawn battle with the drama, Mr Yeats made a violent repudiation, not merely of current civilisation but of life itself, in favour of a supernatural world. But the world of the 'eternal moods', of supernal essences and immortal beings is not, like the Irish peasant stories and the Irish landscape, part of his natural and familiar experience. [46] Now he turns to a world of symbolic phantasmagoria about which he is desperately uncertain. He is uncertain because he has adopted as a technique of inspiration the use of

trance, of dissociated phases of consciousness, and the revelations given in these dissociated states are insufficiently connected with normal experience.

It is, I think, only carrying Mr Richards's complaint a little further to add that Mr Yeats's 'supernatural world' was the wrong supernatural world. It was not a world of spiritual significance, not a world of real Good and Evil, of holiness or sin, but a highly sophisticated lower mythology summoned, like a physician, to supply the fading pulse of poetry with some transient stimulant so that the dying patient may utter his last words. In its extreme self-consciousness it approaches the mythology of D. H. Lawrence on its more decadent side. We admire Mr Yeats for having outgrown it; for having packed away his bibelots and resigned himself to live in an apartment furnished in the barest simplicity. A few faded beauties remain: Babylon, Nineveh, Helen of Troy, and such souvenirs of youth: but the austerity of Mr Yeats's later verse on the whole, should compel the admiration of the least sympathetic. Though the tone is often of regret, sometimes of resignation:

> Things said or done long years ago,
> Or things I did not do or say
> But thought that I might say or do,
> Weigh me down, and not a day
> But something is recalled,
> My conscience or my vanity appalled.

[47] and though Mr Yeats is still perhaps a little too much the weather-worn Triton among the streams, he has arrived at greatness against the greatest odds; if he has not arrived at a central and universal philosophy he has at least discarded, for the most part, the trifling and eccentric, the provincial in time and place.

At this point, having called attention to the difficulties experienced by Mr Pound and Mr Yeats through no fault of their own, you may be expecting that I shall produce Gerard Hopkins, with an air of triumph, as the orthodox and traditional poet. I wish indeed that I could; but I cannot altogether share the enthusiasm which many critics feel for this poet, or put him on a level with those whom I have just mentioned. In the first place, the fact that he was a Jesuit priest, and the author of some very beautiful devotional verse, is only partially relevant. To be converted, in any case, while it is sufficient for entertaining the hope of individual salvation, is not going to do for a man, as a writer, what his ancestry and his country for some generations have failed to do. Hopkins is a fine poet, to be sure; but he is not nearly so much a poet of our time as the accidents of his publication and the inventions of his metric have led us to suppose. His innovations certainly were good, but like the mind of their author, they operate only within a narrow range, and are easily imitated though not adaptable for many purposes; furthermore, they sometimes strike me as lacking inevitability – that is to say, they sometimes come near to being purely *verbal*, in that a whole poem will give us *more* of the same thing, an accumulation, rather than a real development of thought or feeling.

[48] I may be wrong about Hopkins's metric and vocabulary. But I am sure that in the matter of devotional poetry a good deal more is at issue than just the purity and strength of the author's devotional passion. To be a 'devotional poet' is a limitation: a saint limits himself by writing poetry, and a poet who confines himself to even this subject matter is limiting himself too. Hopkins is not a religious poet in the more important sense in which I have elsewhere maintained Baudelaire to be a religious poet; or in the sense in which I find Villon to be a religious poet; or in the sense in which I consider Mr Joyce's work to be penetrated with Christian feeling. I do not wish to depreciate him, but to affirm limitations and distinctions. He should be compared, not with our contemporaries whose situation is different from his, but with the minor poet nearest contemporary to him, and most like him: George Meredith. The comparison is altogether to Hopkins's advantage. They are both English nature poets, they have similar technical tricks, and Hopkins is much the more agile. And where Meredith, beyond a few acute and pertly expressed observations of human nature, has only a rather cheap and shallow 'philosophy of life' to offer, Hopkins has the dignity of the Church behind him, and is consequently in closer contact with reality. But from the struggle of our time to concentrate, not to dissipate; to renew our association with traditional wisdom; to re-establish a vital connexion between the individual and the race; the struggle, in a word, against Liberalism: from all this Hopkins is a little apart, and in this Hopkins has very little aid to offer us.

[49] What I have wished to illustrate, by reference to the authors whom I have mentioned in this lecture, has been the crippling effect upon men of letters, of not having been born and brought up in the environment of a living and central tradition. In the following lecture I shall be concerned rather with the positive effects of heresy, and with much more alarming consequences: those resulting from exposure to the diabolic influence.

III

ASG, 51–63. On p. 59 'wordly' has been corrected to 'worldly'.

Revised from 'Personality and Demonic Possession', *Virginia Quarterly Review*, 10. 1 (Jan. 1934), [94]–103: Gallup C351.

1 I think that there is an interesting subject of investigation, for the student of traditions, in the history of Blasphemy, and the anomalous position of that term in the modern world. It is a curious survival in a society which has for the most part ceased to be capable of exercising that activity or of recognising it. I am persuaded that pretty generally, when that term is used at all, it is used in a sense which is only the shadow of the original. For modern blasphemy is merely a department of bad form: just as, in countries which still possess a Crown, people are usually (and quite rightly) shocked by any public impertinence concerning any member of their Royal Family, they are still shocked by any public impertinence towards a Deity for whom they feel privately no respect at all; and both feelings are supported by the conservatism of those who have anything to lose by social changes. Yet people nowadays are inclined to tolerate and respect any violation which is presented to them as inspired by 'serious' purposes; whereas the only disinfectant which makes either blasphemy or obscenity sufferable is the sense of humour: the indecent that is funny may be the legitimate source of innocent merriment, while the absence of humour reveals it as purely disgusting.

2 I do not wish to be understood as undertaking a defence [52] of blasphemy in the abstract. I am only pointing out that it is a very different thing in the modern world from what it would be in an 'age of faith'; just as a magistrate's conception of blasphemy will probably be very different from that of a good Catholic, and his objections to it will be for very different reasons. The whole question of censorship is now of course reduced to ludicrous inconsistency, and is likely to remain so as long as the morals of the State are not those of the Church. But my point is that blasphemy is not a matter of good form but of right belief; no one can possibly blaspheme in any sense except that in which a parrot may be said to curse, unless he profoundly believes in that which he profanes; and when anyone who is not a believer is shocked by blasphemy he is shocked merely by a breach of good form; and it is a nice question whether, being in a state of intellectual error, he is or is not committing a sin in being shocked for the wrong reasons. It is certainly my opinion that first-rate blasphemy is one of the rarest things in literature, for it requires both literary genius and profound faith, joined in a mind in a peculiar

and unusual state of spiritual sickness. I repeat that I am not defending blasphemy; I am reproaching a world in which blasphemy is impossible.

3 My next point is a more delicate one to handle. One can conceive of blasphemy as doing moral harm to feeble or perverse souls; at the same time one must recognise that the modern environment is so unfavourable to faith that it produces fewer and fewer individuals capable of being injured by blasphemy. One would expect, therefore, that (whatever it may have been at other times) blasphemy [53] would be less employed by the Forces of Evil than at any other time in the last two thousand years. Where blasphemy might once have been a sign of spiritual corruption, it might now be taken rather as a symptom that the soul is still alive, or even that it is recovering animation: for the perception of Good and Evil – whatever choice we may make – is the first requisite of spiritual life. We should do well, therefore, to look elsewhere than to the blasphemer, in the traditional sense, for the most fruitful operations of the Evil Spirit to-day.

4 I regret, for my present purposes, that I have not a more intimate, accurate and extensive knowledge of the English novelists of the last hundred years, and that therefore I feel a little insecure of my generalisations. But it seems to me that the eminent novelists who are more nearly contemporary to us, have been more concerned than their predecessors – consciously or not – to impose upon their readers their own *personal view of life*, and that this is merely part of the whole movement of several centuries towards the aggrandisement and exploitation of *personality*. I do not suggest that 'personality' is an illicit intruder; I imagine that the admirers of Jane Austen are all fascinated by something that may be called her personality. But personality, with Jane Austen, with Dickens and with Thackeray, was more nearly in its proper place. The standards by which they criticised their world, if not very lofty ones, were at least not of their own making. In Dickens's novels, for instance, the religion is still of the good old torpid eighteenth century kind, dressed up with a profusion of holly and turkey, and supplemented by strong humanitarian [54] zeal. These novelists were still observers: however superficial – in contrast, for instance, to Flaubert – we find their observations to be. They are orthodox enough according to the light of their day: the first suspicion of heresy creeps in with a writer who, at her best, had much profounder moral insight and passion than these, but who unfortunately combined it with the dreary rationalism of the epoch of which she is one of the most colossal monuments: George Eliot. George Eliot seems to me of the same tribe as all the serious and eccentric

moralists we have had since: we must respect her for being a serious moralist, but deplore her individualistic morals. What I have been leading up to is the following assertion: that when morals cease to be a matter of tradition and orthodoxy – that is, of the habits of the community formulated, corrected, and elevated by the continuous thought and direction of the Church – and when each man is to elaborate his own, then *personality* becomes a thing of alarming importance.

5 The work of the late Thomas Hardy represents an interesting example of a powerful personality uncurbed by any institutional attachment or by submission to any objective beliefs; unhampered by any ideas, or even by what sometimes acts as a partial restraint upon inferior writers, the desire to please a large public. He seems to me to have written as nearly for the sake of 'self-expression' as a man well can; and the self which he had to express does not strike me as a particularly wholesome or edifying matter of communication. He was indifferent even to the prescripts of good writing: he wrote sometimes overpoweringly well, but always very carelessly; at times his style touches sub-[55]limity without ever having passed through the stage of being good. In consequence of his self-absorption, he makes a great deal of landscape; for landscape is a passive creature which lends itself to an author's mood. Landscape is fitted too for the purposes of an author who is interested not at all in men's minds, but only in their emotions; and perhaps only in men as vehicles for emotions. It is only, indeed, in their emotional paroxysms that most of Hardy's characters come alive. This extreme emotionalism seems to me a symptom of decadence; it is a cardinal point of faith in a romantic age, to believe that there is something admirable in violent emotion for its own sake, whatever the emotion or whatever its object. But it is by no means self-evident that human beings are most real when most violently excited; violent physical passions do not in themselves differentiate men from each other, but rather tend to reduce them to the same state; and the passion has significance only in relation to the character and behaviour of the man at other moments of his life and in other contexts. Furthermore, strong passion is only interesting or significant in strong men; those who abandon themselves without resistance to excitements which tend to deprive them of reason, become merely instruments of feeling and lose their humanity; and unless there is moral resistance and conflict there is no meaning. But as the majority is capable neither of strong emotion nor of strong resistance, it always inclines to admire passion for its own sake, unless instructed to the contrary; and, if somewhat deficient in vitality, people imagine passion to be the surest evidence of vitality. This in itself may go towards accounting for Hardy's popularity.

[56] 6 What again and again introduces a note of falsity into Hardy's novels is that he will leave nothing to nature, but will always be giving one last turn of the screw himself, and of his motives for so doing I have the gravest suspicion. In *The Mayor of Casterbridge* – which has always seemed to me his finest novel as a whole – he comes the nearest to producing an air of inevitability, and of making the crises seem the consequences of the character of Henchard; the arrangement by which the hero, leaning over a bridge, finds himself staring at his effigy in the stream below is a masterly *tour de force*. This scene is however as much by arrangement as less successful ones in which the motive intrudes itself more visibly; as for instance the scene in *Far From The Madding Crowd* in which Bathsheba unscrews Fanny Robin's coffin – which seems to me deliberately faked. And by this I mean that the author seems to be deliberately relieving some emotion of his own at the expense of the reader. It is a refined form of torture on the part of the writer, and a refined form of self-torture on the part of the reader. And this brings me to the point of this lecture, for the first time.

7 I have not so far made it apparent what relation the documents considered in this lecture bear to the subject matter of the last. I was there concerned with illustrating the limiting and crippling effect of a separation from tradition and orthodoxy upon certain writers whom I nevertheless hold up for admiration for what they have attempted against great obstacles. Here I am concerned with the intrusion of the *diabolic* into modern literature in consequence of the same lamentable state of affairs; and it was for this [57] reason that I took the pains at the beginning to point out that blasphemy is not a matter with which we are concerned. I am afraid that even if you can entertain the notion of a positive power for evil working through human agency, you may still have a very inaccurate notion of what Evil is, and will find it difficult to believe that it may operate through men of genius of the most excellent character. I doubt whether what I am saying can convey very much to anyone for whom the doctrine of Original Sin is not a very real and tremendous thing. I can only ask you to read the texts, and then reconsider my remarks. And one of the most significant of the Hardy texts is a volume of short stories, indeed of masterly short stories, which has never received enough examination from that point of view: I mean *A Group of Noble Dames*. Here, for one thing, you get essential Hardy without the Wessex staging; without the scenery dear to the Anglo-Saxon heart or the period peasants pleasing to the metropolitan imagination. Not all of these stories, of course, illustrate my point equally well; the best for my purpose, to which I refer you, rather than take up your time by summarising the

plot, is *Barbara of the House of Grebe*. This is not realism; it is as Hardy catalogues it, 'romance and fantasy' with which Hardy can do exactly what he wants to do. I do not object to horror: *Oedipus Rex* is a most horrible plot from which the last drop of horror is extracted by the dramatist; and among Hardy's contemporaries, Conrad's *Heart of Darkness* and James's *Turn of the Screw* are tales of horror. But there is horror in the real world; and in these works of Sophocles, Conrad and James we are in a world of [58] Good and Evil. In *Barbara of the House of Grebe* we are introduced into a world of pure Evil. The tale would seem to have been written solely to provide a satisfaction for some morbid emotion.

8 I find this same strain in the work of a man whose morbidity I have already had occasion to mention, and whom I regard as a very much greater genius, if not a greater artist, than Hardy: D. H. Lawrence. Lawrence has three aspects, and it is very difficult to do justice to all. I do not expect to be able to do so. The first is the ridiculous: his lack of sense of humour, a certain snobbery, a lack not so much of information as of the critical faculties which education should give, and an incapacity for what we ordinarily call thinking. Of this side of Lawrence, the brilliant exposure by Mr Wyndham Lewis in *Paleface* is by far the most conclusive criticism that has been made. Secondly, there is the extraordinarily keen sensibility and capacity for profound intuition – intuition from which he commonly drew the wrong conclusions. Third, there is a distinct sexual morbidity. Unfortunately, it is necessary to keep all of these aspects in mind in order to criticise the writer fairly; and this, in such close perspective, is almost impossible. I shall no doubt appear to give excessive prominence to the third; but that, after all, is what has been least successfully considered.

9 I have already touched upon the deplorable religious upbringing which gave Lawrence his lust for intellectual independence: like most people who do not know what orthodoxy is, he hated it. With the more intimate reasons, of heredity and environment, for eccentricity of thought and [59] feeling I am not concerned: too many people have made them their business already. And I have already mentioned the insensibility to ordinary social morality, which is so alien to my mind that I am completely baffled by it as a monstrosity. The point is that Lawrence started life wholly free from any restriction of tradition or institution, that he had no guidance except the Inner Light, the most untrustworthy and deceitful guide that ever offered itself to wandering humanity. It was peculiarly so for Lawrence, who does not appear to have been gifted with the faculty of self-criticism, except in flashes, even to the extent of ordinary worldly shrewdness. Of divine illumination, it may be said that probably every

man knows when he has it, but that any man is likely to think that he has it when he has it not; and even when he has had it, the daily man that he is may draw the wrong conclusions from the enlightenment which the momentary man has received: no one, in short, can be the sole judge of whence his inspiration comes. A man like Lawrence, therefore, with his acute sensibility, violent prejudices and passions, and lack of intellectual and social training, is admirably fitted to be an instrument for forces of good or for forces of evil; or as we might expect, partly for one and partly for the other. A trained mind like that of Mr Joyce is always aware what master it is serving; an untrained mind, and a soul destitute of humility and filled with self-righteousness, is a blind servant and a fatal leader. It would seem that for Lawrence any spiritual force was good, and that evil resided only in the absence of spirituality. Most people, no doubt, need to be aroused to the perception of the simple distinction between the spiritual and [60] the material; and Lawrence never forgot, and never mistook, this distinction. But most people are only very little alive; and to awaken them to the spiritual is a very great responsibility: it is only when they are so awakened that they are capable of real Good, but that at the same time they become first capable of Evil. Lawrence lived all his life, I should imagine, on the spiritual level; no man was less a sensualist. Against the living death of modern material civilisation he spoke again and again, and even if these dead could speak, what he said is unanswerable. As a criticism of the modern world, *Fantasia of the Unconscious* is a book to keep at hand and re-read. In contrast to Nottingham, London or industrial America, his capering redskins of *Mornings in Mexico* seem to represent Life. So they do; but that is not the last word, only the first.

10   The man's vision is spiritual, but spiritually sick. The demonic powers found an instrument of far greater range, delicacy and power in the author of *The Prussian Officer* than in the author of *A Group of Noble Dames*; and the tale which I used as an example (*The Shadow in the Rose Garden*) can be matched by several others. I have not read all of his late and his posthumous works, which are numerous. In some respects, he may have progressed: his early belief in Life may have passed over, as a really serious belief in Life must, into a belief in Death.[1] But I cannot see much development in *Lady Chatterley's Lover*. Our old acquaintance, the gamekeeper, turns up again: the social obsession which makes [61] his well-born – or almost well-born – ladies offer themselves to – or make use

---

1. I am indebted to an unpublished essay by Mr E. F. W. Tomlin for the suggestion that this is so.

of – plebeians springs from the same morbidity which makes other of his female characters bestow their favours upon savages. The author of that book seems to me to have been a very sick man indeed.

11 There is, I believe, a very great deal to be learned from Lawrence; though those who are most capable of exercising the judgement necessary to extract the lesson, may not be those who are most in need of it. That we can and ought to reconcile ourselves to Liberalism, Progress and Modern Civilisation is a proposition which we need not have waited for Lawrence to condemn; and it matters a good deal in what name we condemn it. I fear that Lawrence's work may appeal, not to those who are well and able to discriminate, but to the sick and debile and confused; and will appeal not to what remains of health in them, but to their sickness. Nor will many even accept his doctrine as he would give it, but will be busy after their own inventions. The number of people in possession of any criteria for discriminating between good and evil is very small; the number of the half-alive hungry for any form of spiritual experience, or what offers itself as spiritual experience, high or low, good or bad, is considerable. My own generation has not served them very well. Never has the printing-press been so busy, and never have such varieties of buncombe and false doctrine come from it. *Woe unto the foolish prophets, that follow their own spirit, and have seen nothing! O Israel, thy prophets have been like foxes in the waste places.... And the word of the* LORD *came unto me, saying, Son of man, these men have taken their idols into their hearts,* [62] *and put the stumbling-block of their iniquity before their face: should I be inquired of at all by them?*

12 I wish to add a few words of retrospect and summary, partly as a reminder of how little, in the space of three hours, one can undertake to say about such a serious subject as this. In an age of unsettled beliefs and enfeebled tradition the man of letters, the poet, and the novelist, are in a situation dangerous for themselves and for their readers. I tried to safeguard myself, in my first lecture, from being taken to be merely a sentimental admirer of some real or imaginary past, and from being taken as a faker of traditions. Tradition by itself is not enough; it must be perpetually criticised and brought up to date under the supervision of what I call orthodoxy; and for the lack of this supervision it is now the sentimental tenuity that we find it. Most 'defenders of tradition' are mere conservatives, unable to distinguish between the permanent and the temporary, the essential and the accidental. But I left this theory as a bare outline, to serve as a background for my illustration of the dangers of authorship to-day. Where there is no external test of the validity of

a writer's work, we fail to distinguish between the truth of his view of life and the personality which makes it plausible; so that in our reading, we may be simply yielding ourselves to one seductive personality after another. The first requisite usually held up by the promoters of personality is that a man should 'be himself'; and this 'sincerity' is considered more important than that the self in question should, socially and spiritually, be a good or a bad one. This view of person-[63]ality is merely an assumption on the part of the modern world, and is no more tenable than several other views which have been held at various times and in several places. The personality thus expressed, the personality which fascinates us in the work of philosophy or art, tends naturally to be the *unregenerate* personality, partly self-deceived and partly irresponsible, and because of its freedom, terribly *limited* by prejudice and self-conceit, capable of much good or great mischief according to the natural goodness or impurity of the man: and we are all, naturally, impure. All that I have been able to do here is to suggest that there are standards of criticism, not ordinarily in use, which we may apply to whatever is offered to us as works of philosophy or of art, which might help to render them safer and more profitable for us.

Variants from *Virginia Quarterly Review* (1934):
Title Personality and Demonic Possession
2   from what it would] than it would
3   is still alive] was still alive
5   matter of communication] communication
    Landscape is fitted] It is fitted
    Hardy's characters] his characters
    it always inclines to admire passion for its own sake, unless instructed to the contrary; and,] it always inclines, unless instructed to the contrary, to admire passion for its own sake; and
6   is however] is, however,
    – which seems] , which seems
    seems to be] seems to me to be
    to the point of this lecture, for the first time] for the first time to the point of this lecture
7   I have not so far made it apparent what relation the documents considered in this lecture bear to the subject matter of the last. [Not represented in 1934.]
    I was there concerned] I have concerned myself elsewhere
    refer you] refer the reader
    your time] his time to less purpose
    it is as] it is, as
    Conrad and] Conrad, and
    we are introduced] we seem to be introduced
    The tale] It

8 strain] strain of morbidity
whose morbidity I have already had occasion to mention, and [Not represented in 1934.]
sexual morbidity] morbidity and hypertrophy of personality

9 already touched] touched elsewhere
inspiration comes] inspiration comes or what it means
simple distinction] simple difference
his capering redskins] the capering redskins
only the first] but only the first

10 The man's] The intensity of the man's
(*The Shadow in the Rose Garden*)] , *The Shadow of the Rose Garden*,
his late] Lawrence's late
[Between 'progressed:' and 'his early belief':] as Mr E. F. W. Tomlin has suggested, [No fn. in 1934.]
plebeians] plebeians,
other of his] his other

11 Progress] Progress,
condemn it] condemn them
half-alive hungry] half-alive, hungry
hearts] *heart*

12 I wish to] I would
safeguard myself, in my first lecture] safeguard myself
real or imaginary] actual or imaginary
But I left this theory as a bare outline, to serve as a background for my illustration of the dangers of authorship to-day. [Not represented in 1934.]
[After 'a good or a bad one.':] [New para.]

Appendix

ASG, 65–8.

I have after some deliberation called this essay a primer of modern heresy: hinting that it is offered primarily to those who may be interested in pursuing the subject by themselves. I had thought of supplementing it by a graduated Exercise Book, beginning with very simple examples of heresy, and leading up to those which are very difficult to solve; and leaving the student to find the answers for himself. My chief reason for abandoning this project is perhaps the overwhelming abundance of elementary exercises, compared with the paucity of those which can tax the abilities of the really quick and proficient student. I therefore content myself with four examples. No. I is very elementary: countless specimens of the same kind might be found. No. II is slightly, but not much, more advanced. Nos. III and IV are among the most advanced that I can find. A really satisfactory exercise book would require the co-operation of a board of editors. I am not well enough read; and I find to my discomfiture that most of the examples that occur to me hardly rise above the simplicity of No. I. Numerous advanced exercises are possible to those who possess a familiarity with foreign languages.

[66] I

'The barbaric sense of the exceeding sinfulness of sin, with the moral hatred it carried, is giving way to a more natural attitude. Vice offends more from its ugliness than from its sinfulness. Goodness has its appeal in moral beauty rather than in virtue.' – JOHN A. HOBSON: *The Moncure D. Conway Lecture* 1933.

II

'At the end of my life as a teacher . . . I am convinced that it is personality that counts always and all the time. . . .

This question of Latin is a part, and only a part, of what I think is the most important educational question that is now before the country. It is a question which is engaging the attention of the Consultative Committee of the Board of Education at the present moment – the question of what is the right education to give pupils between the ages of 11 and 16½, whose education is not going to be continued beyond that point. Are we giving the right education at the present time? I am pretty certain that we are not.

I would give a boy first a sound education based on English culture, English geography, English history, and English literature, less mathematics, a different kind of science, and I would not attempt to teach him more than one foreign language. I would also try to give him a thorough physical education, and a thorough training of the hand, eye and ear, and I would seek to make that as important as his literary education. In his last years at school I would seek to build on that foundation some under-[67]standing of the modern world, why it is, how it works, and what his place is in it. In that education I do not think that there will be room or time for Latin, but at present we have not formulated anything like that. It is still an ideal.' – Dr Cyril Norwood, addressing the Conference of the Incorporated Association of Preparatory Schools at the Hotel Great Central, Marylebone (*The Times* newspaper of December 21, 1933.)

III

'Character, in short, is an impersonal ideal which the individual selects and to which he sacrifices all other claims, especially those of the sentiments or emotions. It follows that character must be placed in opposition to personality, which is the general-common-denominator of our sentiments and emotions. That is, indeed, the opposition I wish to emphasise; and when I have said further that all poetry, in which I wish to include all lyrical impulses whatever, is the product of the personality, and therefore inhibited in a character, I have stated the main theme of my essay.' – HERBERT READ: *Form in Modern Poetry*, pp. 18–19.

IV

'Any serious criticism of communist philosophy must start by declaring openly how much of its theory is accepted by the critic. I must therefore preface my criticism by saying that I accept the rejection of idealism and the principle of the unity of theory and practice in the sense in which I have expounded it. And since this is the truly revolutionary principle, such an acceptance involves taking [68] one's stand within the tradition of thought which derives from Marx. The negative implications of accepting this fundamental principle go very deep. They include the rejection of all philosophy and all social theory which does not accept this principle, not because of particular objections to their conclusions, but because of a complete break with the assumptions upon which they are based and the purpose which governs their development. They involve the belief that all theory must seek verification in action and adapt itself to the possibility of experiment. They make a clean sweep of speculative thought on the ground that the validity of no belief whatever is capable of demonstration by argument. They involve a refusal at any point to make knowledge an end in itself, and equally, the rejection of the desire for certainty which is the motive governing speculative thought.' – JOHN MACMURRAY: *The Philosophy of Communism*, pp. 62–63.

Le Morte Darthur

Spectator, 152. 5513 (23 Feb. 1934), 278. Signed 'T. S. Eliot'. Gallup C353.

This is the text of *Le Morte Darthur*,[1] printed after Caxton, with no prefaces, introductions or notes, and a very beautiful rubricated piece of book-making indeed. It is for those who appreciate Malory and can afford to possess his book in as grand a form as anyone could wish; and those who enjoy Malory ought to be willing to pay him this honour if they can afford it. I mean no disrespect to this wholly admirable edition in

1. *Le Morte Darthur*. Reduced into Englisshe by Sir Thomas Malory. (Blackwell: The Shakespeare Head Press. 2 vols.)

suggesting that we need three more editions to follow it: (1) a cheap edition of the text; (2) a scholarly edition with a full commentary by some person as learned as Miss Jane Harrison or Miss Jessie Weston; and (3) a children's edition. Such an edition was in my hands when I was a child of eleven or twelve. It was then, and perhaps has always been, my favourite book. I have not come across this, or any similar children's edition, since.

What we are, as a matter of fact, familiar with is a kind of children's edition; but it is a children's edition edited according to the wrong principles. I should like to have an edition of the text made *readable* for children, and somewhat abbreviated; that with which Sir Edward Strachey of Sutton Court provided us is an edition meant to be *safe* for children. The most accessible and convenient text for everybody was actually prepared to this end. Sir Edward announces:

> I do not believe that when we have excluded what is offensive to modern manners there will be found anything practically injurious to the morals of English boys, for whom I have chiefly undertaken this work.

We observe the confusion of *morals* and *manners*. 'Lord Tennyson,' says Sir Edward, 'has shown us how we may deal best with this matter.' Sir Edward believed in the compulsory sterilisation of literature. It is not irrelevant to call attention to the degraded moral conceptions of an age in which an editor of Malory could write:

> The morality of 'Morte Darthur' is low in one essential thing, and this alike in what it says and in what it omits: and Lord Tennyson shows us how it should be raised. The ideal of marriage, in its relation and its contrast with all other forms of love and chastity, is brought out in every form, rising at last to tragic grandeur, in the *Idylls of the King*. It is not in celibacy, though spiritual and holy as that of Galahad and Percivale, but in marriage, as the highest and purest realization of the ideal of human conditions and relations, that we are to rise above the temptations of a love like that of Launcelot or even of Elaine; and Malory's book does not set this ideal of life before us with any power or clearness.

This, one may remark, is the result of the policy of Henry VIII. Sir Edward might as well have observed that the morality of St Paul is low in this one essential thing. He does mention St Paul in this very introduction. And what does he say of St Paul? 'In modern times,' he says, 'St. Paul has been held to be the model of a gentleman.' There is nothing more that one can say.

When one compares the present text with that of Sir Edward Strachey, it is perhaps the more trifling alterations of Sir Edward, just because they are trifling, that are the more irritating. One might mention, however, that his bowdlerising makes the episode of the knight whom Sir Gareth beheads on two different evenings in the hall of Dame Lioness, *completely* unintelligible. But there are places where his tampering is still more fatal. Let us take the birth of Mordred. The Strachey text reads:

> And thither came to him Lot's wife of Orkney ... and she was a passing fair lady, wherefore the king cast great love unto her, and so was Mordred born, and she was his sister, on the mother side Igraine ... But all this time King Arthur knew not that king Lot's wife was his sister.

The true text reads:

> And thyder came to him king Lot's wife of Orkney ... for she was a passyng fayr lady, wherfore the kyng cast grete love unto her, and desyred to lye by her; so they were agreed, and he begate upon her Mordred: and she was his sister on the moders syde Igrayne, &c.

It is a very slight alteration. But the incest of Arthur is the foundation of the plot of the whole book, which is almost meaningless without it. Whether it should be minimised in an edition for boys is a question for dispute; but I feel sure that Sir Edward Strachey regarded it as an 'impurity', instead of as springing from a profound, tribal, Sophoclean morality. It is indeed to Sophocles and his sources that I should compare Malory. He is a kind of crude northern Homer, a good chronicler, organiser and designer, a fine prose writer, just lacking the poet's power over the word.

The morality of the *Morte Darthur*, as I have suggested, is of that primitive kind which belongs to the nature of things as our shallow modern manners do not. This primitive morality was refined by Christianity; but the passing of Christianity has left only the refinement without the morality, as one can already see in the preface of Sir Edward Strachey; and it ends in a 'sense of justice', a humanitarianism, which is finally immoral. To a simpler and truer view of life than ours the moral law is a very real thing, as real and inexorable as natural law – indeed, a part of natural law: the early peoples did not foolishly require, as we do, that morality itself should be moral. Certain acts were sins, and had deadly consequences; and these consequences must follow whether the acts were committed in ignorance or not. They demanded purgation.

It is, perhaps, most perfectly in Sophocles, but legibly also in Malory, that the pattern of responsibility and fatality is woven. Arthur himself is the offspring of sin, though legitimated; but it is his unwitting sin that is the clue to the whole story. It is his incest-born bastard who shall destroy him; and like Laius, still more like Herod, the paragon king attempts by a most-unchristian slaughter of the innocents born on May day to defeat fate. Arthur throughout is a man under doom, at first admonished by the prophetic voice of Merlin, his Tiresias, himself cursed, not by blindness, but by the blind infatuation which ruins him. Arthur remains without legitimate issue, an unhappy man, dedicated, and under the doom giving his warmest love and highest esteem to the known lover of his wife. And they all remain, like the House of Atreus, and the House of Laius, great people. And like Oedipus at Colonus, the doomed and persecuted of Heaven is reserved for great honour from Heaven; Oedipus and Arthur leave the world not like ordinary men. In life it is not Arthur who triumphs in the lists and in adventures; he is always partly the observer, the stranger; but it is he, rather than Launcelot or the saint begotten by a sleight, who dominates the scene.

One of the reasons why the *Morte Darthur* is a permanent source of refreshment, is the degree to which the primitive 'ritual' stories are and are not integrated into the narrative. The inconsequence of many episodes is important, a consistent inconsequence. It is less, certainly, than appears on first reading. Balin and Balan, those pure folk-lore pre-Christian personages, are connected through the sword of Balin, through the Dolorous Stroke, with Galahad and the Sangreal. And the personalities of the Round Table are excellently well balanced: the simple good – Sir Gareth and Sir Pelleas, Sir Tor and other minor figures; the mixed good and evil, like Sir Gawaine, who are human not on the heroic scale; and the gradation from Sir Bors to Sir Percival (whose sister has significance) to Sir Galahad – whom I mentioned as a saint, but who is more properly *angelic*: certainly not simply human, but the offspring of a virgin sacrifice.

I do not wish to suggest that everything in the *Morte Darthur* is right and inevitable. There are plenty of loose ends. The book is anything but self-explanatory, and there was much of which Sir Thomas Malory was ignorant. I pray that during my lifetime someone may bring out an edition, as bulky as Frazer's *Pausanias*, which shall give the natural history of the Questing Beast, and the etymology of the names of all the knights and kings. I accept Sir La Cote Male Taile, but what about Sir Marhaus, and Sir Suppinabiles, and King Bagdemagus, and Sir Meliagrance, Sir Lamorak and Sir Persant of Inde?

The Old and New Testaments, and Homer and Aeschylus and Sophocles and Malory, are books which deserve good printing and binding. This book is accordingly well worth nine guineas, and the extra six shillings to have it in full leather.

Tradition and Orthodoxy

American Review, 2. 5 (Mar. 1934), 513–28. Signed 'T. S. Eliot'. Gallup C354.

Revised from *ASG*, Part 1. Gallup (p. 228) is mistaken in stating that this article was 'Reprinted, with alterations' in *ASG*; *ASG* was publ. by Faber on 22 Feb. 1934.

1 A recent first visit to Virginia afforded me an appropriate occasion to reconsider a subject on which, some fifteen years ago, I wrote an essay entitled 'Tradition and the Individual Talent'. In the South one finds, I imagine, at least some recollection of a 'tradition', such as the influx of foreign populations has almost effaced in some parts of the North, and such as never established itself in the West: though it is hardly to be expected that a tradition here, any more than anywhere else, should be found in healthy and flourishing growth.

2 I have been much interested, since the publication a few years ago of a book called *I'll Take My Stand*, in what is sometimes called the agrarian movement in the South, and look forward to any further statements by the same group of writers. My first, and no doubt superficial impressions of their country – I speak as a New Englander – have strengthened my feeling of sympathy with those authors: no one, surely, can cross the Potomac for the first time without being struck by differences so great that their [514] extinction could only mean the death of both cultures. I had previously been led to wonder, in travelling from Boston to New York, at what point Connecticut ceases to be a New England state and is transformed into a New York suburb; but to cross into Virginia is as definite an experience as to cross from England to Wales, almost as definite as to cross the English Channel. And the differences here, with no difference of language or race to support them, have had to survive the immense pressure towards monotony exerted by the industrial expansion of the latter part of the nineteenth and the first part of the twentieth century. The Civil War was certainly the greatest disaster in the whole of American history; it is just as certainly a disaster from which the country has never recovered, and perhaps never will: we are always too ready to assume that the good effects of wars, if any, abide permanently while the ill effects are obliterated by time. Yet I think that the chances for the re-establishment of a native culture are perhaps better in the South than in New England. The Southerners are farther away from New York; they have been less industrialised and less invaded by foreign races; and they have a more opulent soil.

3 My local feelings were stirred very sadly by my first view of New England, on arriving from Montreal, and journeying all one day through the beautiful desolate country of Vermont. Those hills had once, I suppose, been covered with primeval forest; the forest was rased to make sheep pastures for the English settlers; now the sheep are gone, and most of the descendants of the settlers, and a new forest appeared blazing with the melancholy glory of October maple [515] and beech and birch scattered among the evergreens; and after this procession of scarlet and golden and purple wilderness you descend to the sordor of the half-dead mill towns of southern New Hampshire and Massachusetts. It is not necessarily those lands which are the most fertile or most favoured in climate that seem to me the happiest, but those in which a long struggle of adaptation between man and his environment has brought out the best qualities of both; in which the landscape has been moulded by numerous generations of one race, and in which the landscape in turn has modified the race to its own character. And those New England mountains seemed to me to give evidence of a human success so meagre and transitory as to be more desperate than utter failure.

4 I know very well that the aim of the 'new-agrarians' in the South will be qualified as quixotic, as a hopeless stand for a cause which was lost long before they were born. It will be said that the whole current of economic determinism is against them, and economic determinism is today a god before whom we all fall down and worship with all kinds of music. I believe that these matters may ultimately be determined by what people want; that when anything is generally accepted as desirable, economic laws can be upset in order to achieve it; that it does not so much matter at present whether any measures put forward are practical, as whether the aim is a good aim, and the alternatives intolerable. There are, at the present stage, more serious difficulties in the revival or establishment of a tradition and a way of life, which require immediate consideration.

5 Tradition is not solely, or even primarily, the main-[516]tenance of certain dogmatic beliefs; these beliefs have come to take their living form in the course of the formation of a tradition. What I mean by tradition involves all those habitual actions, habits and customs, from the most significant religious rite to our conventional way of greeting a stranger, which represent the blood kinship of 'the same people living in the same place'. It involves a good deal which can be called *taboo*: that this word is used in our time in an almost exclusively derogatory sense is to me a curiosity of some significance. We become conscious of these items, or conscious of their importance, usually only after they have begun to fall

into desuetude, as we are aware of the leaves of a tree when the autumn wind begins to blow them off – when they have separately ceased to be vital. Energy may be wasted at that point in a frantic endeavour to collect the leaves as they fall and gum them onto the branches: but the sound tree will put forth new leaves, and the dry tree should be put to the axe. We are always in danger, in clinging to an old tradition, or attempting to re-establish one, of confusing the vital and the unessential, the real and the sentimental. Our second danger is to associate tradition with the immovable; to think of it as something hostile to all change; to aim to return to some previous condition which we imagine as having been capable of preservation in perpetuity, instead of aiming to stimulate the life which produced that condition in its time.

6 It is not of advantage to us to indulge a sentimental attitude towards the past. For one thing, in even the very best living tradition there is always a mixture of good and bad, and much that deserves criticism; and for another, tradition is not a matter of feeling alone. [517] Nor can we safely, without very critical examination, dig ourselves in stubbornly to a few dogmatic notions, for what is a healthy belief at one time may, unless it is one of the few fundamental things, be a pernicious prejudice at another. Nor should we cling to traditions as a way of asserting our superiority over less favoured peoples. What we can do is to use our minds, remembering that a tradition without intelligence is not worth having, to discover what is the best life for us not as a political abstraction, but as a particular people in a particular place; what in the past is worth preserving and what should be rejected; and what conditions, within our power to bring about, would foster the society that we desire. Stability is obviously necessary. You are hardly likely to develop tradition except where the bulk of the population is relatively so well off where it is that it has no incentive or pressure to move about. The population should be homogeneous; where two or more cultures exist in the same place they are likely either to be fiercely self-conscious or both become adulterate.[1] What is still more important is unity of religious background; and reasons of race and religion combine to make any large number of free-thinking Jews undesirable. There must be a proper balance between urban and rural, industrial and agricultural development. And a spirit of excessive tolerance is to be deprecated.

---

1. Or else you may get a *caste* system, based on original distinctions of race, as in India: which is a very different matter from *classes*, which presuppose homogeneity of race and a fundamental equality. But social classes, as distinct from economic classes, hardly exist today.

7 We must also remember that – in spite of every means of transport that can be devised – the local com-[518]munity must always be the most permanent, and that the concept of the nation is by no means fixed and invariable.[1] It is, so to speak, only one *fluctuating circle* of loyalties between the centre, the family and the local community, and the periphery of humanity entire. Its strength and its geographical size depend upon the comprehensiveness of a way of life which can harmonise parts with distinct local characters of their own. When it becomes no more than a centralised machinery it may affect some of its parts to their detriment, or to what they believe to be their detriment; and we get the regional movements which have appeared within recent years. It is only a law of nature, that local patriotism, when it represents a distinct tradition and culture, takes precedence over a more abstract national patriotism.

8 So far I have only pronounced a few doctrines all of which have been developed by other writers.[2] I do not intend to trespass upon their fields. I wish simply to indicate the connotation which the term *tradition* has for me, before proceeding to associate it with the concept of *orthodoxy*, which seems to me more fundamental (with its opposite, *heterodoxy*, for [519] which I shall also use the term *heresy*) than the pair *classicism-romanticism* which is frequently used.

9 As we use the term *tradition* to include a good deal more than 'traditional religious beliefs', so I am here giving the term *orthodoxy* a similar inclusiveness; and though of course I believe that a right tradition for us must be also a Christian tradition, and that orthodoxy in general implies Christian orthodoxy, I do not propose to lead the present discussion to a theological conclusion.

10 The relation between tradition and orthodoxy in the past is evident enough; as is also the great difference there may be between being an orthodox Christian and a member of the Tory Party. But Conservatism, so far as it has ever existed, so far as it has ever been intelligent, and

---

1. 'To place the redemptive work of the Christian Faith in social affairs in its proper setting, it is necessary to have clearly in mind at the outset that the consciousness of "the nation" as *the* social unit is a very recent and contingent experience. It belongs to a limited historical period and is bound up with certain specific happenings, theories of society and attitudes to life as a whole.' (V. A. Demant, *God, Man and Society*, p. 146).

2. I should not like to hold any one of them responsible for all of my opinions, however, especially any that the reader may find irritating. I have in mind Mr Chesterton and his 'distributism', Mr Christopher Dawson (*The Making of Europe*), Mr Demant and Mr M. B. Reckitt and their colleagues. I have also in mind the views of Mr Allen Tate and his friends as evinced in *I'll Take My Stand*, and those of several Scottish nationalists.

not merely one of the names for hand-to-mouth party politics, has been associated with the defense of tradition, ideally if not often in fact. On the other hand, there was certainly, a hundred years ago, a relation between the Liberalism which attacked the Church and the Liberalism which appeared in politics. According to a contemporary, William Palmer, the former

> were eager to eliminate from the Prayer-book the belief in the Scriptures, the Creeds, the Atonement, the worship of Christ. They called for the admission of Unitarian infidels as fellow-believers. They would eviscerate the Prayer-book, reduce the Articles to a deistic formulary, abolish all subscriptions or adhesions to formularies, and reduce religion to a state of anarchy and dissolution. These notions were widely spread. They were advocated in numberless publications, and greedily received by a democratic, thoughtless public. . . . Christianity, as it had existed for eighteen centuries, was unrepresented in this turmoil. [Quoted in *Northern Catholicism*, p. 9.]

[520] It is well to remember that this sort of Liberalism was flourishing a century ago; it is also well to remember that it is flourishing still. Not many months ago I read an article by an eminent Liberal divine from which I have preserved the following sentence:

> We now have at hand an apparatus which, though not yet able to discover reality, is fully competent to identify and to eliminate the disproportionate mass of error which has found lodgment in our creeds and codes. The factual untruth and the fallacious inference are being steadily eliminated from the hereditary body of religious faith and moral practice.

And, in order not to limit my instances to theology, I will quote from another contemporary Liberal practitioner, a literary critic this time:

> Aided by psycho-analysis, which gave them new weapons, many of the poets and dramatists of our day have dug into the most perverse of human complexes, exposing them with the scalpel of a surgeon rather than that of a philosopher.

11 At this point I may do well to anticipate a possible misunderstanding. In applying the standard of orthodoxy to contemporary literature my emphasis will be upon its collective rather than its static meaning. A superficial apprehension of the term might suggest the assumption that everything worth saying has been said, and that the possible forms of

expression have all been discovered and developed; the assumption that novelty of form and of substance was always to be deprecated. What is objectionable, from the point of view which I have adopted, is not novelty or originality in themselves, but their glorification for their own [521] sake. The artist's concern with originality, certainly, may be considered as largely negative: he wishes only to avoid saying what has already been said as well as possible. But I am not here occupied with the standards, ideals, and rules which the artist or writer should set before himself, but with the way in which his work should be taken by the reader; not with the aberrations of writers, but with those of readers and critics. To assert that a work is 'original' should be very modest praise: it should be no more than to say that the work is not patently negligible.

12 Contemporary literature may conveniently be divided as follows. There is first that which attempts to do what has already been done perfectly, and it is to this superfluous kind of writing that the word 'traditional' is commonly applied: *mis*applied, for the word itself implies a movement. Tradition cannot mean standing still. Of course, no writer ever admits to himself that he has *no* originality; but the fact that a writer can be satisfied to use the exact idiom of a predecessor is very suspicious; you cannot write satire in the line of Pope or the stanza of Byron. The second kind of contemporary writing aims at an exaggerated novelty, a novelty usually of a trifling kind, which conceals from the uncritical reader a fundamental commonplaceness. If you examine the work of any great innovator in chronological order, you may expect to find that the author has been driven on, step by step, in his innovations, by an inner necessity, and that the novelty of form has rather been forced upon him by his material than deliberately sought. It is well also to remember that what any one writer can contribute in the way of 'originality' is very small indeed, and has [522] often a pitifully small relation to the mass of his writings.

13 As for the small number of writers, in this or any other period, who are worth taking seriously, I am very far from asserting that any of these is wholly 'orthodox' or even that it would be relevant to rank them according to degrees of orthodoxy. It is not fair, for one thing, to judge the individual by what can be actual only in society as a whole; and most of us are heretical in one way or another. Nor is the responsibility solely with the individual. Furthermore, the essential of any important heresy is not simply that it is wrong: it is that it is partly right. It is characteristic of the more interesting heretics, in the context in which I use the term, that they have an exceptionally acute perception, or profound insight,

of some part of the truth; an insight more important often than the indirect perceptions of those who are aware of more, but less acutely aware of anything. So far as we are able to redress the balance, effect the compensation, ourselves, we may find such authors of the greatest value. If we value them as they value themselves we shall go astray. And in the present state of affairs, with the low degree of education to be expected of the public and of reviewers, we are more likely to go wrong than right; we must remember too, that an heresy is apt to have a seductive simplicity, to make a direct and persuasive appeal to intellect and emotions, and to be altogether more plausible than the truth.

14 It will already have been observed that my contrast of heresy and orthodoxy has some analogy to the more usual one of romanticism and classicism; and I wish to emphasise this analogy myself, as a safeguard against [523] carrying it too far. I would wish in any case to make the point that these are not matters with which creative writers can afford to bother over-much, or matters with which they do, as a rule, in practice greatly concern themselves. It is true that from time to time writers have labelled themselves 'romanticists' or 'classicists', just as they have from time to time banded themselves together under other names. These names which groups of writers and artists give themselves are the delight of professors and historians of literature, but should not be taken very seriously; their chief value is temporary and political – that, simply, of helping to make the authors known to a contemporary public; and I doubt whether any poet has ever done himself anything but harm by attempting to write as a 'romantic' or as a 'classicist'. No sensible author, in the midst of something that he is trying to write, can stop to consider whether it is going to be romantic or the opposite. At the moment when one writes, one is what one is, and the damages of a lifetime, and of having been born into an unsettled or a torpid society, cannot be repaired at the moment of composition.

15 The danger of using terms like 'romantic' and 'classic' – this does not however give us permission to avoid them altogether – does not spring so much from the confusion caused by those who use these terms about their own work, as from inevitable shifts of meaning in context. We do not mean quite the same thing when we speak of a writer as romantic, as we do when we speak of a literary period as romantic. Furthermore, we may have in mind, on any particular occasion, certain virtues or vices more or less justly associated with one term or the other, and it is doubt-[524]ful whether there is any total sum of virtues or of vices which may be arrogated to either class. The opportunities for systematic

misunderstanding, and for futile controversy, are accordingly almost ideal; and discussion of the subject is generally conducted by excitement of passion and prejudice, rather than by reason. Finally – and this is the most important point – the differences represented by these two terms are not such as can be confined to a purely literary context. In using them, you are ultimately bringing in all human values, and according to your own scheme of valuation. A thoroughgoing classicist is likely to be a thoroughgoing individualist, like the late Irving Babbitt; so that one should be on guard, in using such terms, against being thoroughgoing.

16 When we press such a term to an exactness which it will not bear, confusions are bound to occur. Such, for instance, is the association sometimes made between classicism and Catholicism. It is possible for a man to adhere to both; but he should not be under the delusion that the connection is necessarily objective: it may spring from some unity within himself, but that unity, as it is in him, may not be valid for the rest of the world. And you cannot treat on the same footing the maintenance of religious and literary principles. I have said that you cannot restrict the terms 'romantic' and 'classical', as professors of literature conveniently do, to the literary context; but on the other hand you cannot wholly free them from that context either. There is surely something wrong when a critic divides all works of art neatly into one group and the other and then plumps for the romantic or the classical as a whole. Whichever you like in theory, it is sus-[525]picious if you prefer works altogether of one class in practice: probably you have either made the terms merely names for what you admire and for what you do not, or you have forced and falsified your tastes.[1] Here again is the error of being too thoroughgoing.

17 I may as well admit at this point that in this discussion of terms I have my own log to roll. Some years ago, in the preface to a small volume of essays, I made a sort of summary declaration of faith in matters religious, political, and literary.[2] The facility with which this statement has been quoted has helped to reveal to me that as it stands the statement is injudicious. It may suggest that the three subjects are of equal importance to me, which is not so; it may suggest that I accept all three beliefs on the same grounds, which is not so; and it may suggest that I believe that they all hang together or fall together, which would be the most serious misunderstanding of all. That there are connections for me I of course

---

1. For instance: two of my own favourite authors are Sir Thomas Malory and Racine.
2. Editor's Note: 'The general point of view may be described as classicist in literature, royalist in politics, and Anglo-Catholic in religion.' (*For Lancelot Andrewes*, p. vii.)

admit, but these illuminate my own mind rather than the external world; and I now see that there was danger of suggesting to outsiders that the Faith is a political principle or a literary fashion, and the sum of all a dramatic posture.

18 From another aspect also I have a personal interest in the clearing up of the use of the terms with which I have been concerned. My friend Dr Paul Elmer More is not the first critic to call attention to an apparent incoherence between my verse and my critical [526] prose – though he is the first whose perplexity on this account has caused me any distress. It would appear that while I maintain the most correct opinions in my criticism, I do nothing but violate them in my verse; and thus appear in a double, if not double-faced rôle. I feel no shame in this matter. I am not, of course, interested by those critics who praise my criticism in order to discredit my verse, or those who praise my verse in order to discredit my opinions in religious or social affairs; I am only interested in answering those critics who, like Dr More, have paid me the compliment – deserved or not does not here matter – of expressing some approval of both. I should say that in one's prose reflections one may legitimately be occupied with ideals, whereas in the writing of verse one can only deal with actuality. Why, I would ask, is most religious verse so bad; and why does so little religious verse reach the highest levels of poetry? Largely, I think, because of a pious insincerity. The capacity for writing poetry is rare; the capacity for religious emotion of the first intensity is rare; and it is to be expected that the existence of both capacities in the same individual should be rarer still. People who write devotional verse are usually writing as they want to feel, rather than as they do feel. Likewise, in an age like the present, it could only be poetry of the very greatest rank that could be genuinely what Dr More would be obliged to call 'classical'; poets of lower ability – that is all but such as half a dozen perhaps in the world's history – could only be 'classical' by being pseudo-classical; by being unfaithful and dishonest to their experience. It should hardly be necessary to add that the 'classical' is just as unpredictable as the romantic, and that most of us would [527] not recognise a classical writer if he appeared, so queer and horrifying he would seem even to those who clamour for him.

19 I hold – in summing up – that a *tradition* is rather a way of feeling and acting which characterises a group throughout generations; and that it must largely be, or that many of the elements in it must be, unconscious; whereas the maintenance of *orthodoxy* is a matter which calls for the exercise of all our conscious intelligence. The two will therefore considerably complement each other. Not only is it possible to conceive

of a tradition being definitely bad; a good tradition might, in changing circumstances, become out of date. Tradition has not the means to criticise itself; it may perpetuate much that is trivial or of transient significance as well as what is vital and permanent. And while tradition, being a matter of good habits, is necessarily real only in a social group, orthodoxy exists whether realised in anyone's thought or not. Orthodoxy also, of course, represents a consensus between the living and the dead: but a whole generation might conceivably pass without any orthodox thought; or, as by Athanasius, orthodoxy may be upheld by one man against the world. Tradition may be conceived as a by-product of right living, not to be aimed at directly. It is of the blood, so to speak, rather than of the brain: it is the means by which the vitality of the past enriches the life of the present. In the co-operation of both is the reconciliation of thought and feeling. The concepts of *romantic* and *classic* are both more limited in scope and less definite in meaning. Accordingly they do not carry with them the implication of abso-[528]lute value which those who have defended one against the other would give them: it is only in particular contexts that they can be contrasted in this way, and there are always values more important than any that either of these terms can adequately represent.

[This article is based on one of the Page-Barbour Lectures given by Mr Eliot at the University of Virginia, 1933]

Variants from *ASG*:

Title [No title.]

1 A recent first visit to Virginia afforded me an appropriate occasion to reconsider a subject on which, some fifteen years ago, I wrote an essay entitled 'Tradition and the Individual Talent'.] Some years ago I wrote an essay entitled *Tradition and the Individual Talent*. During the course of the subsequent fifteen years I have discovered, or had brought to my attention, some unsatisfactory phrasing and at least one more than doubtful analogy. But I do not repudiate what I wrote in that essay any more fully than I should expect to do after such a lapse of time. The problem, naturally, does not seem to me so simple as it seemed then, nor could I treat it now as a purely literary one. What I propose to attempt in these three lectures is to outline the matter as I now conceive it. [New para.] It seemed to me appropriate to take this occasion, my first visit to Virginia, for my re-formulation. In the South one finds] You have here

2 and look forward] and I look forward
My first] May I say that my first
their country] your country
better in the South] better here
The Southerners are farther away] You are farther away
they have been] you have been
they have] you have

5 an almost exclusively] an exclusively
 7 [No new para.]
    fluctuating circle] fluctuating circle
    the centre, the family] the centre of the family
    [After 'abstract national patriotism.':] This remark should carry more weight for being uttered by a Yankee.
 8 I wish simply] I wished simply
    fn. 2 all of my opinions] my opinions
10 [No new para.]
    the former] the former group of Liberals
11 as well as possible] as well as it can be
13 indirect perceptions] inferences
    aware of more, but] aware of more but
14 these are not matters] romanticism and classicism are not matters
    matters with which] with which
    an unsettled or a torpid society] an unsettled society
16 what you do not] what you dislike
18 [After 'adequately represent.':] I propose in my second lecture to illustrate these general reflexions by some application to modern English literature.

Shakespeare Criticism

A Companion to Shakespeare Studies, ed. Harley Granville-Barker and G. B. Harrison, [287]–99. Subheaded 'by | T. S. ELIOT'. Publ. Mar. 1934: Gallup B23.
A missing word has been supplied in para.1 where the text as printed is ungrammatical. In the last para. '*Knocking on*' has been corrected to '*Knocking at*'.

I. FROM DRYDEN TO COLERIDGE

I do not propose in this brief sketch to offer a compendium of all that has been written about Shakespeare in three languages in the period I have to cover. For that the reader may turn to Mr Augustus Ralli's *History of Shakespearean Criticism* (Oxford: 2 volumes). The purpose of a contribution on 'Shakespeare Criticism' to a volume such as this, as it seems to me, should be to provide a plan, or pattern, for the reading of the principal texts of Shakespeare criticism. Such a vast amount there is, such a sum of Shakespeare criticism increasing every day at compound interest, that the student of Shakespeare may well wonder whether he should consume his time over Shakespeare criticism at all. The first step, therefore, in offering a scheme of Shakespeare criticism is to give a reason why the student of Shakespeare should read what has been written about him. The second step is to make points of emphasis to show why he should read certain things first, and other things second; rather than occupy himself industriously reading everything that has been written about Shakespeare with equal attention and in perfect chronological order.

Why then, to begin with, should we read all that has been written about Shakespeare, in three hundred years, merely because we want to understand Shakespeare? Should we not rather just soak ourselves in the poetry and drama of Shake-[288]speare, and produce our own opinions, unaided and unencumbered by antiquity, about Shakespeare? But when a poet is a great poet as Shakespeare is, we cannot judge of his greatness unaided; we need both the opinions of other poets, and the diverse views of critics who were not poets, in order to help us to understand. Every view of Shakespeare is an imperfect, because a partial, view. In order to understand these views, we need something more than a good memory. In order to make a pattern of Shakespeare criticism, we need to have some conception of the function of criticism. It is quite impossible to make anything of the history of Shakespeare criticism, unless we can come to some understanding of criticism in general. We have first to grasp what criticism is, and second to grasp the relation between literary and philosophical criticism on the one hand, and literary and textual criticism on the other. With the history of textual criticism, with our increasing knowledge of Shakespeare, of his times, of his texts, of his theatre, I am not to be concerned; but I am concerned with (among other things) the general formulation of the relation between our literary criticism and our scholarly knowledge. In the history of the criticism of Shakespeare which is primarily or strictly literary and dramatic there is a certain 'progress', but only such progress as is possible as a result of the improved texts, the increased knowledge about the conditions of the Elizabethan stage, about the life of Shakespeare himself, and about the times in which he lived. Otherwise, it would be imprudent to say that we are approximating towards a final goal of understanding, after which there will be nothing new to be said; or retrospectively, to assume that A. C. Bradley's criticism of Shakespeare is 'better' than that of Dryden. Shakespeare criticism will always change as the world changes.

The point is really a very simple one, and easy to accept when our eye is on the history of criticism in general; but when we are confining our attention to the history of the criticism of a single great poet like Shakespeare, it is easy to slip into a different assumption. We find it difficult, of course, to believe that the view of Shakespeare to be taken 100 years hence can [289] be very different from our own. On the other hand, we are inclined to assume that the criticism of Shakespeare written before the nineteenth century is less illuminating than that written since. Neither assumption is quite true. There is undeniably an aspect in which early criticism may be seen as the substructure of that of the nineteenth century. We have to admit that the fuller understanding of Shakespeare's greatness came slowly, just as it comes slowly, I believe, in the life of the individual reader. But Shakespeare criticism cannot be appreciated without some understanding of the time and of the place in which it is written, without allowing for its nearness or remoteness in place or time from the object, and for its inevitable development in the future. The views of Shakespeare taken by different men at different times in different places form an integral part of the development and change of European civilisation during the last 300 years. Furthermore, in this study we should, I think, take an attitude which is represented by the popular word *Gestalt* or, as we might say, 'pattern'. That is, we should not begin by the attempt to decide which Shakespeare critics are most illuminating, and ignore the rest; what we have to study is the whole pattern formed by Shakespeare criticism from his own time to ours. In tracing this pattern, certainly, we must study some critics more closely than others, and we may for practical purposes select certain critics who serve to determine the main outline of the pattern; but it should be the whole pattern rather than the individual critic, in which we interest ourselves.

For this reason I shall not attempt, in this space, a compendious history of the subject. I shall simply select certain critics, according to the principle I have indicated above, and leave the reader to fill in the gaps by his own reading. There are obvious points of triangulation. First, there is the testimony of Shakespeare's contemporaries, of which, making due allowance for personal bias, that of Ben Jonson may be our specimen. Second, there is the criticism of the age of Dryden, regarding which, again, we make due allowance for the singular individual genius of Dryden. This is a period in which there is still a criti-[290]cism of the *acted* play (as Pepys's *Diary* attests); when – so far as the distinction holds – there is still dramatic as well as literary criticism; it is still a period in which criticism is directly in simple relation to the object, in contrast with modern criticism which is necessarily as much in relation to other criticism as to the work of Shakespeare itself. In the time of Pope and his contemporaries we feel at once the greater distance of time between the critic and the object, and we begin to feel that criticism has already to take account of criticism as well as of the object criticised. (This period, by the way, has been somewhat maligned: there is no period in which Shakespeare has not been treated with the greatest respect.) Against this, we must offset the critical views of the French in the eighteenth century, where we find, not so much the conflict of one dramatic type with another, as the conflict of English drama with a critical theory which was *not contradicted* by French practice. The French views of the eighteenth century – for example those of Voltaire, Diderot and La

Harpe – have again to be compared with the other French views of the nineteenth century – as those of Taine and Victor Hugo. Meanwhile we find English criticism modified, during the later part of the eighteenth century, by the development of the sentimental attitude. English criticism of the greater part of the nineteenth century is very largely a development from the work of Coleridge, Lamb, Hazlitt and De Quincey; amongst these the influence of Coleridge is very much the most significant; and the explanation of Coleridge is partly found in the German critical thought of the latter part of the eighteenth century.

The student of Shakespeare criticism will be aware of all these views and developments, will endeavour to appreciate their appropriateness each to its place and time, their relations to each other, their limitations of time and cultural sympathy, and will consequently recognise that at different places and times criticism has different work to do. The contemporary of the poet has both obvious limitations and obvious advantages; he is too near to the object to see it clearly or in perspective; his judgement may be distorted by enthusiasm or prejudice; on the [291] other hand he enjoys the advantage of a freshness unspoilt by generations of other men's views. The later critic has both to try to see the object as if for the first time, without the direction of the criticism which has intervened; and also, as I have said, previous criticism is itself a part of the object of his criticism. Hence the critic's problem becomes for every generation more complicated; but also, every generation has a better opportunity for realising how complicated the problem is. At one time, the critical task may be the elaboration of a kind of criticism already initiated; at another, its refutation; at another, the introduction of a new theory, that is to say the exposition of an aspect hitherto overlooked; or again, it may be to combine and to display the pattern afforded by the diverse voices. And in this Shakespeare pattern everything laudatory must find a place, when it is a true praise not previously sounded; and everything derogatory too, even when blunted by misunderstanding, so long as it evinces the temper of an age or a people, and not merely a personal whim.

Of the contemporary comment upon Shakespeare it is that of Ben Jonson which is best remembered and most quoted; and with justice, as Jonson not only had the finest critical mind of his day, but as a dramatist and poet is of so different a kind from Shakespeare that his opinion has a peculiar interest. We may incline to think that Shakespeare's contemporaries underestimated his accomplishment, and were blind to his genius; forgetting that greatness is in a sense the result of time. It has again and again been illustrated that the opinion of contemporaneity is imperfect; and that even when it shows intelligent appreciation and enjoyment, it is apt surprisingly to elevate some quite insignificant figure above a very great one. Our opinions of our own contemporaries will probably seem grotesque to the future. I believe that if I had lived in the seventeenth century, it is quite likely that I should have preferred Beaumont and Fletcher to Shakespeare; though my estimate of their difference to-day is enough to satisfy the most fanatical Shakespearian. What I wish to do is to remove the *stigma* of being a contemporary, and to deprecate the complacency which attaches to being a member of posterity.

[292] And I certainly do not mean to confound all distinctions, or to allow easily all opinions to be right. Whenever Dryden mentions Shakespeare, Dryden's opinion must be treated with respect. To understand his view of Shakespeare we must read *all* of his critical writing. And in particular, in weighing Dryden's opinions, we must spend some time over his collocation of Shakespeare and Fletcher, we must try to come to a point of understanding at which we *see* why it was natural and proper for him to make this frequent parallel and comparison. That is not so much a matter of wide reading and scholarship, although we must make ourselves very familiar with the plays of Fletcher, and with the plays, as well as the criticism, of Dryden: it is a matter of the exercise of the critical imagination. There are critics who are definitely wrongheaded. Thomas Rymer was a man of considerable learning, and not destitute of taste, when he left his taste to look after itself; but a false theory of what the drama should be, of what he *ought* to like, came very near to paralysing that function altogether, and made him the butt of his own and subsequent times. Nevertheless, I believe that the falsity of his dramatic theory, and the absurdity of the conclusions he drew from it, have had the unfortunate effect – as the extremity of false theorising is apt to do – of sometimes confirming people in their own false opinions merely because they assured themselves too confidently that whatever Rymer did not believe must be right.

As soon as we enter the eighteenth century we feel a change in the atmosphere of criticism; and in reading the criticism itself we are aware that Shakespeare is beginning to be more read than seen upon the stage. Addison calls attention to a point of detail (the crowing of the cock in *Hamlet*) which has probably, we feel, struck him rather in the reading than at a performance; the attention of the eighteenth-century critic in England is rather on the poetry than on the drama. The observations of Pope are of value and interest, because they are by Pope. If other eighteenth-century critics are to be read, it is not so much for their individual contributions, but as a reminder that there was no period in which Shakespeare fell into neglect. There is [293] indeed some development. Shakespeare begins to be written about in greater detail and at greater length, and apart from any more general discussion of the drama; he is, in the eighteenth century, gradually *detached* from his environment, from the other dramatists, and from a time which had become unfamiliar. And it may be mentioned, though this is outside my province, that during the eighteenth century the standard of scholarship and editorship was rising. But the major part of eighteenth-century criticism down to Johnson, and almost all the French criticism of Shakespeare during this period, strike me as unprofitable reading unless we enlarge our interests. The criticism of Shakespeare at any epoch is a most useful means of inducting us into the way in which people of that time enjoyed their contemporary poetry; and the approval which they express of Shakespeare indicates that he possessed some of the qualities that they cultivated in their own verse, and perhaps other qualities that they would have liked to find there. A study of the opinions of Voltaire, La Harpe and Diderot about Shakespeare may help to increase our appreciation of Racine; it is quite certain that we can never make head or tail of these opinions unless we enjoy Corneille and Racine. And I do not mean merely a polite acquaintance with their plays, or a fluent ability to declaim their verse; I mean the immediate delight in their poetry. That is an experience which may arrive late in life, or oftener not at all; if it comes – I am speaking, of course, of Anglo-Saxon experience only – it is an illumination. And it is far from corrupting our pleasure in Shakespeare, or reducing our admiration. Poetry does not do these things to other poetry: the beauty of the one kind only enhances the lustre of another.

To pass from Dryden to Johnson is to make the journey from one oasis to another. After the critical essays of Dryden, the Preface to Shakespeare by Samuel Johnson is the next of the great pieces of criticism to read. One would willingly resign the honour of an Abbey burial for the greater honour of words like the following, from a man of the greatness of their author:

> The poet, of whose works I have undertaken the revision, may not begin to assume the dignity of an ancient, and claim the privilege of [294] established fame and prescriptive veneration. He has long outlived his century, the term commonly fixed as the test of literary merit. Whatever advantages he might once derive from personal allusions, local customs, or temporary opinions, have for many years been lost; and every topic of merriment, or motive of sorrow, which the modes of artificial life afforded him, now only obscure the scenes which they once illuminated. The effects of favour and competition are at an end; the tradition of his friendships and his enmities has perished; his works support no opinion with arguments, nor supply any faction with invectives; they can neither indulge vanity, nor gratify malignity; but are read without any other

reason than the desire of pleasure, and are therefore praised only as pleasure is obtained; yet, thus unassisted by interest or passion, they have passed through variations of taste and changes of manners, and, as they devolved from one generation to another, have received new honours at every transmission.

What a valedictory and obituary for any man to receive! My point is that if you assume that the classical criticism of England was grudging in its praise of Shakespeare, I say that no poet can ask more of posterity than to be greatly honoured by the great; and Johnson's words about Shakespeare are great honour.

Johnson refutes those critics – and only Johnson could do it – who had thought that Shakespeare violated propriety, here and there, with his observation that Shakespeare's 'scenes are occupied only by men, who act and think as the reader thinks that he himself should have spoken or acted on the same occasion'. But a little further Johnson makes another most remarkable (but not sufficiently remarked) observation, to which several subsequent editors and publishers, even to our own time, seem to have paid not sufficient deference:

> The players, who in their edition divided our author's works into comedies, histories, and tragedies, seem not to have defined the three kinds by any very exact or definite ideas.

To those who would divide periods, and segregate men, neatly into classical and romantic groups, I commend the study of this sentence, and of what Johnson says afterwards about the relation of the tragic to the comic. This Preface to Shakespeare was published in 1765, and Voltaire, still writing ten years and [295] more after this event, was maintaining an opposite point of view. Johnson saw deeper than Voltaire, in this as in most matters. Johnson perceived, though not explicitly, that the distinctions of tragic and comic are superficial – for *us*; though he did not know how important they were for the Greeks; for he did not know that they sprang from a difference in ritual. As a poet – and he was a fine poet – Johnson is at the end of a tether. But as a critic – and he was greater as critic than as poet – Johnson has a place comparable to that of Cowley as poet: in that we cannot say whether to classify him as the last of one kind or the first of another. There is one sentence which we may boggle over. Johnson says:

> In tragedy he (*i.e.* Shakespeare) often writes, with great appearance of toil and study, what is written at last with little felicity; but, in his comic scenes, he seems to produce, without labour, what no labour can improve.

This is an opinion which we cannot lightly dismiss. Johnson is quite aware that the alternation of 'tragic' and 'comic' is something more than an alternation; he perceives that something different and new is produced. 'The interchanges of mingled scenes seldom fail to produce the intended vicissitudes of passion'. *'Through all these denominations of the drama Shakespeare's mode of composition is the same.'* But why should Johnson have thought that Shakespeare's comic parts were spontaneous, and that his tragic parts were laboured? Here, it seems to me, Johnson, by his simple integrity, in being wrong has happened upon some truth much deeper than he knew. For to those who have experienced the full horror of life, tragedy is still inadequate. Sophocles felt more of it than he could express, when he wrote *Oedipus the King*; Shakespeare, when he wrote *Hamlet*; and Shakespeare had the advantage of being able to employ his grave-diggers. In the end, horror and laughter may be one – only when horror and laughter have become as horrible and laughable as they can be; and – whatever the conscious intentions of the authors – you may laugh or shudder over *Oedipus* or *Hamlet* or *King Lear* – or both at once; then only do you perceive that the aim of the comic and the tragic dramatist is the same: [296] they are equally serious. So do the meanings of words change, as we inspect them, that we may even come to see Molière in some lights as a more serious dramatist than Corneille or Racine; Wycherley as equally serious (in this sense) with Marlowe. All this is suggested to me by the words of Samuel Johnson which I have quoted. What Plato perceived has not been noticed by subsequent dramatic critics; the dramatic poet uses the conventions of tragic and comic poetry; so far as these are the conventions of his day; there is potential comedy in Sophocles and potential tragedy in Aristophanes, and otherwise they would not be such good tragedians or comedians as they are. It might be added that when you have comedy and tragedy united in the wrong way, or separated in the wrong way, you get sentiment or amusement. The distinction between the tragic and the comic is an account of the way in which we try to live; when we get below it, as in *King Lear*, we have an account of the way in which we do live.

The violent change between one period and another is both progress and retrogression. I have quoted only a few sentences from Johnson's Preface to Shakespeare; but I think they represent the view of a mature, if limited, personality. The next phase of English criticism of Shakespeare is prefaced from Germany. I must add, however, that the influence of German criticism upon English at this point can easily be exaggerated. It is in no wise to belittle the value of this criticism, if we affirm that there was rather a similarity of outlook, and a natural sympathy between the German and the English mind, in approaching Shakespeare, which we do not find with the French critics. It would be rash to assert that the German mind is better qualified to appreciate Shakespeare than is the French; but one less comprehensive generalisation I believe can be made. For the French mind, the approach to Shakespeare has normally been by way of a comparison to Corneille and Racine, if not to Molière. Now for the Frenchman the plays of his classical age are primarily, to this day, plays to be acted; and his memories of them are of the theatre at least as much as of the library. For the Englishman of the nineteenth century the plays of Shake-[297]speare have been dramatic poems to be read, rather than plays to be seen; and for most of us to-day the great majority of the plays are solely literary acquaintances. Furthermore, the French have always had this background of their own great dramatic achievement. But the Germans have never had this background of native authority in the drama; their acquaintance with Shakespeare was formed in the study; and until the reputation of Goethe was firmly established throughout Europe they had no native dramatic author with whom to compare him. For these reasons alone, without any rash generalisations about the Gallic and the Teutonic mind, we should expect the German attitude to be more sympathetic.

But the kind of criticism which arises rather from reading than from attendance at the theatre arose in England spontaneously. The first striking example of this sort of criticism, a remarkable piece of writing which deserves meditation, and which commands our respect whether we agree with its conclusions or not, is Morgann's Essay *On the Dramatic Character of Sir John Falstaff* (1777). For the case which Morgann attempts to make out, I refer the reader to Morgann himself. My point is that Morgann's essay is the first conspicuous member of a long line of criticism dealing with the characters of the personages in the plays, considering not only their actions within the play itself, but inferring from their behaviour on the stage what their general character is, that is to say, how they would behave in other circumstances. This is a perfectly legitimate form of criticism, though liable to abuses; at its best, it can add very much to our enjoyment of the moments of the characters' life which are given in the scene, if we feel this richness of reality in them; and at its worst, it becomes an irrelevance and distracts us from our enjoyment of the play.

The first of the great German critics, Lessing, tended to make of Shakespeare almost a national issue, for it was he who affirmed that English literature, and in particular Shakespeare, was more congenial than French literature and drama to the German taste. The German critics in general insist upon the naturalness and fidelity to reality of Shakespeare's plays. Herder, a critic [298] of considerable understanding, begins to appreciate the existence of something like a poetic pattern, in calling attention to the fitness between the passions of the personages and the scenery in which these passions are enacted. But what interests me in this place is not a detailed valuation of the opinions of the German critics of this period – not even the opinions of the Schlegels and Goethe – but a consideration of the general tendency of their opinions. Neglecting the circumstances in which the plays were written – and indeed the historical information was not available – and paying little attention to their dramatic merits, the Germans concentrated their attention chiefly upon the philosophical significance of character. They penetrate to a deeper level than that of the simple moral values attributed to great literature by earlier times, and foreshadow the 'criticism of life' definition by Arnold. Furthermore, it is not until this period that an element of 'mystery' is recognised in Shakespeare. That is one of the gifts of the Romantic Movement to Shakespeare criticism, and one for which, with all its excesses, we have reason to be grateful. It is hardly too much to say that the German critics and Coleridge, by their criticism of Shakespeare, radically altered the reflective attitude of criticism towards poetry.

The writings of Coleridge upon Shakespeare must be read entire; for it is impossible to understand Shakespeare criticism to this day, without a familiar acquaintance with Coleridge's lectures and notes. Coleridge is an authority of the kind whose influence extends equally towards good and bad. It would be unjust to father upon him, without further ceremony, the psycho-analytic school of Shakespeare criticism; the study of individual characters which was begun by Morgann, to the neglect of the pattern and meaning of the whole play, was bound to lead to some such terminus, and we do not blame Morgann for that. But when Coleridge released the truth that Shakespeare already in *Venus and Adonis* and *Lucrece* gave proof of a 'most profound, energetic and *philosophic* mind' he was perfectly right, if we use these adjectives rightly, but he supplied a dangerous stimulant to the more adventurous. [299] 'Philosophic' is of course not the right word, but it cannot simply be erased: you must find another word to put in its place, and the word has not yet been found. The sense of the profundity of Shakespeare's 'thought', or of his thinking-in-images, has so oppressed some critics that they have been forced to explain themselves by unintelligibles.

I have not spoken of Hazlitt, Lamb and De Quincey; that is because I wished to isolate Coleridge as perhaps the greatest single figure in Shakespeare criticism down to the present day. In a conspectus like the present, only the most salient points can be more than mentioned; and Hazlitt, Lamb and De Quincey, for my present purposes, do but make a constellation about the primary star of Coleridge. Their work is chiefly important as reinforcing the influence of Coleridge; though De Quincey's *Knocking at the Gate in Macbeth* is perhaps the best known single piece of criticism of Shakespeare that has been written. But for the student of Shakespeare criticism, the writing of all of these men is among those documents that are to be read, and not merely read about.

[Samuel Taylor Coleridge, 1772–1834]

Sent to Sir Ivan Charteris, chairman of the trustees of the National Portrait Gallery, on 17 Mar. 1934, as a biographical sketch for the verso of a postcard depicting the 1795 portrait of Coleridge by Peter Vandyke on the recto. Signed 'T. S. ELIOT'. Not in Gallup, but would be C355a.

When five years old had read the *Arabian Nights*. Christ's Hospital and Cambridge. Metaphysician and poet. His life was ill-regulated; weak, slothful, a voracious reader, he contracted an unhappy marriage and much later the habit of taking laudanum. Described his own character in his great 'Ode to Dejection' (1802). The greatest English literary critic, he was also the greatest intellectual force of his time. Probably influenced Newman, Maurice, and the Young Tories; and died as the guest of Mr Gillman of Highgate.

A Commentary

Review of *Évocations* by Henri Massis (1931).
C., 13. 52 (Apr. 1934), 451–4. Signed 'T. S. E.' Gallup C357.

I have been reading (it is not a new book, for it was published in 1931) the *Évocations* (*Souvenirs 1905–1911*) of our friend Henri Massis. The book should be, for anybody, an interesting and valuable document upon a period; but has a more personal interest for me, inasmuch as M. Massis is my contemporary, and the period of which he writes includes the time of my own brief residence in Paris. I remember the appearance of M. Massis's first conspicuous piece of writing; though I was ignorant at the time, as were most people, that the 'Agathon' who attacked the New Sorbonne was a name covering the joint authorship of Henri Massis and Alfred de Tarde. At the beginning of his reminiscences Massis quotes from Péguy: *je vais fonder un parti, le parti des hommes de quarante ans; vous en serez aussi, mon garçon. Un jour, vous serez mûr.* I wonder whether we should make that prediction, with equal assurance, to our juniors to-day.

Younger generations can hardly realise the intellectual desert of England and America during the first decade and more of this century. In the English desert, to be sure, flourished a few tall and handsome cactuses, as well as James and Conrad (for whom the climate, in contrast to their own, was relatively favourable); in America the desert extended, *à perte de vue*, without the least prospect of even desert vegetables. The predominance of Paris was incontestable. Poetry, it is true, was somewhat in eclipse; but there was a most exciting variety of ideas. Anatole France and Rémy de Gourmont still exhibited their learning, and provided types of scepticism for younger men to be attracted by and to repudiate; Barrès was at the height of his influence, and of his rather transient reputation. Péguy, more or less Bergsonian *and* Catholic *and* Socialist, had just become important, and the young were further distracted by Gide and Claudel. Vildrac, Romains, Duhamel, experimented with verse which seemed hopeful, though it was always, I think, disappointing; something was expected of Henri Franck, the early [452] deceased author of *La Danse devant l'arche*. At the Sorbonne, Faguet was an authority to be attacked violently; the sociologists, Durkheim, Lévy-Bruhl, held new doctrines; Janet was the great psychologist; at the Collège de France, Loisy enjoyed his somewhat scandalous distinction; and over all swung the spider-like figure of Bergson. His metaphysic was said to throw some light upon the new ways of painting, and discussion of Bergson was apt to be involved with discussion of Matisse and Picasso.

I am willing to admit that my own retrospect is touched by a sentimental sunset, the memory of a friend coming across the Luxembourg Gardens in the late afternoon, waving a branch of lilac, a friend who was later (so far as I could find out) to be mixed with the mud of Gallipoli. And I know that like all other periods, this period does boil down. Nevertheless, it seems to me that it did provide for the young such experiences as justified Péguy's prediction, *un jour, vous serez mûr*. To-day, such words seem to read like a counsel of perfection. Our occupation with immediate social, political and economic issues to-day is a necessity, but a regrettable one; for it tends to abbreviate and confuse that period of adolescence in which a man is acquiring understanding by submitting himself, in a leisurely way, to one intellectual influence after another. I know that for some natures the diversity of influences of Paris in those days – a real diversity, not merely a division into political groups – was too strong: the gentle Jacques Rivière fell a victim to the opposing forces of Gide and Claudel, and never could make up his mind. Péguy had the ability to combine a variety of doctrines by a force of imagination which sometimes concealed and usually atoned for incoherence. Some, like Ernest Psichari, seem too facile a result of some such formula as: Charles de Foucauld *plus* Rudyard Kipling. But an atmosphere of diverse opinions seems to me on the whole favourable to the maturing of the individual; because when he does come to a conviction, he does so not by 'taking a ticket', but by making up his own mind.

[453] There is something to be said, in these days, for individualism. I do not mean what ordinarily passes by that name, simply a party of folk huddling together to be independent in company. Most 'individualists', I dare say, have never held an opinion contrary to that of the other members of their small immediate society, nor have ever gone into the wilderness for the purpose of making up their minds. A number of eminent Liberals of all three parties have recently signed a manifesto in favour of 'democratic' government. I have considerable sympathy with them, with reference to the recent developments which cause them alarm; but I cannot feel that their convictions are fundamental enough to cut much ice; and the juvenile enthusiasm of their opponents may only be heated to a higher degree by such pronouncements. To surrender individual judgment to a Church is a hard thing; to surrender individual responsibility to a party is, for many men, a pleasant stimulant and sedative. And those who have once experienced this sweet intoxication are not easily brought back to the difficult path of thinking for themselves, and of respecting their own person and that of others.

The intellectual primacy of Paris is not what it was in the days of which I have been speaking; and I cannot expect Paris to mean for young people now what it meant for us *quadrégenaires*. But the very failure of the recent disturbances goes to indicate, amongst other things less hopeful to contemplate, that the French are still individual human beings. There was an emotional upheaval of indignant citizens, who, in order to demonstrate at all, had to sort themselves out into half a dozen warring groups, occasionally united against the police and military; just as in 1910 I remember the *camelots* cheering the *cuirassiers* who were sent to disperse them, because they represented the Army, all the time that they were trying to stampede their horses. Perhaps France will be the last country to be conquered by the mob. A good deal has been said, more by Frenchmen than by foreigners, of journalistic corruption; but perhaps some-[454]thing is to be said for a variety of corruption, if you have newspapers enough, as against uniformity of control in a few hands.

Let us therefore say a word for diversity of opinion. What ultimately matters is the salvation of the individual soul. You may not like this principle; but if you abjure it, you will probably in the end get something that you like less. The world tends now to scramble for its salvation by taking a ticket.

The effort of some of the younger men of letters in Paris – I have in mind the groups of *Esprit*, *L'Ordre nouveau*, *L'Homme nouveau*, and more isolated writers like Thierry Maulnier – show a valuable determination not to surrender individuality to any of the prevailing tendencies of the hour, at the same time that they avoid the Liberalism that still practises its shrill choruses in England. We hope to keep in touch with such current thought in France, and present it from time to time to our readers.

The Story of the Pageant

Publ. in the programme of the *The Rock*
at Sadler's Wells (28 May 1934), p. [7]. Gallup B24.

The Rock is not a pageant in the usual sense. It does not consist of a number of historical scenes or tableaux in order of time. The aim is not merely to remind people that churches have been built in the past, but to employ the historical scenes to reinforce, in appropriate places, the emphasis upon the needs of the present.

The direct action of the play is concerned with the efforts and difficulties of a group of bricklayers engaged in building a modern church. At the beginning of the play they are seen working upon the foundations; later the half-built church is shown. When the builders have finished, decorators of various kinds complete the work, and the church is shown ready for its dedication. And during the course of construction the builders experience difficulties – from poor soil for the foundations, from the fear of lack of money to continue the work, from an agitator and a tumultuous mob, from critics who complain that the church is too ornate, or that it is too 'modern'. Besides the immediate troubles experienced by the group of workmen represented by Bert, Alfred and Edwin, the more general difficulties of the Church in the Modern World are symbolised in the action: the difficulties of the Church opposed, ignored, or interfered with by the secular tendencies of the present age.

A Chorus, as in Greek Tragedy, comments in verse from time to time upon the needs and troubles of the Church to-day, and upon the action. This Chorus opens both parts of the play, and from time to time appeals to 'The Rock', who, though he takes little part in the action, symbolises the permanence and continuity of the Church of God, and its resistance to the forces of evil and dissolution.

After the opening chorus, and some words of encouragement and consolation by 'The Rock', a chant of Builders is heard, followed by a chant of the Unemployed, to which the Builders reply. The light then discovers the modern bricklayers discussing their work and many other things as well. A remark by one of them leads to an 'experiment with time', in which the builders find themselves spectators of the conversion of Sabert, King of London, and his Saxon followers, by the Roman missionary Mellitus. After this scene they resume their work, but under great difficulties: the ground is swampy. To them appears Rahere, the builder of St Bartholomew's, and after reassuring them he and his men give them supernatural aid in the work. They are next confronted by social opposition, in the form of an agitator and a mob; and their momentary conflict with the mob calls up to our memory, as so upon the stage as the following scene, the troubles of Nehemiah in rebuilding the Wall of Jerusalem.

In the second part the building (interspersed with other historical scenes) is completed. A scene of the Reformation reminds us of the dangers of destruction. A group of scenes towards the end recall the dedication of other churches: Westminster Abbey, St Michael Paternoster Royal, and St Paul's. At the end 'The Rock' reappears; and the play is completed by the Bishop's benediction of the audience.

Signed T. S. ELIOT
MARTIN BROWNE

A Commentary

C., 13. 53 (July 1934), 624–30. Signed 'T. S. E.' Gallup C363.

The aims of the English Association are set forth as follows:

(a) To promote the due recognition of English as an essential element in the national education.
(b) To discuss methods of teaching English and the correlation of School and University work.
(c) To encourage and facilitate advanced study in English literature and language.
(d) To unite all those who are interested in English studies; to bring teachers into contact with one another and with writers and readers who do not teach; and to induce those who are not themselves engaged in teaching to use their influence in the cause of English as a part of education.

We may presume that it is to forward one or more of these aims that the English Association has published an anthology of 'modern verse' entitled *The Modern Muse*.

At first sight, these aims appear harmless enough, and even commendable. After a little reflection, considering the four points together, the suspicion creeps into our mind that one or two rather important questions have been begged. We should like, for instance, to make up our opinion as to what is the *due* 'recognition of English', before we commit ourselves to promoting it. We ought indeed to have some notion of what we mean by the 'national education'. Who are the people who should be taught English, and what English, and how much should they be taught, and are they all to be taught the same things and in the same way? And if we aim to 'discuss methods', as we certainly should do, ought we not to aim also at coming to a conclusion? What is meant by 'advanced study'? Who ought to pursue it, and why? And should we not have a fifth point: to 'discuss' the relation of the study of English to other studies?

The absence of these further questions from the agenda does not justify us in coming to any conclusion about the activities of the English Association; but it may perhaps justify us in asking the English Association for some further [625] justification of itself. The most remarkable achievement of the English Association hitherto has been two previous collections of verse, *Poems of To-day*, First Series and Second Series. The Association boasts that the first series has sold 350,000 copies; the second 132,000 copies. And it asserts, also on the jacket of the present volume, that *Poems of To-day* 'has probably had the largest sale, both among the general public and *in schools* (italics ours), of any anthology of modern verse, not only in our lifetime but in the whole history of the publishing of anthologies'. An examination of these three ignoble compilations must lead us to ask the English Association to do something more than justify its existence. Such a request might be made of that comparatively inactive congregation, the Royal Society of Literature. But of the English Association we must ask whether it can show any reason why its meddling with British and American poetry should not be denounced.

The prefatory matter to *The Modern Muse* is more moderate in tone than that of *Poems of To-day*, and does not contain such remarkable specimens of flamboyant bad writing. Nevertheless, it contrives to concentrate a notable amount of nonsense on one page.

> In each of the continents are vast numbers of persons whose mother tongue is English, and it is for the purpose of quickening among these peoples the sense of the greatness of their common heritage

that this collection of contemporary poetry gathered from the four quarters of the globe has been made.

What wandering mind could have conceived such a thought as that! The effect of this queer anthology upon the more lively minds among the 'vast numbers' speaking various English dialects over the 'globe', should be to impress them with the prodigious quantity of junk which our 'common heritage' is accumulating. And a phrase like 'the four quarters of the globe' to appear in an official announcement of the *English* Association! The manifesto then strikes a note of profundity:

> [626] The present century has seen events which have deeply influenced human thought everywhere. The Great War and its consequences have shaken the world from end to end. Such experiences could not fail to find expression in poetry, and the interest in the present volume should be all the greater in that it illustrates these reactions among peoples living in lands far apart but speaking one language.

It is no doubt to illustrate the effect of the Great War and its consequences that the anthologists have included the following address to a mole:

> Did the wonder of the day
> Beat like a voice upon thy shuttered soul
> To tell thee cruelly that thou wert blind,
> And make thee know thyself a little mole
> With pushing snout,
> From worlds of light shut out?

Of course the anthology does anything but illustrate the effects which it pretends to illustrate. For one thing, some of the better poems in the volume were written before the War. For some of the others, it would defy criticism to discover *what* the effects of the War were. More of the poems illustrate merely the fact that bad poets are not really *influenced* by anything, being too obtuse. But in the next paragraph the anthologist unconsciously surrenders all pretence to critical judgement:

> The anthology is intended to exhibit the range and variety of poetry among contemporary writers of English throughout the world. While a standard of excellence has been kept in mind, the main aim has been to make the selection fully representative of the various countries. To this aim must be attributed the presence of poems which are unusual in form, structure, and subject-matter; and it should be remembered under what conditions, geographical, political, and social, they have been written.

This is the most astonishing confession by an anthology-maker that I have ever read. This anthology issued by the English Association does not pretend to be an anthology chosen from among the best poems written in our time. Its [627] aim has been to represent the various countries! And then we are told that it is to *this* consideration that we owe the presence of poems unusual in form, structure and subject-matter. (I wonder what is the distinction intended between 'form' and 'structure'.) Had the anthology aimed at including merely the most excellent poems, we are given to understand, no poems unusual in form, structure or subject-matter would have been chosen.

Another critic has pointed out that several of the most interesting modern poets have been omitted. That seems to me a minor fault in this collection. What is more deplorable is that several of the best modern poets have *not* been omitted. Had they been omitted, the public might less easily be gulled into accepting this anthology. The book might even have provided, for relaxed moments, some innocent merriment. It is the mixture of good and bad that makes the book dangerous. There is a sense in which the word 'catholicity' means something pernicious, and in this sense the book is fully catholic. The editors do not show bad taste: they show no taste at all.

The occasion is much more serious than the appearance of one more bad anthology. This book has a kind of official sanction; and as we are assured that its monstrous predecessors have circulated in schools, there is good reason to believe that this volume will follow them. In compiling a collection of verse for which such vast popularity is anticipated, the English Association should have felt a sense of responsibility towards the public. It should have taken as one of its aims, instead of the brainless balderdash of its preface, the aim of educating the public taste. It might not sell 132,000 copies if it did. Instead, it would perform a public service. It has preferred, in a spirit of addled Imperialism and Anglo-American amity of the most futile kind, to offer a marketable ware to English-speaking people in 'the four quarters of the globe'; and to talk about it in the language used by politicians without policy, whose only programme is to stay in power.

[628] The whole problem of education is involved: in the long run the most important problem of society. We seem nowadays to be committed to the task of giving some sort of education to everybody. Education is a training of the mind and of the sensibility, an intellectual and an emotional discipline. In a society in which this discipline is neglected, a society which uses words instead of thoughts and feelings, one may expect any sort of religious, moral, social and political aberration, and eventual decomposition or petrification. And we seem

to have little to hope from the official representatives of education.

Sir Charles Petrie has written a brisk and readable book on *Monarchy* (Eyre & Spottiswoode, 10s. 6d. net), which is just good enough for one to wish that it might have been better. Perhaps the chief faults of the book are negative: a lack of philosophy and a lack of passion. The result is that the author gives the appearance of preaching, not to the converted, but to those born in the faith; those who like to think about the matter a little, but not too long or too deeply. The book is commended by the publishers as being 'outspoken' (an adjective given popularity by the Dean of St Paul's); and in some matters of detail that is true; yet the total effect is that of something cautious and tentative. Sir Charles gives some interesting information about the actual role of kings in modern European history, but does not concern himself much with earlier writers on the subject. It is refreshing, certainly, to meet a Bt, M.A. (Oxon.), F.R.Hist.Soc. (for this is his title-page description) who is acquainted with the work of Maurras, Benoist, Bainville and Gaxotte. But the name of Chateaubriand occurs only once, in a not very enlightening connexion; and the names of Bonald and de Maistre are not to be found in the index. He mentions that 'of late there has been, in France itself, a very decided reaction' against the Liberal interpretation of history; yet the name of Fusterl de Coulanges, again, is not to be found in the index. And his book is hardly 'controversial' (the other [629] adjective used by his publishers). It is, I fear, more likely to give the impression that royalty is an 'institution worth preserving', rather than a form of government.

This suspicion is increased by the offhand way in which he speaks of dictatorships. His chief ground of objection to dictatorships is that they cannot last, rather than that he finds in them anything essentially incompatible with the principle of kingship. Yet it is possible to argue that, while they do last, they are a violation of that principle. Furthermore, Sir Charles does not distinguish between the two types of dictatorship: those which are merely *de facto*, and exist because, in some peculiar situation in which a country may find itself, no other form of government will for the moment work; and those which create *une mystique* (there is no English equivalent for this useful word of Péguy's). The Roman Empire (with its Imperial deification) lasted a long time; and I see no *a priori* reason why the system of government of Russia should collapse merely because it is a dictatorship. But perhaps Sir Charles would call the Russian government an oligarchy. In any case, what is to be the attitude of a royalist towards any system under which absolute submission to the will of a Leader is made an article of faith or a qualification for office? Surely the royalist can admit only one higher authority than the Throne, which is the Church.

The problem of Church and State, indeed, is quite ignored in Sir Charles Petrie's book; and this omission alone is enough to render it inefficient. It is the distinction of Maurras to have recognised the capital importance of this question, though his method of treating it is open to objection. A purely secular theory of kingship runs the risk of being no more than a theory, based on experience, of what is most expedient. Even on this ground, the author of *Monarchy* might have experimented with new ideas, such as vesting the ownership of land and of the materials of production in the Crown, instead of that questionable proprietor, the nation. He might further have shown how a devotion to the Throne (as distinct from personal devotion to a popular [630] King) may act as a check and balance upon devotion to the party, the party leader, or the State. A young French royalist, Thierry Maulnier, has recently remarked in '1934':

> The law of French society does not consist in an utter devotion (*un dévouement total*) – however enthusiastic and heroic this devotion may be – of the individual to the State, but in the restoration of a right equilibrium and of right relations between the State and the individual.

To which the commentator of *L'Action Française* adds: 'whilst protecting the rights, the duties, the forces and the amenities of the family'.

[*The Oxford Handbook of Religious Knowledge*]

Review of *The Oxford Handbook of Religious Knowledge* (1934).
C., 13. 53 (July 1934), 709. 'Signed erroneously: T[homas]. McG[reevy]': Gallup C364.

This handbook was prepared by a committee, at the request of the Bishop of Oxford, for the use of teachers (of pupils over the age of eleven) in that diocese. But the task has been performed so admirably that the book is to be recommended also to parents for private use, for introducing their children to Bible reading and the Prayer Book: indeed, there are few of the laity who would not find it profitable for themselves.

[*The Mystical Doctrine of St John of the Cross*]

Review of *The Mystical Doctrine of St. John of the Cross*. Being an abridgement of his works as translated into English by David Lewis and revised by Dom Benedict Zimmerman, O.D.C. With an introduction by R. H. Steuart, S.J. (1934).

C., 13. 53. (July 1934), 709–10. 'Signed, erroneously: T[homas]. McG[reevy]': Gallup C365.

The description above indicates the method which has been followed. The abridgement is excellent. For anyone who wishes to make a study of the work of St John (a Spanish writer little known in this [710] country) this is an admirable introduction; and for ordinary educated people, will give all that they need to know. While very few persons ever reach a stage so advanced that they can adopt St John of the Cross as their guide, and must be content to use more elementary manuals of meditation, there is great advantage in acquiring some notion of what are the higher stages of the contemplative life. And this convenient little book can be slipped into the pocket when leaving for the weekend or the summer holidays.

[*A Christian Sociology for To-day*]

Review of *A Christian Sociology for To-day* (an abridged edition of *Faith and Society*) by Maurice B. Reckitt (1934).

C., 13. 53 (July 1934), 710. 'Signed, erroneously: T[homas]. McG[reevy]': Gallup C366.

Faith and Society was, as a matter of fact, much too long a book. Mr Reckitt devoted so much space to an account of various organisations and movements in this field, as to be in danger of defeating his own purpose; the reader might have been tempted to wonder why, with so much attempted, so little seems to have been done. In its present form the book is a necessary addition to any library on the subject, either public or private.

In Sincerity and Earnestness: New Britain as I See It

New Britain (25 July 1934), 274. Signed 'T. S. Eliot'. Not in Gallup, but would be C366a.

I rather wish that these remarks were not to be headed 'In Sincerity and Earnestness', because I should like to think that my sincerity and earnestness could be taken for granted; but that is the Editor's business, not mine.

I suffer, like most of my generation, in not having been brought up to think about politics and economics. (But if we had, we would certainly have been taught wrong.) It seemed that politics could be left to an inferior class of people, actuated by vanity and love of power, who liked politics; and it seemed that economics was a special study for a set of people who were studying it in order to make a living by teaching it to the next generation who were studying it in order to make a living by teaching it, &c.

It is probable that the politicians, bankers, economists, &c., of tomorrow will be the same sort of people as those who pursue these vocations today. They are the best qualified, for the primary reason that they are the sort of people who enjoy working these machines. They probably work the machine as well as it can be worked; and a later generation of them will probably provide the best people to run a better machine. They are moderately efficient at minor repairs and road troubles. But they are the last people to believe that any better machine can be made. That is human nature.

I do not suggest that all vocations will remain the same in New Britain. The Art of Newspaper Proprietorship will be a different art practised by different people; and the Art of Advertising will become a very minor profession indeed.

From the Christian point of view there are two parallel postulates to be made: (1) That the Christian Life is not merely the affair of the individual, and that 'Christian feeling' alone will not make a bad piece of machinery work. (2) A mere change of machinery is not going to get us anywhere without a revival of Christian ideals and Christian ways of living. It is an unpleasant fact to face: but you cannot leave all the work to Professor Soddy, or Major Douglas, or anyone else; you have got to do a lot of work upon yourself.

It is ridiculous to expect the majority of people to lead Christian lives under present conditions. It is extremely difficult even for the very poor and for the stupid; it is almost impossible for the well-to-do and those who pass for intelligent.

As a postscript to point (2), it is unlikely that any change of social machinery which is more than tinkering would fail to modify profoundly our spiritual life. Only, these modifications, even when plausibly offering immediate good, may just as easily work for the worse as for the better.

The Churches cannot, of course, pick out any one political form and maintain that it is essential for the Christian life; but they can and should denounce any political form which is either hostile to or subversive of the Christian Life. Nothing accordingly need be said about the necessary Christian attitude towards Communism, except to repeat the obvious warning against accepting any other form simply because it is anti-Communistic. As for Fascism, we have been told by its English exponent that it 'synthesises' the Nietzschean and the Christian doctrines. The Christian ought to know what to think of a doctrine which 'synthesises' Christianity with something else. And the Christian cannot possibly agree that any simply political reorganisation can be 'the greatest cause and the greatest impulse in the world'.

There is another ground for rejecting Communism and Fascism, which is simply that they do not appear to have any solution, or even any awareness, of our real and urgent economic problems. Indeed, I gather from an article in *The Adelphi* that Social Credit Reform is to be deprecated because it might make people so contented that they would turn the deaf ear to the spiritual consolations of Communism.

While the Churches cannot advocate any particular political system, or any particular economic machinery, they can and should oppose openly all systems that make Christian virtue more difficult of practice. The present system is worse than that: it elevates Christian sin into worldly virtue.

We cannot expect to extirpate the roots of sin, to kill the passions of acquisitiveness and love of power. But we can at least establish some order in which these vices do not receive the sanction of society. We cannot abolish social distinctions; but we can abolish an order in which the distinctions are merely between the wealthy, the well-to-do, the poor, and the destitute.

We must remember that voluntary poverty is a high Christian state; but that involuntary misery or wage-slavery is an anti-Christian state. And in condemning usury and love of power we must avoid the company of people who condemn usury and love of power because they have no inclination towards them, and who condone gluttony and lust because they have a mind to them – inverting the Puritanism denounced in *Hudibras*.

We need both intelligence and passion. Otherwise we are helpless against unintelligent passion. Both Fascism and Communism exhibit a diversion, to material ends, of passion which should only be devoted to religious ends. There are many people of intelligence, goodwill and public spirit who cannot prostitute their emotions in this way, though they lack Christian Faith. These people are with us: but we must remember that it is the Christians who must provide the emotional intensity which is necessary. And we must also remember that it is our Christian duty to think as well as to feel; to think as clearly, as consistently and as thoroughly as we can.

John Marston

Publ., unsigned, in *TLS*, 1695 (26 July 1934), [517]–18: Gallup C367.
Revised in *EE*, and repr. from there in *ED* and *SE* (1951).
See below, pp. 852–61.

The Problem of Education

Harvard Advocate, 121. 1 (Freshman Number 1934), 11–12. Gallup C368.
Attributed to '*T. S. Eliot*' in the Contents. In para. 2, in 'the same problem at the state universities', 'at' has been corrected to 'as'.

At the present time I am not very much interested in the only subject which I am supposed to be qualified to write about: that is, one kind of literary criticism. I am not very much interested in literature, except dramatic literature; and I am largely interested in subjects which I do not yet know very much about: theology, politics, economics, and education. I am moved at the moment to say something on the last of these subjects; so, if my comments appear very scrappy, I can only say that it is hard to start one's own education over again when one is in the forties. I have had some practical experience of education; first, having been educated myself, and in my opinion very badly. Second, I have taught boys of all ages in English schools; I was once an assistant in the Philosophy Department at Harvard; I have conducted Adult Education classes, and I have lectured at Cambridge in England and Cambridge in Massachusetts. I mention these facts because they are what might be considered credentials. But I do not feel that I have learned very much except to appreciate the magnitude of the educational problem. A great many men have taught for many more years than I, and yet are no more qualified to make any general statements about education. Indeed, most of the people engaged in educating seem to have very little conception of the general problem of education for a race and a nation, or of what purpose in a general scheme their own work is serving. They are merely Ford operatives. As for the big executives of education, I suspect that many of them have their minds filled with unexamined assumptions. Yet after feeding and clothing and housing people, the problem of how they should be educated is the most important you have, and perhaps the most difficult. Wherever you begin, you are led on to everything else. The problem of education leads you out to every other, and every other problem leads you back to education.

If what I am concerned about was merely the local problem, the question of what kind of education we ought to have in England, or in America, I should feel certainly that I am too ignorant to have the right to say anything. But I do not consider that there is one problem of education in America and another in England. However different the present systems may appear, I am sure that fundamentally we have one problem, at least in all English speaking countries, and that the things which alarm or depress me in America are equally present and alarming or depressing in England. English education is changing just as American education is changing: with only the trifling difference that the former seems to be going to the devil rather more slowly. The provincial universities, in any case, have much the same problem as the state universities of America: what sort of an education to give when the population to be educated includes almost everybody.

The chief persisting advantages of Oxford and Cambridge over American universities are (1) theological (2) economic.

I cannot attempt to demonstrate here that education, as the finest training of the finest minds, in contrast to the general education of everybody or the special technical training of persons to fill definite social needs, cannot afford to be separated from religion. But I am certain that the theological background – however far back it may be – is the only one that can provide the idea of order and unity needed for education. And I believe that if education is not rearranged by people with some definite social philosophy and some notion of the true vocation of man, the only education to be had will be in seminaries and colleges run by Jesuits. There is a good one in St Louis, Mo. Incidentally, the only two men I know who have had what seemed to me hopeful theories of education and put them into practice, are Father Herbert Kelly of the Society of the Sacred Mission in Nottinghamshire, and Canon Iddings Bell of Providence, Rhode Island. I have no first-hand acquaintance with Canon Bell's frustrated attempts at St Stephen's College, Annandale; and Father

Kelly's system was designed for theological students; but I know of no other ventures in higher education of equal interest to these.

[12] The leading American universities were, of course, originally directed by clergy of definite denominations. They now suffer from the dreadful blight of non-sectarianism, which means substituting a vague Christianity which the modern mind despises, for a precise Christianity which it may hate but must respect. Oxford and Cambridge are to a large extent atheist, but they remain in structure and ceremony foundations belonging to the Church of England. They may lose religion altogether, in time, but they are hardly likely to become non-sectarian; one feels, in their precincts, the sharp division of clerical and anti-clerical which is beneficial to both.

The American universities struck me, in contrast to Oxford and Cambridge, appallingly centralised in administration. That however is not the economic advantage of the latter universities that I have in mind. The English colleges own property; and much of their property is still that kind of property which is the least ignoble to possess: land. The ownership of land in England by individuals is now discouraged by Estate Duties, but ownership of land by colleges is still tolerated. The riches of the Oxford and Cambridge colleges do not, for the most part, consist in shares or debentures of fluctuating or doubtful value. Consequently the two older universities of England are on the whole independent of millionaires. Neither are their methods easily pliable to the theories of any one powerful administrator, like the late President Eliot. A Vice-Chancellor, or the Head of a House, does not have to spend much of his time begging for endowments; nor would he have unlimited control over their use when received. In fact, the two older English universities are not quite so dependent upon an industrial aristocracy as the American: they sprang from and flourished in conditions older than capitalism, and they can perhaps survive it.

When I have mentioned these advantages, and the fact that a classical education, although no longer imposed, is still regarded as normal, I have stated what seem to me the essentials. The other advantages of Oxford and Cambridge are in comparison trivial or irrelevant. I should not care to see American universities imitating Oxford and Cambridge, even to the worm-holes in the system.

Of course there are many details which might be examined. But whom do you want to educate? The answer will depend on your conception of a good society; and so will the sort of education you want to give. The answers depend upon your notion of the place of man in the world, of the relation of a supernatural order, if any, to the natural; they depend upon our answers to all the questions which we tacitly agree not to raise, when we discuss educational matters. You may have a notion of the understanding of certain things as valuable in itself, so that you want a few people in every generation to be educated to understand and value and preserve them. Or you may have a notion of the kind of society you want, and concentrate on whatever seems to subserve the interests of that society. Or you may have a vague notion that a university 'education' confers a social degree, and proceed to overrun the country with gentlemen. Instead we assume at the same time that education is for those individuals who are fine enough to deserve it, that it is for the upper classes, that it is to make everybody a member of the upper classes, that everybody is entitled to the same education, that education is something to give one an advantage over the uneducated, and that education is going to make it possible to get a good job, according to whatever be our notion of goodness in jobs. But once you start to think about education you must go on thinking about your whole social system, and about politics and economics and theology. At any rate I am glad to think that all these subjects in which I am uneducated but interested are fundamentally related.

A Commentary

C., 14. 54 (Oct. 1934), 86–90. Signed 'T. S. E.' Gallup C369.

The annual report of the National Trust for Places of Historic Interest or Natural Beauty grows yearly more impressive. The map of England and Wales is dotted with preserves of the Natural Trust, the greatest success being apparently in the Lake District. And what is remarkable, and most commendable, is the fact that the work has been done by the labour and the benefactions of a considerable number of persons. The total of donations, to the end of 1933, appears to be under three hundred and fifteen thousand pounds, and the list includes a great many individuals; a few years ago, a single American millionaire could have provided the whole sum. It would seem that the kind of work that the National Trust does in preservation has appealed to a general public spirit which is the best assurance of its continuation. Eminent persons so different as Lord Curzon (representing Historic Interest) and Viscount Grey (representing Natural Beauty) have supported it; it has had the invaluable advertisement of the impressive photographs of threatened districts which appear in *The Times*; but what is most important is that it has obviously stirred the feelings of a very large number of people.

I do not in any way depreciate the value of the National Trust, or belittle the generosity of those who have given labour, money and land, in suggesting that the existence of such a society as a permanent and important institution in the country gives rise to curious reflections which may be worth examination. Surely we are living in a very odd and unsatisfactory state of society, when such a struggle has to be carried on to preserve England from destruction and disfigurement. For what is the process going on, the existence of which is tacitly assumed by these worthy efforts? Does it lead to the eventual partition of England into two parts, one overrun and ravaged by human beings, and the other protected from human beings; and are the members of the National Trust satisfied that all is well in proportion to the [87] extent of England which can be acquired for 'preserves'? It is excellent to do what we can in the present state of affairs; but it would be better that those who are making such generous efforts, and who are therefore in a position to come to think in more general terms, should not content their hearts and consciences with the thought that this is all that needs doing. For when such work has to be done, we must acknowledge that we are interfering, in a way never before attempted in history, with natural development; and when natural development has to be interfered with, ought we not to look a little deeper and try to do something about the 'nature' which develops in such an unpleasant way?

What we should be interested to read, besides a list of the properties so far acquired, and some knowledge of their beauties or historical importance, is a detailed account of what, in each case, the several properties have been preserved *from*. What would have happened to the properties? How many of them would have been developed in a reasonable way to satisfy just needs, and how many for purposes which have no justification anywhere? Sometimes, no doubt, the sites have been wanted for putting up houses which could just as well be put up round the corner. But we want to form some notion of the nature of the forces which we may expect to be active in destruction of the beauty of England in the future. We want to know how much is accounted for by causes such as the increase of the population; how much by vandalism; how much by 'speculative building'; how much may be attributed to fundamental defects in the social system. We should like to know the part played by Estate Duties, and whether anything ought to be done about that. The existence of such an institution as the National Trust, and the present necessity for its existence, seems to me to imply some pretty drastic criticism of contemporary society; and we should like all the people interested in the preservation of 'beauty spots' to investigate a state of society in which beauty spots have to be preserved.

It is difficult to be quite whole-hearted in one's support of [88] the National Trust, until one is able to answer such questions. For one thing, we do not want to feel that we are protecting beauty spots against the needs of the people. And for another, the amount of preserving that could be done is quite indefinite. Some parts of England are more beautiful than others; some, because of their natural configuration, are quite exceptional; but there is very little of rural England that is not beautiful and worthy of protection. Some of the wilder and more romantic spots may be quite unsuited for tilth, grazing, or other legitimately profitable uses; these are rightly to be protected against the hotel on the hilltop, the week-end bungalow on the slope, the 'roadhouse' in the valley, the golf course on the downs, the pavilion on the beach. But the beauty of England is not primarily that of the more remote hills and moors which men have not yet found it worth their while to disfigure, but is to be found in the ordinary countryside which is largely the work of generations of humanising labour. And if this cannot be preserved, and preserved *alive*, it is of small good that the land should be dotted with little museums of scenery.

Again, with regard to the preservation of buildings of 'historic interest'. They are not worth preserving because they are 'interesting'. They are worth preserving because they give a conscious reminder of the traditions of a people; and by traditions I do not mean its vainglories, its conceit of itself in its past; but the fact that it has grown in one way and not in another, and that its future growth is determined in certain directions, if any, by its having grown in that way through the past: by the things which are a cause of regret and shame, as well as those which may be a cause for pride. And they are still more worth preserving because of their unconscious effect upon those who live among them. But an accumulation of old buildings, however beautiful, means death unless we can also make beautiful new buildings. Old buildings are dead in so far as we put them to a different use than that for which they were intended. If Christianity disappeared, it would be more sensible to destroy all the [89] churches in England than to preserve them as monuments. (It seems to me inconsistent with the principles of communism to leave standing a building like the Kremlin.) But an age and a society which is sure of itself – not self-consciously cocksure – will neither destroy too much nor preserve too much. Excessive and purposive destruction implies that we deny our natural dependence upon the past, upon the bad as well as the good in it; and excessive preservation implies our lack of confidence in ourselves. While supporting the work of the National Trust so far as it goes, I am apprehensive lest it help to engender a lack of confidence in the future, and consequently a neglect of action about the future. You must have humility, and you must have conviction. Humility and conviction should express our attitude towards the past and towards the future. But for humility people are apt to put defeatism, and for conviction cockiness.

Such work as that of the National Trust seems to belong to a transitional period of society. Either society will somehow rearrange itself in such a way that whatever ought to be preserved exactly as it is, will be in no danger; or the whole business of artificial conservation will be taken over by the State. The latter event is much the more probable, the former the more desirable. The former would require a very different economic basis, and a healthy, settled agriculture, with a proper balance between town and country life; the latter only requires that things continue in their present direction towards State control of everything.

Certain types of building very likely belong to a state of society which we have left behind. The huge country manor, the large town mansion, will very likely disappear except where their beauty or historical value makes their preservation, as some sort of public institutions, desirable. But much of the change of a destructive kind which we are concerned to combat, seems to result from the over-development of town life and the atrophy of the country. It is from a population habituated to town life, a population to which [90] the countryside represents holidays, whether on an elaborate or a simple scale, that the countryside has to be protected, rather than from those to whom the country means the scene of their daily work and life. And it is the continuous re-arrangement of towns to accommodate larger numbers of people with different standards of living than the previous generation, and the efforts of private interests to make money by providing for these larger and more vulgarised populations, that occasion the destruction of buildings of dignity in towns. No one will deny that the central part of London has been growing progressively uglier during the present century. Change is inevitable and necessary; but it is a pity that so many of the most noticeable changes should be made solely for reasons of private profit – and that others should be dependent upon the vagaries of a body like the London County Council. You cannot content yourself, in London, with merely collecting sums to preserve bits here and there. Here, obviously, the problem of preservation cannot be separated from the problem of intelligent building. And for the intelligent appreciation of both problems, we must aim to get at some real understanding of the changes which are taking place in society, an understanding which will distinguish between those which are inevitable and those which should be combated, between those which are beneficial and those which are pernicious. It is as important – to take questions which are actual – to plan wisely for the future development of the Surrey Bank, and to see that the new suburbs in

Middlesex are properly provided with parks and gardens and arranged so that they may grow to be communities, as it is to preserve any part of rural England, or any number of historic monuments. And in this context we have to ask the question whether it is desirable that the large towns should become larger; whether it is healthy that the mind of the whole nation should become urban. And in asking such questions we are questioning all the assumptions of our society for many generations past.

Religious Drama and the Church

rep [magazine of the Westminster and Croydon Repertory Theatres], 1. 6 (Oct. 1934), 4–5. Subheaded 'By T. S. ELIOT'. Gallup C369a.

The possibility of a religious drama depends upon a kind of reciprocity. The dramatists must be able to provide a drama which will be really useful to the Church; and the Church must be ready to make itself useful to those who want to write drama. When I say the Church, I am thinking primarily of those in authority, but I imply also the goodwill of the laity. For the audience must be willing to learn from the playwrights, and the playwrights must be willing to learn from the audience.

I do not think (with all due respect) that religious drama has much to gain from those dramatists, even if they are also poets, who have already established their reputation, and who occasionally consent, out of good nature or an efflux of piety, to write a religious play to order. Plays produced by such writers with such motives may easily have only a superficial varnish of religious interest, or may be sentimental embroidery on conventional Biblical themes, or may innocently present the most dubious theology. The development of religious drama depends upon its being able to appeal, as a task, to the self-interest of younger men who are anxious to write for the theatre.

There are, among the younger poets to-day, several who are definitely interested in the theatre; I think there is even a tendency to regard dramatic form as the consummation of poetic activity. The causes of this tendency are probably complex and are to be found in the social changes which have taken place within our memory. I shall not attempt to explore them; but assuming that a poet to-day wants to write for the theatre, where will he find an opportunity? On the commercial stage there is obviously no opening. The commercial stage has to appeal to the lowest common middle-class denominator; to an audience with no dignified beliefs to give it cohesion, and with the smallest minimum of moral convictions of any kind. Even the plays of Mr Shaw are too good to be nowadays really successful; I should imagine that Mr Noel Coward has about all the intelligence and sensibility that a successful dramatist can afford to be encumbered with. A few years ago Mr Aldous Huxley produced a play (*The World of Light*) which, although founded of course upon a thin and sandy philosophy, had considerable intellectual and dramatic merit: it ran lamely for six weeks; it was taken off, that is to say, at about the moment when plays like *Autumn Crocus* or *Escape Me Never* (both written by women) are just beginning to show promise of triumphant longevity. Mr Huxley made the mistake of trying to appeal to the 'theatre-goers' with something much beyond their intelligence and sensibility. I doubt whether there is anything to be done with the contemporary theatre-going public: you have got to assemble new audiences.

The young dramatist to-day, however, does not want to write a play merely to please a small audience of poetry-lovers many of whom he will know, and the faces of the rest of whom he remembers having seen before and is tired of seeing. The best opportunity that presents itself seems to be the opportunity to appeal to those who are interested in a common cause which the poet and dramatist can also serve. Only a cause can give the bond, the common assumptions between author and audience, which the serious dramatist needs. (This accounts perhaps for the relative *importance* of Mr Shaw's plays at a period which younger people to-day will not remember, and for the unimportance of a new play by Mr Shaw now: he is no longer serving any cause which is actual for us.) There are only two causes now of sufficient seriousness, and they are mutually exclusive: the Church and Communism.

People are born, doubtless, with more or less dramatic talent; but it is certain that this talent will never come to anything without hard work, without a good deal of humbleness and readiness to learn from both producers and actors; without a good deal of give and take, and a willingness, within limits of conscience, to produce what is wanted even if it is not quite what one wants to produce. The writer with dramatic ambitions must be ready to co-operate; but the co-operation that we should get with commercial producers, the kind of lessons that we should learn from professional producers and professional actors, most of whom are quite unable to declaim any kind of [5] verse, is not exactly the kind of co-operation that we want. Religious drama, if those responsible for its production see their opportunity, has a good deal to offer. It has definite limitations: and to see what one can do within a given framework is always stimulating. It can employ actors who have no experience of the professional stage, and who therefore *may*, now and again, be able to pronounce verse properly. It must, for the most part, be capable of being inexpensively produced, which suits our needs, because we do not want our words to be distorted by actors with star personalities or eclipsed by magnificent scenery and costume. And the writer of religious drama may have the satisfaction of breaking the religious conventions in order to expose the religious reality; though he will have to remember that the majority of his audience may be Christians from the surface in, rather than from the centre out, and that a little Biblical pageantry, voiced with a few ambling pentameters, is all that they will come prepared for.

If anything is to be made of religious drama in England, the clergy must help to prepare their faithful – both as spectators and as participants – to understand that there is a common cause to be served, and that the writer also is serving, rather than performing a charity or pursuing a reputation. The appreciation of poetry among members of the Church of England leaves much to be desired. The writer of religious drama must be allowed a considerable degree of liberty and experiment – we have not to paraphrase the mystery plays but to devise new forms. On the other hand, the Church should demand of the men of letters who wish to contribute to its drama, that they have an adequate knowledge of theology; and it should not tolerate the promulgation of unsound doctrine by great poets, or even by poets of great reputation. The Bolsheviks, who apparently take a keen interest in literature, ask no less in the matter of orthodoxy.

I am not suggesting that the future of the drama in England is to be looked for only in churches, in church-halls, and in theatres hired for church-benefit performances. I am only suggesting that it will be for the common benefit if the Church will employ poets, as well as architects, artists and musicians. The plastic arts, incidentally, are in a state of collapse, because of their economic dependence upon a capitalistic prosperity which has become less dependable; and they suffered indeed in their quality from this dependence. The Church has the opportunity, greater now than in the period of industrial expansion, of gathering to itself, of educating and spiritualising, all the potential forces of civilisation. And these forces, gathered in the Church, will consequently radiate out from it. So that we may perhaps come to a time, in which a play as fundamentally Christian and Catholic as *Polyeucte* may be written and may be performed successfully to audiences which will not be consciously attending a 'religious play', because they will be imbued with the Christian and Catholic way of feeling, even when they ask only to be entertained.

John Marston

EE (4 Oct. 1934), 177–95. The other essays are reprinted from *SE*: Gallup A27.

Revised from 'John Marston', *TLS*, 1695 (26 July 1934), [517]–18: Gallup C367.
Repr. in *ED* and in *SE* (1951).

1 John Marston, the dramatist, has been dead for three hundred years. The date of his death, June 25th, 1634, is one of the few certain facts that we know about him; but the appearance of the first volume of a new edition of his works, as well as an edition of his best-known play by itself, is a more notable event than the arrival of his tercentenary.[1] For Marston has enjoyed less attention from either scholars or critics, than any of his contemporaries of equal or greater rank; and for both scholars and critics he remains a territory of unexplored riches and risks. The position of most of his contemporaries is pretty well settled; one cannot go very far wrong in one's estimate of the dramatists with whom Marston worked; [178] but about Marston a wide divergency of opinion is still possible. His greater defects are such as anyone can see; his merits are still a matter for controversy.

2 Little has transpired of the events of Marston's life since Bullen presented in 1887 what has hitherto been the standard edition. The date and place of his birth have been unsettled; but the main facts – that his mother was Italian, that he was educated at Brasenose College and put to the law, that he wrote satires and then plays for a brief period and finally entered the Church – are undisputed. We are left with the unsupported statement of Ben Jonson that he beat Marston and took away his pistol; but, without necessarily impugning the veracity of Jonson, or suggesting that he wished to impress Drummond with his own superiority, having gone such a long journey to talk to him, we may do well to put aside the image of a mean and ridiculous figure which Jonson has left us before considering the value of Marston's work. And before reading the selections of Lamb, or the encomium of Swinburne, we should do better to read the plays of Marston – there are not many – straight through. Did Marston have anything of his own to say or not? Was he really a dramatist, or only a playwright through force of circumstances? And if he was a dramatist, in which of his plays was he at his best? In answering these questions we have, as with no other Elizabethan [179] dramatist, the opportunity to go completely wrong; and that opportunity is an incentive.

---

1. *The Plays of John Marston*, in three volumes, edited by H. Harvey Wood, Volume I (Edinburgh: Oliver and Boyd).
  The Malcontent, edited by G. B. Harrison, The Temple Dramatists (Dent).

3 Dr Wood's first volume includes, besides *Antonio and Mellida* and *Antonio's Revenge*, *The Malcontent*. There are three quartos of *The Malcontent*: Dr Wood tells us that he has followed the second (B in Dr Greg's classification), but has adopted what seemed to him better and fuller readings from A and C. Dr Harrison's text is, he tells us, the 'revised quarto', and he follows the Temple Dramatists principle (certainly the right one for such a series) of modernised spelling and punctuation. Our only complaint against both editors is that they have conscientiously limited themselves, in their notes, to what is verifiable, and have deprived themselves and their readers of that delight in aside and conjecture which the born annotator exploits. Dr Harrison's glossary, for instance, omits some difficult words, but includes others of which the meaning is obvious; one wishes that editors of Elizabethan texts would take as their model that perfect annotator Mr F. L. Lucas in his monumental edition of John Webster. Dr Wood appears to have had the advantage of consulting Dr Harrison's edition; and it must be said that they both refer the reader to Mr Lucas's edition of Webster for fuller information on certain points. Both Dr Wood and Dr Harrison seem to be assured on one critical judgement: that [180] *The Malcontent* is the most important of Marston's plays. Dr Harrison says forthright: '*The Malcontent* is Marston's best play.' Dr Wood says only:

> The best of Marston's comedies and tragedies, and his great tragicomedy, *The Malcontent*, have striking and original qualities. . . . *The Malcontent* is one of the most original plays of its period. . . .

4 It is this assumption that we are privileged to examine.

5 If we read first the two plays with which collected editions, including Dr Wood's, begin – *Antonio and Mellida* and *Antonio's Revenge* – our first impression is likely to be one of bewilderment, that anyone could write plays so bad and that plays so bad could be preserved and reprinted. Yet they are not plays that one wholly forgets; and the second reading, undertaken perhaps out of curiosity to know why such bad plays are remembered, may show that the problem is by no means simple. One at first suspects Marston to have been a poet, with no inclination to the stage, but driven thereto by need, and trying to write to the popular taste; just as a fastidious writer of to-day may produce, under financial pressure, something which he vainly imagines to be a potential bestseller. There is one immediate objection to this theory, even before we have read Marston's later work. It is that there is better *poetry* in these [181] two plays, both in several passages, quotable and quoted, and in the

general atmosphere, than there is in the *Satires*, *The Scourge of Villainy*, or *Pygmalion*. The last of these was apparently an attempt to repeat the success of *Venus and Adonis*, and deserves only the fate of every piece of writing which is an attempt to do again what has already been done by a better man. The first are obviously lacking in personal conviction. The Satire, when all is said and done, is a form which the Elizabethans endeavoured to naturalise with very slight success; it is not until Oldham that a satire appears, sufficiently natural to be something more than a literary exercise. When Donne tries it, he is not any more successful than Marston; but Donne could write in no form without showing that he was a poet, and though his satires are not good satires, there is enough poetry in them, as in his epistles, to make them worth reading. Marston is very competent, and perfectly perfunctory. He wrote satires, as he wrote *Pygmalion*, in order to succeed; and when he found that the satire was more likely to lead him to the gaol than to success, he seems to have taken up, in the same spirit, the writing of plays. And however laboured the first two tragical plays may be, there is more poetry in them than in anything he had written before. So we cannot say that he was a 'poet', forced by necessity to become a 'dramatist'.

[182] 6 The second observation upon *Antonio and Mellida* and its sequel, if we may call 'sequel' a play of such different intent, is that their badness cannot be explained simply by incapacity, or even by plain carelessness. A blockhead could not have written them; a painstaking blockhead would have done better; and a careless master, or a careless dunce, would not have gone out of his way to produce the effects of nonsensicality which we meet. These two plays give the effect of work done by a man who was so exasperated by having to write in a form which he despised that he deliberately wrote worse than he could have written, in order to relieve his feelings. This may appear an over-ingenious apologetic; but it is difficult to explain, by any natural action of mediocrity the absurd dialogue in Italian in which Antonio and Mellida suddenly express themselves in Act IV, Sc. i. The versification, such as it is, has for the most part no poetic merit; when it is most intelligible, as in the apostrophes of Andrugio, it is aiming at a conventional noble effect; but it has often, and more interestingly, a peculiar jerkiness and irritability, as of a writer who is, for some obscure reason, wrought to the pitch of exasperation. There are occasional reversions to an earlier vocabulary and movement, difficult to explain at the very end of the sixteenth century, reversions which to Ben Jonson must have seemed simple evidence of [183] technical incompetence. As in the Prologue to *Antonio's Revenge*:

> The rawish dank of clumsy winter ramps
> The fluent summer's vein; and drizzling sleet
> Chilleth the wan bleak cheek of the numb'd earth,
> While snarling gusts nibble the juiceless leaves
> From the nak'd shuddering branch. . . .

or the line at the beginning of Act II:

> The black jades of swart night trot foggy rings
> 'Bout heaven's brow. . . .

It is not only in passages such as these that we get the impression of having to do with a personality which is at least unusual and difficult to catalogue. Marston's minor comic characters, in these two plays, are as completely lifeless as the major characters. Whether decent or indecent, their drollery is as far from mirth-provoking as can be: a continuous and tedious rattle of dried peas. And yet something is conveyed, after a time, by the very emptiness and irrelevance of this empty and irrelevant gabble; there is a kind of significant lifelessness in this shadow-show. There is no more unarticulated scarecrow in the whole of Elizabethan drama than Sir Jeffrey Balurdo. Yet Act V, Sc. i of *Antonio's Revenge* leaves some impression upon the mind, though what it is we may not be able to say.

> [184] 7 Ho, who's above there, ho? A murrain on all proverbs. They say hunger breaks through stone walls; but I am as gaunt as lean-ribbed famine, yet I can burst through no stone walls. O now, Sir Jeffrey, show thy valour, break prison and be hanged. Nor shall the darkest nook of hell contain the discontented Sir Balurdo's ghost. Well, I am out well; I have put off the prison to put on the rope. O poor shotten herring, what a pickle art thou in! Of hunger, how thou domineer'st in my guts! O for a fat leg of ewe mutton in stewed broth, or drunken song to feed on! I could belch rarely, for I am all wind. O cold, cold, cold, cold, cold. O poor knight! O poor Sir Jeffrey, sing like an unicorn before thou dost dip thy horn in the water of death. O cold, O sing, O cold, O poor Sir Jeffrey, sing, sing!

After this comes a highfalutin speech by Pandulpho, and cries of 'Vindicta!' Balurdo, like the others, is so unreal that to deny his reality is to lend him too much existence; yet we can say of the scene, as of the play, that however bad it is no one but Marston could have written it.

8 The peculiar quality, which we have not attempted to define, is less evident in most of the plays which follow, just because they are better plays. The most considerable – setting aside his work of collaboration –

are *The Malcontent, The Dutch Court-*[185]*esan, The Insatiate Countess,* and *The Fawn.* Of these, the last is a slight but pleasant handling of an artificial situation, a kind of Courtship of Miles Standish in which the princess woos the prince who has come to sue on behalf of his father. The Insatiate Countess is a poor rival of the White Devil; her changes of caprice from lover to lover are rapid to the point of farce; and when the Countess, brought to the block for her sins, exclaims, in reply to the executioner's bidding of 'Madam, put up your hair':

> O, these golden nets
> That have ensnared so many wanton youths,
> Not one but has been held a thread of life,
> And superstitiously depended on.
> Now to the block we must vail. What else?

we may remark (if these lines are indeed Marston's) that we have known this sort of thing done better by another dramatist, and that it is not worth going to Marston for what Webster can give us. *The Dutch Courtesan* is a better play than either of these; Freevill and Malheureux behave more naturally than we expect of Marston's heroes; the Courtesan's villainy is not incredible or unmotivated, and her isolation is enhanced by her broken English; and the heroine, Beatrice, has some charming verses to speak and is not, according to the standards of that [186] stage and age, preposterously mild and patient. Yet the play as a whole is not particularly 'signed' by Marston; it is a theme which might have been handled as well, or better, by Dekker or Heywood. We are looking, not for plays of the same kind and in parts almost as good as those done by other dramatists. To prove that Marston is worth the attention of any but the Elizabethan scholar, we must convince the reader that Marston does something that no one else does at all: that there is a Marston tone, like the scent of a flower, which by its peculiarity sharpens our appreciation of the other dramatists as well as bringing appreciation of itself, as experiences of gardenia or zinnia refine our experience of rose or sweet-pea. With this purpose in mind, we may agree, with reservations, with the accepted view that *The Malcontent* is superior to any of the three other plays mentioned in the foregoing paragraph.

9 The superiority of *The Malcontent* does not lie altogether in more solid dramatic construction. The construction is hardly as close as that of *The Dutch Courtesan*, and the lighter passages have hardly the interest of under-plot which, in the other play, we find in the pranks played by Cocledemoy at the expense of Mulligrub. Marston at best is not a careful enough playwright to deserve comparison with his better-

known contemporaries on this score. He [187] can commit the grossest carelessness in confusing his own characters. Even in *The Malcontent* there appears to be one such lapse. Several of the earlier scenes seem to depend for their point upon Bianca being the wife of Bilioso (a sort of prototype of the Country Wife); but she is not so named in the list of characters, and the words of Ferneze to her in the last scene seem to indicate that Marston had forgotten this relationship.

10   Nor is the character of Malevole really comparable to that of Jacques. In the play of Shakespeare, Jacques is surrounded by characters who by their contrast with him, and sometimes by their explicit remarks, criticise the point of view which he expresses – a point of view which is indeed an almost consciously adopted humour. And while a malcontent drawn by Jonson lacks the depth and the variety which Shakespeare can give by human contrasts, he at least preserves a greater degree of consistency than does Malevole. The whole part is inadequately thought out; Malevole is either too important or not important enough. We may suppose that he has assumed his role primarily as a disguise, and in order to be present at his usurper's court on the easy footing of a tolerated eccentric. But he has the difficult role of being both the detached cynic and the rightful prince biding his time. He takes pity on Ferneze (himself not a very satisfying character, [188] as after his pardon in Act IV he lets the play down badly in Act V, sc. iii by his unseemly levity with Bianca). Yet Malevole, in his soliloquy in Act II, sc. i, which is apparently not for the benefit of Bilioso but intended to express his true thoughts and feelings, alludes to himself as suffering from insomnia because he ''gainst his fate repines and quarrels' – not a philosophical role, nor one to be expected of the magnanimous duke whom he has to be at the end. Whether his sarcasms are meant to be affected railing or savage satire, they fail of their effect.

11   Nor is any of the other characters very much alive. It is possible to find Dr Harrison's praise of Maria, as a 'virtuous and constant wife who is alive and interesting', to be excessive, and to find even Maquerelle deficient in liveliness. The virtue of *The Malcontent*, indeed, resides rather in its freedom from the grosser faults to be expected of Marston than from any abundance of positive merits, when we hold it up to the standard, not of Shakespeare, but of the contemporaries of Shakespeare. It has no passages so moving as the confrontation of Beatrice and Franceschina in *The Dutch Courtesan*, and no comic element so sprightly as the harlequinades of Cocledemoy in the same play. It has, as critics have remarked, a more controlled and even diction. Swinburne does not elevate it to the position of Marston's best play; but he observes that

[189] the brooding anger, the resentful resignation, the impatient spirit of endurance, the bitter passion of disdain, which animate the utterance and direct the action of the hero, are something more than dramatically appropriate; it is as obvious that these are the mainsprings of the poet's own ambitions and dissatisfied intelligence, sullen in its reluctant submission and ardent in its implacable appeal, as that his earlier undramatic satires were the tumultuous and turbid ebullitions of a mood as morbid, as restless and as honest.

We are aware, in short, with this as with Marston's other plays, that we have to do with a positive, powerful, and unique personality. His is an original variation of that deep discontent and rebelliousness so frequent among the Elizabethan dramatists. He is, like some of the greatest of them, occupied in saying something else than appears in the literal actions and characters whom he manipulates.

12 It is possible that what distinguishes poetic drama from prosaic drama is a kind of doubleness in the action, as if it took place on two planes at once. In this it is different from allegory, in which the abstraction is something conceived, not something differently felt, and from symbolism (as in the plays of Maeterlinck) in which the tangible world is deliberately diminished – both symbolism and allegory be-[190]ing operations of the conscious planning mind. In poetic drama a certain apparent irrelevance may be the symptom of this doubleness; or the drama has an under-pattern, less manifest than the theatrical one. We sometimes feel in following the words and behaviour of some of the characters of Dostoevsky, that they are living at once on the plane that we know and on some other plane of reality from which we are shut out: their behaviour does not seem crazy, but rather in conformity with the laws of some world that we cannot perceive. More fitfully, and with less power, this doubleness appears here and there in the work of Chapman, especially in the two *Bussy D'Ambois* plays. In the work of genius of a lower order, such as that of the author of *The Revenger's Tragedy*, the characters themselves hardly attain this double reality; we are aware rather of the author, operating perhaps not quite consciously through them, and making use of them to express something of which he himself may not be quite conscious.

13 It is not by writing quotable 'poetic' passages, but by giving us the sense of something behind, more real than any of his personages and their action, that Marston established himself among the writers of genius. There is one among his plays, not so far mentioned, and not, apparently, widely read or highly esteemed, which may be put forward with [191] the

claim that it is his best, and that it is the most nearly adequate expression of his distorted and obstructed genius: *The Wonder of Women*, otherwise *The Tragedy of Sophonisba*. This is a fairly late play in Marston's brief career, and we have reason to guess that the author himself preferred it to his others. As the 'tragedy which shall abide the most curious perusal' it gives the impression of being the play which Marston wrote most nearly to please himself. Bullen found it 'not impressive', and even Swinburne reserves his praise for a few scenes. Yet the play has a good plot, is well constructed and moves rapidly. There are no irrelevancies and no comic passages; it is austere and economical. The rapidity with which the too-scheming Carthaginians transfer their allegiance from Massinissa to Syphax, his rival suitor for Sophonisba, bringing about an alliance between Massinissa and Scipio, is not unplausible, and keeps the reader in a state of continuous excitement over the fortunes of war. The scene in which the witch Erictho takes on the form of Sophonisba in order to induce Syphax to lie with her, is by no means what Bullen would have it, a scene of gratuitous horror, introduced merely to make our flesh creep; it is integral to the plot of the play; and is one of those moments of a double reality, in which Marston is saying something else, which evidence his poetic genius. And the memor-[192]able passages are not, as in his earlier plays, plums imbedded in suet; they may be taken as giving a fair taste of the quality of the whole play – e.g.

> though Heaven bears
> A face far from us, gods have most long ears;
> Jove has a hundred marble marble hands.

> Nothing in Nature is unserviceable,
> No, not even inutility itself.
> Is then for nought dishonesty in being?
> And if it be sometimes of forced use,
> Wherein more urgent than in saving nations?

> Our vows, our faith, our oaths, why they're ourselves.

> Gods naught foresee, but see, for to their eyes
> Naught is to come or past; nor are you vile
> Because the gods foresee; for gods, not we
> See as things are; things are not as we see.

(This last quotation reminds us of Meredith's line, 'By their great memories the gods are known'; but Marston has the better of it. Swinburne, in spite of his ability to like almost any Elizabethan play that can be tolerated, is less than fair, when he calls *Sophonisba* 'laboured and ambitious', and speaks of 'jagged barbarisms and exotic monstrosities of metaphor'; and his derogatory quotation of the end of Act II does injustice to a passage which is acceptable enough in its context.)

[193] I do not praise gods' goodness, but adore;
    Gods cannot fall, and for their constant goodness
    (Which is necessitated) they have a crown
    Of never-ending pleasures. . . .

The following has a distinct originality:

    Where statues and Jove's acts were vively limned
    Boys with black coals draw the veil'd parts of nature,
    And lecherous actions of imagin'd lust;
    Where tombs and beauteous urns of well-dead men
    Stood in assured rest, the shepherd now
    Unloads his belly, corruption most abhorr'd
    Mingling itself with their renowned ashes.

The following has a fine Senecal ring:

    My god's my arm; my life my heaven; my grave
    To me all end.

And the last words of *Sophonisba*,

    He that ne'er laughed may with a constant face
    Contemn Jove's frown: happiness makes us base.

may be considered as a 'classical' comparison to the 'romantic' vein of Tourneur's

    I think man's happiest when he forgets himself.

14 It is hoped that the reader will see some justification for accumulating quotations from *Sophonisba*, [194] and leaving the other plays unquoted. The quotations are intended to exhibit the exceptional consistency of texture of this play, and its difference of tone, not only from that of Marston's other plays, but from that of any other Elizabethan dramatist. In spite of the tumultuousness of the action, and the ferocity and horror of certain parts of the play, there is an underlying serenity; and as we familiarise ourselves with the play we perceive a pattern behind the pattern into which the characters deliberately involve themselves; the kind of pattern which we perceive in our own lives only at rare moments of inattention and detachment, drowsing in sunlight. It is the pattern drawn by what the ancient world called Fate; subtilised by

Christianity into mazes of delicate theology; and reduced again by the modern world into crudities of psychological or economic necessity.

15 We may be asked to account, in giving this play such high place, for the fact that neither contemporary popularity nor the criticism of posterity yields any support. Well; it may be modestly suggested that in our judgements of Elizabethan plays in general we are very much influenced by Elizabethan standards. The fact that Shakespeare transcended all other poets and dramatists of the time imposes a Shakespearean standard: whatever is of the same kind of drama as Shakespeare's, whatever may be [195] measured by Shakespeare, however inferior to Shakespeare's it may be, is assumed to be better than whatever is of a different kind. However catholic-minded we may be in general, the moment we enter the Elizabethan period we praise or condemn plays according to the usual Elizabethan criteria. Fulke Greville has never received quite his due; we approach Greville, and Daniel, with the assumption that they are 'not in the main current'. The minor poet who hitches his skiff astern of the great galleon has a better chance of survival than the minor poet who chooses to paddle by himself. Marston, in the one play on which he appears to have prided himself, is Senecal rather than Shakespearean. Had the great ship been that of a Corneille or a Racine, instead of a Shakespeare, Marston might cut a better figure now. He spent nearly the whole of his dramatic career writing a kind of drama against which we feel that he rebelled. In order to enjoy the one play which he seems to have written to please himself, we should read Greville and Daniel, of his affinity with whom he was probably quite unconscious, and we should come to him fresh from Corneille and Racine. He would, no doubt, have shocked the French dramatists by his improprieties, and the English classicists as well: nevertheless, he should be with them, rather than with the Shakespeareans.

Variants from *TLS* (1934):

1 dead for] dead
attention from] attention, from
4 [No new para. in *TLS*.]
5 [New para. at 'There is one immediate objection' in *TLS*.]
Villainy, or *Pygmalion*] *Villiainy* or in *Pygmalion*
6 mediocrity] mediocrity,
in Italian] in peculiar Italian
dried peas] dry peas
10 repines] Repines
13 established] establishes
15 Shakespeareans] Shakespearians

What Does the Church Stand For?

Spectator, 153. 5547 (19 October 1934), 560–1. Subheaded 'BY T. S. ELIOT'.
Gallup C370.

I observe that the propounder of the question 'What does the Church stand for?' in your columns uses the terms 'Church' and 'Churches' interchangeably (he speaks of 'different branches of the Christian Churches'), and this raises a doubt in my mind as to what point of view, at least for the purpose of the moment, he is maintaining. And it is very difficult to reply to any criticism of the Church which is made from an unspecified point of view. To discuss the shortcomings of the Church with another person who is inside it is one thing; to defend the existence of the Church against those who are outside of it is quite another. The Church is not a public institution on the same footing as, let us say, the Water Board – an institution the proper functions of which can be discussed by all members of the community on the same assumptions. I cannot conceive such a discussion as you have initiated taking place in a Latin country, where people are either inside the Church or outside; it can take place here because the Church of England is in a vague way accepted by your 'man in the street' as a *kind* of national institution, something maintained, as he supposes, at the public expense, something which has an obligation towards him, although he is unaware of any obligation towards *it*. It is something, of course, that he should feel that the Church should be concerned with *him*. But the man who is neither inside the Church nor outside is a person who has thought nothing out, and therefore a person with whom discussion is impossible; we can consider for purposes of argument only those who hold the Christian Faith, and those who (without necessarily being hostile) hold some other beliefs equally positive.

It is easy to admit, in the abstract, that there must be a profound difference not only between the theories, or between a few ideas which are from time to time consciously in the mind, but between the whole process of life, of those who believe in Christian Revelation of the supernatural order and those who do not. Both classes of people may underestimate the difference. We are apt to assume that we all, at least of one nation and language, have so to speak a large bookful of working beliefs in common, codes of conduct and manners and feeling; and that the Churchman simply has something more, a kind of *appendix* to the book, called Christianity, which contains some more beliefs to which the other man does not subscribe. But from the Christian point of view the appendix is the book, and the book the appendix; and for him even the appendix is not quite the same. You do not carry on business in the same way you do not make investments with the same convictions; for the matter of that, you do not make love in the same way, or enjoy good wine in the same way. I know I am thinking of the ideal Christian, who might be a St Francis, and of the ideal atheist, who might be a Lenin; and I know that such admirable exemplars of thoroughness and reason as St Francis and Lenin are very uncommon; but it clarifies the issues if we concern ourselves with the pure types.

Now if your correspondent was, as I suspect, a Churchman (whether of my communion or not) trying to take the point of view of the 'man in the street', there are two confusions: that of a man taking two points of view at once, and that inherent in the 'man in the street's' point of view. I am assuming, out of good will, that your correspondent's own point of view is not a confused one. The confusion which he appears to have taken on does not prevent him from having something to say that is worth saying; but it is something which needs a good deal of clarification. We must make clear at the start that to justify the existence of the Church in the eyes of the world is from the Church's point of view no more rational than to justify any of the laws of physics, or the primary axioms and propositions of mathematics. The thoughts, words and deeds of individual ecclesiastics may from time to time require a good deal of justification, or even regret; the ecclesiastical organisation and administration may be criticised; the quality and qualifications of men taking orders may be criticised; the quality and the subject-matter of sermons do actually come in for severe criticism which is often deserved. And obviously, the quality of spiritual direction given to individual penitents will vary a great deal. But so long as the Sacraments are provided for the benefit of men, and the services for the glory of God, the Church is doing what is its *essential* business.

Is there not a great [deal] more that the Church might do? There is, as a matter of fact, a great deal more that the Church does do. But one would hardly suspect, from your correspondent's way of putting the matter, that any responsibility rested with the laity. I suspect that the 'man in the street' interprets the parabolic figure of the Shepherd and the Flock too widely, and regards himself for *all* purposes as a Sheep; with no further obligations toward the pastors than those expected of the sheep which we eat as mutton. He is even inclined to murmur that he has looked up and not been fed; he expects, like an ordinary sheep, to have his pasture provided for him without taking the trouble to look up.

Your correspondent seems to envisage a Church weakened by an irresolute Modernism, established upon [561] no theological Rock, and attempting to justify its existence by 'a thousand and one services, which other organizations might do better'. It is for him to provide evidence.

There are no doubt services, such as the provision of better housing, which can be done better by other organisations – such as the State. But after all, your contributor says only, '*might* be done better'; and until they *are* done better, I do not see why the Church should not lead the way; and I see no reason for assuming that the Church, in exerting itself in social activities, is necessarily neglecting its proper business.

A great deal of the criticism which the Church meets comes from such antagonistic sources that it cancels itself out. The two great popular types of criticism may be named Indifference and Meddling. If the Church affirms the primary importance of the spiritual over the temporal, it is accused of indifference to the real problems of the modern world; if it affirms that the Christian Doctrine is incompatible with this or that political doctrine, or with this or that tendency of modern society, if it affirms its attitude towards divorce, or usury, or the treatment of the unemployed, another class of critics, equally numerous, vocal and powerful, will immediately accuse it of meddling with what is not its business. Is the Church which put forth *Rerum Novarum* and *Quadragesimo Anno* 'seeking eagerly' (as your contributor puts it) 'for irrelevant attractions to win ears which are deaf to its doctrines'?

It is difficult to reply to a writer when one does not know upon what facts he bases his generalisations. It is still more difficult when he formulates the problem very differently from oneself. There are at least three problems (1) the attitude, not of the Church toward the laity, but of the Church in the sense in which it comprehends the laity, towards the World, (2) the attitude of the layman, who has to take part in the life of the World as well as in that of the Church, (3) that of the person who is neither for us nor against us. None of them can be dealt with very briefly.

Orage: Memories

A tribute to A. R. Orage. *NEW*, 6. 5 (15 Nov. 1934), 100.
Headed 'T. S. Eliot'. Gallup C371.

I had a feeling of loss when Orage gave up the *New Age* and went to America; I had a feeling of relief when he returned and started the *New English Weekly*; I had a feeling of very deep loss when I read of his death the other day. It was not a personal loss, for my meetings with him, over a period of some eighteen years, had been infrequent and in public places. It is something quite as disturbing as a private loss: it is a public loss.

Many people will remember Orage as the tireless and wholly disinterested evangelist of monetary reform; many will remember him as the best leader-writer in London – on Wednesday mornings I always read through the first part of the *New English Weekly* before attending to any other work. A smaller number will remember him, as R. H. C. of the *New Age*, as the best literary critic of that time in London. Some will remember him as the benevolent editor who encouraged merit and (what is still rarer) tolerated genius. He was something more than the sum of these. He was a man who could be both perfectly right and wholly wrong; but when he was wrong one respected him all the more, as a man who was seeking the essential things and therefore was unafraid of making a fool of himself – a very rare quality indeed. What was great about him was not his intelligence, fine as that was, but his honesty and his selflessness. Most of us have not the self-knowledge to realise how parasitic we are upon the few men of fixed principle and selfless devotion, how the pattern of our world depends, not so much upon what they teach us, but just upon their being *there*. But when a man like Orage dies, we ought to admit that his no longer being *there* throws us, for the time, into disarray; so that a more thorough reorganisation is necessary than we should have believed possible.

Index of Article Titles

This index covers all four volumes in the present edition. Various publications listed here have similar or identical titles or may have appeared more than once in different versions. Publication dates are employed to help distinguish these; articles published separately and as chapters within books are listed both within the book entries and under their own titles.

The *Action Française*, M. Maurras and Mr Ward	Vol. I, page 714
An Address (1952)	IV 63
[Address] (1959)	IV 444
[Address at Mary Institute]	IV 453
Address By T. S. Eliot, '06	II 768
After Strange Gods	II 781
Preface	II 781
I	II 783
II	II 784
III	II 795
Appendix	II 803
The Age of Dryden (*UPUC* 1933)	II 709
[The Aims of Education. 1] (1950)	III 835
The Aims of Education. 2. The Interrelation of Aims (1951)	IV 16
The Aims of Education. 3. The Conflict between Aims (1951)	IV 17
The Aims of Education. 4. The Issue of Religion (1950)	IV 18
The Aims of Education 1 (*TCTC* 1965)	IV 751
The Aims of Education 2 (*TCTC* 1965)	IV 764
The Aims of Education 3 (*TCTC* 1965)	IV 777
The Aims of Education 4 (*TCTC* 1965)	IV 789
The Aims of Poetic Drama (1949)	III 771
The Aims of Poetic Drama (1949)	III 780
An American Critic	I 23
American Critics	II 3
American Literature	I 217
[American Literature and the American Language] (1953)	IV 78
American Literature and the American Language (*TCTC* 1965)	IV 736
American Prose	I 513
Andrew Marvell (1921)	I 358
Andrew Marvell (1923)	I 415
Andrew Marvell (*SE* 1932)	II 492
An Anglican Platonist	III 209
[Anti-Semitism in Russia]	IV 547

868 · INDEX OF ARTICLE TITLES

Apology for the Countess of Pembroke (1932) — II 655
Apology for the Countess of Pembroke (UPUC 1933) — II 700
Appendix (ASG 1934) — II 803
Appendix (ICS 1939) — III 316
Appendix (ICS 1939) — III 316
Appendix I: The Development of Leibniz's Monadism (KEPB 1964) — IV 680
Appendix II: Leibniz's Monads and Bradley's Finite Centres (KEPB 1964) — IV 697
Appendix The Unity of European Culture (NTDC 1948) — III 706
The Approach to James Joyce — III 476
Archbishop Bramhall — I 628
Arnold and Pater (1930) — II 176
Arnold and Pater (SE 1932) — II 564
The Art of Poetry I — IV 413
[*The Ascent of Olympus* by Rendel Harris] — I 200
Audiences, Producers, Plays, Poets — III 64
Augustan Age Tories — I 788
The Author of 'The Burning Babe' — I 504

The Ballet — I 468
Baudelaire (SE 1932) — II 554
[*Baudelaire and the Symbolists* by Peter Quennell] — II 102
Baudelaire in our Time (FLA 1928) — I 800
The Beating of a Drum — I 419
Ben Jonson (1919) — I 266
Ben Jonson (SE 1932) — II 389
Bergson — I 33
Beyle and Balzac — I 229
The Birds of Prey — I 3
Bishop Bell — IV 400
[Books by W. J. Perry] — I 448
Books of the Quarter — I 519
[Books of the Year] — IV 97
Books of the Year Chosen by Eminent Contemporaries — III 838
The Borderline of Prose — I 67
Bradley's *Ethical Studies* — I 678
[*Brahmadarsanam* by Sri Ananda Acharya] — I 165
A Brief Introduction to the Method of Paul Valéry — I 454
A Brief Treatise on the Criticism of Poetry — I 279
[Brief über Ernst Robert Curtius] — IV 119
Britain and America — III 529
Bruce Lyttelton Richmond — IV 476
Building up the Christian World — II 272
Byron (1788–1824) (1937) — III 162
Byron (OPAP 1957) — IV 305

[*The Canary Murder Case* by S. S. Van Dine] — I 667

Catholicism and International Order (1933)	II 672
Catholicism and International Order (*EAM* 1936)	III 82
Charles Péguy	I 41
Charles Whibley (*SE* 1932)	II 613
Charles Whibley: A Memoir	II 242
Charleston, Hey! Hey!	I 569
Chaucer's 'Troilus'	I 510
[Christian Amnesty]	III 579
The Christian Conception of Education	III 417
The Christian News-Letter (1940)	III 352, III 357, III 362
The Christian News-Letter (1941)	III 395
The Christian News-Letter (1942)	III 436
[*A Christian Sociology for To-day*]	II 839
Christianity and Communism	II 247
Christopher Marlowe (*SE* 1932)	II 366
The Church as Action	III 129
The Church's Message to the World	III 162
Civilization: 1928 Model	I 771
The Class and the Élite (1945)	III 553
The Class and the Elite (*NTDC* 1948)	III 645
The Classics and the Man of Letters (1942)	III 441
The Classics and the Man of Letters (*TCTC* 1965)	IV 803
Classics in English	I 47
The Comedy of Humours	I 267
[Commemoration of Irving Babbitt]	III 401
[Comment on a Lecture by Van Wyck Brooks]	III 434
[A Comment on James Thurber]	IV 17
A Commentary (1924)	I 439, I 444, I 449
A Commentary (1925)	I 459, I 465
A Commentary (1926)	I 493, I 497, I 517
A Commentary (1927)	I 544, I 588, I 615, I 621, I 630, I 638, I 654, I 672, I 674
A Commentary (1928)	I 681, I 698, I 713, I 740, I 767, I 812
A Commentary (1929)	II 16, II 38, II 67
A Commentary (1930)	II 84, II 139, II 161, II 177
A Commentary (1931)	II 186, II 192, II 203, II 216
A Commentary (1932)	II 236, II 267, II 278, II 650
A Commentary (1933)	II 656, II 660, II 667, II 674
A Commentary (1934)	II 774, II 829, II 833, II 845

A Commentary (1935)	III 3, III 30, III 49, III 57
A Commentary (1936)	III 66, III 132, III 137, III 145
A Commentary (1937)	III 155, III 168, III 192, III 205
A Commentary (1938)	III 216, III 232, III 237, III 243
A Commentary (1939)	III 262, III 265, III 268
A Commentary (1940)	III 383
Comments by T. S. Eliot	IV 90
Comments on T. S. Eliot's New Play *The Cocktail Party*	III 790
[The Common Market]	IV 538
Concerning 'Intuition'	I 640
Conclusion (*UPUC* 1933)	II 759
Conclusion (*KEPB* 1964)	IV 667
[*Conscience and Christ* by Hastings Rashdall]	I 35
Contemporanea	I 174
Contemporary English Prose	I 411
A Contemporary Thomist	I 113
[Contribution to journal on 'Das Theater ist unersetzlich' ('The theatre is irreplaceable')]	IV 100
A Conversation with T. S. Eliot	IV 707
Correspondence	I 108
Countess Nora Wydenbruck	IV 452
Creative Criticism	I 509
[The Criterion]	I 394
Critical	II 665
Criticism in England	I 233
Cultural Diversity and European Unity (1945)	III 541
Cultural Diversity and European Unity (1946)	III 562
Cultural Forces in the Human Order by T. S. Eliot	III 540
Culture and Anarchy	I 703
Culture and Politics	III 584
Cyril Tourneur (1930)	II 185
Cyril Tourneur (*SE* 1932)	II 417
Dainty Devices	I 735
Dante (*SW* 1920)	I 344
Dante (*SE* 1932)	II 448
Dante as a 'Spiritual Leader'	I 297
Das schöpferische Recht des Regisseurs (The creative right of directors)	IV 125
Découverte de Paris	IV 60
Des Organes Publics et Privés de la Cooperation Intellectuelle	III 489
[*A Defence of Idealism* by May Sinclair]	I 97
The Development of Leibniz's Monadism (1916)	I 41

INDEX OF ARTICLE TITLES

The Development of Leibniz's Monadism (*KEPB* 1964)	IV 680
The Devotional Poets of the Seventeenth Century	II 133
A Dialogue on Poetic Drama (1928)	I 737
A Dialogue on Dramatic Poetry (*SE* 1932)	II 309
Diderot	I 59
Disjecta Membra	I 160
Dr Charles Harris	III 144
Donne in our Time	II 227
Dossier on *Murder in the Cathedral*	IV 54
Dramatis Personae	I 404
'A Dream within a Dream'	III 464
Dryden the Critic (*JDPDC* 1932)	II 641
Dryden the Dramatist (*JDPDC* 1932)	II 632
Dryden the Poet (*JDPDC* 1932)	II 624
The Duchess of Malfi at The Lyric: and Poetic Drama	I 274
The Duchess of Malfy	III 411
Durkheim	I 30
The Early Novel	II 63
[Editorial Notes]	III 261
Education in a Christian Society	III 333
The Education of Taste	I 237
[Edwin Muir] (1959)	IV 404
Edwin Muir: 1887–1959 (1964)	IV 706
Eeldrop and Appleplex, I	I 61
Eeldrop and Appleplex, II	I 89
[*Egoists* by James Huneker]	I 10
[*The Elementary Forms of the Religious Life* by Émile Durkheim]	I 130
[*Elements of Folk Psychology* by Wilhelm Wundt] (1917)	I 51
[*Elements of Folk Psychology* by Wilhelm Wundt] (1918)	I 131
[Eliot interviewed by T. S. Matthews]	IV 716
[Eliot's choice of Books of the Year]	IV 402
Elizabeth and Essex	I 835
Elizabethan Dramatists	IV 548
The Elizabethan Grub Street	II 28
Elizabethan Travellers' Tales	II 53
An Emotional Unity	I 700
English Satire	I 473
The English Situation	III 339
The English Tradition	III 373
English Verse Satire	I 499
Epigrams of an Elizabethan Courtier	I 577
The Epistemologist's Theory of Knowledge (*KEPB* 1964)	IV 612
The Epistemologist's Theory of Knowledge *continued* (*KEPB* 1964)	IV 635
Essays Ancient & Modern	III 71
Preface	III 71

Religion and Literature	III 72
Catholicism and International Order	III 82
The *Pensées* of Pascal	III 94
Modern Education and the Classics	III 106
In Memoriam	III 113
[*Essays of a Catholic Layman in England* by Hilaire Belloc]	II 215
Essays on Elizabethan Drama	IV 121
Euripides and Gilbert Murray: A Performance at the Holborn Empire	I 279
Euripides and Professor Murray (*SE* 1932)	II 323
Experiment in Criticism	II 71
An Extempore Exhumation	I 763
[*Extraits d'un Journal* by Charles du Bos]	II 48
Ezra Pound (1946)	III 574
Ezra Pound (1950)	III 824
Ezra Pound: His Metric and Poetry (1918)	I 133
Ezra Pound: His Metric and Poetry (*TCTC* 1965)	IV 816
[*Fashion in Literature* by E. E. Kellett]	II 222
Fr Cheetham Retires from Gloucester Road	IV 116
[The Festival of Poetry]	IV 544
For Lancelot Andrewes: Essays on Style and Order	I 791
Preface	I 791
Niccolo Machiavelli	I 792
Baudelaire in our Time	I 800
A Note on Richard Crashaw	I 807
A Foreign Mind	I 244
Foreword (1951)	IV 9
Foreword (1952)	IV 56
Foreword (1956)	IV 121
Foreword (1959)	IV 432
Foreword (1960)	IV 458
Foreword to the English Edition	IV 76
A Forgotten Utopia	I 92
Four Elizabethan Dramatists (*SE* 1932)	II 359
Four Elizabethan Dramatists. I A Preface (1924)	I 435
[*Four Quartets*]	III 587
Francis Herbert Bradley (*SE* 1932)	II 575
[*The Free Society* by John Middleton Murry]	III 605
[*The French Renascence* by Charles Sarolea]	I 25
Freud's Illusions	I 832
From Poe to Valéry (1948)	III 721
From Poe to Valéry (*TCTC* 1965)	IV 736
[From *Revelation*, ed. Baillie and Martin]	III 173
From T. S. Eliot	II 655
The Frontiers of Criticism (1956)	IV 119
The Frontiers of Criticism (*OPAP* 1957)	IV 221

INDEX OF ARTICLE TITLES

Full Employment and the Responsibility of Christians	III 534
The Function of Criticism (1923)	I 417
The Function of Criticism (SE 1932)	II 292
Fustel de Coulanges	I 816
The Future of Poetic Drama	III 246
A Game at Chesse	II 104
The Genesis of Philosophic Prose	II 33
Gentlemen and Seamen	I 8
Geoffrey Faber	IV 483
George Herbert	IV 511
I	IV 511
II	IV 519
III	IV 528
George Herbert A Select Bibliography	IV 535
Giordano Bruno	I 45
[*God* by J. Middleton Murry]	II 99
'Goethe as the Sage' (1955)	IV 115
Goethe as the Sage (OPAP 1957)	IV 319
The Golden Ass of Apuleius	I 775
Gordon Craig's Socratic Dialogues	IV 103
Grammar and Usage	I 559
The Great Layman	III 409
[*The Greene Murder Case* by S. S. Van Dine]	I 774
[Greeting to the Asociacíon de Artistas Aficionados]	IV 76
[Greeting to the Staatstheater Kassel]	IV 452
[*Group Theories of Religion and the Individual* by Clement C. J. Webb] (1916)	I 29
[*Group Theories of Religion and the Individual* by Clement C. J. Webb] (1916)	I 37
Hamlet (SE 1932)	II 384
Hamlet and his Problems	I 255
The Hawthorne Aspect	I 184
Homage to John Dryden	I 453
Preface	I 454
Homage to Wilkie Collins	I 562
Homage to Wyndham Lewis 1884–1957	IV 126
Hooker, Hobbes and Others	I 527
Hopousia	III 349
Housman on Poetry	II 678
The Humanism of Irving Babbitt (1928)	I 760
The Humanism of Irving Babbitt (SE 1932)	II 596
Humanist, Artist, and Scientist	I 257
A Humanist Theory of Value	II 87

The Idea of a Christian Society (1939) — III 268
The Idea of a Christian Society (1939) — III 270
   Preface — III 270
   The Idea of a Christian Society I — III 271
   II — III 281
   III — III 293
   IV — III 299
   Notes — III 303
   Appendix — III 316
   Appendix — III 316
The Idea of a Literary Review — I 484
The Idealism of Julien Benda — I 749
If I Were a Dean — II 199
Imperfect Critics: Swinburne As Critic (SW 1920) — I 315
The Importance of Wyndham Lewis — IV 126
In Memoriam (1930) — II 143
In Memoriam (*EAM* 1936) — III 113
In Memory of Henry James — I 116
In Praise of Kipling's Verse — III 436
In Sincerity and Earnestness: New Britain as I See It — II 840
The Influence of Landscape upon the Poet — IV 460
The Influence of Ovid — I 502
Inquiry into the Spirit and Language of Night — III 231
[Interview] — IV 499
[Interview with T. S. Eliot] — IV 504
Introduction (SW 1920) — I 302
Introduction (1926) — I 489
Introduction (1928) — I 708
Introduction (1930) — II 164
Introduction (1930) — II 176
Introduction (1931) — II 216
Introduction (UPUC 1933) — II 686
Introduction (1935) — III 35
Introduction (1936) — III 70
Introduction (1937) — III 167
Introduction (1944) — III 517
Introduction (1948) — III 609
Introduction (NTDC 1948) — III 617
Introduction (1948) — III 721
Introduction (1950) — III 798
Introduction (1950) — III 816
Introduction (1954) — IV 83
Introduction (1958) — IV 384
Introduction: 1928 (1949) — III 749
Introduction by T. S. Eliot (1928) — I 812
Introduction By T. S. Eliot (1952) — IV 31

Introduction to Goethe	II 5
Introductory Essay	II 171
Introductory Note	III 444
Isolated Superiority	I 691
Israfel	I 613
An Italian Critic on Donne and Crashaw	I 475
John Bramhall (SE 1932)	II 528
John Donne	I 407
John Dryden (1921)	I 374
John Dryden (1930)	II 154
John Dryden (SE 1932)	II 503
John Dryden I, II and III	II 199
John Dryden The Poet the Dramatist the Critic	II 624
Dryden the Poet	II 624
Dryden the Dramatist	II 632
Dryden the Critic	II 641
John Dryden's Tragedies	III 467
John Ford (1932)	II 278
John Ford (SE 1932)	II 426
John Marston (1934)	II 842
John Marston (1934)	II 852
John Maynard Keynes	III 554
John Webster	I 694
Johnson as Critic and Poet (OPAP 1957)	IV 277
Kipling Redivivus	I 220
Knowledge and Experience in the Philosophy of F. H. Bradley	IV 555
Preface	IV 555
On Our Knowledge of Immediate Experience	IV 557
On the Distinction of 'Real' and 'Ideal'	IV 570
The Psychologist's Treatment of Knowledge	IV 591
The Epistemologist's Theory of Knowledge	IV 612
The Epistemologist's Theory of Knowledge *continued*	IV 635
Solipsism	IV 657
Conclusion	IV 667
Appendix I: The Development of Leibniz's Monadism	IV 680
Appendix II: Leibniz's Monads and Bradley's Finite Centres	IV 697
[*La guerra eterna e il dramma del' esistenza* by Antonio Aliotta]	I 164
[Lady Margaret Rhondda]	IV 395
Lambeth and Education. The Report Criticised	III 761
L'amitié Franco-Britannique	IV 74
Lancelot Andrewes (1926)	I 517
Lancelot Andrewes (SE 1932)	II 518
Last Words	III 256

The Latin Tradition	II 14
A Lay Theologian	III 322
Le Morte Darthur	II 805
'Le salut de trois grands poètes: Londres: T. S. Eliot'	IV 100
Leadership and Letters	III 736
Leçon de Valéry (1946)	III 554
'Leçon de Valéry' (1947)	III 580
Leibniz's Monads and Bradley's Finite Centres (1916)	I 41
Leibniz's Monads and Bradley's Finite Centres (KEPB 1964)	IV 697
Les Lettres Anglaises	I 608
The Lesson of Baudelaire	I 357
The Letters of J. B. Yeats	I 72
[Letters of Mrs Gaskell and Charles Eliot Norton]	II 672
Lettre d'Angleterre	I 385
Lettres Étrangères (1922)	I 398
Lettres Étrangères (1923)	I 426
The Lion and the Fox	III 212
Literature	IV 79
Literature, Science, and Dogma	I 579
Literature and the American Courts	I 150
Literature and the Modern World	III 24
The Literature of Fascism	I 824
The Literature of Politics (1955)	IV 107
The Literature of Politics (TCTC 1965)	IV 802
The Local Flavour	I 278
London Letter (1921)	I 364, I 369, I 374, I 377
London Letter (1922)	I 382, I 392, I 395, I 398
['Lotze, Bradley, and Bosanquet' by Agnes Cuming]	I 104
M. Bourget's Last Novel	I 83
Man and Society	III 346
The Man of Letters and the Future of Europe	III 522
The Man who was King	I 5
[A Manual of Modern Scholastic Philosophy by Cardinal Mercier]	I 102
Marianne Moore	I 431
Marie Lloyd (SE 1932)	II 584
Marivaux	I 205
Massinger	I 529
Matthew Arnold (UPUC 1933)	II 737
['The Meaning of the Universe' by C. E. Hooper]	I 103
Medieval Philosophy	I 539
[Memoir of Richard Aldington]	IV 817
[Memorial Tribute for Mrs Violet Schiff]	IV 503
[Memorial Tribute for Sylvia Beach]	IV 510

[*Mens Creatrix* by William Temple]	I 75
'The Merry Masque of Our Lady in London Town'	I 840
A Message	IV 88
[Message from T. S. Eliot]	IV 30
[Message to *Merkur*]	III 839
Message to the Anglo-Catholic Congress in London	II 160
The Metaphysical Poets (1921)	I 381
The Metaphysical Poets (*SE* 1932)	II 484
The Method of Mr Pound	I 262
Milton (1947)	III 588
Milton (1948)	III 605
Milton I (*OPAP* 1957)	IV 252
Milton II (*OPAP* 1957)	IV 259
The Minor Metaphysicals	II 149
Miss Harriet Weaver (1961)	IV 496
Miss Harriet Weaver (1962)	IV 501
[Mr Ashley Dukes]	IV 443
Mr Barnes and Mr Rowse	II 41
Mr Charles Williams	III 540
Mr Chesterton (and Stevenson)	I 679
Mr Doughty's Epic	I 25
Mr Harold Monro: A Poet and his Ideal	II 254
Mr Leacock Serious	I 27
Mr Lee Masters	I 44
Mr Lucas's Webster	I 746
Mr Middleton Murry's Synthesis	I 662
Mr Murry's Shakespeare	III 141
Mr P. E. More's Essays	II 11
Mr Reckitt, Mr Tomlin and the Crisis	III 162
[*Mr Shaw and 'The Maid'* by J. M. Robertson]	I 495
Mrs Runcie's Pudding	IV 98
The Modern Dilemma	II 680
Modern Education and the Classics (*EAM* 1936)	III 106
The Modern Mind (*UPUC* 1933)	II 747
Modern Tendencies in Poetry	I 287
Mögen Sie Picasso?	IV 496
More and Tudor Drama	I 532
Murmuring of Innumerable Bees	I 256
The Music of Poetry (1942)	III 434
The Music of Poetry (*OPAP* 1957)	IV 145
Mystic and Politician as Poet	II 143
[*The Mystical Doctrine of St John of the Cross*]	II 839
The Mysticism of Blake	I 651
The Naked Man	I 279
The Nature of Cultural Relations	III 459

The Need for Poetic Drama	III 150
The New Elizabethans and the Old	I 210
New Philosophers	I 180
Niccolo Machiavelli (1469–1527) (1927)	I 621
Niccolo Machiavelli (*FLA* 1928)	I 792
Nightwood	III 173
The Noh and the Image	I 80
A Note (1959)	IV 451
Note (*TCTC* 1965)	IV 723
A Note by T. S. Eliot	III 167
A Note of Introduction	IV 497
A Note on Culture and Politics (*NTDC* 1948)	III 686
A Note on Ezra Pound	I 192
A Note on *In Parenthesis* and *The Anathemata*	IV 101
A Note on Intelligence and Intuition	I 656
A note on *Monstre Gai* by Wyndham Lewis	IV 93
A Note on Poetry and Belief	I 565
A Note on Richard Crashaw (*FLA* 1928)	I 807
A Note on *The Criterion* By T. S. Eliot	IV 818
A Note on the Verse of John Milton	III 137
A Note on Translation	IV 705
A Note on Two Odes of Cowley	III 221
Note sur Mallarmé et Poe	I 525
Notes (1923)	I 410
Notes (1923)	I 418
Notes (*ICS* 1939)	III 303
Notes . . . from T. S. Eliot	III 835
Notes on Education and Culture: and Conclusion (*NTDC* 1948)	III 695
Notes on the Way [I]	III 6
Notes on the Way [II]	III 9
Notes on the Way [III]	III 14
Notes on the Way [IV]	III 19
Notes Towards the Definition of Culture (1943)	III 447
I	III 447
II	III 450
III	III 453
IV	III 456
Notes Towards the Definition of Culture (1948)	III 616
Preface	III 616
Introduction	III 617
The Three Senses of 'Culture'	III 623
The Class and the Elite	III 645
Unity and Diversity: The Region	III 662
Unity and Diversity: Sect and Cult	III 674
A Note on Culture and Politics	III 686
Notes on Education and Culture: and Conclusion	III 695

INDEX OF ARTICLE TITLES • 879

    Appendix The Unity of European Culture   III 706
Notes Towards the Definition of Culture (1962)   IV 502
    Preface to the 1962 Edition   IV 502

Obituary   IV 479
[Obituary Notice for Louis MacNeice]   IV 546
Observations   I 169
The Old Comedy   I 301
On a Recent Piece of Criticism   III 227
On Christianity and a Useful Life . . .   III 250
[On G. K. Chesterton]   III 136
On Our Knowledge of Immediate Experience (KEPB 1964)   IV 557
On Poetry (1947)   III 588
On Poetry and Poets   IV 134
    Preface   IV 134
    I. On Poets   IV 135
        The Social Function of Poetry   IV 135
        The Music of Poetry   IV 145
        What Is Minor Poetry?   IV 158
        What is a Classic?   IV 172
        Poetry and Drama   IV 189
        The Three Voices of Poetry   IV 208
        The Frontiers of Criticism   IV 221
    II. On Poets   IV 236
        Virgil and the Christian World   IV 236
        Sir John Davies   IV 247
        Milton I   IV 252
        Milton II   IV 259
        Johnson as Critic and Poet   IV 277
        Byron   IV 305
        Goethe as the Sage   IV 319
        Rudyard Kipling   IV 339
        Yeats   IV 362
On Reading Einstein   II 179
On Teaching the Appreciation of Poetry   IV 463
On the Distinction of 'Real' and 'Ideal' (KEPB 1964)   IV 570
On the Eve: A Dialogue   I 462
[On the production of *The Confidential Clerk*]   IV 475
Orage: Memories   II 864
'Our Culture'   III 595
[*Outlines of Jainism* by Jagmanderlal Jaini]   I 168
[*The Oxford Handbook of Religious Knowledge*]   II 838
The Oxford Jonson   I 757

The Panegyric by Mr T. S. Eliot   IV 440
Parnassus Biceps   I 667

Paul Elmer More	III 159
[Paul Elmer More, *Selected Shelburne Essays*]	III 70
The *Pensées* of Pascal (*EAM* 1936)	III 94
The Perfect Critic [I] (1920)	I 301
The Perfect Critic [II] (1920)	I 301
The Perfect Critic (*SW* 1920)	I 307
Personality and Demonic Possession	II 780
Philip Massinger (1920)	I 300
Philip Massinger (*SE* 1932)	II 435
[*Philosophy & War* by Émile Boutroux]	I 40
[*The Philosophy of Nietzsche* by A. Wolf]	I 20
The Phoenix Nest	I 568
Plague Pamphlets	I 506
Planning and Religion	III 470
[*The Playgoer's Handbook to the English Renaissance Drama* by Agnes Mure Mackenzie]	I 637
Plays of Ben Jonson	I 628
[*The Poems English Latin and Greek of Richard Crashaw* ed. L. C. Martin]	I 731
'Poet and Saint . . .'	I 608
The Poetic Drama	I 297
Poetry and Drama (1951)	IV 8
Poetry and Drama (1951)	IV 12
Poetry and Drama (*OPAP* 1957)	IV 189
Poetry and Film	IV 6
Poetry and Propaganda	II 107
Poetry and Religion	I 548
Poetry and Religion [II]	I 590
Poetry and the Schools	IV 124
Poetry by T. S. Eliot	III 833
[Poetry Collections and Commentary]	I 111
The Poetry of W. B. Yeats	III 349
Poets' Borrowings	I 731
The Point of View	I 8
Political Theorists	I 623
A Popular Shakespeare	I 488
Popular Theologians	I 602
A Portrait of Michael Roberts	III 795
The Possibility of a Poetic Drama (1920)	I 301
The Possibility of a Poetic Drama (*SW* 1920)	I 333
The Post-Georgians	I 214
The Preacher as Artist	I 270
A Prediction in Regard to Three English Authors	I 435
Preface (*HJD* 1924)	I 454
Preface (1928)	I 778
Preface (*FLA* 1928)	I 791

INDEX OF ARTICLE TITLES

Preface (1929)	II 66
Preface (1931)	II 224
Preface (1932)	II 242
Preface (*UPUC* 1933)	II 685
Preface (*ASG* 1934)	II 781
Preface (*EAM* 1936)	III 71
Preface (*ICS* 1939)	III 270
Preface (1942)	III 426
Preface (1946)	III 558
Preface (*NTDC* 1948)	III 616
Preface (1950)	III 811
Preface (1951)	IV 10, IV 17, IV 18
Preface (1952)	IV 48
Preface (1954)	IV 92
Preface (*OPAP* 1957)	IV 134
Preface (1957)	IV 373
Preface (1959)	IV 448
Preface (1961)	IV 478
Preface (1961)	IV 482
Preface (1961)	IV 494
Preface (*ED* 1963)	IV 548
Preface (*KEPB* 1964)	IV 555
Preface (1965)	IV 719
Preface by T. S. Eliot	III 368
[*Preface to a Christian Sociology* by C. E. Hudson]	III 123
A Preface to Modern Literature	I 422
Preface to the 1928 Edition	I 737
Preface to the 1962 Edition (*NTDC* 1962)	IV 502
[Prefatory Note on James Joyce]	III 779
President Wilson	I 65
[Prizewinners]	I 398
The Problem of Education	II 842
The Problems of the Shakespeare Sonnets	I 574
Professional, Or . . .	I 162
Professor H. H. Joachim	III 242
Professor Karl Mannheim	III 583
Prólogo del autor para la edición española	III 574
Prologue to an Essay on Criticism (1928)	I 683
Prologue to an Essay on Criticism (1928)	I 721
Prose and Verse	I 358
The Prose of the Preacher	II 48
[*The Prospects of Humanism* by Lawrence Hyde]	II 202
The Psychologist's Treatment of Knowledge (*KEPB* 1964)	IV 591
Publishers' Preface	I 780
The Publishing of Poetry	IV 68

Recent British Periodical Literature in Ethics	I 123
Recent Detective Fiction	I 618
Records of the Class	I 473
[*The Reef of Stars* by H. de Vere Stacpoole]	I 50
Reflections on Contemporary Poetry. I.	I 86
Reflections on Contemporary Poetry [II]	I 98
Reflections on Contemporary Poetry [III]	I 105
Reflections on Contemporary Poetry [IV]	I 241
Reflections on the Unity of European Culture	III 554
Reflections on the Unity of European Culture (II) (1946)	III 561
Reflections on the Unity of European Culture (II) (1953)	IV 79
Reflections on the Unity of European Culture (III)	III 561
Reflections on *Vers Libre* (1917)	I 53
Reflections on Vers Libre (*TCTC* 1965)	IV 816
[*Reflections on Violence* by Georges Sorel]	I 77
Religion and Literature (1935) I	II 30
Religion and Literature (*EAM* 1936)	III 72
[*Religion and Philosophy* by R. G. Collingwood]	I 76
Religion and Science: A Phantom Dilemma	II 256
[*Religion and Science* by J. T. Merz]	I 39
[*Religion and Science* by John Theodore Merz]	I 166
Religion without Humanism	II 117
Religious Drama: Medieval and Modern	III 195
Religious Drama and the Church	II 849
Rencontre	I 470
A Reply to Mr Ward	I 743
[Report on Obscene Publications]	IV 376
Reunion: Construction or Destruction	III 514
Reunion by Destruction	III 494
'Rhetoric' And Poetic Drama (*SE* 1932)	II 301
Rhyme and Reason	II 128
Richard Edwards	I 649
A Romantic Patrician	I 220
The Romantic Englishman, the Comic Spirit, and the Function Of Criticism	I 355
The Romantic Generation, If It Existed	I 248
[Rudyard Kipling] (1941)	III 411
Rudyard Kipling (*OPAP* 1957)	IV 339
Rudyard Kipling (1959)	IV 405
The Sacred Wood: Essays on Poetry and Criticism	I 302
Introduction	I 302
The Perfect Critic	I 307
Imperfect Critics: Swinburne As Critic	I 315
The Possibility of a Poetic Drama	I 333

Swinburne as Poet	I 340
Dante	I 344
[The Saddest Word]	IV 99
[Salutation]	IV 401
[Samuel Taylor Coleridge, 1772–1834]	II 829
Saving the Future	III 125
A Sceptical Patrician	I 225
A Scholar's Essays	I 670
['Schopenhauer and Individuality' by Bertram M. Laing]	I 104
Scylla and Charybdis	IV 35
The Search for Moral Sanction	II 261
Second Message to the Anglo-Catholic Congress	II 160
Second Thoughts about Humanism (1929)	II 23
Second Thoughts about Humanism (1929)	II 66
Second Thoughts about Humanism (*SE* 1932)	II 604
Selected Essays 1917–1932	II 284
Tradition and the Individual Talent	II 285
The Function of Criticism	II 292
'Rhetoric' And Poetic Drama	II 301
A Dialogue on Dramatic Poetry	II 309
Euripides and Professor Murray	II 323
Seneca in Elizabethan Translation	II 327
Four Elizabethan Dramatists	II 359
Christopher Marlowe	II 366
Shakespeare and the Stoicism of Seneca	II 373
Hamlet	II 384
Ben Jonson	II 389
Thomas Middleton	II 400
Thomas Heywood	II 408
Cyril Tourneur	II 417
John Ford	II 426
Philip Massinger	II 435
Dante	II 448
The Metaphysical Poets	II 484
Andrew Marvell	II 492
John Dryden	II 503
William Blake	II 513
Swinburne as Poet	II 518
Lancelot Andrewes	II 518
John Bramhall	II 528
Thoughts after Lambeth	II 535
Baudelaire	II 554
Arnold and Pater	II 564
Francis Herbert Bradley	II 575
Marie Lloyd	II 584
Wilkie Collins and Dickens	II 588

The Humanism of Irving Babbitt	II 596
Second Thoughts about Humanism	II 604
Charles Whibley	II 613
Seneca in Elizabethan Translation (1927)	I 649
Seneca in Elizabethan Translation (SE 1932)	II 327
A Sermon	III 598
Seventeenth-Century Preachers	I 765
Shakespeare and Montaigne	I 477
Shakespeare and the Stoicism of Seneca (1927)	I 654
Shakespeare and the Stoicism of Seneca (SE 1932)	II 373
Shakespeare Criticism	II 819
Shelley and Keats (UPUC 1933)	II 727
Short Notices (1918)	I 173
Short Notices (1918)	I 183
Short Reviews	I 121
Shorter Notices	I 177
Should There Be a Censorship of Books?	III 51
The Significance of Charles Williams	III 575
The Silurist	I 645
Sir John Davies (1926)	I 534
Sir John Davies (OPAP 1957)	IV 247
Sir John Denham	I 760
[Social Adaptation by L. M. Bristol]	I 29
The Social Function of Poetry (1943)	III 480
The Social Function of Poetry (1945)	III 541
The Social Function of Poetry (OPAP 1957)	IV 135
Solipsism (KEPB 1964)	IV 657
Some Notes on the Blank Verse of Christopher Marlowe	I 255
Some Thoughts on Braille	IV 60
[Son of Woman by John Middleton Murry]	II 209
The Sources of Chapman	I 572
[A special message about Ezra Pound]	IV 375
[Speech at the Nobel Banquet]	III 719
[Speech to the BBC Governors]	IV 131
Spinoza	I 586
The Spoken Word	IV 12
Stage Studies	I 676
[Statement about The New Leader]	IV 440
[Statement on the Award of the Nobel Prize]	III 719
Stendhal the Romantic	I 534
The Story of the Pageant	II 832
Studies in Contemporary Criticism (1918)	I 197
Studies in Contemporary Criticism (1918)	I 201
Studies in Sanctity. VIII. George Herbert	II 244
A Study Of Marlowe	I 583
[The Study of Religions by Stanley A. Cook]	I 79

Style and Thought	I 157
A Sub-Pagan Society?	III 324
Swinburne	I 279
Swinburne and the Elizabethans	I 255
Swinburne as Poet (SW 1920)	I 340
Swinburne as Poet (SE 1932)	II 518
[T. S. Eliot] (1927)	I 544
[T. S. Eliot] (1942)	III 417
[T. S. Eliot] (1943)	III 446
T. S. Eliot Answers Questions	III 775
T. S. Eliot Nous Dit	III 794
T. S. Eliot on Poetry in Wartime	III 442
T. S. Eliot on the Language of *The New English Bible*	IV 538
T. S. Eliot Talks about his Poetry	IV 396
A Tale of a Whale	I 4
Talk on Dante	III 803
Talking Freely: T. S. Eliot and Tom Greenwell	IV 486
Tarr	I 190
Television is not Friendly Enough	IV 402
[*Theism and Humanism* by A. J. Balfour]	I 15
Thinking in Verse	II 122
[*Thomas Hardy* by H. C. Duffin]	I 22
Thomas Heywood (1931)	II 216
Thomas Heywood (SE 1932)	II 408
Thomas Middleton (1927)	I 621
Thomas Middleton (SE 1932)	II 400
Thomas Stearns Eliot (1917)	I 53
Thomas Stearns Eliot (1921)	I 354
Thomas Stearns Eliot (1935)	III 40
Thomas Stearns Eliot (1940)	III 346
Thomas Stearns Eliot (1950)	III 803
Thomas Stearns Eliot (1960)	IV 471
Thomas Stearns Eliot (1965)	IV 718
Thomas Stearns Eliot Gratulation	IV 79
'Those Who need Privacy and Those Whose Need is Company'	IV 27
Thoughts After Lambeth (1931)	II 192
Thoughts after Lambeth (SE 1932)	II 535
[Three Books by Eugene O'Neill]	I 496
The Three Provincialities (1922)	I 382
The Three Provincialities (1922) (1951)	IV 3
Three Questions	I 391
Three Reformers	I 784
The Three Senses of 'Culture' (NTDC 1948)	III 623
The Three Voices of Poetry (1953)	IV 82
The Three Voices of Poetry (OPAP 1957)	IV 208

To Criticize the Critic (*TCTC* 1965)	IV 724
To Criticize the Critic and other writings	IV 723
Note	IV 723
To Criticize the Critic	IV 724
From Poe to Valéry	IV 736
American Literature and the American Language	IV 736
The Aims of Education 1	IV 751
The Aims of Education 2	IV 764
The Aims of Education 3	IV 777
The Aims of Education 4	IV 789
What Dante Means to Me	IV 802
The Literature of Politics	IV 802
The Classics and the Man of Letters	IV 803
Ezra Pound: His Metric and Poetry	IV 816
Reflections on Vers Libre	IV 816
[To Ezra Pound on his Seventieth Birthday] (1955)	IV 115
[To Ezra Pound on his Seventieth Birthday] (1956)	IV 118
To the Reader	III 521
[*Totem* by Harold Stovin]	III 69
Towards a Christian Britain (1941)	III 390
Towards a Christian Britain (1941)	III 403
[*The Tower* by Hugo von Hofmannsthal]	IV 545
Tradition and Experiment in Present-Day Literature	II 71
Tradition and Orthodoxy	II 809
Tradition and the Individual Talent [I] (1919)	I 255
Tradition and the Individual Talent [II & III] (1919)	I 266
Tradition and the Individual Talent (*SE* 1932)	II 285
A Tribute	IV 91
[Tribute to Aldous Huxley]	IV 721
[Tribute to Ananda K. Coomaraswamy]	III 734
[Tribute to Artur Lundkvist]	IV 118
[Tribute to August Strindberg]	III 735
[Tribute to Charles Maurras]	III 602
[Tribute to Georg Svensson on his 60th Birthday]	IV 706
[Tribute to Giuseppe Ungaretti]	IV 474
[Tribute to John Davidson]	IV 130
[Tribute to Luigi Pirandello]	IV 68
A Tribute To Mario Praz	IV 818
[Tribute to Sir Hugh Walpole]	III 393
[Tribute to Victoria Ocampo]	IV 509
[A Tribute to Wilfred Owen]	IV 705
The Tudor Biographers	II 59
The Tudor Translators	II 23
Turbervile's Ovid	II 8
Turgenev	I 109
The Twelfth Century	I 635

Twenty-One Answers	III 594
Two Studies in Dante	I 781
The Two Unfinished Novels	I 119
[*The Ultimate Belief* by A. Clutton-Brock]	I 39
Ulysses, Order, and Myth (1923)	I 422
Ulysses, Order, and Myth (1964)	IV 551
Un Feuillet Unique	III 802
The Unfading Genius of Rudyard Kipling	IV 435
Unity and Diversity: Sect and Cult (*NTDC* 1948)	III 674
Unity and Diversity: The Region (*NTDC* 1948)	III 662
The Unity of European Culture (*NTDC* 1948)	III 706
[*Union Portraits* by Gamaliel Bradford]	I 61
The Use of Poetry and the Use of Criticism	II 685
Preface	II 685
Introduction	II 686
Apology for the Countess of Pembroke	II 700
The Age of Dryden	II 709
Wordsworth and Coleridge	II 716
Shelley and Keats	II 727
Matthew Arnold	II 737
The Modern Mind	II 747
Conclusion	II 760
The Value and Use of Cathedrals in England To-Day	IV 19
Vergil and the Christian World	IV 19
Verse Pleasant and Unpleasant	I 152
The Very Revd F. P. Harton	IV 401
A Victorian Sculptor	I 155
Views and Reviews [I]	III 43
Views and Reviews [II]	III 46
Views and Reviews [III]	III 55
Views and Reviews [IV]	III 61
Views and Reviews (1940)	III 328, III 331, III 386
Views and Reviews (1941)	III 393
Virgil and the Christian World (*OPAP* 1957)	IV 236
Virginia Woolf	III 390
The Voice of His Time	III 428
Wanley and Chapman	I 479
War-Paint and Feathers	I 260
Was There a Scottish Literature?	I 251
What Dante Means to Me (*TCTC* 1965)	IV 802
What Does the Church Stand For?	II 862
What France Means to You	III 519
What India is Thinking about To-day	I 12

What is a Classic? (1944)   III 521
What is a Classic? (1945)   III 534
What is a Classic? (OPAP 1957)   IV 172
What is Minor Poetry? (1944)   III 533
What Is Minor Poetry? (OPAP 1957)   IV 158
Whether Rostand Had Something About Him   I 251
Whitman and Tennyson   I 541
Why Mr Russell is a Christian   I 632
Why Rural Verse?   I 471
Wilkie Collins and Dickens (1927)   I 635
Wilkie Collins and Dickens (SE 1932)   II 588
William Blake (SE 1932)   II 513
William James on Immortality   I 95
[*The Wine of the Puritans* by Van Wyck Brooks]   I 7
[*With Americans of Past and Present Days* by J. J. Jusserand]   I 49
[*The Women of Trachis*: A Symposium]   IV 99
Wordsworth and Coleridge (UPUC 1933)   II 716
[Works by Conan Doyle and A. K. Green]   II 19
[*The World as Imagination* by E. D. Fawcett]   I 179
The Writer as Artist   III 369
The Writings of Charles Williams   III 598
Wyndham Lewis   IV 127

The Year's Poetry   III 141
Yeats (OPAP 1957)   IV 362